Ornament of the Great Vehicle Sūtras

Ornament of the Great Vehicle Sūtras

Maitreya's *Mahāyānasūtrālaṃkāra*
with Commentaries by
Khenpo Shenga and Ju Mipham

TRANSLATED BY
DHARMACHAKRA TRANSLATION COMMITTEE

Snow Lion
Boston & London
2014

SNOW LION
An imprint of Shambhala Publications, Inc.
Horticultural Hall
300 Massachusetts Avenue
Boston, Massachusetts 02115
www.shambhala.com

© 2014 by Dharmachakra Translation Committee

All rights reserved. No part of this book may be reproduced in any form
or by any means, electronic or mechanical, including photocopying,
recording, or by any information storage and retrieval system,
without permission in writing from the publisher.

9 8 7 6 5 4 3 2 1

First Edition
Printed in the United States of America

♾ This edition is printed on acid-free paper
that meets the American National Standards Institute z39.48 Standard.
♻ Shambhala Publications makes every effort to print on recycled paper.
For more information please visit www.shambhala.com.

Distributed in the United States by Penguin Random House LLC
and in Canada by Random House of Canada Ltd

LIBRARY OF CONGRESS CATALOGING-IN-PUBLICATION DATA

Asaṅga, author.
[Mahāyānasūtrālaṃkāra. English]
Ornament of the Great Vehicle Sūtras : Maitreya's Mahāyānasūtrālaṃkāra
with commentaries by Khenpo Shenga and Ju Mipham / translated by
Dharmachakra Translation Committee.—First edition.
pages cm
Includes translations from Tibetan.
ISBN 978-1-55939-428-4 (hardback)
1. Yogācāra (Buddhism)—Early works to 1800. I. Maitreyanātha.
II. Gźan-phan-chos-kyi-snaṅ-ba, Gźan-dga', 1871–1927.
III. Mi-pham-rgya-mtsho, 'Jam-mgon 'Ju, 1846–1912.
IV. Dharmachakra Translation Committee.
V. Title.
BQ3002.E5D53 2014
294.3'85—dc23
2013047535

Contents

Translators' Introduction	vii
Ornament of the Great Vehicle Sūtras	1
Title and Translator's Homage	4
1. How the Scripture Was Composed	5
2. Establishing the Teachings of the Great Vehicle	21
3. Going for Refuge	41
4. Potential	59
5. Developing the Enlightened Mind	77
6. Practice	109
7. Reality	125
8. Power	145
9. Full Maturation	157
10. Enlightenment	181
Summary of Chapters 1 through 10	261
11. Inspiration	265
12. Investigation of the Dharma	285
13. Teaching	397

14. Practice	429
15. Practical Instructions and Advice	453
Summary of Chapters 11 through 15	489
16. Skillful Means	491
17. Transcendences and Means of Attraction	497
18. Worship, Reliance, and the Immeasurables	571
19. The Factors That Accord with Enlightenment	639
20. The Qualities	777
21. Activity and Perfection	863
Colophons	927
Appendix: A Visual Representation of Mipham's Topical Outline	931
Notes	963
English-Tibetan Glossary	969
Tibetan-English-Sanskrit Glossary	977
Bibliography	987
Index	991

Translators' Introduction

Why is this called the "Great Vehicle of enlightenment"?
Because whoever rides it delivers all sentient beings from
   suffering.
Resembling space, this vehicle is an immeasurable palace;
Granting joy, happiness, and bliss, this vehicle is supreme.[1]

In these few lines, the *Noble Sūtra on Transcendent Insight in Eighteen Thousand Lines* teaches us about the nature, effect, purpose, and benefits of the so-called "Great Vehicle" (Skt. *Mahāyāna*). The sūtras of the Great Vehicle contain many hundreds of thousands of such lines of instruction, each of them contributing to a dynamic framework of teaching and realization—the Great Vehicle—that is intended to yield a buddha's awakening for the sake of all sentient life.

Despite the likely alien and awkward feel of the concepts involved, we might, when hearing a sūtra, experience a quite innocent sense of wonder—a brief moment of almost childlike, delightful surprise, perhaps colored by a subtle tone of promise and potential. In line with the teachings set out in this book, we might say that just such a brief clearing within simple, unprepared wonder is what constitutes the awakening of faith in the Great Vehicle.

But really, we might ask, how could anything worthy of being referred to as "palatial" also be like space? How, if it is both space-like and a palace, could it also be the vehicle of something? And, assuming that it is at all intelligible, how could this supremely odd vehicle lead to anything desirable, let alone universal deliverance and perfect fulfillment for all? We may feel that the reasons to be skeptical or simply dismissive of such fanciful claims are so numerous that we don't even need to state them.

Whatever our reaction may be, for several hundred million Buddhists in this world, the Great Vehicle sūtras are sacred scripture and have been here, in that capacity, since ancient times.[2] Our present treatise, the *Ornament of the Great Vehicle Sūtras,* compares itself to a mirror that reflects this vast body of scripture. The perceptive student of this text will, we are told, gain access to the Great Vehicle's profound view, expansive path, and inconceivable fruition—simply by looking in this one direction. The *Ornament*'s author, who according to tradition is the Buddha's regent, Maitreya,[3] explains in the opening lines:

> When a body, replete with ornaments and naturally endowed
>   with excellent qualities, is reflected in a mirror,
> Those who see it will experience total and supreme joy.
> Likewise, while the well-spoken words of the Dharma are
>   always replete with excellent qualities,
> When their meaning is explained herein, the wise will
>   experience supreme joy. [1.3]

This joy that the wise will feel when encountering the *Ornament of the Great Vehicle Sūtras* is explained in terms of five analogies, and the commentators through the ages have related these five to the contents of the treatise in various ways. Here is how the images are presented in the opening verses:

> Resembling shaped gold, a lotus in bloom,
> And an excellent meal enjoyed when stricken with hunger;
> Like receiving a letter with good news and an open treasure
>   trove—
> Such is the Dharma, which when here explained engenders
>   perfect joy. [1.2]

While these examples will be considered in detail in the commentaries that follow, let us simply notice here how experience with the *Ornament* and its teaching is described in terms of beauty, sensuousness, fulfillment, and marvel. It is, we are told, in the nature of the Dharma of the Great Vehicle to deliver such joy.

For the experience of the spiritual journey to be described in such terms is perhaps not all that unusual. The world's religions typically speak of heaven, or the Great Beyond that awaits the devout, as being something that is supremely desirable. It is perhaps not surprising, then, that the Dharma, which in Buddhism is the path for the attainment of the supreme, is here described in such jubilant terms. Yet, as we listen further, it becomes clear that when our text speaks of the qualities of the Dharma, it is not in fact concerned with a realm that lies entirely beyond the senses. The bodhisattvas' experience with the Dharma is their experience within this very world, "this great mass of nothing but suffering" that, according to Buddhist doctrine, follows from the merciless spinning of the wheels of existence.[4] The bodhisattvas see and live in this world, through insight and compassion, and so their experience is transformed.[5]

Steadfast and wise bodhisattvas, those "whose very nature is compassion," will, we are told, gladly subject themselves to even the most horrifying pains if it is for the benefit of others.[6] They do so happily, indeed ecstatically, if it serves that supreme purpose:

> A bodhisattva free from suffering
> Experiences suffering because of love;
> First there is fear, but upon contact
> There follows utterly intense joy. [XVIII.46]

The text seems to promise that, tangible and concrete, the bliss of the Great Vehicle is potentially there for us to experience in our very next move of compassionate action. And yet, to sense such bliss, we must abandon our otherwise instinctive fear of personal suffering.

The bodhisattva achieves this relinquishment of fear by seeing that its foundations—the perceived opposition between self and other—is entirely artificial and in fact a mere mistake.[7] As long as it remains uncorrected, this cognitive error will have pervasive and catastrophic consequences, but, since none of its elements carry any substance, the delusion of an actual divide between self and other will, as is customary for delusions, vanish as soon as reality is seen.[8]

Such liberating and nondual perception is indeed transcendent, for it goes beyond the reach of thought. But, according to the teaching of the *Ornament*, true transcendence is necessarily also intensely affectionate. Recognizing that "what I am is also what all sentient beings are; what they are is also what I am,"[9] the bodhisattva discovers how fearless love and transcendent bliss are of the same fabric within the experience of insight:

> Suffering due to love
> Outshines all the world's happiness.
> And not even those who have accomplished their objective
>   possess it.[10]
> What could be more wondrous than this? [XVIII.47]

> When the steadfast ones give with love,
> They experience a joy of giving
> Of which the happiness of those experiencing the three
>   realms[11]
> Cannot match even a fraction. [XVIII.48]

Thus, for the author, the true wonder of transcendent bliss is discovered within the simple but deeply meaningful act of giving. Living by such acts of insight and compassion for the infinite sea of embodied beings—for all those whose otherwise separate existences are now understood as inseparable from one's own—the bodhisattvas traverse the path to awakening for the benefit of all. On this accomplishment, our text declares:

> Thus, everywhere throughout the world, the steadfast ones
>   constantly and always
> Achieve the great enlightenment that is hard to achieve, yet is
>   marvelously endowed with supreme qualities:
> The permanent and steadfast refuge for those who have none.
> This is a great wonder, but also not, for they have practiced
>   the way of goodness. [X.50]

What sort of world are we being introduced to here? What might it be like to be a bodhisattva? What does it mean to be a sentient being if this is how things are? If our response to the worldview of the sūtras goes beyond the purely dismissive, we are most likely here to experience a certain sense of wonder. Further, with the last line of the stanza, it seems that our author also wants to convey that, no matter how superhuman or supernatural the bodhisattvas and their enlightenment may appear to be, the authentic journey of the Great Vehicle could begin right here and now for each one of us. Even here—in my own little, private, and so clearly imperfect existence. If I take this message to heart, I will then stand in awe before the bodhisattva, simultaneously humbled and empowered.

ANNOTATION AND EXPLANATION: OUR TWO COMMENTARIES

The teachings of the *Ornament* are a true classic, and through the ages this treatise and its perceived intent have been studied, contemplated, interpreted, and practiced in countless ways by numerous brilliant minds. Hence, the literature that is based on, and inspired by, the *Ornament* is also extremely rich, having developed across the centuries throughout south, east, and central Asia, as well as, more recently, across the globe. For us translators, to work with this treasure of world literature, philosophy, and religion has been as intimidating as it has been gratifying. Hence, despite any and all shortcomings of our work, it is with great joy that we present the *Ornament of the Great Vehicle Sūtras*,[12] accompanied by two influential commentaries, both of which emerged from Tibet in relatively recent times.

Shenphen Chökyi Nangwa (Tib. gZhan phan chos kyi snang ba, 1871–1927),[13] who is widely known as Khenpo Shenga (Tib. mkhan po gZhan dga'), uses the method of interspersing glosses and explanatory remarks between the words of the root text, as is characteristic of an "annotation commentary" (Tib. *mchan 'grel*). This format lets the reader begin the process of unpacking the condensed message of the verses without ever losing sight of them. Shenga's annotation commentary on the *Ornament of the Great Vehicle Sūtras*—which in this book appears right after the root verses, with the words of the root text set apart from the commentary in bold font—draws chiefly on the commentary attributed to the great Indian master Vasubandhu (fl. fourth century CE).[14] Shenga's glosses are thus typically direct quotations from the latter's commentary. As an exponent of the nonsectarian Rimé (Tib. Ris med) movement, Shenga wished aspiring Tibetan scholars to gain a thorough and firsthand experience with the classics of Indian Mahāyāna Buddhism. His commentary on the *Ornament of the Great Vehicle Sūtras* belongs to a set of thirteen annotation commentaries on classical Indian treatises.[15] These commentaries on the "thirteen classics" (Tib. *gzhung chen bcu gsum*) have, across traditional affiliations, become essential to the curriculum in many of the monastic colleges of Tibet, Nepal, Bhutan, and India.

Shenga's commentary speaks with the authority of the ancient masters. It is both weighty and concise, and yet it carries a tone of mystery. In this book, our translation of Shenga's commentary is joined with the explanations found in *A Feast of the Supreme Vehicle*, the great commentary to the *Ornament of the Great Vehicle Sūtras* composed by Ju Mipham (Tib. 'Ju mi pham, 1846–1912).[16] Mipham introduces the original stanzas within the framework of a traditional "topical outline" (Tib. *sa bcad*), and, for each section of root verses, the text of Mipham's actual explanation follows after both the verses and Shenga's commentary on them. See below for an example of how this text is organized.

When reading this book, we recommend frequent reference to the visual representation of Mipham's outline that appears in the appendix. Doing so will help keep track of this intricate system of divisions and subdivisions that structures a traditional Tibetan scholarly text. Please note that the text of the visual outline typically consists of the exact text of Mipham's prose, as he first enumerates the relevant divisions. The headings that initiate the sections of the translation have, on the other hand, typically been simplified in conformity with modern literary conventions. While the simplified headings are, therefore, similar to, but not identical with, the outline text found in the appendix, the headings still carry numbers that exactly tally with those used in the appendix.

It must be noted that in numbering the chapters we have followed the Tibetan translations of the root verses and Vasubandhu's commentary, both of which consider the initial six stanzas of the text to be the first chapter. While this approach is the one taken by the Tibetan commentarial tradition, it differs from the enumeration that is now customary in the academy. The latter considers the Tibetan chapters 1 and 2 to be a single, first chapter, while the Tibetan chapter 21 is split into two chapters.[17]

In Mipham's topical outline, the twenty-one chapters of the *Ornament of the Great Vehicle Sūtras* are aligned with five primary topics—what is to be established, what is to be understood, what is to be contemplated, the inconceivable, and the factors that accord with enlightenment (see the appendix, p. 931)—and each of these five classical themes is itself treated under many subdivisions. Before beginning to read the text, it is helpful to notice that as an upshot of this explanatory structure, the twenty-one chapters are treated at different levels within the topical

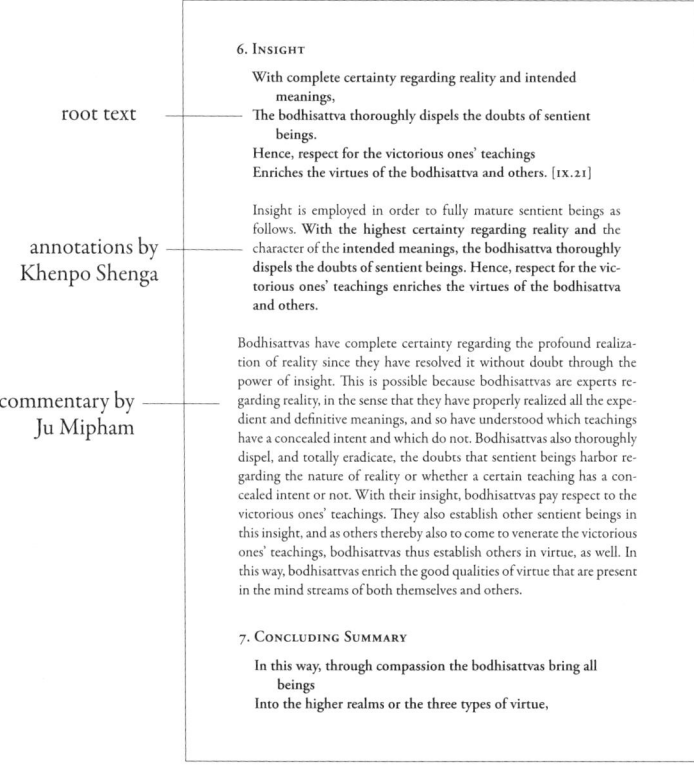

outline. This means that, for example, chapter 5, which is the chapter on developing the enlightened mind, appears as the third section within the context of what is to be understood. This location of the chapter within the topical outline is also reflected in the heading that appears subsequent to the chapter heading on p. 77. Hence, despite the chapter's being the fifth among the twenty-one, the latter heading reads: "3. Developing the Enlightened Mind." Such numbered headings that locate a given chapter within a specific context of Mipham's topical outline should not be confused with the basic numbering of the twenty-one chapters.

As a whole, Mipham's comprehensive authorship can be seen as a celebration of the principles of clarity and depth, for, with little patience for those who "talk much but say little," Mipham writes with a natural elegance that centers on key points (Tib. *gnad*). In *A Feast of the Supreme Vehicle,* Mipham relies on the Indian masters Vasubandhu and, in particular, Sthiramati, who according to Tibetan accounts, was Vasubandhu's direct disciple.[18] Sthiramati authored a vast and extensive subcommentary[19] to Vasubandhu's fairly concise explanations, and while writing *A Feast of the Supreme Vehicle,* Mipham bases himself on Sthiramati's work. In doing so, he wishes, as he says, to present the vast content and deep import of the *Ornament* "in a way that is both lucid and easy to understand."[20]

Shenga's commentary, with its strong focus on the wording of the root verses and its wish to present that basis from which all commentarial traditions grow, leaves many issues wide open to interpretation. Mipham, on the other hand, often goes much further, seeking to explain and provide clear solutions. We believe that this marked difference in method makes the two commentaries excellent companions. While Shenga's commentary maintains a unique closeness to both the root verses and their very first commentary—a feature that would be lost in any other format—Mipham invites us to follow him on a journey of exploration, taking up the issues set forth in the verses and offering his understanding of them in the light of Sthiramati's exposition. We hope that the synergy that we have felt between the root verses and the two forms of commentary might also be sensed in the translations. For those wishing to read the translations alongside the Tibetan originals, cross-referenced editions of the Tibetan texts are available for download at the website of the Dharmachakra Translation Committee (www.dharmachakra.net).

ACKNOWLEDGMENTS

The Ornament of the Great Vehicle Sūtras forms part of the Dharmachakra Translation Committee's larger project of translating "the thirteen great treatises" with their commentaries by Khenpo Shenga, Ju Mipham, and other such influential authors of the Indian and Tibetan Buddhist tradition. As such, Chökyi Nyima Rinpoche conceived and supervised the present work. While I prepared the initial version of the root text and Shenga's commentary, a team of translators—Cortland Dahl, Douglas Duckworth, James Gentry, Hillary Herdman, and Heidi Köppl—who shared the text between them, produced the translation of Mipham's commentary to the first ten chapters. Douglas Duckworth and Gillian Parish subsequently compiled and edited the ensuing translations. While Douglas translated Mipham's commentary on chapters 11 to 17, I prepared the final chapters, and Cortland and I then edited the entire work. Libby Hogg completed a final copy edit before the text was submitted to Michael Wakoff, our editor at Shambhala. Rafael Ortet of the Tsadra Foundation produced the visual representation of Mipham's outline that appears as an appendix to the translation.

We are all very grateful to Khenpo Jampa Dönden who taught the *Ornament of the Great Vehicle Sūtras* at the Rangjung Yeshe Institute in Kathmandu, Nepal, and who so graciously provided transmission for the texts and helped clarify many difficult points. We hope that these translations may serve as a circumstance for the flourishing of the form of engaged and comprehensive textual studies that traditionally takes place within monastic colleges. We likewise hope that such studies of the Buddhist literary heritage may find an increasing relevance within a diverse and expanding field of academic disciplines.

In preparing our translation, we have benefited much from the English version of both the verses and Vasubandhu's commentary, which are part of the Treasury of Buddhist Sciences series,[21] and we wish to express our gratitude to everyone involved in its production. Throughout the translation process, our work was supported by generous grants from the

Tsadra Foundation and the Fonds de Boer de l'Université de Lausanne. We are very grateful for the privilege of this support.

May whatever merit there may be in producing these texts serve to ensure the continuous presence of our source of refuge, Chökyi Nyima Rinpoche, and all others who with their lives give such meaningful form and expression to wisdom and compassion. May all beings find paths that lead from happiness to happiness, and may the world be resplendent with the light of wisdom.

On behalf of the team,
THOMAS H. DOCTOR
May 2013, while listening to the Dharma at Borubudur

MAITREYA'S ORNAMENT OF THE GREAT VEHICLE SŪTRAS

ELUCIDATED BY

Shenphen Nangwa

Annotation Commentary on the
Ornament of the Great Vehicle Sūtras

AND

Ju Mipham

A Feast of the Supreme Vehicle—
An Exposition of the Intended Meaning of the
Ornament of the Great Vehicle Sūtras

Namo Mañjuśrīkumārabhūtāya!

Peerless teacher, king of the Śākyas,
Regent, Ajitanātha, master of the ten grounds,
Noble Asaṅga, accepted by the Regent,
Supreme scholar Vasubandhu, born from Asaṅga's speech,
Glorious Sthiramati, Vasubandhu's supreme disciple,
Assemblies of noble ones, whose lineage succession stems from
    Sthiramati,
And all spiritual teachers who have directly transmitted the goodness
    of this path—
With reverence I pay homage to you all!

In undivided devotion for this feast of the Supreme Vehicle's Dharma
Thus elaborately laid out for all beings in this scripture of the Great
    Regent,
I shall here, with the wish to benefit others, deliver an exposition
That is a feast of the nectar of the Supreme Vehicle.

The great chariot Asaṅga received the *Ornament of the Great Vehicle Sūtras,* one of the five treatises of Maitreya, after attaining the meditative absorption of the stream of Dharma. He received this teaching directly from the mouth of the Regent, the invincible protector, in the Dharma palace of The Joyful Realm.

   Here this exalted scripture will be explained in a manner that is both lucid and easy to understand. The explanation will contain four sections: (1) the meaning of the title, (2) the translator's homage, (3) the meaning of the scripture, and (4) the concluding colophon.

1. The Title

In the Indian language: *Mahāyānasūtrālaṃkāra-nāma-kārikā*

In the Tibetan language: *The stanzas entitled Ornament of the Great Vehicle Sūtras.*[22]

To explain, the Great Vehicle is referred to as such because of seven features that distinguish it as great. This text adorns the Great Vehicle sūtras by elucidating their intent in terms of five rich subjects of the Unexcelled. For this reason, it is entitled the *Ornament of the Sūtras*. The word "stanzas" is used because the text is composed in verse.

2. Translator's Homage

The great translator Kawa Peltsek offered the following translator's homage when he began to render this scripture into Tibetan:

> I pay homage to all the buddhas and bodhisattvas!

3. The Scripture

Accounting for the meaning of the scripture will include an explanation of (1) the way the scripture was composed and (2) the character of the scripture thus composed, that is, the explanation of the treatise itself.

I
How the Scripture Was Composed

The first topic is taught in the following three stanzas:

> The one who knows the meaning reveals the meaning with immaculate speech and immaculate words.
> To liberate from misery, this arises from the compassion for suffering beings that is present in those who have that as their very nature.
> Belonging to the Dharma that teaches the Supreme Vehicle and intended for sentient beings who progress by means of this,
> It explains the five rich subjects of the Unexcelled. [1.1]

> Resembling shaped gold, a lotus in bloom,
> And an excellent meal enjoyed when stricken with hunger;
> Like receiving a letter with good news and an open treasure trove—
> Such is the Dharma, which when here explained engenders perfect joy. [1.2]

> When a body, replete with ornaments and naturally endowed with excellent qualities, is reflected in a mirror,
> Those who see it will experience total and supreme joy.
> Likewise, while the well-spoken words of the Dharma are always replete with excellent qualities,
> When their meaning is explained herein, the wise will experience supreme joy. [1.3]

Who is it that adorns? It is the protector Maitreya, **the one who unmistakenly knows the meaning** of the sūtras. What type of adornment is this? It is an adornment that **reveals the** profound **meaning.** What are the means of adornment? It is done **with immaculate speech** that has qualities, such as being "urbane," **and** with **immaculate words** and syllables that are connected with reasoning. Indeed, if the speech, words, and letters were not pure, the meaning could not be revealed. What purpose does this adornment serve? It serves **to liberate** all sentient beings **from misery.** What causes the adornment? **This arises from the compassion for suffering beings that is present in those** children of the victorious ones **who have that** compassion **as their very nature.** What is adorned, and for whose sake? This ornament can be classified as **belonging to the Dharma that teaches the Supreme Vehicle and** it is **intended for** the benefit of **sentient beings who progress by means of this** Great Vehicle. How many aspects does this ornament encompass? **It explains the five rich subjects,** as they are sound and reasonable, **of the Unexcelled** Vehicle.

The second stanza sets forth the nature of these five subjects, which are explained in such a way as to correlate with the five principles, the three natures, and the three persons. First, the five principles are name, reason, conception, suchness, and nonconceptual wakefulness.

Concerning name, it is established through scripture and reason that phenomena expressed with names do not truly exist in the way they are expressed. **Resembling** the form of **shaped gold** fashioned by an expert goldsmith, the teaching of this treatise clarifies this point.

Reason refers to dependently originating phenomena, as in the case of a seed and its sprout. All phenomena are to be understood and, in that regard, are similar to **a lotus in bloom.**

Conception refers to the mind and mental states of the three realms. When their nature is contemplated correctly, it is like **an excellent meal enjoyed when** one is **stricken with hunger.**

Suchness refers to the intrinsic nature, which is inconceivable to a mind with confined perception. This is **like receiving a letter with good news.**

Nonconceptual wakefulness refers to the wakefulness of the noble ones. It is one's own direct awareness of the thoroughly established, the realized meaning, **and** the essential nature of the factors that accord with enlightenment. In this way, it is like **an open treasure trove. Such is the Dharma, which when here explained engenders perfect joy.**

The five subjects also correlate with the three natures. That which is to be established is that the imputed nature does not exist as imputed. The dependent nature consists of the mind and the mental states, each of which is to be understood. This enables one to contemplate the way in which to accept and reject. The thoroughly established nature is inconceivable, and the character of the thoroughly established is realized as the object of one's own direct awareness [by means of] the factors of enlightenment.

When the five subjects are correlated with the three types of persons, that which is to be established for the inferior person is that the Great Vehicle is the Word of the Buddha. For those who have entered the Great Vehicle, the topics of this vehicle must be understood. The topics of the Great Vehicle should also be contemplated repeatedly, and the causal and resultant entities are inconceivable. Through practicing the path of the Great Vehicle properly, the character of the thoroughly established is realized as the object of one's own direct awareness and the factors of enlightenment.

One may wonder why the Dharma should be adorned, given that it naturally possesses excellent qualities. In order to cast aside such criticism, it is said that, for example, **when a body replete with ornaments and naturally endowed with excellent qualities is reflected in a mirror, those who see it will experience total and supreme joy. Likewise, while the well-spoken words of the Dharma** of the Great Vehicle **are always replete with excellent qualities, when their meaning is explained here in** this treatise, **the wise will experience supreme joy.**

The one who knows the meaning of the Great Vehicle sūtras reveals it to others with immaculate speech and immaculate words, in order to liberate all sentient beings from suffering. The cause for this revelation is compassion, which is his very nature; the teaching arises from the bodhisattva's great compassion for suffering beings.

The method that is taught belongs to the Dharma that explains the Supreme Vehicle. It is presented for those individuals who progress by means of this Supreme Vehicle, meaning the Saṅgha of the Great Vehicle, that is, those sentient beings who progress to the state of fruition by means of the path of the Great Vehicle. The teaching is presented as an elegant discourse, a rich combination of words and meanings imbued with the character of the Great Vehicle. As such, it reveals the five subjects of the Unexcelled Great Vehicle. This fivefold nature of the Great Vehicle Dharma can be compared with (1) earrings and other jewelry fashioned from gold by an expert goldsmith, (2) a lotus in full bloom, (3) a well-prepared meal, eaten when one is stricken by hunger, (4) receiving a letter with good news, and (5) an open treasure trove of various gems.

When the Dharma of the Great Vehicle is explained in this treatise, it evokes a supreme joy in the five rich subjects. That is to say, the treatise clarifies the intended meaning of the Great Vehicle sūtras by means of these five, and it is for this reason that it is called the *Ornament of the Sūtras*. Thoroughly identifying the five is a crucial point since they summarize the meaning of the whole treatise from beginning to end. As this is the case, I will explain them below.

In the present context, the commentary of the great being Sthiramati[23] explains that this treatise elucidates all of the vast and profound conduct of a bodhisattva. There are, he explains, three aspects that summarize the conduct of bodhisattvas: what they train in, how they train, and those who do the training. The first of these three, what the bodhisattva trains in, consists of seven topics: (1) one's own benefit, (2) the benefit of others, (3) reality, (4) power, (5) full maturation of the buddhas' qualities for oneself, (6) full maturation of sentient beings, and (7) unexcelled, perfect enlightenment.

How the bodhisattva trains is explained by six topics: (1) fostering the motivation of the Great Vehicle Dharma, (2) seeking out the Dharma,

(3) teaching the Dharma, (4) practicing the Dharma in accord with the Dharma, (5) adhering to authentic practical instructions and following the teachings, (6) embracing one's physical, verbal, and mental activities with skillful means.

Those who train are the bodhisattvas. Bodhisattvas can be categorized into ten types: (1) those who dwell with the potential, (2) those who have engaged it, (3) those of impure intention, (4) those of pure intention, (5) those of immature intention, (6) those of fully matured intention, (7) those of indefinite realization, (8) those of definite realization, (9) those with one birth remaining, and (10) those in their final existence. According to the scriptures, all of these bodhisattvas are referred to as "bodhisattvas," "great beings," "the wise," and so forth. This is the way in which Sthiramati presents the body of this treatise in accordance with the initial two stanzas.

Consistent with the seven inflections discussed in grammatical texts, the explanation offered in the present context is made in terms of agent, object, instrument, purpose, cause, attribute, and beneficiary. "Purpose" implies the purpose and objective with which something is done. It is thus associated with the fourth inflection and the dative case. In the treatises on linguistics, this is also explained as the "recipient." In other words, it states the purpose or the sake for which something is given. "Cause" relates to the ablative, while "attribute" refers to the sixth inflection and the genitive case. (Some grammar texts call this *hasti*, which denotes a hand or attribute, as in "Pūjadatta's hand.")

In the present context, however, the "beneficiary" does not relate to the fourth inflection. Rather, it refers to the people who have the potential for the Great Vehicle, and who in that sense serve as the supports for the Great Vehicle. Thus, the "beneficiary" is in terms of the seventh inflection and the locative, which some grammarians also refer to as *nimittasapta*,[24] or "the seventh mark."

Emphasizing the direct object, the great commentary explains this by raising the question of which agent adorns which essence, or Dharma. "The one who knows the meaning" is the agent here, while the Great Vehicle sūtras are the basis or essence that is adorned. How so? It is by eliciting knowledge of their meaning that this treatise adorns the Great Vehicle sutras. The direct object, the sūtras, are adorned by the treatise, in the sense that their meaning is revealed. The instrument through which this takes place is indicated by the phrase "with immaculate speech and immaculate words," while the purpose of this adornment can be found in the phrase "to liberate from misery." It is caused by "the compassion for suffering beings that is present in those who have that as their very nature."

What does the treatise belong to? It belongs "to the Dharma that teaches the Supreme Vehicle." This statement illustrates that this treatise and the words of the Great Vehicle relate to one another as part and whole. The person it is based upon is identified with the phrase "for sentient beings who progress by means of this," meaning that it is for the benefit of those who practice the Great Vehicle. It is based on their streams of being, just like birds sitting in a tree. Since what is taught in the great commentary may seem difficult to understand, I have paraphrased it in this short summary to clarify the main points.

To explain further, with an emphasis on the agent, the phrase "the knower of the meaning" refers to the one who knows and sees the intended meaning, as it is, of the entirety of the Great Vehicle's sūtras; the one who has gained correct awareness of this meaning, the invincible protector Maitreya, the regent and lord of the ten bodhisattva grounds. The object of his action, as indicated by the phrase "reveals the meaning," shows that, through the strength of the correct awareness of acumen, his composition reveals the meaning of the sūtras in their entirety. The instrument that brings this about is indicated by the phrase "with immaculate speech and immaculate words." Thus it takes place through pure, expressive speech, which is the correct awareness of Dharma, and through the languages of sentient beings and, hence, by means of correct awareness of definitive words. These are immaculate, in the sense of being without the stains of obscuration.

In terms of purpose, this treatise was composed for the sake of liberating all sentient beings from misery. The motivation, or cause, that prompted it is the great compassion for suffering sentient beings that is present in the Great Regent, the embodiment of insight and compassion. In this way, a sublime cause brought about the composition of this treatise. Among the categories of the Great and Lesser Vehicles, it belongs, or is related, to the Great Vehicle. This is referred to with the words "belonging to the Dharma that teaches the Supreme Vehicle." In terms of the type of people this is for, or those whose streams of being it is based upon, this treatise is for bodhisattvas, sentient beings "who progress by means of this" Supreme Vehicle.

In order to address immaculate speech, we must consider its eight qualities. (1) It is "urbane," as it belongs to the city of liberation and is widely accepted. (2) It is pleasantly resonant and melodiously captivating. (3) It is extremely clear, with excellent phrasing and diction. (4) It elicits comprehension. (5) It is deeply evocative. (6) It has great meaning that is pleasing to the ear, such that those with no previous background in the sublime Dharma are completely inspired by it. (7) It is free from inconsistencies, and therefore agreeable and adored. (8) It is boundless, such that even those who are learned in its extremely vast topics cannot fathom its extent. The first of these eight relates to the purpose of such speech, the following two to its essence, and the remaining five pertain to its application.

Immaculate words also have eight qualities. (1) They are correct words and letters, insofar as they are phrases, words, and letters that are connected in proper sequence. (2) Their meaning is connected with the path of reason, which refers to their being proven, or established. (3) They are consistent, in that the meaning is eloquently explained. (4) They are apt, meaning that these words and letters are clear. (5) They are rich, since they touch the heart. (6) They are fitting, insofar as these words are correctly transmitted to the minds of the audience. (7) They are appropriate, in the sense that they are meaningful words consistent with the Dharma and appropriate to the context. (8) They are an assembly of limbs of exertion, where "exertion" implies the process of gaining learning and achieving consistency, while "assembly of limbs" means that these words embody the authentic view, and so forth. This treatise teaches by means of a discourse that is endowed with these qualities.

What are the implications of the five metaphors that illustrate the nature of the five rich subjects of the Unexcelled? The five subjects are outlined by the great master Vasubandhu as follows: (1) that which is to be established, (2) that which is to be understood, (3) that which is to be contemplated, (4) the inconceivable, and (5) the character of the thoroughly established as it is realized through one's own direct awareness, the very essence of the factors that accord with enlightenment.

The masters have several interpretations of these concise statements. Sthiramati offers three presentations, which correlate them to the five principles, the three natures, and the three persons. To offer a brief explanation of this, the entirety of that which expresses the Great Vehicle is contained in the following five principles: (1) name, (2) reason, (3) conception, (4) suchness, and (5) nonconceptual wakefulness.

"Name" is explained as follows. Sentient beings conceive of all phenomena as if they existed objectively, as expressed by their names. Nevertheless, nothing exists as expressed by mere names. This is what is to be established. "Reason" refers to the reasons for the application of names. In other words, these are the appearances of the objective aspects of the dependent nature and are to be understood as dependent arisings that appear through the power of mind. "Conception" refers to the appearances of the subjective features of the primary mind and mental states, that is, the eight collections of consciousness. This is the actual dependent nature, which is contemplated through a process that determines its mode of being.

These three principles correlate sequentially with the first three metaphors. Suchness, moreover, is the thoroughly established nature, which is inconceivable in the absence of one's own direct awareness of it. Yet, directly realizing suchness on the first bodhisattva ground elicits joy like that of hearing the good news that enlightenment is sure to be attained. The factors that accord with enlightenment, and nonconceptual wakefulness in particular, correlate with the fifth metaphor.

The *Compendium on the Great Vehicle* explains:

> What is the thoroughly established nature? This is to be understood in terms of the four aspects of complete purity: (1) the complete purity of the nature of suchness, (2) the complete purity free from defilements, which is suchness that is free of all obscurations, (3) the complete purity of the path, meaning the factors of enlightenment, the aspect that brings forth the realiza-

tion of suchness, and (4) the complete purity of the focal points that brings forth the development of the path, which refers to the Dharma of the Great Vehicle.

In terms of the three natures, the imagined nature is what is to be established as nonexistent. The remaining four subjects are correlated as follows: that which is to be understood is the dependent nature in the form of the dependent arising of complete purity; that which is to be contemplated is the essence of the dependent nature; the inconceivable is the unchanging thoroughly established nature; and the factors that accord with enlightenment are the unmistaken thoroughly established nature.

In terms of the correlation with the three types of person, it is explained, for example, that the proof of the Great Vehicle's being the Word of the Buddha is taught first, for the sake of individuals who lack understanding, have doubts, or misunderstand. However, the correlation with the three types of person will not be further addressed here, for fear of the length of the discussion.

According to the master Jñānaśrī, it is not reasonable to correlate the meaning of what is to be established and so forth with name, reason, and the rest of the five principles. He explains that there are two correct approaches. In the former, the five subjects are correlated with the words of the opening verses. In the latter, the five are correlated with certain chapters, such as the chapter that establishes the Great Vehicle to be the Word of the Buddha. Jñānaśrī sees this latter approach as that of Vasubandhu. He proceeds to explain that there are three points to be established: (1) the Great Vehicle must be established as the Buddha's Word; (2) the act of going for refuge, taken as the domain of developing the enlightened mind, must be established as supreme; (3) the potential of the Great Vehicle is to be established as the perpetuating cause [of enlightenment]. Likewise, two points are to be understood: (1) cultivating the enlightened mind and (2) the practice of the twofold benefit. In terms of what is contemplated, of the profound and the vast reality, here it is the profound reality that is contemplated. The inconceivable has two aspects: power and full maturation. Finally, the thoroughly established is enlightenment. Jñānaśrī holds that all of this can be understood from the chapter that establishes the Great Vehicle to be the Word of the

Buddha, and also from the passage "like an open treasure trove." This is also how he makes his summary.

Next, he explains that the way one trains is taught in the chapters on motivation up to those on practical instructions. Tying this to the explanation just given, he sees the chapters from motivation up to and including practice as associated with the establishment of the Great Vehicle as the Word of the Buddha. Similarly, the topics that are to be understood are taught in the chapter on practical instructions, and the topics that are to be contemplated are explained in the chapters on the vast skillful means, the means of attraction, the transcendences, the immeasurables, worship, reliance on the spiritual teacher, and so forth, as well as in the chapter on the factors of enlightenment on the path. Finally, the inconceivable is taught in the chapter on the qualities, and the character of the realization of the thoroughly established is taught in the context of completion.

All of these statements are indeed the fine explanations of supreme scholars. However, in order to correlate these principles with the progression of the entire treatise, and for the sake of ease of comprehension, we may explain the issue in the following way. The Great Vehicle is to be established as the Word of the Buddha. As when gold is beaten and formed into jewelry, this establishment will free one from lack of understanding, misunderstanding, and whatever doubts one may harbor about the Great Vehicle's being the Word of Buddha. Thereby one will feel the joy of experiencing the Great Vehicle.

The factors that are to be understood are the unique features of the Great Vehicle. These are addressed in the chapters from refuge up to practice. The Listeners also go for refuge in the three supreme jewels, have the potential of the Lesser Vehicle, generate the mind that is set on a state of peace and happiness for their own benefit, and practice the path of the three trainings. Nevertheless, through understanding in particular how the Lesser Vehicle is surpassed by the Great Vehicle, one acquires an intense delight in the path of the Great Vehicle and so comes to experience the joy of one's mind turning toward the Great Vehicle, like a lotus in bloom.

Having understood the Great and Lesser Vehicles in this way, one enters the Great Vehicle. That which is to be contemplated at this point is the meaning of reality taught in the Great Vehicle, the magical powers belonging to Great Vehicle bodhisattvas, and the manner in which their faculties are fully matured. By contemplating these topics, one will gain certainty regarding the nature of reality and discover the bodhisattva's power to accomplish the twofold benefit, as well as the means for fully maturing the faculties that produce that power. Like eating a meal when stricken by hunger, such a person will experience the joy of attaining the various good qualities that come from understanding reality, accomplishing great power, and maturing one's faculties.

The inconceivable refers to enlightenment. Generally, it is not possible to conceive of the nature of reality as it is, in the absence of one's own direct awareness of it. Nevertheless, there is no contradiction in its being something that one can receive and reflect upon by means of conceptual abstractions. Likewise, there is nothing inconceivable that is superior to the inconceivability of the buddhas' activity, which is enumerated among the four inconceivables. However, through resolving the nature of this inconceivable enlightenment at this stage, one will know upon entering the path of the Great Vehicle that it can be achieved at some point, although not even a mere fraction of its qualities may at present be manifest. This can be likened to hearing or seeing good news in a letter. If one were to receive a letter from a king or another such person stating, "I will give you such and such a gift ...," one would feel joyful and confident that the present would arrive later, despite the fact that the gift would not be there immediately. In sum, enlightenment is the thoroughly established nature that is known and realized by one's own direct awareness. It is, therefore, inconceivable. All the qualities of the path are the causes for the accomplishment of this enlightenment. These are implied by the phrase "the essence of the factors that accord with enlightenment."

Thus, all the chapters that follow the chapter on enlightenment correlate with the metaphor of an open treasure trove. One might think that, since the metaphor of an open treasure trove refers explicitly to enlightenment, it is inappropriate to link this metaphor with the factors of enlightenment. However, this is perfectly fitting. The fully perfected fruition of the factors that accord with enlightenment on the path is enlightenment itself. Hence, enlightenment is what is ultimately to be shown by the metaphor of an open treasure trove. Nevertheless, inconceivable enlightenment is presented here in the context of coming to know that enlightenment through the process of receiving and reflecting on the teachings. Thus, it can be likened to hearing in a letter that you will be given a great chest filled with an infinite number of precious treasures. The powers and other qualities of the path of no more learning are indeed manifest for a buddha, like an open chest filled with every precious treasure. Although, for a person on the path of training, these qualities are not yet manifest, that person can still simply become aware that such qualities exist. Hence, while the nature of enlightenment, as it is, is inconceivable, there is still no contradiction in saying that the inconceivable is to be conceived of.

In this way, one aims for unsurpassable enlightenment, the attainment of which begins with motivation. While practicing the profound and vast path in its entirety, all the various qualities gradually manifest on specific grounds and paths, like various gems falling into one's hands. Likewise, the qualities of the grounds and paths of a bodhisattva develop more and more until one reaches the state of a buddha. At that time, the experience of these qualities is like having an open treasure trove right in front of one. Thus, the open treasure trove refers to the chapters from motivation through the treatment of the qualities of the fruition.

Some people think that since the Buddha's teachings are naturally replete with the qualities of perfect words and meanings, there is no purpose in newly adorning them with treatises. In response, it may be said that a person with a naturally excellent body bedecked with jewelry is already essentially, or naturally, replete with good qualities. Nevertheless, when a reflection of that person's ornamented body appears in a clear mirror, the sight of that body further adorned with beautiful jewelry will engender a rapturous joy in people's minds.

In this way, the Buddha's eloquent teachings are virtuous in the beginning, middle, and end and are replete with perfect words, meanings, and the four qualities of pure conduct. In this way, they are supremely exalted. This treatise gathers the vast meaning of all of the Buddha's various teachings—the Dharmas that are always naturally replete with boundless qualities. It excellently organizes them in a clear sequence, unerringly distinguishing each of the Victorious One's intended meanings by fully distinguishing the aspects of the profound that are otherwise difficult to realize. Consequently, intelligent and wise individuals can easily gain certainty in the meaning of the Victorious One's speech by studying this treatise, thereby coming to feel sublime joy. It is like a mirror that makes the qualities of the beautiful body that is reflected in it clear, and so this treatise is an ornament that elucidates the intention of the sūtras.

2. Explanation of the Treatise

This section has five parts, including explanations of (1) what is to be established, (2) what is to be understood, (3) what is to be contemplated, (4) the inconceivable, and (5) the essence of the factors that accord with enlightenment.

1. Establishing the Great Vehicle to be the Word of the Buddha

The first topic has two parts: (1) a general demonstration and (2) a specific explanation.

1. General Demonstration

The first topic is taught in the following three stanzas:

> Like a medicine with a foul odor,
> Yet of exquisite taste,
> It should be understood that the Dharma is twofold as well,
> For there is the meaning and the letters. [1.4]

> This Dharma is hard, vast, and profound.
> It is difficult to please, just like a king.
> Yet, similarly, if one succeeds in pleasing,
> The riches of supreme qualities will be granted. [1.5]

As with a jewel that is genuine and priceless,
Yet unacknowledged by those not acquainted,
So do the unwise relate to this Dharma.
For others it is different; they cherish it. [1.6]

This was the first chapter of the *Ornament of the Great Vehicle Sūtras*.

Three stanzas explain the benefits of venerating the Dharma. First, the metaphor of medicine shows how the obscurations are eliminated: **Like a medicine with a foul odor, yet of exquisite taste, thus it should be understood that the Dharma is twofold as well, for there is the** profound **meaning and the letters** that carry its intent.

The metaphor of the king explains how one takes possession of the qualities. **This Dharma** of the Great Vehicle **is hard** to practice, as it entails **vast** methods **and profound** knowledge. **It is difficult to please, just like a king. Yet, similarly, if one succeeds in pleasing** it, then, as when the king is pleased, **the riches of all supreme qualities will be granted,** both the mundane and the transcendent.

The metaphor of the jewel shows how the riches of the noble ones are enjoyed. **As with a jewel that is genuine and priceless, yet unacknowledged by those** who are **unacquainted** with jewels, **so do the unwise** who do not understand the way of the Dharma **relate to this Dharma. For others it is different; they cherish it** just like a skillful captain who knows a gemstone when he sees one.

The metaphors presented here are as follows: An excellent medicine can have a foul odor and thus be difficult to bear. Yet, when put on the tongue, this same medicine can have an exquisite taste, cure illnesses, and be extremely healthy for the body. Likewise, the Dharma of the Great Vehicle exists in two forms—meanings, and words composed of letters. To elaborate, in terms of mere words, in the Great Vehicle texts it is said that all phenomena are devoid of essential nature, that one must give away one's head and undergo other great austerities for three incalculable great eons, and that one must remain in cyclic existence. Hearing this, immature, small-minded beings who are inclined toward what is inferior are frightened and discard the Great Vehicle, just as one might throw away a delicious and powerful medicine due to its foul odor. Yet here the problem lies with the person, not with the Dharma of the Great Vehicle.

When properly ascertaining the meaning of this Great Vehicle Dharma through reasoning, one will see that, while all phenomena are empty of their own essence, the conventional principles are nevertheless thoroughly justified. The Great Vehicle does not teach that in terms of convention nothing exists. Rather, things do not exist in the way ordinary beings imagine them to be. The dependent nature exists conventionally, and the thoroughly established nature is the ultimate. It is not taught that things are nothing.

Moreover, regarding remaining in cyclic existence and undergoing austerities, one is able to accomplish these without hardship through special means and insight. Consequently, when one understands the meaning of the Dharma, one will become especially inspired by the Great Vehicle. Therefore, this shows that it is not right to abandon the Great Vehicle on the basis of clinging to mere words and without realizing their depth.

Furthermore, the path of the Great Vehicle involves undergoing vast hardships, gathering immeasurably vast accumulations, and becoming accomplished over a long duration. But these are good qualities of the Great Vehicle, not faults. The reasoning here is as follows. The Great Vehicle Dharma is extremely rare and extremely difficult for anyone other than the noble ones to practice. It is vast, in the sense that the various grounds, transcendences, and so forth, are immeasurable. It is also difficult to comprehend due to its profundity. In a similar way, it is difficult to please great kings through meager deeds. Yet if one pleases a king by successfully carrying out some great act, then one will be rewarded with great wealth and power. Likewise, it is difficult for an inferior person to accomplish the Great Vehicle, yet if one practices through a union of means and insight, then one will receive a wealth of supreme qualities—such as the ten powers, the four fearlessnesses—that will never disappear.

Moreover, even though the Dharma of the Great Vehicle is replete with supreme qualities, a person with inferior insight and inclinations will not understand this. Similarly, a gem of the finest variety may be of inestimable value, yet if it were to fall into the hands of an uncultured individual who is unfamiliar with jewels, this person would not know how to see its real character. Thus, cowherds and other lowly people would not derive any pleasure from it. They may even consider such a gem useless and discard it. Likewise, unwise people do not delight in this Dharma, nor do they consider it to be marvelous. Yet on the other hand, those who are familiar with gems will take delight in a supreme jewel, just as someone who is wise and open minded will cherish and pursue this Great Vehicle.

This concludes the explanation of the first chapter of the *Ornament of the Great Vehicle Sūtras*.

2
Establishing the Teachings of the Great Vehicle

2. Specific Explanation

This section will involve (1) a demonstration of the types of reasoning that overturn misconceptions and (2) instructions on giving up mistaken ideas about the Great Vehicle.

1. Overturning Misconceptions

This topic is taught in the following seven stanzas:

> It was not previously prophesied, and they arose together.
> It is not within the domain yet is established.
> It exists, and if not, that would not exist.
> It is the remedy and means something else—these are the reasons. [II.1]

> The eyes of the buddhas perceive directly,
> They protect the teachings,
> Their wakefulness is unimpeded by time.
> Hence, they could not be indifferent. [II.2]

> It is incomplete, in conflict, and not the means.
> Given that it does not teach in this way
> The Vehicle of the Listeners
> Is not what is known as "the Great Vehicle Dharma." [II.3]

There is conflict in terms of
Intent and the teaching,
Practice, support, and time.
Hence, the Lesser Vehicle is utterly inferior. [11.4]

It applies to its own sūtras,
And appears in its own Vinaya.
As it is profound and vast,
It does not conflict with the intrinsic nature. [11.5]

Logic is dependent, uncertain,
Incomprehensive, relative, and tiresome.
It is held to be reliable by the childish,
And this is, therefore, not within the domain. [11.6]

Because of its vastness and profundity,
Maturation and nonconceptuality,
Its teaching is twofold.
Therefore, it is the means for the unexcelled. [11.7]

Some have gone astray, stating that since this Great Vehicle is not even the Word of the Buddha, it could not possess such qualities. For such individuals, it must be established that the Great Vehicle is indeed the Word of the Buddha. For this reason, the following explanation is offered: If the teaching of the Great Vehicle were an obstacle to the Dharma that arose at a later point in time, then why is it the case that **it was not previously prophesied** by the Buddha that such an obstacle would occur? Similarly, **they,** the Great Vehicle and the Listeners' Vehicle, **arose together.** How then can one be certain that this is not the Word of the Buddha? **It,** meaning this profound and vast Dharma, **is not within the domain** of logicians.

One might then think that this is the teaching of some buddha other than the blessed Buddha Śākyamuni. **Yet if this is the case, it is** thereby indeed **established** as the Word of a buddha. If **it,** that is, the Great Vehicle, **exists,** then it follows that this is it.

And if the Great Vehicle does **not** exist, then **that,** meaning the Listeners' Vehicle, **would not exist** either, for no buddhas would appear without a vehicle for buddhahood.

Furthermore, **it,** the nonconceptual wakefulness that arises when practicing the Great Vehicle, **is** the **remedy** for the afflictions, **and** its teaching, such as that on nonarising, **means something else.** These are the reasons that invalidate the notion that the Great Vehicle is not the Word of the Buddha.

Some might believe that the Buddha was simply not particularly concerned [about the teaching of the Great Vehicle] and that this is why he made no prophecies about it. In response, it is explained that **the eyes of the buddhas perceive directly,** and in this way their wakefulness functions effortlessly. Moreover, **they,** the buddhas, **protect the teachings** and **their wakefulness is unimpeded by time. Hence, they could not be** resting **indifferent**ly.

Others may think that the Vehicle of the Listeners is itself the Great Vehicle, and that therefore great enlightenment can be achieved only through that vehicle. In response, it is explained that, for the listeners, **it,** meaning their vehicle, **is incomplete** in terms of the means to benefit others because the methods taught therein are merely aimed at disenchantment, freedom from attachment, and individual liberation. Practicing a path toward a personal transcendence of suffering **is in conflict** with the accomplishment of complete enlightenment, **and,** moreover, the Vehicle of the Listeners is **not the means** for accomplishing great enlightenment, just as one cannot tap milk from a horn. It is the Great Vehicle that explains the training of a bodhisattva. Therefore, **given that it does not teach in this way, the Vehicle of the Listeners is not what is known as "the Great Vehicle Dharma."**

One may wonder, "Why should there be such a strong conflict between the Vehicle of the Listeners and the Great Vehicle?" **There is conflict in terms of intent,** insofar as listeners desire transcendence of suffering only for themselves **and the teachings** that are presented for precisely that purpose. There is also a conflict in terms of **practice,** which for listeners involves pursuing transcendence of suffering. There is conflict in terms of the **support** of the accumulations of merit and wakefulness, in that for listeners this support is minor, **and** there is conflict in terms of the short duration of **time** [that is devoted to practice in this vehicle]. **Hence, the Lesser Vehicle is utterly inferior.**

Some may argue that since the defining character of the Word of the Buddha is that it applies to Sūtra, appears in the Vinaya, and does not conflict with the intrinsic nature, the Great Vehicle does not meet these criteria because it teaches that all phenomena are devoid of essence. In response, it is explained that the Great Vehicle teaches the training of the enlightened mind and that **it** therefore **applies to its own sūtras. And likewise, it appears in its own Vinaya** because the afflictions of the bodhisattvas are thoughts, and those thoughts are pacified by the Great Vehicle. Finally, **as it is profound** in insight **and vast** in method, **it does not conflict with the intrinsic nature.**

For the following reasons, the Great Vehicle is not within the domain of **logic**ians. Logicians do not themselves see the profound reality. The logician **is**, therefore, slightly **dependent** on the testimony of others. Logic is **uncertain** because its conclusions change over time. It is **incomprehensive,** insofar as it is not concerned with all topics of knowledge. Its perspective is limited to the **relative truth and,** as the logician's confidence is exhausted, it is also **tiresome.** With all these faults, **it is held to be reliable by the childish, and this,** the Great Vehicle, **is, therefore, not within the domain** of logicians.

The Vehicle of the Listeners does not provide the means for accomplishing buddhahood and cannot, therefore, lead to this result, even after a long time. How, then, does the Great Vehicle do this? It is able to do so **because of its vastness** in revealing the superknowledges and other powers **and** because of the **profundity** of the view it teaches. With respect to the **maturation** of sentient beings **and** its nature of **nonconceptuality, its teaching is twofold. Therefore, it is the means for the unexcelled** wakefulness.

Listeners view the three scriptural collections of the Listeners, but not the Great Vehicle, as the Word of the Buddha. They believe that the Great Vehicle was concocted by extremists and logicians after the Buddha's passing as a demonic ploy to harm the doctrine. The Buddha himself taught that it is necessary to distinguish between what is and what is not the Word of the Buddha by distinguishing between dark teachings and great teachings. On this point, he taught:

> That which applies to the Sūtras, which appears in the Vinaya, and which does not contradict the nature of the Abhidharma is the great teaching and thus the Word of the Buddha. Its opposite is dark teachings, the doctrines of demons and extremists.

Given this statement, listeners believe that the Great Vehicle's explanation of the phenomena that comprise the aggregates, elements, and sense sources as being devoid of essence is inconsistent with the explanation in the listeners' sūtras that the aggregates and elements exist.

In the listeners' Vinaya, it is taught that the one who propounds the nonexistence of the Buddha, Dharma, and Saṅgha will incur a downfall. Since these are explained in the Great Vehicle to be nonexistent, its teaching is one that does not appear in the Vinaya.

In the listeners' scriptures, it is explained that dependent origination—which is subject to arising and ceasing—evolves as cyclic existence, and that the reversal of this process brings the transcendence of suffering. In the Great Vehicle, it is explained that all phenomena neither arise nor cease. Moreover, the listeners' texts explain that the transcendence of suffering is achieved upon abandoning the objects, or entities, that are to be abandoned by means of the paths of seeing and cultivation. In the Great Vehicle, it is explained that the objects to be abandoned and the means for abandoning them are devoid of essence, and that all phenomena are the transcendence of suffering by their very nature. Listeners believe that since statements such as these contradict the nature of the Abhidharma, they cannot be the Word of the Buddha.

Listeners believe that their own vehicle, when accomplished by those of inferior faculties for their own benefit, brings about the fruition of a listener. They assert that the same vehicle, when it is practiced for a hundred eons by middling beings, will lead to the fruition of a rhinoceros-like, self-realized buddha. Likewise, they also hold that it is their very vehicle that, when cultivated for three incalculable great eons by superior individuals who can withstand the suffering of cyclic existence, brings about the attainment of a buddha. Thus, they believe that there is no Great Vehicle apart from the Listeners' Vehicle.

Eight ways of reasoning are given in response to these objections:

(1) If the Great Vehicle were not the Word of the Buddha, and were instead something that harms the doctrine, it would have been reasonable for the Buddha to have prophesied it in the past, mentioning that such a thing would occur in the future. Yet he made no such prophecy.

(2) The Great and Lesser Vehicles arose together, while the Buddha was in this world. The claim that the Great Vehicle came later is not definitive.

(3) Since a profound and vast Dharma like this, which teaches the grounds, transcendences, emptiness, and so forth, is not accessible to logicians and extremists, they could not have fabricated it. Even if the grounds, transcendences, and so forth, had been taught by another buddha who had realized them for himself, exactly as they are, then these would still indeed be the Words of a Buddha.

(4) It is widely known that there were three vehicles when the Blessed One, the King of the Śākyas, taught the Dharma to the listeners. This is undisputed. The Buddha himself was the teacher of all three vehicles; he is established as the omniscient teacher of the paths of the three potentials. Therefore, when the treatise says, "It exists, and if not, that would not exist . . . ," this implies that if the term "Great Vehicle" refers to a vehicle that is distinct from that of the Listeners, then by that token the Listeners' Vehicle must exist as well. The existence will thus have been proven of a Listeners' Vehicle, in which one seeks peace for one's own benefit, without relying on the path of the Great Vehicle in order to become a buddha.

(5) If a Great Vehicle that is distinct from the Listeners' Vehicle did not exist, however, then there would likewise be no Listeners' Vehicle. This is also implied by the third line of the first stanza. If there were only a single vehicle, there could not be both Great and Lesser Vehicles. Also, since there would be no such thing as a distinct path that leads to the accomplishment of omniscient buddhahood, nobody could become a

buddha. Therefore, it would be impossible for there even to be a buddha who could teach the Listeners' Vehicle. For there still to be buddhas, it would have to be the case that listeners could also be buddhas, but this is impossible. Consequently, the Listeners' Vehicle would not exist either.

(6) When there is a Great Vehicle, then it is reasonable for the Buddha to teach it when he appears in the world to disciples who have the Great Vehicle potential. This follows because he is omniscient and has the compassion to accept the three kinds of disciples. Therefore, since it is reasonable that the Blessed One himself taught the Great Vehicle, there must be a Great Vehicle. It does indeed exist. Moreover, no Great Vehicle can be perceived other than the Dharma of the unerring teaching of the transcendences, emptiness, and so forth. Therefore, the Great Vehicle is the Word of the Buddha and not the concoction of logicians.

(7) The Great Vehicle Dharma is the remedy for the two obscurations. If it did not exist, then no matter how habituated one might become to the mere realization of the lack of a personal self—that is, the doctrine taught in the Listeners' Vehicle—one would still not be rid of cognitive obscurations. Consequently, there would be no path for attaining omniscient buddhahood.

(8) The teaching that there is no Buddha, no path, no fruition, no arising, no cessation, and so forth, is not a literal negation that applies even to conventional existence. These words have another meaning or intent. For this reason, the Great Vehicle does not contradict the intrinsic nature.

It may seem unclear whether or not the Great Vehicle is a false doctrine when only the fact that the Buddha did not give any prophecy about it is considered. Nevertheless, since buddhas have no attachment or obstruction in relation to all objects of knowledge, they possess the eye of wakefulness that directly perceives all phenomena. Thus it would be impossible for a buddha not to know about such an occurrence. Moreover, buddhas possess unflagging compassion that protects the teachings for the benefit of sentient beings. So, upon seeing that a teaching will come that is harmful to the Dharma, they could not indifferently put this knowledge aside without prophesying such an event. Finally, the wisdom vision of the buddhas is unimpeded and active throughout all three times. For the above three reasons, they could not be indifferent and not foretell the arrival of a teaching that would harm the Dharma.

Furthermore, it is not possible to become a buddha by familiarizing oneself, even for a long time, with the Listeners' Vehicle alone. The path of the Great Vehicle accomplishes the twofold benefit of self and other. In the Listeners' path, however, the activity of benefiting others is incomplete. Frightened by the prospect of remaining in cyclic existence, one develops revulsion and nonattachment in the pursuit of peace; this conflicts with the practice of altruism. Moreover, the means for attaining unsurpassable enlightenment is the wakefulness that realizes the twofold selflessness, along with the great compassion that wishes to free all sentient beings from suffering. Given that these two are the primary means to attain unsurpassable enlightenment, entering the Listeners' Vehicle would be insufficient for that attainment because these means are not taught in that vehicle.

Moreover, the Vehicle of the Listeners is not referred to as the "Great Vehicle" because it is in conflict with the Great Vehicle. There are five points of conflict. (1) The intent of the Vehicle of the Listeners is one of self-concern. Consistent with that intention, (2) its path is taught for the sake of achieving merely one's own personal peace. (3) Its practice involves striving on such a path, and (4) it provides an inferior support because there is no engagement in the two vast accumulations. Finally, (5) the perfect fruition of this vehicle is attained in the short span of three lifetimes. Hence, since the Listeners' Vehicle is inferior to the Great Vehicle in terms of its intent and the rest of these five ways, it is a path that is by nature simply inferior to the Great Vehicle in all regards. How could it be the Great Vehicle?

The criticism that the Great Vehicle does not apply to Sūtra and so forth is senseless. The fact that it does not accord with some of the listeners' sūtras does not prove that the Great Vehicle is not the Word of the Buddha. The sūtras of the listeners' schools are likewise at odds with one another. Thus, if the objection is that the Great Vehicle does not accord with those sūtras that one has accepted, the fault is to be located within one's own intellect, not in the Great Vehicle Dharma. It is through not understanding the profound intended meaning of one's own sūtras that one could maintain that such a conflict exists. The Buddha's earlier and later teachings are not contradictory in meaning.

The three jewels and the phenomena of the aggregates, elements, and sense sources do exist, as mere constructions, or as what is conventionally existent, in the perception of the immature. This is accepted in the Great Vehicle as well. However, those who insist that these phenomena are truly established and undeceiving in every way are unable to realize that all such things are ultimately devoid of their own essence. Therefore, the Buddha taught about things that arise and cease, thorough affliction and complete purification, objects to be abandoned and their remedies, and so forth, but he did so from the perspective of the relative, conventional truth. Even when he did not teach that phenomena are devoid of essence, he did not teach that things are not empty, not devoid of essence, either. Moreover, in the Listeners' Vehicle, he did indeed teach that the five aggregates are as empty and insubstantial as an illusion, stating "forms are like bursting bubbles..." and so forth.

Therefore, in terms of the Great Vehicle itself, which is much more profound and vast than the Listeners' Vehicle, there are scriptural collections of Sūtra, Vinaya, and Abhidharma that teach the Dharma of the three special trainings. Thus, the Great Vehicle applies to its own sūtras. Likewise, it appears in the Great Vehicle's own Vinaya for taming the afflictive factors, and since it unerringly teaches the meaning of the profound and the vast, it does not conflict with the intrinsic nature as taught in the Great Vehicle's Abhidharma.

It might be thought that the earlier statement "it is not within the domain of logic" is inconclusive because clever logicians can produce anything. Yet this is not the case. Logic exclusively analyzes the domain of limited perception, and "logician" refers here to someone who is unable to access the profound meanings that are beyond the range of limited perception. Such logicians rely on the word of others, take evidence of the sort that is perceptible to themselves as reasons, and so forth. They engage merely in conceptual analysis and are uncertain as to the full extent of knowledge, reflecting only upon a limited scope of meaning, proportionate to how much their own intellects can handle. Thus, without encompassing all that there is, meaning all the objects of knowledge, nor understanding the meaning of profound emptiness as it is, their domain is the relative, which is merely what can be understood with the faculties and mind of a stream of being with limited perception. As they attempt to comprehend the profound and vast points of meaning, the confidence of the logicians is exhausted, which is why logic is tiresome and fails to deliver understanding. Logicians are believed to be reliable by childish, ordinary beings. The Great Vehicle, which teaches issues that are extremely profound, hard to realize, and limitlessly vast, is therefore not within the domain of logic.

The Dharma explained by the Buddha embodies the wakefulness of omniscience, and thus transcends all the characteristics of logic described above, such as dependence on others and so forth. In this sense, it is inconceivable. Therefore, it would be impossible for such a teaching to come from the doctrine of a logician or an extremist. The topics that are explained in the Great Vehicle—the paths, transcendences, emptiness, and so forth—have never been seen before within their texts, nor is it possible that they ever will.

It might be argued that if the means required to become a buddha are not taught in the Listeners' Vehicle, they could not be taught in the Great Vehicle either. This argument is addressed in stanza seven. The Great Vehicle teaches the vast Dharma, namely, all things in their multiplicity. This includes the paths, transcendences, and so on. The Great Vehicle also teaches profound emptiness, things as they are. Therefore, the Great Vehicle is both vast and profound. It is vast in that one's stream of being comes to full maturation based on the accumulation of vast merit, and it is profound in that nonconceptual wakefulness manifests through the force of realizing profound emptiness. Unsurpassable enlightenment is attained in this way.

Listeners pursue the pacification of the suffering of cyclic existence for their own benefit. Their understanding is limited to the lack of a personal self. In terms of the wakefulness that realizes things as they are, this understanding is, when compared to the realization of the Great Vehicle, as small as the space inside a mustard seed that has been hollowed out by a bug. In terms of the realization of things in their multiplicity, listeners can, through a preconceived procedure, understand entities that are not cut off from them in terms of distance, time, and features. Even though they do not understand the full scope of the sublime Dharma, from the meaning of just a single stanza of the heart of dependent arising, they can realize selflessness and attain the fruition.

As vast as space, the profound wakefulness of the Great Vehicle is, on the other hand, the nonconceptual transcendent wakefulness that encompasses all objects of knowledge. This is the subject that engages the five fields of knowledge together with the knowledge of the inner meaning, comprising the vast, innumerable teachings of the three vehicles. Likewise, the Great Vehicle's accumulation of merit is as boundless as the water of the ocean, whereas the listeners' accumulation of merit is as meager as the water in a cow's hoof print.

2. Giving Up Misconceptions about the Great Vehicle

This section is taught in the following eight stanzas:

> The fear of wandering beings is unjustified and causes agony
> Because they amass vast heaps of wrongdoing for a long time.
> Lacking the potential, keeping unwholesome company, not having gathered virtue in the past, and not training the mind,
> One is frightened by this Dharma, and so falls short of what is immensely meaningful. [11.8]

> There is no Great Vehicle other than this anywhere; it is extremely profound and in accord.
> It teaches a diversity, and it teaches consistently using numerous means.
> Different from the literal meaning taught, the intent of the Blessed One is extremely profound.
> The wise who examine it properly are not frightened by this Dharma. [11.9]

> Here one begins by receiving teaching, and, based on that, one directs the mind.
> By properly directing the mind, there will be wakefulness and the object, the true nature.

With that comes the attainment of the qualities, and thereby
     wisdom will fully develop.
This is one's own direct awareness. How can one be certain
     when lacking this? [11.10]

"I do not understand." "The Buddha does not know the
     profound."
"Why is the profound not the domain of logic?"
"Why should those who know the profound meaning be
     liberated?"
These are not grounds for fear. [11.11]

If those inspired by the inferior, whose constitutions are
     extremely inferior,
And who are surrounded by inferior company,
Have no interest in this well-spoken Dharma of the profound
     and the vast,
It will thereby have been established. [11.12]

Those who achieve understanding through receiving teaching,
Yet completely disregard reception and
Ignore the boundless diversity, will remain ignorant of it.
How could they be certain? [11.13]

Taking the meaning to be exactly what is literally stated,
One becomes arrogant and intelligence deteriorates.
As even the excellent discourses are rejected,
One will come to ruin with obscurations due to harboring
     anger toward the Dharma. [11.14]

The flaw of mind is toxic by nature.
Inappropriate even when directed at an unfavorable form,
It is obviously so when directed at the Dharma one doubts.
Therefore, being neutral is preferable, for then there is no
     fault. [11.15]

This was the second chapter of the *Ornament of the Great Vehicle Sūtras,* the chapter on establishing the Great Vehicle.

The Great Vehicle is not to be feared. The next stanza explains what problems occur if one does fear it and what causes such fear. **The fear of wandering beings is unjustified and causes agony** in the lower realms **because they amass great heaps of wrongdoing** and experience pain **for a long time** as a result. There are four factors that cause such fear: **lacking the potential, keeping unwholesome company, not having gathered virtue in the past, and not training the mind** in the Great Vehicle. Due to these factors, **one becomes frightened by this Dharma, and so falls short of what is immensely meaningful,** the accumulation of enlightenment.

If it is accepted that there is a Great Vehicle, then **there is no Great Vehicle other than this,** which is taught in scriptures such as the Mother. If it is held that the Listeners' Vehicle is itself the Great Vehicle, then it follows that there would not be any listeners or self-realized Buddhas **anywhere,** for they would all be buddhas. **This is extremely profound,** for it is the path of omniscient wakefulness, **and** the Great Vehicle is also **in accord** with the Lesser Vehicle with respect to the time it was taught, since both were taught when the Buddha was in this world. **It teaches** not only emptiness, but **a diversity** of paths of accumulation. **And,** nevertheless, **it teaches** emptiness **consistently using** the **numerous means** that are set forth in all the different sūtras. **Different from the literal meaning taught,** such as the teaching that all phenomena lack any essential nature, **the intent of the Blessed One is extremely profound.** Hence, there is no reason to fear the Great Vehicle, feeling that one cannot understand it. **The wise who examine it properly are not frightened by this Dharma.**

Here one begins by receiving the **teaching** of the Great Vehicle in depth **and, based on that, one directs the mind** properly. By properly directing the mind, there **will be** subjective **wakefulness,** which is the view that transcends the world, **and the object** of that wakefulness, which is **the true nature** of reality. **With that comes**

the attainment of the qualities of its fruition, **and thereby the wisdom** of complete liberation **will fully develop. This** wisdom **is one's own direct awareness. How can one be certain that the Great Vehicle is not the Word of the Buddha, when lacking this?**

The next verses explain that the four factors that cause fear are, indeed, not grounds for fearing the Great Vehicle: These four are the following thoughts: (1) "**I do not understand this.**" (2) "If even **the Buddha does not understand the profound**, then why is it taught?" (3) "**Why is the profound not the domain of logic?**" And (4) "**Why should only those who know the profound meaning be liberated**, and not logicians?" These four notions **are not grounds for fear.**

Next it is explained how lack of interest itself serves to prove that the Great Vehicle is the Buddha's word: **If those who are inspired by the inferior** path, thinking that it is supreme, **whose constitutions** (that is, the elements of virtue that suffuse the all-ground consciousness) **are extremely inferior, and who are** completely **surrounded by,** and attracted to, **inferior company, have no interest in this,** the Great Vehicle's **well-spoken Dharma of the profound and the vast,** then **it will, thereby, have been established** to be supreme.

The following verses explain that rejecting the Great Vehicle Sūtras without having received them properly is not reasonable: **Those who achieve understanding** of the meaning of the Lesser Vehicle **through** merely **receiving, yet completely disregard** the process of **reception** of the sūtras of the Great Vehicle **and ignore the boundless diversity** of sūtras to be received, **will remain ignorant of it.** How could they be certain that the Great Vehicle is not the Word of the Buddha?

Moreover, teachings must be received in a proper way, for there are faults in not doing so. **Taking the** intended **meaning to be exactly what is literally stated, one becomes arrogant,** thinking of oneself as supreme, **and** since one does not seek the Dharma with the guidance of wise individuals, the eye of one's **intelligence deteriorates.** As, in this process, **even the excellent discourses** of the Buddha Vehicle **are rejected, one will come to ruin** in the lower realms, **with** accumulated **obscurations** that are **due to harboring anger toward the** profound Dharma.

Even if one does not know its nonliteral meaning, it is not reasonable to harbor anger toward the Dharma. On this topic, it is explained that **the flaw of mind,** meaning anger, **is toxic** because it is negative **by nature.** Anger is **inappropriate even when** it is **directed at an unfavorable form** that brings harm. Therefore, **it is obviously so when directed at the Dharma one doubts. Therefore, being neutral is preferable, for then there is no fault.**

Inferior beings have an unjustified fear of the Great Vehicle, which brings them mental anguish and causes them to hate the Dharma. Consequently, they end up amassing vast heaps of wrongdoing, and in the future they will agonize for a long time in the miseries of the hells.

What causes someone to reject the Great Vehicle out of fear in this way? There are four causes: a lack of the Great Vehicle potential; the conditions associated with being influenced by the unwholesome company of people who are hostile to the Great Vehicle; being incapable of interest due to not having gathered virtue in the past; and not training the mind in the profound meaning during one's present lifetime. By disrespecting the Great Vehicle Dharma when encountering it, one falls short of what is immensely meaningful. Therefore, the instruction is to understand these points by all possible means, and thereby guard oneself from these flaws with a vigilant mind.

There is no other vehicle anywhere, at any time, that is superior to the Great Vehicle. This is because its intent is extremely profound and in accord with the mental inclinations of disciples. Alternatively, it can be said to be in accord with all aspects of knowledge.[25] The Great Vehicle teaches a diversity of aspects of the vast Dharma—such as the paths, transcendences, factors of enlightenment, aggregates, elements, sense sources, the correct and the incorrect, and so forth. Its many sūtras consistently teach emptiness and every other permutation of the doctrine with a wealth of words and meanings. Moreover, most of what it teaches through intention and concealed intention is not to be taken literally.

The intent of the Blessed Buddha, therefore, is extremely profound. The learned who have properly examined it are not frightened by this

Great Vehicle Dharma. Instead, they see it to be wondrous and worthy of respect. Hence, the instruction here is that the Great Vehicle is to be examined and not discarded without scrutiny.

It is also possible that, despite having examined it, one may not gain certainty. This happens if one fails to engender even an intelligence that approximates to actual knowledge, not to mention the actual knowledge that comes about through one's own direct awareness. In the context of engaging the Dharma as discussed here, one begins by receiving it. Based on that, one brings to mind the meaning of what one has received. Without having received the teaching of a given topic, it is impossible to contemplate it, or to bring it to mind. Through properly directing the mind, however, the wakefulness of acceptance arises on the grounds of inspired conduct and takes the true meaning as its object. Through that comes the attainment of the noble qualities of the first ground. This, in turn, causes wisdom, or the wakefulness of the ten grounds, to develop fully. Yet only one's own direct awareness realizes the profound, authentic meaning; it is never realized by an intellect with limited perception. Hence, how could the logical intellect deliver certainty in the absence of such direct awareness? Similarly, even if one has ears and the rest of one's senses intact, without eyes one would still not see any forms.

Therefore, even though one may not comprehend the meaning of the Great Vehicle, it is not reasonable to reject it. It is inappropriate to think that since one does not understand it, it must be an inauthentic doctrine. It is because one has not gathered the accumulations that one lacks the fortune to understand the profound meaning, as when a blind person cannot see the sun despite its presence.

It would also be unreasonable to think that since even the Buddha does not know the profound, it lies outside the range of our intellects. While the authentic meaning is obscured from our view, the Buddha has wakefulness free of all obscurations. How could the Buddha not know what we do not understand? The subtle forms that cannot be seen by someone with an eye disease can, in the same way, be seen by those with divine sight.

It should not be thought that the Great Vehicle, though profound, could also be within the domain of logic, for if they had not surpassed mere logical cognition, how would the buddhas achieve profound, manifest enlightenment?

One may then wonder why beings are liberated who know of the profound meaning, which neither arises nor ceases, whereas logicians who examine by means of direct perception and inference are not? Such thoughts are not grounds for fearing the Great Vehicle. If one could be liberated by a thorough analysis of entities using direct perception and inference alone, then we should expect all sentient beings to be already liberated. That, however, is not the case. The notion that one will be bound by strong fixation to entities and liberated by the understanding that entities are devoid of intrinsic nature is indeed reasonable. In light of this, childlike logicians are complete fools when they believe their own intellects to be reliable means of cognition, abandoning as they do so the profound meaning of the Dharma as seen by the great noble ones, for in this way they take their own unreliable intellects as proof and disavow what is reliable cognition. They can be likened to a frog in a well, or to a blind person arguing with someone who can see.

Thus, there are three factors that establish this Dharma, which unmistakably explains the profound and vast meaning, to be the supreme Dharma. It can be established as such if it fails to attract (1) in terms of intention, the interest of those inspired by what is inferior; (2) in terms of cause, those with an extremely inferior constitution or potential; and (3) in terms of condition, those who are completely surrounded by inferior companions who hate the Great Vehicle. Since it is not the domain of the inferior, the extraordinary Dharma is understood by the wise.

For those who have received teaching, and are thereby intellectually capable of performing minor analyses concerning what is reasonable and unreasonable, it is unreasonable to forsake investigation into the profound meaning of what one has yet to understand. In other words, one should not disregard the Great Vehicle without investigating it beyond what one has already studied. Why would one leave the boundless diversity of the Great Vehicle's intended meanings unknown? Indeed, how could one possibly be certain about whether or not it is reasonable, or whether or not it is the Dharma, while still remaining ignorant? Without properly knowing its meaning, one will not be able to ascertain whether it is to be accepted or rejected.

One may erroneously take the meaning of all statements taught in sūtras (such as there being no form, no sound, and so forth) to be exactly what is stated literally without understanding their intent. Believing that one has fully understood or comprehended them, one then becomes arrogant and thinks, "I know what those words mean." Yet because one does not correctly understand their meaning, one's intelligence deteriorates. If one then rejects other excellent discourses as well, one will be ruined by amassing severe obscurations out of hatred for the profound Dharma. The reason for this is that the flaw of mind, hatred, is toxic by nature; it is negative by its very essence. Unlike actions of body and speech, it cannot be altered by motivation or other factors. For this reason, it is even inappropriate to harbor hatred toward something unpleasant, a harmful circumstance, or toward a disagreeable physical thing, such as a half-charred piece of wood. In the listeners' scripture entitled the *Saw-Like Sūtra*,[26] it is taught:

> Monks, if it is inappropriate to harbor anger in one's mind even toward a charred piece of wood, what need is there to mention that it is inappropriate to be angry at a body endowed with a mind?

Likewise, it is obviously unsuitable to harbor anger toward a doctrine about which one is doubtful, without having determined whether or not it is the authentic Dharma. For the Blessed One taught that those who abandon the authentic Dharma of the Great Vehicle will experience the utterly unbearable sufferings of the hell of ultimate torment, repeatedly enduring these sufferings for eons, as numerous worlds form and dissolve. Therefore, for those who want the best for themselves, it is preferable to remain neutral toward any doctrine in which one has neither experience nor interest, avoiding the disparagements of anger and disrespect. Thereby, such problems will not arise.

This concludes the explanation of establishing the Great Vehicle, the second chapter of the *Ornament of the Great Vehicle Sūtras*.

Having established the Great Vehicle to be the Buddha's word in this way, what follows is that which is to be understood—the distinction between the Great and Lesser Vehicles. There are many ways that this topic can be divided. Nevertheless, the distinction is explained in four chapters, from the chapter on going for refuge through the chapter on practice. The reason is that we here find an explanation that covers the distinctive aspirations and applications, including the causal potential and the initial entryway of the path, which is going for refuge.

2. What Is to Be Understood

This section covers: (1) going for refuge, (2) potential, (3) developing the mind, and (4) practice.

3
Going for Refuge

1. Going for Refuge

Refuge is explained in terms of (1) its distinctions, (2) the nature of the distinctive refuge, and (3) a summary.

1. Distinctions

There are two parts in the first section: (1) a brief presentation of the four distinctions and (2) an extensive explanation of their meaning.

1. Brief Presentation of the Four Distinctions

The first part is taught in the following two stanzas:

> Universality, commitment, realization, and outshining—
> These four elements distinguish the supreme vehicle.
> The one who thus goes for refuge in the Jewels
> Is known as supreme among all who take refuge. [III.1]

> First, this determination is difficult,
> And the practice throughout many thousands of eons is difficult as well.
> The purpose is great, for once accomplished, there is benefit for beings.
> Therefore, taking refuge in this Great Vehicle has a supreme objective. [III.2]

The following explanation relates to the distinct way that one goes for refuge in the Great Vehicle: (1) the reference point, which is characterized by **universality**; (2) the essence, which is of the nature of **commitment**; (3) the result, which is of the nature of **realization**; and (4) the accompaniment, which is characterized by **outshining**. **These four elements distinguish** the refuge in the Supreme Vehicle. **The one who thus goes for refuge in the Three Jewels is known as supreme among all who take refuge.**

The following verses are stated in order to inspire. **First, this determination** of thinking "I shall rely on the Three Jewels in order to become a perfect Buddha for the welfare of others" **is difficult. And the practice** of benefiting others **throughout many thousands of eons is difficult as well. Yet their purpose is great, for** once the stage of buddhahood has been **accomplished, there is benefit for numerous beings. Therefore, taking refuge in this Great Vehicle has a supreme objective.**

The refuge of the Great Vehicle excels in four regards: (1) universality, because this refuge is taken to liberate all sentient beings; (2) the commitment, which is to attain buddhahood; (3) the realization of the twofold selflessness; and (4) the way in which one thereby surpasses mundane beings, listeners, and self-realized buddhas. These four general issues distinguish the Supreme Vehicle. Those who thus go for refuge in the Three Jewels in the manner of, or for the sake of, the Supreme Vehicle are said to be supreme in relation to those who seek protection in worldly beings such as Brahma and Īśvara, and to the listeners and self-realized buddhas who take refuge in the Three Jewels for their own benefit. It is difficult for ordinary beings in the first instance to become resolved and committed to the pursuit of buddhahood—complete and unsurpassed enlightenment—in order to free all sentient beings from cyclic existence and establish them in the state of liberation and omniscience. Among the multitude of sentient beings, one who makes such an aspiration, orienting the mind in this way, is exceedingly rare.

After having given rise to the enlightened mind in this way, one must practice giving away one's body, one's enjoyments, and so forth, for many thousands of eons for the sake of attaining unsurpassable enlightenment and completely liberating sentient beings. It is difficult, yet there is great purpose to this, for once one accomplishes unsurpassable enlightenment as a buddha, one will benefit all sentient beings until the end of time. Therefore, those who take up this Great Vehicle as their path and rely upon it as their refuge hold a supreme objective.

2. Extensive Explanation of Their Meaning

In the same order as above, this section proceeds to explain (1) universality, (2) commitment, (3) realization, and (4) outshining.

1. Universality

Those who pursue the liberation of all sentient beings,
Have expertise regarding the vehicles and universal wakefulness,
And know cyclic existence and peace to be of one taste within the transcendence of suffering
Are wise individuals, who should here be known as "universal." [III.3]

Next comes an explanation of the aforementioned quality of universality. (1) There is universality with respect to sentient beings because the children of the victorious ones are **those who pursue the liberation of all sentient beings**. (2) Similarly, there is universality with respect to the vehicles because such individuals **have expertise regarding the** three **vehicles**. (3) There is universality in terms of wakefulness because, in clearly understanding the way that both persons and phenomena are devoid of self, such beings are masters of **universal wakefulness**. (4) Finally, there is also universality regarding the transcendence of suffering because since flaws and good qualities are not conceived as separate, such individuals **know cyclic existence and peace to be of one taste within the transcendence of suffering**. Such beings **are wise individuals, who should here be known as "universal."**

The distinction of universality is fourfold: universality in terms of sentient beings, vehicles, wakefulness, and the transcendence of suffering. Respectively, "universality" refers to those who pursue the liberation of all the infinite number of sentient beings, who thoroughly realize the three vehicles, whose expertise in universal wakefulness realizes the twofold selflessness, and who realize that within the basic field of the transcendence of suffering, cyclic existence and peace are of one taste. Through their insight and compassion, they abide neither in the extreme of existence nor in that of peace. Thus, their transcendence of suffering, or their knowledge, is universal. Wise individuals like these should be known in this context as "universal." Listeners do not possess such qualities.

2. Commitment

There are two parts to the discussion of commitment: (1) the actual commitment and (2) a presentation of the examples of those who possess this commitment.

1. Actual Commitment

> In pursuit of supreme enlightenment with manifold joy,
> Fully undertaking hardship without weariness,
> They become buddhas, equal to all the buddhas.
> Know that such wise individuals have a supreme commitment.
> [III.4]

The meaning of commitment is explained with reference to the following three distinctions. (1) Its distinct aspiration is that of the children of the victorious ones, who are **in pursuit of supreme enlightenment with manifold joy**, contemplating the excellent qualities that are to be attained. (2) Its distinct practice consists of their **fully undertaking hardship without weariness** for a long time. (3) Its distinct attainment is such that **they become buddhas,** equal to all the buddhas. Know that such wise individuals have a supreme commitment.

The distinct aspiration in this vehicle is the intent to pursue supreme enlightenment from the depth of one's heart, rejoicing in the powers, fearlessnesses, and other qualities of buddhahood. The distinct practice involves practicing the path from the grounds of inspired conduct to the tenth ground, throughout which the bodhisattvas embrace suffering, give away their bodies, and fully undertake other such hardships without growing weary. The distinct fruition is to become a buddha, indistinguishable from all the buddhas in both abandonment and realization, and being equal in terms of body, speech, and mind. Know that such wise individuals possess a supreme commitment or promise.

2. Examples of Those with This Commitment

The demonstration of their good qualities includes: (1) the example of the prince and (2) the example of the minister.

1. Example of the Prince

For the one of noble birth, the supreme child of the buddhas,
Mind, insight, accumulation, and compassion
Are like the unequalled seed, mother, abode of the womb, and nursemaid.
Know that this wise individual has a supreme commitment. [III.5]

With a body adorned by various marks,
The bodhisattva has attained the power to mature all beings
And discovered the peace of the buddha's limitless great bliss,
Knowing how to exhibit great means for protecting all beings. [III.6]

They have the empowerment bestowed by great rays of light from all the buddhas

And possess complete and genuine mastery over phenomena.
They know how to display the circle of a buddha's retinue,
And strive, having established the training, to subjugate and
    assist. [III.7]

Here it is explained that one who has this distinct commitment is a supreme child of the victorious ones. **For the one of noble birth, the supreme child of the** fully enlightened **buddhas,** the generation of the **mind** of enlightenment, transcendent **insight,** endowment with the **accumulations** of merit and wakefulness, **and compassion are,** respectively, **like the unequalled seed** from the father, the **mother** who produces the body, the supporting **abode of the womb,** and the **nursemaid** who rears the child. **Know** then that **this wise individual,** this child of the buddhas, **has a supreme commitment.**

The distinct quality of this commitment is expressed in terms of four specific features. (1) A bodhisattva's beautiful form is distinct, **with a body adorned by various marks,** distinguished in clarity, perfection, placement, and so forth. (2) His or her power is distinct because **the bodhisattva has attained the power to mature all beings. And** (3) the bodhisattva's bliss is also distinctive because this individual **has discovered the peace of the buddhas' limitless great bliss.** (4) In **knowing how to exhibit great means for protecting all beings,** the wakefulness of the bodhisattva is distinct as well.

Next it is explained how these beings of noble birth avoid severing the family line of the buddhas. There are four causes that enable one to maintain an unbroken [royal] family line: (1) receiving empowerment, (2), unimpeded mastery, (3) skill in resolving dispute, and (4) subjugation and assistance. Similarly, **they,** the bodhisattvas, (1) **have received the empowerment bestowed by great rays of light from all the buddhas.** Having achieved unimpeded wakefulness, they (2) **possess complete and genuine mastery over phenomena.** Likewise, (3) **they know the way to display the circle of a buddha's retinue** within which questions are raised and answered, **and** (4) they **strive, having established the** bases for the **training, to subjugate** those who do wrong **and** to **assist** those with good qualities.

First, it is explained how the son of a universal monarch can be used as an example of one who has been born into the supreme family of the Buddha. The son of a universal monarch is endowed with four excellent factors: (1) the seed from his father, (2) a mother who is a sublime queen of royal heritage, (3) a womb that is free of illness and other faults, and (3) the nursemaid who raises him. Likewise, bodhisattvas are known as noble children, the offspring of an unbroken line of descendants of the thus-gone ones. Listeners, however, are not known as the children of the Buddha; they are students born from the Buddha's speech.

Bodhisattvas are the supreme children of the buddhas, the blessed ones. They arise from the four qualities of (1) the generation of the mind of unsurpassed enlightenment, (2) the transcendent insight that realizes the absence of self, (3) the possession of the two accumulations of merit and wakefulness, and (4) the compassion that does not neglect any sentient being. Respectively, these qualities are likened to the unequalled (1) father's seed, (2) mother, (3) abode of the womb, and (4) nursemaid. The bodhisattvas who arise from such qualities are wise individuals, who possess a supreme commitment. It is by the power of this commitment to accomplish unsurpassable enlightenment that one is born, like an actual son of a universal monarch, into the family of the thus-gone ones.

Moreover, one who is born the son of a universal monarch has qualities superior to ordinary people. He (1) has a body adorned with special marks, (2) gains control over border regions and takes good care of them, (3) attains the enjoyments of royalty, and (4) is expert in politics and all other fields of learning. Similarly, bodhisattvas have (1) bodies adorned with all of the excellent and beautiful major and minor marks. These surpass the characteristics of a worldly universal monarch by means of three qualities: perfect placement, complete luminosity, and utter perfection. (2) Through the power of their minds, they have attained the power of body and speech such as to fully mature all sentient beings in virtue. (3) They have discovered the pacification of all afflictions and the great bliss of the buddhas, which is infinite because it is never exhausted. (4) They free all sentient beings from suffering and thereby establish them in lasting happiness. Thus, they understand the array of great means for protecting all sentient beings—the immeasurable gates of means and insight—as they are and in their multiplicity.

Furthermore, an actual son of a universal monarch (1) has been empowered by his father as regent, (2) is an expert in strategizing, (3) is an expert in all the skills of body, speech, and mind, and (4) protects his subjects by means of subjugation and support. Likewise, bodhisattvas who have committed to accomplish unsurpassable enlightenment (1) receive, on the tenth ground, empowerment with great rays of light from all buddhas; (2) attain, thereby, the unobstructed wakefulness that expresses itself as the genuine and complete mastery over phenomena, both as they are and in their multiplicity; (3) possess a thorough knowledge of the forms of miracles and displays of Dharma in all the maṇḍalas of a buddha's retinue; (4) maintain the training of superior discipline by subjugating harm-doers and assisting and supporting those who do good.

2. Example of the Minister

> They resemble a great minister because they practice the transcendences,
> Always oversee the array of factors that accord with great enlightenment,
> Always sustain the domains of the triple mystery,
> And always provide for multitudes of beings without interruption. [III.8]

The next stanza explains how, due to this distinct commitment, bodhisattvas can be said to resemble a great minister. A great minister is classified as such for four reasons. (1) He enters among the ladies of the court, and so has experience with the interior. (2) He oversees the entire treasury. (3) He is relied upon in matters of confidentiality. (4) He is in charge of the allocations. They, the bodhisattvas, **resemble a great minister because (1) they practice the transcendences**, (2) they **always oversee the array of factors that accord with great enlightenment** as found in the different sūtras, without forgetting any of them, (3) they **always sustain the** domains of the triple mystery of the body, speech, and mind, **and (4) they always provide for the multitude of beings without interruption.**

Bodhisattvas oversee the Buddha's Great Vehicle Dharma and the mysteries of body, speech, and mind, while listeners do not. They can be likened to a king's most great and reliable minister, who would have four powers: (1) entry into the retinue, including that of the ladies-in-waiting, (2) supervision of the entire treasury, (3) involvement in confidential discussions, and (4) the ability to give orders to others. Bodhisattvas resemble great ministers in the following ways. (1) They enter into the Great Vehicle Dharma, such as the Buddha's doctrine of the ten transcendences, and so forth. (2) They act as stewards, or supervisors, constantly overseeing the treasury of the display, or array, of the factors that accord with great enlightenment. (3) They always uphold the domains of the triple mystery of the Buddha's enlightened body, speech, and mind. In this context we may think of Vajrapāṇi, who always remained in the presence of the Blessed One throughout his career as a bodhisattva, as is taught in the *Sūtra of the Inconceivable Secret*. When he became a buddha, he knew mysteries of the Buddha's body, speech, and mind of which others had no knowledge. (4) Furthermore, bodhisattvas constantly, and without interruption, provide for a multitude of sentient beings.

3. Realization

They have great heaps of merit, are teachers of the three
    worlds, and enjoy the pleasures of existence.
Completely pacifying great masses of suffering, and with the
    bliss of supreme intelligence,
They possess the supreme assembly of numerous qualities, a
    permanent body, and a host of virtues.
Reversing habitual tendencies, they are liberated from
    existence and peace—this is their attainment. [III.9]

The following explanation concerns the bodhisattvas' realization. From the time they become inspired by this Dharma, **they have**

great heaps of merit, while, at the time of engendering the enlightened mind, they **are teachers of the three worlds and enjoy the pleasures of existence** as they intentionally take birth. At the time of clear realization, bodhisattvas accept all sentient beings as themselves. Thus, their attainment involves **completely pacifying great masses of suffering**. **With the bliss of supreme intelligence**, experienced when they gain acceptance of nonarising phenomena, bodhisattvas, at the time of their manifest and supreme enlightenment, become the source of the infinite doctrines of the sūtras and so forth. Hence, **they possess** the attainment of **the supreme assembly of numerous qualities**. Since it is inexhaustible, this is a **permanent body**, embodying **a host of virtues**, such as the powers. **Reversing** all **habitual tendencies** without exception within this body, **they are liberated from existence and peace**, as they remain in neither cyclic existence nor in transcendence of suffering. **This is their attainment.**

The distinct realization of the bodhisattva is, in brief, the realization of the selflessness of persons and phenomena. To elaborate, this involves eight qualities. (1) When one first becomes inspired by the Great Vehicle, one attains great heaps of merit, equal in extent to the reaches of space and sentient beings. (2) When, based on such inspiration, one has brought forth the mind set on unsurpassable enlightenment, one becomes a teacher, exalted over all sentient beings in the three realms. (3) When one intentionally takes birth in existence for the benefit of self and others, one experiences the immeasurable pleasures of existence, the sublime enjoyments of gods and humans. (4) On the first ground, one realizes the basic field of phenomena directly, and so attains the mind of equality regarding oneself and others. One then experiences complete joy through seeing that one is able to accomplish one's own benefit and that of all others. At that time, therefore, one brings about the complete pacification of the great mass of suffering that is experienced by oneself and others. One is thus free from the five sources of fear: lack of livelihood, not being praised, being the center of attention, falling into the lower realms, and death. As one's own suffering is pacified in this way, one will also actively pacify the five sufferings of all other sentient beings as though they were one's own. (5) When attaining the acceptance of nonarising phenomena on the eighth ground, one spontaneously accomplishes the great vision of nonconceptual wakefulness and so abides in the bliss of supreme intelligence. In addition to these five, there are three further attainments when passing beyond the tenth ground and becoming a buddha. These are (6) the body of qualities, which is the complete perfection of the host of all virtues without exception. This body is a boundless assembly of uncontaminated qualities, or of the teachings that appear in the sūtras and the rest of the twelve categories of scripture. Perfect, supreme, and superior to mundane beings, listeners, and self-realized buddhas, this body remains permanent until the end of cyclic existence. Thus, one further attains (7) a thorough reversal of the afflictive and cognitive habitual tendencies and (8) nonabiding transcendence of suffering, complete liberation from the two extremes of existence and peace.

4. OUTSHINING

The wise surpass the gatherings that include the listeners
By means of virtues that are vast, tremendously beneficial,
    infinite, always constant, and inexhaustible.
These virtues are, moreover, the mundane, the supramundane,
    the thorough ripening, and the attainment of mastery.
They are not exhausted by the pacification of the aggregates.
[III.10]

The following section explains how the bodhisattva surpasses others. **The wise surpass the gatherings** of beings **that include the listeners** and the self-realized buddhas **by means of** fundamental **virtues** that are (1) **vast**, (2) **tremendously beneficial**, (3) **infinite, always constant, and** (4) **inexhaustible. These** four types of **virtues are, moreover,** respectively associated with (1) the vast intent of the cultivation of the enlightened mind on **the mundane** path of inspired conduct, (2) the practices of **the supramundane** path, entered upon attaining the path of seeing, and which are greatly beneficial to both oneself and others, (3) **the thorough ripening** of sentient beings that occurs by means of limitless retentions and meditative absorptions on the seven impure grounds, **and** (4) **the attainment of mastery** on the three pure grounds. They, these virtues, **are not exhausted** by the pacification of the aggregates without remainder in the basic field.

The way in which bodhisattvas surpass others is extensively explained in this passage. The wise, meaning the bodhisattvas, surpass the great assemblies of listeners and of self-realized buddhas by means of four virtues. These are as follows: (1) From the grounds of inspired conduct up to the supreme worldly quality, the virtues of the bodhisattvas are, unlike those of the listeners, not oriented solely toward the transcendence of suffering. They also serve as a cause for entering cyclic existence for the welfare of all sentient beings. Therefore, the virtues of the bodhisattvas are vast, and in this way they surpass those of the listeners. (2) Virtues from the first ground up through the seventh bring forth the attainment of unsurpassable enlightenment. Therefore, these virtues are tremendously beneficial and hence they surpass those of the listeners.

(3) On the three pure grounds, nonconceptual wakefulness is spontaneously present. Thus fundamental virtues, like ripening fruit, expand and mature. The infinite qualities of the powers, transcendences, and so forth, also develop, while buddha activities and explanations of Dharma stream forth continuously. Hence, the bodhisattvas surpass the listeners in this way as well. (4) At the stage of buddhahood, the powers, fearlessnesses, unshared qualities, and other perfect, sublime qualities are obtained. These qualities are never exhausted, not even within the basic field that is without any remainder of the aggregates. Hence, in this too, the bodhisattvas surpass the listeners.

In this way, on the grounds of inspired conduct beneath the supreme worldly quality, the virtues of taking refuge in the Great Vehicle consist of the cultivation of the enlightened mind. In terms of the supramundane path from the second up to the seventh ground, these virtues are characterized by the thorough ripening of sentient beings through a pure, superior intent; and on the three pure grounds they consist of the attainment of the four perfect masteries—nonconceptuality and the rest. The virtues of the Great Vehicle are superior because, contrary to the case of the listeners and self-realized buddhas, they are not exhausted when the aggregates are pacified without remainder.

2. The Nature of the Distinctive Refuge

This is a commitment with the wish for the nature of that, and
 it should be understood to arise from compassion.
Omniscient wakefulness ensues from this, as do benefit and
 happiness, and no aversion when facing hardship.
As for definitive emergence, this always has the qualities that
 are relied on in all the vehicles.
Attained through symbols and the intrinsic nature, the way
 that the wise go for refuge is supreme. [III.11]

Going for refuge is explained as follows. The essence of **this** manner of going for refuge **is a commitment** to rely upon the Three Jewels **with the wish** to attain **the nature of that** (that is, the buddha). **And it should be understood to arise from** the cause of **compassion. The omniscient wakefulness** of buddhahood **ensues, as the effect, from this, as do benefit and happiness** for sentient beings **and no aversion when facing hardship**, both of which constitute the function of going for refuge. **As for** the means for **definitive emergence**, the paths of all three vehicles are revealed through this form of refuge. In this way, **this always has the qualities that are relied on in all the vehicles.** The endowment of this form of refuge is that it has the means to bring about such definitive emergence.

This refuge is of two types: the coarse refuge that is **attained through symbols and** the subtle refuge that is attained from **the intrinsic nature**. Hence, **the way that the wise**, meaning the children of the victorious ones, **go for refuge is supreme.**

According to the Great Vehicle, going for refuge involves wishing to become of the nature of the Buddha. In other words, one desires to accomplish the very nature of the buddha to whom one goes for refuge. When taking refuge in this way, one makes an aspiration in which one commits and promises to do just that, thinking, "The Buddha is the protector of all sentient beings. May I, too, in the same way become a buddha in order to alleviate the sufferings of all sentient beings." This is the essence, or nature, of going for refuge. Listeners, on the other hand, go for refuge in the Buddha, Dharma, and Saṅgha in order to protect themselves, thinking, "May I be free from the suffering of cyclic existence." The commitment to become a buddha should be understood to arise from affection, the desire to free all sentient beings from suffering. Therefore, the cause of taking refuge in the Great Vehicle is compassion.

By going for refuge in this way, one progressively accomplishes the ten grounds. At the state of buddhahood, one then attains the omniscient wakefulness that knows all aspects of what can be known. This is the fruitional aspect of refuge. Having become a buddha, one provides benefit and happiness for all sentient beings for as long as space exists. However, even while still in training, bodhisattvas have no aversion whatsoever in the face of undergoing all manner of hardships for the welfare of sentient beings. These are the function of going for refuge. Moreover, Sthiramati's commentary explains that the term "benefit" refers to the material goods and virtues experienced in this lifetime, and the term "happiness" indicates the enjoyments of gods and humans experienced in another lifetime, as well as the transcendence of suffering. There are also other explanations where the term "happiness" refers to high birth in one's present life, whereas "benefit" means the definitive goodness experienced in the future. Similarly, we may also think in terms of temporary happiness and ultimate benefit.

For the distinct individuals who definitively emerge through the Great or Lesser Vehicles, taking refuge always involves all of the excellent qualities that are realized through each of the three vehicles. Such is the endowment of refuge. Taking refuge in the Great Vehicle extends to all three vehicles. This also means that with this refuge one will teach sentient beings who have faith in any of the three vehicles. Impartially, one explains the particular Dharma of the respective vehicle, through which beings will be liberated from suffering and so be able to emerge definitively. Hence, the refuge of the Great Vehicle possesses the qualities relied on by all three vehicles. Although each of the three types of beings relies upon and trusts in his or her own particular vehicle, this Great Vehicle is the refuge and protector of all three types.

There are two categories, or instances of, refuge: (1) the refuge attained through symbols and (2) the refuge attained from the intrinsic nature. The refuge attained from the symbols of one's own spoken commitment and the words in the speech of the preceptor or master is the coarse refuge that is achieved through symbols. The refuge that is attained by the intrinsic nature comes from the direct realization of the character of the intrinsic nature. This realization takes place on the first ground, and from that point on it cannot possibly deteriorate. This is referred to as the profound, or subtle, attainment by means of the intrinsic nature. The same two categories also pertain to the development of the enlightened mind.

Therefore, the way in which wise bodhisattvas go for refuge has six aspects: (1) nature or essence, (2) cause, (3) fruition, (4) function, (5) endowment, and (6) gateway. This form of refuge is superior to that of worldly beings, as well as to the refuge of the supramundane listeners and self-realized buddhas.

3. Summary

The concluding verse offers the following summary:

> Taking refuge in this has a great purpose,
> For unfathomable qualities will be gathered thereby,
> These beings will be embraced by a compassionate intent,
> And the Dharma of the unequaled, great noble ones will flourish. [III.12]

> This was the third chapter of the *Ornament of the Great Vehicle Sūtras,* the chapter on going for refuge.

Taking refuge in this Great Vehicle **has a great purpose, for unfathomable qualities** related to logic, numbers, and time **will be gathered thereby** for one's own welfare. In terms of the welfare of others, **these beings will be embraced by a compassionate intent**, namely, the wish to free beings from suffering. **And**, and as one endeavors accordingly, **the Dharma of the unequaled, great noble ones**, the buddhas and bodhisattvas, **will flourish**.

As just explained, the way in which one takes refuge in the Great Vehicle serves a great purpose. How so? It accomplishes both one's own benefit and that of others. Those who take refuge in this way develop and accumulate unfathomable qualities, progressively accomplishing the grounds and paths up to the attainment of the qualities at the stage of buddhahood. These qualities include the powers and fearlessnesses, as well as unceasing and spontaneously present enlightened activity, and as such they embody the perfection of one's own welfare. For the welfare of others, those who take refuge in the Great Vehicle engage in a peerless practice that is suffused with a compassionate intent on behalf of all the limitless number of beings. This enables them to uphold the Great Vehicle Dharma of the great and noble buddhas and bodhisattvas, spreading it in the ten directions so that beings are established in both temporal happiness and the lasting happiness of liberation. Thus, those taking this refuge embody perfect intent and application.

This concludes the explanation of going for refuge, the third chapter of the *Ornament of the Great Vehicle Sūtras*.

AT THE OUTSET of the path of any of the three vehicles, one goes for refuge. When one trusts a particular path as constituting a path to liberation that is capable of completely overcoming the suffering of cyclic existence, one will also take the teacher of that path and those who have entered that path as supreme sources of refuge. Consequently, one then enters the path. However, those who do not accept the Three Jewels as genuine objects of refuge do not have the fortune to practice this Dharma. This is why taking refuge is explained first.

The Great and Lesser Vehicles are the same in that both involve taking refuge in the Three Jewels. With this in mind, one may wonder why there are three types of individuals who each have their own potential, such that some go for refuge according to the Great Vehicle and some according to the Lesser Vehicle. In order to clarify uncertainties regarding this issue, the chapter explaining potential comes next. Following this, the chapter on developing the enlightened mind is presented since an individual who has supreme potential will cultivate the mind that is directed toward unsurpassable enlightenment. Then, after the discussion of developing the enlightened mind, its practice is addressed because practice is the application of the enlightened mind that has thus been developed.

As for the reason that practice is discussed twice in this treatise, we may note first that, in the context of what is to be understood, practice is simply treated in terms of a general presentation of the differences between the practices of the Great and Lesser Vehicles. The later chapter on practice explains practice as such, that is, practice as distinguished from explanation. With these supplementary remarks in mind, let us continue our reading.

4
Potential

2. Potential

This chapter, which is the second in the section concerned with what is to be understood, will cover (1) an explanation of the presence of potential, (2) an explanation of the lack of potential, (3) a concluding summary of the chapter that praises the potential of the Supreme Vehicle.

1. The Presence of Potential

The first section contains (1) a brief presentation and (2) a detailed explanation of the individual topics.

1. Summary

The summary is taught in the following stanza:

> Existence, supremacy, characteristics,
> Signs, classifications of potential,
> Flaws, benefits, and the two metaphors—
> Each of these is fourfold. [IV.1]

This stanza summarizes the classifications associated with potential: (1) establishing the **existence** of different potentials, (2) showing the **supremacy** of the Great Vehicle potential, (3) the **characteristics** of potential, (4) the **signs** of an activated Great Vehicle potential, (5) the **classifications of potential**, (6) the **flaws** that hinder the development of potential, (7) the **benefits** of potential, and (8) **the two metaphors** of gold and jewels that demonstrate how common and extraordinary qualities develop from the potential. **Each of these** topics **is fourfold.**

The general framework of this chapter addresses (1) the existence of different potentials, (2) the superiority of the Great Vehicle potential, (3) the characteristics of potential, (4) its signs, (5) classifications, (6) the flaws or obscurations associated with an inactivated potential, (7) the benefits derived from potential, and (8) the two metaphors of gold and jewels. Each of these eight points has a fourfold meaning.

2. The Individual Topics

This section has eight parts, following the sequence shown above.

1. Different Potentials

We observe a diversity of elements, interests,
Forms of practice, and fruitions.
It is, therefore, definitively stated
That there is such a thing as potential. [IV.2]

The existence of different potentials is established as follows. **We observe a diversity of elements** of sentient beings. In fact, the elements of beings are infinitely diverse, as explained in the *Sūtra on Numerous Elements*. Since we have to believe that there are such infinitely diverse elements, there must be a distinct potential associated with each of the three vehicles. We likewise observe that the **interests** of sentient beings are different, with some beings having an interest in one specific vehicle from the very beginning. Moreover, even when conditions have aroused such an interest, we will still notice that individuals engage in different **forms of practice, and** also that there are different **fruitions,** for there are inferior, intermediate, and extraordinary forms of enlightenment.

It is therefore definitively stated that there is such a thing as difference in terms of the potential of beings.

The potentials differ, it is said, because there are numerous potentials or elements within the realm of sentient beings. (The words "element," "seed," and "potential" are all synonyms.) In this regard, the elements of sentient beings are dissimilar and can take various forms. While some beings experience mostly desire, others predominantly have anger, dullness, pride, and so on. Some have the potential of a listener, others have that of a self-realized buddha, and some have the Great Vehicle potential. We can thus be certain that there are different potentials. There are also many differences among those sentient beings who, say, have a predominance of desire. The *Sūtra on Numerous Elements* states:

> Think of a pile of myrobalan fruits that is a league high and wide. We may take aside one fruit whenever we see a sentient being with the potential of a listener, or a sentient being with the potential of a self-realized buddha, or a sentient being whose potential is such that the predominant experience is desire, and so on. If we were to count sentient beings and their individual elements in this way, the heap of myrobalan fruits would quickly disappear, but there would still not be an end to the different elements of sentient beings.

The interests of sentient beings also vary widely according to the individual's potential or elemental constitution. There is no limit to the different interests of sentient beings. Similarly, there is no one type of food that will satisfy everyone; some prefer sweet food while others like sour. Sentient beings differ with reference to the path of complete liberation as well. Some have faith in the Listeners' Vehicle but none in the Great Vehicle, for instance, regardless of whether or not they have received teachings from a spiritual teacher. There are also differences in terms of whether or not one has the ability to practice the six transcendences, as well as in terms of the fruition, or resultant liberation. There is the minor enlightenment of a listener, the mediocre enlightenment of a self-realized buddha, and the supreme enlightenment of the Great Vehicle. Since differences in elements, interest, practice, and fruition can be observed, it is said definitively that there are indeed different potentials. If there were not different potentials or elements, we should expect that the latter three, interest and so forth, would also not vary because they would be as uniform as their cause. Yet this is not the case, and so it is established that there are different elements.

2. Supremacy of the Great Vehicle Potential

The virtue of that
Is superior, total,
Greatly beneficial, and not exhausted.
Hence, this potential is declared to be supreme. [IV.3]

The supremacy of the potential of the Great Vehicle is explained as follows. The fundamental **virtue of that** (meaning the potential of the Great Vehicle) **is superior,** for it functions as the remedy of the two obscurations. This potential, moreover, serves as the cause for the **totality** of excellent qualities, such as the powers. It is also **greatly beneficial,** for it brings about one's own and others' welfare, **and** it is **not exhausted** [in a transcendence of suffering] without remainder of the aggregates. **Hence, this potential** of the Great Vehicle **is declared to be supreme.**

The potential, or fundamental virtue of the Great Vehicle serves as the cause for clarity and purity in the absence of the two obscurations. Hence, it is superior to the potential of the Lesser Vehicle. This potential also functions as the cause for perfecting the totality of fundamental virtues, such as the grounds, transcendences, and the ten powers of the final fruition. Since it accomplishes one's own welfare and the welfare of other sentient beings, it serves as the cause for great, virtuous benefit. Virtues such as the powers and fearlessnesses are not exhausted until the end of cyclic existence, even if one were to transcend suffering without remainder of the aggregates. For these four reasons, the potential of the Great Vehicle is declared to be supreme. Since the listeners do not possess these four qualities of virtue, which are superior due to their clarity and purity and so on, their potential does not serve as the cause for such virtues.

3. Characteristics of the Potential

The natural and the developed
Are the support and the supported.
Present while not present,
It should be known to mean "freeing qualities." [IV.4]

The following is an explanation of the classifications that pertain to the potential's characteristics: There is **the naturally** present **po**tential **and the** potential that is **developed**. These **are**, respectively, **the support and the supported**. The naturally present potential is **present** as a causal essence, **while** it is **not present** as a resultant essence. It **should be known to mean "freeing qualities,"** in the sense that it enables one to become free from the ocean of cyclic existence.

The characteristics of this potential are twofold: the naturally present potential and the developed or developing potential. The former is the support while the latter is the supported. Thus, there are four categories. According to the explanations of the Mind Only tradition, "the naturally present potential" refers to the distinctive character of the six sense sources of a particular type of sentient being. Since time without beginning, this potential remains as such by the power of the intrinsic nature. That is to say, its existence is natural; no one has to produce or fabricate it. In this way it holds the seeds for attaining manifest enlightenment. It is held that, by virtue of one's possession of this potential, one will have the fortune to become a buddha and attain unsurpassable enlightenment.

A certain type of stone may possess the element of gold, another the element of iron, and another that of copper. It is held that, just as these elements cannot change from one to another, the same is the case with the potential for buddhahood. In the Mind Only tradition, five potentials are asserted: (1–3) the potentials of the three vehicles, (4) the uncertain potential, and (5) the potential that is completely cut off from liberation.

Our present treatise certainly teaches this fivefold classification, which, in the proper context, will not be refuted even by proponents of the Middle Way. It is taught that until they reach their goal, those who are certain to attain the listener's one-sided peace cannot be stopped, even if the buddhas would try to prevent them. Likewise, when individuals with immense desires do not develop any wish to be free from cyclic existence, it must be the case that even the buddhas are unable to establish them on the path of liberation. Were this not the case, why would there be individuals who achieve the enlightenment of a listener and a self-realized buddha, and why would there be such an infinite number of sentient beings within cyclic existence? Although numerous buddhas have appeared, there are still beings who have not achieved liberation.

When looking at things in the way mentioned above, the assertions of the Mind Only approach are not unreasonable. It is, however, impossible for the fundamental nature of the mind of sentient beings to be anything other than the nonarising and naturally luminous essence of enlightenment. Since this is the intrinsic nature of mind, just as heat is the intrinsic nature of fire, it is impossible for any sentient being not to have this nature. Hence, it is taught that there is no potential that is completely cut off from liberation. Indeed, also in this present treatise we find the stanza, "suchness is present in all without distinction,"[27] which states that all sentient beings have buddha nature. It also declares: "Any mind other than the mind of the intrinsic nature is not luminous—the reference is to the natural."[28] Thus, in its final meaning, the naturally present potential refers to the intrinsic nature of the mind, the abiding reality of the unity of empty clarity, as is taught extensively in the *Supreme Continuity*.[29] Here I shall not elaborate further on these issues.

The "developed potential" refers to the potential when it is truly accomplished. That is to say, when a bodhisattva who possesses the naturally present potential meets with a spiritual teacher, develops the unsurpassable mind of enlightenment, and sets out to engage in the conduct of a bodhisattva, this is called the "developed" or "truly accomplished" potential. Here we may also want simply to enumerate some further ways of explaining these two forms of potential. Thus, "naturally present potential" can refer to someone possessing the bodhisattva potential who enters the Great Vehicle from the very beginning. When individuals of the bodhisattva potential have first entered the Listeners' Vehicle and then only later enter the Great Vehicle through the influence of a spiritual teacher, one speaks instead of the "fully accomplished potential." The term "certain potential" can also refer to the naturally present potential, while "truly accomplished potential" can refer to those with an uncertain potential, which later turns into the certain potential of the Great Vehicle due to the guidance of a spiritual teacher. These uses of the terms are explained in the great commentary.

Furthermore, it is also taught that "potential" has the sense of "cause." When merely possessing the naturally present potential, one's potential is characterized by being merely a cause, without the characteristics of a result. Therefore, considering that it is simply a cause, it is said to be "present [as a cause] while not present [as a result]." The developed potential manifests based on the naturally present potential. In that sense, the developed potential is a result based on the naturally present potential. However, it is also a cause because the subsequent paths manifest from it. The naturally present potential serves as a cause for everything up to the qualities of enlightenment, such as the powers. Based upon it, both path and fruition manifest.

The etymology of "potential" can be explained in the following way: The Sanskrit word that is translated as "potential" is *gotra*; it is a combination of *guṇa*, which means "quality," and *tāra*, which means "liberation." Thus, the meaning should be understood as "freeing qualities." Potential brings forth liberation and the completion of all qualities, from the generation of the mind of enlightenment, inspired conduct and the ten grounds, through to the stage of buddhahood.

4. Signs of Potential

Before the practice, there is
Compassion, inspiration,
Forbearance, and genuine experience with virtue.
These are definitively taught to be the signs of potential. [IV.5]

The signs of an activated potential are explained next. **Before the practice** of undertaking demanding activities, there is a **compassionate** wish to free sentient beings from suffering, an **inspiration** with respect to the profound and vast, a true **forbearance** that enables one to remain unfazed in the face of hardship, **and genuine experience with** the kind of **virtue** that is of the nature of the transcendences. **These are definitively taught to be the signs of** the presence of **potential.**

There are a great number of signs, or marks, of potential. In brief, there are four signs that, when present in individuals, reveal their Great Vehicle potential, just as fire is revealed by smoke. What are these four? (1) Even before entering or engaging in the Great Vehicle—that is, before turning the mind toward supreme enlightenment—compassion spontaneously wells up when seeing the suffering of sentient beings. (2) When merely hearing the vast and profound Dharma of the Great Vehicle, one is naturally inspired, even though one may not understand its meaning. (3) When hearing about the hardships undertaken for the welfare of others, there is no feeling of discouragement. One does not think, "How could this possibly be?" Rather, the teaching is embraced with a sense of wonder. (4) There is a feeling of spontaneous joy in the virtues of the six transcendences and a wish to practice them. These are said to be definite signs of the Great Vehicle potential. Those without such a potential display the opposite signs.

5. Classifications of Potential

Potential may be either certain or uncertain,
Unaffected by conditions,
Or affected by them.
In short, the classification of potential is fourfold. [IV.6]

The classification of potential is explained as follows: **Potential may be either certain or uncertain.** Accordingly, it is either unchangeable and **unaffected by conditions, or,** otherwise, changeable and thus affected by them. In short, the classification of potential is fourfold.

A potential that is entirely certain, in the sense of being either that of the listeners, self-realized buddhas, or bodhisattvas, will definitively lead to the attainment of the respective form of enlightenment. No other enlightenment will be attained, no matter what is done, just as an element of a stone cannot become silver, gold, or any other element. The uncertain potential, on the other hand, can become the potential of whichever of the three vehicles it encounters. It is similar to special types of stone that can be changed into gold, silver, or copper if they are melted, purified, or treated with chemicals. The potential that is certain is said to be unaffected by conditions. Even if a spiritual teacher explains another doctrine, individuals with this potential will not pursue any other enlightenment than the one that is given by virtue of their definitive potential. Those with an uncertain potential, on the other hand, are affected by conditions. Just as a white cloth will absorb red or any other color it encounters, these individuals achieve the result of the path taught by whichever spiritual teacher they encounter.

In brief, there are four classifications of potential. Although this is how it is in general, in the present context, we should understand that there are two because here our concern is with the potential of the Great Vehicle. These two are the certain potential of the Great Vehicle and the uncertain potential, in which case only the influence of particular conditions will prompt the individual to enter the Great Vehicle.

6. Shortcomings of a Potential That Is Not Activated

Habituation to affliction, negative company,
Poverty, and being controlled by other—
In short, it should be understood
That there are four flaws with regard to potential. [IV.7]

The flaws that occur when a potential is not activated are explained next. **Habituation to affliction** without understanding its faults;

keeping **negative**, unvirtuous **company**; suffering from **poverty**, in the sense of lacking material means; **and being controlled by powerful others**—in short, it should be understood that there are four flaws with regard to potential. Even when possessing the potential, these four may keep one from experiencing its qualities.

Although one has the potential, flaws or obscurations may prevent one from engaging in virtuous conduct. In brief, one should be aware of four types of shortcomings: (1) long-standing habituation to attachment, aversion, bewilderment, and other such afflictions; (2) engaging in what is unwholesome due to the influence of negative company; (3) engaging in negative deeds and not doing anything virtuous, due to being deprived of material means; and (4) having no freedom to shun what is negative and do what is virtuous, due to being under the control of others, such as a king, a master, thieves, or bandits.

7. Benefits of Potential

They seldom go to the lower realms
And are freed quickly.
Experiencing little suffering even there,
Saddened, they bring sentient beings to maturation. [IV.8]

The following explanation concerns the benefits of potential. Those who possess the bodhisattva potential may do things that lead to a rebirth in the lower realms. Even so, **they seldom go to the lower realms, and are freed** from them **quickly. Experiencing little suffering even there, saddened, they bring the sentient beings** that have taken birth there **to** complete **maturation** through their compassion.

The benefits, or excellence, of the Great Vehicle potential are as follows. If sentient beings who possess the potential of a listener, or who lack the potential for liberation, engage in the five deeds with immediate retribution or other forms of extreme negativity, they will take birth in the hell realms the moment they die. However, when sentient beings with the bodhisattva potential commit the five deeds with immediate retribution or other such negative actions, they will take birth in hell and experience the consequences of their negativity in the distant future, after many years or eons have passed. The negative results of those with the Great Vehicle potential are not able to ripen as swiftly as in the case of other potentials. This is how it is explained in the great commentary.

The reason for this is that the Great Vehicle potential causes one to feel remorse and embarrassment, not joy, for having committed negative deeds. Hence, it is difficult for them to experience the ripening of negativity as quickly as others. Furthermore, even when individuals with the bodhisattva potential take birth in hell, they do not need to remain there until the life span of a hell being has been completed, as other sentient beings do. Instead, they are quickly freed. They are able to leave the hell realms after experiencing just a small measure of suffering. This was the case with King Ajātaśatru, who had killed his father, a stream enterer, but who experienced the complete ripening of this negative deed with immediate retribution for only as long as it takes to bounce a ball of yarn.

Moreover, while experiencing the miseries of the lower realms, bodhisattvas become saddened by the sight of sentient beings suffering helplessly due to the power of karma. This prompts them to give rise to great compassion for other sentient beings that are just like themselves, and they develop the wish to establish them in virtue and bring them to full maturation. This is exemplified in the life story of Vallabha's "daughter."[30] Conversely, those who do not possess the bodhisattva potential and who experience the miseries of the lower realms must undergo the entire range of excruciating agonies, becoming aggressive toward each other, and so on. These are thus the four excellent qualities of the Great Vehicle potential.

8. Metaphors of Potential

This section explains two metaphors: (1) the gold mine and (2) the jewel mine.

1. Gold Mine

It should be known to be like a gold mine
For it is the abode of limitless virtues;
It is the abode of wakefulness, stainlessness,
As well as the powers. [IV.9]

The potential of the Great Vehicle is explained as being similar to a great gold mine. **It should be known to be like an** excellent **gold mine** that produces abundant, luminous, stainless, and pliant gold. **For it**, the potential, **is the abode of limitless** fundamental **virtues. It is the abode of wakefulness,** and, in the absence of affliction, the abode of **stainlessness, as well as** that of **the** superknowledges and other such **powers**.

As for the first of the two metaphors for potential, it should be understood that the Great Vehicle potential is like the element of gold, or like a great gold mine. An excellent, great gold mine has four qualities. It is (1) the abode or support of an abundance of gold, (2) the abode of luminous gold, (3) the abode of stainless gold, and (4) the abode of pliant gold. Similarly, the bodhisattva potential is the abode of the transcendences, grounds, fearlessnesses, and other limitless virtues. It is just like an excellent gold mine, or source of gold, which yields a hundred thousand measures and is still infinitely rich. Just as the gold that emerges from such a mine is of the finest color, clear and radiant, the bodhisattva potential is the abode, or support, of the luminous wakefulness that unerringly knows the general and specific characters of all phenomena. Moreover, gold from a great mine is free from even the slightest stain or blemish. Even if the gold is fired, its brilliance only increases. Similarly, the bodhisattva potential is free from the stains of afflictive emotions; it is the abode of the transcendence of suffering. Gold from a great mine is pliant, such that even when it is hammered, it does not split apart or break into pieces. Likewise, the bodhisattva potential is the abode of all the powers of superknowledge, ready to be employed in whichever way one desires.

2. JEWEL MINE

It should be known to be like a mine of precious jewels,
For it is the cause of great enlightenment,
And the abode of great wakefulness, superior meditative absorption,
And benefits for numerous sentient beings. [IV.10]

The Great Vehicle potential is also explained as being like a great jewel mine. **It should be known to be like a mine of** genuine, **precious jewels** that are perfect in color, shape, and quantity. **For it is the cause of,** or basis for, **great enlightenment, and the abode of great** fourfold **wakefulness,** the vajra-like meditative absorption and other **superior meditative absorption**s, **and** of **benefits for numerous sentient beings** through bringing them to full maturation.

The bodhisattva potential can also be likened to a mine filled with lapis lazuli, great sapphires, rubies, and other types of precious jewels. Jewel mines have four properties: a mine or source of jewels is not the source of metal or colored glass, but a place where perfect jewels like lapis lazuli, diamonds, and pearls can be found. Likewise, the bodhisattva potential is not the basis or place of the enlightenment of a listener or self-realized buddha. Rather, it is the cause of the great enlightenment free from all obscurations, which occurs right after the vajra-like meditative absorption. Just as supreme jewels are things of radiant colorful beauty, the bodhisattva potential is the source of abundant wakefulness that arises due to the radiant clarity of mirror-like wakefulness and the rest of the four forms of wakefulness. Just as supreme jewels have an exquisite shape, the bodhisattva potential is the abode of all exalted meditative absorptions, such as the heroic gait and the treasury of space. From a jewel mine, limitless and manifold jewels appear, and since the value of supreme jewels is immeasurable, they can be used to sustain many beings. Likewise, the bodhisattva potential is the basis for bringing happiness to multitudes of sentient beings in this life and beyond, that is, forever.

2. Lack of Potential

Some are exclusively and decisively engaged in error.
Some have completely destroyed their positive qualities.
Some lack virtue that is conducive to liberation.
Some possess insufficient virtue, and some lack the cause. [IV.11]

The classifications with respect to a lack of potential are explained as follows. Temporarily unable to pass beyond suffering, **some are exclusively and decisively engaged in error**. Some have, because of their mistaken view, completely **destroyed their positive qualities**, severing their fundamental virtues. Some have accumulated a bit of merit, but **lack the kind of virtue that is conducive to liberation**. **Some possess insufficient virtue** that accords with liberation, for they have not completed the accumulations, **and** there are **some** who are permanently incapable of completely passing beyond suffering. Lacking the very potential for complete transcendence of suffering, they **lack the cause**.

"Lack of potential" can mean either that the cause of liberation is temporarily lacking or that liberation remains permanently impossible. The first situation is explained in terms of four cases. In all four of them, although one does not permanently lack the potential for liberation, at a particular time it is as though one has none because in that situation one is incapable of cultivating the path to liberation. The negation in "lack of potential" hence implies inferiority, just as one might say "I have no children," meaning simply that all one's children are bad.

These four forms of lack of potential are as follows. (1) Even though some individuals have the Great Vehicle potential, they are overwhelmed by afflictive emotions and engage only in negative conduct, committing actions such as the five deeds with immediate retribution. Although they have the potential, they do not have the fortune to completely transcend suffering at this time. Therefore, it is said that they "lack potential" because they are similar to those without any potential. (2) Some individuals are influenced by the condition of an unvirtuous spiritual teacher, and thereby come to harbor wrong views such as the belief that there is no causality of karma or liberation. Because of this, they either completely annihilate the fundamental virtues of all positive qualities or disrupt the fundamental virtues. Until they are free from such views, they lack the potential for liberation. Therefore, at that time they too are said to "have no potential." (3) Some individuals may engage in defiled virtues with the sole objective of experiencing pleasant karmic ripening within cyclic existence, for example, as a god or a human. Since they lack the forms of virtue that are conducive to liberation—those that are embraced by the motivation to seek liberation—they will not actualize the transcendence of suffering for many eons. Hence, they too are said to "lack potential." (4) Furthermore, some individuals may possess a few fundamental virtues that are conducive to liberation, or some inferior virtues, but yet, at that time, may be completely incapable of accomplishing any higher qualities of the type that are born of a mighty and powerful accumulation of merit and wakefulness. Hence, they may be said to "have no potential."

In each of these four cases, individuals are overpowered by forceful negative circumstances, possess a weak cause, and their potential remains inactive, even though they may possess the Great Vehicle potential. Until their situation changes, they remain far from enlightenment. Therefore, when it is said that they "have no potential," this negation implies deficiency. Finally, when the root text speaks of those who "lack the cause," it refers to a case that is different from the aforementioned four. When such individuals are said to "have no potential," it is because they permanently lack the cause for reaching liberation.

3. Concluding Summary of the Chapter That Praises the Potential of the Supreme Vehicle

In conclusion, the treatise praises the supreme potential, stating:

> The great Dharma that explains the profound and vast is
>   taught for the sake of benefiting others.
> Even while not understanding it, they develop tremendous
>   inspiration and bear the practice.
> Their final perfection is supreme, beyond the two.

Know that this is due to the natural presence of bodhisattva qualities and the development of that potential. [IV.12]

Since it produces the tree of enlightenment with its extremely vast qualities;
Since it brings the attainment of bliss and the great pacification of suffering;
And since it provides the fruits of benefit and happiness for oneself and others—
This supreme potential is like an excellent root. [IV.13]

This was the fourth chapter of the *Ornament of the Great Vehicle Sūtras*, the chapter on potential.

A classification with respect to the naturally present and the developed potential is taught next. The Great Vehicle's **Dharma that explains the profound and vast is taught for the sake of benefiting others. Even while not understanding it, they,** the bodhisattvas, **develop tremendous inspiration with respect to it, and they bear the practice** of it without growing weary. **Their final perfection is the attainment of supreme,** great enlightenment **beyond the two,** the Mundane and Lesser Vehicles. **Know that this is due,** first, **to the natural presence of bodhisattva qualities, and** second, to **the development of that potential.**

With reference to the fruition, the superiority of the Great Vehicle potential is explained as follows: **Since it produces the tree of enlightenment with its extremely vast qualities,** which are those of the stage of buddhahood; **since it brings the attainment of** great **bliss and the great pacification of suffering,** with the abundant branches of the ten grounds; **and since it provides the fruits of benefit and happiness for oneself and others** in enlightened activity, **this supreme potential** of the Great Vehicle **is like an excellent root** of a tree.

Since the Great Vehicle teaches the doctrine of emptiness, it is profound. Since it teaches the transcendences, powers, fearlessnesses and so on, it is vast. When those with the Great Vehicle potential are taught, for the benefit of sentient beings, the teachings of the Great Vehicle that explain both the profound and vast, they develop tremendous interest, even when not fully understanding their meaning. They are also able to endure the difficulties of practicing the transcendences. For these reasons, such individuals perfect the two accumulations and, in the end, attain the perfect result that is great enlightenment, which transcends both mundane results and the supramundane fruitions of the listeners and self-realized buddhas. Such attainment is due to the developed potential, which in turn manifests when bodhisattvas endowed with the qualities of the naturally present potential become engaged in truly accomplishing virtue.

In this way, the bodhisattva potential produces the supreme and unsurpassable tree of enlightenment. The powers and the other extremely vast qualities of enlightenment are its trunk, flowers, and so on. It makes all sentient beings attain undefiled, great bliss and pacifies their great miseries, just as the cool shade of a tree soothes the torments of someone suffering from heat and puts the mind and body at ease. Like a tree that bears exquisite fruit, it ripens the fruition that brings happiness and benefit to oneself and all other sentient beings. Therefore, the supreme potential is like an excellent root, steadfast and free of decay.

This concludes the explanation of potential, the fourth chapter of the *Ornament of the Great Vehicle Sūtras*.

5
Developing the Enlightened Mind

3. Developing the Enlightened Mind

Within the section concerned with "what is to be understood," this third section, which is on developing the enlightened mind, will be treated under four headings: (1) the essence of the enlightened mind, (2) its types, (3) its metaphors, and (4) the praise of its benefits.

1. Essence of the Enlightened Mind

> Extremely delightful, vigorous,
> Meaningful, and productive,
> The bodhisattva's mind
> Is a mental state of intention that possesses two objectives.
> [v.1]

Thus are taught the characteristics of the development of the enlightened mind. Initially, one generates the enlightened mind with **extremely delightful** armor-like diligence. As one then applies oneself in perfect accordance with one's armor, the development is extremely **vigorous**. It is also extremely **meaningful** because it benefits both oneself and others, **and** extremely **productive** because it accomplishes great enlightenment. This is a thorough presentation of three types of qualities, in that the first two expressions present qualities of a creative being, while the last two expressions show the qualities of accomplishing the objectives and of thoroughly taking hold of the fruition. **The bodhisattva's mind is a mental state of intention that possesses two objectives,** for it focuses on great enlightenment and on the welfare of sentient beings.

The development of the enlightened mind is endowed with a fourfold greatness and a twofold objective. It is extremely delightful in the sense that one delights in receiving, reflecting, and meditating on the Great Vehicle Dharma with armor-like diligence, and also in taking upon oneself the hardships of practicing the path for the welfare of others for countless eons without turning back. It is extremely vigorous in that one practices in accord with one's donning of the armor of diligence. It is also extremely meaningful insofar as both one's own and others' objectives are perfectly accomplished. Finally, it is extremely productive, referring to the result, the attainment of unsurpassable enlightenment. In this way, the enlightened mind is endowed with four qualities.

In essence, the development of the enlightened mind is an intention, a particular mental state in the mind stream of a bodhisattva. What then is it that this mental state intends? It aims at, and intends to attain, great enlightenment for oneself, just as it also aims at and intends to make sentient beings happy and to benefit them. In other words, it aims at enlightenment and the welfare of sentient beings. Thus, the "development of the enlightened mind" is a mental state in association with primary mind, and it is endowed with these two objectives. In short, the development of the enlightened mind is the intention, aspiration, and pledge to awaken to unsurpassable enlightenment for the welfare of all sentient beings.

2. TYPES

This section treats the various types of enlightened mind in terms of (1) the stages of the grounds, (2) the principles of the root and so on, and (3) its attainment through symbols and through the intrinsic nature.

1. The Stages of the Grounds

The mind is developed on the grounds
Through inspiration, pure superior intent,
And maturation.
Likewise, there is the elimination of obscurations. [v.2]

As regards the various types of enlightened mind, **the mind is developed on the grounds** as follows. On the grounds of inspired conduct, it arises **through inspiration**. On the first seven grounds, it is developed by means of **pure superior intent**. And on the remaining grounds, from the eighth on, it is developed through **maturation. Likewise, there is the elimination of obscurations,** which occurs at the stage of buddhahood.

The following explanation concerns the enlightened mind as developed at the stage of the grounds of inspired conduct and so forth. On the paths of accumulation and joining, which constitute the grounds of inspired conduct, the enlightened mind is cultivated merely through inspired conviction. Therefore, this stage is referred to as the development of the enlightened mind that comes from inspiration.

During the first seven grounds, this stage is called the development of the enlightened mind with pure superior intent. It is referred to as "superior intent" because at this point the mind has reached a state in which self and others are seen to be equal. Hence, the mind has been trained to such a degree that one no longer sees any difference between one's own and others' welfare. It is called "pure" because it is free from the stains of the duality of apprehended and apprehender.

The period from the eighth ground up to the tenth is called the development of the enlightened mind of complete maturation. Since on these grounds one spontaneously attains nonconceptual wakefulness, engagement in the transcendences is effortless and spontaneous. At the stage of buddhahood, it is referred to as the development of the enlightened mind that has eliminated the obscurations since the enlightened mind that has been developed here is free from the two obscurations and their habitual tendencies. This is the final fruition.

2. The Principles of the Root and So On

Concerning the eleven types, which begin with that of the root, the verses state:

Its root is held to be compassion.
The intention is to always benefit sentient beings.
Its inspiration is the Dharma,
And its objective is to seek out the wakefulness of that. [v.3]

Aspiration reaching ever higher,
The vast vow serves as its support.
What blocks the path is the arising and pursuit
Of conflicting factors. [v.4]

The benefits are an increase of virtues
That are the nature of merit and wakefulness.
Constant engagement in the transcendences
Is held to be the definitive emergence. [v.5]

Its culmination is the grounds,
As these are individually reached.
The bodhisattvas' development of the mind
Should be understood decisively in this way. [v.6]

The development of the enlightened mind is determined to be as follows. Its **root**, the four ways that bodhisattvas develop the enlightened mind [taught in the previous stanza], **is held to be compassion**. The **intention** [associated with this development of the enlightened mind] **is to always benefit sentient beings**. Its **inspiration is the Dharma** of the Great Vehicle, **and its objective is to seek out the wakefulness of that**.

Its progression involves **aspiration reaching ever higher**, and **the vast vow** associated with the bodhisattva's discipline **serves as its support**. As for flaws, **what blocks the path is the arising and pursuit of conflicting factors**, that is, mind-sets associated with other vehicles. The **benefits** of developing the enlightened mind are an increase of the fundamental **virtues that are the nature of merit and wakefulness**. The sense of definitive emergence is the constant engagement in the six transcendences. This is held to be the definitive emergence. Its culmination is the grounds, as these are individually reached. The bodhisattvas' development of the mind should be understood decisively in this way.

The root of the cultivation of the enlightened mind is held to be compassion. Out of compassion, one wishes to dispel the sufferings of sentient beings and one aspires toward enlightenment for their sake. If one lacks compassion, one will strive for a transcendence of suffering that is similar to that of the listeners, in which one's own suffering is completely pacified. The intention of this compassion is to always benefit sentient beings, in this life and forever after, until the limits of cyclic existence have been reached. The inspiration for cultivating the enlightened mind is the vast and profound Dharma of the Great Vehicle, while its objective is to strive to fully attain nonconceptual wakefulness, which completely realizes the twofold absence of self. This is done through receiving, reflecting, and meditating on the Great Vehicle Dharma.

When abiding on any particular ground, one ascends to the next ground through aspiration. Aspiration is the vehicle of developing the enlightened mind; it is that which makes it progress, causing one to rise higher and higher.

Maintaining the bodhisattva vows involves the three types of discipline: refraining from negative conduct, gathering virtuous deeds, and benefiting sentient beings. The vows are the support for the development of the enlightened mind. The cultivation of a mind that aspires toward an inferior transcendence of suffering would block the path of the Great Vehicle. It would be a hindrance, or conflicting factor, to a mind that aspires toward supreme enlightenment. If this conflicting factor arises in one's mind and is perpetuated, this will prevent the development of the enlightened mind.[31]

Great compassion that wishes for all sentient beings to achieve the transcendence of suffering constitutes the accumulation of merit. Insight that realizes emptiness, the understanding that ultimately there is nothing that needs to transcend suffering, is the accumulation of wakefulness. The nature of the development of the enlightened mind consists of these two accumulations. The benefit of cultivating the enlightened mind is the increase of meritorious virtue in all possible realms of space, realms of sentient beings, and realms of the world.

Developing the enlightened mind leads to one's emergence from cyclic existence. One definitively emerges from the three realms and attains unsurpassable enlightenment. Constant engagement in the six transcendences is held to be the definitive emergence.

The grounds are the culmination of these developments of the enlightened mind. While on any of the ten grounds, reaching the perfection of a particular ground through practice is said to be the culmination of that particular ground. Reaching the culmination of all ten transcendences—from perfecting transcendent generosity on the first ground up to transcendent wakefulness on the tenth ground—is called the culmination of the ten grounds. Consequently, the development of the enlightened mind that fully accomplishes one of the transcendences establishes the culmination of the transcendence on that ground, while the end of the continuum of the tenth ground constitutes the culmination of the development of the enlightened mind on the path of training. The culmination of the fruition is the stage of buddhahood. In this way, the bodhisattva's development of the enlightened mind can undoubtedly be determined through this elevenfold presentation.

3. Attainment through Symbols and through the Intrinsic Nature

The development of the enlightened mind that is brought about by inspired conduct up to the point at which one attains the supreme mundane quality is known as the enlightened mind "attained through symbols." By the power of one's fundamental virtues and a spiritual teacher, one resolves to cultivate the enlightened mind in accordance with the way in which that commitment is expressed in words. From the first ground, on the other hand, the cultivation of the enlightened mind is said to be "attained through the intrinsic nature."

Moreover, the development of the relative mind of enlightenment refers to setting one's mind on attaining unsurpassable, supreme enlightenment. The ultimate development of the enlightened mind means the realization that one's mind is free from all constructs or, in other words, realization of the truth of the intrinsic nature. These descriptions are similar in meaning; they both refer to nonconceptual wakefulness. With the attainment of the grounds comes the realization of the essential and inseparable unity of the relative and ultimate development of the enlightened mind.

1. Relative Mind of Enlightenment

First, it is explained how one develops the enlightened mind that is acquired through symbols or shown by others:

**Brought about by the power of the teacher, the cause, the fundamental,
Hearing, and familiarity with virtue,
The arising is unstable and stable.
This cultivation of the mind is explained as being taught by others.** [v.7]

Next it is explained how one genuinely cultivates the enlightened mind that arises based on symbols. This development of the enlightened mind may be **brought about by the power of** (1) the spiritual **teacher**, (2) **the cause**, meaning the potential, (3) **the fundamental** virtues associated with the developed potential, (4) embracing the development of the mind by **hearing** any of the many categories of Dharma that are taught, **and** (5) **the familiarity with virtue**, such as studying, retaining, and explaining this Dharma. It should be understood that **the arising** of the enlightened mind **is unstable** in the first case, **and stable** in the case of the other four. **This cultivation of the mind is explained as being taught by others.**

Cultivating the enlightened mind, having been inspired by a spiritual teacher who tells one to develop it, is called (1) "developing the enlightened mind through the power of a teacher." Developing the enlightened mind through the force of the bodhisattva potential is called (2) "developing through the power of the cause." (3) "Developing through fundamental virtues" refers to when the mind turns toward enlightenment in one's present life as a result of having developed the enlightened mind during past lives, having practiced the Great Vehicle Dharma, and having gathered the accumulations of wakefulness. Anyone who develops the enlightened mind through the power of hearing the Great Vehicle Dharma (4) "develops through hearing." For instance, many gods and human beings developed the mind of unsurpassable enlightenment when the Blessed One taught the Dharma in the past. Finally, when one listens to, and reflects on, the Great Vehicle Dharma in one's present life, one (5) "develops the mind of enlightenment by familiarizing oneself with virtue." Of these five, the first is unstable and may revert back, while the latter four are stable. This was the explanation of the five ways of developing the enlightened mind that are taught by others.

2. Ultimate Mind of Enlightenment

Next, the cultivation of the ultimate mind of enlightenment will be taught over seven stanzas.

> The perfect buddhas are served,
> The accumulations of merit and wakefulness thoroughly
>   gathered,
> And nonconceptual wakefulness with regard to phenomena is
>   born.
> Therefore, this is held to be ultimate. [v.8]
>
> With regard to phenomena, sentient beings,
> Their needs, and the highest buddhahood,
> One discovers a mind of equality.
> Hence, this sublime joy is exalted. [v.9]

The following explanation concerns the development of the ultimate mind of enlightenment. That **the perfect buddhas** are served by upholding the Dharma of scripture is the distinction with respect to scripture. Moreover, that **the** two **accumulations of merit and wakefulness** are **thoroughly gathered** is the distinction with respect to practice. The distinction with respect to realization is that **nonconceptual wakefulness with regard to phenomena is born.** Therefore, **this is held to be** the development of the **ultimate** enlightened mind.

At this time, **with regard to phenomena,** one realizes that they are all equally devoid of self. With respect to **sentient beings,** one comes to see oneself and others as equal. Regarding **their needs,** one becomes just as intent on eliminating the suffering of sentient beings as one is on bringing an end to one's own. **And,** with respect to the basic field of phenomena that pertains to **the highest buddhahood, one** comes to see it and oneself as inseparable, and so one **discovers a mind of equality. Hence, this** ground of **sublime joy is exalted.**

On the grounds of inspired conduct, one serves the perfect buddhas for one incalculable eon by making offerings to them; by receiving, reflecting, and meditating on the Dharma; and by thoroughly gathering the two accumulations of merit and wakefulness comprising the six transcendences. These causes give rise to the nonconceptual wakefulness that does not conceive of any dualistic phenomena, such as an apprehended and an apprehender, or that which is permanent or impermanent. A sacred realization such as this is held to be the development of the ultimate or sacred enlightened mind, the attainment of which arises on the first ground. As the attainment is accompanied by sublime joy, this ground is also termed "the Joyous."

That one feels such joy at this time is due to the realization of equality with respect to the aggregates and all other such phenomena, as well as with respect to sentient beings, the actions that are carried out for their welfare, and the truth body of the supreme buddhas. As they attain this mind of fourfold equality, the sublime joy of the bodhisattvas is exalted. Phenomena, self and other, and the buddhas are all realized to be equal, not different, within the nature of the basic field of phenomena. Therefore, by knowing the nature of phenomena, one has no fear of cyclic existence. Moreover, the needs of others are not thought of as different from one's own needs, and one sees that one is accomplishing the welfare of sentient beings. One realizes that one supports all sentient beings and realizes that one is close to the state of buddhahood. This brings about a feeling of sublime joy.

1. Summary

Birth, vastness, delight in this,
Pure intent, expertise in what remains,
And definitive emergence—
Thus it should be understood. [v.10]

The ultimate mind of enlightenment can be understood in terms of six points: **birth, vastness, delight in this, pure intent, expertise in what remains, and definitive emergence**—thus it should be understood.

The ultimate mind of enlightenment should be understood in terms of six points: (1) birth, (2) vastness, (3) delight in this, (4) pure intent, (5) expertise in what remains, and (6) definitive emergence. Following this summary there is an elaborate explanation of each point.

2. Elaborate Explanation
1. Birth

Inspiration with respect to the Dharma is the seed,
And the supreme transcendence is the mother from whom it
    is born.
Emerging from the womb of the bliss of meditative
    concentration,
It is raised by the nursemaid of compassion. [v.11]

Inspiration with respect to the Dharma of the Great Vehicle **is the seed** from the father, **and the** practice of the **supreme transcendence is the mother from whom it is born**. Emerging from the womb of the bliss of meditative concentration, which is its abode, it is, subsequently, **raised by the nursemaid of compassion.**

Concerning the first topic, birth, there are four ways in which the emergence of the enlightened mind resembles birth from a womb within this world. (1) Inspiration with respect to the Dharma of the Supreme Vehicle can be compared to the seed and (2) since the enlightened mind takes birth from the transcendent insight that realizes the emptiness of all phenomena, which is supreme among all the transcendences, this insight can be likened to a mother. Furthermore, (3) the bliss of agility that arises from single-pointed meditative concentration is like a flawless womb, and (4) great compassion can be compared to a nursemaid, for it nurtures the virtuous qualities and offers protection from the abyss of the listeners' transcendence of suffering. Thus, the enlightened mind arises from four such causes.

2. Vastness

**Because of the practice of the ten great aspirations,
It should be known to be vast. [V. 12a–b]**

Because of the practice of the ten great aspirations, it should be known to be vast.

While the listeners cultivate the enlightened mind for their own benefit, the bodhisattvas develop it for the benefit of others as well as themselves. Since they also practice the ten great aspirations, their development of the enlightened mind should be known to be "vast." With the ten great aspirations, one aspires to (1) make offerings to all the buddhas, (2) fully uphold the entire sacred Dharma, (3) fully display the bodies, (4) enter into all fields, (5) perfect all the transcendences, (6) bring all sentient beings to maturation, (7) bring forth buddha fields, (8) be in accord with the objectives of the bodhisattvas, (9) let all activities be meaningful, and (10) attain great enlightenment. In addition to these aspirations, there are hundreds of thousands, indeed countless, associated aspirations.

Moreover, these aspirations are accomplished in relation to ten infinite fields of activity: (1) the realms of sentient beings, (2) the world realms, (3) the realm of space, (4) the extents of the sacred Dharma, (5) the transcendence of suffering, (6) the presence of buddhas, (7) the wakefulness of the buddhas, (8) the reference points of the minds of sentient beings, and (9) the fields of the buddhas' activity of wakefulness. In this way, the aspirations are accomplished to the extent of these infinite fields of activity. Finally, these nine fields can be summarized into (10) the elements that comprise the continuities of the worlds, Dharma, and wakefulness. Such elements pervade time and space without limit, and it should be understood that bodhisattvas display the magical manifestations of their aspirations to the same extent.

3. Delight

> Since there is no weariness during long periods of hardship,
> It should be understood to be delightful. [v.12c–d]

> Since there is no weariness, even during long periods of undergoing hardship, it should be understood to be delightful.

While listeners delight in working merely for their own welfare, bodhisattvas, who work for the sake of both themselves and others, do not feel weary despite having to undergo all manner of hardships, unbearable for others, for the long period of three incalculable eons. Hence, by that token it can be understood that this ultimate mind of enlightenment is delightful.

4. Pure Intent

> Since it is realized that enlightenment is near,
> And since knowledge of the means for that has been discovered,
> The intent should be known to be pure. [v.13a–c]

> Since it is realized that enlightenment is near, and since knowledge of the means for that has been discovered, the intent should be known to be pure.

Listeners attain their fruition by eliminating merely the obscurations that are afflictions. Bodhisattvas realize that the unsurpassable enlightenment in which both obscurations are purified is near at hand. They also discover the means and wakefulness for achieving buddhahood. Hence, their intent is pure.

5. Expertise in What Remains

There is expertise with regard to the other grounds. [v.13d]

There is expertise with regard to the other grounds that still remain to be attained.

Due to their approach to eliminating the contrived and innate afflictions that pertain to the three realms, listeners have expertise merely in the stages of a stream enterer, a once-returner, a nonreturner, and a foe destroyer. When bodhisattvas attain the first ground and so forth, they have expertise regarding the nature of the remaining grounds, their qualities, and how to gradually attain them. Hence, it is said that they have "expertise in what remains."

6. Definitive Emergence

*The mind is perfectly attentive to the principles.
They are precisely known to be thoughts,
And there is no thought with regard to that.
Thus, this should be known to be definitive emergence.
[v.14]*

The mind is perfectly attentive to the principles that pertain to the grounds. How is the mind attentive to these principles? They, the principles pertaining to the grounds, **are precisely known to be** mere **thoughts, and there is no thought with regard to that** understanding of them in this manner either. **Thus, this should be known to be definitive emergence.**

In leaving the previous ground and entering the next, one ascends from one to the next and there is definitive emergence. Thus, on the first ground one perfects transcendent generosity and attains the twelve hundred qualities—seeing a hundred buddhas, and so on. These are the conventional, relative characteristics of that ground.

As one accurately brings those principles to mind, one will comprehend that the characteristics of the grounds are nowhere else; they are simply set forth by one's own thoughts. Without thinking that "they are mind only, mere thought!" one abides within nonconceptual wakefulness and transcends the first ground, entering into the second. This process takes place on the other grounds in the same way. Hence, this is definitive emergence from one ground to the next.

3. Metaphors

The metaphors for the development of the enlightened mind are taught in the following six stanzas:

> The development is like the earth.
> Another is like exquisite gold.
> One is like the waxing moon,
> Another is known to be like fire. [v.15]

> Another resembles a great treasure,
> Another is like a jewel mine.
> Others are known to be like the ocean,
> Like a diamond, and like a great mountain. [v.16]

> One is like the king of medicines,
> While another is known to be like a great friend.
> One resembles a wish-fulfilling jewel.
> Another is like the sun. [v.17]

> Another is like the melody of the gandharvas,
> While yet another resembles a king.

One is like a treasury,
Another is like a highway. [v.18]

It is known as a vehicle.
The development of the mind is like a spring,
Like a sound that is lovely to everyone,
Like the flow of a great river. [v.19]

The development of the mind of the children
Of the victorious ones is said to be like a cloud.
Therefore, as it possesses a wealth of qualities,
That mind is fully developed with joy. [v.20]

The following explanation concerns the great metaphors for developing the enlightened mind. The bodhisattvas' initial **development** of the enlightened mind **is like the earth** because it serves as the foundation for all the qualities of enlightenment, as well as their flourishing accumulation. **Another** way of developing the enlightened mind, namely, the one associated with intent, **is like exquisite gold,** for the intent to bring benefit and happiness to others never changes into anything else. **One** development of the enlightened mind, namely, the one associated with engagement, **is like the waxing moon,** for it increases virtuous qualities. **Another,** associated with superior intent, **is known to be like fire** because it is enriched like a fire consuming special types of firewood.

Another, associated with transcendent generosity, **resembles a great treasure** because it satisfies infinite sentient beings with enjoyments and because it is inexhaustible. **Another,** associated with transcendent discipline, **is like a jewel mine,** for from it all precious qualities emerge. **Others are known to be like the ocean** (as is the case with the development associated with patience) because it is not stirred by anxieties; **like a diamond** (as with the development associated with diligence) because it is so firm that it is indestructible; **like a great mountain** (that is, the one associated with concentration) because it remains unmoved by distractions.

One way of developing the enlightened mind, associated with transcendent knowledge, **is like the king of medicines,** for it completely cures the diseases of the afflictive and cognitive obscurations. Another, associated with the four immeasurables, **is known to be like a great friend,** for it never forsakes any sentient being at any time. One, associated with superknowledges, **resembles a wish-fulfilling jewel,** for it grants whichever result is desired. Another, associated with the four means of attraction, **is like the sun** because it brings the harvest of disciples to complete maturation. Another, associated with the correct awarenesses, **is like the melody of the gandharvas,** as it reveals the Dharma in a way that tames those needing to be trained, **while yet another,** associated with the four reliances, **resembles a king,** because it ensures that nothing is wasted. The one associated with the accumulations of merit and wakefulness **is like a treasury** because it serves as the precious storehouse for the vast accumulations of merit and wakefulness. Another, associated with the factors that accord with enlightenment, **is like a highway,** for it is the path taken by all noble individuals and the one they will continue to take.

Referring to the development associated with calm abiding and special insight, **it is thus known as a vehicle** because it carries one with ease. The development of the enlightened mind associated with retention and acumen **is like a spring,** for it is an inexhaustible source of the words of the Dharma, both those that have been heard and those that have yet to be heard. It holds and yields both those words and their meanings. The development of the enlightened mind associated with teaching the Dharma is **like a sound that is lovely to everyone,** for it is delightful to the ear of those to be trained and who wish for liberation. For the bodhisattvas who reach the [eighth] ground, all activities are integrated inseparably within the single path to be traversed. The development of the enlightened mind that is associated with this is **like the flow of a great river** because the attainment of the acceptance of nonarising phenomena occurs on its own.

The development of the enlightened mind of the children of the victorious ones that is associated with skill in means **is said to**

be like a cloud because all the activities of benefiting sentient beings depend on it, such as the act of dwelling in the Joyful Realm. Therefore, as it is rich and **possesses a wealth of qualities,** that mind is to be **fully developed with joy.**

Twenty-two metaphors apply to the development of the enlightened mind, beginning with the initial generation of the enlightened mind on the grounds of inspired conduct, up to the enlightened mind that is cultivated on the tenth ground. These twenty-two aspects of the development of the enlightened mind contain all the key points of the path of the Great Vehicle. The metaphors are presented in relation to the eighty inexhaustible qualities, such as aspiration and intent.

The first way of developing the enlightened mind is associated with aspiration—an aspiration to achieve unsurpassable, supreme enlightenment. This is the sole basis, or foundation, for producing the full range of qualities of the path—the intention, practice, superior intent, transcendences of the Great Vehicle, all the way up to its skillful means. It is also the basis for its resultant qualities, such as the powers, fearlessnesses, and the unshared qualities. This way of developing the enlightened mind resembles the great earth, upon which all grasses, trees, fruits, and grains must grow.

Based on this, an enlightened mind develops that is different from that of the previous stage. Its excellent intent, to bring benefit and happiness to all sentient beings, is unchanging. It resembles exquisite gold. However much we examine pure gold by melting, cutting, or polishing it, its color and nature will not change. By wholeheartedly practicing the transcendences, an enlightened mind that increases the two accumulations will develop further and further like the waxing moon.

This is followed by the development of an enlightened mind endowed with a superior intent that is able to bear the burden of benefiting sentient beings. It is known to resemble fire, which blazes and flares up naturally as more firewood is added to it. Abiding in the heat of the path of joining, this form of the enlightened mind aspires to achieve all the higher qualities, from the summit stage up to the stage of buddhahood, and as such it causes one to attain all these. (In other texts, the enlightened mind of superior intent is likened to the waxing moon and the metaphor for the practice is fire.) These four are developed by ordinary beings and extend from the initial generation of the enlightened mind up until the supreme quality.

The development of an enlightened mind endowed with transcendent generosity is known to be like a great treasure. In some contexts there are said to be four types of great treasure, such as the conch, lotus, and magnificent lotus, while in others there are said to be nine. In brief, an unending variety of items, such as food and clothing, can be gained from an inexhaustible trove of precious treasures. Likewise, through generosity, limitless sentient beings are satisfied with material goods, Dharma, and so on. The bodhisattva's generosity is never exhausted—even in the field of the transcendence of suffering, within which there is no remainder of the aggregates.

The development of the enlightened mind endowed with transcendent discipline resembles a trove of jewels or a jewel mine. Just as a limitless number of jewels can be found in such mines, all the limitless, precious qualities of the path and fruition of the Great Vehicle spring forth from the bodhisattva's enlightened mind endowed with discipline. These qualities include the grounds, the transcendences, the factors of enlightenment, the powers, and the fearlessnesses. The development of an enlightened mind endowed with transcendent patience can be likened to a great ocean. The ocean remains undisturbed and its depth unstirred, even when it is filled with boats, fish, and sea creatures. Likewise, a bodhisattva's mind, when endowed with patience, remains flawlessly undisturbed in the face of hardships or the malice of others.

Furthermore, the development of an enlightened mind endowed with transcendent diligence resembles a diamond. Just as a precious diamond is unaffected by fire, water, and the like, and just as it cannot be scraped or cut, this enlightened mind developed by a bodhisattva is unharmed by the weapon of laziness. The development of an enlightened mind endowed with transcendent concentration resembles the supreme king of mountains. Just as this mountain cannot be moved by any of the winds from the four directions, a bodhisattva's meditative absorption is not moved by distracted thoughts. The development of an enlightened mind endowed with transcendent knowledge is like the king of medicines or elixirs. By merely seeing, touching, smelling, or tasting this medicine, all sicknesses stemming from wind, phlegm, and bile will be cured. Likewise, receiving, reflecting, and meditating on transcendent knowledge cures all the diseases of the afflictive and cognitive obscurations.

The development of an enlightened mind endowed with the four immeasurables can be likened to a great friend. A great friend will always assist you and never forsake you, whether in times of happiness, sadness, or indifference. Likewise, this mind joyfully helps by alleviating suffering through compassion in painful times. When there is sadness, it brings happiness through love. It promotes constant happiness with joy, and, through equanimity, it promotes nonattachment to happiness and nonaggression in the face of pain. In this way, it enables the mind to remain in naturalness, free from attachment and aversion.

The development of the enlightened mind endowed with the five superknowledges is like a wish-fulfilling jewel, which grants all of one's needs and wishes. By the power of the superknowledges, one can display various miracles, fulfilling all one's wishes and desires as well as those of others. For instance, one can see all forms with the miraculous eye and know the future by understanding the transference of death and birth. Through the miraculous ear one can hear all sounds and, by knowing the minds of others, one can understand the differing mental constitutions of sentient beings. By recalling past existences, one can know one's own and others' previous lives, and through the superknowledge of miracles, one can emanate a variety of bodies.

The development of the enlightened mind endowed with the four means of attraction is known to be like the sun. Just as the sun ripens a whole range of crops, with this enlightened mind one can bring the mind streams of all beings to maturation, universally establishing them in virtue through the four means of attraction. More specifically, one can attract miserly individuals through generosity and thereby establish them in virtue. Likewise, one will speak pleasantly to aggressive individuals, act meaningfully toward dim-witted individuals, and act consistently for those who are proud. Having attracted them in this way, one can then establish them in virtue.

The development of an enlightened mind endowed with the four correct awarenesses that are related to Dharma, meaning, definitive words, and acumen is like the melody of the gandharvas. Endowed with the four correct awarenesses, bodhisattvas explain whatever Dharma or meaning sentient beings wish to understand. Since bodhisattvas' acumen knows no limits, they can correctly answer any question in the respective language of a particular sentient being. In this way, they completely satisfy the minds of sentient beings. This can be likened to the tremendous beauty of the gandharvas' melodies, in that all who hear them feel happy and fulfilled.

The development of the enlightened mind endowed with the four reliances can be likened to a king. Since a king has control over his subjects, they cannot but obey his commands. Hence, his directives will not be wasted. A bodhisattva endowed with the four reliances—which are related to words and their meanings, people and the Dharma, expedient and definitive meanings, and consciousness and wakefulness—correctly knows all the viewpoints explained by the Thus-Gone One and is able to realize the intended meanings of his teachings without letting any of them be wasted. A king, for instance, not forsaking those who serve him well, will lavish power and riches upon them. Those who serve the king poorly, however, will be forsaken, losing power or meeting their demise. Those who merely rely on people, words, expedient meanings, and consciousness will likewise be forsaken. On the other hand, those who rely on the Dharma, the meaning, the definitive meaning, and on wakefulness will ensure that the purport of the Buddha's words is not forsaken.

The development of the enlightened mind endowed with the two accumulations of merit and wakefulness is like a treasury. Just as there are boundless grains and riches in a treasury, there are also immeasurable accumulations of merit and boundless accumulations of wakefulness within the enlightened mind that is associated with them. The development of the enlightened mind endowed with the thirty-seven factors that accord with enlightenment can be illustrated by the example of a highway on which sentient beings, high and low, all travel throughout the past, present, and future. The thirty-seven factors that accord with enlightenment are, in a similar way, the path on which all the listeners, self-realized buddhas, and bodhisattvas of the past, present, and future travel to their own fruition of enlightenment.

The development of the enlightened mind associated with calm abiding and special insight resembles a vehicle, that is, something one rides on or in. Vehicles such as horses, elephants, and chariots carry burdens and bring one to one's desired destination. Likewise, by integrating calm abiding, in which the mind rests one-pointedly free from distraction, with the special insight that unerringly perceives the facts, one realizes without distortion the topics that are to be resolved, namely, all phenomena, as they truly are and as many as they are. This carries one to the destination of the final fruition.

The development of the enlightened mind endowed with complete retention and inexhaustible acumen is like a natural spring. Springs are used by everyone. Yet, no matter how much water is drawn from a spring, it will never run out: the flow of water never stops. Likewise, through the bodhisattvas' attainment of retention, the Dharma does not diminish: they never forget the doctrines they have heard in the past. Due to their acumen, they expand on the Dharma anew. No matter how much they teach of it, there is no end to the Dharma.

Next comes the development of the enlightened mind endowed with the four summaries, or summations of the Dharma. These four are as follows: (1) all conditioned phenomena are impermanent, (2) everything contaminated is suffering, (3) all phenomena are selfless, and (4) transcendence of suffering is peace. The development of an enlightened mind endowed with these four can be likened to words that completely delight the mind. For instance, people are sad when separated from relatives, wealth, and so forth, but if someone tells them that they will meet their relatives again, and find their wealth again, they will feel reassured. The same is the case when someone who fears for his or her life receives words that offer protection. In brief, words that completely delight the mind are words that, when heard, give assurance to the downtrodden or which perfectly convey happy and joyous matters. Likewise, the elixir of the authentic Dharma is the path of peace and transcendence of suffering. Hearing a discourse of the fourfold Dharma yields peace, for in hearing its four summaries, wondrous joy wells up in the mind streams of fortunate beings, as though they were being satisfied by an elixir. This is because it assures them that they will be free from the entirety of suffering in cyclic existence, that they will realize the nature of the authentic Dharma, and that they will attain a state of everlasting happiness.

The development of the enlightened mind endowed with the single path to be traversed is like the flow of a great river. A great river flows effortlessly and naturally empties into an ocean. Likewise, great acceptance of nonarising phenomena is attained on the eighth ground, where nonconceptual wakefulness is always effortlessly and spontaneously present, both during meditative equipoise and the subsequent attainment. When this is achieved, there is equality beyond distinctions as the mind streams and activities of all the bodhisattvas who have reached this ground merge. Consequently, it is called "the single path to be traversed" because, without any effort, one spontaneously accesses all the qualities of a buddha and engages in the activities of bringing sentient beings to full maturation.

The development of the enlightened mind endowed with the skillful means of the children of the victorious one is likened to a cloud. The rain that falls from gigantic clouds allows for various sorts of worldly bounties, such as the crops that grow in the earth's fields. Likewise, bodhisattvas who integrate skillful means with insight display all the enlightened deeds, from descending from the palace in The Joyful Realm through to the transcendence of suffering, and they bring forth numerous beneficial and joyous qualities of the higher realms as well as liberating enlightenment.

In this way, the bodhisattva's development of the enlightened mind, as shown by these twenty-two metaphors, is rich and abounds with qualities. With complete faith and joy, one should fully cultivate this supreme enlightened mind.

4. Praise of Its Benefits

There are eight stanzas that praise the enlightened mind, thereby encouraging one to develop it. The first explains how four kinds of happiness will be thwarted for all those who are deprived of the enlightened mind of the Great Vehicle.

1. Four Kinds of Happiness

> Beings without this development of the mind, which suits the great,

DEVELOPING THE ENLIGHTENED MIND 99

Lack the concern to be of benefit to others, the discovery of
the means to do so,
The meaning of this great intent, and the vision of supreme
reality.
Deprived of this happiness, they proceed to peace. [v.21]

The following explanation takes the form of a rebuke toward those
who do not cultivate the enlightened mind. **Beings without this
development of the mind, which suits the great, lack** four kinds
of happiness: (1) the happiness experienced through **the concern
to be of benefit to others**, (2) the happiness that comes with **the
discovery of the means to do so**, that is, to accomplish the welfare
of others, (3) the happiness of realizing **the meaning of this great
intent**, which is the intended meaning of the profound sūtras of
the Great Vehicle, **and** (4) the happiness of gaining **the vision
of supreme reality**, the fact of the absence of self in phenomena.
Deprived of this happiness, of the kinds explained above, **they
proceed** alone **to** solitary **peace**.

The supreme enlightened mind suits the bodhisattvas and the thus-gone
ones. Listeners and self-realized buddhas—beings who lack the development of the enlightened mind that suits the great, or is greatly beneficial—are deprived of four types of happiness. Bodhisattvas have the
happiness that comes from courageously working for the welfare of other
sentient beings. They establish these others in the perfect abandonment
that is achieved by eliminating the two obscurations and in the perfect
realization that comes with understanding the twofold selflessness.
Since benefiting even a single sentient being in some small way makes
bodhisattvas happier than they would be by attaining their own benefit, it goes without saying that they are happy when establishing others
in perfect realization and abandonment. They experience the supreme,
boundless happiness, free of negativity, that comes from accomplishing
the benefit of countless sentient beings. Yet, listeners and self-realized
buddhas abandon these pursuits, and are thereby deprived of this happiness. Moreover, bodhisattvas feel supreme happiness when they discover
and understand the various means for accomplishing the benefit and

happiness of all sentient beings. When listeners and self-realized buddhas simply understand the means for becoming free from the sufferings of cyclic existence, they experience a joy that is confined; it is not vast like that of the bodhisattvas.

The meaning of the "great intent" expressed in the Great Vehicle is that all phenomena are nonarising and unceasing and that they are naturally free from all constructs. When bodhisattvas come to understand this profound meaning, and when they properly realize the profound viewpoints indicated through words of intent and concealed intent, they feel exceedingly happy. Listeners and self-realized buddhas are deprived of such happiness. They experience the happiness of merely a limited knowledge of the path and the selflessness of persons. Bodhisattvas see the final reality of all phenomena. In other words, they see the most supreme emptiness, the great equality, exactly as it is. Through this, they feel a great happiness that is inexhaustible and equal to space. Listeners and self-realized buddhas, on the other hand, do not experience this happiness because they merely realize the selflessness of persons, while considering entities to exist. Therefore, they do not realize reality as it is.

In this way, listeners and self-realized buddhas do not cultivate the mind of supreme enlightenment, and they are therefore deprived of this fourfold happiness. Free from the appropriated aggregates, they depart for a transcendence of suffering that is a mere pacification of the sufferings of cyclic existence. This shows that it is worthwhile to give up any attraction to the results of the listeners and self-realized buddhas and cultivate instead the mind of supreme enlightenment.

2. No Fear of Pain

The following shows that if one cultivates the ultimate enlightened mind, there will be no fear of, or aversion to, the sufferings of the lower realms and cyclic existence.

> As soon as the wise give rise to the supreme mind,
> Their minds are perfectly on guard against doing wrong to the infinite,

**And, as the two are developed, they are forever in possession of virtue and love,
Joyful in both happiness and suffering. [v.22]**

It may be thought that although one has given rise to the mind of enlightenment, fear of rebirth in the lower realms might lead one to take up the path of the listeners or self-realized buddhas. This is not the case. **As soon as the wise give rise to the supreme mind,** the ultimate mind of enlightenment, **their minds are perfectly on guard against doing wrong,** which would cause harm **to the infinite** host of sentient beings. Therefore, they have no fear of the lower realms. **And, as the two**—virtuous actions and a loving heart—**are developed, they are forever in possession of virtue and love, joyful in both happiness** (because of their virtue) **and** the **suffering** that is experienced when benefiting others (because of their loving heart).

"The wise" refers to bodhisattvas who possess the wakefulness that realizes selflessness. When they cultivate the ultimate enlightened mind, the supreme mind of unsurpassable enlightenment, on the first ground, their minds are immediately fully guarded against committing any faults. They are guarded from activities that are harmful to any of the infinite number of sentient beings and from the limitless dimensions of nonvirtue that occur through the three gateways. Such is their vow of abstinence, which they obtain by the power of the intrinsic nature, and as they will refrain from unwholesome acts in the future, they have no fear of falling into the three lower realms.

Bodhisattvas who cultivate the enlightened mind develop virtue, and they always dwell in virtue due to the expanding streams of their love and compassion toward sentient beings. Since they have love for sentient beings, they are joyful when experiencing happiness but also when encountering pain. Therefore, they are free from fearful aversions. Through the power of virtue, they have joy as they experience an abundance of human and divine delights. By means of their increasing love, they also joyfully accept the experiences of manifold sufferings, such as the heat and cold of the lower realms, for the benefit of other sentient beings who suffer. Always joyful, they never become weary of cyclic existence. Hence, this instruction counsels one never to turn one's back on the cultivation of the enlightened mind and to pursue it joyfully.

3. Never-Diminishing Virtue

> When they accept extreme hardship for the sake of others,
> Without concern for body or life,
> How could the harm that is inflicted by others
> Cause them to engage in negative acts? [v.23]

One might think that bodhisattvas might retaliate when they are hurt by others. This is not so. When they, having reached the bodhisattva grounds, **accept extreme hardship for the sake of others, without concern for** their own **body or life, how** then **could the harm that is inflicted by others** possibly **cause them to engage in** unvirtuous **negative acts** in response?

Sentient beings show a great deal of ingratitude when dwelling in cyclic existence. Since this ingratitude is difficult to bear, one may wonder how it could be that bodhisattvas never get frustrated and that their virtue never diminishes. The compassion of the bodhisattvas who have attained the grounds is such that they cherish others more than they do themselves. They even give up, and have no regard for, their own lives and bodies. For the sake of other sentient beings, they joyfully take on, or accept, agonizing pains, such as giving away their head or limbs, for many eons. When such bodhisattvas are killed or harmed in various ways by others, how could they engage in negative actions in retaliation? This would not make sense, nor does it ever happen. For this reason, one should aspire to cultivate the enlightened mind.

4. Never Turning Back

> Realizing that all phenomena are like an illusion
> And that taking birth is like a trip to a pleasure grove,

They do not fear the afflictions or suffering,
Regardless of whether they are prosperous or poor. [v.24]

One may then wonder whether bodhisattvas might still become arrogant when prosperous, or depressed when impoverished, even if they do not cause harm to others. In other words, one may think that bodhisattvas could revert back after cultivating the enlightened mind. However, by **realizing that all phenomena are like an** optical **illusion, and that taking birth is like a trip to a pleasure grove, they do not fear the afflictions or suffering, regardless of whether they are prosperous or poor.**

However much prosperity or poverty bodhisattvas may experience in cyclic existence, they never turn their backs on the bodhisattva conduct. Bodhisattvas realize that all outer and inner phenomena are like a dream, like an illusion, and so forth. Through the accumulations of merit and wakefulness, they assume birth in the realms of gods and humans for the sake of others, in whatever way they please. They realize that taking another birth after leaving their former body behind is like a trip to an exquisite pleasure grove. As will be explained below, in times of prosperity, they do not fear being fettered by afflictions such as attachment, even if they become the master of gods and humans. As was mentioned earlier, the reason for this is that they see all phenomena as an illusion.

Likewise, when they are impoverished, when death approaches and they have to give up their enjoyments and divine bodies, for instance, bodhisattvas do not fear the suffering of losing these things. This is because they know them to be like an illusion and that birth is similar to a trip to a pleasure grove. Therefore, however much happiness or misery bodhisattvas may experience, they never fall away from the path. Thus, these instructions show that it is reasonable to train on the bodhisattva path.

5. A Trip to a Pleasure Grove

The fifth point is an elaboration on what was just explained, that is, the meaning of the realization that birth is like a trip to a pleasure grove:

Joyfully benefiting others with their qualities,
Willingly taking birth and displaying miracles,
Their joys of ornaments, feasts, supreme grounds, and games
Do not belong to those whose very being is not compassion.
[v.25]

Joyfully benefiting others with their qualities, willingly taking birth as though they are taking a trip to a pleasure grove, **and displaying miracles**, through the five superknowledges, **their joys of ornaments, feasts, supreme grounds, and games do not belong to those whose very being** as bodhisattvas **is not compassion**.

Gods and humans take trips to delightful pleasure groves for four reasons. They do so (1) to bathe and then adorn their bodies with ornaments; (2) to enjoy a whole range of festive food and drinks; (3) to rest in that delightful place, and (4) to play an assortment of games. It is with a desire to experience these four joys that they enter and remain in the pleasure grove. This is similar to how bodhisattvas enter the stream of successive births because as they do so, they become increasingly adorned with beautiful qualities, such as generosity, discipline, retention, meditative absorption, and insight. As though participating in a feast, they enjoy benefiting the sentient beings of the place where they take birth. No matter where they are born, and no matter what their bodily support might be, they are as delighted when they intentionally take birth as when dwelling in the most supreme place. They magically manifest various miracles through the five superknowledges, as when people play a range of joyful games.

In this way, bodhisattvas who successively take birth in existence experience a joy that we can compare to the happiness of worldly beings when they engage in the four activities that are associated with going to a pleasure grove. Bodhisattvas experience the joy of being adorned by the ornaments of excellent qualities, the joy of the feast of benefiting others, the joy of resting in the supremely delightful pleasure grove that supports the benefit of others, and the joy of participating in various games of magical feats. Only bodhisattvas, whose very being is that of compassion, experience these four joys. Since even noble listeners and self-realized buddhas do not experience them, it should go without saying that mundane beings do not either. Therefore, since bodhisattvas who cultivate the enlightened mind possess superior qualities, it makes sense to cultivate the enlightened mind.

6. Never Discouraged

The sixth point states how they do not become discouraged or turn back due to the suffering of giving away their bodies and so forth:

> Diligently benefiting others, the one whose very being is compassion
> Holds even the hell of incessant pain to be joyful.
> When even such a thing is possible, how could those who are supported by others
> Ever fear painful events? [v.26]

This stanza explains how, for these bodhisattvas, even dreadful pain is joyful. **Diligently benefiting others, the one whose very being is compassion holds even the hell of incessant pain to be joyful** when working for the benefit of others, and so he enters this realm with joy. **When even such a thing is possible, how could those who are supported by** the welfare of **others ever fear painful events?**

Realizing that all phenomena are devoid of a self, bodhisattvas are completely free from attachment to their own benefit. For the sake of other sentient beings who have not yet realized this, they nevertheless practice the six transcendences with a constant diligence, seeking to establish those beings in the highest forms of goodness and happiness in both this and all future lives. Since they themselves become miserable when others suffer, bodhisattvas, who have compassion as their very being, will even make the hell of ultimate torment their home if it is for the sake of others. Holding it to be delightful and enjoyable, they do not feel the slightest aversion. How could they ever become intimidated by giving away their limbs and bodies, and by other forms of suffering, when doing so is in support of, or for the sake of, benefiting other sentient beings? Indeed, they gladly accept intense suffering.

At this point, the verses that appear in the translation of Sthiramati's commentary are somewhat different, yet the meaning is the same. Since bodhisattvas possess such marvelous qualities, they are never intimidated by any form of suffering in existence; they take them on with joy, one and all. Therefore, their joy never fades, and they experience no sadness. Hence, it makes good sense to take up the path of enlightenment.

7. No Need for Encouragement

The seventh point shows how bodhisattvas are the great, unacquainted friends of all sentient beings:

> For those whose nature it is always to rely on the teacher of
>   great love,
> And who are pained by the suffering of others,
> To be exhorted by another to work for the welfare of others
> Would be a matter of great shame. [v.27]

The next explanation forbids a bodhisattva from disregarding any sentient being. **For those whose nature it is always to rely on the teacher of great love, and who are pained by the suffering of others**, were it necessary **to be exhorted by another** spiritual teacher **to work for the welfare of others, it would be a matter of great shame.**

When bodhisattvas benefit others, it is not because they have been friends or relatives with them in this life, or that they have been gratified by them in the past with respect, material offerings, or service. Rather, it is their naturally good disposition to feel loving compassion toward other sentient beings. This prompts them to work for the welfare of sentient beings spontaneously, without others having to exhort them. For instance, a student may be guided by a teacher to accept what is right and reject what is wrong. Love and compassion are, similarly, the bodhisattvas' guiding teachers, to which they give constant attention in their mind streams.

Bodhisattvas are pained by the suffering of others, even more so than a mother whose child is sick. Therefore, they take on themselves the responsibility to dispel the sufferings of other sentient beings and to do what brings them to virtue and happiness. If they did not do so by themselves, but had to be urged to do so by others, it would be extremely shameful. Such a thing is in conflict with the way of a bodhisattva. It would be like a wealthy son not giving the slightest thing to his starving mother. If it were necessary for another to exhort the son by saying, "This is your mother! Give her some food!" then even worldly people would consider this extremely shameful. If, in spite of being implored, he still did not give her even a little, he would be called a savage and would be held in complete disgrace. Similarly, the teacher of great love is someone who exhorts, so to speak, and it would hence be extremely shameful if those who rely on great love should not act accordingly.

In this way, bodhisattvas do not need other sentient beings to urge them to act. Since their minds have a naturally loving disposition, they work for the welfare of sentient beings without needing others to encourage them. Indeed, it is impossible for them to forsake the welfare of sentient beings. This implicit praise of their qualities provides an instruction to work for the welfare of sentient beings.

8. Exceptional Diligence

The eighth point instructs bodhisattvas to persevere with exceptional diligence:

> For supreme beings who shoulder the burdens of beings,
> It is not becoming to walk leisurely.
> Numerous are the ties that bind oneself and others—
> This calls for a hundredfold diligence. [v.28]

> This was the fifth chapter of the *Ornament of the Great Vehicle Sūtras,* the chapter on cultivating the enlightened mind.

It might be thought that laziness could occasionally make a bodhisattva give up benefiting sentient beings. Yet, **for the supreme beings who shoulder the burdens of beings, it is not becoming just to walk leisurely** in their undertakings. **Numerous are the ties** associated with affliction, karma, and birth **that bind oneself and others.** Compared with those who practice the Lesser Vehicle, **this calls for a hundredfold diligence.**

Even in this world, people who carry huge loads must walk fast and firmly when they need to travel a long distance. If they are too lax, it will be difficult for them to reach their destination. Bodhisattvas cultivate the enlightened mind to attain great enlightenment in order to liberate all sentient beings into unsurpassable enlightenment. Shouldering the heavy burden of all sentient beings, bodhisattvas, who are supreme among all beings, must reach the destination of great enlightenment just as they have promised. Thus, it is not becoming for a bodhisattva to delay, leisurely entering or traveling the path under the influence of laziness. He or she must quickly muster diligence and so pursue the conduct of the six transcendences, which are the causes of that enlightenment. Even listeners and self-realized buddhas, striving to cut through the ties of karma and afflictions for their own benefit, are quick to develop a diligence that is rapid and without interruption, as when two sticks are rubbed together to start a fire. This enables them to reach the result of their respective enlightenment in three or seven lifetimes. A bodhisattva, however, must dispel the ties of karma and afflictions that are present in both his or her own stream of being as well as in that of all sentient beings. If presently all sentient beings—oneself and everyone else—are entirely fettered by numerous ties, meaning the threefold obscurations of karma, afflictions, and ripening, then it is reasonable for a bodhisattva to generate a diligence that is a hundred times greater than that aroused by listeners.

This concludes the explanation of cultivating the enlightened mind, the fifth chapter of the *Ornament of the Great Vehicle Sūtras*.

6
Practice

4. Practice

Once the enlightened mind has been developed as explained in the previous chapter, one needs to practice in accordance with one's pledge. Therefore, practice is explained as the fourth topic in the context of what is to be understood. This chapter will be covered under three headings: (1) a general presentation of the perfect practice endowed with the twofold benefit; (2) a specific explanation of how to practice for the sake of others; (3) a conclusion that shows the magnificence of this practice.

1. General Presentation of the Perfect Practice Endowed with the Twofold Benefit

That which consists of the great basis, pursuit, and fruition
Is held to be the practice of the children of the victorious one.
It is the constant, authentic practice of great concern, great forbearance,
And accomplishment of great benefit. [VI.1]

The characteristics of the practice are explained next. **That which consists of the great basis,** orienting the mind toward supreme enlightenment, the great **pursuit** of one's own and all others' welfare, **and** the great **fruition** of accomplishing complete enlightenment **is held to be the practice of the children of the victorious one.** **It is,** respectively, the **constant, authentic practice of** the **great concern** for all sentient beings, the **great forbearance** of taking on all suffering, **and** the **accomplishment** that is **of great benefit** for numerous sentient beings.

The practice of the children of the victorious ones is exalted because it is of the nature of the great basis, great pursuit, and great fruition. The great basis unfolds through orienting the mind toward supreme enlightenment, which is the initial thought to liberate all sentient beings into unsurpassable enlightenment. It is called "the great basis" because the basis of the practice is the development of the enlightened mind. This great concern is constant and, in initiating activity for the welfare of beings, it is the virtuous beginning.

The phrase "great pursuit" refers to the generation of boundless joy—from the grounds of inspired conduct through to the tenth ground—which occurs by one's perfecting the qualities of buddhahood oneself and by bringing other sentient beings to maturation. In this pursuit, there is no weariness, but rather great forbearance. Hence, this is the virtuous middle.

Attaining the fruition of unsurpassable, great enlightenment is of perfect benefit to oneself, and it allows one to accomplish the great benefit of all other sentient beings until the end of existence. This is the virtuous conclusion. The listeners and self-realized buddhas lack these three superior elements.

2. A Specific Explanation of the Practice for the Sake of Others

This section has six parts: (1) how to work for the welfare of others, (2) the types of actions for others' welfare, (3) how acting for others' welfare is supreme, (4) exalted, and (5) uninterrupted, and (6) knows no dejection in the face of ingratitude.

1. How to Work for the Welfare of Others

There is a mind of equality toward self and other,
Or, as one cherishes others more than oneself,

A perception of the welfare of others as far more important
than one's own.
Which objectives are then one's own, and which are those of
others? [VI.2]

Those whose nature is compassion
Bring endless torments upon themselves for the sake of others.
These exceed the torture that even the most ruthless worldly
person
Would ever use against his enemy. [VI.3]

The way in which there is no difference between one's own and others' welfare is explained as follows. When developing the enlightened mind attained through symbols and when developing the ultimate enlightened mind, **there is**, for the Bodhisattva, the presence of **a mind of equality toward self and other** that in the first case is presumptive and in the second consists of knowledge. Or, as one cherishes others more than oneself, one has, as a bodhisattva, **a perception of the welfare of others as** being **far more important than one's own. Which objectives are then one's own, and which are those of others?** In other words, there is no difference.

The character of the bodhisattva's altruism is distinguished as follows: **Those** bodhisattvas **whose nature is compassion bring endless torments upon themselves for the sake of others.** They may, for instance, feed others with their own body for an entire eon. **These exceed the** suffering induced by **torture that even the most ruthless worldly person would ever use against his enemy.**

Bodhisattvas have attained a mind of complete equality toward themselves and other sentient beings, or, having come to see others as more lovable than themselves, they have achieved a state of mind that cherishes others more than they cherish themselves. They perceive the practices of giving up afflictions and suffering, and of achieving mundane and supramundane happiness for the welfare of others, to be of paramount importance in comparison with practices aimed at achieving these two ends for their own sake. Which objectives are then their own and which are those of others? They are said to be equal, without any difference.

On the grounds of inspired conduct, bodhisattvas meditate on equalizing and exchanging self and other through compassion and inspired discernment. This enables them to attain a mind of equality toward themselves and other sentient beings. When attaining the first ground, they realize the universally present character of the basic field of phenomena and thereby discover the equality of self and others. "Although I have realized this," they think to themselves, "other sentient beings have not. Therefore they have to roam about in the delusional experience of the long-lasting, agonizing pains that can hardly be endured." With this, they actualize the mind that cherishes others more than themselves. Consequently, those whose nature is compassion bring intense suffering upon themselves for the sake of other sentient beings, giving up their lands, bodies, and so forth. These sufferings exceed the mutilations or any other torture that even the most ruthless worldly person, the most horrible enemy or the greatest butcher, would ever inflict upon an enemy.

2. Types of Actions for Others' Welfare

For those of the lowest, mediocre, and supreme nature,
They elegantly explain, delight, provide entry,
Ascertain the meaning, and thoroughly mature virtues.
Likewise they grant practical instructions, rest, and liberation
   of the mind. [VI.4]

They accomplish special qualities, provide birth into the
   family,
As well as prophecy, empowerment,
And the stage of the thus-gone ones' unsurpassable
   wakefulness.
These are the thirteen ways of benefiting others. [VI.5]

The next section explains how the practice of benefiting sentient beings is divided. Bodhisattvas work in thirteen different ways for the benefit of **those** sentient beings who are **of the lowest, mediocre, and supreme nature,** meaning the individuals who possess any of the three types of potential. (1) **They elegantly explain** [the Dharma] through a display of teaching and expression. (2) They **delight** beings with a display of miracles. (3) They **provide entry** so that the teachings will be accepted. (4) They **ascertain the meaning** for those who have gained entry so that they can overcome their doubts. (5) They **thoroughly mature** fundamental **virtues. Likewise,** to bring about calm abiding and special insight, (6) **they grant practical instructions,** based on which they facilitate the accomplishments of (7) mental **rest and** (8) the **liberation of the mind.** (9) **They** also **accomplish** the superknowledges and other **special qualities.** Furthermore, they (10) **provide birth into the family** of the buddhas on the first ground, **as well as** (11) grant **prophecy** on the eighth ground, and (12) bestow **empowerment** on the tenth. **And,** finally, (13) they establish beings on the eleventh ground, **the stage of the thus-gone ones' unsurpassable wakefulness. These are the thirteen ways of benefiting others.**

One may wonder what the bodhisattvas' different ways of acting for others' welfare may involve. Among the different types of sentient being we may distinguish three potentials. The lowest or least among these three is the potential of the listeners, the mediocre is that of the self-realized buddhas, and the supreme is the potential of the bodhisattvas. Thus, the sentient beings for the sake of whom the bodhisattvas are active can be seen to be of three such natures.

(1) Through the miraculous display of expression, bodhisattvas know the minds of sentient beings, while the miraculous display of teaching enables them to give elegant explanations of the relevant remedies for each individual. Thus, to a desirous person, for instance, they will teach repulsiveness. (2) They arouse faith in extremists and others who lack faith in the teachings by manifesting a display of miracles. This, in turn, causes such people to enter the authentic teachings, through which they will experience delight.

(3) Bodhisattvas cause ordinary sentient beings to uphold the discipline of the five bases of trainings by granting refuge in the Three Jewels.

(4) For those with a potential for one of the three vehicles, they clear away doubts regarding the points that have not been understood, and so bodhisattvas engender certainty regarding the meaning of each respective topic. (5) They lead those who have not matured their fundamental virtues to engage in the conduct of the six transcendences and thereby bring the fundamental virtues of the six transcendences to thorough maturation.

Likewise, (6) they grant scriptural instructions or give practical advice to those who desire meditative concentration, yet lack its quintessential instructions. (7) They enable those who have received guidance in meditative concentration to rest in meditative absorption with a single-pointed mind. (8) For those who lack special insight, they generate insight, letting them develop the intelligence that is required to attain the result of their respective vehicle, and allowing them to completely free their minds from doubts and other obscurations. (9) They endow such individuals with special qualities that they had otherwise not attained before, such as the qualities of the unity of calm abiding and special insight, the superknowledges, the factors of enlightenment, and the spheres of totality. All of these activities are carried out in common, for the welfare of sentient beings belonging to any of the three vehicles.

(10) In terms of the Great Vehicle alone, bodhisattvas allow beings to take birth within the family of the buddhas on the first ground. (11) They also bring about acceptance of nonarising phenomena on the eighth ground. With that achievement, one receives, by the power of the intrinsic nature, the thus-gone ones' prophecy: "At such a time and in such a place, you, noble child, will become a thus-gone one by the name...." Similarly, (12) on the tenth ground, all the buddhas of the ten directions empower one through light rays to be the regent of the buddhas, the kings of the Dharma. Finally, (13) at the stage of buddhahood, there is complete illumination. Thus one is established at the unsurpassable level of a thus-gone one's wakefulness by attaining the four types of wakefulness. These thirteen categories show what is entailed in accomplishing the welfare of others.

3. The Supremacy of Working for the Welfare of Others

Teaching correctly and in harmony with beings,
Absence of conceit and any notion of "mine," expertise,
Patience, discipline, extremely far reach, and inexhaustibility:
Such are the supreme practices of the children of the
victorious ones. [VI.6]

The perfect nature of the bodhisattvas' practice of benefiting others is explained in the following way. **Teaching correctly and in harmony with** individual **beings** who have one of the three types of potential is the sign of excellent teaching. **Absence of conceited** pride is the sign of bringing them delight. **And**, similarly, the bodhisattvas' practice takes place without discord, without **any notion of "mine."** In this way, their magical feats do not become a cause of conceit, and they do not think of those beings whom they have ushered in as being theirs. They have **expertise** in ascertaining the meaning. They also have **patience** when undertaking hardship for the sake of others, which enables them to ripen thoroughly all virtues. They have physical and mental **discipline** concerning the practices of granting practical instructions, letting the mind rest, liberating it, and accomplishing special qualities, for without discipline one cannot advise others, and so on. For those who have taken birth into the family of the buddhas, and [on the grounds] beyond, the practice has **extremely far reach** because those bodhisattvas are capable of causing others to take birth into the family, and so forth. **And** these practices of the bodhisattvas also feature **inexhaustibility** because there is no end to the number of sentient beings that they accept. **Such are the supreme practices of the children of the victorious ones.**

The following passage discusses how these practices benefit others and how they are supreme since they are never wasted. When the Dharma is taught in harmony with the individual beings of the three potentials, it will be of benefit to those who receive it. On this point, the *Jewel Mound Sūtra* states: "It is a mistake for a bodhisattva to explain the vast and profound Dharma to those belonging to the vehicles of the listeners or self-realized buddhas." As stated here, if a teaching is given that is not in harmony with a particular individual's constitution, it will not be meaningful for him or her. Such an act would not be the supreme practice of acting for the welfare of others. Likewise, to explain the Dharma unerringly is to teach the antidotes in the correct manner. Since the three types of potential have varying degrees of attachment and so forth, repulsiveness is taught to a desirous person, loving-kindness to an aggressive individual, the meaning of dependent origination to a dull person, and so forth.

Although one may attain miraculous powers and other excellent qualities, it is the supreme practice for the welfare of others to remain free from conceit in body, speech, and mind, without thinking, "Since I possess these qualities, I am extraordinary." In other words, if one arrogantly makes a show of one's body, praises oneself, and is conceited, one will not achieve much in terms of benefiting others.

While bodhisattvas tame sentient beings and establish them on the path by teaching the Dharma, displaying magical powers, and other such activities, they are not biased, thinking, "This is my disciple whom I have tamed." In other words, they are free from the notion of "mine." As experts in the meaning of the three vehicles, they guide to understanding those who have none. They dissolve the misunderstandings of all those with wrong understanding, and they clear away the doubts of those who have qualms. For the sake of others, they endure the various pains of heat, cold, hunger, thirst, ingratitude, and so on. Disciplined themselves, with restraint of body, speech, and mind, they are able to establish others in discipline as well. As stated in a sūtra: "Unless I am liberated, I will not be able to liberate others. Likewise, unless I am at peace, I will not be able to instill peace in others. Unless I am disciplined, I will not be able to establish others in discipline."

The expressions "extremely far reach" and "inexhaustibility" refer to the practices of the bodhisattvas who have entered the grounds. Bodhisattvas who have attained the grounds accomplish the welfare of sentient beings by establishing them on the grounds as well. Those who enter the grounds, from the first ground up to the stage of buddhahood, have "reached extremely far." Listeners and self-realized buddhas are not able to enter any of those grounds; this can be done only by bodhisattvas. Consequently, bodhisattvas possess a reach that extends far beyond the former. As explained above, when coming to abide on the first ground, bodhisattvas are born into the family of the buddhas. From there, they are capable of helping others take birth into the family of the buddhas as well. Likewise, as their nonconceptual wakefulness matures by receiving the prophecy, they also become able to establish others at the stage of the prophecy. Similarly, by attaining the empowerment themselves, they are able to establish others on that ground as well. When they become buddhas, their omniscient wakefulness also enables them to establish other sentient beings in that state.

The term "inexhaustibility" indicates that the practice of the bodhisattvas can never be exhausted nor come to an end. There are four reasons for this, as follows. (1) Since the sentient beings that need to be liberated are of an inexhaustible number, the enlightened mind that is cultivated for their sake must be so too. (2) Since the enlightened mind is inexhaustible, its intent is also inexhaustible. (3) Since the intent is inexhaustible, so is the compassion that arises from it. (4) Since compassion is inexhaustible, the means and insight for benefiting sentient beings are equally inexhaustible.

Therefore, the practice of the children of the victorious ones is supreme because it is carried out for the welfare of others. These eight principles, such as practicing in harmony with beings, are the means for accomplishing the thirteen ways of benefiting others. (1) By being in harmony with beings and free from error, one accomplishes elegant teaching; (2) freedom from deceit brings delight; (3) absence of the notion of "mine" accomplishes entry; (4) expertise enables one to ascertain the meaning; (5) patience achieves the ripening of virtue; (6) discipline accomplishes the four that begin with practical advice; (7) extremely far reach achieves the final four, beginning with birth in the family; (8) inexhaustibility reveals the qualities in general.

4. How the Practice of a Bodhisattva Is Exalted

This topic is taught in two stanzas:

> The desirous pursue the terrifying,
> Those fond of existence pursue fleeting, perverse enjoyments,
> And those fond of peace are concerned with pacifying their own appropriations.
> Those whose very nature is compassion are constant in pacifying the appropriations of all. [VI.7]

> Deluded beings strive for their own happiness
> And always suffer because of not finding it.
> The steadfast ones are always diligent for the sake of others.
> Accomplishing the welfare of both, they leave suffering behind. [VI.8]

This superiority of the practice of the bodhisattvas is explained as follows. **The desirous pursue the terrifying,** which leads to great physical and mental suffering and causes them to go to the lower realms. **Those fond of existence** in the form and the formless realms **pursue** utterly impermanent, **fleeting, perverse enjoyments.** In terms of the suffering of conditioning, such enjoyments are ultimately suffering. **And those fond of peace,** the listeners and self-realized buddhas, **are concerned with** the means for **pacifying their own** afflictions, the sources of their **appropriation** of suffering. **Those whose very nature is compassion,** the children of the victorious ones, **are constant,** meaning that they do not cease in a transcendence of suffering without any remainder of the aggregates; they are constant **in pacifying** both their own **appropriations** and those **of all** others. **Deluded beings strive for their own happiness, and yet they always suffer because of not finding it. The steadfast ones are always diligent** solely **for the sake of others. Accomplishing the welfare of both** (that is, of self and others), **they leave suffering behind.**

Desirous individuals in the desire realm crave, consume, and indulge in the five sense pleasures. This brings them great fears in their present and future lives. Thus, they pursue the terrifying. Individuals in the higher realms, the form and formless realms, practice a meditative absorption in which the mind is withdrawn inwardly. The joys of their respective grounds and forms of existence do not transcend the suffering of conditioned existence. Yet their attachment to this unstable and fleeting happiness, which is of the delusive nature of cyclic existence, causes them to practice this kind of meditative concentration. Listeners and self-realized buddhas, on the other hand, are drawn to the pacification of the sufferings of cyclic existence. They practice to pacify completely the appropriations of a future existence, merely in their own stream of being.

The practice of the bodhisattvas, whose very nature is compassion, pacifies through insight all appropriations of their own and others' miseries. Out of compassion, bodhisattvas do not forsake sentient beings and constantly work for the welfare of others. Thus, their practice surpasses the mundane practices mentioned above and is superior to the supramundane practice of the listeners and self-realized buddhas.

Ordinary, deluded beings of the world do not consider others' welfare at all. Searching for their own happiness, they diligently pursue a whole range of activities such as farming, business, or the pursuit of women, to the point of utter exhaustion. They perpetually desire their own objectives to be flawlessly and perfectly fulfilled, yet they never find the happiness they seek. Instead, in their present lives they suffer due to heat, cold, hunger, thirst, and other difficult circumstances. They also experience a great deal of physical and mental suffering from searching for what they have yet to acquire, from losing what they have, and so on. In future lifetimes, they will experience numerous forms of suffering, such as those of the lower realms.

The steadfast ones, the bodhisattvas, constantly strive for the welfare of others. In the short term, they bring both themselves and others the experience of all manner of joy in both their present and future lives, and ultimately they achieve nonabiding transcendence of suffering. The great happiness they attain at that time completely fulfills their own welfare and can never be lost. For the sake of others, they carry out unending activities that bring benefit and happiness to the infinite number of sentient beings.

5. Uninterrupted Practice

> When the children of the victorious ones are active,
> All that they experience through the senses
> Is accompanied by fitting and agreeable verbal expressions
> That are formed for the sake of others. [VI.9]

The complete purity of their sphere of activity is explained in this way: **When** bodhisattvas, **the children of the victorious ones, are active,** involved in performing various activities, **all that they experience through the** eyes and other **senses is accompanied by fitting and agreeable verbal expressions that are formed for the sake of others.** This is elaborately explained in the *Sūtra of the Completely Pure Sphere of Activity.*

Others lose their practice when they don't actively pursue it. For bodhisattvas, however, this is not the case. Through the force of cultivating the enlightened mind of aspiration and application, their fundamental virtues increase uninterruptedly, even when they are careless, such as when asleep. They not only benefit sentient beings by practicing generosity and the rest of the six transcendences with body, speech, and mind, but they also practice through the mental impetus of aspiration. This allows them to benefit beings during all activities of walking, moving about, sitting, and sleeping. When the children of the victorious ones perform any activity, partaking of the various experiences of the six faculties, they accompany it with fitting and agreeable expressions of aspiration. By forming aspirations to benefit sentient beings, they are skilled in the means for transforming even neutral activities into acts that benefit sentient beings.

As explained in the *Sūtra of the Completely Pure Sphere of Activity,* when bodhisattvas enter a city, they make the wish that all sentient beings may enter the city of supreme liberation. When setting out on a path, they wish that all sentient beings may set out on the path of the

Great Vehicle. When climbing stairs, they wish for all sentient beings to climb the stairway to liberation. When washing, they form a wish that the karma and afflictions of sentient beings may be washed away. When lighting a fire, they wish that the fuel of the thoughts of sentient beings may be completely burned away by the fire of wakefulness, and so on. As they thus cultivate the qualities of complete purification in a way that is adjusted to the particular activities that they engage in, bodhisattvas ceaselessly benefit others by means of their dedication to, and aspiration for, the happiness and complete liberation of all sentient beings.

6. Not Being Dejected in the Face of Ingratitude

The sixth point explains that bodhisattvas do not feel dejected when their efforts to benefit others are met with ingratitude.

> **Knowing that they are always governed by their flaws,**
> **The wise find no flaw in beings.**
> **"Their inappropriate conduct occurs against their will"—**
> **With this thought, their compassion for beings grows.** [VI.10]

It may be thought that when sentient beings return good with bad, the Victorious One's children might be discouraged from their practice of benefiting others. This is not the case. **Considering that they are always governed by their flaws,** that is, their afflictions, **the wise find no flaw in beings** who act inappropriately. **"Their inappropriate conduct occurs against their will." With this thought, their compassion for beings grows.**

Bodhisattvas are endowed with the insight that unerringly realizes the nature of all phenomena, and they have compassion for sentient beings. Sentient beings, however, constantly cling to a self where none exists. Their minds are helplessly taken over by desire, anger, and bewilderment, which are rooted in ego-clinging. Therefore, wise bodhisattvas do not fault these beings even if the latter beat them, insult them, or harbor wrong views about them. Rather, bodhisattvas understand that against their wishes these sentient beings are helplessly driven to engage in such inappropriate conduct, just like a crazy person who harms others or even kills himself. Therefore, bodhisattvas do not feel dejected or angry toward ungrateful beings. Indeed, their compassion grows as they wish them to be free from such flaws.

3. Conclusion

Next follows the conclusion that shows the magnificence of the practice of the bodhisattvas:

> Outshining all of existence and wandering beings,
> This practice is endowed with supreme peace.
> Enhanced by the accumulation of numerous qualities,
> It constantly attracts beings with a loving intent. [VI.11]

> This was the sixth chapter of the *Ornament of the Great Vehicle Sūtras*, the chapter on practice.

Next follows an explanation of the magnificence of the practice. **Outshining all of** the three realms **of existence and** the five classes **of wandering beings, this practice is endowed with the supreme peace** of nonabiding transcendence. As for the magnificence of its qualities, **this practice is enhanced by the accumulation of numerous qualities,** such as the powers, which are due to the force of the two accumulations. And its magnificence in terms of not forsaking sentient beings lies in the fact that **it constantly attracts beings** through the four means of attraction, motivated **with a loving intent.**

The practice of the bodhisattvas proceeds by outshining the three realms of existence and the five paths of wandering beings. It is endowed with supreme peace, the nonabiding transcendence of suffering, and becomes increasingly enhanced by accumulations of numerous qualities as found in the grounds, transcendences, powers, fearlessnesses, and so forth. Because of its loving intent, it always attracts sentient beings and never forsakes them. As explained above, the practice of the bodhisattvas possesses a fourfold magnificence: (1) it surpasses all beings, (2) it leads to the attainment of nonabiding transcendence of suffering, (3) it enhances all excellent qualities, and (4) it never forsakes sentient beings.

This concludes the explanation of practice, the sixth chapter of the *Ornament of the Great Vehicle Sūtras*.

It was here explained that through practice one will proceed toward the nonabiding transcendence of suffering. However, without realizing reality, one will not be able to gain such accomplishment. Therefore, the explanation of reality follows the chapter on practice.

3. What Is to Be Contemplated

This section has three parts: (1) contemplating the reality that must be realized, (2) contemplating the six superknowledges that one must accomplish, and (3) contemplating the full maturation of one's stream of being, which is the cause for the attainment of all excellent qualities.

7
Reality

1. Contemplating Reality

The first section has three parts: (1) determining the characteristics of reality, (2) determining the lack of the twofold self, and (3) determining the stages in realizing reality.

1. The Characteristics of Reality

> Not existent and not nonexistent, not the same and not different,
> Without origination and destruction, decrease and increase,
> Without becoming pure, it still becomes pure—
> These are the marks of the ultimate. [VII.1]

The following is an explanation of the characteristics of reality. The ultimate is the character of the nondual nature. Therefore, it is **not existent** with any characteristics of the imagined or dependent natures, **and** yet, with respect to the characteristic of the thoroughly established nature, it **is not nonexistent** either. The three natures are **not the same**, that is, they are not one, **and** since the thoroughly established is the dependent nature's being empty of the imagined, they are **not different** either. Furthermore, since the basic field of phenomena is unconditioned, it is **without origination and destruction**. Even when the factors of thorough affliction cease, their intrinsic nature does not **decrease, and,** even as the factors that constitute the remedies **increase**, their intrinsic nature does not. **Without becoming pure,** since by nature it is never afflicted, **it still becomes pure** through being freed of the adventitious afflictions. **These are the marks,** or characteristics, **of the ultimate.**

The characteristics of reality are to be understood by means of one's own direct awareness. These characteristics are free from the four extremes of existence, nonexistence, sameness, and difference. This, in turn, means that the ultimate reality does not exist in the way the characteristics of the imagined and dependent natures would make it seem. Nevertheless, in terms of the characteristics of the thoroughly established nature, the ultimate reality is not nonexistent either. The term "all phenomena" does not refer to anything other than the phenomena of the dependent nature, which are profound, inner, dependent arisings. The concepts of these phenomena being real in the same way that they appear—as a duality of perceiver and perceived—are the imagined nature. Although child-like, ordinary beings believe that such appearances exist in the way that they appear, the dualistic phenomena of apprehended and apprehender have never had any establishment. This is the thoroughly established nature, the ultimate reality, or the way things actually are. The emptiness that implies one thing's being empty of another, in the sense that the latter is absent from the former, exists conventionally because it is established by determinative affirmation.

The so-called imagined and dependent natures are not the same as the thoroughly established nature because they are not indistinguishable from the latter. Yet, since they are also not different, they are not anything other than the thoroughly established nature. This is also stated in the *Sūtra on the Definitive Explanation of the Intent:*

The characteristics of the conditioned realms and the ultimate
Are neither the same nor different.

The imagined nature is an error and does not exist in actuality, whereas the dependent nature is the basis for the imagined nature—the appearance of duality. The thoroughly established nature, on the other hand, is unmistaken and empty of duality. Therefore, these are not the same; they are phenomena and their intrinsic nature.

Yet neither are they different. The dependent nature's lack of the imagined duality of apprehended and apprehender is itself the thoroughly established nature. As there is no other "thoroughly established nature" aside from this, the latter is precisely the intrinsic nature of the phenomena that are the dependent nature. If these two were different, the dependent nature could not be empty of duality in terms of apprehended and apprehender, which would not make sense. Thus, it should be understood that they are not different, in the same way that an impermanent phenomenon is no different from a conditioned phenomenon, or the element of fire is no different from heat.

The ultimate thoroughly established nature has never known any origination, destruction, or cessation. How could there be a cessation of something that, in essence, has never originated from causes and conditions? Throughout the contexts of cyclic existence and transcendence of suffering, the thoroughly established nature does not change from one point to another; it never decreases or increases. It remains just as it is, like the sky that does not increase or decrease regardless of whether there are clouds in it. Reality cannot decrease or increase through a decrease and increase in the factors of thorough affliction and complete purification.

Since its essence is completely pure by nature, it does not become newly pure either. In this sense, it can be likened to the sky, to excellent gold, water, and crystal, all of which are naturally pure. Yet, although there are no stains to be dispelled from these in terms of their nature, the sky can still be cleared of the clouds that cover it temporarily, gold can be cleared of spots, water can be purified, and crystals can be rid of a blemish. Likewise, although pure by nature, the thoroughly established nature can still be divested of stains as the two adventitious obscurations are cleared away. Such is the character of the ultimate, and the ultimate nonduality is therefore taught as (1) neither existent nor nonexistent, (2) neither the same nor different, (3) neither originating nor ceasing, (4) neither increasing nor decreasing, and (5) neither pure nor impure.

According to the Middle Way, all phenomena that appear through the force of dependent origination are not nonexistent conventionally, yet ultimately they are not existent either. Nor are they both existent and nonexistent. Ultimate nonexistence is the intrinsic nature of all conventionally existent phenomena; hence these two are not different from each other in reality. They are nothing more than a mere nominal division, as with fire and its heat or molasses and sweetness. Could we, then, say that reality constitutes a third category that is neither ultimate nonexistence nor relative existence? No, because there is no reliable means of cognition that can establish some third category that is neither identified with phenomena nor with their intrinsic nature of emptiness. Such a third principle could not possibly be the nature, or intrinsic nature, of conventional phenomena.

Therefore, in being free from all four extremes of existence, nonexistence, both, and neither, reality transcends all constructs. It is held to be the indivisible two truths, in which the phenomenon and its intrinsic nature are inseparable, and as such it is realized by one's own direct awareness. This intrinsic nature, free from constructs, is always equality free from origination and cessation, as well as from decrease and increase. Therefore, it does not possess even the slightest mark of duality. It is not pure or impure, and so on.

The Mind Only tradition asserts that all phenomena are nothing more than mere mental perceptions and that the ground of these perceptions exists substantially as the mere clear and aware consciousness that is the dependent nature. If one follows this assertion through to its final conclusion, then that consciousness is asserted to be substantially existent simply in the sense that it is the cause of the appearances of all conventional phenomena. And if this consciousness is not held to have any ultimate substantial existence that is truly established, then it does not at all conflict with the tradition of the Middle Way. On the other hand, if this consciousness is asserted to be ultimately and truly established, then this view does contradict the Middle Way. Indeed, it appears that whether or not there is conflict between the Mind Only and the Middle Way comes down to the analysis of merely this issue.

The corpus of the doctrines of Maitreya and the scriptures of the great chariot, Asaṅga, both teach with a single intent that a person on the grounds of inspired conduct initially understands all phenomena to be merely mind, and next experiences that the mind has nothing to apprehend. Then, at the time of the supreme quality on the path of joining, one realizes that since the apprehended does not exist, neither does the apprehender. Right after this, one directly realizes the truth of the intrinsic nature, which is free from all dualistic fixation. This is taught as being the attainment of the first ground.

As for the way in which appearances are mind only, it is held that the cause of all dualistic appearances that manifest as places, objects, and bodies is the all-ground consciousness, which in conventional terms exists substantially. Yet, since the all-ground consciousness is not established as a duality while still manifesting in various ways, it is said to be like an illusion, and so on. Therefore, from the perspective of this very tradition, it is perfectly reasonable not to see nondual consciousness as a truly established entity and instead to realize that it bears no marks. Consequently, one should understand that the final viewpoint of the chariots of Mind Only and the Middle Way are in harmony.

If this is so, then why is it the case that the masters of the Middle Way refute the Mind Only philosophy? Some blatantly arrogant proponents of Mind Only philosophy assert, when explaining their viewpoint, that external objects do not exist, but that the mind exists substantially. They liken this to the way a rope is empty of being a snake, but is not empty of being a rope itself. These individuals have not understood that this account applies to the conventional. Therefore, this philosophy that fixates upon the ultimate, true establishment of a nondual consciousness is refuted.

Such a refutation, however, does not apply to the viewpoint of noble Asaṅga, who clearly realized the proper path of Mind Only that was set forth by the Buddha. There is nothing unreasonable in making this assertion. Indeed, some learned individuals from the Land of Snow assert that listeners who see the truth also realize the twofold selflessness and that they are, therefore, no different from proponents of the Middle Way in this regard. If this is the case, then it goes without saying that the great chariot, Asaṅga, indeed realized the intended meaning of the Middle Way as well, because he is a noble being.

In general, it is sufficient for proponents of the Middle Way to determine that all phenomena that arise in dependent relation are nonarising. Thus, although it is not necessary for them to accept the tenets of the Mind Only School, we have to keep in mind how two types of dependent arising are taught in noble Asaṅga's *Compendium on the Great Vehicle* and elsewhere: one type of dependent origination has to do with distinguishing the essential nature and the other with distinguishing the desirable and the undesirable. The former explains how appearances develop from the all-ground. This subtle, inner dependent arising is realized by bodhisattvas who are learned in the profound and subtle meaning. Compared to the coarse, outer dependent arising in twelve links, this dependent origination is the subtle one. Correspondingly, the sūtras of definitive meaning and the tantras of profound mantra state that there are no phenomena other than the mind, and that the root of both cyclic existence and transcendence of suffering comes down to the mind. The phenomena of cyclic existence and of transcendence manifest through the power of the mind; if there were no mind, they could not be, either. It is also through the power of mind that the deluded factors of cyclic existence come into being when the afflictions bring about the formation of karma. Moreover, it is the mind that cultivates the insight that realizes selflessness and compassion, thereby accomplishing the path of the Great Vehicle. Having accomplished that path, one becomes a buddha with the nature of the five forms of wakefulness because the eight collections, along with the all-ground, undergo a fundamental transformation. Even listeners and self-realized buddhas achieve their transcendence of suffering and disengagement from existence by means of the mind realizing the absence of a personal self. Therefore, all Buddhists must necessarily agree that the processes of affliction and purification depend on the mind.

The *Manifest Enlightenment of Vairocana*, moreover, explains that, by resolving that the mind has no nature, one will fully realize the path of the Great Vehicle without difficulty, and hence it considers this insight to be the crucial issue on the path. In his *Precious Lamp of the Middle Way*, a treatise that gathers all the key points of the Middle Way, the Master Bhavya, who was widely renowned as a great scholar in India, distinguishes between the Middle Way of Yogic Practice, which is the subtle, inner Middle Way, and the coarse, outer Middle Way, which asserts external objects. He also clearly states that, in the context of practice, the Middle Way of Yogic Practice is more profound and that even Candrakīrti practiced in this way.

Therefore, the Mind Only assertion of a self-luminous, nondual consciousness might be taken to imply a consciousness that, as the final condition of all dualistic mind, itself escapes description in terms of apprehended and apprehender. This would then imply that, as such, it is truly established and not empty of its own essence. Such an assertion is to be negated. However, if one understands that this mind has a nature that from the beginning knows no origination, a self-luminous wakefulness that is free from apprehended and apprehender and is directly experienced in one's perception, then that is to be affirmed, as it is necessarily accepted in both mantra and the Middle Way.

If there were no wakefulness of one's own direct awareness, or no luminous and clear mind, then there could not reasonably be a mind that realizes the truth of the intrinsic nature on the path of training. Also, at the time of the transcendence of suffering without any remainder on the path of no more learning, buddhas would not have omniscient wakefulness; their transcendence of suffering would be no different from that of the Lesser Vehicle, which is similar to the extinction of a flame. So how, then, could one assert that the bodies, wakefulnesses, and activities of a buddha are inexhaustible?

Therefore, it may appear as though the chariots of Mind Only and the Middle Way establish their highways of the profound and vast Dharma through different principles, yet in their final intent they equally reach the expanse of wakefulness. Understanding this integral point yields an extremely fine insight. In brief, reality—the way all phenomena actually are—is in no way confined to either appearance or emptiness; it is a unity that is known through one's own direct awareness. Realizing that this remains unchanged throughout the ground, path, and fruition, one is saved from the abyss of the wrong views that cleave to extremes.

2. THE LACK OF SELF

Second, determining reality involves a proof of the absence of self, by means of reasoning.

1. Establishing the Selflessness of the Person

First, the lack of a personal self is established:

> The nature of the belief in a self does not characterize the self,
> Neither do the negative bases, for their characteristics differ.
> Apart from these two there is nothing; this is a mistake that occurred.
> Liberation is, therefore, the cessation of a mere mistake.
> [VII.2]

A refutation of the mistaken belief in a self follows next. **The nature of the belief in a self does not characterize the self, neither do** the appropriated aggregates that are **the negative bases, for their characteristics differ** from those ascribed to the imagined self. **Apart from these two, there is nothing.** The self does not exist. This **belief in a self is** but **a mistake that occurred.** Hence, as there is no self, **liberation is, therefore, the cessation of** clinging to the self, the nature of which is **a mere mistake.**

Other than being merely a mistaken apprehension that has not been subjected to analysis or inquiry, personal self has no reality. This is because the self is not the belief in a self, it is not the aggregates, and it is not something other than these two either. The nature of the view of the transitory collection, or the belief in a self, is not the self. Since the belief in a self is a mental quality, it is conditioned, impermanent, does not pervade everything, and it performs virtuous, unvirtuous, and neutral actions. Therefore, the belief in a self has different characteristics from those of an extremist's conception of self, which has the characteristics of being unconditioned, permanent, pervasive, and incapable of performing actions.

The five aggregates, which are the basis of the view of the transitory collection, are taught to have neither the nature of the self nor its characteristics. In Sthiramati's commentary, he explains that the "negative" in negative bases refers to the view of the transitory collection, which is the root of all afflictions. Being caught up in that view constitutes these bases of afflictive beliefs, and so the term is "negative bases." Alternatively, the "negative bases" can be understood as the aggregates because they are produced by afflictions and negative tendencies. In some translations, at this point we find the term "bases of the negative." In this case, the term simply refers to the aggregates because they are the bases of suffering and affliction.

In any case, the five aggregates are not the self. As was explained above, they are impermanent, conditioned, nonpervasive, agents of actions, and multiple. Therefore, the aggregates have different characteristics from those of the self, which is believed to arise through its own nature, rather than being newly formed by causes and conditions, as well as being pervasive, permanent, uninvolved in actions, and singular.

Finally, there is nothing that can be referred to as a "self" apart from the subject, which is the belief in the transitory collection, and its object, the five aggregates. This is because an existent self other than these two cannot be observed through any of the reliable means of cognition, perception and inference. This refutation of the self that is imputed by outsiders also negates the conceived object of the innate apprehension of self because sentient beings believe the self to be singular and not multiple. They apprehend it to be one and the same from beginningless time and to the final end. Through investigating such a self in the above-mentioned three ways, one will come to understand that it is merely a superimposition.

If there is no self, then why is it that all sentient beings think that there is one? The self is not conceived of because of any fact that it exists. Although it does not exist, the mere thought that it exists occurs simply as an error or delusion of the mind. This can be likened to perceiving a rope to be a snake or to seeing a young lady in a dream. It might be thought that if there is a self, it makes sense for that self to be bound to cyclic existence by afflictions and to become liberated when cutting through that bondage. If there is no self, however, then who is it that becomes liberated? Without a self, it would be unreasonable to strive to liberate it! It is, however, not the case that one strives to liberate an existent self. For instance, if one is frightened when mistaking a rope for a snake, one will feel relieved when seeing that there is no snake. Similarly, afflictions and karma are accumulated by conceiving of a self where there is none. This, in turn, leads one to a continuous experience of suffering in cyclic existence.

When authentic insight enables one to realize the lack of self, then karma and afflictions will cease to be, and one will be liberated. Therefore, what we refer to as "liberation" is merely the cessation of a mistake, or delusion, in one's mind stream. There is no liberation of an existent self. If there were a self, then ego-clinging could never be averted, and yet, if this ego-clinging is not relinquished, then karma and afflictions cannot cease either. Thus, the continuous engagements in cyclic existence occur due to the attachment to a self.

2. Selflessness of Phenomena

Second, presenting the absence of a self of phenomena, the root text states:

> Based on a mere mistake, beings do not realize
> The continuous nature of suffering.
> While not aware, there is awareness; there is suffering, yet they
>   do not suffer.
> This is the nature of phenomena, and yet it is not that nature.
>   [vii.3]

> When they clearly experience the dependent arising of things,
> Why do beings take recourse to creation by something else?
> How can they fail to see what exists, and instead see what does
>   not?
> What sort of dense darkness is this? [vii.4]

> There is ultimately no difference whatsoever
> Between peace and birth;

Yet it is said that those performing virtuous acts
Bring an end to birth and thereby gain peace. [VII.5]

One might think that if there is no self in reality, then everyone would realize the fact that there is none. Yet this is not the case. Based on a mere mistake, the belief in self, **beings do not realize** that **the continuous**ly abiding **nature of suffering** is in fact devoid of a self. This is because they lack undefiled wakefulness. It might then be thought that, in that case, they would not realize that there is suffering either. Yet **while not aware** of the nature of suffering by means of wakefulness, **there is** an **awareness** of suffering, which is due to the experience of suffering. Since they have not eliminated it, **there is suffering.** Yet all the while **they** nevertheless **do not suffer** because there is no self to undergo any suffering. Since no self exists in the form of a person, there are mere phenomena. Hence **this is the nature of phenomena. And yet** because there is no self in the form of phenomena either, **it is not that,** meaning the nature of phenomena, either.

When they (that is, worldly beings) **witness clearly,** and directly **experience the dependent arising of things, why** then **do beings take recourse to** the idea of **creation by something else** such as the Almighty? **How can they fail to see what exists,** dependent origination, **and instead see what does not,** such as the self? **What sort of dense darkness is this?**

Some may think that if there were no self, there would be no one to attain liberation and no path of liberation. Consequently, there would be no liberation either, and in this way there would be no difference between cyclic existence and the transcendence of suffering. In reply, it is explained that **there is ultimately,** meaning in terms of the absence of self, or in terms of equality, **no difference whatsoever between peace** (that is, transcendence of suffering) **and birth** (that is, cyclic existence). **Yet it is said that those performing** the **virtuous acts** of cultivating the path of liberation **bring an end to birth,** transcend suffering, **and thereby gain peace.**

In this way, based on a mere error, a delusion of the mind, beings believe that both the self and phenomena exist. Due to this delusion, they continuously have to experience various sufferings—birth, old age, and so on. While what they experience is thus simply their minds' delusion, they do not realize this. As will be explained later, they are enveloped by an immense darkness, mistakenly seeing things that do not exist while failing to see those that do.

Since they lack the undefiled wakefulness that realizes that the entities of cyclic existence are suffering and delusion, it is said that they have "no awareness" or "no genuine awareness." On the other hand, since their defiled consciousness mistakenly experiences the sensations of pleasure, pain, and indifference, there is, in that sense, awareness. None of these three sensations is beyond suffering: painful sensations are natural suffering, enjoyable sensations are the suffering of change, and neutral sensations are the suffering of conditioning.

In reality, suffering is not experienced because there is no self that could experience it and because the phenomena that are experienced are not truly real. How is it that they are not real? Although the natures, or essences, of phenomena—which are composed of the aggregates, elements and sense sources—exist as mere appearances, these are like an illusion, a dream, or a mirage. Ultimately there is no essence or nature to these phenomena. They do not, in fact, exist the way they appear. Therefore, they are selfless, empty, and abide as emptiness.

How is this? Outer entities arise from the four elements, seeds, and other such causes and conditions. Inner entities, the aggregates of sentient beings, are also due to various causes and conditions coming together, such as ignorance, formations, and so on. Therefore, it is directly experienced that all outer and inner phenomena are entities that arise based on the coming together of their respective causes and conditions.

Although this is apparent, ignorant fools nonetheless take these entities to be due to something else, for instance an almighty god or the self. Thus they fail to see the fact of dependent arising in entities. While there is no self, no almighty god, and no other creator, what kind of darkness is it, then, that makes them see these things? The darkness that is known in the world obscures that which exists and hinders sight, but it does not make one see things that do not exist. The darkness of ignorance that is present in the mind streams of sentient beings hinders the sight of dependent arising, that which obviously exists as the intrinsic nature of entities, while at the same time it also conjures the sight of an origination that is due to something else that does not in fact exist. What an astonishing, unprecedented darkness this is!

The word "self" can mean person, and hence it also appears in the series of equivalents that otherwise includes "sentient being," "life-force," "person," "being," "individual," and so on. The term "self" is also applied to the nature of phenomena, and hence "the self of phenomena" refers to the nature or essence of phenomena. Extremists are fixated upon a personal self, and they mistakenly claim that self to be subject to bondage and liberation. Listeners are fixated upon the self of phenomena, and so assert bondage and liberation in terms of the essences of phenomena. They are also mistaken because they do not comprehend the nature of phenomena.

According to the Great Vehicle, all phenomena are nondual and, therefore, equal. Yet it is nevertheless reasonable for cyclic existence and transcendence of suffering, bondage and liberation, to occur. Ultimately, or in terms of the abiding reality, there is not the slightest difference between the appearances that manifest as the phenomena of transcendence, meaning the peace of the cessation of everything from ignorance to old age and death, and the appearances of cyclic existence, which is the condition of ignorance giving rise to formation, and so forth, right up to old age and death. Since all phenomena of cyclic existence and transcendence are by their very essence equal, free from origination and cessation, the nature of cyclic existence is itself the transcendence of suffering.

One may then wonder what the difference is between ordinary beings who remain in cyclic existence and noble ones who have achieved the transcendence of suffering. Cyclic existence and transcendence are not different because of any ultimately existent entities of self and phenomena. Rather, they differ in terms of whether or not one realizes how, in fact, there is no essence of self or phenomena. Ultimately, cyclic existence and transcendence are indeed equal. Yet it is explained that by perfecting the cultivation of virtue—that is, by realizing how entities are impermanent, suffering, and selfless—birth in cyclic existence ceases. This is the peace of listeners and self-realized buddhas. When perfecting the path by performing the virtuous acts of the six transcendences and embracing these acts with nonconceptual wakefulness, even birth in a mental body will not occur. Thus, even the subtle imprints of cyclic existence vanish and the nonabiding transcendence of suffering is attained.

3. The Stages of Realizing Reality

The next five stanzas show the stages of realizing ultimate reality:

> When a bodhisattva has thoroughly gathered the accumulations
> Of merit and wakefulness beyond measure,
> The bodhisattva contemplates the Dharma in a most decisive way,
> And thereby realizes that the forms of objects are the result of expression. [VII.6]
>
> Hence, knowing objects to be mere expressions,
> The bodhisattva recognizes that such appearances are mind only,
> And then realizes the basic field of phenomena,
> Free from the characteristics of duality, in direct perception. [VII.7]
>
> Becoming aware that there is nothing apart from the mind,
> The bodhisattva also realizes that the mind does not exist at all.
> Having seen that the two do not exist, the intelligent one abides
> In the basic field of phenomena, which does not contain them. [VII.8]
>
> For the wise, the power of nonconceptual wakefulness
> Always makes everything equal in all regards.
> This clears the wilderness of supported flaws
> Just as a powerful antidote dispels a poison. [VII.9]

The Dharma taught by the Able One is presented well.
Intelligence is directed toward the root, the basic field of
    phenomena.
Those stable in the awareness that what moves in the mind is
    mere thought
Are swift in crossing the ocean of qualities. [VII.10]

This was the seventh chapter of the *Ornament of the Great Vehicle Sūtras,* the chapter on reality.

When a bodhisattva on the path of accumulation **has thoroughly gathered the accumulations** that are of the nature **of merit,** which is means, **and wakefulness,** which is insight—accumulations that are gathered throughout time **beyond measure,** that is, throughout an incalculable eon, and which thereby bring the attainment of the path of seeing—he or she reaches the path of joining. In reliance upon meditative absorption on the path of joining, **the bodhisattva contemplates the** scriptural **Dharma** taught by the Buddha, the topic of his or her studies and reflections, **in a most decisive way, and thereby realizes that the forms of** external objects **are the result of expression,** that is, the result of thought.

Hence, knowing **all objects to be mere** mental **expressions,** the bodhisattva recognizes that such appearances are mind only, and then, attaining the path of seeing, also **realizes the basic field of phenomena, free from the characteristics of** the **duality** of apprehended and apprehender, **in direct perception.**

How does this realization take place? **Becoming aware that there is nothing** to be observed and perceived **apart from the mind, the bodhisattva realizes that the mind as well does not exist at all** because without anything perceived there can be no perceiver either. **Having seen that the two,** apprehended and apprehender, **do not exist, the intelligent one abides in the basic field of phenomena, which does not contain them,** that is, the apprehended and the apprehender.

For the wise abiding on the path of cultivation, **the power of nonconceptual wakefulness always makes everything equal in**

all regards. This clears the wilderness of supported flaws, the characteristics of negative tendencies, **just as a powerful antidote dispels a poison.**

The following is an explanation of the magnificence of ultimate wakefulness. **The Dharma taught by the Able One is presented well.** The **intelligence** of the bodhisattva who enters ultimate wakefulness **is directed toward the root** of the Dharma, **which is the basic field of phenomena.** Thus, the bodhisattva's intelligence is the root attention since it contains the Dharma. **Those stable in the awareness that what moves in the mind is mere thought are swift in crossing the ocean of qualities,** and so they become buddhas.

Through nonconceptual wakefulness that realizes that all phenomena are without a self, bodhisattvas of the Great Vehicle attain their fruition by traversing the paths of accumulation, joining, seeing, and cultivation. This process is explained here, beginning with the path of accumulation, which is the topic of the first three lines. Throughout one incalculable eon, bodhisattvas make offerings to the thus-gone ones as they receive, reflect, and meditate. Thus, they gather the accumulations of merit and wakefulness composed of the six transcendences, the nature of which is beyond measure. In this way, as is also implied in the root text, the bodhisattvas have gathered the accumulations for time beyond measure, and they enter the grounds of the noble ones. The bodhisattvas properly contemplate the character of impermanence, suffering, emptiness, and selflessness, which are the topics taught in the sūtras and other scriptures, and their meditative absorptions of calm abiding and special insight enable them to ascertain these topics beyond all doubt. Thus they gain complete certainty about them.

Since they gather the accumulations in this way and gain confidence in the Dharma through contemplation, bodhisattvas realize that all the features of forms and sounds, pillars and vases, and all other external phenomena are the products of verbal expression. In other words, conceptual thought apprehends things based on names and assumes them to be what they are said to be. Yet the actual essence of an object is inexpressible and beyond names. This realization is called "the wakefulness that has reached the light at the stage of heat." With the particular awareness that all objects are merely verbal expressions, or mere conceptions, bodhisattvas see that objects appear from the mind. This is called "the meditative absorption of the spread of light at the stage of summit."

Bodhisattvas understand that phenomena appearing as something apprehended are not external objects that exist apart from mind; they are no different from the contents of a dream where the mind itself takes on a certain appearance. Thus, their minds fully recognize the nature of mind only. This realization is what is termed "acceptance, the meditative absorption that has partial access to reality" because since at this point they realize that what they apprehend has no nature, they have partial access to the reality that is free from both apprehended and apprehender. Based on this, they will directly realize the basic field of phenomena, free from the characteristics of apprehended and apprehender, and so attain the path of seeing. Before that attainment, during the phase of acceptance, they understand that there are no external objects, that there is nothing apprehended other than mind. Based on that understanding, they then realize that if there is nothing apprehended, then also there is no mind that apprehends because apprehended and apprehender mutually depend on each other. The realization that there can be no apprehender when there is nothing apprehended takes place during the meditative absorption of the supreme quality, which directly precedes the path of seeing.

Thus, immediately after the phase of the supreme quality, the wise actualize nonconceptual wakefulness with the awareness that both apprehended and apprehender lack any nature. By means of their own direct awareness, they now directly realize the basic field of phenomena, free from the marks of the dualistic phenomena of the apprehended and that which apprehends. This brings about the elimination of the afflictive and cognitive obscurations that are to be discarded by the path of seeing. Then, for wise individuals on the path of cultivation that extends from the second to the tenth ground, everything, meaning all outer and inner phenomena, is seen to be always and in all regards equal. This realization occurs through the power of nonconceptual wakefulness.

Without any concepts regarding entities that are apprehended or that apprehend, everything equally becomes nondual. Through this, the afflictive and cognitive obscurations that are based within the bodhisattva's mind stream—or that are supported by the all-ground consciousness of dependent nature—are cleared away. Accumulated from beginningless time, these masses of negative tendencies for dualistic fixation are difficult to recognize and hard to discard. They resemble a vast, dense wilderness. Yet, sprinkling a few drops of a powerful antidote into a vessel with poison can transform all the poison into medicine, and by merely smelling or tasting such an antidote one can be completely detoxified. Hence, in the same way that a powerful antidote does away with poison, nonconceptual wakefulness on the path of cultivation dispels the most subtle, poisonous obscurations that are to be discarded, from their very root, and thereby actualizes the great nonconceptual wakefulness of buddhahood.

The sacred Dharma, as contained in the sūtras and the rest of the twelve branches, is taught by the buddhas, who are capable of refraining entirely from all faulty behaviors of body, speech, and mind. Since this Dharma is virtuous at the beginning, middle, and end, it is presented well. The final root of all the meanings that are revealed by the teachings is the basic field of phenomena. Therefore, to direct one's intelligence toward this root is to focus on the message of all of the sūtras, gathered in one. The intelligence or insight that does so is hence also called the "root attention."

In this way, for the steadfast ones, the bodhisattvas, the continuity of attention and recollection with regard to the basic field of phenomena becomes increasingly exalted during meditative equipoise. During the subsequent attainment, they understand that everything is merely the mind, that there are no other phenomena aside from one's own mere thoughts, and that the mind itself is also without any nature. Swiftly, without delay, they cross over the ocean of the powers, fearlessnesses, and other resultant qualities, and become buddhas. Thus, the verses also teach the path of no more learning.

The phrase, "what moves in the mind," that is found in most editions appears to arise from a spelling mistake. In the great commentary of

Sthiramati and in the *Compendium on the Great Vehicle*, both of which cite this stanza, we instead find the term, "the continuity of recollection."

This concludes the explanation of reality, the seventh chapter of the *Ornament of the Great Vehicle Sūtras*.

8

Power

2. The Six Superknowledges

Having explained the reality that is to be realized, there follows an explanation of the chapter on power. This considers the special qualities that are accomplished and through which others are brought to maturation.

This chapter has seven sections: (1) the essence of power, (2) its cause, (3) its result, (4) its function, (5) its endowment, and (6) its application, or its types, along with (7) an explanation of the magnificence of its qualities.

1. Essence of Power

> Birth, speech, mind, the creation of virtue and nonvirtue,
> The realms, and emergence—these are perceived directly.
> Omnipresent and unimpeded regarding the subdivisions;
> This is the power of having attained stability. [VIII.1]

The following explains the nature of power by enumerating its characteristics.

(1) Knowing the **birth**s of others implies superknowledge with respect to the transference that takes place from death to birth.

(2) Being aware of the **speech** of others is the superknowledge associated with the divine ear.

(3) Knowing the **mind** of others implies superknowledge with respect to the categories of mind.

(4) Knowledge of **the creation of virtue and nonvirtue** means superknowledge concerning previous existences.

(5) Knowing how to reach **the realms** where beings to be trained are present is the superknowledge of the field of miracles.

(6) **And** direct knowledge of the method for definitive **emergence** from cyclic existence is superknowledge with respect to the exhaustion of defilements.

These six domains **are perceived directly** and, as this cognition extends throughout space and time, it is therefore **omnipresent and unimpeded regarding the subdivisions** of the six. **This is the power of** the bodhisattva's **having attained stability,** in the sense of having become indomitable.

When the stanza speaks of "birth," this implicitly includes death, and so it refers to (1) the superknowledge of the divine eye that knows birth and the transference at death. With this superknowledge, one is aware of the places where sentient beings will be born upon their death and transference, and of all that happens to them until they reach the transcendence of suffering.

(2) "Speech" indicates the superknowledge of the divine ear that understands all the languages of sentient beings.

(3) "Mind" refers to the superknowledge of knowing others' minds—the perception of the eighty-four thousand activities and so forth of the minds of sentient beings.

(4) "The creation of virtue and nonvirtue" implies the superknowledge of previous existences, in that it is the knowledge of the results and creations of all virtuous and unvirtuous actions performed by beings since beginningless time, throughout cyclic existence. Thus, one knows where beings were born in previous lifetimes, what kind of karma they gathered, the character of their experiences, how long they lived, and so forth.

(5) "The realms" refers to the world realms where buddhas, bodhisattvas, listeners, self-realized buddhas, and sentient beings dwell. The superknowledge of miracles has to do with being able to reach those realms, without obstruction, so that one can make offerings to the buddhas and be of benefit to sentient beings.

(6) "Emergence" concerns the superknowledge of the exhaustion of defilements, that is, the knowledge of those methods by which one definitively emerges from cyclic existence. Through the power of mastering the six superknowledges, these six domains are perceived directly, as when a fresh amalaki fruit is placed in the palm of one's hand.

The superknowledges of bodhisattvas are superior to those of worldly sages, listeners, and self-realized buddhas. This is because they are omnipresent throughout all the world realms in the ten directions and throughout all times. Moreover, each of the six superknowledges can be developed into an infinite number of subdivisions. When this is done, they extend in a way that is completely unhindered. These are the distinguishing features of the power of those bodhisattvas who have attained stability within the superknowledges, or mastery of them. This shows the nature or essence of these superknowledges.

2. Cause

> When the utter purity of the fourth concentration has been attained,
> Complete embrace by means of nonconceptual wakefulness,
> Along with the mind's being directed to the methods,
> Brings the accomplishment of true power. [VIII.2]

The character of the cause of this power is explained as follows: **When the utter purity of the fourth concentration** that functions as the support **has been attained,** two factors bring about the accomplishment of power, namely, wakefulness and directing the mind. Thus, **complete embrace by means of nonconceptual wakefulness, along with the mind's being directed to the** respective **methods, brings the** bodhisattva's **accomplishment of true power,** that is, of superknowledge—the nature of which is superior to what is achieved by others, such as the listeners and self-realized buddhas.

The cause of superknowledges is explained in terms of three principles.
(1) Concerning the grounds that these powers are based upon, these superknowledges occur once one has attained the meditative absorption

of the fourth concentration. This absorption is exceedingly pure because it lacks the flaws of excessive craving, belief, pride, and doubt, and because one's mastery in the absorptions is such that one can move with flexibility and as one pleases, sequentially or in leaps through the forward and reverse sequences of the absorptions.

(2) Superknowledge is facilitated by its being completely suffused with, or embraced by, nonconceptual wakefulness.

(3) It is accomplished by the proper directing of the mind to the methods for each form of superknowledge. In other words, superknowledge is accomplished by properly directing the mind to those marks that are taught for the purpose of eliciting the specific attainment of each respective superknowledge.

Regarding these methods, the sūtras explain that one who wishes to attain the superknowledge of sight will seek to visualize a light that pervades all of the directions, rendering all forms visible without obstruction. Similarly, one who pursues the superknowledge of miraculous powers should make the body buoyant and capable of transforming into whatever is desired. One who wishes to achieve the superknowledge of hearing should be attentive to the numerous types of sound, letting all sounds be heard. Those who wish to know the minds of others should direct their minds to numerous instances of others' minds, whereby all mental activity will be known. One must focus on previous existences, future situations, the truths, and liberation. In this way, one aspires to, and directs the mind toward, the methods for the accomplishment of each superknowledge.

Based on these causes, one will attain the true power of the six superknowledges. Superknowledges thus attained are those of the noble bodhisattvas, distinguished by being embraced by nonconceptual wakefulness and so forth.

3. Result

> The one who always abides, incomparably and expansively,
> In the noble, divine, and sublime abodes,
> Journeys everywhere to worship thoroughly the buddhas,
> And bring about the purification of sentient beings. [VIII.3]

The result of power is as follows. **The one**, meaning a child of the victorious ones, **who always abides, incomparably and expansively**, to an extent that cannot be fathomed by the listeners and self-realized buddhas, **in the noble** states associated with the three gates of liberation, the **divine** states of the absorptions pertaining to the form and formless realms, **and** the **sublime abodes** of the four immeasurables, **journeys everywhere** throughout the ten directions in order **to worship thoroughly the buddhas, and bring about the purification of** the streams of being of **sentient beings** through teaching the Dharma.

The result of having attained the superknowledges is the state of the noble ones—the three gates of liberation. Similarly, as a result of this attainment, one abides in the state of the four truths, the grounds, the transcendences, and, in particular, within emptiness and the equilibrium of cessation. The result is also the divine abodes of the four meditative concentrations and the four formless absorptions, particularly the fourth concentration. It is likewise the sublime abodes of the meditative absorptions of the four immeasurables and the state of compassion in particular. Because they always abide incomparably and expansively in this way, the state of the bodhisattvas is a superior one. The power of their superknowledges enables them to journey everywhere throughout the ten directions in worship of the buddhas. Through their miraculous powers and other qualities, they inspire sentient beings and thereby engender pure fundamental virtues in their streams of being. For these three reasons, the results of their superknowledges are superior to those of the listeners and self-realized buddhas.

4. Function

The function of the superknowledges is explained next:

> **Bodhisattvas see the entire world as an illusion,**
> **Including its formation and disintegration, and its sentient beings.**
> **Possessing mastery, they manifest whatever is wished for,**

And they present various displays in the most perfect way.
[VIII.4]

Emitting light rays, they make the wretched
Inhabitants of the lower realms depart to the higher.
Shaking them in their lofty and beautiful mansions,
They terrify the demons. [VIII.5]

In the supreme gathering, the bodhisattvas revel
In an infinite display of meditative absorptions.
With creative, incarnate, and supreme emanations,
They are constantly present for the welfare of others. [VIII.6]

With mastery regarding wakefulness,
Bodhisattvas display whatever fields are wished for, and
    thereby accomplish purity.
For those who have not heard them,
They proclaim the buddhas' names, and so unfold further
    realms. [VIII.7]

Next, there follows an explanation of the six activities, beginning with the activities of vision and display. The bodhisattvas see the entire world as an illusion, including its formation and disintegration, and its sentient beings. Possessing the ten forms of mastery, they manifest whatever is wished for, and they present various displays, such as making the ground shake, in the most perfect way.

The activity of light rays involves emitting light rays from one's body, whereby they make the wretched inhabitants of the lower realms develop faith and depart to the higher realms. Shaking them in their lofty and beautiful mansions, they terrify the demons.

The activities of reveling and emanation involve the following. In the supreme gathering, the circle of their retinue, the bodhisattvas revel within equipoise, in an infinite display of meditative absorptions. With emanations present as creative works of art, emanations intentionally **incarnate** to influence others, **and supreme emanations** [that demonstrate the twelve deeds of] abiding in The Joyful Realm and so forth, **they are constantly present for the welfare of others** until cyclic existence is emptied.

The activity of thoroughly cultivating the pure fields is explained as follows. **With mastery regarding wakefulness, bodhisattvas display whatever** buddha fields made of crystal, lapis lazuli, and so forth, **are wished for, and thereby accomplish purity** with respect to the environment. **For those who,** because of their place of birth, **have not heard them, they proclaim the buddhas' names, and so** develop their faith. In this way, bodhisattvas **unfold further realms** of the world where there is no separation [from buddhas].

The superknowledge of sight functions in such a way that one is able to see that all the realms of the world in all the ten directions are devoid of nature—like an illusion, a mirage, a dream, and so forth. This includes the external environment, which begins with its formation and ends in disintegration, along with all its sentient beings.

The activity of displaying miracles is as follows. Those bodhisattvas who have mastered the six superknowledges to the extent that they can accomplish whatever they wish for—that is, those with the ten powers—will manifest whatever methods will be useful in taming sentient beings. This can also be explained as meaning that they bring forth whatever other sentient beings may wish for and are interested in. Thus, they reveal the most perfect display of all sorts of activities—emitting flames, flying, shaking the ground, fitting the entire universe into a mustard seed, and so forth—in a vast and unpredictable array.

The light emitted by bodhisattvas quells the suffering of hell beings, hungry ghosts, animals, and the other wretched inhabitants of the lower realms, immediately upon making contact. As they then gain faith, this immediately makes these beings depart from their previous locations to the higher realms of gods and humans. These light rays also shake the dwellings of the demons, the lofty, beautiful mansions inlaid with numerous jewels. This terrifies the demons and their retinues, causing these demonic minions to cower in fear.

Concerning the activity of reveling, bodhisattvas who have attained power can enter into infinite meditative absorptions, such as the absorption of the heroic gait, the illusion-like absorption, or the absorption of the treasury of space, within the supreme circle of thus-gone ones and foremost bodhisattvas. They fully reveal numerous and immeasurable displays, like the displays of meditative absorption demonstrated by Mañjuśrī, Avalokiteśvara, and others described in the sūtras.

The activity of emanation involves being continually and fully present for the welfare of sentient beings throughout the ten directions by sending forth creative, incarnate, and supreme emanations. An example of a creative emanation is the lute-playing gandharva that the Buddha sent forth, in order to tame the gandharva Pramudita. Incarnate emanations can appear as gods such as Indra. They can also appear with the body of a malevolent spirit, an animal, or any other such sentient being, as they take birth within their respective realms. A supreme emanation is the display of a buddha, who demonstrates manifest enlightenment and the transcendence of suffering, after descending from The Joyful Realm, and so forth.

Creative emanations are called "action emanations" in Sthiramati's commentary. He explains that, having emanated as craftsmen, potters, sitar players, and so forth, they proceed to manifest various forms of art that are of benefit to sentient beings. This great commentary further mentions six activities of superknowledge: (1) the activity of sight, (2) the activity of display, (3–4) the activity of light rays, which both guide beings in the lower realms and frighten demons, (5) the activity of reveling, and (6) the activity of emanation.

Moreover, bodhisattvas with the six superknowledges thoroughly cultivate the buddha fields. Since those with the ten powers have mastered the wakefulnesses, they are able to display buddha fields in the color of crystal, gold, or whatever other colors are wished for, and likewise in whatever shape, design, and dimension sentient beings may desire. Since they manifest realms of such complete purity, these realms are referred to as "thoroughly pure environments." For those in world realms where the names of buddhas are not heard, where the words "Dharma" and "Saṅgha" are not heard either, the bodhisattvas proclaim these words and names. As they hear this, the beings of those realms develop faith, which in turn leads to the unfolding of further buddha realms where the Three Jewels are present. This is explained as the training in purifying the sentient beings that inhabit the worlds.

5. Endowment

Having thus explained the activities, the next teaching explains the qualities of the superknowledges.

> **Like a bird with its wings fully developed**
> **They are indeed capable of maturing sentient beings.**
> **They gain tremendous praise from the buddhas,**
> **And sentient beings find their words worthy of recollection.**
> [VIII.8]

The next section explains the endowment of the superknowledges. **Like a bird** that can fly anywhere it chooses, **with its wings fully developed they**—the children of the victorious ones who possess the superknowledges—**are indeed capable of maturing sentient beings.** Therefore, **they gain tremendous praise from the buddhas,** and all the **sentient beings** who receive their help will **find their words,** those of the children of the victorious ones, **worthy of recollection.**

(1) Those with the superknowledges have the capacity to mature sentient beings. (2) They are the objects of tremendous praise. (3) Their words are worthy of recollection. Just as birds with fully developed wings are able to fly through the sky, going wherever they please without any difficulty, bodhisattvas who have attained the six superknowledges have attained a supreme capacity to bring sentient beings to maturity without any difficulty, magnetizing them with the four means of attraction and establishing them in virtue. When such a bodhisattva properly poses questions to a buddha, the buddha will respond with the words "Noble child, what you have asked is excellent" and offer other forms of praise. Moreover,

since a bodhisattva with superknowledge knows the minds of others, he or she will engage them accordingly, and since the bodhisattvas also delight beings with their miraculous powers and other such qualities, their advice is certainly found to be worth adhering to, such that nobody will ever disregard their instruction.

6. Application or Types

> Six superknowledges, three types of awareness,
> Eight freedoms, eight commands,
> Ten domains of totality, and boundless meditative absorptions
> Constitute the power of having gained stability. [VIII.9]

This section explains the application of the superknowledges. **The six superknowledges, three types of awareness, eight freedoms, eight** domains of **commands, ten domains of totality, and boundless meditative absorptions**—all these **constitute the power of having gained stability.**

The following shows the classifications of superknowledge, or power, and how these are applied for the benefit of sentient beings. The six explained above, from the superknowledge of divine or miraculous sight to the superknowledge of the exhaustion of defilements, constitute the first classification of power. The second comprises the three types of awareness, which contain the superknowledge of previous existences, death and transference, and the exhaustion of defilements. These constitute a second category because together they are the precise knowledge of events in the past, present, and future.

The third category consists of the eight freedoms: (1) seeing form with form; (2) seeing form without form; (3) [seeing] the good or pleasant; (4-7) the freedoms of infinite space and the other formless realms; (8) the absorption of cessation.

The fourth category is the eightfold domain of subjugation. These eight include (1) the command of small outer forms—regardless of their color and whether they are fine, ugly, or exquisite—by means of the perception of inner form; (2) the command of large forms in a similar manner; (3–4) the command of both small and large forms through perceiving inner formlessness; (5) the command of blue; (6) the command of yellow; (7) the command of white; (8) the command of red.

In the fifth category are the ten domains of totality. These include the totalities of (1) earth, (2) water, (3) fire, (4) wind, (5) blue, (6) yellow, (7) white, and (8) red—along with (9) infinite space and (10) infinite consciousness.

These freedoms, totalities, and commands comprise the path of developing excellent skill in emanation by means of meditative absorption. One initially begins with the freedoms, then practices the forms of command, developing further and further with the domains of totality. All of these are divisions of power.

Furthermore, the boundless meditative absorptions of the Great Vehicle, such as the meditative absorption of the heroic gait, the illusion-like meditative absorption, and the treasury of space, are also powers of the bodhisattvas. They constitute a sixth category. All six types constitute the power of the steadfast bodhisattva because all of them are of the nature of capacity and power.

7. The Magnificence of the Qualities of Power

> Wise individuals with supreme mastery
> Empower beings deprived of freedom.
> With true delight in doing what benefits others,
> They participate in existence, indomitable like lions. [VIII.10]

> This was the eighth chapter of the *Ornament of the Great Vehicle Sūtras,* the chapter on power.

Next follows an explanation of the magnificence of these powers. **Wise individuals,** the bodhisattvas **with supreme mastery** of wakefulness, **empower** those **beings** whom the afflictions have **deprived of freedom.** This is the magnificent empowerment. The magnificent joy involves living **with true delight in doing what**

benefits others. Finally, with no fear of the sufferings of cyclic existence, **they participate in existence, indomitable like lions.** This is the magnificent quality of fearlessness.

The chapter concludes by extolling the magnificence of attaining the power of the six superknowledges, showing the magnificent empowerment, the magnificent joy, and the magnificent fearlessness within existence. Having thus accomplished power, bodhisattvas have gained mastery over the ten powers, or the mastery of pure wakefulness. They are therefore referred to as "the wise who have gained supreme mastery." This intelligence, or insight, that they possess is the cause for the empowering of beings. Beings who have fallen under the power of karma and the afflictions are controlled by these factors, and are thus deprived of any freedom in their present lifetime. In other lifetimes as well, they must go wherever their karma and afflictions propel them, regardless of any wishes to the contrary. In this way, they are always deprived of freedom. Nevertheless, since bodhisattvas are their own masters, they can employ their miraculous powers to tame such beings and establish them in virtue. Thereby, these sentient beings gradually attain the same freedom as the bodhisattvas. This is the magnificent empowerment.

Without considering their own welfare, bodhisattvas always take "true joy in doing what benefits others." This is their magnificent joy. Like a lion that is not frightened by any wild animal when roaming through forests, caves, or mountains, bodhisattvas—who have become stable in their mastery—are not frightened by any demons, extremists, and so forth, while they remain in the three realms of existence for the welfare of sentient beings. They do not have even a shred of doubt that they might become tainted by the afflictions, nor do they have the slightest fear of suffering. Thus, with fearless and unshakable confidence, they participate in existence.

This concludes the explanation of power, the eighth chapter of the *Ornament of the Great Vehicle Sūtras*.

9
Full Maturation

3. Full Maturation

Since the bodhisattvas attain their powers and other special qualities by maturing their streams of being, this issue, which is the third among the topics to be contemplated, will now be explained. The explanation of full maturation has two sections: (1) one's own maturation and (2) the maturation of others.

1. One's Own Maturation

The first section has three parts: (1) an overview, (2) an extensive explanation, and (3) a summary.

1. Overview

> Joy, faith, serenity, affection,
> Forbearance, keen intellect, power,
> Unassailability, and possession of the factors—
> The superior presence of these characterizes the full
>   maturation of the children of the victorious ones. [IX.1]

The full maturation of the bodhisattva is summarized as follows: **Joy** with respect to the Dharma of the Great Vehicle; **faith** in those who teach it; **serenity** through pacifying afflictions; **affection** for sentient beings; **forbearance** when undergoing hardships; **keen intellect** through receiving, retaining, and comprehending the three vessels; **power** with respect to what is to be realized; **unassailability** in the face of demons and adversaries; **and possession of the factors** that eliminate the afflictions. It should be understood that **the superior** (indicating magnitude) **presence of these** nine **characterizes the full maturation of the children of the victorious ones.**

The full maturation of the children of the victorious ones is characterized by nine qualities. These are: (1) joy in the Dharma of the Great Vehicle; (2) faith in the spiritual teachers who explain it; (3) serenity in terms of possessing the power of abandonment due to having few afflictions; (4) affection toward sentient beings; (5) patience in undergoing hardships for the welfare of self and others; (6) a keen intellect or sharp mind that is able to uphold unmistakenly the Dharma of the Great Vehicle, through receiving and reflecting upon the grounds of inspired conduct; (7) the power of being unaffected by afflictions and having the ability to realize emptiness, due to having gathered the accumulations to a great extent; (8) being unassailable on the path in the face of demons, extremists, and so forth; (9) possessing the factors that eliminate afflictions, that is, being replete with the five factors of faith, freedom from hypocrisy, freedom from pretense, absence of disease, and a powerful basis or support.

2. Extensive Explanation

The extensive explanation concerns the qualities outlined above.

1. Joy

> The supreme friend and the rest of the three, as well as
>   foremost diligence,
> True perfection, and the gathering of the supreme Dharma—
> These are held to be the characteristics of a compassionate
>   one's full maturation
> For the sake of comprehensively upholding the sacred
>   Dharma. [IX.2]

The full maturation of joy is explained as follows. **The supreme friend and the rest of the three**, that is, (1) following a holy being, (2) listening to the sacred Dharma, and (3) engaging the mind in accordance with it—**as well as** engendering the **foremost**, perfect **diligence**, the **true perfection** of joy through having become free of doubts with regard to the inconceivable domains, **and the gathering of the supreme Dharma,** which refers to protecting the Great Vehicle Dharma by guarding from harm those who have entered it—**these are held to be the characteristics of a compassionate one's**, that is, a bodhisattva's, **full maturation** of true joy **for the sake of comprehensively upholding the sacred Dharma.** Furthermore, the supreme friend and the rest are the cause of the full maturation of joy. Foremost diligence and the rest are the nature of this full maturation, and its function is to gather the supreme Dharma.

The cause for the full maturation of joy is taught as being "the supreme friend," meaning one's spiritual teacher. "And the rest" refers to the two further factors of listening to the Dharma and acting according to its meaning. "Foremost diligence" implies the continuous reception, reflection, and meditation on the Dharma of the Great Vehicle. "True perfection" refers to being free from doubt with regard to the inconceivable, profound principles of the Great Vehicle, as illustrated, for example, by the teaching on "the four inconceivable domains," which refer to the karma of sentient beings, the power of mantra and medicine, the wakefulness of the thus-gone ones, and the experiential domain of a yoga practitioner.

Both true perfection and diligence illustrate the essence or nature of fully mature joy. The function of fully mature joy is to gather the Dharma of the Great Vehicle, the supreme among all Dharmas, on a vast scale and to ensure that it does not decline. Fully mature joy protects the Dharma from decline by safeguarding one's own activities of teaching and practice, as well as those of others. The purpose of fully mature joy, in brief, is to uphold extensively the sublime Dharma of the Great Vehicle. These qualities characterize a compassionate bodhisattva's truly full maturation of joy in the Great Vehicle.

2. Faith

> Knowing the qualities, an undivided mind,
> Swift attainment of meditative absorption, and the experience of its result—
> These are held to be the characteristics of the children of the victorious ones' full maturation
> For the sake of trust in the teacher. [IX.3]

This section presents an explanation of the full maturation of faith. **Knowing the qualities** of the Buddha is the cause of faith. The nature of faith is **an undivided mind**, as one's faith has arisen through knowledge. In terms of its functions, faith brings about the **swift attainment of meditative absorption and the experience of** the results of meditative absorptions, that is, the superknowledges and its other **results**. **These are held to be the characteristics of the children of the victorious ones' full maturation** of true faith **for the sake of trust in the teacher.**

Knowing the qualities of the teacher, the Buddha, is the cause of faith. Having found irreversible faith in the teacher, the mind will be unreserved and unshakable in its appreciation of the teacher. Genuine faith arises when one has attained the first ground, whereupon one understands the Three Jewels and so experiences an undivided faith in them.

This undivided character is the nature of faith. The function of mature faith is that it causes one swiftly to attain the meditative absorptions of the Great Vehicle, such as that of the heroic gait. Mature faith also brings forth the experience of the superknowledges, which are the fruition of those meditative absorptions. The purpose of mature faith is to engender trust in the supreme teacher. These are held to be the characteristics of the children of the victorious ones' full maturation of faith.

3. Serenity

> Complete restraint, elimination of afflictive thoughts,
> Absence of obstacles, and delight in virtue—

These are held to be the characteristics of the children of the
victorious ones' full maturation
That dispels the afflictions. [IX.4]

The full maturation of serenity is explained as follows. The causes of serenity are mindfulness and attentiveness. These qualities bring about **complete restraint** with respect to the sense faculties. The nature of serenity is the **elimination of afflictive thoughts**. In terms of function, it leads to the **absence of obstacles** that impede the cultivation of the remedies **and to delight in virtue. These are held to be the characteristics of the children of the victorious ones' full maturation** of the serenity **that dispels the afflictions.**

The causes of the full maturation of serenity are found in being completely restrained in engaging the objects of the sense faculties and in refraining from embracing negative conduct. This restraint is brought about by maintaining mindfulness and alertness. The elimination of afflictive thoughts is the essence of the full maturation of serenity. Its function is to ensure that there are no obstacles to meditating on the antidotes of afflictive and unvirtuous factors, and that there will be delight in virtue, that is, the activities of the six transcendences. The purpose of the full maturation of serenity of the children of the victorious ones is to dispel the afflictions. These are held to be the characteristics of the perfect and full maturation of serenity.

4. Affection

Natural affection, seeing the suffering of others,
Complete elimination of the mind-set that is inferior,
Distinctive progress, and a body that is supreme among
    beings—
These are the characteristics of the full maturation of affection
    for others. [IX.5]

The following explains the characteristics of the full maturation of affection. The cause of affection is the **natural affection** brought about through the power of the potential, the **affection that arises from seeing the suffering of others**, and the **complete elimination of the mind-set that is** associated with the **inferior** vehicles. Its nature lies in the ever-increasing, **distinctive progress** of maturation, **and** its function is to bring about the attainment of **a body that is supreme among** the forms of **beings**, which occurs on the ground of irreversibility. **These are the characteristics of the thorough maturation of affection for others.**

The causes of the full maturation of affection are the following three factors: (1) a natural increase in affection for sentient beings brought about through the power of one's potential, (2) perception of the observed condition, the suffering of other sentient beings, and (3) the perfect and complete rejection of the mind-set associated with the Lesser Vehicle, that is, the wish for the transcendence of suffering that is achieved by listeners and self-realized buddhas. The nature or essence of the full maturation of affection is its distinctive progress, in the sense that the affection of one who has attained the first ground is superior to that of those on the paths of accumulation and joining; the affection of someone on the second ground is superior to the affection of one on the first ground; and so on. The function of affection is to bring about the attainment of a body that is supreme among beings, meaning a bodily support with qualities that are superior to those of sentient beings, and with the major and minor marks that are attained from the first ground onward. These are the characteristics of the children of the victorious ones' full maturation of affection for others.

5. Patience

Natural steadfastness, analytical meditation,
Remaining unmoved by intense suffering due to cold and the like,
Distinctive progress and delight in virtue—
These are held to be the characteristics of the full maturation
of patience. [IX.6]

The characteristics of the full maturation of patience are explained as follows. The causes of patience are the **natural steadfastness** brought about by the power of the potential, which enables one to endure pain and other difficulties, and **analytical meditation** on the flaws of anger. In terms of its nature, patience involves **remaining unmoved** even **by intense, unbearable suffering due to cold and the like**. **Distinctive progress and delighting in virtue** are its functions. These are held to be the characteristics of the full maturation of patience.

The causes of the full maturation of patience are the forbearing character that comes about through the power of the potential and the natural steadfastness, likewise due to the power of potential, that enables one not to become disheartened when taking on suffering and so forth. Another cause is to meditate, based on having received and investigated the Dharma in accordance with its meaning. Here one meditates on how the harm inflicted by others has originated from one's own karma; how others are not in control of themselves; how all phenomena have originated from causes and conditions and are devoid of a self and a creator; how all phenomena are devoid of nature, being like an illusion; and so forth. The essence of the full maturation of patience is never to be upset, even by intense suffering such as cold, heat, and being mistreated by others, thereby ensuring that one is unperturbed and does not turn away. The full maturation of patience functions to bring about distinctive progress in the development of good qualities It also brings delight in undauntedly embracing the virtues of the six transcendences. These are held to be the qualities of the full maturation of patience.

6. Keen Intellect

> Pure ripening, the mindfulness of not forgetting what has been received and so forth,
> Fully recognizing good and bad statements,
> And the capacity to engender the great mind—
> These are the characteristics of the full maturation of a perfectly keen intellect. [IX.7]

The full maturation of a keen intellect is explained as follows. A keen intellect is caused by the **pure ripening** of factors that are conducive to it. The **mindfulness of not forgetting what has been received and so forth**, even when much time has passed, along with the capacity for **fully recognizing good and bad statements,** constitutes the nature of a keen intellect. **And**, in terms of function, it gives one **the capacity to engender the great mind,** that is, supramundane insight. These are the characteristics of the **full maturation of a perfectly keen intellect.**

The cause of the full maturation of a keen or sharp intellect, "pure ripening," is the possession of a bodily support with complete faculties, endowed with discernment. Such physical and mental qualities manifest, in turn, as a result of the ripening of virtuous acts performed in previous lifetimes, such as acts associated with receiving and reflecting on the sacred Dharma. In essence, mature intellect involves (1) being mindful so that one does not forget the meaning of the teachings that one has received and reflected upon and (2) having the wakefulness that makes it possible to differentiate clearly between statements that are insightful, accurate, and well formed, and statements that are flawed and false. Hence, an intellect that is unerring due to both mindfulness and discernment is termed a "keen intellect." As one enhances the mind with a keen intellect through mundane mindfulness and discernment, this then functions to produce the great wakefulness on the grounds of the noble ones. These are held to be the characteristics of the full maturation of a keen intellect.

7. Power

> The strengthening of the two elements through the two virtues,
> The support being perfectly ready to produce the fruition,
> Accomplishing what is wished for, and superiority in the world—
> These are the characteristics of the full maturation of the attainment of power. [IX.8]

> The full maturation of the attainment of power is explained as follows. **The strengthening of the two** seed **elements** of merit and wakefulness **through the two virtues** of merit and wakefulness is the cause of attaining power. **The support,** the continuum of the aggregates, **being perfectly ready to produce the fruition,** constitutes the nature of the attainment. Perfectly **accomplishing what is wished for and** obtaining a body that is characterized by **superiority in the world** constitute its function. **These are the characteristics of the full maturation of the attainment of power.**

The cause of the full maturation of power is an intensifying engagement in the virtuous accumulations of merit and wakefulness. This brings about a strengthening of the elements, or seeds, of these virtues that are present in the all-ground—like seeds that are ready to grow when they meet with moisture. The nature or essence of the full maturation of power involves the support of the thus-strengthened two elements now being perfectly ready to produce the fruition of the Great Vehicle's noble path. In Sthiramati's commentary, there is mention of "the perfect support for the arising of the fruition." Sthiramati treats this as a reference to the kind of bodily support that is equipped to sustain the attainment of the noble path. In any case, the full maturation of power is that which empowers the support of the noble path.

In terms of function, with the full maturation of power, one has the ability to accomplish whatever is desired, such as the welfare of sentient beings. This, in turn, means that one can accomplish whatever is wished for. Moreover, as one attains an exalted body and perfect enjoyments through merit, and exalted insight through wakefulness, one gains superiority in the world. Possessing this triad of cause, nature, and function characterizes the full maturation of the attainment of power.

8. Unassailability

> A mind that discerns the good Dharma with reason,
> Continuous absence of obstacles from demons,
> Discovery of the extraordinary, and disproof of the position of
>   others—

These are the characteristics of the full maturation of unassailability. [IX.9]

Next follows an explanation of the full maturation of unassailability. The cause of unassailability is **a mind that** correctly **discerns the good Dharma** of the Great Vehicle **with reason**. Once certainty has been gained within one's own vehicle, there is a **continuous absence of obstacles from demons** on the path. This is the nature of unassailability. **Discovery of the extraordinary** realization **and disproof of the position of others** serve as its functions. These are the characteristics of the full maturation of unassailability.

The cause of the full maturation of unassailability is to discern, by means of the four reasonings, the wholesome meaning that is intended by the authentic teachings of the Great Vehicle Dharma, the nature of which is profound and vast. As one thus ascertains their meaning, one discovers a mind free from doubt. The nature of the full maturation of unassailability is the continuous absence of obstacles from demons. Having gained certainty, one is confident in the meaning of the profound Dharma. Consequently, one cannot be led astray from the path by demons, extremists, or anyone else. In terms of function, the full maturation of unassailability enables one to establish the authentic way of the Dharma and to disprove those who take false and deceptive positions. This ability is achieved through the discovery of an extraordinary certainty regarding the meaning of what is taught in the Great Vehicle and elsewhere. In Sthiramati's commentary, it is explained that the "discovery of the extraordinary" refers to the intellect becoming extraordinarily brilliant. The possession of such a cause, nature, and function characterizes the full maturation of unassailability.

9. Factors of Elimination

Accumulation of virtue, the support being fit for diligence,
Delighting in seclusion and supreme virtue—
These are the characteristics of the genuine, full maturation

Of the children of the victorious ones' possession of the factors. [IX.10]

Next follows an explanation of the full maturation of possessing the factors of elimination. **Accumulation of** fundamental **virtue** is its cause, and **the support being fit for** arousing **diligence** is its nature. **Delighting in seclusion** from the afflictions **and the supreme virtue** of the Great Vehicle constitute its function. These are the characteristics of the genuine, full maturation of the children of the victorious ones' possession of the factors of elimination.

In the phrase "the full maturation of possessing the five factors of elimination," "elimination" refers to relinquishing dualistic fixation upon the initial direct realization of the basic field of phenomena. This elimination is facilitated by faith and the rest of the five qualities mentioned above, and the latter are therefore termed "the factors of elimination." The process of fully ripening these five factors, through the attributes of their cause, nature, and function is as follows. Their full maturation is caused by the accumulation of the virtues of merit and wakefulness, which is associated with faith. The "support" in "the support being fit for diligence" refers to the bodily support, for when performing virtue, there is nothing that the body cannot do. This support is the nature of the factors of elimination. Of the five factors, it is associated with absence of disease. The function of the factors of elimination is twofold. (1) There is the supreme and complete delight in the seclusion that comes about by abandoning all diversions, as well as delight in the seclusion of a bodhisattva, which is the supreme seclusion from entertaining selfish concerns and so forth. (2) There is the supreme and complete delight in receiving, reflecting, and meditating on the Dharma of the Great Vehicle, which is a delighting in virtue. Delighting in seclusion corresponds with freedom from hypocrisy and pretense, while delighting in virtue is associated with insight. This way of maturing the five factors of elimination is thus explained as "the characteristics of the genuine, full maturation of the children of the victorious ones' possession of the factors."

3. Summary

The third section has two parts: (1) one's own full maturation and (2) an explanation of the metaphors for maturation.

1. One's Own Full Maturation

> The one who has matured through these nine factors
> Is equipped to bring about full maturation in others.
> The one who embodies the ever-increasing stream of the
>   nature of qualities
> Will always be the supreme friend of beings. [IX.11]

The one who has matured through faith and the rest of these nine factors is a teacher equipped to bring about full maturation in others. The bodhisattva, being one who embodies the ever-increasing stream of the nature of the body of qualities, will always be the supreme friend of beings.

The one who, through delight and the rest of the nine factors outlined above, has fully ripened the qualities of buddhahood within himself or herself will also have the ability to bring about the full maturation of other sentient beings. In this way, through having matured oneself, one will be able to bring about the maturation of others. The one who embodies an ever-increasing stream of the nature of all the qualities of the six transcendences will constantly bring about the maturation of other sentient beings. Hence, such a being is known as the "supreme friend of beings." In this way, the verses show how one's own ripening supports the ripening of others, and how this further serves to increase one's own body of qualities.

2. Explanation of Metaphors for Maturation

> Boils and food are held to be mature
> When they are ready to be drained or enjoyed.

Similarly, it is taught that maturity is present when
The two factors are pacified and enjoyed within their support.
[IX.12]

The divisions pertaining to the full maturation of sentient beings are explained as follows. **Boils and food are held to be mature when,** respectively, **they are ready to be drained** of pus **or** ready to be **enjoyed.** Similarly, it is taught that maturity is present when **the two factors,** meaning the conflicting factors and their remedies, **are** ready to be **pacified and enjoyed,** respectively, **within their support** of sentient beings.

"Maturation" can be likened to boils and food, which are regarded as "mature" when they are ready to be drained or enjoyed, respectively. If an abscess breaks open before having matured into pus, then it will not be possible to drain it, and hence the ailment will not be healed. When it has matured into pus and a boil has formed, however, it is ready to be drained and is referred to as a "mature boil." Similarly, when grapes and other fruit have not yet ripened, or when food is still in the process of being prepared or cooked, these are not ready to be enjoyed. When ripened to the proper extent, however, they are ready to be enjoyed. The supportive five aggregates are, likewise, mature when the factors that are to be eliminated and the factors that serve as their remedies are respectively pacified and enjoyed. When a boil forms after an abscess has matured and filled with pus, the ailment will recede after the pus has been drained. Likewise, afflictions such as attachment, that are associated with this bodily support, will be quelled through the powers that eliminate them. When along with this pacification one is able to employ one's body in a constant cultivation and enjoyment of virtuous factors, as if they were ripe food, one will be referred to as "someone who has fully matured."

One may have experienced joy in the Great Vehicle Dharma, yet if that joy does not mature, one will not be able to embrace the Dharma fully as one receives, reflects, and meditates under the guidance of a spiritual teacher. When joy has fully matured, however, one will indeed be capable of upholding the sacred Dharma. This is equally relevant to the other eight factors treated above. Once they have fully matured, they can directly perform their respective functions. Therefore, as bodhisattvas progress in the full maturation of faith and the other faculties, they bring the qualities of the Great Vehicle's path and fruition to perfection in their own streams of being, while at the same time ripening sentient beings. Hence it is taught that bodhisattvas should persist in cultivating the faculties. It is likewise important to cultivate the faculties in order for them to go from being of inferior to middling quality, and from middling to supreme. Once they have been cultivated, one will realize what was not realized before, and one will achieve what was not previously achieved, such that one's qualities will continue to develop until the stage of buddhahood.

2. Maturation of Others

The discussion of bringing about the maturation of other sentient beings has three parts: (1) types, (2) intention, and (3) application.

1. Types

> The maturation of embodied beings is taught in terms
> Of separating maturation, complete maturation, full maturation,
> Accordant maturation, excellent maturation,
> Realized maturation, constant maturation, and progressing maturation. [IX.13]

The maturation of embodied beings is taught in terms of the following classifications: **separating maturation**, in the sense of separation from the afflictions; **complete maturation** by means of the three vehicles; the **full maturation**, which is superior to that achieved by extremists; **accordant maturation** that is in harmony with those possessing the various types of potential; **excellent maturation** through being respectful; **realized maturation** through having gained excellent realization oneself; **constant maturation** by means of the unmistaken meaning; **and** the incorruptible **progressing maturation.**

The following eight forms of maturation are taught. (1) Separating maturation involves bringing embodied sentient beings to a point of maturation in terms of having separated from attachment and other afflictions. (2) Complete maturation refers to the maturation of all who possess the potential for one of the three vehicles. (3) Full maturation refers to the fact that those matured by the three vehicles do not regress, whereas those who have matured into the higher realms of the mundane path do regress. (4) Subsequent, or accordant, maturation takes place through teaching the Dharma in a way that is appropriate and in accord with the mind streams of disciples. An example of this would be giving a teaching on repulsiveness to someone with attachment. (5) Excellent maturation involves applying oneself diligently, without bias, and with respect for others. (6) Special maturation occurs once one has attained the first ground and then establishes others on that ground. This is also referred to as maturation through realization. (7) Constant maturation is brought about by constantly giving the Dharma taught by the Buddha to sentient beings. (8) Progressing maturation takes place from the grounds of inspired conduct up to and including the tenth ground.

2. Intention

The distinctive intention is as follows:

**The children of the victorious ones, due to their benevolent intent,
Are present here to mature all beings.
No father, mother, or friend is so kind
To children, relatives, or friends.** [IX.14]

**Those who embody love pursue benefit and happiness
With affectionate care for other beings.
People do not even love themselves this much,
Let alone those who are dear to them.** [IX.15]

The children of the victorious ones, due to their benevolent intent, are present here to mature all beings. In the world, **no father, mother, or friend is so kind to** his or her own **children, relatives, or friends. Those who embody love,** the children of the victorious ones, **pursue benefit and happiness with affectionate care for other beings. People do not even love themselves this much, let alone those who are dear to them,** for whom they likewise have no such concern.

Due to their benevolent intent, the wish to establish all sentient beings in temporary and perfect happiness, the children of the victorious ones are present here, within existence, to fully mature all beings. There are no fathers, mothers, or friends in the world who are as well-intentioned toward their own children and friends as this. Even though parents, for instance, have love for their children and are therefore able to be of some temporary, meager benefit in this lifetime, they do not know how to bring forth the wish to establish them in virtue, which is the cause of eternal happiness. Some even bind their loved ones to vice.

When those—whose very nature is love—work for the benefit of other sentient beings, their affectionate wish is to act in a way that brings others happiness, temporarily and forever. Worldly beings do not even love themselves in this way, much less the beings they otherwise hold dear. It is the case, of course, that ordinary beings love themselves. However, while hoping to become happy in their present life, in their delusion they actually incur a great deal of suffering in both present and future lives. These sufferings, for instance, being punished for breaking the law, are brought about by unvirtuous deeds, such as killing or stealing. Likewise, through committing suicide or engaging in unwholesome acts of penance, such as the yogic conduct of dogs and cows, they bring about suffering in both their present and future lives. They do not know the path to lasting happiness, and they fail to find it. The love that bodhisattvas have for all sentient beings is a love that is virtuous in all regards, and it involves wishing for beings' eternal happiness.

3. Application

There are seven stanzas in this section: the first six stanzas concern the maturation brought about by the six transcendences, and the seventh stanza offers a concluding summary.

1. Generosity

> For a bodhisattva, there is no body or enjoyment
> That is not given to others.
> The bodhisattva matures others by helping in two ways;
> Giving equally, they never know enough of the qualities.
>   [IX.16]

This section explains how a bodhisattva fully matures sentient beings with generosity. **For a bodhisattva, there is no body or enjoyment** that one possesses **that is not given to others. The bodhisattva matures others by helping in two ways** that benefit them in both present and future lives. The two ways are (1) the bodhisattva completely fulfills others' wishes without feeling any loss himself or herself and (2) the bodhisattva establishes others in virtue by attracting them with acts of generosity. In this way, **giving** with a mind that regards all recipients **equally, they,** the bodhisattvas, **never know enough of the qualities** of generosity.

Sentient beings are brought to maturation through three forms of generosity: giving all, giving equally, and giving tirelessly. Bodhisattvas do not have even one iota of their own body or enjoyments that they are not willing to give to others if they see that it would help the other person to do so. They give all that they possess. Moreover, their generosity does not simply benefit others by supplying them with the particular thing that is given. It benefits others in this life by completely fulfilling their wishes, and, as it also matures them and establishes them in virtue, which is the cause of the fulfillment of one's wishes, it benefits them in future lives as well. Thus, bodhisattvas establish these beings in lasting happiness by planting the seed of liberation. In this way, generosity matures sentient beings by helping them in two ways, insofar as there are both temporary and lasting benefits. Moreover, this generosity is practiced with equal regard for all. Since there are no biases in terms of the recipients' moral standing, social position, or relation to oneself, they characteristically practice giving equally. Finally, not content with giving a confined number of material things for a certain number of years or eons, a bodhisattva never knows enough of the qualities of generosity, even were he or she to continue giving until the end of cyclic existence.

2. Discipline

> Steadfast, natural, completely nonviolent,
> Inherently delightful, and careful—the bodhisattva establishes others in this.
> Thus benefiting in the two ways, the bodhisattva matures others
> Through a succession of qualities of maturation and the causally linked. [IX.17]

The way in which a bodhisattva fully matures sentient beings through being disciplined is as follows. The discipline of the bodhisattvas remains **steadfast**, even at the cost of their life. Their discipline is also effortless and **natural**, since from the past they are already familiar with the practice. It is also **completely nonviolent** toward others, which implies a discipline of relinquishment. Their discipline is **inherently delightful** as well, which shows their discipline of realization, **and careful**, and thus always free from delusion. **The bodhisattva establishes others in this** fivefold discipline. **Thus benefiting** them **in the two ways**, meaning in both present and future lives, **the bodhisattva matures others through a succession of** mutually supportive, and hence uninterrupted, **qualities of maturation and the causally linked.**

Being "steadfast" involves guarding one's discipline constantly, not just temporarily, for as long as there are sentient beings. This is constant discipline, and so the word "constant" is, in fact, also used in the verses that are contained in the translation of Sthiramati's commentary. "Natural" discipline, on the other hand, is the natural disposition to engage in virtue and to avoid doing what is not virtuous through being accustomed to such discipline from the past. "Complete nonviolence" toward sentient beings involves not performing the ten unvirtuous actions, even in a dream. This complete perfection of discipline is attained on the second ground. Similarly, "inherently delightful" discipline is attained through the intrinsic nature, when one first realizes the truths. This is the attainment of discipline that delights the noble ones. Thus, this form of discipline naturally eliminates unvirtuous factors and clearly realizes the joys of virtue. "Careful" refers to unerring discipline, in which not even the slightest error, mistake, or lapse in conduct occurs.

Adhering to the supreme state of these five forms of discipline, one establishes other sentient beings in them as well. This brings them benefit in two ways, that is, both in their present and future lives, or both temporarily and for eternity. Establishing others in this discipline also brings about a maturation that involves the successive attainment of pleasing physical supports, such as rebirths as gods or humans. Finally, when one successively takes up such discipline in future lifetimes, and so brings about the maturation of others, that is the quality that is causally linked with discipline.

3. Patience

> Seeing those who harm them as benefactors,
> They tolerate even the most severe injuries.
> Knowing the methods, those who tolerate harm
> Cause those who do them harm to experience virtue. [IX.18]

Patience is used in order to fully mature sentient beings in the following manner. **Seeing those who harm them as benefactors, they**, the bodhisattvas, **tolerate even the most severe injuries. Knowing the methods** to mature others, **those who tolerate harm cause those who do them harm to** engender faith, thereby leading them to **experience virtue**.

When a sentient being harms a bodhisattva in one of various ways, including physical attacks or attempts on his or her life, the bodhisattva is able to say: "This being is the cause of the perfection of my patience." In this way, the wise perceive these sentient beings as benefactors, like spiritual teachers. Bodhisattvas tolerate even the most severe harm done against them, even when the flesh and bones of their bodies is being cut into pieces, so why even mention lesser forms of injury?

The method for cultivating patience includes what was just explained, as well as various analyses and other skillful means. Yet it also involves maturing malicious individuals by bringing them temporary and lasting benefit. Through this, those who demonstrate patience when injured mature those who do them harm by letting them experience virtue.

4. Diligence

> Relying on supreme diligence,
> The children of the victorious ones fully mature the gathering of beings.
> For the sake of even a single virtue in the mind of someone else,
> The bodhisattva knows no weariness throughout ten trillion eons. [IX.19]

Diligence is used in fully maturing sentient beings in the following way. Always **relying on supreme diligence, the children of the victorious ones fully mature the gathering of beings. For the sake of** the arising of **even a single virtue in the mind of someone else, the bodhisattva knows no weariness throughout ten trillion eons.**

The children of the victorious ones rely on armor-like diligence and the diligence of application in a way that is irreversible and that involves being insatiable when working for the welfare of sentient beings. Through such diligence, the bodhisattva brings an infinite number of sentient beings to full maturation. When seeing that someone can engender a generous attitude or some other maturing virtuous mind-set for even a single instant, the bodhisattva will work for however long is necessary to make that happen, even for ten trillion eons. All the while, he or she will not feel the slightest bit weary.

5. Concentration

> Having attained supreme mastery of the mind,
> They have thoroughly vanquished the desire for offerings from others.
> Inspiring interest in the teaching of the supreme,
> The bodhisattva completely enriches the virtues of others. [IX.20]

Concentration is engendered in order to fully mature sentient beings in the following way. **Having attained** the essence of mental flexibility, bodhisattvas gain **supreme mastery of the mind** of meditative concentration. Therefore, **they** do not hope for material things and **have thoroughly vanquished the desire for offerings from others. Inspiring interest in the teaching of the supreme** Teacher, **the bodhisattva completely enriches the virtues of others,** inspiring them to develop interest in the teachings.

Bodhisattvas who attain mastery of the mind, or the mental faculty, have gained this through meditative absorption. When they have attained the six forms of superknowledge, and specifically the special meditative absorptions of the buddhas and bodhisattvas, such as that of the heroic gait, bodhisattvas accomplish an unexcelled mastery of the mind. With this achievement, bodhisattvas have thoroughly vanquished all desire for others to make offerings to them, as well as for any other forms of honor and renown based on having these qualities. Without any such concerns at all, bodhisattvas inspire others to become interested in the teachings of the supreme ones, the buddhas, and so they thoroughly enrich the virtues of the transcendences that are present in the mind streams of others. They do so, for example, by showing miracles through the power of their superknowledge, or by using their clairvoyance to teach the Dharma in accordance with the mind streams of others.

6. Insight

With complete certainty regarding reality and intended meanings,
The bodhisattva thoroughly dispels the doubts of sentient beings.
Hence, respect for the victorious ones' teachings
Enriches the virtues of the bodhisattva and others. [IX.21]

Insight is employed in order to fully mature sentient beings as follows. **With the highest certainty regarding reality and** the character of the **intended meanings, the bodhisattva thoroughly dispels the doubts of sentient beings. Hence, respect for the victorious ones' teachings enriches the virtues of the bodhisattva and others.**

Bodhisattvas have complete certainty regarding the profound realization of reality since they have resolved it without doubt through the power of insight. This is possible because bodhisattvas are experts regarding reality, in the sense that they have properly realized all the expedient and definitive meanings, and so have understood which teachings have a concealed intent and which do not. Bodhisattvas also thoroughly dispel, and totally eradicate, the doubts that sentient beings harbor regarding the nature of reality or whether a certain teaching has a concealed intent or not. With their insight, bodhisattvas pay respect to the victorious ones' teachings. They also establish other sentient beings in this insight, and as others thereby also to come to venerate the victorious ones' teachings, bodhisattvas thus establish others in virtue, as well. In this way, bodhisattvas enrich the good qualities of virtue that are present in the mind streams of both themselves and others.

7. Concluding Summary

In this way, through compassion the bodhisattvas bring all beings
Into the higher realms or the three types of virtue,

Manifesting the way of the lesser, the supreme, and the middling.
Thus, for as long as it exists, they enter the world and cultivate it. [IX.22]

This was the ninth chapter of the *Ornament of the Great Vehicle Sūtras,* the chapter on full maturation.

In this way, through the means of great **compassion, bodhisattvas bring all beings** that are to be trained **into the higher realms or the three types of virtue** associated with the three vehicles. The bodhisattvas' training thus involves **manifesting the way of the lesser** approach associated with the grounds of inspired conduct, **the** way of the **supreme** approach that pertains to the eighth ground and beyond, **and the** way of the **middling** approach associated with abiding on the first through the seventh ground. **Thus, for as long as it exists,** which is another way of saying "forever," **they enter into the world and cultivate it.**

In this way, the bodhisattvas' compassion leads to actions for the welfare of beings that bring them to maturation. On the temporary level, it causes these individuals to attain good rebirths as gods and human beings. By encountering bodhisattvas, even people with the cut-off potential are established in the ten virtues, and will thereby temporarily find maturity in pleasant rebirths. "The three types of virtue" are the virtues of the lasting bliss of the three forms of enlightenment. To bring beings into such virtues thus means to establish upon their respective paths those who possess one of the three potentials.

The verses also explain how this process relates specifically to practitioners of the Great Vehicle. In that context, those with a meager amount of the two accumulations are matured on the grounds of inspired conduct, the supreme are brought to maturation on the three pure grounds, and the middling are matured from the first through the seventh ground.

One may then wonder for how long bodhisattvas will be active to bring sentient beings to maturation. Bodhisattvas will enter the world and cultivate it for as long as there is a world. Wherever there is space, there are sentient beings, and bodhisattvas will train sentient beings and bring them to maturation throughout all of space and time. There is no end to their activity.

This concludes the explanation of full maturation, the ninth chapter of the *Ornament of the Great Vehicle Sūtras*.

10

Enlightenment

4. The Inconceivable

The nine forms of maturation are primarily taught in terms of the grounds of inspired conduct. However, from a general perspective, the great enlightenment that is achieved at the end of the continuum of the tenth ground constitutes the final maturation of the bodhisattvas' grounds and faculties. For this reason, great enlightenment is explained after full maturation.

The chapter on enlightenment has three parts: (1) an overview of how enlightenment is the final attainment, (2) an extensive explanation of the nature of enlightenment, and (3) a summary that provides advice for cultivating the enlightened mind oriented toward unsurpassable enlightenment.

1. Overview

The first section is taught in the following two stanzas, and the third stanza explains their meaning:

> Hundreds of immeasurable austerities,
> Accumulations of immeasurable virtue,
> Immeasurable time,
> And exhaustion of immeasurable obscurations—[x.1]
>
> Because of this there are no defilements at all,
> And omniscience is attained.

Like opening a trove of treasures,
This is shown to be buddhahood itself. [x.2]

Hundreds of marvelous hardships have been practiced with austerity.
Throughout long eons, all virtue has been gathered.
All the obscurations of wandering beings are dissolved; even the subtle ones on the grounds are conquered.
This buddhahood possesses great power and can be likened to an open treasure trove. [x.3]

Omniscience itself is explained as involving many **hundreds of immeasurable austerities**, the gathering of the **accumulations of immeasurable virtue**, the **countless time** span of many incalculable **eons, and the exhaustion of immeasurable** afflictive and cognitive **obscurations. Because of this** there is true accomplishment, in which **there are no defilements at all, and omniscience is attained.** This absence of defilements and attainment of omniscience is the essential nature of enlightenment. **Like opening a treasure trove, this is shown to be buddhahood itself.**

Hundreds of marvelous hardships have been practiced with austerity and persistence. **Throughout long,** incalculable **eons, all** the **virtue** contained within the two accumulations **has been gathered. All the obscurations** that are present in the mind streams **of wandering beings are dissolved, and even the subtle ones on the grounds are conquered. This buddhahood possesses great power** to help others **and can be likened to an open treasure trove.**

On the path of the six transcendences, it is said that one performs "hundreds," meaning countless, austerities, such as giving away one's body and possessions. Such austerities are not practiced by listeners or self-realized buddhas. On the performance of immeasurable austerities through discipline, patience, and so forth, a sūtra states:

When piling up the eyes that I have sacrificed for the benefit of beings, the heap is higher than the king of mountains. The blood I have given is more than the oceans in the four directions.

The transcendences, grounds, factors of enlightenment, and so on, allow for the accumulation of immeasurable virtues. One strives for a long time, an immeasurable duration, and one exhausts immeasurable obscurations. No defilements of the obscurations are then left at all, and one attains omniscient wakefulness itself. It is as if a treasure trove full of all sorts of precious substances had been thrown open, directly revealing its contents. That is how the final fruition of buddhahood is explained.

To summarize, there are here "hundreds of austerities," meaning an immense number of different types of highly demanding practices that others are incapable of taking upon themselves. Hence, buddhahood involves "immeasurable austerities." The grounds, the factors of enlightenment, and the transcendences are likewise immeasurable, and a buddha has fully gathered all of these marvelous virtues without exception. These qualities surpass the fundamental virtues of the listeners and self-realized buddhas. Hence, buddhahood is characterized by immeasurable virtues. Moreover, to reach there, one must practice for an immeasurable period of time. That is to say, the time that is required is not measured in terms of shorter, intermediate eons, but in terms of great eons. Moreover, this does not take just one great eon, or even a hundred. Rather, one must practice for a period of three incalculable eons. As this is indeed an extremely long duration, it is incalculable to ordinary minds.

In what sense can the obscurations be said to be incalculable? The obscurations are present in the mind streams of all wandering beings, and they have been forming there during all their lives since time without beginning. These obscurations, moreover, can be either afflictive or cognitive and can be distinguished in terms of their features, reference points, and so on. When discerned in this way, they can be seen to be infinite and innumerable.

All such stains of obscuration are dispelled when the wakefulness that emerges on the ten grounds progressively destroys them, eliminating the particular forms of obscurations that pertain on each ground. Thus one becomes a buddha when even the subtle cognitive obscurations associated with the ground of ignorant habitual tendencies are destroyed by the vajra-like meditative absorption. This is the complete perfection of abandonment and the final realization, in which the perfect qualities of the fruition—such as the powers, fearlessnesses, and unshared qualities—are fully manifest. This attainment can be likened to opening a resplendent treasure trove that has the power to fulfill all needs and wishes.

2. Extensive Explanation of the Nature of Great Enlightenment

This section has two parts: (1) a general presentation of enlightenment by describing its ten qualities and (2) a sixfold presentation of the enlightenment that possesses those qualities, in terms of essence, cause, result, and so forth.

1. The Ten Qualities of Enlightenment

The ten qualities of enlightenment are (1) inconceivability, (2) perfection of the twofold benefit, (3) sublime refuge, (4) transformation, (5) all-pervasiveness, (6) spontaneous and nonconceptual activity, (7) profundity that is difficult to fathom, (8) unchanging essence, (9) immeasurable mastery, and (10) the maturation of sentient beings.

The first two qualities will each be explained in a separate stanza and then treated together in a third stanza.

1. Inconceivability

> All phenomena are buddhahood itself;
> There are no phenomena at all.
> Although of the nature of virtuous qualities,
> Those cannot express it. [x.4]

Suchness is not a nature that is any different from phenomena, and it is the purity of that suchness that distinguishes buddhahood.

Therefore, **all phenomena are buddhahood itself. There are no phenomena at all** that exist as imagined. **Although** this buddhahood is **of the nature of** the transcendences and other such **virtuous qualities, those,** meaning the transcendences and so forth, **cannot** serve to **express** the nature of **it,** meaning the nature of buddhahood, for these qualities do not exist as conceived by the immature.

Buddhahood is inconceivable, for it contains no duality of apprehended and apprehender, or existence and nonexistence. When one is a buddha, the duality of apprehended and apprehender has been relinquished. Buddhahood does not exist along the lines of the imagined nature, the apprehended and the apprehender, and yet it does exist in terms of the thoroughly established nature. Consequently, buddhahood transcends existence and nonexistence. What we refer to as "buddhahood" is suchness devoid of the twofold self and purified of adventitious defilements. On this point, the *Sūtra of the Ornament of the Light of Wakefulness* explains:

> Phenomena, always unborn, are the Thus-Gone One.
> All phenomena are like the Bliss-Gone One.

Likewise, a buddha's body of qualities is free from arising and ceasing. The *Vajra Cutter Sūtra* states:

> Those who see me as form
> And those who hear me as sound
> Have entered the wrong path;
> They do not see me.
> Regard suchness as the Thus-Gone One;
> All the guides are the body of qualities.
> The intrinsic nature is no object of mind;
> Consciousness cannot grasp it.

When assessed in accordance with the abiding reality of suchness, all that appears is of the nature of buddhahood. This is because no phenomenon exists separate from suchness, the basic field of phenomena. If there were something that existed separately, then it would not be the case that all phenomena lack nature and do not arise. Or, we may say that all phenomena are of the nature of buddhahood because no phenomenon whatsoever exists in the way it is imagined by immature, ordinary beings.

Buddhahood comes about by accomplishing the grounds, transcendences, and factors of enlightenment. At the time of buddhahood, the nature of the transcendence of suffering, the transcendences, and the factors of enlightenment, as well as the powers, the fearlessnesses, and all other undefiled, positive qualities are fully present. However, in the way they are conceived of and held as reference points within the imaginary duality of apprehended and apprehender, none of these qualities are descriptive of buddhahood. For example, although buddhahood is of the nature of generosity, none of the marks of duality, such as the notion of a buddha who performs a substantial act of giving for the benefit of substantial recipients, has any bearing on the buddha. Buddhahood is, hence, not within the domain of comprehension for a cognition with imagined, dualistic perception. In this way, buddhahood is characterized by nonduality and is, therefore, inconceivable.

2. The Spontaneous Accomplishment of the Twofold Benefit

> In being the cause of the jewel of the Dharma,
> It is likened to a mine of precious jewels.
> In being the cause of the harvest of virtue,
> It is held to be like a cloud. [x.5]

In being the cause of the jewel of the teachings of the Dharma, it, meaning buddhahood, is likened to a mine of precious jewels. In being the cause of the ripening of the harvest of virtue in the mind streams of those to be trained, it is held to be like a cloud.

The spontaneous accomplishment of the twofold benefit occurs due to the power of buddhahood. The buddhas teach the Dharma of scripture, and they function as the causes and conditions for the limitless, precious jewels of the Dharma of realization—the ten powers, the four fearlessnesses, and so forth. Having perfectly accomplished that which benefits himself or herself, a buddha can be likened to a mine or source of all manner of precious jewels. In being the cause for the ripening of the crops of virtue in all beings, buddhas can be likened to clouds that possess the power to accomplish perfectly all that is of benefit for others.

The next passage explains the meaning of the previous two stanzas:

> **Buddhahood itself either contains all phenomena or is free from them all.**
> **As the vast and expansive Dharma jewels manifest, it is like a mine of precious jewels.**
> **As it rains down the inexhaustible Dharma on beings through excellent statements—**
> **Causing tremendous growth of the fine harvest in beings—it is like a cloud.** [x.6]
>
> **Buddhahood itself either contains all phenomena,** for there is no phenomenon that is different from suchness, **or,** in being free from the imaginary, **is free from them all. As the vast and expansive Dharma jewels manifest, it is like a mine of precious jewels. As it rains down the inexhaustible Dharma on beings through excellent statements—causing tremendously** vast **growth of the fine harvest** of all things virtuous **in beings—it is like a cloud.**

Buddhahood either contains all cognizable phenomena, or is free from all phenomena. When examined from the perspective of things in their multiplicity, suchness can be seen to contain all phenomena because no phenomenon is different from suchness—its intrinsic nature. However, when evaluated from the perspective of things as they are, buddhahood is free from all phenomena because, in suchness, there is no duality of apprehended and apprehender nor any marks of dualistic phenomena.

In this way, nondual buddhahood is like a mine or a source of precious jewels. It is the source of the extremely vast and jewel-like Great Vehicle Dharma of scripture, and it is the source of the extensive and limitless

Dharma of realization, as exemplified by the grounds, transcendences, powers, and fearlessnesses. The Dharma is virtuous in the beginning, middle, and end. Hence, once the meaning of its excellent statements has been realized, there will be an inexhaustible rain of Dharma for all beings until the end of cyclic existence. Alternatively, this passage can be explained in reference to the fact that buddhahood rains down the Dharma that is inexhaustibly diverse. It thereby causes a tremendously vast growth of the virtuous seeds of the stainless and undefiled transcendences. This is like a magnificent harvest for all beings, and hence buddhahood can be compared to a cloud.

3. The Sublime Refuge

This section has three parts: (1) accomplishing one's own benefit, (2) accomplishing others' benefit, and (3) through these two, accomplishing the incomparable refuge.

1. Accomplishing One's Own Benefit

> The entire array of afflictions—
> All misdeeds, as well as old age and death—
> Against all this, the Buddha is always
> The perfect protector. [x.7]

Next follows an explanation of the way that the buddhas are the supreme protectors. **The entire array of afflictions—all misdeeds, as well as** birth, **old age,** sickness, **and death—against all this, the Buddha is always the perfect protector.**

Taking refuge in the Buddha does not offer a merely temporary form of protection. The buddhas are always active as the perfect protectors against ignorance, craving, and all the other afflictions. They also protect one from all defiling actions and flawed conduct, such as the ten nonvirtues and the five deeds with immediate retribution, as well as from old age and the lord of death.

For a buddha, the thorough affliction constituted by the principles of affliction, karmic action, and life, or birth, never occurs. The one who goes for refuge in the Buddha will at some point achieve this resultant refuge and thereby completely perfect his or her own benefit. Therefore, it is taught that buddhahood provides one's own protection. Stricken by fear, worldly beings search for protection by fleeing to mountains or caves. Or they take refuge in mundane kings, in minor mundane gods, in Brahma and Īśvara, and so on. Yet these are incapable of offering such a protection.

2. Accomplishing Others' Benefit

All harmful things, the lower realms,
Nonmethods, the transitory collection,
And the Lesser Vehicles—
Since it saves one from these, it is the sublime refuge. [x.8]

From **all harmful things**, such as disturbances of the mind and contagious diseases; from the states of **the lower realms**, the **nonmethods** that belong to mistaken paths, **the** view of the **transitory collection, and**, for those whose potential is uncertain, from **the Lesser Vehicles—since it saves one from these, it is the sublime refuge**.

Five ways are taught in which the buddhas protect sentient beings. Buddhas protect beings from all worldly harms because, through the blessings of the thus-gone ones, the blind find sight, the deaf will hear, and the mad find their sanity. Manifold diseases, bad harvests, and so on, are all quelled by the mere arrival of a buddha in the region. Those who supplicate a buddha will pacify all their faults. The thus-gone ones also radiate rays of light that extend to the lower realms and the hells. As soon as the light touches the beings in these places, it pacifies all their suffering, causing them to be born in the higher realms. Likewise, hell-beings and the other inhabitants of the lower realms are liberated from their painful condition by recollecting buddhas or hearing their names. And those without a method for liberation—extremists and others who engage in asceticism and mistaken spiritual disciplines—are freed from those paths and established on the path to higher realms and liberation.

Furthermore, buddhas protect others by teaching the selflessness of persons to those who adhere to the view of the transitory collection (the view of "me" and "mine"), thus establishing them in the listeners' and self-realized buddhas' transcendence of suffering. Those of undetermined potential who have entered, or wish to enter, the path of the listeners and self-realized buddhas are established in the Great Vehicle. Thus, they protect such beings from the Lesser Vehicles. For these reasons, buddhas are the supreme refuge for others.

3. Accomplishing Incomparable Refuge

This section has three parts: (1) the actual incomparable refuge, (2) the supreme refuge, and (3) the great refuge. These three are each taught in one stanza.

1. Actual Incomparable Refuge

> The refuge of buddhahood is held to be incomparably supreme,
> For it protects against the different fears, all of the transitory collection, the vehicles,
> The numerous sufferings of the lower realms, the pursuit of nonmethods,
> Birth, death, afflictions, and the lower realms. [x.9]

The refuge of buddhahood is held to be incomparably supreme, for it protects against the different fears, such as that of the degeneration of one's faculties or of being struck by a disease. It also protects against **all of** the view of the **transitory collection, the lesser vehicles, the numerous sufferings of the lower realms, the pursuit of** those **nonmethods** that accomplish neither the higher realms nor liberation, **birth, death,** and so on, attachment and other **afflictions, and** the assembling of the causes for **the lower realms.**

To summarize the meaning explained above, buddhahood is held to be the supreme refuge. It cannot be compared to any of the other things in which worldly beings seek refuge. Buddhahood cannot even be compared with the one-sided peace that is the transcendence of suffering attained by the listeners and self-realized buddhas and that, as such, is an object of refuge that transcends the world. This is because buddhahood is the refuge that offers complete protection. It protects one against all the different frightening and harmful things in cyclic existence, against the view of the transitory collection and other unwholesome views, against the Lesser Vehicles, against the numerous sufferings of beings in the lower realms, against engagement in, or pursuit of, methods that do not lead to liberation, against birth and death, and against all the afflictions and karmic actions that cause birth and death. In some editions, the term "karmic actions" is replaced by "lower realms."[32] In that case, it should be understood to refer to the thorough affliction of karmic actions, such as the deeds with immediate retribution and the ten unvirtuous acts that lead to birth in the lower realms.

2. Supreme Refuge

> An utterly perfect body of the qualities of buddhahood,
> Knowing how to train sentient beings in the sacred Dharma,
> And transcendent love for all wandering beings;
> Buddhahood is held to be the supreme refuge here. [x.10]

With respect to one's own benefit, there is **an utterly perfect body** that is of the nature of the powers and the other **qualities of buddhahood**. With respect to the welfare of others, buddhahood involves **knowing how,** that is, the means, **to train sentient beings in the sacred Dharma, and** there is equal, **transcendent love for all wandering beings.** Thus, **buddhahood is held to be the supreme refuge here.**

Buddhahood is the supreme refuge because it is the twofold perfection of one's own benefit and the benefit for others. Thus, upon becoming a buddha, the three exalted bodies that are the utter perfection of the enlightened qualities of the fruition (such as the powers) are one's own perfect benefit.

In terms of the benefit for others, sentient beings are brought into the sacred Dharma that contains the twelve sections of sūtra and so on, and are then fully trained. The way they are taught the Dharma is liberating because it takes place in accordance with their respective constitutions, abilities, and intentions. Insight is the unobstructed knowledge that is capable of teaching and training beings in this way, and great compassion is the transcendent love that never forsakes anyone. Together, these two accomplish the perfect benefit for others, and, in thus embodying the perfection of the twofold benefit of self and others, buddhahood is held to be the supreme refuge here within existence.

3. Great Refuge

For as long as the world exists,
This protects sentient beings from harm
And provides them with all that is excellent.
Therefore, the Buddha is held to be the great protector. [X.11]

For as long as the world exists, this protects all sentient beings from harm and provides them with all that is excellent. Therefore, the Buddha is held to be the great protector.

Buddhahood is the great refuge. For as long as there are world realms contained within space and time, buddhas will be there to protect and permanently save all sentient beings from harm. Moreover, buddhahood is also held to be the great refuge because it possesses the power to let sentient beings reach all that is excellent, whether mundane or supramundane.

4. Transformation

This section has two parts: (1) the explanation of transformation itself and (2) the superiority of this transformation.

1. Explanation of Transformation Itself

> Buddhahood is the elimination, extremely vast and completely obliterating,
> Of the seeds of the afflictive and cognitive obscurations that for so long have been constantly present.
> It is the attainment of the fundamental transformation with its supreme qualities,
> Accomplished by the path of the utterly pure nonconceptuality and the wakefulness of the extremely vast field. [X.12]

Buddhahood is the perfect **elimination—extremely vast and completely obliterating—of the seeds of the afflictive and cognitive obscurations that for so long have been constantly present,** that is, since beginningless time. **It is the attainment of the fundamental transformation** of the all-ground and the other [collections of consciousness], **with its supreme qualities,** such as mirror-like wakefulness. This transformation is **accomplished by the path of the utterly pure nonconceptuality** that occurs during meditative equipoise **and the** subsequently attained **wakefulness** that is the subject [in the realization] **of the extremely vast field** of all objects of knowledge.

The mind stream has a constant continuity. For a very long time, since beginningless cyclic existence, it has never been separate from the habitual tendencies, or seeds, of the afflictive and cognitive obscurations. The obscurations are eliminated by the sacred supramundane wakefulness that arises from the first through the tenth ground. Such wakefulness, in turn, manifests as the result of the great force of the two accumulations. It is completely nonconceptual and extremely vast, equal to space. On each ground, there are nine stages of wakefulness, such as "the greatest of the great" wakefulness. Since it manifests with all these features, it thoroughly eliminates, or obliterates, all of the obscurations.

Thereby a fundamental transformation occurs. The five aggregates that constitute the subject transform into the completely pure nature of the basic field of phenomena, and the subject, consciousness, transforms into the nature of nonconceptual wakefulness. Alternatively, the fundamental transformation can be understood as fivefold, encompassing (1) transformation of phenomena into the emptiness of utterly pure suchness—the basic field of phenomena, and (2–5) transformation of the eight collections [of consciousness] into the four types of wakefulness.

In brief, all impure appearances—the environment that is the abode, the eight collections of consciousness that manifest as objects, and the appearances of the body—are by nature and from the beginning nothing but reality itself. Covered by the two obscurations, however, their nature is not seen as it is. Yet the obscurations can be eliminated by means of the path, and when that happens the boundless expanse of appearances is now distinguished in terms of its purity. This is what is referred to as "transformation."

In terms of the way things are, there are no dualistic phenomena of apprehended and apprehender. When one does not waver from the realization of equality, there is, in terms of the multiplicity of things, a clear perception of all objects of knowledge. As in an illusion, everything appears distinctly, yet all is equally free from any marks of separation. This fundamental transformation possesses undefiled, positive qualities, such as the powers and fearlessnesses, which the listeners and self-realized buddhas do not have. The attainment is, therefore, completely supreme. This is the very essence of what we refer to as "buddhahood."

During a bodhisattva's meditative equipoise, the complete and utter purity of the nonconceptual state occurs. Through this, all phenomena are realized to be as unobservable as the limits of space. In the ensuing attainment, all the infinite objects of knowledge appear, yet they are seen to be like illusions; this is called "the wakefulness of the extremely vast field" or "the pure mundane wakefulness." Meditative equipoise and ensuing attainment are accomplished by means of the path of cultivation. When one is a buddha, there is no separation between meditative equipoise and ensuing attainment. At that point, the great self-existing, or inconceivable, wakefulness simultaneously sees all phenomena, both as they are and as many as they are.

2. Superiority

This section has two parts: (1) the way in which a buddha's transformation is superior to the transformation of listeners and self-realized buddhas and (2) a tenfold categorization of this superiority.

1. The Superiority of a Buddha's Transformation

> Abiding there, the Thus Gone One sees wandering beings
> As though he were standing on the lofty king of mountains.
> Since he has compassion even for those who are fond of peace,
> Why mention those who are fond of existence? [x.13]

> **Abiding there,** in the basic field free from defilement, **the Thus Gone One sees** all **wandering beings as though he were standing on the lofty king of mountains. Since he has compassion even for those who are fond of peace,** the listeners and the self-realized buddhas, **why mention** that he has compassion for **those who are fond of existence?**

In saying that buddhas are "thus gone," the meaning is that they have completely realized, or "entered into," the abiding way of the basic field of phenomena. Thus, they dwell within the transformation of that undefiled basic field. When looking in the ten directions from the summit of the highest of all mountains, the majestic king of mountains, one can see everything below, whether good or bad, near or far. Likewise, compared with the transformation of the listeners and self-realized buddhas, the transformation of a thus-gone one is both high and greatly elevated. Abiding on the summit of the lofty king of mountains, the completely transformed buddhas see all beings with their great, noble minds. They have great compassion for the listeners and self-realized buddhas, those wandering beings who are deeply fond of their own benefit, the peace of transcendence.

Since beginningless cyclic existence, listeners and self-realized buddhas have forsaken great compassion by not acting for the welfare of their family: sentient beings. Since they lack the insight that realizes the selflessness of phenomena, they are incapable of relinquishing the cognitive obscurations. Consequently, they cannot attain omniscient wakefulness. If the buddhas show compassion even for them, then it goes without saying that they have compassionate love for the beings in cyclic existence, for these are beings who are fond of an existence that is an abode of suffering, and who are therefore not free from the three sufferings.

2. Tenfold Categorization of the Qualities of a Buddha's Transformation

The nature of transformation is accepted in terms of
       engagement, superior engagement, nonengagement,
Reversal, thoroughgoing engagement, duality, nonduality,
Comparability, superiority, and omnipresence.
This is the thus-gone ones' complete transformation. [X.14]

The nature of the thus-gone ones' complete **transformation is accepted in terms of** the following. (1) It is a transformation that entails (1) **engagement** for the welfare of others. (2) It entails supremely **superior engagement** because among all phenomena it remains superior. (3) It entails **nonengagement** with the causes of thorough affliction. (4) It entails **reversal** of thorough affliction. (5) It entails constant, **thoroughgoing engagement** for the welfare of beings. (6) It entails **duality** in the sense of revealing manifest, complete enlightenment and complete transcendence of suffering. (7) It entails **nonduality** through the absence of engagement with either the conditioned or the unconditioned, due to abiding in neither cyclic existence nor in the transcendence of suffering. (8) It entails **comparability** in the sense of resembling the liberation of the listeners and self-realized buddhas. (9) It entails **superiority** of engagement, due to the powers and other qualities of buddhahood. (10) **And it entails omnipresence** in the sense of performing the activity of revealing all the vehicles. **This is the thus-gone ones' complete** and fundamental **transformation.**

The fundamental transformation of buddhas involves the following superior qualities.

(1) Engagement for the benefit of others through constantly performing only that which benefits sentient beings.

(2) Superior engagement, in that this transformation is superior to all mundane qualities, as well as to the supramundane qualities of the listeners and self-realized buddhas.

(3) Nonengagement in the causes that produce afflictive emotions, which for ordinary beings are threefold: proximity of the object, improper mental engagement, and not having eliminated the latent tendencies of the afflictive emotions.

(4) In a buddha's transformation, there is never any engagement in the causes that produce the afflictive emotions. Having attained that transformation, it is impossible for a buddha ever to engage in afflictions or unvirtuous actions. In other words, these engagements are reversed.

(5) Once attained, this transformation will never degenerate for as long as there is cyclic existence, and, since in this way it is always uninterrupted, this is a thoroughgoing engagement. Alternatively, it is known as thoroughgoing engagement because it engages all the phenomena that are antidotes to thorough affliction.

(6) This transformation is also characterized by duality because it enters into the twofold display of manifest enlightenment at the beginning, and transcendence of suffering at the end. Supreme emanation bodies issue forth from the buddha and constantly reveal, in all worlds in the ten directions, the way of great enlightenment for those to be trained.

(7) Ultimately there is no engagement in the duality of cyclic existence and transcendence of suffering. Yet there is engagement in the nondual, through realizing the equality of cyclic existence and the transcendence of suffering.

(8) There is also a comparability, or likeness, with the listeners and self-realized buddhas in terms of the aspect of the mere liberation that is the elimination of the afflictions along with their seeds.

(9) However, the specific transformation of the buddhas is superior to that of the listeners and self-realized buddhas because of its elimination

of the cognitive obscurations and the qualities it possesses, such as the powers and fearlessnesses.

(10) Omnipresence refers to omnipresence regarding the vehicles, meaning that the Dharma of the three vehicles is revealed to sentient beings in accordance with their respective potential, faculties, and inclinations.

This tenfold categorization is held to describe the thus-gone ones' complete transformation. Therefore, since the transformation of the buddhas has the best of all qualities and engages all antidotal qualities, its engagement is seen to be vast.

5. All-Pervasiveness

This section has two parts: (1) the actual quality of all-pervasiveness and (2) dispelling doubts.

1. Actual Quality of All-Pervasiveness

> Just as space is held to always reach everywhere,
> This is also held to be all-pervasive at all times.
> Just as space pervades all forms,
> So does this pervade the entire host of sentient beings. [x.15]

Just as, for example, space is held to always reach everywhere, in all times and places, **this** activity of the buddhas **is also held to be all-pervasive at all times.** That is to say, **just as space pervades** objects such as vases and **all** other **forms, so does this** activity of the buddhas **pervade the entire host of sentient beings.** This is because buddhas have thoroughly accomplished the acceptance of all sentient beings as themselves.

The way that buddhas pervade all things in time and space is as follows. Just as space is asserted to pervade all things, such as pillars and pots, the undefiled basic field of phenomena, which is the transformation of the buddhas, is similarly asserted to pervade all things of the past, present, and future. This is because all the phenomena contained in the three times are never beyond suchness. Moreover, the basic field of phenomena is a natural purity. There is, therefore, no essential distinction between this field in the context of buddhahood and in the context of the state prior to buddhahood. Space reaches everywhere, pervading all material forms without distinction—long and short, white and red, good, bad, and mediocre. Likewise, the basic field of buddhahood reaches the streams of being of the entire host of sentient beings—good, bad, and mediocre—and it pervades them as their intrinsic nature.

Buddhahood is the nature of the basic field of phenomena. It is utterly pure of adventitious defilements. When realizing the omnipresent character of the basic field of phenomena on the first ground, one attains equality of mind regarding oneself and all sentient beings. Here, one comprehends how one is sentient beings and sentient beings are oneself—"that which is me is also that which is sentient beings; that which is sentient beings is also that which is me." This realization of equality without distinctions is then progressively cultivated on the ten grounds. At the time of attaining the state of perfect buddhahood, one completely perfects the realization that the nature of all sentient beings is one's own nature. In doing so, one attains manifest and perfect enlightenment. This is referred to as "pervading the entire host of sentient beings."

2. Dispelling Doubts

> Just as the reflection of the moon
> Does not appear in a broken water vessel,
> The form of the buddhas
> Does not appear to inferior sentient beings. [X.16]

> Just as in some places fire blazes,
> Whereas in others it dies out,
> So also should one understand
> The appearance and disappearance of the buddhas. [X.17]

The buddhas pervade everywhere, yet **just as the reflection of the moon does not appear in a broken water vessel, the form of the** buddhas does not appear to inferior sentient beings. Their own karma and afflictions prevent this from happening.

The next verses consider the way that enlightened activity remains uninterrupted despite the buddhas' transcendence of suffering. Giving an example, the text states: **Just as in some places, namely, where there is fuel, fire blazes, whereas in others,** where there is none, **it dies out, so also should one understand** the places of **the appearance and disappearance of the buddhas.**

If in this way, the nature of the buddhas encompasses all sentient beings and there is no distinction, then why is it that this nature, which is also the intrinsic nature of the minds of all sentient beings, is not always seen? Further, why are the form bodies of the buddhas not seen? It is explained that this is because the mind streams of sentient beings are blinded by obscurations, rendering them unfit vessels for the perception of the buddhas. For example, although the sphere of the moon is in the sky, its reflection will not appear in a broken vessel that holds no water. The inferior mind streams of those sentient beings who have not gathered the accumulations of merit and wakefulness, and who possess afflictions and obscurations as the result of unvirtuous actions, are similar to such a broken vessel that cannot hold water. These mind streams lack the pure water of faith and meditative absorption. Therefore, the nature of the buddhas, and also their form, will not appear to these individuals.[33]

Therefore, seeing or not seeing the form body of a buddha is not due to the buddhas' lack of omnipresence. For those students who have gathered enough accumulations to be able to see a buddha, a buddha will appear. Without these accumulations, there will be no such perception. The form bodies of the buddhas can be likened to fires, which will blaze in places where there is firewood, yet die out and not burn where there is none. The form bodies of the buddhas will appear where there are individuals to be trained, yet at times and places where there are no such individuals, the buddhas will transcend suffering and disappear.

6. Spontaneous and Nonconceptual Activity

The next four stanzas show the way in which buddha activity is spontaneous and nonconceptual, in terms of (1) teaching the Dharma, (2) displaying various activities, (3) acting without interruption, and (4) appearing as development and decline.

> Just as the drum resounds
> Without being beaten,
> So do the victorious ones teach
> Without constructing. [X.18]

> Just as a jewel effortlessly
> Reveals its own luster,
> The buddhas definitively display
> Their deeds without constructing. [X.19]

> Just as all the workings of the world
> Unfold in space without interruption,
> The activities of the victorious ones
> Are unceasing within the undefiled field. [X.20]

> Just as within space
> Activities constantly cease and arise,
> Buddha activities develop and decline
> Within the undefiled field. [X.21]

These verses explain the uninterrupted and spontaneous accomplishment of buddha activity. **Just as the drum** in the Heaven of the Thirty-Three **resounds**, for instance, with the proclamation, "Everything conditioned is impermanent!" **without being beaten** by anyone, **so do the victorious ones teach** in accordance with the constitution of those to be trained, yet **without constructing** any thoughts. **Just as a** precious **jewel** fully and **effortlessly reveals its own luster, the buddhas definitively display their** physical **deeds without constructing** thoughts. **Just as all the workings of the** world, its formation and disintegration, **unfold in space without interruption, the activities of the victorious ones are** unfolding unceasingly **within the undefiled field.** Just as, within space, the activities associated with the formation and disintegration of the world **constantly cease and arise, buddha activities develop and decline,** depending on whether or not there are beings to train, **within the undefiled field.**

The listeners and self-realized buddhas pursue their own benefit and, upon transcending suffering, their activities are interrupted. The activities of the buddhas are carried out for the benefit of others, however, and are supreme in the sense that they are free from conceptual effort, spontaneously accomplished, and uninterrupted. This is just like the great drum that is formed from the merit of the gods. When Indra wants to enjoy the five sense pleasures, this drum emits sounds that are in tune with the enjoyment of the sense pleasures, yet without being beaten by anyone, and when Indra turns away from the five sense pleasures, it will make sounds that are suited to withdrawing from them. When the gods are victorious over the demigods, the drum produces sounds of victory, while for the heedless it manifests declarations of impermanence and so forth. Likewise, the victorious ones, the perfect buddhas, reside in the undefiled field without concepts. They teach effortlessly, without thought constructs such as "I will teach such and such to this and that person," and yet all sorts of explanations of the Dharma unfold in accordance with the specific inclinations of the listeners.

Just as a precious jewel effortlessly shines in all directions all by itself, the buddhas work for the benefit of sentient beings without thinking, or constructing, any motivating thoughts, such as "I will do this and that." Like the jewel, the various deeds of the exalted body, speech, and mind are displayed definitively, and yet they are spontaneously accomplished for the benefit of those to be trained.

Space is present without interruption throughout the formation, abiding, and disintegration of the external environment of the world, and also throughout the actions that are performed by sentient beings, such as staying and going. Likewise, the buddhas reside within the abode of complete purity, the undefiled basic field of phenomena, and, without wavering from that, they perform their activities without interruption throughout the ten directions until the end of time.

Even though their activities are uninterrupted, the buddhas' actions appear to come and go, develop and decline, due to those to be trained. This can be likened to the way that space remains constant throughout time, although external and internal entities arise, abide for some time, and then fade away within it. Things such as forests and households may burn down, what had previously existed will deteriorate, as when a sentient being dies, and at the same time other external and internal entities will be newly formed. Similarly, because of those to be trained, while the buddhas abide within the undefiled basic field of suchness, the activities of their emanating form bodies nonetheless appear to manifest anew, and what had existed before appears to decline.

7. Profundity That Is Difficult to Fathom

The next sixteen stanzas describe the profundity of the field of the buddhas. This section addresses (1) its profound characteristics, (2) its profound abode, and (3) its profound activity.

1. Profound Characteristics

The first topic is fourfold: (1) the characteristics of complete purity, (2) the characteristics of the supreme self, (3) the characteristics of issues not professed in scripture, and (4) the characteristics of complete liberation. These four are shown, respectively, in four verses.

1. The Characteristics of Complete Purity

> There is no difference between earlier and later,
> Yet buddhahood is held to be
> Suchness free from all defilements,
> Neither pure nor impure. [X.22]

Next follows the explanation of the undefiled field's profundity. With respect to the intrinsic nature, **there is no difference** between the earlier context of being an ordinary individual and the later situation of being a noble one, yet buddhahood is held to be suchness that is free from all defilements. It is, therefore, neither pure, as there is no difference between before and after, nor impure, because suchness is later purified of all defilements.

In the suchness of natural purity, there is no difference between earlier and later states. There is no difference between the time when one is an ordinary being and the point at which one is a buddha. In essence, the natural luminosity of emptiness never changes.

Nevertheless, buddhahood is suchness free from all the defilements of the adventitious obscurations. When there are adventitious defilements, on the other hand, this is not referred to as the basic field of the buddhas. Natural purity is pure from the beginning. It is not newly pure. Nor could it later become impure due to adventitious defilements. This is the profound character of purity, which is difficult to understand for those with little insight. Such people may think, "If they are pure from the beginning and free from defilements, then why don't sentient beings become buddhas?" and "If they are buddhas only at a later time, when they have purified the defilements, then there is no natural purity from the beginning."

2. The Characteristics of the Supreme Self

Within pure emptiness,
The buddhas achieve the supreme self of selflessness.
Thus they achieve the pure self,
And are hence the self of great beings. [x.23]

Within pure emptiness, the buddhas achieve the suchness that is the supreme self of selflessness. Thus they achieve the supremely pure self, and hence they are the self that is the realization of great beings.

The pure and natural luminosity of emptiness is completely free from the self-manifestation of the adventitious defilements. In the absence of the twofold self of persons and phenomena, this is the actual nature of things, the supreme nature of the abiding reality, the intrinsic nature or essence itself. In achieving this, the buddhas have achieved a nature that is of complete purity. Thus, [to actualize] the suchness that is the unmistaken way things are is to be "the self of great beings." This self is not the same as the conceived object that is involved when apprehending the twofold self because such a self has no bearing on things as they are. The buddhas, however, have actualized the unmistaken abiding reality, which is the suchness of the twofold selflessness, free from the extremes of existence and nonexistence. That is the supreme self—"the self of great beings."

3. The Characteristics of Issues Not Professed in Scriptures

> Therefore, buddhas do not exist
> Yet neither are they said to be nonexistent.
> Thus, questions regarding the Buddha
> Are held to be indeterminate. [x.24]

Therefore, buddhas do not exist, for they are characterized by the absence of self with respect to both the person and phenomena. **Yet neither are they said to be nonexistent** because they are the very self of complete purity. **Thus, questions regarding the Buddha,** such as whether the thus-gone ones exist or not after death, **are held to be indeterminate.**

Therefore, buddhas do not exist with the nature of either persons or phenomena. Yet, neither can it be claimed that they are nonexistent in terms of the nature of suchness that is beyond constructs. Those whose minds are based on duality understand the buddhas conventionally, in terms of limited streams of being. Thinking in that way, they have asked the Buddha questions like, "Do the buddhas, having transcended suffering, appear again or not? Having transcended suffering, do the buddhas then exist or not?" Questions that in this way are posed from the conceptual standpoint of the two extremes are held to be indeterminate because buddhas transcend the extremes of existence and nonexistence, and the conventions related to appearing or not appearing do not apply to them.

Emanation bodies do appear again and again in the world, manifesting whenever and wherever there are beings to be trained. They appear to whatever extent sentient beings exist. Nevertheless, this does not occur in the same way that a sentient being reappears after dying. One may ask whether or not sentient beings who have died will appear again. Here, however, the question is posed with something like the death and rebirth of ordinary sentient beings in mind, and yet it concerns the Buddha. The buddhas are not actually born, and do not actually appear, because their nature is suchness.

4. The Characteristics of Liberation

> As with the pacification of heat in iron
> And haze before the eyes,
> The buddhas' mind and wakefulness
> Cannot be said to feature existence or nonexistence. [x.25]

As with the pacification of heat in iron and the remedy for **haze before the eyes,** where, respectively, the burning heat and the haze do not exist, yet where the character of their pacification is not nonexistent either, **the buddhas' mind,** which is free from afflictive obscurations, **and** their **wakefulness,** which has overcome the cognitive obscurations, **cannot be said to feature** any **existence** of desire and ignorance **or** any **nonexistence** of liberated mind and insight.

In this way, since the buddhas are of the essence of suchness, their liberation is profound. In the present context, we may use the examples of an iron that has cooled off and eyes that have been cured of their ailment and hence no longer experience vision that is blurred. When an iron has cooled, one cannot say that it possesses pacified heat. While the iron is now cool and its previous heat has ceased and no longer exists, how could the heat's having been pacified be present? This would be as nonsensical as a barren woman's son dying! Yet neither can one say that the iron is not qualified by heat having been pacified because the iron would be hot if not for the fact of heat having dissipated there. The same can be understood in terms of the presence or absence of haze before the eyes.

The liberated minds of the buddhas can be seen as iron where the burning heat of attachment has been pacified, and their insight, the wakefulness of liberation, as being like eyes that have been cured of the haze of ignorance. The pacification of heat and haze, respectively, cannot be said to exist, yet neither can it be said to be nonexistent. When the mind and insight have been liberated, the heat of attachment and the haze of ignorance that were there before have ceased and do not presently exist. Hence, since both are absent, their pacification cannot be said to exist either. And yet, neither can it be said that their having been pacified does not exist because that is what follows in the wake of the liberation of the mind and the liberation of insight. By considering the continuity of mind in relation to the contexts of impurity and purity, we may speak of "elimination" and "liberation." However, when considered in light of the essence of suchness, liberation is there from the beginning. There is, therefore, no new liberation that occurs when buddhahood is actualized.

When free from the afflictions that are to be discarded by the paths of seeing and cultivation, the mind is said to be liberated, and when that liberation of the mind is recognized for what it is, that is termed "liberated insight." This is how it is explained in the commentary. It is also fitting to say that liberated insight is what occurs by eliminating the cognitive obscurations. Thus, the reference is actually to the wakefulness that is liberated from the two obscurations.

2. Profound Abode

> Within the undefiled field,
> Buddhas, like space, have no bodies,
> Yet they proceed from their previous bodies.
> Therefore, they are neither one nor many. [x.26]

Within the undefiled field, buddhas, like space, have no bodies, yet they proceed from their previous bodies, which they had as bodhisattvas. Therefore, they are neither one nor many.

Buddhas, who dwell in the undefiled field, are one and the same, like space, within the truth body of suchness. Consequently, they have no separate, individual bodies, nor are they subject to any clinging to a self. Therefore, they do not make up a plurality of separate buddhas. Yet, when in the past they engaged in bodhisattva conduct, from the grounds of inspired conduct up to the tenth ground, they did so through a multitude of separate bodies. Proceeding from these distinct bodies, we also speak of distinct buddhas, or distinct fruitions of their attainment. Consequently, the buddhas are not one either. Therefore, since the buddhas' singularity and multiplicity within the undefiled field can hardly be comprehended, it is profound.

3. Profound Activity

The profound activity will be addressed in terms of ten distinct activities: (1) the activity of the factors of enlightenment, which is like a jewel mine, (2) the activity of completely maturing sentient beings, (3) the activity of perfection, (4) the activity of teaching the Dharma, (5) the activity of emanating and so forth, (6) the activity of active wakefulness, (7) nonconceptual activity, (8) the activity of seeing various things simultaneously, (9) the activity of inactive wakefulness, and (10) the activity that is common in terms of liberation, yet unique in terms of wakefulness. Having explained these, an eleventh stanza will then summarize the three profundities.

1. The Activity of the Factors of Enlightenment, like a Jewel Mine

> Considering the powers and the other qualities of buddhahood,
> Enlightenment is like a jewel mine. [x.27a–b]

Considering the manifestation of **the powers**, the fearlessnesses, and the other qualities of buddhahood, great **enlightenment is like a jewel mine**.

Great enlightenment, which is the source of the ten powers, the four fearlessnesses, and the other qualities of buddhahood, is like a mine containing a variety of jewels.

2. The Activity of Fully Maturing Sentient Beings

With regard to the crops of virtue in wandering beings,
It is also held to be like a great cloud. [x.27c–d]

With regard to the growth of **the crops of virtue in** the infinite number of **wandering beings, it is also held to be like a great cloud.**

With regard to the ripening of the crops of virtue—that is, the six transcendences—within the streams of being of the wanderers, the activity of ripening is also likened to rain falling from a great cloud.

3. The Activity of Perfection

Since merit and wakefulness are completely perfected,
It is held to be like the full moon. [x.28a–b]

Since the two accumulations of **merit and wakefulness are completely perfected, it is held to be like** the sphere of **the full moon.**

Since the complete perfection of the accumulations of merit and wakefulness reaches a point of culmination at the stage of buddhahood, buddhahood is held to be like the full moon. When the moon is full, there is nothing whatsoever that is lacking; it is perfectly complete. This is also the case with the activity of perfection.

4. The Activity of Teaching the Dharma

Since it shines with the light of wakefulness,
It is held to be like a great sun. [x.28c–d]

Since it shines with the great **light** of the Dharma through the power **of wakefulness, it is held to be like a great sun.**

The buddhas' omniscient wakefulness comprehends all objects of knowledge. It is likened to a great sun because its light rays of Dharma teaching shine on the authentic meaning and make it perceptible within the mind streams of sentient beings in the ten directions. In a single world with four continents, there is only one sun, so there is no reference point for thinking of it as either a big or a small sun. The sun of buddhahood, however, illuminates countless world realms throughout the ten directions, and we might therefore call it a "great sun," thereby likening it to something that has never existed before.

5. The Activity of Emanating and So Forth

Just as the innumerable light rays
Of the sun's orb mingle together as one,
Always performing the same function
Of radiating light in the world, [x.29]

It is also held that the innumerable buddhas
Mingle together within the undefiled field,
Carrying out the same activity
And radiating the light of wakefulness. [x.30]

Just as the innumerable light rays of the sun's orb mingle together as one single power, **always performing the same function of,** for example, ripening crops and dispelling darkness by **radiating light in the world, it is also held that the innumerable buddhas mingle together** as the single body **within the undefiled field, carrying out the same activity** of ripening those to be trained, **and radiating the** great **light of wakefulness.**

The innumerable light rays that shine forth from the orb of the sun all mingle as one without distinction. These light rays always function to produce the same effect, as they serve to ripen crops, dry up mud, and so forth. They also all radiate light in the world. Likewise, abiding in the pure, undefiled basic field of phenomena, buddhas, who by reference to their former bodies may be said to be infinitely many, all mingle beyond distinction within the one taste of the suchness essence of the body of qualities. Their activity is also as one: ripening those to be trained and spreading the light of wakefulness for all sentient beings in the ten directions. When a buddha sends forth emanations, carries out the activity of ripening sentient beings, and so on, the whole infinity of buddhas will also perform that very activity because there are no distinctions in the truth body. Their activities mingle, as their actions, pursuits, and wakefulness are all the same without distinction. In this way, whenever a buddha performs an activity—such as bringing forth emanations, teaching the Dharma, ripening those to be trained, and performing miracles—this act actually embodies the activity of all the buddhas.

6. The Activity of Active Wakefulness

**When, for example, a single ray of sunlight shines forth,
All the others also emerge as well.
Understand that it is the same
With the wakefulness of the buddhas.** [x.31]

When, for example, a single ray of sunlight shines forth, all the others simultaneously **emerge as well. Understand that it is the same with the wakefulness of the buddhas,** for the presence of one is the presence of all. It is, hence, never the case that a particular wakefulness fails to cognize a certain object, or that certain objects are known before others.

For example, when a single ray of sunlight shines forth, all of the other light rays that appear in different places will emerge simultaneously, not earlier or later. Likewise, one should know that when, for the benefit of those to be trained, one among all the buddhas makes a declaration by means of wakefulness, for instance in response to a question, all of the wakefulness that is present in the infinite number of other buddhas will manifest simultaneously, not earlier and not later. All wakefulness will effectively be present within the one wakefulness.

7. Nonconceptual Activity

> When the rays of the sun shine forth,
> There is no sense of ownership.
> Likewise, the wakefulness of the buddhas is active
> Without any sense of ownership. [x.32]

> **When the rays of the sun shine forth, there is no sense of ownership** with respect to the four continents [that they illuminate]. **Likewise, the wakefulness of the buddhas is active without any sense of ownership** with regard to the objects of its activity.

The light rays of the sun proceed wherever they go without any sense of ownership. They do not think, "I will shine here and illuminate this place." Likewise, the wakefulness of the buddhas is active for the benefit and happiness of those to be trained, without any sense of "me" and "mine." Its activity is spontaneously accomplished without conceptuality.

8. The Activity of Cognizing Various Things Simultaneously

> Just as a single ray emitted from the sun
> Illuminates the world,
> The wakefulness of the buddhas
> Reveals all objects of cognition at once. [x.33]

> Moreover, **just as a single ray emitted from the sun illuminates the world** at once, **the wakefulness of the buddhas** engages with and **reveals all objects of cognition at once.**

When a single sunray shines on a particular place, it will simultaneously make all forms that are located at that place be perceptible to the beings who are present there. Similarly, the wakefulness of the buddhas simultaneously illumines all objects of cognition in the ten directions and the three times, so that everything is known at the same time. This knowledge is not limited, as it would be if one first knew some things and later others, or if one knew only some things, and not others. Rather, in the same instant the entire range of objects of knowledge is known in full. This can also be likened to the way that all forms within the range of a clear mirror will appear within the mirror simultaneously, not sequentially.

9. The Activity of Inactive Wakefulness

> It is held that the rays of the sun
> Are obscured by things such as clouds.
> In the same way, the wakefulness of the buddhas
> Is obscured by the flaws of sentient beings. [x.34]

It is held that the rays of the sun are obscured by things such as clouds so that they do not reach everyone. **In the same way, the wakefulness of the buddhas is obscured by the flaws of sentient beings.** That is to say, it is obscured due to a predominance of the five degenerations that render sentient beings unfit receptacles for the buddhas' wakefulness.

Although the rays of the sun radiate everywhere, we agree that the light does not appear when the sun is obscured by clouds, the walls of a cavern, or the like. The light rays of the wakefulness of the buddhas shine everywhere, but the flaws of sentient beings obscure them, and consequently they may not appear. The wakefulness of the buddhas thus becomes inactive due to the faults of its recipients, who then fail to see the emanation bodies of the buddhas, to hear the Dharma, and so on.

10. The Activity That Is Common in Terms of Liberation, Yet Unique in Terms of Wakefulness

> Just as knots are responsible
> For the presence or absence of vivid patterns in fabric,

> So does the driving force determine
> Whether liberated wakefulness is vivid or not. [x.35]

Just as the knots that are tied in it **are responsible for the presence or absence of vivid patterns in a fabric, so does the driving force** of aspirations, conduct, and so forth **determine whether liberated wakefulness is vivid** (as in the case of the buddhas) **or not** (as in the case of the listeners and self-realized buddhas).

Listeners and self-realized buddhas do indeed actualize the undefiled field of liberation from the suffering of cyclic existence. Let us, however, consider the following example. When one is dyeing a fabric in which knots have been tied, the fabric will absorb color only where there are no knots. Hence, when later the knots are untied some places will have been colored while others remain white, and therefore vivid and colorful patterns will have emerged on the fabric. Similarly, it is the driving force of aspiration prayers and the two accumulations that have occurred previously on the path of learning that determine whether or not the vividness of wakefulness will be present within the basic field of liberation. The listeners and the self-realized buddhas are liberated, having exhausted the afflictions that are the root of suffering in cyclic existence. The buddhas are likewise liberated from cyclic existence, for they have exhausted the obscurations of afflictions along with their habitual tendencies. Yet the buddhas have also made prior aspirations, eliminated the cognitive obscurations, and achieved the great wakefulness that is the complete perfection of the two accumulations. Due to all of this, their activity of wakefulness that matures the realms of sentient beings, sending out emanations and so forth, appears continually and without interruption. This is not the case with the listeners and self-realized buddhas.

4. Summary of the Profound Meaning

> This explanation of the buddhas' profound
> Characteristics, abode, and activity
> Within the immaculate field
> Is like a painting on space. [x.36]

This was an **explanation of the buddhas' profound characteristics** (to which four stanzas were devoted), their profound **abode** (the topic of the fifth stanza), **and** the categories of their profound **activity** (set out in the remaining stanzas) **within the immaculate field.** Nevertheless, the undefiled field **is** not a conceptual construction. Therefore, this explanation should be understood to be **like a painting on space.**

The first four stanzas, detailed above, address the profound characteristics of the buddhas, who abide in one taste within the stainless field. The fifth stanza concerns the profound abode, while the remaining ten stanzas relate to the ten profound activities. However, trying to explain buddhahood is as difficult as painting a picture on space. In other words, we may conceptually describe this space-like field, in which all constructs are pacified, as being one way or the other. Yet doing so is similar to trying to create a painting on space; regardless of one's efforts, nothing will stick to space. Nevertheless, it should be understood that for those who have trust in the inconceivable field, it is indeed as if one could make a painting on space. What a wonder this is!

8. The Unchanging Essence

The next section explains how the suchness of the basic field of phenomena does not change:

> **Suchness is present in all without distinction,**
> **Yet when pure**
> **It is a thus-gone one.**
> **Therefore, all wandering beings possess this essential nature.**
> [x.37]

Next it is explained that, while the profound is present in everyone, the profundity of the buddhas is exceptional: **Suchness is present in all without distinction, yet when pure it is a thus-gone one. Therefore, all wandering beings possess this essential nature** of the thus-gone ones.

This suchness, this intrinsic nature of all phenomena, which is their basic field, is from the very beginning present without distinction in the minds of all sentient beings. Yet, when suchness is pure in the absence of adventitious defilements, it is none other than the state of the thus-gone ones. In this way, all wandering beings possess suchness as their naturally luminous, essential nature. This undefiled field of buddha-nature is unchanging, without any increase or decrease throughout the three times. This is why the perfect and completely pure body of the thus-gone ones' wakefulness is permanent, steadfast, peaceful, and unchanging.

9. Limitless Mastery

This section addresses (1) distinctive mastery and (2) the various types of mastery.

1. Distinctive Mastery

> The mastery of the listeners
> Surpasses that of mundane beings,
> While that of the stage of self-realized buddhas
> Surpasses that of the listeners. [x.38]

> Yet that cannot compare to even a fraction
> Of the mastery of the bodhisattvas,
> And that cannot compare to even a fraction
> Of the mastery of the thus-gone ones. [x.39]

> The mastery of the buddhas is,
> In terms of its beneficiaries, locations,
> Manner, extent, and duration,
> Held to be employed in inconceivable and infinite ways. [x.40]

The mastery of the accumulations achieved by the listeners surpasses everything that constitutes the accumulation of mundane beings, while the mastery that is of the stage of self-realized buddhas in turn **surpasses that,** meaning the mastery **of the listeners. Yet that** mastery of the self-realized buddhas **cannot compare to even a fraction,** even a hundredth or a thousandth, **of the mastery of the bodhisattvas, and that,** the mastery of the children of the victorious ones, **cannot compare to even a fraction,** even a hundredth or a thousandth, **of the mastery of the thus-gone ones** who have truly and completely awakened.

The mastery of the buddhas is profound **in terms of** the individuals who are **its beneficiaries,** the **locations** of the world where it is employed, and the **manner** in which, the **extent** to which, **and** the **duration** throughout which it is employed. Therefore, the mastery of the buddhas is **held to be employed in inconceivable and infinite**ly numerous **ways.**

The mastery of superknowledges and the accumulations of wakefulness and merit as achieved by the listeners surpass the mastery of the two accumulations of mundane beings and the superknowledges and so forth that the sages achieve. The mastery at the stage of the self-realized buddhas, in turn, surpasses the mastery of the listeners because it is superior and more extensive. Nevertheless, the mastery of qualities of the self-realized buddhas cannot compare with even a fraction, even a hundredth or a thousandth, of the two accumulations and the superknowledges of the bodhisattvas. This means that no comparison can be made in terms of analogies, enumerations, or causes of their mastery. The bodhisattvas' mastery, moreover, cannot compare with even a fraction of the thus-gone ones' mastery of the limitless qualities of the transcendences, their complete perfection of the two accumulations, superknowledges, powers, fearlessnesses, and so on. Although the bodhisattvas' mastery of qualities is infinite indeed, when measured against the buddhas' mastery of qualities, the difference is as great as the difference between the size of a single subtle particle and that of the infinite realms of the world.

This difference is due to the fact that the completely perfect buddhas' mastery of activity for the welfare of individuals is limitless. It is not carried out for the benefit of one person, a hundred people, or some other finite number of individuals. Rather, it is employed for the welfare of all the infinite number of sentient beings.

The location where it is employed is also beyond measure. Such locations are countless because a buddha's mastery will be applied throughout world realms that extend as far as space. The way it is employed is limitless because their display of creative, incarnate, and supreme emanation bodies and their arrays of skillful means are as immeasurable as the realms of those to be trained. The extent of this employment is immeasurable because a buddha's mastery brings benefit and happiness to all sentient beings. Hence, it cannot be quantified in terms of any limited amount.

Its duration is also limitless, in that buddhas work for the welfare of others as long as sentient beings exist, yet there is no end to sentient beings. In this way, the buddhas' mastery exceeds that of the listeners and self-realized buddhas. It is more profound in terms of its beneficiaries, location, manner, extent, and duration. A buddha's mastery is inconceivable, beyond the domain of thought, and vast—to the extent that the derivable categories of its employment are held to be infinite.

2. The Types of Mastery

The next eight stanzas explain the infinity of this mastery by considering the seven types of mastery that arise from transformation:

> When the five faculties have transformed,
> There is engagement with all objects,
> And each has twelve hundred qualities.
> Such true mastery is achieved. [x.41]

> When the mind has transformed,
> There is engagement in accordance with that mastery.
> Within utterly immaculate nonconceptual wakefulness
> A true mastery is achieved. [x.42]

> When apprehending, including its objects, has transformed,
> There is encounter with whatever is wished for and the
>   capacity to reveal to others.
> Therefore, with respect to the pure fields,
> A true mastery is achieved. [x.43]

When thought has transformed,
There is constant wakefulness and
All activities are unimpeded.
Such true mastery is achieved. [x.44]

When the support has transformed,
There is nonabiding transcendence of suffering
Within the immaculate abode of the buddhas.
Such true mastery is achieved. [x.45]

When intercourse has transformed,
One dwells within the bliss of the buddhas,
And the sight of females is not afflictive.
Such true mastery is achieved. [x.46]

When the identification of space has transformed,
Whatever is wished for manifests.
There is passage, as well as the discernment of form.
Such true mastery is achieved. [x.47]

Thus, within the stainless abode of the buddhas,
There is immeasurable transformation.
Regarding the inconceivable engagement in activity,
It is held that there is immeasurable mastery. [x.48]

When the eye and the rest of **the five faculties have transformed, there is** true mastery in the **engagement with all** of the five types **of objects, and each** of the faculties **has twelve hundred qualities.** To illustrate this using the eye as an example, with the four cardinal directions and adding the zenith and nadir, there are six directions. Each of these six can then be divided further in terms of the ten directions. When enumerating the qualities of the eye, one does not count the eye's perception of form in terms of, for example, the eastern direction. Instead, for each of the remaining four [sense perceptions, a particular quality is enumerated], and the remaining nine directions are treated in the same way. Hence, the number [of qualities associated with the eye and the east] becomes forty. The same is the case with the remaining [five directions] and thus the total [number of qualities associated with the eye] becomes 240. When the same calculation is made for the ears and the rest of the five faculties, there are, in total, twelve hundred qualities associated with the faculties. Such true mastery is achieved.

When the afflicted mind has completely transformed, there is engagement in accordance with that mastery. Within utterly immaculate nonconceptual wakefulness, a true mastery is achieved. When the apprehending that takes the form of the five cognitions associated with the eye and the other sense faculties, including forms and its other objects, has transformed, there is an encounter with whatever is wished for and also the capacity to display to others. Therefore, with respect to the pure fields, a true mastery is achieved.

When thought has transformed, there is constant wakefulness by means of the four correct awarenesses, and all enlightened activities are unimpeded at all times. This true mastery is achieved. When the support, the all-ground consciousness, has transformed, there is nonabiding transcendence of suffering within the immaculate abode of the buddhas, the field free from defilements. Such true mastery is achieved.

When intercourse has transformed, one dwells within the bliss of the buddhas, and the sight of females is not afflictive. Such true mastery is achieved.

When the identification that is involved in the apprehending of space has transformed, whatever is wished for manifests through the treasury of space. There is free passage to anywhere one may want to go, as well as discernment of form, in the sense that one sees it as displaying the characteristics of space. Such true mastery is achieved.

Thus, within the stainless abode of the buddhas, the field free from defilement, there is immeasurable transformation. Regarding the inconceivable engagement in activity for the benefit of others, it is held that there is immeasurable mastery of enlightened activity.

At the time of purity, when the eyes and the other faculties have transformed, each faculty engages with all the objects of the other faculties as well. In this way there are twelve hundred manifest qualities of seeing the forms of all objects. This true mastery is achieved.

Prior to the transformation of the faculties, the eye faculty sees only visible forms and is incapable of determining the domains of the other faculties, such as sound. When transformed, however, the eye faculty can apprehend all forms, sounds, scents, tastes, and textures because it is able to engage all objects of the senses. Concerning these twelve hundred qualities, Sthiramati's commentary states that it is the faculties alone that attain these qualities, and he bases this interpretation on the *Sūtra of the Lord of Retention* and the *White Lotus of the Sacred Dharma*. He also notes how some assert that the intended number of qualities is 112, corresponding with the number of major and minor marks of a buddha, whereas others say that the qualities referred to are those of the grounds. However, since all such explanations do not see the qualities as specific to the sense faculties, Sthiramati finds them inappropriate in the present context, and he instead determines the issue in accordance with the accounts of the abovementioned two sūtras.

Therefore, if we begin by taking the six directions, and then divide each in terms of the ten directions, we may for each of those ten enumerate [the five perceptions associated with] the five objects. If we then take the eye as an example, we will not enumerate its perception of form because that is not an extraordinary quality. Apart from that, however, we will enumerate the eye's perception of sounds, scents, tastes, and textures [as they occur in relation to the six times ten directions]. Counting in this way, we can enumerate 240 qualities of the eye. When adding together such a number for each of the five faculties, we arrive at twelve hundred qualities. This appears to be the way that Sthiramati arrives at the number, twelve hundred.

The *White Lotus of the Sacred Dharma* also states that the corporeal faculties that arise from the merit of upholding the Dharma as taught in that sūtra will apprehend all the forms and other sense objects that are present in all the directions. This appears to be a subject worthy of detailed investigation based on the sūtras, yet in the present context I shall not venture any further.

According to the School of Consciousness, there are no physical faculties or physical objects. We might, therefore, at this point wonder how that school understands the transformation of the faculties? It is taught that:

> The various perceptions of consciousness
> Arise in accordance with their respective seeds.
> It is with reference to this that the Able One
> Has spoken of the various "twofold sense-fields."
> These are taught by the Sage.

As stated here, the six outer and six inner sense sources appear from the habitual tendencies of apprehended and apprehender that exist within the all-ground consciousness. For instance, the inner seed that is the support for the production of the eye consciousness is apprehended as "the eye." The apprehended object manifesting as form to the eye consciousness is called "form." The same relations hold for the other faculties as well. In this way, we may distinguish two types of sense sources in terms of the way things appear: the outer and the inner ones. Transformation consequently occurs when the errors of inner attachments are eliminated by means of unmistaken wakefulness.

The listeners and self-realized buddhas use the term "mind" to refer to the mental faculty of the six consciousnesses that have just ceased. However, "mind" is not viewed in this way by the Great Vehicle tradition; rather, here the afflicted mental cognition is called "mind" and that, in turn, is held to be the support for the mental consciousness, in the same way that the eye faculty is the support for the eye consciousness. When not transformed, this afflicted mind is possessed of the view of self. When free from the apprehension of "me" and "mine," however, it transforms into the wakefulness of equality. At that point it will be engaged in conjunction with the mastery of the five transformed faculties, just as the mind also engages universally in all the sense objects when not yet transformed. Thus, true mastery is achieved within the wakefulness that does not conceive of an apprehended and an apprehender, and which in the absence of afflictive and cognitive obscurations is utterly immaculate.

When both form and the rest of the five objects, as well as the five sense consciousnesses that are the subjects that perceive those objects, have transformed, whatever is wished for can be enjoyed as an object of the sense consciousnesses. One is thereby able to manifest a completely pure field, like the Realm of Bliss. Thus, one achieves a true mastery in revealing whatever is wished for. Moreover, Sthiramati's commentary states that there is transformation both of the six objects, from the objects of form up to phenomena, and of the five sense consciousnesses. Impure sense consciousnesses do not know anything other than their own respective objects, but when they transform, each one knows all objects.

When thought, that is, the mental consciousness, has transformed, there is a wakefulness that is constant and unimpeded in its knowledge of all that can be known. All enlightened activities, such as revealing emanations, are likewise now unimpeded. This true mastery is achieved. When the support, the all-ground consciousness, has transformed, one resides within the immaculate abode of the buddhas. One achieves true mastery in the transcendence of suffering that abides neither in the extreme of cyclic existence nor in that of transcendence.

When intercourse, the meeting of the male and female organs, has transformed, one dwells within the bliss of the buddhas' meditative absorption, which is free from constructs. And there is no affliction of attachment upon seeing females. This true mastery is achieved.

When the identification involved in apprehending space has transformed, whatever one wishes for will be attained from space. Thus, one attains the meditative absorption of the treasury of space. One will also be able to pass unimpededly through space, mountains, rocks, and so on. If one wishes for a particular form to appear, that very form will be manifested out of space. When one does not wish for anything to appear, everything will become as formless as space. This is attained through the meditative absorption that dissolves the body. This is the true mastery that is achieved.

As illustrated by these explanations, the myriad aspects of the objects of knowledge—the appearances of abodes, the appearances of bodies, as well as consciousness, objects, form, and so on—are indeed limitless. Hence, when appearances transform into complete purity, their transformations are also limitless. Therefore, within the immaculate abode of the buddhas, there are immeasurable transformations. The mastery of the qualities of power that accomplish the inconceivable activities that bring benefit and happiness to those to be trained is also held to be immeasurable.

10. Bringing Sentient Beings to Maturation

Having reached the buddhas' immeasurable mastery of qualities, one will be bringing other sentient beings to maturation. This tenth section describes the qualities of that maturation by considering: (1) how it takes place, (2) the persons who are matured, (3) the various means of maturing, (4) the nonconceptual activity that brings maturation, (5) how maturation occurs without partiality, (6) how it is continual maturation from one to another, and (7) how, without ever becoming saturated, maturation is uninterrupted beyond increase or decrease.

1. Way of Maturing

> Here and everywhere throughout the world, the victorious
>   ones' excellent teachings
> Cause beings rich in virtue to proceed to supreme purity,
> While those who have not gathered virtue are made to
>   progress toward the supreme enrichment of virtue.
> Although the immature are thus always matured, everyone is
>   not. [x.49]

This next section explains how the buddhas are the cause of the complete maturation of others. **Here and everywhere throughout the world** where there are beings to be trained, **the victorious ones' excellent teachings cause beings rich in** the development of **virtue to proceed to the supreme purity** of the nonabiding transcendence of suffering, **while those who have not gathered** the **virtue** associated with the Great Vehicle **are made to progress** toward the supreme enrichment of virtue. **Although the immature are thus always matured** by the supreme enrichment of their fundamental virtues, and while those who are mature constantly progress toward the supreme purity that is the stage of buddhahood, **everyone is not** liberated because the world is infinite.

How, we may ask, does one ripen the field of beings to be trained, once one has become a buddha? Wandering beings are brought to maturation across infinite and endless worlds. This does not just happen in a few places, but everywhere in the ten directions. Who is it that ripens them? The victorious ones do. By what method? Through the excellent teachings of the scriptures of the sacred Dharma. How are they matured? Worldly beings whose virtues of the six transcendences are in the process of flourishing from the grounds of inspired conduct up until the tenth ground are matured so that they can achieve increasing purity. In this way they progress toward the supreme purity of the transcendence of suffering. As for those worldly beings who have not previously gathered virtues, or who have not aroused the enlightened mind and have not entered the path, these beings are matured in a way that lets them give rise to the enlightened mind and enter the path. Thus, they progress toward the supreme enrichment of virtue.

In this way, immature sentient beings are continuously brought to maturation, and the enlightened activity that matures sentient beings is never interrupted; it is a constant process. Nevertheless, it is not the case that all sentient beings without exception will become matured to the extent that there are no more sentient beings. There is never any decrease in the number of sentient beings because there is no end to sentient beings. Nor is there any increase because the basic field of phenomena is nonarising. Thus, while all phenomena are devoid of nature, they exist merely in appearance. It is, therefore, impossible that the appearance of thorough affliction and complete purification should ever come to an end.

2. The Individuals Who Are Matured

> Thus, everywhere throughout the world, the steadfast ones constantly and always

> Achieve the great enlightenment that is hard to achieve, yet is
>   marvelously endowed with supreme qualities:
> The permanent and steadfast refuge for those who have none.
> This is a great wonder, but also not, for they have practiced
>   the way of goodness. [x.50]

Thus, everywhere throughout the world, the steadfast ones, on all occasions, constantly and always, achieve the great enlightenment that is hard to achieve, yet is also marvelously, because it is unparalleled, endowed with the powers and other supreme qualities. That enlightenment is the permanent (since it does not change) and steadfast (since it is continuous) refuge for those who have none. This is a great wonder, but also not, for they have practiced the way of goodness, meaning the actions that are conducive to it.

Unlimited numbers of sentient beings are brought to maturation in this way. The steadfast bodhisattvas who are matured everywhere throughout the world, achieve constantly and without interruption, every day and every instant of every day, the fruition of unsurpassable great enlightenment, which is extremely difficult to achieve. They are endowed with the powers and other supreme qualities and, compared to worldly beings, listeners, and self-realized buddhas, they have attained what is truly marvelous. Their attainment is permanent because it lasts for as long as cyclic existence endures, and it is steadfast since it never wanes. This refuge that brings forth the attainment of the transcendence of suffering, pacifying all the sufferings of those who are tormented and have no protection, is thus achieved in each instant of every day, successively and continually by numerous individuals. This is an extremely great wonder! Yet, these completely mature bodhisattvas have attained such a fruition because they have cultivated the mind of enlightenment and practiced the wholesome way of the vast and profound path, meaning the two accumulations composed of the six transcendences. This is, therefore, also not such a great wonder, for a supreme cause yields a supreme result. That is the way things are.

3. Various Means of Maturing

> All at once, a buddha will in some places display the turning
>   of the Dharma wheel through hundreds of means,
> While elsewhere showing birth and nonmanifestation, the
>   manifold deeds of the lives,
> Enlightenment, and the transcendence of suffering.
> Yet all of this a buddha does without wavering from the
>   abode. [x.51]

All at once, a buddha will in some places display the turning of the Dharma wheel through hundreds of skillful **means, while elsewhere,** in various other worlds, **showing birth and nonmanifestation, the manifold** distinctive **deeds of the** succession of lives, manifest **enlightenment, and the transcendence of suffering. Yet all of this a buddha does without wavering from the abode** that is free from defilement.

A buddha will actively ripen sentient beings through numerous means that are employed simultaneously, rather than one after another. In some places, he will turn the wheel of the Dharma, expressing its meaning in many ways, through many hundreds of gateways of the Dharma—such as the teachings of the aggregates, elements, sense sources, dependent arising, the truths, the grounds, and the transcendences. The words a buddha uses to express the Dharma in chapters, verses, and so on, are also diverse in hundredfold ways. Yet at the same time, in some pure fields, that buddha will descend from Tuṣita and teach beings on a Jambu continent. In other realms, he displays nonmanifestation, meaning he does not display the twelve deeds but manifests instead in bodhisattva form. In still other realms, he manifests different activities of birth, in that he displays the deeds of a bodhisattva's succession of lives. In some world realms, he thus demonstrates the activities of transcendent generosity, benefiting others by giving away his body and possessions. By similarly displaying the conduct of transcendent discipline, patience, diligence, concentration, and insight, he thus teaches throughout realms that are of varying degrees of excellence or inferiority.

In some realms, buddhas display the activity of great and unsurpassed enlightenment. In some, they also show the methods for attaining the enlightenment of the listeners and self-realized buddhas. For the purpose of training those to be trained, they display all three enlightenments,[34] while, in some realms, they display the transcendence of suffering. All these acts are displayed simultaneously, not sequentially, yet a buddha never wavers in the slightest from suchness, the completely pure basic field of phenomena that is the undefiled abode, and all his activities are accomplished spontaneously and without effort.

4. Nonconceptual Activity

The buddhas do not form thoughts, such as "I have ripened this being,"
"This one I shall mature," or "I am ripening this one now."
Yet everywhere and always, they do indeed mature
Beings with the qualities of virtue through the three gateways.
[x.52]

When **the buddhas** benefit sentient beings, they **do not form thoughts, such as** "in the past **I have ripened this being," "this one I shall mature** in the future," **or "I am ripening this one now." Yet everywhere and always,** wherever there are beings to be trained, **they do indeed mature** such **beings with** the six transcendences and all **the** other **qualities of virtue, through the three gateways** of the vehicles.

Buddhas do not think, "In the past I matured these embodied beings," "I shall mature this individual in the future," or "I am presently ripening this one." Yet, although free from the efforts of forming thoughts, they mature countless beings through their undefiled qualities of virtue. They do not just do so somewhere and sometimes, but everywhere and always, for as long as there is space and time, by means of the gateways of all three vehicles.

5. Bringing Forth Maturation without Partiality

> Just as the sun effortlessly ripens crops everywhere
> With an abundance of infinite, clear rays,
> So does the sun of the Dharma mature sentient beings everywhere
> With the infinite rays of the Dharma that brings peace. [x.53]

Just as the sun effortlessly ripens crops everywhere with an abundance of infinite, brilliantly **clear rays, so does** the Buddha, the sun that shines with the light **of the Dharma,** thoroughly **mature sentient beings everywhere with the infinite rays of the Dharma that brings peace** in the absence of all suffering.

The sun effortlessly ripens many crops with an abundance of clear light rays that reach everywhere, not just in one direction. Likewise, the sun of buddhahood, which possesses the immeasurable Dharma of the twelve sections of scripture, spreads the abundant light of the Dharma in limitless directions, revealing the path to perfect peace within the transcendence of all suffering. Thus, without partiality, the buddhas bring sentient beings everywhere to maturation.

6. Continual Maturation from One to Another

> Without itself being extinguished, one single lamp
> May cause innumerable other lamps, beyond all measure.
> Likewise, without itself becoming extinct, one single maturation
> Brings about innumerable maturations, beyond all measure. [x.54]

Without itself being extinguished, one single lamp may cause the lighting of **innumerable other lamps, beyond all measure. Likewise, without itself becoming extinct,** without its own qualities disappearing, **one single** full **maturation** of true and complete buddhahood **brings about innumerable maturations,** that is, other buddhas, in a process that is **beyond all measure.**

A limitless and vast array of lamps can be lit from a single lamp. Yet, the original lamp will not become extinguished when it lights many other lamps. Likewise, an immeasurably vast array of mature bodhisattvas will come from a single buddha's perfect maturation. Each bodhisattva, in turn, will then mature a further multitude of bodhisattvas. From those that they have matured, a succession of many others will emerge, passing from one to another, for as long as there is existence. Thus, beings in limitless number are matured. Yet the maturation of the first buddha will never become extinct, and its continuity will never be exhausted.

7. Continuity without Saturation, Increase, or Decrease

> Just as the great ocean neither fills up nor increases
> By the inflow of many great rivers,
> The realm of the buddhas neither fills up nor increases
> By the uninterrupted entry of the pure—what a supreme
>   wonder this is! [x.55]

For example, **just as the great ocean neither fills up nor increases,** or rises, **by the inflow of many great rivers, the realm of the buddhas,** the field free from defilement, **neither fills up nor increases by the uninterrupted entry of the** immaculately **pure** individuals. It always accommodates them, and yet does not increase, since there is nothing beyond it. **What a supreme wonder this is!**

The great world ocean never fills up, even though rivers and streams from different directions constantly and uninterruptedly flow into it. The ocean always accommodates this continual inflow, yet despite those many great rivers emptying into it, the ocean does not increase and rise. Likewise, the realm of the buddhas, the field of undefiled suchness, is neither filled nor does it increase, even though innumerable listeners, self-realized buddhas, and bodhisattvas constantly and uninterruptedly attain purity in the absence of obscuration, thereby entering the transcendence of suffering. What a perfect wonder this is!

2. The Enlightenment That Possesses Those Qualities

Above, ten principles describing the qualities of great enlightenment were explained. Now follows an explanation of that which possesses those qualities, that is, enlightenment itself. Enlightenment will here be considered in terms of its essence and five further principles. Its explanation is divided in terms of (1) the actual presentation of enlightenment and (2) a specific explanation of its applications.

1. Actual Presentation of Enlightenment

The actual presentation is taught in four stanzas:

> It is characterized by the suchness of all phenomena,
> Free from the two obscurations,
> And by an inexhaustible mastery
> Regarding that nature and its observation. [x.56]

> It fully emerges through meditating
> With full knowledge of suchness.
> For all sentient beings, this results at all times
> In the inexhaustible twofold production. [x.57]

> It is active through skillful engagement
> Of the emanations of body, speech, and mind,
> Endowed with the gateways of meditative absorption and
>   retention,
> As well as the two beyond measure. [x.58]

> Its distinct applications are those of nature,
> The perfect enjoyment of qualities, and emanation.
> These are taught to be the purity of the buddhas'
> Basic field of phenomena. [x.59]

The following concerns the essence of the completely pure basic field of phenomena. **It is characterized by the suchness of all phenomena free from the two obscurations,** the afflictive and the cognitive, **and by an inexhaustible mastery regarding that nature and its observation.** That is to say, a realization of the intrinsic nature of the meditative equipoise occurs, without any interruption, as well as a realization of the meditative equipoise by means of the ensuing attainment. Since all of the gateways of reason associated with the Great Vehicle are employed, **it fully emerges through meditating with full knowledge of suchness.** That is the cause of the completely pure basic field of phenomena.

For all sentient beings, this results at all times in the inexhaustible twofold production of benefit and happiness. **It is active through skillful engagement of the emanations of body** that appear in accordance with those to be trained, **of speech** that manifests as the sound of the Dharma, **and of mind,** as when the minds of others are blessed. Its endowment is indicated by stating that it is **endowed with the gateways of meditative absorption and retention, as well as the two** accumulations of merit and wakefulness **beyond measure.** Its distinct applications are those of the **nature** body, **the body of perfect enjoyment of the qualities** of the Great Vehicle, **and the emanation** body. **These are taught to be the purity of the buddhas' basic field of phenomena.**

The topic that is addressed in these four stanzas, when set forth concisely, is the utter purity of the basic field of phenomena. This, therefore, is explained first, followed by mirror-like wakefulness and the rest of the four wakefulnesses. As the *Noble Ground of Buddhahood* states:

> Five principles comprise buddhahood: the purity of the basic field of phenomena, mirror-like wakefulness, the wakefulness of equality, discriminating wakefulness, and the all-accomplishing wakefulness.

The present treatise resolves the nature of these principles in a concise summary.

(1) "Suchness" refers to emptiness free from all extremes. It is the nature of all phenomena contained in the categories of the conditioned and the unconditioned and all defiled and undefiled objects of knowledge. This is because suchness is the unmistaken abiding reality, the perfectly genuine, and the ultimate. While there are no differences whatsoever in terms of their having the nature of suchness, we may nevertheless speak of "phenomena" in reference to different subjects that have this nature.

Although there are no distinctions between the suchness of buddhas and the suchness of sentient beings, the suchness that is the nature of the mind stream of sentient beings, who possess the adventitious defilements of distorted self-appearances, is termed "defiled suchness." Adventitious obscurations can be eliminated, while the intrinsic nature never changes. Therefore, that which we refer to as "the enlightenment of a buddha" is the character of the utterly pure basic field of phenomena once the mind stream of a distinct sentient being has been completely purified of both the afflictive and the cognitive obscurations. Enlightenment is, in other words, transformed suchness.

Furthermore, enlightenment is the attainment of the inexhaustible mastery of the nonconceptual wakefulness that observes the nature of the purity of the basic field of phenomena within meditative equipoise. The wakefulness of the ensuing attainment achieves the inexhaustible mastery of observing that nonconceptual wakefulness. In this way, the ensuing attainment provides the means whereby we may know nonconceptual wakefulness exactly as it is.

In the translation of Sthiramati's commentary, the verses at this point read "knowing the nature and its observation." The phrase "knowing the nature" implies the full knowledge of the nature of the all-ground consciousness of the dependent nature, once this consciousness has been fundamentally transformed. That knowledge is achieved through the wakefulness of ensuing attainment. As for the words, "its observation," this is seen as a reference to nonconceptual wakefulness observing that basic field of phenomena. Although that text thus lays out the wording of the verses differently, the meaning is the same as explained above. This is because, in that text, the attainment of the two inexhaustible masteries is likewise explained in terms of the wakefulness of meditative equipoise and ensuing attainment.

In short, at the stage of buddhahood, there is no alternation between meditative equipoise and the ensuing attainment. A single wakefulness sees things nonconceptually, both as they are and in their multiplicity. This is omniscience. Hence, buddhahood is held to be characterized by the attainment of the inexhaustible mastery of these two aspects of wakefulness. Phenomena and their intrinsic nature are, in this way, not different. At the time of the final transformation, there is effortless and spontaneous cognition of phenomena in all their multiplicity, yet without any wavering from the vision of the intrinsic nature as it is. The mastery of this twofold wakefulness comprises the essence body, or the body of qualities—the character of great enlightenment. This is the essence of great enlightenment.

(2) The cause of the attainment, or actualization, of great enlightenment is as follows. Through resolving the nature of suchness, or emptiness, as taught in the Great Vehicle sūtras, by means of listening, contemplating, and meditating, one trains in gathering the two accumulations on the grounds of inspired conduct. As a result of this training, the direct perception of suchness will occur, and as one thus experiences supramundane wakefulness for the first time, one attains the first ground. After that, and until the end of the continuum of the ten grounds, one continues to train while making full use of the various skillful means. Through this process, buddhahood fully emerges.

(3) The result of enlightenment is the production of lasting and temporary benefit and happiness at all times and for all the infinite number of sentient beings. This fruition will not be exhausted for as long as cyclic existence remains.

(4) In terms of function, enlightenment is active through the skillful functions, or engagements, of emanations that reveal their bodies, that teach the Dharma with exalted speech, and that bring blessings through the enlightened mind. In terms of the skillful activity of the engagements of the exalted body's emanations, this involves the buddhas taming beings by appearing as buddhas, but also by taking the form of various gods, nāgas, and so on. In terms of the exalted speech, sounds of the Dharma either arise directly through a buddha's voice, or otherwise from space, a wall, a tree and so forth. Furthermore, through the blessings of the

enlightened mind, even fools will realize the profound meaning of the Dharma. It was, for example, also the blessings of the enlightened mind that entered Śāriputra and Subhūti and led them to explain transcendent insight. "Engagement" implies activity, and "skillful" refers specifically to being aware of the methods for producing emanations. Alternatively, "skillful" can be understood in terms of the function of the emanations, that is, the various skillful means whereby sentient beings are trained.

(5) The endowments of enlightenment are the limitless meditative absorptions, such as that of the heroic gait and the treasury of space; the limitless gates of retention, such as that of the inexhaustible trove; and the two limitless accumulations of merit and wakefulness. In other words, it entails being endowed with the limitless retentions, meditative absorptions, and two accumulations.

(6) As for its divisions, there are the following. In terms of the essence, there is the nature body or body of qualities. In terms of appearance, there is the body of the perfect enjoyment of the Great Vehicle Dharma. In terms of providing for the welfare of others, there is the emanation body. In this way, we may enumerate distinct applications.

This sixfold presentation describes the purity of the buddhas' basic field of phenomena. The great enlightenment within the pure basic field of phenomena is hence to be understood by means of these six, beginning with essence.

2. The Specific Explanation of the Applications

This section pays specific attention to the various applications, or divisions, that pertain to enlightenment. The discussion will include: (1) an explanation of the three bodies that form the support and (2) an explanation of the four wakefulnesses that are supported thereby.

1. The Support—The Three Bodies

This section has two parts: (1) a brief presentation and (2) an extensive explanation.

1. Summary

> The bodies of the buddhas can be divided
> In terms of the nature body, the perfect enjoyment body,
> And the emanation body.
> The first is the support of the two. [x.60]

The bodies of the buddhas can be divided in terms of the nature body, the perfect enjoyment body, and the emanation body. The first body is the support of the latter two.

As for the types of body that the buddhas possess, their nature body is the body of qualities. When the defilements of the apprehended and apprehender that are present within the all-ground consciousness have been eliminated, the basic field of phenomena is seen as it is. This is known as "mirror-like wakefulness." Considering the suchness aspect of enlightenment, we speak of the "nature body," or "essence body," while in acknowledgment of its wakefulness aspect it is called the "body of qualities." These two are inseparable as phenomena and their intrinsic nature. Therefore, however this may be explained, it must be understood that both are indeed the actualization of the utterly pure and abiding way of unity. It does not work to think of the appearing aspect as being somehow separate. This is the sublime insight that is universally conveyed in all the scriptures.

The perfect enjoyment body consists of the wakefulness of equality that is the transformed afflicted mind and the discriminating wakefulness of the transformed mental consciousness. As such it allows the bodhisattvas on the grounds to experience perfect enjoyment of the Great Vehicle Dharma. The emanation body brings about the maturation of sentient beings in places like the Jambu continent, by displaying the descent from Tuṣita and so on when the five sense consciousnesses have transformed. The first of these, the body of qualities, is the support or basis of the other two because the two form bodies are the expressions of completely pure, great enlightenment, appearing as form to pure and impure beings that are to be trained.

2. Extensive Explanation

This section is divided into (1) an explanation of each of the three bodies and (2) an explanation of their inclusion, equality, and permanence. The first section has three parts: (1) the perfect enjoyment body, (2) the body of qualities, and (3) the emanation body.

1. The Three Bodies
1. Perfect Enjoyment Body

> In all the realms, the perfect enjoyment differs
> With respect to the gathering of retinue, field, name,
> Body, perfect enjoyment of the Dharma,
> And the various types of activity. [X.61]

> **In all the realms** of the world, **the** body of **perfect enjoyment differs with respect to the gathering of** the **retinue** of the children of the victorious ones, the buddha fields, the categories of **name**s, the displays of the **body,** the **perfect enjoyment of the Dharma, and the various types of activity** that correspond with the wishes of the retinue. Thus, different classifications apply to the perfect enjoyment body.

In all the completely pure world realms, the perfect enjoyment body differs in terms of the retinue of bodhisattvas that it gathers, for bodhisattvas with individual names compose the numerous retinues. The fields also differ in color and in their features of crystal, gold, lapis lazuli, and so on. The buddhas of the perfect enjoyment body also bear different names, such as Vairocana and Amitābha, and their bodies are distinct as well. Some are white, for instance, while others are yellow. With respect to the perfect enjoyment of the Dharma, these buddhas teach a variety of principles of the Great Vehicle Dharma. Some explain transcendent insight, others the ten grounds, and so forth. In terms of their activity, their bodies are perceived as large by some and as small by others, depending on the inclinations of the disciple. In this way, the perfect enjoyment body appears in different ways corresponding to the inclinations of those to be trained. There is, therefore, no definite color or other such qualities, and the teachings, such as those of the Great Vehicle, also manifest in numerous ways.

2. The Body of Qualities

The nature body is held to be equal,
Subtle, and connected to that.
With regard to the display of delightful enjoyments,
It is held to be the cause of the mastery of perfect enjoyment.
[x.62]

The **nature body** of all the buddhas **is held to be** entirely **equal** and beyond distinctions. It is considered **subtle** because it is difficult to realize, **and** it is also held to be **connected to that,** that is, to the perfect enjoyment body. **With regard to the display of delightful enjoyments** of the Great Vehicle Dharma, **it is held to be the cause of the mastery of** the **perfect enjoyment** body.

The nature body of qualities is completely equal with no distinctions and with no appearances that conflict with the completely pure nature of the basic field of phenomena, endowed with the twofold purity. It is said to be "subtle" because it is not the domain of listeners and self-realized buddhas. Moreover, the perfect enjoyment body is connected with this body of qualities because the latter causes the appearance of the former. In other words, the manifestation of the enjoyment body is causally linked with the body of qualities. As it appears in this way to the bodhisattvas on the grounds, it shows them how to partake freely of the Dharma of the Great Vehicle's perfect enjoyments. Thus it is held to be the cause of the power, or mastery, of the bodhisattvas' perfect enjoyment of the Dharma because the enjoyment body brings forth the perfect entirety of the Great Vehicle Dharma in the minds of those bodhisattvas who surround it. The outer enjoyment is the completely pure field, and the inner enjoyment is the Great Vehicle Dharma. It is the enjoyment body because it enables the bodhisattvas to partake freely of these perfect enjoyments, just as they please.

3. EMANATION BODY

The immeasurable emanations of the Buddha
Are held to be the emanation body.
The perfection of the twofold benefit
Always rests on the two. [x.63]

As it always displays creativity, incarnation,
Great enlightenment, and transcendence of suffering,
This, the emanation body of the buddhas,
Is the great means for liberation. [x.64]

The **immeasurable emanations of the buddhas** that accomplish the welfare of others **are held to be the emanation body. The perfection of the twofold benefit,** one's own and that of others, **always rests on the two,** the body of perfect enjoyment and the emanation body, respectively.
As it always displays creativity (as when taking the lute to tame Pramudita, the king of the gandharvas), and **incarnation** as a member of a certain class of beings, and **great enlightenment** by means of the supreme emanation body, **and transcendence of suffering, this, the emanation body of the buddhas, is the great means for** the **liberation** of those to be trained.

The emanation body of the buddhas is held to consist of all those immeasurable emanations that train beings in whichever ways are necessary. This does not only include the supreme emanation body, but also emanations in the form of beings such as gods. These are also referred to as emanation bodies. The perfection of the twofold benefit—that is, the perfection of one's own benefit and that of others—rests always and in all regards on these two, the enjoyment body and the emanation body. The buddhas, having fulfilled their own benefit, always reside in the completely pure field with a pure retinue, celebrating the feast of the Great Vehicle Dharma through the perfect body of form, the perfect enjoyment body. By means of the emanation body, the buddhas also bring impure sentient beings to maturation, thereby benefiting them in a perfect way. This [distinction between the form bodies regarding one's own benefit and that of others] is in terms of what is typically the case. Distinctions between one's own benefit and the benefit of others do not apply to the body of qualities, and yet it is the body of qualities that is the support for the arising of the two perfect embodiments of one's own benefit and that of all others.

The ways that the emanation bodies bring benefit to others can be classified in terms of (1) displays of creativity, (2) displays of incarnation, (3) displays of manifest, great enlightenment, and (4) displays of transcendence of suffering. Forever displaying these four, the emanation bodies of the buddhas are the great means for bringing about the complete liberation of sentient beings into the field of the transcendence of suffering. Displays of creativity are displays of artistry: woodwork, pottery, lute-playing, and so forth. Incarnation involves, for instance, descending from Tuṣita and being born into a royal or a Brahmin family. Great enlightenment involves becoming a buddha. In the end, there is the display of passing beyond suffering. This is how it is taught in Sthiramati's commentary, and it has also been explained above.

2. Threefold Explanation of Inclusion, Equality, and Permanence

> It should be known that these three bodies
> Comprise the bodies of buddhahood.
> The three bodies consist of benefit
> For self and others, and also of the support. [x.65]

> With respect to support, realization, and activity,
> They are completely the same.
> In terms of nature, no interruption, and continuity,
> They are indeed permanent. [x.66]

It should be known that these three bodies comprise all of **the bodies of buddhahood. The three bodies consist of benefit for self** through the body of perfect enjoyment **and for others** through the emanation body, **and also of the support** of the former two through the nature body.

With respect to their **support** (because the basic field of phenomena does not differ), **intention** (because the intention of the buddhas does not differ), **and activity** (because the activity is performed in common), **they,** meaning the three bodies of all the buddhas, **are completely the same.** The essential body is permanent **in terms of** its **nature,** the enjoyment body is permanent in the sense that it knows **no interruption, and** the emanation body is permanent in terms of the **continuity** of its display of emanations that, although they may disappear, continue to reemerge. In this way, **they,** the three bodies, **are indeed permanent.**

These three bodies comprise all of the buddhas. The enjoyment body and emanation body manifest one's own benefit and that of others, and the body of qualities is the basis of these two. Everyone and everything is included within the three bodies. That is to say, the bodies of qualities that pertain to all the buddhas are all contained within one; their limitless enjoyment bodies are likewise included within the enjoyment body; and the limitless emanation bodies are contained within the emanation body.

We may say, "all the thus-gone ones are the same," with reference to the following three forms of sameness. (1) Their support or abode is the same because the completely pure, basic field of phenomena is the same as the body of qualities without any distinctions. (2) Their intentions are also the same because the intentions of all the enjoyment bodies constitute a single wish, without any distinctions in terms of quantity or quality, to bring benefit and happiness to sentient beings. (3) Finally, the activities of all the emanation bodies are the same with respect to their training sentient beings and, as explained previously, all the emanations of the buddhas arise as one.

When it is said that "the bodies of all the thus-gone ones are permanent," this implies three forms of permanence, as follows. (1) Since the body of qualities is, by nature, free from arising or ceasing, it is, in terms of its essence, or nature, permanent. (2) The enjoyment body is permanent because it always teaches the Dharma continuously and without interruption. (3) The emanation body is a permanent continuity. Although it may not appear at a given time to some, it is meanwhile appearing to others. It is permanent because it continuously appears in this way until there are no more sentient beings. Therefore, these three bodies of the buddhas are indeed permanent.

2. The Supported—The Four Forms of Wakefulness

This section has four parts: (1) a summary, (2) an extensive explanation of each wakefulness, (3) a demonstration of the cause for attaining such wakefulness, and (4) how the wakefulness of the buddhas is the consummation of all paths.

1. Summary

> Mirror-like wakefulness is unmoving
> And the three types of wakefulness are supported by that.
> These are, precisely, the wakefulness
> Of equality, discernment, and accomplishment of activity.
> [x.67]

Next follows the explanation of the divisions of wakefulness. **Mirror-like wakefulness is unmoving** and serves as the support, whereas **the other three types of wakefulness** move and **are supported by** that mirror-like wakefulness. **These are, precisely, the wakefulness of equality, discernment, and accomplishment of activity.**

The all-ground consciousness transforms into mirror-like wakefulness. This wakefulness never moves from the pure, basic field of phenomena; it abides until the end of cyclic existence, beyond arising or engagement. Three further forms of wakefulness are present within that mirror-like wakefulness and are supported by it. Since they arise and engage, they move. What are these three? They are the wakefulness of equality, which is the transformed afflicted mind; the discriminating wakefulness, which is the transformed mental consciousness; and the all-accomplishing wakefulness, which is the five sense consciousnesses once they have transformed. In this way, the wakefulness of the transformed eight collections of consciousness is exclusively fourfold.

2. Extensive Explanation of Each Wakefulness

This section explains (1) mirror-like wakefulness, (2) the wakefulness of equality, (3) discriminating wakefulness, and (4) all-accomplishing wakefulness.

1. Mirror-Like Wakefulness

> Mirror-like wakefulness involves no "mine."
> It is unconfined, always present,
> Free from delusion regarding the objects of cognition,
> And yet it never turns toward them. [x.68]
>
> Being the cause of all wakefulness,
> It is the great source of wakefulness.
> This, precisely, is the buddha of perfect enjoyment,
> And reflections of wakefulness appear within it. [x.69]

Mirror-like wakefulness involves no "mine." It is unconfined with respect to objects, and, in terms of time, **always present.** Because nothing obscures it, it is **free from delusion regarding the objects of cognition, and yet,** because no features [of objects] exist, **it never turns toward them. Being the cause of all** other types of **wakefulness,** such as the wakefulness of equality, **it is the great source of** all forms of **wakefulness. This, precisely, is the buddha of perfect enjoyment, and** this wakefulness is mirror-like, for **reflections of wakefulness appear within it.**

All forms of knowledge appear within mirror-like wakefulness, and yet this wakefulness knows no sense of "mine." This is due to the fact that it has no concepts of apprehended and apprehender, no concepts of "me" or "I," nor is it involved in the efforts associated with the formation [of karma]. This wakefulness can be likened to a mirror within which all sorts of images can appear. These images are not things that exist in the mirror, and the mirror neither conceives of those images, nor tries to do something to them. Mirror-like wakefulness is not confined in terms of engaging only with certain objects and locations and not with others. Rather, it engages with all objects without any boundaries, and hence is completely unconfined. Since it arises in all of the three times, it is always present. Since it is free from the afflictive and cognitive obscurations, its observation is not deluded with respect to any object of knowledge. It realizes everything in a perfectly precise manner, and yet it never turns toward objects of knowledge, apprehending them conceptually as this or that. Although everything appears, there are no thoughts that conceive of things with separate marks.

Mirror-like wakefulness is the cause of all other forms of wakefulness. Like a great ocean, it is the source of all types of precious wakefulness. This is precisely the buddha of perfect enjoyment because this is what the term ultimately refers to.

Why is this termed "mirror-like wakefulness"? All objects of knowledge appear within this wakefulness, just as any image will appear in a clear mirror. As they appear, they are all seen as equal, exactly as they are. Likewise, whatever form they take is recognized distinctly, and the wakefulness that spontaneously accomplishes the aims of those to be trained manifests as well. Hence, it is called mirror-like wakefulness because the features, or reflections, of the latter three forms of wakefulness arise within it.

2. Wakefulness of Equality

> The wakefulness of equality is held to be
> The pure cultivation with respect to sentient beings.
> Resting in nonabiding peace,
> It is held to be the wakefulness of equality. [x.70]
>
> At all times it is endowed
> With great love and compassion.

In accordance with the inclinations of sentient beings,
It reveals the body of buddhahood. [x.71]

The wakefulness of equality is held to arise. It is taught **to be the pure cultivation** that the bodhisattvas achieve at the time of clear realization, which involves the cognition of equality **with respect to** all **sentient beings. Resting in nonabiding peace** beyond the extremes of existence or peace **is held to be the wakefulness of equality. At all times it is endowed with** the **great love** of wishing happiness for sentient beings **and** the great **compassion** of wanting them to be free from suffering. **In perfect accordance with the inclinations of sentient beings, it reveals the body of buddhahood.** Hence, some sentient beings, for example, will see a thus-gone one as blue, while to others the same buddha will appear to be yellow.

Regarding the wakefulness of equality, the equality of oneself and other sentient beings is initially realized on the first ground and then cultivated up until the tenth ground. The wakefulness of equality is held to be that very realization at the pure stage of buddhahood, subsequent to the final elimination of the subtle habitual tendencies that conceive of an "I" and a "self." One does not abide within the confines, or extremes, of existence or peace, and therefore cyclic existence and transcendence of suffering have become an indivisible equality. Hence, the essence of the wakefulness of equality is the pacification of the perception of duality in existence and peace. At all times, it is endowed with love and great compassion. In terms of its function, the wakefulness of equality serves to reveal a variety of colors, shapes, and other such aspects of the body of buddhahood, all of which manifest in accordance with the individual inclinations of sentient beings.

3. Discriminating Wakefulness

Discriminating wakefulness
Is always unimpeded regarding all objects of knowledge;

Containing the absorptions and retentions,
It is like a great treasure. [x.72]

Within the circle of the retinue,
It reveals all the riches
And rains down the great Dharma
That cuts through all doubts. [x.73]

Discriminating wakefulness is always unimpeded regarding all objects of knowledge. In a single instant it knows them clearly and without effort. **Containing the absorptions and retentions, it is like a great treasure,** from which an abundance of the former is made manifest. **To the circle of the retinue, it reveals all the riches** of the pure field **and rains down the great Dharma** of the profound and the vast **that** simultaneously **cuts through all** their **doubts.**

Discriminating wakefulness is the wakefulness that always knows, without impediment, all the general and specific characteristics of all objects of knowledge. With its limitless meditative absorptions and gateways of retention, it is like a treasure. It functions to reveal the outer riches of the sense pleasures and the inner riches of the Dharma in all the maṇḍalas of a buddha's retinue. It reveals all the perfect outer riches of a pure field, with a ground made of precious gems, a wish-fulfilling tree, rivers of nectar, ornate palaces, and great cloud banks of undefiled forms, sounds, scents, tastes, and textures. It also genuinely and flawlessly reveals the inner riches of Dharma, displaying the general and specific characteristics of the profound and the vast. Thereby, it rains down the magnificent Dharma of the Great Vehicle, which cuts through any doubts that the retinue might have.

4. All-Accomplishing Wakefulness

The all-accomplishing wakefulness
Is at work throughout all realms;

By means of diverse emanations that are immeasurable and
   inconceivable,
It accomplishes the objectives of all sentient beings. [x.74]

It should be understood that the emanations of the Buddha
Are always inconceivable
With respect to the accomplishment of specific deeds,
As well as numbers and fields. [x.75]

The all-accomplishing wakefulness is at work throughout all world **realms. By means of diverse emanations that are immeasurable** in number **and inconceivable** to the mind, **it accomplishes the objectives of all sentient beings. It should be understood that the emanations of the buddhas are always inconceivable with respect to the accomplishment of** diverse, specific deeds, as well as numbers, and fields.

All-accomplishing wakefulness brings forth the diverse array of emanations of body, speech, and mind that appear throughout all the limitless realms of the world. With inconceivable and limitless emanations, it accomplishes the objectives of all sentient beings. As stated above, the emanations of the buddhas are diverse, immeasurable, and inconceivable. The reason for this is that they respond to, and constantly work to benefit, sentient beings who have diverse constitutions, faculties, and inclinations. Buddhas thus train sentient beings by emanating in the form of buddhas for those who will be benefited thereby, but they also take the form of listeners, self-realized buddhas, bodhisattvas, gods, and so on, including any type of sentient being. In short, since these different emanations manifest in a limitless variety, they are indeed diverse. They are also immeasurable because they cannot be counted in the hundreds, thousands, and so on. They are infinite in number.

Concerning the term "fields," the field in which the buddhas train beings is not limited. It is not one field, or a hundred, and so on. Rather, the emanations of the buddhas reveal a display of emanations in fields that are unconfined, limitless, and boundless throughout the ten directions.

These fields exceed the number of grains of sand in the river Ganga. Thus, this wakefulness should be understood to be inconceivable in every way.

3. The Cause for Attaining These Forms of Wakefulness

This section has two parts: (1) the cause of ripening and (2) the cause of attaining complete purity. The first topic is divided further into a discussion of (1) the actual cause of ripening and (2) supplementary topics.

1. The Cause of Ripening
1. The Actual Ripening Cause

> The four forms of wakefulness are brought forth
> Due to retention, equality of mind,
> Genuine teaching of the Dharma,
> And the practice of activities. [x.76]

The causes of these forms of wakefulness are as follows. **The four forms of wakefulness are brought forth**, respectively, **due to retention** of the Dharma that one has received, **equality of mind** with respect to oneself and all sentient beings, **genuine teaching of the Dharma** without concern for material things, **and the practice of activities** for the sake of others.

The cause of attaining the mirror-like wakefulness is reliance on a spiritual teacher when one is an ordinary being, and retention of the Great Vehicle Dharma through listening, contemplating, and meditating. It is explained that, due to this causal process, the all-ground consciousness will gradually transform and become mirror-like wakefulness. Therefore, it is said that mirror-like wakefulness arises due to the retention of the Dharma.

The other three wakefulnesses arise in a similar manner. That is to say, the wakefulness of equality manifests based on having cultivated the mind of equality when still an ordinary being. This cultivation is a training of the mind through developing love for all sentient beings in the same way as one loves oneself. Similarly, at the time of inspired conduct, one teaches other sentient beings the authentic Dharma, completely and flawlessly, just as one has heard it oneself. This serves as the cause for the manifestation of discriminating wakefulness. Finally, all-accomplishing wakefulness arises based on doing for sentient beings that which they would otherwise have to do themselves. In this way, these four causes serve to bring forth perfectly the four kinds of wakefulness. Therefore, to attain these four forms of unsurpassable wakefulness, one must, while still an ordinary being, develop the mind of supreme enlightenment, accomplish the four causal factors to the best of one's capacity, and thoroughly dedicate all of this to the attainment of these forms of wakefulness. Through the unfailing dependent arising of cause and effect, there will be a time when such wakefulness is attained; the causal powers will not go to waste.

2. Supplementary Topics

> Because of different potentials, because a purpose is served,
> Because of fulfillment, and the absence of a first, the buddhas
>   are not one;
> Yet, because there are no differences within the stainless abode,
> They are not many either. [x.77]

The next section explains how the buddhas are neither one nor different from each other. **Because of** the presence of **different potentials** in each of the infinite number of sentient beings who have the potential for buddhahood; **because** of the fact that **a purpose is served** when different bodhisattvas gather the two accumulations; **because of** the **fulfillment** of enlightened deeds that establish numerous sentient beings in enlightenment; **and** because of **the absence of** any **first** buddha—for these reasons **the buddhas are not one.** Such singularity does not make sense. **Yet, because there are no differences within the stainless abode,** that is, the body of qualities within the field free from defilement, **they are not many either.**

One might ponder: "When many different sentient beings attain unsurpassable wakefulness in this way, they will be turning into many different buddhas, each with his or her own stream of being. But does this not then mean that buddhas are actual persons? And since a buddha's aggregates, elements, and sense sources would turn out to be a variety of actual phenomena, these would have to be conditioned and impermanent phenomena. How then can it be right to say that 'noble individuals are distinguished by the unconditioned, and not by the conditioned?' But if, on the other hand, the buddhas are not different from one another, it would serve no purpose when individual sentient beings practice the path to attain the fruition."

As long as there are perceptions that apprehend persons and phenomena, there will be the appearance of persons with separate streams of being and composed of many different phenomena, such as the aggregates and elements. Ultimately, however, phenomena and persons have no essential nature, and this twofold selflessness is emptiness, luminous clarity. Therefore, when this is fully actualized, there is no perception of a nature of either persons or phenomena. Thus, within their enlightenment, the buddhas are of the nature of the basic field of phenomena. They are the body of wakefulness—an inconceivable totality—and they therefore do not bear any of the marks of persons and phenomena that are otherwise apprehended by ordinary minds. Consequently, it is taught that ultimately there is no difference among buddhas, yet conventionally they exist as distinct from each other by way of imputation. This is "because of different potentials . . . ," as is taught in one stanza.

Moreover, some may believe that when one buddha manifests in a given world realm, no other buddhas will appear in any other of the different world realms of the ten directions at that same time. Thus, there can only be one buddha in all of the realms of the world at any one time, and it is that one buddha who benefits beings by emanating in the other different realms.

Others claim that, throughout beginningless cyclic existence, there has been only one buddha, and that it is this single buddha who performs the various buddha activities for the benefit of sentient beings in all of the buddha fields.

Yet others hold that the buddhahood of the final attainment is not singular and that there are accordingly distinct bodies of qualities wherever the conceptions of "I" and "self" have been eliminated and wherever the two obscurations have been dispelled.

None of these one-sided assertions of there being one or multiple buddhas is correct. Throughout the realms of the world there are infinitely many sentient beings who possess the potential to become buddhas, and because all these different potentials, or causes, are present, it does not make sense for there to be only one fruition of buddhahood. This would be like saying that, within a great pile of grains, only one single grain has the potential to produce a sprout, and not any of the others. Food that has been prepared perfectly well will satiate and benefit anyone who eats it, and in the same way any individual who gathers the two accumulations will also experience the result of achieving buddhahood. If there were only one buddha, then there would be no point in many individuals gathering the two accumulations in order to achieve buddhahood. Hence, since this assertion is unreasonable, it is not the case that there is only one buddha.

When the buddhas first engender the unsurpassable enlightened mind, they make a commitment to achieve great enlightenment and establish all beings in that same achievement. This commitment is then to be completely fulfilled at the stage of buddhahood. Yet, if buddhahood were entirely singular, no one apart from the one sole buddha could ever attain buddhahood, and that one buddha would hence not bring even one sentient being into the state of enlightenment. In other words, the initial commitment would remain unfulfilled. This is not correct, however, for the commitment of the buddhas to bring benefit to sentient beings is indeed completely fulfilled, and it is hence not the case that there is only one buddha. The preceding passage repudiates the claim that there is only one buddha in the world and that there are no other buddhas in other worlds.

It is said that in a single world realm a universal emperor and a buddha cannot both appear at the same time. This refers to one world of four continents. The *Compendium on the Great Vehicle* states that a supreme emanation, like the king of the Śākyas, simultaneously appears throughout one billionfold universe. Thus, a buddha emanation will simultaneously enter into the womb, and so forth, within each of the one billion worlds with four continents.

In terms of time, it could not be the case that there is only one buddha from beginningless time because it is not possible to become a buddha without gathering the two accumulations of merit and wakefulness. Moreover, these two accumulations do not arise independently without the involvement of other buddhas who have transmitted the scriptural statements. Therefore, for each of the buddhas there are buddhas before them, and just as cyclic existence is without beginning, there is no first buddha either. Hence, it does not make sense for there to have been only one buddha since beginningless time, and the buddhas do indeed appear in succession. For all of these reasons, there is not just a single one; there are countless buddhas.

Nevertheless, in terms of their attainment of, and abiding within, the basic field of phenomena—the pure, stainless and sublime field that is undefiled by the two obscurations—there is not the slightest difference between the buddhas. Consequently, they are distinguished and classified in terms of the unconditioned suchness that is endowed with the twofold purity. In light of this, and as was also mentioned earlier, neither are there many buddhas. All are of one taste within the basic field of phenomena free from marks, the suchness nature of mere luminous clarity.

2. Cause of Attaining Complete Purity

> Nonexistence is itself
> Held to be perfectly existent.
> The complete absence of observation
> Is held to be the supreme observation. [x.78]

> The complete absence of the idea of meditation
> Is held to be the sublime meditation.
> The attainment of those who have no thought of attainment
> Is likewise held to be supreme. [x.79]

The explanation of the means for entering buddhahood is as follows. The **nonexistence** of that which is of an imaginary nature **is**

itself held to be perfectly existent as the thoroughly established nature. **The complete absence of observation** of that which is of an imaginary nature **is held to be the supreme observation** of the thoroughly established nature. **The complete absence of the idea of** some path of **meditation** that is practiced by someone **is held to be the sublime meditation. The attainment of those who have no thought of** the **attainment** of a result **is likewise held to be supreme.**

The five transcendences, and especially the transcendent insight that purifies the other transcendences, is what brings forth the attainment of omniscience, the self-existing wakefulness of the great enlightenment that is characterized by nonduality. Therefore, this cause, transcendent insight, which brings forth great and perfect wakefulness, is explained next.

The very nonexistence of any of the marks of imagined duality, such as the apprehended and the apprehender, is itself held to be the existence of the ultimate and thoroughly established suchness. This existence is perfect because suchness is true, real, and the way things actually are. This presents transcendent insight in terms of its object.

Nonconceptual wakefulness, the complete and total nonobservation of any of the constructed marks, is itself held to be the supreme observation. This is because it is the insight that resolves the character of the perfectly genuine. Actual nonreferential wakefulness is achieved on the first ground, and the nonobservation that is free from all constructed marks is the pure view of the Great Vehicle. This is why the teachings on transcendent insight state that not seeing any reference point at all is supreme vision.

Meditation is held to be sublime when it does not perceive any features of an apprehended and an apprehender. Since this meditation accords with suchness and the way things are, it is the genuine nonobservation of the three spheres of meditator, object of meditation, and meditation. While this manifests from the second ground up until the tenth, a semblance of it can also occur on the [grounds] of inspired conduct.

The result, the qualities of buddhahood, are naturally beyond observation, and the attainment of those who do not hold any view of a true or real attainment is therefore held to be sublime. Until the fixation of holding on to something to be attained has been eliminated, buddhahood will not be attained. Rather, buddhahood is attained through comprehending the character of nonattainment. On this point, the teachings on transcendent insight state: "Nonabiding is the supreme abiding; nonattainment is the supreme attainment."

In this way, suchness is devoid of all the constructed marks that are associated with qualities of the ground, path, and fruition. It is by knowing this one taste that the fruition, the great wakefulness of the buddhas, will be attained. If one does perceive marks, one is far from the resultant transcendent insight, and so there is no attainment. Yet when one does not conceive of any marks, it is taught that the fruition does not lie far away, but will be attained quickly.

The next two stanzas are as follows:

Arrogant bodhisattvas
Who think of weight, length, and signs,
And consider their own diligence special,
Are said to be "far from enlightenment." [x.80]

It is definitively stated that bodhisattvas
Who consider all that was taught to be mere thought,
And who do not have any thought,
Have attained enlightenment. [x.81]

Arrogant bodhisattvas who think of the buddha as **weighty** in possessing amazing qualities, who entertain the idea of the great **length** of time involved in accomplishing buddhahood, **and** who think of **signs**, in the sense that they hold mental reference points, **and** who **consider their own diligence special** and supreme: such bodhisattvas are in this way involved in maintaining reference points and **are therefore said to be "far from enlightenment." It is definitively stated that bodhisattvas who consider all that was taught** above **to be mere thought, and who do not** even **have any thought** about everything being mere thought, **have attained enlightenment**, for they have attained the acceptance of nonarising phenomena, which is similar to the attainment of enlightenment.

Arrogant bodhisattvas who adhere to a view that holds reference points are far from unsurpassable enlightenment. With respect to the qualities of their guru, the Buddha, they apprehend entities and marks. The word guru means "weighty." This is why Sthiramati's commentary, at this point, speaks of "the perception of diligence in relation to weight, length, and marks." Following Sthiramati, we may then say that while such bodhisattvas see unsurpassable enlightenment as endowed with marvelous qualities, such as the powers, they also perceive it as weighty because it is difficult to achieve. Since it takes three incalculable eons to achieve it, they likewise think of it as distant, and they conceive of an object of meditation that bears marks. They also think that they are vastly superior to others because they arouse diligence for the sake of unsurpassable enlightenment. Arrogant bodhisattvas who maintain such reference points are said to be "far from enlightenment" because they will not find the authentic path to achieve enlightenment until they are free from such reference points and arrogance.

As explained above, all these referential views are mere imputations. They are one's own thought patterns and do not, therefore, capture anything that is of an extra-mental essential establishment. Some, however, realize that all phenomena are their own mind, and yet they do not view and see the mind in terms of entities and marks. In this way, they do not form any reifying thoughts that relate to marks. It is definitively declared that such bodhisattvas will achieve unsurpassable enlightenment because, since they are free of thought, they will quickly gain the acceptance of nonarising phenomena.

4. Showing That the Buddha's Wakefulness Is the Consummation of All Paths

> As long as rivers flow on the surface of the earth,
> They have different locations, and their waters are distinct.
> Containing but little water, they perform their own distinct functions,
> Providing for little water creatures. [X.82]

Upon flowing into the ocean, they all
Share one single location, and as one great water
They perform the same function,
Continuing to provide plentifully for numerous creatures
  living in water. [x.83]

Those steadfast ones who have not yet entered buddhahood
Have distinct supports, and their intelligence differs.
With little realization, they perform distinct activities,
Constantly providing for but a few sentient beings. [x.84]

Once they have entered buddhahood, they all
Share a single support, and their vast realization is one.
Their deeds merge as one, and they constantly provide
  plentifully
For great multitudes of beings. [x.85]

As long as rivers flow on the surface of the earth, they each have their own environment in different locations and their waters are distinct and not mixed together. Containing but little water, they perform their own distinct functions, providing for only a few little water creatures. Upon flowing into the ocean, they all share one single location, being supported upon the ground of gold, and as one great ocean of water they perform the same function, continuing to provide plentifully for numerous large creatures living in water. Likewise, those steadfast ones, the children of the victorious ones, who have not yet engaged or entered buddhahood, have distinct bodily supports and the sharpness of their intelligence differs. With little realization, in the sense that they do not possess omniscient wakefulness, they perform distinct activities, constantly providing for but a few sentient beings. Formerly children of the victorious ones, once they have entered buddhahood, they all share a single support, namely, the body of qualities, and their vast realization of all objects of cognition is one. Their deeds to train sentient beings merge as one, and they constantly provide plentifully for great multitudes of beings.

When one is a sentient being, different mind streams and a variety of different phenomena appear undeniably, due to the influence of one's own conceptualization. Nevertheless, all phenomena are nothing other than mere projections of thought, mere conceptual imputations. There are no objects that exist by virtue of their own individual essence or nature. When thinking is progressively purified by means of nonconceptual wakefulness, the obscuring graspings and fixations gradually fall away. The result is a continuously increasing attainment of that suchness in which the various constructs, such as those of persons and phenomena, have been completely pacified. In this way, one accomplishes equality beyond all distinctions within the basic field of phenomena.

This process can be illustrated by the following example. As long as rivers flow on the surface of the earth and have not yet entered and merged with the great ocean, each flows in its own direction and has its own location. Each contains its own water. Some rivers, such as the Ganga and the Indus, have a great deal of water, while in smaller tributaries, there is less. Nevertheless, compared to the great ocean, the rivers contain little water. The different waters function in their own different ways. Some, for example, cause wind; others, bile; others, phlegm. Sentient beings use them for different purposes, such as irrigation or bathing. River water also supports small creatures such as frogs and tadpoles. When their waters have flowed into the ocean, all the rivers merge into one great ocean that is supported by the golden ground. Hence, they have but a single location, not many different ones. It is difficult to fathom the breadth and depth of the waters of the ocean; they are one in their vastness. All of the ocean's waters are also of one salty taste, they participate in the one motion of ebb and flow, and they constantly support an abundance of life, including large crocodiles and sea monsters, as well as many smaller creatures.

Like the rivers in this example, steadfast bodhisattvas who have not yet entered the stage of final buddhahood have different supports in terms of their respective five aggregates. Their intellects vary in terms of quality, scope, and degree of sharpness. Since they lack the omniscient wakefulness that has eliminated all the obscurations, their realization is very limited compared with that of the buddhas. Their actions are also different because their individual activities, such as generosity, are confined to particular situations. On their respective grounds, they benefit only a few sentient beings. They provide for beings that can be trained by them in particular, but, unlike the buddhas, they do not benefit the entire infinite number of sentient beings in the ten directions.

When all these bodhisattvas have entered the buddhas' completely pure, basic field of phenomena, which is of the nature of mirror-like wakefulness and the rest of the four, their support and abode will have become one. Theirs is the single, pure basic field of phenomena, and there are no different supports in the form of different continua of aggregates. All possess the great realization of directly seeing all objects of knowledge. There is a single omniscient wakefulness without any differences in terms of sharp or dull faculties, and so forth. All of their deeds merge as one beyond differences, and they are constant, never interrupted. Their activity thus provides plentiful and inexhaustible benefit and happiness. It operates on a scale that is boundless and immeasurable because it embraces the infinite multitudes of sentient beings across the ten directions of space.

3. Concluding Advice for Cultivating the Enlightened Mind Oriented toward Unsurpassable Enlightenment

> In this way, since buddhahood possesses incomparably excellent qualities,
> Since it is the cause of benefit and happiness,
> And as it is an inexhaustible source of bliss and virtues of the most sublime kind,
> It is right for the wise to pursue the virtues of the enlightened mind. [x.86]

> This was the tenth chapter of the *Ornament of the Great Vehicle Sūtras,* the chapter on enlightenment.

This stanza shows how it is appropriate to delight in buddhahood. **In this way, since buddhahood possesses** the powers and other

incomparably excellent qualities that constitute one's own perfect benefit, **since it is the cause of** perfect **benefit and happiness** for others, **and as it is an inexhaustible** (even while nothing remains of the aggregates) **source of** undefiled **bliss** (indicating the distinctive state of bliss) **and virtues** (because it contains no evil) that are **of the most** perfectly **sublime kind, it is right for the wise to take up the virtues of the enlightened mind.**

As explained above, buddhahood possesses, in and of itself, undefiled and incomparably excellent qualities—such as the transcendences, the factors of enlightenment, the powers, and the fearlessnesses. For the welfare of other sentient beings, it serves as the cause of benefit and happiness. This fruition is an inexhaustible source of sublime bliss, completely liberated from suffering, and of sublime virtue, completely freed from the misdeeds of suffering. Therefore, this advises the wise that it is right for them to pursue, within their streams of being, the cultivation of the mind that is oriented toward unexcelled, supreme enlightenment.

This concludes the explanation of enlightenment, the tenth chapter of the *Ornament of the Great Vehicle Sūtras*.

Summary of Chapters 1 through 10

At this point, we may wish to summarize the preceding chapters by means of a brief enumeration. The first chapter, which explains how this treatise is an ornament of the Great Vehicle sūtras, contains five stanzas. Establishing the Great Vehicle as the Word of the Buddha is then taught in fifteen stanzas. After that, there are twelve stanzas on refuge, thirteen on potential, and twenty-seven on the development of the enlightened mind. For the topic of practice—accomplishing one's own benefit and that of others—three stanzas show one's own benefit and six stanzas teach the benefit of others. Ten stanzas teach reality, or the true meaning; a further ten are on the subject of power; and twenty stanzas show the full self and others. Enlightenment is taught in eighty-seven stanzas.

> **Beginning, establishment, refuge, potential,**
> **Development of the mind,**
> **Benefit for self and others, reality,**
> **Power, full maturation, and enlightenment.** [XI.1]

Referring to each of the previous chapters, this stanza offers a summary of their content, from the first chapter up to the chapter on enlightenment: **beginning, establishment** of the Great Vehicle as the Word of the Buddha, going for **refuge, potential, development of the mind, benefit for self and others,** the meaning of **reality, power, full maturation, and enlightenment.**

Next follows a summary of the preceding ten chapters. Of the unexcelled five rich subjects, the first four are generally taught in the chapters on establishing the path of the Great Vehicle to be the Word of the Buddha. The subjects taught are: the potential, which is the ground; going for refuge, which is the root of the path; the development of the enlightened mind, which is the distinct intention of the path of the Great Vehicle; the practice, that is, its application; power and full maturation, which are the distinct means of accomplishment; and enlightenment, which is the result of accomplishment. Thus the qualities that ensue from training on the path of the Great Vehicle, as well as its fruition, can be comprehended through these subjects.

While the previous explanations thus lay the foundation, the account that follows will elaborately explain the means for attaining the fruition of unsurpassable enlightenment. The means in this case comprise the essence of the factors that accord with enlightenment. Thus, the teaching that follows will concern the fifth rich and unexcelled subject, and the present stanza summarizes what has been taught up to this point.

When the character of that Great Vehicle into which one is to enter has been explained in general, one will not stray from the path. Rather, one will embark without any doubts, like a galloping horse. It is for this purpose that the first four subjects are taught, beginning with what is to be established. Although the nature of enlightenment is indeed inconceivable, like an open treasure trove, here—in the context of the five subjects—the enlightenment to be attained is also something to be contemplated. For this reason, enlightenment is here associated with the metaphor of receiving a letter that bears good news. Furthermore, although the stage of buddhahood is the actual open treasure trove, the means or cause for actualizing buddhahood is the path of the factors that accord with enlightenment. Therefore, the general term "factors that accord with enlightenment" should not be understood as applying only to the specific thirty-seven factors of enlightenment. It includes everything that is taught in the chapters from inspiration up to and including the activity.

To elicit an understanding of enlightenment and of that which accords with enlightenment, the tenth chapter teaches the realized nature of the thoroughly established—that which is known through one's own direct awareness. Following on from chapter ten, the method or path for accomplishing this enlightenment is taught, and in that sense the topic can be seen to be "the essence of the factors that accord with enlightenment." Moreover, through practicing the factors of enlightenment, one will traverse the ten grounds and attain their distinct qualities. This process culminates with the actualization of the perfect qualities of buddhahood, such as the four immeasurables, the freedoms, totalities, and commands, and the ten powers. In this way, all of the remaining eleven chapters, from the chapter on inspiration to the chapter on conduct, explain this topic—the essence of the factors that accord with enlightenment.

This can be correlated with the similar aspects of the five stages of spiritual practice. Thus, the five chapters from inspiration to practical instructions are concerned with the "basis." The four chapters from skillful means to the factors of enlightenment teach the "development." The chapter on the qualities concerns "the mirror-like." The chapter on activity, together with the stanzas of the concluding summary of the ten grounds, is on "appearance." The stanzas on the qualities of the consummate fruition teach the "support." Having offered this general explanation, there follows the fifth main section—the essence of the factors of enlightenment.

5. The Factors of Enlightenment

This section has four parts: (1) the five chapters of the preliminaries, beginning with inspiration; (2) the four chapters on the main part of practice, beginning with skillful means; (3) the chapters on the temporary qualities, from the chapter on the qualities and up to the explanation of the ten grounds of conduct; (4) the explanation of the ultimate qualities of the perfect fruition.[35] Among the unexcelled five rich subjects, this one—the factors of enlightenment—is like an open treasure trove.

1. Preliminaries

This section has five parts: (1) the chapter on inspiration, which is the cause; the chapters on (2) the investigation of the Dharma, (3) teaching the Dharma, and (4) the practice of the Dharma, which are all concerned with practical application; and (5) as a specific discussion that relates to these first four sections, the chapter on imparting practical instructions and advice.

II

Inspiration

1. Inspiration

When first embarking on the path, it is necessary to cultivate inspiration. As stated in a sūtra: "The Sage taught that the root of all virtuous qualities is inspiration." The allusion here is that the engendering of inspiration is the beginning of all virtuous qualities, and that it is through inspiration that virtue is accomplished. Without inspiration, one would never pursue the cultivation of virtue. Thus, it is necessary to develop inspiration. As taught in the *Jewel Lamp Sūtra:*

> Faith is like a guide that leads one and like a mother who gives birth.
> It protects and increases all positive qualities.
> It dispels doubts and transports one across the river.
> Faith is what reveals the city of bliss.
>
> Faith contains no impurity but makes the mind clear.
> It eliminates pride and is the root of respect.
> Faith is a treasure, a jewel, and the best of feet.
> Like a hand, it enables one to gather virtue.

And:

> Faith delivers one from the paths of Māra.
> It reveals the supreme path to liberation.
> It is the unspoiled seed of the field of qualities.
> Faith produces the tree of enlightenment.

Thus, the first section, the chapter on inspiration, will address four topics: (1) the twenty-six types of inspiration, (2) the sixteen obstacles to inspiration, (3) the benefits of inspiration, and, following on from this presentation of the general types of inspiration, (4) a specific explanation of inspiration in the Great Vehicle. The latter will include (1) a metaphorical teaching on the distinct inspiration that belongs to the Great Vehicle and (2) advice to embrace the Great Vehicle with delight and without being fainthearted.

1. General Enumerations of Inspiration
1. The Twenty-Seven Types of Inspiration

Inspiration can be arisen and not arisen; apprehender and
    apprehended;
Adopted from a friend and from oneself;
Mistaken and unmistaken; perceptible and imperceptible;
Arisen based on words, search, and view; [XI.2]

Susceptible, mixed, and unmixed with conflicting factors;
Inferior and vast; obscured and not obscured;
Diligent and not diligent; gathered and not gathered;
Stable and gone beyond. [XI.3]

What follows is an explanation of **inspiration**, which **can be** divided into inspiration that has **arisen** in the past, inspiration that is arising in the present, **and** inspiration that will manifest in the future—and which thus has **not arisen**. Inspiration can also relate to the internal **apprehender** whereby a focal point is held, **and** it can be related to an externally **apprehended** focal point. There is a coarse inspiration that is **adopted from a friend and** a subtle inspiration that arises **from oneself**. There is a **mistaken** inspiration that is inferior and erroneous **and** an **unmistaken** inspiration that is excellent and true. Inspiration can be close and **perceptible** when the spiritual friend and the other conditions for the arising of inspiration have all come together, **and** it can also be distant and **imperceptible** when these conditions are not present. There is the inspiration that has **arisen based on** the **words** of others, that is, through receiving teachings, the inspiration that occurs as one's own mind **search**es during the process of reflection, **and** the inspiration that manifests through the **view** that regards the meaning single-pointedly through the practice of meditation.

There is also the lesser inspiration that is **susceptible** to the factors that conflict with it, the middling inspiration that is **mixed** with these factors, **and** the great inspiration that is **unmixed with conflicting factors.** There is the inspiration that concerns other vehicles, and which is therefore **inferior, and** the **vast** inspiration that pertains to the Great Vehicle. There is the inspiration that cannot achieve distinction since it is **obscured** by negative conditions, **and** there is another form that is **not obscured** by such conditions. There is inspiration that involves **diligent** application with devoted constancy **and** inspiration that does **not** entail being **diligent.** There is inspiration where the accumulations required for seeing the truth have been **gathered and** another inspiration where they have **not** been **gathered.** Finally, there is the inspiration that is **stable** from the first [through the seventh] ground, **and** the subsequent inspiration that is associated with having **gone beyond** those earlier stages.

In general, the quality of faith that trusts in the truth of karmic causality, in the four truths, and in the three jewels is what is known as the mental state of "faith" or "inspiration." With this mental state, one regards these principles as the way things are. Past, present, and future forms, as well as forms that are near and distant, are thus presented as the aggregate of form. In a similar manner, inspiration can also be explained in terms of its particular instances—its focal points, time, features, and so on.

Faith that has arisen in both the past and the present is called "arisen inspiration." Future faith, on the other hand, is described as inspiration that has not arisen. Inspiration as apprehender is the mental state of inspiration itself—known as "inner inspiration." Inspiration in terms of the apprehended observes an inspiration that has previously arisen, determining it to be something good, savoring and enjoying its flavor. This so-called "inspiration of the apprehended" is also described as "outer inspiration" because it takes another inspiration as its object. The inspiration through training under the guidance of a spiritual teacher is "inspiration adopted from a friend." This is also described as "coarse inspiration." The inspiration that arises from the seed of faithful inspiration within oneself and from the power of one's potential is referred to as "inspiration from oneself." This is also known as "subtle inspiration."

Trust and inspiration in non-Buddhist discourses that teach the existence of self and of sentient beings is mistaken inspiration. It is negative inspiration. Trust and faith in the discourses from the scriptures of the Buddha that teach impermanence, suffering, and the absence of self is, on the other hand, unmistaken inspiration. Such inspiration is excellent. The inspiration that manifests when all of its causes and conditions have come together is called "perceptible inspiration." This is also known as "close inspiration." At the point in time when the causes and conditions of inspiration have not yet come together and when inspiration, therefore, is not yet manifest, it is known as "imperceptible inspiration." Its presence is contingent on the causes and conditions coming together, and so, compared with perceptible inspiration, this is also known as "distant inspiration."

Inspiration that arises from listening to the sacred Dharma is described as "inspiration that has arisen from words," or "inspiration that has arisen based on words." Inspiration that comes from reasoned analysis of the meaning of what has been received is known as the "inspiration of investigation by means of reflection." The inspiration that arises from realizing the meaning by the power of meditation is termed "the inspiration of the view," or "the inspiration through viewing reality."

Even where there is faith, when one is prone to be led onto other paths by demons, extremists, and so forth, one's faith is described as unstable. This is called "susceptible inspiration," which is a lesser form of inspiration. When there is faith, but with intervals of lack of faith, the inspiration is described as mixed. Mixed inspiration is referred to as "middling inspiration." The constant presence of faith alone, without any lack of faith, is said to be "inspiration unmixed with conflicting factors." This is known as "great inspiration."

Inspiration in the Dharma of listeners and self-realized buddhas, which brings about a thorough pacification for one's own benefit, is called "inferior" or "lesser inspiration." Inspiration in the Dharma of the Great Vehicle, which is the path to the nonabiding transcendence of suffering and the spontaneous accomplishment of the twofold benefit, is what is known as "vast inspiration." Beginning with the stage of heat at the level of inspired conduct and continuing throughout the path, there may be inspiration regarding the attainment of extraordinary, higher qualities, yet such inspiration may nevertheless also be obstructed due to afflictions such as attachment. When this is the case, it is known as "obscured inspiration." When, on the other hand, the obstacles are absent, it is known as "unobscured inspiration." Diligence that is endowed with both devoted endeavor and consistency brings about an uninterrupted inspiration called "diligent inspiration" or "endowed inspiration." Inspiration that is not thus endowed is called "inspiration without diligence" or "unendowed inspiration."

Gathering the two accumulations for an incalculable eon on the grounds of inspired conduct serves as the cause for realizing the basic field of phenomena on the first ground. Such inspiration is referred to as the "inspiration of gathered accumulations." Conversely, inspiration that is not endowed with these accumulations is known as the "inspiration where the accumulations have not been gathered." In general, based on the number of accumulations one has gathered, there is a corresponding degree of magnitude and stability in one's inspiration with respect to the Great Vehicle. The inspiration of bodhisattvas on the first to the seventh ground is known as "stable inspiration" because their inspiration does not wane or diminish. The inspiration of bodhisattvas on the pure grounds, from the eighth through the tenth ground, is called "inspiration that has gone beyond." It is described in this way because this form of inspiration is nonconceptual and spontaneously present; it has transcended the grounds that are characterized by effortful practice and thoughts that apprehend marks.

2. The Sixteen Obstacles to Inspiration

Frequent failing to direct the mind,
Laziness, disturbance to spiritual practice,
Negative company, weakness of virtue,
Improper mental activity, [XI.4]

Carelessness, insufficient teaching,
Contentment with one's reception of teaching, and minor
    reflections,
Pride based on mere peace, and lack of familiarity—
These are asserted. [XI.5]

Lack of disenchantment, disenchantment,
Obscuration, lack of diligence,
And not having gathered the accumulations—
These are obstacles to inspiration. [XI.6]

The obstacles to these kinds of inspiration are taught next. Arisen inspiration is hindered when **frequently failing to direct the mind**. Unarisen inspiration is prevented by **laziness**. Inspiration associated with the apprehended and the apprehender is prevented by **disturbances to spiritual practice**, in the sense that apprehended and apprehender are taken to be real. The inspiration adopted from a friend is inhibited by **negative company** since such company corrupts one's perspective. Inspiration one has adopted by oneself is impeded by a **weakness of virtue**. Unmistaken inspiration is hindered by its opposite, **improper mental activity**. Perceptible inspiration is countered by **carelessness**. Inspiration based on words is impeded by **insufficient** reception of the **teaching** of the sūtras of definitive meaning. Inspiration based on investigation is hindered by **contentment with** the extent of **one's reception of teaching and** by being content with only **minor reflections**. Inspiration based on the view is inhibited by the notion that reflection alone is sufficient, as well as by the **pride** that is **based on mere peace**; and both susceptible inspiration and mixed inspiration are hindered by a **lack of familiarity** with the factors that constitute the remedy. **These are asserted** to be the obstacles.

Furthermore, inferior inspiration is hindered by a **lack of disenchantment** toward cyclic existence. Vast inspiration is prevented by extreme **disenchantment**. Unobscured inspiration is prevented by **obscuration**. Diligent inspiration is inhibited by a **lack of diligence; and** inspiration through having gathered the accumulations is precluded by **not having gathered the accumulations**. **These are obstacles to inspiration.** Only sixteen obstacles are enumerated for the twenty-seven categories of inspiration. This is because five of the twenty-seven are themselves obstacles (namely, the inspirations that are mistaken, obscured, deprived of diligence, lacking accumulation, and imperceptible), whereas unmixed inspiration, inspiration of abiding stably, and inspiration that has gone beyond are inherently free from obstacles.

When one predominately or frequently fails to direct the mind through faith in the Dharma, this hinders arisen inspiration. Although inspiration may have arisen in the past, and although it may arise from time to time in the present, if the mind is not engaged in sustaining its continuity, faith will dissipate. Laziness is a hindrance to activating unarisen inspiration because faith will not arise in a lazy person who does not make efforts to engender it. "Disturbance to spiritual practice" is when one brings to mind, and focuses on, a past instance of faith, and so becomes attached to it as an apprehended entity. This obstacle also occurs when, based on a present instance of inspiration as apprehender, one develops attachment to that inspiration, taking it to be an actual apprehending subject. Such obstacles hinder the proper meditative absorption of spiritual practice, within which there is no grasping at any entities in the form of apprehended or apprehender. Thus, this form of obstacle is taught as being a hindrance for both apprehended inspiration and inspiration associated with apprehending.

Negative company, which refers to negative companions and unvirtuous spiritual guides, hinders inspiration adopted from a friend. This is because, even if this form of inspiration was previously present, it will be squandered due to the influence of negative companions who engage in what is not Dharma. Thus, if one is taken in by negative company, the inspiration that comes from the instructions of a spiritual friend will not arise.

Weakness with respect to the accumulation of the fundamental virtues is the hindrance to the inspiration that arises from oneself. This is because one will not be inspired by the Great Vehicle Dharma and so forth if great virtue has not been gathered, even though one may otherwise have the potential and possess the seed of inspiration. Improper mental activity, which involves thinking in terms of permanence, happiness, purity, and a self, becomes a hindrance to unmistaken inspiration because such activity misunderstands the meaning of impermanence and so on. Furthermore, carelessness hinders perceptible inspiration, which otherwise arises from an absence of attachment, aversion, and bewilderment, and from the condition of diligence. These four conditions are referred to as heedfulness, while attachment, aversion, bewilderment, and laziness are described as carelessness because they hinder heedfulness.

If one listens only to teachings that explain limited issues, as when listening only to the sūtras of expedient meaning and not those of definitive meaning (such as the Dharma of emptiness), this will hinder the inspiration that is based on words. If one does not know the meaning of a given teaching because one has never heard it, one will not develop with respect to that teaching. Moreover, those who have not studied the topics of the definitive meaning will experience fear and will lack inspiration with respect to issues such as profound emptiness.

The inspiration that is based on investigation will likewise be hindered in those who are content only to receive teachings, without also feeling the need to reflect and meditate, and in those who do not feel the need to receive very much in the way of teaching due to being content with only a small amount of learning. The reason for this is that the inspiration derived from the insight of reflection is not developed, or only developed very little, and therefore this vast, full, and complete inspiration cannot arise. One may reflect on the meaning of what one has studied, but only slightly, being content with minor reflections without any extensive consideration. This hinders, as before, the inspiration based on investigation, which arises through reflection. In short, in both cases the inspiration from reflection does not arise, or arises very little, because one is content with receiving and reflecting on the teachings to a lesser degree. This creates an obstacle to complete perfection.

The pride based on mere peace involves being content just with calm abiding, without cultivating special insight. This arrogant form of contentment is based on the simple pacification of thoughts that are outwardly distracted. This obstructs the inspiration that is based on the view, or the inspiration that arises from meditation, because, without special insight, mere calm abiding does not bring realization of the truth. Furthermore, if one is content with reflection alone, one will not engage in meditation. This is also an obstacle to the inspiration that is based on the view. "View" comes from the word *dṛś,* meaning "to see." Thus, it refers to seeing the authentic meaning with a mind in meditative equipoise.

The phrase "lack of familiarity . . . ," refers to the following. If one does not become familiar with inspiration and does not integrate it into one's mind stream, this will become an obstacle to both susceptible inspiration and mixed inspiration. When one's mind stream is not accustomed to inspiration, it will be susceptible to external circumstances. This will be the case even when one does have inspiration, and there will be periods of faith mixed with times without faith. Conversely, when this lack of integration has been averted, one will become accustomed to being inspired, and, as a result, it will be difficult for one's inspiration to be swept away by circumstances and for there to be periods where faith is absent. Therefore, the obstacle to these two forms of inspiration is a lack of familiarity in one's mind stream.

A lack of disenchantment in cyclic existence hinders the inspiration that is based on the Lesser Vehicle. This is because if one is attached to cyclic existence and not disenchanted by it, one will not pursue peace. Conversely, being thoroughly disenchanted by cyclic existence hinders inspiration in the context of the Great Vehicle. This is because one's dissatisfaction with cyclic existence will urge one to leave it behind completely. One will strive for one's own peace, as listeners do. Moreover, regarding obscuration, those hindrances that were explained above in the context of obscured inspiration are also the ones that hinder unobscured inspiration. Lack of diligence hinders diligent inspiration, while not having gathered the accumulations is a hindrance to the presence of the inspiration that occurs through having gathered the accumulations.

In this way, only sixteen obstacles are explained. Five of these (the mistaken, imperceptible, obscured, lack of diligence, and lack of accumulation) are situations where one is seized by conflicting factors, and thus there is no need to specify separate obstacles. Since three forms of inspiration (unmixed inspiration, the inspiration of abiding stably, and inspiration that has gone beyond) constitute the remedy that it is free from obstacles, these three have no obstacles. Finally, the inspirations associated with the apprehended and the apprehender, as well as the susceptible and mixed inspirations, share a single obstacle. Thus, subtracting ten, there are sixteen obstacles all together.

One can also enumerate eighteen obstacles by separately counting the two types of contentment (that is, with receiving teaching and with minor studies) as they relate to the inspiration inspired by reflection, or by separately counting the contentment with mere reflection and the pride of mere peace as they relate to the inspiration arisen from meditation. Yet, in consideration of what they hinder, it is good to enumerate the obscurations in terms of these sixteen categories. Without correlating them with the specific forms of inspiration, we may also make the general observation that since all sixteen factors obscure the different types of inspiration, they are all to be rejected.

3. The Eleven Benefits of Inspiration

Vast merit, absence of regret,
Mental bliss, great bliss,
No dissipation, stability,
Gaining distinction, [XI.7]

Manifest realization of the Dharma,
Supreme accomplishment of the welfare of self and others,
And the agility of superknowledge—
These are the benefits of inspiration. [XI.8]

The benefits of inspiration are explained as follows. Inspiration that arises in the present brings **vast merit**. Past inspiration is associated with the **absence of regret**. The inspirations based on the apprehended and apprehender entail **mental bliss** and the **great bliss** of physical agility that is due to the presence of meditative absorption. Inspiration produced by a spiritual teacher entails **no dissipation,** and inspiration produced by oneself has **stability.** Unmistaken inspiration, perceptible inspiration, inspiration derived from receiving teaching, reflecting, and meditating, as well as the lesser and the middling forms of inspiration, are all associated with the continuous process of **gaining distinction.** Great inspiration entails **manifest realization of the Dharma.** The **supreme accomplishment of the welfare of self and others** is associated with, respectively, the inspiration pertaining to the Lesser Vehicle and the inspiration known as vast inspiration. **And the agility of superknowledge** is the benefit of positive factors associated with the absence of obscuration, with diligence, with having gathered the accumulations, with stability, and with having gone beyond. **These are the benefits of inspiration.** There are no benefits of the inspirations associated with being mistaken, with being deprived of diligence, with not having gathered the accumulations, and with imperceptibility. Moreover, no benefit is explained for the inspiration associated with the future because it has not yet arisen.

Present inspiration develops immeasurably the vast merit of faith in the Dharma. Past inspiration prevents one from having regrets in the present because one's prior inspiration with respect to the Great Vehicle Dharma is of a virtuous nature. In not being attached to the apprehended entity as such, one partially recognizes reality by realizing that there is no nature in that which is apprehended, and the attainment of meditative absorption brings mental bliss. The inspiration associated with realizing the lack of nature of an apprehender carries the great bliss of the meditative absorption that occurs at the stage of the supreme quality, or during the subsequent meditative absorption. As for the inspiration adopted from a friend, if the circumstances do not bring any obstacles, one will achieve qualities of virtue that will not dissipate. If inspiration produced by oneself is free from obstacles, fundamental virtues will not wither and will instead become stable. And, as mentioned before, when discordant factors do not obstruct unmistaken inspiration, perceptible inspiration,

inspiration that arises based on words, inspiration through investigation, inspiration based on the view, susceptible inspiration, and unmixed inspiration, these forms of inspiration will all gain distinction as their qualities will be continuously enhanced. Great unmistaken inspiration thus arises from middling unmistaken inspiration, and so on.

When an inspiration unmixed with conflicting factors is thus free from obstacles, all phenomena will be realized directly, and the first ground will be attained. In the Lesser Vehicle, the peace of transcendence that constitutes one's own welfare will be attained when the obstacles to the relevant inspiration are absent. In the Great Vehicle, when free from the obstacles to inspiration, the objectives of self and others will be perfectly achieved. When unobscured inspiration, diligent inspiration, the inspiration through having gathered the accumulations, the inspiration of abiding stably, and the inspiration through having gone beyond are all free from the circumstantial impediments, the qualities of the agile forms of superknowledge will be attained. The first three inspirations produce exceptionally sharp faculties. The latter two will swiftly bring the attainment of omniscient wakefulness.

Thus, these eleven categories describe the benefits of inspiration. There is no explanation of the benefits of mistaken inspiration, imperceptible inspiration, future inspiration, obscured inspiration, inspiration without diligence, and inspiration without having gathered the accumulations. As for these, the possible benefits are included in the various benefits of faith in general. Yet because, for instance, a future inspiration has not yet arisen and because the inspirations that are mistaken and so forth carry obstacles, there is no specific enumeration of the benefits of these forms of inspiration. Hence, knowing them to be the benefits of faith in general, one should cultivate faith.

4. Inspiration with regard to the Great Vehicle

This section presents (1) teaching by means of metaphors and (2) advice to enter the Great Vehicle wholeheartedly and with joy.

1. Teaching by Means of Metaphors

In the desirous, it is like a dog,
In meditative absorption, it resembles a turtle,
In those who benefit themselves, it is like a slave,
And in those who benefit others, it resembles a king. [XI.9]

It is like a dog that is always hungry, that suffers, and can never get enough,
Like a turtle, completely withdrawn in the water,
Like a slave who constantly moves with a frightened, fearful demeanor,
And like a king who rules the land by decree. [XI.10]

Thus, the different inspirations of the frivolous, the introverted,
Those who benefit themselves, and those who benefit others, should always be distinguished.
Having properly seen that what pertains to the Great Vehicle is supreme,
The steadfast should always pursue that to the highest degree. [X.11]

Furthermore, **in the desirous, it,** meaning inspiration, **is like a dog,** whereas **in** those who possess mundane **meditative absorption, it resembles a turtle. In those** listeners and self-realized buddhas **who benefit themselves, it is like a slave, and in those** children of the victorious ones **who benefit others, it resembles a king.**

That is to say, in these beings **it,** that is, inspiration, **is** respectively **like a dog that is always hungry, that suffers, and can never get enough** of eating; **like a turtle** that lies with its limbs **completely withdrawn in the water; like a slave who,** apprehensive of his master, **constantly moves with a frightened** and **fearful demeanor** to obtain food and clothing for himself or herself; **and like a king who rules the land by decree** that is in accord with the scriptures.

Thus, the different inspirations of, respectively, **the** beings of the desire realm who are deprived of sense pleasures, tormented by suffering, insatiable with respect to wealth and riches, and **frivolous** in their pursuit of sense pleasures; **the** beings who cultivate the mundane meditations associated with the form and formless realms and who remain **introverted,** as their minds are withdrawn in meditative absorption, without being aware of the general and specific characteristics of phenomena; **those who** are listeners and self-realized buddhas, constantly fearful and frightened by cyclic existence, **benefit themselves** by applying effort to limited practices for their own welfare; **and those who** are children of the victorious ones and who benefit **others** with their vast waves of activity that employ means and knowledge—the different inspirations of all of these **should always be distinguished. Having correctly seen that what pertains to the Great Vehicle is the supreme** form of inspiration, **the steadfast should always pursue that** inspiration, associated with the Great Vehicle, **to the highest degree.**

The inspiration of desirous beings in the desire realm, who are attached to the five outer sense objects and their enjoyment, resembles a dog. The inspiration of those on the grounds of withdrawn equipoise, where outward distractions are given up through mundane meditative absorptions in the form and formless realms, can be compared to a turtle. The inspiration of listeners and self-realized buddhas, which is directed at their own achievement of liberation from the suffering of cyclic existence, is slave-like. The bodhisattva's inspiration to benefit all other sentient beings is comparable to a king.

The next section of the root text elaborates on the meaning of these metaphors. Thus, the first form of inspiration is likened to a dog because a dog is always hungry. Feeling famished and deprived of food, it experiences torment and is never satisfied with whatever food it obtains. The second form of inspiration is compared to a turtle. Due to their fear of others, turtles lie in the water with all of their limbs withdrawn. The third form of inspiration is likened to the slave of a king or similar figure. Afraid of contradicting the words or thoughts of their master, slaves always carry out the master's tasks with a frightened and fearful demeanor.

Finally, the fourth form of inspiration is compared to a king, who governs by decree, and so rules his realm just as he wishes.

Beings in the desire realm resemble a dog because they are constantly preoccupied with, and distracted by, outer sense pleasures. Thus, they roam about, helplessly driven by their desires. Next, distracted by the taste of the two higher realms, there are beings whose inspiration is turtle-like. Rather than turning their minds toward the profound nature and the vast qualities of what is to be realized, they simply remain withdrawn and introverted due to fear. Moreover, listeners, who make great efforts to fulfill their own benefit alone, dread the sufferings of cyclic existence. They are concerned lest the slightest transgression of the trainings of the Thus-Gone One, who is the king of the Dharma, will be at odds with the methods for liberation from cyclic existence. Thus, they fear that it will obscure the path of liberation and cause them to encounter an unpleasant result in the future. Fearfully, they hence make great efforts in applying the methods for individual liberation so that they will swiftly be free from cyclic existence. In this sense, their motivation and demeanor can be likened to that of a slave.

As for the inspiration of bodhisattvas, just as a king has power over his land due to having gathered accumulations in the past, the power of their great insight and compassion allows bodhisattvas to dwell in cyclic existence, yet remain unstained by its faults. Thus, they do not dwell in the extreme of a one-sided peace. Rather, they transcend the state of peace, endowed with power over both cyclic existence and the transcendence of suffering. Thus, they perfectly benefit all sentient beings, both themselves and others, for now and for eternity.

In this way, the bodhisattvas' inspiration is supreme and surpasses the inspiration associated with the mundane realms (that is, the desire realm and the two higher realms), as well as the transcendent states of the listeners and self-realized buddhas. Therefore, among the various inspirations of sentient beings, the bodhisattvas' inspiration of constant faith in the Great Vehicle is clearly superior. Knowing this, one should properly see that the Great Vehicle teachings of the Buddha are superior to the others, and one should enter them with faith. A steadfast bodhisattva must always pursue this inspiration that is directed toward the Great Vehicle Dharma to the highest degree.

2. Advice to Enter the Great Vehicle Wholeheartedly with Joy

This section has three parts: (1) entering the Great Vehicle without dejection, (2) entering it with joy because great merit proceeds from doing so, and (3) entering it based on a demonstration of three qualities.

1. Entering the Great Vehicle without Dejection

> Beings of the human kind—
> Infinitely many, and in each and every instant—
> Attain complete enlightenment.
> Therefore, do not entertain dejection. [XI.12]

Next follows a refutation of dejection. **Beings of the human kind—infinitely many, and** moreover, **in each and every instant**—continue to **attain complete enlightenment. Therefore, do not entertain dejection.**

"In the Great Vehicle, one needs to give away one's head, limbs, and so forth, while on the path, and it is necessary to adopt the austerity of not fearing the sufferings of cyclic existence. Therefore, although one will achieve the result of a buddha with all the marvelous qualities that come from doing so, this vehicle is the domain only of certain great beings. How could an ordinary human being like me accomplish something like that?" One should not be disheartened based on such thinking. In terms of support for the accomplishment of enlightenment, beings with a human body are supreme, even compared to the gods. Furthermore, there are not just a few humans that become buddhas. There are infinitely many. And this does not simply happen occasionally, or once in a while. In each and every moment, including this present one, there are infinitely many bodhisattvas in the boundless worlds throughout the ten directions who achieve unsurpassed, perfect enlightenment.

Therefore, one should not be dejected, thinking "I cannot attain enlightenment." Rather, think as follows: "I was born as a human being just like them. Beginning with inspired conduct, they trained progressively and gained the power of insight and compassion, knowing the sufferings of cyclic existence to be illusory. Once the power of the great compassion that never forsakes sentient beings is perfected, I will not perceive the enlightened activities as hard. Not only that, I will experience a great and immaculate joy that is unrivaled by any worldly pleasure, a joy that accomplishes buddhahood, the great objective. If I act like them, why shouldn't I too become a buddha? I will, because the great bodhisattvas were also ordinary sentient beings like me at first. But they achieved enlightenment by practicing the Great Vehicle."

2. Entering the Great Vehicle because Great Merit Proceeds from This

When one feeds others, merit develops,
Yet when one is eating, it does not.
Likewise, by teaching the Dharma
That supports the welfare of others, [XI.13]

Great merit, just as taught in the sūtras,
Will be attained.
Yet that is not the case when the Dharma
That supports one's own welfare is taught. [XI.14]

These verses explain what distinguishes the merit of inspiration. **When one feeds others, merit develops, yet when one is** oneself **eating it does not** develop. **Likewise, by teaching the** Great Vehicle **Dharma that supports the welfare of others,** exceedingly **great merit, just as taught in the sūtras** of the Great Vehicle, **will be attained. Yet that is not the case when the** Lesser Vehicle **Dharma that supports one's own welfare is taught.**

In the beginning, one may have gained only a slight measure of inspiration with respect to the Great Vehicle Dharma. Yet, such inspiration will nevertheless result in immeasurable benefits. What need, then, is there to mention that practicing the Great Vehicle Dharma correctly will yield tremendous results? Why is the Great Vehicle Dharma so beneficial? The reason is that this is the Dharma that explains how to benefit others. Giving food to other sentient beings increases one's merit, yet there is no merit to be gained from one's own eating. There is, in the same way, great merit in teaching the Great Vehicle Dharma, which supports the welfare of other sentient beings, just as there is great merit in aspiring to the way of the Great Vehicle oneself. This is all just as taught in the sūtras. For example, compared to offering infinite realms completely filled with the seven precious substances to the thus-gone ones, it is more beneficial to explain just one verse of the Great Vehicle Dharma to others. Although teaching the Lesser Vehicle Dharma, which supports one's own welfare, will also produce fine benefits, these do not compare with those that are gained from teaching the Great Vehicle.

3. Three Qualities

> Hence, the Dharma of the great noble ones is extensive,
> And when the wise constantly develop strong inspiration,
> It creates unceasing great merit, enhancement,
> And unfathomable qualities, thereby turning them into great beings. [XI.15]

This was the eleventh chapter of the *Ornament of the Great Vehicle Sūtras,* the chapter on inspiration.

This section explains the results of inspiration. **Hence,** the focus of inspiration, **the Dharma of the great noble ones, is extensive** and vast, **and when the wise** bodhisattvas **constantly develop strong inspiration** with respect to that Dharma, **it creates** an **unceasing** flow of **great merit** as the result of individual effort. Also, an **enhancement** of inspiration takes place as the result that resembles the cause, **and,** as the ripening result, **unfathomable qualities** issue forth, **thereby turning them into great beings,** into buddhas.

In this way, the Dharma of the path of the noble beings of the Great Vehicle is extensive and vast. Since wise bodhisattvas constantly engender great inspiration in this Dharma, vast merit issues forth uninterruptedly. Such inspiration will develop further and further, up through the tenth ground. Finally, as great beings endowed with unfathomable qualities, bodhisattvas attain unsurpassed enlightenment.

This concludes the explanation of inspiration, or faith—the eleventh chapter of the *Ornament of the Great Vehicle Sūtras*.

12

INVESTIGATION OF THE DHARMA

2. Investigation of the Dharma

It is not enough merely to be inspired by the profound and vast Dharma of the Great Vehicle. Rather, by means of the insights gained from learning, reflecting, and meditating, one must investigate the Dharma that inspires. Hence, as one must receive abundant teaching and gain certainty in the meaning of what is taught, the chapter on the investigation of the Dharma is taught after the chapter on inspiration. There are five sections in this chapter: (1) the Dharma that is investigated, (2) how the mind is directed in the investigation, (3) specific types of investigation, (4) the outcome of investigation, and (5) a summary.

1. The Dharma

The first section has two parts: (1) a thorough investigation of the Dharma of scripture, which must be explained, and (2) an investigation of the actual Dharma, which is to be realized.

1. The Dharma of Scripture

This section has three parts: (1) thoroughly investigating the teachings themselves, which are the focal points, (2) thoroughly investigating the meaning of the teachings, thereby discovering the focal points, and (3) thoroughly investigating the way that the mind is directed during such investigation.

1. The Teachings Themselves

The following four stanzas describe the objects that serve as the focal points for the three types of insight:

> There may be either three or two vessels,
> Yet, they are held for nine reasons in terms of what they contain.
> Through imprints, realization, pacification, and full
>   realization,
> They bring about liberation. [XII.1]

> Sūtra, Abhidharma, and Vinaya
> Are held to be summarized in four topics.
> The wise gain complete omniscience
> By comprehending these topics. [XII.2]

> Bases, characteristics, phenomena, and meanings—
> It is Sūtra because it proclaims these.
> In being oriented toward, persistent, overpowering,
> And eliciting realization, it is Abhidharma. [XII.3]

> The Vinaya is so called because it addresses downfalls,
> Occurrence, reemergence, and definitive emergence,
> As well as the person, formulation,
> Elaboration, and ascertainment. [XII.4]

There may be either three vessels, that is, the Sūtras, Vinaya, and Abhidharma, **or two,** when specified in terms of the lesser and the supreme vehicles. Yet, **they are held** to be threefold **for nine reasons in terms of what they contain,** that is, all topics of knowledge.

Sūtra is the remedy for doubt. The sūtras are taught for the sake of developing certainty in topics where one harbors doubts. The Vinaya is the remedy for being bound by the two extremes. It prevents one from being bound by the extreme of desire and overindulgence by prohibiting negative actions. As it permits actions that are not negative, it also prevents one from being bound by the extreme of hardship and exhaustion. Finally, the Abhidharma is the remedy for the belief in the supremacy of one's own view because it unerringly teaches the characteristics of phenomena.

Sūtra teaches all three trainings. The Vinaya, on the other hand, enables one to accomplish discipline and mental training because one who is disciplined will have no regrets and so forth, and will hence gradually achieve meditative absorption. The Abhidharma enables one to accomplish the training in insight because it allows one to discern the meanings of the teaching without error.

The sūtras also present Dharma teachings and their meanings, whereas the Vinaya accomplishes them because as one diligently tames the afflictions, both the teachings and their meanings will be realized. The Abhidharma engenders the expertise to understand decisively the discourses that relate teachings and their meanings.

All of this, in turn, enables one to be liberated from cyclic existence. Liberation is brought about **through** the imprints that are created in the mind when learning the Dharma; through the **realization** of the meaning of the teachings due to contemplating them; through the **pacification** of afflictions by calm abiding; and finally, through the **full realization** of the intrinsic nature by means of special insight. In this way, **they,** meaning the three vessels, **bring about liberation** from cyclic existence.

Sūtra, Abhidharma, and Vinaya are each individually **held to be summarized in four topics. The wise,** that is, the bodhisattvas, **gain complete omniscience by comprehending these topics.** A listener can achieve the exhaustion of defilements even by understanding the meaning of a single stanza.

These four topics that pertain to the three vessels are the **bases** of the teacher and the retinue, the **characteristics** of the two truths, the **phenomena** of the aggregates, elements, and sense sources, **and the meanings** intended by the statements that speak of existence and nonexistence, and so forth. **It is Sūtra because it proclaims these.**

In teaching the four truths, the factors of enlightenment, the gateways to liberation, and so forth, the Abhidharma is **being**

oriented toward the transcendence of suffering. It is also **persistent,** because it specifies whether each of the various phenomena are physical, demonstrable, and so forth. Likewise, it has the capacity for **overpowering** opponents' arguments with debates and the bases of debate, **and** it is also capable of **eliciting** the realization of the sūtras' meaning. Hence, **it is Abhidharma.**

The Vinaya is so called because it addresses the five classes of **downfalls;** the pathways for the **occurrence** of these downfalls; the **reemergence** from a downfall by means of reflection (that is, not by means of punishment); **and** the sevenfold process of **definitive emergence.** These seven are: (1) confession; (2) acceptance of punishment, as when generosity training is accepted in relation to the previous occurrence of an unconcealed downfall from the path; (3) relaxation of an otherwise prescribed training through a specified exception; (4) suspension, in the sense of a congregation of the Saṅgha suspending a point of training; (5) sex-change, which has implications for the unshared downfalls; (6) special realization of the features of the fourfold summary of the Dharma; and (7) the accomplishment of the intrinsic nature that, based on seeing the truths, renders even the most subtle of the subtle downfalls nonexistent. **As well as** the above, it addresses the four topics of (1) **the person** from whom one receives the trainings; (2) the Teacher's **formulation** of a certain training, subsequent to the Teacher having been informed about a given person's flaws and having hence called a gathering of the Saṅgha; (3) the **elaboration** of points of the training that have hitherto been formulated concisely; **and** (4) the precise **ascertainment** of what does and does not constitute a downfall.

The focal points are the teachings of the Buddha, the vessels of the Dharma. The term "vessel" comes from *piṭaka*. The teachings are designated in this way because many meanings to be known are contained within them. In Magadha, this term also refers to a large measuring vessel that can hold several smaller vessels within it. In a similar manner, these vessels contain the numerous expressed meanings that are to be understood. The vessels can be divided into three—Sūtra, Vinaya, and

Abhidharma—or otherwise into two—the Bodhisattva Vessel of the Great Vehicle and the Listener Vessel of the Lesser Vehicle. In terms of etymology, a "vessel" is referred to as such because it contains numerous meanings, as mentioned before.

There is also an expanded twelvefold division of the teachings, which has been taught as follows:

There are discourses, songs, prophecies, poetry, purposeful expressions, narrations, narratives, parables, past-life stories, elaborate teachings, marvels, and doctrinal discourses.

From among these, the fully elaborate teachings and the past-life stories belong to the Bodhisattva Vessel, while most of the rest are common to the listeners and the Great Vehicle. There are also some among these categories that belong predominantly to the Listener Vessel. All of the twelve are contained in the three vessels.

It is said that the framework of the three vessels is accepted for nine reasons—three based on what is rejected, three on what is to be trained in, and three on what is to be known. The first relates to dispelling the afflictions: the Sūtra vessel is the antidote that dispels the afflictions of those harboring doubt regarding the phenomena of the aggregates, elements, and sense sources. In showing exactly what are the general and particular characteristics of phenomena (that is, phenomena such as the aggregates, elements, sense sources, dependent arisings, the truths, the grounds, and the transcendences), the sūtras thereby dispel the doubts of those who suffer due to a lack of precise knowledge of the nature of those characteristics.

The Vinaya is the antidote that dispels the subsidiary afflictions that tie one to the two extremes—the extreme of desire and overindulgence on the one hand and the extreme of austerity and weariness on the other. It bans negative worldly behaviors in order to prevent one from acting as if one were a householder, frivolously engaging in negative actions while partaking of various possessions and enjoyments out of desire. Such actions are prohibited as defeating downfalls, downfalls, remainders, faults, and so on. Certain possessions, such as one's own begging bowl and Dharma robe, are not negative. Hence, these items are permitted.

Some extremists engage in severe ascetic practices. They lie in ashes or thorns, they fast or go naked, they practice the austerities of a dog or cow. In so doing, they bring suffering and hardship upon their bodies. As an antidote to this, all the material conditions that sustain the body and are not evil are permitted for all ordained individuals. On this point, it is said, "Disciplined and educated monks are permitted to enjoy foods with hundreds of tastes, clothes worth hundreds of thousands, and beautiful houses with many windows." These wonderful enjoyments can be enjoyed without negativity as long as one harbors no attachment to them, no conceit. Conversely, even if one eats rotten food and wears clothes from the trash, if one is attached and conceited about this, then such acts become negative. In this way the Vinaya is the antidote to the two extremes because one gives up negative material circumstances while still enjoying those that are not negative.

The Abhidharma is the antidote to the arrogance that can arise regarding one's view. The "arrogance of one's view" refers to when one studies just a little bit, becomes full of pride and attached to a faulty discipline, and then does not seek to study further with spiritual teachers. Through a decisive and correct understanding of the general and particular characteristics of the phenomena that are taught in the Abhidharma, the arrogance associated with the various distorted views and disciplines will be given up.

In terms of the trainings, with regard to the special training in discipline, there is the perfect discipline that pertains to individual liberation and is held in common with the Lesser Vehicle, and there is the [unique] discipline that pertains to the Great Vehicle. The latter category includes restraint from flawed actions, the gathering of virtuous qualities, and working to benefit sentient beings. As for the special training in attention, there are the eight meditative absorptions of the form and formless realms that the two vehicles hold in common, as well as the unique meditative absorptions such as the heroic gait of the bodhisattva. In terms of the special training in insight, there are the four noble truths that the two vehicles hold in common and the nonconceptual wakefulness of the Great Vehicle that is unique.

Sūtra teaches all three of the trainings. The Vinaya teaches the trainings of discipline and meditative absorption because if one acts according to the teachings of the Vinaya, one's discipline will be flawless. By being disciplined, without regrets and so on, one will progressively attain meditative absorption. The Abhidharma brings about a decisive understanding of the general and particular characteristics of phenomena, and it thereby produces an insight that consists of the authentic knowledge of the characteristics of phenomena.

In terms of what is to be known, it is said that the Sūtras present "Dharma teachings and their meanings." "Dharma teachings" refers to the presentation of both names and their meanings. "Dharma teachings" can also refer to the expositions of the aggregates, elements, sense sources, and so forth, whereas "meanings" refers to the four intentions and the four concealed intentions. Alternatively, "Dharma teachings" can be understood to refer to the ten virtues that cause one to achieve the higher realms and "meanings" to the thirty-seven factors of enlightenment and so forth that cause one to achieve the transcendence of suffering. It is further said that "the Vinaya allows one to accomplish Dharma teachings and meanings." That is because these two will be accomplished—actualized or practiced—through persevering in taming the afflictions. The Abhidharma presents Dharma teachings and meanings without error, thereby eliciting clear ascertainment and expertise.

One may wonder what the purpose is of investigating these three vessels. Well, one thoroughly investigates and gains experience in them by means of the three forms of insight. Through study, the imprints of the path of liberation are placed in one's stream of being. Reflection allows the meaning that has been studied to be realized, as one gains certainty. Finally, through meditation, distracting thoughts will be pacified within calm abiding, and one's mind stream will be liberated by the special insight that completely realizes the nature of things.

One may then wonder how many topics are presented in the three vessels, or what their etymology is. When summarized, the Sūtra, Abhidharma, and Vinaya are said to contain four topics. Wise bodhisattvas achieve omniscience by training in the path and knowing well the entirety of the three vessels of the Great and Lesser Vehicles. Listeners, on the other hand, do not seek omniscience. Lacking the knowledge of the three vessels, they attain the wakefulness that knows the nonarising and exhaustion of their own path. This they can attain by understanding the meaning of even a single verse that shows the mere selflessness of persons.

The four topics mentioned above are as follows:

(1) The basis, meaning a narrative foundation, or source of the sūtras. It is the "basis" in that it presents first, the place of exposition, such as Śrāvastī, second, the way the Blessed One spoke, and third, the beneficiaries of the exposition, such as those who requested the teaching.

(2) The characteristics of the two truths.

(3) The Dharma teachings of the aggregates, sense sources, and dependent arising.

(4) The meanings of these teachings, differentiated in terms of the intended meaning and the concealed meaning, and so on.

"Sūtras" are referred to as such in consideration of the fact that these four topics are taught concisely in the sūtras. "Sūtra" is a term that literally implies a guided teaching of all such meanings, carrying also the sense of a concise summary.

Abhi means manifest, and *abhimukha* means facing. The Abhidharma faces in the direction of the transcendence of suffering in that it enables one to gain unerring certainty in topics such as the truths, the factors of enlightenment, and dependent origination. Moreover, each of the teachings is clearly presented and repeatedly distinguished in a variety of categories such as form, the formless, the defiled, and the undefiled. Also, by means of reason, it completely overpowers objectors, entering into debates and presenting an elaborate discourse. It elicits realization and understanding through reason and through ascertainment of the meaning of the Sūtras. For these reasons, it is called "Abhidharma."

Vinaya is "that which tames." In this regard, there are five downfalls: (1) defeating downfalls, (2) partially defeating downfalls, (3) serious downfalls, (4) downfalls, and (5) offenses to be individually confessed. Alternatively, these five are (1) defeats, (2) remainders, (3) downfalls, (4) offenses to be individually confessed, and (5) faults. The cause of downfalls, or the reason that they arise, is fourfold—not knowing their characteristics, the afflictions, carelessness, and not respecting the trainings. Reform, or reemergence from downfalls, is effected by the mind, with remorse, and with the resolve never to fall into the given fault again.

There are seven aspects to emerging from downfalls, or to definitive emergence. (1) Individual confession, which is to confess by admitting the relevant fault in the presence of a specific number of monks, such as one or four.

(2) Acceptance of the punishment, which implies acting without concealing the defeat, and confessing, with remorse, what one has done. This also involves accepting a punitive course of action, such as sitting at the end of the line or being the last to get food and then subsequently retaking the precepts.

(3) Specified exemption, which involves, for instance, the specific permission to take food in the afternoon when travelling, even though the Blessed One has prohibited eating food after noon.

(4) Easing, which specifically refers to when the Blessed One spoke to Ānanda: "When I pass entirely beyond suffering, remember that the minor precepts among the bases of training should be eased." When the Buddha was about to pass away, Ānanda was overwhelmed with grief and did not ask him how this instruction was to be understood. Later, Mahākāśyapa and others among the compilers of the teachings asked him why he had not inquired further, and thus he was reproached. Sthiramati's great commentary explains that the Sarvāstivādins point to the declaration that "the minor precepts should be eased," and based on that, they teach that the minor precepts *can* be eased. Other than that, he explains, the Saṅgha has nevertheless not actually eased any of the precepts.

(5) Transformation, or sex-change. A monk has four defeating downfalls, while a nun has eight, and in this way there are different defeats and downfalls for monks and nuns. Hence, someone who goes from being a monk to a nun may, while still a monk, have sustained a downfall that is not common to both monks and nuns. Since such a downfall is only to be confessed by monks, it need not be removed through a ritual of confession and so forth, as it will be automatically relinquished by virtue of having become a nun. If a nun undergoes a sex-change, the same principles apply, mutatis mutandis.

(6) Relinquishment through authentic realization, which involves seeing, with insight, the meaning of the fourfold summary of the Dharma (that all conditioned things are impermanent and so on). Subtle faults are thereby expunged.

(7) Definitive emergence through attaining the intrinsic nature. By the power of the intrinsic nature, one's vision of the truths frees one from previous minor faults and precludes one's engagement in them in the future.

The "Vinaya" is classified as such in relation to these four issues. An alternative enumeration of the four issues considers, instead, the following:

(1) The persons in relation to whom the precepts have been formulated, such as Suddhodana in the case of the original prohibition of sex acts.

(2) The precepts themselves, as when, having been informed by the monks about a certain person's conduct, the Blessed One declared, "From now on such conduct is not permitted."

(3) The divisions of the precepts, as when a certain precept is given a detailed treatment, being subdivided into further categories.

(4) The ascertainment of the exact extent and character of the five classes of downfalls.

The preceding discussion has been concerned with the Dharma of scripture, which serves as the focal point.

2. The Meaning of the Teaching, the Discovery of the Focal Points

> The focal points are held to be the Dharma,
> The inner, the outer, and both.
> Through the two realities, the two are discovered,
> And through the absence of a focal point in terms of the two.
> [XII.5]

> With respect to the meaning taught, the expression of mind
>   becomes very bright,
> For it is clearly understood
> That whatsoever appears as meanings is due to expression,
> And the mind abides in names. [XII.6]

> With the three cognitions that result from listening and the
>   rest,
> The focal point of the Dharma is discovered.

The discovery of the three focal points
Depends entirely on what was just explained. [XII.7]

This section concerns the pursuit of the discovery of **the focal points**. The focal points **are held to be the Dharma** of the three vessels as follows: the constituents of **the inner** apprehender as contained in the physical body and its faculties, the sensations, the mind, and phenomena; the bodies and so forth that comprise **the outer** apprehended; **and** the suchness of **both** the apprehended and the apprehender. **Through the** absence of a focal point in terms of **two** distinct outer and inner **realities**, the focal points pertaining to **the two**, that is, the outer and the inner, **are discovered. And through the absence of a focal point in terms of the two** realities, the focal point of suchness is discovered.

The discovery of the focal point of the Dharma comes about through three types of cognition that arise from study, reflection, and meditation. When listening to the Dharma, one places the mind on the words of the Dharma in one-pointed equipoise. **With respect to the meaning,** just as it is **taught, the expression of mind,** that is, thought, **becomes very bright** as inspiration develops based on having gained certainty. **For,** through the cognition that is based on reflection, **it is clearly understood that whatsoever appears as meanings is** all **due to** the mind's **expression.** Hence, one comes to see that "these are nothing more than expressions of the mind!" **And,** with the cognition that arises through meditation, **the mind** then **abides in** the intrinsic nature of the four **names,** the vision that is the absence of a focal point in terms of the two types of self.

With the three cognitions that result from listening and the rest, the focal point of the Dharma is achieved. Therefore, **the discovery of the three focal points** that pertain to the outer, the inner, and suchness **depends entirely on what was just explained,** that is, the discovery of the focal point of the Dharma.

"The discovery of the focal point" refers to the focal point becoming directly perceptible. That is to say, having pursued the focal points of the Dharma teachings, one subsequently finds them and so clearly resolves their precise significance. The objects that are the focal points are fourfold:

(1) The features of the Dharma teachings that are contained in the vessels of the Great Vehicle and are the objects observed by the threefold insight of study, reflection, and meditation.

(2) The inner, meaning the aggregates that belong to one's own stream of being, or the six inner, apprehending sense sources.

(3) The outer, meaning the six outer, apprehended sense sources that are not comprised within one's stream of being;

(4) The factors that comprise both the inner and outer, meaning the phenomena of thorough affliction and complete purification.

Of these, through properly observing a twofold reality with regard to the entities of an outer apprehended and an inner apprehender, a twofold reality is discovered that does not observe any inner or outer entity. When the suchness of the outer is realized, the outer focal point is discovered, and when the suchness of the inner is directly known, the inner focal point is discovered.

Furthermore, when it is discovered that there is no apprehended object other than the mind, this is the time of acceptance. When it is discovered that there is no apprehender either, this is the supreme quality. When the suchness of both is discovered, exactly as it is, then no duality of apprehender-apprehended is observed. In this way, suchness is manifest with the attainment of the first ground. At that time, one discovers the focal points of both the outer and the inner, as well as the suchness that is the lack of any focal point with respect to all phenomena. At the time of heat and crown, or summit, the intrinsic nature has not been directly discovered, and hence it is taught that its focal point has at that time likewise not yet been discovered. However, it seems that by thinking in terms of a cognition that is free from doubt and takes place by means of an object universal, the latter focal point could still be considered as being discovered directly at that stage. Emptiness has no divisions, yet, out of dependence on the way in which it is realized by the subject, we may apply distinct conventions and so speak of the discovery of the focal points of the inner, outer, or both.

The way that the discovery of the focal point of the Dharma takes place is as follows. "The expression of mind" refers to the expression of the conceptual mind. With respect to the Dharma vessels of scripture, it is said that this expression "becomes very bright" as the mind finds faith and seizes on the meanings taught by scripture, just as they are. This is what is meant by the discovery of the focal point of Dharma through the insight that arises through receiving teachings.

That is to say, when the preceptors and masters teach the Dharma, one directs one's aural faculties and listens, placing one's attention on the meaning that is conveyed. For instance, when hearing a phrase of teaching such as "the nature of all these names, phrases, and letters is merely apparent to the mind," one knows this to be the case and holds it to be that way. Through the insight from contemplation, one discovers the focal point that is the clear understanding that while phenomena such as pillars and vases are merely imputations based on the habitual patterns of the expression of one's mind, their essential reality is inexpressible. Thus one comprehends that there are no objects beyond one's own concepts.

In the context of insight through meditation, the root text refers to mind by speaking of "names" as distinguished from "form," thereby implying the totality of mind and mental states. In short, all phenomena appear to the mind, are imputed by the mind, and are simply set forth by the power of the mind. There is no "other" apart from this, and thus all is mind only. This mind itself abides within suchness, within empty, luminous clarity, devoid of any of the focal points that are associated with the duality of apprehended and apprehender. Thereby, meditative insight allows one to discover the focal point of the Dharma.

In this way, the focal point of the Dharma of the vessels is discovered through the threefold insight that arises through study, contemplation, and meditation. First, one hears the words and understands the meanings of the expressions in one's mind. Next, one gains certainty by contemplating these meanings. Finally, by meditating, one gains the three experiences described above and so discovers the focal points of the meaning of the sacred Dharma. As was explained earlier, the discovery of these three focal points of the outer, inner, and both depends fully on the discovery of the observation of the Dharma. That is, if one studies the Dharma and contemplates its meaning but does not meditate, there is no way to realize the suchness that is the nonobservation of the phenomena of the outer, inner, and both.

3. Investigating the Way That the Mind Is Directed

Having discovered the focal points in this way, one should discover meditative absorption by directing the mind again and again. This is explained as follows:

> The three potentials; endeavors;
> Supported by the challenged and the unchallenged;
> That which induces motivation;
> That which engenders strong intention; [XII.8]
>
> The lesser and complete,
> With and without expression;
> Associated with cognition;
> Spiritual practice endowed with cause and nature; [XII.9]
>
> Observing integration
> And observing the distinct,
> Which are fivefold and sevenfold;
> Fivefold complete cognition; [XII.10]
>
> Features associated with meditation,
> Which are fourfold and thirty-seven;
> Of the nature of the twofold path;
> The twofold benefit; reception; [XII.11]
>
> Application; and mastery;
> The nature of the small and the vast—
> These ways that spiritual practitioners direct their minds
> Are held to constitute the nature of all. [XII.12]

Eighteen ways in which spiritual practitioners direct their minds are enumerated as follows:

(1) The distinct directing that is characteristic of those definitively possessing the **three potentials.**

(2) The directing that is associated with the **endeavors** that bring about the elimination of factors to be discarded in the context of realization.

(3) The two types of directing the mind that are specified with reference to their support, that is, that which is **supported by the challenged,** namely, householders, **and** supported by **the unchallenged,** that is, those who have fully emerged.

(4) **That** directing of the mind **which induces motivation** through the recollection of the qualities of the three jewels.

(5) **That** directing of the mind **which engenders strong intention** to accomplish the qualities of the jewels.

(6) The directing of the mind that is based on meditative absorption, that is, **the lesser and complete,** which pertains to the preparatory stages and the main parts.

(7) The directing of the mind **with and without expression,** as found respectively in the meditative absorptions that possess concept or discernment and the meditative absorptions that are free from both.

(8) The directing of the mind that is **associated with cognition,** referring to the **spiritual practice** of calm abiding and special insight that is **endowed with cause** (the insight arising through study and reflection) **and nature** (the insight arising from meditation).

(9) The directing of the mind that involves **observing integration,** that is, observing (1) one sūtra alone, (2) summarizing verses, (3) an outline, (4) the extent of one's own comprehension, and (5) the range that is to be explained to others, **and** the directing that involves **observing the distinct,** that is, the observations of (1) names, (2) phrases, (3) syllables, (4) the absence of a personal self, (5) the absence of a self in phenomena, (6) the material phenomena of the body, and (7) the immaterial phenomena of sensations and so forth, **which is,** then, **fivefold and sevenfold** in the way just indicated.

(10) The directing of the mind that is associated with **the fivefold complete cognition**—complete cognition in terms of (1) the basis

for complete cognition, which is suffering; (2) the meaning that is thoroughly cognized, which is impermanence, suffering, and so forth; (3) the complete cognition itself, which is the path; (4) the result of complete cognition, which is liberation; and (5) the full awareness of this liberation, the vision of liberated wakefulness.

(11) The directing of the mind that concerns **features** that are **associated with meditation, which are fourfold**—meditation, either as characterized by (1) features of the absence of a personal self, (2) features of the absence of a self in phenomena, (3) features of witnessing that absence on the path of seeing, and (4) features of cognition on the path of cultivation, or otherwise as characterized by the two types of acceptance and the two types of understanding—**and** also **thirty-seven:** the four applications of mindfulness, the four authentic eliminations, the four bases of miraculous power, the five faculties, the five powers, the seven aspects of enlightenment, and the eight aspects of the noble path.

(12) That directing of the mind that is enumerated in consideration of the fact that all these ways of directing the mind are **of the nature of the twofold path** of calm abiding and special insight, and as such are contained within that twofold path.

(13) The directing of the mind associated with **the twofold benefit**, that is, the benefits related to overcoming negative tendencies and to clearing away the marks associated with views.

(14) The directing of the mind associated with the **reception** of practical instructions based on having achieved the meditative absorption of the stream of Dharma.

(15) The directing of the mind in terms of the five **application**s that pertain to the sphere of meditative absorption, that is, the application associated with (1) knowledge of enumerations, which refers to the knowledge of the enumeration of names, phrases, and letters; (2) knowledge of the bases, which extends to the application of the finite set of fifty letters and the infinite extent of names and phrases; (3) knowledge of thorough conceptuality, whereby objects are understood based on names, and names are understood based on objects; (4) gradual understanding, which concerns a comprehension of objects that is preceded by the comprehension

of names; (5) realization, which itself contains eleven principles: (1) the realization of the adventitious nature of words and objects that occurs on the path of accumulation; (2) the realization of the mental nature of the reasons that are appearing objects that occurs on the stages of heat and summit; (3) the realization without any observation of apprehended objects that occurs at the stage of acceptance; (4) the realization that is devoid even of observation as such, which occurs with the supreme property; (5) the realization of the basic field of phenomena that occurs on the path of seeing. These five pertain to the stages of realization. In terms of what is realized, two principles are enumerated (6–7), namely, (6) the realization of the absence of a personal self and (7) the realization of the absence of a self in phenomena. In terms of the support (8–9), there are the realizations associated with the intent of (8) the Lesser Vehicle and (9) the Supreme Vehicle. Finally (10–11), two factors are enumerated in terms of the means that bring about realization: (10) authentic view, which brings about a realization of the principles of one's own realization, and (11) authentic realization, through which there is realization of the principles that pertain to the means for conveying that realization to others.

(16) Utter purity in the absence of the afflictive obscurations, utter purity in the absence of the cognitive obscurations, and utter purity in the application of **mastery** in terms of the accomplishment of qualities.

(17) **The nature of the small** benefit in relation to the Lesser Vehicle.

And, (18) **the vast** benefit in relation to the Great Vehicle.

These ways that spiritual practitioners direct their minds are held to constitute the nature of all ways that the mind can be directed.

There are eighteen ways in which spiritual practitioners direct their minds. Of these eighteen (the directing of the three potentials and the directing associated with endeavors and so forth), first there follows a short teaching with respect to the three potentials. The remaining enumerations then present an extensive explanation of the characteristics of the ways in which those possessing the three potentials direct their minds.

(1) "The three potentials" thus refers to the three potentials of listeners, self-realized buddhas, and bodhisattvas. Those who definitively possess the potential of the listeners direct their minds to the focal points of the Dharma of the four truths, while those who definitively possess the potential to become self-realized buddhas do so with respect to the observation of dependent origination, which is the Dharma of their particular path. Those who are of definitive bodhisattva potential direct their minds to the focal point of the twofold absence of self.

(2) The directing of the mind that is associated with endeavors is indicated by the term "endeavors," which in turn refers to working to gather the accumulations. The cause of attaining the first ground is the directing of the mind toward the accumulations of merit and wakefulness for an incalculable eon on the grounds of inspired conduct.

(3) The directing of the mind to the types of support, or context, is taught by the phrase "supported by the challenged and unchallenged." The challenged support, or context, refers to the context of being a householder. Due to their many worldly activities, the training of householders in directing the mind is challenged. Those who have fully emerged are just the opposite; they have a supportive context that is unchallenged.

(4) The directing of the mind that induces motivation is indicated by the phrase "inducing motivation." Motivation is induced by recollecting the Buddha. Thus one recollects (1) that the blessed buddhas have mastery over all phenomena with their superknowledge that is unobstructed throughout all world realms; (2) that the permanent body of the thus-gone ones is always immaculate; (3) that since they have relinquished all the afflictive and cognitive obscurations, the thus-gone ones are not subject to negativity; (4) that all deeds of the thus-gone ones are spontaneously accomplished and uninterrupted; (5) that the thus-gone ones have dominion over the great, undefiled enjoyments of the pure buddha fields and so forth; (6) that the thus-gone ones are untainted, unstained by the faults of the eight worldly concerns; (7) that through the methods of demonstrating manifest enlightenment and the transcendence of

suffering, the thus-gone ones ripen and liberate sentient beings and thus serve a tremendous purpose.

(5) The directing of the mind of intense aspiration is taught by the phrase "engendering strong intention." After recollecting the Buddha, one should engender a strong intention as one finds trust in the Buddha as the consummate refuge, free of all faults and replete with all good qualities, spontaneously accomplishing the twofold benefit, and endowed with the three bodies. One likewise develops trust in the authentic Dharma as the actualization of the path and the cessation; and in the spiritual community as those who have entered the authentic path, are crossing the swamp of cyclic existence, and are perfect recipients of offerings. Trusting in these points, one engenders a powerful intention.

(6) The directing of the mind to the domain of meditative absorption is taught by the phrase "the twofold lesser and complete support, with and without expression." The support is twofold because the transitional preparatory stage of the first concentration is a lesser support, whereas the support of the meditative absorption of the main part, from the first to the fourth concentration, is a complete support, or abode. The preparatory stage for the main part of the meditative absorptions and the ordinary main part of the first meditative absorption are said to be with expression because they involve both concept and discernment. They are classified as "with expression" because concept and discernment are the factors that motivate speech. The special main part of the first meditative absorption has discernment but no determination, yet it is nevertheless included in the category classified as "with expression." The meditative absorptions from the second concentration onward, on the other hand, are free from concept and discernment and are hence "without expression." In Sthiramati's commentary, it is said that the preparatory stage and the first concentration possess concept and discernment, that the second concentration and the intermediate concentration lack concept but possess discernment, and that the third and fourth meditative concentrations are without both concept and discernment.

(7) The directing of the mind that is associated with cognition is taught in the line "Associated with cognition, spiritual practice endowed with cause and nature." At this point, Sthiramati's commentary reads,

"Fully endowed with wakefulness, spiritual practice has the nature of the cause." Directing the mind associated with cognition is a mental activity that is associated with, or fully endowed with, wakefulness, or the cognition that arises from meditation. That cognition is itself of the nature of spiritual practice, or of calm abiding and special insight, and it is endowed with its cause, which is the nature of insight arising from study and reflection. In short, the directing of the mind that is associated with cognition is the spiritual practice of the meditation of calm abiding and special insight, arising from stainless causes in the form of study and reflection.

(8) The directing of the mind toward the focal point of integration is taught by the phrase "observing integration" and the term "fivefold." There are five aspects to directing the mind toward the focal points of integration: (1) observing integration within the sūtras, (2) observing integration within purposeful expressions or summarizing verses, (3) observing integration within the prologue, (4) observing integration within comprehension, and (5) observing integration within exposition. To elaborate, this refers to (1) directing the mind on a general summation of the meaning taught in the sūtras, such as the *Sūtra on the Ten Grounds*, (2) directing the mind to a summary of the meaning taught within each chapter, (3) observing a general structure by way of an outline (for instance, by way of prologue, scriptural meaning, and concluding summation), (4) condensing the subject matter that one has comprehended into concise points that are to be cultivated in meditation, and (5) explaining the subject matter to others by way of a similar concise presentation. In brief, this refers to the directing of the mind toward the meaning of the sūtras, their intermediate purposeful expressions or summarizing verses, and the summarizing prologue, and likewise to directing the mind by integrating the meanings of all that is studied and explained.

All of the meanings taught in the Great Vehicle sūtras are subsumed within the profound and the vast. In summary, observing integration with respect to the profound meaning is to comprehend, for instance, that the profound meaning is contained within the suchness free from the constructs of dualistic phenomena, such as apprehended and apprehender, and self and other. Likewise, it is to understand that this is always how it is, regardless of the amount of elaboration that may be used when accounting for the way things appear. As for the phenomena of the vast, one observes their integration by understanding them to comprise the ground, path, and fruition, and by further knowing the ground to be composed of the two truths, the path of the two accumulations, and the fruition of the two bodies.

(9) Observing difference, or the distinct, is taught by the phrase "observing the distinct" and later by the term "sevenfold." There are seven aspects to observing the distinct: (1) observing names, such as "pillar" and "pot"; (2) observing phrases, like "long pillar" or "new pot," which include qualifiers that are applied to names; (3) observing letters, like *a* and *ka,* which is the observation of the syllables that are the bases for the formation of words. One focuses on these, as a threefold division of the means of expression, for the sake of determining the complete set of phrases, names, and letters found in a given sūtra, along with their meanings. Yet, none of the treatises, whether mundane or transcendent, are beyond the nature of names, phrases, and letters. While they do reveal meanings, this occurs because of the mind's investing them with such referential power. Thus, knowing that all names, phrases, and letters come from the mind and are merely imputed by the mind is the gateway to the inexpressible.

As for the expressed meaning, in terms of the thoroughly established nature, it is the twofold observation of (4) the absence of a personal self and (5) the absence of a self in phenomena. In terms of the dependent nature, (6) those aspects of it that appear as something apprehended (that is, the phenomena that have physical form) are observed to be multiple and impermanent, and the body is observed to be unclean and a support for suffering. (7) The aspects that appear as something that apprehends (that is, the minds and mental states, which do not have physical form) are observed to be suffering and impermanent.

(10) The directing of the mind that is associated with ascertaining complete cognition is taught by the phrase "the fivefold complete cognition." The observation of this meditative absorption involves five forms of complete cognition. These five are: (1) the complete cognition of the basis, which is the four truths, (2) the complete cognition of the meaning, which is impermanence and the rest of the sixteen aspects, (3) the complete means of cognition, which comprise the two paths of seeing

and cultivation, (4) the result of complete cognition, which is liberation, and (5) full awareness of that liberation, which is the wakefulness that beholds liberation.

Furthermore, by observing the bases, which are the five appropriating aggregates, one understands them to be of the nature of suffering, impermanence, no-self, and emptiness. The full understanding of this is achieved by means of the eight aspects of a noble one's path, as these occur on the paths of seeing and cultivation. These paths result in the relinquishment of the afflictions and, thereby, the mind is liberated. With this liberation comes the vision of wakefulness. Thus, this cognition is in fact the complete knowledge of the four truths.

(11) The directing of the mind that concerns features associated with meditation is shown by the phrase "features associated with meditation, which are fourfold and thirty-seven." The four features that meditations possess, or are endowed with, are as follows: (1) the feature of the absence of a personal self; (2) the feature of the absence of a self in phenomena; (3) the feature of seeing; (4) the feature of cognition. As for the first, meditating with the understanding that the five aggregates have the four qualities of impermanence and so forth is a meditation that even the listeners engage in. Concerning the second, meditating on the fact that all phenomena lack intrinsic nature is the meditation of the bodhisattvas. Regarding the third, "seeing" refers to witnessing the eight acceptances within the sixteen moments of wakefulness. As for the fourth, "cognition" includes the features of the eight cognitions within those sixteen moments. Alternatively, "seeing" can also refer to calm abiding, and "cognition" to special insight.

The thirty-seven features of meditation are the thirty-seven factors that accord with enlightenment. Of these, the four applications of mindfulness involve being aware of the impurity of the body, the pain of sensation, the impermanence of mind, and the absence of self in all phenomena. The first authentic elimination is to meditate with the feature of full attainment, meaning to develop those aspects of the three special trainings that have not yet arisen. The second authentic elimination is to meditate with the feature of stability, and so to expand and further increase the qualities of the three trainings that have already arisen. The third authentic elimination is to meditate with the feature of removal, in the sense that one strives to relinquish what has arisen in terms of factors that conflict with the three trainings. The fourth authentic elimination is to meditate with the feature of the antidote. That is to say, one meditates on repulsiveness, love, and interdependence to ensure that whatever negativity and nonvirtue that has so far not arisen will not do so in the future either.

Next are the four bases of miraculous power: intention, which is directing the mind toward the antidote to complacency; diligence, which is directing the mind toward the antidote to distraction and doubt; attention, which is directing the mind toward the antidote to agitation by taking firm hold of the mind; and discernment, which is the antidote to dullness and faintheartedness.

As for the five faculties, faith is the directing of the mind by way of trust; diligence takes the form of striving; mindfulness is characterized by absence of forgetfulness; meditative absorption expresses itself as abiding mind; and insight manifests as discernment. The five powers consist in directing the mind in a way that destroys the factors that conflict with the five faculties.

Concerning the seven aspects of the path of enlightenment, enlightenment is the nature of the wakefulness that is aware of exhaustion and nonarising, while mindfulness and the rest of the seven are the aspects of enlightenment. Alternatively, enlightenment can be described as the nondual wakefulness through which one attains the path of seeing; the seven factors of mindfulness and so on are then its aspects. These seven, also described as the "training in the complete illumination of enlightenment," consist of the following seven aspects: mindfulness, which is absence of forgetfulness; full discernment of phenomena, which means knowing them without error; diligence that delights in virtue; joy that has the nature of a delighted mind; agility in the sense of flexibility; equanimity that abides evenly; and the meditative equipoise of the resting mind.

Regarding the eightfold noble path, authentic view is known as "training with the feature of freedom from doubt." The basic field of phenomena has been realized free from doubt, or with certainty, on the first ground. One then trains in this very realization, again and again, on the path of cultivation. Authentic thought is called "training with the feature of understanding the ground of complete purification." Study, reflection, and meditation progressively develop through the grounds of inspired conduct, and the basic field of phenomena is thereby directly realized on the first ground. This is called the "ground of complete purity." Arising from meditative equipoise, one subsequently understands that through complete purification one has realized the basic field of phenomena, just as it is.

Authentic speech is known as "training with the feature that brings others to authentic awareness." Authentic activity is "training with the feature of entering the discipline of those who aspire to become noble ones." This is the discipline that delights the noble ones. Authentic livelihood is "training with the feature of living in moderation," with few possessions and rejecting any corrupt means of sustenance. Authentic effort is "training with the feature of being accustomed in the path of attainment due to previous training." As a result of having trained from the stages of inspired conduct up to the first ground, one achieves exceptional diligence on the first ground, and as one continues the training throughout the ten grounds, this diligence is distinguished even further.

Authentic mindfulness is "training with the feature of not forgetting the marks of abiding in the Dharma." The "Dharma" here refers to the basic field of phenomena. As one abides one-pointedly within this, dullness or agitation may occur, yet they can be dispelled through the three marks that serve as remedies. The training in authentic mindfulness has the feature of not forgetting these three marks—that of abiding calmly, of fully seizing or uplifting, and of equanimity. Meditating on the mark of calmly abiding pacifies agitation. Meditating on the mark of uplifting pacifies feelings of dullness and lethargy by fully seizing. Finally, when there is neither slackness nor agitation, one brings to mind equanimity and lets the mind be natural without wavering.

Authentic meditative absorption is "training with the feature of the transformation of the meditation that is free from marks." Without dullness or agitation, one no longer requires any of the three marks, thus attaining the compassion that is characterized by one's meditation having been effortlessly transformed.

(12) The directing of the mind to the nature of the twofold path is taught by the phrase "being of the nature of the twofold path." This med-

itation has the nature of the twofold path of calm abiding and special insight. Based on the nondistraction of calm abiding, the objects of the special insight that fully discerns phenomena will be realized just as they are.

(13) The directing of the mind to goodness or benefit is shown by the phrase "the twofold benefit." This form of directing the mind is divided in terms of two beneficial features: it dispels negative tendencies, and it dispels wrong views. There are also two types of negative tendencies: (1) those of body—performing unvirtuous deeds such as killing, taking what is not given, sexual misconduct, and lying; and (2) those of mind—stirring the mind with the causes of unvirtuous actions, which are attachment, anger, and bewilderment.

These negative tendencies can be dispelled by directing the mind to the lack of a self in phenomena and by comprehending this absence. By comprehending the lack of a personal self, the five views will be dispelled. These five are the view of the transient collection, extreme view, wrong view, the view of holding one's own view as supreme, and the view of holding one's discipline as supreme.

(14) The directing of the mind to the authentic reception of the teachings of practical instructions is taught with the word "reception." By generating the enlightened mind, those who possess the potential for the Great Vehicle attain the meditative absorption of the stream of Dharma on the grounds of inspired conduct. From the buddhas and bodhisattvas, they thus receive the practical instructions on the meditative absorption for attaining the first ground, and they subsequently retain those instructions. This is the directing of the mind to authentic reception.

(15) The directing of the mind to application is taught with the word "application." The result of receiving practical instructions is to apply them on the path. There are five forms of application: Once one has received, within the sphere of meditative absorption, practical instructions that belong to the sūtras or another one of the twelve sections of scripture, one trains in (1) the application of understanding numbers, which concerns the knowledge of the numbers of names, phrases, and letters, as well as the numbers of ślokas and the like that are contained in the particular instruction. This is combined with (2) the application

of understanding the features of the bases or extents, which concerns the character of the means of expression, that is, the names, phrases, and letters. Letters are the root or origin of all names and phrases. Since there are only fifty of them in the alphabet, letters are understood to be finite. Names and phrases, however, are understood to be infinite, as there is an abundance of them in scriptures such as the *Sūtra on Transcendent Insight in One Hundred Thousand Lines,* and there are hundreds of thousands of sūtras. Hence, the bases or extents are limitless. Further, there is (3) the application of understanding through conceptuality. This concerns the way a person or a mental activity may concern itself with a name such as "pot," for instance, and its referent, which in this case would be a bulbous vessel that holds water. The name and its referent are related such that, having received practical instruction or something similar, one may think that "this is the name of that" or "that is what this refers to." Based on the linguistic-universal that is associated with the name, the features of the actual object appear to the mind. By conceiving of that which appears to the mind as if it were the actual object, the name comes to imply its referent. Thus one conceives of the referent. Similarly, when seeing the actual object, one applies the name to the object universal, and so one conceives of the name by thinking that it belongs to the object. (4) The application of gradual understanding concerns the way the designation of various names, such as "pot," "cloth," "person," and "horse," becomes customary in the world. When these names are expressed accurately and in the proper sequence, they appear to the mind in a way that allows one to conceive of the relevant meaning. Thus, one realizes meanings based on names that appear in the mind. The application of the understanding of numbers and the aforementioned other three applications of understanding are all means for discovering the focal points of the Dharma on the path of accumulation.

(5) The application of full realization occurs on the path of joining and beyond. This application involves eleven principles, and the realization of these principles is thus called "the application of full realization." These eleven include four principles that pertain to the path of joining, one that pertains to the path of seeing, and a further division of six: two that pertain to what is realized, two that pertain to the supreme and

the inferior, and two that pertain to a division within the subsequent attainment.

Of the four principles that pertain to the path of joining, the first has to do with the stage of heat. While there is no essential relationship between names and objects, names are associated with objects, and objects are associated with names. Thus the notions of "the name" and "the meaning of the name" are simply the result of mental imputation. This understanding as it occurs on the stage of heat is known as "fully realizing that names and objects are adventitious." At the stage of summit, one realizes that there is no essence of an apprehended or an apprehender in the phenomena that otherwise appear in a dualistic manner—as if there really were an apprehended and an apprehender. Phenomena are fully realized as mere marks that manifest, or appear, that way, as if real, due to the dependent nature, that is, the mind and mental states. As one thus realizes them to be, for example, like the double moon that appears when one applies pressure on the eyeballs, this is known as "fully realizing the marks of appearance." "Mark" refers here to the cause of appearance, and the term thus indicates that at this stage one comprehends that the mind is the cause of appearance.

At the stage of acceptance, one does not conceive of the six objects, or six bases, (from form to phenomena) and instead one fully realizes the absence of focal points in terms of an apprehended. This is known as "fully realizing the absence of objective focal points." At the stage of the supreme quality, one understands that there is no nature to the six collections of consciousness that apprehend and observe the six objects. Thus this is "fully realizing that the observed is not observed." Subsequent to this realization of the absence of any focal points in terms of the duality of apprehended and apprehender, one attains the path of seeing and so realizes the intrinsic nature that is free from the duality of apprehended and apprehender, the omnipresent basic field of phenomena. This is "fully realizing the basic field of phenomena."

That which the listeners realize on their path of seeing is the lack of a personal self. They directly realize the mere absence of a personal self in relation to the five aggregates and thereby achieve the fruition of a stream enterer. Bodhisattvas realize not only the absence of a personal self on their path of seeing but also perceive the five aggregates to be illusion-like and devoid of nature. Thus, they fully realize the lack of self in phenomena. The full realization with small intent concerns that of the listeners' four fruitions (of stream enterer and so forth) and that of the self-realized buddhas. This is because these individuals are concerned merely with their own welfare and do not realize the absence of self in phenomena. The full realization of the intent of great beings, which is vast, concerns that of the bodhisattvas on the ten grounds and that of the thus-gone ones. This is because these great beings act for the welfare of themselves and others and completely realize the twofold selflessness.

"Fully realizing the array of comprehended qualities" concerns the realization of the array of the twelve times one hundred qualities, such as beholding the faces of a hundred buddhas in a single instant. These qualities are attained on the first ground, due to the realization of the basic field of phenomena as it occurs on the path of seeing. This is also realization by means of the authentic view.

"Fully realizing the array of qualities" concerns the realization in which one comprehends the further expanding array of the twelvefold qualities, from a hundred to a thousand and so forth. This occurs as particular qualities of realization in the process of cultivation from the second ground up to the tenth. Thus, this is the authentic realization of those who are on the path of cultivation. According to Tibetan commentaries, these last six correspond solely to the path of cultivation, but it is hard to see how this can be reconciled with Vasubandhu's and Sthiramati's viewpoint.

(16) The directing of the mind to mastery is taught with the word "mastery." Here there are three types: (1) directing the mind to mastery in the purity of the absence of afflictive obscurations, (2) directing the mind to mastery in the purity of the absence of both the afflictive and the cognitive obscurations, and (3) directing the mind to mastery in the accomplishment of the distinctive qualities. As for the first, attachment and other such afflictions obstruct liberation and the transcendence of suffering. Thus, in realizing the absence of a personal self, these afflictions are relinquished through the paths of seeing and cultivation and do not arise again. This, in itself, is also achieved by the listeners. Concerning

the second, the cognitive obscurations, which consist of the concepts that ascribe true nature to dualistic phenomena, obstruct the wakefulness of omniscience. By the path of the Great Vehicle, one eliminates both afflictive and cognitive obscurations so that they do not arise again. Finally, as one relinquishes that which obstructs the attainment of the special qualities—such as the six superknowledges, the powers, and fearlessnesses—and thus accomplishes these qualities, one gains mastery in the utter purity of the full accomplishment of excellent qualities.

(17–18) The last two of the eighteen ways of directing the mind are (17) directing the mind to the listener's path of the Lesser Vehicle and (18) directing the mind to the bodhisattva's vast path of the Great Vehicle.

These eighteen ways in which spiritual practitioners direct their minds are held to comprise all possible ways of directing the mind within the entirety of the Great and Lesser Vehicles.

2. The Actual Dharma That Is to Be Realized

This section has eleven parts: (1) the investigation of reality, (2) the investigation of the illusion-like, (3) the investigation of objects of cognition, (4) the investigation of thorough affliction and complete purification, (5) the investigation of mere cognition, (6) the investigation of characteristics, (7) the investigation of liberation, (8) the investigation of essencelessness, (9) the investigation of the acceptance of nonarising phenomena, (10) the investigation of the intent of teaching a single vehicle, and (11) the investigation of the five fields of knowledge.

1. The Investigation of Reality

> Always free from duality, the support for delusion,
> And the natural, entirely beyond expression and mental
>   construction—such is reality.
> Considered what is to be understood, eliminated, and the
>   stainless nature, this is to be purified.
> Like the sky, gold, and water, this is held to be pure, free from
>   afflictions. [XII.13]

In wandering beings there is nothing but that,
Yet in their delusion about this, all beings without exception
Abandon the existent and become attached to the nonexistent.
What is this dense delusion of the world?! [XII.14]

The following explanation concerns the investigation of reality. The imaginary is **always free from** the **duality** of apprehended and apprehender, while the dependent is **the support for delusion, and the natural is entirely beyond expression and mental construction. Such is reality.** The first is **considered** as **what is to be understood,** the second what is to be **eliminated,** and the third is held to be **the stainless nature.** Thus, **this is to be purified** of the adventitious stains. **Like the sky, gold, and water, this** natural purity **is held to be pure, free from afflictions.**

In wandering beings there is nothing but that, the characteristics of the basic field of phenomena, **and yet, in their delusion about this** intrinsic nature, **all beings without exception abandon the existent** intrinsic nature **and become attached to the nonexistent** apprehended and apprehender. **What is this dense delusion of the world?!**

The investigation of the reality of the phenomena of thorough affliction and complete liberation is known by means of the three natures: the imaginary, the dependent, and the thoroughly established. The imaginary nature is characterized by the appearance of a duality of apprehended and apprehender, where there is none. The dependent nature serves as the support or basis for the delusion of this dualistic appearance of apprehended and apprehender, while in fact there is no such duality. The nature that can never be expressed in words and is free from conceptual constructs is the thoroughly established. This is reality, the abiding condition of all phenomena. It is the unconstructed nature free from dualistic phenomena that is to be realized in one's own direct awareness.

In this way, the imaginary nature should be known not to exist, just as a snake does not exist in a rope. The impure dependent nature should be eliminated, meaning that the appearances of duality that exist within the dependent nature are to be eliminated. As for the adventitious stains within the thoroughly established nature, which itself is held to be naturally stainless, these are to be eliminated. The natural stainlessness of the thoroughly established nature refers to its essence. Like the natural purity of the sky and of gold, and like the natural clarity of water, it contains in its essence from the beginning no impurity. Yet, just as clouds can appear in the sky, mud can cover gold, and dirt can be present in water, there are adventitious afflictions that obscure the thoroughly established nature, in which case it is not manifest. When it is free from afflictions, its utter purity is manifest.

If we consider this in terms of the way things ultimately are, there is nothing but the thoroughly established nature within the constitution of wandering beings (that is, within the subjects who are the bearers of the intrinsic nature). Yet, while everything indeed abides as the identity of the intrinsic nature, beings in the three realms do not realize this. Completely deluded concerning this reality, they are instead attached to dualistic phenomena. As a result, they completely abandon their own thoroughly established, fundamental nature and become instead attached to that which is nonexistent and imaginary. Now, what is this deep and dense delusion of the world?

2. The Investigation of the Illusion-like

The false imagination is explained
To be like a magical illusion.
The delusion of duality is explained
To be like the features of an illusion. [XII.15]

Just as those are not there,
So the ultimate is asserted.
Just as those are observed,
So the relative is asserted. [XII.16]

When that is not there,
Its causes are clearly perceived.

Likewise, upon fundamental transformation,
The false imagination is perceived. [XII.17]

Just as mundane individuals, free from delusion,
Act as they please with respect to its causes,
So do those who persevere in the vows and are free from delusion
Partake with delight in the fundamental transformation. [XII.18]

There are such features there,
Yet there are no such things.
With regard to illusions and so forth,
This is the way existence and nonexistence are explained. [XII.19]

Within that, the present is not nonexistent,
And the absent is not existent.
With respect to illusions and the like, it is also explained
That existence and nonexistence are not different. [XII.20]

Likewise, appearances of duality are there,
But entities are not.
Hence, with respect to form and so forth,
There is both existence and nonexistence. [XII.21]

Within that, the present is not nonexistent,
And the absent is not existent.
With respect to form and so forth, it is also explained
That existence and nonexistence are not different. [XII.22]

Assertions are for the sake of negating
The extremes of exaggeration and denigration
And for the sake of preventing
The journey by means of the Inferior Vehicle. [XII.23]

The causes of delusion and delusion
Are held to be awareness of form
And awareness without form.
When one does not exist, the other does not either. [XII.24]

Apprehending the form of an illusory elephant
Is a delusion with reference to which one speaks of duality.
There is no actual duality there,
And yet a duality is observed. [XII.25]

Apprehending the form of a skeleton
Is a delusion with reference to which one speaks of duality.
There is no actual duality there,
And yet a duality is observed. [XII.26]

The phenomena that characterize delusion
Are, in that same way, existent and nonexistent.
Because existence and nonexistence are thus not different,
Existence and nonexistence are like an illusion. [XII.27]

The phenomena that constitute the remedy
Are, in that same way, not existent, existent, and not existent.
Therefore, the characteristics are taught
To be nonexistent and like an illusion. [XII.28]

An illusory king may be defeated
By another illusory king.
In that way, those children of the victorious ones
Who see phenomena have no pride. [XII.29]

The supreme and perfectly awakened buddhas teach again and again
That conditioned things should be understood to resemble illusions, dreams, mirages, reflections,
Optical illusions, echoes, the moon's reflections in water, and emanations.

Respectively, these are asserted with reference to the six, the six, the two, the six, the two sets of six, and the three. [XII.30]

The next teaching considers the investigation of the illusion-like reality. **The false imagination is,** as the dependent nature, **explained to be like** a stick, a dirt clod, or some other thing that has been subjected to a spell, thereby creating **a magical illusion**. **The delusion of** the **duality** of apprehended and apprehender **is asserted to be like the features of** the horses, elephants, and other things in **an illusion.**

Just as those horses and so on **are not there** within the illusion, so **the ultimate is explained** in terms of the absence of the imaginary characteristics of duality within the dependent nature. **Just as those** illusions of elephants and so forth **are observed, so the relative** existence of the imaginary nature **is asserted.**

When that illusion **is not there,** the nature of **its causes**—sticks and the like—**are clearly perceived. Likewise, upon fundamental transformation, the false imagination is** fully **perceived** in the absence of dualistic delusions.

Just as mundane individuals who are **free from delusion act** freely and **as they please with respect to** sticks and **its other causes, so do those** noble individuals **who persevere in the vows and are free from delusion partake** freely and **with delight in the fundamental transformation.**

There are such features of horses, elephants, and the like **there,** meaning where the stick and so forth is, **yet there are no such things** as horses and so forth. **With regard to illusions and so forth, this is the way** that the **existence** of their appearances **and the nonexistence** of the things they seem to be **are explained.**

Within that, the present appearance of a horse or an elephant **is not nonexistent, and yet the absent** entity, such as an elephant, **is not existent. With respect to illusions and the like, it is, therefore, also explained that existence and nonexistence are not different. Likewise, the appearances of duality are there** within the false imagination, **but** dualistic **entities are not. Hence, with re-**

spect to form and so forth, there is both an **existence** of appearances of duality **and** a **nonexistence** of any dualistic entities.

Within that, the present appearance of duality **is not nonexistent and** yet **the absent** dualistic entity **is not existent. With respect to form and the like, it is also explained that existence and nonexistence are not different** because the very existence of the appearance of duality does not exist in terms of actual dualistic entities.

One may wonder what the purpose is of speaking in terms of existence and nonexistence. These **assertions are** made **for the sake of negating the extremes of exaggeration,** as one knows the nonexistent to be nonexistent, **and denigration,** as the existent is seen to be existent; **and,** as one understands that there is no difference between existence and nonexistence, the assertions are also made **for the sake of preventing** the disenchantment that would lead one into **the journey by means of** the path of **the inferior vehicle.**

The causes of the **delusion** pertaining, for example, to blue and other such forms, **and** the **delusion** that pertains to forms like visual cognition, **are held to be,** respectively, **awareness of form and awareness without form. When one,** namely, the awareness of form, **does not exist, the other,** that is, the awareness without any form, **does not either** because its cause is then missing.

Apprehending the form of an illusory elephant is a delusion with reference to which one speaks of a duality of apprehended and apprehender. Contrary to the appearance, however, **there is no actual duality** of apprehended and apprehender **there, and yet a duality** of apprehended and apprehender **is observed.**

Likewise, **apprehending the form of a skeleton is a delusion with reference to which one speaks of a duality.** Yet, in this case as well, **there is,** contrary to the appearance, **no actual duality** of apprehended and apprehender **there, and yet a duality** of apprehended and apprehender **is observed.**

The phenomena that characterize delusion and that are, in essence, conflicting factors **are, in that same way, existent** as precisely false imagination **and nonexistent** in terms of an apprehended and an apprehender. **Because existence and nonexistence are**

thus not different, existence is not the case and nonexistence is not the case either. The characteristics are all like an illusion.

The phenomena that constitute the remedy, such as the applications of mindfulness, are, in that same way, not existent as apprehended by the immature, yet existent as taught by the Buddha; and, with respect to the Buddha's displaying the twelve deeds, they are not existent in the way they appear to the immature. Therefore, the characteristics are taught to be nonexistent and like an illusion.

For example, an illusory king may be defeated by another illusory king. In that way, those children of the victorious ones who see all the phenomena that constitute the discards and their remedies have no pride based on either of these.

The blessed ones, who are supreme among beings and who are perfectly awakened buddhas within the equality of all phenomena, teach again and again in the various sūtras that conditioned things are comparable to illusions and so forth. Such things should be understood to resemble illusions, dreams, mirages, reflections, optical illusions, echoes, the moon's reflections in water, and emanations. Respectively, these are asserted with reference to the six inner sense sources, which appear as a self, a living being, and so forth, although they do not exist as such; the six outer sense sources, which, although not real, appear to be encountered entities; the two, (that is, mind and mental states), since they are the basis for delusion; the two sets of six, that is, the six inner sense sources, because they are the reflections of past actions; and the six outer sense sources, because they are like a shadow of the inner sense sources; and the three that consist of the Dharmas that are taught, the qualities that are supported by meditative absorption, and the wholehearted acceptance of birth within existence in accordance with one's wishes.

While not existent in reality, all the phenomena of dualistic appearance lack intrinsic nature due to the fact that they exist merely in experience, just like illusions and other such examples. Using such things as pebbles, magicians conjure up illusory appearances like horses and elephants, through the power of a mantra. Likewise, the cause of dualistic appearances is the false imagination, which is explained as being the dependent nature, that is, the mind and mental states that appear as the apprehended and apprehender. The features of the illusory appearances of horses, elephants, and so forth (such as their bodies, limbs, and colors), appear as if they were real entities. It is the same with the delusion of the duality of an apprehended and apprehender that constitutes the imaginary nature. Although they do not exist, there is nevertheless the delusional perception of an apprehended and an apprehender. The delusional appearances of this dualistic nature are the imaginary, which can be likened to the mistaken perception of a rope as if it were a snake.

Just as there are no horses or elephants in the pebbles and sticks that the magician uses to conjure them, there has never been any duality within the intrinsic nature, which is the ultimate, the abiding reality. Since this is the undistorted nature of all phenomena, it is called the "thoroughly established." The way that all dualistic appearances are held to be relative can be understood by considering the way the magician's substances are observed to be horses, elephants, and so on, through the power of mantra. When the experience as tainted by the illusionist's mantra no longer occurs, and when the deluded perceptions of horses, elephants, and so forth, are hence no longer there, then the pebbles and sticks that cause these perceptions are clearly observed. In the same way that horses and elephants are then no longer perceived, when dualistic habitual tendencies have been eliminated and the all-ground consciousness has been transformed, duality is no longer observed. Rather, the reality of the thoroughly established is then observed by the wakefulness of meditative equipoise. Just as the pebbles and sticks are seen, in the wakefulness of the subsequent attainment, the false imagination (the dependent nature itself) that causes these dualistic appearances is observed, and the three realms are realized to be mind only.

Worldly beings whose vision has not been altered by the magician's substances and mantras do not perceive the illusory horses and elephants, and they are hence not subject to delusion. They can therefore act as they please with respect to the simple pebbles and sticks. Likewise, those who persevere in the vows and are without delusion—those who have attained the path that is the remedy to delusion—have transformed the deluded perceptions of dualistic fixation. They partake with delight in the pure dependent nature, meaning that since they see it to be like an illusion, they act freely without fixation, fear, and so on.

The mere appearances of the features of the illusory horses, elephants, and so forth, are present in relation to their causes, such as pebbles or sticks. Yet no actual entities of horses and elephants are present at all. In this way, since the appearances are there, as in dreams, they cannot be said to be nonexistent. On the other hand, such things *can* be said not to be existent when considering the fact that they are not there in the way they seem to be. Thus they cannot be said to be existent, either.

One may then think that since it is not possible for something to be both existent and nonexistent, or neither existent nor nonexistent, we must certainly assert either one of these options. However, the appearance of an illusion exists as a mere appearance. Hence, it is not nonexistent. If it were nonexistent, then no horse, elephant, and so forth, would appear and there would then be no basis for classifying the illusion as false. Yet, the entities that appear to be there are nonexistent. They never existed, because if they did, they could not be proven to be false; they would be actual horses and elephants. Therefore, when considering, for example, the appearance of an illusion, we must conclude that, with reference to this single basis, there is no difference between existence and nonexistence. Existence and nonexistence are not contradictory in this case. Rather, this is appearance and emptiness combined.

Likewise, the mere appearance of duality exists within the dependent, yet the entities that appear in this way do not exist as a real duality. Thus, external forms and sounds and so on merely exist as appearances, yet it is taught that they do not exist in the way that they appear. Why? Because their mere appearance, as such, is not nonexistent, whereas the objects, such as forms, that appear to be there have in fact never existed—just as in the case of the appearance of a double moon. Therefore, with respect to forms and so on, neither existence nor nonexistence is predominant. As just explained, they are joined without any difference between them. Thus they are held to resemble the examples of illusions.

This teaching of indistinguishable existence and nonexistence—existence in terms of the presence of mere appearance and nonexistence in terms of the absence of that which appears to be there—is the path of the Middle Way because it refutes the extremes of exaggerating the imaginary as if it were existent and denigrating the dependent nature, which is the basis for appearance, as if it were nonexistent. Thus *Distinguishing the Middle from Extremes* also teaches: "The false imagination exists. In it, the two do not exist. . . . This is the path of the Middle Way."

When this is realized, dualistic phenomena may appear, yet they will be known to have no nature, like the appearances in a dream. As a result, there is no fear of cyclic existence nor any attachment to the transcendence of suffering. Therefore, this realization also prevents beings from entering the extreme of peace by fleeing toward the peace of transcendence—having pursued it through the Lesser Vehicle, out of fear for the suffering of cyclic existence. Thus, this path is asserted to be free from the two extremes.

While there is no duality, the cause of the delusion of duality and the delusion itself are asserted to be the awareness of form and awareness without form. The cause of delusion is the awareness that arises with the features of the five faculties and five objects, the forms that appear as if they were separate from mind. In a dream, forms such as horses, elephants, and women appear to be accessible to one's senses, but they are actually one's own cognition appearing in the form of an apprehended entity. However, when this is not understood, the apprehended entities are believed to be separate from cognition and thus the appearances of external objects serve as the causes of delusion. The essence of delusion is awareness without form. It consists of the six collections of consciousness (such as the eye consciousness) that apprehend a duality of apprehended and apprehender.

In this way, while the delusion of duality does occur, there is no apprehended object separate from an apprehender. Thus, without the other part in the dichotomy, the apprehender cannot exist either. These two are established in dependence on one another: without one the other cannot be there either. In reality, the case is therefore emptiness—devoid of anything apprehended and anything that apprehends.

One may wonder: "Since in this way there is no physical faculty of the eye and so on, and no physical object, there are no causes for sense cognition. Hence such consciousness could not reasonably arise. Nevertheless, the apprehended and apprehender undeniably appear. How can this be?"

Two examples show how it is reasonable that duality appears, even while there is no duality. The first example is accepted by the world and the second by the treatises.

The first example is this: When an illusory elephant is seen, since the consciousness apprehends an appearance of what is not in fact an object, this appearance is a delusion. From the deluded perspective, there is said to be both the apprehended form of the elephant and the consciousness that apprehends it. Both what is apprehended and the apprehender, however, do not exist in the way they are apprehended. From the perspective of the world, it is merely the deluded mind's observation of the two that exists.

The second example, taken from the treatises, is this: When spiritual practitioners who meditate on repulsiveness accomplish clear appearance, they directly perceive skeletons while in fact there are none. This perception is a delusion, and thus one merely speaks of an apprehended object and an apprehender. For the apprehender of the appearance of the skeletons, there is, despite the appearance, no actual apprehended object that is distinct from that which apprehends it. Nevertheless, the mental states that observe the two—apprehended and apprehender—undoubtedly exist.

As is the case with these examples, while the appearances of thorough affliction and complete purification within the dependent do not exist as an established duality, it is taught that they exist as mere dualistic appearances. Therefore, the conflicting factors of thorough affliction and the phenomena characterized by delusion—all that is comprised within karma, the afflictions, and the former's ripening—merely exist as deluded perceptions, as in the case of the aforementioned examples, and they do not exist as conceived by immature beings. There is, therefore, no difference between existence and nonexistence. Existence and nonexistence are not in conflict. To exist as mere appearance while not actually existing is to be like an illusion.

The phenomena that function as remedies—the Dharma that is explained in the sūtras and so forth, as well as the applications of mindfulness, the transcendences, and so forth, that constitute the path, along with the powers and so forth that are the qualities of fruition—all of these do not exist in the dualistic manner that immature beings imagine. Yet they do exist as mere appearances. Since they appear, but do not exist as they appear, they are devoid of essence or characteristics, and it is therefore taught that they are like illusions. The *Transcendent Insight* teaches: "All phenomena are like an illusion and a dream. Even the transcendence of suffering is like an illusion and a dream."

One may wonder: "If the factors of thorough affliction are like an illusion, and if that is also the case with the factors of complete purification, then how can illusion-like factors of complete purification eliminate illusion-like factors of thorough affliction?"

A magician may conjure a show where a weak illusory king and his retinue are defeated and banished by another, more powerful illusory king with *his* retinue. Similarly, the all-ground consciousness is like a kingdom wherein reigns a weak king—the afflicted mind with the view of self and so on, surrounded by its retinue of mental states. As long as the remedy has not arisen, the weak king rules over all the phenomena of thorough affliction. Nevertheless, a more powerful illusory king—the mind of complete purification with its insight into selflessness and its virtuous nature of faith and so forth—may, together with its retinue of mental states, completely expel the factors of thorough affliction. Thus this more powerful king comes to rule the realm of the transformed all-ground, through the mastery over all undefiled qualities.

In this way, the children of the victorious ones see all the phenomena of thorough affliction and complete purification to be like an illusion, in that they appear while still being empty of an apprehended and an apprehender. Thus they do not develop the pride of thinking, "I have eliminated thorough affliction and developed complete purification."

The following explanation concerns the meaning of the Buddha's statement that all phenomena are like the eight examples of illusion. The buddhas are perfectly awakened: they are the ones with supreme and complete knowledge, superior to the listeners and self-realized buddhas. Thus the translation of the root text found in Sthiramati's commentary also refers to them as "the buddhas with supreme knowledge." "Perfectly awakened" implies here that they have awakened from the sleep of ignorance and have an expanded intelligence regarding the objects of knowledge. Thus the word *buddha* carries the sense of realization, and it can be applied both as a noun and as an adjective. Hence, there is no superfluous repetition in saying, "the perfectly awakened buddhas." Therefore, these teachers, the perfectly awakened buddhas, have in the sūtras and so forth taught that all conditioned phenomena should be known to be like illusions, dreams, mirages, reflections, optical illusions, echoes, the reflections of the moon in water, and similar to emanations.

In general, all phenomena are unreal appearances, so any of these examples is suitable. However, to be more specific, the inner sense sources are like an illusion. Illusory people, horses, or elephants do not possess faculties, a self, sentience, or a life force; yet they appear as if they were sentient beings with faculties, life force, and mind. The appearances of sentient beings with eyes and the rest of the six inner sense sources can likewise be seen not to possess any life force, not to be persons, and so forth. Moreover, form and the rest of the outer six sense sources are like a dream. In a dream, one can have the perception of enjoying the forms, sounds, smells, tastes, textures, and mental phenomena that pertain to a woman, man, or otherwise. Yet, it should be known that all the while there are no objects separate from the mind.

"The two" refers to the mind and mental states, which are like a mirage. With a mirage, from a distance one has the perception of water, blue and shimmering; yet, as one approaches, there is nothing there. Likewise, the mind and mental states have perceptions of various phenomena, such as pillars, vases, men, women, blue, yellow, white, and red, and fixate upon them as such. When these phenomena are analyzed, however, they are found to be multiple, impermanent, and so forth. There is no whole object at all on which to fixate.

"The two sets of six" refer to the two sets of six inner and six outer sense sources, which are like a reflection and an optical illusion. The inner sense sources are like a reflection. Based on one's physical form, its reflection appears on the surface of a mirror. Likewise, while the six sense sources indeed appear, they are unreal like a reflection. They are, so to speak, the reflections of the habitual patterns of the actions that were carried out by the six sense sources in previous lifetimes. The outer sense sources, however, are like optical illusions. An optical illusion occurs when one's vision becomes distorted due to certain conditions. Such illusions may take many forms. A heap of stones may be mistaken for a man, for instance, or two moons may be perceived when the eyes are pressed; one's shadow can be mistaken for another being; floating hairs can appear; and mountains may appear to move when seen from a boat. Yet, in this context, it is taught that the specific example is that of the shadow. Just as a shadow appears based on a body, an umbrella, or the like, the outer sense sources appear like shadows based on the inner sense sources. From the all-ground consciousness, the inner sense sources of the eye and so forth arise. From these inner sense sources, the appearances of the outer sense sources then arise, taking the form of objects.

"And the three" refers to (1) the Dharma that is taught, (2) the mind abiding in meditative absorption, and (3) the body with which one willingly takes birth in existence. Respectively, these three correspond to the three examples of echoes, reflections of the moon, and emanations. All Dharma that is taught is like a reflection. Echoes do not exist as actual sounds, yet they can still be heard as objects of the ear. All Dharma that is explained occurs in a similar manner.

Moreover, when the moon's reflection appears in clear water, there is not any actual moon present there. Similarly, when one abides one-pointedly in meditative absorption, there is no pollution due to distracted thinking, and so this resembles clear water. Thus, whatever the meditation—whether it be mindfulness of the four truths, or the development of the totalities, subjugations, and so forth—the reflections of the contents of one's meditation will be clearly manifest.

As for intentionally accepting birth, like an emanation appearing in one place and then another without attachment or aversion, a bodhisattva continues from one lifetime to the next for the welfare of sentient beings, accepting birth without attachment or aversion.

3. The Investigation of Objects of Cognition

> False imagination, neither correct
> Nor false, not conceptual,
> Not conceptual and not nonconceptual—
> This characterizes all objects of cognition. [XII.31]

Next, when investigating the objects of cognition, we see that they are as follows: **false imagination, neither correct nor false** (which includes everything up through the factors conducive to ascertainment), **not conceptual** (namely, in the case of suchness and the supramundane wakefulness), and **not conceptual and** yet **not nonconceptual** either (which is the case with the subsequently attained mundane wakefulness). **This characterizes** and contains **all objects of cognition.**

In brief, objects of cognition can be designated as either mundane phenomena or supramundane phenomena. The term "false imagination" refers to all dualistic thinking in the three realms, which is not in accordance with the basic field of phenomena or the attainment of nonconceptual wakefulness. The phrase "neither correct nor false" concerns the period when ordinary beings begin to receive and reflect upon the sacred Dharma. Thus this includes all the proper intentions for the Dharma that are present on the grounds of inspired conduct and beyond, up to the supreme quality. Since all of these involve thinking in terms of apprehended and apprehender, they are not correct. Yet, since they are in accordance with the realization of the basic field of phenomena and supramundane wakefulness, serving as their cause, they are not false either. When the root text says "nonconceptual," it refers to the nonconceptual character of the object, that is, the basic field of phenomena, and to its subject, the supramundane wakefulness. Both of these are devoid of concepts such as those of an apprehended and an apprehender. The phrase "not conceptual and not nonconceptual" refers to the mundane wakefulness that is attained in the wake of the nonconceptual wakefulness of the meditative equipoise. This form of wakefulness observes the basic field of phenomena and nonconceptual wakefulness, and, since it therefore does not operate in terms of the duality of apprehended and apprehender, it is not a form of thinking. Alternatively, this is not conceptual because, in being attained subsequent to the nonconceptual equipoise, it does not engage in dualistic grasping. Yet, since this wakefulness conceives of all the particular and general characteristics of all phenomena without mixing anything up and while seeing them to be like illusions and mirages, it is not nonconceptual either.

These four categories are said to comprise all objects of cognition. There are no phenomena other than simply the mind, and these four contexts of the mind, along with the basic field of phenomena, comprise all objects of cognition.

4. Investigation of Thorough Affliction and Complete Purification

> The two appear from their own element,
> And, together with ignorance and affliction,
> Engaged thoughts emerge
> While being devoid of dual substance. [XII.32]
>
> Upon the attainment of the special focal point,
> There is abidance and possession within their own natural element.
> Hence, there is engagement with the reality free from dualistic appearance,
> As in the case of the hide and the arrow. [XII.33]

The following explanation concerns the investigation of thorough affliction and complete purification. **The two**, the apprehended and the apprehender, **appear from their own element**, the all-ground consciousness, **and together with**, and accompanied by, **ignorance and affliction, engaged thoughts emerge, while being devoid of** any **dual substance** of apprehended and apprehender.

Upon the attainment, or discovery, **of the special focal point** of the Dharma as it was explained above, **there is abidance** (which on the grounds of inspired conduct occurs by means of an object universal, and on the path of seeing via direct perception) **and possession** (as familiarity is achieved on the path of cultivation) **within their own natural element** (that is, within the suchness of the various thoughts). **Hence,** when fundamental transformation occurs, **there is engagement with the reality** of thought **free from dualistic appearance, as in the case of the hide** (thus referring to the pliability that ensues from the absence of conceit) **and the arrow** (which becomes straight by being heated in fire). These two examples pertain to the liberation of attention and insight that occurs through calm abiding and special insight, respectively.

Next follows an investigation of the characteristics of thorough affliction, including affliction, karma, and birth, or ripening. Likewise, there is an investigation of the element of complete purification, which contains the path of noble individuals and the transcendence of suffering. The terms "element," "seed," and "cause" have a similar meaning. One's natural element is the all-ground that retains the habitual patterns of duality. The dualistic appearances of apprehended and apprehender emerge from this all-ground. As these appear, there arise the thoughts of consciousnesses that are involved in the apprehending of forms and other such objects, together with the ignorance of not knowing the nature of entities and other afflictions, such as attachment. Again and again, birth within cyclic existence occurs in this way. When dualistic appearances occur, they are devoid of any dual substance in the form of an apprehended and an apprehender. From the beginning, there are not two different things. Rather, it is due to the mind's delusion that dualistic appearance and dualistic fixation occur, and it is due to this that cyclic existence is established. In this way one investigates the nature of thorough affliction.

As for the investigation of the character of complete purification, a person who attains the special focal point of the Dharma on the stage of inspired conduct will, as explained above, on the first ground, come to abide within the mind of the dependent nature's natural element, or abiding reality, which is the basic field of phenomena. On the grounds of the path of cultivation, one possesses this realization and so pursues the spiritual practice endowed with calm abiding and insight. Thus, within the absence of the apparent duality of apprehended and apprehender, reality is accessed to an ever-greater extent through to the stage of buddhahood.

The minds of sentient beings are tainted by the delusion of dualistic appearances and dualistic conceptions. Due to this, they are unable to bring forth a mind that is free from afflictions and an insight that is free from ignorance. The bodhisattvas actualize both of these freedoms because they realize nonduality and they possess the meditative equipoise of calm abiding and special insight whereby nonduality is acknowledged. This can be illustrated by two examples. The mind is like a hide that has become hardened and inflated because of exposure to alcohol or the like. Yet just as hide can be softened with water and oil, the mind can be made pliable with calm abiding. Likewise, wrong views, such as the views of self or of permanence and annihilation, are like a crooked arrow that steers the mind into conflict with the way things actually are. This can be straightened with the heat of special insight. By steering the mind away from the path of error, one will accomplish the unmistaken path and in the end, at the stage of buddhahood, attain a liberated mind and liberated insight that will never know decline.

5. The Investigation of Mere Cognition

It is held that the mind appears as duality,
And that it likewise appears as attachment and so forth,
As well as faith and so forth.
No afflictions or virtuous qualities exist. [XII.34]

Mind appears as diversity
And is active with various features.
Since it appears in this way there is existence and yet none.
Hence this is not related to things. [XII.35]

The investigation of mere awareness is as follows. **It is held that the mind appears as** the **duality** of apprehended and apprehender **and that it likewise appears as** afflictions, such as **attachment and so forth, as well as faith and so forth.** Apart from that, **no afflictions or virtuous qualities exist.**

Mind appears as the **diversity** of afflictions and factors such as faith, **and it is** simultaneously **active with various expressions** such as faith and diligence. **Since it,** meaning the mind itself, **appears in this way,** as all of this, **there is existence, and yet** also **none,** because apart from that no characteristics of things can be found. Hence, this is not related to things that may be afflictive or virtuous.

For some adherents to this position, "mind only" is the assertion that in the end mind and mental states are all that there is, and that there are hence no external phenomena. Thus, the "only" in "mind only" is seen as a denial of forms but not of mental states. For others, "mind only" negates the existence of both forms and mental states. The present verses can be explained along the lines of both of these interpretations. According to the first, "mind" refers to the all-ground and the rest of the eight collections of consciousness, together with the mental states. These factors appear as the duality of apprehended and apprehender, and apart from this appearance there are no external objects. According to the second approach, the mind itself appears as the duality of apprehended and apprehender. Other than this, they say, there are no mental states, and no apprehended or apprehender. Sthiramati refers to both of these interpretations. According to the first, the mind and mental states are separate substances, while the second position is clearly an approach that does not hold them to be distinct substances.

Furthermore, afflictive and virtuous qualities are nothing other than the mind, for it is the mind that appears as afflictive qualities, such as attachment and anger, or as faith, diligence, and so forth. In this way, the mind, the all-ground itself, appears as various apprehended phenomena, and it is active with various features of apprehending. Since in this way the apprehended and apprehender appear to the mind, there is existence in the sense of mere appearance. Yet in reality none of this exists as it appears. Hence this is not related to things that exist separately from the mind. Since all phenomena are merely appearances to the mind, all prove to be mind only.

6. The Investigation of Characteristics

For the benefit of sentient beings,
The buddhas teach
By distinguishing bearers of characteristics,
Characteristics, and that which is characterized. [XII.36]

The mind, along with its views,
Its contexts, and the unchanging
Are, in short, the bearers of the characteristics.
When discerned, they are limitless. [XII.37]

The reasons conceived of as objects that accord with
    expressions,
The habitual tendencies associated with those,
And the appearances of objects based on those:
These are characteristics of the imaginary. [XII.38]

That which appears as object and name
In accordance with name and object,
And serves as the reason for false imagination:
This is the characteristic of the imaginary. [XII.39]

Having the three and the three appearances,
The characteristics of the apprehended and the apprehender,
This false imagination
Is the characteristic of the dependent. [XII.40]

Nonexistence and existence,
The sameness of existence and nonexistence,
No peace, peace, and nonthought
Are the characteristics of the thoroughly established. [XII.41]

Based on the focal point of the Dharma of causal concordance,
The mind is directed correctly,
Abides in the field of the mind,
And sees how the object is existent and nonexistent. [XII.42]

Within that, one is perfectly equal.
The noble potential is utterly stainless.
Equal, superior, without decrease, and without increase—
These are its characteristics [XII.43]

The next section concerns the investigation of the characteristics. For the benefit of sentient beings, the buddhas teach by distinguishing **the bearers of characteristics,** that is, the five bases of the objects of cognition, the **characteristics** of the three natures, **and that which is characterized** by the fivefold spiritual practice.

The mind (differentiated in terms of that which appears as something that apprehends, namely, consciousness, and as something that is apprehended, that is, form), **along with its views** (thus indicating the mental states), **its contexts** (that is, the nonassociated formations), **and the unchanging** and unconditioned—these are, in short, the bearers of the characteristics. When discerned, they are limitless. The reasons that are **conceived of as objects that accord with** nominal **expressions, the habitual tendencies associated with those** expressions, **and the appearances of objects** (that is, objects that manifest unaccompanied to those who have no knowledge of language and accompanied by a name to those who do know language, and which are **based on those** habitual tendencies)—these are the characteristics of the imaginary.

That which appears as object and name in accordance with name and object, and serves as the reason for, and observation of, the false imagination—this is the characteristic of the imaginary.

Having the three appearances of abode, object, and body, **and the three appearances** of mental cognition, apprehension, and thought, which are respectively **the characteristics of the apprehended and the apprehender**—this false imagination is the characteristic of the dependent.

The **nonexistence** of any imaginary phenomena **and** the existence of that nonexistence; **the sameness of existence and nonexistence** in the absence of any difference between the two; **no peace** from adventitious afflictions; **peace because of natural purity; and nonthought** in the absence of mental constructs—these **are the characteristics of the thoroughly established.**

Based on the focal point of the Dharma of causal concordance (that is, the Dharma of the scriptural teachings, the Buddha's account of his own comprehension of the four truths), **the mind is directed correctly** toward the object of one's aspiration; the mind **abides** one-pointedly in meditative absorption with**in the** mirror-like **field of the mind; and** it **sees,** with respect to the appearances, exactly **how the object,** that is, the intrinsic nature, **is existent and nonexistent** in terms of being empty of the imaginary.

The support is fundamental transformation, the undefiled field. **Within that, one is perfectly equal** to the other noble ones. This is **the noble potential, which is utterly stainless.** In terms of liberation, there is **equal**ity with the listeners and the self-realized buddhas, but this liberation is also **superior** in the following ways: (1) the absence of afflictions includes their habitual tendencies; (2) its complete purity is superior with respect to the completely pure realm; (3) there is superiority in terms of its body because the body of qualities is attained; (4) its enjoyment is superior since there is uninterrupted engagement with the perfect enjoyments of the Dharma within the circles of the retinues; (5) its activity is superior, as the emanations that abide in The Joyful Realm and so forth bring benefit to beings. This also is **without decrease** upon the cessation of the factors of thorough affliction **and without increase** as the factors of complete purification arise. **These are its characteristics.**

The buddhas arouse in sentient beings the insight that is free from any delusion with regard to the nature of the objects of cognition. In order to benefit them, they explain by means of an analysis of bearers of characteristics, characteristics, and that which is characterized. All bearers of the characteristics of the three natures, or three essences, are included in just five bases of objects of cognition: the basis of form, the basis of the primary mind, the basis of its accompanying mental states, the basis of nonassociated formations, and the basis of the unconditioned. The basis of form comprises the five faculties and the five objects—the ten sense sources that are forms. The basis of the primary mind consists of the eight collections of consciousness. The basis of the mental states contains the fifty-one mental states. The nonassociated formations are set out in the enumeration of twenty-three that begins with attainment, nonattainment, and so forth. There are four unconditioned bases: analytical cessation, nonanalytical cessation, space, and suchness.

In the root text, the term "mind" refers to the basis of mind, while the phrase "along with its views" concerns the mental states plus the five faculties and five objects. When the mind views objects, it requires the complete triad of object, faculty, and mental activity. Thus the mind, directed toward the features of its object, implies the basis of the mental states, while the five faculties and their five objects—forms, sounds, scents, tastes, and textures—further involve the basis of form. "Its contexts" refers to the contexts of the mind, mental states, and forms—contexts in which the basis of nonassociated formations are imputed. The latter include everything that pertains to conditioned phenomena and yet is neither matter nor mind. This category includes attainment, nonattainment, equal fortune, being alive, being a person, and so forth. The term "the unchanging" concerns that which is not causally conditioned—which is free from arising, abiding, and disintegrating. Thus it refers to the basis of the unconditioned—that which is of an essence that never turns into anything else. In short, these five bases contain the bearers of characteristics; there are no phenomena that are not comprised within these five. Thus, these five are established as the bearers of the characteristics of the three natures.

According to Sthiramati's commentary, the term "mind" refers to the mind that appears as the five faculties and five objects that are apprehended, as well as in the form of the six collections of consciousness that apprehend the former faculties and objects. Sthiramati also sees the phrase "along with its beliefs" to be a reference to the clear and stimulated mental states that engage with objects. In some translations, the phrase "that which is characterized" takes the place of "the bearers of characteristics," thus referring to that which is characterized by the three characteristics. Both versions can, however, be seen as conveying the same understanding.

When the bearers of characteristics are further divided, the divisions turn out to be limitless because each subdivision itself covers innumerable particularities. Each of the categories of mind, form, and so on, can be divided with reference to the different continua of sentient beings, as well as in terms of distinct times and locations. Hence the number of subdivisions is just as infinite as the number of objects of cognition.

In short, these five bases for characteristics each have three characteristics, or natures: the imaginary, the dependent, and the thoroughly established. These three are, respectively, the aspect of the dualistic appearance of phenomena, the cause of this appearance, and the aspect of nonduality. The character of the imaginary is described as follows. While there are no external objects, the expression of names such as "pillar" or "vase" produces a mere conceptual appearance, which is nevertheless treated as if there were an objective entity. As one thinks "this is a pillar" or "this is a vase," conceiving of such things as if they were actual facts, such identifications serve as the causes for the manifestation of the imaginary. These conceptions of names and marks therefore constitute one aspect of the characteristic of the imaginary.

The habitual tendencies associated with these constructs are also included within the imaginary; these serve as the causes of the false imagination. The ripening of habitual tendencies from beginningless time brings about manifest appearances of objects such as pillars, vases, and elephants. Those who know language apprehend these as mixed with names; those who do not know language do not impute any names, yet the objects appear nevertheless as suited to be mixed with names. This too is the imaginary nature. In short, the various phenomena of dualistic appearance are the constructs of activated habitual tendencies. From these habitual tendencies appear the various phenomena of duality that are then apprehended in terms of names and marks and conceived of as if they actually were what they seem to be. This is what characterizes the imaginary.

The etymology of the term "imaginary" is explained in the line "That which appears as object and name in accordance with name and object." A name such as "vase" gives rise to the appearance of an entity that takes the form of a bulbous object. Although the object is not seen directly, the presence of an objective bulbous entity is nevertheless apprehended, based on the mere expression of the name "vase." Thus the name functions as the cause of the false imagination. Whenever a bulbous entity is seen, it will then be treated as an entity that has a name, and so one will think, "This is a vase." Thus the object also becomes a cause for the false imagination. Actually, there is no essential relationship between names and objects at all. Names are adventitiously superimposed by thought upon objects that appear to bear marks. Thus, whenever a given name is recollected, the features of the relevant object will also appear to the mind, and so objects are also superimposed upon names. In this way, as conception mixes names and the marks of objects, various phenomena are apprehended as belonging to distinct types. This, then, is the reason for the false imagination, and in this way the mind of dualistic grasping imputes a variety of separate objects and subjects. Such are the characteristics of the imaginary.

The characteristics of the dependent are referred to in the line "Having the three and the three appearances." The first three appearances concern apprehended forms—the threefold appearances of abode, objects, and body. The latter three appearances refer to the apprehending mind and mental states—the threefold appearances of mental cognition, apprehension, and thought. The term, "abode" refers to the appearance of the world environment. "Objects" refers to the six external objects of forms, sounds, scents, tastes, textures, and phenomena. The appearance of the "body" includes the six faculties of eye, ear, nose, tongue, body, and mental faculty. The appearance of "mind" refers to the afflicted mind, which observes the all-ground and takes it to be a self. "Apprehension" includes the five sense consciousnesses, from the eye consciousness to the body consciousness. "Thought" points to the mental consciousness, which determines various objects and conceptualizes them. The last three appearances are characterized by being aspects of the apprehender, while the first three appearances bear the characteristics of the apprehended.

All these six appearances are due to the element of the habitual tendencies that are present within the all-ground consciousness. Whenever those tendencies awaken, those things will appear, as in a dream. They are not established as any actual duality of apprehended and apprehender at all, and yet they appear as a duality. Thus all minds and mental states of the three realms are false imagination, and it is this that is the characteristic of the dependent nature. The *Journey to Laṅkā* states:

The body, enjoyments, and common abode,
These I explain to be mind only.

In this way, the basis for all the appearances of internal and external phenomena is the all-ground consciousness and the minds and mental states of the seven collections of consciousness that accompany it. These are what is referred to as "the dependent." They are referred to as such because they appear as dualistic phenomena in dependence on the conditioning of the habitual tendencies of thorough affliction.

The thoroughly established is characterized by emptiness, the basic field of phenomena. Within it, there are no characteristics of the imaginary, the entities of the apprehended and apprehender. It exists with the characteristics of suchness and of being empty of duality. Due to the nonexistence of duality, it exists as suchness, while, due to the existence of suchness, there is no existence of duality. Whether it is expressed as existent or nonexistent, there is no difference in meaning; the import is alike and the same. Duality is negated by exclusion and suchness is established by determination. Likewise, when suchness is established by determination, duality is negated in the manner of exclusion. In this way existence and nonexistence carry the same meaning and are not different.

In terms of its being mixed with adventitious stains, there is no peace, while, from the point of view that the essence of the thoroughly established is naturally pure and luminously clear, there is peace. Not being within the domain of logic, it is free from all dualistic constructs and hence it is nonconceptual. These are the characteristics of the thoroughly established.

To show and make it known that these three characteristics are borne by the five groups of bearers, the five stages of spiritual practice are shown. These five are known as (1) the basis, (2) the development or placement, (3) the mirror-like, (4) the appearance, and (5) the abode or support. Through these five, it can be understood, as it must, exactly how the aspects of the imaginary are present as mere imputations in relation to phenomena. In a similar manner, the dependent, that is, the false imagination that appears as duality and is to be eliminated, and the thoroughly established, that is, the intrinsic nature that is the basis for purification, will be known as they are. Thus, all three natures will be clearly explained and introduced as the objects of one's mind.

The five stages of spiritual practice are explained as follows. The buddhas comprehend the lack of the twofold self. Their teaching of this fact of the absence of self in the twelve branches of scripture is referred to as the "Dharma of causal concordance." Since this teaching is in accord with the Dharma of realization that the buddhas have comprehended, or because it is the cause for attaining it, it is known as the "Dharma of causal concordance." Beginning on the path of accumulation, anyone who wishes to realize reality must first listen carefully to the scriptural teachings of the Dharma that accord with the realization of the basic field of phenomena. Based on that, one must contemplate its meaning and become familiar with it through meditation. The focal points involved in this process are referred to as "the basis." They are the basis or source for the later stages of the spiritual practice, and they are the initial cause of entering the teachings. Next, the words "the mind is directed correctly" indicate the product or development of that basis. Thus, at the time of heat on the path of joining, phenomena are seen to be inexpressible through the experience that arises from the meditation of properly directing the mind. At the time of the summit, objects are understood to be like an illusion. At the time of acceptance, one realizes that nothing is apprehended. Finally, at the stage of supreme quality, one sees that there is no apprehender. Progressively, one's certainty in suchness grows increasingly firm and clear. This is referred to as the "developed basis" because from this emerges the path of seeing. Alternatively, since one places the mind in the proper direction, it is also called "placement." Thus, this is also the placement in the mind of the habitual tendencies for the realization of supramundane qualities.

The mirror-like stage is referred to with the phrase "abides in the field of mind." The field of the mind of the dependent nature is suchness free from duality. Thus, directly abiding within this refers to the occasion of the first ground. Just as a reflection clearly appears within a mirror, this wakefulness clearly and directly perceives all phenomena within the nature of suchness. Some people explain "mirror-like" to refer to the duration between the greater path of accumulation and the supreme quality, when emptiness is realized by means of the features of an object universal. However, it is better to see this as referring to the context of the first ground, as explained in Sthiramati's commentary.

The stage of appearance is presented with the phrase "seeing how the object is existent and nonexistent." This pertains to the supramundane wakefulness that occurs from the second to the tenth ground. This wakefulness sees the existent as existent and the nonexistent as nonexistent, while the nature of all entities appears to it in an undistorted way. The words "the object is existent" concern the existence of that which has the characteristics of the relative, that is, the dependent, and the existence of that which has the characteristics of the ultimate, namely, the thoroughly established. These two are seen to be existent. The imaginary is apprehended by the deluded mind and so is seen to be as nonexistent as a rabbit's horn.

The abode or support is taught in the stanza that begins "Within that, one is perfectly equal. . . ." At the stage of buddhahood, all phenomena become equality. As they enter the undefiled field, all the buddhas are equal in body, speech, and mind, and it is likewise understood that all phenomena are of one taste within the essence of great equality.

Furthermore, the natural purity that is the reality of the basic field of phenomena is the way that all phenomena actually are. This reality is referred to with the expression "the noble potential," which is to say "buddha-nature," and it is also known by the term "the perfectly genuine." When the basic field is freed from the stains of the two obscurations, a transformation into utter purity occurs. In the mere sense of liberation through the elimination of the afflictive obscurations, this attainment is equal to that of the listeners and self-realized buddhas—because they also achieve such freedom from affliction. Nevertheless, there are five distinctions that show how this liberation is superior to that of the listeners and self-realized buddhas. Moreover, within the basic field of phenomena, there is no decline due to a cessation of thorough affliction, and there is no increase in terms of the development of complete purification. Thus, there is no wavering from the equality that does not increase, decrease, diminish, or develop. This is the abode or support of peace.

Liberation is a universal support. Thus, listeners and self-realized buddhas also become liberated from cyclic existence. Since buddhas also achieve this form of liberation, they are all equal in this regard, yet a buddha's liberation is distinguished by five superior features. Their liberation is superior in terms of the buddhas' (1) purity, (2) completely pure field, (3) attainment of the body of qualities, (4) complete enjoyment of the

Great Vehicle Dharma, and (5) benefit to sentient beings by means of their emanation bodies and uninterrupted enlightened activity.

Concerning the first, that is, purity, since the listeners and self-realized buddhas have not eliminated the cognitive obscurations, they do not possess the purity achieved by the buddhas. Moreover, although they have relinquished the seeds of the afflictions, they have not eliminated their subtle habitual tendencies. While they are free from the afflictions, even after becoming foe destroyers, they still retain aspects of the imprints of affliction. Due to the imprints from having previously been a monkey, for instance, one foe destroyer jumped around like a monkey, and because of the imprints of having previously been a prostitute, another foe destroyer had the habit of looking into mirrors and at the surface of his begging bowl in order to see his face. Buddhas do not have even the most subtle habitual tendencies of the two obscurations, and so they are superior in purity.

The buddhas cultivate their fields. They are able to establish a completely pure field with a ground of precious gems, wish-fulfilling trees, and streams of nectar, and so forth. Listeners are not able to do this. Hence, the buddhas are superior with respect to the complete purity of their fields.

The buddhas realize the twofold absence of self and thereby attain the body of qualities, the great equality of suchness. The listeners and self-realized buddhas, however, possess nothing more than a body of liberation within the realization of the absence of a personal self. The buddhas attain bodies that consummately and without interruption enjoy the Great Vehicle Dharma together with their retinues of bodhisattvas on the ten grounds for as long as existence remains. The listeners and self-realized buddhas, in contrast, have nothing like this. Finally, through a display of emanations of body, speech, and mind, such as supreme emanation bodies, the buddhas uninterruptedly perform enlightened activities that bring benefit and happiness to all sentient beings until the end of time.

Of the five stages of spiritual practice presented here, the first four are causal practices, whereas the fifth is the resultant stage. "Spiritual practice" refers here to the integration of calm abiding and special insight. Furthermore, these five stages of spiritual practice show how the three characteristics are borne by the five classes of bearers. Thus they serve to explain three issues: the way immature beings impute duality with respect to the phenomena of the five aggregates, the unconditioned, and suchness; the way these phenomena appear as duality; and the way they are in fact devoid of duality.

Some people say that forms and nonassociated formations are imaginary, the mind and mental states are dependent, and the unconditioned is the thoroughly established. However, it is not quite right to correlate these specifically to the five bases. Each of the five bases has all three characteristics, and so there are, for example, imaginary forms, dependent forms, and forms as distinguished by the intrinsic nature, that is, the intrinsic nature of form. One should know that this threefold division applies to them all.

7. The Investigation of Liberation

Because the seeds have been transformed,
The appearances of abode, object, and body
Have turned into something else:
The undefiled field, the omnipresent basis. [XII.44]

Mental cognition, apprehensions, and thought—
Because these have changed,
There is a fourfold mastery of nonconceptuality,
The fields, wakefulness, and activity. [XII.45]

There are four masteries
Upon three grounds, beginning with the Immovable.
One contains two masteries,
And the others one each. [XII.46]

The wise also become aware of the twofold absence of self throughout existence.
With equal understanding, they access reality through apprehension.

Then, because their minds abide there, not even that appears.
This nonappearance is liberation, supremely free from focal
   points. [XII.47]

When through accumulation there is a basis and development,
Perception takes place in terms of names only.
One only sees names and so, by that perception,
One will later not see that either. [XII.48]

Mind, possessing negative tendencies,
Is held by the shackles of belief in a self.
Thus, it is thoroughly engaged,
Yet due to inner abiding, it is held to turn back. [XII.49]

Next follows the investigation of liberation. Because the seeds have been transformed, the consciousnesses that constitute the appearances of abode, object, and body have turned into something else: the undefiled field, which is liberation. This is the omnipresent basis for listeners, self-realized buddhas, and buddhas alike.

The defiled mental cognition, the apprehensions of the five sense cognitions, and the mental consciousness of thought—because these have changed, there is a fourfold mastery of nonconceptuality, the pure fields, the four forms of individual self-aware wakefulness, and the activity of great superknowledge.

There are four masteries upon three grounds, beginning with the Immovable. One ground, the Immovable, contains two masteries, and the others contain the attainment of one mastery each.

Further principles of liberation are explained as follows. The wise also become aware of the twofold absence of self throughout the phenomena of existence. With equal understanding (that is, knowing that, just as the imaginary person does not exist, imaginary phenomena do not exist either), they access the reality of mere awareness through the understanding of mere apprehension. Then, because their minds abide there, not even that reality of mere awareness **appears** either. **This nonappearance is liberation, supremely free from focal points.**

In terms of other principles of liberation, **when through** the power of having gathered the **accumulations** in the past **there is a basis** (that is, extensive exposure to the teachings of scripture) **and development** (the correct directing of the mind), then the **perception** of all the appearances of objects **takes place in terms of names only. One only sees names** (that is, the four aggregates other than form) **and so, by that perception, one will later not see that either** because when there is no object, there cannot be any awareness of it either.

Other principles of liberation include the way the **mind, possessing** the obscuring **negative tendencies, is held by the shackles of belief in a self. Thus it is thoroughly engaged** in cyclic existence, **yet, due to inner abiding** in mind only, **it is held to turn back** from cyclic existence.

Liberation is the elimination of the afflictions and suffering, and the attainment of the transcendence of suffering as accomplished through the path of noble individuals. The present investigation of liberation takes the form of an analysis of the method whereby one attains the transcendence of suffering. The habitual tendencies associated with the afflictive and cognitive obscurations, or the various habitual tendencies of duality, are present in the all-ground consciousness. Hence, it is also referred to as the "the entirety of seeds." When the all-ground that otherwise possesses these seeds is divested of the stains of duality, it transforms, and hence the threefold phenomena that appear from it likewise undergo transformation. The abode (the appearances of an environment), the objects (the appearances of the six objects), and the body (the appearances of the six faculties) thus all transform. When this happens, impure environments with ravines, thorny abysses, and so on, will no longer appear. Instead, a world environment that is of the nature of precious jewels will appear, filled with undefiled and delightful objects to be enjoyed by the senses, such as wish-fulfilling trees and pools of nectar. The body will become like that of the Buddha, with each faculty performing the function of all the others. This completely pure and perfect body, which is like a vajra, has twelve hundred qualities and limitless powers.

The transformed all-ground is the undefiled field, the universal abode or support of liberation. As such, it permeates all the qualities of transformation. Alternatively, its serving as the universal support can be explained with reference to the fact that the listeners, self-realized buddhas, and bodhisattvas all enter this field of liberation. The transformations of the afflicted mind, the apprehending five sense consciousnesses, and thought (the mental consciousness), all lead to the following four masteries. (1) When the afflicted mind transforms, there is mastery over nonconceptuality. When transformation has not yet occurred, the all-ground is believed to be a self. Once it has transformed, the all-ground is nonconceptual, so it will at that point also be observed as such, thereby yielding the mastery of nonconceptuality. (2) When the apprehending five senses transform, no ordinary, impure realm appears. Instead, there is mastery over completely pure fields. (3-4) When thought, meaning the mental consciousness, transforms, there is mastery over both wakefulness and activity. Since the four correct awarenesses are attained, there is mastery over wakefulness. And, through the power of superknowledge, mastery over enlightened activity is attained. This is all as explained above, in the context of transformation.

These four masteries are achieved on three grounds, beginning with the eighth, the Immovable. Upon the eighth ground, two are achieved—namely, mastery over nonconceptuality and mastery over the fields. On the ninth and tenth grounds, respectively, mastery over wakefulness and mastery over activity are accomplished. Hence, each of these two grounds is held to be endowed with one mastery.

Further principles of liberation are elaborated as follows. Wise bodhisattvas comprehend the one taste of the twofold absence of self (in terms of both persons and phenomena) that pertains to all phenomena throughout the three realms of existence, or to all the phenomena that there are. Knowing the absence of the imaginary twofold self clears away the extreme of superimposition. Yet the realization of no-self does not just concern an exclusive emptiness in the mere sense of absence. The illusion-like dependent nature is not separate from the suchness of the thoroughly established, which is empty of the twofold self. Knowing these to be equal clears away the extreme of denigration. Understanding the middle path in this way, bodhisattvas uphold it by means of mind only and thus they access reality. In this way, they familiarize their minds again and again with reality.

This way of directing the mind to reality by means of mind only is characteristic of the stages from heat through acceptance. As one abides in the awareness of mind only, one recognizes that, while apprehended objects appear, they lack any essence of the apprehended. In the same way, one will realize that, while the apprehending mind alone appears, there is no apprehender as such. At this point, the meditative absorption of the supreme quality is achieved, and so the apprehender is not perceived either. When both the apprehended and apprehender are seen to be equally unestablished, dualistic constructs are not perceived at all and one is liberated from all forms of conceptuality. This is the wakefulness of the noble ones, supremely free from all focal points, and as such the unmistaken thoroughly established nature.

There are further principles of liberation. Once one has gathered the two accumulations for an incalculable eon, there comes a point at which, in one's present life, one possesses both (1) the basis of the accumulations of having studied, contemplated, and meditated on the Great Vehicle Dharma and (2) the ground of development that results from correctly directing the mind to impermanence, suffering, emptiness, and selflessness during the phases of inspired conduct. Based on these causes, at the time of attaining the stages of heat and summit on the path of joining, one sees that all phenomena are merely imputed by the mind by means of names. As there are thus no real objects, one sees them all as mere concepts.

In this way, one understands that none of the phenomena imputed by thought exist and that, therefore, there are no external objects other than names (thus referring to the mind and mental states of the four aggregates that are distinguished as "name" in juxtaposition with "form"). This is the time of attaining acceptance on the path of joining, the point at which one sees that there are no external objects, apprehending only names, or only mind. Later, at the time of the supreme quality, even this is not seen. In this way, when there is no duality of apprehended and apprehender, the mirror-like and appearances arise, and, in the end, at the stage of buddhahood, equality and liberation are attained.

Yet more principles of liberation are taught. Thus, when the root text speaks of "mind," it refers to the all-ground consciousness and so forth—the phenomena of mind and mental states. This mind possesses negative tendencies, and thus there are both physical negative tendencies, which involve committing unvirtuous acts like killing, as well as mental negative tendencies of attachment, anger, and bewilderment. Alternatively, we may enumerate two forms of negative tendencies by referring to the habitual tendencies of the afflictive and cognitive obscurations. The cause of negative tendencies is the belief in a personal self and the belief in a self in phenomena. Belief in self shackles the mind and brings it into cyclic existence. In short, due to clinging to the twofold self, the mind gets embroiled in the accumulation of the habitual tendencies associated with the afflictive and cognitive obscurations. For as long as this clinging to the twofold self has not been relinquished, habitual tendencies are gathered in the mind and one continues to engage in cyclic existence.

Concerning the line "yet due to inner abiding, it is held to turn back": how does the mind abide inwardly? The distracted mind that is attached to the apprehended is brought to settle within itself and is thus authentically placed in inner calm abiding. Seeing that there is nothing apprehended, one realizes that the apprehending mind is all that there is. When the mind is seen to be nonexistent as well, one becomes free from the duality of apprehended and apprehender. Thereby none of the imprints of negative tendencies will be accumulated, and the mind is turned back from its involvement in cyclic existence. This is liberation.

These four sets of principles of liberation have here been taught concisely in an evolving succession, just as in Sthiramati's commentary. Sthiramati's explanation does not proceed any further than this. Nevertheless, the first set of principles, which is presented with reference to transformation, explains the essence of liberation. The second set explains liberation from the perspective of the path that leads to it. The third set explains how the stages of liberation occur, and the fourth set shows that the presence or absence of liberation depends upon the mind.

When bound, it is the mind that is bound; when liberated, it is the mind that is liberated.

According to extremist outsiders, liberation happens because of the power of the Almighty. According to the Jains, liberation is physical. Such accounts of liberation do not make sense. Without leaving the shackles of the mind behind, liberation will never be possible, and so "liberation" refers to the relinquishment of the bondage of clinging to the twofold self. Thus, liberation has here been investigated by means of four sets of principles.

8. The Investigation of Essencelessness

They do not exist as themselves or with their own nature;
They do not abide by their own nature;
And they do not exist as apprehended.
Therefore, it is held that they have no essential nature.
[XII.50]

The former are the supports of the latter.
Hence, with reference to the absence of essential nature,
Absence of arising, absence of cessation, peace from the beginning,
And the natural transcendence of suffering—are all established. [XII.51]

The next section concerns the investigation of the absence of essential nature. **They**, that is, phenomena, **do not exist as themselves**, because they depend on conditions, **or with their own nature**, because phenomena that have now ceased will never recur with their own nature. **They do not abide by their own nature**, because they are momentary (thus, three features of essencelessness are correlated with three characteristics of conditioned phenomena), **and they do not exist as apprehended** by the immature either. **Therefore, it is held that they have no essential nature.**

Furthermore, the absence of arising and so forth is established on this basis. That is to say, **the former are the supports of the** latter. Hence, with reference to the absence of essential nature, the **absence of arising** is also established, and when there is nothing that arises this also implies the **absence of cessation**. Moreover, that which does not arise and does not cease is **peace from the beginning, and** peace from the beginning is **the natural transcendence of suffering.** Thus, these **are all** successively **established.**

The sūtras state that all phenomena are without essence and naturally the transcendence of suffering. This can be explained in the following way, by means of the three natures. All phenomena are included within the three natures—the imaginary, the dependent, and the thoroughly established. The dependent nature is the continuity of the impermanent mind and mental states that appear as duality. The dependent consciousness thus bears the three characteristics of the conditioned: arising, abiding, and ceasing. Yet, since phenomena of the past have already ceased, they do not have any essence of their own; future phenomena, at the present time, have likewise not arisen. Therefore they do not exist in terms of their own identity. Finally, the phenomena that are present now do not remain for a second moment subsequent to their own essential establishment. Hence, no entities, or essences exist. This analysis of the lack of essence in terms of arising and ceasing is similar to the one that the listeners employ when they expound the meaning of emptiness and essencelessness.

Furthermore, pointing to the way the dependent nature is devoid of any essence of arising, the root text states "not as themselves," thereby indicating how these dependently arisen appearances of the dependent do not arise by way of their own essences. Since they arise in dependence upon the gathering of causes and conditions, their arising is without essence. Thus the dependent nature can be seen to be devoid of essence. This also serves as a refutation of the Enumerators, who claim that all things arise because of the existence of the primary principle, and that if the effect did not thus exist at the time of its cause, production would be unreasonable. "Not with their own nature" points to the fact that once entities have ceased, they do not arise again with their former identity. This shows that, apart from the mere cessation of a given entity, there is no such thing as a state of having disintegrated. Hence the Enumerators are wrong when they say that disintegrated entities never become nothing and that they instead remain dormant within the expanse of the primary principle.

The line "They do not abide by their own nature" concerns the fact that all phenomena that have arisen in the present do not remain for a second moment. Hence, this statement shows their lack of abiding. Extremists do not assert momentary disintegration but a disintegration that happens anew after a phenomenon has arisen and remained for its duration. This line rejects that position.

The line "They do not exist as apprehended" considers the imaginary appearance of duality and the imputations of duality that take place in relation to that appearance—that is, mistaken concepts such as duality, purity, bliss, permanence, and the self. As when a rope is taken to be a snake, these are all simply the conceived objects of a deluded mind. There is nothing more to them than this. That which the mind takes to be the case does not correspond with any fact at all. Therefore, all of this is without essence. In this way, it is held that the imaginary and the dependent are devoid of essence.

Essencelessness, nonarising, and so forth, make up a sequence where the former principles establish the latter. That is to say, nonarising is proven by lack of essence because something that is devoid of essence cannot reasonably arise. Likewise, when there is no arising, there cannot be cessation; and, without arising or cessation, peace must be primordial—no one can produce it anew. With peace from the beginning, suffering and its origin become impossible, and so the natural transcendence of suffering is established.

In this manner, essencelessness is shown in three ways with respect to the dependent nature and in one way in terms of the imaginary nature. We can therefore conclude that all phenomena that appear in a dualistic manner are devoid of essence. That which is thoroughly established is therefore that all phenomena are devoid of arising and ceasing; they are peace from the beginning and thus the natural transcendence of suffering. For this reason, although the dependent appears to arise and cease, and appears to be produced from the dependent emergence of the gathering of causes and conditions, it does not arise in terms of any essence of its own. As for the imaginary, its very characteristics are unarisen and essencelessness, and since the thoroughly established ultimate nature abides from the beginning, it is not of any essence that arises or ceases. Thus it can be understood how the teachings on absence of essence, nonarising, and so on, are delivered with a view to the three natures.

9. The Investigation of the Acceptance of Nonarising Phenomena

> Beginning, self, other,
> Own characteristics, self, change,
> Thorough affliction, and the distinct—
> This is how the acceptance of nonarising phenomena is explained. [XII.52]

Next follows the investigation of the acceptance of nonarising phenomena. There is no original **beginning** to birth within cyclic existence. Yet that which was previously born is not it**self** born again, nor is something **other** born that did not exist earlier. Since the imaginary has no particular characteristics, it does not arise in terms of its **own characteristics**. The dependent does not arise by it**self**. The thoroughly established is unconditioned and is, hence, unarisen in the sense that it does not **change**. For a foe destroyer who has attained the knowledge of exhaustion, there is no arising of **thorough affliction, and**, in terms of **the** body of qualities, there is no arising of anything **distinct** from what was previously the case. **This is how the acceptance of nonarising phenomena is explained.**

The sūtras speak of "the attainment of acceptance of nonarising phenomena." What does this term denote? It is the mind's acceptance of the eight features of nonarising. These eight are described as follows.

(1) First, as regards the acceptance of the absence of a beginning, it is not reasonable to believe in the origin of cyclic existence, thinking that at some point it arose for the first time. Cyclic existence was not created by someone like the Almighty or Brahma. From beginningless time, cyclic existence has emerged as the continuity of the twelve links of depen-

dent origination, with one life following after the other, again and again. Hence, as one finds no origin, to accept that there is no beginning is to attain the acceptance of that fact.

(2) Moreover, what has taken birth in cyclic existence is not itself born again. Once that which has come into being ceases, it becomes nonexistent. Hence it is not reasonable for it to be born again. Thus to accept that what was already born is not reborn is the second principle.

(3) "Other" concerns the way that only the well-known aggregates, elements, and sense sources arise within cyclic existence. Something unprecedented, that is, something not included within the aggregates, elements, and sense sources, will never arise. Likewise, no previously nonexistent sentient being will ever be born. This is the third principle.

(4) The imaginary is nonarising in terms of its own characteristics. Like the horn of a rabbit, the imaginary does not arise. To accept this form of nonarising is the fourth principle.

(5) The dependent does not arise by itself because it arises in dependence on causes and conditions. The acceptance of this form of nonarising is the fifth principle.

(6) The thoroughly established is unarisen in the sense that it does not change. The acceptance that it never changes, like space, is the sixth principle.

(7) The noble foe destroyers achieve the wakefulness of exhaustion after having eliminated the entirety of the afflictions that are to be discarded by the paths of seeing and cultivation. The seventh principle is the acceptance of the fact that thorough affliction will never arise again.

(8) Finally, the eighth principle concerns the distinct knowledge of exhaustion and nonarising that pertains to the fact that the two obscurations do not recur within the buddha's body of qualities. Alternatively, this principle can also be seen to concern the fact that, for each of the buddhas, their body of qualities is of the same nature, beyond any difference. It is not the case that the body of qualities that was attained by a certain buddha of the past is in any way distinct from the body of qualities that is accomplished by some later buddha. There is no difference or discord in the way that the body of qualities manifests. To accept this absence of distinct arising is the eighth way of accepting nonarising.

Thus, the acceptance of nonarising phenomena is taught with reference to these eight principles.

In general, there are three categories related to how the acceptance of nonarising phenomena is attained, namely, lesser, middling, and greater. When acceptance is attained on the path of joining, the fact of nonarising is accepted by way of an object universal. This is the lesser acceptance. At the time of the first ground on the path of seeing, nonarising is directly realized. This is the middling acceptance. At the time of the complete maturation of nonconceptual wakefulness on the eighth ground, one does not waver from the meaning of the nonarising of all phenomena, throughout both meditative equipoise and subsequent attainment. This is the attainment of the greater acceptance of nonarising phenomena. Because the irreversible bodhisattvas on the eighth ground have attained this greater acceptance, the buddhas grant them their prophecy, which is why the eighth ground is known specifically as the "ground of prophecy." However, in order to serve particular purposes, the buddhas may also prophesy the future enlightenment of those abiding with the potential or who have just generated the enlightened mind. The term "acceptance of nonarising phenomena" is primarily explained as the acceptance of the fact that since no phenomena exist apart from the basic field of phenomena, no phenomena have ever arisen.

10. Investigation of the Intent behind the Teaching of the One Vehicle

> Because phenomena, absence of self, and liberations are the same;
> Because of different potentials;
> Because of the achievement of the two intents; because of emanation;
> And because of the consummate—for these reasons the vehicles are one. [XII.53]

> In order to lead some
> And to sustain others,

The perfect buddhas teach those uncertain
That the vehicles are one. [XII.54]

Uncertain listeners are of two kinds
For some have seen the objective of that vehicle, while others have not.
Of those who have seen it, some are free
And some are not free from desire—these are inferior. [XII.55]

Since the two who have attained the path
Of the noble ones take up existences,
They are in possession
Of inconceivable birth. [XII.56]

Some thoroughly accomplish birth
By the power of their aspirations.
Others thoroughly accomplish by means of emanations
Because they possess nonreturn. [XII.57]

Since, for the two, the selfish mind
Repeatedly emerges,
They are fond of transcendence
And are therefore held to be slow realizers. [XII.58]

Those who have not accomplished the objective are born
When there is no buddha and pursue emanation.
They apply themselves to concentration
And, on that basis, attain true enlightenment. [XII.59]

Next follows an investigation of the teaching that the vehicles are one. **Because** there are not different **phenomena** to reach; because the persons that travel, such as the listeners, are not different in terms of **the absence of self; and because** the **liberations are the same; because of** the fact that individuals with **different** indeterminate **potentials** achieve the same fruition of the great vehicle;

because of the achievement of the two intents (the first intent being a buddha's accomplishment of a mind that does not distinguish between himself or herself and all sentient beings, and the second having to do with the fact that some with the determinate listener's potential, who in the past have engaged in the accumulation of enlightenment, may, by the power of a buddha, gain a small measure of the buddha's realization of the lack of difference between self and other); **because of** the buddha's display of **emanations** in the form of listeners for the benefit of beings; **and because of** the **perfection** of the destination of buddhahood—**for these reasons, the vehicles are one.**

Considering the reasons outlined above, the buddhas teach that the vehicles are one **in order to lead some** listeners whose potential is uncertain, **and to sustain others,** that is, bodhisattvas whose potential is uncertain. Thus, **the perfect buddhas teach those of uncertain** potential **that, in the end, the vehicles are one.**

Moreover, **uncertain listeners are of two kinds, for some have seen the objective** (that is, the truths) **of that vehicle, while others have not. Of those who have seen it, some are free** from the desire associated with the realm of desire **and some are not free from** that **desire. These** two **are inferior** because of their slow realization.

Since the two who have seen the objective and **attained the path of the noble ones take up existences, they are in possession of inconceivable birth** because undertaking birth upon the path of the noble ones is an inconceivable domain.

Some, namely, those who are not free from desire, **thoroughly accomplish birth** in accordance with their wishes **by the power of their aspirations. Others,** that is, those who are free from desire, will **thoroughly accomplish** others' welfare **by means of emanations because they** are in **possession** of the meditative absorption of **nonreturn** to the realm of desire.

Since, for the two types of listeners who have previously acquired familiarity, **the selfish mind** of disenchantment **repeatedly emerges, they are** especially **fond of transcendence, and are therefore held to be slow realizers.**

Concerning the way that a single individual attains three fruitions, it is explained that **those who have not accomplished the objective,** and hence are on the path of training, **are born when there is no buddha and pursue emanation.** Thus **they apply themselves to concentration and, on that basis** of emanation, finally **attain true enlightenment.** With these three situations in mind, in the *Śrī Mālā Sūtra* the Blessed One gives the example of a fire fed by dung becoming a fire fueled by grass, and then a fire fueled by wood. Thus, he explains, someone who has become a listener may become a self-realized buddha, and then, finally, a completely awakened buddha.

Some sūtras teach that there are three vehicles, while others say that there is one. What is the purpose of this? With regard to the sūtras, some carry definitive and others expedient meaning. In the Mind-Only tradition, it is held that the teaching of three vehicles is definitive, whereas the teaching of a single vehicle is expedient and thus given with a certain intention. So, in terms of the latter tradition, what is it that is intended by the statement that, in the end, there is only one vehicle?

Seven concerns lie behind this teaching, and thus the point is not to deny that there are three vehicles of the path and three forms of resultant enlightenment. Rather, the following should be considered:

(1) The intrinsic nature of those who practice the three vehicles, as well as the nature of the paths and fruitions, is always the same. All are in this way nothing other than the single basic field of phenomena.

(2) This teaching also concerns the fact that the individuals who enter the path are all equally devoid of a personal self.

(3) It considers the way that all three vehicles result in the same fruition, in the sense that they all provide liberation from karma, afflictions, and suffering.

(4) Furthermore, this teaching is intended for those of an uncertain potential who, on the paths of listeners and self-realized buddhas, have entered those respective vehicles, so that they can instead enter the Great Vehicle.

(5) The teaching is also given for the purpose of accomplishing two types of intent: (1) the intent with respect to a buddha for whom all

other sentient beings are equal to him or her; (2) the intent of those who are in possession of the listener's potential, who previously engaged in bodhisattva activities but are now inclined to give up those activities. As the Thus-Gone One grants them his assurance, they will think, "I, too, will become a buddha," and so they will temporarily discover [the lack of difference between self and other].

(6) Moreover, the Buddha, intending to train beings by this method, has demonstrated the way to transcend suffering through the Listeners' Vehicle, saying, for instance: "Hundreds of times I have completely transcended suffering through the Listeners' Vehicle." Thus, the teaching of the oneness of the vehicles may also be made simply in consideration of the fact that emanations of the Buddha and actual listeners both appear to attain the transcendence of suffering through the Listeners' Vehicle. Similarly, bodhisattvas may emanate as listeners, yet instead of actualizing the listener's transcendence of suffering, they become buddhas.

(7) Finally, the perfect vehicle is only the Great Vehicle and none other.

Hence, in consideration of this, it is said that there is only one vehicle, not three. The great commentary contains an extensive explanation of this issue, but I fear that elaboration would only make it more difficult to comprehend. Here I have therefore summarized the essential points for ease of understanding.

The purpose of teaching that there is a single vehicle is to guide listeners and self-realized buddhas with uncertain potential toward the Great Vehicle and to keep others who are bodhisattvas with uncertain potential from turning away from the Great Vehicle. The latter may have entered the Great Vehicle, but when they see the faults of sentient beings—noticing how, within cyclic existence, sentient beings respond with harm even when they are benefited; how they hurt others even though no one has hurt them; and how beings hurt other beings for no reason at all—such bodhisattvas may become saddened by cyclic existence and inclined to enter into the listeners' transcendence of suffering. Hence, it is said to be for the sake of those of uncertain potential that the perfect buddhas teach that there is but one vehicle. When it is explained to them that even after achieving the goal of having entered the listener's path, it will still be necessary to enter the Great Vehicle, the bodhisattvas will feel that they should enter this Great Vehicle from the beginning and never abandon it. They will not then turn away from the bodhisattva path.

The listeners with an uncertain potential have previously practiced the activities that are particular to listeners and, consequently, developed the listener potential. There are two kinds of listeners with an uncertain potential who enter the Great Vehicle and then become buddhas—(1) those who have seen the truths, which is the objective of their vehicle (the stream enterers, once-returners, and nonreturners) and (2) those who have not yet seen the truths, and who thus are ordinary individuals at the level of inspired conduct. Among those who have seen the truths, there are those who are free from the desires of the desire realm (the nonreturners) and those who are not yet free from the desires of the desire realm (the stream enterers and the once-returners). Regardless of whether they are free of those desires, whenever listeners of uncertain potential who have seen the objective of their vehicle enter the Great Vehicle, their faculties are dull, and it takes them a long time to achieve the fruition of buddhahood. Therefore, they are inferior to ordinary beings who enter the Great Vehicle.

Now, noble listeners turn their back on existence and attain that path of the noble ones whereby one will no longer be born in existence. When, on the other hand, such beings enter the Great Vehicle, they need to take birth in cyclic existence and accomplish accumulation, maturation, and cultivation throughout three incalculable eons. How, we may then wonder, is it possible for those who have attained that which exhausts existence to take birth again subsequently in cyclic existence? When listeners of uncertain potential have seen the truths, they may, regardless of whether they are free from desires, nevertheless not actualize the listeners' fruition. Instead they may, by the power of aspiration, transform the undefiled karma that they attained on the path of noble ones (and which is otherwise the remedy for existence in the three realms), so that it becomes the cause of again taking birth in existence. Thus they are in possession of the type of birth that is inconceivable to logicians. Through this, they continue to be born in cyclic existence again and again, engaging in the practices of accumulation, maturation, and cultivation.

The path of the noble ones causes one to turn away from cyclic existence; it is the remedy that brings an end to existence. So how, we may wonder, is it possible for that to become a cause of birth in cyclic existence? And indeed, it is not the path of the noble ones that alone produces birth in cyclic existence. However, nonreturners possess afflictions associated with the higher realms, and stream enterers and once-returners have in addition to this not exhausted the afflictions that belong to the desire realm and that are discards upon the path of cultivation. The commentary here states that these individuals can therefore dedicate their noble path to birth within cyclic existence. Thus, with the afflictions serving as causes, they are eventually born within cyclic existence.

The undefiled karma attained on the path of the noble ones never changes into something defiled; it is impossible for the undefiled to become defiled, or for virtue to become negativity. Yet it is possible to give up a prior intention to pursue the transcendence of one's own suffering by means of the undefiled path that relinquishes cyclic existence. Thus, through the power of taking up the aspiration to be born in cyclic existence, one can come to possess this inconceivable birth, whereby the listener's fruition will then not be actualized. This type of birth takes place on the strength of the mind's aspiration and because of the power of undefiled karma. It is, therefore, unlike ordinary birth. Hence, this is known as the attainment of inconceivable birth.

As for the listeners of uncertain potential who are not free from the desires of the desire realm, the buddhas may make them lose interest in their path of special insight, which is otherwise in accord with the transcendence of suffering, in that it involves the perception of cyclic existence as suffering and transcendence as peace. Instead, the buddhas will establish them on the path of great compassion, which is directly concerned with cyclic existence. Out of compassion, they then embrace birth within cyclic existence and become completely dedicated to existence. Since they are noble ones who have seen the meaning of the truths, they are not helplessly reborn in cyclic existence due to karma and afflictions in the same way as ordinary beings are. Instead, they embrace inconceivable birth.

Such beings are born in two ways, depending on whether or not they are free from the desires of the desire realm. Those who are not free from such desires are either stream enterers or once-returners. Out of compassion, these individuals aspire to be born in any way that may be of help to suffering sentient beings. Through the power of their aspirations, they are actually born in accordance with their wishes, and they then gather the accumulations by bringing benefit and happiness to sentient beings, thereby ultimately attaining buddhahood. As for those who are free from the desires of the desire realm, since they have attained the stage of no return to the realm of desire, they do not themselves take birth there. However, they display birth in the desire realm through emanations brought forth through meditative equipoise. Thereby they gather the accumulations and attain buddhahood.

Whether or not they are free from the desires of the desire realm, the minds of those who have seen the truths of the listeners' path are, due to the imprints of continuous training in the past, strongly inclined to take delight in their own welfare. Since these individuals are fond of transcendence, they are held to be slow to realize the fruition of the Great Vehicle. Those of the Lesser Vehicle who have not accomplished the objective of seeing the truths, and who are either ordinary beings with an uncertain potential, or listeners of the buddhas on the grounds of inspired conduct, may enter the Great Vehicle. Then, when their lives as human beings of the desire realm are over, they may be born as long-living gods in the desire realm. Having thus lived among the gods of longevity, they may again take birth in the desire realm, at a time when an enlightened teacher is no longer in the world, and his teachings have disappeared. Having been born there, they may, out of a lack of interest in the objects around them and through the power of previous familiarity with the words of the buddhas, actualize the noble path without a master, as if they were self-realized buddhas. Wishing to bring forth emanations, they strive with the objective of attaining the concentrations of the form realm. Based on the attainment of concentration, they will manifest emanations and bring benefit to sentient beings in the three realms. Perfecting the accumulations of merit and wakefulness, they eventually attain true enlightenment. The *Śrī Mālā Sūtra* gives the example of fire that spreads, in the end consuming the whole country. This metaphor illustrates the three contexts of first becoming a listener, then a self-realized buddha, and, in the end, a perfect buddha.

According to this tradition that accepts the finality of the three vehicles, those with uncertain potential can enter the Great Vehicle and become buddhas, but those with a listener potential that is certain, rather than uncertain, can never become buddhas. Therefore, forget about the possibility of those of the "cut-off" potential ever achieving buddhahood; they do not even have the fortune to accomplish the enlightenment of a listener or a self-realized buddha. This tradition also accepts that when the listener foe destroyers achieve transcendence of suffering without remainder, they have no chance of entering the Great Vehicle because the continuity of their five aggregates has been broken completely.

Proponents of the Middle Way assert that since all sentient beings have buddha nature, they are also all able to become buddhas. There are no beings without this potential because the nature of mind is luminous clarity; since the stains are adventitious, these obscurations can be shed. Therefore, when the listeners and self-realized buddhas attain the fruitions of enlightenment that pertain specifically to their own respective vehicles, they may for a while remain within their transcendence of suffering that is without remainder. Yet they will nevertheless be aroused by the light rays of the thus-gone ones and so emerge from the field of cessation. Accepting inconceivable birth, they will complete the accumulation, maturation, and cultivation, and so also become buddhas. This is what one will ultimately find to be the case, and this is also the teaching of the *Supreme Continuity*.

In consideration of the different constitutions, faculties, and intentions of sentient beings, the sūtras teach both of the above two traditions. In terms of the temporary context, no one can deny the existence of three vehicles that each have distinct paths and fruitions. Moreover, the case is similar regarding the issue of the so-called "cut-off" potential. This, therefore, is how the present issue should be explained.

11. The Investigation of the Five Fields of Knowledge

Unless they pursue the five fields of knowledge,
Even supreme noble beings will not become omniscient.
They therefore apply themselves to these so that they may
   conquer and provide for others,
And so that they themselves will know everything. [XII.60]

The next investigation concerns the fields of knowledge. **Unless they pursue the five fields of knowledge**—(1) the inner knowledge, (2) medicine, (3) linguistics, (4) reasoning, and (5) arts and sciences—**even** the members of the **supreme** among the three classes of **noble beings will not become omniscient**. This is because, generally speaking, these five are the causes of omniscience. **They**, the bodhisattvas, **therefore apply themselves to** mastering these five. **In particular, they** pursue linguistics and reasoning, **so that they may conquer** those who have no devotion; **and** they pursue medicine and the material arts and sciences to **provide for others** who are already devoted. **And**, with respect to the inner knowledge, they apply themselves **so that they themselves will know everything** that is taught in the three vessels.

Bodhisattvas of the Great Vehicle cut through superimpositions regarding the nature and manifestation of all things. Thus they gain accomplishment and achieve omniscience. Bodhisattvas must, therefore, pursue the knowledge of all things. The listeners who wish for peaceful happiness may, through the realization of the meaning of just one stanza of teaching, actualize the path that cuts through the root of existence and so attain their fruition. Yet, such listeners do not engage the vastness of the fields of knowledge. All mundane and supramundane topics of knowledge can be contained, as follows, within a simple enumeration of just five fields of knowledge.

(1) Topics such as poetry or philosophy must be understood based on the words whereby they are expressed. Therefore, the treatises on linguistics, or on the knowledge of language, are concerned with the correct presentation of the relationships of grammar and so forth that are relevant with respect to names, phrases, and letters.

(2) The treatises on reasoning, or on reliable means of cognition (which includes inference and perception), pursue the correct and unmistaken understanding of the meanings that are conveyed.

(3) The treatises on the mundane arts and sciences may, in terms of the body, be concerned with physical exercise, penmanship, or other crafts. With respect to the voice, they may, for example, address the seven melodies, or be concerned with religious or political rhetoric. In terms of

the mind, these treatises may pursue the distinction between what is upheld by the world as opposed to what is rejected by it. As exemplified by those devoted to the eightfold analysis, there are numerous treatises on the mundane arts and sciences.

(4) The treatises on medicine, or the knowledge of longevity, elicit expertise with respect to the causes of illness, the nature of illness, the remedies that alleviate illness, and the factors that prevent illness. Thus, these treatises generally show how, based on diet, lifestyle, and so forth, it is possible to cure the problems that ensue from surpluses, depletions, or imbalances within the natural constitutions of wind, bile, and phlegm, as found within the body. As for their various types, some among these treatises on the eight aspects of medicine are specifically concerned, for example, with the treatment of children or women. Others describe the healing of ailments caused by the temporary influence of external factors, such as poison, weapons, or spirits. Some treatises address the restoration of virility, so as to enhance semen and the experience of pleasure. Still others discuss the procedures for rejuvenation and the promotion of longevity by means of, for example, the extraction of essences through contact with someone who enjoys good physical health.

(5) The treatises on the inner knowledge, or the authentic sacred Dharma, teach without error the nature of the objects of cognition, just as they are and as many as they are. Thus they explain the path to the lasting happiness of liberation and omniscience. All the scriptures, including those of the five lesser fields of knowledge, are included within these five categories. Unless he or she diligently pursues expert knowledge of these five fields, even a supreme noble being (in the sense of being superior to those of the Lesser Vehicle) will never become omniscient. Why is this? Because to be omniscient is to know all objects of cognition, and all objects of cognition are contained within the five fields of knowledge. Therefore, it is impossible to be omniscient without knowing these five.

Moreover, those with the Great Vehicle potential have sharp faculties by nature, as well as vast intentions and broad intelligence. Thus, even on the grounds of inspired conduct, they pursue the knowledge of all objects of cognition as contained within the five fields, while dedicating their pursuit to the attainment of omniscient wakefulness. By the power of harmonious causal relationships, they accustom themselves with such practice throughout extremely many lifetimes. Once they have reached the grounds, the power of meditative absorption and wakefulness enables them to know whatever objects of cognition there are without any difficulty, and they familiarize themselves with such knowledge over innumerable lifetimes. Noble ones of the Great Vehicle exhibit a particular diligence with respect to the five fields of knowledge and become expert in them. It should be understood that they could not possibly lack expertise in the five fields. Please do not develop the pathetic idea that it is only after becoming a supremely noble being that one needs to take up training in the fields of knowledge.

The excellent insight, on the path of training, that ensures that one is not deluded regarding the five fields of knowledge may be referred to as "omniscient knowledge of the fields of learning." It is just like saying that "all medicine has been gathered" or "everybody has arrived," when just wishing to refer to the totality of what is relevant in a given situation. However, it is only by the perfection of such causal factors within a buddha's direct perception of all objects of cognition, as included in the five fields of knowledge, that one is fully qualified for the title "omniscient one."

Bodhisattvas strive to benefit beings, and they achieve the ability to do so by gaining knowledge of the five fields. It is with this altruistic objective in mind that they pursue omniscience. In order to conquer extremists and others who promote mistaken teachings, they train in the fields of linguistics and reliable means of cognition. In order to provide for sentient beings, both in general and individually, they train in medicine as well as in the arts and sciences. Finally, to ensure that they themselves may come to know genuinely all phenomena, exactly as they are and as many as they are, they train in the inner knowledge, the sacred Dharma. In this way, bodhisattvas wholeheartedly pursue the knowledge of the five fields.

The *Sūtra on Repaying Kindness* explains how it is necessary to study the sūtras and the others among the twelve sections of the sacred Dharma, the knowledge of reasoning or causes, linguistics, medicine, and the arts and sciences of the world. The sūtra then goes on to say:

If bodhisattvas do not train in the five fields of knowledge, they will never attain the omniscient wakefulness of unexcelled and completely perfect enlightenment. Therefore, in order to achieve unsurpassable enlightenment, one should train in the five fields of knowledge.

2. How the Mind Is Directed in the Investigation

The explanation of how the mind is directed in the investigation sets out the way the mind is directed to develop the element of the transcendences:

> There is joy through the observation of the cause,
> Recollecting the support,
> Wishing for the universal fruition,
> And aspiring in perfect accordance with enlightenment. [XII.61]

> Because of the four powers, there is joy,
> Definitive absence of weariness,
> And the four practices associated
> With conflicting factors and remedies. [XII.62]

> There is inspiration, true reception,
> The intention to be generous to others,
> Armor, aspiration prayer,
> Manifest joy, and creative mind. [XII.63]

> With respect to generosity and the rest of the six,
> There is attainment of power, maturation, worship, and reliance.
> In these there is supreme and true delight.
> There is also love. [XII.64]

> About that which was not done or poorly done,
> There is shame and regret.
> There is joy in the objective and weariness is considered the enemy.
> There is establishment and intelligence of expression. [XII.65]

Generosity and so forth are the support for complete
 enlightenment;
Not the Almighty or the like.
With respect to the two,
There is correct awareness in terms of flaws and good qualities.
 [XII.66]

There is joy through recollecting accumulation;
Perception of the great objective;
And the wish for spiritual practice, nonconceptuality,
Retention, and encounter. [XII.67]

There is the attainment of the power
Of relinquishing the seven mistaken ways of apprehending.
There are the four notions
Of the amazing and the unamazing. [XII.68]

There is equanimity toward sentient beings,
Perception of the great being,
Hoping for the reward of others' qualities,
Wishing for the three, and continuity. [XII.69]

Because of practicing in accordance with the Buddha's teaching,
The mind does not dwell on this side.
Hence, regarding beings who are inferior and who flourish,
There is displeasure and delight. [XII.70]

Regarding artificial and authentic training,
There is absence of faith and faith.
The mind is directed without acceptance,
And there is joy in the prophecy and the certainty. [XII.71]

There is seeing of future lives,
Intent on engagement, regarding as equal,
And, because of having accessed the supreme qualities,
Ascertainment of oneself as supreme. [XII.72]

These ways of directing the mind
Toward virtues caused by the ten transcendences
Bring forth a constant development
Of the bodhisattva element. [XII.73]

There next follows an investigation of the development of the element of the transcendences. **There is** the element that develops when one experiences the **joy** that occurs **through the observation of the cause,** the potential for the Great Vehicle, within oneself. This development continues through **recollecting the** presence of the **support** for the transcendences, which is the enlightened mind; through **wishing for the universal fruition** of the transcendences for all sentient beings; **and** through directing the mind in terms of one's **aspiring in perfect accordance with** the **enlightenment** that is achieved by all the buddhas of the three times as they realize the intrinsic nature of the transcendences. It should be understood that the progression of the stages is always of this kind.

Because of understanding that one possesses **the four powers** of (1) eliminating the factors that conflict with the transcendences, (2) fully maturing the accumulations, (3) benefiting self and other, and (4) supplying the ripened and concordant result in the future, **there is joy.** Likewise, there will be a **definitive absence of weariness** when one experiences suffering and the ingratitude of others while pursuing buddhahood for the benefit of both self and others. **And the four practices** for the attainment of enlightenment that are **associated with conflicting factors and remedies** will unfold. These four are (1) overcoming the individual conflicting factors, such as stinginess, (2) rejoicing in the remedies, such as generosity, (3) supplicating the buddhas to teach the Dharma of the six transcendences, and (4) dedicating everything toward enlightenment.

Beginning with devotion, **there is inspiration** with respect to the words and meanings that concern the transcendences. Beginning with the investigation of the Dharma, there is **true reception,** from the spiritual teacher, of the Dharma that concerns the transcendences. Beginning with teaching, there is **the intention to be generous to others** with the Dharma. Beginning with the practice, there is the donning of the perfectly complete **armor of generosity** and so forth, as well as the donning of armor for the sake of the practical instructions. There is **aspiration prayer** for the sake of encountering the circumstances for the perfection of the transcendences. There is **manifest joy** because of having previously practiced generosity, and so forth. The latter three ways of directing the mind are associated with the explanation of the instructions. **And,** finally, there is the continuous directing of the **creative mind** toward the practice of the transcendences. This latter way of directing the mind is explained in terms of the possession of skillful means.

The four ways that the mind is directed with delight are as follows. Since each of the six transcendences includes all of the others, **with respect to generosity and the rest of the six there is** (1) **the attainment of power;** (2) the **maturation** of sentient beings through the four means of attraction that are of the essence of the transcendences; (3) **worship,** which in the case of generosity is by means of possessions and veneration, and in the case of the remaining five takes place through practice; **and** (4) **reliance** on a spiritual teacher for the sake of flawless instruction. **In these there is supreme and true delight.**

There is also the directing of the mind through **love,** which involves the four immeasurables: (1) love in terms of the practice of generosity and the rest, (2) compassion for sentient beings who remain stingy and so forth, (3) joy for those sentient beings who possess generosity and the rest, and (4) the equanimity of wishing them to be free from thorough affliction.

The next section concerns the way in which there is shame. **About that which was not done** in terms of generosity and so forth, or about that which was done to a certain extent but not completely, **or** about that which was **poorly done** (that is, done incorrectly)—**there is shame and** then quickly **regret** so that one may be able to make the right choices. **There is** stable and undistracted **joy in the objective** (that is, generosity and the rest) **and,** while engaged in these, **weariness is considered the enemy. There is** endeavor in the **establishment** of the treatises that teach the six transcendences, **and** there is **intelligence of expression** as one wishes to teach these treatises in a way that is adjusted to the recipients.

As for the directing of the mind that is associated with the support, it is explained that **generosity and so forth are the support for complete enlightenment.** Its support is **not the Almighty or the like.** Hence, this implies that one should rely on the Dharma and not the person, as well as the rest of what is taught in the four reliances. As for the directing of the mind through the correct awarenesses, it is explained that **with respect to the two**—stinginess versus generosity, and so forth—**there is correct awareness in terms of flaws and good qualities.**

There is joy through recollecting that **the accumulation** of merit and wakefulness is engendered by practicing generosity and so forth. There is **perception of the great objective,** that is, generosity and the other factors that are conducive to enlightenment, which are seen to bring about its attainment. **And,** moreover, there is **the wish for** the **spiritual practice** that consists of the meditation of calm abiding and special insight, the wish for **nonconceptuality** beyond the three spheres, the wish for the **retention** of the words and meanings that are associated with teaching the Dharma of the six transcendences, and the wish to **encounter** the spiritual teacher who is the condition for the perfection of the transcendences.

There is the attainment of the power of relinquishing, by means of the remedies of the three meditative absorptions of emptiness and the rest, and of the four summaries of the Dharma, namely, **the seven mistaken ways of apprehending,** which are: (1) holding the imaginary, which is nonexistent, to be existent; (2) believing that cyclic existence, which is riddled with flaws, holds desirable qualities; (3) believing that the transcendence of suffering, which holds desirable qualities, does not hold such qualities; (4) believing conditioned things to be permanent and (5) pleasurable; (6) taking phenomena to be a self: (7) believing that the transcendence of suffering is not peaceful.

There are the four notions of the amazing, and four **of the unamazing.** The four notions of the amazing are concerned with: (1)

the vastness of the transcendences, (2) the length of time, (3) the absence of hope for a reward, and (4) a lack of interest in ripening. The four notions of the unamazing involve considering that: (1) since the causal transcendences are vast and long lasting, they accomplish the resultant buddhahood; (2) with the presence of such long-lasting vastness, the mind will be in equanimity with respect to self and others; (3) since the mind does not take delight even in the offerings proffered by Indra, it will not have any hope for common rewards; (4) since the mind is unimpressed even when attaining a body and enjoyments that exceed anything in the world, it is no wonder that it does not take any interest in ordinary ripening.

With generosity and so forth, **there is equanimity toward sentient beings,** as one provides for them without considering some near and others distant. There is the **perception of the great being** who benefits sentient beings with generosity and so forth. As one establishes others in the six transcendences, there is a **hoping** and wishing **for the reward of others'** streams of being—in terms of their becoming endowed with the **qualities** of generosity and so forth. There is a **wishing for the three,** namely, (1) the final ground of the bodhisattvas, (2) the final ground of buddhahood, (3) the accomplishment of the welfare of others. **And** there is meaningful **continuity,** as one engages in generosity and the other transcendences at all times.

Because of practicing generosity and so forth without error and **in accordance with the Buddha's teaching, the mind does not dwell on this side.** Hence, **regarding beings who are inferior and** those **who flourish** in their endeavor, **there is** respectively **displeasure and delight.**

Regarding the **artificial and** the **authentic** training in the transcendences, **there is,** respectively, **absence of faith and faith.** The **mind is directed without acceptance** of the conflicting factors, such as stinginess. **There is joy in** the attainment of **the prophecy** that concerns one's perfection of the transcendences at a particular time. **And** there is likewise joy in the attainment of abidance on **the** ground that is characterized by **certainty** in terms of the transcendences.

There is the seeing of the fact that once one has become a bodhisattva, one must pursue generosity and so forth in all **future lives**. Furthermore, there is the **intent on engagement** in the transcendences together with the other bodhisattvas, **regarding** oneself **as** their **equal**. **And, because of having accessed the supreme qualities** that are associated with the six transcendences (such as, in the case of generosity, generosity with the Dharma), there is an **authentic ascertainment of oneself as supreme**.

In conclusion it is said that **these ways of directing the mind toward virtues caused by the ten transcendences bring forth a constant development of the bodhisattva element**.

First, by observing the cause, the mind is directed to joy. After this, there follows the directing of the mind to recollecting the support, to the wish for universal fruition, to aspiring in perfect accordance with enlightenment, to consummate joy, to nonaversion, to the elimination of conflicting factors and the accomplishment of the remedies, to inspiration, and so forth, right up to the directing of the mind to oneself as being supreme. These ways of directing the mind develop the element of the transcendences in one's stream of being.

As for the first of these, the root text describes "joy through the observation of the cause." Bodhisattvas dwelling with the potential first investigate whether they possess within themselves the buddha potential—the capacity or potential that enables one to accomplish the six transcendences. Upon observing the presence of the cause that expresses itself as the wish to engage in the transcendences and attain buddhahood, they think, "I have the good fortune of becoming a buddha," and so—again and again—they direct their minds toward this fact with joy. Thereby the seed of the transcendences within the all-ground develops. Likewise, "recollecting the support" concerns the way in which those dwelling with the potential later generate the mind of unsurpassable enlightenment—the basis or support of the transcendences. Acknowledging this, they think with joy, "by generating the enlightened mind, I will perfect the transcendences," and so they recollect the support, the enlightened mind. Recollecting the enlightened mind with insight causes the element of the transcendences to develop.

Next, "wishing for the universal fruition" has to do with those who are practicing the six transcendences and are ripening the results of the transcendences. Their wishes are not only for their own sake, but for others as well. As they thence direct their minds by means of dedication, they develop the element of the transcendences.

"Aspiring in perfect accordance with enlightenment" refers to the aspiration: "Just as all the buddhas of the past, present, and future manifest unsurpassable enlightenment through the practice of the six transcendences, may I too attain manifest enlightenment by practicing the six transcendences." This likewise causes the element of the transcendences to develop.

These aforementioned ways of directing the mind—(1) to the joy of observing the cause, (2) to recollecting the generation of the enlightened mind, (3) to training in the transcendences with the wish to share their results with sentient beings, and (4) to attaining the unexcelled—all serve to develop further and further the seeds of the transcendences that already exist in the element of the all-ground consciousness. It should be noted, also, that the subsequent ways of directing the mind are ways of developing the element of the six transcendences. They are, moreover, presented in the order in which they are employed.

In the following section, the words of the scripture will receive a concise explanation.[36] The line "because of the four powers, there is joy" refers to the way, explained below, in which seeing that one possesses the four powers has the effect of directing the mind to joy. Similarly, the line "definitive absence of weariness" indicates the way in which noticing one's power to perfect a buddha's qualities completely and to bring sentient beings to maturity will direct the mind to a definitive absence of sadness. "With conflicting factors and remedies" refers to practicing, free from weariness and for the sake of accomplishing unsurpassable enlightenment, the elimination of stinginess and those other factors that conflict with the transcendences, while cultivating generosity and the other remedies. Thus arises a set of four ways of directing the mind.

The four powers are: (1) the power or ability to eliminate the factors that conflict with the transcendences; (2) the power to mature the accumulations of the transcendences, which are the remedies; (3) the power to benefit self and others; (4) the attainment of the ability to accomplish the transcendences at a future time, through the concordant and ripened effects.

What is understood by the power to eliminate conflicting factors? Generosity is seen to have the power to eliminate stinginess. In the same way, each of the other transcendences can eliminate its conflicting factor. Respectively, these conflicting factors are: flawed discipline, anger, laziness, distraction, and misguided intelligence. In terms of ripening the accumulations, one sees how the merit and wakefulness of the transcendences are accumulated and matured. Generosity, discipline, and patience accumulate merit, while insight and meditative absorption accumulate wakefulness. Diligence is involved in the accumulation of both.

How does this benefit self and others? Acts of generosity, carried out with joy and free of remorse, bring benefit to self both in the present and in the future. The act of giving also benefits others. Likewise, discipline and patience ensure that others are not harmed. With diligence, others' welfare is accomplished. By the power of concentration, others' sicknesses, bad harvests, and so forth, are overcome. Teaching the Dharma with insight brings benefit to others. It goes without saying that these practices also benefit self.

How do the concordant and ripened effects occur in the future? Generosity brings great riches. Discipline yields the attainment of a human or divine body. Through patience, one will achieve a beautiful, splendid retinue. Diligence brings the fulfillment of all actions. Concentration accomplishes a healthy body and an agile mind. Through insight, one becomes learned in all fields of knowledge. These are the ripened effects. As for the concordant effects, no matter where one is born in one's future lives, one will be fond of the practices of generosity and so forth, and so one will accomplish one's own benefit and bring others to maturation. These are the four powers.

Directing the mind to the absence of weariness concerns not becoming weary when working to bring sentient beings to maturity through the four means of attraction, as well as not becoming weary when involved in perfecting or completing the maturation of one's own enlightened qualities. The latter takes place by means of listening to the sacred Dharma and so forth, and through following a spiritual teacher. As one thus abides by the transcendences and establishes others in them as well, the ingratitude of others, together with whatever suffering may come about—such as heat, cold, hunger, thirst, or exhaustion—none of these cause one to grow disheartened. Instead one will practice the Dharma without conceit.

There are four ways of directing the mind in the practice of eliminating the conflicting factors and accomplishing the remedies. (1) If any of the negative actions from stinginess to misguided understanding occur, that is, the factors that conflict with the transcendences, one confesses each of them. (2) One rejoices in the practices of generosity and the other remedies whenever they are accomplished by either self or others. (3) One supplicates the thus-gone ones to turn the wheel of the Dharma on the profound and vast qualities of the transcendences. (4) One completely dedicates all fundamental virtues, such as those of confessing, rejoicing, and supplicating, to the attainment of unsurpassable enlightenment. On this topic, a sūtra states:

> "I individually confess all of my evil actions. I rejoice in all the fundamental virtues. I invoke and supplicate all the buddhas. May I and others attain true, supreme, and unexcelled wakefulness!"

Inspiration and true reception are also taught as being ways of directing the mind that cause the element of the transcendences to develop. "Inspiration" implies the directing of the mind by means of inspiration. This brings forth clarity in the mind regarding the Dharma teachings of the six transcendences and the meanings that these teachings reveal. "Dharma and meanings" refers to the Dharma teachings whereby the six transcendences are expressed and to the actual six transcendences themselves, that is, the subject matter of those teachings. Alternatively, "Dharma" can refer to the causal six transcendences and "meanings" to their results. In brief, this is the directing of the mind by means of trusting in the six transcendences as the foundation for all perfection, maturation, and cultivation—as well as trusting in the limitless qualities of their fruition. Having cultivated faith in this way, "true reception" concerns the directing of the mind to the pursuit and genuine reception of the teachings on the six transcendences. "The intention to be generous to others" implies directing the mind to the joy of giving this Dharma to others, or to the intention of doing so. These three ways of directing the mind belong to the context of the Dharma being explained.

"Armor" refers to directing the mind in such a way as to don the armor of the limitless practice of the transcendences. "Aspiration prayer" has to do with directing the mind in an aspiration to be able to practice the transcendences powerfully and without interruption throughout all lives, by means of the coming together of the conditions—in terms of one's spiritual teacher, one's associates, one's body, one's possessions, and so forth—for the perfecting of the transcendences. "Manifest joy" concerns wholeheartedly directing the mind to manifest joy in the practice of the transcendences, which in all lifetimes is the cause of attaining unsurpassable enlightenment. These three ways of directing the mind have to do with applying the instructions on the transcendences in the intended way.

Next follows the directing of the mind that is endowed with skillful means. "Creative mind" concerns directing the mind to the perfection of training in the transcendences. This not only involves one's own actual training, but also includes a sense of rejoicing in, taking delight in, and relishing the practices that are accomplished by others.

The four ways in which the mind is directed with delight is taught in the lines "with respect to generosity and the rest of the six..." down to "in this there is supreme and true delight." These four ways are: (1) directing the mind to delight in the attainment of the power of the six transcendences, (2) directing the mind to delight in the complete maturation of sentient beings, (3) directing the mind to delight in making offerings to the thus-gone ones, and (4) directing the mind to delight in following a spiritual friend.

For the first, directing the mind to delight in the attainment of the ability to practice the transcendences, there are thirty-six aspects—as each of the transcendences has six divisions, from the generosity of generosity to the generosity of insight, and so on. Thus, for example, the generosity of generosity includes the actual giving of various things, as well as the aspect of benefiting others at that time. The implicit sense of restraint from harmful action, of doing what is virtuous, and of benefiting sentient beings—is the discipline of generosity. There is also patience in the sense of enduring harm, and diligence in the efforts applied. There is concentration when considering that the mind is single-pointed without being derailed by conflicting factors. There is insight because one unmistakenly understands, in terms of the relative, what the causes and effects of the transcendences are, while ultimately embracing them with the nonobservation of the three spheres.

The second way of directing the mind with delight, "maturation," refers to delight in the complete maturation of sentient beings. This takes place by practicing the six transcendences through the four means of attraction. The third way, "worship," refers to the directing of the mind to delight in worshiping the thus-gone ones. Thus, in terms of transcendent generosity, one brings them material offerings and pays homage, while, with respect to the other five transcendences, one worships the buddhas by engaging in those practices. "Reliance" teaches the fourth way of directing the mind, which is to delight in following a spiritual teacher who unerringly teaches the Dharma of the transcendences. As one directs the mind with genuine and supreme delight to these four—the transcendences, the four means of attraction, worship, and reliance—the element of the transcendences develops.

Next follows directing the mind with love, which in the root verses is referred to with the word "love." This includes love, compassion, joy, and equanimity, just as they will be explained below in the discussion of the four immeasurables. In that context, compassion is not just pity for those who dwell with the factors that conflict with the six transcendences and for those who experience suffering as the result of these factors. Rather, with compassion, one strives, to the best of one's capacity, to clear away their suffering. As one seeks to rid them of conflicting factors and establish them in the transcendences, one pursues wholeheartedly the causal factors that will prevent the experience of suffering. Love is the wish for sentient beings to be happy, but this is not simple love: it establishes others in the transcendences, which are the causes of happiness. Joy means to have heartfelt joy whenever sentient beings are in possession of the causes of happiness—the six transcendences—or whenever they feel the resultant happiness itself. With that joy, one then establishes them in the virtues of the transcendences, which serve as causes to ensure that they do not subsequently separate from happiness. Equanimity is to be free from attachment and aversion. Hence, this involves wishing that those who are happy may be free from attachment and that those who suffer, for example, from being robbed of their possessions, may not develop aggression. It also involves teaching the Dharma of the transcendences since that Dharma is free from attachment and anger.

Directing the mind with shame is taught with the line "about that which was not done or poorly done, there is shame or regret." The transcendences that have never been done, have not been completed, or were done with miserliness or an attitude related to the lesser paths are known as inferior or poor actions. For these, there is shame and remorse. "There is joy in the objective" refers to the stable direction of the mind as it is directed to the joy of one-pointedly and continuously practicing the transcendences without distraction. "Weariness is considered the enemy" concerns the directing of the mind to the absence of weariness, in which case one thinks, "weariness is the enemy because when engaging in generosity and the other transcendences, feeling weary without wanting to practice is an obstacle to the attainment of unsurpassable enlightenment."

"There is establishment" refers to directing the mind with the wish to protect sentient beings by means of the teachings of the Dharma related to the six transcendences. This also involves establishing disciples in the treatises that explain the scriptural teachings. It is therefore also known as "directing the mind to establishment." This subject can be learned from the chapter on the factors of enlightenment. "Intelligence of expression" concerns directing the mind so as to teach intelligently in accordance with the distinctive character of the individual sentient beings who are the recipients of the teaching. Thus, this is described as knowing the mental abilities of the world. Below, in the chapter on the factors of enlightenment, the knowledge of the truths of the world's arising and fading will be taught. That, however, is in terms of ultimate knowledge.

Next it is taught that "generosity and so forth are the support for complete enlightenment, not the Almighty or the like." This line shows that generosity and the rest of the six transcendences are the support for complete enlightenment, not the Almighty, Brahma, and so on. This is the directing of the mind to the supported, and this way of directing the mind arises from the insight that is endowed with the four reliances.

The line "with respect to the two, there is correct awareness in terms of flaws and good qualities" concerns the directing of the mind to discrimination in the sense of correctly distinguishing, by means of the correct awareness of meanings, between the faults of the conflicting factors (such as becoming impoverished due to the conflicting factor that is miserliness) and the good qualities that ensue from their remedies, such as generosity. This is also known as "directing the mind to understanding."

Joy through recollecting the two accumulations is taught with the line "there is joy through recollecting accumulation." Generosity, discipline, and patience are the accumulation of merit; insight and concentration constitute the accumulation of wakefulness. Diligence constitutes the pursuit of the training in these and the relinquishment of their opposites. To recollect in this way how the accumulations are gathered is to direct the mind toward the joy that occurs through recollecting the accumulations.

Directing the mind through seeing the great objective is taught with the words "perception of the great objective." Generosity and the other transcendences are of the nature of the factors of enlightenment, and great enlightenment is the fulfillment of nonconceptual wakefulness. Since generosity and the other transcendences are the cause of attaining great enlightenment, one attains great enlightenment by completely perfecting them. Thus, they are perceived as great objectives.

"Spiritual practice" implies directing the mind to spiritual practice in the sense of training in the integration of calm abiding and special insight in order to completely perfect the six transcendences. "Nonconceptuality" concerns directing the mind with the wish for nonconceptuality. Nonconceptual wakefulness is the method for completely perfecting the transcendences, and this way of directing the mind serves to bring forth that wakefulness. Alternatively, directing the mind with the wish for nonconceptuality can be understood as the accomplishment of nonconceptual practice that ensues from the wish to engage in the transcendences nonconceptually. The present discussion of the two accumulations up through nonconceptuality can be seen to correlate with the treatment of these issues in the chapter on the factors of enlightenment.

"Retention" concerns directing the mind to retaining the transcendences. Thus, by the power of retention, one forgets neither the Dharma teachings whereby the transcendences are conveyed, nor the conveyed transcendences as such. "Encounter" refers to directing the mind to attaining the conditions. Thus one prays with the wish to meet, wherever one is born, spiritual teachers and other such favorable conditions for completely perfecting the transcendences.

The root text further states that "there is the attainment of the power of relinquishing the seven mistaken ways of apprehending." This involves directing the mind to the attainment of the power that ensues from the relinquishment of seven distorted ways of cultivating the transcendences. These seven distortions are relinquished by means of the three meditative absorptions and the four seals of Dharma. As for the three meditative absorptions, these serve as remedies for the three mistaken views: (1) taking the delusional phenomena of the imaginary, which do not exist, to exist; (2) taking the faulty phenomena of cyclic existence to have good qualities, such as permanence; (3) taking the transcendence of suffering, which is in possession of excellent qualities, to have no such good qualities. Thus the third misperception takes the transcendence of suffering to be an abyss—the extinction of the self—just as imagined by immature beings. Against these views, the meditative absorptions of emptiness, wishlessness, and absence of marks are, respectively, the remedy. Moreover, apprehending conditioned phenomena as permanent, defiled things as happiness, phenomena as self, and the transcendence of suffering as not peaceful—these are respectively remedied by the four summaries of the Dharma. The latter state that (1) all conditioned phenomena are impermanent, (2) all defiled things are suffering, (3) all phenomena are empty and devoid of self, and (4) the transcendence of suffering is peace.

All the above ways of directing the mind serve to develop the element of the transcendences. Moreover, all six—from inspiration to manifest joy—are treated elaborately in the six chapters on inspiration, the investigation of the Dharma, explanation of the Dharma, practice, practical instructions, and teaching. Likewise, "the creative mind" is explained in the chapter on skillful means; the six of generosity and so forth are discussed in the chapter on the attainment of power as well as in the section on the six transcendences that is to be found in the chapter on the transcendences; and the maturation of sentient beings is addressed in that chapter's section on the four means of attraction. Worship, reliance, and love correspond to the progression in the chapter on worship, reliance, and the immeasurables, whereas the progression from shame to the relinquishment of the seven ways of misapprehending follows the structure of the chapter on the factors that accord with enlightenment.

Next, the explanation of the two ways of directing the mind to the amazing and the unamazing are taught in the line "there are the four notions of the amazing and the unamazing." There are four ways of directing the mind to the notions of the amazing, just as there are four ways of directing the mind to the notions of the unamazing. Directing the mind to these will also develop the element of the six transcendences. In fact, at the end of the enumeration of all of these ways of directing the mind so as to develop the ten transcendences, stanza seventy-three states, "These ways of directing the mind toward virtues caused by the ten transcendences . . ." The message of that stanza pertains to all the enumerated principles, and therefore it need not be stated explicitly for each one of them.

What are the four notions of the amazing?

(1) In the chapter on the qualities, this is taught in the first and second stanzas. Thus, it is amazing to be able to train in the transcendences while being intent on relinquishing even that which is hard to relinquish, namely, one's own body. And yet, for the sake of one's practice of generosity, one will indeed relinquish, or give up, one's own body. Likewise, for the sake of discipline, one relinquishes whatever perfection there may be in terms of one's body, family, and so forth. Thus, for each of the transcendences all the way up to and including nonconceptual insight, there are amazing features.

(2) As for the amazing duration, it is a wonder that one is able to develop the idea of practicing the vast activities of the transcendences for three incalculable eons.

(3) As one practices the six transcendences, it is amazing that one does not hope to receive something in return in this life.

(4) It is likewise amazing that one does not hope for any future ripening, either. Further amazing issues are explained in the third stanza of that same chapter.

As for the four notions of the unamazing:

(1) When rice grows where rice is planted, that is not amazing, but it is simply the way that dependent and causally conditioned entities emerge. It is, therefore, also not quite so amazing that the cause that is the practice of limitless transcendences brings about an effect that manifests as limitless qualities of enlightenment.

(2) It would be amazing to benefit others in the same way as one benefits oneself if at the same time one were to keep holding oneself and others in different esteem. Yet, when the notion of self has been relinquished through a long process of cultivating its remedy, so that one now instead sees oneself and others as equal, it is not so amazing that one benefits sentient beings in the very same way as one benefits oneself.

(3) Bodhisattvas have no desire for rewards in the form of offerings and veneration, even if they were rendered by gods such as Indra or Brahma, who are supreme among ordinary sentient beings. Rather, they perceive such things to be as uninteresting as a gob of spit. How, then, could they possibly have any hope for a reward of this type, when out of love they are acting to benefit sentient beings? It is no wonder that they do not hold the slightest hope for a reward such as this, in return.

(4) Neither is it amazing that bodhisattvas do not hope for a ripened result. Bodhisattvas do not desire mundane ripening because it is certain that they will attain the supramundane three bodies and the undefiled bliss.

Next, "equanimity toward sentient beings" concerns the practice of establishing all sentient beings in the transcendences, seeing them all as equal without feeling near to some and far from others. This is directing the mind toward practice, which is also taught in the sixth stanza of the chapter on the qualities. "Perception of the great being" refers to the way that only happiness and benefit, and not even the slightest harm, can ensue from the practice of the six transcendences. Thus, the bodhisattva is seen, in six different regards, as a great being who grants nothing but happiness and benefit to all sentient beings. This way of directing the mind to observe the great being is taught in stanzas eight and nine in the chapter on the qualities, which explain how bodhisattvas benefit sentient beings. It is also explained in the subsequent stanzas of that chapter, which present seven examples—that of a mother, a father, a relative, and so on—as further illustrations of the way in which bodhisattvas bring benefit.

"Hoping for the reward of others' qualities" concerns the hopes of the bodhisattvas, which are fulfilled if they succeed in establishing others in the transcendences. When others thus come to possess qualities of the six transcendences, bodhisattvas think: "These sentient beings have benefited me." Bodhisattvas hope only for the qualities of others in return for their efforts; they do not wish for anything else. They feel that sentient beings must, by every means possible, come to possess the qualities of the transcendences. Whenever a sentient being thereby matures, that sentient being will have fulfilled the hopes of the bodhisattvas. This is known as "directing the mind to the wish for a reward," and it is the supreme way of repaying the kindness of the bodhisattvas. Their kindness is being repaid when sentient beings whom the bodhisattvas have established in the transcendences subsequently come to possess the qualities of the transcendences. Nothing else will repay the bodhisattvas' kindness, and they do not hope for anything else in return. This is also taught in stanzas twenty-four and twenty-five in the chapter on the qualities.

"Wishing for the three" refers to directing the mind toward hope or wishing. That which is wished for is threefold: (1) that all sentient beings may achieve the consummate stage of a bodhisattva, (2) that they may all achieve the final stage of buddhahood, and (3) that the welfare of sentient beings may be achieved. The first accomplishment is held to be that of bodhisattvas who have perfected the entire training from transcendent generosity on the first ground, which is the ground of generosity, all the way up to the transcendent wakefulness on the tenth ground. The second wish concerns the attainment of the consummate fruition of a buddha who has passed beyond the tenth ground. The third wish regards the benefit and happiness that the buddhas and bodhisattvas bring forth for all sentient beings. In the chapter on the qualities, this is taught in the twenty-sixth stanza.

"Continuity" refers to the practice of the transcendences being uninterrupted like the continual flow of a river, rather than practiced only sometimes, and at other times not. This is directing the mind to continuity. Thus, the bodhisattvas practice to ensure that the import of the teachings and instructions is not wasted. This is taught in stanza twenty-seven of the same chapter.

The next statement is: "Because of practicing in accordance with the Buddha's teaching, the mind does not dwell on this side." This refers to practicing the transcendences purely and in precise accordance with the Buddha's teachings. From the beginning of one's studies and reflections, when the mind of enlightenment has been brought forth for the first time, and all the way through to the achievement of buddhahood, one must muster diligence in the practice of the transcendences—without ever interrupting the training. To do so is to direct the mind in the manner of genuine endeavor. This is the teaching of the twenty-eighth and twenty-ninth stanza in the former chapter. The line "the mind does not dwell on this side" indicates that although one practices generosity and the rest, the mind does not dwell within the mundane domain, or "on this side," with desires for results in the form of enjoyments within cyclic existence or the like. In the commentary, this single line does not appear to be correlated with any particular explanation in the chapter on the qualities. It is therefore plausible that it should be joined with what has been taught above. Please consider whether that is warranted.

Next follows the statement: "Hence, regarding beings who are inferior and who flourish, there is displeasure and delight." This refers to seeing those whose practice of the transcendences is inferior, in the sense that it has declined, as uninspiring. As such, it is directing the mind by way of displeasure. On the other hand, seeing those sentient beings as inspiring who flourish and develop in the practices of generosity is to direct the mind by way of delight. In the chapter on the qualities, this is taught in stanzas thirty and thirty-one.

Likewise, "regarding artificial and authentic training, there is absence of faith and faith." This shows, on the one hand, how faith is absent when there is a cultivation of the six transcendences that is contrived and like a reflection. Thus, the mind is directed by way of lack of inspiration. When generosity is artificial, it is impure—a pretense of generosity—and the same holds for the rest of the transcendences, up to and including insight. With respect to the authentic cultivation of the transcendences, there is, on the other hand, faith: this is the directing of the mind by way of inspiration. These two are taught in the thirty-second and thirty-third stanza.

"The mind is directed without acceptance" shows how, when a factor that conflicts with the transcendences, such as miserliness, occurs in one's own mind stream or that of another, it is not accepted and is instead conquered by a remedy endowed with insight. This is the directing of the mind to nonacceptance, as taught in the thirty-fourth stanza of the chapter on the qualities.

As for "prophecy," the thus-gone ones may declare: "Noble Child, after such and such time you will perfect the transcendences, become a buddha, and achieve unsurpassable enlightenment." Wishing for, or taking delight in, the obtainment of that sort of prophecy is held to be the directing of the mind to prophecy. Alternatively, this can also be understood as the wish to achieve the eighth ground, which is the ground of prophecy. As for the nature of prophecy, this can be understood in a number of ways in relation to specific persons and times, just as it is taught in stanzas thirty-five to thirty-seven in the chapter on the qualities.

"Joy in the certainty" concerns directing the mind to the wish to abide upon the ground of certainty. Regarding this, there are two wishes: the wish for certain enjoyments and the wish for a certain birth. As for the first, upon perfecting transcendent generosity and attaining the first ground, one will attain twelve times one hundred qualities and so be able to perceive one hundred buddhas, be active in one hundred fields, and so on. These qualities are enhanced on each ground, and at the time of the tenth ground, when transcendent wakefulness is perfected, there is mastery of ineffable and inconceivable powers that extend throughout as many realms as there are particles in the world. Thus one also accomplishes the mastery of expert insight into the five fields of knowledge. As for the wish for certain birth, this means wishing to attain the tenth ground and become a bodhisattva who is in his or her final life. This part is taught in the thirty-eighth stanza.

The phrase "there is seeing of future lives, intent on engagement" concerns directing the mind to engagement through seeing what is coming in the future. Having generated the mind of enlightenment, one wishes for unsurpassable enlightenment, the cause of which is the transcendences. Seeing that in every lifetime one needs to practice these, there is an intention or mental direction to train continuously in the six transcendences in this life, also. Through practicing like that, one will witness the concordant result that takes the form of also training in the transcendences in future lives. Intent on seeing this happen, one then practices the transcendences. "Regarding as equal" concerns the directing of the mind to thinking in terms of equality. Thus one thinks: "As I continually train in the transcendences, I shall become equal to other bodhisattvas in body, speech, and mind."

The line "because of having accessed the supreme qualities, ascertainment of oneself as supreme" concerns directing the mind to the ascertainment of oneself as supreme. Here, one acknowledges the way in which one will attain the stage of a bodhisattva and a buddha by practicing the supreme path of the transcendences. As one thus enters into the Dharma of the supreme path and fruition, one will become superior even to those who are supreme among sentient beings, including also the listeners and self-realized buddhas. As the bodhisattvas in this way observe the ten transcendences, or as they direct their minds to the virtues that arise from the causal factors that are composed of the qualities of the transcendences, the element of the ten transcendences continually develops within their streams of being. These last three ways of directing the mind correspond to stanzas thirty-nine to forty-two, which teach the following: what is to be done without a doubt; what is to be done constantly; and the character of the foremost, supreme pursuits with respect to the transcendences. From here on, no further ways of directing the mind are taught. The reasons for this are set out as follows. The discussions of the Dharma, the truths, reasoning, and the vehicles that appear in the chapter on the qualities are included within this chapter on investigating Dharma, as well as elsewhere. Moreover, what follows in the chapter on the qualities, after these four topics, is a praise of the bodhisattva. The chapter on activity, from its discussion of the signs through to the grounds, is simply a description of various occasions on the path. Finally, the stanzas on the qualities of the fruition concern the qualities of enlightenment, which have already been discussed. It is, therefore, not necessary to formulate further specific ways of directing the mind. From the directing of the mind in terms of "joy through the observation of the cause" to "the ascertainment of oneself as supreme," there are, generally speaking, if one omits some internal subdivisions, altogether fifty-one principles enumerated. Since all these ways of directing the mind are taught in order to develop the element of the transcendences, they appear to be an outline of the entire scripture from beginning to end. Thus, the seven—beginning with "joy through the observation of the cause"—provide a general summary of the meaning of the ten chapters from refuge up to enlightenment. In particular, "observing the cause" concerns the potential, while "recollecting the support" relates to the foundational, inner support of the path, which is the mind of enlightenment. Moreover, since the sources for the reception of the enlightened mind are the three jewels, which serve as the outer support for the path, the recollecting of the support also includes refuge. Similarly, "directing the mind to enlightenment" includes the content of the chapters on reality and enlightenment, while the remaining four ways of directing the mind implicitly contain the subject matter of the chapters on power, maturation, and practice. Thus, although they do not correspond to the progression of the chapters, it appears that their subject matter is all included. From the directing of the mind to inspiration and onward, the progression follows that of the chapters in the manner explained above.

3. Specific Types of Investigation

Expansion, superior intent, and greatness
Are held to be the investigations of the steadfast ones.
These involve discards,
Involve no discards, and, likewise, mastery. [XII.74]

The investigations of the bodhisattvas
Are held to be lacking body, in possession of body,
The attainment of body, the completion of body,
Frequent pride, subtle pride, and the absence of pride. [XII.75]

In terms of divisions that pertain to investigation, there is the investigation of the **expansion** of inspiration that takes place through studies on the levels of inspired conduct. There is also the pure **superior intent**, which occurs through familiarity with the stream of the gateway of the Dharma, or through realizing the equality of self and others on the seven impure grounds, **and** there is **greatness** in the case of those who have attained the pure grounds. These **are held to be the investigations of the steadfast ones.** These investigations respectively **involve discards** through seeing, **involve no discards** through seeing, **and, likewise, mastery.**

The investigations of the Dharma that are carried out by **the bodhisattvas are held to be lacking** the **body** of qualities when they occur as a result of receiving teachings and reflecting. On the other hand, they are held to be **in possession of** the **body** of qualities when, on the grounds of inspired conduct, a mere semblance of nonconceptuality arises through meditation. Moreover, they are held to be **the attainment of body** on the seven impure grounds and to be **the completion of body** on the three pure grounds. They are also held to involve **frequent pride** on the grounds of inspired conduct, **subtle pride** on the first seven grounds, where the mere defiled mental cognition has not been abandoned, **and the absence of pride** upon the remaining grounds.

The Dharma includes the Dharma of scripture that is to be explained, as well as the Dharma of realization that is to be understood. There are thirteen specific principles that account for the way this Dharma is investigated.

(1) "Expansion" pertains to the stages of the grounds of inspired conduct, up to the supreme mundane quality, when one is an ordinary being who is beginning to listen to, and reflect upon, the sacred Dharma. This is called "expansion" because the seed of liberation is being developed.

(2) At the time of the supreme mundane quality, one discovers the meditative absorption of the stream of the gateways of the Dharma. From this time on, and from the first through the seventh ground, the context is called "possessing the superior intent" because the twofold selflessness is realized, and one has discovered the mind of equality with respect to self and other.

(3) The realization of the Dharma from the eighth to the tenth ground is called "greatness" because nonconceptual, spontaneously present wakefulness is attained. These three categories that are realized are held to constitute the steadfast bodhisattva's investigation of the Dharma.

(4) On the grounds of inspired conduct, up to the supreme mundane quality, the bodhisattvas have obstacles in the form of discards; their minds are not stable, they are influenced by association with virtuous and evil company, and they have not relinquished the two obscurations.

(5) From the first through the seventh ground, however, they no longer have these obstacles in the form of discards.

(6) The realization of the Dharma from the eighth to the tenth ground is associated with "mastery" because here there is spontaneously present mastery of nonconceptuality, superknowledge, and the cultivation of buddha fields. In this way, there is a threefold division by reference to the discards.

A fourfold division of the bodhisattva's investigation of the Dharma can be made in terms of their attainment.

(7) An ordinary being on the paths of accumulation and joining, up until acceptance, does not attain the nonconceptuality that is causally linked with the body of qualities; thus, there is no body of qualities.

(8) Nevertheless, duality is relinquished at the time of the supreme mundane quality, so an aspect of the body of qualities is discovered; hence, there is possession of body. This account is in keeping with that of the great commentary. Some say that the absence of the body of qualities pertains to the stages up to the middling path of accumulation on the grounds of inspired conduct. According to them, the possession of body occurs when, subsequent to the attainment of the meditative absorption of the stream of the Dharma on the greater path of accumulation, one discovers a semblance of nonconceptual wakefulness (which is the cause of the body of qualities) on the four stages of the path of joining.

(9) From the first to the seventh ground, the truth is directly seen by nonconceptual wakefulness through the involvement of effort. This is the discovery or attainment of the body.

(10) Finally, from the eighth to the tenth ground, nonconceptual wakefulness is effortless and spontaneously present; thus, the body is completely perfected.

There is also a threefold division based on the presence or absence of pride.

(11) There is frequent pride when one is an ordinary being, up to the time of the supreme quality.

(12) From the first through the seventh ground, there is subtle pride because on the first ground the imputed aspects of pride have been eliminated and, from the second ground, innate pride is also increasingly overcome.

(13) Since nonconceptual wakefulness is completely mature on the eighth through to the tenth ground, it is held that on those grounds there is no pride.

4. The Outcome of Investigation

This section has two parts: (1) the accomplishment of qualities and (2) the relinquishment of discards.

1. Accomplishment of Qualities

> The steadfast ones' Dharma is, in terms of form and the
>   formless,
> The cause of marks, the absence of disease,
> The mastery of superknowledges
> And inexhaustibility. [XII.76]

The next section concerns the purposes of the investigation. **The steadfast ones'** investigation of the **Dharma is, in terms of form and the formless,** respectively, **the cause of marks** and signs **and the** cause of the **absence of** the **disease** of the afflictions. It is also the cause of **the mastery of superknowledges and inexhaustibility** because its continuity is not interrupted even if suffering is transcended without remainder of the aggregates.

The result of the steadfast ones' investigation of the Dharma can be distinguished in terms of form, that is, body, and the formless—which refers to mind. The qualities of form include the accomplishment of the thirty-two major marks with their subsidiary features—the eighty minor signs. These are accomplished through receiving the Dharma, as well as reflecting and meditating on it. Likewise, as for the formless—the four aggregates of feelings, identifications, formations, and consciousness—these suffer from the disease of afflictions such as desire and anger. The causal factor that cures that disease is understanding the Dharma and practicing it because all the afflictions that are the discards of the paths of seeing and cultivation will then be utterly pacified. Moreover, the attainment of the mastery of superknowledges also arises in dependence upon the Dharma. Finally, when even in the transcendence of suffering without remainder, the qualities of the powers and so forth are still inexhaustible, this likewise is due to diligence in the Dharma. Thus, by seeking the Dharma and practicing it, one attains the qualities that are associated with form, the formless, the quelling of the disease of the afflictions, mastery, and inexhaustibility. The *Sūtra Requested by Brahma* states:

> Possessing four qualities, the bodhisattva investigates the Dharma. Since these four are rare, they are considered to be jewels. Since they cause an end to disease, they are thought of as medicine. Since they cause the bounty of superknowledge, they are held to be wealth. And since they are the cause of inexhaustibility, they are considered to be transcendence of suffering.

The Dharma is rare and hard to encounter. Yet if one does find it, it is deeply fulfilling, like a jewel that grants whatever is wished for. In the present context, this jewel-like preciousness is thought of in terms of the major and minor marks, which are like a beautiful and pure jewel, rare in the world. Just as medicine eliminates disease, the nectar of the Dharma heals what other medicines cannot; it is seen to be the great medicine that pacifies the disease of the afflictions. Worldly wealth is insignificant, limited, and runs out. Yet, through the sacred Dharma one will attain the perfect powers of superknowledge and so forth. As it yields the attainment of inexhaustible masteries, the Dharma is thought of as wealth. This sacred Dharma is the remedy that brings a complete end to all sufferings of birth, aging, and so on. Hence the Dharma is considered to be eternal happiness. It is the transcendence of suffering that, when attained, is everlasting and inexhaustible, being of the nature of peace, relief, happiness, and auspiciousness.

2. Relinquishment of Discards

> Existence, nonexistence, exaggeration, denigration,
> Oneness, multiplicity, nature, distinction,
> And the attachment to name and entity as such—
> These thoughts are to be abandoned by the children of the victorious ones. [XII.77]

The investigation of thoughts is as follows. As the remedy for thoughts of **existence**, it is, for example, taught that "the bodhisattva cannot be seen in accordance with reality" and, as a remedy for thoughts of **nonexistence**, we find teachings such as "the bodhisattva exists precisely as the bodhisattva." Thoughts that are **exaggeration** are remedied by statements such as "Śāriputra, form is empty due to the essential nature of form," while thoughts that are **denigration** are countered, for example, by "this is not because of emptiness." Thinking in terms of **oneness** is remedied by teachings such as "that which is the emptiness of form is not form," and thoughts of **multiplicity** are overcome by, for example, the statement that "form is nothing other than emptiness." Against thoughts that conceive of a characteristic **nature**, there are remedying teachings such as "that which is form is name only," and the idea of **distinction** is remedied by teachings such as "form does not arise and does not cease; it knows neither thorough affliction nor complete purification." **And, the attachment** to the idea of an entity that is captured by means of its **names** is remedied by teachings such as "names are artificial," **and** the attachment to a name that corresponds with a referent **entity as such** is countered by teachings such as "the bodhisattvas do not perceive any names in accordance with reality; and, because they do not perceive any names in accordance with reality, they have no such attachments either." **These thoughts are to be abandoned by the children of the victorious ones.**

Ten discards are relinquished by investigating the Dharma. These are the ten distracting thoughts that, as taught in the *Transcendent Insight,* are factors that conflict with the realization of reality:

> Children of the victorious ones, who investigate the Dharma, must relinquish ten thoughts through knowing the meaning of the Dharma. These ten are the four thoughts of existence, nonexistence, exaggeration, and denigration, as well as the thought of oneness, the thought of multiplicity or difference, the thought of an essential nature of phenomena, the thought of distinctions of phenomena, the thought of meanings captured by words, and the thought of words corresponding to meanings.

The *Transcendent Insight in One Hundred Thousand Lines* teaches: "Although there are bodhisattvas, the bodhisattva cannot be seen in accordance with reality." Holding the meaning of "emptiness" to be that phenomena are nonexistent in conventional terms would be a nihilist understanding of emptiness. Such a view is to be dispelled. On the other hand, the appearances of dependent arising, which are the dependent nature, do exist, and the ultimate and thoroughly established nature exists as their intrinsic nature. This is rightly conceiving of what exists as existent; hence, it is not an extreme. The sūtra states that "although there are bodhisattvas, the bodhisattva cannot . . ." The initial qualifier shows how the extreme of nonexistence is dispelled through the assertion of an individual that is present, conventionally, as a dependently arisen appearance.

However, if the individual were held to exist along the lines of the imaginary nature, that is, in the way that ordinary, immature beings believe it to exist, then that would imply the extreme of existence. Such a belief is therefore countered by saying that "the bodhisattva cannot be seen in accordance with reality." While there does appear to be an individual, there is no entity of a self because no self can be observed that is either the same as or different from the aggregates. Having in this way taught the absence of a personal self, the remaining statements all concern the absence of a self in phenomena.

The remedy that dispels the extremes of exaggeration and denigration is taught with statements such as: "Form is empty by its own essential nature; not because of emptiness." Phenomena such as form appear the way they do, but since they have no essence of their own, they are said to be empty in terms of their essential nature. Thus, form is taught to exist as mere imputation, which in turn dispels the exaggeration of ascribing ultimate existence to form. The teaching that this is "not because of emptiness" dispels the denigration involved in thinking that the emptiness of the thoroughly established nature does not exist. Such a belief ensues from the failure to distinguish correctly between what does and does not exist. Since this is a holding on to the idea of the nonexistence of everything, it is a view of denigration. In consideration of this, the sūtra therefore teaches that "things do not exist, nor are they nonexistent," thereby refuting both of the above extremes. Thus, the position that is particularly singled out for refutation here is the one that, without asserting anything, instead just randomly denies everything.

The remedy for the thought of oneness is taught by statements such as: "That which is the emptiness of form is not form; that which is form is not emptiness." Thus, the sūtras address the entities of form and so on versus their intrinsic nature of emptiness. The imagined and the thoroughly established are not one and the same because the former does not withstand analysis and is the domain of a deluded mind, while the latter does withstand analysis and is the domain of a mind that is free from delusion.

The remedy for the thought of difference is presented with the statement: "Emptiness is form. Form is emptiness. There is no form other than emptiness. There is no emptiness other than form." The various entities, or the appearances of duality, themselves abide as emptiness. There is no separate emptiness that exists apart from them. As with fire and its heat, emptiness is the very nature of these phenomena. As taught in the *Sūtra on the Definitive Explanation of the Intent*:

> The characteristics of the conditioned realms and the ultimate
> Are neither the same nor different;
> Those who conceive them as the same or different
> Are engaged in error.

Thus, the sūtra teaches how a distinct set of four faults ensues from the idea of oneness and another set of four from the concept of difference.

The remedy for thinking in terms of the nature, for example, of a thing like a vase, as well as the distinctive qualities that such a thing may possess (such as the vase's impermanence)—is taught with the statement: "That which is form is name only." We may speak of "that which is capable of being form" or "that which is characterized by experience," and we may say that "earth is solid" or "water is wet." Yet, other than simply as set forth by means of names and linguistic signs, there is nothing at all that exists in this way by virtue of any essence, characteristic, identity, or nature.

The remedy for the thought of difference is taught in the following way: "Form does not arise and does not cease, it knows neither thorough affliction nor complete purification." This applies to all phenomena. Ultimately, phenomena lack any essence whatsoever, so all the distinctions of arising and so forth are void.

One might think that when a name such as "vase" is spoken, the name captures a referent entity with which it is associated. One might think that objective entities (such as a vase) can be conceived of as they actually are, by means of their respective names. The remedy for such thoughts is presented in the statement: "Names are artificial and fake." There is no essential relationship between a name and its referent, yet an object comes to be implied when, for the sake of communication, immature beings employ strictly adventitious signs while at the same time conceiving of an object that corresponds with its name. When an object is seen, the object itself is held to be exactly that which the name expresses. Thus, while the minds of immature beings superimpose names onto objects, there is, actually, no object expressed, and the name that is the means of expression is not established as real, either. All phenomena are inexpressible, beyond words; therefore, they are not even observed to be names only.

5. Summary

Thus, the virtuous intelligence, with intense diligence,
Investigates the twofold intrinsic nature, including suchness,

And manifests, therefore, always as the teacher of beings,
Like an ocean full of excellent qualities. [XII.78]

This was the twelfth chapter of the *Ornament of the Great Vehicle Sūtras,* the chapter on the investigation of the Dharma.

The concluding verses express the magnificence of the investigation of the Dharma. Thus, **the virtuous intelligence** (the aspect of intent), **with intense diligence** (the aspect of application), **investigates the twofold intrinsic nature** (referring to the relative and ultimate truths), **including suchness, and** so the child of the victorious ones **manifests, therefore, always as the teacher of beings, like an** enormous **ocean full of excellent qualities.**

The subject matter of this chapter is summarized by way of expressing the magnificence of the investigation of the Dharma. Hence, the intelligence that observes all the phenomena of the profound and the vast possesses tremendous means of virtue that are endowed with the transcendences. With intense diligence that is free from laziness, faintheartedness, or delusion, it investigates the Dharma. Examining the intrinsic nature of the two truths of the ultimate and relative, it unerringly ascertains and genuinely realizes this intrinsic nature, just as it is. (At this point the translation in Sthiramati's commentary uses the expression "observes the intrinsic nature that is endowed with the two truths.")

Pursuing the Dharma in this way, the bodhisattva always manifests as the teacher of beings—someone who, without error, explains the fine statements of the Dharma to others. Like an enormous ocean containing masses of water and all manner of jewels, the bodhisattva's stream of being is saturated with the excellent qualities of the path and fruition.

This concludes the explanation of the twelfth chapter of the *Ornament of the Great Vehicle Sūtras,* the chapter on the investigation of the Dharma.

13
Teaching

3. Teaching the Dharma

There are five sections in this chapter on explaining the Dharma to others: (1) showing that it is reasonable to teach others the Dharma without stinginess, (2) the purpose of teaching the Dharma, (3) the way to teach the Dharma, (4) the nature of the Dharma that is taught, and (5) a concluding summary.

1. It is Reasonable to Teach Others the Dharma without Stinginess

> The lives of the steadfast ones and their enjoyments, acquired with great hardship and yet futile,
> Are always, most happily and in full, passed on to suffering beings.
> What need then is there to speak of the expansive Dharma, that constant source of benefit,
> Which is not obtained with hardship, and which, when given, is not depleted but enriched? [XIII.1]

By way of prohibiting stinginess in the Dharma teacher, it is explained that **the lives of the steadfast** children of the victorious **ones and their enjoyments, acquired with great hardship and yet futile, are always, most happily and in full, passed on to suffering beings. What need then is there to speak of the expansive Dharma** of the Great Vehicle, **that constant source of benefit,** which, at a time when the teachings remain, **is not obtained with hardship, and which, when given, is not depleted but enriched?**

Bodhisattvas discover the Dharma by investigating it. Once they have understood it, free from error, they explain it without stinginess to sentient beings, thereby perfecting the transcendences for themselves and bringing other sentient beings to maturation. Since there is no other better means to accomplish perfection, one must by all means teach.

Stable bodhisattvas acquire their bodies or lives by having gathered great accumulations of virtue in the past, while the great number of enjoyments they experience arise from great hardships, such as those endured when journeying on the sea. They know that all possessions will be exhausted in the end; they are devoid of any essence and cannot be relied upon. For this reason, bodhisattvas will always happily pass on the domains they rule and vast enjoyments as material offerings in a way that completely fulfills the wishes of the recipients—sentient beings who suffer.

The sacred Dharma is vast and expansive; it is never exhausted. It is a constant source of benefit for beings in this and all other lives. Hence it is unlike material offerings; we can rely on it, and it is truly meaningful. When a Buddha has appeared in the world and his teachings remain, it is easy to obtain the Dharma for those who pursue it; it does not require the great hardship one must endure when, for example, going on a sea voyage in pursuit of material wealth. Moreover, even when one is extremely generous with it, there is no risk that the Dharma that is present within one's stream of being might thereby become depleted. On the contrary, it will expand and become enriched whenever one gives it away to others. Hence, there is no need to mention that bodhisattvas do not hesitate to give the Dharma to sentient beings. Having investigated the Dharma, they definitely teach it to others.

2. Purpose of Teaching the Dharma

As it is the object of individual awareness, the Blessed One did
  not teach the Dharma.
The embodiment of compassion, like the giant snake, by

    means of the reasoned exposition of the breath-like
    Dharma,
Draws beings to his own Dharma and establishes them truly
    within
The pure, vast, universal, and inexhaustible mouth of perfect
    peace. [XIII.2]

The meditation of those who possess spiritual training is,
    therefore, not meaningless;
Hence, the teaching of the bliss-gone ones is not meaningless
    either.
Meditation would serve no purpose if hearing alone would
    make one see reality;
Teaching would be meaningless if even without hearing one
    would enter the meditation. [XIII.3]

As it is the object of the wakefulness of **individual** direct **awareness, the Blessed One did not teach the Dharma** that he had realized to others. In which case, what then did he teach? Think of the example of the great snake, the *ajagara*, which while asleep emits a stream of saliva. Any living being that touches this stream of saliva will be held by it and then consumed by the snake once the snake has woken up. Similarly, the blessed Buddha, who is **the embodiment of compassion, like the giant snake, by means of the reasoned exposition of the breath-like Dharma** contained in the twelve sections of the scriptural teachings, **draws** those **beings** who are to be trained **to his own Dharma** of realization **and establishes them truly within** the bliss of **the pure** (in the absence of the two obscurations), **vast, universal** (since it is the attainment of all the buddhas in common), **and inexhaustible mouth of perfect peace** that is beyond constructs.

    The meditation of those who possess spiritual training is, therefore, not meaningless because based on it, they realize the Dharma that is the object of one's individual awareness. **Hence, the teaching of the bliss-gone ones is not meaningless either** because it leads beings to their intrinsic nature. **Meditation would**

serve no purpose if hearing alone would make one see the reality of absence of self; and **teaching would be meaningless if even without hearing one would enter the meditation** on the reality of absence of self.

The ultimate Dharma of realization, which is accessed by the noble ones with individual direct awareness, lies beyond the domain of words and letters. Yet, in order to attain this Dharma of realization, the Dharma of scripture is taught by means of words and letters. Moreover, without studying and contemplating the Dharma of scripture, one will never be able to attain the Dharma of realization. Thus, the Blessed One has taught the Dharma of scripture, which is the domain of receiving teachings and reflecting on them, as the means for actualizing one's own direct awareness. Since the Dharma of realization is an object of direct awareness within the mind streams of the noble ones, this Dharma cannot be directly taught to those who lack such direct awareness. Rather, the noble ones' Dharma of realization is to be individually and directly realized in one's own awareness. In this sense, the blessed buddhas have not taught the Dharma that takes the form of words and letters because that which is known by one's own direct awareness cannot be shown as it is in words and letters. It is referred to as "the object of one's own direct awareness" because it is beyond all the world's expressions, thoughts, examples, and arguments. This is unlike worldly knowledge; it is not like knowing about conditioned phenomena such as pillars and vases, or unconditioned phenomena like space. Hence, suchness is that which is realized by the direct awareness of those who possess the noble ones' wakefulness. If even the domain of those who have attained mundane concentration is inconceivable to those who have not, there is no need to mention that the domain of supramundane wakefulness is not the domain of mundane studies and so forth.

One may wonder, then, how it can be declared in the profound sūtras that the Buddha explained the nature of the object of one's own direct awareness—the definitive meaning as he had realized it in his own awakened mind? The Blessed One, as the embodiment of compassion for sentient beings, is compared to a great snake. The giant snake, called the *ajagara,* is said to be so large that its back can support ploughed fields and flowing rivers. From the mouth of the snake comes a fluid that streams like a river and when wild deer drink from this, thinking it is a river and not saliva, they die. When the snake then inhales, the animals are brought into its mouth.

The Buddha is said to be like that giant snake. Possessing the four reasonings, he explains all issues without error and in a perfectly reasonable and cogent way. In this regard, scriptural teachings can be seen to be like the snake's breath because they have the power to draw beings in. The twelve sections of the scriptural teachings of Dharma catch the host of beings to be trained, who are like the wild deer in the metaphor, and pull them into the Buddha's own authentic path of Dharma. Thus, in the end they become truly established within, as it were, the "mouth of the Buddha," that is, the complete transcendence of suffering and its origin, which is the body of qualities. The body of qualities is supreme purity because it is free from the two obscurations. With its vast qualities of the powers and so forth, it is supreme bliss; since it is the universal body that is common to all the buddhas, it is the supreme self, the great nature; and, because it can never be exhausted, it is the transcendent, supreme permanence.

The perfect object of one's own direct awareness is the buddha body of qualities, and no sentient being has ever gained enlightenment by taking the body of qualities to be just as it is taught in words. Nevertheless, the Dharma of scripture, the unmistaken teaching on the profound reality and the factors of skillful means, is the cause for realizing this ultimate body of qualities. This is because, by following the path of listening, reflecting, and meditating free from error, one's own direct awareness that is the wakefulness of the noble ones will undeniably be attained.

Once this wakefulness has flawlessly recognized the inconceivable reality that is the object of one's own direct awareness, one will, in the end, thereby also actualize the enlightened wakefulness of the body of qualities. Thus, while the object of one's own direct awareness cannot be directly expressed by words, it can, based on the Dharma of scripture, be expressed indirectly. Therefore, the meditation is not meaningless of those who possess the spiritual training endowed with calm abiding and special insight, for the wakefulness of one's own direct awareness comes about based on it.

Just as there is a point to meditation, there is also a point to the Dharma taught by the bliss-gone ones in the sūtras and elsewhere, because it enables one to meditate free from error. Non-Buddhists, who lack the path of meditation on reality, are not able to accomplish the path of liberation through their meditations on the self and so on. Rather, one must listen to the Dharma teachings that reveal the real condition of things without error, such as teachings on meditation in the context of absence of self. Having gained certainty about their meaning through reflection, one then meditates in accord with what one has understood, and so one's own direct awareness that perceives reality will become manifest. Otherwise, if it were the case that the facts of the absence of self and so on could be seen directly, simply upon hearing about them, then this alone would be sufficient for liberation, and the process of accustoming oneself to those facts through meditation would accordingly be meaningless. Likewise, if, on their own, people were to begin the meditation on matters such as the absence of self without even having listened to the Dharma teachings that explain them, then the teachings of scripture would also be meaningless and serve no purpose.

Nevertheless, this is not the case. In order to attain the wakefulness of the noble ones—one's own direct awareness that realizes the intrinsic nature exactly as it is—one must first hear the sacred Dharma, then gain certainty about its meaning through reflection, and then also meditate one-pointedly on the ascertained facts. In this way, the insight that arises from listening to the Dharma is the beginning of everything. The teachings of scripture—that is, the Dharma that is listened to and explained—are therefore deeply meaningful and serve a great purpose.

3. How to Teach the Dharma

This section considers: (1) the way that bodhisattvas teach the Dharma and (2) the way that buddhas teach the Dharma.

1. The Way Bodhisattvas Teach the Dharma

This section has three parts: (1) enumerating the ways of explanation, (2) the excellent meaning, and (3) the excellent words.

1. Enumerating the Ways of Explanation

The teaching of a supreme heroic being
Comes from scripture, realization, and mastery.
Emerging from the mouth and all sorts of form,
It even arises from space. [XIII.4]

The next section concerns the ways in which the teachings are given. The Dharma **teaching of a supreme heroic being comes from** the Buddha's **scripture,** his or her own **realization** of the nature of things, **and** the **mastery** that is attained on the pure grounds. **Emerging from the mouth,** trees, **and all sorts of forms, it even arises from space.**

Three ways to teach the Dharma are enumerated in this section. On the grounds of inspired conduct, bodhisattvas base their explanations on scripture, explaining in the same way that they themselves have heard from spiritual teachers—other bodhisattvas and buddhas. From the first to the seventh ground, they explain by the power of their realization of the basic field of phenomena. On the three pure grounds, they explain the Dharma with the mastery of spontaneously accomplished nonconceptual wakefulness and superknowledge. Moreover, on the eighth ground and beyond, the blessings of their attained masteries will cause Dharma explanations to emerge in song from their own mouths and those of others, as well as through sounds of music. The sounds of Dharma being explained will likewise emerge from all types of form, such as walls and musical instruments, for example. The sounds of the Dharma teachings will even emerge from space.

2. Excellent Meaning

A teaching that is vast, free from doubt,
Trustworthy, and reveals the twofold reality—
This is what is known
As the bodhisattva's excellent teaching. [XIII.5]

The teaching of the supreme bodhisattva
Is gentle, free from conceit, untiring,
Clear, diverse, reasoned,
Comprehensible, unconcerned with material things, and universal. [XIII.6]

On the excellence of the teaching, it is said: **A teaching that is vast**, based on extensive learning, **free from doubt** due to great insight, **trustworthy** because the three gateways are free from negative factors, **and** which **reveals the twofold reality** of the thorough affliction associated with suffering and its origin and the complete purification of cessation and the path—**this is what is known as the bodhisattva's excellent teaching** of the Dharma.

Moreover, **the teaching of the supreme bodhisattva is gentle** in its way of offering replies, and it is **free from conceit** based on either the praise of others or the bodhisattva's own ability to prove, by means of scripture and reasoning, the issues that are otherwise hard to fathom. It is **untiring**, and since it does not conceal what is to be explained, it is **clear** in presenting the complete message. Without repetition it presents **diverse** principles, and since it does not conflict with the genuine means of reliable cognition, it is **reasoned**. It is **comprehensible** because the words and letters conform with the conventions of the world. It is **unconcerned with material things, and** as it reveals all three vehicles, **it is universal**.

Due to their extensive learning, bodhisattvas teach and elucidate vast issues that are connected with the Dharma. Since they themselves have no doubts regarding the Dharma, they can dispel the doubts of others. Because they themselves abide by the Dharma, their words can be trusted. They are pleasant to listen to and agreeable. As they teach in this way, they reveal the twofold reality in terms of thorough affliction and complete purification. The bodhisattvas' excellent Dharma teaching characteristically possesses such qualities, just as is also stated in the *Sūtra Requested by Brahma*:

With extensive learning, one explains the sacred Dharma on a vast scale to ensure that it remains in the world for a long time. As one trains in the Dharma, and teaches it, one's own insight is sharpened further, and the doubts of others are dispelled. Abiding by the Dharma oneself, one will behave as a holy being, and one's words will be held with respect and in esteem. Since one teaches the ways of thorough affliction and complete purification, or the relative and the ultimate, as they relate to the nature of the four truths, one's teaching is deeply meaningful.

Furthermore, there is also a set of nine principles that are characteristic of excellent teaching. The supreme bodhisattva's Dharma teaching is (1) gentle, for even if others seek to refute them, bodhisattvas do not respond with any harsh words. (2) Even when they receive honor and praise, they will not harbor any conceit. (3) They are untiring, for while teaching the Dharma, they feel no weariness. (4) They explain the teachings clearly, disclosing the issues completely, without concealing anything that should be explained. (5) While covering numerous issues, their teaching is free from repetition. (6) It is reasoned because it does not stand in any conflict with reliable means of cognition. (7) Since the teachings are expressed by means of words and letters that are renowned in the world, they are highly comprehensible. (8) Because bodhisattvas have relinquished the desire for honor or gain, they have no concern for material things. Finally, (9) since they are learned in all the vehicles, bodhisattvas teach in a way that is universal, in the sense that they explain the subject matter of all three of the vehicles. In possessing such qualities, the teaching of the bodhisattvas is one of excellent meaning.

3. Excellent Words

The words of the child of the victorious ones are not subdued,
But delightful, well spoken, established,
Appropriate, without concern for material things,
Proportionate, and far reaching. [XIII.7]

Teaching, explanation,
Accordance with the vehicles, delight,
Acceptance, appropriateness,
Definitive emergence, and accordance—[XIII.8]

In short, such are
The excellent letters of the supreme bodhisattvas. [XIII.9a–b]

On the excellence of the words, it is taught: **The words of the children of the victorious ones are not subdued** for they reach everywhere in the circle, but they are **delightful** to the ear, and as they clearly account for their meaning, they are **well spoken**. They are **established** because they provide access to the relevant meaning. They are **appropriately** adjusted to the various contexts of the world. They are spoken **without concern for material things**. They are **proportionate** since they do not cause weariness among the audience, **and**, as they are inexhaustible, they are **far reaching**.

Next, regarding the excellence of the letters, it is taught: **Teaching** with words and letters that do not contradict reason, **explanation** in accordance with the teaching, **accordance with the** three **vehicles, delight** through statements made without anxiety, expression as per the world's **acceptance, appropriateness** through teaching individually in accordance with those to be trained, **definitive emergence, and accordance with** the transcendence of suffering—**in short, such are the excellent letters of the supreme bodhisattvas.**

The words with which the children of the victorious ones explain the Dharma are (1) not cowed or subdued. They are not spoken so softly that some people can hear them while others cannot; they reach everywhere in the circle. (2) The words are also pleasant, gentle, and delightful to the ear, while to the mind they are reasonable and compelling. (3) They are well spoken and eloquent, as they are lucid words that elicit comprehension of their meaning. (4) If words that are not well established in the world are expressed, others do not understand, but when words and phrases that are indeed established in the world are spoken, meaning is conveyed. The bodhisattvas' words are in this way "established." (5) They are also taught in accordance with the mind streams of those to be trained, as appropriate. Hence, they are suited to the audience. (6) Their words are not spoken out of an interest in honor and gain. On the contrary, they are expressed with neither concern for nor dependence on material things. (7) If there is an excess of words, teachings become tiring, so the bodhisattvas' words are proportionate and measured for the sake of easy retention. Likewise, (8) their words are far reaching, imbued with an inexhaustible capacity for vast explanation.

In the sūtras, it is said that the words explained have eight qualities—pervasiveness, excellence, lucidity, conveyance, suitability, independence, proportion, and inexhaustibility. These correspond with the above explanation.

Although not depending on gain and honor is a mental quality, here it seems to be invoked in consideration of the way the words are not influenced by impulses to teach those who bring gain and honor, or to despise and refrain from teaching those who do not.

There are also eight good qualities concerning the way these words are explained. These are as follows: (1) When the teaching is concise, the overall meaning of the words is easy to grasp; (2) the subjects are also explained in detail so that their import can be ascertained; (3) the explanation is in accord with the vehicles, so disciples possessing any one of the three potentials will be taught the corresponding vehicle; (4) the teaching is easy to listen to since it is delivered without mixing up the sequence of words, letters, or meanings; (5) the words and letters used in the teaching are well known and established; (6) the teaching is, in whichever way called for, appropriately adjusted to the mind streams of the disciples; (7) it reveals the Dharma of the path of the noble ones, the definitive emergence from the three realms; (8) it is the Dharma that accords with the eightfold path of the noble ones. Such are, in short, the excellent letters of the supreme bodhisattva.

The sūtras teach the following eight excellent qualities of the letters: (1) possession of reasonable words, (2) possession of reasonable letters, (3) adherence, (4) full accord, (5) acceptance, (6) accord, (7) full accord, and (8) fulfillment of the accumulations for attaining learning. These principles can be applied to what was explained above. Thus (1–2) the words and letters that are endowed with the reasoning of the threefold reliable means of cognition convey teachings that are concise, as well as detailed explanations of that which was taught concisely. (3) The words and letters adhere to the vehicles, (4) are true in the sense that they are presented in a way that does not mix them up, and they are gentle and not hard to listen to because they are in full accord with the mind. (5) They are also established and generally accepted, and can hence readily be understood. (6) They are appropriate in the sense that they accord with the individual recipients. (7) Since they teach the path of the noble ones, they follow in full accord with the transcendence of suffering. (8) When it is said that they fulfill the accumulations for attaining learning, the following should be understood. Those who possess learning are the seven types of individual from the stream enterer to the foe destroyer of entry. The "fulfillment of the accumulations" refers to the perfection of the accumulations associated with their respective paths of seeing and cultivation. Thus, this accords with the noble eightfold path. This is how the correlation is explained in the great commentary.

2. How the Buddhas Teach the Dharma

The speech of the Bliss-Gone One is infinite,
Consisting of the inconceivable sixty qualities. [XIII.9c-d]

Speech and words that are extremely reasonable,
Presenting, distinguishing, and cutting through doubt,
With many repetitions for those who understand
By indication and through elaboration, [XIII.10]

This teaching of the buddhas
Is beyond the three spheres.
Moreover, it should be known to be
Free from the eight defects. [XIII.11]

Laziness, incomprehensibility,
Failing to take an opportunity, uncertainty,

Failing to cut through doubts,
Failing to do so in a lasting way, [XIII.12]

Weariness, and stinginess—
These are held to be defects of discourse.
Because it is free of those,
The teaching of the Buddha is unsurpassable. [XIII.13]

The speech of the Bliss-Gone One is infinite, consisting of the inconceivable sixty qualities that are taught in the *Sūtra of the Inconceivable Secret*. Considering the magnificent nature of this teaching, the following qualities are enumerated: expressive **speech and** labeling **words that are extremely reasonable,** briefly **presenting** classifications, **distinguishing** distinct features, **and cutting through doubt** by means of commentary. **With many** clarifying **repetitions—teaching** through brief summary **for those who understand by indication, and** explaining comprehensively and completely for those who understand **through** a teaching of **elaboration—this teaching of the buddhas is beyond the three spheres** because the buddhas do not apprehend any reality with respect to the means of teaching (speech and words), the mode of the teaching (the features of presenting and so forth), or the recipients of the teaching (those who understand through indication and elaboration).

Moreover, it should also **be known to be free from the eight defects.** These eight are (1) refraining from teaching due to **laziness,** (2) **incomprehensibility** due to lacking clarity of expression, (3) **failing to take an opportunity** to teach, (4) **uncertainty** because of a failure to ascertain the given issue, (5) **failing to cut through** present **doubts,** (6) **failing to do so in a lasting way,** (7) failing to teach again and again because of **weariness, and** (8) teaching incompletely because of **stinginess—these are held to be defects of discourse. Because it is free of those, the teaching of the Buddha is unsurpassable.**

The voice of the bliss-gone ones' Dharma teaching has an infinite and inconceivable melody, but, in short, it is endowed with the sixty aspects of melodious speech, just as taught in the *Sūtra of the Inconceivable Secret*. Each of these aspects also has infinite qualities of melodious speech, so that the buddhas' speech is inconceivable. The sixty aspects are as follows.

(1) Just as grass, trees, and other types of vegetation are brought forth and enriched by water, the speech of the buddhas serves to bring forth and enhance the fundamental virtues of sentient beings. Thus, the exalted voice is gentle and rich. (2) Like the soft garments of the gods, which are delightful to touch, the mere sound of a buddha's voice brings happiness to the mind within the very same life. Thus, the exalted voice is soft. (3) In teaching the two truths, dependent origination, the factors of enlightenment, and so forth, it is delightful. (4) It is also compelling because it does not make use of the words and letters of ordinary cowherds, or the like. Rather, it consists of the words and letters of gods and noble beings.

(5) The voice of the buddhas is pure because it is attained subsequent to nonconceptual wakefulness, the great supramundane wakefulness that is free from the two obscurations. (6) Since it is free from latent afflictions, it is flawless. (7) In making clear use of words and letters that are established in the world, it is perfectly lucid. (8) As it possesses the power to dispel the negative views of extremists and the like, it is indomitable, or powerful. (9) When applied as taught, it brings deliverance beyond the three realms. Hence, it merits being listened to. (10) Because the speech of a buddha cannot be refuted by opponents, it is indomitable. (11) Since it delights the mind of the listener, it is pleasant. (12) Because it subdues desire and all other afflictions, it is subjugating. (13) Regarding the training, it is not forceful. This is because, unlike severe commands such as the extremists' reliance on the five fires, the teaching of the buddhas is conveniently applied. (14) Because it shows the methods of confession, restoration, and so forth, in the event of a downfall, it is neither impractical nor harsh.

(15) Teaching the three vehicles, it thoroughly tames beings of various potentials. (16) As the speech of buddhas is delightful and gentle, one will not want to let go of it. Instilling keen and undistracted interest, it

is gratifying to the ear. (17) Such speech fosters meditative absorption. Thus, its pliancy satisfies the body. (18) Its special insight satisfies the mind. Cutting through the pains of doubt, it is gratifying to the heart, and, without either lack of understanding or misunderstanding, it thus produces (19) joy of the heart and (20) happiness. (21) When put into practice as taught, the teaching of the buddhas lets one attain the fruition without fail. Hence, since there will be no regrets based on the sense that one's listening to it served no purpose, such teaching is free from anguish. (22) Since it is the basis for perfect insight through listening, it provides knowledge of everything. (23) As the source of perfect insight through reflection, it calls for awareness. (24) Providing thorough accounts without holding anything back, it elucidates completely.

(25) Those who have accomplished their own welfare are the eight categories of persons consisting of stream enterers and so forth, as well as bodhisattvas of the ten grounds and thus-gone ones. The noble listeners and bodhisattvas witness the attainment of their own welfare by means of the voice of the thus-gone ones. As it produces joy, the speech of the buddhas is joyous. (26) Wishing to accomplish their own welfare, ordinary beings, who have not yet done so, enter into the teachings of the thus-gone ones. Thus, the enlightened voice is thoroughly delightful. (27) The basic field of phenomena that is to be individually cognized, the nonconceptual wakefulness, and the factors of enlightenment are all inconceivable. As it reveals these inconceivable factors, the speech of the buddhas delivers knowledge of everything. Alternatively, this aspect of the enlightened voice can also be understood in terms of its delivering teachings on the following four inconceivable topics: (1) the activities that accomplish various external entities, (2) the field that is accessed through the meditative absorption of spiritual practitioners, (3) the field that is accessed by the thus-gone ones, and (4) the powers of medicine and mantra. (28) Since the voice of the buddhas teaches the vast topics that are to be contemplated, such as the aggregates, elements, grounds, and transcendences, it engenders awareness.

(29) The enlightened speech is reasonable, for its expression is endowed with the three reliable means of cognition. (30) Its teaching is in harmony with the minds of its recipients. Hence, since it thus accords with their mind streams, it is relevant. (31) Although the same

issue may be taught in many different ways, the voice of the buddhas is not repetitive. The phrases that make up the various enumerations found in the sūtras, for example, each carry their own separate points for understanding.

(32) The voice of the buddhas intimidates opponents and extremists, just like the roar of a lion is frightening to deer. Thus, they cannot withstand the roar of the declaration of the absence of self, and other such teachings of the buddhas. (33) It is also said that, within the circle of the assembly, this speech resounds like the trumpeting of an elephant. Here it is explained that the example is not the type of elephant that is found in this world of humans. Rather, the reference is to elephants such as Airāvata,[37] the elephant of the gods, whose trumpeting is never meek or unclear. (34) The voice of the buddhas is also likened to the rumbling thunder of a dragon. The commentary explains this with reference to the fact that a buddha's voice does not sound overly loud when one is nearby, nor is it ever hard to hear when one is at a distance. Thus, always balanced, it resembles the "sound of the clouds," or the thunder of dragons. (34) In the realm of the nāgas, the words of the nāga king are always received as delightful and authentic by his subjects. Similarly, since, gods, demigods, and others will pay heed to the voice of a buddha, it resembles the voice of the king of the nāgas. (35) Among all the voices of sentient beings, that of the gandharvas is the most delightful. Hence, the voice of the buddhas is compared to the song of the kinnaras and gandharvas.

(37) The voice of the kalaviṅka bird is captivating, for it is unbroken and becomes more melodious, the more that one listens to it. Since it is continuous and becomes ever more enrapturing, the voice of the buddhas is also likened to the kalaviṅka's song. (Some have here claimed that the example builds on the fact that when one has become fond of the kalaviṅka's song one will want to continue listening, even when the bird has stopped singing. Thus, they say, if one has once listened to the voice of a buddha, one will want to do so again.) (38) The voice of Brahma is never fragmented, but gentle and extended. Similarly, when a buddha speaks there is never any shortness of breath. (39) The civacivaka bird is known for its auspicious tune. If, while in the pursuit of something, one hears the song of this bird it is a sure sign that one will accomplish all that

one wishes. Likewise, hearing the buddha's speech is the auspicious sign of one's attainment of all aims that transcend the world, because, when one has heard the teachings, this will lead to the accomplishment of all aims in the future. (40) Because his words are genuine, everyone respects and abides by the commands of Indra. Similarly, no one can break the command of a buddha. (41) The sound of the drum of the gods brings defeat for the demigods and victory to the gods. Hence, when hearing it, the demigods will flee by themselves. The buddhas are victorious in the face of all demons and attackers. When they turn the wheel of Dharma, whoever hears their teaching will, similarly, defeat all demonic forces.

(42) Even when praised by the whole world, including the gods, a buddha will not develop pride. Hence, a buddha's voice is free from arrogance and conceit. (43) Nor do they become reticent, for if demons, extremists, or others criticize their teachings and declare them wrong, this will not influence a buddha. (44) The term *vyākaraṇa* covers communication and linguistic determination. In the present context, the term refers to the way buddhas definitively point out all issues pertaining to the past, future, or present. Alternatively, it may be understood in terms of the way their voice ascertains all topics within the fields of learning in accordance with [the rules] of communication, or the way their voice abides by all the principles of grammar, adhering to the characteristics of proper sentence structure and the systems for communication.

(45) With unfailing mindfulness, a buddha's voice never treats a given issue insufficiently. Conversely, free from forgetfulness, it always flawlessly covers the various topics of the teachings. (46) Teaching all activities involved in bringing forth, increasing, and perfecting fundamental virtues for the benefit of those to be trained, it is never incomplete. (47) Free from craving for material gain, respect, and so on, it is unattached, or as certain editions have it, it is undaunted. (48) When teaching the Dharma within the assembly, a buddha speaks without any fear of demons, or the like. Thus, his voice is free from weakness, or undaunted (as it again appears in certain editions). (49) The mind of a buddha never becomes weary of teaching the Dharma, nor does a buddha ever feel any physical discomfort from teaching. In this way, they speak with thorough joy. (50) Exhaustively comprehending all fields of learning, they

answer any question without hindrance. Thus, as it teaches all issues extensively and comprehensively, the voice of the buddhas is described as vast, or pervasive.

(51) Their voice is free from misdeeds because for those sentient beings who have not given rise to roots of virtue and are involved in misdeeds, it elicits understanding of the way to accomplish one's objectives. (52) It is also continuous and constant because the teaching of the Dharma is delivered always and without interruption. (53) It is rich, engaged, and sophisticated, as it explains elaborately, reveling in an abundance of words, phrases, and letters. (54) It delivers every word perfectly because each statement that a buddha makes will be heard by gods, nāgas, humans, animals, spirits, and so on, each in their individual language. (55) When a buddha speaks, the words will be understood by sentient beings in accordance with their specific wishes. Thus, it pleases and gratifies everyone's senses. (56) Whatever the buddhas propose, they will uphold all the way to perfection, without ever giving up and letting their declaration be wasted. Thus, their voice is irreproachable. This quality can also be understood in terms of the definitive character of a buddha's speech. When teaching that a given path leads to a given fruition, no sentient being will be able to object and deny that this is indeed the case. (57) The voice of a buddha is unchanging and immutable as it benefits others because whenever the time is right for a certain sentient being to be helped, the buddhas will always respond, without any delay. (58) The speech of the buddhas is also stable and unhurried, for it never expresses itself with excessive or inappropriate speed. (59) Those in the presence of a buddha will all hear the words of the teachings delivered at a perfect volume, clearly and exactly. This, however, is also the case with those who are present at a distance from the teacher, and even with individuals to be trained who are located beyond exceedingly many universes. Everyone hears just as well as those who are present right in front of the buddha, and so a buddha's voice resounds throughout the assembly. (60) Finally, unhindered in teaching the Dharma, the buddhas make use of all things as examples and so they reveal all meanings. Thus, their voice is endowed with all supreme features.

It is said that there are eight ways in which the speech of the Buddha teaches the Dharma: (1) presenting the essence of an object, as with nouns and expressions such as "pillar," and explaining the distinctive qualities of such objects by means of phrases, such as "the pillar is impermanent"; (2) teaching through reliable means of cognition in a way that is extremely logical, and is hence an explanation that fully "possesses the meaning" or "possesses the root"; (3) briefly presenting; (4) elaborately explaining the issue that was briefly presented; (5) cutting through doubts by means of reasoning; (6) repeatedly using various arguments to prove points; (7) explaining for those who comprehend through brief indication; and (8) explaining for those who understand through elaborations. These eight are derived from the sūtras, which may state that such and such an issue has been "named," "set forth," "discerned," "provided with commentary," "made clear," "shown," and "thoroughly explained." To someone who follows the teachings based on faith, the Buddha may explain by means of demonstrative nouns and phrases that show the distinctive qualities of their referents, as when, for example, saying that "all conditioned phenomena are impermanent." To someone who follows the teachings based on reason, such a teaching is then proved by reasoning. Thereby it is provided with "root" or facticity, thus showing that the statement has been made through reliable means of cognition. With a mere brief presentation, the general structure of the subject matter is set forth, and its significance is then expanded on and discerned in detail. To cut through doubts, there is commentary. To ensure that the meaning is understood without error, further principles of elucidation are brought forth and applied repeatedly, thereby producing perfectly clear comprehension. The essential meaning is shown in brief to those who understand through indication. For those who understand through elaboration, there are extensive presentations, which are comprehensive teachings or thorough accounts.

The first two principles are the means of expression; the following four (presentation and so on) are the manner of expression; and the last two concern the audience to whom the teaching is expressed. In this manner, the eightfold way in which the buddhas teach the Dharma is free from the three spheres of the agent of teaching, the activity of teaching, and the recipients. Since the buddhas have reached the culmination of nonconceptual wakefulness, they do not observe those spheres when teaching the Dharma. Hence, their teaching is extremely pure.

Moreover, one should know that the Buddha's Dharma teaching is free from the eight defects of discourse. These eight are as follows. (1) The laziness of being attached to sleep and not taking joy in explaining the Dharma. (2) Incomprehensibility despite one's teaching the Dharma, which may be due to either one's own lack of precise realization or one's failure to teach clearly in terms of both words and content. (3) Not taking the opportunity to teach the Dharma because of feeling disinclined. (4) Uncertainty, or lack of definitive meaning, which occurs when one fails to teach the definitive meaning and instead teaches the expedient. Alternatively, this can refer to a situation where others fail to ascertain the meaning of the teaching because the teaching lacks detail. (5) Teaching the Dharma but failing to cut through the doubts and reservations of those to be trained. (6) Failure to consider, from numerous angles and by numerous means, those issues about which there is no longer doubt—so as to fully determine them. (7) Weariness because one takes teaching the Dharma as a burden. (8) Being stingy with the Dharma and concealing it. In the context of discourse, these are held to be faults and, because the Buddha's explanation of the Dharma is free from these defects, it is declared to be unexcelled.

The latter eight are the factors that conflict with the former eight. Thus: (1) as the Buddha presents the teaching, there is no laziness. (2) As the teaching is related to reasoning, its meaning is understood. (3) The opportunity is taken and a brief presentation is provided. (4) Uncertainty is dispelled through elaborate explanation. (5) Doubts are cut through. (6) The method of teaching is persistent. (7) Without weariness, the teaching is delivered elaborately to those who gain understanding thereby. (8) To those who can understand through indication, it is granted without stinginess. While the two sets thus correlate, it seems that Sthiramati's commentary does not make this connection explicit.

4. The Nature of the Dharma That Is Taught

This section has two parts: (1) the general characteristics of the Dharma and (2) the specific explanation of the intent and concealed intent.

1. General Characteristics of the Dharma

Faith, joy, and intelligence—since it causes these,
This Dharma is virtuous.
Endowed with the twofold meaning, it is easy to comprehend,
And it teaches a pure conduct that possesses four qualities.
   [XIII.14]

Possession of that which is not shared by others,
Complete elimination of the afflictions of the three realms,
Essential purity, and purity in the absence of stains—
Thus it is held to be a pure conduct that possesses four
   qualities. [XIII.15]

The next section is concerned with the excellence of meaning. First arises **faith**, as one feels trust in the message one hears. Next, when reflecting on what was heard and decisively examining it with reasoning, one experiences **joy** as one comes to see that one is indeed capable of attaining this. And finally, at the time of meditating, the **intelligence** that sees in perfect accordance with reality arises. **Since it causes these** qualities to occur, **this Dharma is virtuous** in the beginning, middle, and end. It is of excellent meaning, for it is **endowed with the twofold meaning** of the relative and of reality itself. Its various means of expression are also excellent, and so **it is easy to comprehend**. And, moreover, **it teaches a pure conduct that possesses four qualities**: (1) **possession of that which is** unique and **not shared by others**, (2) **complete** cultivation of the remedies that bring about the **elimination of the afflictions of the three realms**, (3) **essential** absence of defilement and, hence, complete **purity**, (4) **purity in the absence of** the adventitious **stains** and, hence, complete purification. **Thus it is held to be a pure conduct that possesses four qualities.**

What, we may wonder, is considered to be "sacred Dharma"? That which is in possession of three virtues, two excellences, and four qualities is held to be the scriptural teaching of the Thus-Gone One, the sacred Dharma.

That is to say, listening to the Dharma causes the faith of conviction to arise. Thus, the Dharma is virtuous in the beginning. When one reflects on it, it produces joy through the discovery of certainty. Hence, it is virtuous in the middle. At the time of meditation, it is the cause for genuine intelligence, and therefore it is also virtuous at the end. In this way, the sacred Dharma is nothing but virtuous and excellent throughout the beginning, middle, and end.

The two excellences imply an endowment with excellent meanings and excellent words. The first refers to the fact that the sacred Dharma fully and flawlessly delivers that which is to be understood, namely, the meaning of the relative and ultimate truths. The possession of excellent words is in terms of the Dharma being taught through perfect words and letters that are in tune with the terminologies established in the world. Because of this accordance, the words are easy to understand and easy to retain.

The Dharma of scripture teaches the path of the noble ones, which is endowed with four qualities of pure conduct. "Pure" in this context refers to the transcendence of suffering, just as the sūtras speak of "attaining purity, coolness, the transcendence of suffering." Hence the path of the noble ones, which causes one to attain the transcendence of suffering, is referred to as "pure conduct." This path has four qualities, as follows. (1) It is unique because only this Dharma possesses such noble qualities. They are not shared with others, such as the non-Buddhist extremists. (2) The path of the noble ones completely relinquishes the entirety of the afflictions of the three realms. Hence, it is also thoroughly complete. The mundane paths, on the other hand, may lead to the summit of existence—but from there one will have to return. In terms of the permanent elimination of all the afflictions, such paths are therefore still incomplete. (3) The path of the noble ones is naturally pure, like space or a crystal. As it is by nature undefiled, it is thoroughly pure. (4) Finally, by this path, the adventitious stains are removed and do not arise again. Hence, as it transforms the mind into the nature that is free from defilement, it is also thoroughly purifying. These are asserted to be the four qualities of pure conduct.

2. Specific Explanation of the Intent and Concealed Intent

The thus-gone ones teach the Dharma in accordance with the constitutions, capacities, and inclinations of those to be trained. There ensue, therefore, numerous teachings that are given with a specific intent or a particular concealed intent. If, without properly knowing the intent of a given teaching, one holds on to what is literally expressed, one will not realize the genuine and definitive meaning of that teaching. Not only that—one will also misunderstand its expedient meaning, thinking that the words mean just what they say, when in fact the meaning requires interpretation. Hence, it is extremely important to differentiate these correctly. The present section will, for this purpose, include (1) an explanation of the four concealed intents, (2) an explanation of the four intents, and (3) an explanation of the eight intents with respect to remedies, along with the benefits of such teaching.

1. The Four Concealed Intents

Concealed intent on access,
Concealed intent on characteristics,
Concealed intent on remedies,
And concealed intent on change—[XIII.16]

Thus, relating to the listeners, the essential nature,
The overcoming of flaws,
And the profundity of expression,
The concealed intent is fourfold. [XIII.17]

On the enumeration of concealed intents, it is taught as follows. (1) **Concealed intent on access** is when, for the sake of letting listeners with an indeterminate heritage gain access to the Great Vehicle, it is taught that, for example, form exists. (2) **Concealed intent on characteristics** is when, keeping in mind the three characteristics of the imaginary and so forth, it is taught that all phenomena are devoid of essential nature, that they have not arisen, and so forth.

(3) **Concealed intent on remedies** is when the intent is to overcome flaws. (4) **Concealed intent on change** refers to a teaching that considers profound expressions. **Thus, relating** respectively **to the listeners, the three essential natures, the overcoming of the eight flaws, and the profundity of expression, the concealed intent is fourfold.**

The four concealed intentions concern (1) the entry of particular individuals, (2) the characteristics of phenomena, (3) the remedies to overcome the flaws in the stream of being of those to be trained, and (4) the alteration of the meaning of words and letters into something other than what is established in the world. These four will next be explained in succession.

(1) Intending the entry into the path of liberation for listeners who are unable to access the absence of a self in phenomena, the Buddha teaches that phenomena that lack a personal self, such as the aggregates, do exist. Such statements are simply made with a view to the nonexistence of the imaginary person and the conventional existence of the dependently arisen phenomena that constitute the dependent nature.

(2) The teachings on the lack of essential nature, nonarising, and so forth, do not mean to say that conventionally existent phenomena are utterly nonexistent and that they do not appear to arise and cease. Rather, the concealed intent relates to the characteristics or the essential nature of the ultimate, and it can thus be explained in terms of the teaching of the imaginary, dependent, and the thoroughly established natures. The essence or characteristic of the imaginary is total nonexistence; thus, the imaginary has no characteristics. Based on dependent minds and mental states, there appear places, objects, and bodies that seem to arise and cease, yet these appear due to the dependent arising of causes and conditions. There is no arising or ceasing in terms of their own essential nature, and so they have no essence of arising. The thoroughly established nature is the absence of essential nature—in the sense that it is by nature the transcendence of suffering, peace, emptiness, and the ultimate.

(3) Like the former, the concealed intent on remedies serves to overcome the flaws in an individual's stream of being. An example of this can be found in statements such as: "In the past, when I was the Buddha

Vipaśvin . . ." This will be explained below, in the context of the eight intents with respect to remedies.

The concealed intent on change is when, in consideration of a profound issue, the words that are used to address that issue are not to be understood literally. An example of this can be found in the following declaration:

> Know the meaningless to be meaningful,
> Abide in the inverted,
> Be completely struck by affliction,
> And you will achieve true enlightenment.

If the words of this statement were taken literally, they would present the causes for not attaining enlightenment. Yet, the word *sāra* applies to both distraction and what is lacking in essence or meaning. The prefix *a* is a negation, so *asāra* can also mean without distraction. Thus the message of the sentence becomes that the training in special attention should be known or realized as being meaningful. Moreover, thoughts of purity, bliss, permanence, and the self are inverted ways of grasping at entities. By inverting those graspings themselves, one will abide in the training in special insight that is an awareness of impermanence, suffering, impurity, and no-self. Finally, by letting oneself be struck by the afflictions of taking on hardships for the welfare of sentient beings for a long time, one will in the end achieve true enlightenment. In the great commentary, the first three lines are correlated with inspired conduct, the path of seeing, and the path of cultivation. However, independently of such a correlation, they may also be understood in terms of meditative absorption, insight, and diligence. These, then, are the four concealed intents.

2. The Four Intents

> Equality, another meaning,
> Another time,
> And individual inclinations—
> This is known as the fourfold intent. [XIII.18]

The enumeration of intents is explained as follows. (1) When, for example, the Buddha says, "At that time I myself was the Buddha Vipaśvin," his intent is to convey the **equality** of the truth body. (2) When it is taught, "all phenomena are devoid of essential nature; they have no arising" and so forth, the intent is to convey **another meaning**. (3) The intent on **another time** is when, for example, it is taught that "whoever directs prayers toward the Realm of Bliss will be born there." (4) The intent on **individual inclinations** is when the same root of virtue is praised for some and reviled for others, who would otherwise be content with lesser virtue. This is to be **known as the fourfold intent**.

(1) Considering the equality of the truth bodies of all the buddhas, our teacher, the king of the Śākyas, has, for instance, said: "At that time I myself was the Buddha Vipaśvin." (2) Similarly, being aware of another meaning, namely, the ultimate, he has taught: "All phenomena are devoid of essential nature. Without arising and without ceasing, they are peace from the beginning and naturally the transcendence of suffering." (3) Likewise, with a view to another time, the Thus-Gone One has, for the benefit of lazy beings who fail to cultivate any fundamental virtues, said that by merely praying to be born in Amitābha's pure field, one will indeed take birth there. This statement concerns the fact that one will be born there in some future lifetime. (4) Finally, considering the individual inclinations of beings, the Buddha may, for example, praise generosity for those who can be greatly generous, while to others who are content with just a minor amount of giving, he may treat generosity with contempt, or as not very remarkable. For others again, who believe that generosity alone is sufficient, and who hold generosity alone to be supreme, he shows it to be inferior to discipline, which he will then praise instead. These are the four intents. Teachings given with such intents occur extremely frequently. A selection of examples can be found in the *Compendium on the Great Vehicle*.

3. The Eight Intents with Respect to Remedies, along with the Benefits

Disdain for the Buddha and the Dharma,
Laziness, contentment with the insignificant,
Pride, engagement with desire,
Regret, and return of those uncertain—[XIII.19]

These are obscurations of sentient beings,
And the supreme vehicle is taught as their remedy.
Thereby, all of the obstructing
Flaws will be overcome. [XIII.20]

Whoever, in word or meaning, upholds
And applies himself or herself to these two stanzas
Is a supremely intelligent being
Who will attain ten different qualities: [XIII.21]

Exhaustive development of the element,
Supreme joy at the time of death,
Birth in accordance with his or her wishes,
Perfect recall of previous lives, [XIII.22]

Meeting with buddhas,
Hearing the supreme vehicle from them,
Devotion endowed with intelligence,
The two gateways, and swift attainment of enlightenment.
[XIII.23]

These two stanzas summarize the extremely vast sūtras of the Great Vehicle and their benefits. (1) The obscuring flaw of **disdain for** the Capable One, **the Buddha**, is remedied by teachings such as: "at that time I myself was . . ." **and** (2) the obscuring flaw of disdain for **the Dharma** is remedied by the teaching that "only after one has venerated as many buddhas as there are grains of sand in the river Ganga will the realization of the Great Vehicle arise." (3) The obscuration of **laziness** is remedied by the teaching: "those who direct their prayers toward the Realm of Bliss . . ." (4) In order to remedy **contentment with the insignificant,** generosity and so forth are praised at some times and reviled at others. (5) In order to remedy **pride** about one's personal physique or powers, there are teachings that extol the bodies and powers of various buddhas. (6) So as to remedy **engagement with desire** based on attachment to the excellences of the three realms, there are praises of various pure realms. (7) As a remedy of intense **regret,** it is taught that "even if one harms buddhas or bodhisattvas, one will go to the higher realms." (8) **And,** as a remedy of the **return** to the inferior vehicle **of those** bodhisattvas whose potential is **uncertain,** there is the teaching that, in the end, the vehicles are one.

These, the aforementioned, **are obscurations of sentient beings, and the supreme vehicle is taught** by the Buddha **as their** remedy. Thereby, all of the eight **obstructing flaws** that beings face **will be overcome.**

Whoever, in word or meaning, without forgetting them, **upholds and** so with recollection **applies himself or herself to these two stanzas is a supremely intelligent being who will attain ten different qualities.** As the obscurations disappear, one attains devotion to the great vehicle and so there will be: (1) an **exhaustively** complete **development of the element,** (2) the attainment of **supreme joy at the time of death,** (3) the ability to take **birth in accordance with one's wishes,** (4) **perfect recall of** one's **previous lives** throughout all one's lives, (5) **meeting with** truly and completely awakened **buddhas,** (6) **hearing** the Dharma of **the supreme vehicle from them,** (7) a **devotion** to that Dharma that is **endowed with intelligence,** (8–9) **the two gateways of** meditative absorption and retention, **and** (10) **swift attainment of** true **enlightenment.**

(1) Some might think: "The life of the king of the Śākyas, who appeared when the life span was a hundred years, was relatively short, as he did not remain in the world for more than eighty years. His outer environment was also impure, and the sentient beings to be trained by him possessed

the five degenerations. Buddhas such as Vipaśvin, however, came at a time of excellence during the age of perfection. Therefore, such buddhas are superior to our Teacher." As a remedy to such disdain for a buddha, the Buddha has said: "At that time I myself was the Buddha Vipaśvin." While the Buddha has in mind here that, in terms of the body of qualities, all buddhas are equal, without any qualitative difference between them, the disciples will, when hearing this, think that "Buddha Vipaśvin was none other than our Teacher," and so not hold one as superior to the other.

(2) As for disdain for the Dharma, some might think: "The Brahmanical Vedas are the religion of those of high birth, such as Brahmins and royalty. They are not for outcastes. The Buddha's Dharma can, on the other hand, also be practiced by those of inferior birth, all the way down to the outcastes." Hence, thinking that the Dharma is easy to come by, they might frown upon it. As a remedy for this, it is taught that only if one venerates as many buddhas as there are grains of sand in the river Ganga, will one begin to comprehend the Great Vehicle Dharma. In this way, the Buddha shows that unless one has gathered such vast accumulations, it will be hard to gain realization. Accordingly, when disciples hear this, they may give up the disparaging thought that the Dharma is easy to come by.

(3) Lazy individuals who cannot bring forth the slightest virtue are told that if they pray to be born in the Realm of Bliss, they will indeed be born there. Similarly, there are teachings that explain that if one just remembers the name of the thus-gone one Vimalacandra, one will attain unsurpassable enlightenment; or that if one just recites one single incantation, all negative karma—such as that of the five deeds with immediate consequences—will be purified. As one accumulates the fundamental virtues that ensue from reciting such prayers, recalling such names, or reading such incantations, one will, at some point, certainly be born in the Realm of Bliss, attain enlightenment, and so forth, just as it is taught. And, based on such practices, even lazy individuals will gradually become more diligent and so give up their indolence.

(4) As a remedy to contentment with insufficient fundamental virtues, the Buddha may, for instance, praise discipline for someone who is content with only generosity, and so give an appearance of being critical

of generosity, treating it as inferior to discipline. Another example of this would be teachings that exalt undefiled virtues as being superior to mundane, defiled virtues.

(5) Some sentient beings have become proud and infatuated, based on their bodies and possessions. As a remedy to such pride, there are praises for the exalted bodies of the buddhas and bodhisattvas, as well as for their extensive enjoyments. When hearing such praises, beings who are otherwise proud may think that, no matter how excellent mundane enjoyments and bodies may be, there is nothing great about them. (6) For those with attachment to the inferior enjoyments of the world, the five sense pleasures, the remedy is to praise and describe in detail the limitless blissful enjoyments of the Buddha's pure fields. Thereby, those who are attached to the defiled enjoyments of cyclic existence, which are of the nature of suffering, may come to see such pleasures as putrid vomit and instead develop renunciation.

(7) Some sentient beings have harmed buddhas and bodhisattvas out of ignorance. Recalling this later, they may think: "I have done something terribly wrong; I am going to the lower realms!" Their minds are tormented with regret, and this obstructs their proper practice of virtue. As a remedy to this, it is therefore taught: "Even harming a buddha or bodhisattva will make one go to the higher realms!" When they hear such teachings, their regret is cast away, and so they may think: "If even harming buddhas and bodhisattvas will lead me to be born in the higher realms, then there is no need to mention what will happen if I do good for the buddhas and bodhisattvas!" Thus they will develop faith and progressively bring forth fundamental virtues. The result of harming a buddha or a bodhisattva is certainly the experience of suffering, yet the power of buddhas' and bodhisattvas' prayers will at some point make the perpetrator connect with the happiness of the higher realms and beyond. Hence, such statements are made in consideration of such states of affairs and for the sake of providing a remedy.

(8) Bodhisattvas of an uncertain potential may formerly have performed the practices of a bodhisattva, but a spiritual teacher who is a listener, or the like, may cause them to take up the practices of the Listeners' Vehicle, so relinquishing their bodhisattva activity. As a remedy for those who thus are inclined to turn their back on the Great

Vehicle, the Buddha may state that "in the end, also the listeners attain buddhahood," thus declaring that the vehicles are all one. As they hear such teaching, those who otherwise wished to attain the transcendence of suffering through the Listener's Vehicle will also pursue the practices of the Great Vehicle.

In this way, these eight—showing disdain for the Buddha, the Dharma, and so on—consist of the obscurations of sentient beings, and the teachings of the Great Vehicle serve as their remedy. Thus, the eight remedies that are taught in the supreme vehicle—and which have here been explained—function to eliminate the obscurations of an individual, or to overcome all the flaws that hinder his or her entry into the supreme vehicle. Those who, in word or meaning, retain the two stanzas on the eight remedies that eliminate the eight obscurations, if they memorize their words and fully apply themselves to their meaning, will, as supremely intelligent beings, achieve ten qualities.

What are these ten qualities? (1) Because of having devotion and faith in the Great Vehicle, there will be an exhaustively complete development of the potential, or the element. (2) At the time of death, one will be endowed with supreme joy. These two qualities are experienced in this life, whereas the remaining eight will be experienced subsequently. (3) Thus, after dying, one will take birth wherever one pleases. (4) In all one's lives, one will remember one's past lives. (5) One will meet teachers who are buddhas, and (6) one will hear teachings on the supreme vehicle from those buddhas. (7) One will have devotion to the Great Vehicle and (8) possess the intelligence that realizes the definitive meaning. (9) One will attain the two gateways: the gateway of meditative absorptions, such as that of the heroic gait, and the gateway of retentions, such as that of the inexhaustible treasury. (10) In the end, one will swiftly attain unsurpassable enlightenment.

5. Summary

Thus, with excellent intelligence, free from weariness, and loving,
In high esteem, and aware of the excellent means,
The Bodhisattva teaches well.

Explaining among the people, they shine like the sun.
[XIII.24]

This was the thirteenth chapter of the *Ornament of Great Vehicle Sūtras,* the chapter on teaching.

Regarding the benefits of the teaching, it is said: **Thus, with excellent intelligence,** bodhisattvas teach in an unmistaken way. **Free from weariness,** they explain again and again **and** so, with **loving minds,** have no concern for material things. Speaking words that are suited to be taken to heart, they are held **in high esteem, and** they are **aware of the excellent means** for beneficially training those who are to be trained. Thus, **the bodhisattva teaches well.** Explaining among the multitudes of **people, they shine like the sun.**

Finally, there follows a concluding summary, which extols the excellent qualities that are associated with teaching the Dharma. Relying on the excellent intelligence that enables one to explain the Dharma in an unmistaken way, bodhisattvas teach constantly and without weariness. They do not teach for honor or gain, but out of love for sentient beings. Such bodhisattvas are highly respected in the world as learned and holy, and as masters of the six transcendences. They know the excellent ways and means for teaching the Dharma, knowing which Dharma teaching should be given to whom and so forth. Bodhisattvas explain the sacred Dharma well. When they teach, they shine like the sun in the midst of the crowds of beings. The sun brings warmth, ripens the crops, and so forth, and in the way that they benefit beings, bodhisattvas can, hence, be compared to the sun.

This concludes the explanation of the thirteenth chapter of the *Ornament of the Great Vehicle Sūtras,* the chapter on teaching.

14

Practice

4. Practice of the Dharma

Having in this way investigated the Dharma and studied it extensively, one needs to practice the Dharma. Thus, this chapter has three parts: (1) a general presentation, (2) a detailed explanation, and (3) a summary.

1. General Presentation

> Regarding the two, the wise, by means of three
> That are not mistaken and are not correct,
> Thoroughly understand the twofold absence of self
> With respect to persons and phenomena. [XIV.1]
>
> Then, understanding the facts, they realize
> That the Dharma is like a boat;
> When the notion that receiving teaching is paramount has
>   been relinquished,
> It is referred to as "understanding the Dharma." [XIV.2]
>
> With an ordinary being's knowledge
> The two are understood accordingly.
> In order to complete the knowledge,
> They thoroughly practice the Dharma through attunement.
>   [XIV.3]

Next, upon the first ground
The bodhisattva, being of the nature of that
And equal to all, attains the unsurpassable
Wakefulness beyond the world. [xiv.4]

Having genuinely exhausted all afflictions
That are to be eliminated through seeing,
They, in order to eliminate cognitive obscuration,
Thoroughly apply themselves to meditation. [xiv.5]

By practicing the combination
Of classifying and nonconceptual wakefulness,
They likewise practice the concordant Dharma
On the remaining grounds. [xiv.6]

Regarding the two (that is, the absence of self in terms of a person and the absence of self in terms of phenomena), **the wise, by means of three** meditative absorptions (the meditative absorption of emptiness with respect to the nonexistent imaginary nature, the meditative absorption of the absence of wishes in terms of the existent dependent nature, and the meditative absorption of the absence of marks regarding the existent thoroughly established nature) **that are not mistaken,** since they facilitate supramundane wakefulness, **and** that **are not correct** either, because they are essentially mundane—by means of all of these, the wise come to **thoroughly understand the twofold absence of self with respect to persons and phenomena.**

Then, understanding the facts, as they have attained the meditative absorption of the stream of Dharma, **they realize that the Dharma** of scripture **is like a boat. When the notion that receiving teaching is paramount has been relinquished,** and they hence engage in reflection, **it is referred to as "knowing the Dharma."**

With an ordinary being's knowledge of meanings and Dharma teachings, **the two** aspects of absence of self **are,** as explained before, **understood accordingly. In order to complete the knowledge** and attain the path of seeing, **they** then **thoroughly practice**

the Dharma through attunement with the path of seeing on the path of joining.

Next, upon the first ground, the bodhisattva, being of the nature of that first ground and being equal to all in abiding upon it, attains the unsurpassable wakefulness beyond the world.

Having attained the first ground and thereby genuinely exhausted all afflictions that are to be eliminated through seeing, they, in order to eliminate cognitive obscuration, thoroughly apply themselves to the meditation of the path of cultivation from the second ground onward.

The cognitive obscurations are thus eliminated. By practicing the unbroken combination of continuously shifting between the wakefulness of the ensuing attainment (which is classifying, since it discerns the essences of the particular grounds, along with the relevant discards and qualities to be attained) and the nonconceptual wakefulness of the equipoise, they likewise practice the concordant Dharma on the remaining grounds in a sustained practice of gaining familiarity.

In the sūtras, practice is taught under five headings: (1) thoroughly understanding the facts, (2) thoroughly understanding the Dharma, (3) practicing the Dharma by attuning oneself to it, (4) entry in accord, and (5) engaging in the concordant Dharma.

(1) As for the first of these five, a wise bodhisattva who is on the grounds of inspired conduct is "not mistaken and not correct" regarding the two truths, or regarding the nonexistent imaginary versus the dependent and thoroughly established, both of which exist. That is to say, someone on the grounds of inspired conduct is in accord with reality and with the realization of the twofold absence of self. Therefore, compared to others with mundane minds, such bodhisattvas are not mistaken, and thus not incorrect. And yet, because their minds are still mundane, they are also not correct when compared to those with supramundane minds. In this way, they can be said to be "not mistaken and not correct."

On the grounds of inspired conduct, the twofold absence of self with respect to persons and phenomena is thoroughly known by means of the meditative absorptions of emptiness, absence of wishes, and absence of marks. With the meditative absorption of emptiness, one comprehends that persons and phenomena are merely imputed through names, marks, symbols, and conventions, and so the imaginary is known to be emptiness devoid of essence. Thereby one understands that the personal self does not essentially exist as something that is apprehended or as something that apprehends. Likewise, the phenomena of form, sound, and so forth, are also understood to be devoid of the essence of something apprehended or something that apprehends. In this way, it is thoroughly understood that the two types of self have never in fact existed and that they are, therefore, just like the horns of a rabbit.

The basis for the appearance of duality is the false imagination, the mind and mental states that constitute the dependent nature. These are conventionally existent. Thorough affliction and the various sufferings of cyclic existence are an undeniable and incontrovertible reality. It would not make sense for anyone to say that they do not exist. If they did not exist, it would be completely impossible to classify something as thorough affliction and something else as complete purification. Yet, no one disputes the reality of both cyclic existence and transcendence. Although in this way the dependent nature exists, it is also flawed because it is the false imagination—the abode of suffering and afflictions such as attachment. Thus, by means of the meditative absorption of the absence of wishes, one will correctly understand the nature of the false imagination, seeing that it is nothing to place one's hopes in and aspire toward.

The thoroughly established is the nature that is empty of duality and the twofold self. Thus, like heat in fire and wetness in water, it exists from the beginning as the intrinsic nature of all phenomena. If this did not exist, the twofold self and duality would exist instead. Hence, the intrinsic nature—that which is thoroughly established—exists, but without any of the marks of dualistic construction at all. Thus, the thoroughly established nature is, by means of the meditative absorption of the absence of marks, understood to be the complete pacification of all concepts associated with word and thought.

This, then, is to understand thoroughly the facts of existence and nonexistence, or the two truths. In this way, one will understand what is nonexistent and what is existent with respect to both the relative truth of the imaginary and dependent natures and the ultimate truth that is the thoroughly established nature.

(2) Understanding the Dharma means to know the subject matter taught in the sūtras and so forth. The entirety of the Dharma that, in scripture, is expressed in the form of groups of names, phrases, and letters is meant to elicit the understanding of their subject matter. For example, to cross a body of water one needs a boat, but, once one is across, the boat has served its purpose, and one is no longer exclusively dependent on that vessel. By understanding that the Dharma, which takes the form of indicatory names, phrases, and letters, is like a boat, one will give up the notion that listening to the words of the teachings alone is sufficient. Instead, one will focus on generating the insight that arises from reflecting on their meaning. This is what is entailed in "understanding the Dharma."

(3) Practicing the Dharma by attuning oneself to it refers to when, as an ordinary being on the grounds of inspired conduct, one has gained an understanding of the facts of the Dharma, based on the insights that are gained from study and reflection. Having thereby become neither mistaken nor correct, as explained above, one realizes the twofold selflessness as if one were seeing its reflection, or, in other words, by means of an object universal. That very cognition must then be completely perfected and purified, and so turn into the nature of supramundane wakefulness. To achieve that, one therefore meditates further, from the stage of heat through to the level of the supreme quality. In this way, one practices the Dharma by attuning oneself to it.

(4) Entry in accord refers to the practice of the bodhisattvas on the first ground, known as the Joyous. At this stage, the bodhisattva becomes equal to all who have attained abidance within the nature of the path of seeing. Such bodhisattvas have all achieved the supramundane, nonconceptual wakefulness that is unexcelled and superior to that of the listeners and self-realized buddhas. By directly realizing the character of the intrinsic nature, one thoroughly and flawlessly enters the grounds of the bodhisattvas, and thus the practice is known as that of "entry in accord."

(5) Practicing the concordant Dharma concerns the practice on the path of cultivation. Having already attained the path of seeing, the

afflictions to be relinquished through seeing are already all exhausted. Yet, in order to eliminate the cognitive obscurations, one must apply oneself thoroughly to meditation from the second through the tenth ground. The wakefulness that eliminates the obscurations takes two alternating forms. During the subsequent attainment, pure mundane wakefulness cognizes and classifies the full multiplicity of things, whereas, during the meditative equipoise, nonconceptual wakefulness knows the space-like intrinsic nature, just as it is. By practicing these two in continuous alternation, a continuum emerges that extends from the second through the remaining grounds. Since this practice is in accord with that which has already been seen, it is known as the "concordant Dharma." Thus the practice is presented in general by means of the five categories taught in the sūtras.

2. Detailed Explanation

Next, the detailed explanation will cover: (1) the conditions for practice, (2) the essence of practice, and (3) the examples that demonstrate the way to practice.

1. The Conditions for Practice

> The place of practice of the wise
> Is well equipped, a good dwelling,
> A good ground with good company, and it is endowed
> With qualities that delight a spiritual practitioner. [XIV.7]

> The bodhisattva whose learning is great,
> Who sees the truth, is skilled in teaching,
> Possesses love, and is not weary,
> Is to be known as a great holy being. [XIV.8]

> Excellent focus, excellent adherence,
> Excellent means, definitive emergence,
> And excellent application—
> This explains the nature of genuine commitment. [XIV.9]

Joy, being born with leisure,
Freedom from disease, meditative absorption, and
 discernment—
The cause of these
Is the production of merit in the past. [XIV.10]

On dwelling in a favorable place, and on the rest of the four wheels, it is taught: **The place of practice of the wise is well equipped,** in the sense that the necessities for maintaining life can be obtained with little hardship. It is **a good dwelling** with an absence of thieves and such. It is **a good ground,** meaning that one will not be likely to fall sick there, and one is **with good company,** that is, individuals who abide by a discipline and a view that is in accord with one's own. **And,** since, for example, during the day there are few causes of commotion and defilement, and during the night there is little noise, **it is** a place that is **endowed with qualities that delight a spiritual practitioner.**

The bodhisattva whose learning, in terms of the scriptural teachings, **is great** and **who,** in terms of the qualities of realization, **sees the truth,** who **is skilled in** the ways of **teaching** the Dharma, who **possesses love** while being uninterested in material wealth, **and** who has given up idleness and **is not weary**—that bodhisattva **is to be known as a great holy being.**

Excellent focus, that is, keeping the Great Vehicle Dharma in mind; **excellent adherence** to the gathering of the two accumulations; **excellent means** such as thoroughly seizing and thoroughly resting, in the eventuality that dullness or agitation occur; **definitive emergence** onto the higher paths without being content with the lower ones; **and excellent application** with constant diligence and respect—this explains the nature of genuine commitment.

As merit has been attained in past lives, there is **joy** wherever one presently remains. As a result of **being born with leisure,** one succeeds in following a holy person. There is **freedom from disease,** and there is **meditative absorption and discernment** through various insights. **The cause of these is the production of merit in the past.**

The conducive conditions for practice are known as the four great wheels. These are (1) a conducive place to stay, (2) the support of holy beings, (3) one's own excellent aspirations, and (4) karmic affinity from the past. When endowed with these four, one's practice will be excellent. Regarding the location, the wise stay in a place of practice that is well equipped in the sense of there being ample provisions. They stay in good dwellings, without uncouth people and wild animals, where the land and water are agreeable and do not cause illness, where the ground is good, meaning that there is no leprosy or other contagious diseases, and which is amenable to the mind. While remaining in such locations, one should have good and virtuous company, consisting of people whose discipline and views are in harmony with one's own. There should be no thorns to concentration, meaning no obstacles to spiritual practice, such as travelers coming during the day or the sound of disturbing noises at night. In the absence of such obstacles, the place should display delightful qualities. By staying in such a location, spiritual training will flourish. Yet, places where the opposite of the above is the case will present obstacles to practice. Therefore, one should begin by carefully investigating one's location and not just start a practice anywhere.

Relying on a holy being as a companion is the supreme condition for all good qualities. What are the typical characteristics of a holy person? Such individuals are bodhisattvas who have entered the Great Vehicle and are endowed with extensive learning in the Dharma of scripture. As for the Dharma of realization, he or she will have comprehended the truths and thus seen their meaning. These beings are also skilled in explaining the Dharma to others, and they have love for others, without becoming weary when benefiting them. One should rely on such holy beings and know them to be great teachers of virtue.

As for the third great wheel, one's own excellent aspirations, the individual who practices should seek out the Great Vehicle Dharma and orient his or her mind by means of the threefold insight, thereby possessing excellent focus. Without being content with minor fundamental virtues, one should perfectly adhere to the practice of gathering the accumulations of merit and wakefulness to the best of one's capacity. Noticing the faults in the mind when distraction and agitation occur, one relinquishes them through directing the mind to the marks of calm abiding. When becoming discouraged or depressed, one thinks of the qualities of the buddhas and bodhisattvas, the benefits of meditative absorption, and the general and specific characteristics of phenomena. Thereby, one's mind is uplifted, and one can proceed to overcome one's discouragement by meditating on the marks of special insight. Whenever there is neither dullness nor agitation, one may then meditate on the mark of equanimity—abiding within that state without wavering. As, in this way, one cultivates the spiritual practice of meditating on the marks of calm abiding, special insight, and equanimity, one becomes endowed with excellent means.

Moreover, without being content with merely one's present state, one applies oneself to higher and higher stages of the grounds and paths—excellently and definitively emerging onto these. Likewise, one's constant practice on the path by means of calm abiding and special insight is of the nature of excellent application. Thus, to be endowed with the aforementioned five excellences is to possess the armor of aspiration, or the commitment of a one-pointed mind to its genuine aim. This is what is implied by "one's own excellent aspirations."

Finally, due to having brought forth merit in the past, one will (1) remain in favorable places and there meet with spiritual teachers and the Dharma, through which the mind finds joy. (2) Likewise, one will be born with the leisure of being free from the eight inopportune states, (3) have a body that is free from disease so that one can practice the Dharma, (4) possess the meditative absorption of a flexible mind, and (5) be endowed with the insight that discerns the meaning of the two truths. The cause of these five endowments is the merit of past lives. If presently such results are perceptible, we can be certain about the existence of such merit—just as fire can be inferred from the presence of smoke.

2. The Essence of Practice

The essence of the practice of the Great Vehicle is insight beyond focal points and great compassion that does not forsake sentient beings. This will be explained next by means of (1) a short summary and (2) an expanded analysis.

1. Short Summary

Apart from the basic field of phenomena,
There are no phenomena.
The buddhas have therefore realized that deliverance
Is attachment and the rest. [XIV.11]

Apart from the basic field of phenomena,
There are no phenomena.
Thus, the wise hold this to be the intent
Of the teaching on thorough affliction. [XIV.12]

Because attachment and the like
Are themselves engaged correctly,
A complete liberation from them occurs—
And through that one definitively emerges from them. [XIV.13]

Excruciating pains of life in hell for the sake of sentient beings
Do not in any way harm the child of the victorious ones.
Yet the various virtuous thoughts that condition the inferior
     vehicle, holding peace and existence to be good and bad—
These are harmful for the wise. [XIV.14]

For the wise, remaining in hell can never
Obstruct the stainless wide awakening.
With the thoroughly cooling thoughts that benefit oneself in
     other vehicles,
One may be thoroughly at ease; yet there is that obstruction.
[XIV.15]

Definitive emergence beyond affliction is nothing but the afflictions themselves. **Apart from the basic field of phenomena, there are no phenomena.** Hence, the definitive emergence beyond attachment and so forth is achieved by cultivating the observation of the intrinsic nature of attachment and the rest. **The buddhas** have therefore realized that deliverance from attachment and the other afflictions **is itself attachment and the rest.**

Apart from the basic field of phenomena, there are no phenomena. Thus, the wise hold this to be the intent of the Buddha's **teaching on thorough affliction,** which declares that ignorance and manifest enlightenment are identical.

Because the intrinsic nature of **attachment and the like are themselves engaged correctly, a complete liberation from them occurs** (that is, from attachment and so forth), **and through** becoming familiar with **that,** meaning the intrinsic nature of attachment and so forth, **one definitively emerges from them.**

The next stanzas concern the way to give up directing the mind in the way that the listeners and self-realized buddhas do. The **excruciating pains of** living a **life in hell for the sake of sentient beings do not in any way harm the children of the victorious ones. Yet the virtuous thoughts that condition** the mind toward entering **the inferior vehicle, holding peace and existence to be good and bad—these are harmful for the wise. For the wise, remaining in hell can never obstruct the stainless wide awakening. With the thoroughly cooling thoughts that benefit oneself in other vehicles, one may be thoroughly at ease; yet there is that obstruction** that prevents complete enlightenment.

The first three stanzas of this section show how insight beyond focal points does not engage in any purposeful elimination of the afflictions based on seeing cyclic existence as flawed. The last two stanzas show how abandoning sentient beings and entering into peace on one's own is in conflict with the practice of the Great Vehicle. Here these stanzas will be treated in one section.

Those on the inferior path hold afflictions to be existent by nature, and they believe that one attains the transcendence of suffering by exhaustively eliminating them by means of the path. They hold strongly to the notion that cyclic existence has flaws and that the transcendence of suffering has good qualities. Thus, they reject the former in order to enter the latter.

Bodhisattvas realize that the afflictions themselves do not have any nature, and so they are skilled in the methods for gaining liberation by means of the afflictions themselves. Endowed with nonconceptual wakefulness, bodhisattvas act without rejecting cyclic existence. Yet, they do not become stained by the flaws of cyclic existence. In the end, they attain the transcendence of suffering that abides neither in existence nor peace. Thus, through insight beyond reference points, nonconceptual wakefulness, they realize the equality of cyclic existence and transcendence of suffering.

The *Transcendent Insight in One Hundred Thousand Lines* states: "I do not teach any deliverance from desire that is something other than desire." The same is also said with regard to bewilderment and anger. The statement that desire itself delivers one from desire, and that there is no other deliverance, is made with a specific intent. What this means is that no phenomenon is anything other than the basic field of phenomena. It is certain that the abiding reality, essence, or nature of all phenomena is the suchness of the basic field. Apart from the basic field of phenomena, there are no phenomena in the least. Therefore, with this realization, the buddhas have said that deliverance from desire and so forth is identical with those very same afflictions. Recognizing that the nature of the afflictions is in this way pure from the beginning, one will know how affliction is self-liberated, meaning liberated by affliction itself, and one will not need to look for any other remedy.

If there were an affliction that by its own nature was something other than liberation, no one could ever achieve liberation from it; it could never be eliminated. Therefore, in the sūtras of definitive meaning that belong to the Vehicle of Characteristics, it is taught that all phenomena are, from the beginning, neither bound nor liberated. As for the resultant Vehicle of Mantra, we find, for example, the following statement from the chapter on the purity of spiritual practice within the two-part *Hevajra Tantra*:

Suchness is declared to be
The purity of all things.

And likewise:

The pure nature of self-awareness—
Liberation does not occur by means of any other purity.

Thus we find here precisely the same essential point conveyed.

It is similarly also taught that ignorance and manifest enlightenment are identical. Since there are no phenomena besides the basic field of phenomena, thorough affliction is seen to be of the essence of natural enlightenment. Wise bodhisattvas know that this is how the buddhas see it, and so they make their assertions along such lines. In the same way, the sūtras also teach that "the afflictions are the vajra-bases of enlightenment."

It may then be thought that if the afflictions themselves bring deliverance from affliction, then why aren't all sentient beings, who are already experiencing the afflictions, not also already liberated? Such a question shows that the intended meaning of these teachings has not been properly understood. Sentient beings do not understand the real condition of desire and so forth, and they are instead bound by attachment to the marks of such afflictions. The bodhisattvas, on the other hand, understand that the real condition of afflictions such as desire is nothing other than the nature of the basic field of phenomena, and so they experience the afflictions accordingly. That is why they are freed from ordinary, afflictive attachment and the like, and it is indeed the case that deliverance from affliction is nothing other than the afflictions themselves. The bodhisattvas do not perceive any entities or marks with respect to desire and the like, and so they become neither attached nor aggressive.

Therefore, by realizing the nature of afflictions such as desire, one recognizes the facts of their primordial exhaustion and nonarising—this is how the great enlightened wakefulness that knows exhaustion and nonarising is attained. For the listeners and the self-realized buddhas, however, desire and so on exist by virtue of their own essences to begin with, and enlightenment is attained when, at some point, one has brought them to exhaustion so that they do not arise again. That sort of enlightenment is a bewilderment with respect to the nature of reality. As stated in the *Ornament of Manifest Realization:*

While phenomena do exist,
The Teacher has brought obscurations regarding the knowable to
  exhaustion—
This claim by others
I consider a joke.

Likewise, in the verses on the profound body of qualities from his *Compendium on the Great Vehicle*, the noble Asaṅga states:

Endowed with the great means,
The afflictions are the factors of enlightenment;
And cyclic existence, likewise, is the intrinsic nature of peace.
Therefore, the Thus-Gone One is beyond the domain of thought.

Here it is taught that cyclic existence itself is the transcendence of suffering and that the afflictions are the factors, or path, of enlightenment. These points are thus also made clearly in the Vehicle of Characteristics because unless one realizes with insight that this is the case, one will not be able to achieve the great enlightenment that is beyond the extremes of existence and peace. The reason that the Resultant Vehicle presents a swift path to buddhahood is that it explicitly and without concealment explains the exceptional means that accord with this realization.

The second part of this section shows how the means for not rejecting sentient beings are also the means for achieving great enlightenment. For the sake of sentient beings, the bodhisattvas may undergo the otherwise excruciating pains of being boiled, burnt, and so on in the realms of hell. This does not harm the bodies or minds of the children of the victorious ones at all, nor is there harm done that could obstruct them on the path of the Great Vehicle. Instead, this causes the bodhisattvas to don the armor of knowing things to be like an illusion, having intense compassion for sentient beings.

The potential obstructions to the path of the wise bodhisattvas are the various ideas that are seemingly virtuous, namely, the thoughts that are concerned with entering the path of the Lesser Vehicle because of the belief that the peace of transcendence is good while cyclic existence is flawed. When wise bodhisattvas remain in hell, the mere suffering of being there can never obstruct the great wide awakening, the vast qualities of the powers, and so on, that are attained within the absence of the stains of the two obscurations. The life story of Vallabha's "daughter" illustrates this point well.[38] Yet in other vehicles, one is concerned with the path and result of the listeners and self-realized buddhas, wishing for a thorough cooling of the afflictions and suffering, to one's own exclusive benefit. Whereas for a while one may thus rest thoroughly at ease, this obstructs the attainment of great enlightenment. Such a situation is similar to that of someone who, having entered the Great Vehicle, gives up cultivating the enlightened mind due to the ingratitude of others, and so instead actualizes the transcendence of suffering that is associated with the listeners' and self-realized buddhas.

2. Expanded Analysis

The next teaching once more explores insight free from focal points, followed by a discussion of great love. We begin with the first of these two.

> No phenomena and yet observation,
> No thorough affliction and yet purification—
> These should be known to be comparable
> To such things as illusions and space. [XIV.16]

> In a well-made painting, there is no high and low,
> And yet there seems to be.
> Likewise, while the false imagination never contains the two,
> It seems that they are there. [XIV.17]

> When murky water clears up,
> Clarity is not produced from that;
> Rather, it is simply free from impurities.
> That is also exactly how it is with the purity of one's own mind. [XIV.18]

> The mind is held to be constantly luminous;
> It is rendered unfit by the adventitious flaws.

Any mind other than the mind of the intrinsic nature
Is not luminous—the reference is to the natural. [XIV.19]

Bodhisattvas treat all sentient beings
As if they were their only child.
Feeling great love from the marrow of their bones,
They always wish to help them. [XIV.20]

As they benefit sentient beings,
They may be attached but incur no downfall.
It is hatred that is always
Opposed to all sentient beings. [XIV.21]

The pigeon, with unparalleled love,
Lies embracing its young ones;
Just as hatred is precluded there, so it is
With the loving ones and their children, embodied beings.
    [XIV.22]

Because they have love, anger is precluded;
Because they pacify, ill will is precluded;
Because they bring help, deceit is precluded;
And because they bring satisfaction, terror is precluded.
    [XIV.23]

The way to give up fear about that which is pure by nature is explained next. In actuality, **no phenomena** of apprehended and apprehender exist, **and yet** for the immature there is an **observation** of something apprehended and something that apprehends. Likewise, within the basic field of phenomena there is, by nature, **no thorough affliction, and yet** there may still be future **purification**. These issues may be frightening to the immature, yet they **should be known to be comparable to such things as illusions**, which—although not really there—nevertheless appear to the deluded, **and space**, which may become free from clouds.

Also, in a well-made painting, there is no division in terms of high and low, and yet there seems to be. Likewise, while the false imagination never contains the two, the apprehended and the apprehender, it seems that they are there despite their nonexistence.

When murky water clears up, clarity is not newly produced from that, that is, the murkiness. Rather, it is simply the case of that which is pure by nature having become free from impurities. That is also exactly how it is with the natural purity of one's own mind, which is present in the absence of adventitious stains.

Therefore, the mind is held to be constantly luminous; it is rendered unfit by the adventitious flaws. Any mind other than the mind of the intrinsic nature, that is, the mind of the dependent nature, is not luminous. Hence, when speaking of luminosity, the reference is to the natural mind.

Next, it is explained how no downfall is sustained from the arising of desire. Bodhisattvas treat all sentient beings as if they were their only child. Feeling great love from the marrow of their bones, they always wish to help them. As they benefit sentient beings with great love, they may become attached, but they will incur no downfall. It is hatred in the mind stream that is always opposed to providing for all sentient beings.

The pigeon, with unparalleled love, lies embracing its young ones. Just as anger is precluded there, so it is with the loving ones, the children of the victorious ones, and their children—embodied beings.

Because they have love, anger is precluded; because they pacify, ill will is precluded; because they bring help, deceit is precluded; and because they bring joy and, thereby, satisfaction, terror is precluded.

Feeling that it is contradictory for all phenomena to be ultimately nonexistent and yet observed as mere appearances, immature beings fail to comprehend the nature of things. Instead, they develop fear. In the same way, they also perceive a contradiction between the natural nonexistence of the afflictions and the purification of the adventitious stains. Frightened, they hence become disinclined to pursue the Great Vehicle. When something like that happens, it is because one has failed to understand the profound intended meaning. Once that is understood, there is no such contradiction. How so? These phenomena exist as mere appearances but do not truly exist as they appear; they are like illusions or dreams. Thus, they can be observed conventionally. Ultimately there are, however, no marks to observe. One should therefore know these phenomena to be like space. There is, for this reason, no conflict between observation and nonobservation.

To illustrate this, we may think of a skilled painter who knows well the methods and techniques of his art. Mixing colors and carefully painting various forms, he creates an impression of depth and height, and there appear to be arms, legs, faces, and so forth—even though none of these things is actually there. Similarly, without properly realizing the way things are, it seems to the false imagination that there is a duality in terms of apprehended and apprehender, although in fact there are no such two different things. That which seems to be the case can, in other words, be different from that which actually is the case. Hence, while things are actually nonexistent, they may nevertheless still seem to be there. There is no contradiction in that.

Neither is there any conflict between, on the one hand, purity being natural and, on the other, purity coming to appear only later, once the stains have disappeared. Water is naturally pure when not mixed with any particles, and when water is muddied, it is not the case that particles and water have fused to the extent that they cannot be separated. Thus, while the water is always just water, it can still appear murky. When it clears up, it is just the nature of the water that was there before, which has now become manifest; the purity is not some newly arisen product of murky water. Its clearing is simply a matter of the water becoming free of the adventitious stains that were polluting it. Likewise, while the nature of the sky above us is always pure openness, it may still either contain or be free of clouds. We may also think of the example of gold being extracted from ore. Although the gold itself is always just gold, it nevertheless does seem to undergo two different states—one that is crude and another that is refined. As demonstrated by these examples, the purity of one's own mind may appear pure just as it may appear impure.

Moreover, we hold that in its basic character, or abiding reality, the mind is always by nature stainless, luminous clarity. The afflictions of directing the mind improperly, such as attachment, are adventitious flaws; it is not the case that they cannot be removed from the fundamental nature of the mind. Yet, when present in the mind, they make it unfit and defiled. Thus, any mind other than the luminous clarity, which as the mind's intrinsic nature is not subject to pollution, should be known to be thought and false imagination. Such a mind is not luminous clarity. Rather, when speaking of the mind of the stainless intrinsic nature, or of the wakefulness of luminous clarity, the reference is to the mind's nature—the fundamental unity of clarity and emptiness.

The second part of this section concerns the great love that does not forsake sentient beings. Bodhisattvas cherish sentient beings as a mother loves her only child, with uncontrived, great love from the marrow of her bones. Constantly wishing to benefit sentient beings, bodhisattvas never turn their back on them. When working to help someone, a bodhisattva might become attached to that sentient being, but the bodhisattva does not, thereby, incur the fault of a downfall. Such attachment causes one to hold sentient beings to be "mine," but it does not make one reject them. For those who abide by love and cultivate the enlightened mind, anger is the factor that is completely incompatible with the practice of constantly holding all sentient beings to be "mine." Developing anger causes one to reject them and begin to harm them. This is why the sūtras teach that for a bodhisattva, one instant of a hateful mind is a bigger flaw than several eons of recurring faults of attachment. One takes care of sentient beings through love, and it is said that when one becomes attached to sentient beings in this way it is not an affliction. A householder bodhisattva may be attached to children, spouse, and so forth, but since that does not conflict with love, such attachment does not in any way cause a downfall from the bodhisattva training.

For example, pigeons have more desire than other birds, and they have great love and attachment for their offspring. From the time when their eggs hatch, until the wings of their offspring have fully developed, they lovingly embrace their young and cover their bodies with their wings.

For them, developing anger at their offspring is completely precluded, so that does not happen. The same is the case when bodhisattvas, out of love for embodied sentient beings, treat others as their own children. Since they love them and wish happiness for them, anger—the cause of ill will—is in their case precluded. Since they wish to pacify the suffering and afflictions of sentient beings, ill will and hate is precluded. Because they wish to benefit sentient beings with their own bodies and enjoyments, trickery and deceit are precluded. Since bodhisattvas satisfy sentient beings with joy, and since just seeing or hearing a bodhisattva will protect one from fear,[39] the terrors of physical punishment and so on are also precluded.

For this reason, the supreme bodhisattva practice consists of great uncontrived love and compassion, free from deceit or pretense and without ever turning one's back on sentient beings. It also requires nonconceptual insight, which ensures that one does not take existence and peace to be separate things.

3. Showing the Way of Practice through Examples

As with the sick and excellent medicine,
They enter cyclic existence.
As with the doctor and the sick,
They practice for sentient beings. [XIV.24]

As with a servant that is useless,
They practice on themselves.
Like merchants with their merchandise
They practice for those who desire. [XIV.25]

Like dyers with their fabric,
They practice the activities.
As with a father and his young son,
They practice without hurting sentient beings. [XIV.26]

Like a man in pursuit of fire and his sticks,
They are engaged in constant practice.

Like a trustworthy person, they continue
With superior intent the practice to perfection. [xiv.27]

Like a magician, they practice
With insight into the objects of cognition.
This is held to be the way and the occasions
Of the bodhisattva's practice. [xiv.28]

On the principles of practice it is taught that, **as with the sick and** the **excellent medicine** that they rely upon for healing, **they,** while aware of its misery, nonetheless **enter cyclic existence** for the benefit of others. **As with the** skilled **doctor and the sick, they practice** with compassion **for** the sake of **sentient beings** who are stricken by the disease of the afflictions.

As with a servant that is punished because he **is useless** at work, **they practice on themselves** in order to shape their own minds well. **Like merchants with their merchandise,** for whom there is no thing that is not for sale, **they practice** the way of giving away all things **for** the sake of **those who desire** wealth and enjoyments.

Like dyers working **with their** soaked **fabric, they practice the activities** of body, speech, and mind. **As with a father and his young son,** where the former is tolerant of the latter's ingratitude, **they practice without hurting** those **sentient beings** who, conversely, harm them.

Like a man in pursuit of fire and his sticks, which he uses to produce fire by friction, **they are engaged in** a **constant** and continuous **practice** of engendering virtuous qualities. **Like a trustworthy person,** a minister who does not treat the royal treasury as his own, **they continue, with superior intent, the practice** through **to perfection** of the training, without relishing the tastes of meditative absorption.

Like a magician who has no attachment to his own creations, **they practice with** unerring **insight into** all of **the objects of cognition. This is held,** by means of reasoning, **to be the way and the occasions of the bodhisattva's practice.**

For the sake of unsurpassable enlightenment, bodhisattvas willingly take birth in cyclic existence. They eliminate the suffering of sentient beings and provide them with benefit and happiness, having no attachment to cyclic existence. Just as the sick eagerly pursue good medicine to eliminate their illnesses, bodhisattvas are aware of the suffering of cyclic existence but still gladly accept it. Even though a medicine may be pungent or bitter, it is relied upon in order to eliminate disease. Likewise, bodhisattvas happily take on cyclic existence so that they can cure all the diseases of the two obscurations and achieve the great enlightenment that spontaneously accomplishes the twofold benefit. In this way, they enter, and do not relinquish, cyclic existence.

A virtuous doctor with a loving mind gives medicine to his or her suffering patients in order to heal them of their ailments. Likewise, in order to cure the afflictions of sentient beings, bodhisattvas dispense the medicines of the sacred Dharma and do all they can to bring benefit.

A haughty servant may not work or do what is asked unless he or she is coerced, for example, through physical punishment. Similarly, when one is in the grip of the afflictions, one is like a savage, and so, whenever an emotion such as weariness about serving sentient beings may occur, one should direct the mind in the proper way, persistently striking at one's own unwholesome mind. This is similar to the way that one tames a wild horse, as taught in the *Jewel Mound Sūtra*.

To support their children and retinue, merchants may seek to turn a large profit, even when selling insignificant goods. Likewise, bodhisattvas use whatever desirable objects they have as the "merchandise of generosity," thus gathering excellent enjoyments and pleasures of the five senses, which they then fully donate to sentient beings for the sake of their benefit and happiness.

Dyers diligently soak their fabrics again and again so that the colors may be absorbed by the cloth. This illustrates the bodhisattvas' discipline, as they apply themselves in body, speech, and mind to purify and wash away the ten unvirtuous actions and fully accomplish the ten virtuous ones.

A young boy, still a child, may be unruly and misbehave in various minor ways, yet his father will not get angry with him and will instead just love him more. Likewise, in their bewilderment, sentient beings make various mistakes, yet, in response, bodhisattvas do not harm them or get angry. Instead, they practice the development of inexhaustible compassion.

When rubbing sticks together to make fire, one must persist without interruption until the fire starts. Likewise, bodhisattvas constantly practice with great diligence, never giving up, until they reach the culmination of virtue.

A trustworthy person may be put in charge of the royal treasury and all the property of the royal household, yet he will not be tempted to take anything that is in his custody and use it for his own purposes, even if he is free to do so. Likewise, until they have perfected the meditative absorptions of the training in special attention, bodhisattvas will not pause to relish the taste of meditative absorption. Instead, they will carry through to complete perfection of the practice.

Applying various mantras and substances, magicians create the illusion of many different things, such as horses and elephants; yet they know that the things they perceive are merely appearances and not really there. Likewise, bodhisattvas practice the transcendences; yet they practice with insight into the unity of the two truths that is the nature of all phenomena. This account that makes use of examples is held to capture the way of the bodhisattvas' practice.

3. SUMMARY

Thus, always and with great diligence,
They pursue the twofold maturation.
Gradually, by means of the supreme intelligence, stainless and without concept,
They proceed to the unsurpassable practice. [XIV.29]

This was the fourteenth chapter of the *Ornament of the Great Vehicle Sūtras*, the chapter on practice.

The following explanation considers the way in which the practice is thoroughly purified of the three spheres. Thus, always and with

great diligence, they pursue the twofold maturation of themselves and others. **Gradually, by means of the supreme intelligence,** which is **stainless** because of the realization of the twofold absence of self **and without** any **concept** of the three spheres, **they proceed to the unsurpassable practice** at the stage of buddhahood. Here it should be understood that since there is no concept of a practitioner, an object of practice, or an activity of practice, the practice is thoroughly purified of the three spheres.

As has been explained, bodhisattvas always practice the transcendences with great diligence. Striving in the practice of the two accumulations, or the maturation of themselves and others, they progressively advance from the path of accumulation through to the culmination of the tenth ground. Thus achieving the supreme intelligence that does not conceptualize the three spheres and that is free of the stains of the afflictive and cognitive obscurations, they fully proceed to the attainment of unsurpassable enlightenment.

This was an explanation of the fourteenth chapter of the *Ornament of the Great Vehicle Sūtras,* the chapter on practice.

15
Practical Instructions and Advice

5. Practical Instructions and Advice

Since the cause of practice is the imparting of practical instructions and advice, these will be explained next. Their treatment will cover: (1) how to obtain practical instructions, (2) how to direct the mind to practical instructions, (3) how to traverse the path, and (4) the immense benefits of practical instructions.

1. How to Obtain Practical Instructions

With deliverance over an incalculable eon,
And the increase of devotion,
The qualities of virtue are perfected,
Like rivers flowing into the sea. [xv.1]

Thus, having gathered the accumulations,
The children of the victorious ones are already purified.
With clear knowledge and virtuous minds,
They fully commit themselves to meditation. [xv.2]

At that time, within the stream of Dharma,
They receive from the buddhas
Vast practical instructions for the attainment
Of calm abiding and expansive wakefulness. [xv.3]

What follows is an explanation of the way that practical instructions are given. **With deliverance over an incalculable eon** of gathering the accumulations, **and** with **the** continuous **increase of devotion, the qualities of virtue** permeate and **are perfected, like rivers flowing into** and filling **the sea.**

Thus, having gathered the vast accumulations, the children of the victorious ones who are thoroughly trained in the vows of the bodhisattvas **are already purified. With clear** unmistaken **knowledge** of the meaning of the scriptures **and** with **virtuous minds** that are free from the five obscurations, **they fully commit themselves to** the **meditation** on the nature of reality.

At that time, within the meditative absorption of **the stream of Dharma, they receive from the buddhas vast practical instructions** that reveal the profound and the vast **for** the sake of both **the attainment of calm abiding and** the expansive wakefulness of special insight.

Gathering the accumulations for an incalculable eon on the grounds of inspired conduct serves to deliver one onto the first supramundane ground. This process is one of continuously increasing devotion to the path of the Great Vehicle. Like the rivers in the four directions all flowing into the great sea, the virtues consisting of the accumulations of merit and wakefulness will completely perfect the qualities in one's stream of being. Then, at the end of the stage of the supreme quality, one enters the flawless grounds of the noble ones. Yet before this, since the children of the victorious ones, as just mentioned, have already been purifying their streams of being over many prior eons, they will already be in possession of pure discipline. They have extensively studied the vast and profound Dharma, and they know its meaning clearly, just as it is. On the path of joining, they thus fully apply themselves to meditation with the virtues of a flexible mind that is dissociated from the five obscurations. Possessing the good fortune to comprehend the wakefulness of the first ground due to their gathered accumulations, they attain at that time the meditative absorption of the stream of the gateways of Dharma.

The meditative absorption of the stream of Dharma takes place when, within meditative equipoise, one is able to receive limitless practical instructions on the sacred Dharma from innumerable buddhas, retaining the stream of words and meanings without interruption. Those with sharp faculties attain this meditative absorption on the greater path of accumulation. There are some, however, who explain that this attainment occurs at the time of the supreme quality. In any case, after this meditative absorption has been attained, its distinctive qualities will continue to develop further and further. As they abide within the meditative absorption of the stream of Dharma, bodhisattvas will receive—from supreme spiritual friends, that is, the buddhas, the blessed ones—a limitless abundance of practical instructions that are imbued with the meaning of many hundreds of thousands of sūtras. These instructions concern the attainment of extremely vast and expansive calm abiding and extremely expansive wakefulness of special insight. Thus, they have the power to bring forth the wakefulness of the noble ones on the first ground.

2. Directing the Mind to Practical Instructions

This section has two parts: (1) directing the mind in contemplation; (2) directing the mind in meditation.

1. Directing the Mind in Contemplation

Initially, the one who persists in the vows
Relates to the Dharma of the sūtras and so forth
That explore the nondual meaning,
By placing the mind on the names of these sūtras and so forth. [xv.4]

From there on, they gradually
Distinguish the categories of the words
And within each
Determine the meanings correctly. [xv.5]

Once the meanings have been ascertained,
The Dharma is thoroughly summarized.

For the sake of achieving the objectives,
Subsequently, there is aspiration toward them. [xv.6]

With the expressions of the mind,
It is continuously sought for and examined.
While the mind is directed without expression,
It should nevertheless examine through one taste. [xv.7]

The summary of names of the Dharma
Should be known to be the path of calm abiding.
The path of special insight should be known
To be an examination of the meaning. [xv.8]

The path of unity should be known
To be the integration.
The dull mind is seized
And agitation pacified. [xv.9]

Thus, when there is balance with that focus,
One rests in equanimity.
This should be approached
Through constant and devoted application. [xv.10]

Among the six types of attention, the root attention is as follows. Initially, **the one who persists in the vows**, that bodhisattva, **relates to the Dharma of the sūtras and so forth** (that is, the Dharma of the twelve sections of the scriptural teachings) **that explore the nondual meaning** (the meaning of the nonduality of the apprehended and that which apprehends), **by placing the mind on the names of these sūtras and so forth**, such as, for example, the *Sūtra on the Ten Grounds*.

From there on, they gradually distinguish, with the attention of subsequent discernment, **the categories of the words and**, with the attention of clear discernment, **within each they determine the meanings** and the letters **correctly**. Thus there is enumeration, measurement, understanding, and discerning understanding. "Enumeration" refers to the comprehension of the categories. Thus one notices, for example, that form includes eleven sense sources, or that there are six forms of sensation. "Measurement" means to comprehend these categories in a way that neither exaggerates nor denigrates. "Understanding" is the understanding that takes place through reliable means of cognition. "Discerning understanding" refers to a discerning understanding of the meaning of enumeration and the rest. Letters are discerned in two ways: in combination where they have meaning and in isolation where they do not.

Once the meanings resolved by means of the former attentions **have been ascertained** with the attention of ascertainment, the meaning of **the Dharma** that was discerned by means of the first three attentions, such as, for example, the ten grounds, **is** then **thoroughly summarized** by means of the summarizing attention. Then, **for the sake of achieving the** diligently pursued **objectives**—objectives that may relate to meditative absorption, its total completion, the results of spiritual training, engagement, or gaining distinction—**subsequently there is aspiration toward them** by means of the aspiring attention.

One may think, "What occurs here is an observation of nothing but the mind itself; nothing is observed apart from the mind!" Yet, regardless of whether one in this way understands it to be the mind only, nothing is observed apart from the mind, and the six attentions are therefore classified as focal points.

With the expressions of the mind, it (that is, the object of the meditative absorption) **is**, at the time of both the preparatory stage and the ordinary main part of the first concentration, **continuously** to be **sought for**, using both conception and discernment; **and**, at the time of the special main part, it is to be **examined** with discernment alone. Beyond the second concentration, there is neither concept nor discernment. **While the mind is** thus **directed without expression, it should nevertheless examine through the one taste** within meditative concentration.

The summary of names of the Dharma, such as the *Sūtra on the Ten Grounds,* **should be known to be the path of calm abiding.** The path of special insight should be known to be an examination of the meaning.

The path of unity should be known to be the integration of calm abiding and special insight. **The dull mind** that suffers from torpor and so forth **is seized** by focusing on the qualities of the Buddha and so forth, **and** the mind's **agitation is pacified** by contemplating, for example, the suffering of cyclic existence.

Thus, when without dullness and agitation, **there is balance with that focus, one rests in equanimity. This** ninefold sequence **should be approached through constant and devoted application.**

Having received practical instructions, bodhisattvas who persist in the vows hold initially in mind the mere names of the Dharma teachings that are found in the sūtras and the other categories within the twelve sections of scripture. Specifically, they concern themselves with the scriptures that clearly teach and reveal the facts of nonduality, showing the nondual reality that is devoid of apprehended and apprehender, or free from existence and nonexistence. This includes sūtras such as the *Sūtra on the Ten Grounds, Journey to Laṅkā,* and the *Moonlamp Sūtra*. Placing the mind on the mere title of such a sūtra is "the root attention." From there, those who persist in the vows gradually examine and discern all the words of the given sūtra, beginning with "Thus I have heard..." and continuing all the way through to the end, without leaving anything out. In this way, one notices how many chapters the sūtra has, how many stanzas there are, and how many letters. This is called "the attention of subsequent discernment" or "the subsequent attention."

Concerning the line "And within each, determine the meanings correctly...," there is nothing wrong with expanding this into: "And within each *sūtra,*..." Yet, according to Sthiramati's commentary, one has to expand it into: "And within each *one's own direct awareness*..." In any case, what is implied here is that after discerning the words of a given sūtra, one must identify and understand their meanings through a process of concerning oneself with both the expressed meaning and the words that are the means for their expression. With respect to the meanings, four principles thus become relevant: enumeration, measurement, understanding, and discerning understanding.

The first principle has to do with enumerating, for example, the five aggregates, the eighteen elements, and the twelve sense sources. In this way, one may then, for instance, further enumerate the eleven categories within the aggregate of form, which consists of ten sense sources together with the imperceptible forms that are a part of the element of phenomena. Or, one might similarly distinguish the six types of sensation that are the result of gathering and contact, and that are enumerated with reference to the six faculties that pertain to the eye and so forth, up to the mind. In short, this is the investigation of the subject matter of the teachings by means of categorical enumeration. "Measurement" is to avoid incorrectly extending or shortening the enumerations but instead to determine the exact numbers. Thus, it involves evaluating and contemplating the particular characteristics of the enumerations. "Understanding" is to apply reliable means of cognition so as to comprehend with reason why the various enumerated phenomena, such as form, are classified the way they are. "Discerning understanding" involves discerning the particular and general characteristics of the subject matter treated in the previous three ways. In short, one is aware of the enumerations of the categories of phenomena; one calculates the relevant numbers without mistake; one investigates with reason why they are enumerated in exactly the way they are; and one distinguishes the particular and general characteristics for each of the enumerated types of phenomena.

Letters are the means of expression. In isolation, letters such as *a* do not convey any meaning. Yet, meaning is expressed when several such letters come together to form a word, and such words in turn form phrases, and many such phrases form a continuum of speech. Letters are to be analyzed for meaning and the lack of it. This is done by what is called "the attention of clear discernment."

"Once the meanings have been ascertained..." refers to the "attention of ascertainment." Here the topics, enumerations, divisions, and characteristics of the treated subject matter are correctly ascertained through insight. Thus, definitively, four attentions serve to ascertain, not just roughly but in detail, the words and meanings of the Dharma that is contained in the sūtras and so on.

The line "the Dharma is thoroughly summarized" refers to the knowledge of the way in which the entire meaning of a sūtra, from beginning to end, can be subsumed and condensed into a concise key point. One may, in the same way, also reach such a conclusion regarding the teaching of all of the sūtras, thereby coming to the clear understanding that "this alone is their concise, essential meaning."

For example, one may think that "all of the vast exposition of the ten grounds that is found in the *Sūtra on the Ten Grounds* can be categorized as a teaching on the ten grounds; hence the subject matter that is contained under the title *Sūtra on the Ten Grounds* is simply that." Thus one produces a summary based on the root attention. That which brings forth such a concise summary of the entire meaning of a teaching is known as "the summarizing attention." In short, while the teachings of the sūtras are extensive, some concern the excellent qualities of the path, some consider the sequences on the path, others treat its fruition, yet others explain what is discarded by means of it, and so on. All of these issues must indeed be understood. Yet, what one does here is to summarize the essential meaning of the teachings into concise and clearly comprehended key points for the purpose of one's current spiritual training. Once one has become free of doubts in this way with respect to the subject matter of the sūtras, one pursues the objectives taught in the sūtras, such as the ten grounds, with the wish to achieve them directly, oneself. When someone engaged in spiritual training thus aspires with a strong yearning, thinking, "I shall achieve this objective," it is known as "the aspiring attention."

By means of these six attentions, one thus correctly directs the mind toward the meaning of the sūtras and the other categories within the sacred Dharma of scripture. This process involves a further eleven ways of directing the mind. These are presented in the four stanzas that begin with the words, "With the expressions of the mind..." The term "expressions of the mind" refers here to mental conceptions. The mental consciousness mixes name and meaning to arrive at expressed notions of the meaning of things. That which is aware of such conceptually formulated meanings is the conceptual mind, which can be employed in a continual investigation of the words and meanings of the scriptures, through conception and discernment. This way of operating may be practiced by the mind that has attained either the transitional preparatory stage or the ordinary main part of the first concentration. The concentration that involves conception but not discernment is called "the intermediate concentration." This concentration pertains to the mind that has attained either the distinctive main part of the first concentration or the second concentration. Thus, one examines the object of the meditative absorption within these states. Upon attaining the third and fourth concentration, since there is at this stage neither concept nor discernment, the way the mind is directed cannot be expressed in terms of conception and discernment. Nevertheless, the examination is now to be conducted by means of the one taste of meditative absorption. These three (directing the mind with conception and discernment and so on) are divisions that distinguish essentially distinct minds.

Merely focusing the mind on names and phrases is also included within the six types of attention. Thus one may place the mind on the mere words in the summary of a given sūtra's complete meaning. For example, one may keep as focus the term "transcendent knowledge," considering it to be a concise summary of all the elaborate subject matter taught in sūtras such as the *Transcendent Insight in One Hundred Thousand Lines*. Such practices should be known to belong to the path of calm abiding. The path of special insight, on the other hand, involves the examination of the meaning of the sūtras through the four principles of enumeration, measurement, and so on. Finally, the path of the unity of calm abiding and special insight consists of summarizing both words and meanings.

When calm abiding and special insight are not integrated, calm abiding observes names and phrases while special insight observes meanings. Once the two have been united, names and meanings are, however, no longer observed in separation. Instead, with word and meaning combined into one, they are equally accessed and observed by both calm abiding and special insight. These ways of directing the mind to calm abiding, special insight, and their unity are a threefold division that is made from the perspective of the path.

There is also a threefold differentiation that is made with regard to the focal points, namely, the division in terms of the following three marks: the mark of calm abiding, the mark of comprehension, and the mark of equanimity. When the mind is agitated and dispersed, contemplating the faults of distraction and cyclic existence will make the mind rest evenly without being scattered outwardly; this is directing the mind to the mark of calm abiding. When the mind becomes lethargic and dull, it is directed to the mark of special insight. By keeping in mind the qualities of the Buddha or of meditative absorption, or by directing the mind to the particular and general characteristics of phenomena, the mind is fully seized and protected from dullness. In this way, the dull mind should be uplifted. Agitation accords with special insight, and special insight therefore cannot dispel agitation. Instead, the mind must be directed to calm abiding. Since lethargy, dullness, and sleep are in accord with calm abiding, they need, on the other hand, to be dispelled by special insight. Thus, while a dull mind is thoroughly apprehended by directing the mind to the mark of special insight, agitation is pacified by directing it to the mark of calm abiding. When the mind is balanced without agitation or dullness, one directs it to equanimity and, without wavering from that, one leaves the mind in this state.

All such meditation should be practiced continuously with a mind that is directed by means of devoted and constant application. Thus one employs the aforementioned ways of directing the mind, not just occasionally, but constantly, doing so with a joyful and reverent commitment to the path.

2. Directing the Mind in Meditation

Having directed the mind to the focus,
The mind is not distracted from the continuum,
Distraction is realized quickly,
And the mind is summoned once more. [xv.11]

The wise individual increasingly
Gathers the mind within.
As the qualities are seen,
The mind is tamed within meditative absorption. [xv.12]

As the defects of distraction are seen,
Lack of joy is pacified.
The occurrence of covetousness, mental discomfort, and so forth,
Is likewise pacified. [xv.13]

The one who persists in the vows
Applies the mind,
And attainment occurs naturally.
Through familiarization with that, there will be no formation. [xv.14]

When body and mind
Have thereby attained great agility,
This should be known to involve directing the mind.
When that is then enhanced, [xv.15]

The development reaches far
And so there will be abidance in the main part.
The pursuit of superknowledges
Brings training and supreme pliability. [xv.16]

As the superknowledges achieved through concentration
Become fully accomplished,
There is, for the sake of venerating and receiving
Innumerable buddhas,
A journey throughout the world realms. [xv.17]

Having served and worshipped
Innumerable buddhas for innumerable eons,
The result of service and worship
Is the supreme pliability of the mind. [xv.18]

Then, in the prelude to purity
Five benefits are attained,
And with that, one becomes
An unexcelled pure vessel. [xv.19]

The negative tendencies of the body
Are with each instant brought to exhaustion.
Body and mind are at all times
Replenished by means of agility. [xv.20]

The light of the Dharma is always
Realized without interruption.
Unimagined marks of the genuine
Are fully perceived. [xv.21]

In this way, to perfect the body of qualities,
And for the sake of purification,
The wise do in all regards
Always embrace the causes. [xv.22]

The ninefold way of settling the mind is taught next. Having firmly directed the mind to the focus for meditative absorption (1. settling the mind), the mind is not to be distracted outwardly, away from the continuum of meditative absorption (2. subsequent settlement). Whenever it occurs, one makes sure that distraction is realized quickly and the mind is summoned back into meditative absorption once more (3. definitive settlement). The wise individual increasingly gathers the mind one-pointedly within (4. superior settlement), and, as the qualities of meditative absorption are seen, the mind is tamed by abiding within meditative absorption (5. taming). As the defects of distraction are seen, lack of joy in meditative absorption is pacified (6. pacification). The occurrence of covetousness, mental discomfort, and so forth, is likewise pacified (7. thorough pacification). The one who persists in the vows applies the mind, and the attainment of the remedy occurs naturally (8. bringing into one continuum). Through familiarization with that type of formation, there will be no formation and, since dullness and agitation do not occur, one arrives at meditative absorption (9. equipoise).

When the body and mind of the bodhisattva have thereby become pliable and have attained great agility, this should be known to involve directing the mind in the eleven ways. When that elevenfold directing of the mind is then enhanced, the development reaches far, and so there will be abidance in the main part of concentration. The pursuit of superknowledges brings training in concentration and thereby the attainment of **supreme pliability**.

As the superknowledges achieved through concentration become fully accomplished, there is—for the sake of venerating innumerable buddhas and for the sake of receiving the authentic practical instructions of those **innumerable buddhas—a journey throughout the world realms,** embarked upon by the bodhisattva.

Having thus served and worshipped innumerable buddhas for innumerable eons, the result of service and worship is the supreme pliability of the mind, in terms of its capacity for meditative absorption.

Then, with superior intent **in the prelude to** the **purity** of the first grounds, **five benefits are attained** by the bodhisattva. **And with that, one becomes** of the nature of **an unexcelled pure vessel** for the Great Vehicle. The five benefits are as follows. (1) **The negative tendencies of the body,** which make one unable to bear applying oneself to virtue physically, **are even with each instant brought to exhaustion.** (2) **Body and** (3) **mind are at all times replenished by means of** an **agility** that allows one to do as one pleases. (4) **The light of** insight into **the Dharma** of the sūtras and so forth **is always realized without interruption.** (5) In dreams and so forth, **unimagined marks of the** attainment of **genuine** superior intent **are fully perceived. In this way, to perfect the body of qualities** upon the tenth ground **and for the sake of** the **purification** of all obscurations upon attaining buddhahood, **the wise do, in all regards, always embrace the causes,** that is, the gathering of the accumulations. It should be understood that the former three are associated with calm abiding, whereas the latter two pertain to special insight.

Insight through contemplation alone will not enable one to actualize the qualities of the path. Thus, one needs to meditate one-pointedly. Moreover, initially the mind of the desire realm does not rest evenly within and will not settle even for a moment. Indeed, it moves like lightning, the wind, and the clouds. The thoughts that, like waves in the ocean, are difficult to stop will nevertheless gradually be subdued by the nine methods for letting the mind rest. The way to achieve the meditative absorption of genuine settling within is as set out below.

First, the mind is placed on a given focal point, so as to focus one-pointedly on that. Although placed in this way, the mind may not stay even for a moment and may instead roam elsewhere. With mindfulness, one then tries to continue to stay with the earlier focus for as long as one can without being distracted. When the mind is brought to settle in this way but is nevertheless unable to stay very long and is distracted, this is to be recognized quickly. With the thought, "I have been carried away by distraction," one must again bring the mind back to the earlier focus. By again and again familiarizing oneself with the practice in this way, one sustains the continuity of the abiding mind.

When the wise are able to remain for just a little while, they become firmly committed. They train again and again in letting the mind settle inwardly on the previous mental focal points. This is known as "subsequent settlement." (3) Then, if the mind abides a little longer than before, one will begin to perceive the qualities of the mind's abiding within. Hence one will feel, "I must by all means achieve the meditative absorption of mental rest!" And so, in a delighted pursuit of meditative absorption, one will practice to tame one's own mind.

The distracted thoughts of the untamed mind now become tamed through the joy experienced in meditative absorption. As, in this way, one pursues meditative absorption with joy, one is able to let the mind rest on a number of different focal points. When, in the process, one becomes distracted due to past habits, one thinks, "Distraction does great harm; it is like a robber that strips me of meditative absorption. Since I see the flaws of distraction, I will not fall under its sway, but will strive to achieve meditative absorption, the root of all good qualities." Thinking thus, the cause of distraction—which is not taking joy in meditative absorption—is pacified. This is the sixth stage of mental abiding, which is called "pacifying."

By striving in this way, the mind will rest much better than before. However, at times, covetousness, mental discomfort, and the like, as well as subsidiary afflictions such as laxity and agitation, will arise. If one falls under their power, one will likewise fail to accomplish meditative absorption, and so these factors are potentially extremely problematic. If, however, one does not fall under their sway, one will accomplish the meditative absorption that is the basis for the distinctive qualities of the superknowledges and so forth. Realizing this, one says to oneself, "I will under no circumstances entertain these negative thoughts," and so one pacifies them through discernment, the application of a remedy, or not paying them any attention. This is known as "thorough pacification."

Next, the mind of the one who strives in the vows will apply effort in the eighth stage of conditioning the mind to rest. By the power of increasing familiarization, this stage of mental rest is accomplished naturally. This is because, as one applies concerted effort, no other thoughts can interfere, and one will be able to stay with the focus. This is the stage that is described as "involved in formation." As one's familiarity with the state of mental abidance that involves formation develops further, there is finally no longer any need to put forth particular effort. The mind will, instead, naturally rest on the focal point, without effort and beyond formation. This is the last of the nine stages of mental abiding. It is also described as the single-pointed mind of the desire realm that is in accord with meditative absorption.

These nine methods for achieving the abiding mind are mentioned in a sūtra:

> To settle, to settle completely, to gather and settle, to settle thoroughly, to tame, to pacify, to pacify thoroughly, to bring into one continuum, to be in meditative absorption or equipoise.

Beyond formation, the mind abides naturally. As one becomes familiar with that state, the body and mind of the spiritual practitioner become agile and pliant. The body will feel light and extremely blissful; hence it can be employed in the cultivation of virtue. There will also be an experience of the mind's being immaculately clear and permeated with joy, thereby enabling it to work with virtuous focal points. As this development goes from its lesser to middling stages, a great agility is attained that is fine, like a shadow, and pure. Combined with the directing of the mind that distinguishes subtle from coarse features, such agility and pliability bring about the attainment of the first concentration.

Meditative absorption further develops as one directs the mind in this way, so as to eliminate successively the greater, middling, and lesser afflictions of the desire realm. Such enhancement of the practice enables the spiritual practitioner to move far beyond the lower grounds and to attain abidance within the main part of the first concentration. By means of directing the mind in a way that distinguishes subtle from coarse features, the process of development continues up to the main part of the fourth concentration.

Thus, until this point, the explanation has been concerned with the way to accomplish meditative absorption. What follows is a demonstration of the good qualities that are associated with the attainment of meditative absorption.

Upon attaining the main part of the fourth meditative concentration, one will pursue superknowledges. This practice serves to purify the afflictions of craving, belief, and doubt that are predominant on, and specific to, the main part of meditative concentration at that particular level. This brings about a supreme pliancy. This pliant concentration, in turn, enables one to attain the five superknowledges, such as that of magical emanation. By accomplishing these, the spiritual practitioner can travel throughout the world realms of the ten directions to make offerings to innumerable buddhas and to listen to the sacred Dharma.

In this way, one venerates and serves innumerable buddhas for innumerable eons. In this context, an "innumerable eon" is not of the same order as , for example, three incalculable eons. Rather, here the phrase "innumerable eons" refers to an uncountable number of eons. Thus, the reference to innumerable eons is to be seen as an indication of the power of the mind and its attainment of meditative absorption. Having venerated the sacred field of the buddhas in the ten directions in innumerable ways, the mind of the spiritual practitioner who possesses pure intention becomes supremely pliant and can be engaged in any way he or she pleases. Thus, bodhisattvas, as a prelude to their accomplishment of the first ground, attain five benefits that are signs of their coming accomplishment.

The first of these good qualities is the pliancy of mind. It turns one into a perfect vessel for the actualization of the wakefulness of the first ground, which is superior to that of listeners and self-realized buddhas, and which is unsurpassable. Negative tendencies of the bodhisattva's body—such as monkey-like restlessness because of the mind's lack of discipline and the failure to engage the body in acts of virtue because of sensations of physical heaviness and discomfort—are all exhausted, moment by moment, due to his or her attainment of pliancy. In other words, this is the purification of the habitual, negative tendencies that are present in the all-ground and that are associated with lack of pliancy in body and mind. This is the first good quality.

The second good quality is agility, which constantly permeates body and mind. To illustrate pliancy and agility, we may think of someone washing fabric with detergent. The water of calm abiding cleanses the body to make it pliant, and one is permeated with the bliss of the agility of body and mind.

The third quality is the continuous and uninterrupted realization that manifests as the light of insight into the meaning of the sacred Dharma. Thus, one's realization is free from any incompleteness in terms of knowing only certain teachings and not others.

The fourth quality is the clear perception of the signs and marks of attaining the noble grounds, including when such signs and marks were not anticipated or conceived of before. They include, for example, the body not harboring parasites, one's dreaming of taking a bath or receiving the prophecy from the buddhas, as well as the dream signs of attaining the ten grounds that are taught in the *Sūtra on the Ten Grounds*. These latter two qualities are signs that ensue from special insight.

The fifth quality consists of the way in which the wise fully embrace the causes of perfect abandonment and realization, always and in all regards. They do this in order to attain the final realization that is the complete perfection of the body of qualities and to overcome the discards of the two obscurations. This fifth quality has aspects of both calm abiding and special insight.

In his commentary, Sthiramati explains the five benefits as (1) the exhaustion of negative tendencies of body and mind, (2) the permeating bliss of the body's agility, (3) the permeating bliss of the mind's agility, (4) the uninterrupted light of the Dharma, and (5) the vision of the genuine marks. Thus Sthiramati enumerates the five by counting physical and mental agility separately. Fully embracing the causes for perfecting the body of qualities and attaining purity, he refers to as "complete embrace." Here, the explanation of the five benefits has followed the *Compendium on the Great Vehicle*.

Up to this point, the discussion in this chapter on practical instructions has been concerned with the way in which an ordinary being, abiding on the grounds of inspired conduct, attains the Dharma and the associated qualities.

3. Traversing the Path

As a bodhisattva of this kind
Rests in equipoise,
There is no perception of objects
Aside from the expressions of the mind. [xv.23]

To increase the light of Dharma,
The steadfast one musters diligence in all regards.
As the light of Dharma increases,
One abides in mind only. [xv.24]

Since all appearances of objects
Clearly manifest as the mind,
This is the time of the relinquishment
Of the distraction of the apprehended. [xv.25]

Then only the distraction
Of an apprehender remains.
At this point, the unimpeded meditative absorption
Will be reached quickly [xv.26]

For the relinquishment of the apprehender
Follows in the wake of it.
These should be understood to be,
Respectively, heat and so forth. [xv.27]

Then, beyond the world,
They attain the unsurpassable wakefulness—
Nonconceptual, stainless,
And free from dualistic grasp. [xv.28]

This is their fundamental transformation
And so this is held to be the first ground;
Following an unfathomable eon,
This is utter purity. [xv.29]

As the basic field of phenomena
Is here clearly realized to be equality,
There constantly occurs toward all beings
An understanding that they are the same as oneself. [xv.30]

With respect to all sentient beings,
The perception is equal in terms of absence of self,
Suffering, objective, and nonexpectation of reward.
Moreover, one is like the other children of the victorious ones.
    [xv.31]

All conditioned phenomena within the three realms
Are the false imagination—
This they see by means of the nondual nature
Of utterly pure wakefulness. [xv.32]

Seeing the very essence of that which is devoid of the two,
They have become free of the discards.
Hence, they are definitively said
To have "achieved the path of seeing." [xv.33]

Knowing the emptiness of the nonexistent
As well as the emptiness of the existent,
And the natural emptiness,
They are said to be "knowers of emptiness." [xv.34]

The ground for the absence of marks
Is taught to be the genuine exhaustion of thoughts.
For the absence of wishes,
It is the false imagination. [xv.35]

It is held that, for the child of the victorious ones,
All of the different factors that accord with enlightenment
Are always attained together
With this path of seeing. [x.36]

As a bodhisattva of this kind rests his or her mind in equipoise, there is no perception of objects aside from the mere expressions of the mind. It is on the stage of heat that a bodhisattva thus perceives that what appear as the particular and shared characteristics of phenomena are nothing but the mind's expressions.

Then, on the stage of summit, **to increase the light of Dharma,** the steadfast one musters diligence in all regards. As the light of Dharma increases, one abides in mind only. Since all appearances of objects clearly manifest as the mind, this is the time of the relinquishment of the distraction of the apprehended and the stage of acceptance. Then, only the distraction of an apprehender remains. At this point, the **unimpeded meditative absorption,** which is the stage of the supreme mundane quality, **will be reached quickly,** for the relinquishment of the apprehender follows in the wake of it. These should be understood to be, respectively, the four stages of **heat and so forth.**

Then, beyond the world, they attain the unsurpassable **wakefulness,** which is **nonconceptual** in the absence of thoughts of an apprehended and apprehender, **stainless** since the discards that occur through seeing are gone, **and free from dualistic grasping** in terms of object and subject.

As they have attained the supramundane, **this is their fundamental transformation and so this is held to be the first ground. Following an unfathomable eon,** one incalculable eon, **this is the** perception of the **utter purity** of the basic field of phenomena. **As the basic field of phenomena is here,** upon this ground, **clearly** realized to be equality, there constantly occurs toward all beings an understanding that they are the same as oneself in five ways.

With respect to all sentient beings, the perception is one of equality of self and others. This equality is **in terms of** the **absence of self** that is the case for both oneself and others, the lack of distinction between one's own **suffering** and that of others, the **objective** that one has to benefit both oneself and others, **and** the **nonexpectation of a reward,** just as if one were to benefit oneself with enjoyments. **Moreover, one's** own realization **is** seen to be **just like** that of **the other children of the victorious ones.**

All conditioned phenomena within the three realms are merely **the false imagination.** Having seen **this, they see by means of the nondual** (that is, devoid of apprehended and apprehender) **nature of utterly pure wakefulness,** which transcends the world.

Seeing the very essence of that, the basic field of phenomena, **which is devoid of the two,** apprehended and apprehender, **they become free of** the afflictions, which are **the discards** in this context. **Hence, they are definitively said to have "achieved the path of seeing." Knowing the emptiness of the** imaginary nature, which is **nonexistent** in terms of its own characteristics, **as well as the emptiness of the** dependent nature, which is **existent** in terms of its own characteristics, **and the natural emptiness** of the thoroughly established nature, which is the very essence of emptiness, **they are said to be "knowers of emptiness." The ground for the absence of marks is taught to be the genuine exhaustion of thoughts. For the absence of wishes, it** (that is, the ground or the observation) **is the false imagination. It is held that, for the child of the victorious ones, all of the different factors that accord with enlightenment,** such as the applications of mindfulness, **are always attained together with this path of seeing.**

Bodhisattvas who have achieved distinctive calm abiding and special insight on the path of accumulation will rest in equipoise through one-pointed meditative absorption. Aside from the expressions of the mind, they do not perceive any external objects that are separate from mind. This is the context in which the light of the stage of heat is attained.

In order to develop further the attainment of the light of Dharma, the steadfast bodhisattva must arouse a thoroughgoing diligence. The light develops and expands at the time of the summit. By bringing forth diligence in this way, the light of the Dharma greatly develops, and there cease to arise appearances of actual entities in the form of external objects. Thus, one abides in mind only. This can be likened to the way one may recognize the appearances in a dream to be dream. Similarly, forms and whatever else appears as objects are simply seen to be the perceptions of the mind; there are no actual external objects.

At this time, one gives up the distractions of apprehending external objects such as forms, and they no longer appear. Thus, for the spiritual practitioner, only the distraction or thought of an apprehender—the thought that the mind exists—remains. This is the time of the meditative absorption of acceptance, which has partial access to reality. Yet, at that point, one thinks, "If nothing is apprehended, then how can there be an apprehending mind?" Thus, quickly realizing that the two must be on an equal footing, one soon reaches the unimpeded meditative absorption that immediately precedes the path of seeing. In other words, this is the time of the supreme quality—the "immediately preceding" meditative absorption. In the wake of the realization that there are no apprehended objects, which occurs at the stage of acceptance, this latter meditative absorption likewise relinquishes the distraction of the apprehender, thereby providing immediate access to the first ground. Hence, this meditative absorption of the supreme quality is also known as the "immediately preceding" meditative absorption. In this way, there is a fourfold progression, as explained above, that belongs to the path of joining—with its stages of heat and so on.

Next, it is taught how the path of seeing is achieved immediately after the supreme quality. Here the bodhisattva who has attained the supreme quality attains the unexcelled, supramundane wakefulness that is superior to that of the listeners and self-realized buddhas and that perceives free from the concepts of the three spheres. This wakefulness is stainless because it is free from the afflictions to be discarded through seeing. Since it has relinquished the notions of apprehended and apprehender, it is free from dualistic grasping. The sūtras here speak of "the attainment of the immaculate and stainless Dharma eye that sees the Dharma." It is immaculate in the sense of being free from duality. It is stainless because it is free from the discards of the path of seeing. Alternatively, we may say that acceptance is immaculate in being the unimpeded path of the antidote to the afflictive and cognitive obscurations, while wakefulness is stainless because it is the path of liberation. The words "that sees the Dharma" imply that the intrinsic nature, the suchness of all things, is here seen by the eye of wakefulness, just as it is.

In this way, there occurs a fundamental transformation of the all-ground of the bodhisattva who thus gives rise to nonconceptual wakefulness. It is this transformation that is held to be the first ground of the noble ones. How long does it take to attain the first ground? Those who experience such transformation and abide on the first ground have engaged before in limitless bodhisattva practices for an incalculable eon on the grounds of inspired conduct. It is through this process that they attain the grounds of the noble ones. Once they have attained the first ground, they will no longer be stained by the defects of cyclic existence in any way, and they have hence become extremely pure.

As for the special qualities of attaining the grounds, the direct realization of the basic field of phenomena allows one to see all phenomena—such as those associated with ordinary beings and with noble beings—to be equal and without difference. Hence, when the first ground is attained, one continually acknowledges that sentient beings and oneself are equals, or the same, and without the slightest difference. Five types of equality are thus realized: (1) the equality of the lack of self in all beings; (2) equality in the sense that all suffering of all beings who are afflicted by bewilderment must equally be overcome; (3) equality in terms of the objective to eliminate the origins of karma and the afflictions in all beings; (4) equality regarding the nonexpectation of a reward. (When one enters the path and achieves the fruition, one benefits oneself—yet one does not expect to be rewarded. Similarly, just as they do not expect to be rewarded when benefiting themselves, bodhisattvas, when benefiting other beings by establishing them in the truth of cessation, have no expectation of any reward.) Finally, (5) there is equality in terms of the abandonment and realization of oneself and all other children of the victorious ones who thus have attained the first ground.

Having thus explained the special way of acting for the benefit of others, the next verses are concerned with distinctive realization through insight. With the pure mundane wakefulness of subsequent attainment, bodhisattvas on the first ground see all conditioned phenomena in the three realms (such as the five aggregates in the form and desire realms and the four aggregates of the form realm) to be merely the false imagination—the minds and mental states that arise within the continua of sentient beings. Thus they see that there are no phenomena other than mind and mental states. This insight accords with the *Sūtra on the Ten Grounds*, which declares: "O children of the victorious ones, these three realms are mind only."

This perception takes place by means of nonconceptual wakefulness, which is completely purified of obscurations and free from duality. Now, nonconceptual wakefulness does not observe self or other, or even mind only. It is like the field of space—pure and without duality. Hence, when it is said that the above realization takes place "by means of" nonconceptual wakefulness, it refers to the manner of seeing of the wakefulness that is subsequently attained. It perceives that while there are no phenomena other than mind, the mind itself appears in various ways—like the experiences in a dream or like the appearance of an illusion. Bodhisattvas who achieve the path of seeing perceive directly the very essence of the thoroughly established nature, free from duality. This vision frees them from the discards, through seeing, and at this point they are accordingly said to have "achieved the path of seeing." Furthermore, the achievement of the path of seeing is also known as the threefold knowledge of emptiness. In subsequent attainment, the pure mundane wakefulness, or the wakefulness that discerns the objects of cognition, knows the imaginary to be the emptiness of the nonexistent, as represented in the example of a rope that is perceived to be a snake. Likewise, the dependent, although not existent with the characteristics that immature beings impute onto it, nonetheless exists as the basis of appearance. The characteristics of the dependent nature, therefore, are known to be the emptiness of the existent. Since the thoroughly established is from the beginning free from the duality of apprehended and apprehender, it is known to be natural emptiness. Thus, with these insights, those on the path of seeing are called "knowers of emptiness."

Having in this way explained, from among the three meditative absorptions, the meditative absorption of emptiness, the next topic is the focal point or ground of the meditative absorption of the absence of marks. This is declared to be the truth of cessation, the complete exhaustion of the thoughts of the marks of this and that, concerning all phenomena from form up to the transcendence of suffering. As stated in the *Concise Abhidharma Treatise:*[40]

The defining characteristic of the truth of cessation is the ceasing of thought within suchness by means of the truth of the path.

Finally, the observation or ground of the meditative absorption of the absence of wishes is the false imagination, the impure dependent nature. The false imagination is the support of the seeds for the afflictive and cognitive obscurations. It is the cause for numerous sufferings such as birth and aging; hence, it is not observed as something to wish for.

It is held that when the children of the victorious ones achieve the path of seeing—which is of the nature of the sixteen moments of acceptance and knowledge—they always and invariably achieve all the manifold qualities of the path that are factors of enlightenment. Such factors include the applications of mindfulness and the rest of the thirty-seven, together with the path of seeing. The reason for this is that when one first attains the undefiled, supramundane path, those qualities that one previously cultivated on the grounds of inspired conduct—such as the applications of mindfulness and the four correct eliminations—now come to their complete ripening and are pure. Furthermore, it is at this point that all the abilities for actualizing the higher path of cultivation are also attained.

1. Praising the Amazing Qualities of the First Ground

The one whose mind realizes that wandering beings
Are merely conditioned phenomena, the selfless unfolding of suffering,
Gives up the meaningless view of self
And discovers the deeply meaningful view of the great. [xv.37]

Without any view of self, they regard selves,
Without any suffering, they suffer intensely.
As with one's relation to oneself when benefiting oneself,
They bring all benefits, but without the expectation of reward.
[xv.38]

While their minds have been freed by supreme liberation,
They are bound for a very long time due to endless ties.
Although they see no end to suffering,
They apply themselves and act. [xv.39]

Worldly persons cannot bear their own suffering for one lifetime;
Why even mention the combined suffering of others
For as long as the world exists—that is unthinkable.
With the bodhisattvas, the case is entirely different. [xv.40]

With joy and love for sentient beings,
The children of the victorious ones are tirelessly active—
This is a great wonder within the worlds of existence.
Yet, since sentient beings are the same as themselves, it is also no wonder. [xv.41]

The next explanation concerns the greatness of the bodhisattva's path of seeing. **The one** who abides on the path of seeing, and **whose mind,** by the power of insight, **realizes that wandering beings are merely conditioned phenomena—the selfless** (since they are devoid of a self of person or phenomena) **unfolding of suffering—gives up the meaningless view of** a self in relation to the transient collection **and** instead **discovers the deeply meaningful view of the great** mind that realizes the equality of self and others. **Without any view of** a **self of their own, they regard all** sentient beings **as selves. Without any suffering** of their own produced by karmic action and affliction, **they suffer intensely** due to compassion for others who suffer. **As with one's relation to oneself when** one is **benefiting oneself** without any hope for a reward, they bring all benefits to others **but without the expectation of any reward**. While their minds have been freed by the supreme liberation that is achieved upon the path of seeing of the unsurpassable vehicle, **they are bound for a very long time, due to the endless ties** that are present in the minds of all sentient beings. **Although they see no end to suffering,** since the realms of sentient beings are as infinite as space, **they apply themselves** for the sake of liberating sentient beings from suffering, **and** so they **act** in a way that benefits immeasurably many beings. **Worldly persons cannot bear** just **their own suffering for one lifetime; why even mention** that they cannot bear **the combined suffering of others for as long as the world exists—that is unthinkable. With the bodhisattvas, the case is entirely different** because as long as there is a world, they are able to take upon themselves the combined suffering of all sentient beings. **With joy** (wishing that sentient beings may never lack happiness) **and love for sentient beings** (wishing them benefit and happiness), **the** noble **children of the victorious ones are tirelessly active** in order to provide for sentient beings. **This is a great wonder within the worlds of existence. Yet, since** all **sentient beings are** viewed as **the same as themselves, it is also no** such great **wonder.**

The next section contains praises for the amazing qualities of the first ground. By the power of insight, one's mind realizes that all wandering beings are merely conditioned phenomena, empty of the twofold self. Reliant on others, they are dependent arisings that emerge through the formative conditions of ignorance and so forth. It is, likewise, understood that the self of the one who experiences is nothing more than the unfolding of the three sufferings through the power of the ripening of karma and affliction. Hence, giving up the meaningless view of self that is of the nature of delusion, bodhisattvas discover the view of the great equality of self and other—which is deeply meaningful since it involves benefiting infinite numbers of sentient beings. While lacking the view of self, they nevertheless view other beings as themselves. That is to say, while they themselves have achieved the direct perception of the fact that the two types of self have no establishment, they know that sentient beings do not realize this. In their deluded individual perceptions, they experience all sorts of sufferings just as if self and other actually existed. Bodhisattvas take these sentient beings as their own, and so, without ever turning their back on them, they strive until the end of time to rid all beings of their dream-like suffering.

Since bodhisattvas themselves are free from defiled phenomena, they do not suffer. Other sentient beings, however, suffer enormously. Hence, like a mother whose child is sick, they take it as their duty to dispel the suffering of the infinite number of sentient beings. Having attained the grounds, the bodhisattvas tirelessly accept the sufferings of others because they are themselves free from the five fears. These five are the fears of lacking sustenance, of being speechless (as when, for example, one is unable to recite verses), of the ingratitude of those around oneself, of birth in the lower realms, and of death. The bodhisattvas on the first ground are beyond these five fears.

Just as one expects no reward from oneself when one does something that benefits oneself, bodhisattvas expect no reward for all that they do to benefit other sentient beings. In having attained the wakefulness of the first ground, they are endowed with the distinctive realization of the Great Vehicle, and hence with supreme liberation. Yet, while their minds are thus free from the discards through seeing, the ties that result from the load of their commitment to benefit others are endless—just as endless as the number of sentient beings. Until the end, they will not put down the load that they have taken upon themselves, and so, since the duration is endless, they are indeed bound for a long time. Although they do not see any final end to the suffering of sentient beings, they nevertheless wholeheartedly practice for as long as there is suffering, diligently applying themselves to eliminate the misery of sentient beings. Therefore, as they take birth in cyclic existence, their personal striving in the transcendences, and their activities to establish others in the transcendences as well, are truly amazing.

One may as well forget about taking on the sufferings of limitless beings: mundane beings are not even able to carry the burden of their own suffering for a single lifetime. If they are not able to bear their own suffering, then why even mention that they would not be able to bear the combined sufferings of all others, without exception, for as long as the realms of the world exist. To their minds, this is not conceivable even for an instant.

Bodhisattvas are just the opposite. Although they do not have to accept any suffering for their own benefit, they possess the power that makes them gladly accept limitless sufferings for the welfare of sentient beings. Therefore, the joy and love that children of the victorious ones feel from the marrow of their bones for the infinite number of sentient beings, the way they strive and practice for their benefit, the way they do not become weary in the face of ingratitude, and so on, is truly a wonder within this world of existence. Yet, on the other hand, since they have attained a mind of equality and sameness with regard to self and other, it is not really such a great wonder. Neither do we consider it a wonder when someone does what benefits himself or herself.

2. The Path of Cultivation and Path of Consummation

From there on, upon the remaining grounds,
The path of cultivation,
They practice for the sake
Of cultivating the twofold wakefulness. [xv.42]

Nonconceptual wakefulness
Perfects the qualities of buddhahood,
While the other, describing in complete accordance,
Ripens sentient beings. [xv.43]

At the end of two incalculable eons,
Cultivation comes to perfection.
Having reached the end of cultivation,
The bodhisattva is empowered. [xv.44]

With the attainment of the vajra-like meditative absorption,
Indestructible to thought,
Comes the final, fundamental transformation
In the absence of the stains of obscuration. [xv.45]

Abiding in that which is active
For the benefit of all sentient beings,
They gain the omniscient wakefulness
Of the unsurpassable stage. [xv.46]

The next teaching explains the path of cultivation. From there on (that is, from the attainment of the path of seeing), **upon the remaining** nine **grounds** that compose **the path of cultivation, they practice for the sake of cultivating the twofold wakefulness** in relation to the qualities of buddhahood and sentient beings. How so? The **nonconceptual wakefulness** of equipoise **perfects the qualities of buddhahood** that pertain to oneself, **while the other,** the wakefulness that is involved in **describing** the objects of cognition **in complete accordance** with the way they are, **ripens sentient beings.**

At the end of two incalculable eons, the path of **cultivation comes to perfection.** Having reached the end of the path of cultivation, the bodhisattva is **empowered** by the great rays of light. With the attainment of the vajra-like meditative absorption, which is by nature **indestructible to** latent **thought, comes the final, fundamental transformation in the absence of the stains of** the twofold **obscuration,** including the habitual tendencies. **Abiding in that** wakefulness of buddhahood, **which is active for the benefit of all sentient beings** and thus accomplishes the objectives of others, **they gain the omniscient wakefulness of the unsurpassable stage.**

Following the attainment of the first ground, the remaining nine bodhisattva grounds, from the second to the tenth, compose the path of cultivation. Since both the nonconceptual wakefulness of meditative equipoise and the pure mundane wakefulness of subsequent attainment are cultivated here, the afflictive and cognitive obscurations are purified. Moreover, since nonconceptual wakefulness perfects the qualities of buddhahood (such as the ten powers and four fearlessnesses), it ripens oneself. The other wakefulness, that of subsequent attainment, ripens others through accurately describing all things in their multiplicity, thus also explaining issues such as the characteristics and qualities of the ten grounds. Hence, these forms of wakefulness are explained with reference to complete enlightenment and the teaching of the Dharma to sentient beings.

Furthermore, the path of cultivation is perfected after two incalculable eons, and the culmination of the tenth ground is also the culmination of the path of cultivation. The process from the second to the seventh ground is known as "cultivation that involves formation," which requires one incalculable eon. The eighth to the tenth grounds are together known as the "cultivation without formation," and this requires another incalculable eon. At the end of the path of cultivation, when abiding on the tenth ground, the bodhisattva is empowered as a regent of the King of Dharma by the great rays of light from the buddhas of the ten directions. Based on this, he attains the vajra-like meditative absorption, which cannot be destroyed by thoughts that apprehend marks.

By completely uprooting the subtle habitual tendencies toward the dualistic appearance of apprehended and apprehender, the final fundamental transformation occurs. In being free from the two obscurations and their habitual tendencies, this is the great abandonment that is free from the stains of any of the obscurations. Abiding upon the eleventh ground of no more learning, in order to benefit all sentient beings for as long as space exists, one then carries out the great enlightened activity that accomplishes numerous benevolent deeds. Here, one manifests great compassion that is supreme among beings, and one is endowed with the great realization that directly knows all objects of cognition simultaneously and without any obscuration. Thus, bodhisattvas attain the unsurpassable stage that is endowed with the triple greatness.

4. The Immense Benefits of Practical Instructions

Thus, constantly beholding the able ones, so difficult to behold,
And always satiated with the buoyant brightness,
That arises by the power of peerless learning,
How could they not attain the great objective? [xv.47]

To those abiding in the gateway of Dharma,
The thus-gone ones always grant direct instruction.
As if pulled by their hair, they are powerfully delivered
Out of the wilderness of error and established in enlightenment. [xv.48]

The buddhas always duly praise authentic engagement toward one's own objective, whereas they spurn flawed practices.
For sentient beings who perfectly pursue abidance and discernment,
They show what is to be abandoned and relied on in this teaching of the Bliss-Gone One.
What the obstacles and the aids to this vast spiritual training are—this the victorious ones will always correctly reveal. [xv.49]

With perfectly pure vision, enlightenment beyond thought,
They outshine the entire world.
Illuminating in every way even the greatest darkness,
To wandering beings they are like the rising, brilliant sun. [xv.50]

Thus, constantly replenished by the virtuous accumulations,
The supreme being who constantly obtains magnificent practical instructions from the able ones
Will attain the truly vast mind of meditative absorption
And proceed to the far side of the ocean of excellent qualities. [xv.51]

This was the fifteenth chapter of the *Ornament of the Great Vehicle Sūtras*, the chapter on the practical instructions and advice.

On the magnificent nature of practical instructions, it is taught: Thus, as explained before, the bodhisattvas abiding within the stream of Dharma are **constantly beholding the able ones, so difficult to behold, and always satiated with the buoyant brightness that arises by the power of** their **peerless learning** through listening to the Great Vehicle Dharma, **how could they not attain the great objective? To those** children of the victorious ones who are **abiding in the gateway of Dharma, the thus-gone ones always grant** directly manifest practical **instructions. As if** they were being **pulled by their hair** to protect them from falling into a precipice, **they are powerfully delivered,** by the strength of compassion, **out of the wilderness of error and established in** the supreme state of **enlightenment.**

In terms of the training in special discipline, **the buddhas always duly praise the authentic engagement** in the discipline of a bodhisattva **toward one's own objective, whereas they spurn flawed practices,** teaching the methods whereby such errors can be overcome. In terms of the training in special attention and special insight, **for sentient beings who perfectly pursue abidance and discernment, they show what is to be abandoned,** such as dullness and agitation, **and relied on,** such as directing the mind toward the features of calm abiding, **in this teaching of the Bliss-Gone One.** What the obstacles and the aids to this vast spiritual training in calm abiding and special insight **are—this the victorious ones will always correctly reveal.**

With the final **perfectly pure vision, enlightenment beyond thought, they,** those children of the victorious ones who have obtained practical instructions, **outshine the entire world. Illuminating in every way even the greatest darkness** of ignorance, along with its seeds, **to wandering beings they are like the rising, brilliant sun.** Thus, with his or her own continuum **constantly replenished by the virtuous accumulations, the supreme being who constantly obtains the magnificent practical instructions** of the Great Vehicle **from the able ones will attain the truly vast mind of meditative absorption, and** in this supreme way **proceed to the far side of the ocean of** the excellent qualities that are attained upon the grounds and paths.

As explained in this chapter on practical instructions, sentient beings who have sufficiently gathered the accumulations will, despite their still impure streams of being, still constantly behold the buddhas, the able ones who are so difficult to behold, and hear from them the unparalleled practical instructions of the Great Vehicle Dharma. By the power of the inspiration that arises from proper learning, the bodhisattva's stream of being is always satiated. How could they not attain the great objective that is behind the practical instructions and advice? Without a doubt, they will have no difficulty in attaining great enlightenment, thereby fulfilling the greatest objective.

To those abiding in the meditative absorption of the gateway of the Dharma, the thus-gone ones grant practical instructions constantly and directly. The way this takes place can be compared to a powerful individual who rescues people drowning in water or in a swamp, unable to get out by themselves. Grasping them by their hair, he or she will easily pull them out and bring them to a dry spot. Thus, with their blessings and teaching of practical instructions, the thus-gone ones pull beings out of the dense wilderness of the errors of cyclic existence, bringing them to unsurpassable enlightenment with the power of compassion.

The distinction between practical instructions and advice is as follows. Practical instructions are special, newly revealed pith instructions that deliver to their recipients the methods for eliminating what is to be eliminated and attaining what is to be attained. Moreover, as for the Buddha's teachings, since these are given with the knowledge of, and in accordance with, the constitutions, capacities, and inclinations of those to be trained, it is certain that they will serve their purpose. Advice, on the other hand, is given to those who have already received practical instructions. It consists of detailed and persistent subsequent teachings that allow the recipients to ascertain the full import of the instructions.

A bodhisattva may be constantly in pursuit of his or her specific objectives, and continuously involved in training in the special discipline that consists of restraining oneself from negative actions, gathering virtuous qualities, and benefiting beings. To such bodhisattvas, the buddhas will say, "Well done, noble child," thus uplifting them with praise, and pointing out the good qualities of such training. In the same way, wherever discipline is lost, they will criticize such flawed practices, showing their faults. For sentient beings on the grounds of inspired conduct, who excellently pursue the training in the unwavering mind of special meditative absorption and the thorough discernment of phenomena with special insight, they explain what the factors are that conflict with such training, and how such faults are to be avoided. In the same way, the buddhas will also explain what the concordant factors are, and how one should rely on such positive factors. Thus, granting instructions and advice, the victorious ones always and correctly reveal which factors are obstacles and which factors are conducive qualities, in the context of the vast and expansive spiritual practice of calm abiding and special insight, within the teaching of the Bliss-Gone One.

In this way, bodhisattvas receive flawless practical instructions and advice on the trainings in discipline, meditative absorption, and insight. They are taught what these trainings essentially are, as well as what the obstacles and conducive factors are that relate to them. Through such teaching, the bodhisattva enters the three trainings, relinquishes the respective conflicting factors, and relies on those that are conducive. Thus, they achieve the vast and expansive spiritual practice of calm abiding and special insight. Proceeding from ground to ground, they gain the vision of the wakefulness that is completely purified of the afflictive obscurations. Likewise, they attain the nonconceptual supramundane path of supreme enlightenment that is the remedy for the cognitive obscurations associated with the concepts of the three spheres. They outshine the entire world, including the listeners and self-realized buddhas. Having gained the power to dispel completely the great darkness of the afflictive and cognitive obscurations, they shine for beings like the rising sun. The mundane sun cannot shine in places such as caves, where its light is impeded by other things. Yet, since the teaching of the Dharma dispels the darkness of ignorance, the bodhisattva is like a great unprecedented sun—one that rises to illuminate all of the world in the ten directions, with its magnificent and brilliant light.

Through the constant gathering of the virtuous two accumulations, one's own continuum is replenished, just as the sea is filled by the rivers. The supreme bodhisattva who thus always receives extensive practical instructions directly from the able ones, the perfect buddhas, attains an ever more expansive mind of extremely vast meditative absorption, endowed with special insight. Thus, advancing from the first ground to the stage of buddhahood, he or she will proceed to the far side of the ocean of limitless qualities.

This concludes the explanation of the fifteenth chapter of the *Ornament of the Great Vehicle Sūtras*, the chapter on practical instructions and advice.

Summary of Chapters 11 through 15

The summary consists
Of great inspiration, investigation of the Dharma,
Teaching of the Dharma, practice,
And the practical instructions and advice. [XVI.1]

The summary consists of great inspiration, investigation of the Dharma, teaching of the Dharma, practice of the Dharma, *and the practical instructions and advice.*

At this point, a stanza appears that makes us aware that the previous five chapters, which concern the way that one enters the grounds of the noble ones, serve as a general outline of the entire fifth rich topic—the essence of the factors that accord with enlightenment. This topic will be further explained below, in the chapters that are specifically concerned with skillful means, the transcendences, worship, reliance, the immeasurables, and the factors that accord with enlightenment. The previous five chapters, as mentioned above, have provided an outline of the topic of the factors that accord with enlightenment. (1) One begins their cultivation by bringing forth a vast inspiration. This is followed by (2) one's investigation of the meanings that are conveyed in the discourse of the Dharma as contained in the vast and profound scriptural teachings. Having thus discovered the Dharma, one (3) explains it to others and (4) takes up the meaning of the Dharma in practice. Finally, for one's practice to gain distinction, one must (5) receive practical instructions and advice.

2. The Actual Factors of Enlightenment

This section has six parts. First is the discussion of (1) the means for embracing the factors that accord with enlightenment, that is, the chapter on skillful means. After that follow three chapters that concern the factors that are thus to be embraced. These chapters are: (2) the chapter on the transcendences and the means of attraction; (3) the chapter on worship, reliance, and the immeasurables; (4) the chapter on the factors that accord with enlightenment. Finally, there are (5) the chapter on the qualities that are based on those factors and (6) the chapter that presents the associated activities, the contexts of the grounds, and the final culmination of the factors.[41]

16

Skillful Means

1. Skillful Means

This section has two parts: (1) the actions embraced by skillful means and (2) a three-part explanation of the skillful means that embrace them.

1. Actions Embraced by Skillful Means

> Forests, embodied beings, mountains, and rivers
> Are always supported by the ground;
> It is taught that, similarly, for the virtues of generosity and so forth
> The three actions of the wise are always the basis. [XVI.2]

On the method for motivation, it is taught: Things partaken of, such as **forests**, and the **embodied beings** who partake of them; stable things, such as **mountains, and** unstable ones, like **rivers**— are all alike in **always** being **supported by the ground. It is taught that, similarly, for the virtues of generosity and so forth** (that is, the virtues of the transcendences, the factors of enlightenment, and so forth), **the three actions of** the body, speech, and mind of **the wise** children of the victorious ones **are always the basis**.

The great earth always and in all regards serves as the support of the forests, embodied beings, mountains, and rivers. All solid things in the external world, as well as the fluctuating embodied beings that inhabit it, are thus supported by the great earth. Likewise, generosity and the thirty-seven factors that accord with enlightenment are always supported by the threefold actions of the body, speech, and mind of the wise bodhisattvas. In short, among all the various possible virtuous qualities, there is none that is not supported by body, speech, and mind. Thus, the basis of all virtuous qualities is said to be the actions of body, speech, and mind.

2. Skillful Means of Embracing

As they exert themselves in extremely difficult tasks
That are of diverse character and take many eons to complete,
The children of the victorious ones do not get discouraged
    from action,
Which is of the nature of body, speech, and mind. [XVI.3]

Those who wish themselves well guard their bodies
From poison, weapons, lightning bolts, and enemies;
The children of the victorious ones similarly turn their
    threefold acts
Away from the two inferior vehicles. [XVI.4]

Always nonconceptual, they never conceive
In terms of agent, object, and action.
Therefore, as they embrace the authentic methods,
Their perfectly pure acts are infinite and transcendent. [XVI.5]

This was the sixteenth chapter of the *Ornament of the Great Vehicle Sūtras*, the chapter on the possession of skillful means.

In the account of the method for rising above obstacles, first it is explained how weariness is abandoned in the Great Vehicle: **As they exert themselves in extremely difficult tasks,** such as giving away the flesh of their own bodies, **that are of diverse character,** since they are composed of the six transcendences, **and that take many eons to complete, the children of the victorious ones do** not get discouraged from action, which is of the threefold nature of body, speech, and mind.

On avoiding directing the mind to the approach of the inferior vehicle, it is said: Those who wish themselves well guard their bodies from poison, weapons, lightning bolts, and enemies. The children of the victorious ones similarly turn their threefold acts of body, speech, and mind away from the two inferior vehicles.

Always nonconceptual, they, the children of the victorious ones, never conceive in terms of the three spheres. Thus, they do not think of themselves as an agent, or of the six transcendences as objects of practice, and they do not conceive of any action associated with practice. Therefore, as they embrace the authentic methods, their perfectly pure acts are infinite and transcendent.

The next three stanzas are concerned, respectively, with not being discouraged, not directing the mind to an inferior path, and adopting the way of nonconceptual wakefulness. Bodhisattvas engage in extremely difficult tasks of all possible kinds, as they give away their bodies and possessions, accomplish the benefit of sentient beings, and accept the ingratitude of others. Furthermore, their mission takes many eons to complete because they must continue their endeavor for three incalculable eons. The great beings, the children of the victorious ones, thus don the magnificent armor of diligence, and, without ever becoming inclined to turn away from cyclic existence, they persist in their activities, which are of the nature of body, speech, and mind. Due to their potential and their affinity with virtuous qualities from the past, they never become depressed or weary. Moreover, as when fuel is added to fire, they naturally and insatiably engage their three gates in the accumulations of merit and wakefulness. This shows how they avoid weariness.

Those who wish themselves well will seek to guard their bodies from lethal poisons, weapons, lightning bolts, or the army of the enemy. They will strive to avoid such threats. Likewise, in body, speech, and mind, the children of the victorious ones turn away from the lesser vehicles of the listeners and the self-realized buddhas. None of the actions of their three gates is performed for the sake of the result of the lesser vehicles.

Why? Because the lesser vehicles involve strong self-concern, whereby compassion for sentient beings is forsaken. Likewise, because they fail to realize fully the twofold absence of self that is a fact with respect to the objects of cognition, the wakefulness of these vehicles is incomplete. Therefore, since the paths of the lesser vehicles conflict with the path to great enlightenment, entering them would, for a practitioner of the Great Vehicle, be like falling into a great abyss.

Bodhisattvas always pursue the knowledge of the real condition of the objects of cognition. This they do through the realization of the twofold absence of self, and therefore they do not conceive of any phenomena. Hence, when they persist in practices such as generosity, they do not apprehend any of the three marks. Thus, they do not believe that they themselves are the agents who engage in virtue, that there is an object that is given, or that there is an act of generosity that is practiced. This is the result of their being naturally accustomed to the insight that does not observe the three spheres. With this kind of wakefulness, one never loses heart when faced with the suffering of sentient beings, their ingratitude, or the length of time that is required for the practice. Having realized equality, they never perceive any marks of faults or good qualities in terms of existence and peace; nor do they conceive of an actual self and other, in the way that ordinary beings do. Since their fundamental virtues are not polluted by the bewilderment of clinging to marks, their virtues are accomplished purely. Among the limitlessly many skillful means of the Great Vehicle, this nonconceptual wakefulness is the main, sacred principle.

Whatever qualities of the path they may cultivate, such as generosity, bodhisattvas embrace those practices with the skillful means of nonconceptual wakefulness. All the virtuous acts of generosity and so forth that they engage in, through their three gates, therefore become completely pure. Thus, as their infinite, limitless qualities become transcendent, they attain buddhahood. The complete purity of generosity and all the other limitless practices of the vast and profound are accomplished through the transcendent insight of nonconceptual wakefulness. It is when they are embraced by such insight that they are referred to as "supramundane transcendences." Not even listeners and self-realized buddhas possess such insight, so it should go without saying that mundane beings do not, either.

To summarize the meaning of the chapter on the possession of skillful means into a single quintessential instruction, we may cite the victorious Longchenpa:

> If fundamental virtues are embraced by the three excellences, they all become the path of the Great Vehicle.

These three excellences are (1) the excellent preparation of generating the enlightened mind, (2) the excellent main part free from reference point, and (3) the excellent conclusion of dedication. Within these three, the three factors that we discussed above are included—not growing weary with the path of the Great Vehicle, giving up directing the mind toward the Lesser Vehicle, and embracing one's endeavors with nonconceptual wakefulness. Thus, if they are embraced by this essential key point, all of the bodhisattvas' paths of virtue, their practices of generosity, and so forth, by means of body, speech, and mind, will certainly be the path of the Great Vehicle.

This concludes the explanation of the sixteenth chapter of the *Ornament of the Great Vehicle Sūtras,* the chapter on actions with skillful means.

17
Transcendences and Means of Attraction

2. The Transcendences and Means of Attraction

This chapter on the transcendences and means of attraction has three parts: (1) the six transcendences that perfect the qualities of buddhahood, (2) the four means of attraction that ripen other sentient beings, and (3) the conclusion of those two.

1. The Transcendences That Perfect the Qualities of Buddhahood

This section has two parts: (1) a brief presentation in the form of a summary and (2) an elaborate explanation of the latter's import.

1. Summary

> Their enumeration, characteristics, sequence,
> Etymologies, process of training,
> Analysis, summary, conflicting factors,
> Qualities, and mutual ascertainment—this is how they are known. [XVII.1]

The topics in the context of the transcendences are presented as follows: Their fixed **enumeration**, the **characteristics** of the six transcendences, their **sequence**, **etymologies**, **process of training**, analysis, summary, how to separate from **conflicting factors**, praises of their **qualities**, and their **mutual ascertainment**—this is how they are known.

All of the practices of the Great Vehicle Dharma are comprised within the six transcendences. The central part of the path comes down to just this. Therefore, what is achieved by the teachings on the means of attraction, worship, service, and the immeasurables is the provision of a wealth of perspectives on precisely this practice of the six transcendences. Thus, the gateways of the Dharma manifest in limitless ways.

Here we begin with the presentation of the Dharma of the six transcendences, which will include: (1) the fixed enumeration of the six transcendences, (2) their specific characteristics, (3) their sequence, (4) the specific etymologies of "generosity" and the rest, (5) the way to cultivate the qualities of the transcendences, (6) the internal divisions within the six transcendences, (7) the way that all positive qualities are comprised within the six transcendences, (8) the elimination of the factors that conflict with them, (9) the qualities of the transcendences, and (10) their mutual ascertainment in terms of the presence of each transcendence—such as generosity—within the others. Hence, this tenfold enumeration provides the structure for the following explanation.

2. Elaborate Explanation

This section has ten parts, following the ten topics in the summary: (1) fixed enumeration, (2) characteristics, (3) sequence, (4) etymologies, (5) process of training, (6) analysis, (7) summary, (8) separation from conflicting factors, (9) qualities, and (10) mutual ascertainment.

1. Fixed Enumeration

Enjoyments, excellent body,
Retinue, and excellent perseverance for the truly elevated.
Never being under the control of the afflictions,
And being unmistaken about the course of action. [XVII.2]

Diligent pursuit of the welfare of others
Is accomplished by giving, abstaining from harm, and
    patience.
Abidance and liberation, along with their basis,
Bring about all that is beneficial for oneself. [XVII.3]

No destitution, nonviolence,
Tolerance of aggression, no weariness with activity,
Engendering joy, and excellent speech—
Thus the objectives of others are their own. [XVII.4]

No fondness for pleasures, complete devotion,
No weariness with respect to the two,
Spiritual training, and nonconceptuality—
The entire Great Vehicle comes down to just this. [XVII.5]

These are the path of nonattachment to objects,
Avoiding the distraction of trying to obtain them,
Not forsaking sentient beings, development,
And the thorough purification of obscurations. [XVII.6]

The Victorious One has taught the six transcendences
With reference to the three trainings:
The first three, the final two that make two,
And the one that is included in all three. [XVII.7]

The explanation of the enumeration is as follows: Generosity brings **enjoyments**, discipline an **excellent body**, patience brings **retinue, and** diligence involves the **excellent perseverance** that accomplishes all activities. Thus, these four are the factors **for** the accomplishment of **the truly elevated**. The latter two accomplish what is definitively good because **never being under the control of the afflictions** is the result of concentration, **and being unmistaken about the course of action** by means of true and exact knowledge is the result of insight.

The bodhisattva's **diligent pursuit of the welfare of others is accomplished by giving** away all enjoyments (generosity), **abstaining from harm**ing others (discipline), **and** bearing the harm done by others (**patience**). As for the subsequent three, the mind's **abidance** (concentration) **and liberation** (insight), **along with their basis** (diligence), **bring about all that is beneficial for oneself.**

Through one's generosity, others will not be lacking what they need and thus will experience **no destitution**. With discipline, there will be **nonviolence**. Through patience, one is able to have **tolerance of aggression;** diligence facilitates virtuous action and so ensures that there is **no weariness with activity;** concentration involves **engendering joy** through the power of miraculous displays and so forth; **and** with insight comes the **excellent speech** that answers questions—thus, for the bodhisattvas, **the objectives of others are their own.**

Moreover, bodhisattvas who practice generosity are unattached and therefore have **no fondness for pleasures**. With discipline, they pursue with **complete devotion** the trainings to which they have committed themselves. Through patience and diligence, they have **no weariness with respect to the two** (that is, bearing the suffering that may have arisen from sentient or insentient causes and applying themselves to what is virtuous). Through the final two, they will also give rise to the **spiritual training** of the meditation of calm abiding **and** to the **nonconceptuality** of special insight. Thus, **the entire** path of the **Great Vehicle comes down to just this.**

These are, likewise, as follows. Generosity is **the path of nonattachment to objects** because as one becomes accustomed to giving, there will be no attachment. Discipline is the path of **avoiding the distraction of trying to obtain them** because when abiding by the vows of a fully ordained monk, none of the distractions will occur that are associated with the endeavor of trying to obtain things. Patience is the path of **not forsaking sentient beings** because by virtue of patience, one will not become discouraged—no matter how much suffering is inflicted. Diligence is the path of the **development** of virtue, for it serves to enrich further the fundamental virtues. **And, finally, concentration and insight are the path of the thorough purification of obscurations,** for they purify the afflictive and cognitive obscurations.

The Victorious One has taught the six transcendences with reference to the three trainings. With the first three transcendences, he has explained the training in special discipline. That is to say, through generosity one will become uninterested in pleasures, and so one will take up genuine discipline. Discipline will, in turn, ensure that one observes the four teachings of a spiritual practitioner, and one will thereby be capable of patience. **The final two** transcendences, concentration and insight, **are the two that make** up the other **two trainings**—in special attention and special insight, respectively. **And diligence is the one that is included in all three** trainings because it serves as an aid to them all.

Of the four reasons for the fixed enumeration, the first is that the six transcendences are taught with reference to the accomplishment of the truly elevated and the definitive good. Generosity brings excellent enjoyments within one's lifetimes in cyclic existence. Discipline provides an excellent support in the form of a human or divine body. From patience, one gains an excellent retinue. From diligence, one develops excellent perseverance in activities. These four bring about the accomplishment of the truly elevated. Due to concentration, one's mind stream becomes gentle and the afflictions are suppressed, ensuring that one does not fall under their power. With insight, one will know what to accept and reject in general. As one comes to know the four truths, the factors that conflict with the transcendences, and the remedies of those factors, one will, with respect to cyclic existence and the transcendence of suffering, set out on an unerring course of action. Concentration and insight are hence concerned with the definitive good. In this way it can be understood why there are exactly six transcendences. More are not necessary and less would not be enough.

The second reason that there are six transcendences has to do with the way that bodhisattvas accomplish the objectives of self and others. First we will consider the benefit of others.[42] When bodhisattvas fully exert themselves for the sake of sentient beings, they help others by acts of giving, while with discipline, they avoid bringing harm to anyone through killing, taking what has not been given, and so forth. Moreover, because of their patience, bodhisattvas will help others rather than retaliating if someone harms them. This primarily constitutes their accomplishment of the benefit of others.

Concentration is the support of liberation. For instance, when the mind is resting in equipoise, it may definitively see the true nature. Insight, on the other hand, is that which specifically brings about liberation. "Along with their basis" refers to the basis of these two, which is diligence. It is by rousing diligence that the mind will enter meditative equipoise and accomplish special insight. These three bring about all that is beneficial for oneself.

Thus there are six transcendences, three factors that accomplish the benefit for others and three that accomplish one's own benefit. Furthermore, bodhisattvas mainly act for the benefit of others without concern for their own benefit. Thus, they also accomplish the benefit of others by means of all six transcendences. With generosity, they give the impoverished whatever they need and thus provide for sentient beings, such that they are not lacking provisions. Through discipline, they avoid being violent toward sentient beings. Due to patience, they endure other beings' aggression without getting angry. Because of diligence, they do not tire of helping others. Concentration affords them superknowledge of what is hidden and enables them to bring forth miraculous displays that inspire and delight the minds of beings. And, with insight, they eloquently express the sacred Dharma. Thus they accomplish the benefit of others, and benefiting others is the supreme way of benefiting oneself. Although one may diligently strive to benefit oneself alone, one cannot achieve great enlightenment by doing this. When striving for the sake of others, however, all one's own aims will naturally be fulfilled, even on the temporary level, and in the end, one will attain unsurpassable enlightenment. Hence, the benefit of self and others will be automatically accomplished by means of these six transcendences.

The third way that all the practices of the Great Vehicle bodhisattvas are comprised within the definitive enumeration of the six transcendences is as follows. Without fondness for any of the inner or outer sense pleasures, bodhisattvas have no attachment, as there is nothing that they will not give away. Since they are completely devoted to the training in discipline, they are not stained by even the slightest flaw in terms of conduct. Through patience as well as diligence, they are tireless, despite the harm inflicted by sentient beings and the difficulties that their endeavors involve. With patience, they endure any amount of harm done by sentient beings, as well as the various difficulties of their tasks, and through diligence, they endlessly strive to benefit sentient beings, undertaking all their difficult endeavors for long periods of time without ever growing weary. Alternatively, their lack of weariness can be understood in terms of the way they tirelessly gather the two accumulations of merit and wakefulness by means of patience and diligence: through patience they eliminate the conflicting factors and with diligence they apply the remedies. Finally, with concentration, they abide one-pointedly in the true spiritual training and, through insight, they do not conceive of any marks at all. These latter two are, respectively, calm abiding and special insight. Comprising all the topics of the Great Vehicle without anything lacking, everything is included within these six transcendences, and so the Great Vehicle comes down to these alone.

The fourth enumeration concerns the three special trainings. Generosity is the path of nonattachment to the five sense pleasures; everything is given away. Transcendent discipline is the path of avoiding the distractions that ensue from wanting to acquire the objects of desire. This keeps one from participating in a great deal of distracting worldly activities. Patience is the path of not forsaking sentient beings, despite their ingratitude and harmful actions. Diligence is the path that further develops the accumulation of virtue. Finally, concentration and insight constitute the path that purifies the obscurations: concentration purifies the afflictive obscurations while insight mainly purifies the cognitive ones. Or, concentration is the path that alleviates the two obscurations through suppression, while insight is the path that uproots them.

In this way, the Victorious One taught the six transcendences with reference to the three special trainings. The first three—generosity, discipline, and patience—compose the special training in discipline. Generosity, the path of nonattachment, is the cause of discipline. Discipline itself is the essence of the path of restraint, and it is assisted by the path of not forsaking sentient beings, which is patience. With these three, one will genuinely be able to uphold discipline. The last two—concentration and insight—involve two trainings because while concentration is the special training in meditative absorption, insight is precisely the special training in insight. One of the transcendences, namely, diligence, is included in all three trainings. Since all the other five have to be practiced with the diligence of devoted and constant application, it is clear that diligence in the transcendences belongs to all three trainings. Thus, the enumeration of the transcendences is definitive.

2. Characteristics

Generosity is the breakdown of the conflicting factor,
Possession of nonconceptual wakefulness,
Complete fulfillment of all wishes,
And the threefold maturation of sentient beings. [XVII.8]

Discipline is the breakdown of the conflicting factor,
Possession of nonconceptual wakefulness,
Complete fulfillment of all wishes,
And the threefold maturation of sentient beings. [XVII.9]

Patience is the breakdown of the conflicting factor,
Possession of nonconceptual wakefulness,
Complete fulfillment of all wishes,
And the threefold maturation of sentient beings. [XVII.10]

Diligence is the breakdown of the conflicting factor,
Possession of nonconceptual wakefulness,
Complete fulfillment of all wishes,
And the threefold maturation of sentient beings. [XVII.11]

Concentration is the breakdown of the conflicting factor,
Possession of nonconceptual wakefulness,
Complete fulfillment of all wishes,
And the threefold maturation of sentient beings. [XVII.12]

Insight is the breakdown of the conflicting factor,
Possession of nonconceptual wakefulness,
Complete fulfillment of all wishes,
And the threefold maturation of sentient beings. [XVII.13]

Next follows an explanation of the different characteristics. The **generosity** of the bodhisattvas **is the breakdown of the conflicting factor** of miserliness. It is a **possession of nonconceptual wakefulness** through the realization of the absence of self in phenomena. It is the **complete fulfillment of all wishes** because it delivers whatever is wished for. **And**, having attracted beings, generosity accomplishes **the threefold** (in terms of the three vehicles) precise **maturation of sentient beings.**

The **discipline** of the bodhisattvas **is the breakdown of the conflicting factor** of faulty discipline. It is a **possession of nonconceptual wakefulness** through the realization of the absence of self in phenomena. It is the **complete fulfillment of all wishes** because, with respect to others, one shows genuine restraint of body and speech. **And**, as discipline creates appreciation, it is **the threefold** (in terms of the three vehicles) precise **maturation of sentient beings**, in accordance with their capacities.

The **patience** of the bodhisattvas **is the breakdown of the conflicting factor** of anger. It is a **possession of nonconceptual wakefulness** through the realization of the absence of self in phenomena. It is the **complete fulfillment of all wishes**, as one tolerates those who do harm. **And**, as patience creates appreciation, it is **the threefold** (in terms of the three vehicles) exact **maturation of sentient beings**, in accordance with their capacities.

The **diligence** of the bodhisattvas **is the breakdown of the conflicting factor** of laziness. It is a **possession of nonconceptual wakefulness** through the realization of the absence of self in phenomena. As it serves as the aid of virtue, it is the **complete fulfillment of all wishes. And**, as diligence creates appreciation, it is **the threefold** (in terms of the three vehicles) precise **maturation of sentient beings**, in accordance with their capacities.

The **concentration** of the bodhisattvas **is the breakdown of the conflicting factor** of distraction. It is a **possession of nonconceptual wakefulness** through the realization of the absence of self in phenomena. As concentration engenders appreciation through the performance of miracles and so on, it is the **complete fulfillment of all wishes and,** having thus created appreciation, it is **the threefold** (in terms of the three vehicles) precise **maturation of sentient beings,** in accordance with their capacities.

The **insight** of the bodhisattvas **is the breakdown of the conflicting factor** of misguided intelligence. It is a **possession of nonconceptual wakefulness** through the realization of the absence of self in phenomena. As insight cuts through doubts, it is the **complete fulfillment of all wishes, and,** as insight creates appreciation, it is **the threefold** (in terms of the three vehicles) precise **maturation of sentient beings,** in accordance with their capacities.

In this section, four characteristics for each of the six transcendences are taught in one stanza each. The characteristics are presented as follows. Generosity is characterized by the breakdown of its conflicting factor, which is miserliness, because the absence of miserliness provides the motivation for being generous. It is aided by the possession of the nonconceptualization of the three spheres, due to realizing the absence of self in persons and phenomena. Thus, one does not observe any nature of a giver, a substance given, or a recipient of generosity. The way in which generosity takes place is such that it completely fulfills all the wishes of the receiver. Its function is to attract sentient beings and establish them in the three final fruitions by bringing them to maturation on the path that accords with their respective potential, whether it be that of the listeners, the self-realized buddhas, or the Great Vehicle.

Just as there are four characteristics for generosity, the same is the case with discipline. The latter is the breakdown of the conflicting factor that takes the form of faulty discipline, and it is aided by the embrace of nonconceptual wakefulness, such that there is no observation of an individual upholding discipline, an act of discipline, or of practices undertaken. By upholding discipline, one does not act in a way that harms other sentient beings; instead, one fulfills their wishes completely. Since discipline creates appreciation, sentient beings are attracted, and they too become established in discipline. Thus, there ensues the threefold maturation within the three vehicles.

Patience is the breakdown of the conflicting factor of anger. It possesses the nonconceptual wakefulness that does not observe the three spheres of one who is being patient, the act of patience, and the object of patience. Since it does not return harm with harm, it completely fulfills the wishes of others. By means of patience, sentient beings are established in the three vehicles and are brought to the threefold maturation.

Diligence is the breakdown of the conflicting factor of laziness. It possesses the nonconceptual wakefulness that does not observe the three spheres of a diligent one, the act of diligence, and what is accomplished. Since it benefits sentient beings by assisting them in their endeavors and so forth, it completely fulfills all their wishes. Diligence also brings beings to the threefold maturation in the three vehicles.

Concentration is the breakdown of the conflicting factor of distraction. It possesses the nonconceptual wakefulness that does not observe a meditator, the act of meditating in concentration, or an object of meditation that is concentrated upon. It completely fulfills the wishes of sentient beings with miraculous displays and superknowledge. The threefold maturation of beings is also brought forth by means of concentration.

Insight is the breakdown of the conflicting factor of misguided intelligence. It possesses the nonconceptual wakefulness that does not observe an individual, an act of insight, or what is established thereby. By cutting through doubts and the like, it completely fulfills the wishes of others. It brings beings to the threefold maturation by means of the three vehicles.

3. Sequence

> The subsequent ones arise based on the previous ones,
> They go from inferior to supreme,
> And from the coarse to the subtle;
> This is the reason for their sequence. [XVII.14]

The next explanation concerns the structure of the sequence. **The subsequent ones arise based on the previous ones** because if one is not interested in pleasures, one can truly take up discipline, and when endowed with discipline, one becomes patient. Diligence, moreover, is aroused on the basis of patience, and it is through diligence that meditative absorption is produced. Finally, when the mind abides in equanimity, one comes to know reality as it is. They (generosity and the rest) also compose a sequence that **goes from the inferior to the supreme, and from the coarse to the subtle** because while the earlier ones are comparatively easy to enter and to practice, they become increasingly difficult. **This is the reason for their sequence.**

There are three reasons behind the sequence of the transcendences. The first is that the subsequent transcendences arise based on the previous ones. If one is attached to various pleasures, one will not be able to give up one's household and adhere to discipline; but without attachment, one can do so. Hence, generosity that is not attached to pleasures is explained at the outset because it serves as the cause of discipline. People who are habituated to negative ways cannot bear criticism and the like, but those who can restrain themselves from negative conduct can also accept such challenges. Hence, since it is the cause of patience, discipline is explained after generosity. Without being able to endure at all the hardships of heat, cold, hunger, thirst, and so on, one will not be able to muster diligence. Since, on the other hand, a patient person can muster diligence, patience is taught after discipline. When possessing constant diligence in virtue, one will be able to settle the mind in the concentration of equipoise. Thus, diligence is explained after patience. Finally, when one possesses the meditative absorption of a mind resting in equipoise, the insight that genuinely knows the noble truths will arise, and therefore concentration is explained after diligence. Therefore, while concentration serves as a cause, the insight that sees the meaning of the truths is its effect. For this reason, insight is taught subsequent to all the other practices, which themselves arise in a causal sequence as explained above.

Another reason for the sequence is that the earlier transcendences are inferior to the latter, which are supreme in comparison. The inferior ones are thus stated prior to those that are superior. While in the world we find acts of generosity, it is more rare to meet someone who in body, speech, and mind is guarded against engagement in negative actions. In this way, generosity can be seen to be inferior to discipline. Likewise, it is more difficult to endure harm done by others than to refrain from doing negative actions oneself, and it is even harder to be constantly diligent in virtuous actions than it is to be patient. Moreover, while one may be diligent in a range of pursuits, it is more difficult to tame one's mind with meditative absorption. Similarly, even if one has achieved the meditative absorptions of the form and formless realms, it is still more difficult to accomplish the insight that sees the meaning of the truths.

The sequence is also laid out in this way because the easier practices involve more affliction than those that are harder and that involve less affliction. The various qualities of the transcendences likewise increase from generosity up to insight. Moreover, the transcendences are also outlined in terms of coarse and subtle, with the coarse ones taught first and the subtle ones later. The coarse transcendences are easier to engage in and practice, while the subtle ones are more difficult. Generosity can be practiced in various ways, by the likes of kings and ministers and all the way down to servants and outcastes. Thus, generosity is simple to understand, coarse, and easy to begin practicing. Compared with that, the practices of discipline and patience, and so forth, all the way to insight, become by nature more and more subtle. They go from being comparatively simple to increasingly demanding. This, too, is a reason for the structure of their sequence.

4. Etymologies

They are taught to be the eradication of poverty,
Attaining coolness, exhaustion of anger,
Joining with the supreme, seizing the mind,
And knowledge of the ultimate. [XVII.15]

Next follows the account of the etymologies. **They are taught to be the "eradication of poverty"** in the case of generosity, **"attaining coolness"** from the torments of the afflictions in the case of discipline, **"exhaustion of anger"** with respect to patience, **"joining** with the supreme" in the case of diligence, "seizing the mind" in the context of concentration, and "knowledge of the ultimate" with respect to insight.

Why is "generosity" referred to as such? "Generosity" comes from the Sanskrit word *dāna: dā* implies poverty" and the *na* has the sense of eradicating. Thus, generosity refers to that which eradicates poverty. When wealth is given away, the poverty of the receiver is eradicated in this life while the poverty of the giver is also eliminated—because, in future lifetimes, he or she will achieve plenty of wealth without having to lack anything. Likewise, the Sanskrit term for discipline is *śīla*. *Śī* carries the sense of coolness and *la* that of attaining or getting, and thus we arrive at "attaining coolness." Possessing discipline, one will not have to suffer punishment at the hands of the law, or any other such torments of this life that result from attachment to objects. In the future, one will not be born in the lower realms but instead will live as a god or a human being. In the end, one will attain the soothing bliss of the transcendence of suffering. The Sanskrit word for patience is *kṣānti: kṣān* has the sense of exhaustion and *ti* implies "to make happen." Hence, patience refers to that which exhausts anger in one's mind stream.

Vīrya is the Sanskrit term for diligence. *Vī* carries the meaning of "supreme" or "true" while *rya* indicates practice. Hence, since it makes one practice the true, supramundane virtues, diligence is the "practice of the supreme." Concentration is a translation of the Sanskrit term *dhyāna*. The *ya* subscript is equal to a *ra*, so the term is the same as *dharana*, which means "to hold." Concentration is, therefore, when the mind is held to its inner observation without being distracted outwardly. Insight is the term for the Sanskrit word *prajñā: pra* is a prefix that means "superior," and, given that *pra* can be seen as an abbreviated form of the term *paramārtha*, "the ultimate truth," *pra* means "ultimate truth," while *jñā* means "to know." Hence, insight is "knowledge of the ultimate."

This explanation relates to the *meaning* of these terms and is a special way of explaining them through the use of their abbreviated and augmented forms in Sanskrit. Yet, it should be understood that the etymology of "generosity" and other such standard, direct translations[43] from the Sanskrit can be explained in the above way, as well.

5. The Process of Training

All of the training is taught
To be based on entities,
Directing the mind, intent,
Skillful means, and mastery. [XVII.16]

The next explanation concerns the various forms of training. **All of the training is taught to be based on** the following principles.

First, the training based on **entities** includes that which is: (1) based on the cause, which refers to the training that occurs through an affinity with the practice of the transcendences, by the power of the potential; (2) based on maturation, that is, the training that is accomplished by the power of having an excellent body; (3) based on aspiration, that is, training by the power of past aspirations; (4) based on discernment, the training in the transcendences that is accomplished by the power of insight.

Next follows the training that is based on **directing the mind**: (1) directing the mind with devotion to all the sūtras that teach the transcendences; (2) directing the mind with relish, that is, relishing the attainments of the transcendences, seeing them to be excellent qualities; (3) directing the mind by rejoicing, as one rejoices in the generosity and so forth of all sentient beings in the world; (4) directing the mind with true delight, as one takes delight, specifically, in the future training in the transcendences that is to be carried out by oneself and others. Thus, the training in the transcendences can be divided in terms of the way the mind is directed.

The divisions of the training that are based on **intent** are: (1) insatiable intent, (2) vast intent, (3) joyous intent (4) grateful intent, (5) stainless intent, and (6) virtuous intent.

Finally, there is the training in the transcendences that is based on the **skillful means** of nonconceptual wakefulness **and** the training that is based on **mastery**. The latter includes the training that is based on (1) mastery of the accomplishment of the bodies, (2) mastery of the activities that tame those to be trained, and (3) mastery in teaching the six transcendences.

How does one train in the transcendences, from generosity to insight? Each of the six involves a fivefold process of training or cultivation. Thus we have training that is based on, or supported by, (1) entities, (2) directing the mind, (3) intent, (4) pure methods, and (5) mastery. In this context, "entities" has the sense of facts or substances. There are four types of training that in this way are based on the entities of (1) the cause, (2) maturation, (3) aspiration, and (4) discernment. As for the first, the power of the causal bodhisattva potential will make one take delight in the practice and cultivation of the six transcendences, such as giving, without having to be encouraged by another person, no matter where one is born. Based on this, one will practice any and all of the transcendences.

Training based on maturation occurs due to having affinity with the practice of the transcendences from the past. Based on such affinity, one will possess a bodily support that allows one to spontaneously engage in them during one's present life. The third, the training that is based on aspiration, consists of the practice of the six transcendences that ensues from having made aspirations such as "Wherever I am born, may I practice generosity without any attachment to my body or enjoyments." The fourth, the training based on discernment, is when, for example, one practices generosity based on having understood, through intelligent inquiry, that enjoyments and possessions are unreliable and futile. Thus this refers to the correct practice of the transcendences, based on knowledge of their qualities.

The second type of training is based on four ways of directing the mind. (1) Directing the mind with devotion involves believing in, and having devotion toward, the teachings of the six transcendences as taught in the Great Vehicle sūtras; thereby, the element of the transcendences is developed. (2) Directing the mind with relish has to do with truly delighting in one's past accomplishments of generosity and so forth, regarding these recollected deeds as good qualities and thinking, "Well done!" (3) Directing the mind to rejoicing involves taking joy and delight in the accomplishment of the transcendences that takes place in the world realms throughout the ten directions, just as one does with respect to one's own accomplishment. (4) Directing the mind to true delight is to take delight in the practice of the transcendences with the thought "May I and others practice the transcendences in the future, wherever we may be born."

The third type of training is sixfold, based on intent: (1) the insatiable intent or the intent that does not grow content, (2) the vast intent, (3) the joyous intent, (4) the grateful intent, (5) the stainless intent, and (6) the virtuous intent.

The first—insatiable intent—also has four subdivisions. To illustrate this with generosity, there is (1) insatiability with respect to the giving of things. If it is to the benefit of just one sentient being, and if it brings that individual to maturation, one will not think that one has done enough even if one gives that single being as many world realms as there are grains of sand in the river Ganga, all filled with the seven precious gemstones. There is also (2) insatiability with respect to giving the body. For the sake of a single sentient being, one may in every moment sacrifice as many of one's own bodies as there are grains of sand in the river Ganga and still not think, "I have sacrificed that many bodies—now it is enough." Likewise, there is (3) insatiability with respect to time. When giving away one's bodies and enjoyments in the way just described, one does so throughout as many eons as there are grains of sand in the river Ganga without a single moment of interruption. Still, one does not think, "I have given this many inner and outer entities throughout that many eons—this suffices." Finally there is (4) insatiability with respect to sentient beings. For a single sentient being to be ripened and established in unsurpassable enlightenment, one may, as just explained, fill as many world realms as there are grains of sand in the river Ganga with the seven precious gemstones, and give them away, and one may sacrifice the same number of bodies for so many eons, all for the sake of that one sentient being. The same is the case with two sentient beings, or with three—this commitment is there for all sentient beings, as many as there are. Thus, if we imagine the fictional situation that all beings have become buddhas, even then there would be no thought that this is enough. That is how far bodhisattvas train their minds in cultivating this attitude that does not grow content.

Second is the vast intent, which is the wish to be able to practice generosity such as this, and so on, continuously, without a single moment of interruption, all the way up to the attainment of the heart of enlightenment.

Third is the joyous intent. This involves thinking, in a joyous frame of mind, "These sentient beings who have been attracted by the likes of generosity, and who have in this way been ripened, are my companions in the attainment of unsurpassable enlightenment!" Thus, with appreciation for sentient beings, who are the domain of benefit, one considers them extremely kind and regards them with love.

The fourth is the grateful intent. When benefiting sentient beings, bodhisattvas do not think, "I have benefited those beings." Rather, they look at sentient beings with the thought "Those sentient beings have benefited me because without sentient beings to benefit, I would not be able to perfect the accumulations that bring about unsurpassable enlightenment. Yet, by serving them, I will achieve unsurpassable enlightenment. They have done me tremendous good!"

The fifth is the stainless intent. Bodhisattvas benefit others in this way through generosity and so on, yet without expecting any reward or hoping for the ripened result of birth in the higher realms. They do it for the benefit of sentient beings, without any attachment to their own welfare.

Finally, the sixth is the virtuous intent. Bodhisattvas perform extensive generosity and so on without wanting to experience the results of this themselves; they completely dedicate the fundamental virtue of their actions to the result that all beings may attain unsurpassable enlightenment.

This was a description of the way that this sixfold intention applies to generosity, but one trains in the same way with respect to the other transcendences, from discipline through to insight. We may imagine that the billionfold realms of the world are on fire and that there are no sources of relief—such as water that could extinguish the fire—to be found anywhere. Imagine having to suffer there, not just by means of one body, but by having bodies equal in number to the grains of sand in the river Ganga. Imagine having to suffer there for the duration of not just a finite number of eons, like a hundred or a thousand, but while living under such circumstances for as many eons as there are grains of sand in the river Ganga. In such a context, one then practices discipline, not just in terms of one activity, but in every moment throughout the four activities of going, staying, sleeping, and moving about. Thus, one masters innumerable aspects of the practice, all the way up to the discipline of the attainment of unsurpassable enlightenment. Yet, even having completely perfected the training in discipline, one will still not think, "The practices of discipline have been perfected, this is sufficient." The situation is similar in the case of insight, which can likewise be explained along the lines of insatiable insight, vast insight, and so forth.

The fourth type of training is based on skillful means. Whichever of the transcendences is practiced, one does not observe the practice in terms of the three spheres, and so we may in this way speak of the threefold skillful means. In fact, skillful means consists of embracing the practice with nonconceptual wakefulness because this ensures that all the ways of directing the mind—as well all the qualities of buddhahood—will be accomplished and free of stains.

Fifth is the training based on mastery. When mastery is achieved on the three pure grounds, the activities of the transcendences are spontaneously accomplished without effort. Based on this, one will finally discover the perfections of body, speech, and mind at the stage of buddhahood and so spontaneously engage in the transcendences for the benefit of sentient beings. Thus, there ensues the threefold mastery of body, activity, and teaching. The first comprises the mastery of the body of qualities and the body of perfect enjoyment, while the second is the mastery of the emanation body, and the third the mastery of the speech that teaches the Dharma.

6. Analysis

An inconceivable number of internal divisions pertain to the transcendences, but here each of them will be analyzed concisely in terms of six components. For each transcendence there are two stanzas that explain these six components.

> Giving things
> Based on the intent associated with the fundamentals
> Brings about an excellent body and enjoyments,
> Providing for both, as well as completion; [XVII.17]

A possession of those who are not stingy,
It is the granting of Dharma, material things, and freedom
   from fears.
Fully comprehending such generosity,
The wise practice it authentically. [XVII.18]

With six aspects and the embrace of the intent on peace,
It brings happy states and the attainment of stability.
Support, peace, and absence of fear—
It is the possession of the accumulation of merit, [XVII.19]

Attained through the use of symbols and by the intrinsic
   nature,
And thus present in those who possess the vows—
Fully comprehending such discipline,
The wise practice it authentically. [XVII.20]

Tolerance, disregard, and knowledge—
It is caused by compassion and reliance on the Dharma.
Explained in terms of five benefits,
It accomplishes the objectives of both. [XVII.21]

Always in possession of the foremost austerity,
It is asserted to be of three types.
Fully comprehending such patience,
The wise practice it authentically. [XVII.22]

Genuinely delighting in virtue
Is based on faith and aspiration.
It brings the development of the qualities of mindfulness and
   so forth,
Remedies thorough affliction, [XVII.23]

And is in possession of the qualities of nonattachment and so
   forth.
It is of seven types.

Fully comprehending such diligence,
The wise practice it authentically. [XVII.24]

It is mind resting within,
Based on mindfulness and diligence.
It creates delight,
And involves mastery of superknowledges and abodes. [XVII.25]

The foremost among all good qualities,
It is of three types.
Fully comprehending such concentration,
The wise practice it authentically. [XVII.26]

The authentic and thorough discernment of the objects of cognition,
It is based on meditative absorption
And is utterly free from affliction,
Providing sustenance through insight and excellent explanation. [XVII.27]

Supreme among all qualities.
It is of three types.
Fully comprehending such insight,
The wise practice it authentically. [XVII.28]

The explanations that follow are an analysis of the transcendences. The essence of generosity is **giving things** for the sake of the various recipients. As for its cause, generosity is **based on the intent** that is **associated with** nonattachment and **the** other **fundamentals.** In terms of result, generosity **brings about** an **excellent body and** excellent **enjoyments. Providing for both** oneself and others, **as well as** bringing about the full **completion** of the accumulations for great enlightenment—these are the functions of generosity. As **a possession of those who are not stingy, it is,** in terms of its application, **the granting of Dharma, material things, and freedom** from fear. **Fully comprehending such generosity, the wise** children of the victorious ones **practice it authentically.**

The essence of discipline is explained **with** reference to **six aspects:** (1) intact discipline, (2) the discipline of definitive emergence, (3) the discipline that dissolves even the slightest flaw, (4) the excellent ritual, (5) the excellent sphere of activity, and (6) the authentic engagement with the bases of training. **And,** moreover, the cause of discipline is **the embrace of the intent on** attaining peace. As its result, **it brings** the achievement of **happy states and the attainment of** mental **stability.** In terms of function, discipline serves as the **support** for all good qualities, delivers **peace** in the absence of the torments of the afflictions, **and** accomplishes an **absence of** the **fears** that otherwise ensue from taking the lives of others, and so forth. **It is the possession of the accumulation of merit** through an authentic engagement in the activities of body, speech, and mind. The application of discipline is divided in terms of the vows for individual liberation, which are **attained through the use of symbols, and** the vows of concentration and the undefiled vows, which are attained by **the intrinsic nature. And thus,** with respect to the support for the application of discipline, it is **present in those who possess the vows** just mentioned. **Fully comprehending such discipline, the wise** children of the victorious ones **practice it authentically.**

The essence of patience is **tolerance** in the face of those inflicting harm, **disregard** for suffering, **and** the patience that takes the form of ascertainment of the Dharma through **knowledge** of the nature of reality. **It,** meaning patience, **is caused by compassion and** brought to perfection through **reliance on** discipline and listening to **the Dharma.** The result of patience is **explained in terms of five benefits:** (1) little resentment, (2) little divisiveness, (3) much pleasure and happiness, (4) death without regrets, and (5) birth into the happy states of the higher realms of the world. In terms of function, **it,** that is, patience in its three forms, **accomplishes the objectives of both** self and others. Patience is **always in possession of the foremost** and supreme **austerity.** In terms of its application, **it is asserted to be** the case that those who have patience are in possession of three types of it. Fully comprehending such patience, the wise practice it authentically.

Genuinely delighting in virtue is the essence of diligence. In terms of cause, diligence is based on confident faith and enthusiastic aspiration. In terms of result, it brings the development of the qualities of mindfulness, meditative absorption, and so forth, while, with regard to function, it remedies thorough affliction. And, regarding its possession, diligence is in possession of the qualities of nonattachment, absence of anger, and so forth. As for its application and in terms of those who possess it, it is of seven types because there is a quality of diligence associated with each of the five consciousnesses that emerge within the training in discipline, and there is a quality of diligence associated with each of the mental consciousnesses that emerge in the context of, respectively, the training in attention and the training in insight. Fully comprehending such diligence, the wise children of the victorious ones practice it authentically.

As for the essence of concentration, it is the mind resting one-pointedly within. As for its cause, it is based on the mindfulness that ensures that the focus is not forgotten and on the diligence that takes delight in concentration. Regarding the result, it creates meditative delight, and its function is explained by showing that it involves mastery of superknowledges and of the abodes of the noble ones, the gods, and the sublime. The possession of concentration is the foremost among all good qualities, and so it is also taught that "meditative absorption is the foremost among all good qualities." Regarding application, the concentration that is present within those who possess it is asserted to be of three types: concentration that involves conception and discernment, concentration within which there is no conception but merely discernment, and concentration within which there is neither conception nor discernment. Fully comprehending such concentration, the wise children of the victorious ones practice it authentically. The authentic and thorough discernment of the objects of cognition, such as the five fields of knowledge, is the essence of insight. As for its cause, it is based on the mind's abiding one-pointedly in **meditative absorption, and**, in terms of result, it **is utterly free from affliction. Providing sustenance through insight and excellent explanation** of the Dharma is the function of insight. Regarding its possession, insight is **the supreme among all qualities**. As for its application, the insight that is present within those who possess **it is** asserted to be **of three types:** mundane insight, inferior supramundane insight, and supreme supramundane insight. **Fully comprehending such insight, the wise** children of the victorious ones **practice it authentically.**

As for the analysis of generosity, the nature or essence of generosity is the giving of things, both external and internal, to the field of qualities, the field of benefit, and the field of suffering. Its cause, or basis, is attention—in the form of the three fundamental virtues of nonattachment and the rest. Its result is the attainment of an excellent body and enjoyments. Its function is to benefit others and to bring about the attainment of great enjoyments for oneself in another birth. It thereby provides for both oneself and others. Material offerings and the gift of Dharma perfect the accumulations of merit and wakefulness. As for its possession, generosity is inextricably in possession of the absence of stinginess. It is divided into three: giving the Dharma, which consists of explaining the words and meanings of the scriptural teachings without error; material generosity, which is the giving of internal and external things; and granting protection from fear, which is to guard others from the fears of kings, thieves, fires, floods, and so forth. Bodhisattvas, fully comprehending such generosity in terms of its essence, cause, and so forth, practice it authentically.

The essence of discipline has six aspects: (1) abiding by discipline, (2) the excellent ritual, (3) the excellent sphere of activity, (4) restraint through adhering to the vows of individual liberation, (5) regard for even the smallest misdeed with trepidation, and (6) authentic engagement with the bases for training. The first of these refers to the genuine upholding of discipline. The second involves maintaining the Dharma robes and so forth according to scripture, ensuring that one does not become an object of scorn from the perspective of sacred beings. The third is to give up the five inappropriate spheres of activity (prostitution, butchering, selling alcohol, and so forth). The fourth relates to the discipline of definitive emergence. The fifth is to remain unblemished by even minor infractions. Finally, the sixth is to engage with the complete set of bases for training.

The cause of discipline is when one is seized by the wish for full emergence and peace. Its result is the attainment of the higher realms and freedom from regrets. As one in this way becomes happy in this life, it also facilitates the accomplishment of the mind's resting in meditative absorption. Its function is to serve as the foundation for all virtuous qualities, just as the great earth is the foundation for all harvests. It also pacifies the torments of the afflictions, does away with the fear of evil, blood revenge, and so forth, in this life, and dispels the fears of the three lower realms in other lives. As for its possession, it consists of the accumulation of merit that ensues from one's three gates being in a virtuous state. In terms of its applications, or types, there is the discipline that is acquired through symbols. This is the vow of individual liberation, received from the preceptor and ritual master through the procedure of supplication and request. Further, there is the discipline that is acquired through the intrinsic nature, which comprises the vows of concentration and the undefiled vows. Such discipline is supported by individuals who adhere to the vows, and it is not found elsewhere. Fully comprehending such discipline, the wise practice it authentically.

The essence of patience is to remain tolerant when one is harmed by sentient beings. It involves forbearance in the sense of completely disregarding suffering and being able to accept the profound Dharma's meaning without fear. Its causes are, respectively, compassion for sentient beings, whereby one is able to tolerate harm without being disturbed, adhering to the discipline, and the study of the Dharma. In terms of result, patience is explained to have five benefits: (1) one is free from grudges because one does not engage in fights, (2) there is little disharmony because one has many friends, (3) one is happy in body and mind in this life, (4) one experiences joy at the time of death, and (5) one proceeds to a happy destination after death.

Patience enables one to remain happy while not aggravating others; thus, benefiting oneself and others is the function of patience. Patience is in possession of the foremost among all the good qualities associated with the practice of austerities. Patience is held to be of three types, which have already been stated in the context of its essence. Fully comprehending such patience, the wise practice it authentically.

The essence of diligence is a genuine delight in virtuous qualities. In terms of its cause, diligence is based on devoted inspiration and faith in virtuous qualities and on the aspiration to accomplish them. Its result is the continuous development of all good qualities, such as mindfulness. Its function is to provide remedies for the thorough afflictions, and its possession is an endowment of all pure qualities of nonattachment and so forth.

Diligence is taught as being sevenfold. In terms of its object, there are three forms of diligence (1–3) that relate to the three trainings. In terms of its essence, there are two further divisions, namely, (4) the diligence of body and (5) the diligence of mind. With regard to its application, there are, finally, (6) devoted application and (7) constant application. An alternative categorization into seven types of diligence is also taught. The latter is enumerated by counting the five instances of the mental state of diligence that arise in the company of the five senses. These pertain to the training in special discipline and are associated with the body. In addition to these five, there are two that accompany the mental consciousness and pertain to the trainings in, respectively, special attention and special insight. Fully comprehending such diligence, the wise practice it authentically.

The essence of concentration is to rest one-pointedly within, undistracted by outer objects. In terms of its cause, concentration is based on the mindfulness of not forgetting the focal point and on the diligence of continual meditation. Its results are the bliss of agility in body and mind, as well as the production of that bliss associated with birth in the higher realm of form, beyond the sufferings of the desire realm. Its function is mastery over the superknowledges, such as that of miraculous display, as well as mastery over the abodes of the gods, the sublime, and the noble ones. The abodes of the gods are the four concentrations and the four formless absorptions. The sublime abodes are the four immeasurables. The abodes of the noble ones are the three gates of liberation and so forth. As for its possession, concentration is endowed with the foremost among virtuous qualities because gaining control of the mind allows for the accomplishment of special qualities. Further, it serves as the support for liberation and liberated wakefulness. As for its applications, concentration is the possession of those who cultivate it, not of others. Those in possession of concentration can be divided into three groups in relation to the character of the remedy they apply. As explained above, for some the remedy involves both conception and discernment, for others discernment but not conception, and for yet others there is neither conception nor discernment. Divided in terms of its qualities, concentration involves joy up through the second concentration, bliss on the third, and equanimity from the fourth and beyond. Fully comprehending such concentration, the wise practice it authentically.

The essence of insight is the authentic and thorough discernment, without error, of all objects of knowledge, as they are and however many there are. In terms of cause, the insight that sees the meaning of the truths is based on meditative absorption. Its result is freedom from thorough affliction. Mundane insight temporarily alleviates afflictions. The supramundane insight of the listeners and self-realized buddhas eliminates latent afflictive obscurations. The insight of the Great Vehicle realizes the twofold absence of self and also eliminates the latent tendencies of both afflictive and cognitive obscurations. As for its function, it is insight that, on a temporary level, sustains life by providing the knowledge of worldly means of sustenance, such as business and agriculture. More important, insight provides the sustenance of the vast and profound Dharma, keeping the fundamental virtues alive so that, in the end, one attains the everlasting state of great enlightenment. Thus, by the true sustenance of insight and through excellent explanations to others, one achieves the sustenance of virtue.

As for its possession, insight is endowed with all the qualities of transcendent insight, the supreme vessel of all Dharma. As stated in the Mother:[44] "Transcendent insight is sacred among the transcendences; it is the primary one, the special one." Regarding its foundational applications, insight is the endowment of the person who possesses it, not of any others. As for the types of insight, here these are made with respect to the principal form of insight. Thus, there is the mundane insight that is present up through the supreme quality, the lesser supramundane insight of the listeners and self-realized buddhas, and the great supramundane insight of the bodhisattvas. Fully comprehending such insight, the wise practice authentically.

7. SUMMARY

All of the positive qualities should be known
To be distracted, composed, or both.
They are thoroughly contained
In three pairs of transcendences. [XVII.29]

The explanation of the summary follows next. **All of the positive qualities** associated with generosity and so forth **should be known to be distracted, composed, or both** distracted and composed. As such, **they are thoroughly contained in three pairs of transcendences,** namely, the first two, the final two, and the middle two.

All the good qualities of the grounds, the transcendences, the factors of enlightenment, the gathering of virtues, and so forth, are comprised within the six transcendences. In short, all virtuous qualities can be subsumed within the following three aspects of virtue: virtue that belongs to the context of being distracted and not composed; virtue within the context of equipoise; and virtue, such as patience or diligence, that may or may not be associated with equipoise. From among these three, the virtuous, positive qualities that do not belong to the context of equipoise include the first two transcendences, generosity and discipline. Generosity is performed by means of the body and is not of the essence of composure. Discipline includes the vows of individual liberation, concentration, and the undefiled vows. The seven vows of individual liberation consist of abandonment by means of body and speech. They are not of composure because they are not of a mental nature. Concentration and insight contain virtuous qualities of composure. Concentration is the very nature of composed equipoise. This includes also the vows of concentration and the undefiled vows. As for insight, the insight of study and reflection is included within what is not composed, while the insight of meditation is included within what is composed because it constitutes special insight.

Patience and diligence are included in the category of that which is not composed, when they are employed in the context of generosity and discipline. Conversely, when they are involved in cultivating calm abiding and special insight, patience and diligence do belong to the category of the composed.

8. Separation from Conflicting Factors

Concerning the separation from conflicting factors, each of the six transcendences will be addressed in one stanza in the following passage:

> The generosity of the bodhisattvas
> Is unattached, free from attachment, knows no attachment.
> Nor is it in any way attached,
> For it is unattached, free from attachment, and knows no attachment. [XVII.30]

> The discipline of the bodhisattvas
> Is unattached, free from attachment, and knows no attachment.
> Nor is it in any way attached,
> For it is unattached, free from attachment, knows no attachment. [XVII.31]

> The patience of the bodhisattvas
> Is unattached, free from attachment, and knows no attachment.
> Nor is it in any way attached,
> For it is unattached, free from attachment, knows no attachment. [XVII.32]

The diligence of the bodhisattvas
Is unattached, free from attachment, and knows no
  attachment.
Nor is it in any way attached,
For it is unattached, free from attachment, knows no
  attachment. [XVII.33]

The concentration of the bodhisattvas
Is unattached, free from attachment, and knows no
  attachment.
Nor is it in any way attached
For it is unattached, free from attachment, knows no
  attachment. [XVII.34]

The insight of the bodhisattvas
Is unattached, free from attachment, and knows no
  attachment.
Nor is it in any way attached,
For it is unattached, free from attachment, knows no
  attachment. [XVII.35]

Now follows the explanation of the separation from conflicting factors. The generosity of the bodhisattvas is unattached to possessions, free from the attachment of procrastination, and it knows no attachment in the form of contentment. Nor is it in any way attached to a reward, for it is unattached to ripening, free from attachment in the form of latent conflicting factors, and it knows no attachment to distractions.

The discipline of the bodhisattvas is unattached to faulty discipline, free from the attachment of procrastination, and it knows no attachment in the form of contentment. Nor is it in any way attached to a reward, for it is unattached to ripening, free from attachment in the form of latencies, and it knows no attachment to distractions.

The patience of the bodhisattvas is unattached to anger, free from the attachment of procrastination, and it knows no attachment in the form of contentment. **Nor is it in any way attached** to a reward, **for it is unattached** to ripening, **free from attachment** in the form of latencies, and it **knows no attachment** to distractions.

The diligence of the bodhisattvas is unattached to laziness, **free from** the **attachment** of procrastination, **and** it **knows no attachment** in the form of contentment. **Nor is it in any way attached** to a reward, **for it is unattached** to ripening, **free from attachment** in the form of latencies, and it **knows no attachment** to distractions.

The concentration of the bodhisattvas is unattached to distractions regarding the objects, **free from** the **attachment** of procrastination, **and** it **knows no attachment** in the form of contentment. **Nor is it in any way attached** to a reward, **for it is unattached** to ripening, **free from attachment** in the form of latencies, and it **knows no attachment** to distractions.

The insight of the bodhisattvas is unattached to misguided intelligence, **free from** the **attachment** of procrastination, **and** it **knows no attachment** in the form of contentment. **Nor is it in any way attached** to a reward, **for it is unattached** to ripening, **free from attachment** in the form of latencies, and it **knows no attachment** to distractions. Distraction is of two kinds, for there is distraction in terms of the way the mind is directed (this refers to fondness for other vehicles), as well as conceptual distraction (which implies thinking within the three spheres).

The bodhisattva's generosity is free from seven conflicting factors. What are these? Not being able to give because of attachment to the objects one possesses is a conflicting factor. Having given up this attachment, bodhisattvas are unattached to possessions. When someone comes to ask them for something, they do not delay and procrastinate. Instead, they give right away. Thus they are free from attachment in the form of procrastination. Without partiality in the form of thoughts such as "I shall just give such and such," or "I shall just give to so and so," or "I shall give for such and such a period only," they know no attachment in the form of contentment. Their generosity has no bounds in terms of things, places, times, and sentient beings.

Bodhisattvas are not attached in any way to a reward for their generosity; they are unattached in the sense that they have no desire for the ripening that takes the form of great enjoyments in the future. They are also free from attachment in the form of the latent tendencies of miserliness and attachment, the factors that conflict with generosity. They give while being completely free from the polluting influence of miserliness. They know no attachment to the distractions that are related to the way the mind is directed and that are associated with thought. The reason is that they have given up the mental activity of dedicating their generosity and so on to the attainment of the enlightenment of the listeners and self-realized buddhas, and they have abandoned the thoughts that observe the three spheres.

Likewise, the bodhisattva's discipline is unattached to faulty discipline. It is free from the attachment that is procrastination, and it knows no attachment in the form of contentment with whatsoever is limited. It is in no way attached to a reward for being disciplined, nor does it involve harming others and so forth. It is unattached to defiled ripening, free from attachment in the form of afflictive latencies, and knows no attachment to thoughts that direct the mind to inferior paths or that perceive a reality of the three spheres.

The bodhisattva's patience does not contain attachment in the form of anger that upsets the mind stream and leads to acts that harm others. It is free from the attachment of procrastination without being able immediately to tolerate harm. It knows no attachment to a mere limited patience. It does not in any way anticipate help from others in reward for having been patient with them, nor does it become attached to ripening, as when one thinks, "If I cultivate patience, in the future I will have an excellent physical appearance and a large retinue." It is free from attachment in the form of the latent tendencies of anger, which is its conflicting factor. It knows no attachment to the distractions associated with directing mind and thought.

The bodhisattva's diligence is unattached to manifest laziness. It is free from the attachment that involves procrastination without swiftly engaging in the pursuit of virtue. It knows no attachment to limited diligence. It is in no way attached to a personal reward for being diligent in benefiting others. It is unattached to ripening that may take the form of successful future projects. It is free from attachment to the latencies of laziness, its conflicting factor. It knows no attachment in the form of directing the mind to inferior paths or thoughts of the three spheres.

The bodhisattva's concentration is unattached to manifest distraction. It is free from the attachment that makes one procrastinate, as when one thinks, "When should I meditate?" It knows no attachment to contentment with limited concentration. It is in no way attached to a personal reward for being concentrated for the sake of benefiting others. It is unattached to ripening, such as freedom from illnesses or birth in the higher realms, and is free from attachment to the latent tendencies of distraction, its conflicting factor. It knows no attachment to the distractions of directing the mind to inferior paths or the thoughts of the three spheres.

The bodhisattva's insight is unattached to manifest misguided intelligence, as with the views of permanence and annihilation. It is free from attachment to procrastinating when it comes to such things as serving or attending a spiritual friend, or engaging in study and contemplation. It knows no attachment to minor insight. It is in no way attached to a reward for oneself when teaching the Dharma to others. It is unattached to ripening and therefore does not harbor thoughts such as "If I develop insight now, I shall become learned in the future." It is free from attachment to the latent tendencies of misguided intelligence. It knows no attachment in the form of dedication to the inferior forms of transcendence of suffering and the distractions of thoughts that believe in a reality of the three spheres.

9. Qualities

When meeting someone in need, the children of the buddhas
   will always give away even their own lives.
Out of compassion they do not hope for reward from others,
   nor do they aim at cherished results.
With their generosity they establish all beings in the three
   kinds of enlightenment,

And, as their generosity is embraced by wakefulness, it
    remains inexhaustibly in the world. [XVII.36]

The children of the buddhas always abide by the triple
    discipline, the nature of guarding and persevering.
They feel no fondness for the higher realms, and when truly
    attaining them, do not become attached.
With their discipline they establish all beings in the three
    kinds of enlightenment,
And, as their discipline is embraced by wakefulness, it remains
    inexhaustibly in the world. [XVII.37]

The children of the buddhas tolerate what is extremely
    difficult to endure and likewise accept all the injuries of
    humanity,
Not for the sake of the higher realms, not because they are
    incapable, not out of fear, and not because they perceive a
    benefit.
With unexcelled patience they establish all beings in the three
    kinds of enlightenment,
And, as their patience is embraced by wakefulness, it remains
    inexhaustibly in the world. [XVII.38]

The children of the victorious ones display incomparable
    diligence, the nature of armor and application;
Overcoming their own and others' afflictions and
    accomplishing true enlightenment.
With their diligence they establish all beings in the three kinds
    of enlightenment,
And, as their diligence is embraced by wakefulness, it remains
    inexhaustibly in the world. [XVII.39]

Endowed with numerous meditative absorptions, the children
    of the victorious ones practice all forms of concentration.
Abiding by the highest bliss of meditation, they
    compassionately rely on inferior births.

With their concentration they establish all beings in the three
kinds of enlightenment,
And, as their concentration is embraced by wakefulness, it
remains inexhaustibly in the world. [XVII.40]

The children of the victorious ones know reality and the
entirety of the objects of knowledge.
As their minds do not become attached to the transcendence
of suffering at all, what need is there to mention cyclic
existence?
With their wakefulness they establish all beings in the three
kinds of enlightenment,
And, as their wakefulness embraces sentient beings, it remains
inexhaustibly in the world. [XVII.41]

Vastness, freedom from materialism,
Great purpose, and inexhaustibility—
These should be known as four qualities
Present throughout generosity and so forth. [XVII.42]

Next follows the explanation of the qualities of the transcendences. First, regarding the vastness of generosity, it is explained that, when meeting someone in need, the children of the buddhas, the bodhisattvas, will always give away even their own lives. Next, on the way this generosity is free from materialism: out of compassion they do not hope for any reward from others in this life, nor do they aim at cherished results in terms of enjoyments in future lives. Regarding its great purpose: with their generosity they establish all beings in the three kinds of enlightenment in accordance with the individual capacities of beings. And in terms of its inexhaustibility: as their generosity is embraced by non-conceptual wakefulness, it remains inexhaustibly in the world until the attainment of buddhahood.

Concerning the vastness of discipline, it is taught that the children of the buddhas always abide by the triple discipline, which is of the nature of (1) guarding against conflicting factors and

(2) **persevering** in the accumulation of virtue, and (3) **benefiting sentient beings.** In terms of the way this discipline is free from materialism: **they feel no fondness for the higher realms, and when truly attaining them, they do not become attached.** In terms of its great purpose, **with their discipline they establish all beings in the three kinds of enlightenment** in accordance with the individual capacities of these beings. **And,** regarding its inexhaustibility, **as their discipline is embraced by** nonconceptual **wakefulness, it remains inexhaustibly in the world** until the attainment of buddhahood.

On the vastness of patience, it is explained that **the children of the buddhas tolerate what is extremely difficult to endure** with the patience of complete disregard for suffering, **and they likewise accept all the injuries of humanity** with the patience of endurance. In terms of the way in which their patience is free from materialism, they are patient, **not for the sake of the** resultant **higher realms, not because they are incapable** of striking back at those who cause harm, **not out of fear, and not because they perceive a benefit** in the form of a reward. Regarding its great purpose, **with unexcelled patience they establish all beings in the three kinds of enlightenment, and** in terms of its inexhaustibility, **as their patience is embraced by** nonconceptual **wakefulness, it remains inexhaustibly in the world** until the attainment of buddhahood.

Concerning the vastness of diligence, it is taught that **the children of the victorious ones display** an **incomparable diligence,** which is of **the nature of armor and application.** In terms of the way their patience is free from materialism, they display this diligence for the sake of **overcoming their own and others' afflictions and accomplishing true enlightenment.** Regarding its great purpose, it is taught that **with their diligence they establish all beings in the three kinds of enlightenment** in accordance with their individual capacities. **And,** on its inexhaustibility, it is taught that, **as their diligence is embraced by** nonconceptual **wakefulness, it remains inexhaustibly in the world** until the attainment of buddhahood.

On the vastness of concentration, it is explained that, **endowed with** infinitely **numerous meditative absorptions, the children of the victorious ones practice all forms of concentration**. In terms of its being free from materialism, **abiding by the highest bliss of meditation, they compassionately rely on inferior births** and so take birth in the desire realm in order to benefit beings. Concerning its great purpose, **with their concentration they establish all beings in the three kinds of enlightenment** in accordance with the individual capacities of beings. And, regarding its inexhaustibility, **as their concentration is embraced by** nonconceptual **wakefulness, it remains inexhaustibly in the world** until the attainment of buddhahood.

On the vastness of insight, it is explained that **the children of the victorious ones know reality and the entirety of objects of knowledge**. In terms of its being free from materialism, **as their minds do not become attached to the transcendence of suffering at all, what need is there to mention cyclic existence?** In terms of its great purpose, **with their wakefulness they establish all beings in the three kinds of enlightenment** in accordance with their individual capacities. And concerning its inexhaustibility, **as their** compassionate **wakefulness embraces sentient beings, it remains inexhaustibly in the world** until the attainment of buddhahood.

In summarizing these stanzas it is said: **vastness, freedom from materialism, great purpose, and inexhaustibility—these should** therefore **be known as four qualities** that are **present throughout generosity and so forth.**

Each of the transcendences is taught in terms of possessing four qualities: vastness, freedom from materialism, great purpose, and inexhaustibility. When the children of the victorious ones, the bodhisattvas, meet someone in need, they are even able to sacrifice their lives, so there is no need to mention that they will give away other things. Their generosity is not just occasional, either, but a constant giving that takes place until the end of cyclic existence. Such is its quality of vastness.

Since their generosity is solely motivated by compassion, wishing to benefit others, they have no concern for a personal reward. Neither do they seek some pleasant ripening in the future as the result of their generosity. Thus it is free from materialism. Attracting them with generosity, they establish all beings in whichever of the three enlightenments they are individually inclined to pursue. This shows the great purpose of their generosity. Finally, since their generosity is embraced by wakefulness that does not conceive of the three spheres, it is unlike the generosity of mundane beings, which is exhausted once it has ripened its result in cyclic existence. This generosity is not even exhausted in the attainment of the transcendence of suffering, as would be the case with a listener or a self-realized buddha. Subsequent to their attainment of the great transcendence of suffering that is neither confined to cyclic existence nor to transcendence, their generosity remains inexhaustibly in the world for as long as the world exists; such is its quality of inexhaustibility.

The children of the victorious ones always, until the attainment of great enlightenment, abide by the complete threefold discipline, which is of the nature of restraint from negative actions, gathering virtuous qualities, and striving to benefit others. This is its quality of vastness, which is lacking in the listeners and so on. While they have no desire for the results of discipline, the bodhisattvas do attain the higher realms, but without becoming attached to the happiness there. Such is its quality of being free from materialism. Their discipline's quality of the great purpose is that it establishes all beings in the three enlightenments. As their discipline is embraced by nonconceptual wakefulness, it remains as an inexhaustible treasure in the world; this is its quality of inexhaustibility.

The children of the victorious ones pursue both the ripening of sentient beings and their own perfection of the qualities of buddhahood. To achieve that, they do what is extremely difficult to do, for they intentionally take birth in cyclic existence for an extremely long time, endure all injuries of humanity, and disregard the pains of heat, cold, hunger, thirst, and so on. In this way, their patience is vast. Moreover, bodhisattvas do not cultivate patience for the sake of happiness in the higher realms, nor are they patient because of being unable to retaliate. Indeed, they possess the power of superknowledge. They are not patient out of fear either since they are free from the five fears, nor are they patient because they see that to be of some benefit to themselves. Thus, their patience is free from materialism. Unexcelled patience establishes all beings in the three enlightenments, which is its great purpose. As their patience is embraced by wakefulness, it remains inexhaustibly in the world, which is its quality of inexhaustibility.

The diligence of the children of the victorious ones has the nature of an armor-like intent and an application that follows through with this intent in practice. Since it is not mixed with affliction, it is superior to mundane diligence. Since it realizes the twofold absence of self and accomplishes the twofold benefit of self and other, it is superior to the diligence of the listeners and self-realized buddhas. It is an incomparable effort because this diligence is hard to fathom in terms of time and space. Such is its quality of vastness. As it breaks down one's own accumulated afflictions as well as those of others, and as it brings forth the attainment of true enlightenment, it is free from materialism. Since it establishes all beings in the three enlightenments, it is of great purpose. As the bodhisattva's diligence is embraced by wakefulness, it remains inexhaustibly in the world, which is its quality of inexhaustibility.

The children of the victorious ones possess many forms of meditative absorption, such as the heroic gait, and they practice, for example, the fourth concentration, as well as the freedoms, totalities, and commands. Hence their meditative absorption is vast. They abide in the perfect bliss of concentration, yet without savoring it, and out of compassion they take up inferior births in the desire realm. Such is the freedom from materialism. Moreover, as their concentration establishes all beings in the three enlightenments, it is of great purpose. And, as their concentration is embraced by wakefulness, it remains inexhaustibly in the world, which is its quality of inexhaustibility.

The bodhisattvas completely know reality as it is, as well as the entirety of objects of knowledge, as many as there are. Thus their insight is vast. If they do not even become attached to the transcendence of suffering, then there is no need to mention that they do not develop attachment to cyclic existence either. Instead, they have realized all appearances of cyclic existence and the transcendence of suffering to be like an illusion in terms of the relative and as equality in terms of the ultimate. In this way, their insight is free from materialism. This very wakefulness establishes all beings in the three enlightenments, which is its quality of great purpose. Since this wakefulness does not abide in the extremes of existence or peace, it is essentially inseparable from great compassion. Thus embracing sentient beings, it remains in the world without ever becoming exhausted. As it is never interrupted and always pervasive, it possesses the quality of inexhaustibility. In this way, transcendences such as generosity should all be known to possess four qualities: vastness, freedom from materialism, great purpose, and inexhaustibility.

Furthermore, it will now be explained how the qualities of the six transcendences are pure. This will include (1) an explanation of the way they are superior, (2) an explanation of the way they are supreme, (3) an illustration of their pure qualities through a praise to generosity, and (4) a specific explanation of the qualities of diligence.

1. The Way They Are Superior

The perfect joy of those in need, upon sight,
Their displeasure, and their prayer,
Are by the loving benefactors
Always surpassed with their special possession. [XVII.43]

The loving ones are always more than happy
To offer sentient beings
Their own lives, possessions, and spouses.
What need is there then to speak of their observing restraint?
    [XVII.44]

The noble ones have no concerns and are of balanced mind.
Fearless and loving, they give away everything.
How could they ever speak to others
With hurtful and inappropriate words? [XVII.45]

The loving ones wish to benefit equally.
They are horrified by the suffering of others.
As they exert their minds so as to influence sentient beings,
They are extremely far from the three flaws of speech.
    [XVII.46]

Universally generous, compassionate,
And skilled regarding the phenomena of dependent
    origination,
How could they possibly adhere
To any of the mind's afflictions? [XVII.47]

Whenever the loving ones are hurt
Or suffer for the benefit of others,
They think of it as helpful and find joy.
For them, what is there to be patient about? [XVII.48]

Without regarding others as others,
They always love others much more than themselves.
Undertaking hardship and abiding by love—
Such diligence is not difficult, but extremely difficult.
    [XVII.49]

In three cases concentration is held
To yield little happiness and personal happiness, to be
    attached,
To be subject to deterioration and exhaustion, and to involve
    delusion.
For the bodhisattvas, the case is the opposite. [XVII.50]

Like groping in the night and a lamp under cover,
Such are the three cognitions.
The compassionate ones' knowledge is unequalled,
Like the rays of the sun. [XVII.51]

The following teaching concerns the purity of the qualities of the six transcendences. The **perfect delight of those in need,** upon having taken **sight** of a benefactor and being given all that they wish for to their hearts' content, **their displeasure** when failing to encounter such a benefactor and remaining dissatisfied, **and their prayer** to be able to meet such a benefactor and have all their wishes fulfilled—all these **are by the loving benefactors always surpassed with their special possession** of joy upon seeing a recipient and so forth.

The loving ones, the children of the Victorious One, **are always more than happy to offer sentient beings their own lives, possessions, and spouses**. What need is there then to speak of their **observing restraint** and abiding by the threefold discipline of the body: giving up taking the lives of others, stealing, and the sexual misconduct of engaging with someone else's spouse?

Lies may be told for one's own sake because one is concerned about one's own body and life, or for the sake of others, for loved ones for whom one feels affection. The reason may also be fear—fear of a monarch, for example. Finally, lies may be spoken for the sake of wealth and material things. **The noble ones, however, have no concerns** for their own body and life **and are of** a **balanced mind** with regard to all sentient beings. It is taught:

Neither in terms of losing one's livelihood, nor due to death,
    defamation, the lower realms, or an audience,
Do they ever feel any fear—they are undaunted.

Thus, free of the five fears, they are **fearless and loving, and so they give away everything** that they possess. **How, then, could they ever speak to others with hurtful and inappropriate words?**

The loving ones **wish to benefit** all sentient beings equally—how could they possibly create divisions among friends? Affectionately, **they** wish to dispel the suffering of others to the extent that they **are horrified by the suffering of others**. How could they possibly speak harsh words that give others pain? As **they** thoroughly **exert their minds so as to influence sentient beings**, how could they engage in idle talk? **They are**, therefore, **extremely far from the three flaws of speech**.

Intent on giving away all possessions, they are **universally generous**; wishing to free others from suffering, they are **compassionate**. And, they are also **skilled regarding the** causal and resultant phenomena of dependent origination. How could they possibly adhere to any of the mind's three afflictions?

Whenever the loving ones, the children of the victorious ones, have to endure harm and suffering, whenever they **are hurt or** have to **suffer for the benefit of others, they think of it as** a harm that is **helpful** because it serves as the cause for the perfection of patience, **and** in their suffering they find a rare **joy. For them, what** challenging hardship **is there to be patient about** with respect to harm and suffering?

Without regarding others as others, they always love others much more than themselves. Undertaking hardship for the sake of others **and abiding by love**—such **diligence** of the bodhisattvas **is not difficult, but extremely difficult.**

Concentration differs in the case of mundane beings, listeners, self-realized buddhas, and bodhisattvas. Thus, **in** the context of the first **three cases, the concentration** of mundane beings **is held to yield little happiness** because it involves defilement, **and** the listeners and self-realized buddhas practice meditation for their own **personal happiness.** In these three cases, concentration is also held **to be attached** because mundane beings are attached to the transient collection, whereas listeners and self-realized buddhas are attached to the transcendence of suffering. Concentration is also seen **to be subject to deterioration** in the case of mundane beings **and** to **exhaustion** in the other two cases. **And,** in all three cases, concentration is held **to involve delusion,** which is afflictive in the first case and nonafflictive in the latter two. **For the bodhisattvas,** concentration yields abundant happiness, and happiness for both themselves and others. It does not involve attachment; it neither deteriorates nor is exhausted, and it does not involve delusion. Hence, here **the case is the opposite** of what was mentioned above.

As for the differences between the three forms of insight, the insight of ordinary individuals is **like groping in the** darkness of **night**—its object is small, not perceptible, and not clear. **And,** in the case of the listeners and self-realized buddhas, cognition is like a **lamp** that has been placed **under** a **cover**—its object is partially perceptible, but not very clear. **Such are the three cognitions** of ordinary beings, listeners, and self-realized buddhas. **The compassionate ones' knowledge is unequalled, like the rays of the sun,** for here all objects are perceptible, and it is utterly free of stain.

This section begins with a praise of generosity. When people in need see a benefactor, they are happy, just as they are happy when their wishes are fulfilled and they are given what they want. Yet, they are not happy when they do not meet any benefactors and their wishes therefore remain unfulfilled. Hence, they will always pray to encounter benefactors and be given what they wish for. Loving bodhisattva benefactors are happy when they see beings in need and are able to give to them, but they are not happy when this is not the case. They, therefore, pray to find beings in need and to be able to provide them with what they wish for. In all these ways, the bodhisattva always surpasses the needy. That is, the bodhisattva is much more happy when seeing someone in need than someone in need is when seeing a benefactor, and a bodhisattva's joy in being able to give is far greater than the joy of someone in need when having his or her wishes fulfilled and so forth. Therefore, the bodhisattva's generosity is of superior purity.

The quality of pure discipline is explained next. With loving hearts, bodhisattvas will always relinquish their lives, enjoyments, and spouses to sentient beings without the slightest unhappiness and with great joy. Thus, why should they not be able to refrain from selfishly taking lives, stealing, and engaging in sexual misconduct? Thus, they possess pure discipline free from the three nonvirtues of body.

The noble bodhisattvas have no concern for their bodies or their lives. They regard all sentient beings equally and are free from the five fears. Hence, they do not fear punishment from the arm of the law and so on. With loving concern for all embodied beings, they give away all their possessions, so how could they tell lies? How could they speak any untrue or false words meant to deceive and hurt others? Lies are spoken either to save one's life, or out of affection—to make one's family happy, for example—or they are told with an unbalanced mind—to harm one's enemies, for instance. One might also lie out of fear of a king or thieves, for example, or out of fear that one will otherwise lose one's spouse or wealth. Yet for the bodhisattvas there are no such causes for lying, and so they do not lie.

Likewise, wishing, with loving concern, to benefit all sentient beings equally, they are horrified when another person suffers, and they wish this would never happen. They strive one-pointedly to tame the afflictions of beings. They are, in this way, extremely far from the three forms of flawed speech. How, then, could they engage in divisive talk, which arises from not having the same concern for everyone, regardless of whether they are one's friends? How could they speak any harsh words, which are based on the wish to see others suffer? How could they engage in idle chatter, which feeds the afflictions?

The compassionate ones give all their possessions to others, and they are experts regarding the dependent arising of phenomena. How could they possibly adhere to mental afflictions such as covetousness, ill will, and wrong view, which are the products of attachment, anger, and bewilderment? For example, it is not reasonable for someone who gives away all his or her possessions to covet the possessions of someone else. And so on and so forth—the reasons are obvious.

Pure patience is addressed next. When loving bodhisattvas are harmed by others or suffer in order to benefit another, they think: "This is the method for perfecting patience, the cause of supreme enlightenment!" Without perceiving it as harm or suffering, they find joy in the situation, seeing it as supremely beneficial and delightful. For the bodhisattvas there is nothing difficult to bear in what is otherwise considered "unbearable," because they do not perceive it as unbearable. For a fish, similarly, there is nothing unbearable about swimming through water, and for the deer that bathes in fire there is likewise nothing challenging about staying in fire.[45]

Regarding the purity of their diligence, it is explained how the bodhisattvas do not perceive others as others because they realize the equality of self and other. Although they realize the facts of this equality, when they observe other beings who have not realized this, they nevertheless feel a constant love for those other beings that exceeds the love they have for themselves. They undertake unfathomable hardships for the welfare of sentient beings, and so possess great love. Because of that love, their tremendously diligent activity for the welfare of others is not difficult in the slightest. Yet, for all others—mundane beings, listeners, and self-realized buddhas—such a frame of mind that is able to exchange oneself with others and go through trials for the welfare of others is extremely difficult to achieve.

In terms of pure concentration, the concentrations that are accomplished by worldly beings, listeners, and self-realized buddhas yield little happiness compared with the bodhisattva's concentration. That of mundane beings is defiled happiness. Although the concentrations of the listeners and self-realized buddhas are undefiled, they satisfy only one's own stream of being; they do not satisfy others. Mundane beings take it that there is a self, and so they desire happiness in cyclic existence. The listeners and self-realized buddhas, on the other hand, desire the happiness of the transcendence of suffering for themselves alone. Worldly beings are attached to cyclic existence, whereas listeners and self-realized buddhas are attached to peace. The bliss of mundane concentration deteriorates, and the concentration of the listeners and self-realized buddhas is exhausted when nothing remains of the aggregates. Mundane beings do not eliminate either of the two obscurations, while listeners and self-realized buddhas fail to eliminate the cognitive obscurations. They are thus all held to be deluded.

The bodhisattvas' concentration is just the opposite of this. It has six distinctive qualities, for it is: (1) saturated with vast happiness, (2) employed for the benefit of others, (3) in possession of nonconceptual wakefulness that is not attached to existence or peace, (4) free from deterioration since it arises in all lifetimes, (5) not exhausted in a field without remainder of the aggregates, and (6) free from delusion since it eliminates both of the obscurations.

The qualities of pure insight are explained last. The mundane insight that arises when receiving teachings, contemplating, and meditating can be likened to searching for something on a dark night by groping for it with one's hand. In the context of mundane insight, one comes to an understanding of the features of reality, such as impermanence and suffering, merely through the use of inference, while there is no direct perception. The insight of listeners and self-realized buddhas, on the other hand, is like a lamp under a cover. If a lamp is put in a box or placed in a cave, it illuminates only that limited area. Likewise, the insight of listeners and self-realized buddhas merely dispels the afflictions because their realization of the absence of self involves only seeing that no person exists in relation to the five aggregates of their own stream of being. A third kind of cognition is that of the compassionate bodhisattvas. This is like sunlight, shining in all directions. It is unequalled because it completely realizes the twofold absence of self just as it is, while also being clearly aware of all phenomena of thorough affliction and complete purification, as many as there are. Thus, it eliminates the two obscurations and realizes the two truths.

2. THE WAY THEY ARE SUPREME

Generosity is held to be supreme
In terms of its support, substance,
Reason, dedication, cause,
Wakefulness, field, and states. [XVII.52]

Discipline is held to be supreme
In terms of its support, substance,
Reason, dedication, cause,
Wakefulness, field, and states. [XVII.53]

Patience is held to be supreme
In terms of its support, substance,
Reason, dedication, cause,
Wakefulness, field, and states. [XVII.54]

Diligence is held to be supreme
In terms of its support, substance,
Reason, dedication, cause,
Wakefulness, field, and states. [XVII.55]

Concentration is held to be supreme
In terms of its support, substance,
Reason, dedication, cause,
Wakefulness, field, and states. [XVII.56]

Insight is held to be supreme
In terms of its support, substance,
Reason, dedication, cause,
Wakefulness, field, and states. [XVII.57]

What follows is an explanation of the supreme qualities. **Generosity is held to be supreme in terms of its support,** which is the bodhisattva, and its **substance,** that which is given. It is supreme in terms of material gifts, as the life force is given; supreme in terms of the gift of fearlessness, as protection from the fears of the lower realms and cyclic existence is granted; and supreme in terms of the gift of the Dharma, because the teaching of the Great Vehicle is delivered. The **reason** for generosity, the compassionate motivation, is also supreme, and so is the **dedication** to the great enlightenment toward which generosity is directed. The same goes for the **cause** of generosity, which is affinity with transcendent generosity from the past, as well as the **wakefulness** that embraces generosity free from the three spheres, and the **field** of generosity. The field comprises: (1) those in need, (2) those suffering, (3) the exposed, (4) those lacking support, and (5) those in possession of excellent qualities. The first four are mentioned here in order of their increasing excellence. The fifth field is excellent in the absence of the other four. **And,** finally, generosity is also supreme in terms of its **states,** which are inspiration, directing the mind, and meditative absorption. "Inspiration" refers to inspiration with respect to the sūtras of the Great Vehicle. "Directing the mind" involves considering one's own generosity to be a virtue, rejoicing in the generosity of others, and being truly delighted by one's own generosity and that of others. Meditative absorption concerns the mastery of meditative absorptions, such as that of the treasury of space.

Discipline is held to be supreme in terms of its support, which is the bodhisattva, and its **substance,** the bodhisattva vow to be observed. The **reason** for discipline, the compassionate motivation, is also supreme, and so is the **dedication** to the great enlightenment toward which discipline is directed. The same goes for the **cause** of discipline, which is affinity with transcendent discipline from the past, as well as the **wakefulness** free from the three spheres, with which discipline is embraced, and the **field** upon which discipline relies, namely the Great Vehicle Dharma. **And**, finally, discipline is also supreme in terms of the **states** within which one trains in discipline.

Patience is held to be supreme in terms of its **support**, which is the bodhisattva, and its **substance**, being patient with the rude and the weak. The **reason** for patience, the compassionate motivation, is also supreme, and so is the **dedication** to the great enlightenment toward which patience is directed. The same goes for the **cause** of patience, which is affinity with transcendent patience from the past, as well as the **wakefulness** free from the three spheres, with which patience is embraced, and the **field** upon which patience relies, namely the Great Vehicle Dharma. **And**, finally, discipline is also supreme in terms of the **states** within which one trains in patience.

Diligence is held to be supreme in terms of its **support**, which is the bodhisattva, and its **substance**, the diligent practices of the transcendences and the relinquishment of their conflicting factors. The **reason** for diligence, the compassionate motivation, is also supreme, and so is the **dedication** to the great enlightenment toward which diligence is directed. The same goes for the **cause** of diligence, which is affinity with transcendent diligence from the past, as well as the **wakefulness** free from the three spheres, with which diligence is embraced, and the **field** upon which diligence relies, namely the Great Vehicle Dharma. **And**, finally, diligence is also supreme in terms of the **states** within which one trains in diligence.

Concentration is held to be supreme in terms of its **support**, which is the bodhisattva, and its **substance**, the meditative absorptions of the bodhisattvas. The **reason** for concentration, the compassionate motivation, is also supreme, and so is the **dedication** to the great enlightenment toward which concentration is directed. The same goes for the **cause** of concentration, which is affinity with transcendent concentration from the past, as well as the **wakefulness** free from the three spheres, with which concentration is embraced, and the **field** upon which concentration relies, namely, the Great Vehicle Dharma. **And,** finally, concentration is also supreme in terms of the **states** within which one trains in concentration.

Insight is held to be supreme in terms of its support, which is the bodhisattva, and the **substance** from which it arises, which is suchness. The **reason** for insight, the compassionate motivation, is also supreme, and so is the **dedication** to the great enlightenment toward which insight is directed. The same goes for the **cause** of insight, which is affinity with transcendent insight from the past, as well as the **wakefulness** free from the three spheres, with which insight is embraced, and the **field** upon which insight relies, namely, the Great Vehicle Dharma. **And,** finally, insight is also supreme in terms of the **states** within which one trains in insight.

The way the six transcendences are supreme can be understood in terms of eight supreme qualities. These are the supreme (1) support, (2) substance, (3) reason, (4) dedication, (5) cause, (6) wakefulness, (7) field, and (8) states. Because the transcendences possess these eight, they are endowed with the qualities of transcendence, authenticity, and supremacy.

As for generosity, the support is supreme because the benefactor is not like an ordinary being or a listener, but a bodhisattva. The substance or nature of the bodhisattva's generosity is also supreme when compared with that of the listener. The latter will give slight material gifts in the form of food, clothes, and so on; they will grant the Dharma gifts of the listener's scriptures; and they will offer protection from the harms that one may encounter in this life. The bodhisattvas' generosity, however, is limitless. This can be appreciated from the fact that they give away vast numbers of possessions and enjoyments that are otherwise extremely difficult to part with, relinquishing even their own heads and limbs, and offering the protection of the Great Vehicle, thus establishing beings in great enlightenment beyond the extremes of existence and peace.

The reason for their generosity is a motivation that is unlike the aspiring faith of the listeners. Mainly, their generosity comes from compassion upon seeing the suffering of sentient beings. Their dedication is supreme as well, for they do not dedicate their generosity to the achievement of the happiness of gods and humans, nor to accomplishing the enlightenment of listeners or self-realized buddhas. Instead, their generosity is dedicated to the attainment of complete and unsurpassable enlightenment of all beings. The cause of the bodhisattvas' generosity is found in the habitual tendencies that are present within the all-ground. From previous lifetimes, bodhisattvas thus have an affinity with generosity as embraced by the three fundamental virtues of nonattachment and so forth. This causes them to continue with such practices, wherever they are born in the present. These habitual tendencies can be compared to a seed, which serves as a perpetuating cause, while the bodhisattvas' reasons, or motivation, for compassion are comparable to the accompanying cooperative conditions of water, earth, and so on. Supreme wakefulness ensures that their practice of generosity is embraced by the nonconceptual wakefulness that does not observe any of the three spheres in relation to generosity.

As for the field of generosity, this includes: (1) the field of those in need, which concerns those who have a little wealth, but still ask for more, like Brahmins and merchants; (2) the field of those who suffer, such as the sick; (3) the field of the unprotected, those lacking food and clothing, for example; (4) the field of those who do wrong, such as those committing evil acts for the sake of property; and (5) the field of good qualities, which includes beings who are in possession of qualities such as discipline and insight. While the way of the world and the way of the listeners is primarily concerned with the field of good qualities, the compassion of the bodhisattvas makes them consider the field of those in pain as most important. They give in order to eliminate suffering, and especially to eliminate the causes of suffering. At the same time, they also give to those endowed with good qualities and the rest of the five fields in many different ways.

Within the field of those who suffer, the lowliest and those who are in the greatest pain will be the superior recipients of generosity. Thus, it is more beneficial to give to one poor person than to many rich people, and the more poor the recipient, the better the effect. Even better is giving to a starving spirit, and better yet is giving to a starving spirit whose throat is obstructed. In terms of the field of good qualities, it is best to give to the most exalted. Thus, compared with giving to innumerable ordinary beings, it is better to give to someone who is endowed with discipline.

When moving from listeners, to self-realized buddhas, to bodhisattvas, and finally to buddhas, the field likewise becomes increasingly exalted. Thus, the bodhisattvas who consider the welfare of others more important than their own will be especially generous to those who partake of the causes and effects of suffering, and in this way the field of their generosity is supreme.

In terms of the states, that is, the states within which giving is done, there are three: the state of inspiration, the state of directing the mind, and the state of meditative absorption. Here we may keep in mind what was explained before in the context of the investigation of the Dharma. Directing the mind with inspiration concerns directing the mind according to the Great Vehicle Dharma that teaches the transcendences. The state of directing the mind concerns savoring previous acts of generosity and so on, thinking, "Well done!" It also involves rejoicing in others' generosity and delighting in one's own future generosity and that of others. Meditative absorption concerns, for example, giving by means of the mastery of the treasury of space. It includes, as well, the mastery of bringing about the welfare of others, which occurs through the discovery of the three bodies at the stage of buddhahood. In this way, by means of the eight aspects of support and so forth, the bodhisattva's generosity is held to be supreme in comparison with both mundane generosity and the generosity of the listeners and self-realized buddhas.

From discipline to insight, the supreme qualities of the transcendences differ on two out of the eight points: the divisions of the bases and the respective fields. The latter refers to the particular aspect of the Great Vehicle Dharma that one observes and in which, consequently, one establishes others—rather than in the Dharma of the listeners. Apart from these two, the remaining six among the eight supreme qualities remain the same for all of the transcendences. Hence, discipline has as support the bodhisattvas who uphold it. Its substance, however, consists of the threefold nature of discipline: refraining from negative actions, gathering virtuous qualities, and working to benefit sentient beings. Its reason is compassion for sentient beings, and it is dedicated toward unsurpassable enlightenment. Its cause is affinity with discipline from previous lives, and it is embraced by nonconceptual wakefulness. Its field is the Great Vehicle Dharma that one observes and in which one establishes sentient beings. Discipline is upheld from within the three states of inspiration, directing the mind, and meditative absorption.

The substance of patience is the triple practice of enduring harm, having disregard for suffering, and the patience of certainty in the Dharma. The others are the same as before, and so the root text declares: "Patience is held to be supreme in terms of its support, substance, reason, dedication, cause, wakefulness, fields, and states." Likewise, in the case of diligence, the substance is armor-like diligence, applied diligence, and the diligence that accomplishes the benefit of sentient beings. The substance of concentration, on the other hand, comprises the concentration of a happy present life, the concentration that accomplishes superknowledge, and the concentration that accomplishes the benefit of sentient beings. Finally, the substance of insight is understood in terms of insight that knows the relative truth, insight that knows the ultimate truth, and insight that accomplishes the benefit of sentient beings. It should also be noted that the triads given in the context of the supreme substances, or natures, of the six transcendences are each enumerated in the order of lesser, middling, and supreme.

3. Showing the Pure Qualities through a Praise of Generosity

The bodhisattva's generosity is such
That, for the sake of the happiness of a single being,
Even eons of harm will be the cause of joy.
It is needless, then, to speak of different cases. [XVII.58]

The reason that embodied beings wish for wealth
Is precisely what the steadfast ones grant to beings.
People want wealth for the sake of their bodies.
This is exactly what the steadfast ones relinquish hundreds of
   times. [XVII.59]

When even giving away one's body causes no anguish to the
   mind,
What need is there then to speak about inferior substances?

This is the way that they transcend the world,
And the joy they experience thereby is the highest. [XVII.60]

When, to the delight of the needy, the wise give away everything,
The joy that they thereby experience
Is not felt by those in need,
Who receive all that they wish for. [XVII.61]

When the wise have given away all that they own and have no wealth,
They consider themselves prosperous.
Their sense of being wealthy is not shared
By recipients in possession of perfect enjoyments. [XVII.62]

When the wise have fully satisfied the needy with their excellent generosity,
They think of them as benefactors in a way
That is not matched by the recipients' acknowledgment
Of their benefactors, the causes of their wealth. [XVII.63]

As if partaking of the perfect fruit of a tree along the road,
Embodied beings harvest wealth and possessions
And enjoy them without a second thought;
None other than the bodhisattva experiences the pleasures of relinquishing all to them. [XVII.64]

The bodhisattva's generosity is such that, for the sake of the happiness of a single being, even eons of harm done to him or her will, because of his or her compassion, be the cause of joy. It is needless, then, to speak of different cases where many beings come to experience happiness, or where throughout many eons he or she is also benefited.

The reason that embodied beings wish for wealth is precisely what the steadfast ones grant to beings. People want wealth for the sake of their bodies, and this body is exactly what the steadfast ones relinquish to others, hundreds of times.

When even giving away one's body causes no anguish to the mind, what need is there then to speak about enjoyments of inferior substances? This is the way that they, the children of the victorious ones, transcend the world, and the joy they experience thereby, that is, by means of undergoing that type of suffering, is the highest among all that transcends the world. When, to the delight of the needy, the wise bodhisattvas give away everything, including their own life, the utter joy that they thereby experience is not felt by those in need, who otherwise to their hearts' content may have received all they wish for.

When the wise bodhisattvas have given away all that they own and have absolutely no wealth, they consider themselves prosperous. Their sense of being wealthy is not shared even by recipients who have gained all that they wished for and who are now in possession of perfect enjoyments. When the wise children of the Victorious One have fully satisfied the needy with their excellent generosity, they consider the recipients to be their own benefactors in a way that is not matched by the recipients' acknowledgment of their benefactors, the bodhisattvas, as the causes of their wealth.

As if plucking and partaking of the perfect fruit of a tree along the road, embodied beings harvest the wealth and possessions of the child of the victorious ones and enjoy them without a second thought. None other than the bodhisattva experiences the pleasures of relinquishing all to them.

The qualities of generosity are described next. The bodhisattvas' generosity is such that, for the sake of the pleasure of one sentient being, they will give away all their possessions and for several eons undergo the sufferings of constant toil and destitution. They will do this with joy and without despair. Needless to mention, they will also be delighted in other cases, such as when they are able to bring benefit and happiness to many beings through gifts of the Dharma or material things, or when they themselves are benefited in the process and gain happiness for a long time. Such is the power of their loving concern for sentient beings.

Embodied beings treasure their body and life passionately. They hold on to them dearly, and it is with their body and life in mind that they wish for wealth. Now, that which beings in this way cherish so dearly is exactly what the steadfast bodhisattvas, from their side, will freely relinquish to other beings. Such is the quality of the bodhisattvas' nonattachment. Beings wish for wealth, searching for it and hoarding it, for the sake of their bodies and lives. The steadfast bodhisattvas, on the other hand, give away their bodies to others hundreds of times. When their minds are still free of suffering, even upon having sacrificed their own bodies and lives, there is no need to mention that they will not become weary by giving away inferior, external substances that are generally easy to part with. Such is the quality of their lack of weariness.

The supreme joy, free from all weariness, that is experienced by the bodhisattvas upon giving up their bodies and lives is a quality that transcends what any mundane being can experience. It is higher, even, than the supramundane joy of the noble listeners and self-realized buddhas; these do not possess such joy. As bodhisattvas practice their generosity without interruption, they are not only free from sadness but are also in possession of supreme joy.

The wise give away their body and all their possessions to those who are in need. When they see that the recipients of their generosity become happy, they will notice that what they did has been of benefit to the needy. The joy that the bodhisattvas thereby feel is unmatched by the joy of those in need when they receive all that they wanted from the bodhisattvas. Such is the love that the bodhisattvas have for their field.

Having given away all their possessions, those of great wakefulness, the bodhisattvas, will no longer be in possession of any wealth, for a while. Yet they think: "I have turned my wealth into a treasury of generosity!" Thus they consider themselves prosperous. This, the bodhisattvas' sense of being wealthy, is not shared by those in need when they receive vast and perfect enjoyments from the bodhisattvas. This is because they still suffer from stinginess and will keep holding on to their wealth. Such is the quality of the way in which bodhisattvas perceive the ever-increasing results of their generosity.

The wise give in a way that is proper and good, fulfilling the wishes of others with respect and without conceit. In this way, they satisfy the needy to their heart's content by giving them whatever they want, including their own bodies and enjoyments. Bodhisattvas consider those sentient beings who have been satisfied in this way to be their benefactors, thinking: "These beings help me in my training to perfect the transcendences and attain unsurpassable enlightenment!" Those in need will, even when they receive vast amounts of wealth, not consider the kindness of their benefactors, the causes of their gain, in a way that matches the bodhisattva's perspective.

Many beings, without any hesitation or fear, may enjoy the perfect fruit of a magnificent tree that stands along the roadside, eating as much as they can. Embodied beings in the same way partake of the vast wealth of the bodhisattvas, thinking: "There is nothing that he will not give." They have no hesitation and so they take what the bodhisattvas offer with pleasure and delight. If they were to hold on to wealth, the bodhisattvas would not be happy, but, by giving it to others, they are full of joy and partake of inexhaustible enjoyments. Only bodhisattvas can be this way: nobody else. Thus, these last two stanzas concern the quality of definitiveness.

The above stanzas explain the distinctive features of the way in which bodhisattvas, out of compassion, practice giving in order to benefit others. However, this also serves to illustrate the way in which they practice the other transcendences, such as discipline. In essence, the transcendences are all, equally, endeavors that are undertaken for the sake of others out of great compassion.

4. Specific Explanation of the Qualities of Diligence

This section has two parts: (1) a brief presentation and (2) an extensive explanation.

1. Brief Presentation

> The divisions with regard to its being foremost, to its cause,
> and to its function;

The divisions of its features and support;
And the divisions of the remedy against the four obstacles—
It is clearly taught that diligence should be known through
   these. [XVII.65]

The divisions with regard to its being foremost, to its cause, and to its function; the divisions of its features and support; and the divisions of the remedy against the four obstacles—it is clearly taught in the sūtras that diligence should be known through these.

As for diligence, the thus-gone ones have clearly taught that it should be understood in terms of its being the foremost and supreme among the transcendences, as well as in terms of its cause, in terms of the divisions of its functions, its features, its support, and its providing the remedies against the four obstacles.

2. Extensive Explanation

Among all virtues diligence is supreme,
For their attainment follows from it.
With diligence one gains perfect ease at once.
It accomplishes all that transcends the world, as well as the
   world. [XVII.66]

Diligence delivers what is wished for within existence.
With diligence purification is attained.
Through diligence one transcends the transient collection,
   gains liberation.
Diligence brings buddhahood, supreme enlightenment. [XVII.67]

Moreover, there is diligence in decrease and increase,
Control of liberation, elimination of conflicting factors,
Entry into reality, total transformation,
And what is ascertained as "diligence of the great objective,"
   which is held to be distinct. [XVII.68]

Diligence of the initial goodness, and then,
Diligence of correct entry and application;
As well as undaunted, unshakable, and insatiable diligence—
All these features the buddhas have taught. [XVII.69]

In terms of the individuals who apply themselves to the three vehicles,
For some, intent and intelligence are feeble, whereas for others they are extremely vast.
Their inferior, mediocre, and supreme diligence
Is respectively held to be of small and great purpose. [XVII.70]

The diligent are not defeated by wealth.
The diligent are not defeated by affliction.
The diligent are not defeated by weariness.
The diligent are not defeated by attainment. [XVII.71]

Among all virtues, diligence is supreme, for their attainment (that is, the attainment of all virtuous qualities) **follows from it**. **With diligence, one gains perfect ease at once** (that is, in this present life). **It accomplishes all** happiness **that transcends the world, as well as** all happiness that is **of the world**.

The next stanza further explains the function of diligence by distinguishing between mundane and supramundane accomplishments. **Diligence delivers what is wished for** in terms of the pleasures **within existence** in the realm of desire. **With diligence, purification** of the afflictions of the realm of desire **is attained**, thus allowing one to enter the mundane concentrations. **Through diligence one transcends the transient collection** and **gains** the foe destroyer's **liberation. Diligence brings buddhahood**, the stage of **supreme enlightenment**.

Moreover, as for the features of diligence, **there is**, in the context of the four correct exertions, a total of two forms of **diligence** that are involved **in the decrease** of unvirtuous qualities, **and** two that are engaged in the **increase** of pure ones. The diligence in gaining **control of** the path of **liberation** occurs at the time of the five faculties. Diligence in **elimination of conflicting factors** is associated with the five powers. Diligence in **entry into reality** is specific to the seven aspects of enlightenment. Diligence of **total transformation** belongs to the eight aspects of the path. **And,** finally, there is also **what is ascertained as "diligence of the great objective," which,** in being the very essence of the six transcendences, the cause of the accomplishment of one's own objectives and those of others, **is held to be distinct** from the previous ones.

There is also the **diligence of the initial goodness,** which is the armor that one dons, **and then** subsequently the **diligence of correct entry** into, **and application** of, the path. These forms of diligence are taught, **as well as** the diligence that is **undaunted** by even the most extensive issues to be realized, the diligence that is **unshakable** in the face of suffering due to heat or cold, **and insatiable diligence,** which does not rest content with just a small measure of realization. **All these features, the buddhas have taught.**

Next, **in terms of** the supports, that is, **the individuals, who** diligently **apply themselves to the three vehicles, for some** the compassionate **intent and the intelligence** of insight **are feeble, whereas for others they are extremely vast.** Their inferior (in the case of the listeners), **mediocre** (in the case of the self-realized buddhas), **and supreme** (in the case of the bodhisattvas) **diligence is respectively held to be of small and great purpose** because the first two accomplish only their own benefit, whereas the latter accomplishes both one's own happiness and that of others.

On the way in which diligence serves as the remedy for the four obstacles, it is taught: **the diligent** children of the victorious ones **are not defeated by** attachment to the essence of **wealth; the diligent are not defeated by the affliction** of obsessive attachment to the enjoyment of pleasures; **the diligent are not defeated by weariness** when they practice generosity and the rest; **the diligent are not defeated by** feeling content with a minor **attainment** of generosity and so on.

It is first explained that, among all the virtuous merits, diligence is supreme. Second, the reason for this is set forth. Why is it supreme?

Because, based on diligence, all the accumulations of virtue will subsequently be attained. Without diligence, no positive or virtuous qualities at all would be accomplished because the extent of the accumulation of virtue depends upon the extent of one's diligence. One may think: "Since concentration and insight are the factors that actually destroy the afflictions, would they not be supreme?" Indeed, they are the supreme factors, but without mustering diligence, neither of them would arise. Thus, the cause of all virtuous qualities is diligence, and from this point of view, it is supreme.

Third, is the division of its functions. By exerting diligence, one comes at once, that is, within this life, to be supremely happy. Even ordinary beings of the world witness its effects in this life because by diligently pursuing respective methods, sicknesses are healed, poverty is alleviated, and so forth. Likewise, through exertion in calm abiding and special insight, one can in this life also perceive the qualities of concentration and special insight.

Diligence accomplishes all good qualities, whether mundane or supramundane, that are attained in this or in future lives. Through diligence in performing the ten mundane virtues, one achieves the pleasant results of the happiness of gods and humans within the desire realm of existence. By striving with diligence in the meditative absorptions of the form and formless realms, one attains a temporary purification of the afflictions of the lower realm of desire. Thereby, one attains birth within the realms of the four concentrations or the four formless absorptions. Based on diligence in meditating on the meaning of the four truths and on dependent arising, one transcends the view of the transient collection and achieves the liberation that is the listeners' and self-realized buddhas' transcendence of suffering. By arousing diligence in the Great Vehicle Dharma, one becomes a supremely enlightened buddha.

The third topic is the divisions of its features. Diligence endowed with the four correct exertions is the intermediate stage of the path of accumulation. Thus, this is diligence in the following: (1) pacifying whatever nonvirtue has arisen, (2) dissipating flaws by not allowing whatever nonvirtue that has not arisen to arise, (3) bringing forth the virtues that have not yet arisen, and (4) developing those that have. Diligence endowed with the five faculties is the diligence that is in control of liberation. The diligence of the five powers is the diligence that eliminates the conflicting factors. The diligence of entry into reality occurs in the context of genuine enlightenment, while the authentic exertion on the path of the noble ones, which is the cause for fundamental transformation, takes place in the context of the eightfold path of the noble ones. Diligence in pursuing the practice of the transcendences is known as "the diligence of the great objective, the attainment of buddhahood." Because such diligence is superior to that of the listeners and self-realized buddhas, it is set aside and distinguished as the "diligence of the great objective."

Furthermore, the diligence of the initial virtuous intent is the diligence of devoted application, whereas the diligence of correctly following through on one's commitment is the diligence of constant application. This twofold division is in terms of the essence of diligence. There is also the diligence that is undaunted in accomplishing the vast path and fruition, the diligence that is unshaken by conflicting factors, and the diligence that is insatiable in applying the remedies. The divisions of all these forms of diligence were taught clearly by the buddhas.

Fifth is the division of diligence in terms of the support. When listeners, self-realized buddhas, and bodhisattvas strive on the paths of the three vehicles, they possess an intent and insight that is, respectively, feeble, mediocre, and extremely vast. Therefore, their diligence should also be understood to be, respectively, inferior, mediocre, and supreme. This, in turn, is how we distinguish three types of diligence with respect to its supports. Among these three, the first two are held to be of little purpose because they are mustered merely for one's own benefit. Since the latter is aroused for one's own benefit and that of all others, it is held to be the diligence of the great objective.

The sixth issue is the division of diligence in terms of its serving as the remedy for the four obstacles. These four are the obstacles of (1) declining wealth, (2) afflictions, (3) weariness, and (4) loss of previously attained good qualities. These are all to be relinquished through diligence. The diligent are not defeated by wealth because through diligence, they accomplish the causes of it. The diligent are not defeated by afflictions because their remedy is produced by it. The diligent are not defeated by weariness in the practice of generosity and the rest because their diligence is insatiable. The diligent are not defeated by the attainment of excellent qualities because with the power of diligence they will not rest but will carry their practices through to the stage of buddhahood.

10. Mutual Ascertainment

The transcendences are mutually ascertainable because within each transcendence all the others are included as well.

With reference to their mutual inclusion, divisions,
The Dharma, and the reasons,
The six transcendences can
Be seen as ascertained. [XVII.72]

The following explanation concerns the way in which the transcendences can be mutually ascertained. The six transcendences can be ascertained **with reference to their mutual inclusion.** That is to say, with respect to fearlessness, generosity subsumes discipline and patience because the latter two accomplish the giving of fearlessness. Generosity with the Dharma includes concentration and insight because it is through those two that the Dharma is given. Both the former types of generosity contain diligence because diligence is instrumental in both of them. Similarly, the discipline of gathering virtuous qualities subsumes generosity and all of the rest.

The ascertainment in terms of **divisions** concerns the way in which one can, for example, be generous in terms of instilling discipline in the streams of being of others. Thus, there are six divisions, from the generosity of generosity up to and including the generosity of insight. Ascertainment with respect to **the Dharma** considers the way in which transcendences such as generosity subsume the sūtras and so forth that express them, while, reciprocally, the sūtras and so forth contain that which is expressed by them, that is, transcendences such as generosity. **And, the** ascertainment of the transcendences that relates to their **reasons** regards the way in which generosity is a reason for engagement in discipline and the other four. It is when one is uninterested in pleasure that one takes up discipline and so forth. Discipline is also a reason for engagement in generosity and the other transcendences because when one has genuinely accepted the vows of a fully ordained monk, one will relinquish all possessions and become endowed with patience and the rest. Moreover, the genuine acceptance of the discipline of gathering virtuous qualities is the reason for generosity and so forth. By extension, it should also be understood that each of the six transcendences individually includes all the others. Therefore, in these ways the **six transcendences can be seen as ascertained.**

While generosity and so on are each distinguishable conceptually, they also each in essence inherently include all the rest. Therefore, they are mutually ascertainable, which will here be explained by pointing out that (1) the six transcendences are mutually inclusive, (2) each of the six can itself be divided into six, (3) the presence of one involves by nature the presence of the rest, and (4) each of the six serves as the reason or cause of the others. In these four ways, the six transcendences can be ascertained as mutually inclusive.

Let us consider the case of generosity. When adopted, generosity eliminates stinginess. Yet it also contains the discipline of working for the benefit of beings, and, in terms of patience, it involves the practice of bearing with inappropriate responses to generosity and of accepting the relinquishment of one's possessions. Furthermore, generosity contains the diligence of devoted and constant commitment to giving. It contains the concentration of one-pointed practice without falling prey to distractions in the form of conflicting factors. Finally, generosity contains insight in terms of comprehending, for example, the characteristics of pure versus impure generosity. Moreover, giving by means of the meditative absorption of the treasury of space is an aspect of generosity that consists of concentration. When one attracts disciples by being generous and then subsequently gives them the gift of the Dharma, that is insight. The bodhisattva's transcendent generosity is also embraced with nonconceptual wakefulness and thus possesses the insight that realizes the nature of things. The latter is true with respect to all the transcendences.

As for discipline, all the transcendences are inclusively practiced within the discipline of gathering virtuous qualities. Upholding discipline for the benefit of others is ultimately also generosity, and by possessing discipline, one will naturally be patient when harmed by others. Being disciplined also implicitly requires diligence, and, when the mind is one-pointedly focused on discipline, that is concentration. Comprehending the principles of discipline, such as what is and is not a downfall, is insight into things in their multiplicity, and the knowledge of discipline beyond the focal points of the three spheres is insight into things as they actually are.

When one is patient for the benefit of others, when one brings benefit to others by means of patience, when one accepts the practices of giving—these are ways of being patient that also include generosity. Patience, as such, is restraint from the negative act of anger. It is the gathering of the virtues of the foremost austerity. The aspect of exerting oneself in the practice of patience is diligence. Moreover, gladly accepting suffering while training in the transcendences is a form of patience that includes all other transcendences. The aspect of the mind abiding one-pointedly and unperturbed is concentration, whereas insight is included in the patience of ascertaining the Dharma, in knowing how to cultivate patience, and in realizing that there is no nature of patience. As for diligence, this practice accompanies all the others, and thus it has an aspect of each of them.

Concentration that accomplishes activities includes all the other transcendences. In the sense that concentration benefits others, it is generosity. Considering the attainment of the vows of concentration, it is also discipline. Concentration is patience insofar as one is not disturbed by distractions. It also involves the diligence of devoted and constant application, as well as the insight that takes the form of an analysis of the four bases of miraculous power. Just as in the previous cases, concentration also involves insight into the way things are and their full multiplicity.

As for insight, all the other transcendences are subsumed within the insight of skillful means. Insight allows for the practices of generosity, discipline, patience, diligence, and concentration. Without it, they cannot be practiced.

As for their divisions, each of the transcendences can be divided into six aspects, such as the generosity of generosity. Thus we arrive at thirty-six in total, as was explained in the context of the investigation of the Dharma. When one abides by the six transcendences, the respective six aspects of establishing others in them is generosity. Likewise, being free from the six conflicting factors, such as stinginess, is discipline, and the six aspects of endurance of the difficult practices are patience. The six aspects of delight are diligence, the six aspects of not being distracted from the focus are concentration, and the six aspects of not conceiving of the three spheres are insight. Alternatively, within a single mind of generosity, we may determine aspects of eliminating conflicting factors, practicing the remedy, delight, nondistraction, and discernment; all six are inextricably present. The same completeness can be noticed with respect to the other transcendences, such as discipline, whereby each involves, for example, the intention to give for the benefit of others.

The phrase "with reference to ... the Dharma" appears to teach that the scriptural Dharma instructions on the transcendences, as their means of expression, contain the subject matter of the transcendences and, further, that the transcendences, as the expressed subject matter, in turn comprise all the scriptural teachings of the Great Vehicle. If we consider this inclusion in terms of the intrinsic nature of the relative, all the other transcendences can be found to be included within each of the others, in the same way that the four elements, which serve as its cause, will be fully present within a single resultant material form. Likewise, when embraced by the ultimate, nonconceptual wakefulness, each of the transcendences will, within the emptiness endowed with all supreme features, be of one taste with the others. The *Gathering of Precious Qualities* similarly explains how transcendent insight arises as equal taste by providing the example of the shadow of ten billion trees and so forth on Jambudvīpa.

Concerning the phrase "with reference to ... the reasons," if one is not attached to pleasures, one can succeed in upholding discipline. Likewise, if one has discipline, one can be patient with the harms inflicted by others. If one has patience, one can arouse diligence. Diligence, in turn, will enable one to rest the mind in equipoise, and if one can rest in equipoise, one will come to see in accordance with reality. Moreover, if one engages in any one of the transcendences, such as generosity, it is certain that it will help accomplish all the others as well. There is, in this way, nothing within the practices of the individual transcendences that does not also contribute to the accomplishment of all the others.

2. The Four Means of Attraction That Ripen Other Sentient Beings

The four means of attraction will be discussed in terms of their (1) essence, (2) definitive enumeration, (3) function, (4) divisions, and (5) benefits.

1. Essence

> As for generosity, the same holds.
> Teaching, bringing acceptance, and one's own consistent engagement
> Are held to be pleasant speech, meaningful action,
> And consistency with the meaning. [XVII.73]

Next follows an explanation of the four means of attraction. (1) **As for generosity, the same** as was taught in the context of the transcendences **holds** with respect to the means of attraction. (2) Pleasant speech is understood as being the **teaching** of generosity and so forth. (3) Meaningful action implies **bringing** others to an authentic **acceptance** of generosity and so forth. (4) Being in harmony with the meaning involves **one's own consistent engagement** in that which one has brought others to accept. Hence, these **are held to be pleasant speech, meaningful action, and consistency with the meaning.**

(1) Generosity, as a means of attraction, is as explained in the context of transcendent generosity; it is no different from that. (2) Pleasant speech is to explain correctly and to teach to others the particular and shared characteristics of the six transcendences. (3) When one thereby establishes sentient beings in the practical experience of the six transcendences, that is meaningful action. (4) Finally, when one practices the transcendences in the same way as one has encouraged other sentient beings to do, that is consistency with the meaning. Thus, teaching, bringing acceptance, and one's own concordant engagement concern the last three of the means of attraction.

2. Definitive Enumeration

The means for benefiting,
Comprehension, engagement
And consistent engagement—
These are to be known as the four means of attraction.
[XVII.74]

Generosity with material things constitutes **the means for benefiting** others. Pleasant speech, in particular, is the means for bringing about **comprehension** in those who have no understanding or who have doubts. Meaningful action is the means for **engagement** with the transcendences. **And** consistency with the meaning implies one's own **consistent engagement** in that which one has taught to others. **These are to be known as the four means of attraction.**

The first of the means of attraction is generosity, which is the method for benefiting others in terms of their physical situation. This may be done, for example, by dispelling heat, cold, hunger, or thirst. Pleasant speech is the method for bringing about an unmistaken comprehension of the transcendences in another's mind, having dispelled his or her lack of understanding, misunderstanding, and doubt regarding the characteristics of the transcendences. Meaningful action consists of the methods for encouraging others to engage in the practice of the transcendences, whereas consistency with the meaning is the method for encouraging others to engage in such practice again and again. That is to say, when teachers of the Dharma embody the Dharma, those whom they have established in the Dharma will eagerly follow through in their own practice of the Dharma. Therefore, as one gathers sentient beings into a circle to be trained, the method for ripening them is the four means of attraction; no more are needed, and fewer would not be enough.

3. Function

The first creates vessels,
The second, devotion,
With the third, there is practice,
And with the fourth, thorough training. [XVII.75]

The first creates vessels since others thereby become capable of listening to the Dharma. **The second** brings **devotion** to the Dharma since all doubts are settled. **With the third, there is practice** of the Dharma, **and, with the fourth, thorough training** in that practice.

The first means of attraction causes sentient beings to become vessels of the Dharma. When sentient beings are benefited by the material generosity of a bodhisattva, they come to like their benefactor and this, in turn, makes them ready to listen to his or her words. The second, pleasant speech, brings devotion to the Dharma that is truly endowed with the transcendences, while the third, meaningful action, brings forth the concrete practice of the transcendences. The fourth, consistency with the meaning, causes the practice of the transcendences to be continual and free from stains.

4. Divisions

This section has two parts: (1) a twofold division and (2) a threefold division.

1. Twofold Division

In terms of material things and the Dharma,
Which includes the Dharma as focal point and so forth,
The four means of attraction are held
To be included in two. [XVII.76]

In terms of material things, which contain the first means of attraction, **and the Dharma, which includes** the subsequent three—with reference to **the Dharma as focal point and so forth** (thus indicating also the Dharma as practice and the Dharma as thorough training)—**the four means of attraction are** thereby **held to be included in two.**

There are two forms of attraction: material attraction and Dharma attraction. Dharma attraction involves the three principles of the Dharma as focal point and so forth. Thus, whereas generosity constitutes the material attraction, the other three means of attraction constitute Dharma attraction. Thus, it is held that the four means of attraction are included within two, and that the Dharma attraction is subdivided further into three.

Within the Dharma attraction, there is the Dharma as focal point, the Dharma as practice, and the Dharma as purity. The first of these refers to the Dharma of the sūtras and so forth that is endowed with the six transcendences; this Dharma is explained by means of pleasant speech. Next, the Dharma as practice is undertaken by means of meaningful action; and the Dharma as thorough training is accomplished by acting in consistency with the meaning of the teachings. This latter ensures that the stains of factors such as miserliness, which conflict with the transcendences, are dispelled.

2. Threefold Division

In terms of divisions, it should be understood
That there are the inferior, middling, and supreme attractions;
The generally unsuccessful, the successful,
And the in-all-regards successful. [XVII.77]

In terms of divisions pertaining to the means of attraction, **it should be understood that there are the inferior** means of the listeners, the **middling** means of the self-realized buddhas, **and the supreme** means of the bodhisattvas' **attractions**. Moreover, there are **the generally unsuccessful** means of attraction practiced by those who are on the grounds of inspired conduct, **the generally**

successful ones that are practiced by those who have gained access to the grounds, **and the in-all-regards successful** means of attraction practiced by individuals on the eighth ground and beyond.

In terms of divisions, the listener's four means of attraction are inferior because they are not employed for the benefit of others. The self-realized buddha's attractions are of middling quality because the faculties of self-realized buddhas are superior when compared to those of the listeners, yet inferior when compared to those of bodhisattvas. The bodhisattva's four means of attraction are known to be supreme because they are practiced for both one's own benefit and that of others. The division in terms of inferior, middling, and supreme means of attraction can also be understood with reference to the way in which the bodhisattvas themselves will establish beings in the vehicles of the listeners, self-realized buddhas, and bodhisattvas.

Moreover, the means of attraction can also be divided with reference to the one who attracts others. Bodhisattvas on the grounds of inspired conduct gather and mature beings through the four means of attraction, yet in doing so they mature only a few, and are otherwise for the most part unsuccessful. The reason for this is that such bodhisattvas have not seen the real condition of phenomena and they do not know the specific inclinations and so forth of sentient beings. When bodhisattvas on the first through the seventh ground practice to bring sentient beings to full maturation through the four means of attraction, they are mostly successful; yet there are still a few that are not ripened. Bodhisattvas on the eighth, ninth, and tenth ground gather and mature beings through the four means of attraction, and in doing so successfully ripen everyone. None of their efforts are in vain.

5. Benefits

> Those involved in attracting a retinue
> Genuinely follow this way.
> This accomplishes, in all regards, the aims of all
> And is extolled as the excellent method. [XVII.78]

All attraction that took place in the past,
That comes about in the future, or which occurs right now
Is of this kind, and hence,
This is the path of ripening sentient beings. [XVII.79]

Those involved in attracting a retinue must genuinely follow this way. This accomplishes, in all regards, the aims of all and is extolled by the buddhas as the excellent method. All attraction brought about by children of the victorious ones **that took place in the past, that comes about in the future, or which occurs right now is of this kind, and hence, this is the** single, universally traversed **path of ripening sentient beings.**

When gathering a retinue, bodhisattvas will take an approach that thus accomplishes all the objectives of sentient beings and is clearly extolled by the buddhas as the excellent and irreplaceable method. Therefore, when sentient beings in the past were attracted by buddhas and bodhisattvas, it was due to these four means. The same is the case with the sentient beings who will be attracted in the future, and those who are being attracted right now. Without exception they are attracted by these four means. Hence, it is certain that the four means of attraction are the single path for the maturation of all sentient beings.

3. Conclusion to the Preceding Two Topics

Thus, with a mind always unattached to pleasures,
They have gone to the other side of peace, restraint, and endeavor.
Those who so abide, not conceiving of any existence, objects, or marks,
Are the ones who attract the hosts of sentient beings.
[XVII.80]

This was the seventeenth chapter of the *Ornament of the Great Vehicle Sūtras,* the chapter on the transcendences and attractions.

In conclusion it is taught: **Thus, with a mind always unattached to pleasures** because of their generosity, **they have gone to the other side of peace** through the pacification of nonvirtue by means of discipline, through **restraint** against anger because of patience, **and** through **endeavor** in virtuous qualities by means of diligence. **Those who so abide** with a one-pointed mind due to concentration, **not conceiving of any existence, objects, or marks** of being clean, and so forth, **are the ones who** can **attract the hosts of sentient beings.**

With a mind that is always unattached to pleasures, bodhisattvas practice generosity. They also have discipline, which pacifies the paths of unvirtuous action caused by attachment and so on. With patience they ensure that their stream of being is not disturbed by anger. While in possession of transcendent diligence, their minds abide within inner meditative absorption that is free from external distractions. They possess the insight that does not conceive of any marks of existence, neither internally in the five aggregates nor externally in phenomena such as form. The bodhisattvas who themselves have matured in this way will attract hosts of sentient beings, ripening them with the four means of attraction.

This concludes the explanation of the seventeenth chapter of the *Ornament of the Great Vehicle Sūtras,* the chapter on the transcendences and attractions.

18

Worship, Reliance, and the Immeasurables

3. Worship, Reliance, and the Immeasurables

The present chapter on worship, reliance, and the immeasurables is concerned with (1) worshipping the buddhas, (2) relying on a spiritual teacher, (3) cultivating the four immeasurables, and (4) summarizing those topics.

1. Worshipping the Buddhas

This section begins with an account of the nature of worship.

1. The Nature of Worship

With the most buoyant mind,
And in order to perfect the two accumulations,
Offerings of clothing and so forth
Are presented to the buddhas, whether manifest or not.
   [XVIII.1]

"May the coming of the Buddha be meaningful."
With this prayer,
And without any holding of the three as reference points,
The worship of the Buddha is perfected. [XVIII.2]

Next, the explanation turns to the aspects of worship. **With the most buoyant mind,** which is the reason for worship, **and,** in terms of the dedication, **in order to perfect the two accumulations** of merit and wakefulness, **offerings** of entities such as **clothing and so forth are presented to the buddhas,** who are the basis for worship, **whether** they, the buddhas, are **manifest or not.**

"**May, in my case, the coming of the Buddha be meaningful**": By having **this prayer,** which is the cause, **and,** by the power of making it **without any holding of the three**—that is, agent, object, and act of worshipping—**as reference points** (thereby implying wakefulness), **the worship of the Buddha is perfected.**

Motivated by the most buoyant mind of faith and for the purpose of perfecting the two accumulations, one worships the field of the buddhas with various offered substances, including Dharma robes, alms bowls, parasols, banners, and flowers. The things that are offered are also understood to include one's praises of the buddhas, listening to the Dharma, and so forth. If this takes place at a time when a buddha has come to the world in the form of a supreme emanation body, the offerings are made to this manifest buddha. If the time is such that a buddha does not reside in the world, one instead brings to mind the buddhas. Thus, in front of sculptures, paintings, stupas, and suchlike, one brings forth offerings to the buddhas who are not manifest.

"The Buddha enters the world, and so we encounter and worship the Buddha; may this become deeply meaningful for me and all sentient beings!" When such prayer is made without observing any marks of (1) the field of the Buddha, (2) a worshipping self, and (3) a substance of offering, then the worship of the Buddha is thoroughly perfected. Thus, one stands before the buddhas of the ten directions, praying to worship them constantly with infinite offerings, so that one oneself and all sentient beings may complete the two accumulations. When such worship takes place within the state of the ultimate nonobservation of any of the three spheres, then the worship is said to be exact and perfect.

2. Types of Worship

There is also the ripening of
The infinite number of sentient beings,
The means of substance and mind,
Inspiration, aspiration, [XVIII.3]

Love, patience,
Genuine practice,
Turning toward the bases, realization,
Liberation, and suchness. [XVIII.4]

Worship is explained
By its reason, dedication,
Entity, support, cause,
Wakefulness, field, and foundation. [XVIII.5]

Cause and effect,
Oneself and others,
Material things, veneration, and practice—
These are twofold. [XVIII.6]

Worship is minor and great,
With pride and without pride,
And asserted with reference to
Application, lives, and aspiration. [XVIII.7]

Worship of the Buddha through one's own mind is supreme
As there is inspiration regarding the Dharma, aspiration, mastery,
Full embrace by the skillful means of nonconceptuality,
And engagement with the single objective of all. [XVIII.8]

With respect to the various types of worship, **there is also the ripening of** the field, that is, **the infinite number of sentient beings,** because the process of sowing the seeds of the two accumulations in sentient beings can likewise be understood as worship. Similarly, in terms of the foundation, there is worship through **the means of substance**, which includes clothing and so forth, **and mind**, which involves directing the mind by way of relishing, rejoicing, and taking delight. Moreover, worship includes **inspiration** with respect to the Great Vehicle; **aspiration** toward and development of the enlightened mind; **love** for sentient beings; **patience** when enduring the pains of hardship; **genuine practice** of the six transcendences; unerringly **turning toward the bases** by directing the mind in accordance with phenomena; **realization** in accordance with the way the bases truly are, which is achieved by means of the view of the path of seeing; the **liberation** from afflictions that is achieved by the listeners, **and** the power of **suchness** free from stains that is accomplished by the followers of the Great Vehicle. Thus, as shown above, **worship is explained by** specifications in terms of **its reason, dedication, entity, support, cause, wakefulness, field, and foundation.**

Next, a different classification is taught: Past worship is the **cause and** present worship is the **effect.** Likewise, present worship is the cause and future worship is the effect. Also, worship that one performs by **oneself** is inner worship, **and** the worship that one causes **others** to engage in is outer worship. Worship by means of **material things** and **veneration** is coarse, **and** worship through **practice** is subtle. **These are twofold** classifications.

Worship is minor when it relates to substance and an inferior frame of mind, **and** it is **great** and excellent in the opposite cases. Moreover, worship **with** the **pride** of thinking "I am" is inferior, **and** worship **without pride** is excellent. **And,** worship is **asserted with reference to** (1) its **application,** which is distant when related to the future and close when engaged in immediately; (2) the **lives** involved, because when worship is interrupted for a period of several lifetimes, the wish to worship is distant, but when the wish concerns the immediately subsequent life, it is close; **and** (3) **aspiration,** which likewise may be distant or close depending on whether the aspiration concerns the future or the present.

One may wonder, "Which of these is the supreme way to worship the Buddha?" **Worship of the Buddha through one's own mind is supreme, as there is,** as follows: **inspiration regarding the Dharma** of the Great Vehicle; **aspiration** (that is, intent in terms of relishing the taste, rejoicing, delighting, being insatiable, vastness, joy, benefiting, being uncovered, and virtuous); **mastery** of the treasury of space and other such meditative absorptions; **full embrace by the skillful means of** the wakefulness of **nonconceptuality; and engagement with the single objective of all** the great bodhisattvas as one's activity merges with theirs.

Engaging in the infinite ripening of sentient beings is enumerated among the categories of worship because benefiting sentient beings is the supreme offering to delight the thus-gone ones. Moreover, when it comes to activities such as making beings intent on worshipping the buddhas and bringing them actually to do so, the foremost activity is that of ripening sentient beings by teaching the Dharma. Hence, such activity is performed while perceiving it to be an offering that delights the thus-gone ones.

There is also worship through the offering of various material substances such as Dharma robes or flowers, as well as worship that is mental and hence not dependent on substance. These, then, are two distinct categories of worship. When making divisions in terms of mental worship, we arrive at the following nine principles, from inspiration to suchness:

(1) Inspiration does indeed imply bringing the buddhas to mind. Hence, as brightness is engendered, it also implies wishing to bring them all manner of mundane and supramundane offerings that may or may not be in one's possession. Here, however, inspiration is the first within the triad of inspiration, aspiration, and mastery. It is thus understood to be the mental offering of inspiration with respect to the meaning of those sūtras of the Great Vehicle, which teach the Dharma of worshipping the thus-gone ones. "Aspiration" has the aspects of (1) relishing, (2) rejoicing, (3) taking delight, (4) insatiability, (5) vastness, (6) joy, (7) benefiting, (8) freedom from affliction, and (9) virtuousness. All of these are mental. Respectively, they are (1) to relish both the recollection of past worship and the noticing of present worship; (2) to rejoice in

the offerings made by others; (3) taking delight in the future worship performed by both oneself and others; (4) being insatiable as the offerings are made beyond restrictions and limits concerning that which is offered, the recipients, and the time of offering; (5) developing vast aspiration since one wishes to worship continuously and without interruption through to the heart of enlightenment; (6) considering sentient beings, the field that is to be matured, with love and joy; (7) wishing to benefit all sentient beings through one's worship; (8) being free from affliction as one has no attachment, pride, or suchlike, and since one does not wish for any defiling results; and (9) having the virtuous intent whereby worship is dedicated to the unsurpassable enlightenment of all sentient beings. As for the third principle, "mastery," this refers to the worship of the thus-gone ones that is performed, for example, on the basis of the meditative absorption of the treasury of space. This form of worship is also mental.

Next, (2) aspiration is based on having brought forth the mind of unsurpassable enlightenment. It consists of the prayer to accomplish one's own welfare and that of others, wherever one may be born throughout one's lives, along with the prayer to worship the thus-gone ones similarly, with limitless offerings. This worship is likewise mental. It is, alternatively, also known as "steadfastness." (3) The loving heart that wishes to dispel the suffering of sentient beings is also an offering to the thus-gone ones, as is (4) the patience of gladly accepting the suffering of heat, cold, hunger, thirst, exhaustion, and the like for the sake of ripening oneself and others.

One worships the thus-gone ones by (5) genuinely practicing the six transcendences. The same is the case when (6) one discerns things, having correctly directed the mind toward the bases—the meanings of impermanence, suffering, emptiness, and absence of self. (7) The genuine view that arises with the attainment of the first ground, and which thus comprehends the inherent nature of things and directly realizes the twofold absence of self, is likewise an offering to the buddhas. (8) The listeners' liberation from the afflictive obscurations is their worship of the buddhas. When the bodhisattvas gradually accomplish the grounds and transcendences, that too is worshipping the buddhas. The latter culminates in the attainment of unsurpassable enlightenment due to (9) suchness, having become free of the two obscurations. That attainment, again, is a form of worshipping the buddhas. Thus we arrive at a distinct enumeration of nine forms of worship.

There is also an eightfold division in terms of the nature of worship: (1) reason, which refers to focusing, with a thoroughly inspired mind, on the buddhas as the sacred field—the perfection of all good qualities; (2) the complete dedication of the ripening of worship toward unsurpassable enlightenment by means of the perfection of the two accumulations; (3) the supports, or bases, which are the buddhas, the objects of worship; (4) the entities of worship, that is, the various material or mental offerings; (5) the cause, which is the prayer that the buddhas may manifest and that one may thus encounter and worship them; (6) wakefulness in the absence of observation of the three spheres; (7) the infinite field of the sentient beings for whose sake one worships; and (8) the foundations of worship—the substantial entities and mental states that are involved in worship.

One may at this point wonder what the difference is between entity and foundation. Since the person who possesses inspiration and the other principles mentioned above is in any case also taught implicitly, one may indeed ask oneself whether there is any difference. Hence, these eight are a concise summary of the principles taught in the first to the fourth stanzas.

Worship can be further divided in terms of past causal worship and present resultant worship, or present causal worship and future resultant worship. As it emerges in such causal conformity, we can thus classify worship in terms of the three times. There is the worship one gives by oneself, as when one offers one's own head or limbs, or when one listens to the Dharma, contemplates it, and so on. This is also known as inner worship. On the other hand, when one inspires others to worship, or when one offers one's things, such as one's Dharma robes, this is known as worship in terms of others, or as outer worship.

Some forms of worship occur through the offering of material things such as Dharma robes, meals, or bedding. Other kinds of worship take the form of veneration, as when one prostrates, joins the palms of one's hands, makes gestures of welcome, or rises from one's seat. Both of these are known as lesser, or coarse, types of worship. Alternatively, worship through practice, as when one listens to the sacred Dharma, contemplates it, or trains in it, are classified as great, or subtle, worship.

Practice itself is minor, or inferior, worship when it takes place along the lines of the Lesser Vehicle. The practice of the Great Vehicle, on the other hand, is great, or excellent, worship. (It appears that this line, 7a, can also be seen as conjoined with what was said before, without any isolated significance.)

Worship that has not been embraced by the wakefulness that is free from the observation of the three spheres is worship with pride. Once it has been embraced by nonconceptual wakefulness, it is worship without pride. These two categories are also known as the lowest and the highest forms of worship.

Worship is also twofold in terms of its application. Thus, when worship is left to be engaged in at some future time, it is distant. When it is engaged in instantly, upon recollection, it is close worship. There is a similar distinction based on whether worship is interrupted by subsequent lives. That is to say, if worship does not occur until after a period involving two or more lives, it is distant, whereas if it follows immediately, in the next life, it is close. Also, when there is the aspiration to engage in worship in this life, it is close worship, but when the aspiration concerns all one's future lives, it is distant worship.

Finally, supreme worship is distinguished in the following terms: its observation, which implies inspiration with respect to the Dharma of the Great Vehicle; its aspiration, which refers to the nine qualities (from relishing, rejoicing, and so on, to virtuousness); the mastery of worship through the attainment of meditative absorptions, such as that of the treasury of space; its being fully embraced by the skillful means of nonconceptuality beyond the three spheres; and its engagement with the single objective of all the great bodhisattvas. The latter occurs from the eighth ground onward, whereupon wakefulness is accomplished spontaneously and without effort. Hence, when one bodhisattva worships, all other bodhisattvas who reside there will join the worship by way of their activities merging into one. As all such bodhisattvas practice by means of their shared objective, their worship is superior to that of the whole world, including also that of the listeners and self-realized buddhas.

2. Relying on a Spiritual Teacher

Second, following a spiritual teacher will be discussed in terms of (1) the way to follow a spiritual teacher, (2) the relevant divisions, and (3) the distinctions of supreme reliance.

1. The Way to Follow a Spiritual Teacher

This first section includes (1) a brief presentation and (2) an elaborate explanation.

1. Brief Presentation

> Reliance is explained
> In terms of support, bases, marks,
> Dedication, cause, wakefulness,
> The pure field, and abode. [XVIII.9]

The next explanation concerns the various aspects involved in following a spiritual teacher. **Reliance on a spiritual teacher is explained in terms of support, bases, marks, dedication, cause, wakefulness, the pure field, and abode.**

Reliance on a spiritual teacher will be explained in terms of (1) the characteristics of the support, the spiritual teacher; (2) the bases, or entities, by means of which one follows such a teacher; (3) the marks of reliance; (4) the objectives of the dedication; (5) the causes of practice [in relation to] the spiritual teacher; (6) the ensuing skill in terms of wakefulness; (7) the purification of the field that consists of the environment and its inhabitants; and (8) the abode within which one rests while following the spiritual teacher.

1. Characteristics

> One should follow a spiritual teacher who is gentle, at peace,
> thoroughly at peace,

Possesses superior qualities, is diligent, rich in terms of
scripture,
Realized with respect to reality, skilled in teaching,
Loving in nature, and has relinquished weariness. [XVIII.10]

With respect to the support, **one follows a spiritual teacher who is gentle**, in the sense of abiding by the training in discipline, **at peace**, as he or she abides by the training in meditative absorption, and **thoroughly at peace**, meaning beyond the afflictions by adhering to the training in insight. This teacher is someone who **possesses superior qualities** when compared with oneself, **is diligent** in the pursuit of the welfare of others, has received no small measure of teaching and so is **rich in terms of scripture**, who is **realized with respect to reality** in the sense of having comprehended it, who is **skilled in** the unimpeded **teaching** of Dharma without any concern for material things, who is **loving in nature, and** who is constantly involved in Dharma teaching and so **has relinquished weariness**.

One should follow spiritual teachers who have self-control, in the sense of adhering to the training in special discipline, and who hence are gentle, being in control of their senses. Such teachers should also adhere to the training in special meditative absorption and so be at peace, free from afflictions and distractions. Finally, with special insight they should be thoroughly at peace, beyond afflictions and thoughts. The teacher one follows should moreover possess qualities that are superior to one's own because there is little benefit in following someone who is either equal or inferior to oneself in terms of discipline, learning, and so forth.

One's teacher should be diligent in teaching and the like, and he or she should have listened to the sacred Dharma in abundance, thereby having become rich in terms of scripture. Regarding the Dharma of realization, he or she should have resolved and realized the essential reality of the four truths, dependent origination, emptiness, and other such issues. The teacher should also be an expert in clearly explaining the Dharma by skillfully combining names, words, and syllables. Teachers to be relied upon are those who have love for the ones who come under their influence, their students. They should not have any weariness, for weariness would either make them disinclined to teach, cause them to teach unclearly, or otherwise make them teach only a little, lacking constancy and persistence.

2. BASES

> Following the teacher with veneration, material things,
> Reverence, and practice are the bases for following.
> [XVIII.11a–b]

The bases relate to **following the** spiritual **teacher** in certain ways: **with veneration**, praising his or her genuine qualities, offering prostrations, and so on; with the offering of **material things** such as Dharma robes; with **reverence**, for example, washing the teacher's feet; **and** by means of **practice** of that which he or she teaches. These **are the bases for following** the spiritual teacher.

Second, once one has found a spiritual teacher, the basis for following such a teacher is proper veneration in body, speech, and mind. In terms of one's body, this means, for instance, to offer prostrations, going forth to welcome the teacher, accompanying the teacher when he or she leaves, respectfully rising from one's seat, and regarding the teacher with a smile on one's face and the look of joy in one's eyes. Similarly, one offers verbal veneration in the form of praise, and by speaking in accord with the words of the teacher, speaking with affection and respect, and so forth. Finally, the mind venerates the teacher by being buoyant and possessing faith. Material things are also employed when following the teacher. That is to say, one offers whatever things the teacher may need, such as Dharma robes or bedding. Moreover, following a teacher with reverence implies serving the teacher by, for example, washing and massaging his or her body. As one accomplishes all appropriate tasks, in these ways one relies on the teacher through the use of outer entities.

Furthermore, one should listen to, reflect on, and meditate in accordance with the spiritual teacher's explanation of the Dharma. When one thus practices the Dharma in accordance with the Dharma, this is known as "reliance by means of inner entities." In these ways, one should rely on the spiritual teacher by means of outer and inner entities. This is what is meant by the "bases of reliance."

3. Marks

> The wise wish to understand the Dharma
> And in a timely manner go respectfully before the teacher.
> [XVIII.11c–d]

As for the marks, **the wise wish to understand** all of **the Dharma and** so, when the time for listening to the Dharma has come, **in a timely manner go respectfully before the teacher.**

The third issue of the signs, or marks, has to do with the understanding of the signs of following a teacher. Just as they faithfully follow their spiritual teacher, wise disciples rely on the Dharma that is the topic of their studies. They abandon all negative mind frames such as disdain, deceit, and the wish to find errors. Instead, with the wish to thoroughly understand the Dharma, they go before their teacher whenever the time for listening to the Dharma is right. That is to say, they do not approach the teacher when he or she is training in meditative concentration, having a meal, or the like. They come when the time for listening to the Dharma is right. Gentle and subdued in body and mind, they come before the teacher with respect and yearning for the Dharma. Never do they behave in ways that are disrespectful or arrogant.

4. Dedication

> Without any wish for respect and acquisitions,
> One brings forth a full dedication to practice. [XVIII.12a–b]

The dedication involved in following a bodhisattva spiritual teacher is such that, **without any wish for respect and acquisitions, one brings forth a full dedication** to the process of following the teacher, a dedication that is directed toward the **practice** of all the points that he or she teaches.

Fourth, as for the dedication, one may ask: "With what objective does one rely on a spiritual teacher?" or "What is it that one, in doing so, wishes for and applies oneself to?" When following a spiritual friend, there is absolutely no concern for the respect and acquisitions that may otherwise be obtained as the result of following learned or famous people, including becoming learned or famous oneself. There is no inclination to dedicate one's efforts to such pursuits. Rather, one follows the spiritual teacher with the heartfelt wish to practice the Dharma of the three trainings just as the teacher explains it. "By following this person, may I listen to, reflect upon, and train in the Dharma; may I practice the noble path and fully realize the truth of the intrinsic nature!" Dedicated to these concerns and objectives, one follows the spiritual teacher.

5. Cause

> The steadfast one who practices in accordance with the teaching
> Will be truly delighting the mind. [XVIII.12c–d]

Regarding the cause, **the steadfast one who practices in accordance with the teaching** received from the spiritual teacher **will be truly delighting the mind** of the spiritual teacher.

Fifth, when the spiritual teacher's mind is delighted, then that is a cause of his or her teaching. As it hence is a cause that makes the following of one's teacher meaningful, good and steadfast disciples will practice and gain experience by following their teacher's instructions, thereby truly delighting their teacher's mind.

6. Wakefulness

> Becoming learned and realized with respect to the three vehicles,
> One persists in the practice of one's own vehicle [XVIII.13a–b]

In terms of wakefulness, training with a view to **becoming learned and realized with respect to all of the three vehicles, one persists in the practice of one's own** bodhisattva **vehicle.**

Having listened to the Dharma that their spiritual friends teach, the bodhisattvas become learned in the three vehicles and so gain realization of the three vehicles with their own mind. Thus, wakefulness is discovered in reliance on the spiritual friend. Having become learned concerning the three vehicles, the bodhisattvas do not practice the Listeners' Vehicle or that of the self-realized buddhas. Their vehicle is the Great Vehicle, and hence, for the sake of accomplishing their objectives and that of all others, they persist in the practices that bring about the attainment of great enlightenment.

7. The Pure Field

For the sake of fully maturing limitless beings
And for the sake of bringing forth the pure fields.
[XVIII.13c–d]

One follows the spiritual teacher **for the sake of fully maturing limitless sentient beings,** the field of those to be trained, **and for the sake of bringing forth the pure** buddha **fields.**

One relies on the spiritual friend to purify, on the inner level, the sentient beings who inhabit the world. Thus, one listens to the Dharma and so forth for the sake of bringing limitless sentient beings to full maturation. Moreover, one also relies on the teacher with the objective of purifying the external environment of the world. One thus relies on the teacher and listens to the Dharma for the purpose of fully bringing forth the perfectly pure fields. The latter refers to the exquisitely adorned buddha fields, featuring, for example, a ground made of precious stones, wish-fulfilling trees, and rivers of elixir.

8. Abode

The spiritual friend is to be followed well for the sake of
    obtaining
One's share of the Dharma and not of material things.
    [xviii.14a–b]

Regarding the abode, **the spiritual friend is to be followed well for the sake of obtaining one's share of the Dharma and not** in order to obtain a share **of material things**.

"Abode" here refers to the specific way of directing one's mind. If at some point the possessions of, for example, one's parents or siblings are passed on in the family, there may be a particular share of the inheritance to which one is entitled, and to which one lays claim, expressing a particular wish. Similarly, bodhisattvas follow their spiritual teachers so that they can qualify for their share of the sacred Dharma. They do not do so for the sake of obtaining a share of material things. Although bodhisattvas may be attracted by means of material things, there is never anyone among them who listens to the Dharma primarily for the sake of material things, while considering the Dharma to be of secondary importance. This is due to the character of their "abode."

2. Divisions of Reliance

The wise should follow the spiritual teacher through the cause
    and effect,
Adhering to the gateway of Dharma [xviii.14c–d]

In the outer way, by listening, and through the inner spiritual
    training,
With pride and without pride.
The way in which the wise follow a spiritual teacher
Takes place in terms of lives, application, and aspiration.
    [xviii.15]

The next explanation concerns the divisions of reliance. **The wise should follow the spiritual teacher through** the **cause,** which takes the form of reliance on a spiritual teacher in the past **and** the resultant **effect,** which is the present reliance on such a teacher. Similarly, one's present following of a spiritual teacher serves as the cause for the effect, which will be the following of such a teacher in the future. **Adhering to the gateway of Dharma** refers to becoming familiar with the meditative absorption of the stream of Dharma, which is an inner mode of following a spiritual teacher. One follows teachers **in the outer way** through, for example, venerating them by offering material things. Likewise, the coarse level of following is **by means of listening and** the subtle level is **through the inner spiritual training,** which consists of reflection and meditation. When this is done **with pride** it is inferior, **and without pride** it is excellent. **The way in which the wise follow a spiritual teacher takes place in terms of** (1) the interval of **lives** involved, because when the intent to follow a spiritual teacher is interrupted by several lifetimes, it is distant, whereas it is close when concerned with the immediately subsequent life; (2) **application,** which is distant when related to practices in the future and close when concerned with what follows immediately; **and** (3) **aspiration,** which may be distant as a wish for the future or close in the sense of being a concern for this present life.

The way in which the wise rely on spiritual teachers can be divided in terms of cause and effect. Reliance in the past serves as the cause for present reliance. Likewise, present reliance on a spiritual teacher is the cause for reliance in future lives. Thus, reliance on a spiritual teacher can be divided in terms of past, present and future. Moreover, inner reliance is when one practices in accordance with the oral instructions received from one's spiritual teacher, thus following the teacher by attaining the meditative absorption of the gateway of Dharma. It is also inner reliance when one follows buddhas and bodhisattvas in accordance with the realization of one's spiritual teacher. Outer reliance, on the other hand, is when one's reliance is in terms of material wealth and the like.

When one follows a teacher by simply listening to the sound of his or her Dharma teaching, it is coarse or crude because here the mind moves externally toward the mere sound of another. Alternatively, when endowed with the spiritual practice of comprehension through reflection or meditation, one's reliance is subtle or fine because in such cases there is inner attention to the meaning of the teachings. Also, when there are reifying concepts that take the form of thinking, "I rely on such and such," there is possession of pride, which is inferior. When, on the other hand, one does not apprehend any marks of oneself, the spiritual teacher, or the acts of following, it is known as "relying on the spiritual friend with a mind free from pride," which is the supreme way of following a spiritual friend.

In relation to lives, application, and aspiration, the way that the wise follow a spiritual teacher can also be considered to be either close or distant. Thus we have a set of six ways of following the teacher. First, reliance on the teacher in the present life is close reliance. When, on the other hand, the reliance is interrupted and only resumes after several lives, it is distant. Likewise, distant application occurs if one's reliance on the spiritual teacher follows at a future time within the present life, or if, in a future life, one does not immediately follow a spiritual teacher, but only in a life subsequent to that. Close application, conversely, is when one follows the teacher right away in the present life, or when in a future life one's practice of relying on a teacher continues without interruption. With respect to aspiration, the case is similar. When one aspires to follow and subsequently does follow the teacher in the present life, it is close aspiration; when the aspiration is in terms of reliance in future lives, it is distant. These three are simply distinguished with reference to one's physical support, one's practice, and the force of one's wishes and aspirations.

3. The Distinctions of Supreme Reliance

Following the spiritual teacher through one's own mind is supreme
As there is inspiration with respect to the Dharma, intent, mastery,
Full embrace of the skillful means of nonconceptuality,
And engagement with the single objective of all. [XVIII.16]

Following the spiritual teacher through one's own mind's becoming learned in the meaning of the Great Vehicle **is supreme**, as there is **inspiration with respect to the Dharma** of the Great Vehicle, there is **intent** (in terms of relishing the taste and the rest of the nine forms of intent), there is **mastery** of meditative absorption, **full embrace of the skillful means of** the wakefulness of **nonconceptuality, and engagement with the single objective of all** the great bodhisattvas, as one's activity mingles with theirs.

The supreme way of following a spiritual friend takes place through one's own mind. This encompasses reliance in terms of (1) inspiration with respect to the Dharma of the Great Vehicle, (2) the nine types of intent that were explained above, and (3) the attainment of the mastery of meditative absorption. The latter allows one, for example, to offer an infinite number of enjoyments through the meditative absorption of the treasury of space and to recollect words and meanings flawlessly by means of retention. One's reliance on a spiritual friend may also be (4) fully embraced by the skillful means of nonconceptuality, and from the eighth ground onward it will (5) engage the single objective of all bodhisattvas, in the sense that one's activities will merge with theirs. The presence of any of these five principles will qualify one's reliance on the spiritual teacher as supreme.

3. The Immeasurables

Third, the account of the four immeasurables is divided in terms of (1) an explanation of the four immeasurables and (2) the specific treatment of compassion.

1. Explanation of the Four Immeasurables

This section explains the immeasurables in terms of their (1) essence, (2) focal points, (3) divisions, (4) effects, (5) conflicting factors, and (6) qualities.

1. Essence

The sublime abodes of the steadfast ones have abandoned the
conflicting factors,
Are in possession of nonconceptual wakefulness,
Engage with the three focal points,
And thoroughly ripen sentient beings. [XVIII.17]

The next explanation concerns the investigation of the immeasurables. **The sublime abodes of the steadfast ones**, the bodhisattvas, **have abandoned the** four **conflicting factors and are in possession of** the remedy, which is **nonconceptual wakefulness.** They **engage with the three focal points**, namely, sentient beings, phenomena, and the absence of observation, **and** they **thoroughly ripen sentient beings.**

The four immeasurables of the bodhisattvas possess four characteristics. That is to say, within the streams of being of steadfast bodhisattvas, the four sublime abodes—love, compassion, joy, and equanimity—are characteristically (1) free from their respective conflicting factors, which are the wish to cause harm, hostility, frequent displeasure, and disturbance in the form of attachments and aversions. They are also (2) accompanied by nonconceptual wakefulness, and they (3) observe the three focal points that are sentient beings, phenomena, and the absence of focal point. Finally, (4) their function is to thoroughly ripen sentient beings without ever abandoning them.

In the case of love, the first characteristic is the absence of the wish to cause harm and the corresponding presence of the loving wish for sentient beings to encounter happiness. The second characteristic refers to the lack of observation of anyone cultivating love, any sentient being that is an object of love, and any love that is to be cultivated. The third distinguishing feature is the engagement with the three focal points. The love in the minds of ordinary beings and extremists is one that holds oneself and sentient beings to be existent. This is love of the type that observes sentient beings. In the case of the listeners and self-realized buddhas, there is no such thing as a "self" or a "sentient being" at all.

Nevertheless, love arises based on the observation of the mere conglomeration of phenomena that comprise the five aggregates, which are seen as manifold, impermanent, and painful. The love of those bodhisattvas who have entered the grounds, and the love of the buddhas, does not observe any sentient beings, or even any phenomena, in terms of the ultimate. Yet, although everything is empty by nature, the buddhas realize that sentient beings, whose essence is emptiness, experience illusion-like suffering in the form of delusional individual perceptions. Hence, while not having any focal point, they carry out limitless activities for the benefit of sentient beings.

The *Grounds of Yogic Practice* explains that the four immeasurables that involve simply observing sentient beings are common to ordinary beings, extremists, listeners, self-realized buddhas, bodhisattvas, and buddhas. Love and so forth that involve observing phenomena, on the other hand, are common to listeners, self-realized buddhas, bodhisattvas, and buddhas. Finally, it is explained that love without focal point is uniquely present in bodhisattvas and buddhas.

In the *Sūtra Taught by Akṣayamati,* it is taught that, to begin with, the love of a bodhisattva who engenders the enlightened mind is the love that observes sentient beings because such a bodhisattva has not yet had any direct perception of the twofold absence of self. In the case of bodhisattvas who have entered the activities of the first through the seventh ground, it is the love that observes phenomena because the bodhisattvas on those grounds have direct perception of the utterly pure, basic field of phenomena. Finally, with the eighth ground comes the achievement of acceptance of nonarising phenomena. Hence, it is taught that from there on love does not hold any focal point. It arises without any involvement in thoughts or efforts.

2. Focal Points

> Thus, for the steadfast ones, these thoroughly engage
> With those who are wishing for happiness, who are tormented
>   by suffering,
> Who are happy, and who are afflicted;
> With treatises; and with the suchness of those. [XVIII.18]

Because its object is suchness,
Because of purity through the attainment of peace,
And because of the two activities and the exhaustion of afflictions—
For these reasons love has no focal point. [XVIII.19]

Here one may wonder what these three focal points are. Thus, for the steadfast ones, these qualities of love and so forth thoroughly engage, in terms of the focal point of sentient beings, with those who are wishing for happiness in the case of love, those who are tormented by suffering in the case of compassion, those who are happy in the case of joy, and those who are afflicted by attachments and aversions in the case of equanimity. In terms of the focal point of phenomena, the four engage with the treatises in which those very qualities are explained. And with respect to the absence of focal point, they thoroughly engage with the suchness of those sentient beings and phenomena.

It should be understood that the absence of focal point takes place for four reasons. Because its observed object is suchness; because of the strengthening of its character and subsequent purity, the latter coming about through the attainment of peace in the absence of thought upon having gained acceptance of nonarising phenomena; and because of the two activities of body and speech, which are engendered by love and yet do not involve focal points; and because of the exhaustion of afflictions, which otherwise involve focal points—for these reasons love has no focal point. The same is the case with the remaining three immeasurables.

The steadfast bodhisattvas' four qualities of love and so forth have as their focal point sentient beings who wish to be happy. Love takes the form of wishing that they might find happiness. Compassion observes them to be miserable due to their suffering, and consequently wishes them to be free from suffering. Joy observes sentient beings who experience happiness, and thus manifests as the wish that they may not be separated from happiness. Equanimity observes sentient beings who suffer from afflictions. That is to say, it observes sentient beings who develop attachment when they experience pleasant sensations or when they meet friends and the like, and who feel aversion when having painful sensations or when they encounter enemies and the like. It then manifests as the wish that sentient beings may not experience such afflictions and instead come to abide in equanimity, free from attachment and aversion. Thus it is explained how the four qualities observe particular groups of sentient beings.

Love that observes phenomena focuses on the genuine treatises and sūtras of the Great Vehicle, which teach these four immeasurables. Consequently, it observes sentient beings as merely conditioned phenomena. Finally, love that has no focal point observes and accesses the suchness, devoid of apprehended and apprehender, of the observed four types of sentient beings and the Dharma of the Great Vehicle.

There are four reasons why love and the other three qualities can be characterized as "free from focal point." (1) The love that observes the suchness of persons and phenomena is love free from focal point because it observes neither persons nor phenomena, nor does it observe anything as outer or as inner. (2) At the time of attaining acceptance of nonarising phenomena on the eighth ground, thoughts and efforts are thoroughly pacified. This brings about the final strengthening of the seeds of the four immeasurables. Hence, without efforts, thoughts, or discernments, they are spontaneously perfected and become utterly pure. This is also a reason that love and so forth are referred to as "free from focal point." (3) Since loving acts of body and speech occur in causal accordance with love and yet pertain to the aggregate of form, such acts are also classified as love free from focal point. Finally, (4) the love of the noble ones is known as free from reference point because such beings have brought attachment, aversion, and the other afflictions to exhaustion. Because the afflictions are tight apprehensions based on a special focus on objects, they are known as "the mind's focal points." Thus, for example, the sūtras speak of "the end of focal points when the knots of the mind are abandoned." Since in the case of the noble ones, there are no such focal points, love and the other four qualities can therefore be classified as free from focal points. Thus, there are four reasons that show how love has no focal point.

3. Divisions

These are known as mutable and immutable,
Relished with attachment and not so relished.
The bodhisattvas thoroughly abide in those
That are immutable and free from attachment. [XVIII.20]

Not of the nature of equipoise, lesser,
Mediocre, belonging to inferior grounds,
Of an inferior mind-set, and involved with pride—
These are inferior while others are superior. [XVIII.21]

As for love and so forth, **these are known as mutable** when their quality may degenerate **and immutable** when they will remain or develop further. When **relished with** an **attachment** to the bliss of meditative absorption, they are known as "afflicted," **and** when they are **not so relished** with attachment, they are "free from affliction." **The bodhisattvas thoroughly abide in those** qualities of love and so forth **that are immutable and free from attachment.**

When these four qualities pertain to the realm of desire, they are **not of the nature of equipoise** and are, therefore, inferior. Among those qualities of love and so forth that *are* of the nature of equipoise, some are **lesser** and others **mediocre. Belonging to inferior grounds,** some qualities thus pertain to levels that, from the perspective of the levels that follow them, are inferior. Moreover, love and so forth are qualities **of an inferior mind**-set in the case of the listeners and self-realized buddhas, **and** they are **involved with pride** as long as the acceptance of nonarising phenomena has not yet been achieved. All of **these** types enumerated here **are inferior, while others,** that is, the opposite cases, **are superior.**

When love and the other three are subject to future degeneration and deterioration, they are referred to as "mutable." When, on the other hand, they will remain or develop further, they are known as "immutable" since they will not degenerate. One may have attained meditative absorption within the four immeasurables, yet if one relishes one's meditative absorption with attachment, holding it to be supreme to the extent that one does not pursue higher qualities, one's state of mind is afflicted. Alternatively, if there is no such relish, and if one does not hold the meditative absorption to be supreme, then the four are known as "immeasurables free from affliction." Of these four divisions, the bodhisattvas abide in those that are immutable and free from the attachments of relishing meditative absorption and holding it to be supreme. They do not abide in those that are mutable and afflicted.

Furthermore, in terms of the ways in which the immeasurables may be divided, those immeasurables that are based on the mind of the desire realm, and which hence are not of the nature of equipoise, are known as lesser immeasurables. The immeasurables that pertain to the form and formless realms are, on the other hand, classified as qualities of equipoise. The first concentration includes three realms: the Realm of Brahma, the Realms of Those Close to and Who Extol Brahma, and the Realm of the Great Brahma. The second concentration spans the three realms that begin with Lesser Light, and within the third concentration, there are the three that begin with Lesser Virtue. Finally, in addition to the three realms that begin with Cloudless Light, the fourth concentration also has the five pure abodes; thus it spans eight realms in total. In the Realm of Brahma, the four immeasurables are lesser, in the Realm of Those Close to Brahma they are mediocre, and in the Realm of the Great Brahma they are great. In this way the immeasurables that are of the nature of equipoise can be classified as lesser, mediocre, and greater. Moreover, both the lesser and mediocre can be subsumed in the lesser, and so we arrive at a twofold division in terms of the lesser and the greater.

When the root text says "belonging to inferior grounds," it refers to the divisions that relate to the immeasurables that belong to either inferior or superior grounds. For example, the cultivation of the four immeasurables that takes place on the grounds of inspired conduct is inferior and lesser when compared with what occurs on the first ground, and in terms of such a comparison the latter is hence classified as superior and greater. On the other hand, compared with the superior four immeasurables that are manifest in someone abiding on the second ground, those of the first ground are inferior, and so on, and so forth. This is the way the immeasurables are classified by mutual comparison as either greater or lesser in relation to the grounds.

The root text also speaks of "the inferior mind-set," thereby alluding to the lesser four immeasurables that are present in listeners and self-realized buddhas, who do not accomplish the welfare of others. Moreover, from the first to the seventh ground, the four immeasurables are involved with the pride that is associated with conceptual efforts, and for that reason they can be classified as lesser. In this way, we see that the four immeasurables can be classified as inferior, and hence lesser, if they are present in a mind that is not in equipoise, or if they are present in a lesser or mediocre mind of equipoise. It is the same if they are lesser in comparison with higher grounds, if they are based on an inferior mind-set, or if they are involved with pride. On the other hand, they may be referred to as "greater" if they are present in a mind in equipoise, if they are greater in comparison with lower grounds, if they are present in those whose mind-set is not inferior (that is, bodhisattvas and buddhas), or if they belong to the three pure grounds (the eighth and above) upon which conceptual efforts no longer hold sway.

4. Effects

The wise who remain in the sublime abodes
Will always take birth in the realm of desire.
Through this they perfect the accumulations
And mature sentient beings. [XVIII.22]

Never parting from the sublime abodes,
They are free from conflicting factors.
Even if, while negligent, they perceive the intolerable,
It will still not make them change. [XVIII.23]

The wise bodhisattvas who remain in the causal factor of the sublime abodes will, as an effect of maturation, always take birth in the realm of desire. Through this, that is, their training in the immeasurables, they perfect the accumulations as a ruled effect, and in terms of the effect of individual effort, they mature sentient beings. **Never parting from the sublime abodes** is the effect of causal accordance, and the fact that **they are free from the conflicting factors** that prevent the training in the immeasurables is the effect of separation. As for the sign, **even if, while negligent, they perceive the intolerable** object—that which functions as the **condition** for the conflicting factors, such as the wish to cause harm—**it will** still **not make them change.**

Generally, the cultivation of the four immeasurables results in a birth in the form realm. However, the wise bodhisattvas who reside constantly in the sublime abodes have achieved tremendous flexibility of mind and mastered inconceivable meditative absorptions. Therefore, as an effect of maturation, they always take birth in the desire realm for the benefit of sentient beings. The ruled effect of their immeasurables is that they perfect the accumulations of merit and wakefulness. Moreover, bodhisattvas endowed with the four immeasurables will let those sentient beings who have not yet entered these teachings enter them. Those who have already entered, they will continue to ripen, further and further. This is the effect of individual effort, or individual strength, an effect that they diligently produce through their four immeasurables. Having familiarized themselves with the four immeasurables in this life, the bodhisattvas will, as an effect in accord with its cause, never separate from the sublime abodes in future lives. The fact that their four immeasurables are free from the wish to cause harm and the other three conflicting factors is an effect of separation.

The next concerns the sign of having perfected the cultivation of the sublime abodes. During a period when bodhisattvas do not purposely train in the cultivation of the four immeasurables, they may not pay any special attention, and so end up being negligent. Yet even if during such a time they should perceive a condition that would otherwise be intolerable, it will still not cause any deterioration of their love, or of the other three qualities. This is the sign and mark of having cultivated the sublime abodes to the extent that one is free of the factors that conflict with them. (This account of the marks may be seen as an aside to the effects, and so be included within the present subsection on the effects. Alternatively, it could also be considered a distinct issue, in which case it would be the fifth among seven topics to be treated in the context of the immeasurables.)

5. Conflicting Factors

The bodhisattva who wishes to cause harm,
Is hostile, feels displeasure,
Or wishes to harm and gain pleasures
Encounters numerous flaws. [XVIII.24]

Their afflictions destroy themselves, sentient beings, and their discipline;
They fall back, become impoverished, and are disparaged by protectors and by the teacher; [XVIII.25]

They encounter reproach and disgrace, take birth in unfree states,
Lose what they have and do not yet have, and incur great suffering of the mind. [XVIII.26]

As for the faults, **the bodhisattva who,** lacking sublime abidance, **wishes to cause harm, is hostile, feels displeasure, or wishes to harm and gain pleasures, encounters numerous flaws** by way of such conflicting factors. How are such flaws encountered? **Their afflictions destroy** the happiness of such bodhisattvas **themselves,** they destroy the life and enjoyments of **sentient beings, and** their afflictions also destroy **their discipline,** thereby bringing about the destruction of both self and others. Since such bodhisattvas are haunted by regret, **they fall back** from happiness, and since others have no faith in them, they **become impoverished** and reviled by others. They end up being **disparaged by** the gods who are **protectors** of the teachings, **and** they will be scorned **by the teacher. They encounter reproach** since those who are skilled in maintaining the life-style of Brahma criticize them intensely, **and** wherever they go, they experience **disgrace.** Moreover, in future lives they will **take birth in unfree states.** As they **lose what they have** in terms of love and the rest, their negative deeds will proliferate in this life, **and** since they also fail to obtain what they **have not yet** obtained in terms of those qualities, negative deeds will increase in their future lives as well. **And** so they **incur great suffering** and agony **of the mind.**

The flaws that ensue from a lack of the four immeasurables are explained next. Wishing to harm is the factor that conflicts with love. Wanting sentient beings *not* to be happy, one instead wishes them to suffer and so intends to harm them through acts of killing, beating, and the like. Hostility that expresses itself in physical violence and so forth is the factor that conflicts with compassion. In terms of joy, the conflicting factor is the irritation and displeasure that arises due to envy when encountering happy sentient beings. Finally, being prone to anger when encountering painful sensations, enemies, and the like, and being subject to craving when experiencing pleasant sensations, being with friends, and so forth, is what constitutes the factor that conflicts with equanimity.

The presence of these conflicting factors will make one encounter numerous problems that are painful for both body and mind. Afflictions such as hostility and the wish to harm will make one do evil deeds, such as taking the life of another. In the present life, this will make one likely to be killed or imprisoned oneself, and in future lives one will be born into painful existences, such as hell, and so be destroyed by suffering. Moreover, such afflictions will also bring harm to the lives, enjoyments, spouses, and so on, of others. Hence these afflictions also destroy other sentient beings.

Those with such afflictions will also fall from the discipline that they may have otherwise adopted correctly. In this way, these afflictions also destroy discipline. Finally, those possessed of such afflictions will think: "Deprived of the path of the noble ones, I have lost the path to the higher realms; I have entered the path of mundane evil beings, the path that leads to the lower realms.... I am destroyed!" Thinking like this, in agony or with regret, they fall into hopelessness and depression. Their previous benefactors will also identify those with corrupted discipline as doers of evil who should not be supported, and with such thoughts in mind, they will then no longer provide them with anything. As others will also revile them, not considering them worthy of any offerings, they will become impoverished, finding it hard to obtain Dharma clothing, food, drink, or other necessities. Even if they were protected by gods and others in the past when they maintained their commitments, they will now instead be attacked and no longer offered protection. They will even become the objects of the scorn that our Teacher has expressed in various ways in the Vinaya scriptures and elsewhere, declaring that, for example, "such a person is not suited to be a monk, he has fallen from spiritual practice; he has acted like a donkey, and is comparable to a dead corpse." By the force of the intrinsic nature, such people will also incur reproach and criticism from those who maintain the life-style of Brahma, as the latter will not find the former to be suitable companions. Thus, they have to face punishment, expulsion, and the like. In all of the ten directions, their bad reputation will spread, as it becomes known that "this person has fallen from the discipline and done negative deeds."

Not only will those whose discipline has collapsed have to experience abundant suffering in this life, in the future they will take birth in the hells and other unfree states. They will lose whatever they had otherwise accomplished in terms of learning, discipline, the four immeasurables, and so forth. As they will be unable to attain what they still needed to attain in terms of good qualities, and since they will moreover lose whatever they had, they will be tormented by regrets and will experience unbearably great suffering and agony of the mind. These are the flaws that follow from the proliferation of afflictions, which is due to a lack of the remedying qualities of love and the remaining immeasurables.

6. Qualities

> All these flaws are not incurred by those
> Who adhere to love and the others.
> Without affliction they will, for the benefit of sentient beings,
> Never relinquish cyclic existence. [XVIII.27]

> Toward sentient beings, the intent of love and the others
> Thus arises in the children of the victorious ones.

> This is unlike what any sentient being could possibly feel
> Toward a precious, only child. [XVII.28]

All these flaws are not incurred by those who adhere to love and the others among the four immeasurables. Based on their intent, without affliction they will, for the benefit of sentient beings, never relinquish cyclic existence. Toward all sentient beings the intent of love and the others thus arises in the children of the victorious ones. This is unlike what any sentient being could possibly feel toward a most precious, only child.

None of the flaws stated above are ever sustained by those who genuinely adhere to love and the others among the four immeasurable qualities. For those who possess such four immeasurables, the power of their insight will ensure that they do not become stained by afflictions such as desire. Hence, they do not become afflicted. Nevertheless, because of their compassion, they will, for the benefit of sentient beings, never relinquish cyclic existence. On the contrary, they will take birth within it and bring sentient beings to maturation. The way that the children of the victorious ones bring benefit and happiness to sentient beings by the power of their minds' immeasurable qualities of love and so forth is not matched by any ordinary sentient being. No father or mother could possibly give rise to this type of love toward their only child, no matter how gifted, adorable, and in need of help it might be.

2. On Compassion in Particular

Second, the specific explanation of compassion has nine subsections. The first of these presents the ten focal points of compassion.

1. Compassion's Ten Focal Points

> Those who are ablaze and under the power of enemies,
> Who are tormented by suffering and enveloped in darkness,
> Who have embarked on the path hard to travel,
> Who are thoroughly tied by great chains, [XVIII.29]

Who are attached to great food mixed with poison,
Who are entirely deprived of the path,
Who have strayed from the path, and who have little strength—
Toward such beings there is compassion. [XVIII.30]

The next section addresses the divisions of the focal points of compassion. **Those who are ablaze** with the fire of craving in the realm of desire, **and** those who are **under the power of enemies** of Dharma practice, [such as] the demon of the divine child; those **who are tormented by** the **suffering** of hell, and so forth, **and** those such as butchers, who are **enveloped in** the **darkness** of delusion; those **who have embarked on the path** that is **hard to travel,** in the sense that they will not become subject to the complete transcendence of suffering; the extremists, **who are thoroughly tied by** the **great chains** of various negative views; those **who are attached to** the afflictive bliss of equilibrium as though **to great food mixed with poison;** those with excessive pride, **who are entirely deprived of the path;** those of the undetermined class, **who have strayed from the path** and entered the Lesser Vehicle; **and** those bodhisattvas **who have little strength** because of not having perfected the accumulations—**toward such beings there is compassion.**

When bodhisattvas observe (1) the sentient beings of the desire realm, who are ablaze with the fire of craving for the five sense pleasures, compassion wells up in them as they think: "Alas, these beings are helplessly consumed by the fires of insatiable desire." Similarly, their compassion fully arises based on their observation of the following categories of beings:

(2) Those who have adopted virtuous practices but then later give them up as they fall under the power of obstacle-making demons, the enemies of virtue.

(3) Those who are tormented by the unbearable sufferings of the three lower realms and those who, although they are born in the higher realms, are nevertheless overcome by the sufferings of birth, old age, sickness, death, and so on.

(4) Butchers, hunters, thieves, and others who engage in negative acts such as killing with body, speech, and mind, without knowing that the effects of those negative deeds will be, for example, the sufferings of hell.

(5) Those whose potential is disconnected and whose minds therefore never turn toward liberation and who thus roam through cyclic existence during endless lifetimes and have hence embarked on the path that is hard to travel.

(6) The extremists who, standing outside these teachings, are thoroughly tied by the great chains of negative views, such as those of "I" and "mine."

(7) Those who perceive the mere equilibria of the form and formless realms to be liberation and bliss, and are thus attached, as though to exquisite food mixed with poison, and who—despite being happy in their present situation—will eventually fall, having still not transcended cyclic existence.

(8) The extremists who, for the sake of liberation, for example, torment themselves with the five fires or commit suicide by jumping off cliffs; who perceive mistaken discipline and yogic activity to be the path, and who hence are entirely deprived of the path.

(9) Listeners and bodhisattvas of uncertain potential, who are on the paths of listeners and self-realized buddhas, and who despite having embarked on the path of liberation are thus nevertheless on an inferior path, disconnected from the path of the Great Vehicle, whereby one accomplishes both one's own objectives and those of others.

(10) Those who have entered the path of the Great Vehicle but who, lacking conducive conditions and being under the power of obstructive conditions, are unable to practice correctly and hence have little strength.

Thus, the compassion of the bodhisattvas can be divided into ten different types with reference to these ten focal points.

2. The Effects of Focusing on Sentient Beings with Compassion

> The elimination of hostility, the seeds of supreme enlightenment,
> The production of happiness and torments, the cause of the desired,

And the supply of the very nature—the children of the
victorious ones who rely
On this Dharma are not far from enlightenment. [XVIII.31]

With the elimination of hostility, compassion causes an effect of separation. With the seeds of supreme enlightenment, it brings about a ruled effect. Through the production of happiness for others and one's personal torments for the sake of others, it engenders an effect of individual effort. In being the cause of the desired, it produces an effect of maturation, and with the supply and superior development of the very nature of compassion in the future, it creates an effect of causal accordance—the children of the victorious ones who rely on this Dharma of compassion that possesses these effects are not far from unsurpassable enlightenment.

Second, what are the effects that are obtained based on observing sentient beings with compassion? As the effect of separation, those who have compassion will give up hostility, which otherwise expresses itself in various acts of violence against sentient beings. The ruled effect is that the two accumulations, which are the seeds of supreme enlightenment, will be gathered. Compassion also enables one to free other sentient beings from suffering and give them happiness, and in order to see that happen one will joyfully accept various torments such as heat, cold, and exhaustion. That is the effect of individual effort. Those who have compassion will also be able to take birth precisely as they wish, which is an effect of maturation. In this way, compassion serves as the cause of the desired. If one has accustomed oneself to compassion in past lives, compassion will continue to grow and become continuous throughout one's coming lives. That compassion supplies its very nature or essence in this way is an effect of causal concordance. For the children of the victorious ones, who rely on these five qualities of compassion, unsurpassable enlightenment is not far away. They will achieve it quickly.

3. Compassion Endowed with Insight

Compassion and supreme wakefulness
Make known all features of suffering within cyclic existence,
Including its absence of identity.
This brings neither weariness nor any damage through flaws.
[XVIII.32]

With love that sees the world as the nature of suffering,
Both suffering and the means
For its complete elimination are understood correctly.
This brings pity but not weariness. [XVIII.33]

Regarding their nondwelling in cyclic existence and the transcendence of suffering, it is explained that, for the bodhisattva, **compassion and supreme wakefulness make known all features of suffering within cyclic existence, including its** natural **absence of** any **identity** of its own. **This brings neither weariness nor any damage through flaws.** As for the thorough understanding of cyclic existence, **with a love that sees the** entire **world as the nature of suffering, both suffering and the means for its complete elimination are understood correctly. This brings** compassionate **pity but not weariness.**

Next the functions of compassion endowed with insight are explained. With supreme wakefulness, the bodhisattvas who possess great compassion discern all inner and outer phenomena within the three realms of cyclic existence, seeing them to be impermanent, the threefold suffering, and the inner mind. As they thus comprehend an abundance of features of suffering, they also know such suffering to be empty and devoid of self. Hence, they do not become weary of the sufferings of cyclic existence and instead compassionately act for the benefit of others.

Cyclic existence is flawed and full of problems due to suffering, such as old age, sickness, and death, and due to desire, anger, and other afflictions. Yet, because of their insight, the bodhisattvas remain unharmed by it all. With love for others, they see the triple suffering of the entire world to be similar to their own suffering. Knowing suffering and its causes, they also become aware of, and understand correctly, the path for eliminating it along with its cessation. They are not indifferent to the suffering of others, as they see it with compassionate pity. Yet since they also know the means for dispelling suffering, this does not bring them any weariness.

4. Divisions

> This love of those whose very nature is compassion
> Is fourfold because it is natural, has investigated,
> Has achieved familiarity in the past,
> And is an attainment of purity where the conflicting factors
>   fall away. [XVIII.34]

The investigation of the types of compassion is as follows. **This love of those whose very nature is compassion is fourfold because it** (1) **is natural,** in terms of, for example, the distinctive potential, (2) **has investigated** the benefits and defects that ensue from either possession or lack of compassion, (3) **has achieved familiarity** with compassion **in the past,** and (4) **is an attainment of** the path of the noble ones, the **purity** that is manifest in the absence of desire, **when the conflicting factors** in the form of hostility fall away.

The love of the bodhisattvas, whose very nature is compassion, may be divided in four ways. (1) By virtue of their potential, their love is natural, meaning their very nature is compassion. (2) Their love may also be based on investigation because it arises through training the mind in contemplating issues such as the following: the excellent qualities of compassion versus the flaws that ensue from a lack of compassion; how sentient beings continue to be helplessly tormented by the three types of suffering; how they have all been one's own friends and loved ones innumerable times; how although sentient beings all equally wish to be happy and to avoid suffering, their wishes stand in complete contrast to what they actually do. (3) The compassion of the bodhisattvas can also be seen as based on their having familiarized themselves with compassion in the past. (4) Finally, their compassion may be distinguished as an attainment of purity in the absence of hostility, the wish to harm, and other such conflicting factors. This latter type of compassion is attained in the absence of the desire that leads to the arising of attachment or aversion. In this way, the four types are distinguished in terms of nature, investigation, familiarization, and the attainment of freedom from desire.

5. The Distinctive Qualities of Great Compassion

As the fifth point, the presentation of the qualities of compassion is divided into explanations of (1) the actual distinctive qualities of great compassion and (2) the examples that illustrate them.

1. The Actual Qualities of Great Compassion

> If it is not equality, eternity, superior intention,
> Means for accomplishment, freedom from desire, and absence
>   of focal point,
> Then it is not love,
> And where there is no love, there is no enlightenment.
>   [XVIII.35]

If it is only a concern for those who are experiencing feelings of pain, and so **not** a love that acknowledges the **equality** of all sentient beings, if it is not present for **eternity** and instead ends in the exhaustion of the aggregates without any remainder, if it is not a **superior intention** that occurs due to the realization that self and others are all the same, if it is not a **means for accomplishment** that protects from suffering, if there is no **freedom from desire** because the conflicting factor of hostility has not been overcome, **and** if there is no **absence of focal point** because of the attainment of acceptance of nonarising phenomena, **then** in those cases, **it is not love, and where there is no love, there is** no bodhisattva and **no enlightenment**.

If compassion is not unbiased, then it is not great compassion. Rather, such a compassion is like that of ordinary beings, listeners, and self-realized buddhas. That is to say, if one has compassion for those sentient beings who experience the suffering of suffering in its manifest form, yet has none for those who experience pleasurable or neutral sensations, then one's compassion is not unbiased and is therefore not great compassion. The bodhisattvas recognize that no defiled experience, whether it is enjoyable, painful, or neutral, is beyond the framework of the three sufferings. Therefore, while they have compassion for those beings who suffer in the Hell of Incessant Pain, the bodhisattvas have, to the very same extent, compassion for all other sentient beings, up to and including those who are at the summit of existence. Hence, this is referred to as "great compassion."

Ordinary beings have compassion sometimes, but at other times not. Listeners and self-realized buddhas, on the other hand, do have compassion; yet, when nothing remains of their aggregates, their compassion is also extinguished and comes to an end. Since such compassion is not constant, it is not "great compassion." On the path, the compassion of the bodhisattvas emerges without interruption and knows no end, even within the field of the transcendence of suffering, wherein nothing remains of the aggregates. Their compassion is therefore eternal, great compassion.

There is also a compassion that lacks the superior intent, whereby one takes upon oneself the burden of benefiting everyone. This is the case when worldly beings feel compassion for their friends and others whom they think of as "mine," in a way that is mixed up with their own personal objectives. It is also the case if compassion goes out only to those from whom one benefits personally. Finally, the compassion of the listeners and self-realized buddhas is also of this kind because since they lack the realization of the sameness of self and others, they have no intention of carrying the burden of benefiting others. In all of these cases, the compassion is not what is known as "great compassion." However, once the bodhisattvas have achieved the first ground, they have directly realized the intrinsic nature within which self and other are equal. This has repercussions for their intent, and so they will no longer see any difference between benefiting self and benefiting others. Possessing this superior intent that accepts the burden of benefiting others, their compassion is "great compassion."

If when seeing suffering sentient beings, there is compassion in the mere sense of a loving affection, without any actual means for protecting others from suffering, then that is not great compassion. This is the case with the listeners and self-realized buddhas, who have simple compassion for all sentient beings, yet are not active in a way that actually protects them. The compassion of the bodhisattvas is great, however, for they bring benefit and happiness to sentient beings for as long as cyclic existence remains.

Although sentient beings have compassion for those whom they feel close to, it is not always so because at times they also become angry with them. They also have anger toward their enemies, and in these ways their love is not free from affliction. As for noble listeners and self-realized buddhas, although they do not possess any manifest anger, they still have not eliminated the subtle imprints of anger. Hence, the compassion of such beings is not what is known as "great compassion." The bodhisattvas, however, overcome the desire that is associated with the imprints of anger and hostility—the factors that conflict with compassion. Theirs is great compassion.

Compassion that is not free from the fixation of the marks of the three spheres is not great compassion, either. Once endowed with nonconceptual wakefulness, however, it is what is known as "great compassion." (This point is taught as relevant to the eighth ground and above, where nonconceptual wakefulness has fully matured, although there is nothing wrong with understanding it to apply to noble bodhisattvas in general.) The perfection of this great compassion of the bodhisattvas is the great compassion of the buddhas, the spontaneously present great compassion free from focal points that is present at the ground of buddhahood.

Thus, that which is not equal, eternal, and the rest of the six qualities is not great love, and not great compassion. On the contrary, great compassion is that which does display these six distinctive qualities. Hence, whoever lacks such great love is, accordingly, not a "bodhisattva of great compassion."

2. The Illustrating Examples

Compassion, patience, attention,
Aspirations, births, and the maturation of sentient beings—
From the initial root to the final, supreme fruition,
This is the great tree of compassion. [XVIII.36]

If there were no root of compassion,
There would not be the patient acceptance of difficult tasks.
If the wise were not to accept suffering,
They would not be attentive for the benefit of beings.
[XVIII.37]

A mind that lacks attention
Will not make aspirations
For virtuous and pure rebirths.
Without the attainment of excellent births,
There can be no maturation of sentient beings. [XVIII.38]

Love is that which waters compassion;
Through happiness while suffering, the tree grows;
By correctly directing the mind
The branches will expand; [XVIII.39]

The continuous stream of aspirations
Will make the leaves change and renew themselves;
And the accomplishment of the two conditions
Will bring the flowers and the meaningful fruition. [XVIII.40]

Next it is shown how **compassion** resembles a tree. Compassion is the root and **patience** the trunk. The branches are **attention** for the sake of benefiting others. The leaves are the **aspirations** toward taking excellent rebirths. The flowers are those **births, and** the fruits are **the maturation of sentient beings**. From the initial root to the final, supreme fruition: this is the great tree of compassion.

If there were no root of compassion, there would not be any patient acceptance of difficult tasks for the benefit of others. If the wise were not to accept suffering, they would not be attentive for the benefit of beings. A mind that lacks attention for the welfare of others **will not make aspirations for virtuous and pure rebirths**. Without the attainment of excellent births, there can be no maturation of sentient beings.

It should be understood that **love is that which waters compassion**. Likewise, **through** the **happiness** that is attained **while** one is **suffering** for the sake of others, **the tree grows** to develop the wide trunk of patience. **By correctly directing the mind** in accordance with the Great Vehicle, **the branches** of attention to the benefit of others **will expand**. Similarly, when **the** end of one aspiration leads to the beginning of another, this **continuous stream of aspirations makes the leaves change and renew themselves, and the accomplishment of the two conditions** (that is, the inner condition that is the ripening of one's own stream of being and the outer condition that is the ripening of those of others) **brings the flowers** of meaningful births **and the meaningful fruition** of fully matured sentient beings.

A fine, great tree has (1) a root, (2) a trunk, (3) branches, (4) leaves, (5) flowers, and (6) fruit. These six can be used to illustrate great compassion. Respectively, they represent (1) the great compassion that wishes to protect all sentient beings from suffering; (2) the ensuing patience in carrying out difficult tasks for the benefit of others; (3) the attention that is directed toward the various skillful means for accomplishing the welfare of sentient beings; (4) the aspiration to be reborn, in all one's lives, into a context where one's body, enjoyments, company, and environment will be of benefit to sentient beings; (5) the ensuing numerous lives that are all lived in ways that bring benefit to oneself and others; and (6) the thorough maturation of sentient beings that is the result of living such lives.

The great compassion that is the first of these six is like a root for the remaining five. As the root of all bodhisattva qualities, it precedes them all. The *Sūtra Taught by Akṣayamati* explains:

Venerable Śāriputra, this is how it is. Just as the faculty of the life force precedes one's exhaling and inhaling, the bodhisattva's great compassion precedes the authentic practice of the Great Vehicle.

And from the noble *Sūtra of Gaya Mountain:*

Compassion is the root of the enlightened mind; sentient beings are its focal point.

The final maturation of sentient beings is exemplified by the ripening of the most excellent fruits. Hence, this is the great tree of compassion. From the root of great compassion grows forth the trunk of patient endurance of numerous sufferings for the benefit of sentient beings. From the trunk of patience grow the branches of attention to the means for freeing sentient beings from suffering. The branches of attention to skillful means, in turn, produce the leaves of aspiration. Since one life alone would be insufficient to provide for the limitless number of sentient beings, one prays to take innumerable births. From the leaves of aspiration appear the flowers of willful births for the benefit of sentient beings, and from those flowers emerge the fruits, the full maturation of sentient beings. Thus, great compassion is praised through comparison with a magnificent tree.

Next, this example receives an expanded explanation, beginning with an account of the way in which all the other qualities depend on the root. If there were no root, none of the other parts of the tree, from its trunk to its fruits, could come about either. Likewise, were it not for the root of great compassion, it would be impossible to bear, or gladly accept, hardship for the benefit of sentient beings. That can be seen from the fact that unless it is of benefit to their relatives, or to others for whom they care, worldly beings will not accept difficult tasks for the sake of others. Likewise, listeners or self-realized buddhas do not struggle for the sake of others. The bodhisattvas, on the other hand, are compelled by great compassion to accept hardship for the sake of sentient beings without ever forsaking them.

Now, if the wise were not to accept suffering for the sake of others, they would not have any reason to be attentive with respect to the different means for benefiting sentient beings. Without such acceptance, they would not be capable of applying such means, even if they did possess them, and they would hence not have any reason to be attentive to such means either. Someone who lacks attention with regard to the welfare of others will, moreover, not make aspirations to take birth in ways that are beneficial to sentient beings and unblemished by negative deeds. Such a person will not be able to bring forth pure aspirations free from the influence of selfish mental activity. The aspirations that bodhisattvas make, on the other hand, are aimed at benefiting sentient beings, and it is through such aspirations that they take birth within cyclic existence. This, for example, is unlike the way in which mundane beings may engage in virtue with the wish to experience the pleasures of the higher realms. It is also different from the listeners' and self-realized buddhas' relinquishment of birth within cyclic existence.

Thus, by the power of their aspiration, the bodhisattvas take birth here in existence. Yet when doing so, if they were not to achieve rebirths that are excellent in terms of being able to benefit sentient beings, then the bodhisattvas would fail to bring sentient beings to maturation. Either they would be unable to do so because of being born the way worldly beings are, namely, as the result of the ripening of karmic actions, or otherwise they would fail to benefit beings in the same way as listeners and self-realized buddhas fail, whose succession of lives come to an end. Therefore, without the root of great compassion, none of the other five factors, from the trunk of patience to the fruits of the maturation of sentient beings, could possibly manifest.

The next verses explain the way everything else grows forth from the root. A tree's root strengthens and grows when it is moistened by water, allowing everything from trunk to fruit to manifest. Likewise, love is that which waters compassion, or as Sthiramati's commentary says, "love is the irrigating water, the water that saturates compassion." Some commentaries here take "that which waters" to be a reference to the fine strings of root with which a tree extracts moisture from the soil, as in the saying "the tree's growing is due to its feet drinking." In other words, "that which waters" is seen to imply, as it were, the root of the root, and such a reading may indeed be warranted. Yet in that case what we are talking about is nothing other than the root itself, and the verses of the present context are an account strictly of compassion. Love and compassion are, by the nature of things, mutually inclusive, such that once one is present, the other will be too. Hence, let us not think that compassion itself is not really the root but that the actual root is love. Rather, let us see love as the contributing factor that makes the root of compassion grow, that it is "the irrigating water, the water that saturates compassion," as the commentary explains. Considering that certain root texts read, "Love is the cause of compassion," and taking into account the explanation of the commentary, this latter reading seems to be the better one. Hence "that which waters" appears to allude to images of fine roots soaking up water, a root that extracts water, or a root that is being watered and saturated.

Therefore, love is that which waters compassion because it is what makes it grow. The loving mind is like water to the root of compassion, for it saturates and expands it. While with compassion one perceives suffering sentient beings and wishes to free them from pain, love will, in turn, make one see them as the most beloved and endearing children, and so one will want to do something to benefit them and make them happy. If a child is sick, its parents will strive to see the child cured and happy. Whatever hardship they may encounter in that process, they will not think of this as suffering. Rather, once they know that a certain method, such as reliance on a particular medicine, is helpful to their child, they will pursue that method with a great sense of joy. Similarly, while the bodhisattvas, those who love sentient beings, work for the benefit of others, they may experience suffering in both the body and mind, yet their loving wish to benefit others will prevent them from seeing such suffering as suffering. Rather, acknowledging that it is for the benefit of others, they will see such suffering as the most excellent pursuit, and so consider it happiness. There is, therefore, nothing they cannot bear, and so the trunk of patience grows wide and tall.

From the wide, tall trunk of patience grow the branches of attention to the means for benefiting others. As one correctly brings to mind an infinite number of skillful means—the twofold absence of self, the superknowledges, the principles such as form that are included within the two truths, and so forth—an abundance of great branches of attention to the benefit of others grow forth. On this basis, a continuous stream of great aspirations always to bring benefit and happiness to sentient beings emerges over countless lives. The leaves of aspiration are small to begin with, yet as the tree sheds them and produces new ones, the foliage becomes greater and more excellent with each change and renewal. In this way, the two conditions that bring, respectively, the flowers of one's own lives and the fruits of the maturation of others will be accomplished by aspiration. Thus, the flowers of one's own lives come to blossom in a way that allows each of them to serve as the support for the fruition, the maturation of innumerable sentient beings.

A tree grows to produce flowers and fruit due to its own perpetuating causal forces combined with certain cooperating conditions, such as earth and water. When the bodhisattvas take birth and mature sentient beings, it is, similarly, due to their own aspirations, along with the presence of sentient beings—the objects of their aspirations.

6. A Praise of the Qualities of Compassion

This section is divided in terms of (1) a general, threefold presentation and (2) a specific account of the challenges of realization.

1. Threefold General Presentation

First it is explained how compassion produces great qualities.

1. The Great Qualities of Compassion

> As great compassion is the source of good qualities,
> Who would not be compassionate to sentient beings?
> They may suffer, but since it is due to love,
> The bliss they experience is immeasurable. [XVIII.41]

Accounting for the qualities of compassion, it is said: **As great compassion is the source of all good qualities, who would not** take up the training in being **compassionate to sentient beings?** As for the children of the victorious ones, **they may suffer** for the sake of others, **but, since it is due to love, the bliss they experience** because of that suffering **is immeasurable**.

Compassion is the source of all the infinite number of excellent qualities, such as the ten powers and four fearlessnesses. So, who would not give rise to compassion for sentient beings? Indeed, it is reasonable to do so. One might think, "Compassion for sentient beings makes one suffer for their sake, and that is hard to bear." Yet that is not so. One may come to suffer for the sake of others, but since the suffering of a bodhisattva is due to compassion, it is unlike any other kind of suffering. It has been brought forth by love and is, in other words, a suffering that step by step brings all suffering to an end. Indeed, this is the source of a bliss unparalleled by, and superior to, the whole world, and to the listeners and the self-realized buddhas.

2. The Qualities of Nonattachment

The minds of the loving ones possessed of compassion
Are not even attracted to peace;
It is needless, then, to mention that they do not
Become attached to worldly pleasures or their own lives.
[XVIII.42]

On the absence of attachment, it is said that **the minds of loving ones**, the children of the victorious ones, who are **possessed of compassion are not even attracted to** the **peace** of the transcendence of suffering. **It is needless, then, to mention that they do not become attached to**, or dwell on, **worldly pleasures or their own lives**.

One might wonder whether one would not become bound by strong grasping, due to attachment to sentient beings, when giving rise to compassion. Yet that is not the case. The minds of the loving ones, the bodhisattvas possessed of compassion, are not even attached to the listeners' and self-realized buddhas' transcendence of suffering. Since they do not even dwell on that, there is no need to mention that they do not become attached to mundane defiled happiness or to their own bodies and life force, as mundane beings do. Therefore, they do not have attachment toward anything within cyclic existence or the transcendence of suffering.

3. The Special Qualities

There is no love that is free from evil
And beyond the world.
The affectionate love of the wise is free from evil
And beyond the world. [xviii.43]

The world is based on the turbulent waves of suffering
And the great darkness of unknowing.
How could that which is the means for guiding the world
Possibly not be free from evil? [xviii.44]

Not even those destroyers of the enemy, who on their own
    attain enlightenment,
Possess this love for the world;
It is needless, then, to mention the case of others.
How could this not be beyond the world? [xviii.45]

On the special quality of love embraced by compassion, it is said that **there is no love** from parents and so forth **that is free from evil and beyond the world**, for in the case of mundane beings, compassion is not free from evil and it is of the world. On the other hand, **the affectionate love of the wise is** indeed **free from evil and it is beyond the world. The world is based on the turbulent waves of suffering and the great darkness of unknowing.** Now, **how could that which is the means for guiding the world** onto the path of enlightenment **possibly not be free from evil?** In the world, **not even those destroyers of the enemy, who on their own attain enlightenment, possess this love. It is needless, then, to mention the case of others.** That is to say, it is certain that listeners and mundane beings do not possess it either. **How could this** love then **not be beyond the world?**

In the world, a mother, for example, may love her child. Yet there is no love in the world that is free from evil and beyond the world. On the contrary, attached to their children and the like, worldly people will engage in negative acts for their sake. Similarly, as they become angry with those who are against their loved ones, the love of worldly people is mixed with afflictions. It is, hence, never completely free from evil. Likewise, since it involves the bewilderment of apprehending selves in the form of persons and phenomena, their love is not beyond the world. The love of the wise bodhisattvas, however, arises out of affection for sentient beings, and it is therefore both free from evil and beyond the world.

How is the bodhisattva's love free from negativity? Well, in the great river of cyclic existence, beings of the world are cast about by the turbulent waves of the resultant triple suffering; and such beings are supported by the causal great darkness of unknowing with respect to the noble truths. How could the bodhisattva's compassion and love, which are the means whereby the beings of the world are guided into liberation, possibly *not* be free from evil? Indeed, among all that is free from evil, their compassion and love are supreme.

How, then, is the bodhisattva's love beyond the world? In the world, self-realized buddhas with sharp faculties manage on their own to actualize and perfect the wakefulness that knows exhaustion and nonarising. Yet even such destroyers of the enemy do not possess this love of the bodhisattvas. There is no need, then, to mention the case of others, such as listeners and mundane beings. How could this love of the bodhisattvas not then be beyond the world? Since it lies even beyond the transcendent listeners and self-realized buddhas, there is no need to say that it is beyond the world.

2. The Challenges of Realization

Next follows an extensive explanation of the statement that "suffering for the sake of others brings bliss."

1. Elaborate Explanation

A bodhisattva free from suffering
Experiences suffering because of love;
First there is fear, but upon contact
There follows utterly intense joy. [XVIII.46]

Suffering due to love
Outshines all the world's happiness,
And not even those who have accomplished their objective
    possess it.
What could be more wondrous than this? [XVIII.47]

When the steadfast ones give with love,
They experience a joy of giving
Of which the happiness of those experiencing the three realms
Cannot match even a fraction. [XVIII.48]

For the benefit of sentient beings, they will not give up
That cyclic existence, which by nature is suffering.
Why then should the compassionate ones not,
For the sake of others, accept suffering? [XVIII.49]

The loving ones' compassionate
Generosity and resourcefulness
Cause the happiness of affection, successful care,
And capability to constantly increase. [XVIII.50]

"Expand, increase,
Fully ripen with compassion and enjoy;
Carry forth and lead!"
Thus, as it were, compassion instructs the weak. [XVIII.51]

Those who, due to compassion, are brought to suffer because
    of suffering,

How could anything but the arising of happiness make them
   happy?
Thus the loving ones create their own happiness
By giving happiness to others. [XVIII.52]

The compassionate always act
Like a teacher to their own generosity:
"My own happiness is unimportant, let enjoyments be
   enjoyed by others.
Otherwise, since there is no difference, I will not be happy
   either." [XVIII.53]

"Their happiness makes me happy.
My gifts, including their effects, are to be given away to
   sentient beings.
If you have something to do for me, then see to it that they
Experience the most tremendous effect." [XVIII.54]

"The giver does not wish for enjoyments
And yet encounters plentiful and excellent enjoyments.
I do not wish for happiness,
But will in this way let my generosity be continuous."
   [XVIII.55]

"See how, because of constant love, I give away
Whatever is in my possession.
Realize, then, that for me
The effects of this are of no concern."[XVIII.56]

"If I were not to give away the effect that is attained as your
   result,
I would not be truly delighting in generosity.
If generosity is absent for even an instant,
There is no true delight in generosity." [XVIII.57]

"You do not give your fruits to those who do nothing,
And since therefore you look for reward, you are inappropriate for me.
I have no concern for your rewards
And completely give away your fruits to others." [XVIII.58]

On fear and joy, the following is explained: **A bodhisattva**, wishing for all sentient beings to be **free from suffering, experiences suffering** in his or her own stream of being **because of love**. First, meaning on the grounds of inspired conduct, **there is fear,** which is due to not yet having realized the sameness of self and others and not yet having encountered the intrinsic nature of suffering. **But upon contact,** on the grounds of superior pure intent, **there follows utterly intense joy.** On the way that suffering through love outshines happiness, it is explained that the bodhisattvas' **suffering due to love outshines all the world's happiness,** and, since **not even those** noble destroyers of the enemy, **who have accomplished their** own **objective** while abiding by pure conduct, **possess it,** what need is there to mention the case of anyone else? Hence, **what could be more wondrous than this?**

On the benefits of giving through compassion, it is said that **when the steadfast ones give with love, they experience a joy of giving of which the happiness of those experiencing** the happiness found within **the three realms cannot match even a fraction.**

On the acceptance of suffering through love, it is said: **For the benefit of sentient beings, they will not give up that cyclic existence, which by nature is suffering. Why then should the compassionate ones not, for the sake of others, accept** their own **suffering?**

The next is an account of the way in which love causes an increase in three qualities, which have three results. In all their lives, **the** bodhisattvas make three qualities increase. They develop affinity with (1) compassion and hence become **loving ones** who engage in **compassionate (2) generosity; and** so, through generosity, they develop (3) **resourcefulness.** These three respectively **cause the** threefold **happiness** (that is, compassion causes the happiness of

affection, generosity allows one to experience the joy of providing **successful care** to sentient beings, **and,** as one provides this based on resourcefulness, there is the happiness associated with **capability) to constantly increase.**

The next stanza concerns taking delight in generosity. "Let compassion, the cause of generosity, **expand;** let minor generosity increase and grow vast; may you **fully ripen** sentient beings **with compassion and** so **enjoy** the happiness of the benefactor; may you **carry forth** the accumulations of great enlightenment **and lead** ahead into great enlightenment!" **Thus, as it were,** the **compassion** of the bodhisattvas **instructs** and inspires **the** ones who are **weak** in their generosity.

On the way that the happiness of others becomes one's own, it is explained: As for **those who, due to** the power of **compassion, are** themselves **brought to suffer because of** the **suffering** of others, **how could anything but the arising of** the **happiness** of others serve as a cause to **make them happy? Thus, the loving ones create their own happiness by giving happiness to others.**

On the way that love instructs generosity, the following is explained: **The compassionate always act like a teacher,** giving instructions **to their own generosity.** Thus they will speak to their generosity, saying, "**My own happiness is unimportant, so let the enjoyments** that result from generosity **be enjoyed by others,** let them be enjoyed by sentient beings. **Otherwise, since there is no difference** between my own happiness and that of others, **I will not be happy either. Their happiness makes me happy; my gifts, including their effects, are to be given away to sentient beings.** Therefore, **if you,** O generosity, **have something to do for me** in terms of a rewarding effect, **then see to it that they,** that is, sentient beings, **experience the most tremendous effect.**

The giver does not wish for enjoyments and yet encounters plentiful and excellent enjoyments. Such is the intrinsic nature of things. Now, **I do not wish for happiness** through enjoyments, **but** since I do wish for uninterrupted generosity, **I will in this way let my generosity be continuous.** I have no other motive. **See how, because of constant love, I give away whatever is in my**

possession. Realize, then, O generosity, **that for me** the enjoyments that are **the effects of this** giving **are of no concern.**

If I were not to give away to sentient beings **the effect that is attained as your result,** that is, as the result of generosity, **I would not be** a bodhisattva **truly delighting in generosity.** Because, if the mind-set that is intent on **generosity is absent for even an instant, there is no true delight in generosity. You, O generosity, do not give your fruits to those who do nothing** in terms of generosity, **and since, therefore**—that is, since you only give to those who engage in generosity and not to others—**it appears that you look for a reward,** in that way **you are inappropriate for me. I have no concern for your rewards and** so **completely give away your fruits** as well—that is, the fruits of generosity—**to others.**

When bodhisattvas are themselves temporarily free from suffering, love makes them experience mental suffering for the sake of others. Or, to go by the account of the commentary, bodhisattvas will themselves experience mental suffering for the sake of others, out of love, so that they may free others from suffering. Yet none of this is intimidating to a bodhisattva. People who lack courage will feel terrified when thinking, in detail, about the sufferings of sentient beings. In fact, they can hardly do so. They will think, "Just as sentient beings are infinite, their suffering is infinite too. Who could possibly dispel that suffering?" They will think of the practices of giving away one's head and limbs, and as they then imagine the ingratitude and perverse reactions of sentient beings, they will find it unbearable. Likewise, they will think of birth, old age, sickness, and death, and of all the different pains that will have to be experienced when thus taking birth in cyclic existence. When they think of the great numbers of suffering sentient beings, and of then having to take on those sufferings themselves, they will feel that there could not possibly ever be a time when they themselves would be liberated from suffering. Yet there is no reason for such dejection. Those who suffer out of love for sentient beings may initially, on the grounds of inspired conduct, feel a sense of fear because such beings have not yet achieved the mind of equality in terms of self and other, and they have yet to realize the emptiness of cyclic existence and its sufferings. Therefore, the sūtras also explain that, to begin with, those who possess the bodhisattva potential should not be taught exclusively, or primarily, about life and suffering within cyclic existence. Rather, they should learn about compassion and illusion-like phenomena, and one should teach them by praising the qualities of the buddhas and bodhisattvas. Yet "upon contact," as the root text says, with the first ground of the noble ones, they will realize the omnipresent character of the basic field of phenomena, and so they attain the mind of equality toward self and other. Out of love, they will then gladly accept even the actual suffering of hell in order to protect others from suffering. Yet, because it is to the benefit of others, their acceptance of suffering turns out to be nothing but the cause of great bliss.

Such a bliss as theirs is not the possession of any god or human of the world. Nor is it known by any listener or self-realized buddha. As it is the supreme and most excellent bliss, the suffering that is engendered by love outshines all the world's happiness. Such bliss is not even known to the listeners and self-realized buddhas who have accomplished their own benefit. What greater wonder could there possibly be than this?

Once the grounds have been attained, there is thus no longer any fear of suffering. On the grounds of inspired conduct, on the other hand, the bodhisattvas contemplate the full nature of cyclic existence, knowing it to be great suffering. In this context of being both a bodhisattva and an ordinary being, the power of the potential and the force of factors such as aspiration will make one consider issues such as the beginning and end of cyclic existence to be inconceivable, yet without thereby arriving at the realization of mind. Thus, one will be thinking of the way one and other sentient beings—since time without beginning and until now—have been exposed to so many forms of suffering. Although there has been happiness at times, such happiness makes no difference whatsoever in the present moment, and the future, moreover, is endless. The realms of sentient beings are endless as well, and the manifestations of new buddhas and bodhisattvas likewise. Thus, the confines of time, space, sentient beings, and suffering are all inconceivable. Nevertheless, understanding that these are also all similar to an illusion, one commits oneself to learning from all the buddhas and bodhisattvas, and so pledges to enter vast bodhisattva activity, throughout time and space, within all of the realms of sentient beings. Having brought forth this armor-like mind, one prays to the buddhas and bodhisattvas for success and dedicates all fundamental virtues to this objective. Thus one becomes irreversible on the path of the Great Vehicle, and will soon be confirmed within fearlessness.

Steadfast bodhisattvas give with love; they give purely to benefit others and have no hope for rewards or karmic ripening. Thus, they do not hold on to things as their own, and instead give them away to others. Whenever an act of giving for the benefit of others is completed, there ensues a joy that far surpasses that of experiencing the pleasures of the three realms. All such pleasures cannot compare to even a fraction of the bliss of giving as it arises in the exalted mind stream of a bodhisattva. It may thus seem that the bodhisattvas suffer for the benefit of others. Yet not only are their mind streams free from suffering; when giving away their bodies and enjoyments, they experience a joy to which no amount of happiness in the world can compare.

Out of love, and for the benefit of sentient beings, the bodhisattvas do not relinquish cyclic existence, although it is of the very nature of suffering. Why, then, should the compassionate ones not, for the sake of other sentient beings, happily accept the suffering of others and take it upon themselves? Indeed, they gladly take on all the suffering of others.

The next verses read, "The loving ones' compassionate generosity and resourcefulness cause the happiness of affection, successful care, and capability to constantly increase." Here it is explained how compassionate giving brings an increase in three causal factors: compassion, generosity, and resourcefulness. Thus, when one practices generosity, the power of compassion will cause a continuous increase in one's compassion, generosity, and enjoyments throughout all one's lives. This, in turn, will lead to a threefold resultant happiness.

First, when compassionately intent on ridding sentient beings of their suffering, and subsequently being generous with a commitment to establish them in happiness, bodhisattvas experience a distinctive happiness that is born from their affection. It is as when a mother provides her child with food and wealth: her affectionate love will make her likewise feel happy.

Second, generosity causes a joy to arise that comes from being able to provide sentient beings with care. Thus, when a bodhisattva sees that his or her generosity is indeed beneficial to sentient beings, an extraordinary happiness is born in the noble mind stream of that bodhisattva. The strength of this happiness makes the bodhisattva ready to relinquish enjoyments and possessions without any sense of loss.

Third, when they have the power thus to benefit sentient beings, this capability will make their happiness grow. If one is deprived of resources, one may have the wish to be generous and yet be unable to fulfill the hopes of those in need. Therefore, when they notice that they are capable of giving the needy what they wish for, bodhisattvas experience the rise of a special joy.

In this way, the joy and happiness of the bodhisattvas increase proportionally with the extent to which they benefit others. Therefore, clearing away the suffering of others and accepting suffering for oneself become, for the bodhisattvas, sources of personal happiness. Even giving away their own body and enjoyments is, for them, not painful because it is felt as happiness.

When a bodhisattva in this way practices generosity, it is as if his or her compassion is giving instructions to someone who lacks familiarity with generosity, and who is therefore weak in terms of its practice. It is as if a lazy person were being admonished by a great friend: "Don't be lazy . . . act like this!" Thus, in the context of the practice of generosity, the bodhisattva's compassion calls: "Let compassionate giving take many forms! May it expand and grow vast! Let your resources, which come about through the ripening of generosity, increase as well! May sentient beings thoroughly mature through your generosity! Give the happiness of full satisfaction to those in need, and so enjoy the happiness of perfect generosity! In this way, give happiness to yourself and all others! Let others carry forth the accumulation of merit and wakefulness! Step by step, lead everyone to the stage of unsurpassable enlightenment!"

Envious beings feel upset when they see others happy, and they like it when others are unhappy. The case of the bodhisattvas is just the opposite because the suffering of others becomes their own pain. When they are unable to dispel the suffering of others, how could anything else possibly make them happy? Their attitude is just like that of a mother whose beloved child has been struck by an illness. In this way, the loving ones work actively to bring happiness to others, and the happiness that they thereby succeed in creating for others is precisely what makes them happy. When a mother searches for a medicine, applies it, and sees that her child is cured, the happiness of the recovered child is precisely what makes the mother happy herself. Similarly, the bodhisattva Vimalakīrti declared: "Until all sentient beings have been healed of their diseases, I will not be cured either."

Next there follows an elaboration on the teaching of nonattachment that was given above. The compassionate bodhisattvas always act as teachers to their own generosity, telling it what to do, and how to do it. Thus they tell their generosity that whatever things they possess are of no interest to them and that therefore their own wealth and enjoyments should be given away for the sake of others' happiness. (The commentary here explains that compassion, as the teacher, instructs the disciple, which is generosity, and—since this is not much different, and yet a simpler way to understand the verses than the previous way of reading them—it would seem that the latter interpretation is permissible as well.)

One may give away one's possessions and so make others happy with them, yet all the while being generous because of a wish to achieve the results of generosity for oneself. That is not the way of a bodhisattva. Bodhisattvas do not consider their own benefit as being any different from the benefit of others. The suffering of others therefore becomes their own, and when others are happy, that will make them happy as well. Hence, they also make the prayer that any wealth that they may obtain as the result of being generous may come to ripen as enjoyments for others, and with this prayer they give their possessions to others. Bodhisattvas feel that if the results of their generosity cannot ripen as other's enjoyments, they would rather not receive any results of generosity themselves either. This is because what benefits them is none other than what benefits others. Bodhisattvas give up self-cherishing as if it were poison and instead let affection for others grow stronger and stronger. Hence they instruct their generosity, saying, "My gifts, including the effects that ensue from giving them, are all to be given to sentient beings. Therefore, O generosity, if you can do something for me, such as providing me with enjoyments, then make sure that all these sentient beings come to experience the most tremendous effect. That would be of great benefit to me." Instructing their generosity in this way through compassion, they give away their gifts along with the karmic results of giving them. The way that they relinquish even the results of their generosity, giving them to others, is heartfelt because bodhisattvas who have no attachment to their own welfare are not interested in acquiring wealth. That they nevertheless will encounter an abundance of wealth and excellent possessions is due to the intrinsic nature of the emergence of cause and effect in dependent origination.

Bodhisattvas thus make it clear that they have no wish for the kind of happiness that ensues from defiling enjoyments. "All that I wish for," the bodhisattva declares, "is to be able to continue to provide for sentient beings throughout all my lives. See how with love I do not use my possessions for personal enjoyment but instead give them all entirely to others. That should make it clear to you, O generosity, that I am not interested in any of your results. If you were to offer only the particular things that are given to others, and yet keep for me the resources that ensue as the effects of generosity, I would not be a bodhisattva who, taking true delight in generosity, gives away everything without becoming attached to what I might gain in the future. The reason for this is that if one feels disinclined or uninterested in being generous for even a moment in this life, one will be lacking that true delight in compassionate giving that is aimed at benefiting others. Since, O generosity, you do not give your fruits to those who have not been generous, it appears that you look for a reward. If indeed that is the case, you will not appeal to me. O generosity, if in fact you do not look for reward, then neither should you hold back the effects of your ripening as mine alone, but distribute them entirely among others." Thus, in the form of a speech of compassion delivered to generosity, the text shows how to train one's mind by wholeheartedly giving away one's body, enjoyments, and fundamental virtues without any attachment to personal gain.

2. Summary

Next there follows a praise that summarizes the qualities of compassionate generosity.

Based on love, the generosity of the children of the victorious ones
Is free from evil, of pure basis,
Ushers in happiness, is protective,
Undiscriminating, and unstained. [XVIII.59]

Based on love, the generosity of the children of the victorious ones
Is total, vast, of the best quality, constant,
Joyful, without concern for material things, pure,
And committed to enlightenment and virtue. [XVIII.60]

With a mind satiated by the threefold pleasure,
The loving one experiences the joy of complete relinquishment;
No one who partakes of enjoyments can experience
A delight that is comparable to this. [XVIII.61]

As for the way that giving takes place through love, the following is explained: **Based on love, the generosity of the children of the victorious ones is free from evil** because it takes place without harming others. It is **of pure basis** because they abstain from giving poison, weapons, alcohol, and so forth. It **ushers in happiness** because those who are gathered through generosity are directed toward virtue. It **is protective** since it does not cause harm to those who surround the bodhisattva. It is **undiscriminating**, for without looking for somebody else to give to, the bodhisattva is generous whenever somebody is understood to be in need or destitute, even if that person does not ask for anything; **and** it is **unstained** because it takes place without any hope for a reward or karmic ripening.

Likewise, **based on love, the generosity of the children of the victorious ones is total** because both inner and outer things are given. It is **vast** since things are granted in abundance. It is **of the best quality** because that which is given is excellent. It is **constant** since it occurs again and again. It is **joyful** without any deliberation in terms of whether or not one will be able to give away. It is **with-**

out concern for material things because there is no hope for a reward or for karmic ripening. It is **pure** because what is given away is something useful, **and** it is **committed to** the **enlightenment and virtue** of those who are gathered through it.

On the special joy of giving, it is taught: **With a mind satiated by the threefold pleasure**—the pleasure of giving, the pleasure of providing for others, and the pleasure of gathering the accumulations for enlightenment—**the loving one experiences the joy of complete relinquishment; no one who partakes of enjoyments can experience a delight that is comparable to this.**

There are six features of the way in which the children of the victorious ones practice generosity out of love.

(1) Generosity should be carried out in a way that is free from evil. One might, for example, give away things that one has obtained through robbery; one might go hunting and then subsequently be generous with the meat of the beings that one has killed; or one might give to a beggar while at the same time hurtfully disparaging him and making fun of his hunger. However, practices such as generosity should be undertaken well and correctly, in a way that does not harm others.

(2) The bases for the bodhisattvas' generosity are pure because they do not give away things such as poison or weapons without having investigated the context, and they do not give away any impure things. Instead, having properly examined the context, they give things that are pure and proper.

(3) The bodhisattvas' generosity is beneficial because, as they thereby attract sentient beings, they also establish them in virtuous practices. Hence, for the sentient beings who receive it, the bodhisattvas' generosity ushers in the resultant happiness of the higher realms and liberation in future lives.

(4) Generosity can be harmful to those who surround one, such as family or staff. This is the case if, for example, one gives away all one's things without leaving anything for them. Extreme cases of this type of harm would ensue if one were to give away one's spouse or children, while at the same time knowing that they were not themselves happy about this, or that indeed it would be causing them great pain. Another such

extreme case would be if one were to offer family or staff to flesh-eating demons or other such evil beings. In short, since the generosity of the bodhisattvas is not harmful to those who surround them and depend on them, it is also protective.

(5) Their generosity is likewise undiscriminating because, when a bodhisattva has understood that someone is in need, he or she will, even if not asked to do so, personally provide the relevant being with whatever may be helpful without looking any further. Neither do bodhisattvas discriminate with respect to the field of merit, thinking, "I shall give to these but not to those." Rather, their giving is balanced and impartial.

(6) Finally, since they do not hope for any reward or karmic ripening, their generosity is unstained and unattached.

The above six features are enumerated with reference to the absence of flaws. There next follow nine features, such as totality, which concern the possession of positive qualities. (1) Total generosity implies that there is nothing at all, neither without nor within, that bodhisattvas will not relinquish. (2) The bodhisattvas' generosity is also vast because what is given is neither small in stature nor little in quantity. Instead, bodhisattvas offer numerous and vast gifts. (3) Their generosity is, furthermore, of the best quality because they do not give things that have been damaged, have expired, or cannot be enjoyed. Rather, what they give is excellent and exquisite, possessing the best colors, shapes, and scents. (4) Without occurring only at certain times and not others, their generosity is constant and continuous. (5) It is also joyful because bodhisattvas are free from stinginess and so they readily and without hesitation give to whomsoever is in need. (6) Neither is it concerned with material things because there is no expectation of reward or future ripening. (7) It is pure because, as already explained in the context of the "pure basis," only pure entities are given. (8) It is dedicated to enlightenment because, instead of dedicating their generosity to the attainment of the pleasures of the higher realms or to the listeners' and self-realized buddhas' transcendence of suffering, they dedicate it to the attainment of unsurpassable enlightenment for the benefit of all. Thus their generosity is committed to enlightenment. (9) Finally, it is also dedicated to virtue because—as was explained above when considering the beneficial nature of their generosity—when the generosity of bodhisattvas attracts sentient beings, it causes them to become dedicated to, and established within, virtue.

The next stanza is on the special joy of giving. Here it is explained that the loving bodhisattva's mind is satiated by three pleasures—the pleasure of giving, the pleasure of providing for others, and the pleasure of gathering the accumulations for enlightenment. The happiness of one who obtains and partakes of enjoyments cannot be compared to that of the bodhisattva, who experiences the joy that comes about through the complete relinquishment of all possessions. Moreover, the commentary here understands the phrase "no one who partakes of enjoyments" to refer to those who are the recipients of the bodhisattva's generosity. These recipients, it is then further explained, cannot possibly experience a joy that is comparable to that of their bodhisattva benefactor. We could similarly see the phrase as a reference to those who partake of exquisite enjoyments in the higher realms. Neither can they ever experience a joy that is comparable to that felt by the bodhisattva in giving. Thus the *Gathering of Precious Qualities* also states:

> The one who gives away the four continents, with all their fine ornaments,
> Will experience a joy that is not known by the one who receives them.

7. The Causes of Compassion

> There is love for the stingy, love for those who do wrong,
> Love for the disturbed, love for the careless,
> Compassion for those caught by the objects,
> And compassion for those with misguided ideas. [XVIII.62]

> From pleasure, pain, and their cause
> Comes the bodhisattva's compassion.
> From the cause, spiritual teacher, and nature
> Comes the bodhisattva's compassion. [XVIII.63]

The next explanation concerns the way the transcendences are practiced by means of compassion. **There is love for the stingy and miserly; love for those who do wrong,** meaning those whose discipline is flawed; **love for the** ones **disturbed** by anger; **love for the careless** and lazy; **compassion for those caught** and distracted **by the objects** of their desires; **and compassion for** the extremists, **those with misguided ideas.** As compassion thus arises in them, bodhisattvas practice the transcendences in order to overcome those conflicting factors.

The conditions for compassion are taught next. **From** sensations **of pleasure, pain, and their cause,** which is neither enjoyable nor painful, **comes the bodhisattva's compassion.** These sensations serve as the observed condition because they bring forth the three forms of suffering: the suffering of change, the suffering of suffering, and the suffering of conditioning. **From the cause,** which is the all-ground consciousness containing the seeds of compassion; from the **spiritual teacher,** who explains the Great Vehicle; **and** from the **nature** of the previous consciousness, which has ceased, and from which the subsequent consciousness emerges—from these three, which respectively are the causal, ruling, and immediately preceding condition, **comes the bodhisattva's compassion.**

Compassion extends to sentient beings who lack the practice of the transcendences. The bodhisattvas have love for those whose mind streams are seized by stinginess and avarice, and who are thus unable to part with the smallest thing. Explaining to them about the problems of miserliness and the fine qualities of generosity, the bodhisattvas will establish such beings in the Dharma of giving. Certain sentient beings are of such a negative disposition that they quite naturally do wrong and evil, taking the lives of others, and so forth. With love for such beings, the bodhisattvas teach them the Dharma of discipline and consequently establish them in it. Likewise, with love for those beings whose minds are disturbed by anger, the bodhisattvas will teach them about the flaws of anger and the virtues of patience, and so establish those beings in patience. Some beings are fond of ordinary activities and are therefore prevented by laziness from practicing virtue. With love, the bodhisattvas will teach such beings the Dharma of diligence that overcomes laziness, and so establish them in diligence. To those who are caught up in the objects of the five pleasures and so are constantly distracted, the bodhisattvas will compassionately teach the Dharma of concentration and establish them within it. Finally, to those suffering from the misguided beliefs that the defiling aggregates entail permanence, self, purity, or bliss, the bodhisattvas will compassionately teach the flaws of such misguided intelligence and instead establish them in true insight.

The bodhisattva's compassion arises based on four conditions. First, we will consider the observed condition. All sensations of defiling pleasure within the three realms are pervaded by the suffering of change; all sensations of pain are pervaded by the suffering of suffering; and all neutral sensations are pervaded by the suffering of conditioning. Hence, all sensations are nothing more than the three types of suffering, and the bodhisattvas' compassion arises upon this observation.

The commentary understands the root text's mention of "their cause" as a reference to the latent tendencies of the three sufferings. Since these latent tendencies are karmic imprints, they are of neutral sensation, and until they have been eliminated, pleasure and pain will arise, again and again. Hence these latent tendencies constitute the subtle suffering of conditioning. We may also read "their cause" as referring to the suffering of conditioning in the sense that this suffering serves as the cause of the defiling aggregates that involve sensations of pleasure and pain. However this may be, what is in effect being pointed out here is that the compassion of the bodhisattvas arises based on the observation of sentient beings who are in possession of three types of suffering.

The causal condition of their compassion comprises the habitual tendencies for loving affection that are contained within the all-ground. These tendencies are due to experience with compassion in previous lives. The ruling condition for the arising of compassion is to listen as the sacred Dharma is taught by a spiritual teacher. Finally, whenever one instant of compassionate mind gives way to another, the nature of the previous instant serves as the immediately preceding condition for the subsequent one. This is the way in which the bodhisattva's compassion arises based on the causal as well as the other two conditions.

8. The Distinctive Equality

The next section describes the distinctive equality of the bodhisattva's compassion.

The compassion of the bodhisattva
Should be understood to be equal
Because of its orientation, practice, freedom from desire,
Absence of focal point, and purity. [XVIII.64]

On the greatness of compassion, it is taught: **The compassion of the bodhisattva should be understood to be equal because of its orientation,** as it acknowledges that, regardless of the way the three sensations may be felt, they are all in any case the nature of suffering; because of its wish to free sentient beings from such suffering; because of the ensuing **practice** of the means for protecting them from suffering; because of the **freedom from desire,** which is the result of having eliminated the conflicting factors; because of the **absence of focal point** in terms of the three spheres; **and** because of the **purity** that follows from the attainment of the acceptance of nonarising phenomena upon the eighth ground.

The bodhisattva's compassion is characterized by equality. Worldly beings have compassion for their friends but not for their enemies. They do not feel compassion for someone who is unimportant to them either. Listeners and self-realized buddhas have compassion for suffering beings, but it does not always arise in the same way, and so their compassion is not equal. The compassion of the bodhisattva arises, as was explained above, without perceiving any difference between all sentient beings who are in possession of the three types of suffering, whether they live at the summit of existence or in the hell of incessant pain. In this way, the arising of the great compassion of the bodhisattvas is characterized by equality.

Therefore, since the bodhisattvas' orientation is equal, with universal concern for all sentient beings, so is their compassion. Just as they work to save sentient beings in hell, so equally do they strive to protect those all the way up to the summit of existence. Hence, their practice is also one of equality. Furthermore, their compassion is equal because the bodhisattvas are free from desire, having neither attachment nor aversion with respect to any type of sentient being, and because it is a compassion that does not involve any focal points. Without observing any marks in terms of oneself, sentient beings, or compassion, the bodhisattvas realize the way that everything is of one taste within emptiness. On the eighth ground, their insight—which in this way does not hold any of the focal points of the three spheres—becomes effortless and free from shifting marks. Hence, the equality of their compassion can also be understood with reference to the purity that follows this achievement.

9. On Supreme Compassion

**Supreme love and so forth are cultivated in one's own mind
And are due to inspiration with respect to the Dharma,
Intent, mastery,
Nonconceptuality, and oneness. [XVIII.65]**

Supreme love and so forth, that is, the four immeasurables, **are cultivated in one's own mind and are due to inspiration with respect to the Dharma** that teaches them, to **intent** in terms of relishing the taste and so forth, to the **mastery** of meditative absorption, to being embraced by **nonconceptuality, and** to the **oneness** of the activities of all the great bodhisattvas.

In general, the cultivation of love and the other qualities of the four immeasurables is also found among the gods of the form realm as well as among the listeners and self-realized buddhas. The way that bodhisattvas cultivate the four immeasurables is, nevertheless, supreme. When in their own mind they cultivate love and so forth, the bodhisattvas do so in a way that surpasses all others because their practice is constantly evolving. The habitual tendencies that they created for cultivating love and so forth in past lives enable them to continue the practices in their present and future lives with an ever-increasing excellence. They likewise possess a tremendous inspiration and faith with respect to the sūtras that teach the Dharma of the four immeasurables. They are in possession of the ninefold intent that was explained above. They have mastery of meditative absorption. In particular, from the eighth ground onward, they have gained a mastery of love and the other immeasurables that is effortless and spontaneously accomplished. Moreover, when bodhisattvas train in love and the rest of the four, they embrace their practice with the wakefulness that does not conceive of any marks of a subject involved in training in the immeasurables, or of sentient beings related to in the training, or indeed in any act of training as such. Finally, from the point at which they attain the eighth ground, their activities merge and mingle as one with the deeds of all the bodhisattvas who reside at the same level. Thus, their practice is supreme in these regards as well.

4. Concluding Summary

> Thus, the mind thoroughly brightens toward the blessed ones,
> While worship is perfectly continuous with substances and great veneration;
> The spiritual teacher, possessing numerous qualities and effectively helpful, is followed,
> And with love for wandering beings, there is accomplishment in all regards. [XVIII.66]

> This was the eighteenth chapter of the *Ornament of the Great Vehicle Sūtras*, the chapter on worship, reliance, and the transcendences.

Now follows a summary of the sequence and qualities of the worship, reliance, and immeasurables that were explained above: **Thus, the mind thoroughly brightens toward the blessed ones,** while **worship is perfectly continuous** over a long time **with substances** such as those of the Dharma robes **and** through the authentic practice of **great veneration. The spiritual teacher—possessing numerous qualities,** such as gentleness, **and** being **effectively helpful** with loving care—**is followed, and with love for wandering beings** because of the training in the four immeasurables, **there** is accomplishment of both one's own welfare and that of others **in all regards.**

As explained above, the mind brightens toward the buddhas, the blessed ones, as one develops the trust that their nature is of inconceivable qualities. Thus one brings them material offerings, such as Dharma robes, garments, flowers, and parasols; and one venerates them with prostrations, praises, circumambulations, and so on, as well as through practice in accordance with their instructions. Such worship is, moreover, not just occasional, but continuous, and through it one attains all mundane and supramundane accomplishments for one's own benefit and that of all others.

In terms of the spiritual teacher, one should follow someone who is endowed with the qualities that were discussed above, as well as those explained in the sūtras and other scriptures. It is taught that by following such a teacher one will oneself attain the full abundance of all the teacher's infinite qualities. One will attain all accomplishments by following such a teacher, who is beneficial in this and in all other lifetimes. Likewise, when with loving affection for all wandering beings one acts through immeasurable love, compassion, joy, and equanimity for the benefit of sentient beings, there will be accomplishment in all regards.

The commentary explains that while worship and reliance primarily accomplish one's own welfare, the four immeasurables are first and foremost a means for accomplishing the welfare of others. In general, however, each of the three is a means for accomplishing the welfare of both.

This concludes the explanation of the eighteenth chapter of the *Ornament of the Great Vehicle Sūtras,* the chapter on worship, reliance, and the immeasurables.

19
THE FACTORS THAT ACCORD WITH ENLIGHTENMENT

4. THE FACTORS THAT ACCORD WITH ENLIGHTENMENT

The topic of the present chapter, the factors that accord with enlightenment, is primarily meditation. This topic may be addressed by explaining (1) [the framework for cultivating the factors of enlightenment],[46] (2) the essence of the factors of enlightenment, (3) the factors that distinguish them, [and (4) a summary].[47] The first issue will be explained by accounting for the way one adheres to the discipline to which one has committed, how one receives teachings and contemplates the teachings, and how one gathers the accumulations. Thus, this section will begin by explaining how (1) conscience, (2) steadfastness, and (3) indefatigability ensure that one does not stray from the path. On that basis, it will next be shown how learning is acquired through (4) knowledge of the treatises and (5) knowledge of the world. This, in turn, will lead to the explanation of the way in which one gathers the two accumulations by means of the pure insight that arises through reflection. Such reflection, moreover, takes place by means of (6) the four reliances, (7) the four ways of correct awareness, and (8) the two accumulations.

1. THE FRAMEWORK FOR CULTIVATING THE FACTORS OF ENLIGHTENMENT]
1. CONSCIENCE

The first of the above topics, conscience, will be addressed in terms of the following sections: (1) the characteristics of conscience, (2) its bases,

(3) its types, (4) the flaws that ensue from a lack of conscience, (5) the benefits of conscience, (6) a praise to those who are endowed with conscience, (7) the signs of possessing conscience and embarrassment, and (8) the character of supreme conscience.

1. The Characteristics of Conscience

The conscience of the steadfast ones has abandoned the
 conflicting factor,
Is in possession of nonconceptual wakefulness,
Focuses on the lesser absence of negativity as its object,
And matures sentient beings. [XIX.1]

The next explanation takes the form of an investigation of conscience. In essence, **conscience** is that which **has abandoned the conflicting factor** of the lack of conscience. As its contributing factor, it **is in possession of nonconceptual wakefulness** beyond the three spheres. In terms of its focal point, it **focuses on the** mental state of conscience, which pertains to the **Lesser** Vehicle and is an **absence of negativity, as its object and,** with respect to its function, it **matures sentient beings** by establishing them in its own form of conscience.

Conscience and embarrassment emerge through the relinquishment of their conflicting factors, namely, lack of conscience and lack of embarrassment. Moreover, conscience is related to oneself whereas embarrassment is related to others. Hence, the bodhisattva's conscience expresses itself in the thought: "Abandoning one's training in the Dharma of the Great Vehicle to pursue the conduct of listeners and self-realized buddhas would not be right for me, being a bodhisattva." Embarrassment, on the other hand, is being concerned about disparagement from other bodhisattvas. Such is the nature of conscience and embarrassment. Their contributing factor is nonconceptual wakefulness, and, once embraced by this wakefulness, there is no observation of any of the marks of oneself, others, or the qualities of conscience and embarrassment.

The focal point is entry into the Lesser Vehicle because the prospect of doing so gives rise to shame. Although pursuing the vehicles of listeners and self-realized buddhas does not involve negativities in the form of personal afflictions, it is nevertheless a pursuit of solely one's own benefit. In all matters pertaining to the intent, practice, and fruition, therefore, it is vastly inferior to the way of the Great Vehicle. Hence, as they focus on the Lesser Vehicle, bodhisattvas will conscientiously turn away from its point of entry. The function of the bodhisattvas' conscience and embarrassment is the maturation of sentient beings.

Such conscience and embarrassment is exclusively the possession of the steadfast ones, the bodhisattvas. Listeners and self-realized buddhas are not concerned even for their own friends among sentient beings; they will forsake them to pursue their own private peace and happiness. With this in mind, a tantra teaches:

> Not even attached to their own children—
> Such is the inferior fortune of the listeners.
> Bringing happiness to all sentient beings—
> Such is the excellent fortune of Śrī Vajrapāṇi.

In this way, the listeners and self-realized buddhas possess less than the bodhisattvas in terms of conscience and embarrassment.

2. The Bases of Conscience

> An increase of the factors
> That conflict with the six transcendences
> And a decrease in the remedies
> Cause the bodhisattvas to feel unbearable shame. [XIX.2]

> If the steadfast ones become lazy
> In terms of relying on the six transcendences
> And partake of factors that accord with affliction,
> This also causes them shame. [XIX.3]

An increase of stinginess and the other factors that conflict with the six transcendences, and a decrease in the remedies, that is, the six powerful transcendences, cause the bodhisattvas to feel unbearable shame. If the steadfast ones become lazy in terms of relying on the six transcendences in their stream of being and instead partake of uncontrolled sense doors and other such factors that accord with the arising of affliction, this also causes them shame.

What are the bodhisattvas conscientious about? If they notice that factors such as stinginess, which conflict with generosity and the rest of the six transcendences, are increasing within their mind stream, or if they see that the power of the remedies, that is, generosity and so on, is decreasing, then this is, for the bodhisattvas, a matter of unbearable shame. In the world, people of high and lofty birth may feel shame about engaging in the conduct of base people, yet if a bodhisattva notices that stinginess and so on are developing, while generosity and so forth are diminishing, the sense of shame will be far greater. This is what is known as "conscience with respect to increase and decrease."

"Conscience with respect to engagement and disengagement" relates, on the one hand, to the event of steadfast bodhisattvas falling prey to laziness, and so disengaging from the practice of cultivating the six transcendences in their stream of being. It likewise has to do with the situation of bodhisattvas showing insufficient restraint of their six senses as they encounter phenomena that further the arising of afflictions such as desire and anger. They thence become engaged in the pursuit of attractive objects of the five senses. Such situations are therefore also the basis for the conscience of the bodhisattvas.

3. Types of Conscience

> Not of the nature of equipoise, lesser,
> Mediocre, belonging to inferior grounds,
> Of an inferior mind-set, and involved with ego—
> These forms of conscience are inferior, while others are
>   superior. [XIX.4]

The next section concerns the difference between inferior and superior conscience. When it pertains to the realm of desire, conscience is **not of the nature of equipoise** and is therefore inferior. Of the forms of conscience that *are* of the nature of equipoise, some are **lesser** and others **mediocre**. Some **belong to inferior grounds**, that is, they pertain to levels that are inferior from the perspective of subsequent levels. Moreover, the conscience of the listeners and self-realized buddhas is **of an inferior mind-set, and** conscience is **involved with ego** as long as the acceptance of nonarising phenomena has not yet been achieved. All **such forms of conscience are inferior, while others**, that is, the opposite cases, **are superior.**

Next the qualitative distinctions of the various types of conscience are discussed. Conscience and embarrassment as found among the beings of the desire realm are not of the nature of equipoise and, in this regard, are therefore inferior. As for the conscience and embarrassment that are associated with the composure of the form and formless realms, these are themselves divided in terms of lesser, mediocre, and superior forms. Both the lesser and the mediocre can, however, as a whole be classified as lesser. The conscience and embarrassment that are found on the grounds of inspired conduct, on the first ground, and so on, are each superior when compared with the preceding stages and inferior in comparison with the subsequent ones.

Moreover, the conscience and embarrassment of listeners and self-realized buddhas, who are solely involved in the pursuit of their own welfare, belong to an inferior mind-set. When manifest on the first through the seventh ground, conscience and embarrassment are "involved with ego," in the sense that they involve the arrogance that is associated with the marks of effort. In this regard, these forms of conscience and embarrassment are to be classified as "inferior" or "lesser."

The superior, greater forms of conscience and embarrassment include, on the other hand, the qualities that belong to the realms of equipoise. Their superiority increases, moreover, from ground to ground. Conscience and embarrassment as found in the Great Vehicle are also superior. The qualities of conscience and embarrassment that are manifest on the eighth and remaining two grounds are free from the grasping at a self and are spontaneously accomplished through nonconceptual wakefulness. Due to their effortless and spontaneous presence, they are classified as great and special.

4. Flaws in the Case of Lack of Conscience and Embarrassment

> The wise who lack embarrassment and are incorrect
> Will take in afflictions, develop anger,
> Have no concern, and be proud,
> Thereby destroying sentient beings as well as discipline. [xix.5]

> They will suffer from remorse
> And receive little respect;
> Hence, by the hosts of faithful nonhumans as well as the Teacher,
> Such people will be ignored. [xix.6]

> Reviled by the children of the victorious ones
> In accord with the Dharma,
> The world will speak poorly of them in this life,
> While in others, they will be born unfree. [xix.7]

> Thus, they will lose what they have and what they have not yet
> Obtained in terms of virtuous qualities.
> Thus dwelling in misery,
> Their minds will be deprived of ease. [xix.8]

On the difference in terms of flaws and good qualities, the following is explained: **The wise who lack embarrassment and are** involved in thoughts that constitute **incorrect** ways of directing the mind **will take in afflictions** themselves, **develop anger** toward others, **have no concern** for sentient beings, **and be proud** without any respect for others. **Thereby** such bodhisattvas will be **destroying sentient beings as well as** their own **discipline. They** will fall from happiness and **suffer from remorse, and,** as others have no faith in them, they will **receive little respect. Hence, by the hosts of faithful nonhumans,** that is, the hosts of gods who are inspired by the teachings, **as well as** by **the Teacher,** who upon examination will determine that this person is not a vessel for the teachings, **such people will be ignored.** Reviled **by the children of the victorious ones,** who act **in accord with the Dharma, the world will speak poorly of them in this life, while in others they will be born** into **unfree** states. **Thus, they will lose what they have and what they have not yet obtained in terms of virtuous qualities.** Negativities will proliferate in both this life and in the worlds that follow after this. **Thus dwelling** constantly **in misery, their minds will be deprived of ease.**

If a wise bodhisattva enters into error due to lack of conscience and embarrassment, then attachment, aggression, and other such afflictions will arise and be uncritically accepted. Due to anger, one will engage in evil acts, such as taking the lives of others. Since one's discipline will deteriorate, one will bring harm upon both oneself and others. With no concern for virtuous and altruistic practices, one will become lazy and careless. Suffering from the flaws of pride, one will destroy discipline within one's own and others' streams of being. This, in turn, will cause one to feel remorse and anguish, and so one's happiness will crumble. Likewise, when others notice that one lacks good qualities, they will grant only little in the way of either respect or wealth. Because of one's lack of conscience and embarrassment, one will not be given any special attention, and instead will be ignored by the hosts of nonhumans who have faith in the teachings and who guard the virtuous, as well as by the Teacher himself. As they note one's misdeeds, one will be reviled by the children of the victorious ones who are in accord with the Dharma. In this life, the people of the world will speak poorly of one, and in future lives, one will be born into the unfree states of the lower realms and so on. Therefore, one will lose both what one had previously obtained in terms of virtuous qualities within one's stream of being, and also what one had yet to obtain. Coming thus to dwell in physical pain and mental discomfort, one will be unable to rest at ease.

5. The Benefits of Conscience and Embarrassment

The children of the victorious ones endowed with conscience
Will not incur any such flaws.
Skillful, they are always born well
Among gods and humans. [XIX.9]

With conscience, the wise swiftly
Complete the accumulations for perfect enlightenment;
The children of the victorious ones will not
Tire as they mature sentient beings. [XIX.10]

Forever free from discordant factors
And in possession of the remedies,
The children of the victorious ones endowed with conscience
Will thus obtain these qualities. [XIX.11]

The children of the victorious ones endowed with conscience will not incur any such flaws. Skillful, they are, as a ripened effect, **always born well among gods and humans. With conscience, the wise will,** as a ruled effect, **swiftly complete the accumulations for perfect enlightenment.** As for the effect of individual effort, **the children of the victorious ones will not tire as they mature sentient beings.** Moreover, as the effect of separation, they will be **forever free from** the **discordant factors** associated with lack of conscience, **and** as the effect of causal accordance, they will always be **in possession of** the **remedies** that are associated with this sense of conscience. **The children of the victorious ones endowed with conscience will thus,** as described above, **obtain these qualities.**

The children of the victorious ones who are endowed with conscience and embarrassment will incur none of the flaws mentioned above. Skilled as they are, they will, as a ripened effect, always take excellent birth among gods and humans, and as a ruled effect, they will quickly complete the accumulations for unsurpassable enlightenment. Children of the victorious ones who are in possession of conscience and embarrassment will, as an effect of individual effort, ripen sentient beings while never growing weary. As for the effect of separation, they will be forever free from the discordant factors, lack of conscience, and lack of embarrassment. Their constant possession of conscience and embarrassment is, in contrast, the effect of causal accordance. The children of the victorious ones who are endowed with conscience will obtain such qualities.

6. Praising Those Who Possess Conscience and Embarrassment

The childish may wear the finest clothing,
Yet without shame they are stained by flaws.
Wearing their sense of shame, the children of the victorious ones
May go uncovered, but they have no staining flaws. [XIX.12]

Children of the victorious ones, who are in possession of shame,
Like the sky, cannot be tarnished by anything.
Within the gathering of children of the victorious ones,
They are beautifully adorned by their sense of shame. [XIX.13]

Conscience makes the bodhisattvas
Care like a mother for those to be trained;
Conscience is also the capable protector
Against all the flaws of cyclic existence. [XIX.14]

The childish may wear the finest and most expensive clothing on their body, yet lacking the mind's sense of shame, they are stained by flaws. Wearing their heart's sense of shame, the children of the victorious ones may physically go naked and uncovered, but since they have no staining flaws, they are delightful to behold. Children of the victorious ones, who are in possession of shame, like the sky, cannot be tarnished by anything that is of a mundane character. Within the gathering of children of the victorious ones, they are beautifully adorned by their sense of shame. Because of their conscience, the bodhisattvas would feel shame if they were to neglect sentient beings. Hence, in this way **conscience makes the bodhisattvas care like a mother for those to be trained**, and, while one remains within cyclic existence, **conscience is also the capable protector**, which guards one's mind against **all the flaws of cyclic existence**.

Childish ordinary beings may bathe and adorn their bodies with clothes made of the finest fabric, beautifully colored, and of excellent design. Yet, since their minds lack conscience and embarrassment, they are nevertheless stained by the flaws of attachment and so on. Those stains will not be erased by clothing. The children of the victorious ones are dressed in conscience and embarrassment; even if they are not covered by any clothing on the outside, they will, by nature, nevertheless be free from stains. This stanza shows how, at the time of resting in the spiritual practice of inner equipoise, conscience and embarrassment serve as remedies for the arising of afflictions.

Bodhisattvas endowed with conscience and embarrassment are just like space, which cannot be stained by clouds, dust, or the like. Hence, when they enter a city, for example, they will naturally be in possession of conscience and embarrassment, and so will not be covered by the stains of the eight mundane concerns. Also, within the gathering of companions who themselves are children of the victorious ones, adhering to a similar view and conduct, the bodhisattvas will be beautifully adorned by their sense of conscience and embarrassment. With harmonious conduct, they are extremely beautiful to behold. Ornaments made of jewels and other precious substances are of no comparison. With their conscience, the bodhisattvas would feel ashamed and embarrassed to neglect sentient beings. They have intense love for those who are to be trained, and so they bring sentient beings to maturation. Like a mother toward her child, they regard all sentient beings with loving affection. Failing to protect them and abandoning them would be a matter of shame.

The bodhisattvas' conscience and embarrassment are like cavalry, war elephants, and infantry—an army in four divisions that protects the realm and the land. They protect against all hostile armies because, within cyclic existence, the bodhisattvas are active for the benefit of beings. Their conscience and embarrassment will successfully protect them from any flaw in the form of attachment and so on. None of the flaws of affliction can affect them.

7. The Signs of Conscience and Embarrassment

Eager acceptance of all,
Complete detachment from all,
Disengagement from all, and engagement with all—
These are the marks of shame in those who possess it. [XIX.15]

In terms of the intent, there is **eager acceptance** of all good qualities and **complete detachment from all** flaws. In terms of practical application, there is **disengagement from all** flaws and **engagement with all** good qualities—these are the marks of shame in those who possess it.

There are four signs of possessing conscience and embarrassment. Two have to do with intent, namely, (1) eager acceptance of all aspects of good qualities, such as generosity and discipline, and (2) complete detachment from all possible flaws, such as lack of conscience, lack of embarrassment, attachment, and aversion. There are also two that are associated with application, namely, (3) disengagement from all flaws and (4) engagement with all good qualities. Wherever any of these four manifest in a person, it is a sign that he or she is in possession of conscience and embarrassment.

8. On Supreme Conscience and Embarrassment

The supreme presence of shame is cultivated in one's own mind,
And is due to inspiration with regard to the Dharma,
Aspiration, mastery,
Nonconceptuality, and oneness. [XIX.16]

The supreme presence of shame is cultivated in one's own mind, and this is due to inspiration with regard to the Dharma of the Great Vehicle, and it is due to **aspiration** (that is, intent in terms of relishing the taste, rejoicing, delighting, being insatiable, vastness, joy, benefiting, being uncovered, and virtue). It is due to **mastery** of the treasury of space and other such meditative absorptions, due to being fully embraced by means of the wakefulness of **nonconceptuality, and** it is due to the **oneness** that ensues when one's own activities merge with those of all the great bodhisattvas.

The supreme cultivation of conscience and embarrassment takes place in one's own mind. That is to say, rather than being intimidated by the thought of the reaction of others, it does not matter to the bodhisattvas whether others should know of any faults they may have because such flaws would be the cause of shame and embarrassment to the bodhisattva himself or herself. This type of conscience and embarrassment is explained in the commentary as supreme.

Moreover, the supreme cultivation of embarrassment displays five features: (1) Inspiration with regard to the Great Vehicle Dharma's teaching on conscience and embarrassment; (2) the manifestation of the ninefold aspiration that was explained above; (3) mastery of meditative absorption or, alternatively, effortless and spontaneously accomplished mastery on the eighth ground and beyond; (4) nonconceptuality with respect to oneself, others, and the phenomena of conscience; and (5) joining within the oneness of the activities that are performed by all the bodhisattvas on the pure grounds. Such is the foremost and supreme cultivation.

2. Steadfastness

The explanation of this topic will include: (1) a brief presentation and (2) an elaborate explanation.

1. Brief Presentation

**The steadfastness of the bodhisattvas
Relates to its characteristics,**

Divisions, and immutability,
Which are superior to those of anyone else. [XIX.17]

The next explanation concerns the investigation of steadfastness. **The steadfastness of the bodhisattvas** relates to its **characteristics, divisions, and immutability, which are superior to those of anyone else** (that is, any self-realized buddha, listener, or ordinary individual).

The courageous steadfastness of the bodhisattva can, by considering its superior characteristics, types, and immutability, be distinguished from that of any worldly being, listener, or self-realized buddha.

2. Elaborate Explanation

Next, each of the distinctive features mentioned above will be explained.

1. Characteristics

Diligence, meditative absorption, and insight
Are held to be courage, fortitude, and steadfastness
Because, with these three, the bodhisattvas
Fearlessly enter into action. [XIX.18]

Faintheartedness, restlessness, and bewilderment
Cause fear of the activities.
Therefore, the threefold naturalness is known
By the name of "steadfastness." [XIX.19]

Diligence, meditative absorption, and insight are held to be courage, fortitude, and steadfastness because, with these three, the bodhisattvas fearlessly enter into action for the welfare of others. How, one may wonder, do they enter into fearless action by means of these three? Well, **faintheartedness,** for one, causes anxiety about the activities since one fails to find delight in them. Secondly, **restlessness** of mind prevents the mind from assuming its natural repose, thereby producing fear, **and,** in the case of **bewilderment,** one will fear the activities because one is unaware of the means for performing them. Hence, these three will **cause fear of the activities, and, therefore, the threefold naturalness** of diligence and the rest **is known by the name of** "steadfastness." Using the word "naturalness" here is meant to show that these qualities do not require deliberation.

Diligence, meditative absorption, and insight are held, respectively, to be undaunted courage, unswerving fortitude, and the steadfastness of incontrovertible knowledge. By means of these three, the bodhisattvas fearlessly pursue the practice of the path, and were it not for these three, they would tremble. Those who lack diligence experience a fainthearted lack of confidence, thinking that they will be unable to practice the conduct of the bodhisattvas. Those lacking meditative absorption experience the anxiety of restless thought, as they are unable to rest the mind single-pointedly. Bewildered and deprived of a precise understanding of enlightened activity, those who lack insight experience fear, being at odds about how to proceed. Such lack of confidence and so forth will prevent them from freely engaging with the objectives of the bodhisattvas. Thus, they will feel dread due to a sense of being incapable. Hence, these three types of fear will be remedied by diligence, meditative absorption, and insight. The latter three constitute a triple naturalness of knowledge and spontaneous presence, which in being indomitable in the face of conflicting factors is also known by the name of "steadfastness." Thus, the characteristic of steadfastness is a supreme stability that in the absence of faintheartedness and so on expresses itself as diligence without any need for deliberation and effort, as well as in the form of natural, nondeliberate, and spontaneously accomplished meditative absorption and insight. It should also be noted that in the basic constitution of the minds of even beginners, there is a natural quality of undauntedness that allows one to enter into action. Depending on the context, that simple quality can also be referred to by terms such as "innate diligence."

2. Divisions

Nature, aspiration,
No concern,
The ingratitude of sentient beings,
Learning the profound and the vast, [XIX.20]

Taming those difficult to tame,
The inconceivable body of the victorious ones,
Numerous hardships,
No relinquishment of cyclic existence, [XIX.21]

And no affliction there—
As steadfastness arises in the steadfast ones,
It has no equal anywhere,
And so among the steadfast, they are held to be supreme.
[XIX.22]

Steadfastness of **nature** relates to the potential, while steadfastness of **aspiration** occurs through the generation of the enlightened mind. For one's own welfare, there is the steadfastness of having **no concern** for one's own body and life, and for the benefit of others, there is steadfastness in terms of bearing **the ingratitude of sentient beings**. The fearless steadfastness that pertains to **learning the profound** is due to the realization of the nature of reality. There will not then be any anxiety concerning the intrinsic nature, which is profound and hard to realize, **and**, as one attains the power of superknowledges and so forth, neither will there be any fear while learning **the vast** methods. Untiring steadfastness in **taming those difficult to tame** relates to the full ripening of sentient beings, and as one devotes oneself to supreme enlightenment, there is the steadfastness of devotion to **the inconceivable body of the victorious ones**. There is also the steadfastness of undertaking **numerous hardships**, the steadfastness of **no relinquishment of cyclic existence** since one purposely takes birth there, **and** the steadfastness of no affliction while one then remains there. As steadfastness thus arises in the steadfast ones, it has no equal anywhere, and so among the steadfast, they are held to be supreme.

The first set of divisions that pertains to steadfastness is eightfold.

(1) Steadfastness of nature refers to the elements of diligence, meditative absorption, and insight that are due to the power of the potential. These allow one to enter the activities of the bodhisattvas without the fears of faintheartedness and so forth.

(2) Steadfastness of aspiration arises through the prayer "As I have given rise to the mind of enlightenment, may I never turn back or away from the activities that bring about the attainment of great enlightenment and the complete liberation of all sentient beings." By the power of this aspiration, one will be unwavering and steadfast, wherever one is born. The aspirations of the bodhisattvas are infinite, emerging through to the ground of buddhahood. Yet, the root of them all is the initial engendering of the enlightened mind. Once one has formed this first aspiration toward enlightenment, all other prayers will emerge based on it in a continuous development, each more steadfast than the one before.

(3) Steadfastness of no concern implies having no concern, regard, or fear for one's own body and life in the pursuit of one's own benefit.

(4) Steadfastness in bearing the ingratitude of sentient beings is the steadfast absence of weariness in the face of ingratitude while pursuing the benefit of others.

(5) Steadfastness of learning the profound is a fearless interest in the nature of profound emptiness, which is primordially beyond arising and ceasing.

(6) Steadfastness of power is an unswerving interest in the practice of the vast qualities of the superknowledges, powers, fearlessnesses, and so on.

(7) Steadfastness of tirelessness refers to the practice of taming beings whose afflictions are extremely rampant, and who therefore can hardly be tamed, over long periods of time and by numerous means, without ever letting them down.

(8) Steadfastness of true enlightenment is the mind's irreversible resolve to attain the inconceivable qualities of the three bodies of the vic-

torious ones—the body of qualities, the enjoyment body, and the emanation body.

Subsequent to this eightfold division, there follows an enumeration of three forms of steadfastness. (1) Steadfastness of undertaking hardship is to practice limitless forms of austerities for the sake of unsurpassable enlightenment. (2) Steadfastness of knowingly taking birth consists of avoiding the relinquishment of cyclic existence and instead, through compassion, fully accepting numerous forms of birth for the benefit of others. (3) Steadfastness of no affliction is to remain in cyclic existence without being stained by its flaws, the afflictions. All these forms of steadfastness that emerge in the streams of being of steadfast bodhisattvas are unlike the steadfastness of worldly beings, listeners, and self-realized buddhas. Among all steadfast ones, the steadfast bodhisattvas are thus held to be supreme.

3. Immutability

> Like a butterfly, the feathered one,
> And the ocean to the king of mountains,
> So the steadfast remain unshakable in the face
> Of negative company, suffering, and hearing the profound.
> [xix.23]

Like a butterfly, like the feathered one, that is, the garuḍa, and like the waves of the ocean to the king of mountains, so the steadfast bodhisattvas remain unshakable in the face of negative company, suffering, and hearing the profound.

The wings of a butterfly, the strong wings of the feathered garuḍa, and the waves of the great ocean cannot shake the king of mountains. These three can be used as examples to illustrate how steadfast bodhisattvas remain unshakable and unperturbed in the face of, respectively, negative company, numerous forms of suffering, and hearing the profound Dharma of emptiness and the absence of self.

3. Indefatigability

The indefatigability of the bodhisattvas has no equal.
It arises in relation to three bases—
Insatiable learning, great diligence, and suffering—
And is based on conscience and steadfastness. [XIX.24]

This strong aspiration toward great enlightenment,
This indefatigability of the wise,
Relates to the grounds that are held to be
Incomplete, complete, and absolutely complete. [XIX.25]

The investigation of indefatigability follows next. **The indefatigability of the bodhisattvas has no equal** anywhere, as can be understood by considering its bases, support, and essence. **It arises in relation to three bases** (because it expresses itself as an **insatiable pursuit of learning,** as a **great diligence** of long-lasting efforts, **and** as indefatigability in the face of the **suffering** of cyclic existence), **and it is based on conscience and steadfastness,** which both serve to dispel fatigue. The essence of **this** indefatigability is a **strong aspiration toward great enlightenment,** as one tirelessly applies oneself to the three bases. As for its divisions, **this indefatigability of the wise relates to the grounds that are held to be incomplete** (that is, the grounds of inspired conduct), **complete** (the first seven grounds), **and absolutely complete** (the final three).

The indefatigability of the bodhisattvas is unparalleled by listeners and self-realized buddhas. It arises in relation to three bases, or entities. (1) Indefatigability with respect to learning or investigating the Dharma consists of an insatiable pursuit of learning from spiritual teachers. (2) Indefatigability of great endeavor involves arousing vast diligence, as if one were to produce fire by rubbing pieces of wood together over a period of three innumerable eons. (3) Indefatigability when facing the painful is to gladly accept numerous forms of suffering for the benefit of sentient beings. These three principles thus present three entities or objects in respect of which there is indefatigability.

The causes, sources, or bases of indefatigability are the qualities of conscience and embarrassment discussed above. The essence or nature of indefatigability is an intense aspiration toward great enlightenment. Such indefatigability of the wise can be divided in terms of the grounds that provide the contexts of the path. Thus, on the grounds of inspired conduct, indefatigability is incomplete because weariness occasionally occurs. One has not yet attained the mind of equality with respect to self and others. On the first seven grounds, however, indefatigability is complete because weariness does not occur at all. Finally, on the three pure grounds, indefatigability is effortless and spontaneously present, and hence absolutely complete. Thus there are held to be three divisions.

4. Knowledge of the Treatises

The steadfast ones' knowledge of treatises
Is superior in terms
Of basis, objective, activity,
Characteristics, inexhaustibility, [XIX.26]

And the authentic accomplishment of the fruition.
Comprising the gates of meditative absorption and retention,
It matures sentient beings
And upholds the sacred Dharma. [XIX.27]

The steadfast ones' knowledge of treatises is superior in terms of its **basis** because it encompasses the five fields, which are the knowledge of (1) the inner meaning, (2) reasoning, (3) linguistics, (4) medicine, and (5) arts and sciences. Its **objective** is also superior, for it involves one's own welfare and that of others. As for **activity**, the first field of knowledge becomes the basis for one's own practice and for the consequent teaching of others. With the second, one comes to comprehend fully any errors there may be with respect to the first, and one will eliminate any attack from opponents. By relating to the third field of knowledge, one will be able to make excellent, definitive statements and elicit faith in others. By means of the fourth, one thoroughly heals the diseases of others, and with the fifth one makes distributions to others. The superior **characteristics** consist of the way in which the five bases are listened to, retained, verbally refined, investigated by the mind, and realized through perception. There is also superiority in terms of the **inexhaustibility** of knowledge, which transcends the cessation within which there is no remainder of the aggregates. Likewise, **the authentic accomplishment of the fruition,** that is, the omniscient knowledge of all phenomena, is superior. **Comprising the gates of meditative absorption and retention, it** thoroughly **matures sentient beings** through meditative absorption **and upholds the sacred Dharma** by means of retention.

The steadfast bodhisattvas' knowledge of the treatises is the comprehension of the five fields of knowledge. This is also known as "knowledge of the corpus." The five fields of knowledge are, as explained above, concerned with (1) the inner meaning; (2) *tarka*, or logic, as a reliable means of cognition—the knowledge of reasoning and argumentation; (3) communication and linguistics, (4) medicine, and (5) arts and sciences. Learning from spiritual teachers who are expert masters of these five fields, the bodhisattvas reflect upon them to gain certainty, and they also offer explanations to others. All objects of knowledge are contained within the five fields, and the bodhisattvas pursue knowledge of everything. Hence, based on the wish to become omniscient, they develop knowledge of the treatises.

Knowledge of the five fields, as such, is also found among worldly beings, listeners, and self-realized buddhas. Yet, keeping in mind the six features of the bases of knowledge and so on, it is clear that the bodhisattvas' comprehension of the treatises is special. These six features are as follows:

(1) In terms of the bases or entities of the knowledge of the treatises, listeners pursue a limited subject within the field of knowledge of the inner meaning, namely, the absence of personal self. They do so for the sake of their own liberation, and without any greater interest in the full field of subject matters that are treated in the scriptural teachings of the Great Vehicle. If there are such differences with respect to the knowledge

of the inner meaning, then this is obviously also the case in terms of the other fields as well.

Bodhisattvas pursue omniscient wakefulness and accomplish the welfare of boundless sentient beings. It is for these reasons that they study all the vast fields of learning and teach them to others. Thus they concern themselves with the three vehicles that pertain to the inner meaning, and they become expert regarding the words and phrases that are the media of expression. With knowledge of the affixes and declensions, the concise and expanded letters, and so forth, they become unimpeded in their expert application of these principles just as they are taught in the treatises on linguistics. Endowed with excellent and definitive words, they convey meaning in a way that is free from all shortcomings. The imparted meaning, moreover, is established in accordance with reliable means of cognition in the form of perception, inference, and scripture. Thus, they refute and establish the positions that either can or cannot be supported by reliable means of cognition, and in this way they bring forth inalienable certainty about meanings and facts. In the field of medicine, they pacify all diseases of embodied beings, balancing their constitutions and providing them with means for longevity. Active within the fields of numerous beneficial arts and sciences, they provide for sentient beings, while also teaching these same methods to others.

In short, the bodhisattvas practice for the benefit of both self and others. Thus they begin by listening to the treatises, or the corpus of scripture, associated with the five fields of knowledge. Next, they take in the words that they come to hear, memorizing them so that they are able to recite them. On this basis, they examine the nature of the meanings of the words until they comprehend them free from error. Discerning between what is right and wrong, they will thus also teach others correctly. In this way, the bodhisattvas' concern for the five fields is special with respect to its bases or entities.

(2) As for the objective of the knowledge of the treatises, listeners and self-realized buddhas persist in all the various points of training primarily for their own benefit. Bodhisattvas, on the other hand, consider benefiting others more important, and so their objective is also superior.

(3) As for the associated activities, listeners gain knowledge of only the inner meaning that is conveyed within their own corpus of scripture,

and so they accomplish their own welfare. Bodhisattvas gain expertise regarding the inner meaning as taught within all three vehicles. While they themselves enter the Great Vehicle, they also teach it to others who share the same potential. To beings who have the potential of a listener or a self-realized buddha, they will accordingly teach the relevant vehicle. The case is similar with respect to the knowledge of reasoning and the rest of the five fields because the bodhisattvas work to benefit others in these contexts and actively teach the treatises to others. Hence, their knowledge of the treatises is superior also with regard to activity.

(4) As for the characteristics, listeners are concerned with a confined issue taught in the context of the knowledge of the inner meaning—namely, the absence of a self in the form of a person. Thus they learn only a few treatises, memorizing their words and so on. The bodhisattvas pursue the knowledge of the inner meaning as comprised within the three vehicles, and they likewise acquaint themselves with however many treatises there are on linguistics, reliable means of cognition, medicine, and the arts and sciences. Thus, they listen insatiably; they retain, refine, investigate, and gain realization. Their knowledge of the treatises is superior in terms of these five characteristics.

(5) A listener's knowledge of the treatises will be exhausted when nothing remains of the aggregates. Conversely, a bodhisattva's knowledge of the topics of the five fields will not come to an end even within the field that is without such remainder. Thus, also in this regard, the bodhisattva's knowledge is superior.

(6) As for the results, the listeners' knowledge of the treatises does not yield omniscience, but when the bodhisattvas gain expertise in the five fields, they dedicate it to the attainment of omniscience. By the power of that dedication, they attain the fruition of the wakefulness that is aware of all objects of knowledge.

The bodhisattvas' knowledge of the treatises on the five fields comprises the media of meditative absorption and retention. In some cases, their expertise in the five fields is thereby either of the nature of meditative absorption—embraced by meditative absorption, or connected with meditative absorption—or being of the nature of retention—embraced by retention, or otherwise connected with retention. Composed in this way of meditative absorption and retention, their knowledge of the fields can also be seen to be twofold. Having gained mastery of meditative absorptions such as that of the heroic gait, they are readily able to comprehend any learned treatise toward which they direct their equipoise, and so they bring sentient beings to maturation. By the nature of retention, they are able to recall flawlessly the words and meanings contained in the treatises on the five fields that they have received throughout extremely many lifetimes. In this way, they retain all of the scriptural traditions of the sacred Dharma as contained within the five fields of knowledge.

Since it is supported by meditative absorption, the bodhisattvas' knowledge of treatises matures sentient beings by means of the threefold miraculous power of miracles, expression, and teaching. Meanwhile, by means of retention, they uphold the knowledge of the four fields of communication and so on. Yet, in particular, through retention they ensure that the knowledge of the inner meaning, that is, the sacred Dharma, remains present in the world without ever waning. Such is the twofold function of their knowledge of the treatises.

5. Knowledge of the World

The steadfast ones' knowledge of the world constitutes,
Through body, speech, and mind,
The knowledge of the truth,
And is hence superior to others. [XIX.28]

The steadfast ones always smile,
And they speak truthfully
So as to turn sentient beings into vessels
And enable them to practice the sacred Dharma. [XIX.29]

It is held that the worlds
Always arise due to two truths
And fade away due to two truths.
Hence the knower of this is termed "knower of the world."
[XIX.30]

For the sake of their pacification and attainment,
The wise apply themselves to the truths.
Because they possess knowledge of the truths, the wise
Are definitively declared to be "knowers of the world."[XIX.31]

The steadfast ones' knowledge of the world constitutes, through body, speech, and mind, the knowledge of the means for influencing sentient beings and the knowledge of the four truths, and it is hence superior to that of any others. How, one may wonder, do they then employ their body and other factors? The steadfast ones always show a radiant smile, and they speak truthfully without deceit. In terms of the purpose of these two, they do this so as to turn sentient beings into vessels for the Dharma and enable them to practice the sacred Dharma. What is the significance of the phrase "knowledge of the truth"? It is held that the worlds always arise due to two truths—namely, the truth of suffering, which is that which arises, and the truth of the origin, which is that by means of which this arises—and fade away due to two truths—that is, the truth of cessation, which is the worlds' having faded, and the truth of the path by means of which they fade. Hence, the knower of this is termed "knower of the world" because of having knowledge of the world's arising and fading.

Regarding the function of the knowledge of the world, it is for the sake of their pacification (in terms of suffering and its origin) and their attainment (with respect to cessation and the path) that the wise apply themselves to the knowledge of the truths. Because they possess knowledge of the four truths, the wise are definitively declared to be "knowers of the world."

The steadfast bodhisattvas' knowledge of the world consists of an awareness of the character of body and speech, as well as insight into the four truths by means of the mind. It is, therefore, superior to the knowledge of the world that mundane individuals, listeners, and self-realized buddhas can arrive at. Here it might be thought: "Knowledge of the conventions of the world is merely a matter of allowing body and speech to be in accord with others, so such knowledge is also found among ordinary worldly beings. Moreover, the listeners and self-realized buddhas also have knowledge of the four truths. How, then, can the bodhisattvas' knowledge of the world be superior?" There is, in fact, an extremely great difference since in those cases knowledge of the world does not serve to mature other beings in the way that it does for the bodhisattvas.

The knowledge of the world is threefold. It is a knowledge of the conventions of the world, the arising of the world, and the cessation of the world. As for the knowledge of the world's conventions, this is further discernible in terms of the understanding of those bodily and verbal conventions that are in accord with the world. Regarding the bodily conventions, bodhisattvas will delight everyone—high, low, or in between—with a bright smile and a countenance that is free from any sign of displeasure. As they thus express sincerity and joy, they are appreciated by others. As for their speech, it is taught that, while their words contain nothing unreasonable, they are also warm and delightful. Thus, their verbal expressions are rich, genuine, and well sounding. Since their physical conduct is agreeable to those who encounter them, it prepares others for the comprehension of the truths, and as they employ their voice to communicate the sacred Dharma, it enables others to practice the sacred Dharma. It is for this purpose that the bodhisattvas pursue the knowledge of the bodily and verbal conventions of the world.

As for the bodhisattva's mind, it has knowledge of the world's arising and dissolution—a knowledge of the facts of the world. It is held that the world of the environment and the world of sentient beings always arise based on two truths, namely, the truth of origin and the truth of suffering. Thus, the term "world" comes to refer to the production of the resultant truth of suffering by the causal truth of the origin. The world, moreover, fades and ceases in terms of the truths of cessation and the path. As the causal factors associated with the origin are eliminated by the truth of the path, the world that is of the nature of resultant suffering comes to an end. Thus, the truth of cessation is that within which resides the world's having ceased, whereas the truth of the path consists of that which brings about this cessation. This knowledge is referred to as "knowledge of the world." Hence, knowledge of the world's arising is knowledge of the impure dependent nature, whereas knowledge of the world's cessation is knowledge of the pure dependent nature. Furthermore, knowledge of the sixteenfold nature of the truths and the three gateways of liberation constitutes knowledge of all three natures. Since they thus know the conventions of the world as well as the four truths that are associated with the ultimate, the wise bodhisattvas have knowledge of the two truths and are therefore referred to as "knowers of the world." In this way, they possess knowledge of the realms of the world and all associated matters of life span, happiness, sorrow, rise, decline, and so forth. They also have knowledge of all the manners and ways of the world, as herein indicated with reference to their mastery of the physical and verbal conventions that accord with the world. Likewise, being aware of the world's arising and the factors that bring that about, they know the relative truth of the world; and, with knowledge of the truths of the path and cessation, they also have knowledge of the ultimate truth. Thus, by means of the two truths, they know the entire world without exception.

Some say that knowledge of the four truths constitutes actual knowledge of the world, whereas knowledge of the conventions of body and speech refers to the context of motivating body and speech through one's knowledge of the world. Thus they claim that the latter type of knowledge of the world is an instance of applying the name of a cause to its effect. Alternatively, it may be claimed that since knowledge of the conventions of body and speech serves to bring forth knowledge of the world in others, it could be referred to as knowledge of the world by naming the cause after its effect. However, since the context here is knowledge of the world, and because knowing the world also includes knowing the conventions of body and speech, it is not inappropriate to see the latter knowledge as actual knowledge of the world.

6. The Four Reliances

> There are the corpus of the Buddha's teaching,
> The intended meaning,
> The definitive meaning endowed with reliability,
> And its ineffable attainment. [XIX.32]

> Rejection, literalism,
> Mistaken identification of the real,

And an attainment that involves expression—
Thus their refutation is shown. [XIX.33]

Inspiration, discernment,
Correct reception from others,
And ineffable wakefulness—
From these the steadfast ones will not fall. [XIX.34]

The next explanation concerns an investigation of the reliances. As for the characteristics of the reliances, **there are** the following: (1) Rather than relying on a person, one relies on **the corpus of the Buddha's teaching,** that is, the teaching given by the victorious ones and their offspring; (2) instead of relying on their words, one relies on **the intended meaning;** (3) rather than taking the support of the expedient meaning, one relies on **the** principles of the **definitive meaning,** which are **endowed with** the **reliability** supplied by the teacher, who is a perfectly authoritative person; **and,** (4) with respect to the definitive meaning, one does not rely on consciousness, but instead on **its ineffable attainment** through the wakefulness of realization, which transcends the world.

These refute (1) the person who is involved in **rejection** of the corpus of the Dharma, (2) **literalism** with respect to the intended meaning of the teachings, (3) a **mistaken identification of the real,** based on getting the expedient and definitive teachings mixed up, and (4) **an attainment** of knowledge **that involves expression** and, hence, is not one's own direct awareness. **Thus their refutation is shown.**

Respectively, the following benefits ensue: **inspiration** with respect to the corpus of Dharma, **discernment** of the intended meaning, perfectly **correct reception** of this meaning **from others, and ineffable wakefulness** beyond the world. **From these, the steadfast ones will not fall.**

The four reliances are taught so that flaws such as primary reliance on a person or exact adherence to the literal mode of the scriptural teachings can be avoided.

(1) Rather than relying on the words of separate individuals, one relies on the teachings that were spoken by the Blessed One, the Buddha, and which are contained within the corpus of scripture. This is relying on the Dharma rather than on a person.

(2) In terms of the scriptural teachings, one should not take at face value those teachings that are given with a concealed intent, such as, "One's own father and mother are to be slain." Instead, one must rely on the meaning rather than the words.

(3) As for the meaning, it may be either expedient or definitive. Hence, one should rely on the meaning that is definitive because it is supported by cognitive means that are reliable in the final investigation of things. For example, teachings that declare the existence of phenomena such as persons and aggregates are of expedient meaning, whereas teachings on the lack of an essential nature convey the definitive meaning. In this way, one should rely on the profound nonduality that is the purport of the profound sūtras of the Thus-Gone One. Such nonduality is also the subject matter of the clarifying investigations of his regent, Maitreya, as well as of the explanations of the great chariots, Asaṅga and Nāgārjuna, both of whom were prophesied by the Victorious One.

(4) Finally, one should not rely on the object universal that is associated with the definitive meaning of the sūtras and the object of the conceptual mind; nor should one rely on the features of dualistic grasping that are the object of the eight consciousnesses. Instead, one should rely on that meaning which, in being free from dualistic grasping, is ineffable and the object of one's own direct awareness—the field that becomes accessible through the attainment of nonconceptual wakefulness.

The *Sūtra Taught by Akṣayamati* thus explains that considering the personal self and phenomena to be of an existent nature is to have reliance on the person, whereas realizing that the two are devoid of a nature is reliance on the intrinsic nature. It likewise speaks of words as "mundane phenomena" as opposed to meanings that are "supramundane phenomena," and it refers to relative phenomena as "words," while describing all ultimate phenomena as "meanings." Similarly, those sūtras that explain how one enters the path can be considered to be of expedient meaning, whereas those that explain how one enters the fruition are of definitive meaning. Likewise, sūtras that teach the relative are expedient, whereas those that teach the ultimate are definitive.

What, then, is meant by "consciousness" [when here we are instructed to rely on wakefulness rather than consciousness]? The consciousness of sentient beings in the desire realm is supported by the aggregate of form; for those in the form realm, it is supported by the aggregate of sensation; in the three lower sections of the formless realm, it is supported by the aggregate of identification; at the summit of existence, it is supported by the aggregate of formation. Thus, consciousness is associated with, and supported by, form and the other three aggregates, and it is taught that when all types of consciousness that rest on those aggregates are understood to be emptiness, consciousness becomes nonconceptual wakefulness.

The purpose of the teaching of the four reliances is presented next.

(1) Certain individuals may, in accordance with their own personal concerns, reject the authentic Dharma taught by the Buddha, declaring that it is not the word of the Buddha and not genuine Dharma. The first of the four reliances is taught in order to avoid such a rejection or denigration of the true Dharma.

(2) The second reliance enables one to avoid misunderstandings along the lines of, for example, the instruction to kill one's father and mother.

(3) Based on the third reliance, one will avoid errors in the form of the misidentification of statements, that is, taking what is of an expedient nature to be definitive instead. For example, the Buddha speaks of "the person who is an ordinary individual," "the person who is a destroyer of the enemy," and "the person who is a self-realized Buddha." He has likewise said that "one person will, once he appears in the world, benefit the whole world—that person is the Thus-Gone One." If one is not aware that such statements are made in consideration of the relative truth and that their meaning is provisional, one could come to the conclusion that there is such a thing as a substantially existent person.

(4) Finally, the profound nondual meaning that is the object of one's own direct awareness is inexpressible. Nevertheless, some take it to be an object of the consciousness that is polluted by the habitual tendencies of duality and also associated with expressions. The fourth of the reliances

is taught to refute such misunderstandings. Thus, this explanation of the four reliances serves as a refutation of the misunderstandings about them.

The next issue is the function, or the qualities, of the four reliances. The first ensures that one's interest in the Dharma of scripture does not wane, and the second that the same is the case with regard to one's discernment of the meaning of its statements. Due to the third reliance, one will not fail to receive, from external spiritual teachers, the exact teaching of the sūtras that are of definitive rather than expedient meaning. Finally, the fourth reliance ensures that the steadfast bodhisattvas never fall from the ineffable wakefulness that transcends the reach of thought.

7. The Fourfold Correct Awareness

In being the knowledge of categories, characteristics,
Words, and wakefulness,
The fourfold correct awareness
Of the bodhisattvas is held to be supreme. [XIX.35]

The teaching and the means of teaching
Of those diligently exerting themselves in teaching
Consists of the pair of Dharmas and meanings
Taught exclusively through words and knowledge. [XIX.36]

The Dharma presented and explained,
The two thoroughly attained,
And opponents responded to—it is for these reasons
That correct awareness is fourfold. [XIX.37]

Having gained individual direct awareness regarding equality,
Thorough knowledge follows.
As all doubts are cut through,
This is known as "correct awareness." [XIX.38]

Next follows the investigation of correct awareness. The relevant characteristics are as follows: **In being the knowledge of** the categories that pertain to every instance of subject matter, the knowledge of general and particular **characteristics** of phenomena, the knowledge of definitive **words** in the languages of various lands, **and** the knowledge of unimpeded **wakefulness, the fourfold correct awareness of the bodhisattvas is held to be supreme.**

The definitive enumeration is as follows: **The teaching and the means of teaching of those** children of the victorious ones who are **diligently exerting themselves in teaching** the Dharma **consists of the pair of Dharmas and meanings,** which are **taught exclusively through** definitive **words and** the **knowledge** of acumen. **The Dharma** and its meaning are briefly **presented and** then elaborately **explained;** the teaching through words is given so that **the two,** Dharmas and meanings, can be **thoroughly attained** by those who listen to it; **and** the teaching through knowledge takes place so that **opponents** are **responded to—it is for these reasons that correct awareness is fourfold.**

The etymology is as follows: **Having** by means of supramundane wakefulness **gained individual direct awareness regarding** the **equality** of all phenomena, **thorough knowledge** of enumerations and so forth **follows** during the subsequent attainment. **As,** in terms of the function of this, **all doubts are cut through, this is known as "correct awareness."**

(1) Correct awareness of the teachings of Dharma consists of knowledge of the various categories of the Dharma, such as the virtuous as opposed to the unvirtuous, or the defiled and the undefiled. This also includes awareness of the ways in which a particular subject matter may be referred to by means of several appellations, as when ignorance is spoken of in terms such as closed-mindedness, bewilderment, unknowing, darkness, or dense darkness. Similarly, wakefulness may be spoken of as just that, yet it may also be termed insight, awareness, intelligence, or illumination. Thus, this is the knowledge of names and categories.

(2) Correct awareness of meanings is the unmistaken knowledge of the particular and general characteristics that pertain to the meanings of words.

(3) Correct awareness of definitive words lets the knowledge of words extend beyond one single language. Thus it brings knowledge of the ways in which syllables combine to form words, words aggregate to form phrases, and phrases carry meaning in the languages of gods, nāgas, humans, gandharvas, and demigods. Thus, it is an exact knowledge of grammar and syntax.

(4) Correct awareness of acumen involves the unimpeded ability to provide clear answers to whatever questions may be asked. Thus one also responds to critical arguments and, even if one were to explain for an eon about the meaning of a single teaching, one would, due to the attainment of wakefulness, never run out of resources. As they possess such flawless knowledge, it is held that the fourfold correct awareness of the bodhisattvas is beyond comparison with that of the listeners and self-realized buddhas.

While the first stanza in this section has thus presented the characteristics of the four forms of correct awareness, the following two explain their definitive enumeration. When bodhisattvas diligently exert themselves in teaching others the Dharma, we may distinguish between the subject matter of their teaching and their means for teaching that subject matter. In that regard, correct awareness of Dharma and correct awareness of meaning together compose the subject matter of their teaching. Moreover, their means of teaching this subject matter are nothing more than correct awareness of definitive words and correct awareness of acumen. In this context, Sthiramati's commentary states:

> Here, Dharma is taught through names, the meanings of which are pointed out.

Thus it is explained that correct awareness of meaning consists of the concise presentation of a given Dharma teaching, whereas the subsequent discernment and explanation is correct awareness of Dharma. With correct awareness of definitive words, one causes the attainment of knowledge of both Dharmas and meanings because through this awareness, one elicits comprehension of words as well as meanings as one communicates in the respective languages of various realms. Finally, relying on acumen, one inquires into the opponent's position, debates its rationale, and presents replies. Hence, the enumeration of the four forms of correct awareness is definitive; there could not be three or five.

As for the cause of this fourfold correct awareness, during equipoise one rests in one's own direct awareness of the equality of all phenomena. Following this equipoise, by means of the subsequently attained wakefulness, one then gains a thorough knowledge of Dharma and the rest of the four. Here, the corresponding two lines of the root text[48] can also be seen as explaining the etymology of the four types of correct awareness. In the Sanskrit word *pratisaṃvidyā, prati* means "distinct," thus referring to one's own direct awareness of nonconceptual wakefulness. Moreover, as it connotes equality and that which is correct, *saṃ* indicates suchness. Finally, *vidyā* is knowledge. Hence, following the direct perception of nonconceptual wakefulness, the pure mundane wakefulness that is subsequently attained will thence teach Dharmas, meanings, and so forth, to others, thereby causing comprehension and knowledge.

In terms of their function, the four types of correct awareness cut through doubts with respect to every aspect of the vast issues pertaining to the aggregates, elements, sense sources, and so on, as well as those concerning the profound matters of emptiness and so forth. It is for this reason that they are termed "correct awareness."

8. The Two Accumulations

The accumulations of the bodhisattvas
Are unequaled merit and wakefulness;
With one comes elevation within cyclic existence,
And with the other one participates in cyclic existence free
    from affliction. [XIX.39]

Generosity and discipline are the accumulation of merit,
And insight is wakefulness;
The other three belong to both,
But all five are also the accumulation of wakefulness. [XIX.40]

With the continuous accomplishment of cultivation,
One practices virtue again and again;

These accumulations of the steadfast ones
Accomplish all objectives. [XIX.41]

For the sake of access, absence of marks,
Spontaneous accomplishment,
Empowerment, and perfection,
The steadfast ones practice the accumulations. [XIX.42]

The following explanation concerns the accumulations. First, regarding their essence, **the accumulations of the bodhisattvas are** of the nature of **unequaled merit and wakefulness. With one,** the accumulation of merit, **comes elevation within cyclic existence, and with the other,** the accumulation of wakefulness, **one participates in cyclic existence free from affliction.**

The two accumulations subsume the six transcendences in the following way: **Generosity and discipline are the accumulation of merit, and insight is** the accumulation of **wakefulness; the other three**—patience, diligence, and concentration— **belong to both, but it must be understood that all five** transcendences **are also the accumulation of wakefulness** when they are embraced by insight.

The etymology is as follows: **With the continuous,** as indicated by the Sanskrit *sam,* **accomplishment of meditation,** as conveyed by *bhā,* **one practices virtue again and again,** as implied by *ra,* which means to practice again and again. As for their function, **these accumulations of the steadfast ones accomplish all objectives,** both those of self and others.

The divisions pertaining to the accumulations are the following. On the grounds of inspired conduct, the accumulations are gathered **for the sake of access** to the grounds. From the first through the sixth ground, the purpose is to attain the **absence of marks** upon the seventh ground. On that seventh ground, the accumulations are gathered for the sake of achieving the **spontaneous accomplishment** of the eighth and ninth ground. On those two grounds, the accumulations are then directed toward the attainment of **empowerment** upon the tenth ground, **and** on the tenth ground, the accumulations serve to accomplish the **perfection of buddhahood. Thus the steadfast ones practice the accumulations** with these objectives.

The bodhisattvas' two accumulations consist of merit and wakefulness. As before, the two accumulations of the listeners and self-realized buddhas cannot compare with those of the bodhisattvas. Thus the *Jewel Mound* teaches:

> Consider the bodhisattvas' accumulation of wakefulness to be like the space of the sky in the ten directions. Consider the listeners' accumulation of wakefulness to be no more than the space of a cavity dug out by a worm in a sesame seed. Consider the bodhisattvas' accumulation of merit to be like the water of the sea in the four directions. Consider the accumulation of the merit of the listeners to be like the water left in the imprint of a hoof.

When by the power of their two accumulations the bodhisattvas embrace birth within cyclic existence, one of the two, namely, the accumulation of merit, will make them gain the fine attainments of the truly elevated realms within cyclic existence. Thus they take birth as Indra, Brahma, a universal emperor, or the like. Meanwhile, the other one of the two, the accumulation of wakefulness, will ensure that they engage with cyclic existence without being stained by any of its flaws.

The two accumulations subsume the six transcendences and the six transcendences likewise comprise the two accumulations. Generosity produces perfect wealth, whereas discipline makes one attain an excellent bodily support as a god or a human. These two both belong to the accumulation of merit. The final one among the transcendences—insight—constitutes, on the other hand, the accumulation of wakefulness because with insight all phenomena are realized as emptiness, and one will thereby not be stained by affliction.

The remaining three transcendences of patience, diligence, and concentration belong to both the accumulation of merit and the accumulation of wakefulness. In this way, the patience of being unaffected by harm and of gladly accepting suffering are both contained in the accumulation of merit, whereas the patience of the ascertainment of the Dharma is contained within the accumulation of wakefulness. Similarly, diligence in helping others plow their fields, do business, and so on, is of the nature of merit, whereas diligence in following a spiritual teacher, and in receiving, contemplating, and training in the sacred Dharma is included within the accumulation of wakefulness. As for concentration, that which is involved in the mundane realms of concentration and in the formless realms, as well as the undefiled concentration that is employed for the benefit of others—all of these belong to the accumulation of merit. The concentration that serves as the support for the meditative absorption of nonconceptual wakefulness, on the other hand, is contained within the accumulation of wakefulness.

All five transcendences of generosity and so on are also included in the accumulation of wakefulness, once they are dedicated to the attainment of omniscient wakefulness, or once they are embraced by the insight that does not observe the three spheres. Furthermore, confession of evil, rejoicing in merit, and requesting the turning of the Dharma wheel are included in the accumulation of merit, and this is also the case, for example, with the three classes of meritorious entities that ensue from generosity, discipline, and meditation. Factors such as serving, accompanying, venerating, and receiving teaching from a spiritual teacher constitute causes and conditions whereby acts become included in the accumulation of wakefulness.

In terms of etymology, "accumulation" implies a sustained cultivation of merit that is based on having accomplished a continuous affinity with such practice. In the Sanskrit word *sambhāra, sam* is short for *samtatyā*,[49] which means "continuous," *bhā* stands for *bhāvana*, or "cultivation," and *ra* is short for *āhara*, which means "accomplishing." Thus the word "accumulation" implies the continuous cultivation of the virtues of generosity and the rest of the six transcendences, thereby leading to the accomplishment of the three bodies of a buddha. The accomplishment of one's own and all others' objectives constitutes the function of the accumulations that are practiced by the steadfast bodhisattvas.

Next the divisions that pertain to the accumulations are discussed. The practice of gathering the accumulations that one engages in as an ordinary being on the grounds of inspired conduct, up through the stage of the supreme mundane quality, is a practice that is undertaken for the sake of accessing and attaining the grounds. From the first[50] to the sixth ground, the accumulations are undertaken to reach and attain the absence of marks on the seventh ground. This seventh ground is associated with the absence of marks because once it has been attained, the Dharma teachings of the sūtras and so on will no longer be kept in mind and conceived of as teachings that carry distinct meanings. On the seventh ground, the accumulations of merit and wakefulness are practiced for the purpose of attaining the spontaneous presence of the two accumulations that is characteristic of the eighth and ninth grounds; and on those latter two grounds, the accumulations are, in turn, gathered for the sake of receiving empowerment as the Dharma regent of the buddhas on the tenth ground. Finally, the two accumulations that are practiced on the tenth ground serve to bring forth the consummate attainment of perfect buddhahood. In this way, the steadfast bodhisattvas practice the accumulations of merit and wakefulness.

2. The Essence of the Factors of Enlightenment

Next, the essence of the process of cultivation, or of the path, will be explained in terms of (1) an elaborate explanation of the thirty-seven factors of enlightenment and (2) a summary discussion of calm abiding and special insight. As for the first, the thirty-seven factors are taught in seven sets, of which the first deals with the applications of mindfulness.

1. Elaborate Account of the Thirty-Seven Factors of Enlightenment
1. The Four Applications of Mindfulness

The wise practice the applications of mindfulness
By means of fourteen features
That render them unequaled
And superior to any others. [XIX.43]

Support, remedies,
Engagement, focal point,

Directing the mind, and attainment—
Thus their practice is superior. [XIX.44]

Accordance, harmonious engagement,
Thorough knowledge, birth,
Magnificence, supremacy, training,
And true accomplishment—these are different. [XIX.45]

With respect to the applications of mindfulness, it is said: The wise children of the victorious ones **practice the applications of mindfulness by means of fourteen features that render them unequaled and superior to any others.** What are these fourteen features?

(1) The **support**, which is their reliance on receiving the Dharma of the Great Vehicle, their reflecting on it, and their meditation based on it.

(2) The **remedies**, for since they engage with the phenomena of body and so forth by way of the absence of self, [their practice is beyond] the four errors as well as their remedies.

(3) As explained in *Distinguishing the Middle from Extremes,* their way of **engagement** with the four truths is both personal as well as one that includes others.

(4) Their **focal point** involves the bodies, and so forth, of all sentient beings.

(5) Their **directing the mind** transcends any focal point in terms of the body and so forth.

(6) **And**, without any wish either to separate or not separate from the body and so forth, they practice for the sake of the **attainment** of the nonabiding transcendence of suffering. Thus their practice is superior. There is also:

(7) The way their applications of mindfulness are in **accordance** with the transcendences since they serve as the remedies against the factors that are in conflict with the transcendences.

(8) Their **harmonious engagement** of mundane beings, listeners, and self-realized buddhas by way of training in harmony with them.

(9) Their **thorough knowledge** of the body being like an illusion since it is perceptible yet unreal, of sensation being dream-like since it is devoid of any essence of experience, of the mind being like space because it is natural luminosity, and of phenomena resembling clouds since they are adventitious.

(10) Their willingly taking **birth** as universal emperors, and so forth, and still, despite their superior bodies and sensations, being able to remain free from affliction.

(11) Their **magnificence**, which is due to their naturally sharp faculties and that means that even at the time of the lesser applications of mindfulness, their practice is exalted.

(12) The **superiority** that is due to their accomplishment in the practice and whereby their practice is spontaneously accomplished in terms of merging and further merging on the eighth ground and above.

(13) Their extremely high level of **training**, making them immune to the exhaustion of the aggregates without remainder.

(14) **And**, finally, their **true accomplishment** upon the tenth ground and perfect buddhahood. **These are** a **different** set of superior features.

The four applications of mindfulness are, respectively, concerned with body, sensations, mind, and phenomena. The wise bodhisattvas' practice of these four can be seen to be unequaled by listeners and self-realized buddhas in fourteen different ways, and so the bodhisattvas' practice of the applications of mindfulness is superior to that of anyone else. The fourteen superior features are enumerated as follows: (1) support, (2) remedy, (3) engagement, (4) focal point, (5) the directing of the mind, (6) attainment, (7) accordance, (8) harmonious engagement, (9) thorough knowledge, (10) birth, (11) quality or magnificence, (12) supremacy, (13) training, and (14) fruition, or true accomplishment.

These fourteen may be explained as follows:

(1) When the listeners practice the four applications of mindfulness, they do so through learning, reflecting, and meditating based on the listeners' vessels of scripture. The bodhisattvas, on the other hand, learn,

reflect, and meditate based on the scriptural vessels of the Great Vehicle. Hence, their support is superior.

(2) With respect to the remedies, the listeners are mindful of the body as unclean, sensation as painful, the mind as impermanent, and all phenomena as empty of personal self. Thus they practice in order to remedy the mistaken notion of purity and the other three errors. The bodhisattvas, however, realize that the body and so on are devoid of both of the two types of self. Thus they meditate on the four applications as being suchness free from all marks of purity or impurity, pleasure or pain, and so on.

(3) By thus understanding the body and the other three categories to be empty, they gradually engage with the four truths of suffering, origin, cessation, and the path, as is explained in *Distinguishing the Middle from Extremes*. As for the superior way that they conduct their practice, whereas listeners practice the four applications of mindfulness so that they themselves can access the four truths, the bodhisattvas practice with a view to the engagement of both themselves and others.

(4) Concerning the distinctive focal point, listeners meditate by primarily focusing on their own body and so on, whereas the bodhisattvas observe the bodies and so forth of themselves and all others.

(5) In terms of the directing of the mind, listeners bring to mind that the body is impure and so on, and so their practice bears the marks of a remedy. The bodhisattvas do not observe any marks, neither of discards nor of remedies, and hence the way they direct their minds is distinct.

(6) Regarding the special attainment, listeners meditate in order to separate from an impure body, painful sensations, and so on. As a result, they therefore also merely attain the severing of the continuum of the aggregates. The bodhisattvas meditate neither to be free from those factors, nor not to be free from them. Since the body and so forth are devoid of nature, they do not observe the four bases as something from which to be either free or not free. Hence, at the point of attaining the fruition, they will not separate from the three bodies of buddhahood but will separate entirely from the impure bodies and so forth that come about due to karma and affliction. This distinguishes their attainment.

(7) Since the bodhisattvas' practice of the applications of mindfulness is in accord with the six transcendences, it is also distinguished in

terms of accordance. As they realize that the body and the other three bases resemble illusions and have no nature, they have no attachment to bodies and enjoyments, inner and outer entities. Thus, free from attachment, their mindfulness is in accord with the practice of generosity. Likewise, without attachment to body and wealth, the bodhisattvas assume and observe pure discipline. With pure discipline, they are able to abide in the patience of not responding to beating with beating, as well as in the rest of the four precepts of a spiritual practitioner. Endowed with patience, they will practice the transcendences, arousing diligence free from weariness. Diligent, they are able therefore to accomplish the concentration of an undistracted mind. Abiding in equipoise, they are able to attain the special insight that realizes the general and particular characteristics of all phenomena. While the practice of the bodhisattvas accords in this way with the six transcendences, the listeners cultivate only the factors of enlightenment as such. They are unable to accustom themselves to the six transcendences over long durations of time.

(8) As for the bodhisattvas' distinctive harmonious engagement, worldly beings as well as listeners and self-realized buddhas are indeed able to practice the simple application of mindfulness with respect to the body and so forth. The bodhisattvas, however, distinguish themselves by abiding in their practice while also teaching the applications of mindfulness to worldly beings, listeners, and self-realized buddhas in whichever way that may accord with the distinct mind-sets of their disciples. This is their distinctive subsequent engagement.

(9) With their distinctive thorough knowledge, the bodhisattvas realize that while the body does appear, it is not real in the way it appears, and that it therefore resembles a magical illusion. As for sensations, the bodhisattvas recognize that these are just like the experience of pleasure and pain in a dream; they do not involve any actual entities at all. They realize that the thoroughly established, intrinsic nature of the mind is natural luminosity, similar to space. They understand that all the phenomena of thorough affliction and complete purification are adventitious, just like clouds and haze that may appear and disappear within the space of the sky. Thus, the phenomena of affliction and purification do not have any bearing within the basic nature of the mind, and yet, like reflections in a mirror, they may temporarily appear by the power of

conditions. Thus the bodhisattvas' applications of mindfulness are distinguished by their thorough knowledge of the nature of the body and so forth.

(10) With reference to birth, the listeners practice the applications of mindfulness in order to avoid birth within cyclic existence. Bodhisattvas are not born by the force of the karmic actions and afflictions that are associated with attachment to cyclic existence. Nevertheless, as Indra, Brahma, or the universal emperor, they knowingly take possession of fine bodies and possessions and, when active in this way for the benefit of others, they do not experience afflictive attachments. Likewise, while accepting ordinary or inferior births as animals and the like, they do not experience dejection, decline, or affliction. Thus their way of taking birth is distinctive.

(11) As for the distinctive magnificent quality, the faculties of bodhisattvas are naturally sharp. Hence, they train in the applications of wakefulness for the benefit of both themselves and others and by means of insight into the absence of the self of persons and phenomena. While they are still ordinary individuals who have trained for just a short duration of time, their practice may, because they are not yet noble beings, be classified as lesser. Yet compared with the listeners' applications of mindfulness, it is nevertheless elevated and magnificent.

(12) Concerning the feature of supremacy, upon attainment of the eighth ground, the training in the four applications of mindfulness is fully complete. Effortless and spontaneously accomplished, the practice is characterized by a merging and further merging with that of other bodhisattvas, and in this regard their practice is supreme. When a bodhisattva on the eighth ground practices the four applications of mindfulness, all other bodhisattvas on that ground will be doing so too, and when other bodhisattvas are practicing them, he or she will equally be doing the same. It is with respect to this relationship that the terms "merging" and "further merging" are applied, conveying the sense of fusion through sharing a single objective. Alternatively, as explained in the commentary, "merging" can refer to the initial instant of attainment of the eighth ground, subsequent to the seventh. "Further merging" begins then with the second moment and lasts until one has entered the ninth ground.

(13) The distinctive sense of training has to do with the way that the bodhisattvas practice the applications of mindfulness. It is embraced in their case by the great compassion that never forsakes sentient beings and the great insight that realizes both forms of the absence of self. Thus, their practice is elevated above that of listeners and self-realized buddhas.

(14) Their distinctive, true accomplishment of the fruition also sets the bodhisattvas' applications of mindfulness apart from those practiced by listeners and self-realized buddhas. Whereas the latter attain the level of a stream enterer and the rest of the four fruitions, the bodhisattvas' applications of mindfulness lead to their attainment of the ten grounds and the ground of buddhahood. Thus, their practice is also distinguished by its superior results.

2. The Four Authentic Eliminations

The steadfast ones' authentic eliminations
Cannot be matched by embodied beings;
These are cultivated as the remedy
For flaws in the application of mindfulness. [xix.46]

Fully partaking of cyclic existence,
Discarding the obscurations,
Discarding the directing of the mind,
Entering the grounds, [xix.47]

Abiding without marks,
Obtaining prophecy,
Thoroughly ripening sentient beings,
Becoming empowered, [xix.48]

Thoroughly cultivating the fields,
And reaching perfection—
With these objectives the wise bodhisattvas
Cultivate the remedies for the conflicting factors. [xix.49]

Based on aspiration, one engages
In spiritual practice endowed with its features.
All of the authentic eliminations
Are definitively referred to as "remedies." [XIX.50]

Next, with a view to investigating the authentic eliminations, first their general characteristics are taught. **The steadfast ones' four authentic eliminations cannot be matched** by other **embodied beings. These are cultivated as the remedy for flaws,** that is, the conflicting factors, **in the** training in the **application of mindfulness** described above. Thus, this training ensures that (1) flaws that have presently not arisen do not arise in the future, (2) flaws that have now occurred are overcome, (3) remedies that have not yet arisen are brought to arise, and (4) remedies that have already arisen are brought to increase.

The relevant divisions are as follows: **fully partaking of** the perfections of **cyclic existence** while remaining free from thorough affliction, **discarding the** five **obscurations** in the context of concentration, **discarding the directing of the mind** that is associated with the listeners and self-realized buddhas, **entering** the first as well as **the** remaining **grounds, abiding without marks** on the seventh ground, **obtaining prophecy** upon the eighth, **thoroughly ripening sentient beings** on the ninth, **becoming empowered** by the great light rays on the tenth, **thoroughly cultivating the fields** on all those three grounds, **and reaching perfection** on the ground of buddhahood. **With these objectives the wise bodhisattvas cultivate** the correct eliminations, which serve as **the remedies for the conflicting factors.**

It is taught that "one aspires, exerts oneself, arouses diligence, thoroughly upholds, and genuinely and thoroughly rests." As conveyed by these words, it is **based on aspiration** that **one engages** and exerts oneself **in** the **spiritual practice** of calm abiding and special insight. This practice is **endowed with its features** of calm abiding, thoroughly seizing, and equanimity. How, one may wonder, does this practice take place? By arousing diligence in terms of the development of the remedies for the factors that conflict with calm abiding and thoroughly seizing, that is, afflictive dullness and agitation, respectively. Thus, because they relate to authentically seizing through insight, and thoroughly seizing by means of calm abiding, and resting in equanimity through having attained the level of equality, **all of the authentic eliminations are definitively referred to as "remedies."**

The bodhisattvas' four authentic eliminations cannot be matched by other embodied beings, such as listeners and self-realized buddhas. Practiced for the benefit of all sentient beings, the practice of the bodhisattvas is superior in terms of both the essence and the objects of the application of mindfulness. As for the four authentic eliminations, these are cultivated as the specific remedies of the flaws that are the factors conflicting with the four applications of mindfulness. In this way, the authentic eliminations serve to remedy and eliminate the flaws that otherwise hinder the bodhisattvas' application of mindfulness—distinguished by their support and the rest of the fourteen features. Thus, while the support for the bodhisattvas' application of mindfulness constitutes receiving, reflecting, and meditating on the Dharma of the Great Vehicle, the flaw that conflicts with this support is precisely the lack of reception, reflection, and meditation based on the Great Vehicle Dharma. The same relationship holds for the remaining features. In terms of the remedy for listeners and self-realized buddhas, the conflicting factor takes the form of the marks of purity, bliss, permanence, and self, whereas, with respect to the authentic accomplishment of the bodhisattvas, the conflicting factor is lack of attainment of the ten grounds and the ground of buddhahood.

Having in this way provided a brief presentation of the authentic eliminations, what follows next is an account of their internal divisions. When, here in cyclic existence, the bodhisattvas take on a corporeal existence as Indra, Brahma, a universal emperor, or the like, they do so in such a way that they fully partake of the finest enjoyments. They practice the four authentic eliminations to ensure that they do not fall under the power of afflictions such as attachment but instead remain unstained by affliction. The four eliminations are also practiced in order to shed the five obscurations—(1) the pursuit of pleasure, (2) the wish to harm, (3) sloth and torpor, (4) restlessness and regret, and (5) doubt—and to discard the ways of directing the mind that are concerned with the results of the inferior vehicles of listeners and self-realized buddhas rather than with those of the Great Vehicle.

Likewise, one practices the four authentic eliminations for the following purposes: eliminating the phenomena that obscure one's ability to ascend above the grounds of inspired conduct and so enter the first ground and beyond; eliminating the flaws that from the second through the sixth ground hinder the attainment of the absence of marks that is associated with the seventh ground; eliminating the flaws that are obstacles to one's attainment of prophecy on the eighth ground; eliminating the obscurations that hinder one's attainment of the four correct awarenesses on the ninth ground, along with one's attainment of the ensuing full maturation of sentient beings as one teaches them the Dharma; eliminating the obscurations that prevent one's empowerment as the regent of the thus-gone ones on the tenth ground; eliminating the obscurations that hinder the accomplishment of the purification of buddha fields on the pure eighth, ninth, and tenth grounds; and eliminating obscurations in the form of factors that conflict with the attainment of the final, eleventh ground of buddhahood. From the grounds of inspired conduct through to the end of the continuity of the ten grounds, the wise bodhisattvas thus cultivate the four authentic eliminations as the remedy of the factors that conflict with the path. As for the way they do so, a sūtra teaches:

> One aspires, exerts oneself, arouses diligence, thoroughly seizes, and genuinely and thoroughly rests.

Thus it explains their cultivation in terms of five maxims. While the first of these, aspiration, functions as the support for diligence, the remaining four constitute its nature. Hence, one exerts oneself in, and applies oneself to, the spiritual practice of calm abiding and special insight based on the aspiration to (1) prevent the arising of whatever nonvirtue has not arisen, (2) eliminate whatever nonvirtue has arisen up to the present time, (3) bring forth whatever virtue has not yet arisen, and (4) enrich the virtue that is already present.

When practicing calm abiding and special insight in this way, certain negative tendencies may manifest. Some of these, such as dullness and torpor, accord with calm abiding, whereas others, such as agitation and distraction, accord with special insight. At times, however, neither of these forms of negative tendency will be present and the mind instead assumes a natural mode of rest. With mindfulness and alertness, one then notices whenever negative tendencies manifest, and one directs the mind to whichever of the three marks of calm abiding, uplifting, and equanimity is appropriate. This is what is known as "cultivating the three marks" in the context of the so-called arousing of diligence in terms of the fourfold formation and the three marks. By means of these three marks, one then thoroughly seizes the mind, allowing it to assume its natural mode free from dejection or agitation. Without leaving that state, the mind is to be authentically and thoroughly settled. If dejection, sleepiness, or torpor should arise, one awakens from such states by directing the mind toward the qualities of the thus-gone ones and the bodhisattvas, or the qualities of meditative absorption. In this way, one directs the mind toward the marks that uplift it. If the mind becomes preoccupied with sense pleasures or outer entities, thereby becoming agitated and distracted, one instead contemplates the defects of cyclic existence and the faults of distraction, thereby bringing the distracted mind under control. As one then inwardly directs the mind toward the marks of calm abiding, its tendency to stray toward the objects is pacified. Once the mind has in this way become free from dejection and agitation, it should be directed toward the marks of equanimity and allowed to settle within the latter state. At that point, no further remedy should be formed.

In this way, one thoroughly seizes the mind by means of the three marks. With the mark of calm abiding, the mind is seized free from agitation. With the mark of uplifting, or of special insight, it is seized free from dejection and dullness. With the mark of equanimity, it is seized within that very state of freedom from dullness and agitation. Hence, in this context, diligence is practiced with respect to the three marks, and the three marks are the means for seizing the mind. When through the repeated application of such means the mind is seized, it will also gain flexibility, thereby reaching a state of rest that is effortless and natural. This is the fruition, the authentic and thorough rest.

While there are also other ways of accounting for the sūtra's five maxims, here the explanation has followed Sthiramati's commentary. Since all of the authentic eliminations that are practiced in the context of these five serve to overcome their respective conflicting factors, they are all definitively referred to as "remedies."

3. The Four Bases of Miraculous Power

The steadfast ones' bases of miraculous power
Possess supreme characteristics and are four in number.
They arise for the sake of the accomplishment
Of one's own and all others' objectives. [XIX.51]

Support, divisions,
Means, and full accomplishment—
These are held to constitute a thorough classification
Of the steadfast ones' bases of miraculous power. [XIX.52]

Based on transcendent concentration,
The types and the means are four;
The full accomplishment is explained
To involve six features. [XIX.53]

The first engenders effort,
The second contributes,
The third places,
And the fourth is the remedy. [XIX.54]

Vision, instruction,
Reveling by way of abidance,
Aspiration, mastery, and attainment of qualities—
Such is the cultivation. [XIX.55]

The investigation of the bases of miraculous power begins with their brief presentation: **The steadfast ones' bases of miraculous power possess supreme characteristics and are four in number.**

They arise for the sake of the accomplishment of one's own and all others' objectives, mundane as well as supramundane. **Support, divisions, means, and full accomplishment**—these are held to constitute a thorough classification of the steadfast ones' bases of miraculous power.

Next follows the explanation. While all are **based on transcendent concentration, the** four **types** of bases of miraculous power are (1) intention, (2) diligence, (3) attention, and (4) discernment, **and the means are four** in number. Moreover, **the full accomplishment is explained to involve six features.** The means for completing the four meditative absorptions involve eight applications that serve to eliminate conflicting factors. These are (1) intention, (2) effort, (3) faith, (4) agility, (5) mindfulness, (6) alertness, (7) attention, and (8) equanimity. Among these eight, intention, effort, and faith constitute **the first** of the four means, which **engenders effort.** When there is faith and inspired pursuit, this will generate effort. **The second** of the four means **contributes** and consists of agility. **The third** means includes mindfulness and alertness and **places** the mind because, due to the first, the mind will not be distracted from the focal point, and due to the second, any such mental distraction will be clearly noticed. **And, finally, the fourth** means, which constitutes attention and equanimity, **is the remedy** for the primary and subsidiary afflictions.

The full accomplishment consists of the following: (1) **vision,** which refers to the accomplishments of the fleshly eye, the divine eye, the eye of insight, the eye of Dharma, and the buddha eye; (2) **instruction** by means of the six superknowledges, which thus involves going to a particular location and instructing the beings there based on knowledge of their languages, minds, past paths, and future paths so as to bring them thereby to deliverance; (3) **reveling** in the display of numerous emanations and so forth **by way of abidance** in meditative concentration; (4) reveling by means of superior **aspiration**s, as is taught extensively in the *Sūtra on the Ten Grounds;* (5) the tenfold **mastery, and** (6) the **attainment of** the **qualities** of the powers, fearlessnesses, and the unshared buddha qualities. **Such is the cultivation.**

The steadfast bodhisattvas' bases of miraculous power are characterized by an endowment with qualities that are supreme compared with the listeners and self-realized buddhas. The four bases of miraculous power are (1) intention, (2) diligence, (3) attention, and (4) discernment. They are known as bases of miraculous power because the possession of these four brings the mastery of miraculous powers, such as the ability to fly through the sky. Since they arise for the sake of the accomplishment of all one's mundane and supramundane objectives and those of all sentient beings, they are superior to the bases of miraculous power possessed by the listeners and self-realized buddhas. The steadfast bodhisattvas' bases of miraculous power are held to be classifiable with reference to their support, divisions, means, and full accomplishment. In terms of support, they emerge through transcendent concentration. That is to say, affinity with the four immeasurables brings a flexibility of mind that, along with the perfectly pure attainment of the first, second, third, and fourth concentrations, will mean the accomplishment of superknowledges.

Four divisions pertain to the bases of miraculous power, just as there are four means. Thus, intention, diligence, attention, and discernment are divisions that are made at the level of essence. The confidence that all phenomena are empty and devoid of self engenders delight and respect, and so arouses diligence. Such diligence will, in turn, bring forth the attainment of the one-pointed resting of the mind in meditative absorption. In other words, with the intent to accomplish the four correct eliminations, one applies them with devoted diligence and so attains one-pointed mind. Alternatively, we may also say that diligence, as a basis of miraculous power, refers to the attainment of one-pointed mind through the diligence of constant application of the four authentic eliminations. In short, while the intention to attain meditative absorption is the cause, the arousing of diligence based on this is the actual means for accomplishment.

Attention constitutes actual calm abiding. Based on the habitual tendencies from having practiced calm abiding in past lives, one will, in one's present life, be able to attain the mind of one-pointed rest with minimal effort. It is this latter attainment that is the meditative absorption of attention. Discernment, on the other hand, constitutes special insight. This is the attainment of a one-pointed mind free from doubt as a result of intelligently investigating the instructions as one receives them. In short, all four factors of intention, diligence, attention, and discernment are concurrent within the meditative absorption of one-pointed focus.

As for the four means of accomplishing the bases of miraculous power, these are actually a summary of the eight applications that serve to eliminate the five flaws that otherwise prevent the accomplishment of meditative absorption. The eight applications that thus serve to eliminate flaws are (1) intention, (2) effort, (3) faith, (4) agility, (5) mindfulness, (6) alertness, (7) attention, and (8) equanimity. When, to begin with, one's faith is directed toward the attainment of meditative absorption, one will develop the intention to accomplish it, and based on this intent, one will apply effort. Hence, if there is effort, then faith and intention must have preceded it—and for this reason all three can be subsumed within the category of effort, which in this sense is the means of delighted exertion. The second means for accomplishing the bases is agility. With the attainment of physical and mental flexibility, the factor of agility serves to facilitate the accomplishment of meditative absorption. Since mindfulness and alertness function in the same way, they are contained in a single means of accomplishment, namely, the undistracted placement of the mind upon its focal point. Finally, attention and equanimity constitute the fourth means, which serves as the remedy for thoughts and affliction.

Next, the sixfold full accomplishment that is supported by the four bases of miraculous power is explained.

(1) Full accomplishment of vision involves the five eyes, as follows. (1) Through the maturation of the training in the four bases of miraculous power, the fleshly eye will perceive all coarse and subtle forms within a billionfold universe. (2) The perception of the miraculous eye, which is also known as the divine eye, arises due to having cultivated any of the concentrations, from the first to the fourth. In a way that surpasses the fleshly eye, it thus sees all coarse or subtle forms throughout the ten directions and the three times. Moreover, (3) the insight eye of the noble ones perceives the intrinsic nature of suchness, whereas (4) the eye of Dharma knows the words and meanings of all the scriptural teachings

contained in the sūtras and so on without any impediment. Finally, (5) the buddha eye sees directly all cognizable phenomena of the three times, both as they are and in their multiplicity.

The perception of the fleshly eye may cover the distance of one league, a hundred leagues, the extent of Jambudvīpa, and right up to the full extent of a billionfold universe. The fleshly eye of a buddha, however, perceives all forms within the worlds of the ten directions. As for the divine eye, this may be the result either of karmic action or of meditation practice. The first is the type of eye that gods are born with due to their past actions, an extremely bright faculty that clearly perceives all forms near and far. The divine eye that manifests through meditation is an attainment of spiritual practitioners who practice concentration. As such, it is an extremely bright faculty that manifests as a transformation of the elements that belong to the practitioner's particular realm of concentration. Perceiving the deaths and transferences of sentient beings in the past, as well as the destinations of their future births, it cognizes past, future, and present forms. The Dharma eye is aware of the particular and general characteristics of phenomena and is capable of cognizing the streams of being of individuals who are either at the same or a lower level than one. The buddha eye sees all phenomena free from any attachment or impediment. Further classifications of the five eyes can be learned from the commentary.

(2) The full accomplishment of instruction involves the six superknowledges. When, through the bases of miraculous power, one receives the scriptures of instruction from the thus-gone ones and also shares such scriptures with other sentient beings, the cause of this is one's accomplishment of superknowledges based on concentration. While (1) the superknowledge of miracles will afford unhindered passage to buddha fields and realms of sentient beings, (2) the divine eye will grant the perception of the exalted forms of the buddhas and the bodies of sentient beings. (3) By means of the divine ear, one will hear the speech of thus-gone ones and the voices of sentient beings. (4) With knowledge of the minds of others, one is aware of the various thoughts of sentient beings. And (5) through the knowledge of previous existences, one knows the settings of one's own past lives and those of all others, as well as the relevant future destinations. Finally, (6) with the superknowledge of

the exhaustion of defilements, one is aware of both the presence and the disappearance of afflictions within one's own mind stream and those of all others. Thus, receiving the scriptural instructions from the bliss-gone ones, one also teaches them to others.

(3) As for the full accomplishment of reveling by way of abidance, this is a reveling in the display of miracles and emanations within the circles of the thus-gone ones and elsewhere.

(4) The full accomplishment of aspiration is the practice of taking birth as gods, humans, and so on, in accordance with one's aspirations. The ability to do so is accomplished by the wakefulness that arises by the power of aspiration. Thus, taking birth and acting as one pleases, one revels in diverse practices for the benefit of others. As is taught in the *Sūtra on the Ten Grounds*, "it is not easy to describe" the qualities of the body, the qualities of the mind power, and the qualities of the melodious speech that are the possession of bodhisattvas, who in this way take birth by the power of aspiration.

(5) The full accomplishment of mastery concerns the attainment of the ten masteries. These are as follows: (1) The mastery of life refers to the ability to remain for as long as one wishes, having blessed the formations of one's life span by the power of cultivating the four bases of miraculous power. (2) Mastery of the mind is the ability to enter, as one pleases, the equipoise of the immeasurable meditative absorptions of the Great Vehicle. (3) Mastery of material things enables one to rain down at will from the sky whatever material things may be beneficial to sentient beings. (4) Mastery of karmic action consists of the ability to produce various emanations of body and speech. It also implies being able to bless karmic actions so that instead of producing rebirth in a given realm or world they instead bring rebirth in a different realm or world. (5) Mastery of birth is the ability to dwell in the concentrations of the form realm and, without losing such concentration, to take birth in the desire realm for the benefit of sentient beings. (6) Mastery of wishes is an ability, for example, to turn earth into gold and water into nectar. (7) Mastery of aspiration, as illustrated by the ten great aspirations of the first ground, is the full accomplishment of bringing forth innumerable great aspirations so as to be able to accomplish perfectly one's own welfare and that of all others. (8) Mastery of miracles implies an ability

to bring forth a boundless display of miraculous feats—such as bursting into flames, flying through the sky, and sending forth rays of light—in order to engender faith in sentient beings. (9) Mastery of wakefulness is the full perfection of the fourfold awareness of Dharmas, meanings, definitive words, and acumen. (10) Mastery of Dharma consists of the ability to employ the words, phrases, and syllables of the Dharma teachings of the sūtras and so forth in a way that is satisfying to the minds of sentient beings.

Regarding the causes of the ten masteries, the first three are accomplished through the perfection of transcendent generosity. That is to say, generosity with respect to fearlessness, the Dharma, and material things will, respectively, accomplish the masteries of life, mind, and necessities. The masteries of karmic action and birth are, on the other hand, achieved through the perfection of transcendent discipline. As the actions of body and speech are purified, one will succeed in sending forth various emanations of body and speech, and through completely pure discipline, one will be able to take birth according to one's wishes. With the perfection of transcendent patience, one will avoid upsetting the minds of sentient beings and will instead be agreeable to them. Thus one will gain mastery in bringing forth whatever they wish for, just exactly as they wish. By the power of perfecting transcendent diligence, one will gain mastery of aspirations because one's previous endeavors for one's own benefit and that of all others will ensure that one is subsequently able to see all such aspirations fulfilled. Moreover, with the perfection of transcendent concentration comes a mastery of the mind that allows one to display miracles in whichever way one wishes, and the masteries of wakefulness and the Dharma will be attained through the perfection of transcendent insight.

Finally, when the root text speaks of the "attainment of qualities," this refers to (6) the full accomplishment of the attainment of qualities. This consists of the accomplishment of the perfect qualities of a buddha's ten powers, four fearlessnesses, eighteen unshared qualities, and so on. Thus, based on the four bases of miraculous powers, one cultivates a full accomplishment that is sixfold.

4. The Five Faculties

Enlightenment, conduct, supreme learning,
Calm abiding, and special insight—
These should be known as the bases for faith and the rest
In the context of accomplishing the objectives. [XIX.56]

Next follows the investigation of the faculties. With regard to the faculty of faith, its basis is its focal point: unsurpassable **enlightenment**. The basis for the faculty of diligence is the bodhisattva **conduct**. In the case of the faculty of mindfulness, the basis is the **supreme learning** contained in the Great Vehicle. The basis for the faculty of meditative absorption is **calm abiding, and** in terms of the faculty of insight, the basis is **special insight**. Thus, **these should be known as the bases for faith and the rest in the context of** the latter faculties **accomplishing** their specific **objectives**.

The five faculties are those of (1) faith, (2) diligence, (3) mindfulness, (4) meditative absorption, and (5) insight.

As for the first of these, (1) faith can be divided in terms of conviction, inspiration, and aspiration. Conviction consists of the acknowledgment of facts such as the unfailing relationship between karmic actions and their results; inspiration is the mind's sharp brightening as it is inspired by the qualities of the three jewels; aspiration is the wish for accomplishment that ensues from seeing that one is actually capable of attaining the transcendence of suffering and practicing the path. Alternatively, faith can be seen as fourfold: (1) having gained conviction in the consequences of karmic actions, one refrains from evil even at the cost of one's life; (2) with faith in the conduct of the bodhisattvas, one becomes uninterested in other vehicles; (3) having found faith in the Dharma of dependent origination, the profound emptiness that has the nature of absence of self and the three gateways of liberation, one crushes all latent views; (4) with faith in all the vast qualities of buddhahood, such as the powers and fearlessnesses, one practices in order to accomplish them free from doubts and hesitation. This is how the *Sūtra Taught by Akṣayamati* characterizes the faculty of faith.

The qualities that are the objects of one's faith will be accomplished by (2) the faculty of diligence, which is of the nature of the four authentic eliminations. Moreover, (3) mindfulness ensures that the qualities that are cultivated with diligence are not forgotten, and so the faculty of mindfulness consists of the attainment of the four applications of mindfulness. (4) The faculty of meditative absorption is the attainment of the equipoise of the four concentrations and the four formless realms. Thus, while the faculty of mindfulness ensures that attention to the qualities does not decrease, the faculty of meditative absorption allows the mind to settle upon them in a one-pointed and continuous fashion. Finally, (5) the faculty of insight cognizes the specific and general characteristics of the qualities that are held single-pointedly by the faculty of meditative absorption, and it comprehends the four noble truths.

Based on this general presentation, we may next consider the bases of the five faculties, in the sense of their supports or focal points. The basis or focal point of the faculty of faith is enlightenment. Thus, focusing on the inexhaustible wakefulness of the fruition of the Great Vehicle, or on the enlightenment that is the nondual wakefulness of the first ground, one experiences faith with a resolve to accomplish these qualities. The faculty of diligence focuses on the bodhisattva conduct that comprises both the special discipline associated with the grounds and transcendences and the discipline of special insight. The faculty of diligence thus observes and practices these two aspects of discipline. The faculty of mindfulness retains one's learning of the Great Vehicle, accurately and without forgetting anything, just as one has received it, absorbed it, and comprehensively resolved it by means of words. Moreover, the faculty of meditative absorption that is associated with inspired conduct focuses on the way to attain the distinctive calm abiding of the first ground. The faculty of insight, on the other hand, is focused on the attainment of the nonconceptual wakefulness that is the special insight of the first ground. Hence, since they are observed in this way, enlightenment and so forth serve as the focal objects of faith and the rest of the faculties.

These are referred to as the five faculties because they rule the accomplishment of all objectives associated with complete purification. Thus, faith, diligence, mindfulness, meditative absorption and insight control, respectively, the attainments of enlightenment, bodhisattva conduct, learning of the Great Vehicle Dharma, calm abiding, and special insight. Alternatively, we may understand their being termed "faculties" as a reference to the fact that they bring about a natural attainment of all such objectives.

5. The Five Powers

> Faith and the rest bring access to the grounds,
> But are held to be associated with thorough affliction;
> Because the conflicting factors have weakened,
> This set is nevertheless known as "powers." [XIX.57]

> On the stages of acceptance and supreme property, **faith and the rest** of the five qualities **bring access to,** and attainment of, **the grounds, but** since they are not supramundane they **are** still **held to be associated with thorough affliction. Because the conflicting factors have weakened, this set is nevertheless known as "powers."**

Once faith, diligence, mindfulness, meditative absorption, and insight can no longer be repressed by their respective conflicting factors, they are referred to as "powers." Hence, access to the first ground of the noble ones is attained due to the strength of these five powers. Yet, although it is thus the steady increase of these powers that is directly responsible for the attainment of the grounds of the noble ones, the powers are themselves not free from the discards that are to be eliminated through seeing. Since they are in this way associated with affliction, they belong to the grounds of ordinary individuals. As for the distinction between faculties and powers, although the five powers are also mundane, they are nevertheless distinguished from the five faculties, as the latter are still prone to obstruction due to lack of faith, laziness, forgetfulness, distraction, and misguided intelligence. When the force of those conflicting factors has weakened, so that they can no longer subdue the remedying five factors of faith and so on, then those very factors of faith and so forth will be referred to as "powers."

6. THE SEVEN ASPECTS OF ENLIGHTENMENT

The seven aspects of enlightenment are, respectively, mindfulness, discernment of phenomena, diligence, joy, agility, meditative absorption, and equanimity.

(1) Mindfulness is associated with calm abiding. It ensures that the actualization of the thirty-seven factors that accord with enlightenment, which occurs by means of practice and experience, is not forgotten but remains clearly present in the mind.

(2) As regards the insight that discerns phenomena, this is the special insight on the path of seeing that is aware of the qualities of thorough affliction that are to be eliminated, as well as the qualities of complete purification that are to be adopted.

(3) Diligence allows for the appropriation of the special qualities that arise on the stages that follow, and it accomplishes the elimination of the flaws that would otherwise prevent their attainment.

(4) Joy is the supreme delight of body and mind when, on the first ground, the universally present nature of the basic field of phenomena has been realized directly and the discards through seeing have been relinquished. The presence of this joy is the reason that the ground is named "the Joyous."

(5) Agility ensues in the absence of the negative tendencies that otherwise leave body and mind inflexible. Agility of the body means physical fitness; mental agility allows the mind to access the focal points without hindrance.

(6) Meditative absorption is the mind's one-pointed observation of the suchness of the basic field of phenomena.

(7) Equanimity is the natural immutability that manifests in the absence of all flaws of dullness and agitation. It is like a brilliant sea, free from waves and pollutants.

Among these aspects, discernment of phenomena, diligence, and joy are aspects of special insight, whereas agility, meditative absorption, and equanimity belong to calm abiding. Mindfulness is associated with both and is therefore universal.

Here, the classification of these seven aspects will be explained in terms of (1) their temporal context, (2) the type of knowledge they involve, (3) their own character, and (4) their fivefold categorization.

1. Temporal Context

> The classification of the aspects of enlightenment
> Is held to pertain to those who have entered the ground.
> [XIX.58a–b]

The classification of the aspects of enlightenment is held to pertain to those who have entered the ground of the Joyous.

On the grounds of inspired conduct, there is also a presence of mindfulness, insight, and so on; yet, on those earlier stages they do not qualify for the name "aspects of enlightenment." Conversely, the factors of mindfulness and so on that are present in the streams of being of those who have entered the flawless grounds of the noble ones—factors that are thus attained on the first ground—are indeed classified as aspects of enlightenment.

2. The Contents of Their Knowledge

> Because they have realized
> That phenomena and all sentient beings are equality.
> [XIX.58c–d]

Those entering the grounds do so **because they have realized that phenomena** are equality devoid of the two selves **and that all sentient beings are equality** without any notion of difference between oneself and sentient beings.

The significance of their being referred to as aspects of enlightenment is explained next. Mindfulness and so on are termed "aspects of enlightenment" because they constitute the direct cognition of the equality that is the nature of enlightenment. As such, they realize that the phenomena of the origin of suffering as well as all sentient beings are in fact the equality of primordial enlightenment due to their pure intrinsic nature, which is naturally unborn from the beginning. The supramundane ultimate mind of enlightenment is actualized at the point of realizing this.

Alternatively, we may also say that, during equipoise, the equality of all phenomena is realized through the recognition of the space-like absence of any self in the form of a person or phenomena. Meanwhile, the ensuing attainment is the occasion where the equality of self and others is realized beyond distinctions, along the lines of the following recognition: "What I am is also what all sentient beings are. What they are is also what I am. Just as I pacify my own suffering, I must pacify the suffering of all sentient beings!"

3. The Character of the Seven

> For the conquest of objects of knowledge not yet conquered,
> Mindfulness is fully active;
> With their thorough discernment, they crush
> All the marks of thought. [XIX.59]
>
> With diligence they apply themselves
> So that they may quickly know all without exception.
> As the light of Dharma spreads,
> Their joy is always on the increase. [XIX.60]
>
> Escaping all obscurations,
> They gain the bliss of agility.
> Through meditative absorption, they experience
> The fulfillment of all wishes. [XIX.61]
>
> With equanimity they abide throughout,
> Just as they please;
> Abiding in subsequent attainment and nonconceptuality,
> They abide always supreme. [XIX.62]

Bodhisattvas endowed with such qualities
Are likened to universal monarchs;
Resembling the seven jewels,
The aspects of enlightenment are their constant retinue.
[xix.63]

Next, it is shown how the aspects of enlightenment resemble the wheel and the rest of the seven jewels. **For the** sake of the **conquest of objects of knowledge** that have **not yet** been **conquered, mindfulness,** as an aspect of enlightenment, **is fully active,** just as the precious wheel of the universal monarch that travels to places not yet visited. **With their thorough** and complete **discernment** of phenomena, **they,** the bodhisattvas, **crush all the marks of thought** just like the precious elephant crushes any attack. **With diligence they,** the bodhisattvas, **apply themselves so that they may quickly know all** that is to be realized **without exception.** This is similar to the way that the precious steed moves swiftly across the wide earth to the shores of the ocean. **As** the bodhisattvas arouse diligence, and as **the light of Dharma spreads** thereby, **their joy is always on the increase,** just as when the special light of the precious jewel delights the universal monarch. **Escaping all** the **obscurations** in the form of negative tendencies, **they gain the bliss of agility** as body and mind become workable. This resembles the way the precious lady lets the universal monarch experience joy. **Through meditative absorption, they experience the fulfillment of all wishes,** just as the wealth of the universal emperor is accomplished by the precious householder. **With equanimity,** that is, nonconceptual wakefulness, **they,** the bodhisattvas, **abide throughout** all occasions **just as they please. Abiding in** the supreme **subsequent attainment,** which allows them to attain all that is to be attained and eliminate all that is to be eliminated, **and** abiding in the supreme **nonconceptuality,** both of which thereby become effortless, **they abide always supreme.** This resembles the way that the precious general directs his armies.

In conclusion it is said: **Bodhisattvas endowed with such qualities are likened to universal monarchs** because, resembling the seven jewels, the aspects of enlightenment are their constant retinue.

Next are explained the seven aspects of enlightenment. For example, just as there are seven precious features characteristic of the realm of a universal emperor, there are also seven aspects that characterize the enlightenment of a bodhisattva who directly realizes the enlightenment of primordial nonarising. When a universal emperor appears in the world, the merit of that emperor will bring forth (1) a thousand-spoked precious wheel. Perfectly rounded and sparkling brightly, this wheel is made of divine substances and produced by the artisan of the gods. Like a second sun, it will ascend into the sky, and when the emperor with his armies follows the course that the wheel takes in the sky, they will, wherever they go, immediately be welcomed by the rulers of the land, residing in fortresses and castles. As soon as the emperor appears, everyone will consider themselves his subjects, and so he is victorious throughout all realms not previously visited and that were not previously under his dominion. Such is the power of what is known as "the precious wheel."

Likewise, the emperor possesses (2) a precious elephant, which is like a snow mountain, flying in the sky. Perfectly shaped and endowed with excellent strength, it is magnificent to behold and indeed worthy of great kings. With its perfect prowess, it can crush all enemy armies.

(3) As for the emperor's precious steed, it is of a pure, blackish blue color, like the neck of a peacock. Stunningly perfect in terms of color and physique, this all-knowing horse will easily cover the distance all the way to the shore of the farthest ocean and back again, all within the time that it takes for a man to have his meal at daybreak. It has the most excellent qualities that a mount could possibly possess.

(4) The emperor's precious jewel fulfills all wishes. Made of the most exquisite lapis lazuli, its dark blue color and design are splendid. Like a sun, it illuminates the land within a mile's distance, and while it is cooling to the touch during hot weather, it emits warmth during times of cold. Merely touching this jewel heals all diseases, and in barren places

and deserts, the jewel will become a source of excellent streams. Fulfilling all aims, it is endowed with perfect powers.

(5) The precious empress is of supreme beauty. Endearing to behold, the mere sight of her brings joy. With few afflictions, she is faithful and so on, and with the highest reverence for the emperor, she is captivating to the mind. Her excellent ways and mode of conduct are enthralling to everyone. From her lips and body emerges a divine fragrance, and the touch of her body is supreme, bestowing coolness, warmth, and so on, depending on what one wishes for. She possesses these and all other such excellent qualities.

(6) The precious master of the household need only stretch out his hand and all riches will appear; his wealth equals that of Vaiśravaṇa. Whatever the emperor orders he will accomplish, and he is endowed with the most perfect qualities of all who carry internal responsibilities.

(7) The precious protector of all, known also as the precious minister or the precious general, is both courageous and steadfast. Endowed with perfect power, he subjugates adversaries, and he is expert in knowing when to let the army advance and when to retreat. He takes care of those who do well and punishes those at fault. Perfectly capable of fulfilling the emperor's wishes and of subduing the enemy, he does so, just as instructed.

The preceding seven can be taken as illustrative examples of the following.

(1) When the bodhisattvas attain the first ground, their mindfulness that recollects their previous training in the Dharma on the grounds of inspired conduct conquers the obscurations that otherwise, on the former grounds, had hindered their direct knowledge. In that sense they can be said to conquer objects of knowledge because they defeat the discards through seeing and attain the direct perception of that which is to be known. In this way, the bodhisattvas' mindfulness can be likened to the precious wheel that grants the universal emperor victory in all the lands that he visits.

(2) On the first ground, the bodhisattva's insight fully discerns phenomena, and as it realizes the absence of self with respect to both phenomena and persons, it crushes all marks. In this regard, it is like the precious elephant that crushes the enemy armies.

(3) With the diligence of the bodhisattvas on the first ground, one aims to realize and accomplish quickly all the special qualities associated with superknowledge and so forth. Active in this way, the bodhisattvas' diligence can be likened to the precious steed that swiftly delivers its rider to the desired destination.

(4) With the attainment of the first ground, there is direct realization of the nature of reality. When the Dharma beyond the world is spreading its great light in this way, body and mind will be constantly nourished by joy. This resembles the luminous, precious jewel that dispels the darkness.

(5) On the path of liberation of the first ground, one escapes—or is completely liberated from—the factors that are to be discarded through seeing. With inflexibility simply no longer possible, one attains the bliss of agility. This can be likened to the delight that the emperor experiences by the touch of the precious queen.

(6) As an aspect of enlightenment, meditative absorption accomplishes all the qualities associated with superknowledge and so forth, and it fulfills all wishes and objectives to the heart's content. Hence, this is comparable to the precious master of the household, who brings forth whatever riches the emperor may wish to employ.

(7) The enlightenment aspect of equanimity allows the bodhisattvas of the first ground to abide always as they please—free from dullness and agitation, attachment and aversion, and all other such root and subsidiary afflictions—perfectly at ease. During the ensuing attainment, their pure mundane wakefulness will accomplish the welfare of sentient beings. This wakefulness also allows them to attain the qualities of the higher grounds that they have yet to achieve, as well as eliminate those flaws that they still need to eliminate in order to leave the lower grounds behind. During equipoise, they abide completely unsupported within nonconceptual wakefulness. Thus, equanimity will constantly uphold the supreme bodhisattvas' constant abidance. (Note that in the context of the supreme bodhisattvas' constant abidance, the root text [line XIX.19] that appears in Sthiramati's commentary reads; "Thus, their abidance always makes them supreme.")

Therefore, equanimity can be compared to the precious general, who brings the four armies together so as to vanquish and expel those who are to be driven out, while gathering and taking care of those who are to be kept together. In this way, the general will eventually establish a place of peace, free from violence and harm. The general's activity in terms of dispelling and keeping together illustrates the workings of the pure mundane wakefulness, which adheres to what is to be adopted and rejects what is to be discarded. The general's eventual standing at ease, free from harm, is an image of the nonconceptual wakefulness that is at rest within the complete pacification of all focal points.

As they employ and master these seven aspects of enlightenment, the bodhisattvas are likened to the universal emperor. Resembling the seven precious features that are characteristic of the latter's rule, the aspects of enlightenment are the bodhisattvas' constant retinue.

4. Their Inclusion in Five Categories

They are the aspect of nature and the aspect of basis;
The third, the aspect of definitive emergence;
The fourth, the aspect of benefit;
And the three that are aspects of freedom from affliction.
[xix.64]

Next is explained the sense in which **they**, that is, the aspects of enlightenment, are "aspects." Fully discerning phenomena is **the aspect of nature** because this is the essence of enlightenment, **and** mindfulness is **the aspect of basis** since everything emerges based on it. **The third**, diligence, is **the aspect of definitive emergence**, for it provides an unbroken continuity up to completion. **The fourth**, joy, is **the aspect of benefit** insofar as it brings happiness of mind, **and** agility, meditative absorption, and equanimity are **the three that are aspects of freedom from affliction**. These three are, respectively, the agent whereby freedom from affliction is attained, the support for this attainment, and the freedom from affliction as such.

The way that the seven aspects can be included in five categories is as follows.

(1) The full discerning of phenomena constitutes the aspect of nature because this discernment is the essence of the realization of enlightenment.

(2) Next, mindfulness is the aspect of basis. The affinity that is achieved through repeated recollection of the teachings at the time of inspired conduct culminates in the mindfulness that is present at the great stage of the supreme quality. It is through such mindfulness that the full discernment of phenomena, as well as the other aspects, emerges.

(3) Diligence is the aspect of definitive emergence. It is through the power of diligence that one is able to go beyond the grounds of inspired conduct and emerge definitively on the first ground. Thus, the mindfulness and diligence that are specific to the first ground are the final fruition of the mindfulness and diligence that were present on the grounds of inspired conduct.

(4) At the time of attaining the first ground, joy is the aspect of benefit that is associated with the realization of the basic field of phenomena because such realization engenders extraordinary joy.

(5) Agility, meditative absorption, and equanimity constitute the aspect of freedom from affliction. As body and mind attain agility, one is freed from the negative tendencies that are associated with the afflictive obscurations. Thus, agility is not only that which frees from affliction but also the state of freedom from affliction. Meditative absorption is the basis upon which one attains freedom from the afflictions because subsidiary afflictions such as dullness and agitation are dispelled when one abides in meditative absorption. Equanimity is the essence of freedom from affliction because when resting at ease within equanimity there are no afflictions at all.

7. The Eight Aspects of the Noble Path

Beyond that, one applies oneself
In harmony with the realization;
Thus one correctly realizes the principles
And engages with those principles. [XIX.65]

The threefold action is purified.
That which is to be known, the path,
And the special qualities—
One cultivates the remedies for that which obscures them.
[xix.66]

Next, the aspects of the path are discerned. Beyond that, meaning subsequent to the attainment of the aspects of enlightenment, **one applies oneself in harmony with the realization** that occurred during the equipoise, and so the authentic view takes the form of thinking, "This is what I have realized!"

Thus, with authentic thought, **one correctly realizes the principles** of the means for revealing that realization to others, **and one engages with** the corpus of scriptural teachings, the sūtras and so forth, in relation to **those principles.** Furthermore, **the threefold action is purified through** authentic speech, activity, and livelihood, while by means of tireless, authentic effort one cultivates, over a long period of time, the remedy for **that which** obscures what **is to be known.** Moreover, authentic mindfulness is cultivated as a remedy for that which obscures **the path.** Thus, as it prevents dullness or agitation with respect to the features of calm abiding, thorough seizing, and equanimity, it is employed for the sake of the direct perception of the path. **And,** finally, authentic meditative absorption is cultivated as the remedy for that which prevents the manifestation of **the special qualities.** Thus **one cultivates the remedies for that which obscures them,** that is, the factors just mentioned.

The eightfold noble path consists of authentic (1) view, (2) thought, (3) speech, (4) activity, (5) livelihood, (6) effort, (7) mindfulness, and (8) meditative absorption.

(1) As for the authentic view, this is the aspect of focusing and meditating on the equality of the basic field of phenomena, empty of any self in the form of a person or phenomenon, just as it was realized directly by the insight that discerns phenomena on the path of seeing.

(2) Authentic thought is caused by authentic view. It conceives of, and wishes for, the causes for deliverance beyond the three realms—special discipline, attention, and insight. It likewise concerns itself with the absence of such afflictions as the pursuit of pleasure and the wish to cause harm.

(3) Authentic speech offers explanation to others, based on what has been comprehended with authentic view and authentic thought. It is free from the faults of speech—lying, harsh words, divisive talk, and idle chatter.

(4) Authentic activity is engagement with the path of liberation, based on having given up killing and other such faults of the body.

(5) Authentic livelihood consists of the relinquishment of all flawed means of livelihood, such as those based on flattery and hypocrisy.

(6) Authentic effort, based on authentic view, thought, livelihood, and activity, is the continuous process of cultivating the path of the noble ones so as to eliminate the two obscurations that are to be discarded through cultivation.

(7) Authentic mindfulness avoids forgetfulness and keeps the meaning of the Dharma clear in the mind.

(8) Authentic meditative absorption is one-pointed equipoise within the suchness of the basic field of phenomena.

As for these eight, one must, in the context of the path of conduct, abide by authentic speech, activity, and livelihood. When resting within meditative equipoise, one should meditate by means of calm abiding and special insight. In that context, authentic view, thought, and effort belong to special insight. Authentic view is precisely that which constitutes special insight, whereas thought and effort serve as its retinue. Authentic mindfulness and meditative absorption pertain to calm abiding because, while meditative absorption is the actual calm abiding, mindfulness is its retinue.

In the root text, this eightfold path is taught in stanzas 65 and 66. It is explained that, subsequent to the attainment of the first ground, the eight aspects of the noble path are to be cultivated on the second ground and beyond, as follows.

(1) With authentic view, one thus applies oneself in perfect accordance with the realization of the twofold absence of self that takes place

with the full discernment of phenomena serving as a factor of enlightenment. Thus, authentic view is the realization of, and meditation upon, the basic field of phenomena.

(2) With the comprehension of the nature of reality that is afforded by authentic view, authentic thought arrives at clear and specific principles. Such classification also takes place in relation to the corpus of scripture that teaches the nature of reality, that is, the principles of the Dharma of the sūtras and so forth that describe and indicate reality by means of names, phrases, and letters. Hence, authentic thought is the means for one's own comprehension of the purport of those principles, and it is also the means for conveying one's understanding to others—therein discerning the principles of scripture free from any errors about the intended meaning.

(3–5) Speech, activity, and livelihood serve to purify the threefold karmic action.

(6) Based on authentic effort throughout two incalculable eons, one cultivates the remedy of cognitive obscurations.

(7) Authentic mindfulness is cultivated as the remedy for that which obscures the path. When cultivating the path of calm abiding and special insight, dullness and agitation are the factors that obscure this path. When they occur, mindfulness can clear them away as one recollects the marks of calm abiding, thoroughly seizing, and equanimity, as explained above.

(8) Authentic meditative absorption serves to remedy that which obscures special qualities, such as those of the six superknowledges treated in the chapter on power.

2. Summary in Terms of Calm Abiding and Special Insight

Based on genuine rest,
Mind is placed within mind
And fully discerns phenomena;
Hence, this is calm abiding and special insight. [xix.67]

These are held to be universal, partial,
Not partial, and the cause.
Realization, definitive emergence,
Absence of marks, nonformation, [XIX.68]

Complete purification, and total purity—
The steadfast ones' spiritual practice of calm abiding and
    special insight
Is universally present on these grounds
And accomplishes everything. [XIX.69]

Next follows the investigation of calm abiding and special insight. Based on the meditative absorption of **genuine rest, mind is placed within mind and fully discerns phenomena**. Hence, it should be understood that **this is calm abiding and special insight**. As for calm abiding and special insight, **these are held to be** of **universal** importance for the accomplishment of all excellent qualities. As such, they are held to be **partial** when practiced individually, **not partial** when practiced simultaneously, **and the cause** of attainment upon the grounds of inspired conduct. **Realization** on the first ground, **definitive emergence** on the sixth, **absence of marks** on the seventh, **nonformation, complete cultivation of the buddha fields, and the total purity** of attaining buddhahood on the remaining three grounds— **the steadfast ones' spiritual practice of calm abiding and special insight is universally present on these grounds** as the cause of attainment, **and** it hence **accomplishes everything** in terms of one's own aims and that of all others.

The term "genuine abidance" refers to the undefiled fourth concentration of the form realm. On this basis, the mind is "placed within mind" with the recognition that there are no phenomena beyond what is set forth by the mind. When the mind dwells on this one-pointedly, that is calm abiding. Based on such calm abiding, special insight is the unmistaken knowledge of the essential reality of all phenomena—the nonconceptuality of their thorough discernment. Thus, in brief, are taught the characteristics of calm abiding and special insight in the Great Vehicle.

Next follow the divisions that pertain to calm abiding and special insight. The latter two are universally present throughout all practice and cultivation of the excellent qualities. As such, they are indispensable for anyone wishing to cultivate the factors of enlightenment, attain the concentrations and meditative absorptions, accomplish the superknowledges, and so on. Thus, their qualification as "universal" is due to the fact that for all aspects of training, these two constitute the main part. In the case of the practice of the four equilibria of the formless realm, however, these two are classified as "partial" because these states feature a predominance of calm abiding while still suffering from an insufficient element of special insight. Similarly, the first, second, and third concentrations of the form realm are predominantly special insight, with deficiency in terms of calm abiding. They are hence said to be characterized by a "partial" presence of calm abiding and special insight. Yet, when the two are integrated and practiced without either one of them being predominant, their cultivation is "not partial." This is the case when calm abiding and special insight are practiced in the context of the fourth concentration.

The calm abiding and special insight meditation that is associated with the stages of inspired conduct is held to be the cause for the attainment of the first ground. On the first ground itself, the two are known as "the calm abiding and special insight of realization" because this is the time when the universally present, basic field of phenomena is realized. From the second through the sixth ground, calm abiding and special insight are associated with definitive emergence because on those grounds all marks are gradually relinquished and one thus emerges definitively upon the seventh ground. Upon that seventh ground, they are known as "calm abiding and special insight without marks" because here all the various Dharma teachings of the sūtras and so forth are not treated in terms of distinct marks. Rather, one practices them as being of one taste and devoid of marks. On the eighth, ninth, and tenth ground, one practices the "calm abiding and special insight of nonformation" because on those stages the practice is effortless and spontaneously accomplished. Moreover, upon these three pure grounds, calm abiding and special insight are also referred to as "complete cultivation of the buddha fields." Since on those same levels one is accomplishing the total purity of buddhahood, divorced of the two obscurations and their habitual tendencies, they are also classified as "calm abiding and special insight of total purity."

In this way, the spiritual practice of calm abiding and special insight that is based on the different grounds extends throughout all stages of the path. It is universally present from the grounds of inspired conduct through to the tenth ground. In this way, calm abiding and special insight accomplish all one's own aims as well as those of others, as the lower stages successively give rise to the higher ones.

3. The Factors That Distinguish the Cultivation of the Factors of Enlightenment

The treatment of the factors that distinguish the cultivation of the factors of enlightenment will include: (1) skill in means, which allows for the unfailing accomplishment of great aims with little hardship; (2) complete retention of Dharma teachings previously received; (3) aspiration whereby excellent qualities will be attained in the future; (4) meditative absorption and the four summaries that ensure the purity of the path.

1. Skillful Means

> Perfection of buddha qualities,
> Thorough maturation of sentient beings,
> Swift attainment, accomplishment of activities,
> And skill in not severing the continuum of the path—[XIX.70]
>
> Upon all the grounds of the bodhisattvas,
> The means are incomparable.
> Thus, based on their skill in means,
> They accomplish all objectives. [XIX.71]

What follows is the investigation of skillful means. The means for the **perfection of buddha qualities** is nonconceptual wakefulness. For the **thorough maturation of sentient beings**, they are the four means of attraction. For the **swift attainment** of buddhahood, the means are confession, rejoicing, supplication, and dedication. For the **accomplishment of activities,** the means are meditative absorption and retention. **And skill in not severing the continuum of the path** is accomplished through the nonabiding transcendence of suffering. **Upon all the grounds of the bodhisattvas, the means are incomparable** since they possess these five features. **Thus, based on their skill in means, they accomplish all objectives.**

The qualities of buddhahood include those of the grounds, transcendences, and factors that accord with enlightenment. They are associated with the path, as well as the powers, fearlessnesses, and so forth—through to omniscience—that constitute the fruition. The means for perfecting all these qualities is nonconceptual wakefulness, for in not observing any marks in relation to the qualities of the path or the fruition, it perfects them all. As the *Transcendent Insight in One Hundred Thousand Lines* states:

> If you wish to completely perfect transcendent generosity, you must train in transcendent insight.

And so it proceeds, through to declaring:

> If you wish to attain omniscient wakefulness, you must train in transcendent insight.

The means for bringing about the thorough maturation of sentient beings are known as the four means of attraction because, through these four, one raises sentient beings out of negative states and establishes them in virtuous ones. On the means for quickly attaining the superknowledges and accomplishing manifest buddhahood, it is taught in a sūtra:

> One must confess all evil, rejoice in all merit, supplicate all the buddhas, and pray: "May I attain unsurpassable, supreme wakefulness, and so attain buddhahood."

Thus, the four means are confession, rejoicing, supplication, and dedication. Next, the means for the accomplishment of activities are retention and meditative absorption. Through retention one recollects the words and meanings of the Dharma without forgetting them, thereby accomplishing one's own welfare; with the various miraculous displays of meditative absorption, one achieves the welfare of others.

Finally, having skill in not severing the continuum of the path is to ensure that the progeny or family line of the thus-gone ones remains unbroken. Thus, this is the path of the nonabiding transcendence of suffering, composed of insight and compassion. With insight, one will not be confined to the extreme of cyclic existence, and due to compassion, one will not remain in the extreme of peace. Moreover, each of these two means is fully contained within the integrated unity of relative and ultimate enlightened mind. Implicitly, this unity includes all other means as well. Hence, the unity of the relative and ultimate enlightened mind is the supreme and singly sufficient skillful means.

Therefore, these five aspects of skillful means pertain universally to the bodhisattvas' grounds of inspired conduct, as well as to all the ten grounds. Preventing entry into the lesser vehicles and bringing about the accomplishment of the Great Vehicle's path and fruition, these means cannot be matched by any methods of the world, the listeners, or the self-realized buddhas. Expert in such means, the bodhisattva easily accomplishes all the objectives of both self and others.

2. Retention

The retentions based on ripening,
Familiarity with learning, and meditative absorption
Are lesser and greater;
The greater are threefold. [XIX.72]

Regarding the wise who have not entered, and those who have,
The retentions of those abiding on impure grounds
Are lesser and middling,
While on the pure grounds they are great. [XIX.73]

As they again and again
Fully rely on these,
The bodhisattvas constantly
Reveal and retain the sacred Dharma. [xix.74]

In terms of an investigation of **the retentions,** there are those that are attained **based on ripening** from the past, others that are attained based on **familiarity with** extensive **learning** in this life, **and** others again that are achieved through the power of **meditative absorption.** Among these, the first two types **are** the **lesser** ones, **and** the third is the **greater.** Moreover, **the greater** retentions **are threefold.** What do the three consist of? **Regarding the wise who have not** yet **entered** the grounds **and those who have** entered them, **the retentions of those abiding on impure grounds are lesser and middling, while on the pure grounds they are great. As they again and again fully rely on these** gateways of retention, **the bodhisattvas constantly reveal** the sacred Dharma to others **and retain the sacred Dharma** in themselves.

The retentions allow the bodhisattvas to retain, by means of special applications of mindfulness and insight, all words and meanings of the scriptural teachings without letting anything go to waste. Moreover, the retentions also cause teachings that one has not yet heard to appear to the mind in both word and meaning, and they bring forth the attainment of the factors of enlightenment.

As for the attainment of retention, one type of retention is the result of ripening. Here the accumulation of virtue that was accomplished in past lives by familiarizing oneself with the sacred Dharma, worshipping it, bearing it, reading it, and so forth, expresses itself in the present as an ability to absorb the words and meanings of a given teaching, simply by having the teaching explained once. Another form of retention is accomplished through a lifestyle of abundant learning as one receives explanations from numerous spiritual teachers in one's present life. When one thus becomes able to retain the words and meanings that are explained by buddhas, bodhisattvas, preceptors, masters, and so forth, this is what is referred to as "retention based on familiarity with learning."

The power of familiarity with meditative absorptions, such as those of emptiness and the absence of marks, also yields the ability to retain a given teaching simply by hearing it once. This is what is known as the "retention of meditative absorption." Retention through ripening and learning are lesser accomplishments; retention through meditative absorption is the greater achievement. As for the latter greater retention, this itself has three levels. Those wise ones who have not yet entered the grounds of the noble ones, and who are thus still at the stage of inspired conduct, possess a lesser form of retention that arises through meditation. The medium level of this retention occurs on the seven impure grounds, and the greater retention through meditation is accomplished on the three pure grounds. These, then, are the divisions that pertain to retention.

As for its function, when the bodhisattvas continuously rely on the three retentions that are achieved from ripening and so forth, they will, thereby, be able to reveal the sacred Dharma constantly to others, as this will ensure that they also retain both words and meanings themselves.

3. Aspiration

The steadfast ones' aspiration
Is attention accompanied by intention;
Motivated by wakefulness,
It is unequaled upon all the grounds. [XIX.75]

It should be known to serve as cause,
Because accomplishment follows from mind only.
While, due to mind, it does indeed carry fruit,
It accomplishes the aims of the future. [XIX.76]

Diverse and magnificent up to enlightenment,
From one ground to the next,
It becomes increasingly pure,
Accomplishing in full the bodhisattva's aims for self and
    others. [XIX.77]

Next follows the investigation of aspiration. **The steadfast ones' aspiration is attention accompanied by** the assisting factor of **intention**. It is **motivated by** the wish to attain **wakefulness**, and in that sense wakefulness is its basis. In terms of the grounds, **it is** present in a way that is **unequaled** by any other type of aspiration **upon all of the grounds**. As for the divisions, **it should be known** that, due to mind only, aspiration carries results in this life as well as the fulfillment of wishes in the future. Thus, aspiration should be known **to serve as the cause, because** in this way **accomplishment follows from**, and in accordance with, that which is merely **mind only. While** aspiration is **due to mind, it** (aspiration) **does indeed carry fruit** because **it accomplishes the aims of the future** in accordance with one's wishes.

On the grounds of inspired conduct, aspirations are **diverse and**, once the grounds have been attained, they become **magnificent** because here the ten great aspirations are formed in a process that continues **up to enlightenment**. Thus, **from one ground to the next, it** (that is, aspiration) **becomes increasingly pure, accomplishing in full the bodhisattva's aims for self and others**.

The aspiration of the steadfast bodhisattvas is an attention that takes the form of a wish to attain a specific fruition, such as great enlightenment, and it is accompanied by the intention to pursue that. The object of aspiration is the excellent cognition of wakefulness, which serves as the motivating factor. In other words, rather than wishing to attain defiling entities for one's own benefit, the mind is motivated by, and intent on, special wakefulness, and so words of aspiration are expressed to that effect. This is hence the cause as well as the essence of aspiration. Let us note that at this point the great commentary explains the statement "motivated by wakefulness" as referring to aspiration either caused by nonconceptual wakefulness or dedicated toward the attainment of such wakefulness.

When it is said that aspiration is "unequaled upon all grounds," that is a reference to the grounds of aspiration. None of the aspirations that the bodhisattvas make throughout all the different contexts of inspired conduct and the ten grounds can be matched by the aspirations of mundane beings, listeners, or self-realized buddhas. Concerning the qualities of aspiration, it should be understood that aspiration is the cause of both one's own welfare and that of others. In this life, one's own aims and that of others will be achieved through aspirations, and the same is the case throughout all future lives. Even if one does not do anything by means of body and speech toward the attainment of those aims, they will nevertheless be accomplished by means of the aspiring mind only. Results will be yielded in this life in conformity with the intents and wishes of the aspiring mind, and also all future objectives will be accomplished based on aspiration.

As for the divisions of aspiration, in the context of the grounds of inspired conduct, the aspirations of the bodhisattvas are diverse because at this time they have not gained realization of the universally present characteristics of the basic field of phenomena. When they perceive the various harms of cyclic existence, they wish to pacify each and every one of them, and they likewise focus on the excellent qualities one by one, wishing to attain them. Accordingly, they form distinct aspirations to benefit sentient beings in various ways in the future.

The various conflicting factors are also diverse at this stage. Once bodhisattvas enter the first ground, their aspirations become magnificent because they then practice the ten great aspirations. Through all the subsequent stages, from the second ground and beyond, they continue this practice and so their aspirations become increasingly vast, distinguished, and pure.

Concerning the function of aspiration, the bodhisattvas accomplish both their own benefit and that of others on the basis of aspiration. This can be gauged from the following sūtra passage:

> It is no simple task to put into words the way that the aspirations of a bodhisattva, who is endowed with the force of merit, will accomplish their own benefit and that of others by means of limitless bodies, limitless rays of light, and limitless miraculous acts.

4. Meditative Absorption and the Fourfold Summary of the Dharma

Next we turn to the explanation of (1) the subject, the three meditative absorptions, and (2) the object that is to be understood by means of the former, that is, the fourfold summary of the Dharma.

1. The Three Meditative Absorptions

> The sphere of activity of the threefold meditative absorption
> Consists of the twofold absence of self,
> The support for the grasping of self,
> And its so-called lasting and thorough pacification. [XIX.78]
>
> Since in essence this is the apprehending of the apprehended,
> It should be known to be threefold—
> Nonconceptuality, turning away,
> And possession of great joy. [XIX.79]
>
> In terms of thorough knowledge, abandonment,
> And direct perception,
> The meditative absorption in emptiness and the rest
> Are widely known to have three objectives. [XIX.80]

Next follows the investigation of the three meditative absorptions. In terms of **the sphere of activity of the threefold meditative absorption**, it is explained that, in the case of the meditative absorption in emptiness, the activity sphere **consists of the twofold absence of self**, that is, the absence of self in terms of persons and phenomena. For the meditative absorption in absence of wishes, it consists of **the support for the grasping of self**, that is, the five appropriated aggregates, **and** in the case of the meditative absorption in absence of marks, **its** sphere of activity is the **so-called lasting and thorough pacification** of that support, that is, the transcendence of suffering. **Since, in essence, this** meditative absorption **is the apprehending of these** three **apprehended** spheres of activity,

it should, corresponding with those three spheres, **be known to be threefold.** Thus, the meditative absorption in emptiness is characterized by **nonconceptuality** in terms of persons and phenomena, the meditative absorption in absence of wishes is characterized by its **turning away** from the bases for the grasping of self, **and** the meditative absorption in absence of marks is in **possession of great joy** with respect to the thorough pacification of those bases for such grasping. **In terms of** the **thorough knowledge** of the absence of self, the **abandonment** of the basis for grasping at a self, **and** the **direct perception** of the thorough pacification of that basis, **the meditative absorption in emptiness and the rest are widely known to have three objectives.**

The three meditative absorptions of emptiness, absence of wishes, and absence of marks are the foremost factors of the path. As such, their spheres of activity or observation are as follows. For the meditative absorption in emptiness, the activity sphere is the twofold absence of self, that is, the nonexistence of imputed persons and phenomena. The meditative absorption in absence of wishes engages the five aggregates of the perpetuation of defilement, that is, the dependent nature's appearances of dependent origination that, in turn, serve as the support for grasping as if the two selves existed. As for the meditative absorption in absence of marks, its sphere of engagement is the lasting and essential absence of the two selves within the basis or support for their imputation. Thus it engages with the thoroughly established pacification of all marks. These, then, are the three fields as observed by the three meditative absorptions, and the three meditative absorptions are thus classified as such due to their apprehension of these three objective fields. In other words, there are three meditative absorptions because there are three such uncommon observations.

Next, the features of the three meditative absorptions are explained. As for the meditative absorption in emptiness, it bears the features of an absence of the thoughts that are associated with the two selves. The meditative absorption in the absence of wishes takes the form of a detached turning away from the five aggregates of appropriation without putting one's hopes in them. This is due to having seen them to be impermanent and the basis for numerous sufferings. The meditative absorption in the absence of marks bears the features of trust and great joy in the basic field that is the complete pacification of all marks and suffering, the ultimate truth.

The enumeration of the three meditative absorptions is definitive. The meditative absorption in emptiness serves to thoroughly recognize the primordial nonexistence of the two imputed selves. The meditative absorption in absence of wishes is cultivated for the sake of relinquishing the impure dependent nature, which is the support for the apprehending of the two selves. And the meditative absorption in the absence of marks provides direct perception of the thoroughly established truth of cessation. In this way, the meditative absorption in emptiness and the rest are widely known to have three objectives.

2. The Four Summaries of the Dharma
[1. Concise Explanation]

With the wish to benefit sentient beings,
And as the cause of meditative absorption,
A fourfold summary of the Dharma
Is taught to the bodhisattvas. [XIX.81]

For the steadfast ones, these four
Carry the meaning of absence,
Thought, nothing but imagination,
And the complete pacification of thought. [XIX.82]

The following is an investigation of the summary of the Dharma. **With the wish to benefit sentient beings, and as the cause of** the threefold **meditative absorption, a fourfold summary of the Dharma is taught to the bodhisattvas.** "All that is conditioned is impermanent" and "all that is defiling is painful" are thus taught as the causal entity for the meditative absorption in absence of wishes. "All phenomena are empty of self" likewise pertains to the meditative absorption in emptiness, and "passing beyond suffering is peace" is associated with that of the absence of marks.

Here one may wonder: "What is the meaning of impermanence and the other issues, including peace?" Hence, **for the steadfast ones, these four carry** meanings that are to be explained in the following way. Impermanence carries **the meaning of** the absence of the imagined characteristics, whereas the meaning of suffering is inauthentic **thought,** that is, the dependent characteristics. The meaning of the absence of self is **nothing but imagination.** Here the emphatic "nothing but" implies that, while the imagined self does not exist, there is nevertheless mere imagination. Hence, the meaning of the nonexistence of the imagined characteristics is explained as the meaning of absence of self. **And finally, the meaning of peace is the complete pacification of thought,** that is, the thoroughly established characteristics of the transcendence of suffering.

With the wish to benefit sentient beings in the most supreme way, the incomparable teachers, the buddhas, teach a fourfold summary of the entire Dharma that serves as the cause of the meditative absorptions in emptiness and so forth. These four summations, or fundamental keypoints, are as follows: (1) All conditioned things are impermanent, (2) all defiled and conditioned things are suffering, (3) all phenomena are devoid of self, and (4) the transcendence of suffering is peace.

How, then, do these four become the cause of the three meditative absorptions? The statements that all conditioned things are impermanent and that all conditioned things are suffering are explained as the cause for the actualization of the meditative absorption in the absence of wishes. The reason for this is that if one understands that conditioned things are impermanent and that they are of the nature of suffering, one will come to see these things as if they were the teeth of a saw or a poisonous meal. As one thus becomes detached and withdraws one's trust in conditioned things, the meditative absorption in the absence of wishes will be actualized. The summary that teaches the absence of self with respect to all phenomena is the cause for accomplishing the meditative absorption in emptiness. When one understands that the self of the person and of phenomena are both simply imaginary and devoid of any actual establishment, this understanding will bring forth the meditative absorption in emptiness. The summary "the transcendence of suffering is peace" functions as the cause of the meditative absorption in absence of marks. That is to say, as one rests in the equipoise of the primordial peace of the thoroughly established nature, which one must realize by one's own direct awareness, one actualizes the truth of cessation—the transcendence of suffering within complete pacification of all marks of construction.

What, one may wonder, is meant by the teaching on impermanence, suffering, absence of self, and peace? For the steadfast bodhisattvas, the meaning of these four summaries is as follows. That which is impermanent is something that does not remain for a second moment upon arising. Hence, impermanent means "not lasting." The Sanskrit word for impermanence, *anityatā,* consists of *nityatā,* which means "permanence," combined with the negation *a.* Hence, it means impermanence in the sense of absence of permanence. At this point, the great commentary remarks:

> The impermanence that is realized by the bodhisattvas is not just in terms of arising and ceasing. Rather, what they comprehend is the constant absence of the imagined two selves.

There do seem to be things that go in and out of existence, but since ultimately nothing arises, how could there be anything that is destroyed? Since there are no such things, there is no basis for the grasping on to permanence, and so one will not give rise to any wishes in that regard either. This analysis is obviously undertaken in terms of the ultimate.

Next, that which is mere thought is explained to be suffering. The suffering of cyclic existence is simply the mistaken imagination of something that is apprehended and something that apprehends. This, therefore, is the meaning of suffering. Furthermore, absence of self implies that while the imputed nature appears as something apprehended and something that apprehends, both apprehended and apprehender, as well as persons and phenomena, are nothing but imagination, and therefore not real in the way imagined. Finally, as regards the meaning of peace, all thoughts of marks will be completely pacified once one has gained perfect familiarity with the knowledge of the thoroughly established nature.

2. Proof of Impermanence and Absence of Self

The next section presents proof of (1) impermanence and (2) absence of self. The first will be covered by means of (1) a general presentation and (2) a specific explanation.

1. Proof of Impermanence
1. General Presentation

> The reasons are inappropriateness, causal arising,
> Conflict, its own lack of remaining,
> Nonexistence, definitive characteristics,
> Pursuit, cessation, [XIX.83]
>
> Observation of transformation,
> Cause and effect,
> Embrace, master,
> And concordance in terms of purity and sentient beings.
> [XIX.84]

The meaning of impermanence is to be understood in terms of the momentary disintegration of the dependent characteristics, and to fully prove this the next section will analyze momentariness. The **reasons** that are thus supplied to establish impermanence in the sense of momentariness **are** the following.

There would be an **inappropriateness** in terms of conditioned things continuously emerging, unless they are momentary. Things do indeed emerge continuously, but that would be impossible if they did not arise and cease from one moment to the next. It might be thought that this continuous emergence relates to things that remain for a certain distinct length of time, that is, a time that is subsequent to what was there before and prior to that which follows after. But in that case there could not be any immediately subsequent emergence because there would not be any continuity. Moreover, it is also not reasonable for that which has arisen to remain, without this continuity, until a certain other time. Why?

Because of the **causal arising** of all conditioned things. If, upon its arising, a thing were to endure into some other time, it would, in order to do so, undoubtedly have to depend on a cause. Without such a cause, it would be causeless from the very beginning. It could not, however, subsist by the power of the initial cause because that cause has already played out its role as cause. Moreover, we cannot observe any other cause either. Therefore, without doubt it must be understood that "each of the successive instants has its own distinct cause."

It might then be argued: "That which required a cause and has already come into being does not do so once more. Rather, that which has come into existence ceases at some other point in time, and not just upon arising." But what, then, is it that makes it cease at that point? It would be unreasonable to claim that nothing other than the cause was responsible for its arising, as well as bringing about its cessation, because arising and ceasing are **conflict**ing qualities. That claim would also be in conflict with both scripture and the way spiritual practitioners direct their minds.

Moreover, if a conditioned thing that has arisen were to remain at a different point in time, what would make it do so? Is it the thing itself, or is it certain other causes? The first does not make sense because of **its** (thus referring to the thing itself) **own lack of remaining,** and the second option is not the case either because of the **nonexistence** of such causes. There are no entities that do not disintegrate in an instant because when the Blessed One declared that conditioned things are impermanent, he was referring to their **definitive characteristics**. If there were something that did not come to an end upon its mere arising, this would mean that it was, at the time of being present, to some slight extent *not* impermanent, and impermanence would then not be a definitive characteristic of conditioned things.

It might be thought: "If every instant were the arising of something that never existed before, we would not be able to identify any of it as this or that." Yet that is not the case because such identification occurs exclusively from the mind's **pursuit** of similar things, as in the example of the magician's tools. We can know this because of the **cessation** of things. That which remains exactly as it was cannot cease in the end either because then there is no difference from the first moment. Also, if things were not undergoing change from the very beginning, there could not be any **observation of transformation** in the end either, and yet we do observe such transformation. Likewise, the eyes and so forth are the **causes** of momentary mind, **and** all conditioned things are the **effects** of the mind.

One may then wonder: "It is proven that they are momentary, but what makes it clear that conditioned things are the effects of the mind?" The faculties with support are **embraced** by the mind. The mind, in turn, is the **master** of the conditioned. Thus, for example, the Blessed One also taught that "this world is guided and led by the mind; it is governed by the emerging mind" and "name and form arise with consciousness as the condition." **And** likewise, it is taught that "the monk endowed with concentration and miraculous powers has gained mastery over the mind. Thus, if he were to visualize this tree as gold, it would turn out in just that way." This shows **concordance in terms of** the mind of **purity. And,** similarly, there is also a concordance in terms of **sentient beings** because for those sentient beings who have performed negative deeds, the external entities will be of an inferior kind, while for those who possess merit, they are excellent. Thus, it has been established that, regardless of their type, all conditioned things are momentary.

In the next two stanzas, fourteen reasons are set forth to prove the thesis that all conditioned things are impermanent from one moment to the next. The first of these reasons is "inappropriateness." Conditioned things come about due to causes and conditions, and until their continuum has come to an end, they display a continuous emergence, like the flow of a river. As previous moments cease and subsequent moments follow, they thus emerge uninterruptedly. If they were not momentary, it would not be appropriate, or reasonable, for things to arise in such continuities of varying length.

Here it may be objected: "That is not inappropriate because once an entity has arisen in the initial moment, due to the coming together of causes and conditions, it will not immediately cease. Rather, it will remain for days, months, or years, until it finally encounters the circumstances for its destruction." Yet if, on such an understanding, we assume that a thing thus manifests in the initial moment, it will turn out to be uncaused in the second moment and beyond. Since the initial moment of manifestation does not immediately give rise to a continuity, it would follow that the arisen entity immediately ceases. It is necessary to account for the cause of the given thing's remaining into a second moment and so on, as well as for the cause of its destruction. However, the cause that first produced the entity cannot be responsible for its supposed remaining for days, months, and so on, because both cause and effect are momentary. The illustrative example of the river is helpful here because the flow of the river is due to an uninterrupted supply of new water. If that supply of new water is cut, the flow of the river will end as well. Similarly, the continuity of the burning flame of the oil lamp is due to the causal factors of its wick and fuel. Until it is exhausted, the fuel will keep turning into a flame, and so what emerges is always new. If the causal fuel runs out, the resultant flame will immediately die out as well, just as the initial moment of flame will not yield any duration unless further casual fuel is supplied.

At this point, some commentators offer an explanation along the lines of "lack of initial disintegration implying final changelessness." Thus, they explain the present issue by arguing that, unless disintegration occurs with every moment, the present entity could never cease to be. Yet, while the point is not unwarranted, one should understand the subject matter as set out above, in accordance with the commentary.

Others say, "For as long as the given thing remains the same, it does not require any further causes. It is exactly the cause that originally brought the thing into existence that is responsible for its remaining." Yet that is not so because the cause that gave rise to the given thing's initial moment will already have ceased once that thing has been produced; it could not possibly be contributing, therefore, to the thing's remaining throughout several moments. Hence, there cannot possibly be any entities that are not momentary. This is similar to claiming that a certain entity's remaining is due to the influence of a barren woman's child. If something that is not momentary could be produced by causes, this would also mean that permanent entities could come into being. Yet, such an assertion is utterly unreasonable and unsupportable. If it is believed that a given thing is originally produced by a cause and that it then subsequently remains and is finally destroyed without any need for another cause, then why, we may ask, should the thing not also arise without cause to begin with since both its remaining the same and its ceasing to be do not require any further causes.

It may be that one denies the causeless arising of the initial moment because such arising is refuted by the reliable cognitive means of direct perception. Yet, just as the initial moment thereby requires its cause, so will each moment in the sequence that makes up the given continuity. That is what is implied by the root text's use of the phrase "causal arising." If, once a thing has arisen, it remains continuously, then it is also thereby established that each moment of entity within that continuity is established by the one before it. No causes can be observed other than that.

There are others who say: "Once something has been produced by the cause that is responsible for its coming into being, it need not be produced again and again. Rather, that which was produced remains as it arose, as the same thing, for a certain period. For as long as that period lasts, no arising and disintegration of distinct, momentary entities takes place, and no other cause is required for the thing's remaining either." That this idea is unreasonable will be shown through the following criticism. If things do not disintegrate immediately upon their arising, but only after some time, we may seek to specify whether that which later disintegrates is something that previously remained, free from momentary destruction, or whether that which so disintegrates was previously participating in a process of momentary disintegration. If, along the lines of the first alternative, the thing remains without any momentary disintegration, then it cannot disintegrate later either. It will have to remain forever because the nature of remaining is divorced from the nature of disintegration. If, on the other hand, the given entity is of the nature of disintegration, then it cannot also possess the nature of permanence and endurance in time, and so it turns out to disintegrate with the very first moment. It could not possibly remain intact for a certain duration.

Moreover, if things arise, remain for some time, and only then cease, the cause of their cessation will have to be explained. It might then be suggested that what causes a given thing to cease is precisely the same as what causes it to arise. Yet, that is contradictory. Arising implies the presence of an entity, whereas cessation is the absence of entity. If those two were to have the same cause, that cause would be responsible for both the presence and the absence of entity, and it makes no sense for two incompatible factors to be caused by the same thing. Light and darkness, heat and cold; such pairs of opposites could similarly not be the product of the same cause.

When here the root text speaks of "conflict," the implication is that if we were to deny that without lasting for a second moment things cease upon their arising, claiming instead that things remain permanent as the same identical things for a certain period of time, then our argument would be in conflict with both scripture and reasoning. How so? In the scriptures that express the voice of the Blessed One, we hear:

> Conditioned things are like an illusion produced by causes and conditions. They disintegrate, being subject to arising and ceasing. They are temporary because once they have arisen they do not last for more than a moment. Their duration is short, for they are destroyed as soon as they arise.

In terms of reasoning, the durability of things is in conflict with the direct perception of spiritual practitioners. Such practitioners, who meditate and direct their minds by means of the four noble truths, see all conditioned things as characterized by momentary arising and ceasing. Hence they feel weary of them and become detached, thereby gaining liberation and the transcendence of suffering. If they were to see things as suggested by the opponent, they would not feel weary, would not become detached, would not gain liberation. Similarly, while ordinary beings of the world do experience weariness when they recognize the facts of cessation and impermanence at death, they do not feel weary until then. Thinking in terms of the way things remain, they are not saddened by the entirety of conditioned things, and they do not become detached.

The root text also states "its own lack of remaining" as a reason for inferential criticism. Let us assume that conditioned things do not disintegrate as soon as they arise, and that they hence remain for a while. Would they so remain by their own power, or by the power of other causes and conditions? In the first case, we should expect all entities to remain forever, but there is not a single conditioned thing that goes on and on until the end of time. The reason for this is that, in terms of their essence, conditioned entities disintegrate from one moment to the next, and, as for their continuities, these will be destroyed whenever a condition for such to occur is encountered. As for other causes and conditions that could make conditioned things last, no such factors can be identified through reliable means of cognition. That we fail to identify such causes is due to the fact that conditioned things do not remain for a second moment once they have come into being.

As for the root text's mention of "nonexistence," others may claim: "For as long as they remain, things do not require any other causes to do so. Exactly that which came into being will remain until it meets with the cause of its destruction. For example, a piece of iron will remain metallic blue and devoid of heat until it encounters fire. Yet, whenever that happens, the bluish color and the absence of heat will disappear, and instead redness and heat will emerge. Similarly, the ceramic vase will remain as it is until it is struck by the hammer, at which point the vase will be destroyed, giving way to shards instead." This is unreasonable, however. Things disintegrate by themselves; there is nothing extraneous that causes their destruction. How so? For example, when someone throws a stone up into the sky, the arms and so on serve as the causes for that to happen. Yet the stone does not need any other causes for falling down to the ground. It does so by itself. All conditioned things similarly disintegrate by themselves as soon as they have been produced by their individual causes. They do not require any other causal factors for that to happen.

Even before they encounter fire and the hammer, the blue iron and the shape of the vase will already disintegrate of their own accord, from one moment to the next. Hence, it is not the fire and the hammer that destroy them. Rather, the perpetuating causes of the final instants of iron and vase, along with the cooperating conditions of the fire and the hammer, give rise respectively to the contexts of the red hot metal and the shards. If one thinks, "now the metal is red," and "now the vase has been destroyed," continuing to believe that the metal and the vase endure, then that delusion is due to the uninterrupted sequence of things that resemble each other. There is nothing there that actually lasts. We may point out to opponents that were we to paint something on the iron and the vase, they would not then claim those paintings to be the causes of the destruction of the iron and the vase. Nevertheless, it is indeed the case that the contexts of unpainted iron and vase cease, giving way instead to the contexts of painted iron and vase. This is what is understood by individuals who are learned regarding the characteristic impermanence of iron and vases.

Therefore, when things turn out in different ways, it is because of differences among their particular causes. When, on the other hand, those causes resemble each other, they can produce a sequence of things that are of a similar kind. Yet, whether diverse or seemingly the same, there is not the least difference in terms of things being momentary. It is impossible to observe any nonmomentary entity that participates in different contexts. Examples such as the boiling and evaporating of water, or the breaking of a vase into shards that are then ground to dust, will, if we examine them well, all simply go to show that momentary entities can encounter certain conditions whereby their contexts change. They are certainly not examples of nonmomentary things being destroyed by extraneous causes. It is just as when a potter uses his hands, a stick, and so forth, to make ceramic vases out of clay. When the vase is produced, the original, raw context of the clay is destroyed, just as the formative acts of the hands and so on signify cessation and destruction.

We may also ask whether the thing that is subject to causes of destruction is itself of the essence of disintegration, or whether it is of an essence that is not disintegration. If the thing is of an essence that is other than disintegration, then it cannot be destroyed by the causes of destruction, and if it is disintegration in and of itself, it does not need anything else in order to be destroyed. Furthermore, if an entity is allegedly destroyed by the cause of its destruction, does this mean the product of that cause is the exact same former entity, or does the cause of destruction instead produce some other entity? If the product of the cause of destruction is the very same entity, then the cause of destruction *produces* the former entity rather than destroying it. Alternatively, if the cause of destruction brings forth some entity other than that, then it does not affect the former entity in the slightest. Similarly, by way of illustration, the production of yarn does not imply the destruction of a pillar.

The root text also speaks of "definitive characteristics," thereby indicating that all conditioned things can be equally ascertained as bearing the characteristics of impermanence. It is not the case that while some are impermanent others are not, and there are no conditioned things that are both permanent and impermanent, just as there are none that are neither permanent nor impermanent. There are no such differences. Hence, the Blessed One has decisively declared: "All conditioned things are impermanent." If things were first permanent and then impermanent, they could be said to be both permanent and impermanent. Yet such a thing is not possible because it is the way of all conditioned things to disintegrate from one moment to the next. There are no exceptions to this, just as heat is always the nature of fire.

Next the text speaks of "pursuit." Some say, "If things were impermanent in the sense of existing only in the moment, then all things would be entirely new. How could it then be possible to recognize something that one has seen before? Since we do indeed notice that 'I have seen such and such before,' it must be the case that things remain without constantly being destroyed." Yet, having the impression of seeing what one has seen before does not mean that one is actually looking at the same thing. The impression is simply a delusion that is based on the mind's continuous pursuit of one similar thing after another. For example, if an illusionist juggles several pebbles from one hand to the other, rapidly and without interruption, then it will appear to the observer as though there is just one stone that is being thrown up into the air by one hand and caught by the other. Likewise, in a river, the water of the previous moment is gone and replaced by new water in the next. However, because such moments look alike, one may think, "I have crossed this river before; now I shall do so again," or "I shall be crossing this river for the first time."

The mention of "cessation" has to do with the following objection: "As long as that which we saw earlier and that which we see later are not observed to be different objects of perception, then how can it be right to say that what is there later differs from what was there before?" To this it is replied that the two are not the same since by the intrinsic nature of things the previous instants of entity have all ceased. If the entity that was there in the initial moment were also remaining now, just as it was before and without ceasing, then it could not end later either. Just as the entity that was seen in the first instant would still be here in the present moment, it would have to be there in all future moments too because it can never then be anything other than a thing that is not momentary.

In the context of "the observation of transformation," it is explained that if things were not momentary and if in essence they remained for a while, then it would never be possible to observe any transformation beyond what was seen in the initial instant. Nevertheless, in terms of inner entities, the bodies of sentient beings change. We notice the transformation from infant to youth, to young adult, to adult, to elderly, and to aged with white hair and wrinkles. As for outer entities, homes and household articles go from being freshly made to becoming old, for instance, and we observe a contrast between the thing as it was then and as it is now. It is certain that this process of transformation begins already in the initial instant. If there were no change from the first moment to the second, change would be precluded later on as well. Hence, since we do indeed observe transformation, it is certain that there is change with each moment.

Let us imagine that someone keeps watching the body of a young person without distraction. The watcher will not discern any process of aging from instant to instant, nor will he or she do so from day to day. Yet when at some point some crude change is seen, such as the person's hair having gone white, the watcher can infer that this change has been underway over years, months, weeks, days, and instants. The change has, in other words, been taking place gradually. It is not the case that the observed person remained unchanged for some time and then, all of a sudden, turned out the way he or she looks now. All external entities in the same way undergo subtle, momentary change. There is the example of milk turning into yogurt. The sour taste here emerges in a process that occurs gradually with each moment. We cannot observe any change other than that which occurs on a momentary basis. Now, because we do not observe subtle change with every moment, and because each moment of entity looks like the one that was there before, people get the idea that it is one and the same thing that they see. That is how worldly people end up with the delusional belief that things last.

Regarding "cause and effect," proponents of permanent entities may argue: "However much we analyze, we will still not be able to determine such subtle change in direct perception. Instead, we perceptually determine things to be exactly the same. How, then, should it be possible to find trust in the statement that things change with each moment?" Now, these things are all the effects of causes, and they arise from the way in which their individual series of former causes give rise to an emerging series of later effects. Hence they are established as momentary. If the causes were not momentary, the effects could not be either. Yet, since the effects *are* momentary, so were their causes. A permanent cause cannot produce any effect, just as space does not yield flowers or vases. Likewise, a permanent effect cannot be produced by any cause, just as space is not a possible product of flowers or anything else. Therefore, when things function as cause and effect, it is because of their momentary nature. If they were not momentary, they would not change and could not therefore serve as causes or effects.

Based on such general considerations, we may next specifically examine the consciousness that is associated with the eye and other faculties. All consciousness emerges based on the four conditions, and there is therefore universal agreement among everyone, from buddhas to extremists, that consciousness manifests with instantaneous speed. Nobody holds that the mind is permanent. Now, the causes of such consciousness are the faculties and the objects of form and so forth, just as is taught in the sūtras: "Visual consciousness arises based on the eye and form." Therefore, since conditioned things serve to produce an effect—consciousness—that is established as momentary, those productive causes—that is, the conditioned things—will have to be momentary as well. If, at this point, others should claim that it is permanent, conditioned things that are giving rise to impermanent moments of mind, we may point out that if nonmomentary things can produce things that are momentary, then that which is permanent must also be capable of producing that which is impermanent. Yet this does not make sense, as can be learned from the example of space not being able to produce vases.

Therefore, it is established that the causes of mind are just as momentary as the mind itself.

Moreover, all conditioned things are also the effects of the mind. It is because of habitual tendencies left in the mind that it appears as though there are external objects. Beyond that appearance, there are no external objects. There is no such thing as a self-sufficient external entity that is not due to karmic action as accumulated by the mind. It is therefore also established that, just as the causal mind is momentary, the resultant conditioned entities are momentary as well.

One may then wonder: "How can we know that conditioned things are the effects of the mind, and how can we know that since the mind is momentary, conditioned things will have to be momentary as well?" It is in reply to such concerns that the root text says, "embrace, master, and concordance in terms of purity and sentient beings," thereby supplying the final four reasons. As regards the first of these, "embrace," the five sense faculties are, along with the general structure of the body that supports them, the outcome of factors that are embraced by consciousness. Hence it is established that they are the effects of the mind. In which sense can the productive factors be said to be embraced by consciousness? It is only through the embrace of consciousness entering the womb and collapsing there that the semen and blood of father and mother can combine into an embryo that gradually develops into the full body of a fetus that is in possession of the faculties. When consciousness enters and merges with the semen and the blood, it collapses. Unless that happens, the most subtle embryo and the further stages of development cannot possibly take place. Thus, the body follows the mind and is embraced by the mind. It is taught in a sūtra:

> Ānanda, unless consciousness collapses within the mother's womb, the impurities of father and mother cannot bring forth the subtle embryo and the further stages of development.

Moreover, if the mind is hurt, the body will be hurt as well, and if the mind is delighted, the body too will feel excellent. This further shows how the body follows the mind. Likewise, if it is separated from the mind, the body becomes insentient and will begin to decay. Therefore, since they are embraced by the mind, conditioned things are the effects of the mind.

When the root text speaks of the "master," it refers to the mind's being in control of—or the master of—conditioned things. The latter are therefore the mind's effects. In which way can the mind be seen to be the master? The Blessed One teaches:

This world is directed by the mind, driven on by the mind.

Based on what the mind thinks, the body follows suit. The body is directed and driven on by the mind. Hence, if the mind becomes desirous, the body will follow along. As the body is aroused, it will act accordingly—smiling, laughing, and so on, in a way that changes its previous appearance. If the mind turns angry, the body will again change its appearance—casting angry glances, frowning, clenching the fists, and so on. In this way, conditioned entities are mastered and controlled by the mind. As a further scriptural argument, we may also allude to the Thus-Gone One's statement that "due to the condition of consciousness, there is name and form." Without consciousness, there would be no context of name and form, and without the latter, there would be no six sense sources and so forth.

As for "concordance in terms of purity," spiritual practitioners may, for example, due to their mastery of pure mind, let earth appear as gold if they so wish. In this way, their mastery of meditative absorption allows them to change the features of things according to their wishes. Thus the sūtras contain abundant references to "monks who have attained concentration" and so forth. For this reason, conditioned things can be seen to be effects of the mind. The root text also speaks of "concordance in terms of . . . sentient beings," thereby referring to the way in which the realms of the world are brought forth by the accumulated virtuous or unvirtuous actions of sentient beings. Since conditioned things follow in accordance with the minds of sentient beings, those who have engaged in unvirtuous acts will encounter crops that are of inferior color, scent, taste and so on, and things such as gold will appear to them as charcoal, for example. Those who have performed virtuous deeds, on the other hand, will perceive grains and the like that are of exquisite color, scent, and taste, and to them even inferior things will appear as jewels, for example. It is, hence, clear that conditioned things are the effects of the mind. Therefore, since the mind that causes them is momentary, the conditioned entities that it causes could not reasonably be held as permanent. Indeed, they are understood to be momentary. Thus, two stanzas explain the momentary impermanence of conditioned things without any specification in terms of outer or inner entities.

2. Specific Explanation

Second, it will be explained how (1) all inner conditioned entities are impermanent and (2) how the same also holds for outer entities.

1. The Impermanence of Inner Entities

Initial, growing,
Development, supportive entities,
Change, thorough maturation,
Inferiority and superiority, [XIX.85]

Clear light and unclear light,
Movement to another place,
With seeds, without seeds,
And birth in the form of a reflection—[XIX.86]

These are fourteen modes of life.
When considering them, differences in cause and size,
Meaninglessness and impossibility of development,
Impossibility of support, [XIX.87]

Impossibility in the case of remaining,
Lack of initial disintegration implying final changelessness,
Impossibility of inferiority and superiority,
As well as clear light and unclear light, [XIX.88]

No moving, impossibility of remaining,
Of finality, and concordance with mind—
These all go to show
That all conditioned things are momentary. [XIX.89]

The next section concerns the momentariness of inner conditioned things. All that is conditioned is impermanent because (1) the **initial** entity of self undergoes a process of (2) **growing**. It undergoes (3) **development** due to food, sleep, pure conduct, and equilibrium. There is also change in terms of (4) the **supportive entities** of the eyes and so forth that support consciousness. (5) **Change** of the facial complexion occurs due to attachment and so forth. (6) **Thorough maturation** takes place as one remains in the womb, becomes an infant, a youth, an adult, and an aged person. As one takes birth in the lower or higher realms, the situations are marked by (7) **inferiority and** (8) **superiority**. Those inhabiting the realms of (9) **clear light**, such as Delighting in Emanation, produce emanations in accordance with their wishes, **and** those characterized by (10) **unclear light,** such as humans, have specific ways of partaking of sense objects. Following the cessation of a life, there is the (11) **moving to another place,** and all forms of life—except the final aggregates of a foe destroyer—come (12) **with the seeds** of previous actions. The final aggregates of the foe destroyer are, on the other hand, (13) **without seeds, and** there is also, in the case of those who meditate on the freedoms, (14) **birth in the form of a reflection**—of fire, for example, due to the power of meditative absorption. These are fourteen modes of life.

When considering them, beginning with the initial mode of life, the **differences in** terms of the various **causes** is a proof of momentariness. If there were no distinct causes, the lack of such causes would make it impossible to observe any distinct emergence of future conditioned phenomena, **and** the fact that there is an increase in **size** is thus also proof of momentariness. If conditioned things were not momentary, this would also result in the **meaninglessness and impossibility of development** because everything would remain just as it was. If things were not momentary, changing with *every* moment, there could not be any development of qualities into different fields. Development would remain permanently impossible. The absence of momentariness would also necessitate **the impossibility of** something serving as **support** because if the support is at rest neither can the supported *not* be at rest. Life undergoing change and life maturing would likewise be an **impossibility in the case of remaining**, and the **lack of initial disintegration** would be **implying final changelessness**. Just as with life undergoing change and life maturing, there would be an **impossibility of inferiority and superiority, as well as** of **clear light and unclear light**. Without momentariness, there would be **no movement** from one place to another, **and** this would then also imply the **impossibility of** any **remaining**.

It should be understood that proceeding, as characterized by unimpeded birth in a different place, has numerous causes. It can be due to the power of mind, as in a situation where desire is present. It may be propelled by past actions, as in the case of existence between two lives. It may be due to propelling, as with an arrow. It may be due to a relationship, as in riding and the crossing of waters. It may come from pursuit, as when grass is pushed ahead by the wind. It may be due to the nature of things, as in the case of wind moving straight ahead, fire ascending, and water falling. It can also be due to powers, as in the case of movements caused by mantras and medicine, the movement of iron by means of a magnet, and movements caused miraculously by those who possess such powers.

The momentary nature of conditioned things can also be seen from the fact that life with and without seed cannot involve abiding, in which case there would be an impossibility **of finality; and** momentariness is likewise established by the fact that birth as a reflection takes place in **concordance with** the **mind**. Thus, **these** facts **all go to show that all conditioned things are momentary**.

Next follow five stanzas that prove the momentary impermanence of all inner entities, which is to say the mind and the subsidiary mental states, along with the body. First, the fourteen modes of life—the initial life, the growing of life, the development of life, and so forth—will be explained, and subsequently those fourteen will be subjected to fourteen arguments of reliable cognitive means—from the argument associated with cause, size, and so on, through the argument of concordance with the mind—so as to prove thereby that all inner conditioned entities are momentary.

(1) Thus, the initial life is the consciousness that enters the mother's womb subsequent to the cessation of the consciousness associated with death. This is the consciousness that collapses in the womb, together with the semen and blood. As such, it is the first moment of linkage with a new life. The cessation of consciousness associated with death and the arising of consciousness associated with birth occurs in a way that resembles the tipping of the arms of a scale. This process is, therefore, momentary.

(2) Growing life begins with the second moment upon the entry of consciousness into the womb, and it continues through stages of the oval shape, the oblong shape, the lumpy shape, and so forth. In a continuous process of growth, the previous states are relinquished, giving way to new ones with each moment.

(3) The development of life has to do with the four causes of physical development: food, sleep, wholesome activity, and meditative absorption. The former three pertain to the realm of desire, and the fourth is associated with the form realm. Based on these causes, the body overcomes weakness and develops. (Note that in place of wholesome activity, such as massage, the commentary here instead mentions pure conduct.) This causal process of physical development is momentary; something permanent could not possibly increase and expand.

(4) Life as associated with the supportive entities concerns the constitution of the six faculties of the eyes and so forth that support visual consciousness and the rest of the six consciousnesses. These are also momentary because they produce effects in the form of momentary consciousness. It has already been explained that whatever is a cause or an effect must also be momentary because something that does not change in the moment cannot reasonably be a cause or effect.

(5) Changing life concerns the way in which the arising of desire and so forth causes changes in the appearance of the body. Those changes also manifest on a momentary basis.

(6) Thorough maturation of life is the life process whereby the newborn grows through infancy, develops the ability to walk, becomes a youth capable of participating in sports, becomes an adult with fully developed physical and mental powers, begins to lose the youthful vigor, becomes an elderly person, and becomes aged with white hair and an entirely wrinkled face. It should be understood that this process of ripening comprises a continuous string of moments.

(7–8) Regarding inferiority and superiority, life in the three lower realms is inferior, whereas life as a human or a god is superior. Without any certain pattern, beings in the lower realms are reborn into the higher ones, and those in the higher realms take birth in the lower ones. Likewise, beings may be born within the same class that they belonged to before, as when humans take birth among humans, or they may take birth within any class other than the one they belonged to previously. All these instances of impermanence occur in a succession of moments, and something permanent could not possibly turn out in a multitude of different ways.

(9) Life as luminosity concerns two among the six classes of the gods of the desire realm, namely, those belonging to the two realms of Delighting in Emanation and Control over the Emanations of Others. Other than those two classes, this category also includes the gods of the form and the formless realms. The enjoyments and equilibria of these gods depend on merely their own mind, and they can thus access them as they please. For this reason, they are, as a whole, referred to as "the gods of luminosity." As for the way that they access enjoyments and so forth, the gods of Delighting in Emanation imagine divine females of whichever complexion, shape, dress, and ornamentation they wish. As in this way they merely think of them, they will bring forth emanations of such females and have pleasure with them. Similarly, the goddesses of that realm will imagine their ideal males, thereby bringing forth such male emanations so that they can enjoy themselves with them. The gods of the realm of Control over the Emanations of Others wish to partake of other gods and goddesses, along with their enjoyments, and for that reason they send forth emanations and enjoy themselves according to their wishes. With their control of the mind, the gods in the form and formless realms are, similarly, able to enter and accomplish

whichever equilibrium of meditative absorption they desire. None of all this would be possible if permanent things were involved, and it should therefore be understood that all of this happens by the power of momentary mind.

(10) Life in the absence of luminosity refers to life in all realms other than those just mentioned. This refers to the remainder of the desire realm, from the Joyful Realm of the gods right down to and including hell. Life in these realms is said to be characterized by an "absence of luminosity," due to the fact that the beings there do not experience the fulfillment of whatever desires come to their minds. Since the minds and possessions of the beings in these realms also turn out in various ways, they should all be understood to be impermanent from one moment to the next. Generally, the sentient beings of the three realms migrate without any certainty as to their realm. Thus, gods of clear light may be born into contexts of unclear light, whereas beings of unclear light may become gods of clear light. On any particular level, a sentient being thus takes birth in numerous ways, which again goes to show that sentient beings are impermanent and that their streams of being are of a momentary nature.

(11) Life in the sense of proceeding to another place concerns the process of migration to a different place subsequent upon death. Below the form realm, this element of not remaining and instead proceeding into something different is also relevant with respect to the body. All such migration happens through the occurrence of a sequence of moments; none of these phenomena would be possible with permanent entities.

(12) Life with seeds is life that involves the seeds of the latent afflictions that lead to birth in the three realms. With the exceptions of the foe destroyer with remainder, who has eliminated all the afflictions that are to be discarded through seeing and cultivation, and the final moment of that foe destroyer's aggregates, this category otherwise includes foe destroyers of entry, nonreturners, once-returners, stream enterers, and all ordinary beings of the three realms. All of these possess the seeds of the afflictions, and hence the emergence of the continuity of their five aggregates can be classified as one that is "with seeds." As their lives are in that way made up of causal and resultant phenomena, they are all established as being momentary.

(13) Life without seeds is life that does not involve the seeds of birth within cyclic existence. Except for the final moment of the aggregates of a foe destroyer with remainder, who is on the verge of entering the field without remainder, the aggregates are always a succession of causes and effects. As for foe destroyers with remainder, these do not possess any seeds of rebirth, yet they are still in possession of the remainder of the aggregates, which is a consequence of their actions in the past. Thus their life continues on a momentary basis until they enter the field without remainder. Subsequent to that final moment of the remainder of their aggregates, there will no longer be any birth for them, as they have then entered the field without remainder. Yet, as long as they are alive, their life is of momentary nature. Since they were previously in possession of seeds, and since later they no longer possess any, they are impermanent and therefore also momentary.

(14) Life in the form of a reflection concerns individuals who have, for example, cultivated the eight freedoms. By the power of their meditative absorption, such individuals will clearly experience mental reflections manifesting as objects that take the form of shapes and colors of blue, yellow, white, and red. Such appearances reflect the power of these individuals' affinity with meditative absorption, and since they were not there to begin with yet later they appear, they are impermanent. Moreover, since they emerge due to the evolving meditation that takes place within a stream of momentary mind, they are established to be momentary. The present category also includes all clear appearances that emerge due to one's having trained, for example, in the meditation of seeing things to be dream-like, or of perceiving them to be unattractive. All of these are mere mental appearances and should be understood to be impermanent.

Thus the fourteen forms of life are impermanent and should be known to be momentary. The initial life is the cause of the different later stages, such as the oval shape and so on. It is, therefore, a momentary occurrence. As for the later stages, these unfold gradually in a causal sequence where each of the different stages is required for the manifestation of the subsequent ones. If any one of them were missing, none of the following stages could occur because they would then be lacking their distinct cause. Life, therefore, is momentary from its very first instant. The oval shape emerges out of the initial moment, and the former, in turn, gives rise to the oblong shape, and so on, in an unbroken chain of different causes and different effects that arise and cease in sequence.

Since it is characterized by an increase in terms of size, shape, and features, growing life is also a momentary process. Likewise, if the body were permanent, there could be no change beyond the initial situation, which would render it meaningless to rely on factors such as food in order to develop the body. Therefore, since it is undeniable that food and so on does develop the body, the latter is established as being impermanent with each moment. The eye consciousness and so on that are supported by the entities of their respective faculties are also of a momentary, impermanent nature. That is how they can reasonably manifest the way they do. That which is permanent cannot possibly serve as support; the permanent does not need the support of anything at all, and the permanent cannot reasonably give rise to a distinct effect. Therefore, since visual consciousness and so on do not arise unless they are supported by their respective faculties, it is established that both the supportive faculties and the supported consciousnesses are impermanent in every moment.

One might then wonder why permanent faculties should not be capable of supporting impermanent consciousness. Just as, without a horse or some other mount, there cannot be a rider, so—if the supports stay as they are, without turning into anything else—the supported consciousnesses cannot move or change either. Similarly, if cotton fabric is burned, the blue color that it supports will be burned along with it, and in this way that which supports and that which is supported cannot be distinguished in terms of the impermanence of their characteristics.

It is, undeniably, the case that afflictions such as desire change the appearance of the body, and that life undergoes maturation from one context to the next, as, for example, when an infant grows into a young child. Such change and maturation would be impossible to observe in the event that things remained permanent. They could then not reasonably change from the exact way that they were before. It is, therefore, established that these things are momentary.

One might wonder what problem there should be in things remaining permanent for a while, without being momentary. Yet, something enduring in this way is extremely problematic. If things did not disintegrate with their very first moment, and instead endured exactly as they were in that initial moment, then the implication is that they would remain like that forever. They could never come to a point of change. Just as a given thing did not change with its initial moment, it could not do so at any later point in time either. Everything would turn out to be completely permanent, and such a scenario is extremely unreasonable because we do not observe things to be forever permanent.

One might think that "for a while things remain as they are without changing, and then at some point they come to an end." With that idea, a thing may—without changing—remain for an instant, a minute, a day, a month, a year, or an eon. Then, at the end of the given period, it ceases. Yet in that case it makes no sense that things can have different durations because whenever something has come into being, it will allegedly remain for some time as it was in its initial moment. Its final moment before destruction would, therefore, never arrive. If the thing that has just come into being and the thing that is just about to disintegrate are one and the same, there are only two possibilities: either the thing that has just arisen is just about to cease (as must be the case with the thing that is just about to disintegrate) or otherwise the thing that is just about to disintegrate will remain for a certain time (as must be the case with the thing that has just arisen). What else could be possible, given that the two are held to be the same thing? Therefore, however long it takes from the moment that something arises until the moment that it comes to an end, we can infer that the thing in question is different for each of the moments that make up the given period. This reasoning of the "lack of initial disintegration implying final changelessness" is the primary one, and all the key issues of the other arguments are contained within it.

The commentary treats the "impossibility in the case of remaining" as the proof that pertains both to life as change and to life as maturation. It then sees "lack of initial disintegration implying final changelessness" as an alternative proof of the same. In this way, the commentary explains how the changes of the body that take place due to desire and so forth would be impossible if the body were not momentary, remaining instead just as it was. It then further argues that the maturation from infant to youth, and so on, will make sense only where impermanent moments arise and cease one after the other. It is in this latter context that the commentary states that if things did not disintegrate from the very beginning, they could not do so later, in which case they would remain permanent without ever disintegrating. However, although the commentary thus applies the arguments in sequence, this does not seem to make any actual difference.

Likewise, our observation of inferior and superior lives is also explicable only if we assert that all entities involved are impermanent from one moment to the next. If impermanence were not the case with each moment, there could not reasonably be any changes in the end either, and then there could not be any differences between the base and the highly distinguished. The same goes for the distinction between clear and unclear light. This can all be understood from the reasoning that has been supplied, and we shall therefore not venture into further elaboration or repetition here.

As for the impossibility of proceeding from one place to another, the implication is simply that such a movement is impossible unless there is a continuity of instants. Here we shall, however, provide a summary of the commentary's account. If a fire breaks out in dry grass, it may seem as though it moves straight from one hill to another. Yet in fact the fire is a process of combustion that goes on over a series of moments and in relation to distinct blades of grass. Likewise, when a person takes birth in cyclic existence, or when someone moves from one location to another, such birth takes place in terms of the continuity of the aggregates, and the movement that occurs is merely an uninterrupted sequence of instantaneous aggregates. There is absolutely no such thing as a "walker" who is enduring and moves from one place to another.

It might be thought, "A walker is one who makes the conditioned entities move to a new location. The mover decides, 'I want to go to that place,' and so sets the conditioned entities of the body in motion in a way that accomplishes a passage to that particular location. If there were no walker, there could not be any act of walking because actions do not take place where there are no agents." Here we may ask whether the action that is the movement of conditioned entities to a new location occurs only after its alleged cause, that is, the walker, has come into being, or whether that action takes place without having been thus brought about. If the first is thought to be the case, then—while the so-called "walker" exists—the conditioned entities may be at rest and may not have moved anywhere at all. How, then, could that person be a walker? At this point it might be denied that conditioned entities are at rest, and it could instead be argued that they are, by nature, in movement. But how could there then be a substantial walker involved, who is something other than the entities of the walking?

Another reasoning is as follows. Does the walker move the conditioned entities to their new location while remaining where it is, or does it do so while itself being in that new location? In the first case, how could the walker make the conditioned entities go to their destination while itself remaining where it is and not moving anywhere? This would be akin to saying that the horse which carries its rider to the destination does so without itself moving anywhere. In the second case, when the walker is at the new location, having already gone there, the conditioned entities are still where they were, without having gone anywhere. How could the former then make the latter move, given that they remain apart from each other? Thus, a horse that is in the east could not be carrying a human being that is in the west.

Regarding conditioned things and their mover, we may also ask whether the latter comes into being first, and then subsequently moves the conditioned things, or whether instead the conditioned things are there first, and are subsequently moved; or indeed whether conditioned things are moved by a mover that is simultaneous with them. In the first case, the mover is present while the moved objects are still absent. What then could the former be moving? Similarly, one cannot be raising a child if no child has been born. In the second case, that which is being moved is present, but the mover is not. This, too, makes movement impossible, just as people cannot be carried by a horse that has not yet been born. In the third case, the two arise simultaneously, just like the right and left horns of a cow. In that case, one cannot be the cause of the other's movement, and instead the two will be moving along on an equal footing. There is then no sense whatsoever of the mover—or walker—being the one that makes the conditioned entities move.

So-called movement, therefore, is a name that is applied when—due to the continuity of the momentary five aggregates—there is a passage from one place to another. The five aggregates are also themselves referred to as "the mover" or "the walker" because, other than the appearance of movement that is due to the continuity of conditioned entities, there is no "mover" or "walker." Know, therefore, that there is no whole that is of any substance other than its parts. Here I have thus summarized the discussion that takes place in the commentaries of Vasubandhu and Sthiramati. Apart from the kind of movement that takes place in terms of a stream of instants, there is no "mover" and no "moving." It should, therefore, be understood that movement is momentary.

As for the various types of movement from one place to another, these are numerous. Movement may be due to mental causes, as when the mind, because of its being habituated to the movement of conditioned things, intends to walk and thereby causes the body to walk. It may also be due to past action, as when, for example, a sentient being between two lives enters a mother's womb. It may also be caused by a propelling force, as when an arrow is shot at a target. Movement may likewise occur due to a particular relationship, as when both horse and rider move from one place to another, or when a current of water carries a raft along with it. Movement through stirring is when, for example, grass or leaves are taken by the wind and moved along, whereas movement by the nature or essence of things is like when the wind blows from one place to another, when fire ascends, or when water descends down into a basin. Movement may also be due to powers. Such powers may be associated with a mantra, as when a practitioner of mantra travels by the power of mantra. They may likewise be due to a substance, as when one travels to a certain destination because of having drunk a medicine or applied an ointment on the body, or when a magnet pulls a piece of iron upward or straight ahead. Movement from one place to another can also be due to miraculous powers. All such instances of going and coming should be understood to be momentary.

That which possesses the seeds of cyclic existence must take birth in terms of a series of arising and ceasing instants, and it is therefore reasonable to hold such life to be impermanent in the sense of being momentary. That which remains without arising and ceasing cannot hold seeds, nor could it have had any seeds earlier. All phenomena that involve seeds are therefore established to be momentary. Moreover, when the continuum that holds the seeds of cyclic existence is conquered by the path and hence transformed into that which does not hold any seeds, then this too can only reasonably occur to a momentary mind. A nonmomentary, enduring essence of mind could never reach the final moment of the remainder of the foe destroyer's aggregates. Neither could it go from first holding seeds to later not holding any, nor could it first involve birth and then subsequently not be involved in birth either. Hence, the arising of the aggregates that do not contain any seeds of cyclic existence is also established to be momentary. Finally, as for the reflections that appear as the objects of meditative absorption, since they adhere to the mind, they too are established to be impermanent. Therefore, all inner conditioned entities are merely a stream of momentary factors.

2. The Impermanence of Outer Entities

The elements and the six objects
Are declared to be momentary
Because of evaporation, increase,
Movement by nature, increase and decrease, [XIX.90]

Relation with the former elements,
The four types of change,
Color, smell, taste, and tactility being similar,
Rendering them similar to them, [XIX.91]

Function in dependence on fuel,
Increase observed,
Accordance with the mind, and inquiry.
Therefore, the external is also momentary. [XIX.92]

The next section concerns the proof that outer conditioned entities are momentary. The four **elements** (earth and the rest) **and the six objects** (color, smell, taste, tactility, sound, and the forms that belong to the sense source of phenomena) **are declared to be momentary because of** the following characteristics. Water is characterized by **evaporation** and **increase**, whereas wind is in **movement by nature** and it undergoes **increase and decrease**.

Earth partakes of a **relation with the former** two **elements** and undergoes the **four types of change.** These four are (1) due to karmic action, that is, change that occurs based on the different karmic actions of sentient beings; (2) due to harm, as when change follows from digging, and so forth; (3) due to the elements, as when earth is scorched by fire; (4) due to the passage of time, as when earth changes depending on the period that has elapsed. In the case of **color, smell, taste, and tactility,** their **being similar** to earth and their other causes is also what is **rendering them similar to them** in terms of momentariness. Fire is momentary because it **functions in dependence on fuel.** With respect to sound, **increase is observed,** which shows that it is of a momentary nature. The forms that belong to the sense source of phenomena are what they are in **accordance with the mind, and** there is also the issue of **inquiry. Therefore, the external is also** established to be **momentary.**

In terms of the issue of inquiry, one may wonder, "How does one construct the proof that all conditioned things are momentary?" Here one should ask those who deny such momentariness why it is that while they do accept that conditioned things are impermanent, they do not accept that they are momentary. They may then reply: "Because we do not apprehend any such impermanence in every single moment."

To this we answer: "Such a thing as a burning oil lamp is for you most certainly established as something momentary. Yet, when it remains unmoving, you do not apprehend it that way. Now, why do you not also deny that the burning lamp is momentary?"

They may then answer: "Because, after a while, we no longer apprehend it in the same way as we did to begin with."

"Why," we then ask, "do you then not draw the same conclusion about other conditioned things?" Here they may reply that this is because things such as burning lamps differ from other conditioned things. Yet there are two types of difference: essential difference and difference in terms of emergence. If they hold that the burning lamp differs in terms of its essence, it can still be used as an example. The exclusive nature of a given thing cannot be used as an example of that thing. That would be like employing fire as an example of fire, or taking cow as an example of cow. If, however, it is held that the difference is in terms of emergence, something such as the burning lamp may indeed be used as an example because it is thoroughly accepted as an instance of the momentary. Moreover, just as one would not accept that the one who rides the mount is traveling while the mount stands still, it does not make sense that while the eyes and so forth are present the consciousness that is supported by them is in constant movement.

Next follow three stanzas that establish the impermanence of outer conditioned entities. Here it will be explained how the four elements of earth, water, fire, and wind, the objects of form, sound, smell, taste, and tactility, and the imperceptible forms that belong to the source of mental objects are all indeed momentary.

As regards water, it may flow in streams and rivers or be found in ponds, lakes, pools, and so on. In winter and spring, or at times of drought, such water gradually dwindles and dries up, whereas in the summer various factors such as rain cause it to swell and increase. Hence, water is impermanent because it increases and decreases. If it were of a nonmomentary lasting essence, it could not possibly do so.

Wind will by nature not remain in one place without moving, and since it thus moves here and there in different directions, it is something momentary. Wind may also gain strength or weaken, and it is therefore momentary. Something permanent could not reasonably move and go through stages of increase and decrease. Earth manifests from a basis in water and wind. Since it participates in such relationships, and because it undergoes the four transformations, earth is established to be by nature impermanent and momentary. How, we may wonder, does earth arise based on water and wind? When the world first forms, the wind element manifests as movements in space. From the wind element manifests water, and as rain falls continuously, the world's ocean forms. When the water is stirred by the wind, this creates a foam from which the world's foundation, its central mountain, and its four continents manifest. Hence, the element of earth emerges from water and wind. Therefore, both the causal and resultant factors that emerge in this continuum are momentary.

Four types of change can be observed with respect to the earth element. (1) Change is observed in terms of the particularities of karmic actions, and so sentient beings who—due to an accumulation of wholesome actions—live as gods will experience the ground as soft and supple, like cotton, whereas sentient beings who—because of negative actions—are born in hell will perceive the ground as extremely hot and made of burning iron. These latter beings may also perceive the ground to be rocky, thorny, and so on. Similarly, in the realm of humans, crops and so forth will not grow at times when the soil has not been plowed and otherwise prepared. Yet, once it has been properly prepared, the earth may yield a fine harvest. (2) Change also occurs when holes and cavities are dug and the earth is struck with hammers, sickles, and so on.

(3) Change of the earth element can likewise be observed when it is burnt by fire, leveled by wind, or eroded by water. (4) Finally, change due to time refers to different appearances over time. Thus, for example, the ground produces excellent grains and so forth during an age of excellence, yet during bad times, it will yield only inferior harvests. Similarly, while green grass and the like will grow forth in summer, in winter the landscape becomes pale, icy, and so on. Moreover, certain places that used to be uninhabited later become densely populated, and what used to be a bustling city may become deserted with time. These are all examples of the fourth type of change.

These four types of change occur by way of a continuity of moments, and each moment that thus arises will be manifesting in a way that is different from the others. If, on the other hand, there were some nonmomentary lasting essence, we would never be able to witness it changing. Therefore, when we perceive earth the way we do, it is because it arises differently with each moment, and hence the element of earth is also established as momentary. As for color, smell, taste, and tactility, these are the transformations of the four elements, and so they can be said to be similar to them. Being related to the elements in this way, they are also similar to the elements in terms of their being momentary.

Fire, in turn, is dependent on fuel. Fire burns only if there is fuel and otherwise it does not. It follows that if there is plenty of fuel, there will be plenty of fire, and with only a little fuel, there will be only a little fire. Thus, fire is established to be momentary and, just as fire is momentary, so is its fuel. Fire burns due to its gradual consumption of fuel, and if fire could continue to burn while its fuel remained unaffected, then how could there ever be an end to fire and fuel? Yet, if its fuel runs out, there will no longer be any fire, and so these two emerge in a gradual process of causal and resultant moments. As long as the supply of causes continues, so will the resultant fire. Yet, without cause, no effect will appear. Thus, all entities appear in an unbroken continuity of causes and effects.

One may argue here that it would be reasonable to refer to fire in the context of the four elements, and only then proceed to the consideration of color and so on. In this way, one could feel that there is an awkwardness in the sequence followed here. Yet it is taught that while either approach amounts to the same in terms of the expressed meaning, the present choice of sequence has been made for stylistic reasons. Moreover, while the elements and their transformations all arise and cease from moment to moment, the latter are the effects of the former and each of the effects manifest in a way that conforms with the character of its respective causes. Hence, the example of fire and fuel is employed to illustrate this.

Some may hold sound to be permanent, arguing that since sound never exists by virtue of a continuity in the same way that color and so on do, it remains permanent for as long as it is heard, without being momentary. Yet that is not the case because we do, for example, observe an increase in sound that may be due to the efforts of an agent. The sound of a bell, for example, can be heard to gradually diminish. Hence, it is established that sound is momentary. If until it has disappeared there were but a single sound that is not momentary, then such sound could not reasonably increase or decrease. Therefore, sound is momentary, just as the syllables that are carried by the breath of the person who applies efforts to speak can be heard to arise and cease in a gradual way.

The imperceptible forms that belong to the sense source of mental phenomena are, for example, the vows of individual liberation, the vows of concentration, and the undefiled vows. While these do not comprise perceptible physical or verbal factors, they are nevertheless concomitant with the mind and so they will not arise unless there is a mind to support them. Therefore, since the mind that causes them is impermanent, the resultant imperceptible forms are likewise established to be momentary.

Next, the root text mentions "inquiry." Worldly beings and extremists do accept that conditioned things are impermanent, in the sense that they disintegrate in the end. Yet, for as long as this disintegration has not been directly perceived, as when a human being dies or a vase breaks, they hold that in essence things remain, without being momentary. Thus one may inquire as to why it is that, on the one hand, these opponents accept that at some point things become impermanent and yet, on the other, they deny that impermanence occurs with each moment. To this, they may reply that their denial of momentary impermanence is due to the fact that while they perceive the final disintegration of conditioned things, they do not perceive any momentary disintegration before that. Thus one again inquires, asking them first to notice how, with respect to something like a flame of fire, or a stream of water, Buddhists and non-Buddhists will all agree that whatever was there in the previous moment will have ceased in the present moment, and that, therefore, what is there now is something new. Yet, if we look at a river from a distance, or if we watch a burning lamp where there is no wind, our senses do not register any momentary disintegration. Why, we may then inquire, do you not deny that what is being looked at is something that is of a momentary nature?

When asked in this way, the opponent may reply: "It is only from a distance that the river appears to be one thing, because once we are on the banks of it, we do not see one river but new water all the time. In the case of the burning lamp, flames of fire rise from their base and move upward until they are exhausted and disappear at their summit, all the while being replaced by new flames that behave in the same way. When in the end the fuel is exhausted, we see that the flames become shorter and then finally cease. In other words, we do not constantly see exactly what was there before, and so we should not deny that what we are looking at is of a momentary nature. The case is very different, however, with pillars, vases, houses, mansions, persons, stones, rocks, and so on, because such things do not diminish and instead we can leave them aside for years and months, and then revisit them, finding them just as they were. In those cases we do not witness any momentary disintegration."

Again, we may then ask: "Is it not the case that once something such as a pillar or a vase has appeared, its color, shape, and so on, will continue to undergo change due to the influence of conditions? Why should we then not say that it keeps turning into something else until finally it encounters a condition that brings about its actual destruction? Hence, since that is how vases and pillars exist, why would they not be momentary in the same way that a burning lamp is?"

To this it may be replied: "The characteristics of a burning lamp differ from those of other conditioned things, such as pillars and vases. A burning lamp is hot and gives light; it is unstable and arises and ceases from one moment to the next. That is how we perceive the characteristics of a lamp. In the case of something like a pillar or a vase, we are looking at something that, once it has been produced, will continue to perform its function of supporting beams and holding water for as long as it exists. In other words, since we perceive something that has solid and stable characteristics, this is unlike what we found in the context of the lamp's flame."

In that case we must explain that while it is established both to us and others that all conditioned things have their own particular and uncommon characteristics, this does not mean that all conditioned things are not characterized by momentary impermanence. To explain why that is so, we must first distinguish between two types of conflicting characteristics: characteristics that are in conflict at the level of the essence of things and characteristics that are in conflict with respect to the way things emerge. As an example of the first, we may mention the conflict that exists between the heat that is the nature of fire and the wetness that is the nature of water. As for different emergence, the opponent may wish to say that because such a thing as the flame of an oil lamp arises and ceases from moment to moment, it emerges in a way that is unlike other conditioned things, such as vases—which come into being, remain for some time, and only then disintegrate. In that case, we will concede that lamps, vases and so on, are of their own distinct nature. Yet this does not mean that they do not emerge in a way that is equally momentary in all cases. On the contrary: for the opponents, the flame of the lamp is established as momentary, and we may use that as an example to illustrate how all other conditioned things, including vases, are established as momentary too.

When it comes to examples, it will not do to use lamp light as an example when seeking to establish lamp light, or the cow as an example when wanting to establish the cow, because in those cases the proposed example is the very same as that which is sought to be established. Yet, when two things are by nature not identical, one can be used to show the emergence and presence of a quality that is shared with the other, and so we may say that "the sun is like a fire" or "a cow is similar to a buffalo." In just that way, while things such as vases, on the one hand, and the flame of the lamp, on the other, do have their own particular characteristics, we can show all of them to be in possession of the general characteristic of momentary impermanence. The mere fact that these things have diverse features does not mean that while some of them disintegrate with the moment, others might remain for a while and only disintegrate later. In terms of their momentary disintegration, all conditioned things are not different in any way at all.

Moreover, what the opponents specifically argue is that the essence of the lamp remains without being momentary and that it thereby gives rise to a gradual succession of one momentary flame after another. They also claim that things such as pillars and vases are not momentary: while in essence they remain just as they are, their effects in terms of supporting beams, holding water, and so forth, are no different throughout last year, this year, and the next. We may therefore ask the opponents to think of the situation of a man riding a horse in order to get from one place to another. Does the horse then stay where it is while only the man goes to the new location? To this they may reply that within the world such a scenario is impossible, and that indeed the man and his horse proceed together.

In that case, we will respond as follows: "According to you, the very essence of the lamp is not momentary, but it produces momentary flames. Things such as vases you also hold to remain immutable, all the while performing their functions of holding water and so on. Likewise, in considering the eyes and the rest of the five faculties, you claim that while they stay as they are, without any fluctuation, they give rise to visual consciousness and so on. Yet if there is no movement at the level of the cause, there cannot be any movement at the level of the effect either. If indeed you hold that, in the above cases, the thing that causes the effect remains just as it was, without any movement, then how is that any different from claiming that the rider travels onward while the horse remains where it is? Moreover, as regards the essence of the lamp, its burning occurs through a continuous supply of oil that is gradually consumed by the flames. When all of the oil has been consumed and exhausted, the flames will die out and the wick turn into ashes. If instead the wick were to remain, beyond arising and ceasing, the lamp's burning could never bring an end to the wick nor would the flames ever die out. Yet, since none of this is the case, both cause and effect are momentary. Therefore, understand that the functioning of things such as pillars and vases and the arising of sense consciousness based on the senses are examples of momentary causes and momentary effects in exactly the same way as the burning lamp."

At this point, the opponents may ask why, given the momentary nature of all that is conditioned, mundane beings cannot determine the impermanence of all such things to the same extent that they can with a burning lamp. Yet, when the perception of mundane beings is not able to determine that all conditioned things are momentary, it is not because only some things are, while others are not. Something like a flash of lightning, a water bubble, a cloud, a burning lamp, or a cascade of water does not last long, and even while they appear, they keep shifting. Therefore, it is easy to understand that they are impermanent. Things such as pillars, vases, rocks, mountains, and diamonds, however, are in fact just as momentary. Yet, as long as what is manifest is similar to what was there just before, then that uninterrupted similarity can serve as the cause of delusion, and so the mind errantly comes to believe that its objects endure. Indeed, things cannot in any way last for more than a moment.

Sentient beings who are possessed by the causes of delusion and whose intellectual powers are weak will believe in a way that runs counter to the actual nature of things, and so they make the error of conceiving of conditioned things in terms of purity, bliss, permanence, and self. Similarly, those suffering from cataracts will see the conch to be yellow, and when at night one looks at a firebrand that is quickly spun around, it will appear to be a flaming wheel. Likewise, to those with poor vision, a multicolored rope may at dusk appear to be a snake.

Therefore, because there is such a thing as mistaken mind, it is also established that there is cyclic existence, and, because the insight that is in possession of reliable means of cognition can dispel mistaken mind, it is also undeniably established that there is complete purification as well. If there were no such thing as a mind in error, then all the perceptions of mundane beings would be factual. In that case, either everyone would be liberated from the beginning, or otherwise nobody could ever attain liberation. Hence, since neither is the case, there is no deception in the existence of both thorough affliction and complete purification. Let us, therefore, not hold the extent and nature of mundane perception to be the decisive issue. By taking the support of the path of authentic reasoning, the light of intelligence will fully unfold.

Hence, for the reasons that have been given from evaporation and increase through to inquiry, all outer conditioned things can be understood to be momentary. The account that has been given here serves as a clarifying, comprehensive summary of the master Sthiramati's elaborate explanations on the purport of Vasubandhu's commentary.

2. Proof of the Absence of Personal Self

> The person should be considered existent nominally
> And not substantially.
> It is unobserved, mistaken,
> Thorough affliction, and the cause of affliction. [XIX.93]

> Since two flaws ensue,
> It cannot be said to be identical or different;
> The aggregates would be the self,
> And the self would be substantial. [XIX.94]

> If it were substantial, the need for its being inexpressible
> Would have to be expressed;
> Inexpressibility in terms of oneness and difference
> Does not make any sense if not for any need. [XIX.95]

When considering the characteristics, the perception of the world,
As well as the treatises,
It would not be right to say that, like fire and fuel,
They cannot be determined to be two, because those are indeed two. [XIX.96]

Consciousness arises with the presence of two;
That is no condition since it would serve no purpose.
Hence, from the one that sees
To the one that is liberated—it is not that. [XIX.97]

If there were a single master,
Impermanence and the undesired would not occur,
Its characteristics would have to be established,
And this would invalidate the triple complete enlightenment. [XIX.98]

Because there are three flaws,
The acts in terms of seeing and the rest are not self-arisen,
The person is not a condition for those activities,
And it is devoid of the activity of seeing and so forth. [XIX.99]

Because of not being an agent, because of impermanence,
And because of simultaneous and constant engagement,
The functions in terms of seeing and the rest
Could not possibly be self-occurring. [XIX.100]

Accordingly, that which abides and disintegrates could—
Because of prior nonexistence, impermanence,
And the nonexistence of any third option—
Not serve as a condition.[XIX.101]

Thus all phenomena are devoid of self
And ultimately empty.
The observation of a self is, hence,
Exclusively taught to be a flaw. [XIX.102]

The particular distinctions between
The contexts of thorough affliction and complete purification,
The application, and the particularities of the continuity
Are shown clearly by means of the person. [XIX.103]

The view of self need not be generated;
Familiarity with that runs since time without beginning.
If there were a person, everyone would either
Be effortlessly liberated or not liberated at all. [XIX.104]

In terms of the proof of the absence of a personal self, **the person should be considered existent nominally, and not substantially** existent. How should we understand this lack of substantial existence with respect to the person? By recognizing that, unlike form and so forth, **it is unobserved**. Moreover, in the absence of any self, the idea of "myself" is entirely **mistaken**. We can realize this by acknowledging that, in being characterized by the affliction of the view of the transitory collection, "I" and "mine" are **thorough affliction. And** we can understand that this is the case by considering how attachment and the other afflictions arise as the result of these ideas, and how they are, hence, **the cause of affliction**.

One may also wonder: "Should the so-called self be said to be identical with or different from what is referred to as 'form and so forth'?" **Since two flaws ensue, it cannot be said to be identical or different.** What are those two flaws? If they were identical, **the aggregates would be the self**, and if they were different, **the self would be substantial**. Therefore, since the person is of nominal existence, it is not to be declared, and this in turn establishes it as being an indeterminate issue. Those who, with their assertion of a substantial self, fall outside the scope of our Teacher's words should be addressed in the following way: **If it were substantial, the need or reason for its being asserted as inexpressible would have to be expressed.** The assertion of the self's **inexpressibility in terms of oneness** with, **and difference** from, the aggregates **does not make any sense if** it is **not** set forth **for any need** or reason.

It might be argued, "It is just like the case of fire and fuel, which likewise cannot be seen as different or not different." Yet, this is not correct. Fuel consists of the element of earth and so forth, and fire is the fire element. Therefore, **when considering** the way in which **the characteristics** of the two differ, **the** way they are different in the **perception of the world, as well as** the way they are considered in **the treatises** (for the Blessed One does not speak of any inexpressibility of fire and fuel either), **it would not be right to say that "like fire and fuel, they cannot be determined to be two,"** because those, fire and fuel, **are indeed two** different things.

It may be objected: "In everything from seeing to knowing, there is a person involved who performs these acts. That person, who is the agent, the consumer, the knower, and the one who is liberated, is nothing if not existent." Now, is that person then someone who in essence exists as a condition for the production of consciousness, or is that person the producer of the ruling condition and other such conditions?

Consciousness arises with the presence of two factors: sense faculty and object. **That is no condition since it would serve no purpose.** Hence, from the one that sees to the one that is liberated—**it is not that. If there were a single master,** a producer of the conditions, the **impermanence** of the occasion of the mind being happy **and the arising of the undesired** occasion of suffering **would not occur.** Moreover, if the person had any substantial existence, **its** function and **characteristics would have to be established** in the same way that we, in the case of the eye, for example, specify the act of seeing and the existence of a subtle form. **And also, if the person were held to be substantial, this would invalidate the** notion of the Buddha's **triple complete enlightenment** (that is, true and complete enlightenment that is profound, exceptional, and transcendent of the world). If the realization were of a person, there would be nothing at all in the way of a true and complete enlightenment that is profound; there would not be anything exceptional when compared to the extremists; nor would there be any sense of being free from the world either. That way of grasping is the understanding of all mundane people; it is the obsession of the extremists, and it has long been marked by cyclic existence.

Furthermore, if from seeing to cognizing it is the person who experiences, we may ask whether in seeing and so forth the person performs a function, and, if so, whether that function is self-occurring and adventitious, or whether it is produced with the person serving as a condition. **Because there are three flaws** that follow from such an account, **the acts in terms of seeing and the rest are not self-arisen.** Similarly, since three flaws would follow, **the person is not a condition for those activities. And**, if the person is not active, **it is devoid of the activity of seeing and so forth**, and is hence not the seer. As for the three flaws, if the act of seeing and so forth and the resultant visual perception were adventitious and uncaused, then, **because of** the person in that case **not being an agent**, the person could not be actively involved in anything from seeing to consciousness. Moreover, if they were adventitious, they would not depend on anything, and hence would be permanent. Therefore, **because of** their **impermanence,** we can understand that seeing and so forth are not adventitious and self-occurring. **And**, finally, **because of** the **simultaneous and constant engagement** that would be the consequence if the activities were permanent, **the functions in terms of seeing and the rest could not possibly be self-occurring.**

If, alternatively, it is held that the person is a condition for these functions, we may examine whether, in that case, the person is a condition that remains, disintegrates, or both. **Accordingly, that which abides and disintegrates could** not be a condition **because**, in the case of a constantly abiding condition, as explained above, the function could not ever be absent since the very possibility of a **prior nonexistence** of its condition is ruled out. On the other hand, disintegration implies **impermanence, and the nonexistence of any third option** must likewise be taken into account. Hence, that which remains, disintegrates, or both remains and disintegrates could **not serve as a condition. Thus all phenomena are devoid of self and ultimately empty. The observation of a self is, hence, exclusively taught to be a flaw.**

"Why," it may be objected, "do we find statements such as 'There is a person who carries the burden' if there is not any substantially existent person?" The term "person" is employed in order to facilitate an understanding of **the particular distinctions between the contexts of thorough affliction and complete purification,** to promote the understanding of the fact-based **application** of the terms "thorough affliction" and "complete purification," **and** to engender knowledge of **the particularities of the continuity** of afflicted or purified aggregates. Those issues **are shown clearly by means of the** term "person."

The view of self need not be generated by means of a teaching that speaks of "the person" because that view has been present since the beginning. When the teachings speak of persons, it is not for the sake of a familiarization with that view because **familiarity with that runs since time without beginning. If there were a person, everyone**—that is, all sentient beings in cyclic existence—**would either be effortlessly liberated** since they grasp in a way that does not conflict with that, **or** otherwise the noble ones would **not** be **liberated at all** by virtue of not apprehending a self.

The present account focuses on what is hard to comprehend within the fourfold summary of the Dharma. Hence, the verses have explained impermanence by first treating it in terms of nonexistence, and then secondly in the sense of momentariness. In the context of the latter understanding of impermanence, the verses first present fourteen general proofs of momentary impermanence. This is followed by fourteen principles that prove, in particular, the momentary nature of inner conditioned entities. After this, as the explicit teaching, comes a set of ten principles that specifically prove the momentary character of outer entities. As for the present issue, proving the absence of self with respect to the person, the previously supplied proof of the impermanence of the five aggregates has already shown implicitly that there is no such thing as a singular, personal self. Nevertheless, mundane people and extremists believe that there is an agent who carries the burden of the aggregates and who exercises control. With this in mind, they speak of "the self," "the vital principle," "the person," or "the doer," whom they understand to be the one that maintains the unbroken continuity of the aggregates. Considered to be in possession of numerous strengths, this individual is also referred to as the "the powerful one," "the master of powers," or the "powerful ruler of beings." Held to be the doer of actions, it is also termed "the potent agent" or "progenitor's descendent." These and other names are used in this way to refer to an existent self. This self, in turn, is held to be the basis for bondage and liberation.

Also within our own group, schools such as the Saṃmitīyas hold that the self exists. They point to the fact that the Blessed One himself has spoken of "the person who is an ordinary being," "the person who is a stream enterer" and so on, just as he has said that "one person will, once he appears in the world, bring benefit and happiness to the whole world—that person is the thus-gone one." Based on such scriptural passages, they argue that all sentient beings have a self. If they did not, they ask, then who is it that is bound within cyclic existence and who is it that is liberated? Who is it that accomplishes what benefits oneself and others, and who is it that embarks on the path? In this way, they argue that the self does indeed exist.

As for the extremists, some hold the self to be of the same size as the body. Some hold it to be mental, and others understand it to be matter. For some it possesses form, while for others it does not. In such ways, there are numerous assertions, yet they generally all consider the self to be permanent and singular. Based on this concept, they then construct various teachings concerning a self that is in control, is the agent of actions, and so on. The Saṃmitīyas within our own group do hold the self to exist substantially, yet they deny that it is either the same as, or different from, the aggregates. Hence, they assert that it is neither permanent nor impermanent, and so forth. The root text begins this section by declaring such assertions to be wrong. The person and the self should be considered to exist merely as a convention that is based on the five aggregates. It is in consideration of this nominal existence that the Blessed One has followed the ways of the world, and so spoken of persons that may be anything from ordinary beings to buddhas. That is not to say that the self or person exists substantially, or ultimately, or by its own essential nature. This way of showing the person to be existent at the nominal level but not existent in terms of substance avoids both the flaws of holding the person to be inappropriate, even in terms of convention, and of taking it to be existent in terms of substance.

What tells us that the self does not exist substantially? Well, if it did so exist, we would have to be able to observe it by means of a reliable means of cognition—either perception or inference. Therefore, since neither of these can provide the observation of the self, the self does not exist substantially. The self cannot possibly be perceived by means of the eyes or by any other of the six faculties. Nor can it be observed through the consciousness that is associated with the eyes and so on. Here, others may object: "The mere fact that the self cannot be observed by means of the eyes and visual consciousness, or by means of any of the other five faculties and the associated consciousnesses, does not mean that the self does not exist. Mind and mental states are not observed by the five sense consciousnesses, but since they are observed by the mental consciousness, we do accept that they exist. Likewise, we who accept the existence of the self make our assertion based on the mental observation of the self. This observation is, moreover, confirmed by the Blessed One, who states that "in this present life one observes and speaks of a self."

To this, we reply that the observation of the self is mistaken in the sense that something that is not there is taken to be there, just as when a colored rope is observed as a snake. Hence it is not the case that mental perception sees the self as existent. The Blessed One did not state that a substantial self is observed by a reliable means of cognition. Rather, he said that while there is no self, one believes that there is, and so while maintaining a mental observation of self, one also speaks of that so-called self.

Again, the proponents of an existent self may argue: "A self that has never had any existence could not reasonably be observed by the mind. Yet the minds of all sentient beings do, nevertheless, observe that there is a self. How, then, could we say that the observation of the self is mistaken?" Now, for the observation of self to be free from error, it will have to be free from flaws as well. The view of self is, however, by nature flawed. It is itself of the essence of thorough affliction, and it functions as the cause of all other afflictions too. It is, therefore, clear that it is mistaken. Observing a self constitutes that view of the transitory collection that among the six root afflictions belongs to the affliction of view. Desire and everything else that is characterized by affliction develops from there, and so it is this that establishes the cyclic existence that is of the nature of numerous sufferings. As it is flawed in this way, the observation of self is mistaken.

It may further be objected that while the view of the self is thus characterized by thorough affliction, it is nevertheless not mistaken. Yet, unless it is mistaken, it could not reasonably be afflictive. That which is affliction, as illustrated, for instance, by the view of permanence and the view of annihilation, is also that which is mistaken. Moreover, that which is free from affliction is also free from error, for example, the cognition of the impermanent and the unclean. When mistaken thoughts of purity, bliss, permanence, and self are dispelled by the path of the realization of impurity, suffering, impermanence, and absence of self, this brings about the attainment of complete purification within the absence of all flaws, just as when the eye is healed and is no longer subject to the mistaken perceptions that follow from the flaws of an eye disease.

Again, the proponents of self may argue: "Even for you, who hold persons to be nominally existent, the imputation of a person cannot reasonably occur without any basis for it. Therefore, what is, for you, the basis for speaking of persons?" When we speak of a person, it is not because there is any substantial person that we then label accordingly. The name is simply applied to the five aggregates of appropriation. As a sūtra teaches:

> Whenever any spiritual practitioner or Brahmin speaks of "I" or "mine," it is simply an imputation based on the five aggregates of appropriation.

With an approach that considers the person to exist substantially, the person and the aggregates will have to be asserted to be either one with, or distinct from, each other. This is because, in relation to a given substance, an entity that exists substantially must be of a substance that is different from the former, or otherwise it must turn out that, in fact, it is of the same substance as the former. Thus, for example, the vase is different from the substance of the yarn, yet it is identical with its own vase substance. An imputed person, however, does not exist as a substance that is different from the aggregates. Moreover, since the two are not different in terms of being simply the basis for imputation and the imputation as such, the person and the aggregates are not identical either.

Two flaws, which will be explained next, render unwarranted any qualification of the person and the aggregates as identical or distinct. The person or self on the one hand, and the aggregates on the other, are therefore neither the same nor different and distinct. What are these two flaws? If the aggregates and the self were the same, the aggregates would be the self, and yet if they were different, it would follow that the self was of a substance different from the aggregates. What, we might then wonder, would be problematic about that? If the aggregates were the self, then either the self would—just like the aggregates—be multiple and impermanent, or otherwise the aggregates would—just like the self—be singular and permanent. If, alternatively, the self were different from the aggregates, we would have to be able to observe it apart from them. It would likewise follow that the aggregates involved in gathering karmic action and the aggregates associated with the resultant pleasure or pain could not have any relation to the self.

The Saṃmitīyas profess a variant of the assertion of self. Although they hold the Buddha to be their teacher, they do not adhere to his teaching on the absence of self. Instead they hold the self to be substantially existent. We may, therefore, charge them with the following: "If the self exists as a substance, is it then the same or different from the aggregates? Your claim that it cannot rightly be seen as either the same or different, or permanent or impermanent, must be substantiated. If it does not serve a particular need, or consider a specific reason, then such an assertion should not be made. Mere words are not sufficient to establish a philosophical position."

When charged in this way, the Saṃmitīyas may say: "The self and the aggregates are not the same because we must accept that the self remains within cyclic existence after the five aggregates have ceased. Yet neither are the two different because that which accumulates karmic action and which experiences its ripening is nothing other than the aggregates. Moreover, the self could not be permanent because it is born into numerous different lives. On the other hand, neither could it be impermanent because the self has been the same since beginningless time. It is not that there are many selves that arise and cease. Therefore, we assert, among other things, that the self that is the support for karmic action and its results must exist as a substance that cannot be stated as identical with, or different from, the aggregates. For example, fire and fuel are not one because fuel alone does not perform the function of burning, nor does fire fulfill the task of fuel. Nevertheless, the two are not different because it is indeed fuel that turns into fire, and fire is never observed under any other circumstances."

The opponents in this way hold that "the self and the aggregates are both substantially existent, yet they cannot be said to be either the same or different." This position, however, does not serve any purpose and is devoid of reason. It is misguided imagination, making no sense at all. How so? For example, if having asserted that the pillar and the vase are established as distinct substances, one says that "these two are not the same," then that statement has already established them as different. It certainly does not work to go on to say "and they are not different either." Likewise, having claimed that the self and the aggregates are both substantial, the reasonable course is to claim, from that point on, that they are not the same. To add that they are not different, or not distinct, not only serves no purpose but is also in extreme contradiction of one's prior statement. This is just like claiming that the pillar is no different from the vase.

The opponents appear to be concerned that, by holding the self and the aggregates as different from each other, a problem will arise in terms of our failing to find any doer of karmic actions, or any experiencer of their results, apart from the aggregates themselves. Fearing such consequences, they then opt for the idea that the self and aggregates are not different. Yet, they have not thereby escaped the aforementioned flaws that are associated with the assertion of an identical nature of the substantial self and the substantial aggregates. If, intimidated by those flaws, they then qualify their assertion, saying "but we do not assert that they are the same," this expressed commitment to their difference will immediately make their own acceptance of sameness fall apart. Such a position that rests on a direct contradiction is not only useless but also tremendously flawed. If the self must be held to be substantial, it makes sense to declare it either identical with, or distinct from, the aggregates, but it could not possibly contain a substance that is neither the same as, nor different from, the aggregates. Neither is there any mention of such a substance in scripture, nor can it be established by reasoning either.

Therefore, when we notice that there is something wrong, both with the assertion that the self and the aggregates are the same and with the claim that they are different, this is because the self does not exist by virtue of any substance. Its existence is merely nominal, as stated above. And a self that is asserted to be a mere imputation should not be held to be either the same as, or different from, the aggregates. The opponents, however, have failed to comprehend this. Instead, while holding the self to be a substance, they teach that it should be declared neither one with, nor different from, the aggregates, neither permanent nor impermanent, and so forth. Such contradictory, mere verbiage does not in any way contribute to the establishment of the support for the experience of karmic consequences.

As for the proposed example—fire and fuel as neither the same nor different—this does not make any sense either. Fire and the wood that feeds it have different characteristics because whereas fire is burning and hot, the wood is neither of these. It is characteristically solid and can be used in numerous ways. Hence, in terms of their characteristics, fire and fuel are different. The world also perceives these two to be different because there may be firewood lying where there is no fire, a flame may be lifted by the wind over a long distance without any fuel, and sparks may fly from iron, stone, or the like. If we consider the corpus of treatises, fire is one among the four elements, whereas fuel is an elemental transformation that is primarily constituted by the adhesiveness of water, the solidity of earth, and the movement of wind. It therefore does not work to say that "the self and the aggregates are neither the same nor different, just like fire and fuel," because fire and fuel are distinct substances.

Next, the extremists' conception of the self is refuted. The extremists claim: "The self exists by virtue of being the one that sees, hears, smells, tastes, touches, and is aware of mental phenomena. The self is also the agent of virtuous and unvirtuous actions, just as it is the one that experiences their ripening and partakes of the objects. It is also the self that gains liberation from the courage, matter, and darkness that bind sentient beings. How can you deny that the self exists?" Other than the self, everything else that the extremists mention here exists, from the seer through to the one that is liberated. The self, however, is not in any way engaged in seeing and so on. Why not? To answer this question, we will first ask: Is the self a condition that, along with the faculties and objects, is indispensable for the arising of seeing and so forth, or is it like a ruler or master, by the power of which the faculties and other conditions must be aroused before they can engage in acts such as seeing?

The first could not be the case because whenever conditions such as the eyes and the other faculties and form and the other objects are present, visual consciousness and the rest of the six consciousnesses will arise on that basis. No further condition is required, and since we do not observe any other productive condition to be involved, we can conclude that the self is not a condition for the arising of consciousness. The former two factors are themselves capable of producing cognitively capable consciousness. Hence, no extraneous condition in the form of a self is required because such a cause would serve no purpose. Similarly, when fire rises from fuel, there need not be any water around. Therefore, that which sees forms is consciousness, and the same goes for all the other principles up to the one that is liberated; it is different sorts of consciousness that are referred to as "the seer" and so on. From the seer through to the one that is liberated, none of these are the self because we do not observe any seeing self and so forth, apart from consciousness.

The opponents may, however, take the alternative position and so argue: "When object, faculty, and cognition come together, seeing and so forth become manifest by the power of the self. Were it not for the self, there would be no such experiences." Yet, if the self were such a powerful master, free to partake of the enjoyments of the senses, then we would expect this ruler of experience to make sure that enjoyable possessions were not lost but partaken of always. Yet, that is not how things are. It would also make sense for this ruler of experience to make sure that something painful would never occur and that pleasure would never wane. But since there is no sentient being that does not encounter suffering, it must, therefore, be understood that there is no self that is in control. As faculties and objects meet, the force of karma produces all sorts of enjoyable and unpleasant situations, and the coming together of conditions brings different forms of pleasure and pain. This is definitely not due to the wishes or blessings of the self. Please, therefore, understand that—

from the seer to the one that is liberated—none of these are the self.

The teaching of an existent self has further faults. If there were such a thing as a substance of the self, it would be necessary to specify its functions and characteristics. For example, we may say that the function of the eye faculty and visual consciousness is to engage in acts of seeing and that the eye faculty characteristically is a buoyant form, whereas visual consciousness is the cognition of blue and so forth. We would also have to state something of this sort with respect to the self's function and characteristics. Yet, since the self does not exist substantially, it cannot be observed by a reliable means of cognition, just as the child of a barren woman and the horn of a rabbit cannot be observed. Hence, it is impossible to talk about any true function or characteristics of such a self. If instead one states the functions and characteristics of the aggregates as if they were the qualities of the self, then that makes for a mistaken and unwholesome philosophical system. Perforated by hundreds of logical inconsistencies, such a position invites exhaustion in whoever assumes it.

Moreover, if the self existed, it would have to be seen by the Buddha, because the Buddha has insight into all that can be known. One might then believe that because he speaks of "ordinary persons," "noble persons," and so on, the Buddha does indeed see the self of the person, yet we have already explained the significance of such statements. If one nevertheless insists that those references do mean that the Buddha perceives a substantial self, then such a claim will run counter to the principle of the Buddha's triple complete enlightenment. The latter is enumerated in terms of the profound, exceptional, and world-transcendent character of a buddha's complete enlightenment. First, such an enlightenment is described as profound because of the realization of the absence of self in phenomena. Second, it is considered exceptional because of the realization of the absence of a personal self, which is a realization not shared with non-Buddhists. Finally, this comprehension of the twofold absence of self is to be found nowhere in the world, and so a buddha's complete enlightenment is also described as transcendent of the world. Alternatively, a buddha's complete enlightenment is profound, exceptional, and transcendent because of the realization of, respectively, the nonexistence of the imaginary, the conventional existence of the dependent, and the natural peace of the thoroughly established.

In fact, the absence of the two selves cannot be grasped by the mind of confined perception of mundane beings. The buddhas realize it, then teach it to others; yet, if they were to perceive an existent self, their vision would not be superior to that of mundane beings. It would not be profound, or exceptional, and it would not be beyond the world, and thus the claims to the contrary would not be valid.

Further errors in terms of the assertion of a substantially existent self become apparent by inquiring in the following way. This allegedly substantial self that sees, hears, and so on—when it wishes, for instance, to see, does it then do so without having to apply any effort to open the eyes, or must it make such efforts in order to see? Neither of these options is reasonable because both entail three flaws, as will be explained next. It is not the case that the self accomplishes the acts of seeing in a way that is self-arisen and effortless. Yet, neither is the self a condition for those acts by making efforts to open the eyes, listen in the right direction, and so on. Seeing is engaged in by consciousness based on the faculties and the objects, and the self is not involved in any acts of seeing or hearing and so forth.

To explain the above, if acts of seeing and so forth were self-arisen and not undertaken by the self, then the self could not be the agent of those acts, precisely because they are then not carried out by the self but occur by themselves. Moreover, seeing and so forth are occasional events and are therefore impermanent and brought about by causes. They could not reasonably be uncaused and self-occurring, therefore. Were they self-occurring and causeless, they would be permanent acts, and yet that possibility is excluded by the reliable, cognitive means of perception. If those acts were to occur uncaused, they would also all be simultaneous, precisely because uncaused effects are not causally dependent, and they would occur forever. Therefore, seeing and so forth cannot possibly be self-occurring and effortless.

Nor is the self a condition for seeing, hearing, and so on. Would the self then function as a permanently active condition for seeing and hearing? Or would it instead function as an impermanent, active condition for those acts? Or would it perhaps serve as a condition for them in a way that is both permanent and impermanent? The first would not work because if the self were to function as a permanently active condition for seeing and so on, it would always remain exactly as it was. Being always active, in this way, as the condition for seeing and so on, it would also have to exist as involved in seeing prior to the coming together of faculty and object, prior to the eye's engagement in the act of seeing. However, when seeing, hearing, and so forth, have not yet taken place, there is nothing that engages in those acts either, and so there cannot be a self that is a permanently active condition for those acts.

The second option is not feasible either. If the self is a condition that is active on an impermanent basis, then its function is not always there. As whatever took place previously comes to an end and is impermanent, the same must be the case with the agent that is involved. The agent too must be impermanent because there are distinct occasions in terms of the presence and absence of activity. Finally, any third option, meaning something that both is and is not impermanent, is entirely impossible. Permanent and impermanent are directly contradictory, and so, if one of them is not the case, then the other surely is, and there cannot be any third option in between. While this type of analysis can also be made in terms of a permanent versus an impermanent self, it seems more convenient to undertake it with reference to a permanent or impermanent activity of the self.

Thus, the absence of self has been established by means of reasoning endowed with reliable means of cognition. Next, in a discussion that is addressed to those within our own group who believe in a self, it will—by means of the reliable, cognitive means of scripture—be established that there is no self. The Blessed One has taught that all phenomena are devoid of self. Where do we find this teaching? Within the fourfold summary of the Dharma, where it is stated that "all phenomena are devoid of self." Likewise, in the sūtra of the listeners that is entitled *Ultimate Emptiness*,[51] the Buddha declares that "in terms of the ultimate truth, all phenomena are empty." Moreover, within one of the listeners' *Long Discourses,* in the section on commencement and so on where the five miracles initiated by the five are explained, it is stated that "five flaws will ensue from the view of self." Thus, it is also explained:

Virtuous and negative karmic actions will bring enjoyable and painful ripening, respectively. Thus, there will be birth and engagement within cyclic existence in the manner of the twelve links of dependent origination. Yet, other than in terms of such conventions of the Dharma, there is no person who discards present aggregates in order to appropriate different ones.

Thus, the observation associated with the belief that the self exists substantially is explained to be a flaw, and it is entirely in conflict with the words of the Buddha. The five flaws referred to above are the following:

(1) The first, "the view of the self and of the life-force," refers to the belief that the self is the life-force. Here one believes that the person is an existent substance, in contradiction of the facts of the absence of a self and of anything that belongs to a self.

(2) The second flaw is "the lack of any difference from the extremists." That is to say, the extremist view of an existent self and the view that takes the self to be substantially existent are no different.

(3) Third is "the pursuit of a mistaken path." The path of the transcendence of suffering and liberation is a process of meditation based on impermanence, suffering, emptiness, and absence of self. Views about a self and a person are not the path of liberation. They are the path of birth within cyclic existence and the lower realms, a path of error.

(4) The fourth is referred to as "the mind's lack of access to emptiness." Emptiness is the absence of a self and of something that belongs to it. The views that believe in a substantially existent self are in discord with emptiness, and so the minds that adhere to such views will be unable to access emptiness. As it is taught, such a mind will have no concern for, will not pay any attention to, will not meditate upon, will not have any faith in, will not abide by, and will not be inspired by emptiness.

(5) The fifth flaw is a "lack of training in the noble qualities." As long as one believes that the self exists as a substance, one will not be able to rely on the paths of seeing and cultivation. Hence, one will be unable to eliminate the afflictions and actualize the transcendence of suffering.

Those who teach the self's substantial existence may argue: "The Blessed One's sūtras speak of "the person who has understood all," "the person who understands all," "the person who has shed the burden," "the person who is a follower of faith," "the person who is a follower of the Dharma," and so on. In other words, the sūtras teach with reference to an abundance of different types of individuals. If there were no substance of the person, what would be the point of all these different categories of persons? Therefore, because the sūtras do indeed teach them, the person exists substantially."

These various categories of individuals are not taught in order to show that such persons exist by virtue of a substance. Instead, they are a means for understanding the differences between the contexts of thorough affliction and complete purification, and for distinguishing the various particularities of these two contexts. As a term or convention, "person" is thus applied as a pedagogical means for explaining first what thorough affliction and complete purification refer to, and then to explain further the various specifics of these processes. All these various persons do not exist as distinct substances. As regards the way that the term "person" is applied, one speaks of "a person that is in possession of thorough affliction" when the stream of the five aggregates is in possession of the factors of thorough affliction. In this way, one may use the term "person" to refer conveniently to all the factors that pertain in a given situation. That is all there is to it. Such references in the sūtras are not meant to indicate that there is a person existing as a substance apart from the factors that make up the continuity of the afflicted aggregates. The sūtras also speak of "a person endowed with complete purification," referring to a possession of the factors of complete purification.

As for abiding within the stream of thorough affliction, there are numerous particular instances. Hence, depending on whether the level of affliction is minor, medium, or great, we see that conventions such as "a person of minor desire," "a person of medium desire," and "a person of great desire" are used. The teachings in the same way refer to distinct "persons" that are qualified by anger or any of the other afflictions. Similarly, because there are lesser, medium, and greater levels of complete purification, we also hear, for example, of "the person that has attained the lesser path." Based on the presence of decidedly virtuous or unvirtuous activity, there is likewise mention of persons that are characterized by virtue and evil. Therefore, there are persons that engage in thorough affliction and in complete purification, persons that are in possession of either of those two, persons that are without either, persons of sharp faculties and of dull faculties, persons that carry the burden of suffering and its origin, persons that have attained cessation by means of the path and so shed the burden, persons that abide on the path of accumulation and so forth, persons of inspired conduct, ordinary individuals, bodhisattvas and buddhas—as well as the further subdivisions in terms of those that have entered the four fruitions, those that have attained the first ground, and so forth. Without all these different categories of persons, all the corresponding instances of specific factors and qualities could not be distinguished. It must, therefore, be understood that in all these cases, the reference is to the continuity of the five aggregates, and among these, primarily consciousness. This is why the teachings speak of persons as qualified in terms of the Dharma.

If the Blessed One were to make use of all these categories of persons in order to show that there is a person that exists substantially, then these teachings would serve to bring forth that view of self. Yet the view of self need not be generated because every sentient being has always had it. Neither could it be the case that, while everyone has had this view of self since beginningless time, in order for this to be purified it is necessary to develop focus and meditate upon the "self"—so that one will finally be able to perceive it directly and thereby gain liberation. The teaching of a substantially existent person could not have been given for the sake of a process of developing familiarity with the self because the process of familiarization with the self has been going on since time without beginning. This is exactly what everyone within cyclic existence has been becoming familiar with, all the while. And yet, not only does this not bring liberation, it is the very root of bondage within cyclic existence. Therefore, the Blessed One's teaching by means of the word "person" could not be due to an intention to let others develop the view of self. Nor could it be for the sake of letting others meditate upon it. Why, then, should the Buddha teach that the person is substantially existent? Such a teaching would not serve any purpose.

If the view of the self is something that the Buddha must elicit in sentient beings, then it must be the case that this view yields effortless liberation for everyone. Alternatively, if this view is not to be elicited, and if the Buddha instead refutes it, then it will have to be the case that those who adhere to the view of self cannot be liberated. No other options are available. Hence, if the person or self were definitively of substantial existence, then any sentient being who believes in it would not be deluded. All such sentient beings would, therefore, reasonably be liberated from the beginning without having to apply any efforts on the path. Nobody, however, is liberated until they have realized the absence of self, and therefore since the view that the self exists substantially is bondage, it must be refuted rather than established and elicited.

If the self were existent by virtue of its own essence, then nobody would be able to refute it on the path of reason, and nobody would be able to relinquish the grasping of this irrefutable self. Yet, attachment to that which one considers "I" and "mine," as well as hostility toward others, will remain so long as there is grasping at self. This, in turn, renders the dissolving of the afflictions impossible. Karmic actions will hence be accumulated by the force of the afflictions, and so cyclic existence will go on forever, like a revolving waterwheel, without there ever being a chance for liberation. It is, therefore, absolutely impossible that the Thus-Gone One should have taught that the self exists substantially because the Buddha's speech reveals the methods of liberation. The fundamental reason that the Buddha's teaching is superior to the views of mundane beings and extremists is that it expresses the view of the twofold absence of self, and it should therefore be understood that a substantially existent self is not taught anywhere throughout the teachings of scripture.

[4.] Concluding the Chapter

> Thus, always in possession of these qualities,
> The bodhisattvas do not
> Reject that which benefits themselves
> Yet accomplish the welfare of others. [XIX.105]

> This was the nineteenth chapter of the *Ornament of the Great Vehicle Sūtras,* the chapter on the factors that accord with enlightenment.

Thus, always in possession of these qualities of conscience and so forth, **the bodhisattvas**, by means of their insight, **do not reject that which benefits themselves, yet** by means of their compassion, they also **accomplish the welfare of others.**

In conclusion to the chapter, it is explained that the bodhisattvas are always in possession of the qualities that ensue from cultivating the factors that accord with enlightenment. These have been explained here, from conscience through to the teaching on absence of self. In this way, bodhisattvas do not reject the perfect abandonment and the realization that benefits themselves, yet they also benefit others by establishing them, too, within abandonment and realization.

This concludes the explanation of the nineteenth chapter of the *Ornament of the Great Vehicle Sūtras,* the chapter on the factors that accord with enlightenment.

20

The Qualities

5. The Qualities

The present chapter, as mentioned earlier, is concerned with the qualities of the bodhisattvas who bring into their experience the subject matter from the chapter on inspiration through to the chapter on the factors of enlightenment. This chapter thus includes (1) a discussion of the qualities of practice and (2) a presentation of the qualities in combination with praise. The first section is divided into (1) a general presentation of three qualities, (2) a specific explanation of the practice of the transcendences by way of the twelve principles, from repaying kindness through to the foremost pursuits, and (3) an explanation of the qualities of expertise in reference to the way they explain the Dharma.

The first of these three sections is itself concerned with three issues: (1) the qualities of causal concordance, (2) the qualities of connection, and (3) the qualities in terms of concern for sentient beings. The first of the three, causal concordance, is taught in stanzas 1 to 2. It is explained how, when the bodhisattvas have familiarized themselves with the paths of training for a long time, their mind streams become of the essence of the path, and how those aspects of the path that have already arisen are thus made stable, while those not yet arisen are brought to manifestation and increase.

As for the qualities of connection, these are presented in stanza 3. Collectively, the first three stanzas thus concern the wondrous nature of the qualities of the bodhisattvas. Subsequent to these three, stanza 4 explains how those qualities are not in fact amazing because it is no wonder that excellent causes give rise to excellent effects. As it thus praises the causal qualities as well, this stanza is concerned with the excellent qualities.

The qualities in terms of concern for sentient beings are taught in stanzas 5 to 7, which explain the mind of equality, and in stanzas 8 to 23, which explain the resulting benefits. Thus, in accordance with the flow of the scripture, the explanation that follows here will address the qualities of (1) the wondrous, (2) the not wondrous, (3) the mind of equality, (4) bringing benefit, (5) repaying kindness, (6) hoping, (7) not wasting, (8) authentic practice, (9) decline and progress, (10) the reflection and the genuine, (11) taming, (12) prophecy, (13) certainty, (14) the indubitable, (15) constant practice, (16) the foremost pursuits, and (17) teaching the Dharma.[52]

1. Qualities of Practice
1. The Wondrous Qualities

> Completely relinquishing one's own body
> And perfections for the sake of commitments,
> Tolerating the weak,
> Arousing diligence [xx.1]

> Without concern for body and life,
> Not dwelling in the bliss of concentration,
> And insight without thought—
> These are held to be the wonders of the wise. [xx.2]

> Birth into the family of the thus-gone ones,
> And the thorough attainments of
> Prophecy, empowerment, and enlightenment
> Are likewise considered great wonders. [xx.3]

On the wonders, it is stated: **Completely relinquishing one's own body** in the context of generosity **and** completely relinquishing the **perfections** of the kingdom and so forth **for the sake of** the **commitments** of discipline, **tolerating the weak** who inflict harm when practicing patience, **arousing diligence without concern for**

> **body and life, not dwelling in the perfect bliss of concentration, and insight without any thought of the three spheres—these are held to be the great wonders of the wise. Birth into the family of the thus-gone ones** on the first ground, **and the thorough attainments of prophecy** on the eighth ground, **empowerment** on the tenth, **and enlightenment** upon the ground of buddhahood—all these **are likewise considered great wonders.**

The wondrous qualities are those associated with the practice of the six transcendences. Why are they wondrous? Because such practices are not found among ordinary beings, listeners, and self-realized buddhas. In fact, such practices are impossible for anyone but a bodhisattva. Hence, they are a cause of amazement. Ordinary beings, listeners, and self-realized buddhas may be generous with food, clothing, and other such things, but only bodhisattvas will relinquish their own bodies in such extreme abundance. That practice is found among bodhisattvas and not found among others.

Likewise, in order to observe their vows of discipline, the bodhisattvas are completely ready to relinquish, give up, and renounce the perfect enjoyments of the likes of a universal emperor as if they were a mere gob of spit. Unlike mighty and powerful kings, they lovingly bear any amount of harassment from the side of the weak, beggars, outcastes, and so on. Without any concern for their own body or life, they arouse diligence. Even when they attain the supreme bliss of the four realms of concentration, they do not dwell on this with relish. On the contrary, they return to the realm of desire, and so take birth even in the three lower realms. Although they have attained the insight that discerns the characteristics of all phenomena, they do not conceive of any marks either of phenomena or of their insight into phenomena. Such are the wondrous qualities of the wise bodhisattvas.

As for the results of this distinguished practice of the transcendences, on the first ground, they achieve, for the first time, the nonconceptual wakefulness that is beyond the world. Thus they are born into the family of the thus-gone ones. When on the eighth ground, they achieve the effortless and spontaneously accomplished nonconceptual wakefulness, they attain the prophecy from all the buddhas, and on the tenth ground, they are empowered as regents of the buddhas. These three are known as results in the context of training. Upon the ground of buddhahood, they gain unsurpassable enlightenment. Since in this world not even the likes of listeners and self-realized buddhas attain such qualities, they are indeed considered great wonders.

2. How These Qualities Are Not Wondrous

> Free from attachment and with a loving heart,
> Having accomplished supreme meditation
> And with their mind of equality,
> It is no wonder that they practice like this. [xx.4]

Next it is shown why these are not a cause of wonder. They practice generosity **free from attachment, and with a loving heart** they accomplish discipline and patience. **Having accomplished supreme meditation** on the eighth ground (thereby enabling them to embrace diligence and the other two by way of nonformation and nonconceptuality), **and with their mind of equality** in terms of self and other, **it is no wonder that they practice** the transcendences **like this**, for they will be as untiring in accomplishing the welfare of others as they are in achieving their own.

Such qualities are truly wondrous when compared with those of worldly beings, listeners, and self-realized buddhas. However, if we consider the immensity of the concern and the conduct that the bodhisattvas master, then why shouldn't they accomplish something of this sort? It is no wonder that they do. That is what is explained in the present stanza.

Since they see pleasures such as those of the universal emperor to be just like a sewer, it is no wonder that the bodhisattvas have no desire for conditioned things and give away both outer and inner entities. Similarly, since they possess the great loving heart that wishes to free all beings from suffering, they observe the discipline of refraining from taking the lives of others. They are patient with others because they have trained their minds to hold others more dear than themselves. They arouse diligence because they engage effortlessly, as when fire meets fuel, in the practice of supreme meditation. Having attained the mind of equality with respect to self and others, they know no weariness while active to benefit others. They do not relish their concentrations, and with insight, they do not conceive of any marks. Since this is how the bodhisattvas work, it is no great wonder that they are born into the family of the thus-gone ones and that they gain all the qualities up to and including those of unsurpassable enlightenment. If that is how they are, then why should they not also achieve such results? Indeed, it is the nature of things that they will.

3. The Mind of Equality

The love of the wise
For sentient beings
Is unlike that which sentient beings
Have for themselves, their spouse, children, or friends. [xx.5]

No partiality toward those with wants,
Discipline that is never damaged,
Forbearance in all regards,
Great diligence for the sake of all, [xx.6]

Constantly virtuous concentration,
And nonconceptual insight—
Thus, the bodhisattva's mind of equality
Is to be understood in terms of these. [xx.7]

Next, the character of the mind of equality is explained. **The love of the wise** bodhisattvas for **sentient beings is unlike that** love **which sentient beings have for themselves, their spouse, children, or friends.** When they practice the transcendences, the bodhisattvas know, in terms of their generosity, **no partiality toward those with wants,** they possess a **discipline that never is damaged,** even in the slightest, and they show **forbearance in all**

regards concerning place, time, and sentient beings. With **great diligence** they practice **for** their own benefit and that of others, and for **the sake of all** virtues. They **constantly** abide by **virtuous concentration, free from affliction and nonconceptual insight** beyond the three spheres. **Thus the bodhisattva's mind of equality is to be understood in terms of these,** that is, the transcendences.

The wise bodhisattvas have tremendous love for sentient beings. Suffering, anguishing sentient beings, however, do not have love for themselves. Disturbed, they sometimes even take their own lives, eat poison, and so on. At times they also get angry with their spouses, children, and friends, and they may beat them and so on. Nor do they maintain their love throughout all lifetimes. The love of a bodhisattva is not like that.

The bodhisattvas have accomplished the mind of equality toward all sentient beings. They do not give only to their own family and the like, without also giving to others. They are not partial. Hence, when someone is out to get something, they respond generously without making any differences as to who is a friend and who is not, who is poor and who is not, and so on. They are always equally disciplined, free from any natural or accepted nonvirtue, whether severe or minor, and they are always equally patient regardless of the place, time, and the beings involved in the situation. For the sake of all sentient beings, they arouse unbroken great diligence, and they never fall from virtue, including that of the undefiling concentrations. With insight, they constantly discern all phenomena without mixing anything up, and yet they are also perfectly free from any focal points in terms of the three spheres. With such equality, the bodhisattvas engage, free from imbalance or partiality, in the practice of the six transcendences. This is the way to understand their mind of equality.

4. The Qualities in Terms of Bringing Benefit

This section will consider (1) the benefit by means of the six transcendences and (2) seven examples that illustrate the way they bring benefit.

1. Benefiting by Means of the Six Transcendences

Turning them into vessels,
Establishing them in discipline,
Tolerating harm,
Being active for their benefit, [xx.8]

Leading them into the teachings,
And cutting through their doubts—
These are held to be the way in which the wise
Bring benefit to sentient beings. [xx.9]

On the way that the bodhisattvas bring benefit, the following is explained. By being generous, bodhisattvas work on **turning them** (that is, sentient beings) **into vessels**. Once that has happened, they will engage in **establishing them in discipline** while **tolerating** any **harm** that is done to themselves, thus **being active for their** followers' **benefit**. By means of miracles and so forth, they will be **leading them into the teachings, and** they will be **cutting through** all **their doubts**. These are held to be the way in which the wise bring benefit to sentient beings.

The bodhisattvas' generosity turns sentient beings into vessels for virtuous practice. When, for example, beings are prevented from practicing the Dharma due to a lack of food, clothing, and so on, the bodhisattvas will provide them with what they wish for. Thus, satisfying them and making them happy, the bodhisattvas establish sentient beings in the Dharma. While they observe their own discipline, the bodhisattvas will also establish others in various forms of discipline. Regardless of how they are harmed by others, the bodhisattvas will be tolerant, practicing whatever is helpful to others without any difficulty. With their displays of miracles by the power of concentration, they lead those to be trained into the authentic teachings, and by the power of insight they cut through the doubts of all beings, teaching them the Dharma of the three vehicles. These are held to be the ways in which the wise bring benefit to sentient beings

2. Seven Examples of Benefit

Always do they uphold sentient beings
With their mind of equality.
They let them take birth on the grounds of the noble ones
And enhance their virtue, [xx.10]

Fully save them from misdeeds,
And bring them learning.
Thus, by these five activities the children of the victorious ones
Are like mothers to sentient beings. [xx.11]

In sentient beings
They always engender faith.
They train them in special discipline and so forth
And let them reach liberation, [xx.12]

They supplicate the buddhas
And eliminate their obscurations.
Thus, by these five activities the children of the victorious ones
Are like fathers to sentient beings. [xx.13]

That which cannot be taught
They keep secret from sentient beings.
Criticizing flawed training
While praising excellence, [xx.14]

They grant instructions
And drive away the demons.
Thus, by these five activities the children of the victorious ones
Are like relatives to sentient beings. [xx.15]

With their own minds free from delusion
Regarding thorough affliction and complete purification,
They grant all possible excellence,
Both in terms of the world and what lies beyond it. [xx.16]

Tireless and unshakable,
They constantly wish for benefit and happiness.
Thus, by these five activities the children of the victorious ones
Are like friends to sentient beings. [xx.17]

To ripen sentient beings,
They always abide by diligence,
Express genuine deliverance,
Tolerate ingratitude, [xx.18]

And provide the two excellences
With expertise about the means.
Thus, by these five activities the children of the victorious ones
Are like servants to sentient beings. [xx.19]

Wishing for the attainment
Of acceptance of nonarising phenomena,
They teach all vehicles and apply themselves
For the sake of the accomplishment of spiritual practice.
    [xx.20]

Their countenance is beautiful, and they have no concern
For benefit and ripening in return.
Thus, by these five activities the children of the victorious ones
Are like teachers to sentient beings. [xx.21]

Exerting themselves for the benefit of beings,
They bring the accumulations to completion,
And those who have gathered the accumulations they quickly
    release,
Letting them eliminate the conflicting factors. [xx.22]

They provide excellence that is
Of the world and beyond it.
Thus, by these five activities the children of the victorious ones
Are like preceptors to sentient beings. [xx.23]

Now it will be shown how their beneficial activity is comparable to that of a mother, as well as other examples. **Always do they,** the children of the victorious ones, **uphold sentient beings with their mind of equality,** as if they were carrying them within their womb. **They let them take birth on the grounds of the noble ones,** which is similar to a mother giving birth to her child, **and enhance their virtue,** which is comparable to a mother breastfeeding, nourishing, and rearing her child. As they **fully save them** (that is, sentient beings) **from misdeeds,** it is as if they were protecting their child from a precipice, **and** insofar as they **bring them learning,** as when a mother teaches her child to speak, they **thus** benefit sentient beings. Hence, **by** virtue of **these five activities, the children of the victorious ones are like mothers to** all **sentient beings.**

In sentient beings they always, as if they were supplying their semen, **engender faith,** the seed of the noble one's body. As if they were teaching them crafts, **they** provide the circumstances for them to **train themselves in special discipline and so forth, and,** like a father who finds a suitable wife for his son, they **let them reach** the bliss of **liberation. They supplicate the buddhas** on their behalf, as when a father arranges instruction for his child from a true master, **and** causes them to **eliminate their obscurations,** just like a father who cancels his child's debts. **Thus, by** virtue of **these five activities, the children of the victorious ones are like fathers to** all **sentient beings.**

That definitive meaning, which cannot be taught to immature sentient beings, **they keep secret from** such **sentient beings** in the same way as relatives keep secret that which needs to be kept secret. **Criticizing flawed training,** just as one relative will criticize the bad behavior of another, **while praising excellence** in the training in the same way as relatives praise each other's good conduct, **they grant instructions** for the sake of realization, as when a relative provides help and guidance in various practical situations, **and they drive away** the activities of **the demons** in the way that relatives will offer protection from dangerous situations. **Thus, by virtue of these five activities, the children of the victorious ones are like relatives to sentient beings.**

With their own minds free from delusion regarding thorough affliction and complete purification, just like a friend who knows clearly the way to achieve benefit and happiness, **they grant all possible excellence, both in terms of the world,** like a friend who brings happiness, **and what lies beyond it,** like a friend who brings benefit. They are **tireless** in the face of difficult tasks, like a friend who never becomes upset, **and** hence **unshakable.** Like a truly benevolent friend, **they constantly wish for benefit and happiness. Thus, by** virtue of **these five activities, the children of the victorious ones are like friends to** all **sentient beings.**

To ripen sentient beings they always abide by diligence, like an industrious servant, **and,** like a trustworthy servant, they **express** words of **genuine deliverance.** In the same way that a servant tolerates scolding and beating, they **tolerate ingratitude, and,** like a servant who successfully accomplishes all tasks, they **provide the two excellences** (mundane and supramundane) **with expertise about the means** for accomplishing them, just as a servant possesses expertise and skill. **Thus, by** virtue of **these five activities, the children of the victorious ones are like servants to** all **sentient beings.**

Wishing for the attainment of acceptance of nonarising phenomena, just like a well-educated teacher, **they teach all** the three **vehicles,** just as a teacher explains what he himself knows, **and they apply themselves for the sake of the accomplishment of** the **spiritual practice** of calm abiding and special insight, in the same way as the teacher makes his students learn fast. **Their countenance is beautiful** and gentle in the same way as the teacher's, **and they have no concern for** material **benefit and** karmic **ripening in return. Thus, by** virtue of **these five activities, the children of the victorious ones are like teachers to** all **sentient beings.**

Exerting themselves for the benefit of beings, like a preceptor who provides the initial ordination for deliverance, **they bring the accumulations to completion,** as when the full ordination is bestowed; **and those who have gathered the accumulations they quickly** bring to **release, letting them eliminate the conflicting factors,** as when the preceptor explains the way to remain free from faults. They provide material **excellence that is of the world and Dharma excellence that is beyond it. Thus, by** virtue of **these five activities, the children of the victorious ones are like preceptors to** all **sentient beings.**

Here we shall follow the flow of the verses, clarifying the seven examples along the way. Bodhisattvas are always in possession of a mind of equality that is equally loving and compassionate with respect to all beings. Never letting anyone down, they always uphold and support sentient beings for as long as there is cyclic existence, just like a mother who carries her child within her womb. As for the term "grounds of the noble ones," it refers to all stages, from the path of seeing to the path of no more learning, within both the Great and the Lesser Vehicles. Since they lead beings to take birth on these noble grounds, bodhisattvas are like a mother as she gives birth to her child. Since they enrich the mundane and supramundane virtues of sentient beings, they are also similar to a mother as she nourishes her child by feeding it milk and food, bathing it, massaging it, and so on. Bodhisattvas protect all beings from the suffering of the lower realms and so on, as well as from the karmic accumulations of misdeeds that cause such suffering. In that way they resemble a mother as she protects her child from falling into an abyss, a precipice, and so on. Since they teach beings the Dharma and bring them learning, they also resemble a mother when she teaches her child names, phrases, gestures, and conventions. Hence, by virtue of these five activities, the children of the victorious ones are like mothers to all sentient beings.

Similarly, always acting so that faith in the three supreme ones may arise in sentient beings, the bodhisattvas supply the cause for the attainment of the body of the three vehicles. In this way they resemble a father who supplies his semen to allow a child to be born. As they train sentient beings in special discipline and the rest of the three special trainings, they resemble a father who instructs his child in the crafts and conduct that accord with their family. In letting sentient beings reach complete liberation from the suffering of cyclic existence, they are like a father who finds a spouse that suits his child, thereby letting the child reach happiness. For the sake of sentient beings, the bodhisattvas supplicate the buddhas not to pass beyond suffering but to turn the wheel of Dharma and so forth. In this way, they resemble a father who, for the sake of his child's health and success, makes arrangements with rulers, friends, and so on. As they work to bring about the elimination of the afflictive and cognitive obscurations in the mind streams of sentient beings, they are like a father who takes over and cancels the unpaid debts and so on that are burdening his child. Thus, by virtue of these five activities, the children of the victorious ones are like fathers to all sentient beings.

Small-minded beings should not be taught the profound, vast, and inconceivable matters that are conveyed in the Great Vehicle because if this happens, they will eventually give up the Dharma out of fear. For this reason, the bodhisattvas keep such teachings secret and do not give them to such beings. This resembles the way that certain matters are not communicated that may put the health and success of others within the family at risk. Instead, they are kept secret from relatives. The way that the bodhisattvas criticize others and point out their errors when they notice that someone is not maintaining the triple training is similar to the way in which one relative will criticize and try to stop another when noticing that the other is doing something that is not sensible. On the other hand, when they see sentient beings endowed with the excellent qualities of the three trainings, the bodhisattvas will praise them and respectfully support them to ensure that they do not lose those qualities. This resembles the way relatives appreciate and praise each other's well-done works. So that sentient beings can realize the noble path, the bodhisattvas offer them key points of practical instructions that serve as the means for gaining such realization. This is like the way one family member instructs and helps the others by explaining to them how things are done at both outer and inner levels. The way that the bodhisattvas clearly point out for sentient beings the obstacles that hinder them on the path, such as deceptive sense pleasures and negative company, resembles the way relatives protect each other from enemies, imprisonment, thieves, floods, fires, and other such harms. Thus, by virtue of these five activities, the children of the victorious ones are like family to all sentient beings.

The bodhisattvas remain aware of what is and is not meaningful when it comes to benefiting sentient beings and making them happy. With their own minds free from delusion, they have unmistaken knowledge of both the factors of thorough affliction as subsumed within the truths of suffering and its origin as well as the factors of complete purification that belong to the truths of cessation and the path. This knowledge they convey to sentient beings in the form of instruction. This, in turn, resembles the way friends, based on their own understanding, will tell each other what will be helpful for the other person to do, and what he or she should refrain from doing. Thus, the bodhisattvas exhaustively and completely grant to sentient beings all manner of mundane happiness, such as that of Brahma, Indra, and the universal emperor, as well as all supramundane happiness up to and including that of buddhahood. This is similar to the way friends will provide each other with whatever may be of benefit to their health and success in either the immediate or the long term. For the benefit of sentient beings, bodhisattvas constantly remain free from weariness in the same way that friends do not tire in taking care of each other. Bodhisattvas will never be shaken or harmed by demons, difficult trials, and so on, when they are involved in benefiting sentient beings. This can be likened to the way a loyal friend cannot be swayed by divisive talk and so forth and has unshakable affection. Bodhisattvas never waver in their constant wish for sentient beings to gain the benefits of transcendent qualities as well as the happiness of mundane qualities. This resembles the way dear friends always wish for the other's benefit in the long term and their happiness on the immediate level. Thus, by virtue of these five activities, the children of the victorious ones are like friends to all sentient beings.

The bodhisattvas constantly apply themselves with diligence, without hesitation, to bring sentient beings to maturation. In this way, they are like a faithful servant who, with delight and free from laziness, always pursues the tasks that are given by the employer. To sentient beings, the bodhisattvas always explain the authentic path of deliverance beyond all suffering, and so they resemble a fine servant who never lies and always conveys what he or she has seen and heard to the employer. Sentient beings bring numerous harms on bodhisattvas and act in inappropriate ways, repaying their benefit with harm. Since bodhisattvas patiently bear all this, they are like a servant who tolerates the employer's beatings and harsh words, and on top of that adheres to the employer's words. Bodhisattvas grant all mundane and supramundane excellences to sentient beings, and so they are like a servant who always fulfills the employer's wishes to the letter. The bodhisattvas are skilled in gathering the accumulations of merit and wakefulness so as to enable sentient beings to attain all mundane and supramundane perfections. In this way, they are like a servant who is skilled in quickly carrying out the wishes of the employer. Thus, by virtue of these five activities, the children of the victorious ones are like servants to all sentient beings.

When on the eighth ground the bodhisattvas have attained the acceptance of nonarising phenomena, they naturally wish for all sentient beings to attain the same, thus resembling a learned and extremely knowledgeable teacher as he or she accepts students. In the way that they teach all three vehicles in accordance with the mind streams of those to be trained, they resemble an expert teacher who teaches whatever topic inspires the students. As they pursue the spiritual practices of calm abiding and special insight, they resemble a fine teacher who brings learning to the students quickly and without delay. Never angry or involved in unvirtuous conduct, the bodhisattvas appear with a smile and a beautiful countenance. In this way, they are like a kind teacher who always gives instruction with a smile and gentle words. Although they benefit beings, the bodhisattvas do not expect beings to benefit them in return, and they are not concerned to receive any karmic ripening from having done so. In this way, they resemble a teacher who lovingly instructs his or her students in the Dharma, but without any concern for material things. Thus, by virtue of these five activities, the children of the victorious ones are like teachers to all sentient beings.

Exerting themselves tremendously for the sake of all sentient beings, the bodhisattvas bring to completion the two accumulations of those sentient being who have not yet completed them. In this way, they resemble a preceptor who lets his disciples fully emerge, leaving the household behind to become homeless, and who grants them the training in spiritual practice. In the way that they bring swift release at the level of the fruition to those who have gathered the accumulations, they resemble a preceptor who lets his disciples complete the approach to become fully ordained monks. The bodhisattvas cause sentient beings to eliminate the factors that conflict with the path of the six transcendences, the attainment of liberation, and the transcendence of suffering. As they tame beings in this way, they are like a preceptor who teaches his disciples the violations, remnants, transgressions, and so forth, and lets them eliminate any flaws. As they provide sentient beings with both mundane and supramundane excellences, they resemble a preceptor who benefits disciples with material things as well as the Dharma. Thus, by virtue of these five activities, the children of the victorious ones are like preceptors to all sentient beings since they benefit them all.

5. Repaying the Kindness

> No attachment to possessions,
> Flawless discipline,
> Grateful recognition,
> And application of the practice—[xx.24]
>
> These are the ways
> In which embodied beings
> Established in the six transcendences
> Repay the kindness of the bodhisattvas. [xx.25]

On the way that kindness is repaid, the following is explained. Pursuing the practice of generosity with **no attachment to possessions**, observing **flawless discipline**, practicing patience with **grateful recognition** of one's bodhisattva benefactors, **and application of the practice**, so that with joyous diligence the calm abiding and special insight of concentration and insight are accomplished: **these are the ways in which embodied beings**, whom the bodhisattvas have **established in the six transcendences**, themselves **repay the kindness of the bodhisattvas.**

The bodhisattvas benefit sentient beings by establishing them in the transcendences. When sentient beings then practice the transcendences flawlessly, this repays the bodhisattvas' kindness. Bodhisattvas give their possessions to sentient beings and make them prosperous. As for repaying their kindness, if the sentient beings who receive a bodhisattva's gifts do not become attached and instead are generous with their wealth and enjoyments, then the bodhisattva will notice this. As he or she sees that the recipients of his or her generosity are now actively benefiting sentient beings, the kindness of the bodhisattva is being repaid. Similarly when the bodhisattvas have established beings in discipline, their kindness in doing so is repaid when sentient beings observe flawless discipline. When bodhisattvas are hurt in different ways, they do not think of this as harm. Instead, they know this to be the cause of patience, and so they look upon the harm-doers as benefactors. Recognizing this, they abide in patience, thereby also establishing others in patience. When those sentient beings who have thus themselves developed patience are able to bear the harm of others, the bodhisattvas' kindness is being repaid. Likewise, as the commentary explains, when bodhisattvas establish beings in the practices of diligence, concentration, and insight, the kindness of the bodhisattvas is thereby repaid. The beings who have thus been helped by the bodhisattvas are themselves active in these same ways.

What this all amounts to is that when embodied beings engage in the six transcendences, they are doing good to the bodhisattvas in return for the good that they themselves have received from the bodhisattvas. Such practice of the transcendences fully satisfies the hearts of the bodhisattvas. Other means of repayment, such as material things, are not what the bodhisattvas want. Wishing to repay the kindness of the bodhisattvas, sentient beings should therefore themselves practice the transcendences. The bodhisattvas will notice this and feel that "these beings have benefited me." They will acknowledge all that is done to this end. This, also, is among the special qualities of the bodhisattvas, the fact that they do not hope for material things.

6. The Qualities of Hope

> They always wish for increase and decrease,
> Full maturation of sentient beings,
> Gaining distinction upon the grounds,
> And unsurpassable enlightenment. [xx.26]

The next verse shows their prayerful intent. **They,** the bodhisattvas, **always wish for** the following five factors: the **increase** of the transcendences **and decrease** of the factors that conflict with them, the **full maturation of sentient beings, gaining distinction upon the grounds, and unsurpassable enlightenment.**

The bodhisattvas have five hopes. They hope and wish: (1) "How may the six transcendences best increase in my stream of being and in those of all others?" and (2) "How may the factors that conflict with the six transcendences best be made to decrease and diminish in my stream of being and in the streams of being of all others?" Hoping and wishing, they likewise declare: (3) "Those sentient beings who have no faith I shall bring to faith; those who have faith I shall establish in virtue; those engaged in virtue I shall bring to full maturation." The bodhisattvas also hope and wish for (4) a continuous process of gaining distinction upon the ten grounds, ascending from the first ground to the second, and so forth, up to the tenth ground. Further, they wish for (5) going beyond the ten grounds and attaining unsurpassable enlightenment. Other than these five, the bodhisattvas do not have the slightest hope for mundane excellence or the path and result of listeners and self-realized buddhas. Such are the qualities of their wishes and hopes.

7. Not Letting Go to Waste

> By means of abandonment of fear and true generation,
> Cutting through doubts
> And instructions for practice,
> The children of the victorious ones let nothing be wasted.
> [xx.27]

Teaching on the way that their practice is not wasted, it is said: **By means of** (1) the **abandonment of fear** of the profound and vast Dharma **and** (2) the **true generation** of the enlightened mind; with respect to (3) **cutting through doubts** regarding the ways to bring forth the enlightened mind, **and** in terms of (4) teaching the **instructions for** the **practice** of the transcendences—by these means **the children of the victorious ones let nothing be wasted**, practicing, as they do, for the benefit of others.

Next, it is explained how their practice is not wasted. Listeners and self-realized buddhas pursue only their own benefit, and since they do not benefit others, their practice is wasted. Mundane beings act based on various hopes that are largely fruitless, and so their efforts are wasted as well. However, since the bodhisattvas have unmistaken and excellent hopes, whatever they do becomes successful and nothing is done in vain.

Four practices are in this way never wasted. (1) In an atmosphere of fear of the profound and vast Dharma of the Great Vehicle, the bodhisattva's practice of the Great Vehicle would be wasted. Yet since the bodhisattvas have themselves given up fear and since they dispel fear in others, their practice of the Great Vehicle is not in vain. (2) If the bodhisattvas were to give rise to the enlightened mind with a wish to attain mundane excellence or the path and result of the listeners and self-realized buddhas, their practice of the Great Vehicle would be wasted. Yet that is not how bodhisattvas develop the enlightened mind. Since they authentically develop both their own minds and the minds of all sentient beings toward unsurpassable enlightenment, their true generation of the enlightened mind does not deteriorate and is, hence, not wasted.

(3) If, once one has given rise to the enlightened mind, one has insufficient knowledge, for example, about the means for accomplishing enlightenment, the ensuing doubts might make one fall back from the practice of developing the enlightened mind, in which case the practice would be wasted. Yet, since the bodhisattvas cut through doubts about the path and fruition of the Great Vehicle, their practice is not wasted. (4) Their practices would be wasted if the bodhisattvas did not themselves apply and teach the instructions on the spiritual practices of the buddhas, the bodhisattvas, the grounds, the transcendences, and calm abiding and special insight. Yet, since the bodhisattvas apply the practical instructions flawlessly to their own experience, and since they also teach them to others, they are not wasted. Hence, these four constitute the bodhisattva qualities of not letting practice be wasted.

8. The Qualities of Authentic Practice

Generosity without expectation,
Discipline free from wishes for future lives,
Patience that tolerates all,
Diligence from which good qualities emerge, [xx.28]

Concentration that is not formless,
And insight endowed with means—
These six transcendences
Are the authentic practice of the steadfast ones. [xx.29]

On the authentic practice, the following is taught. **Generosity without expectation** of a reward or karmic ripening, **discipline free from wishes for** the pleasures of the higher realms in **future lives, patience that tolerates all** harm-doers and suffering, **diligence from which good qualities** both of the world and beyond the world **emerge, concentration that is not a formless** meditative absorption, **and insight endowed with** the **means** of compassion—**these six transcendences are the authentic practice of the steadfast ones.**

The bodhisattva who in this way does not allow practice to be wasted applies himself or herself flawlessly, correctly, and authentically to all activities of body, speech, and mind. Although they fulfill the wishes of the needy and destitute by means of their completely unreserved triple generosity, bodhisattvas do not harbor any expectations or hopes about being benefited in return in this life. Nor do they hope thereby to become wealthy in future lives. Such is their authentic practice of generosity. Likewise, without any wish for a rebirth within the higher realms of cyclic existence, they observe discipline for the sake of attaining unsurpassable enlightenment. Not only do they refrain from physically or verbally retaliating against those who harm them, but in their minds there is no anger at all, and so they are universally patient in body, speech, and mind. The bodhisattvas tolerate everything, no matter which sentient being it is, high or low, who harms them, and regardless of the degree of harm that is caused. In terms of their diligence, they do not apply themselves just to certain transcendences and certain vehicles. Rather, with the diligence of the Great Vehicle, they apply themselves toward the perfection of the qualities of the paths and fruitions of all of the vehicles. Thus they arouse the diligence from which all excellent qualities emerge. Likewise, although they have attained the meditative absorptions of the four concentrations and the four formless realms, the bodhisattvas do not take birth in the realms without form because from such realms the buddha qualities cannot be perfected and sentient beings cannot be brought to maturation. Instead they take birth in the form and desire realms. In particular, having been born into the realm of desire, they accomplish vast perfection and maturation. For a bodhisattva, lack of means and lack of knowledge both amount equally to bondage. Therefore, combining the insight that knows phenomena to be emptiness and the compassion that employs the four means of attraction, they bring sentient beings to complete maturation. This is insight endowed with skillful means, and it is in this way that the steadfast bodhisattvas correctly and authentically practice the transcendences. Thus the *Noble Jewel Mound* teaches:

> Generosity that does not hope for ripening, discipline that is not confined to any form of birth within cyclic existence, patience that does not harbor anger toward any sentient being, diligence that genuinely gathers all fundamental virtues, concentration that is free from the veils of the formless realms, and insight that is fully mature due to the possession of the skillful mastery of the four means of attraction.

9. Downfall and Progress

> Attachment to enjoyments, faults,
> Pride, indulgence,
> Relishing the taste, and thoughts—
> These cause the decline of the steadfast. [xx.30]
>
> The opposite is the case
> With bodhisattvas abiding by their remedies.

> Hence, those are to be known
> As the factors that bring progress. [xx.31]

On the factors that cause decline and progress, it is said: **Attachment to enjoyments, faults** in terms of discipline, **pride, attachment to indulgence, relishing the taste, and thoughts of the three spheres—these cause the decline of the steadfast. The opposite is the case with bodhisattvas abiding by their six remedies. Hence, those** remedies of the bodhisattvas **are to be known as the factors that bring progress.**

The distinction between the factors that bring decline and those that bring progress relates to the factors that, by association, cause one's practice of the six transcendences to deteriorate versus those factors that by association cause one's practice to develop and flourish. Bodhisattvas who adhere to authentic practice experience a decline and decrease in the factors that conflict with the six transcendences. Meanwhile, the qualities of the remedies increase like the waxing moon. To distinguish the factors of decline from those of increase, it is taught that if one's attachment to enjoyments renders one unable to be generous, this will cause transcendent generosity to decline. Likewise, if one's commitment to the subtle points of the training is impaired or deteriorates, this will lead to a decline in terms of transcendent discipline. It causes patience to decline when, out of pride, one refrains from venerating preceptors and individuals with excellent qualities, or when from one's own side one feels opposed to showing acts of respect. Remaining attached to the extreme of indulgence signifies a decline in diligence. Relishing the taste of concentration brings a decline in transcendent concentration. Observing marks due to the thoughts that are attached to substantial entities causes a decline in the insight that is free from the observation of marks. Thus, these six cause the transcendences of the steadfast bodhisattvas to decline.

Next, the causes of progress are the remedies for the former factors: not being attached to enjoyments, having an unimpaired discipline, not being proud, not being attached to indulgences, not relishing the taste of concentration, and not conceiving of marks of entities. Bodhisattvas who abide by these factors turn away from the factors of decline. The former are therefore to be known as the auspicious factors that bring progress and the enrichment of the six transcendences.

10. The Reflection and the Genuine

> Pretense, hypocrisy,
> Showing a nice face,
> Sporadic engagement,
> Subdued body and mind, [xx.32]
>
> And perfect expertise in teaching—
> Divorced from practice,
> These are explained to be
> The bodhisattvas' falsity.
> The opposite, thorough engagement,
> Is taught to be their authenticity. [xx.33]

On the distinction between artifice and genuine practice, it is taught as follows. A hollow **pretense** while not being able to give genuinely; **hypocrisy** for the sake of making a good impression; **showing a nice face** while actually being upset; **sporadic engagement** in virtue without being able to maintain it; giving a false impression of **subdued body and mind; and** even **perfect expertise in teaching**, based on linguistics and reasoning—**divorced from** the **practice** of the transcendences, **these are explained to be the bodhisattvas' falsity,** for they are not the actual qualities of pure bodhisattvas. **The opposite, thorough engagement** with the six transcendences, **is taught to be their authenticity.**

The distinction between the reflection and the true describes the ways one can lose the actual six transcendences and instead arrive at a mere reflection of them. A mere reflection of generosity is a pretense and a show. For example, this is the case if one claims to be practicing generosity with respect to both inner and outer things, and yet does not give anything, or if while engaged in giving one in fact secretly takes.

Likewise, this occurs if one hypocritically maintains an appearance of observing spiritual discipline while in fact continuously engaging in things that run counter to one's commitments; if while angry and intolerant of others one shows a beautifully patient face and speaks gentle words; if while not having any sense of continuous diligence one sporadically makes a great show of diligence in public gatherings and the like; if one stays in places of seclusion, giving up speaking and appearing to be subdued, while in fact one's mind does not rest peacefully and is consumed by distractions; if without having any sound insight into the meaning of the Dharma of the three vehicles one gives credit to words and relies on a knowledge of grammar, reasoning, and so on, to come up with all sorts of claims and positions, acting like an excellent scholar to an audience of fools—all these are instances of being divorced from the proper practice of the six transcendences. They are, therefore, taught as being false versions—mere reflections—of the bodhisattvas' practice of the six transcendences.

As for the genuine transcendences, these are the opposite of the six reflections. They consist of the sincere, uncontrived, and thorough practice of everything from genuine generosity to the unmistaken insight into the characteristics of phenomena. Therefore, when the bodhisattvas practice the transcendences, they do not pretend or act as if they are. Without hypocrisy or negligence, they practice the genuine transcendences, and so the quality of their practice is like that of pure gold. This account that distinguishes between faults and genuine qualities thus serves to point out the qualities of the pure remedies in the absence of the aforementioned flaws.

11. The Qualities of Taming

> On all the grounds, the wise
> Accomplish the practices of generosity and so forth.
> Thereby they tame the six
> Conflicting factors in sentient beings. [xx.34]

The manner in which the bodhisattvas tame beings is ascertained in the following way: **On all the grounds, the wise accomplish** the practices of generosity and so forth. Thereby they tame the six **conflicting factors** that respectively prevent the six transcendences **in sentient beings.**

Bodhisattvas who abide by the qualities of the genuine practice of the transcendences are capable of taming the factors that conflict with the six transcendences within the streams of being of others. Who are the individuals that are capable of doing this? They are the wise bodhisattvas. In which context do they bring about such taming? Throughout all the ten grounds. What are their means for taming? The qualities that are associated with the practice of generosity and the rest of the six transcendences. Who are the beneficiaries? Sentient beings. What is being tamed? Miserliness and other such factors that conflict with the six transcendences, as well as factors of decline and pretense.

12. The Prophecies

In terms of the person and time, the prophecies
Regarding the wise are twofold.
There is prophecy of enlightenment, of prophecy,
And another, referred to as "great," [xx.35]

Which is due to having gained acceptance of nonarising,
Having relinquished pride and efforts,
And having become of the same nature
As all the buddhas and bodhisattvas. [xx.36]

Likewise, it is held to encompass the field, name,
Time, and name of the aeon,
The retinue, and the remaining
Of the sacred Dharma. [xx.37]

The investigation of prophecy is as follows: **In terms of the person** (who may be someone possessing the potential, who has given rise to the enlightened mind, who is directly present, or who is not directly present) **and time** (which may be specified as a particular duration or referred to indefinitely in terms of the future in general), **the prophecies regarding the wise are twofold. There is the prophecy of enlightenment,** just as there is the prophecy **of** another buddha's **prophecy, and** there is, moreover, also **another** form of prophecy, **referred to as "great," which is due to having gained acceptance of the nonarising** phenomena on the eighth ground. Such prophecy thus follows from **having relinquished the pride** of thinking "I shall become enlightened" **and the efforts** applied in that pursuit, **and** it is due to **having become of the essence of all the buddhas and bodhisattvas** because of the elimination of the defiled mental cognition and the grasping of a self that is due to the defiled mental cognition. **Likewise, it,** meaning prophecy, **is held to encompass the** character of the **field** of enlightenment and the name of the future buddha, the duration of **time** before the enlightenment **and name of the aeon** in which it occurs, **the** extent of **the retinue, and the remaining of the sacred Dharma.**

Regarding the individuals who receive prophecies based on their being endowed with extremely pure qualities of the transcendences, we may distinguish between prophecies as received by particular persons and prophecies that concern a certain time. Thus the wise bodhisattvas' prophecies regarding their attainment of unsurpassable enlightenment are twofold.

Four types of people receive prophecy: (1) those with the potential, (2) those who have set the mind on enlightenment, (3) those who are directly present, and (4) those who are not immediately present. In the first case, the individuals who are prophesied to awaken to unsurpassable enlightenment have not yet set their minds on enlightenment, yet they nevertheless have the potential for, and the seeds of, the six transcendences. In the second case, the prophecy is given to someone who has barely given rise to the enlightened mind. In the third, a buddha addresses a person present in the retinue and declares that at a given time in the future that person will become a buddha known by such and such name. In the fourth case, a buddha speaks of a person who is not present in the manifest retinue, thus making the audience aware of the existence of a bodhisattva by a certain name who is present in a different buddha field. Explaining that, in the future, this person will be known by the name of such and such, the buddha explains how at that time this individual will attain unsurpassable enlightenment. Examples of this fourth category are the prophecies concerning Nāgārjuna and Asaṅga. In terms of time, there are two types of prophecies because either a definite number of eons or lifetimes prior to the given person's attainment of unsurpassable enlightenment may be specified, or there may be a general reference to the person's enlightenment in the future.

Another pair of categories with respect to prophecies relates to whether a buddha, in person, prophesies the individual's attainment of great enlightenment, or whether the buddha instructs him or her that he or she will receive the prophecy of a buddha known by such and such a name in the future. Moreover, that which is known as "the great prophecy" is what bodhisattvas of the eighth ground receive following their attainment of the acceptance of nonarising phenomena. Its greatness lies in the fact that it is received based on the relinquishment of arrogant pride, the relinquishment of the marks of effort, and without taking one's own stream of being to be distinct from all the buddhas and the bodhisattvas on the pure grounds. Thus, the prophecy is attained by having become of the nature or essence of all the buddhas and great bodhisattvas. The bodhisattvas who achieve the eighth ground realize that "without a doubt I will attain enlightenment," and—along with their own prophecy of their enlightenment—they also receive it from all the buddhas. Therefore, this is known as "the great prophecy" or "the prophecy of greatness."

In terms of the categories of prophecy, there are also prophecies of the name of a given bodhisattva's buddha field, the name that he or she will be known by as a buddha, the time of his or her enlightenment, the name of the eon during which his or her enlightenment will occur, the extent of his or her retinue upon becoming a buddha, and the character and duration of the Dharma that he or she will teach as a buddha.

13. CERTAINTY

For the wise,
Excellence, life, absence of weariness,
Constant practice,
No decline in meditative absorption,
And spontaneously accomplished acceptance
Are all definitively attained. [xx.38]

On the definitive attainment, it is taught: **For the wise, excellence** in terms of enjoyments is assured by generosity, and because of discipline, they may take up a given **life** in accordance with their wishes. Likewise, **absence of weariness** is assured by patience, **constant** virtuous **practice** will be the effect of diligence, concentration will ensure that there is **no decline in** their **meditative absorption, and** with insight comes the **spontaneously accomplished acceptance** of nonarising phenomena. These **are all definitively attained.**

Next, the qualities of doubtless certainty are explained. Bodhisattvas aspire to attain unsurpassable enlightenment, and they are not interested in temporary enjoyments and so forth. Nevertheless, it is a matter of fact that until their final attainment of great enlightenment, they will, throughout all their lives, continue to gain the results of the six transcendences. Thus, because of their authentic practice of the six transcendences, the wise bodhisattvas will, wherever and whenever they are born, always obtain excellent enjoyments as the result of their generosity, such as those of Brahma, Indra, and the universal emperor. As the fruition of their discipline, they are certain to attain life as a god, human or otherwise—in complete accordance with their wishes. As a result of their patience, they will definitely not become weary due to suffering while benefiting others. Due to their diligence, they are always certain to practice and familiarize themselves with virtuous qualities. As the fruition of their concentration, there will definitely never be any decline in their attainment of meditative absorption. Having attained the powers of superknowledge by the strength of their concentration, they will also be certain to act for the benefit of others by means of miraculous powers and so on. As for their insight, it is certain that it will result in the attainment of the acceptance associated with the spontaneous accomplishment of nonconceptual wakefulness. Thus, since they have indisputably attained the proximate nonconceptual wakefulness while on the lower paths, the actual attainment will certainly, beyond doubt, occur upon the eighth ground.

14. The Unquestionable Imperatives

> Offerings, genuinely assuming the training,
> Compassion, virtuous practice,
> Heedfully dwelling in solitude,
> And never having enough of the meaning of what one learns—
> On all the grounds these are without a doubt
> To be engaged in by the steadfast ones. [xx.39]

> On the definitive activities, it is said: **Offerings** to the Jewels and so forth, **genuinely assuming the training**, remaining undisturbed by means of **compassion**, delighting in **virtuous practice**, **heedfully dwelling in solitude, and never having enough of the meaning of what one learns—on all the grounds these** six **are without a doubt to be engaged in by the steadfast ones**, the bodhisattvas.

Next follow the divisions of the unquestionable imperatives. It is taught that these concern the factors that are indispensable for the attainment of unsurpassable enlightenment. These factors are unquestionable in the sense that one cannot afford to be disengaged from them. They are as follows: As a particular form of generosity, bringing actual or imagined offerings to the thus-gone ones is an unquestionable imperative. Ensuring that there is no decline in the discipline that one has genuinely assumed is likewise indispensable and an unquestionable pursuit. The same is the case with the cultivation of patience that is based on the compassionate wish to dispel the suffering of sentient beings; diligence in cultivating mundane and supramundane virtues; heedful and unpreoccupied, dwelling in solitude for the sake of the attainment of concentration;

insatiability, in the pursuit of excellent insight, with respect to the meaning of the sūtras and the other aspects of the scriptural teachings that one receives from one's spiritual teacher. In all contexts of the grounds, these practices are unquestionably necessary for the steadfast bodhisattvas.

15. The Constant Practice

> Knowing the flaws of attachment,
> Keeping check on delusions,
> Joyfully accepting suffering,
> Practicing virtue, [xx.40]
>
> Avoiding the relish of bliss
> And not conceiving of marks—
> On all the grounds these are constantly
> To be engaged in by the steadfast ones. [xx.41]

On the constant practice, it is taught: **Knowing the flaws of attachment** and hence being unattached, **keeping check on** the **delusions** of one's stream of being, **joyfully accepting** all **suffering**, constantly **practicing virtue, avoiding the relish of** the **bliss** of meditative absorption, **and not conceiving of marks** of the three spheres—**on all the grounds these** six **are constantly to be engaged in by the steadfast ones.**

Six practices must be carried out constantly, not just periodically, in order to perfect the six transcendences. (1) To perfect transcendent generosity, one must always be aware of the flaws of attachment to the pleasures of the five senses. The pleasures of existence are impermanent, like a cloud or a flash of lightning. If one becomes attached to them, they turn into a source of suffering, like a poisonous meal, a pit of fire, the edge of a razor, or a nest of vipers. Thus one must always keep in mind that they are unreliable, like an illusion or a dream. (2) In terms of discipline, one must keep a check on one's delusion and be cautious about it since it expresses itself in negative conduct of body, speech, and mind. (3) Karmic actions and afflictions leave sentient beings no freedom of choice whatsoever, and so they are tossed about by the waves of the three types of suffering. Bringing this to mind again and again, one must don the armor of great compassion and so train in joyfully accepting suffering for beings' sake. (4) Since the lazy do not accomplish even any worldly matters, there is no need to mention that they do not get anywhere in terms of that which transcends the world. On the other hand, since even the level of the buddhas will be accomplished by those who arouse diligence, there is no need to mention all the other things they can achieve. Understanding diligence to be an indispensable root of all virtuous qualities, one must continuously cultivate and practice all mundane and supramundane virtues. (5) If the mind is distracted, one will not be able to accomplish the qualities of virtue; thus, concentration is indispensable. Nevertheless, if one relishes the bliss of concentration and becomes attached to it, that too will become a cause of bondage. Therefore, although one practices concentration, one must always avoid any fascination with its taste; this will ensure that one's concentration does not decline. (6) Foremost among all the transcendences is the insight that is aware of all phenomena, both as they truly are and in their multiplicity. Hence, such insight is indispensable. Nevertheless, from form to omniscient enlightenment, there is not a single phenomenon that bears any marks of its own fundamental character or essence. Conceiving of entities and marks with respect to these phenomena, therefore, means failing to realize the fact of their intrinsic nature. As this produces stains that obscure the nature of all that is to be known, one must abide by nonconceptuality, not conceiving of any marks of something apprehended or an apprehender. This will bring transcendent insight to perfection. On all the grounds, these six practices are to be engaged in constantly by the steadfast bodhisattvas.

16. The Foremost Pursuits

> Granting the Dharma, the discipline of purity,
> Attaining acceptance of nonarising,
> Arousing diligence in the Great Vehicle,
> Abiding by compassion in the final one,
> And insight—these are held to be the wise ones'
> Foremost pursuits in terms of the transcendences. [xx.42]

> On the foremost pursuits, it is taught: **Granting the Dharma** in terms of generosity; **the discipline of purity** with respect to discipline; the patience of **attaining acceptance of nonarising**; diligence, in the sense of **arousing diligence in** the Dharma of **the Great Vehicle**; the concentration of **abiding by compassion in the final one** of the four concentrations; **and** nonconceptual insight—**these are held to be the wise ones' foremost pursuits in terms of the transcendences.**

Regarding the foremost or supreme pursuits, these constitute the supreme and most excellent factors within each of the six transcendences. Thus, when bodhisattvas are endowed with these, they too become supreme and most excellent. The supreme pursuits are as follows. Among the three kinds of generosity, granting the Dharma is the foremost or supreme way of giving. While generosity in terms of material things and protection will bring mundane happiness, generosity with the Dharma also accomplishes supramundane perfection. That is why we find statements such as this one from the noble *Vajra Cutter:*

> Somebody may fill the billionfold universe with the seven precious substances and then make a gift of it all. Yet if someone declares and explains just one four-line stanza from this sūtra, the merit will expand infinitely more.

From among the vows for individual liberation, concentration and the undefiled vows, the undefiled vows are supreme or foremost because these constitute the utterly pure discipline that delights the noble ones. In terms of patience, the acceptance of nonarising phenomena, which among the three types of patience belongs to that of definitively realizing the Dharma, is the foremost type. Compared with all the diligence of worldly beings, listeners, and self-realized buddhas, the diligence that is aroused with respect to the practice of listening to, reflecting on, and meditating on the Dharma of the Great Vehicle is supreme or foremost. Among the four concentrations, the fourth is characterized by a balance of calm abiding and special insight. Hence, to remain in that balance while possessing infinite compassion is supreme among all forms of concentration. Finally, with respect to the former five transcendences, that of transcendent insight is supreme or foremost. Thus, for example, the Mother[53] teaches:

> If you wish to bring transcendent generosity to perfection, then train in this transcendent insight.

These are held to be the wise bodhisattvas' foremost pursuits in terms of the transcendences.

17. Teaching the Dharma

This section explains classifications with respect to (1) the Dharma that is to be taught, (2) the meaning that is to be fully comprehended, (3) the infinite qualities of the bodhisattvas that teach, (4) the effects of teaching, and (5) the summary of Great Vehicle Dharma.

1. The Dharma That Is to Be Taught

With respect to benefiting sentient beings, numerous divisions can be made in terms of temporary and ultimate benefit. Foremost among them all, however, is teaching the Dharma to sentient beings so that they thereby gain liberation. Hence, the categories of the teachings will be considered next. In order to explain the Dharma, the bodhisattvas must first themselves receive abundant teachings of the profound and vast Great Vehicle Dharma, and they must flawlessly ascertain the meanings of the teachings they receive, thereby gaining the qualities of expertise. Unless they do that, they will be unable to explain the Dharma in a way that considers the diverse constitutions, capacities, and inclinations of sentient beings. This is just as it is taught in the *Commentary on Reliable Means of Cognition:*

> If the cause and effect of the method remain hidden,
> It will be difficult to explain.

Here "the effect of the method" refers to the truth of cessation, and the cause of that is the truth of the path. Thus, if knowledge of these is lacking, so that these remain hidden, one will be unable to point out clearly what constitutes the path and fruition of liberation. Thus, the fourfold classification of the Dharma is taught next.

Now, we might wonder whether this material has already been covered in the chapter on investigating the Dharma, and whether, therefore, teaching the same thing here might be repetitive. Yet, the present context is the qualities of the bodhisattvas, and so the topic here regards the qualities of their expertise with respect to the four classifications of the teachings. Hence, although the subject matter is not any different from what was covered earlier, it will be approached differently, and the text will also supply a special summary of points to be understood. Hence, not only is there no superfluous repetition, but the following section is also very meaningful.

Bodhisattvas who possess the supreme qualities of the practice of the six transcendences, as explained above, will be aware of the means for taming sentient beings. With such knowledge, they will therefore also teach those means to sentient beings. Thus, having emerged as teachers, they will expertly explain four topics of the Dharma. These are the classifications of (1) the Dharma, (2) the truths, (3) reasoning, and (4) the vehicles.

1. Classification of the Dharma

> The fields of knowledge are classified
> By means of the distinctions in the sūtras and so forth.
> On all the grounds, these are known
> As "the steadfast ones' classification of the Dharma."[xx.43]

In the context of the fourfold classification, the classification of the Dharma is presented first. **The five fields of knowledge are classified by means of the distinctions in the sūtras, the hymns, and so forth. On all the grounds, these are known as "the steadfast ones' classification of the Dharma."**

The five fields of knowledge—the field of the inner knowledge, linguistics, valid means of cognition, arts and sciences, and the field of medicine—are laid out as such by means of distinctions found in the sutras, the prophecies, the teachings in verse, and the rest of the twelve sections of scripture. Throughout the grounds of imaginative conduct and the ten grounds of the noble ones, these are known as "the steadfast bodhisattvas' classification of the Dharma."

We may wonder what is the sense of "classification," here. Let us take the example of linguistics. Words that are composed of letters receive affixes, declensional marks, and so on, thereby undergoing transformations. The classifications of these changes were in the past explained by the buddhas, bodhisattvas, and great sages, and they are presented in the treatises on the interpretation of verbal signs. Hence, when the bodhisattvas explain and classify for the sake of others, they too make use of those same classifications.

As for the knowledge of argumentation, the classification is in terms of the three reliable means of cognition—perception, inference, and scripture—whereby probanda that are manifest, hidden, or extremely hidden may be evaluated. In terms of medicine, there are the categories of the means for maintaining a healthy body as well as the four remedying factors—diet, lifestyle, medicine, and treatments—that are to be employed in the case of sickness.

The arts and sciences operate with numerous classifications for learning and gaining skill through the use of body, speech, and mind. They include, for example, the knowledge of mathematics, astrology, the eight typologies, and so on. They likewise involve elements of linguistics, such as the scriptures on poetics that classify the ornaments of verse, prose, and their combination with a view to the aesthetics of word and meaning. There are, as well, the scriptures on literary composition that determine the weight of the letters in a verse. The arts and sciences are also concerned with songs in various languages, as well as with dance and drama. We also find here the treatises on synonymy that correctly classify equivalent references to the same meaning. With respect to the knowledge of the inner meaning, here the classifications that are set forth and explained free from error concern the individual paths and fruitions of the three vehicles.

At this point, one may wonder: "Is the subject matter of the sūtras and the rest of the twelve sections of the scriptural teachings not the inner knowledge? If it is, then why is it said here that the scriptural teachings explain the other fields of knowledge? Indeed, the verses say that 'the fields of knowledge are classified by means of the distinctions in the sūtras and so forth.' How could the other five fields of knowledge be included within the sūtras and so on?" Now, the twelve branches of the scriptures of the Buddha are indeed primarily concerned with the knowledge of the inner meaning. Yet, they also include the other four among the five fields as supplements because the extremely vast sūtras of the Great Vehicle flawlessly explain the issues that pertain to all phenomena, both as they are and in their multiplicity. It is, hence, by no means the case that the sūtras of the Great Vehicle do not address the five fields of knowledge. Indeed, it is impossible to determine the full extent of the Buddha's words on the Great Vehicle. Therefore, since the buddhas teach the five fields, the classifications that they deliver thereby are received and internalized correctly by the bodhisattvas. The bodhisattvas, in turn, emanate forth in a timely manner, and so they appear as great sages and Brahmins possessing the five superknowledges, thus passing on these teachings for the benefit of sentient beings in innumerable ways. The *Jewel Lamp Sūtra* explains:

> So that those who appear in the world will quickly gain knowledge,
> They teach beings who do not know the ways of activity
> Matters such as the plowing of fields, ways of doing business,
> As well as the various crafts of the world.

> Practices that neither harm nor damage,
> That bring happiness to sentient beings and that are praised by the learned,
> All sorts of reasoning, powers, medicine, and treatises—
> These the sages will fully explain.

That which interests the world, including the gods,
The truly exalted practices of the sages,
The spiritual disciplines, austerities, and difficult challenges—
All this the skillful ones will fully explain.

Those engaged in extremist practices,
Performing the penance of Gautama, remaining silent,
Going naked without clothes while engaged in virtuous
     practice—
All these the extremist masters will skillfully teach.

The sūtra likewise declares:

Thus, through all sorts of skillful means,
They benefit those who roam and wander in the world.
Unattached to the world, like a lotus in the water,
They cause happiness and faith as they travel.

As masters of poetry and discourse;
As dancers, drummers, and musicians;
As beautiful dancers, adorned with jewelry and holding garlands;
And as illusionists—thus they display an abundance of forms.

They turn into citizens, mayors, and universal emperors;
Captains, business people, and householders;
Monarchs, ministers, priests, and messengers;
Doctors and authors of fine treatises of the world.

In the hermitage they become magnificent trees.
They turn into medicine, jewels, and inexhaustible treasure,
Into wish-fulfilling jewels and wish-fulfilling trees,
And into guides for those who fear losing the way.

Thus, filling the infinite realms of the ten directions, the miraculous manifestations of the buddhas and bodhisattvas know no bounds. All incontrovertible treatises on the five fields of learning are in this way also taught by the power of the buddhas and bodhisattvas. The *Supreme Continuity* explains:

> In short, throughout the entire world without exception,
> The cause of happiness for gods and beings on earth
> Manifests pervasively, filling the realms,
> And is taught to be supported by the melody.

Thus it explains the qualities of the melody of the enlightened voice, just as they are. Therefore, the belief that linguistics and so on are not the Buddha's teaching and that they instead exclusively belong to non-Buddhist contexts betrays an extremely narrow perspective. Subsequent to the teachings of buddhas and bodhisattvas of the past, many treatises on communication and the like have indeed been composed by both non-Buddhist and Buddhist scholars. Yet the mere fact that the author is non-Buddhist obviously does not mean that the learned content of a treatise therefore also must be non-Buddhist, just as its author's being Buddhist, of course, does not guarantee that the subject matter of a certain treatise is Buddhism. Four among the fields are common fields of knowledge, and so it does not make sense to qualify their subject matter as either non-Buddhist or Buddhist.

Nevertheless, it is also quite pointless to mention that certain issues pertaining to the fields of learning are uniquely Buddhist in the sense that they are not recognized among non-Buddhists. Examples of such matters are the proof of the authenticity of the teacher and the teaching as developed in the *Compendium on Reliable Means of Cognition* and the Seven Treatises on Valid Means of Cognition; the secret symbols of the thus-gone ones as taught in Mantra; the means for dispelling physical agitation as taught independently of the maturation and liberation of Mantra in, for example, the *Tantra of Essential Elixir;* the dances and melodies as found in the rituals of secret mantra; the aesthetics for depicting, for example, sacred bodies; and the astrological correlations of the orbits of the planets and the number of breaths that pertain to the central channel as taught in *The Wheel of Time*'s chapter on the external world.

As for examples of non-Buddhist treatments of the inner meaning, we may mention the meditations leading to the absorptions of the form and formless realms, the yogic practices associated with the vital winds as taught by the Followers of Īśvara, and the meditations on the reality of nāda and the thatness of the self as practiced by The Nude. Nevertheless, such practices are undertaken in a way that is divorced from the realization of the absence of self. Hence, while they may indeed bring temporary miraculous powers and other minor attainments, they are not the path of liberation. They are, therefore, by no means the authentic knowledge of the inner meaning, and they do not transcend the world. The voice of enlightenment reveals the path beyond the world, and hence its teaching comprises the genuine knowledge of the inner meaning. Therefore, since the knowledge of the inner meaning resolves the character of all phenomena, as they are and in their multiplicity, communication and all the other disciplines constitute its supplements.

The teaching of the buddhas is boundless and endless, yet, even in terms of the sūtras that these days are apparent in the Noble Land and in Tibet, there are abundant treatments of grammar and so forth. For example, when scriptures such as the *Sūtra on the Definitive Explanation of the Intent* explain dependency, efficacy, and the rest of the four principles of reasoning, they provide an exhaustive account of the science of reasons and arguments. As for linguistics, when the sūtras state, for example, that "it is form because it is obstructive," or "sensation is of the nature of experience," they thereby explain the proper application of definitive words. They do this not only in Sanskrit, but also with regard to the use of definitive words in all the infinite languages of sentient beings. Likewise, when it is taught that "the voice of the Thus-Gone One is excellent expression," the implication is that it employs nouns with the proper declensional affixes to produce excellent and definitive words—words that are, furthermore, expressed in a perfect register of poetic moods by means of physical ornamentation and other such exquisite examples, ornaments, and flavors of poetics. Thus, every statement of the teachings displays infinite variations of proper poetic examples. In terms of astrology, this is taught explicitly in the *Tantra of the Wheel of Time*, and throughout the sūtras we also encounter instances of dance, song, crafts, typology, and so on. The way the bodhisattvas practice the arts and sciences within the framework of the transcendences is explained in, for example, the *Sūtra of the Great Display*.

Thus, it should be understood that all issues pertaining to the fields of learning are contained within the sūtras of the Great Vehicle. The buddhas are aware of all that may bring temporary or ultimate benefit and happiness to those who are to be trained. Hence, given the circumstance of beings who are to be trained and who request instruction, there is nothing that the buddhas will not teach and explain. The bodhisattvas, in turn, receive and internalize the teachings by means of their perfect recall, and they will pass the teachings on whenever the time calls for it. Thus, all matters of knowledge pertaining to the way things are and the way things appear emerge based on the words of the buddhas.

2. Classification of the Truths

The classification of the truths
Is based on seven types of suchness. [xx.44a–b]

The next explanation concerns the classification of the expressed meaning, the truths. There are seven types of suchness: (1) cyclic existence is the suchness of engagement, (2) the three natures are the suchness of the characteristics, (3) the fact that all phenomena are mere awareness is the suchness of awareness, (4) the truth of suffering is the suchness of abidance, (5) the truth of origin is the suchness of wrong engagement, (6) the truth of cessation is the suchness of purity, and (7) the truth of the path is the suchness of genuine practice. Thus, **the classification of the truths is based on seven types of suchness.**

The truths are classified with reference to the seven types of suchness. Suchness is of seven kinds: (1) The suchness of engagement comprises the continuous engagements within cyclic existence. That is to say, karmic formation occurs based on the condition of ignorance. As one link gives rise to another, all twelve links of dependent origination emerge in an unbroken continuity. This is the beginningless and endless process of engaging in cyclic existence.

(2) The suchness of the characteristics concerns the characteristics of the imaginary, the dependent, and the thoroughly established. The duality of the apprehended and the apprehender do not exist as imagined. The dependent consciousness that is the cause or basis for the mistaken appearance of such duality exists conventionally. Finally, the lack of establishment of the apprehended and the apprehender within the dependent is the intrinsic nature and, as such, thoroughly established.

(3) The suchness of awareness concerns the way all conditioned and unconditioned phenomena are nothing more than the mind. As taught in the *Sūtra on the Ten Grounds:*

> Listen, O children of the Victorious One, these three realms are mind only!

Thus, since all phenomena come down to nothing but the mind, they are established as awareness.

(4) The suchness of abidance refers to the nature of the three types of suffering, the continuous presence of the phenomena of cyclic existence. (5) The suchness of wrong engagement is the truth of origin as characterized by karmic action and afflictions. Thus, it consists of the mistaken production of the nature of suffering. (6) The suchness of purity is the truth of cessation. It is referred to as such in consideration of its being free from the flaws of suffering and its origin. (7) The suchness of genuine practice is the truth of the path, whereby the truth of cessation is accomplished free from error.

Due to the suchness of engagement, abidance, and wrong engagement, all sentient beings are alike and equal. With respect to the suchness of the characteristics, the characteristics of the dependent and the thoroughly established render all phenomena alike and equal. Moreover, the suchness of awareness is contained within the dependent. The *Sūtra on the Definitive Explanation of the Intent* explains the suchness of the characteristics exclusively in terms of the twofold absence of self. Hence, according to this sūtra, the suchness of the characteristics pertains to the thoroughly established nature. In terms of the suchness of purity, the enlightenments achieved by listeners, self-realized buddhas, and buddhas are all taught as being alike and equal because all three are alike in terms of their attaining the mere truth of cessation. Finally, because of the suchness of genuine practice, all aspects of listening to, reflecting on, and meditating on the authentic Dharma are all alike and equal. That is how the issue is explained in the *Sūtra on the Definitive Explanation of the Intent*.

In this way, engagement with, and abidance within, cyclic existence comprise the truth of suffering, with its four features of impermanence and so on. Wrong engagement is the truth of the origin, which involves the four features of full arising and so forth. The thoroughly established nature, free from adventitious stains, is the truth of cessation—with its four features of cessation, peace, and so on. Genuine practice is the truth of the path that involves the four features of path, reason, and so forth. Awareness comprises the eight collections of consciousness. When the impure dependent consciousness keeps the imaginary as its focal point, there then occurs the forward arising of the links of dependent origination. In this context, the aspect of abidance within cyclic existence is the truth of suffering, while the aspect of mistaken engagement pertains to the truth of origin. However, the aspect of the pure dependent consciousness that practices the path through the observation of the thoroughly established nature is contained within genuine practice. This is why *Distinguishing the Middle from Extremes* considers the suchness of awareness to belong to the thoroughly established nature. Finally, the suchness of the thoroughly established nature that is free from adventitious stains is the truth of cessation.

Although none of the commentaries brings it up at this point, the five types of being are also distinguished in relation to the three natures. The five types of being are (1) name, (2) reason, (3) conception, (4) suchness, and (5) genuine wakefulness.

(1) Name refers to the use of names such as "pillar" and "vase" and the subsequent understanding of such designated phenomena. As such, these names comprise the imaginary nature.

(2) Reason is the objective appearance of the dependent nature. This principle consists of the appearance of phenomena, such as a bulbous shape for example, that seem to display marks and reasons for the use of names.

(3) Conception is the aspect of the eight collections that appears to apprehend.

(4) Suchness is the unchanging thoroughly established nature.

(5) Genuine wakefulness is the subject of suchness, which is also termed the "unmistaken thoroughly established nature." The latter term is derived by naming the subject after its object. This is done in consideration of the fact that, with genuine wakefulness, the way things appear is also the way they actually are. In this way, the *Journey to Laṅkā* declares:

> The five types of being and the three natures,
> The eight collections of consciousness,
> And the two meanings of selflessness
> Summarize the entire Great Vehicle.

Thus, these are the Dharma's great summations.

3. The Four Types of Reasoning

> The classification of reasoning and vehicles
> Is fourfold and threefold. [xx.44c–d]

The classification of reasoning and the classification of **vehicles** is, respectively, **fourfold and threefold.**

At this point we find a brief presentation of the next two topics: reasoning and the vehicles. Here it is explained that these are, respectively, classified as four and three. We begin with the four types of reasoning:

> Correctly directing the mind,
> The authentic view, possession of the fruition,
> Discernment by reliable means of knowledge, and the
>   inconceivable—
> These are known as the four principles of reasoning. [xx.45]

As for the reasoning of dependency, by **correctly directing the mind** toward all three vehicles, one arrives—in dependence on that and by that circumstance—at **the authentic view** that transcends the world. Next, in terms of the reasoning of efficacy, once the authentic view of the path of seeing has arisen, one is in **possession of the fruition**, which is the efficacious process of eliminating the discards through seeing. The reasoning of valid proof consists of **discernment by reliable means of knowledge**, such as perception, **and the** reasoning of the intrinsic nature concerns the **inconceivable** facts. Hence, one should not think, for example, "Why does the authentic view arise based on correctly directing the mind?" or "Why does the elimination of afflictions follow as the fruition?" Thus, **these are known as the four principles of reasoning.**

The four reasonings are: (1) the reasoning of efficacy that makes one aware of which causes produce which effects; (2) the reasoning of dependency that estimates which effects depend on which causes; (3) the intrinsic nature of the relative, such as fire's being hot and water's being liquid, and the intrinsic nature of the ultimate, the emptiness of all phenomena; and (4) the reasoning of valid proof that, by means of direct perception and inference, carries out evaluations in accordance with the way things actually are.

As for the reasonings of efficacy and dependency, on the grounds of imaginative conduct one correctly directs the mind toward the facts of the twofold absence of self. Since doing so ushers in the authentic view that sees the truth of the intrinsic nature, one thus comes to possess the fruition. That is to say, the authentic view of the path of seeing is in possession of the fruition of liberation and the transcendence of suffering. Therefore, the reasonings of efficacy and dependency are here distinguished with reference to the following. Respectively, there are specific causes producing specific effects, and there is the causally dependent character of the resultant effects. Such relations between cause and effect pertain to dependent origination without deception, just as sprouts grow from live seeds. The cause effectively functions to produce the effect, and so the manifestation of the effect follows the manifestation of the cause. The effect, in turn, also depends thus on the cause, and in the absence of the latter the former will hence have to disappear as well. That which through reliable means of cognition discerns and realizes the appropriate and reasonable nature of these principles is the reasoning of valid proof. Finally, while in relative terms there is no deception with respect to the appearance of produced and productive factors, no such marks can be observed in terms of the ultimate and inconceivable intrinsic nature. Such is the reasoning of the intrinsic nature. Thus, the four reasonings are here exclusively set forth in relation to the authentic path. Based on the present treatment, one can, by implication, further understand how the four reasonings are employed in all other cases as well.

4. Classification of the Three Vehicles

In terms of the differences
In intent, explanation,
Engagement, accumulations, and accomplishment,
The vehicles are held to be threefold. [xx.46]

In terms of the differences in their motivating **intent**, the **explanation** of the corpus of teaching, the **engagement** in the practices, the gathering of the **accumulations, and** the **accomplishment** of the fruition, **the vehicles are held to be threefold**. The vehicle of the listeners is inferior, that of the self-realized buddhas is mediocre, and the Great Vehicle is supreme. The Dharma is explained in accordance with the specific intentions and wishes, and the practices are, in turn, engaged in according to the way the Dharma is explained. Furthermore, the way the accumulations are gathered depends on the practices, and the authentic accomplishment conforms to the character of the accumulations.

The three vehicles—those of the listeners, self-realized buddhas, and bodhisattvas—can be classified as such, based on dividing the five factors of intent and so forth in terms of their lesser, medium, and greater manifestations. The listeners' intent is of lesser quality because they merely wish to realize the absence of a personal self and thereby quickly gain merely their own liberation. In consideration of their intent, the thus-gone ones only teach the listeners about the absence of a personal self, the suffering of cyclic existence, and so on. Thus, they teach them a lesser Dharma of the four truths. Attuning themselves with this teaching of the lesser Dharma, the listeners also engage themselves in a lesser way over a period of three or seven lifetimes. In accordance with the quality of their engagements, they also achieve a lesser accumulation of merit and wakefulness. Finally, through such lesser accumulations, they accomplish the lesser enlightenment of a listener. These considerations serve to classify the vehicle of listeners.

The capacity of the self-realized buddhas is of a medium quality. Unlike the listeners, they are capable of realizing a one-and-a-half absence of self and of cultivating this realization for a hundred eons. As they thus possess a capacity and an intent that is of medium strength, the thus-gone ones teach them a Dharma that concerns the arising and reversal of the links of dependent origination and the illusory nature of that which appears to be apprehended. Since their practical engagement and accumulation is also superior to that of the listeners, they too are classified as medium level. In terms of its being the transcendence of suffering, the fruition of the self-realized buddhas is not any different from that of the listeners. Yet, when considering the types of superknowledge that the self-realized buddhas achieve, there is a difference. For example, whereas the miraculous eye of a listener foe destroyer perceives only as far as a millionfold universe, the miraculous eye and ear of a foe destroyer who is a self-realized buddha sees all forms and hears all sounds within a billionfold universe. Hence, since the faculties of a self-realized buddha are sharper than those of a listener, and since the former's realization and miraculous powers surpass those of the listener, the self-realized buddha's fruition is classified as superior.

With their supreme capacity, the bodhisattvas are able to realize the twofold absence of self. Moreover, with insight and compassion they focus on the welfare of others. Hence, they are capable of benefiting both themselves and others; their intent is vast. The profound and vast Dharma explanations that they receive concern the Great Vehicle. Since they engage themselves in the practice of those teachings, they accomplish the twofold benefit. Gathering the accumulations of merit and wakefulness, they finally accomplish the vast fruition of unsurpassable enlightenment. This is how the path and fruition of the Great Vehicle are classified. In this way, the vehicles are held to be threefold. Both the sevenfold greatness and the summary of the Great Vehicle are explained below.

2. The Meaning That Is to Be Comprehended

Names and entities are, upon investigation,
Seen to be mutually adventitious.
The two designations are here
Investigated as just that. [xx.47]

All are unobservable,
Hence, the fourfold authentic wakefulness
Accomplishes on all the grounds
The objectives of the steadfast ones. [xx.48]

Support, enjoyments, and seeds
Are the causes of bondage;
Mind and mental states,
Along with their supports and seeds, are bound here. [xx.49]

The marks that are placed in front
And those that are present by themselves
Are all destroyed by the wise one
Who attains supreme enlightenment. [xx.50]

Knowledge that witnesses suchness,
Elimination of dualistic grasping,
And direct perception of the body of negative tendencies—
It is held that the wise one accomplishes exhaustion. [xx.51]

The wakefulness witnessing suchness
Practices without distinction.
The direct perception of the facts of existence and nonexistence
Is known as "the mastery of thought." [xx.52]

> For the childish, the genuine is obscured
> And so falsity appears everywhere;
> The bodhisattvas dispel that
> And so reality appears everywhere. [xx.53]
>
> That which is known as the nonappearance and appearance
> Of the meaningless and the meaningful
> Is fundamental transformation.
> Since one can do as one pleases, this is liberation. [xx.54]
>
> The vast object is in all contexts
> The similar appearance of things that are distinct.
> As it is an obstacle, this is to be given up
> By means of thorough knowledge. [xx.55]

Next follows an explanation of the investigation. The relationships between **names and entities are, upon investigation, seen to be mutually** and reciprocally **adventitious. The two designations,** that is, those of essence and distinctions, which are applied with respect to those relationships, **are also here investigated as just that,** being merely adventitious. From the perspective of the knowledge of phenomena that is in perfect accordance with reality, **all four—names, entities, essences, and distinction—are unobservable.** Hence, **the fourfold authentic wakefulness** that cognizes in accordance with reality **accomplishes on all the grounds the objectives of the steadfast ones,** the bodhisattvas, on their own behalf as well as on that of others.

One may wonder: "In that case, what is it that binds one to cyclic existence?" The **support** in the form of the world vessel, the **enjoyments,** which are the five objects of form and the rest, **and** the **seeds** of the all-ground consciousness **are the causes of bondage. Mind and mental states, along with their supports** (the eyes and so forth) **and** accompanied by **the seeds** (meaning accompanied by the all-ground), **are bound here.**

One may wonder: "In that case, what are the means of liberation from cyclic existence?" The **marks that are placed in front** as the imagined focal points of the practices of receiving teachings, reflecting, and meditating **and those** natural focal points **that are present by themselves** without having to be deliberately imagined **are all destroyed by the wise one, who attains supreme enlightenment.** The wakefulness of **knowledge that witnesses** the thoroughly established **suchness, the elimination of dualistic grasping** whereby the imaginary is fully understood, **and the direct perception of the body of negative tendencies**, which yields the full knowledge of the dependent—**it is held that,** by means of these cognitions, **the wise one accomplishes** the **exhaustion** of perpetuated misfortune.

The listeners perceive a distinction between the presence and absence of marks. They then direct their minds toward the field devoid of marks and enter the equilibrium devoid of marks. In the case of the bodhisattvas, however, **the wakefulness** that is **witnessing suchness practices without** any **distinction** in terms of presence and absence of marks because it does not see any marks aside from suchness. **The direct perception of the facts of existence and nonexistence**—which are, respectively, suchness and the marks of the two selves—**is known as "the mastery of thought,"** in the sense that all aims are accomplished just as they are conceived.

For the childish, the perception of **the genuine is obscured and so** the **falsity** of the apprehended and apprehender **appears everywhere. The bodhisattvas dispel that** falsity **and so reality appears everywhere. That which is known as the nonappearance and appearance of,** respectively, **the meaningless** marks of the apprehended and apprehender **and the meaningful** suchness **is fundamental transformation, and since one can do as one pleases, this is liberation.**

On the methods for accomplishing the pure field, it is taught: **The vast** external **object of the world vessel is in all regards the similar appearance of things that are distinct. As it is an obstacle** to the complete purification of the buddha field, **this,** meaning the thought that "such and such is such and such," **is** to be **given up by means of thorough knowledge.**

Next, we turn to the classification of the meaning of the Dharma that is to be fully comprehended. Here one must gain expertise in explaining four topics and, as one thus becomes skilled in the verbal teaching of the Dharma to sentient beings, one will give them the opportunity to investigate and comprehend the meaning and characteristics of the Dharma. The four topics to be investigated are: (1) names, (2) referents, or entities, (3) designations with respect to essences, and (4) designations with respect to distinctions. These are the topics that are under investigation on the grounds of imaginative conduct.

Names are, for example, "vase"[54] or "blanket," and their referents are such things as a bulbous entity that holds water or a piece of fabric that is composed of yarn. Immature beings here take the name to be that which it refers to, just as they believe that the referent is the name. Thus, they think as if name and referent were connected by their very essence. Wise individuals, however, understand that the mutual relations between names and entities are adventitious. The name is an adventitious designation given to the object by thought, just as thought adventitiously conceives of the name as if it were the object. Hence, when investigated, the name is seen to be like a substitute or a loan. If the name were not just an adventitious designation, the mere manifestation of the name would also be the manifestation of the object. The two could not be separated. Hence, if name and object were in this way of the same nature, the destruction of the entity of the vase would also reasonably imply that the designation "vase" was destroyed at the same time and, therefore, is now gone. Yet after the vase has been broken, the name still stays on. Similarly, when a householder becomes ordained, his name changes, but the entity to which it applies does not. Moreover, there is no restriction as to what can possibly be called what. Therefore, know that, apart from what is supplied through merely adventitious symbolic designations, there is no essential relationship between name and referent. With this realization, it will be understood how the designations in terms of essence (as when a bulbous vase-essence is understood based on the word "vase") and in terms of distinctions (as when it is specified that the vase is, for example, long or impermanent) are both adventitious.

Alternatively, Sthiramati's commentary at this point explains that "the two designations" refer to the understanding that designated particulars (such as solid earth and liquid water) and distinctions (as when all earth, water, and so forth, is qualified as being impermanent, suffering, defiling, undefiling, and so forth) are both mere words, without either of them being established by virtue of any essences as such. Regardless of which interpretation we adopt, the twofold designation with respect to essence and distinctions is here investigated in terms of its being adventitious. The key issue, then, is that the mind designates by temporarily connecting name and referent. When the latter is investigated, we find that there is no singular and substantial whole by the name of "vase." Rather, the name is given in relation to aspects such as the vase's opening and midsection, and since each of these can themselves be further split, all the way down to the most subtle particles, the demolishing of the parts does not lead to the establishment of any distinctions either. Therefore, whether we think of essences or distinctions, all are merely nominal imputations; nothing is established by any objective essence. Thus, one arrives at the realization that the existence of all these phenomena is mere imputation.

Investigating in this way brings, as explained in these nine[55] stanzas, a fourfold thorough knowledge. Based on having carried out the above fourfold investigation at the level of imaginative conduct, four thorough cognitions will arise on the path of seeing. That is to say, as names, referents, essences, and distinctions all turn out to be unobservable, there arise four aspects of authentic wakefulness that cognize things in perfect accordance with reality. These comprise knowledge that is in perfect accordance with reality and is based on the accomplishment of the investigation of (1) names, (2) referents or entities, (3) natures or essences, and (4) distinctions. Thus, one essentially recognizes that all names are devoid of entity, empty, and unobservable. Likewise, with respect to vases and all other entities, with respect to the individual essences and particular characteristics of all entities, and with respect to the arising, ceasing, and all other such distinctive qualities of entities, one realizes that everything is devoid of nature, that all is empty, and that none of this can be observed. With such fourfold thorough knowledge, the wise bodhisattvas eliminate discards and attain realizations throughout the ten grounds, and so they accomplish their own objectives as well as those of all others. At this point the commentary explains that while the first half of stanza 47 provides the defining characteristic of this thorough cognition, the second half shows its function.

The fourfold authentic wakefulness also liberates from the bondage of karmic actions. That which binds is here composed of the following: (1) the support or abode, meaning the marks of the world vessel that appear as the objects observed by the all-ground consciousness; (2) the marks of the enjoyments that are the six objects as accessed by the six consciousnesses; and (3) the causes or marks of the entirety of seeds, meaning the all-ground consciousness. Thus, bondage occurs due to these three marks, or causes, of bondage. These three factors thus bind "here" (meaning either "here, within cyclic existence" or "here, in the present situation") the following coexistent aspects: (1) the mind of the eight collections of consciousness and the fifty-one mental states, such as sensation, identification, and contact and (2) the supports in the form of the six sense faculties, from that of the eye up to and including that of the mind, along with the structure of the physical body that supports those faculties. Thus, as the latter category contains the aggregate of form, that which is bound is composed of the five aggregates. This bondage is accompanied by the seeds. That is to say, bondage is due to the possession of seeds. The habitual tendencies associated with the marks of the support and the enjoyments have been accumulated in the all-ground and, until one is rid of these habitual tendencies, liberation will remain impossible.

The next verses explain how one gains liberation by means of identifying the way in which bondage occurs. The practice of listening to, contemplating, and meditating on the Dharma involves focusing on certain marks, such as those of a decaying corpse, or a skeleton, and one's previous focus on such marks makes them reappear to oneself later. Other marks do not appear as the result of having purposely placed them before one. Instead, these emerge spontaneously due to the beginningless thought processes of sentient beings within cyclic existence. Hence, without having to do anything in particular for them to appear, marks of various phenomena, such as pillars and vases, appear and become naturally present before one as the objects of the mind. The wise bodhisattvas recognize that, regardless of whether or not they are purposely imagined, all such marks have no existence. As they thereby destroy all the marks of focal points, they cut through bondage and attain supreme enlightenment.

As for the way they destroy these two marks, first, the bodhisattvas acknowledge that the mentally imputed appearance of the marks of a skeleton, for example, are in the end but a mental appearance. Thus they demolish the appearance through the recognition that there is nothing that exists by virtue of an objective essence, though it may seem to be otherwise. They then expand this recognition to include vases and any other entities that appear to them. In the end, all are but apparent to the mind and mental states; there is nothing that exists by virtue of any nature or essence of its own. They then train by accustoming themselves to this understanding.

Listeners and self-realized buddhas destroy the thoughts of purity, bliss, permanence, and self in relation to the aggregates. They then train in the understanding of impurity, suffering, impermanence, and the absence of a personal self. Thereby, they attain the enlightenment of a listener or self-realized buddha. Bodhisattvas, on the other hand, demolish the very essences of persons and phenomena, rendering them void beyond observation. By training in this recognition, they attain unsurpassable enlightenment. As for the way they are thereby freed from bondage and attain liberation, this occurs through the thorough knowledge of the characteristics of the three natures, as this brings about the elimination of the afflictive and cognitive obscurations that are present in the all-ground consciousness. The cognition, or wakefulness, that observes the basic field of phenomena, which is the suchness of all phenomena, makes the characteristics of the thoroughly established nature directly perceptible. The elimination of grasping in terms of the duality of apprehended and apprehender, or in terms of the selves of persons and phenomena, lays bare the characteristics of the imaginary nature. By directly perceiving the unmistaken nature of the all-ground consciousness that composes the body or collection of the negative tendencies, which take the form of afflictive and cognitive obscurations, the dependent nature becomes directly perceptible. As they make the characteristics of the three natures manifest in this way, the wise bodhisattvas accomplish the exhaustion of the afflictive and cognitive obscurations that are present in the all-ground consciousness of the dependent nature. It is held that they are thereby freed from all bonds.

Here one might wonder: "Noble listeners are in possession of the genuine cognition that has demolished the four errors, so in what way would theirs be any different from the bodhisattvas' authentic cognition that has broken down the marks of dual focal points?" Yet, compared to the way the listeners meditate based on the absence of marks, the bodhisattvas' way of meditating is superior. From the perspective of their wakefulness that observes suchness, there is no observation of any distinction between cyclic existence and the transcendence of suffering. The reason is that the basic field of phenomena, which is the nature of both cyclic existence and the transcendence of suffering, has always been the transcendence of suffering. Thus they realize that there are no differences in terms of a cyclic existence that is to be given up and a transcendence of suffering that is to be embraced. Cyclic existence is, itself, the transcendence of suffering. Fully comprehending that all phenomena are empty, their practice of meditation is therefore superior to that of the listeners. As stated in the *Sūtra Taught by Akṣayamati*:

> The basic field of phenomena, the field of cyclic existence, the field of the transcendence of suffering, the field of sentient beings, and the field of all the teachings—all of these are equal. How so? Because they all are, equally, emptiness. Hence, they are equal.

The listeners observe a distinction in terms of the marks of cyclic existence and the transcendence of suffering that is devoid of marks. As cyclic existence involves the suffering of birth, aging, sickness, death, and so forth, they perceive it as marked by a lack of peace and so they wish to relinquish it. Thus, seeing the transcendence of suffering to be peace beyond all marks of suffering and flaws, they wish to make it manifest. The bodhisattvas, however, meditate on all marks as being beyond difference within the basic field of phenomena. Once their practice has been thoroughly accomplished, they directly witness the primordially existent, thoroughly established nature, empty of duality. As they also directly perceive the primordial nonexistence of the imaginary marks of duality, they thereby achieve the authentic cognition in which existence and nonexistence are directly manifest. As a result of that, they are able to bring forth whatever they wish. Hence, if they think "May the empty sky produce a rain of helpful articles," it happens exactly as they wish. This is what is known as "the mastery of thought."

It may be objected that if cyclic existence, by nature, is itself the transcendence of suffering, all sentient beings ought to be beyond suffering from the very beginning. Yet, although the transcendence of suffering is the nature of cyclic existence, the habitual tendencies for conceiving of selves and phenomena obscure the minds of childish ordinary beings so that they fail to perceive the genuine suchness that is the primordial transcendence of suffering. When suchness is thus obscured, the falsity of duality appears everywhere, just as when someone suffering from visual distortions perceives hair tufts, or somebody mistakenly sees a rope as a snake. The bodhisattvas, however, do not grasp anything as being of the nature of selves and phenomena, and in this way, they dispel the appearance of a duality in terms of something apprehended and something that apprehends it. Hence, to them, the nondual reality of suchness appears everywhere. Similarly, those with healthy eyesight do not perceive any hair tufts; nor do those whose mental consciousness is not in error believe that a rope is a snake.

Therefore, without having to do anything to that effect, childish beings do not perceive the existent but see instead the nonexistent. The bodhisattvas, on the other hand, do not have to pay any attention in order to avoid perceiving the meaningless marks of the apprehended and the apprehender; nor do they have to apply themselves purposely to witness that which is meaningful, that is, suchness. Because of this latter nonappearance and appearance, the bodhisattvas experience that which actually exists and not the nonexistent. Thus they attain what is known as the "fundamental transformation" of the all-ground consciousness of the dependent nature. Since that which has attained fundamental transformation in this way is free from all the bondage of marks, the bodhisattvas can do as they please, and hence this is referred to as "liberation." This is just as when a person has been freed from her ties and is free to do as she pleases. The sky-like mind that has attained fundamental transformation is, similarly, no longer governed by attachment and the other afflictions, and so it is free to do as it pleases, or whatever it likes.

At this point one may wonder: "Although the mind may be freed from all bonds in this way, how could the present perception of a vast external world possibly be halted? The marks of such a location cannot possibly come to an end." To address this concern, an explanation of the way in which the buddha fields are cultivated follows next. The features of an external world appear due to the habitual tendencies present in the all-ground element for the perception of an external world. Thus, the all-ground consciousness observes the features of the aspect of the apprehended, which appear as if they were an external world. Just as with the experience of an environment in a dream, everything is but an appearance of something apprehended and something that apprehends. Beyond this, there is no separate world vessel constituted by external entities. Therefore, the continuous and uninterrupted experience of a vast world that appears to be external is due to the emerging continuum of the momentary all-ground consciousness. That is why there appears to be a world vessel that features a supportive ground and so forth. For as long as the marks of such an appearance are present, and for as long as one conceives of, and is attached to, such a world, for that long, too, the pure buddha fields cannot manifest. Instead, there will appear an ordinary world, and there will be obstacles to the cultivation of a buddha field.

Here it may be objected: "Let us assume that the wide earth and the rest of this world environment appear to the momentary all-ground consciousness without there being any external objects. How, then, could it be that this world remains accessible in such a stable way to the sentient beings who inhabit it? Why is there no difference between what we saw before and what we see now?" In reply, it is explained that while the supportive ground and all the other elements of the world are momentary, these discrete instants make up a temporal succession where the subsequent ones resemble those that came before. Because of this, the mind mistakenly believes itself to be accessing the same things. Likewise, beings who are born in the present world possess habitual tendencies that ensue from similar karmic actions. These mutually resembling habitual tendencies therefore cause each individual to experience things in a way that accords without divergence with the way things seem to all others who possess the same type of tendencies. It is, therefore, also based on changes in the mind's habitual tendencies that the features of the world appear to change. Thus, for example, subterrestrial beings may perceive dungeons that extend below the ground. Hence, for as long there appears to be, and for as long as one conceives of, an actual external world, such appearances and conceptions will be an obstacle to the perception of the pure buddha fields.

What, then, can be done to bring forth the pure fields of the buddhas? If one believes that the appearance of a world with a wide ground and so forth is in accord with fact, and if one develops attachments based on such beliefs, then that will obstruct the experience of the perfectly pure realms. Therefore, having fully understood that this is a hindrance, one must give up grasping at the marks of such a world and instead rest in the suchness that is beyond marks. Through this one will accomplish the complete purification comprising the exquisite ground, adornments, and all the other excellent features of the pure buddha fields.

3. The Infinite Qualities of Bodhisattva Teachers

> To be thoroughly matured, completely purified,
> Attained, suited for maturation,
> And authentically explained—
> These are, in the case of the wise, unfathomable. [xx.56]

The next explanation is an investigation of the unfathomable. The realm of sentient beings is the entity that is **to be thoroughly matured,** while the world vessel is to be **completely purified.** The field of phenomena is to be **attained,** the realm of those to be trained comprises those **suited for maturation, and** the means for taming are to be **authentically explained. These are, in the case of the wise, unfathomable.**

The limitless qualities of the bodhisattvas who teach the Dharma are here presented in terms of five principles.

(1) Bodhisattvas who have gained liberation from the bondage of marks through genuine wakefulness are active in order to bring sentient beings throughout the realm of space to complete maturation. They ripen those with the potential of listeners, self-realized buddhas, or bodhisattvas by means of their respective vehicles. They mature those who are of uncertain potential through whichever among the three vehicles is the most effective. And those whose potential is cut off they lead to maturation in the higher realms, by establishing them in the ten virtues. In this way, the objects of their complete maturation are unfathomable.

(2) The objects of the bodhisattvas' complete purification are unfathomable. They completely purify the world vessel so that it is free from ravines, thorns, dirt, or any other impure entities. Instead, in the beautiful and perfectly pure buddha fields that they cultivate, the ground is made of precious substances, rivers of elixir flow, wish-fulfilling trees grow, and so forth. Likewise, the realms of the world extend unfathomably, like a brocade tent, as far as the field of space.

(3) The objects of their attainment are unfathomable as well. With respect to virtuous and unvirtuous entities, they give up what is unvirtuous and instead actualize undefiling virtuous qualities, such as the ten powers and four fearlessnesses. In this way, the qualities of their attainment are unfathomable.

(4) Those suited for maturation are likewise limitless. Except for individuals whose potential is cut off, this category includes everyone who is in possession of one of the four types of potential for liberation, and who is thus suited for maturation by means of the three vehicles. How does this category of those suited for maturation differ from the category of those who are to be matured? Everyone, regardless of whether they are endowed with the potential for liberation, is to be ripened, yet only some are suited for lasting maturation, in the sense that they can mature into liberation. That is the whole difference.

(5) That which is to be authentically taught and explained is also unfathomable. Sentient beings are to be trained by means of the methods taught through the Dharma, yet since the gateways of teachings, such as the contemplation of the repulsive (for those suffering from attachment) and the cultivation of love (for the benefit of those who are aggressive), are inconceivably diverse, they are unfathomable as well.

Thus these five categories explain who is to be ripened, in which realm, in terms of which attainments, by possessing which potential, and by means of which gateway of Dharma teaching. Hence, as taught here, these five principles render the wise bodhisattvas unfathomable.

1. The Effects of Dharma Teaching

Birth of the enlightened mind,
Acceptance of nonarising,
The inferior stainless eye,
The exhaustion of defilement, [xx.57]

The long-lasting presence of the sacred Dharma,
Knowledge of particularities, cutting through, and
    enjoyment—
These are to be known as the fruits
Of the teaching of the wise ones who are committed to that.
    [xx.58]

Next, the results of the explanation are investigated. Among those who are in the retinue of the bodhisattvas committed to teaching, some experience the **birth of the enlightened mind**, some gain **acceptance of nonarising**, others accomplish **the Inferior Vehicle's stainless eye**, and still others attain **the exhaustion of defilement**. Some bring about **the long-lasting presence of the sacred Dharma** as they uphold it, and those who had no **knowledge of** the **particularities** develop such knowledge. Those who were unsure will experience the **cutting through** of their doubts, **and** those who are certain will experience the great **enjoyment** of tasting the sacred Dharma, free from negativities. **These are** hence **to be known as the fruits of the teaching of the wise ones who are committed to that,** that is, committed to the explanation of the Dharma.

Eight effects of the explanation of the Dharma are explained next. When the Dharma of the Great Vehicle is taught, some beings will (1) set their minds on unsurpassable enlightenment and (2) some will gain acceptance of the nonarising reality. When the Great Vehicle is taught, some individuals who are on the grounds of imaginative conduct will gain acceptance of nonarising phenomena by means of an object universal. That type of partial engagement with reality is a lesser acceptance. The actual attainment of the acceptance of nonarising phenomena occurs when one directly realizes reality on the first ground. Compared with the acceptance that occurs on the eighth ground, this acceptance is nevertheless classified as intermediate. On the eighth ground, nonconceptuality is accomplished spontaneously. This attainment is referred to as the greater acceptance. The sūtras testify to these attainments, and so a sūtra may specify that when a certain teaching of the Dharma was given, a number of individuals set their minds on unsurpassable enlightenment, attained acceptance of phenomena in accord with the Dharma, attained the path of the noble ones, or gained acceptance of nonarising phenomena.

(3) When the Dharma of the listeners is taught, some attain the stainless Dharma eye with respect to phenomena. This is an attainment that is inferior to the Great Vehicle's path of seeing. (4) Others attain the level of a foe destroyer through the final exhaustion of defilements. The attainment of the Dharma eye refers to the listeners' path of seeing. This is referred to as such because it is the manifestation of the wakefulness that is like an eye of the Dharma, perceiving the four truths. Because the eightfold acceptance serves as their remedy, this eye is free from the dust of the afflictions. Because the eightfold cognition is liberated from the factors that are to be discarded through seeing, this eye is also stainless. Once the eye of the Dharma, free from dust and stainless, has been attained, one will have entered the stream of liberation from the factors that are to be discarded through seeing. Those who have thus gained the listeners' path of seeing can then rely on the Dharma to eliminate the discards of the afflictions through cultivation. Thereby eliminating the afflictions associated with the various levels of the three realms, they will bring all afflictions to exhaustion. Hence, with the attainment of the wakefulness that knows exhaustion and nonarising, they gain the stage of a foe destroyer. Thus the sūtras may also specify that when a certain Dharma teaching was given, there were beings who thereby gained

the vision of phenomena through the dustless and stainless eye of the Dharma, just as they may mention that there were beings who gained liberation from all defilements without appropriation.

Whether it is the Dharma of the Great or the Lesser Vehicle that is explained, whenever someone teaches the Dharma it serves (5) to ensure its long-lasting presence in the world and (6) to enable those who were previously not aware of the particular and general characteristics of phenomena to gain knowledge of these. Likewise, (7) whatever doubt there was about them will be dispelled. Thus, without any lack of knowledge or doubt, beings will become certain about the import of the Dharma, thereby (8) coming to experience the joy of partaking of the enjoyments of the sacred Dharma free from negativities. These are the fruits of the teaching of the wise ones who are committed to the activities of explaining the Dharma.

5. Summary of the Great Vehicle Dharma

The vast focal point,
The twofold practice,
Wakefulness, the arousing of diligence,
Skill in means, [xx.59]

Great authentic accomplishment,
And the great buddha activity—
As it possesses such greatness,
It is definitively referred to as the "Great Vehicle." [xx.60]

There is potential, inspiration with respect to the Dharma,
Engendering the mind,
Practicing generosity and the rest,
Entering the flawless, [xx.61]

Thoroughly ripening sentient beings,
Cultivating the fields,
Nonabiding transcendence of suffering,
Supreme enlightenment, and the display. [xx.62]

Within an investigation of the Great Vehicle, it is said: The Great Vehicle maintains a **vast focal point** constituted by the vast Dharma of the sūtras and so forth. It is also characterized by **the twofold practice**, which accomplishes both one's own objectives as well as those of others. At the time of realization, there is the **wakefulness** that comprehends the absence of a self in the form of persons or phenomena. The Great Vehicle likewise characteristically involves **the arousing of** devoted and constant **diligence** throughout innumerable eons; **skill in** the **means** for avoiding the complete relinquishment of cyclic existence while still remaining free from thorough affliction; **great authentic accomplishment** of the powers, fearlessnesses, and unshared buddha qualities; **and the great buddha activity** that again and again displays manifest enlightenment and the transcendence of suffering. **As it possesses such greatness, it is definitively referred to as the "Great Vehicle."**

Next, there is a summary of the full significance of the Great Vehicle. Thus **there is:** possessing the **potential** of the Great Vehicle; **inspiration with respect to the Dharma** of the Great Vehicle; **engendering the mind** of supreme enlightenment; **practicing generosity and the rest** of the transcendences; **entering the flawless** first ground of the bodhisattvas; **thoroughly ripening sentient beings** through the eighth ground; **cultivating the fields** on the three grounds of irreversibility; accomplishing the **nonabiding transcendence of suffering** beyond dual extremes on those same grounds; manifesting **supreme enlightenment** on the ground of buddhahood; **and** revealing **the display** of the Dharma.

The next topic concerns the special qualities and summation of the Great Vehicle. Seven special features make the Great Vehicle superior to the Lesser Vehicle.

(1) Concerning the vast focal point of the Great Vehicle, listeners focus on the three vessels of their own Listeners' Vehicle. Bodhisattvas, on the other hand, observe the limitless Great Vehicle vessels of the profound and the vast.

(2) Moreover, their great practice is distinguished from that of the listeners, who accomplish merely their own benefit. The practice of the bodhisattvas benefits both themselves and others.

(3) With their great wakefulness, the bodhisattvas distinguish themselves from the listeners, who merely realize the absence of a personal self. The former realize the absence of self in terms of both persons and phenomena.

(4) While listeners muster diligence for a period of only three or seven lives, bodhisattvas practice with diligence throughout three incalculable eons. Hence they possess great diligence.

(5) Listeners fear cyclic existence and, therefore, pursue peace and happiness beyond cyclic existence. Hence, they lack the mastery of skillful means. With their compassion, bodhisattvas do not abandon cyclic existence. Yet, due to their insight, they nevertheless remain untainted by the afflictions. They are thus like lotus flowers growing from dirt and in this way they are masters of skillful means.

These five features distinguish the causal or path aspects of the vehicle that enable travel.

(6) Once the listeners have attained the foe destroyer's fruition, having gained simply the associated totalities, commands, and superknowledges, everything will come to exhaustion without any remainder of the aggregates. The bodhisattvas, on the other hand, accomplish the fruition of the Great Vehicle that involves the limitless and utterly inexhaustible qualities of the powers, fearlessnesses, and so forth. Such is their great authentic accomplishment.

(7) While listeners gain the level of a foe destroyer, they do not manifest complete enlightenment, and they do not turn the wheel of Dharma and so forth. When the bodhisattvas have gained complete buddhahood, they will take up residence in the palace of the Unexcelled Realm, enter into the womb, gain complete enlightenment, and so forth. Since in this way they will display activity for as long as there are sentient beings, their buddha activity is great. These latter two principles distinguish the qualities of the vehicle of fruition within which they travel. Thus, as it is endowed with this sevenfold greatness, it is definitively referred to as the "Great Vehicle."

Next follows a summary of the Great Vehicle. The teaching of the sūtras of the Great Vehicle, such as the *Transcendent Insight in One Hundred Thousand Lines* and the *Great Ornament of the Buddhas,* is infinite. Nevertheless, there are eight (or ten) principles that characterize their limitless subject matter as "the Great Vehicle." These principles are as follows: (1) the existence of the potential or element of the Great Vehicle, (2) inspiration with respect to the Dharma of the Great Vehicle based on the presence of this potential, (3) engendering the mind of unsurpassable enlightenment due to the power of inspiration. These three factors pertain to the occasion of remaining with the potential. (4) Once the enlightened mind has been brought forth in this way, one practices generosity and the rest of the six transcendences on the grounds of imaginative conduct. (5) When, from there, one advances to the first ground and experiences the wakefulness beyond apprehended and apprehender, one gains entry into the flawless supramundane grounds of the noble ones. (6) From the second to the seventh ground, one employs the Dharma of the factors of enlightenment and the transcendences in order to elicit faith in sentient beings who lack it and to ripen the virtues of those who already possess it. (7) On the three pure grounds, one accomplishes the purity of the world vessel and its inhabitants and so cultivates the buddha fields. Due to insight, one does not remain in cyclic existence. Because of compassion, one does not dwell in peace. Thus, one practices the nonabiding transcendence of suffering within the realization of the equality of existence and peace. (8) Having gone beyond the ten grounds, one attains the three exalted bodies upon the ground of buddhahood. Having thus attained supreme enlightenment, one will reveal the display of buddha activities, including the manifestation of complete enlightenment. Thus, eight principles are enumerated. Yet since the last two of these eight can each be seen to involve two principles, the above can also be enumerated as ten principles.

2. The Qualities in Combination with Praise

Having in this way explained the seventeen principles of the qualities of the bodhisattvas' practice—from the wondrous qualities through the presentation of the Dharma—the bodhisattvas' qualities will next be explained, along with praise. This will involve (1) a presentation of the types of bodhisattvas—the objects of praise—and (2) the actual praises.

1. Types of Bodhisattvas

Some possess inspiration,
Others superior pure intent.
Some engage with marks, some with absence of marks,
And some with nonformation.
These five are understood to be
The bodhisattvas of all the stages. [xx.63]

On the categories of bodhisattvas, it is explained as follows. **Some,** meaning those who are on the paths of accumulation and joining, **possess inspiration. Others** who are on the first ground are endowed with **superior pure intent. Some,** who are abiding on the second up to and including the sixth ground, **engage with marks. Some,** meaning those who are abiding on the seventh ground, engage **with** the **absence of marks. And some,** who are on the grounds above the seventh, engage **with nonformation. The five are understood to be the bodhisattvas of all the stages,** from that of devoted application through to the tenth ground.

Those on the eleven grounds—the ten grounds plus the grounds of imaginative conduct—are all referred to as "bodhisattvas." By considering their various contexts, these bodhisattvas may be considered to be of five kinds.

(1) Those on the grounds of imaginative conduct have not gained direct perception of the universally present characteristics of the basic field of phenomena. Nevertheless, because they have faith and trust in the basic field of phenomena, they are classified as those who possess inspiration.

(2) The bodhisattvas who have entered the first ground are known as those with superior pure intention. Having realized the universally present characteristics of the basic field of phenomena, they have attained

the mind of equality with respect to self and others. They therefore abide by the superior pure intent, whereby one shoulders the burden of accomplishing the welfare of others. They have also attained the purification of the obscurations that are to be eliminated through seeing.

(3) Bodhisattvas from the second to the sixth ground are those who engage with marks. On the second ground, they engage with the marks of discerning the various vehicles of listeners, self-realized buddhas, and bodhisattvas. Next, on the third, they engage with the marks of the innate view of the transient collection. On the fourth ground, they perceive the marks of the truths of suffering and its origin as harmful, whereas the truths of cessation and the path are seen as peaceful. On the fifth ground, they pursue various arts and crafts, conceiving of their marks, and on the sixth ground, they conceive of the marks of the evolving and the reversal of dependent origination.

(4) Bodhisattvas on the seventh ground are known as those who are free from marks because at this point they have relinquished all the marks that occurred on the grounds below.

(5) On the eighth ground of irreversibility, as well as on the ninth and tenth ground, they are referred to as bodhisattvas who engage with nonformation because on these grounds they accomplish their objectives and that of all others by means of their effortless and spontaneously present meditative absorption of nonconceptuality.

Thus, it can be understood that these five contexts provide the distinctive qualities of the bodhisattvas who dwell on all the grounds.

2. Praise to the Bodhisattvas

This section contains praises that play on the meaning of the term "bodhisattva." These stanzas contain praises of (1) the bodhisattvas' indomitable courage as they practice the causal transcendences and (2) their resultant realization of enlightenment. The first of these sections presents praises in terms of (1) the nine principles that begin with the joy of enlightenment and (2) the epithets of the bodhisattvas.

1. The Nine Principles

Free from attachment to pleasures, pure in the three activities,
Subduing anger, appropriating supreme qualities,
Not moving away from the Dharma, seeing the profound reality,
And endowed with the joy of enlightenment—such are bodhisattvas. [xx.64]

Wishing to benefit, not wanting to harm,
Happily accepting harm from others,
Steadfast, heedful, possessing vast learning,
And pursuing the welfare of others—such are bodhisattvas. [xx.65]

Aware of the flaws of possessions,
Not attached to enjoyments, never holding a grudge,
Expert about the marks of spiritual practice, free from negative views,
And thoroughly abiding within—such are bodhisattvas. [xx.66]

Loving and conscientious,
Accepting suffering, not attached to their own happiness,
Relying on mindfulness as the primary, of the nature of utter equipoise,
And unshakable regarding the vehicles—such are bodhisattvas. [xx.67]

The dispeller of suffering, not the creator of suffering,
Tolerating suffering, fearless about suffering,
Free from suffering, not conceiving of suffering,
And acknowledging suffering—such are bodhisattvas. [xx.68]

Displeased with phenomena, delighting in natural phenomena,
Scorning phenomena, persisting with phenomena,

Mastering phenomena, being unobscured about phenomena,
And relying on phenomena—such are bodhisattvas. [xx.69]

Heedful about possessions, heedful about the definitive,
Heedful about protecting, heedful about virtue,
Heedful about bliss, heedful about the Dharma,
And heedful about vehicles—such are bodhisattvas. [xx.70]

Shamed by disrespect, shamed by minor faults,
Shamed by impatience, shamed by decline,
Shamed by diffusing, shamed by a lesser view,
And shamed by other vehicles—such are bodhisattvas. [xx.71]

Here and beyond, equanimity,
Engagement in formation, possession of mastery,
Appropriate teaching, and the great fruition—
By these means the bodhisattvas serve. [xx.72]

Their generosity is **free from attachment to pleasures**. Their discipline is **pure in the three activities** of body, speech, and mind. With their patience, they practice the **subduing** of anger. With their diligence, they are engaged in **appropriating supreme qualities**. With their concentration, there is **not** any **moving away from** the **Dharma** that is the focal point. They give rise to the insight of **seeing the profound reality**, and their aspiration is based on being **endowed with the joy of enlightenment**. Such are bodhisattvas.

Wishing to benefit others without any concern for their own body and life, **not wanting to harm, happily accepting harm from others, steadfast**ly undaunted in the face of suffering, **heedful** so as to be constantly free from attachment to the bliss of concentration, **possessing vast learning** with respect to the corpus of teaching, **and pursuing the welfare of others**—such are bodhisattvas.

Aware of the flaws of material **possessions; not attached to enjoyments,** having abandoned attachment; emerging as a practitioner; **never holding a grudge** because of having been made to suffer; **expert about the marks of** the **spiritual** meditation practice of calm abiding, thoroughly upholding, and equanimity; **free from negative views; and thoroughly abiding within** the teaching of the sūtras of the Great Vehicle—**such are bodhisattvas.**

Loving and conscientious, accepting all **suffering, not attached to their own happiness, relying on mindfulness as the primary** so as to abide in equipoise, being **of the nature of utter equipoise** within nonconceptual wakefulness, **and unshakable regarding the vehicles** of others—**such are bodhisattvas.**

Exerting themselves as **the dispeller of** the **suffering** of others, **not** acting as **the creator of suffering** for others, **tolerating** any amount of **suffering** for themselves, **fearless about suffering** when pursuing the happiness of others, **free from suffering** because of being free from the desire for pleasures, **not conceiving** of the three spheres **of suffering, and acknowledging** the **suffering** of cyclic existence without rejecting it—**such are bodhisattvas.**

Displeased with the **phenomena** of miserliness, abiding in the discipline of **delighting in natural phenomena, scorning** the **phenomena** of anger, **persisting with** the **phenomena** of virtue, **mastering** the **phenomena** of equilibrium, **being unobscured** and free from ignorance **about phenomena, and** joyfully adhering to and **relying on** the **phenomena** of supreme enlightenment—**such are bodhisattvas.**

Heedful about possessions, they train in generosity. **Heedful about the definitive** points of training, they pursue those. They are **heedful about protecting** their own minds and the minds of others from anger. **Heedful about** the practices of **virtue; heedful about** the **bliss** of concentration; **heedful about the Dharma** of knowledge in complete accordance with reality; **and heedful about** other **vehicles,** so as to not enter them—**such are bodhisattvas.**

Bodhisattvas are **shamed by** any **disrespectful** disparagement of those who make a request, they are **shamed by** even **minor faults, shamed by impatience, shamed by** a **decline** in their practice, **shamed by** the mind **diffusing** toward objects, **shamed by a lesser view** that fails to realize the absence of self in phenomena, **and shamed by** an entry into **other vehicles**—**such are bodhisattvas.**

All these verses provide different sorts of characteristics of bodhisattvas with reference to their practice of the six transcendences and their aspiration toward great enlightenment.

Being generous, bodhisattvas benefit others **here** in this life **and**, through discipline, their help extends **beyond** this life and accomplishes birth in the higher realms. With patience, beings come to rest in **equanimity**; diligence brings **engagement in** the **formation** of factors that assist others in virtue; through concentration comes the **possession of mastery** of miracles and so forth; insight yields the **appropriate teaching** of the absence of self with regard to all phenomena; **and,** upon the attainment of buddhahood, they benefit others through **the great fruition. By these means the bodhisattvas bring benefit.**

Without attachment to the pleasures of the five senses, the bodhisattvas practice transcendent generosity by completely relinquishing all outer and inner entities. Their discipline is pure because their activities of body, speech, and mind are free from nonvirtue. By being patient, they subdue anger. With diligence they appropriate supreme qualities. Through one-pointed concentration, they do not move away from the Dharma. With insight they see the profound reality that is devoid of the two selves. Thus, taking delight in the attainment of the resulting great enlightenment, the bodhisattvas practice the six transcendences for the sake of, and with dedication to, this attainment. Hence, they are known as "bodhisattvas endowed with the joy of enlightenment," and thus the present stanza is a praise of the qualities of the pure transcendences.

Similarly, bodhisattvas wish to benefit sentient beings with their generosity. By being disciplined, they want to avoid even the slightest harm to the lives and possessions of others, just as they are anxious to refrain from deceiving others by not being truthful, or in any other way harming others by means of their three gateways. With patience they gladly accept harm from the side of others, and through diligence they do not turn back but remain steadfast in their joyous persistence. Remaining in solitude, free from either distractions or attachments to the flavor of concentration, they carefully accomplish concentration. With insights of vast learning, they diligently pursue the welfare of other sentient beings. In every context of their practice of the transcendences, therefore, they benefit sentient beings, while at the same time dedicating their practice to the final accomplishment of unsurpassable enlightenment for the benefit of all sentient beings. This praise to the bodhisattvas thus specifically considers the way in which they benefit others.

The bodhisattvas are aware of the flaws of holding on to possessions. They know that possessions are pointless, impermanent, painful, and illusory. They are aware that attachment to them leads to life in the lower realms and that such attachment is a hindrance for the attainment of both mundane and supramundane perfections. Aware of all such flaws, the bodhisattvas practice generosity. Without any attachment to possessions and enjoyments, they relinquish their household so as to emerge definitively. Abiding by spiritual discipline, and without harboring any grudge, they remain patient when others harm them. They diligently engage in the spiritual practice of calm abiding and special insight, according to the Great Vehicle. Thus, whenever they practice one-pointed meditative absorption, they are expert in the application of the triple marks of calm abiding, uplifting (which is also known as thoroughly upholding), and equanimity. Through their insight, free from the view of the self and other negative views, they remain in the foremost inner rest. In this way, the bodhisattvas are praised with reference to their ability to dwell thoroughly in the genuine, inner rest.

The bodhisattvas lovingly extend their generosity to suffering sentient beings, while with conscientiousness they abide by spiritual discipline. Their patience allows them to happily take on suffering, as when others harm them, for example, and without any attachment to sleep, idleness, or other selfish pleasures, they diligently work for the welfare of others. Constantly relying on mindfulness as the primary factor, they do not fall under the power of distractions, and as they are always endowed with insight into the equality of all phenomena, free from the extremes of existence and nonexistence, they remain in the nature of utter equipoise. Thus, the minds of the bodhisattvas will not be carried away from the Great Vehicle, and so this praise concerns their qualities in terms of being unshakable on the path of the Great Vehicle. We may note that Sthiramati's commentary sees these stanzas as structured so that in each stanza the first three lines concern the practice of the six transcendences, while the fourth line explains the dedication to unsurpassable enlightenment.

With generosity, they dispel the suffering of others. Through discipline they refrain from killing, stealing, and other such acts that make sentient beings suffer. They patiently tolerate their own suffering, while for the benefit of others they enter cyclic existence, working for the welfare of others with fearless diligence. Having gained the meditative absorption of concentration, they are free from the suffering of the desire realm and free from mental displeasure, while due to their insight, they do not conceive of any marks of suffering. Such are the bodhisattvas who acknowledge and accept suffering. This praise thus considers how the bodhisattvas do not abandon the suffering of cyclic existence, and how they do not become weary of it.

The bodhisattvas are displeased with the phenomena of miserliness, yet they delight in the flawless and natural qualities that constitute the phenomena of discipline. Scorning the phenomena of anger, they diligently engage with the phenomena of virtue. By the power of the meditative absorption that masters phenomena, they gain mastery of the mind. Free from all darkness that obscures phenomena, they are endowed with insight. Such are the bodhisattvas, as they rely on the phenomena of the genuine. In this way, this praise shows how the bodhisattvas do not consider material things to be of primary concern, and how they instead rely on the sacred Dharma.

Having possessions without giving them to others and seeking instead to accumulate and protect them is to be heedless about one's possessions, because in the end they will be exhausted. Therefore, giving them to others, thereby making sure that they serve a good purpose, is to be heedful about one's possessions. Failing to be on guard against associated and natural evils is to be heedless about them. Therefore, to ensure through discipline that one's three gateways are subdued and free from the flaws of associated or natural evils is to be heedful of subduing. (Some editions here read "heedful about the definitive," yet it is better to follow the translation contained in Sthiramati's commentary, which instead reads "heedful about subduing." There are also texts that here read "heedful about the sides," yet that is simply a typographical error.)

Failing to tolerate harm from others and instead seeking to retaliate is to be heedless, because in this way one fails to guard both one's own mind and the minds of others. Bodhisattvas do not become agitated when hurt by others, and instead of retaliating they will do good to those who harm them. Thus they are heedful, protecting their own minds and those of others through patience. One is heedless if, due to laziness, one fails to accomplish virtuous qualities. Heedfulness in terms of diligence means to ensure that one does not, due to laziness, fail to practice what is virtuous and that one instead practices mundane and supramundane virtues. Heedfulness with respect to bliss means to be free from craving for the taste of attaining the bliss of concentration. It is heedless to conceive of phenomena while believing them to be delightful, having a self, and not being empty. Being heedful in terms of insight is, on the other hand, to realize that phenomena are impermanent and so forth. This is the way that the bodhisattvas pay heed, correctly directing their minds to the Great Vehicle. Thus the present verses praise their qualities in terms of heedfully practicing the six transcendences.

It is shameful if when somebody makes a request, one does not respond by giving, or one gives but disrespectfully, showing a displeased expression or scolding the supplicant. Even the mundane world considers it shameful if a wealthy person entirely refuses to give and instead scolds those who are in need. Bodhisattvas have, for their part, taken the vow to give everything to others, with compassion. Therefore, if a beggar appears, it would not be becoming for a bodhisattva to be displeased and decline the request. To do so would be shameful. Moreover, since bodhisattvas fearfully shun even minor associated or natural evils, sustaining even a minor such flaw would be shameful. For bodhisattvas who practice tolerating harm and suffering, to become impatient with a harm doer, ending up agitated, would be shameful. Bodhisattvas arouse vast and continuous diligence. Hence, if their practice of virtue should decline due to laziness, that would be shameful. Bodhisattvas accomplish the mastery of mind that involves limitless equilibriums and meditative absorptions. Therefore, it would be shameful for them to remain absorbed in physical business while the mind diffuses and is distracted toward outer objects. Finally, bodhisattvas are insightful by nature; they possess the insight that realizes the twofold absence of self, just as taught in the Great Vehicle. If they were to have a lesser view that sees only the absence of a personal self, or if they were not free from the views that perceive marks of phenomena, that would be shameful. Therefore, considering it shameful to do so, the bodhisattvas do not enter or practice other vehicles, meaning the vehicles of listeners and self-realized buddhas. Thus, this stanza praises the bodhisattvas for not wishing for any other vehicle.

All these ways of practicing the six transcendences are primarily undertaken for the benefit of others. Hence, all of these praises can be seen as highlighting the qualities of the bodhisattvas as they practice to benefit others. With their generosity, the bodhisattvas benefit the destitute in this life, providing them with enjoyable things. Their practice of generosity and so on also serves to gather beings around them so that they can be established in discipline. Thus, their practice also benefits sentient beings in a way that extends beyond the present world. When, through patience, the mind stream of the bodhisattvas does not become upset, and when consequently the bodhisattva does not retaliate but rests in equanimity, then that also benefits others. With diligence the bodhisattvas assist others in virtue, or engage in its formation, while through concentration they benefit others with their attainment of the mastery of the qualities associated with superknowledges and so forth. Finally, by means of their insight, they teach the five fields of knowledge—in particular that of the inner meaning as taught in the three vehicles—in a way that is perfectly adjusted to the inclinations of the students. As the result of their practices of the transcendences, the bodhisattvas attain the great fruition of buddhahood, thereby benefiting sentient beings throughout space. They are thus engaged in benefiting all beings in terms of both the cause and effect of doing so. (We may note that in Sthiramati's commentary, this last stanza is seen as a concluding summary.)

2. The Epithets of the Bodhisattvas

They are bodhisattvas, great beings,
The wise, supremely clear,
Children of the victorious ones, ground of the victorious ones,
Conquerors, shoots of the victorious ones, [XX.73]

Powerful ones, supremely noble ones,
Captains, supremely renowned ones,
Compassionate ones, greatly meritorious ones,
Masters, and possessors of Dharma. [xx.74]

There are sixteen synonyms of "bodhisattva." Because of their constant focus on enlightenment and sentient beings they are called **"bodhisattvas,"** and since they are endowed with the sevenfold greatness, they are referred to as **"great beings."** They are **"the wise"** because of their realization of the profound and vast meanings. They are **"supremely clear"** since they realize the nature of the objects without error. They are **"children of the victorious ones"** because they are the offspring of the latter. They are the **"ground of the victorious ones"** in consideration of their perfect insight. They are **"conquerors"** because they have the power to crush the conflicting factors. They are the **"shoots of the victorious ones"** due to their great compassion. They are the **"powerful ones"** since they can destroy the power of the demons. They are **"supremely noble ones"** because of their excellent realizations. They are **"captains"** because they lead wandering beings. They are **"supremely renowned ones"** due to their fame. They are **"compassionate ones"** because they are governed by compassion. They are **"greatly meritorious ones"** since they have gathered the two accumulations in abundance. They are **"masters"** as they master excellent qualities, **and** they are **"possessors of Dharma"** because they have given up doing what is not of the Dharma.

The epithets of the bodhisattvas are given with reference to their qualities, and since the epithets in this way are descriptive of the nature of the bodhisattvas, they also serve as an enumeration of the bodhisattvas' qualities. Beginning with the name "bodhisattva" itself, there are sixteen such epithets that are commonly applicable to all bodhisattvas.

(1–2) They are known as "bodhisattvas" because they have one-pointed faith in the profound issue that is to be comprehended, that is, the nature of the twofold absence of self. Alternatively, "bodhisattva" can also be understood in terms of their steadfast concern for the accomplishment of unsurpassable enlightenment. On the other hand, they are called "great beings" because they master great powers. Thus, they may, for example, be capable of revealing the stages of formation and disintegration that pertain to a billionfold universe within a single hair follicle of their body. Alternatively, we may say that, while "bodhisattva" indicates their wish to attain unsurpassable enlightenment, "great being" shows their intent to deliver all sentient beings from the suffering of cyclic existence and establish them in the transcendence of suffering. Or again, they are called "bodhisattvas" because they are not tainted by any of the flaws of cyclic existence, and they are "great beings" because their great compassion causes them to arouse infinite diligence for the benefit of sentient beings. Or yet again, they are "bodhisattvas" because, in practicing to accomplish unsurpassable enlightenment, they give rise to the enlightened mind, and they are "great beings" because they are endowed with the sevenfold greatness that was explained earlier. In this way, the names "bodhisattva" and "great being" are simply different conceptual distinctions that apply to the same individuals, and so both are equally applicable to all bodhisattvas.

It is also possible to use the term "bodhisattva" to refer to someone on a given ground and then, correspondingly, to characterize those who have attained a higher ground than this as "great beings." Similarly, those who have given rise to the enlightened mind in terms of inspired conduct may be called "bodhisattvas," whereas the noble ones who have attained the grounds may be referred to as "great bodhisattvas." Or, those on the seven impure grounds may be termed "bodhisattvas," while those on the pure grounds are seen as "great beings." Whatever the case may be, the term "bodhisattva" refers to someone who practices the challenging causes of unsurpassable enlightenment, the transcendences, in an infinite way, and who accomplishes the challenging fruition, unsurpassable enlightenment, with an undaunted fortitude of mind.

(3) Because the bodhisattvas have insight into the profound and the vast, they are also known as "the wise." (4) Because they explain the import of the profound intent while spreading the light of Dharma in the ten directions, they are referred to as the "supremely clear" or "supremely splendid." (5) Since they uphold the unbroken lineage of the

thus-gone ones and are born into the family of the buddhas, they are the "children of the victorious ones." (6) Because they are the cause of buddhahood, they are the "ground of the victorious ones." (7) Since they conquer the afflictions within their own streams of being and that of others, they are known as "conquerors." (8) Because they are the cause, as it were, of the leaves, flowers, and fruits of buddha qualities—such as the three bodies, the powers, and the fearlessnesses—they are referred to as the "shoots of the victorious ones." (9) Likewise, the bodhisattvas are capable of taming the demons and moving beyond the ground of ignorant habitual tendencies. For this reason they are known as "powerful ones," strong and unparalleled heroes. (10) Because they are the greatest wonder in the world, they are referred to as "supremely noble ones." (11) They are called "captains" because they lead wandering beings, who are otherwise confined to the ocean of cyclic existence, toward the city of the transcendence of suffering. (12) They are also referred to as "the ones of great fame," or "the supremely renowned ones" because the renown of their qualities spreads throughout the worlds in the ten directions. (13) Because they possess great compassion that never lets any sentient being down, they are known as "the compassionate ones." (14) Since they possess infinite fundamental virtues, they are "greatly meritorious ones." (15) Because they master all mundane and supramundane excellences, they are "lords." (16) Because they are endowed with undefiled qualities free from any evil, they are known as the "possessors of Dharma." Thus, as illustrated by these sixteen renowned primary epithets, the bodhisattvas are known by numerous names, such as "the fearless ones," "the heroes," "the steadfast," and "the supreme among sentient beings."

2. The Resultant Realization of Enlightenment

Next, in line with the explanation of the meaning of the term "bodhisattva," as understood with respect to both the cause and the resultant realization of enlightenment, we will consider (1) the actual praised qualities and (2) the divisions that pertain to these qualities.

1. The Actual Qualities of Realization

Excellent realization of reality, proper realization of the great
    aim,
Universal realization, constant realization,
And realization of the means—
For these special reasons, they are known as "bodhisattvas."
    [xx.75]

Realizing the self, realizing the subtle view,
Realizing variegated awareness,
And realizing that all is the false imagination—
Because of such realization, they are known as "bodhisattvas."
    [xx.76]

Realizing the unrealized, realizing the subsequent realization,
Realizing the absence of entities, realizing emergence,
And realizing the lack of realization—
Because of such discriminating realization, they are known as
    "bodhisattvas." [xx.77]

Realizing the lack of reality, realizing ultimate reality,
Realizing all reality, and realizing the entire reality;
Realizing the object of realization, the basis of realization, and
    the realization—
Because of such realization, they are known as "bodhisattvas."
    [xx.78]

Realizing the accomplishment, realizing the abode,
Realizing the womb, realizing the stages,
Realizing thorough realization and the dispelling of doubts—
Because of such realization, they are known as
    "bodhisattvas."[xx.79]

They are also referred to as "bodhisattvas" in consideration of five factors that distinguish their realization. **Excellent realization of** reality, which is devoid of a self in the form of persons or phenomena; **proper realization of the great aim** for both oneself and others; **universal realization** of all objects of knowledge; **constant realization** free from exhaustion even when the complete transcendence of suffering is displayed; **and realization of the means** for training those to be trained—**for these special reasons they are known as "bodhisattvas."**

Realizing the all-ground that is the basis for the defiled mental cognition's apprehending of a **self; realizing the subtle view** of self, the defiled mental cognition; **realizing** the **variegated awareness** of the six collections of consciousness; **and realizing that all** of the former **is the false imagination**—it is **because** they are in possession **of such realization** that **they are known as "bodhisattvas."**

Realizing the unrealized, that is, ignorance; **realizing the subsequent realization,** that is, the remedy of the former by means of aware wakefulness; **realizing the absence of** the **entities** imagined by way of the imputed nature; **realizing** the **emergence** of the dependent nature; **and realizing,** in terms of the thoroughly established nature, **the lack of realization** of the intrinsic nature as it follows from the dualistic view of apprehended and apprehender—it is **because** they are in possession **of such discriminating realization** that **they are known as "bodhisattvas."**

Realizing, despite their appearance as two, **the lack of reality** of the duality of apprehended and apprehender; **realizing** the **ultimate reality** of the thoroughly established nature; **realizing all** that is of the nature of the imagined **reality** of the apprehended and the apprehender; **and realizing the entire reality** of all objects of knowledge; **realizing the object of realization, the** sense faculty that is the **basis of realization, and the** consciousness of **realization**—it is **because** they are in possession **of such realization** that **they are known as "bodhisattvas."**

Realizing the accomplishment of a buddha's enlightenment; **realizing the abode** of residence, The Joyful Realm; **realizing** the way of entry into **the womb; realizing the stages** of taking birth and so forth; **realizing** the turning of the Dharma wheel, which is the means for **thorough realization** in others **and the dispelling**

of their **doubts**—it is **because** they are in possession **of such realization** that **they are known as "bodhisattvas."**

The bodhisattvas' realization is (1) an excellent realization of reality because they recognize the absence of self in terms of phenomena and persons. It is also (2) the proper realization of the great aim because their realization accomplishes their objectives and that of others. It is (3) a universal realization, for it encompasses all objects of knowledge, whether they be conditioned or unconditioned, defiled or undefiled. (4) Their realization is not just present for a while, only to disintegrate later. Rather, the bodhisattvas' wakefulness is active even within the field that contains no remainder of the aggregates. It is, therefore, a realization that is constant throughout time. (5) It is a realization that recognizes all the infinite means for taming beings. Thus the bodhisattvas are aware of which emanation and which Dharma teaching will be effective in terms of taming a given sentient being. The bodhisattvas are known as such because of their possession of these five special qualities. The word *bodhi* means comprehension and *sattva*[56] refers to the sentient. Hence, these praises explain the etymology of the term *bodhisattva* by showing, in general, what it is that the bodhisattvas are sentient of and what it is that they comprehend.

Four aspects of their realization are also explained.

(1) Within the triad of mind, mental cognition, and consciousness, "mind" refers to the all-ground consciousness that is composed of seeds. All the appearances of environment, objects, and bodies manifest from this, and the bodhisattvas' knowledge or realization of that consciousness is known as the "realization of the self." The term "self" does not capture anything beyond the continuum of momentary all-ground consciousness, which emerges as a stream of being. It is this consciousness that serves as the focal point of the introverted defiled mental cognition, as it takes that focal point to be a self.

(2) "Mental cognition" refers in this context to the defiled mental cognition, which observes the all-ground consciousness and thereby gives rise to the thought of "myself." It is accompanied by the five ever-present mental states, along with the view of self, the attachment to self, the bewilderment of self, and the pride of self. Present throughout all occasions

of virtuous, unvirtuous, and neutral mind, it is of an nonobscuring and indeterminate nature. The exact realization of this defiled mental cognition is referred to as the realization of the subtle view because the subtle root of the view of the transient collection, which is the cause of all negative views and afflictions, is found in this mental cognition.

(3) "Realizing the variegated awareness" refers to the knowledge of the nature of the six collections of consciousness. This is the knowledge of the six forms of consciousness (from that of the eye through to the mental consciousness) that emerge based on object, faculty, and the directing of the mind. These six are concerned with their individual spheres of objects, such as forms, and are accompanied by mental states. As such, they may be virtuous, unvirtuous, or neutral, just as they may involve all sorts of sensations. The knowledge of this is known as the realization of the variegated awareness.

(4) It thus becomes clear that all eight collections of consciousness are involved in the conception of apprehended and apprehender, whereas in fact no such duality exists. Hence, all of this is simply the false imagination, the dependent nature. The bodhisattvas are referred to as such because they realize, in the four ways just described, how all eight collections of consciousness are like an illusion or a dream. Thus, this account describes the bodhisattvas' realization of the way conventional reality appears.

Moreover, bodhisattvas are known by that name because of their realization of the following five issues that are relevant to the realization of the two truths.

(1) A bodhisattva realizes that which was not realized previously, while still a mundane being. This realization, which takes place by means of space-like nonconceptual wakefulness free from focal point, is known as "realizing the unrealized." On the other hand, (2) the bodhisattvas realize that all phenomena are like illusions and so forth, by means of the subsequently attained wakefulness that is their "realizing the subsequent realization." Alternatively, (1) "realizing the unrealized" can be understood as the bodhisattvas' realization of the evolving of ignorance and so forth. In that case, (2) "realizing the subsequent realization" will refer to their realization of the reversal of the links of dependent origination, as the cessation of ignorance brings the cessation of formation, and so forth.

Moreover, (3) when bodhisattvas realize that actual entities are nonexistent and imaginary, that is known as realizing the absence of entities, and (4) when they comprehend that all appearances of apprehended and an apprehender emerge due to the momentary dependent nature, that is known as realizing emergence. Finally, (5) the bodhisattvas' realization of that which remains unknown to ordinary, childish beings—that is, the thoroughly established intrinsic nature that is devoid of duality—is their realizing the lack of knowledge and lack of realization.

There is a further set of five principles that pertains to the realization of the two truths. (1) All appearances of apprehended and apprehender emerge from the dependent consciousness. When there is attachment to these appearances, there will be a continuous experience of suffering. The bodhisattvas, however, realize that the apprehended and the apprehender have no reality. This is their realization of the lack of reality. (2) Moreover, when they realize the thoroughly established nature free from duality that is realizing the ultimate reality, and (3) when they comprehend that all appearances of duality are merely imaginary, that is realizing all of the reality of the appearances of the apprehended and the apprehender. (4) The bodhisattvas' total realization of the multiplicity of phenomena—such as aggregates, elements, and sense sources—is their realization of the relative, and (5) their realization that is free from any observation of the three spheres—in terms of the object, basis (or agent) and act of realization—is their realization of the ultimate. Bodhisattvas are known by that name because they realize, in these five ways, the three natures and the two truths.

The following five principles serve as reasons that the bodhisattvas receive their name. (1) The bodhisattvas' realization of the accomplishment of unsurpassable enlightenment refers to their realization of the actualization of the three exalted bodies in the Great Unexcelled Realm. (2) Their realization of the abode is their understanding of the way of remaining in the Joyful Realm as a bodhisattva in one's final existence, while thus benefiting the gods. (3) The bodhisattvas' realization of the womb refers to their knowledge of entry into a mother's womb in Jambudvīpa, thus benefiting the sentient beings there. (4) Their realizing the stages concerns their knowledge of emerging from the womb, enjoying the pleasures of the five senses among the palace retinue, leaving in secrecy to take ordination, undergoing austerities, and demonstrating enlightenment at the vajra seat by means of the emanation body. (5) Realizing the turning of the Dharma wheel refers to their dispelling the doubts of all sentient beings subsequent to their attainment of enlightenment. These five realizations are reasons that the bodhisattvas are referred to as such. They are enumerated with reference to the bodhisattva in his or her final existence—aware of the way to actualize great enlightenment in the Unexcelled Realm, based on the enjoyment body, and aware of the way to subsequently demonstrate the way of great enlightenment in Jambudvīpa, through the emanation body.

2. The Division of the Qualities of Realization

> The wise possess a mind of the attained, unattained, and
>   thoroughly abiding,
> Realization and subsequent realization,
> Discriminating discernment and ineffability, where "I" is
>   destroyed and "I" is involved,
> Intelligence that is immature and truly mature. [xx.80]

With respect to their realization, **the wise possess,** in terms of time, **a mind of the attained** past, **unattained** future, **and thoroughly abiding** present. Considered in terms of the inner and outer, there is, respectively, **realization** by oneself **and subsequent realization** due to others. Concerning the coarse and the subtle, there is **discriminating discernment,** which is realization through receiving teaching and reflecting, **and** there is the **ineffability** of realization arising from meditation. Distinguished in terms of the inferior and supreme, there is realization **where the "I" is destroyed** from the eighth ground onward, **and** realization where the "I" **is involved** on the seven lower grounds. Finally, when considered from the perspective of the distant and the close, they possess **intelligence that is immature** on the first nine grounds **and truly mature** on the tenth.

This was the twentieth chapter of the *Ornament of the Great Vehicle Sūtras,* the chapter on the qualities.

Next, the bodhisattvas are presented in terms of their eleven forms of knowledge. The bodhisattvas are referred to as such due to their knowledge and realization of the following eleven principles: (1–3) the three times, (4–5) the inner and outer, (6–7) the coarse and the subtle, (8–9) the inferior and the excellent, and (10–11) the close and the distant.

(1) The wise bodhisattvas' knowledge of past phenomena is referred to as "knowledge of the attained" or "knowledge of the acquired" because the phenomena of the past have already attained their own individual essences. (2) Realization of the phenomena that are to come into being in the future, on the other hand, is called "knowledge of the unattained" because such phenomena have not yet been attained in the present, or become established in terms of their individual entities. (3) Realization of present phenomena is knowledge of the "thoroughly abiding" because such phenomena have occurred and not yet ceased.

(4) When the bodhisattvas with their own minds realize impermanence, suffering, and so forth, then such internal cognition is an inner realization by their own wakefulness. (5) Conversely, when the teaching of an extraneous spiritual teacher serves as the cause of knowledge, this is subsequent realization due to external conditions. (6) The mind that discerns the particular and general characteristics of phenomena, through being based on words and phrases, is of a coarse nature, whereas (7) the mind that is settled ineffably within inner equipoise, free from thought, is serene.

(8) On the seventh ground and below, there is still an involvement with the subtle cause for grasping, namely, the "I." Hence, the "I" is involved in the intelligence that manifests at these stages, which in turn qualifies those stages as the ordinary and inferior path. (9) On the eighth ground and above, nonconceptual wakefulness is spontaneously present, and there is, therefore, not even the slightest cause for grasping in terms of an "I." This, then, is the excellent wakefulness within which the "I" has been destroyed. Alternatively, we may say that (8) on the stages of imaginative conduct, there is a realization where the "I" is involved because

on those stages, the thoughts of apprehended and apprehender have not yet been relinquished, whereas (9) it is on the grounds of the noble ones, which are free from the thoughts of apprehended and apprehender, that the "I" is destroyed.

(10) On the seventh ground and below, intelligence has not yet become mature because the effortless and spontaneously present nonconceptual wakefulness has still not been attained. This is also known as "the distant mind." (11) On the eighth ground and above, intelligence is referred to as "truly mature" because nonconceptual wakefulness is now spontaneously present without any need for effort. This is also described as "close intelligence" because it is near the attainment of the ground of buddhahood. Alternatively, (10) we may see the intelligence of the grounds of inspired conduct as immature and (11) that of the noble grounds as mature.

This concludes the explanation of the twentieth chapter of the *Ornament of the Great Vehicle Sūtras,* the chapter on the qualities.

21

Activity and Perfection

6. Activity and Perfection

The present chapter on activity and perfection explains (1) the signs of a bodhisattva, (2) the way that bodhisattvas accept birth, (3) their attainment of the grounds, and (4) their perfect qualities as presented through praise.

1. The Signs of a Bodhisattva

> Love, pleasant speech,
> Steadfastness, openhandedness,
> And definitive explanation of the profound intent—
> These are signs of the wise. [XXI.1]
>
> In terms of embracing, achieving interest,
> Absence of weariness, and the twofold magnetizing,
> It should thus be known that, in relation to intent and
>   application,
> Five signs are differentiated. [XXI.2]

The discernment of the signs is as follows. **Love** that embraces sentient beings, **pleasant speech** so that sentient beings achieve interest in the teaching of the Buddha, **steadfastness** that prevents weariness in the face of demanding activities, **openhandedness** that delivers material things, **and**, in terms of the gift of Dharma, definitive explanation of the profound intent: these are signs of the wise.

In terms of **embracing** with love, **achieving interest** through pleasant speech, **absence of weariness** by means of steadfastness, **and the twofold magnetizing** through material things and the Dharma, **it should thus be known that, in relation to intent** (in the case of the first) **and application** (in the case of the other four), there are **five signs** that **are differentiated**.

Just like smoke is a sign of fire, there are five signs that accord with the practice of the six transcendences that manifest in all bodhisattvas. Based on these signs, an individual can accordingly be identified as a bodhisattva, and will henceforth be counted among them. These five are (1) the loving embrace of sentient beings, (2) pleasant speech in both matters of the world and the Dharma, (3) undaunted steadfastness that braves any amount of terror and suffering in the pursuit of the welfare of others, (4) unabashed openhandedness in the constant practice of generosity, and (5) definitive explanation of the intent of the scriptural teachings. These five are signs of a wise bodhisattva. Sentient beings are embraced with compassion, interest is achieved by means of pleasant speech, and steadfastness ensures that suffering does not cause weariness. Moreover, openhandedness and the explanation of the profound intent ensure that one gathers sentient beings by material means and by means of the Dharma. Thus, it should be understood that while the first of the five has to do with intent, the remaining four are aspects of the application. This is the way to understand the five signs.

(1) As regards the nature of compassion, this includes both intent and practice. The intent raises the mind above nonvirtue and directs it toward virtue with the wish to do well to others. It likewise involves the wish to establish beings in the happiness of the higher realms, having dispelled their suffering in the lower realms and so forth. The aspect of practice is based on the former intent to bring benefit and happiness. It consists of one's involvement in body, speech, and mind so as to benefit sentient beings and give them happiness. An individual who is in possession of such qualities is known as a "compassionate bodhisattva."

(2) The nature of pleasant speech involves two aspects because such speech may be employed in the contexts of mundane convention or the explanation of the Dharma. The former is itself twofold. For instance, speech that is universally appreciated involves making people happy by greeting them with a smile and inquiring about their well-being, while speech that is thoroughly appreciated involves making people happy by speaking in a way that will, for example, enable them to extend their bloodline, expand their circle of friends, increase their wealth, or enhance their harvests. With respect to the Dharma, pleasant speech is the explanation of the Dharma of the transcendences, factors of enlightenment, and so forth, in a way that brings sentient beings to the higher realms and liberation.

(3) Steadfastness is based on the powers of meditative absorption, diligence, and insight. It takes the form of a patience that is undaunted in the face of any amount of suffering and fear. Unperturbed and powerful, it will not retreat.

(4) Openhandedness involves vast generosity and a generosity free from affliction. The first of these involves giving away internal entities, such as one's own head or legs, and external entities that encompass even the enjoyments of the realm of the universal emperor. Hence, there is no need to mention that one will also be generous with other possessions. This way of giving is not meager, but vast. Generosity free from affliction means to avoid giving anything, such as poison or weapons, that will have a harmful effect in the present or the future. Rather, one gives away pure entities without stinginess or expectation of a reward.

(5) The nature of definitively explaining the intent is endowed with the four aspects of correct awareness. Thus, it involves correctly realizing the intent, concealed intent, and so forth, and the exact explanation of the profound meaning.

(1) The five fields of compassion are: those who suffer, those engaged in killing and other misdeeds, the careless, those who have assumed a wrong view, and those who have not relinquished latent affliction. Thus, these five fields include all sentient beings. (2) The five supports, or fields, of pleasant speech are: inquiring about people's well-being and other such speech that is thoroughly appreciated; speech that delights,

as one expresses oneself in a way that allows others to have more friends and enjoyments; reassuring speech, whereby one protects others from fear; timely speech, as one commits oneself to accomplishing the objectives and activities of others, even without being requested to do so; and the truly resolving speech that delivers the Dharma of the methods for attaining the higher realms and liberation.

(3) There are also five bases of steadfastness: the suffering of cyclic existence, the ingratitude of sentient beings, long durations of time, attacks from opponents, and the training in maintaining vast commitments. (4) Likewise, the five bases, or supports, for openhandedness are: vast giving (as explained above), unbiased giving, giving with respect, giving free from affliction, and giving without any expectation of reward or karmic ripening. Finally, (5) there are also five supports, or fields, of the definitive explanation of the intent. With respect to the profound appearance of the Thus-Gone One's sūtras that are endowed with emptiness, there is the evolving and reversal of dependent origination. In terms of the Vinaya, there is expertise with regard to the downfalls and the restoration of vows. There are the particular and general characteristics of phenomena; the discernment of the words and sentences, including their intent, as they appear in the sūtras; and the practice distinguishing and setting apart the words of the Dharma teachings.

(1) The effects of compassion are long life, absence of enemies, happy circumstances, and future birth in the higher realms. (2) As the effect of pleasant speech, one will give up the four verbal misdeeds. Thus, as one achieves pure speech throughout all lives, one's words will be worthy of recollection. (3) Steadfastness has the result that one will not fall back from the type of discipline that one has accepted. With patience, one will be able to exchange oneself with others, and over one's coming lives, the bodhisattva practices will be brought to irreversible perfection. (4) Openhandedness allows one to benefit others in this life. As a result, one will gain vast enjoyments in future lives and perfect the accumulations for enlightenment. (5) As regards the result of explaining the profound intent, one will, through teaching the three vessels, dispel the lack of understanding, the misunderstanding, and the doubts of others, and in future lives one will become an expert in the five fields of knowledge.

The sequence of these five signs is due to the fact that compassion serves as the cause of pleasant speech. When one speaks pleasantly out of compassion, one will not become depressed by the suffering of cyclic existence and will instead develop steadfastness. Thus one will bring beings to maturation as one gathers material things and explains the intent of the Dharma teachings. These five signs are included within the six transcendences as follows.

(1) Compassion is the trained state that is achieved through the four immeasurables and is based on the seed of the potential. Hence, compassion belongs to transcendent concentration. (2) Pleasant speech involves refraining from harsh words and such. In that regard, it is included in discipline. The aspect of speaking the words of the Dharma, however, belongs to insight. (3) Steadfastness is included in three of the transcendences, namely, transcendent diligence, patience, and insight, whereas (4) openhandedness belongs to transcendent generosity, and (5) the explanation of the profound intent is contained within transcendent concentration and insight. As for the functions of the five signs, these have already been explained in accord with the treatise's explicit teaching.

Thus, by possessing the first three of the five signs, one develops the final two in the form of a superior intent on behalf of sentient beings. As one thinks "I shall establish them in the transcendence of suffering with remainder," that is superior intent with respect to benefiting beings because this state of mind carries the benefit of freedom from the damages of affliction. While thinking "I shall establish them in the transcendence of suffering without remainder," that is superior intent with regard to happiness because such a mind is endowed with the happiness of freedom from birth, old age, and all other such forms of suffering. In this way, compassion and the rest of the five signs can be seen to be included within a superior intent of benefit and happiness. As for the divisions that are relevant with respect to such superior intent, these will be explained below, when in stanza 6, the root text speaks of the "impure, pure, and extremely pure." The functions of this superior intent will be taught in stanza 7.

2. The Bodhisattva's Acceptance of a Birth

Bodhisattvas will always
Become universal monarchs
And so as householders
Benefit sentient beings. [XXI.3]

On all the grounds, the wise
Obtain ordination by receiving it,
Just as they obtain it by the power of the intrinsic nature.
Moreover, they also display ordination. [XXI.4]

Those who are ordained
Possess limitless qualities;
Those who persevere in the vows are therefore
Superior to householder bodhisattvas. [XXI.5]

On all the grounds, the steadfast ones'
Wishes for beautiful results beyond,
Engagement with virtue within this life,
And the transcendence of suffering
Are impure, pure, and extremely pure.
This is the assertion regarding their intent for sentient beings.
 [XXI.6]

On all the grounds, the wise
Embrace beings by means of aspiration,
The mind of equality,
Being the ruler, and magnetizing a retinue. [XXI.7]

It is held that the wise
Will be born because of karmic action,
Yet also by the power of aspiration,
Meditative absorption, or mastery. [XXI.8]

In terms of the various supports, it is taught that **bodhisattvas will always become universal monarchs, and so as householders benefit sentient beings. On all the grounds, the wise obtain ordination by receiving it from the preceptor and the ritual master, just as they obtain it by the power of the intrinsic nature. Moreover, they also display ordination** by means of the emanation body.

Among bodhisattvas, **those who are ordained possess limitless qualities. Those who persevere in the vows are therefore superior to householder bodhisattvas.**

The bodhisattvas' superior intent is fivefold. That is to say, **on all the grounds, the steadfast ones'**, that is, the bodhisattvas', **wishes for** all sentient beings to enjoy **beautiful results beyond** is (1) superior intent in terms of happiness. Their wish for sentient beings' **engagement with virtue within this life** is (2) superior intent in terms of benefit; **and** when they wish that sentient beings achieve **the transcendence of suffering,** such wishes are of the nature of these two types of superior intent. In the case of bodhisattvas who have not yet entered the grounds, their wishes **are** (3) **impure;** for those who have entered the grounds they are (4) **pure; and** the wishes of bodhisattvas abiding on the grounds of irreversibility are (5) **extremely pure. This is the assertion regarding their superior intent for sentient beings.**

On all the grounds, the wise embrace sentient **beings.** This they do **by means of aspiration,** that is, the enlightened mind, and at the time of manifest realization, they embrace sentient beings by means of **the mind of** the **equality** of self and other. Having become universal emperors, they embrace sentient beings through **being their ruler, and,** having turned into spiritual masters of sentient beings, they embrace them by **magnetizing a retinue.**

It is held that when **the wise** accept rebirth, those among them who abide on the grounds of inspired conduct **will be born** in the desire realm **because of** their **karmic action**s. Yet there are **also** others, namely, those abiding on the grounds, who will be borne **by the power of** their **aspiration** to ripen sentient beings, because of their **meditative absorption** whereby they do not wish for rebirth in the higher realms, **or because of their mastery** of emanations, which allows them to take birth in the Joyful Realm and elsewhere.

Next follows the explanation of the way the bodhisattvas continue to take birth. The superior intent of the bodhisattvas is supported by love and compassion. Thus, unlike the listeners, they do not turn their back on cyclic existence. Rather than relinquishing cyclic existence, they accept taking birth for the benefit of sentient beings again and again. In doing so, they take many forms, among which those of householders and ordained individuals are the primary ones. Thus, under certain circumstances, bodhisattvas will invariably take birth as householders in the form of universal monarchs. Living such lives, they benefit sentient beings by maturing them in virtue. Likewise, on the first ground and beyond, bodhisattvas obtain ordination, receiving it from the preceptor and ritual master through request and the remaining parts of the fourfold procedure. By the power of the intrinsic nature, they also obtain the undefiled vows, and may, moreover, display the way of receiving ordination by means of an emanated body.

Due to their being distracted, attached, or aggressive, householders possess an abundance of afflictions and sufferings. Ordained individuals, on the other hand, are endowed with infinite qualities that are opposed to these flaws. Thus it is said that they have crossed over the swamp, crossed over the river, crossed over the garbage dump, crossed through the flames, and so forth. In this way, they are, as taught by the Buddha, praised in numerous ways. Those bodhisattvas who persevere in the vows are therefore in possession of a support that is superior to that of householder bodhisattvas.

The bodhisattvas' acceptance of birth within cyclic existence is caused by their superior intent in terms of bringing benefit and happiness to sentient beings. Hence, this superior intent is explained next. On the grounds of inspired conduct, as well as on the ten grounds, the steadfast bodhisattvas have the wish for other sentient beings to reach the happiness of beautiful and delightful results that lie beyond the world or are to be attained in future lives. Such is their intent to bring about happiness. In terms of their intent to be of benefit, they wish for beings to engage with virtues free from affliction within the present life. Their wish that sentient beings may attain the final transcendence of suffering with and without remainder is, as explained above, an expression of their intent regarding both happiness and benefit. Thus, their wish to establish beings in happiness is superior intent in terms of happiness, and their wish to free beings from suffering is superior intent with respect to benefiting others. In short, it is their wish to bring temporary and ultimate benefit and happiness to all sentient beings that is referred to as "superior intent."

As for the divisions of this superior intent, on the grounds of inspired conduct, the intrinsic nature has not yet been realized in direct perception. The attachments to apprehended and apprehender that are to be discarded through seeing have therefore not yet been relinquished. Hence, this is the stage of "impure superior intent." However, from the first through the seventh ground, there is "pure superior intent," and on the three pure grounds of irreversibility, the superior intent is described as "extremely pure." Such are the assertions with respect to the bodhisattvas' superior intent on behalf of sentient beings. The reason that the eighth ground and above are referred to as "grounds of irreversibility" is that the attainment of the eighth ground renders it impossible to regress back into a framework of effort. Thus, with regard to sentient beings, we may distinguish two types of superior intent, namely, that of benefit and that of happiness. In terms of the stream of being of the individual bodhisattva, on the other hand, there are three types of superior intent: the impure, the pure, and the extremely pure. Considering each of these enumerations, we may thus speak of five divisions in the context of superior intent.

Based on superior intent, sentient beings will be gathered; such is the function of superior intent. Concerning the way beings are gathered by means of aspiration, on the grounds of inspired conduct, the bodhisattvas will embrace sentient beings by developing the enlightened mind and forming aspirations. They do this based on the perception that all beings must be established within the field of the transcendence of suffering. With the attainment of the first ground, the bodhisattva also achieves the mind of equality with respect to himself or herself and all sentient beings. Thus they embrace sentient beings, gathering them by means of the mind of equality. As their ruler, gathering sentient beings has to do with becoming the powerful ruler of a realm, for example, as a universal emperor. In that position, one can gather sentient beings by benefiting them through material means and establishing them in the activities of the ten virtues. Finally, gathering sentient beings through guiding a retinue concerns becoming a master or preceptor for a community of students, thus gathering sentient beings by teaching them the Dharma. Hence, bodhisattvas embrace sentient beings by gathering them in these four ways.

There are four causes for the bodhisattvas' acceptance of birth. The birth of wise bodhisattvas on the grounds of inspired conduct is primarily caused by karmic actions. Since such bodhisattvas have not yet gained mastery over their own minds, it is not certain whether they will be born precisely as they wish and aspire. Although at times they may indeed be born in accord with their aspirations, it is for the most part due to having performed the acts of gathering the accumulation of virtue that they take birth in a place that is beneficial to both themselves and others. Birth by the power of aspiration, on the other hand, is the case with those bodhisattvas who have entered the first or second ground. By the power of their aspirations, such bodhisattvas will, in accordance with their wishes, take birth as gods, beasts of burden, freely roaming herbivores, starving spirits, hell beings, or in whatever form will enable them to benefit sentient beings. If harvests fail, so that beings are plagued by hunger and thirst, they may thus assume the body of a fish or an elephant in order to satisfy sentient beings with their own flesh. Likewise, during an age of disease, for example, a bodhisattva may be born as a being whose body has the power to heal illness when consumed. In this way, they may then cure sentient beings of their disease by letting them eat their bodies. They may also, for example, assume the physical form of a master of knowledge mantras, or of a great doctor, and so pacify various diseases for sentient beings. So they take birth in numerous ways, as can be learned from, for example, the *Sūtra That Explains the Secret of the Thus-Gone One's Body*.[57]

From the third through the seventh ground, bodhisattvas take birth by means of meditative absorption. As their minds of meditative absorption become extremely flexible, they attain the four concentrations; yet, rather than consequently being born into the realm of form, they instead take birth within the realm of desire. Due to their meditative absorption, they do this in whichever way they wish. Finally, since on the eighth, ninth, and tenth ground, the bodhisattvas gain mastery of the modes of birth and the gateways of teaching, it is held that, while dwelling there, they take birth by the power of mastery. Thus, they may display the way of taking birth by means of an emanation body, having entered the womb from the Joyful Realm. In this way, they manifest numerous forms of birth. Accordingly, in the context of explaining the eighth ground, the *Sūtra on the Ten Grounds* presents the attainment of the ten masteries in the following way:

> Having accomplished the practice of wakefulness with respect to the body, they are blessed with life throughout an inexpressible number of ineffable eons. Thus they gain mastery in terms of life. As they enter into the wakefulness of the meditative absorption of utter realization, they attain mastery of the mind. As they display the blessing of lavishly adorning and decorating all the realms of the world with a range of ornaments, they attain mastery of material things. As they display the blessing for karmic maturation in a timely fashion, they attain mastery of karmic actions. As they manifest births in all the realms of the world, they attain mastery of birth. As they display the attainment of enlightenment in whichever buddha field and at whatever time they may want to, they attain mastery of wishes. As they show all realms of the world to be filled with buddhas, they achieve mastery of aspiration. As they display miracles and magical feats throughout all buddha fields, they attain mastery of miracles. As they manifest the thus-gone ones' powers, fearlessnesses, unique buddha qualities, and excellent marks and signs, they attain mastery of wakefulness. As they reveal the light of the Dharma beyond extremes and center, they attain mastery of the Dharma.

While bodhisattvas on the grounds of inspired conduct may indeed take birth by the power of aspiration, in the majority of cases they do so due to the force of karmic deeds. Similarly, on the first and second ground, bodhisattvas may indeed be born due to meditative absorption, yet for the most part their birth is due to aspiration. From the third through the seventh ground, birth occurs through meditative absorption, and on the pure grounds, it is due to mastery. When the bodhisattvas take birth throughout numerous realms by the power of the four causes, the latter differences occur in correspondence with their attainment of a lesser, medium, or greater level of purity of mind.

3. The Attainment of the Grounds

Next, the explanation of the grounds upon which the bodhisattvas dwell will include (1) a brief presentation and (2) an elaborate explanation.

1. Brief Presentation

> Characteristics, persons, trainings,
> Aggregates, accomplishment, signs,
> Etymology, and attainment—
> Such is the treatment of the abodes and grounds. [XXI.9]

Next, there follows a summary of the way in which the abodes and grounds are discerned. **Characteristics, persons,** the three **trainings,** the undefiled **aggregates,** the difference between **accomplishment** and lack of accomplishment of the grounds, the **signs** of having attained the grounds, **etymology, and** the **attainment** of the grounds—**such is the treatment of the abodes and grounds.**

The ten grounds will be explained in terms of the following eight issues: (1) characteristics, (2) persons, (3) trainings, (4) aggregates, (5) accomplishment, (6) marks or signs, (7) etymology, and (8) attainment. These eight topics will serve to explain where one dwells, or the principle of a ground as such. Just as the great earth supports the existence and growth of both sentient beings and insentient entities such as grass and trees, the grounds of the bodhisattvas are referred to as such because, corresponding with their gradually increasing attainment of pure minds, these grounds support all the emerging excellent mundane and supramundane qualities.

2. Elaborate Explanation
1. The Characteristics of the Grounds

Having arrived at the supreme realization of emptiness,
One dwells upon the nondissipation of karmic actions.
Having abided in the thoroughly enjoyable concentrations,
One next takes birth into the realm of desire. [XXI.10]

From there, the factors of enlightenment
Are thoroughly dedicated to the realms of cyclic existence.
As the mind is free from afflictions,
One thoroughly ripens sentient beings. [XXI.11]

As one purposely takes birth,
One is safeguarded against the afflictions.
Connected to the single traversed path,
The path is universally ascertained to be devoid of marks. [XXI.12]

Spontaneously established within the absence of marks,
One cultivates the fields.
Beyond that, the ability to ripen sentient beings
Will be accomplished. [XXI.13]

There are meditative absorptions and retentions,
And enlightenment is perfectly pure.
The characteristics of the grounds
Are to be understood by these principles. [XXI.14]

The explanation of the characteristics is as follows. **Having arrived at the supreme realization of** the **emptiness** of persons and phenomena, **one** understands, on the second ground, the various paths of virtuous and unvirtuous karmic actions, as well as their respective fruitions, and so one **dwells upon the nondissipation of karmic actions.** Upon the third ground, **having abided in the thoroughly enjoyable concentrations** of the bodhisattvas, **one** next takes birth into the realm of desire without wavering from those concentrations. **From there, on the fourth ground, there is vast abidance within the factors of enlightenment,** yet these **are all thoroughly dedicated to the realms of cyclic existence.** On the fifth ground, there is vast abidance by the four noble truths. **As the mind is** therefore **free from afflictions, one thoroughly ripens sentient beings** by means of treatises and the development of numerous arts and sciences. Upon the sixth ground, there is vast abidance by means of dependent origination. **As one thus purposely takes birth** within existence, **one is** all the while **safeguarded against the afflictions. Connected to the single traversed path,** which is the eighth ground, **the path** of the seventh ground **is universally ascertained to be devoid of marks.** Beyond formation, one is, upon the eighth ground, **spontaneously established within the absence of marks,** and so **one cultivates the fields.** Beyond that eighth ground, **the ability to** thoroughly **ripen sentient beings** through the mastery of correct awareness **will be accomplished,** and so one is able to mature sentient beings under all circumstances. On the tenth ground, **there are** perfectly pure gateways of **meditative absorptions and retentions, and** on the eleventh ground, the ground of buddhahood, **enlightenment is perfectly pure** in the absence of all cognitive obscurations. The characteristics of the grounds are to be understood by these principles.

On the first ground, bodhisattvas attain direct perception of the absence of self with respect to both persons and phenomena, and this supreme realization of emptiness is the characteristic of the first ground. The *Sūtra on the Ten Grounds* explains the attainment of the first ground in terms of "steadfastness of intent and superior intent, discernment through the power of mind and wakefulness, and the realization of the three times as equality." Steadfastness of mind ensues from the realization of the absence of personal self, while the steadfastness of superior intent is achieved through realizing that there is no self in terms of phenomena. Furthermore, realizing that there is no personal self brings discernment by the power of mind, while comprehending, through insight, that there is no self in terms of phenomena brings discernment by the power of wakefulness. Finally, the realization of the characteristic single flavor of all entities of the three times within emptiness is what is known as "the realization of the three times as equality."

Once the first ground has been attained in this way, the second will follow. Upon that ground it is seen how virtuous and unvirtuous acts bring about, respectively, the maturation of delightful and painful effects, without any dissipation. Consequently, the bodhisattva will solely pursue the avenues of the ten virtues at all times, without following any path of nonvirtue even in his or her dreams. It is for this reason that the characteristic of the second ground is said to be the nondissipation of karmic actions. Upon this ground, one has irreversibly retreated from any form of killing, or other such misdeeds. Since there is not even any thought of hostility in the mind, there is no need to mention that; nor does one physically engage in any harmful acts either. Instead, as taught in the *Sūtra on the Ten Grounds,* one will think: "The ten avenues of unvirtuous action are the universal source of the lower realms, distress, and downfalls for all sentient beings. Therefore, as I abide by the true practice of virtue, I shall establish all other beings in such practices as well."

Having remained in the thoroughly enjoyable realms of the four concentrations, it is a characteristic of the third ground that one subsequently takes birth in the realm of desire without one's previous state of concentration thereby becoming impaired. As the sūtra teaches:

> Thus, without any interruption, the wakefulness of the thus-gone ones perceives in accordance with reality. As it is realized that these conditioned entities are associated with extensive harms, there arises an even greater concern for sentient beings. This concern takes ten forms: (1) concern for those sentient beings who have no protector and support . . .

From there on, the sūtra explains how, as they hear and ascertain these teachings of the Dharma in their own minds, the bodhisattvas will set out alone for a place of solitude and in such a place practice to accomplish the first, second, third, and fourth concentration. Thus, the sūtra explains in detail how the bodhisattva gives rise to the concentrations, freedoms, and so forth.

The characteristic of the fourth ground is that the factors that accord with enlightenment are actualized through insight, thereby generating a compassionate dedication to cyclic existence. Here, some may object: "The factors that accord with enlightenment are the path of deliverance from cyclic existence. Therefore, how could they bring dedication to cyclic existence, and how could they possibly become its cause?" To that we may reply that when not dealt with skillfully, poison can indeed cause death. Nevertheless, by treating it in a skillful way, poison can be turned into medicine. Similarly, when not embraced through the methods of great compassion, the cultivation of the factors of enlightenment is indeed the cause for emerging from cyclic existence. Yet, once embraced by great compassion, the cultivation of these factors will become the cause of birth within cyclic existence. Bodhisattvas who do not turn their back on cyclic existence cultivate the factors of enlightenment with great compassion, and so they practice them for the benefit of sentient beings. Instead of making them turn their backs on cyclic existence, this will, in fact, cause them to turn toward it. Thus, they will, explains the commentary, be thoroughly dedicated to cyclic existence. In this context, the sūtra contains passages such as the following:

> O children of the victorious ones, the bodhisattva on this bodhisattva ground known as The Radiant has become thoroughly trained, alert, and mindful. Having relinquished mundane attachments of the mind along with mental discomfort, he or she will remain mindful of the inner body. . . . Such bodhisattvas are supported by the fulfillment of their past aspirations, made with concern for all sentient beings. Thus, they are endowed with great love that leads to great compassion.

For the fifth ground, it is taught that the characteristic is freedom from afflictions of the mind, leading to the thorough ripening of sentient beings. Endowed with meditation on the four noble truths, one is free from afflictions such as desire, and one has become an expert in the corpus of teachings and the fields of knowledge. Thus, one matures sentient beings by means of the three vehicles. The sūtra teaches:

> As the bodhisattvas give rise to the power of mindfulness, intelligence, and the wakefulness of realization, their minds cannot be turned back. Thus, in perfect accordance with reality, they come to see that "These are the truths of the noble ones!"

Likewise:

> As they exert themselves in investigating the Dharma that carries distinctions, they will also accomplish all that the world holds in terms of language, literature, calculations, and law. They will research natural resources and medicine. They will dispel demons of drought, oblivion, and evil influence. They will know how to neutralize poisoning and the employment of zombies. They will bring joy through mantra, dance, speeches, music, and stories. Thus, they bring benefit and happiness to all sentient beings and, endowed with compassion, they practice in order to establish sentient beings in the final qualities of buddhahood.

On the sixth ground, the bodhisattvas purposely take birth within cyclic existence out of concern for sentient beings. As they meditate on dependent origination, they ensure that they are free from and untainted by the afflictions. This is how the characteristic of the sixth ground is set forth. That is to say, bodhisattvas on the sixth ground are not compelled to take birth in the three realms as a result of the force of karmic actions and afflictions. On the contrary, due to vast accumulations of merit and wakefulness, they take birth with unwavering mindfulness and alertness into the various worlds for the benefit of beings. In this way, they take birth in exact accordance with their particular intentions, and since they repeatedly abide in the meditation on dependent origination, they will also be guarded against, and unblemished by, the afflictions. As the sūtra teaches:

When they regard all phenomena in this way, they will, preceded by compassion, consider the emergence and disappearance of the world. Concerning all of that, incorrect mental engagements and the attachment to the self give rise to the formation of karma . . .

Thus, the sūtra initiates an elaborate discussion of this issue.

The characteristic of the seventh ground is set forth in terms of its relation to the single traversed path and the universal ascertainment of the absence of marks. "The single traversed path" refers to the eighth ground because, until that ground has been reached, the streams of being of the individual bodhisattvas still contain their own distinct efforts and so forth, and their paths are, in this sense, not the same. Upon the eighth ground, however, nonconceptual wakefulness is spontaneously accomplished within equality, and there is therefore no longer any apprehension of marks in terms of either efforts or distinct streams of being. Hence, their paths have become one, as when many rivers become of one taste within the ocean. That which is connected to the single traversed path is therefore the seventh ground because the attainment of the eighth ground follows in its wake. Moreover, upon the seventh ground, the bodhisattvas comprehend the meanings of the Dharma teachings contained in the sūtras and so forth to be all of one taste beyond marks. Hence, this is also the path of the universal ascertainment of the absence of marks. On this, the sūtra teaches:

> O children of the victorious ones, this is how it is. Think, for example, of an afflicted and impure world versus a world of extreme purity. To cover the distance between them, nothing will do but the great power and strength that comes from aspiration, skillful means, insight, and superknowledge. Similarly, O children of the victorious ones, it is only the great power and strength that comes from aspiration, skillful means, insight, and superknowledge that can make one reach the point at which the activities of the bodhisattvas merge—the point of complete purity. Just maintaining the wish to reach there will not be enough.

Thus, the sūtra explains the issue of being connected to the single traversed path. On the decisive ascertainment of the absence of marks, it further declares:

> At the time of dwelling on the seventh ground, one emerges, free from the marks of the limitless acts of the body and free from the marks of the limitless acts of the voice. One is thoroughly purified, free from the marks of the limitless acts of the mind. With the acceptance of nonarising phenomena, one emerges in limitless illumination.

The eighth ground's characteristic is presented with reference to the spontaneous accomplishment of the absence of marks, unstirred by efforts, and to the cultivation of buddha fields. On the eighth ground, nonconceptual wakefulness that is free from marks has been spontaneously accomplished without effort. Thus, one cultivates both the environment and the inhabitants of the buddha fields. The sūtra states:

> O children of the victorious ones, the bodhisattvas who are endowed with this acceptance will, as soon as they have accomplished the bodhisattva ground of The Unwavering, attain the profound abode of the bodhisattvas. This abode is hard to recognize and is unadulterated, free from all marks, a limitless return from all the grasping of identification. Unimaginable to any listener or self-realized buddha, it is both secluded and the manifestation of all that is secluded. O children of the victorious ones, this is how it is. Think of a monk who possesses miraculous powers . . .

The sūtra continues to explain at length how the entry into the equilibrium of cessation is free from moving thoughts and identifications, and how this, then, constitutes freedom from all the efforts of identification and is the transcendence of all acts. If a man falls asleep and dreams that he is carried away by a great river, he may apply great efforts to escape. Yet, the moment he wakes up, he is freed from all such effort.

Likewise, one may apply great efforts to save sentient beings, who are being carried off by the four rivers of affliction. Nevertheless, as soon as the eighth ground has been attained, one will have separated from all the movements of effortful pursuits. Until a seafaring ship has reached the ocean it has to be deliberately kept in motion. Once it has reached the sea, however, it will be pulled along by the wind currents, and so circle the sea without having to be purposely kept moving. Likewise, the sūtra further explains, once the bodhisattvas have come to the eighth ground, they effortlessly enter into omniscient wakefulness in a way that could not be achieved through any of their previous, deliberate activities. As for the way these bodhisattvas cultivate buddha fields, for example, without any effort and by the power of their spontaneously accomplished nonconceptual meditative absorption, the sūtra describes this in the passage that begins: "Limitless accomplishment of lives, limitless cultivation of buddha fields, limitless maturation of sentient beings..."

Subsequent to the attainment of the eighth ground, there follows the ninth. Its characteristic is set forth with reference to the fourfold correct awareness, which elicits an unimpeded ability to teach the Dharma in a way that thoroughly ripens sentient beings. The sūtra explains this elaborately in passages such as the following:

> Those on the bodhisattva ground of Excellent Intelligence work as great teachers of the Dharma, and they protect the treasury of the thus-gone ones' Dharma. With respect to the wakefulness that takes the form of Dharma teaching, they possess an infinite skill. Hence, they teach the Dharma through the practice of the bodhisattvas' correct awareness of words. Through correct awareness of Dharma teachings, they realize the specific characteristics of the various teachings. They realize the divisions that pertain to the Dharma teachings with correct awareness of meanings. Through correct awareness of definitive words, they teach the Dharma without mixing anything up. By means of correct awareness in terms of acumen, they realize, without interruption, the streams of being that are conducive to the teachings.

The tenth ground is characterized by the attainment of infinite gateways of meditative absorption and retention. That is to say, when the tenth ground is attained, limitless meditative absorptions of the bodhisattvas, such as "the stainless" and "illumination of the great vehicle," will be accomplished. These meditative absorptions are classified as the cause, or basis, for the manifestation of abundant qualities of superknowledge and so forth. Similarly, infinite gateways of retention, such as "the inexhaustible trove" and "the retention of the limitless gateways," will also be gained, and through these the bodhisattvas uphold both the words and meanings taught by the buddhas without anything being forgotten. They are referred to as "gateways" because they are the cause for the diverse teaching of Dharma to sentient beings. The sūtra explains:

> O children of the victorious ones, the bodhisattva who possesses this wakefulness and attains empowerment will have the direct perception of the meditative absorption of the bodhisattvas that is known as "the stainless" . . .

It continues:

> . . . will have the direct perception of the meditative absorption of the bodhisattvas that is known as "the perceptual manifestation of the buddhas of the present."

Likewise, it explains:

> These gateways of the bodhisattvas' freedoms and so forth are attained as innumerably and infinitely many hundreds of thousands of gateways.

The sūtra then proceeds to characterize the attainment of meditative absorptions and retentions in a similar way.

The characteristic of the eleventh ground, the ground of buddhahood, is set forth with reference to the perfectly pure nature of the great enlightenment that possesses the wakefulness of exhaustion and no further arising. This wakefulness is due to the elimination of the two obscurations along with their imprints. As taught in the *Definitive Explanation of the Intent:*

> The first and second grounds are attained by eliminating the negative tendencies that are present in the shell. When conquering the negative tendencies that are present in the juice, the third is accomplished. When the latent negative tendencies that are present in the essence have all been fully eliminated to the point where nothing remains, then that is what I declare to be the ground of buddhahood.

The characteristics of all the grounds, from the first through to buddhahood, can thus be understood from the principles provided in this section.

2. Persons

Next follows the presentation of the categories of persons dwelling on the grounds.

> The bodhisattvas possess pure view,
> Perfectly pure discipline, and equipoise.
> They have given up pride regarding the Dharma, streams of being,
> And the distinction between thorough affliction and complete purification. [XXI.15]
>
> They attain instantaneous wakefulness, equanimity,
> Cultivation of fields, skill in ripening sentient beings,
> Great power, the body that is perfectly complete,
> Skill in definitive display, and empowerment. [XXI.16]

Next, the persons who abide on the grounds are discerned. The **bodhisattvas** who abide on the first ground **possess pure view** because they have attained the wakefulness that serves to remedy the views of persons and phenomena. Since bodhisattvas on the second ground are free from even the most subtle delusions in the form of downfalls, they possess **perfectly pure discipline, and** because those on the third ground have attained incorruptible concentration and meditative absorption, they are endowed with **equipoise.** On the fourth ground, **they have given up pride regarding the Dharma** and do not conceive in terms of different Dharma teachings found in sūtras and so forth. On the fifth ground, the practice of the bodhisattvas takes place by means of the tenfold equality of pure mind and intention, and so they relinquish the pride of thinking in terms of different **streams of being.** The tenfold equality includes conceiving of equality with respect to (1–3) the pure qualities of the buddhas of the three times, (4) pure discipline, (5) pure mind, (6) pure dispelling of views, doubt, and regret, (7) knowledge of what is and is not a path, (8) knowledge of the path, (9) the progressive cultivation of the factors of enlightenment, and (10) thorough ripening of the mind. On the sixth ground, there is vast abiding within the suchness of dependent origination, **and** the pride related to conceiving of a **distinction between thorough affliction and complete purification** is thus relinquished. By the power of abiding beyond marks, **they attain,** on the seventh ground, the **instantaneous wakefulness** that enables them to cultivate, with every moment, all of the thirty-seven factors of enlightenment. Since they have spontaneously accomplished the abiding in the absence of marks and because they merge with all bodhisattvas who have entered the grounds of irreversibility, those on the eighth ground accomplish **equanimity** and the **cultivation of buddha fields.** Bodhisattvas on the ninth ground possess **skill in** the thorough **ripening of sentient beings.** On the tenth ground, bodhisattvas attain great superknowledge and are thus endowed with **great power.** Suffused by the infinite gateways of meditative absorption and retention, they attain **the body that is perfectly complete.** They have gained the **skill of** the **definitive display** of emanations that reside in the Joyful Realm, and so forth, **and** hence they receive **empowerment** from all the buddhas.

An individual on the first ground is referred to as "a bodhisattva who possesses pure view" because such a person has gained the nonconceptual wakefulness that realizes the twofold absence of self. Someone on the second ground, however, is classified with reference to his or her possession of perfectly pure discipline. This is because such a person remains untainted by even subtle flaws or downfalls. Those on the third ground are persons who constantly rest in equipoise. Hence, regardless of where they are born, their attainment of concentration and meditative absorption will not wane.

A person on the fourth ground is someone who has given up pride regarding the Dharma. Here it must be understood that, at the time of the third ground, one's respect for, and investigation of, the Dharma is sustained by an extremely analytical insight that allows one to spend both day and night listening to the Dharma, examining the Dharma, contemplating the Dharma, and practicing in accord with the Dharma. There is no external or internal entity whatsoever that one will not be able to give away for the sake of the Dharma. Likewise, with respect to the teachers of the Dharma, there is no form of veneration and respect that one will not practice. Considering the Dharma and the Dharma teacher to be rare and very hard to come by, one shows them tremendous reverence and heartfelt devotion, without the slightest bit of disrespect or conceit. For example, let us assume that someone were to say: "Watch! Here before you is a great mass of fiercely burning flames of fire. Give your body to the flames, and go through the torment! I shall then teach you words of the Dharma. I shall then explain to you the Buddha's teaching, the training in the activities of the bodhisattvas." Now, even if the whole billionfold universe were consumed by raging fire, a bodhisattva of this kind would be ready, for the sake of a single word of the Buddha's teaching on the training in bodhisattva activity, to throw himself or herself into the depth of such masses of fire, all the way from the world of Brahma. Hence, there is no need to mention that such a person will have no qualms about ordinary bonfires. He or she will therefore exclaim: "Even if I have to endure all the pain of sentient beings who live in hell, I shall indeed pursue the Dharma. No need to mention, then, that I can keep company with flames."

Now, at the time of the fourth ground, the bodhisattva realizes that this pursuit of the Dharma with such fierce concern is a distraction and a source of conceit. With this realization, therefore, they devote themselves primarily to the cultivation of the factors of enlightenment and in this way overcome the pride of thinking "Diligently do I pursue the Dharma." Hence, such bodhisattvas are known as "persons who have given up pride with regard to the Dharma."

Bodhisattvas on the fifth ground are "persons who have given up pride in terms of different streams of being" because such bodhisattvas have attained the tenfold equality of pure intention. Thus they comprehend that when considering their pure characteristics, there are no differences with respect to either the streams of being or the qualities of the thus-gone ones of the three times. Hence, they are free from the pride that concerns different streams of being. In the context of the fifth ground, the *Sūtra on the Ten Grounds* explains the tenfold equality of pure intention in the following way:

> O children of the victorious ones, once a bodhisattva of the fourth ground has fully completed the path that is specific to that ground, he or she will enter the fifth bodhisattva ground. Entry upon that ground is gained through a tenfold equality of the mind with respect to purity. Thus, this encompasses pure intent with respect to the qualities of the buddhas of the past, the qualities of the buddhas of the future, the qualities of the buddhas of the present. Similarly encompassed are discipline, mind, view, and the dispelling of views, doubts, and regrets. Likewise, there is purity and equality with respect to the knowledge of what is and is not a path, the knowledge of the diligent elimination, the progressive cultivation of the factors of enlightenment, and the thorough maturation of sentient beings.

Thus, with respect to the pure enlightened qualities of the buddhas of the past and so forth, the bodhisattvas who have attained the fifth ground develop the following intent: "Before long, we too shall attain such purity of the buddha qualities as are associated with factors such as the three trainings."

When dwelling on the sixth ground, the bodhisattva is referred to as a "person who has given up pride in terms of a distinction between thorough affliction and complete purification." At the time of this ground, the attainment of the tenfold equality of phenomena brings the realization of the emptiness of dependent origination. Thus, one realizes that within emptiness there is no duality in terms of negative factors—the condition of ignorance leading to formation, and so forth—and the positive factors that accomplish the cessation of the negative factors. Instead, all are seen to be of one taste as the characteristics of nonarising emptiness. With this realization, the arrogance of perceiving a difference between affliction and purification will be absent. The tenfold equality of phenomena, which is taught to be the means for gaining access to the sixth ground, is set forth as follows:

> All phenomena are equality free from marks, equality free from characteristics. Likewise, all phenomena are nonarising, nonoccurring, void, pure since the beginning, free from mental construction, beyond acceptance and rejection. They are equal to an illusion, a dream, an optical illusion, an echo and an emanation. They are all equally neither something nor nothing.

On the seventh ground, the bodhisattva is known as a "person whose mind is capable of the instantaneous cultivation of the factors that accord with enlightenment, the causes that produce all buddha qualities." As the sūtra teaches:

> O children of the victorious ones, when abiding upon the bodhisattva ground of The Far Reaching, the bodhisattva perfects the ten transcendences and the four means of attraction. The four abodes, the thirty-seven factors of enlightenment, the three gateways of liberation—in short, all of the qualities of the aspects of enlightenment—are perfected within one instant.

Bodhisattvas on the eighth ground are "persons who rest in equanimity and accomplish cultivation." Since, in their case, the meditative absorption that precludes any recurrence of marks has been accomplished spontaneously, they remain in equanimity without any effort. Thus they also cultivate utterly pure buddha fields. Just as taught in the sūtra, they are now effortless like a ship that sails without any need for effort once it has entered the ocean, and they display the blessing of lavishly adorning and decorating all the realms of the world with all types of ornaments.

When dwelling on the ninth ground, the bodhisattva is classified as a "person who has skill in ripening sentient beings." With their accomplishment of the fourfold correct awareness, such bodhisattvas have become great teachers of the Dharma, and so they bring sentient beings to maturation. On the tenth ground, bodhisattvas are "persons who have attained great power of superknowledge; whose bodies of retentions and meditative absorptions, causing the attainment of the body of qualities, have become perfectly complete; who have skill in definitively displaying the deeds of enlightenment, such as residing in the palace of the Joyful Realm, entering the womb, and so forth, all the way through to attaining manifest enlightenment; and who receive empowerment by the great light rays of all the thus-gone ones." The sūtra explains these issues elaborately with passages such as these:

> They attain hundreds of thousands of superknowledges. Hence, depending on what is wished for, they can bless a narrow world to become a wide one, or a wide world to turn into a narrow one. . . .
>
> They possess the ten gates of freedom, as well as innumerable hundreds of thousands of further freedoms. This also is the case with their gateways of meditative absorption and retention. . . .
>
> With their blessings, the bodhisattvas on this Cloud of Dharma can, within a single world, carry out all the deeds of the thus-gone ones—from residing in the palace of the Joyful Realm, moving from there, entering the womb, and so forth, all the way to displaying great enlightenment, responding to requests, turning the wheel of Dharma, and the stage known as the great transcendence of suffering. At the same time, all such deeds of the thus-gone ones are performed in exact accordance with

the inclinations of sentient beings, and in precisely the way that is necessary for taming them. . . .

A strong and perfectly qualified son of a universal emperor may be placed upon a golden throne and, accompanied by a display of manifold ornaments as well as song and music, receive on the crown of his head the water of the ocean from a golden vase. Thus he becomes empowered and will from then on be a king who has received the royal anointment on the crown of his head. Likewise, as soon as this is actualized, upon a great and regal lotus flower of jewels that is as vast as a billionfold universe . . . the bodhisattva will be empowered by the great light rays of the buddhas, the blessed ones, and so, at that very moment, will turn into a bodhisattva who has received the empowerment of the mastery of wakefulness.

Thereby, the bodhisattva perfects the ten grounds and is henceforth a truly and completely enlightened buddha.

3. The Trainings

The third topic is an explanation of the way in which bodhisattvas perfect the three trainings on the ten grounds.

> Having thoroughly realized the intrinsic nature,
> They here subsequently train
> In special discipline, attention, and insight.
> The sphere of engagement through insight is twofold: [XXI.17]

> The real nature of phenomena and the processes that ensue
> From the lack of knowledge and knowledge of that.
> This being the sphere of engagement through insight,
> It is encountered on two grounds. [XXI.18]

> Additionally, there are four results
> Of the trainings and meditations.
> Absence of marks and the presence of formation—
> Abiding in that is the first fruition. [XXI.19]

The same without formation,
Along with the pure fields,
Is held to be the second fruition.
The accomplishment of the maturation of beings [XXI.20]

And the accomplishment of the meditative absorptions and retentions
Are held to be authentic fruitions.
These four fruitions
Are supported by four grounds. [XXI.21]

The principles of the trainings follow next. **Having thoroughly realized the intrinsic nature** of suchness upon the first ground, **they here subsequently train in special discipline** on the second ground, **in special attention** on the third ground, **and** in special **insight** on the fourth. **The sphere of engagement through insight is twofold** in relation to the fifth and sixth ground. On the fifth ground, **the real nature of phenomena**, that is, the truths of suffering and so forth, are encountered; **and** on the sixth ground, **the processes** of the forward and reverse dependent origination that respectively **ensue from the lack of knowledge and the knowledge of that** nature of the truths are realized. **This being the sphere of engagement through insight, it is encountered on two grounds. Additionally, there are four results of these trainings and meditations. Absence of marks and the presence of formation**—the **abiding in that, upon the seventh ground, is the first fruition. The same without formation, along with the pure** buddha **fields, is held to be the second fruition,** or the eighth ground. **The accomplishment of the** thorough **maturation of beings** on the ninth ground (which is the third fruition) **and the** thorough **accomplishment of the meditative absorptions and retentions** on the tenth ground **are held to be authentic fruitions. These four fruitions are supported by four grounds.**

The direct realization of the intrinsic nature that occurs on the first ground serves as the basis for the purification of all aspects of the bodhisattvas' training. Thus, based on that realization, they practice, for example, the training in special discipline on the second ground. Since they do so to the extent that flawed discipline does not occur even in their dreams, there is no need to mention that they steer clear of such flaws in general. Hence, upon this ground, their discipline becomes extremely pure. On the third ground, they practice special attention and so attain a concentration and meditative absorption that do not wane. On the fourth, fifth, and sixth ground, their training primarily involves insight. On the fourth ground, the bodhisattvas gain a distinctive insight through the cultivation of the thirty-seven factors of enlightenment. Moreover, the field to which this insight applies is twofold. Hence, on the fifth ground, their training concerns the suchness of all phenomena and the four noble truths. On the sixth, however, they consider the way in which a lack of knowledge of the nature of dependent origination will manifest as the unfolding of ignorance and so forth, whereas insight into the nature of dependent origination brings the cessation of ignorance, formation, and so forth, by the power of wakefulness. Thus, on the fifth and sixth ground, respectively, the field of their insight concerns the four noble truths and dependent origination.

Practicing the trainings during the ensuing attainment and cultivating nonconceptual wakefulness during the equipoise, the bodhisattvas additionally attain four fruitions. The first of these is the state of resting in the absence of marks while still being involved in formation, which is characteristic of the seventh ground. On the eighth ground, however, the absence of marks is spontaneously accomplished, free from formation, and one thus genuinely cultivates the buddha fields. This is the second fruition, whereas the third is the maturation of sentient beings, which takes place on the ninth ground, through one's teaching of the Dharma by means of the fourfold correct awareness. Finally, the fourth fruition consists of the supreme accomplishment of meditative absorptions and retentions that occurs on the tenth ground. As the pinnacle of all the grounds, the latter fruition is supreme. Thus, these four fruitions are supported by the four grounds from the seventh through the tenth.

4. The Aggregates

Next follows an explanation of the way the bodhisattvas cultivate the five undefiled aggregates on the grounds.

> Having thoroughly realized the intrinsic nature,
> The aggregate of discipline is here subsequently cultivated.
> Next the aggregates of meditative absorption
> And insight are cultivated. [XXI.22]
>
> The remaining ones consist of the disappearance
> Of the four obscurations, as well as the obscuration of impediment.
> They are thus the cultivation
> Of liberation and liberated wakefulness. [XXI.23]

The classification of the aggregates is as follows. **Having thoroughly realized the intrinsic nature,** which is the support for the undefiled aggregates, on the first ground, **the aggregate of discipline is here subsequently cultivated** upon the second ground. **Next, the aggregates of meditative absorption and insight are cultivated,** respectively, on the third and the fourth through the sixth ground. **The remaining ones** (that is, the seventh, eighth, ninth, and tenth ground) **consist of the disappearance of the four obscurations** that cover the four fruitions referred to previously, **as well as the obscuration of impediment,** which hinders the accomplishment of the ground of buddhahood. **They are thus** the occasions of **the cultivation of liberation and** the purification of **liberated wakefulness.**

The thorough realization of the intrinsic nature that occurs on the first ground is the basis for all the undefiling aggregates. Hence, based on the former realization, one cultivates and purifies the aggregate of discipline upon the second ground. Beyond the second ground, one cultivates the aggregate of meditative concentration on the third, and the aggregate of insight on the fourth, fifth, and sixth ground. On the remaining four grounds, from the seventh through the tenth, one cultivates the aggregate of liberation from the four obscurations. The latter four comprise the hindrances for attaining the four fruitions that were explained in the previous section: absence of marks, absence of formation, the maturing of sentient beings, and the attainment of meditative absorption and retention. Thus, the four obscurations are the subtle occurrence of marks, efforts, failing to achieve the correct awareness that matures sentient beings, and failing to gain mastery of meditative absorption and retention. As they progress through the seventh to the tenth ground, the bodhisattvas are freed from the obscurations associated with those four conflicting factors. Thus, the bodhisattvas experience the disappearance of even the most subtle manifestation of marks and so forth, and in this way, they cultivate the aggregate of liberation. Finally, by means of the path without impediment that pertains to the vajra-like meditative absorption, they conquer the deluded habitual tendencies for dualistic experience, the subtle obscurations that otherwise prevent the attainment of the ground of buddhahood. Hence, since they are thus freed even from the obscurations that hinder the cognition of all phenomena, they cultivate the aggregate of liberated wakefulness. In this way, the cultivation of the aggregate of liberation is associated with the seventh through the tenth ground, whereas the aggregate of liberated wakefulness belongs to the ground of buddhahood.

Here it might be argued: "Liberation is the unconditioned cessation that is based on analysis and within which the obscurations have been eliminated. Therefore, how could one rightly classify liberation as an aggregate?" The commentary replies to that objection, stating that *vimukti*, the Sanskrit term for liberation, carries the sense of both relinquishment and inspiration. Thus, in the present context, it is the latter sense of inspiration that is implied. Although there is freedom from all conditioned engagements, the effortless wakefulness beyond action is nevertheless spontaneously present. Hence, this is not comparable to emptiness in the sense of annihilation—the existential negation that is associated with the exhaustion of the factors to be discarded. Rather, the reference is to the qualities of elimination that belong to liberated wakefulness. It is, therefore, appropriate to classify liberation as an aggregate as well.

5. Accomplishment

The fifth topic is the presence versus the absence of accomplished qualities on the grounds.

> All the grounds should be known
> To be unaccomplished and accomplished.
> Those accomplished are, moreover, also
> Held to be unaccomplished and accomplished. [XXI.24]
>
> The accomplishment should be understood to occur
> By directing the mind in accord with the classifications,
> Thereby knowing that it is thinking,
> And not having any thoughts about that. [XXI.25]
>
> Because they are the objects of individual direct awareness,
> And because they are the objects of the buddhas,
> Meditation and accomplishment transcend,
> Upon all the grounds, that which is conceivable. [XXI.26]

Next follows the classification in terms of accomplishment. **All the grounds should be known to be unaccomplished** (which is the case with the grounds of inspired conduct since there the intrinsic nature has not become manifest) **and accomplished** (which is the case with the attained grounds).

Those accomplished are, moreover, also held to be unaccomplished (in the case of the first through the seventh ground, because they involve formation) **and accomplished** (in the case of the eighth ground and beyond since those grounds are free from formation). When it is explained that the first ground and beyond are accomplished, **the accomplishment should be understood to occur by directing the mind in accordance with the classifications** of the corpus of the teachings, **thereby knowing that it** (that is, the ground) is one's own **thinking, and not having any thoughts about that** (that is, about it being one's own thinking).

Moreover, both the meditation and the accomplishment that pertain to the grounds are inconceivable. That is to say, **because they are the objects of the individual direct awareness** of the bodhisattvas **and because they are the objects of the buddhas, both meditation and accomplishment transcend, upon all the grounds, that which is conceivable.**

All eleven grounds (counting the grounds of inspired conduct along with the other ten grounds) can be contained within the two categories of the unaccomplished and the accomplished. That is to say, although the grounds of inspired conduct are referred to as such, they do not belong to the grounds of the noble ones. Hence, they can be seen as unaccomplished since at this stage the universally present characteristics of the basic field of phenomena have not yet been realized. These grounds are thus not accomplished in terms of the perception of the truth. From the first ground and beyond, the grounds should be known as accomplished because with the perception of the truth of the intrinsic nature, these are all accomplished as noble and supramundane grounds.

By considering the different extents to which excellent qualities are present upon them, the ten accomplished grounds can themselves further be understood in terms of the unaccomplished and accomplished. Thus, since the seven impure grounds involve effort to the extent that the spiritual training in the absence of marks has not yet become a spontaneous presence, those seven can be seen to be unaccomplished. The three pure grounds will then, because of the effortless and spontaneous accomplishment of the spiritual training in the absence of marks, be classified as accomplished.

The grounds of the noble ones in general, as well as each specific one in particular, are accomplished through an awareness of the grounds' respective qualities, the flaws of the factors to be discarded upon them, and the good qualities that are to be cultivated upon them. One must therefore direct one's mind to these factors and qualities, just as they are presented in the teachings, until they are clearly present in one's mind. Thus, "directing the mind in accord with the classifications" means bringing to mind the qualities of the next ground, as well as the teachings whereby one accomplishes those qualities. For example, to accomplish the first ground, one directs one's mind toward the qualities of the first ground and the practices upon it that are engaged in. Directing the mind in this way will, therefore, also be a way of bringing to mind the causal qualities that are present on the first ground and that lead to the attainment of the second ground. The sūtra explains the way to direct one's mind to the qualities of the first ground in passages such as the one that begins: "O children of the victorious ones, those sentient beings who have gathered extremely many fundamental virtues, who have gathered extremely vast accumulations..."

As regards the way of directing the mind to the first ground and the causes for the attainment of the second, the sūtra teaches:

> O children of the victorious ones, the bodhisattvas who in this way have trained intensively on the first ground become inspired by the second. Thus, a tenfold intent arises in their minds. What are the ten aspects of this intent? They are the intent of honesty, the intent of gentleness, the intent of physical flexibility...

Alternatively, "directing the mind in accord with the classifications" can also be understood in terms of being attentive to, and keeping in mind, the groupings of names, phrases, and letters.

Now, when one is involved in the accomplishment of a given ground by directing one's mind to the classifications that pertain to it, the ground and its classifications are all simply one's own mind taking on that appearance. The grounds are not established as anything other than the mind. Since they are nothing but one's own thinking, one will thus recognize that they are not established as apprehended objects. Moreover, in the absence of anything apprehended, there can be no subjective apprehending either. With that knowledge, one will hence not have any thoughts about an apprehending mind either. Thus, one must gain insight beyond apprehended and apprehender. As one thus comprehends the mind-sets of the different grounds, knowing them to be merely one's own mind, and understanding that there is neither anything apprehended nor anything that apprehends, one will accomplish each one of them. As this practice is the same for each of the grounds, this is the knowledge for accomplishing all of them. Such practice and such accomplishment, however, are inconceivable to ordinary beings. Hence, since the successive grounds are the objects of the individual self-awareness of the classes of noble beings who attain them, and since the classifications that pertain to the grounds are, moreover, issues that belong to the activity sphere of the buddhas, the whole process of meditating and gaining accomplishment from one ground to the next transcends what is conceivable to ordinary beings, listeners, and self-realized buddhas. This is just as taught in the *Great Ornament of the Buddhas:*

> Just as the path of a bird flying in space
> Is extremely hard to see and impossible to account for,
> The grounds of the bliss-gone ones' children
> Cannot be comprehended as the objects of mind and thought.

6. Signs

The explanation of the signs of attainment includes accounts of (1) the signs themselves and (2) the grounds that bear them.

1. The Actual Signs

> Appearance, inspiration,
> No faintheartedness, no deficiency,
> Independence from others,
> Clear realization of all, [xxi.27]

> A mind of equality toward everyone,
> Not being led, absence of attachment,
> Knowledge of skillful means, and birth in the retinue—
> Throughout, these are held to be the signs. [xxi.28]

> They do not lack motivation, are unattached, free from
>   hostility, have no anger, are free from laziness,
> Have no thoughts other than love and compassion, have
>   intelligence that is free from negative thoughts and
>   thinking,

Have intelligence that is free from distractions, are not
    brought down by pleasures, not hurt by suffering,
Follow the spiritual teacher, persist in learning, and diligently
    worship the teacher. [XXI.29]

Knowing the supreme methods, they fully gather all of the
    extremely vast virtues
And share them with others in dedication to complete
    enlightenment every single day.
Born in excellent places, they always do good, sporting with
    qualities of superknowledge.
Such children of the buddhas are to be known as superior
    to everyone; they are treasuries of excellent qualities.
    [XXI.30]

The signs of having entered the grounds are discerned as follows. **Appearance** of the qualities of the relevant grounds, **inspiration** with respect to the grounds upon which one has not yet entered, **no faintheartedness** with respect to the profound and vast topics, **no deficiency** when undergoing hardship on the path, **independence from others** in the context of acquiring the qualities of the individual grounds, **clear realization of** the way to accomplish **all** of the grounds, recognizing the sameness of oneself and others with **a mind of equality toward everyone, not being led** astray due to pleasant or unpleasant words, **absence of attachment** to the perfections of universal emperors and so forth, **knowledge of** the **skillful means** for attaining buddhahood due to the absence of observation of the three spheres, **and** constant **birth in the retinue** of a buddha—**throughout** all of the grounds, these are held to be the bodhisattva's **signs.**

Next, the signs of having attained the transcendences are discerned. **They do not lack** the **motivation** to practice the transcendences and are free from the factors that conflict with the transcendences. Thus, they **are unattached, free from hostility** toward sentient beings, **have no anger, are free from laziness, have no thoughts other than love and compassion,** and **have** intelligence that is free from the negative thoughts of essences and the thinking in terms of particularities. As a sign of transcendent skillful means, they have intelligence that is free from the distractions that ensue from directing the mind in the way of the other vehicles. They are not brought down by attachment to pleasures. When facing difficulties and undertaking hardship, they are not hurt by suffering but remain unstoppable in their practice. They follow the spiritual teacher, persist in learning, and diligently worship the teacher. Knowing the supreme methods for dedicating virtue toward complete enlightenment, they fully gather all of the extremely vast virtues accumulated in the three times and share them with other sentient beings in dedication to complete enlightenment every single day. As a sign of transcendent aspiration, they are born in excellent places where buddhas and bodhisattvas reside. As a sign of transcendent power, they always do good, and as a sign of transcendent wakefulness, they are sporting with the qualities of great superknowledge. Such children of the buddhas, who are endowed with these signs, are to be known as superior to everyone; they are treasuries of excellent qualities.

Just as one may know the presence of water based on the presence of waterfowl, or the presence of fire based on smoke, there are also signs and marks whereby the attainment of the grounds can be recognized. The five such signs explained earlier are the marks of bodhisattvas in general, regardless of whether they have attained the grounds. What follow here are ten signs that are specific to bodhisattvas remaining on the grounds.

(1) The first mark or sign is the clear appearance, in direct perception, of the factors to be given up, accepted, or meditated upon, within the relevant grounds of attainment. This also includes the inspiration to attain the grounds that lie beyond.

(2) Due to one's perception of the truth, there is freedom from fear and faintheartedness with respect to the profound and vast Dharma.

(3) Since one's mind does not suffer from any deficiency when it comes to facing the hardships and sufferings associated with, for example, heat, cold, or exhaustion, or having to sacrifice one's head or limbs, there is a sense of total irreversibility in one's freedom from weariness.

(4) While one's individual ground has already been realized by the power of the two accumulations, one will not have to rely on others in order to attain those that remain. Thus, one enjoys independence from others with respect to the explanation of the relevant principles of the teachings and the meditation on their meaning.

(5) When attaining the first ground, one also gains, along with that, an expert realization of the principles that are involved in accomplishing the remaining grounds. Due to having remained in nonconceptual wakefulness during the equipoise, one gains the pure mundane wakefulness of the ensuing attainment, and thereby the knowledge of the means for accomplishing all the remaining grounds. Thus, someone on the first ground will have expert knowledge with respect to honesty, gentleness, and the rest of the ten factors that are the means for entering the second ground; but they will also possess expertise regarding pure intent, imperturbability, and the others among the ten factors that are taught as the means for accessing the third ground—and so forth. In this way, an extremely thorough understanding of the classifications of the means for entering all the successive grounds is present upon all the grounds in general. That is the fifth sign.

(6) A mind of equality is achieved that does not make any difference between oneself and the infinity of all sentient beings.

(7) Bodhisattvas on the grounds are endowed with excellent accumulations of merit, and due to their accumulations of wakefulness, they realize that all phenomena are emptiness. This makes them unsusceptible to attachments or aversions toward anything at all. Thus, praise does not give them pleasure, and absence of praise does not make them dejected or disheartened. They are, therefore, not governed by circumstance and cannot be led astray.

(8) Those who have entered the grounds are endowed with the supramundane practices of the buddhas and bodhisattvas. Seeing even the enjoyments of beings such as Brahma, Indra, and the universal emperor to be like filth, they have no craving for any of them. Relinquishing such enjoyments, they give them to others and emerge definitively.

(9) With nonconceptual wakefulness that does not conceive of the three spheres, they have direct knowledge of the means for accomplishing unsurpassable enlightenment.

(10) Except when, by the power of their aspirations, they take birth into realms where no buddha resides, they are born throughout all their lives into the circle of a buddha's retinue.

The above ten signs are all held to be borne universally by all bodhisattvas dwelling on the grounds. Moreover, sixteen marks of accomplishment of the transcendences also manifest on each of the grounds. Since there is never any lack of motivation to practice the ten transcendences on the grounds, it is taught that, in general, the grounds are characterized by supreme motivation. Specifically, however, (1) on the first ground, the bodhisattvas attain pure transcendent generosity. They are, therefore, unattached to their bodies and enjoyments. (2) With the attainment of pure transcendent discipline on the second ground, the bodhisattvas will not engage in any of the ten nonvirtues, not even in their dreams. Hence, they are free from hostility and resentment toward others. (3) On the third ground, transcendent patience is completely purified, and there is, therefore, a complete absence of anger. (4) On the fourth ground, the purification of transcendent diligence ensures the absence of laziness. (5) On the fifth ground, the bodhisattvas are endowed with the four immeasurables of pure transcendent concentration. Hence, they have no thoughts other than those of love and compassion. (6) The complete purity of transcendent insight is attained on the sixth ground. On this ground, bodhisattvas do not fall prey to negative and errant thoughts, such as those of the inferior intellect as it conceives of purity, bliss, permanence, and self. Nor can such bodhisattvas be brought down in any way due to clinging to things as real. In this way, six marks are enumerated with reference to the six transcendences.

Although the ten transcendences, from transcendent generosity to transcendent wakefulness, are paired with the succession of the ten grounds, this is done in consideration of the way in which the individual transcendences are predominant upon the various grounds. All ten transcendences are indeed practiced on each of the grounds. The way the remaining six qualities are derived is not obvious in the great commentary, and they appear, therefore, to be enumerated in somewhat different ways by the various other commentaries.[58] Nevertheless, (7) on the seventh ground, the bodhisattvas attain the purification of transcendent skill in means, which indicates that they are free from distractions that take the form of the mind-set of listeners or self-realized buddhas. (8) On the eighth ground, they gain the purity of transcendent power; they will therefore not be brought down by attachment to pleasure or be harmed by suffering. Instead, without moving from the equality of their spontaneously accomplished nonconceptual wakefulness, they will take on the forms of Brahma, Indra, a universal emperor, and so forth. Thus, although in an instant they may make manifest as many bodies as there are particles in the world, they do not give rise to any thoughts. (9) On the ninth ground, they follow, by means of transcendent aspiration, buddhas and bodhisattvas as their spiritual teachers. Thus, they persist in learning all the gateways of the Dharma, and throughout all the realms of the ten directions, they diligently worship the teachers, the buddhas—with infinite arrays of offerings of flowers, incense, and so forth.

(10) On the seventh ground, with knowledge of the supreme means for accomplishing buddhahood, the bodhisattvas bring about an extremely vast gathering of all the merit they and others have accumulated throughout the three times. Sharing this merit with all sentient beings, they dedicate it to unsurpassable and perfect enlightenment every single day. (11) Moreover, by the power of aspiration, they take birth in excellent places. With transcendent power, they overcome the conflicting factors and succeed in constantly doing nothing but good. Although these latter three qualities of dedication, aspiration, and power belong primarily to the seventh, ninth, and eighth grounds, birth in excellent places and the constant engagement in virtue are here counted as one. (12) On the tenth ground, transcendent wakefulness is purified, and so the bodhisattvas will revel in the qualities of superknowledge. Thus they may show a single subtle particle permeating all of the realms of the world, just as they may make all the world's realms appear to be contained within a single particle. In ways such as these, they playfully engage in numerous miraculous displays. Since the child of the buddhas who abides on the tenth ground possesses tremendously vast qualities in terms of meditative absorption, retention, and so on, he or she should be known to be superior to all other bodhisattvas and a treasury of excellent qualities. As explained, the transcendences predominate on their respective grounds, and the signs of their qualities therefore manifest with a corresponding predominance. Nevertheless, all ten transcendences are practiced on

each of the ten grounds, and there are, therefore, aspects of all sixteen marks present throughout the ten grounds.

2. The Grounds

Next, the qualities of the grounds that bear these qualities are explained.

> On all the grounds and in all regards,
> The benefits for the wise
> Are held to be of a fivefold nature
> In relation to calm abiding, to special insight, and to both.
> [XXI.31]

Next, the benefits are discerned. **On all the grounds and in all regards, the benefits for the wise,** the bodhisattvas, of having attained the transcendences are to be understood to involve five aspects: (1) bringing to exhaustion, moment by moment, the entire basis for negative tendencies; (2) fully achieving the joy of the Dharma that ensues in the absence of the notion of differences; (3) fully knowing the limitless and perfectly unbroken light of Dharma upon all the grounds; (4) engaging with the reasons in accordance with the context of purity, without conceptualizing them; and (5) progressively taking hold of the perfect causes so as to fully accomplish the body of qualities. Thus, the benefits **are held to be of a fivefold nature in relation to calm abiding** (as with the first two benefits), **to special insight** (as with the third and fourth benefit), **and to both** (as in the case of the final benefit).

On all ten grounds of the noble ones, the respective benefits for the wise bodhisattvas can, in all regards, be enumerated in terms of five factors—two that are based on calm abiding, two that are based on special insight, and one that is based on both calm abiding and special insight. As for the two based on calm abiding, (1) the first is a momentary and continuous process that is achieved due to the flexibility of the mind of calm abiding. This serves to conquer and exhaust all of the imprints of the afflictive and cognitive obscurations that otherwise make up the support for negative tendencies. Although the calm abiding and special insight that are present on the grounds of inspired conduct do cause the marks of negative tendencies to wane, they are not capable of completely uprooting them. From the first ground onward, however, those tendencies are, with each moment, continuously eliminated from their root. (2) As the bodhisattvas rest one-pointedly within the absence of marks, they are free from all notions of phenomena that differ in terms of having form or being formless, being conditioned or unconditioned, and so forth. The accompanying experience of joy in the Dharma is what constitutes the second benefit.

Whereas the first two benefits are both associated with calm abiding, the next two belong to special insight. (3) Although all phenomena are of one taste within the absence of marks, the bodhisattvas attain the light of Dharma that illumines all objects of knowledge within the ten directions and the three times. Thus they attain the Dharma light that clearly and distinctly reveals the infinite principles taught in the Dharma of scripture. (4) Although not conceptualized, the reasons are directly manifest in a way that accords with the context of purity. (5) In terms of both calm abiding and special insight, the benefit is liberation with respect to elimination and an increase in possession of the causes of the body of qualities with respect to realization.

The essence of these five benefits has also been explained above. Since the five are cognized in the individual experience of the bodhisattvas, they can also be enumerated among the signs. Since it ends with the explanation of the third of these five benefits, [the extant version of] Sthiramati's commentary is incomplete.

7. Etymology

Next follows the explanation of the etymology of the names of the grounds.

> Seeing that enlightenment is near
> And that the welfare of sentient beings can be accomplished
> Produces great joy;
> Hence, this is known as the Joyous. [XXI.32]

Since the stains of flawed discipline and effort are
    relinquished,
It is known as the Stainless.
As the great light of Dharma unfolds,
It is called the Radiant. [XXI.33]

On this ground, factors that accord with enlightenment
Are like a flaming light.
Therefore, as the two are burned away,
It is known as the Flaming. [XXI.34]

Sentient beings are thoroughly ripened,
And one's mind remains guarded;
As it is hence hard to conquer for the wise
It is known as Hard to Conquer. [XXI.35]

Based on transcendent insight,
Both cyclic existence and the transcendence of suffering
Are here manifest.
Hence, it is known as the ground of the Manifest. [XXI.36]

Connected with the single traversed path,
It is known as Far Reaching.
Unmoved by either identification,
It is referred to as the Unshakable. [XXI.37]

Endowed with the excellent intelligence of correct awareness,
This ground is Excellent Intelligence.
Like clouds, the two pervade the field of space.
Thus it is the Cloud of Dharma. [XXI.38]

With joy they constantly abide
In the practice of all sorts of virtue;
Therefore, the grounds of the bodhisattvas
Are held to be abodes. [XXI.39]

To liberate the innumerable sentient beings from fear,
These immeasurable ones support
A continuously increasing development;
Hence, they are held to be grounds. [XXI.40]

Next, the names of the grounds are explained. Seeing that complete enlightenment is near and that the welfare of sentient beings can be accomplished produces great joy; hence this ground is known as the Joyous. Since the stains of flawed discipline and the stains that consist in the effort of having to search for the Great Vehicle because the mind is engaged in other vehicles are all relinquished, it is known as the Stainless. As one pursues limitless Dharma by the power of meditative absorption and because the great light of Dharma unfolds toward others as well, it is called the Radiant. On this ground, factors of realization that accord with enlightenment are like a flaming light. Therefore, as the two obscurations are burned away, it is known as the Flaming. Sentient beings are thoroughly ripened, and one's mind remains guarded against affliction in the face of ingratitude and so forth. As both of these trainings are mastered, it is hence hard to conquer for the wise. Therefore it is known as Hard to Conquer. Based on transcendent insight, both cyclic existence and the transcendence of suffering are here manifest as equality. Hence, it is known as the ground of the Manifest. Connected with the single traversed path of the eighth ground, it is known as the one that is Far Reaching, beyond marks. Unmoved by either identification—neither by the identification of marks nor by the identification of the absence of marks involving effort—it is referred to as the Unshakable. Being primarily endowed with the excellent intelligence of correct awareness, this ground is Excellent Intelligence. Like clouds, the qualities that are attained by the two—retention and meditative absorption—pervade the support and the field of space; thus it is the Cloud of Dharma. With joy they constantly and on all occasions abide in the practice of all sorts of virtue; therefore, the grounds of the bodhisattvas are held to be abodes. To liberate the innumerable sentient beings from fear, these immeasurable ones, that is, these immeasurable qualities, **support a continuously increasing development; hence they,** that is, these abodes, **are held to be grounds.**

(1) Once the first ground is accomplished, the attainment of unsurpassable enlightenment is certain, and so enlightenment is near. Seeing that this is the case, and that they are capable of accomplishing the welfare of sentient beings, the bodhisattvas experience great joy. This is the reason that the first ground is named the Joyous. (2) On the second ground, the stains that take the form of flawed discipline and efforts in directing the mind according to the Lesser Vehicle all disappear. Hence, this ground is known as the Stainless. (3) Since, on the third ground, one attains infinite qualities by the power of meditative absorption and since one is able to spread the great light of Dharma for others, this ground is known as the Radiant.

(4) On the fourth ground, the bodhisattva's cultivation of the factors that accord with enlightenment is like a flaming light that burns away the afflictive and cognitive obscurations. Hence, since it burns up the two obscurations, the ground is known as the Flaming. (5) On the fifth ground, while thoroughly maturing sentient beings by means of the realization of the four truths, one patiently bears with their ingratitude and keeps one's mind guarded. Since both of the latter practices are difficult to pursue, this ground is hard to conquer for the wise. Hence, it is known as the Hard to Conquer.

(6) On the sixth ground, the nature of cyclic existence (comprising the forward arising of the links of dependent origination) and of the transcendence of suffering (as achieved through the reversal of these links) become manifest based on transcendent insight. Thus the bodhisattvas of this ground dwell neither in cyclic existence nor in the transcendence of suffering. Hence, this ground is known as the Manifest.

(7) The seventh ground is connected to the single traversed path that occurs on the eighth. Therefore, since, as the preliminary to the eighth ground, it occurs right before it, this ground is known as the Far

Reaching. (8) The eighth ground is not affected either by the identification of marks that occurs up to and including the sixth ground, or by the effortful identification of the absence of marks that occurs on the seventh. Upon this eighth ground, nonconceptual wakefulness is spontaneously accomplished, and for this reason it is referred to as the Unshakable. (9) On the ninth ground, the bodhisattvas are endowed with the excellent and extraordinary intelligence of the four forms of correct awareness. Accordingly, this ground is known as Excellent Intelligence. (10) As when a great cloud fills the sky, on the tenth ground, vast clouds of limitless gateways of retentions and meditative absorption fill the mind stream's basic field of phenomena. Hence, this is known as the Cloud of Dharma.

The bodhisattvas abide upon these ten grounds. Yet in what sense, we may wonder, do the grounds thus serve as the bodhisattvas' "abodes"? On each ground, the bodhisattvas always and in all regards abide, with great joy, by the practices of the diverse and infinite virtues that consist of the gradual accomplishment of the two accumulations. It is for this reason that the grounds of the bodhisattvas are referred to as abodes. And why are they termed "grounds?" The Sanskrit *bhūmi* denotes that which functions as the support for sentient beings, greenery, forests, and all other such things of the world. Thus, it is the ground that supports and protects one from the fear of falling, just as it becomes the basis for moving from one place or object to another. The grounds of the bodhisattvas, similarly, support the innumerable beings who are to be trained, providing them with an abode free from fear. Moreover, the immeasurable qualities of the succession of the grounds also provide the support for a continuously increasing development. It is for these reasons that the abodes of the bodhisattvas are termed "grounds."

8. Attainment

> The attainment of the grounds is fourfold
> In terms of the inspired,
> Entry into the activities,
> Realization, and accomplishment. [XXI.41]

In order to inspire and to tame
Embodied beings who are motivated
By both the Great
And the Inferior Vehicle,
The four activities of the steadfast ones
Have been explained by relying on the sūtras. [XXI.42]

The discernment of the attainment follows next. **The attainment of the grounds is fourfold in terms of the inspired conduct** with respect to the qualities explained above, the ensuing **entry into the activities** (that is, the ten Dharma activities and so forth), the thorough **realization** of the ultimate, **and** the **accomplishment** upon the grounds of irreversibility.

The activities are discerned as follows. **In order to inspire and to tame embodied beings who are motivated by both the Great and the Inferior Vehicle, the four activities of the steadfast ones have been explained by relying on the sūtras** of the Jewel Mound. Thus, the activities associated with the transcendences have been explained for the sake of those motivated by the Great Vehicle, while the activities related to the factors that accord with enlightenment have been taught in consideration of individuals motivated by the Inferior Vehicle. The activities that are connected with the superknowledges have been explained in order to inspire both of the above types, and the activities related to the thorough ripening of sentient beings have been taught so that both types may mature.

Four aspects of the attainment of the grounds are enumerated in reference to the following contexts: (1) inspired conduct as one gains inspiration with respect to the meaning of the Great Vehicle, (2) engaged inspired conduct as one enters into the ten Dharma activities, (3) realization of the meaning of the Dharma as it arises upon the first seven grounds of realization, and (4) accomplishment upon the three pure grounds due to the effortless presence of nonconceptual wakefulness. Thus, the four aspects of attainment are enumerated in terms of inspiration, conduct, realization, and accomplishment.

When the activities that accord with the factors of enlightenment are enumerated in detail, they turn out to be infinite. In sum, however, embodied beings who are motivated by the Great Vehicle are taught the activities of the six transcendences, whereas those motivated by the Lesser Vehicle are primarily taught the activities associated with the factors of enlightenment. Moreover, the activities of the superknowledges are taught to inspire beings of both categories, and the activities of the four means of attraction are taught for the sake of taming and maturing those to be trained. Thus, the present treatise explains the four activities of the bodhisattvas in a way that follows the teaching of the *Sūtra Requested by Ratnacūḍa*.

4. The Qualities of Perfection

Having thus concluded the explanation of the qualities of the path—the essence of the factors that accord with enlightenment—the treatise offers verses of praise for the qualities of great enlightenment. These qualities of the fruition, the subject of a previous chapter, are here praised in consideration of their perfect attainment once the ten grounds have been traversed. The teaching begins with praises of the four immeasurables, continues through the qualities of the six transcendences, and concludes with two stanzas on the characteristics of the ground of the buddhas.

1. The Four Immeasurables

> You who have love for sentient beings,
> Who are intent on their meeting, their separating,
> Their never separating, and their benefit and happiness—
> To you, I prostrate. [XXI.43]

Among the qualities of the Buddha, first the immeasurables are discerned. To begin with they are referred to in general ("**You who have love for sentient beings**"), followed by love ("**who are intent on their meeting** with happiness"), compassion ("intent on **their separating** from suffering"), joy ("intent on **their never separating** from happiness"), **and** equanimity ("intent on **their benefit and happiness** in the absence of affliction")—"**to you, I prostrate.**"

The line "You who have love for sentient beings" considers, in general, the Buddha's love for sentient beings. Thereafter, the verses refer specifically to the Awakened One's infinite love that wishes for sentient beings to meet with happiness, infinite compassion that wishes them to be free from suffering, and infinite joy that wants them never to separate from happiness. Together, these three constitute the enlightened intent that is directed toward happiness. Infinite equanimity is the wish that sentient beings may be free from the afflictions of attachment and aversion, thus attaining equanimity. In this way, with utmost veneration of body, speech, and mind, homage is paid to "you," the Buddha, the one who is intent on bringing about benefit and happiness for all sentient beings.

2. Freedoms, Commands, and Totalities

Able One, definitively free from all obscurations,
You command the entire world,
And your wakefulness pervades all objects of knowledge—
I prostrate to you, whose heart is free. [XXI.44]

Next follow the freedoms and the sources of the commands and totalities. "**Able One,** Blessed One, your eight freedoms are **definitively free from all obscurations**; with **your** eight commands you hold **command of the entire world**; and as **your wakefulness** of totality **pervades all objects of knowledge,** it is free from obscuration. **I prostrate to you, whose heart is free** from obscuration."

There are eight freedoms, from the freedom of the physical that regards the physical up to the freedom of cessation. The commands are also eight in number and include the command over smaller external forms by considering them to be internal forms. Through these eight, one gains command over shapes and colors. Finally, ten totalities are enumerated with reference to earth, water, wind, space, consciousness, blue, yellow, white, and red. Thus, the freedoms, commands, and totalities constitute the path for training in bringing forth emanations by means of meditative absorption. This path can be seen to be initiated by means of the freedoms, applied through the commands, and accomplished with the totalities. In the case of a buddha, however, all three are spontaneously accomplished within the essence of nonconceptual wakefulness, and a buddha's freedoms, commands, and totalities are of a quality that is superior to what can be accomplished by mundane beings, listeners, or self-realized buddhas. The freedoms mastered by the Able One, the Buddha, are thus not only free from the specific factors that conflict with the various freedoms but are definitively free from both of the two obscurations and their associated habitual tendencies. Likewise, the Buddha's commands wield mastery not only of shape and color but of the entire world. As for the Victorious One's totalities, these do not merely encompass the objects of a limited nature by means of, for example, the appearance of earth, because the wakefulness of the Buddha pervades all objects of knowledge. Therefore, homage is paid to the one whose heart is free from all obscurations associated with equilibrium, affliction, and cognition.

3. Absence of Affliction

> Conqueror of the afflictions
> Of all sentient beings,
> You conquer afflictions and have love for afflictions—
> To you, I prostrate. [XXI.45]

Then, on the absence of affliction: "**Conqueror of the afflictions of all sentient beings, You conquer** the **afflictions** of those afflicted, **and** you **have** special **love for** those who suffer from **afflictions—to you, I prostrate.**"

A buddha's freedom from affliction is likewise special. Whereas listeners and self-realized buddhas protect themselves from the arising of the afflictions of sentient beings, the thus-gone ones' freedom from affliction possesses the power to conquer the afflictions of all sentient beings without exception. Therefore, here, homage is paid to the one who conquers afflictions for the sake of afflicted sentient beings and who thus has love for every being struck by affliction.

4. Knowledge Arising from Aspiration

> Spontaneously present and free from attachment,
> Unhindered and constantly in equipoise,
> You answer all questions—
> Homage to you. [XXI.46]

The knowing that arises from aspiration is explained next. **Spontaneously present** without any effort **and free from** all forms of **attachment, unhindered** in knowing all that can be known **and constantly in equipoise, you answer all questions**, dispelling all doubts—**homage to you.**

When a listener is, for example, asked a question by someone, he or she may purposely concentrate and rest in equipoise and on that basis display much knowledge in response. Nevertheless, listeners do not possess unimpeded insight into all that can be known, and they are not constantly in equipoise or capable of replying to all questions. A buddha's knowledge out of aspiration can, on the other hand, be distinguished from that of the listeners in five ways. The knowledge of a buddha is (1) spontaneously present without any effort; (2) unattached in the sense that it is free from the habitual tendencies associated with affliction, or in the sense that it does not depend on entering into equipoise; (3) free from the cognitive obscurations and thus unhindered in knowing all that can be known; (4) present within unwavering and constant equipoise; and (5) capable of yielding a reply to all possible questions raised by sentient beings. Hence, homage is here paid to the one whose knowledge is distinguished in these five ways.

5. Correct Awareness

> Regarding the subject matter to be explained, the support and the supported,
> And the means for the explanation, the speech and the knowledge,
> Your intelligence can never be hindered—
> Homage to you, excellent teacher. [XXI.47]

> On correct awareness: **Regarding the subject matter to be explained, the supporting** Dharma **and the supported** meaning, **and the means for the explanation, the speech** of definitive words **and the** confident **knowledge, your intelligence can never be hindered. Homage to you, excellent teacher** of the sacred Dharma.

Next, the four correct awarenesses are praised. Serving as support, the Dharma upholds the supported, that is, the meaning. These two, the Dharma and its meaning, constitute what is to be explained. The means of explanation, on the other hand, is the speech of definitive words that can be understood in the languages of all sentient beings, together with the inexhaustible confidence of knowing all that can be known. Homage is paid to the excellent teacher of the sacred Dharma, who thus explains with an intelligence that can never be impeded.

6. The Six Forms of Superknowledge

> Moving to sentient beings and knowing their conduct,
> You teach, in their own languages,
> About coming, going, and deliverance—
> Homage to you, excellent instructor. [XXI.48]

> On the superknowledges: **Moving,** with miraculous power, **to** the **sentient beings** who are to be trained **and knowing their** mind's **conduct** by means of the knowledge of the minds of others, **you teach** them **in their own languages** by means of the

superknowledge of the divine ear. You teach them **about their coming** from elsewhere **and going** back elsewhere by means of the divine eye, **and** you also instruct them about their **deliverance** by way of the knowledge of the exhaustion of defilements. **Homage to you, excellent instructor.**

With the superknowledge of miracles, the Buddha travels wherever there are beings to be trained. Through knowledge of the minds of others, he is aware of the eighty-four thousand modes of mental conduct of beings. By the power of the superknowledge of the divine ear, he teaches everyone in their own language. He explains to them where they come from with knowledge of past events. By means of the divine eye, he shows them where they will be going to in the future. With knowledge of the exhaustion of defilements, he teaches them the way of deliverance from cyclic existence. Thus, homage is paid to the excellent instructor.

7. The Marks and Signs

> **When corporeal beings see you,**
> **They recognize you as a holy being;**
> **Homage to you, toward whom fervent faith**
> **Arises simply upon sight.** [XXI.49]

On the adornment of marks and signs: **When corporeal beings see you, they recognize you as a holy being. Homage to you, toward whom fervent faith arises simply upon sight.**

The Buddha possesses the thirty-two marks and the eighty signs of excellence. Thus, when corporeal beings see him, they recognize his perfection, thinking, "This is a holy being!" Thus, homage is paid to the one for whom fervent faith arises simply upon sight.

8. The Fourfold Complete Purity

> **Master of assuming, abiding, and relinquishing;**
> **Emanation and transformation,**

Meditative absorption and wakefulness—
Homage to you. [XXI.50]

On the fourfold complete purity: Because of the complete purity of your support, you are the **master of assuming, abiding** by, **and relinquishing** the body. Due to your complete purity of observation, you master the **emanation** of the nonexistent **and** the **transformation** of the existent. Your completely pure mind masters **meditative absorption, and** with completely pure insight, you master **wakefulness. Homage to you.**

Through the complete purity of his support, the Buddha masters the art of purposely assuming a new physical support, abiding by it, or relinquishing the conditions for continued life. Due to his purity with respect to observations, he masters the art of emanating that which did not previously exist and transforming what already does exist. With his purity of mind, he masters meditative absorption, and his completely pure insight masters inconceivable wakefulness. Hence, homage is paid to the master of such purity.

9. The Ten Powers

You conquer the demons who entirely deceive sentient beings
With respect to means, protection,
Purity, and deliverance through the Great Vehicle—
Homage to you. [XXI.51]

On the ten powers: Without exception **you conquer** all of **the** hosts of **demons**—those **who entirely deceive sentient beings with respect to** the **means** for rebirth in the higher realms, **protection** from cyclic existence, the **purity** of the transcendence of suffering, **and** the **deliverance** that takes place **through the Great Vehicle. Homage to you.**

With knowledge of what is fact and nonfact, the buddhas have the power to distinguish between cause and noncause. In this way, they conquer the demons that create deceptions with respect to what causes, or serves as the means for, birth in the higher and lower realms. Thus they destroy deceit, such as when demons teach that violent sacrifice is a cause for rebirth in the higher realms, when in fact it is not. Likewise, by the power of their knowledge of karmic ripening, they show how it is impossible for someone like the Almighty to grant any protection without depending on the force of karma, and so they conquer the deceptions of the demons with respect to the sources of refuge. The buddhas also possess the power of knowing all forms of concentration as associated with thorough affliction and complete purification. With this power, they conquer the demons that otherwise deceive with respect to purification, presenting the mere attainment of the form or formless realms as if it were purity and liberation from cyclic existence.

With the remaining seven powers, the buddhas conquer the demons who deceptively distort the nature of the deliverance that takes place by means of the Great Vehicle. Thus, with the powers of knowing all elements, interests, and faculties, they are aware of the various potentials, types of faith, and the manifestation of factors such as faith in the beings who are to be trained. In this way, these three powers carry knowledge of the factors that distinguish the various beings who are to receive teaching. Moreover, by the power of knowing past contexts and the power of knowing death and transference, the buddhas possess knowledge of the supports for the path, while also being aware—due to the power of their knowing all paths—of the essence of the path. Finally, with the power of knowledge of the exhaustion of defilement, they are aware of the result of the deliverance. As they also transmit all of this knowledge to those who are to be trained, they thus conquer those demons that deceive beings by distorting the character of the deliverance that takes place through the Great Vehicle. Thus, homage is paid to the one who possesses these ten powers.

10. The Four Types of Fearlessness

The wakefulness, elimination, deliverance, and hindrances,
Which pertain to the welfare of self and others,

You declare without being disturbed by extremists or others—
Homage to you. [XXI.52]

On the four fearlessnesses: **The wakefulness, elimination, deliverance, and hindrances, which pertain to the welfare of self and others, you declare without being disturbed by extremists or others. Homage to you.**

Buddhas are not afraid of acknowledging that they have accomplished their own objectives and so they declare their possession of omniscient wakefulness. They have, likewise, no qualms about acknowledging that by eliminating the two obscurations they have accomplished perfect elimination. Nor are the buddhas afraid of revealing the path for the benefit of others, and so they correctly show the path of deliverance from cyclic existence, just as without any fear of exposing the hindrances on the path, they point out the obstacles that obstruct the path of liberation from cyclic existence and the character of the obstructive factors, such as the view of self or attachment. In this way, the buddhas teach with a voice of truth and authenticity. Even if they should be accused of falsity by gods, demons, Brahma, spiritual practitioners, or Brahmins, they will never be disturbed by any such attack that runs counter to the Dharma. Thus, homage is paid to the ones who possess such fearlessness.

11. Nothing to Guard

Without anything to guard yet without forgetfulness,
You speak readily within the assembly;
Free from the two afflictions, you gather the circle—
Homage to you. [XXI.53]

On the freedom from observance and the application of mindfulness: **Without anything to guard** in terms of the conduct of your body, speech, and mind, **yet without** any **forgetfulness** because of the constant composure of your realized mind, **you speak readily within the assembly. Free from the two afflictions** of attachment and anger, **you** fully **gather the circle. Homage to you.**

The exalted body, speech, and mind are entirely free from any flaw. The buddhas, therefore, do not have anything at all to conceal or hold back, worrying that others might discover something, and so they have nothing to keep secret or guard in terms of their conduct of body, speech, and mind. At the same time, they do not know any forgetfulness, as when a mistake occurs and one purposely has to regain equanimity. Thus, undaunted like lions, they readily reveal the Dharma within the circle of the assembly. They are neither attached to those who listen to the Dharma, nor opposed to those who do not, and so they remain mindful with neither clinging nor aversion toward anyone. Hence, homage is paid to the one who has eliminated the afflictions of attachment and aversion and thus fully gathers the circle of the retinue.

12. Defeating the Habitual Tendencies

> All-Knowing One, as you move or remain,
> You are at all times free
> From any conduct that is not omniscient—
> Homage to you, possessor of the ultimate. [XXI.54]

On the complete defeat of the habitual tendencies: **All-Knowing One, as you move** through a town **or remain** composed in meditative absorption, **you are at all times free from any conduct that is not omniscient. Homage to you, possessor of the ultimate.**

Whether moving through a town to share merit or the like, or whether resting in inner composure, an omniscient one is at all times free from any conduct that is not precisely what an omniscient one should do. Hence, when proceeding forth, residing, or engaged in any other aspect of their conduct, the buddhas perceive and remain aware of everything. For them, there is no context that is not equipoise. They never engage in any conduct that is deluded and not of perfect wakefulness. Thus there is nothing at all that could be considered a flaw of theirs. Thus, homage is paid to the one who possesses "omniscience" in the ultimate sense.

While the foe destroyers among the listeners may be free from the afflictions, they have not eliminated their habitual tendencies. Therefore, when on a journey, they might, for example, encounter a mad elephant or have to face a chariot, or a snake might bite their feet, or they may get lost in a dense forest. Likewise, at times they may jump up like a monkey or break out in loud laughter that sounds like the neighing of a horse. Thus, while for them there is the possibility of various forms of conduct that fall short of full discernment, this is never the case with a buddha.

13. Freedom from Bewilderment

> Acting for the benefit
> Of sentient beings without any delay,
> Your deeds are always beneficial—
> Homage to you, who do not know bewilderment. [XXI.55]

On the freedom from bewilderment: **Acting for the benefit of sentient beings without any delay, your deeds are always beneficial. Homage to you, who do not know bewilderment.**

The buddhas act for the benefit of beings without any delay, always doing exactly what is beneficial for whomsoever is in need. Homage is therefore paid to the one who without any bewilderment thus acts for the welfare of beings.

14. Great Compassion

> Throughout the six times of day and night,
> You regard the entire world with discernment;
> Possessor of great compassion,
> Who is intent on benefiting—homage to you. [XXI.56]

On the great compassion: **Throughout the six times of day and night you regard the entire world with discernment,** noticing whoever is in decline and whoever is successful. **Possessor of great** compassion, who is always intent on benefiting—homage to you.

By means of a sixfold diligence throughout day and night, the buddhas remain constantly aware of all that takes place in the worlds of the ten directions. Thus, seeing all that are in decline and everyone that prospers, the buddhas are concerned to benefit all beings with exactly what will be helpful to them. While this is the essence of how great their compassion is, it functions so as to benefit every sentient being. Thus, homage is paid to the one who is intent on benefiting beings.

15. The Eighteen Unshared Qualities

Due to your conduct, realization,
Wakefulness, and activity, you are the master
Of all listeners and self-realized buddhas—
Homage to you. [XXI.57]

On the unshared qualities: **Due to** the six unshared qualities that are subsumed in **your conduct**, that is, (1) the absence of error with respect to the body, (2) the absence of any impediments of speech, (3) the mind's not knowing forgetfulness, (4) the mind's never lacking equipoise, (5) the mind's being free from distinct identifications, and (6) the mind's being free from any unexamined, neutral rest; due to the six unshared qualities that are included in your **realization**, that is, the Buddha's never undergoing any decrease in terms of (1) intent, (2) diligence, (3) mindfulness, (4) meditative absorption, (5) insight, and (6) liberation; due to the three unshared qualities that pertain to your **wakefulness**, that is, the unattached and unhindered cognition of all objects in the three times; and due to the three unshared qualities that are subsumed in your **activity**, that is, the activities of body, speech, and mind, which are preceded and carried out by means of wakefulness, **you are the master of all listeners and self-realized buddhas— homage to you.**

(1) The buddhas' bodies are free from error. (2) Their voices are free from all impediments. (3) Their minds are endowed with unwavering mindfulness. Hence, a buddha's mind is (4) never without equipoise but (5) free from distinct identifications, and it (6) never enters a neutral state that is divorced from full discernment. While these six qualities are thus distinguished with reference to a buddha's conduct, the next six pertain to realization. Thus, for the buddhas, there is never any decrease in their powers of (1) intent, (2) diligence, (3) mindfulness, (4) meditative absorption, (5) insight, and (6) liberation. (We may note that some texts here omit meditative absorption and instead count the wakefulness that witnesses liberation as the sixth quality. Both interpretations are in accord with their own sūtra sources.)

Furthermore (1) a buddha's wakefulness engages with the past, free from either attachment or impediment, and the same is the case in terms of (2) the present and (3) the future. These three qualities are thus enumerated in terms of the wakefulness of the buddhas. Finally, three qualities are specified with reference to their activities of (1) body, (2) speech, and (3) mind because each act of a buddha's body is preceded by, and is in accord with, wakefulness, and the same is the case with their activities of speech and mind. These eighteen qualities are the unique possession of the buddhas. Hence, homage is paid to the one who possesses these eighteen qualities that are not shared by any listener or self-realized buddha.

16. Omniscience

> With the three bodies, you have, in all regards,
> Attained great enlightenment;
> Dispeller of all the doubts of sentient beings—
> Homage to you. [XXI.58]

On the wakefulness of omniscience: **With the three bodies, you have, in all regards, attained great enlightenment. Dispeller of all the doubts of sentient beings—homage to you.**

With their attainment of the three bodies, the buddhas have gained the great enlightenment that is endowed with the supreme among all qualities, that is, true omniscience. Having attained the body of qualities, the buddhas have achieved true enlightenment with respect to the profound field of the twofold purity. Moreover, with their achievement of the body of perfect enjoyment, they have gained true enlightenment with respect to the extraordinary four types of wakefulness. Having accomplished the emanation body, they have also achieved true enlightenment in terms of supramundane activities that benefit sentient beings as far as space abounds. Together, the two form bodies are known as the "true enlightenment with respect to the vast." Homage is therefore paid to the one who, having attained such enlightenment, consequently dispels all the doubts of sentient beings.

17. Perfection of the Six Transcendences

> Free from grasping, free from flaws,
> Unsullied and beyond abiding,
> Unwavering and free from constructs regarding any
>   phenomenon—
> Homage to you. [XXI.59]

On the perfection of the six transcendences: **Free from grasping** at enjoyments, **free from** any **flaws** of the actions of the three gates, **unsullied** by mundane phenomena and suffering, **and beyond abiding** within lesser realizations, **unwavering** without any distraction **and free from constructs regarding any phenomenon**, any object of cognition—**homage to you.**

In the case of the buddhas, transcendent generosity has been perfected in the absence of any grasping. Likewise, since they are free from any flaw, their transcendent discipline has also reached perfection, and because their stream of being is completely unsullied, their transcendent patience is perfect as well. Moreover, since they are never indifferent to the aims of sentient beings, they have perfected transcendent diligence.

Because they never waver from meditative absorption, their transcendent concentration is also perfect. Because they are free from constructs regarding any phenomenon, the same is the case with their transcendent insight. Homage is paid to the one who has thus perfected the six transcendences.

18. Summary of the Buddha Ground

With ultimate accomplishment,
You have emerged definitively beyond the grounds.
Supreme among all beings,
You are the liberator of all beings. [XXI.60]

Possessing inexhaustible qualities beyond compare,
You appear in the worlds and maṇḍalas,
And yet to gods and humans,
You remain imperceptible. [XXI.61]

Still, by the power of that, there arises,
In accordance with the fortune of those to be trained
And for as long as there is existence,
The continuous flow of activities. [XXI.62]

This was the twenty-first chapter of the *Ornament of the Great Vehicle Sūtras*, the chapter on activity and perfection.

The characteristics of buddhahood are discerned as follows: **With ultimate accomplishment** (which is the essence of buddhahood, the essence body), **you have emerged definitively beyond the grounds** (the cause of buddhahood). Having become **supreme among all beings** (which is the effect), **you are the liberator of all beings** (thus showing the activities of buddhahood). **Possessing inexhaustible qualities beyond compare** (the endowment of buddhahood), **you appear in the worlds** as the emanation body **and** in the **maṇḍalas** of the victorious ones as the body of perfect enjoyment, **and yet to gods and humans,** your body of qualities

remains imperceptible. In this way, the functioning of the threefold body can be discerned.

Still, by the power of that, that is, by the power of the body of qualities, **there arises, in accordance with the fortune of those to be trained and for as long as there is existence, the continuous flow of** the **activities** of the body of qualities.

The characteristics of the ground of buddhahood are discerned in the following way. First, the essence of the buddha ground is the accomplishment of the ultimate objective, or reality, which is great enlightenment endowed with both natural purity and the purity that manifests in the absence of the adventitious stains. The cause of such enlightenment is the emerging definitively and perfectly beyond all of the grounds, and its effect is a forever unfailing supremacy among all sentient beings. The way it serves as the liberator of all sentient beings constitutes the function of buddhahood. Moreover, its endowment consists of its inexhaustible possession of excellent qualities such as the powers, and thus the endowment of listeners and self-realized buddhas cannot compare to it. Its applications, or divisions, are specified in terms of the emanation bodies of the buddhas that appear in impure worlds, the enjoyment bodies that are also manifest to pure disciples within the maṇḍalas of the buddhas, and the body of qualities that is seen only by the Buddha and not ever by any god or human.

While the above is in fact the end of our treatise, at this point an additional stanza has been supplied by those who are expert in arranging the auspicious coincidence for benefiting beings. Therefore, by the power of the body of qualities, there nevertheless arises, in accordance with the fortune of those to be trained and for as long as the realms of existence remain, a continuous flow of the activities of the body of qualities.

This concludes the explanation of the twenty-first chapter of the *Ornament of the Great Vehicle Sūtras,* the chapter on activity and perfection.

4. Colophons

The final, fourth section contains the concluding colophon. This colophon is followed by the colophon of the translators.

> This completes noble Maitreya's composition *Ornament of the Great Vehicle Sūtras*.
>
> *The translation was prepared, edited, and finalized by the Indian preceptor Śākyasiṁha and the great editor of lotsawas, the bandhe Paltsek. Later it was slightly modified and again finalized by the paṇḍita Parahita, the great Brahmin Sadjana, and the lotsawa-monk Loden Sherab, based on fine exposition. The final śloka has been entered, in accordance with what can be found in other scriptures, as a circumstance for increasing the benefits for beings.*
>
> This completes noble Maitreya's composition *Ornament of the Great Vehicle Sūtras*. The translation was prepared, edited, and **finalized** at the time of the early spread of the teachings **by the** Indian preceptor Śākyasiṁha and the great editor of lotsawas, the *bandhe* Kawa **Paltsek,** who was one among the 108 lotsawas. Later it was slightly modified and again finalized by the paṇḍita Parahita, the great Brahmin Sadjana, and the lotsawa-monk Loden Sherab, based on fine exposition. The final *śloka* has been entered, in accordance with what can be found in other scriptures, as a circumstance for increasing the benefits for wandering **beings.**
>
> Within the Dharma ocean of the Early Translations, the basis for these annotations is found in the commentary by the second

Buddha, Vasubandhu. Relying on the lamp of the speech of Orgyen Tendzin Norbu, an expert in the study of the excellent statements of the Noble Land, the annotations were written by the vagabond bandhe known as Shenphen Jampé Gocha. May it be virtuous!

Ema!
This treatise perfectly gathers the Dharma way of the Great Vehicle, so hard to obtain even by the accumulations of numerous eons.
Authored by the regent, Maitreya, this treatise, when taught and received,
Delivers the full goodness of the explanation and reception of all of the Great Vehicle Dharma.
The great chariot teaches in the same way as in the *Ground of the Bodhisattvas*,
And so, in order to let this nectar feast of the Great Vehicle Dharma
Reach a limitless number of beings,
The present commentary was composed with the utmost respect for the supreme teaching
And the wish to be of benefit to others.
By the bright white moonlight of the virtue of these efforts,
May the youthful kunda flowers of the minds of wandering beings open,
And, as the delightful voice reaches everywhere,
May all the mind's murkiness clear away in beings.
Throughout all my lives, may I as well,
Before the delighted utpala eyes of Mañjuśrī and the Regent Maitreya,
Enter the ocean of activities of the victorious ones' children.
Thus, as the infinitely many beings that pervade as far as space
Set out firmly on the path of the supreme vehicle,
May they all cross the ocean of accumulation, maturation, and cultivation,
Thus gaining the stage of the one who sees all.

In the summer of the Iron Pig year, while observing seclusion and reciting the knowledge mantra of the Noble Lord of Wakefulness, I, Mipham Jamyang Gyatso, wrote these concise clarifications

based on the commentary of the great master Sthiramati. The composition took place during the breaks between sessions for a period of about forty days.
Let this be of excellent virtue!
Maṅgalam.

APPENDIX:

A Visual Representation of Mipham's Topical Outline

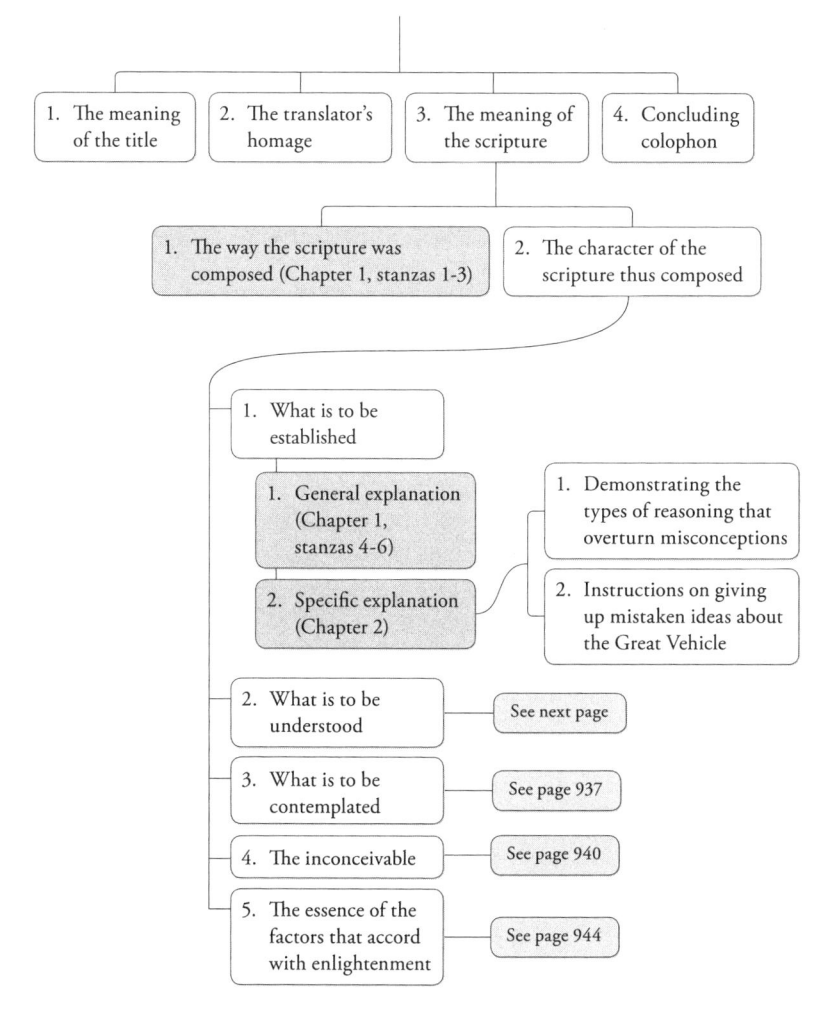

1. The meaning of the title
2. The translator's homage
3. The meaning of the scripture
4. Concluding colophon

Under "3. The meaning of the scripture":
1. The way the scripture was composed (Chapter 1, stanzas 1-3)
2. The character of the scripture thus composed

Under "2. The character of the scripture thus composed":

1. What is to be established
   1. General explanation (Chapter 1, stanzas 4-6)
   2. Specific explanation (Chapter 2)
      1. Demonstrating the types of reasoning that overturn misconceptions
      2. Instructions on giving up mistaken ideas about the Great Vehicle
2. What is to be understood — See next page
3. What is to be contemplated — See page 937
4. The inconceivable — See page 940
5. The essence of the factors that accord with enlightenment — See page 944

APPENDIX

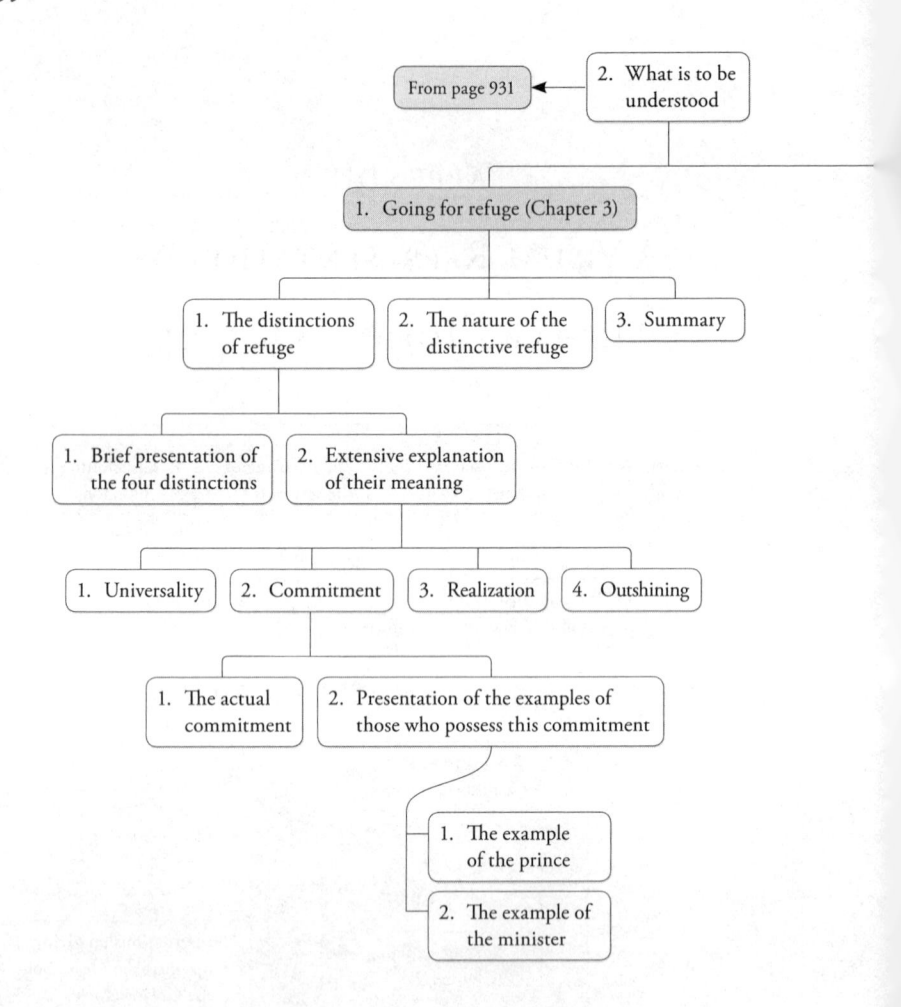

```
From page 931 ← 2. What is to be understood
                    │
                    ├─ 1. Going for refuge (Chapter 3)
                         │
                         ├─ 1. The distinctions of refuge
                         │    │
                         │    ├─ 1. Brief presentation of the four distinctions
                         │    └─ 2. Extensive explanation of their meaning
                         │         │
                         │         ├─ 1. Universality
                         │         ├─ 2. Commitment
                         │         │    │
                         │         │    ├─ 1. The actual commitment
                         │         │    └─ 2. Presentation of the examples of those who possess this commitment
                         │         │         │
                         │         │         ├─ 1. The example of the prince
                         │         │         └─ 2. The example of the minister
                         │         ├─ 3. Realization
                         │         └─ 4. Outshining
                         ├─ 2. The nature of the distinctive refuge
                         └─ 3. Summary
```

A VISUAL REPRESENTATION OF MIPHAM'S TOPICAL OUTLINE

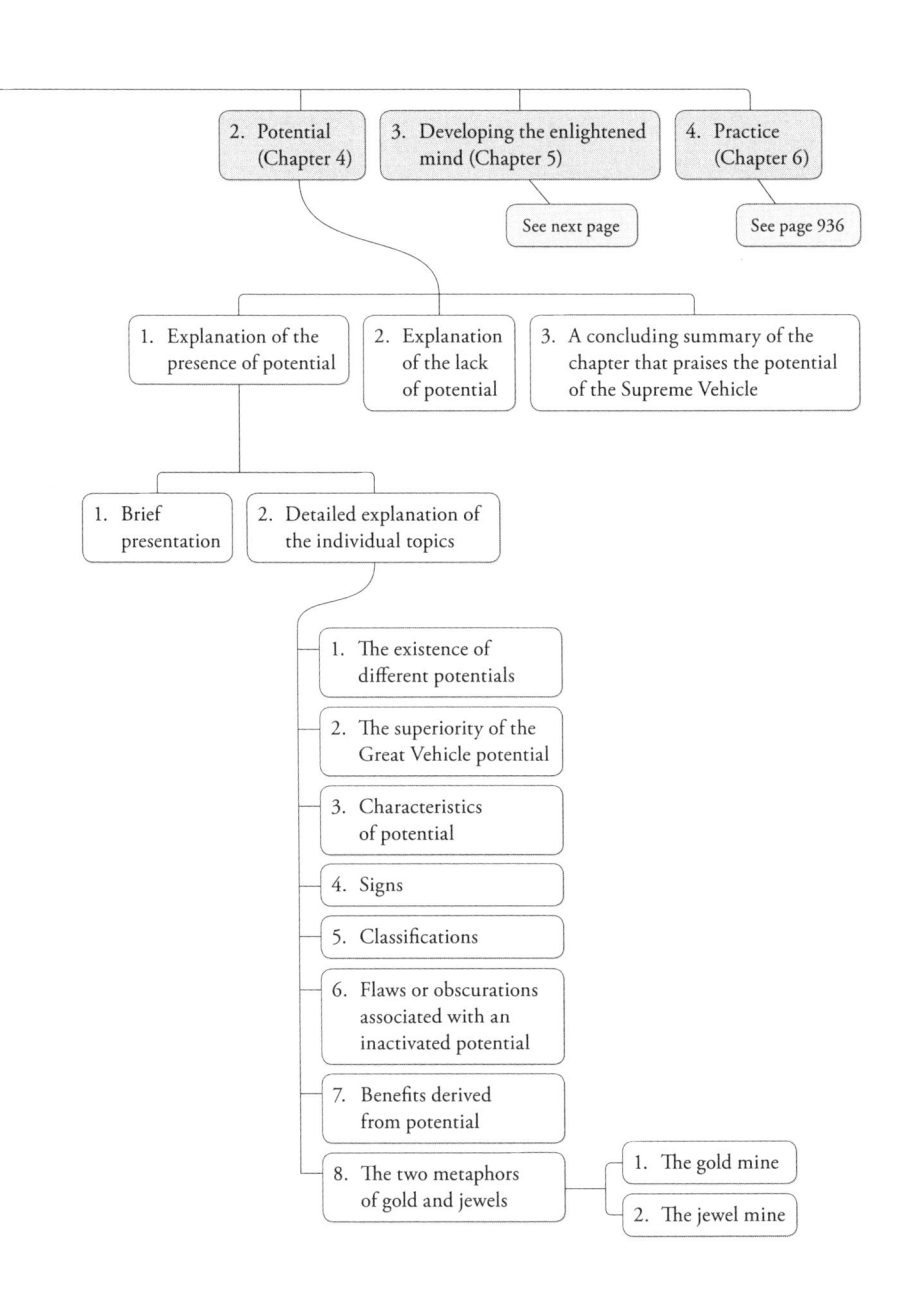

- 2. Potential (Chapter 4)
- 3. Developing the enlightened mind (Chapter 5) — *See next page*
- 4. Practice (Chapter 6) — *See page 936*

2. Potential (Chapter 4)

1. Explanation of the presence of potential
2. Explanation of the lack of potential
3. A concluding summary of the chapter that praises the potential of the Supreme Vehicle

1. Explanation of the presence of potential

1. Brief presentation
2. Detailed explanation of the individual topics

2. Detailed explanation of the individual topics

1. The existence of different potentials
2. The superiority of the Great Vehicle potential
3. Characteristics of potential
4. Signs
5. Classifications
6. Flaws or obscurations associated with an inactivated potential
7. Benefits derived from potential
8. The two metaphors of gold and jewels
   1. The gold mine
   2. The jewel mine

APPENDIX

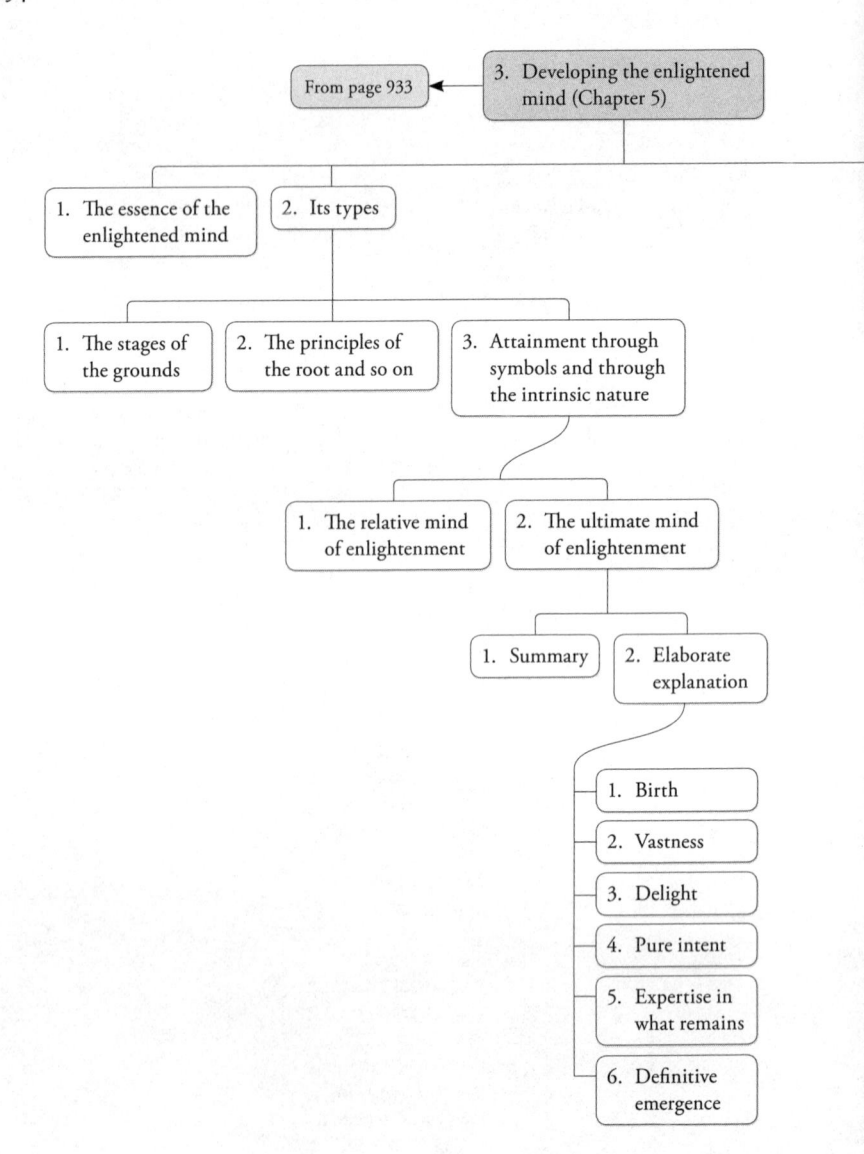

- **3. Developing the enlightened mind (Chapter 5)** [From page 933]
  - 1. The essence of the enlightened mind
  - 2. Its types
    - 1. The stages of the grounds
    - 2. The principles of the root and so on
    - 3. Attainment through symbols and through the intrinsic nature
      - 1. The relative mind of enlightenment
      - 2. The ultimate mind of enlightenment
        - 1. Summary
        - 2. Elaborate explanation
          - 1. Birth
          - 2. Vastness
          - 3. Delight
          - 4. Pure intent
          - 5. Expertise in what remains
          - 6. Definitive emergence

A VISUAL REPRESENTATION OF MIPHAM'S TOPICAL OUTLINE 935

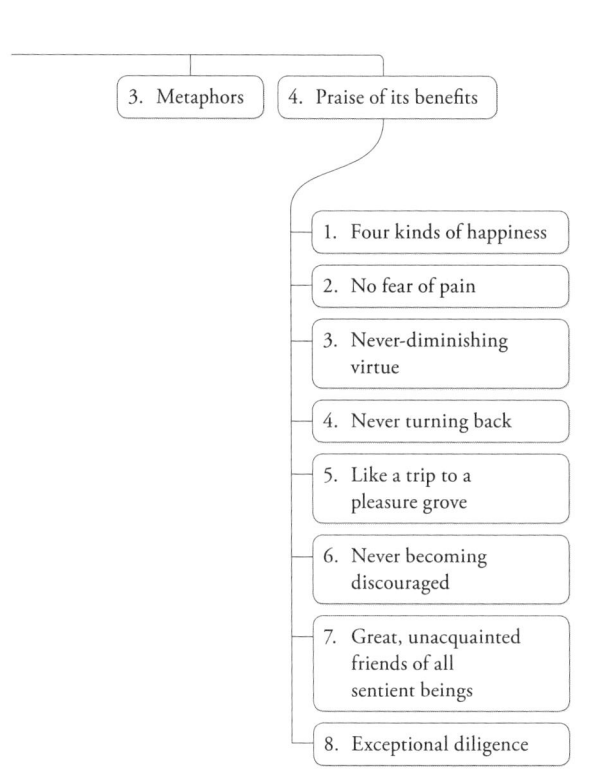

- 3. Metaphors
- 4. Praise of its benefits
    - 1. Four kinds of happiness
    - 2. No fear of pain
    - 3. Never-diminishing virtue
    - 4. Never turning back
    - 5. Like a trip to a pleasure grove
    - 6. Never becoming discouraged
    - 7. Great, unacquainted friends of all sentient beings
    - 8. Exceptional diligence

```
                    ┌─────────────────┐     ┌──────────────────────────┐
                    │ From page 933   │◄────┤ 4. Practice (Chapter 6)  │
                    └─────────────────┘     └──────────────────────────┘
                                                         │
        ┌────────────────────────────┬───────────────────┴───────────────────┐
┌───────────────────────────┐  ┌──────────────────────────┐  ┌──────────────────────────┐
│ 1. General presentation   │  │ 2. Specific explanation  │  │ 3. Conclusion that shows │
│    of the perfect practice│  │    of how to practice    │  │    the magnificence      │
│    endowed with the       │  │    for the sake of others│  │    of this practice      │
│    twofold benefit        │  │                          │  │                          │
└───────────────────────────┘  └──────────────────────────┘  └──────────────────────────┘
                                           │
                               ┌───────────┘
                               │
                    ┌──────────┴────────────────────────┐
                    │ 1. How to work for the            │
                    │    welfare of others              │
                    ├───────────────────────────────────┤
                    │ 2. The types of actions           │
                    │    for others' welfare            │
                    ├───────────────────────────────────┤
                    │ 3. How acting for others'         │
                    │    welfare is supreme             │
                    ├───────────────────────────────────┤
                    │ 4. How acting for others'         │
                    │    welfare is exalted             │
                    ├───────────────────────────────────┤
                    │ 5. How acting for others'         │
                    │    welfare is uninterrupted       │
                    ├───────────────────────────────────┤
                    │ 6. How acting for others'         │
                    │    welfare knows no dejection     │
                    │    in the face of ingratitude     │
                    └───────────────────────────────────┘
```

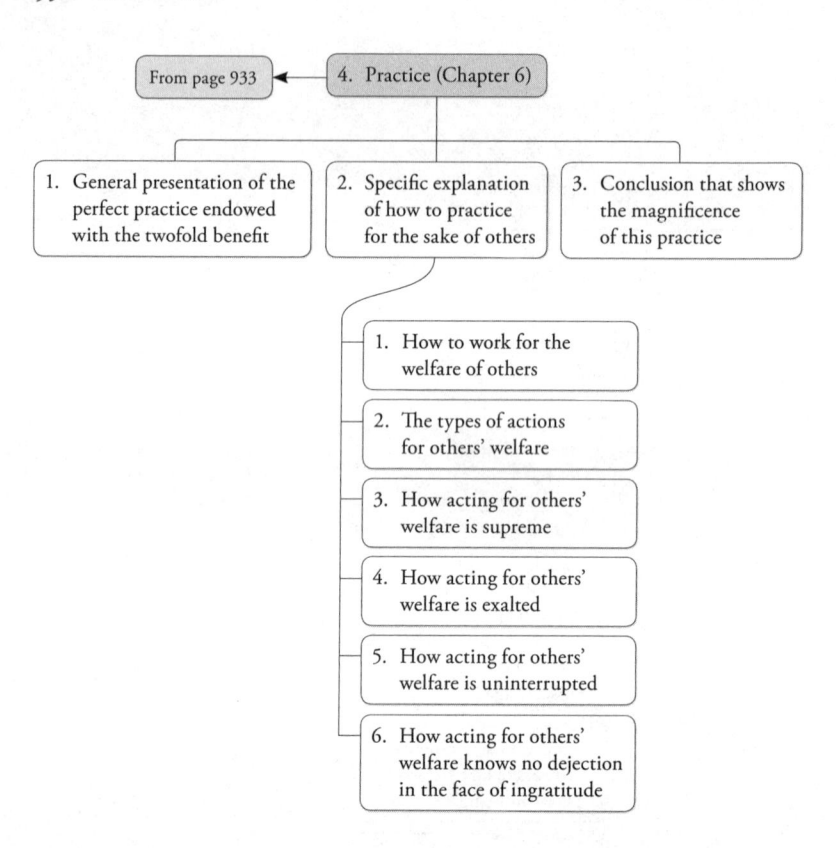

A VISUAL REPRESENTATION OF MIPHAM'S TOPICAL OUTLINE

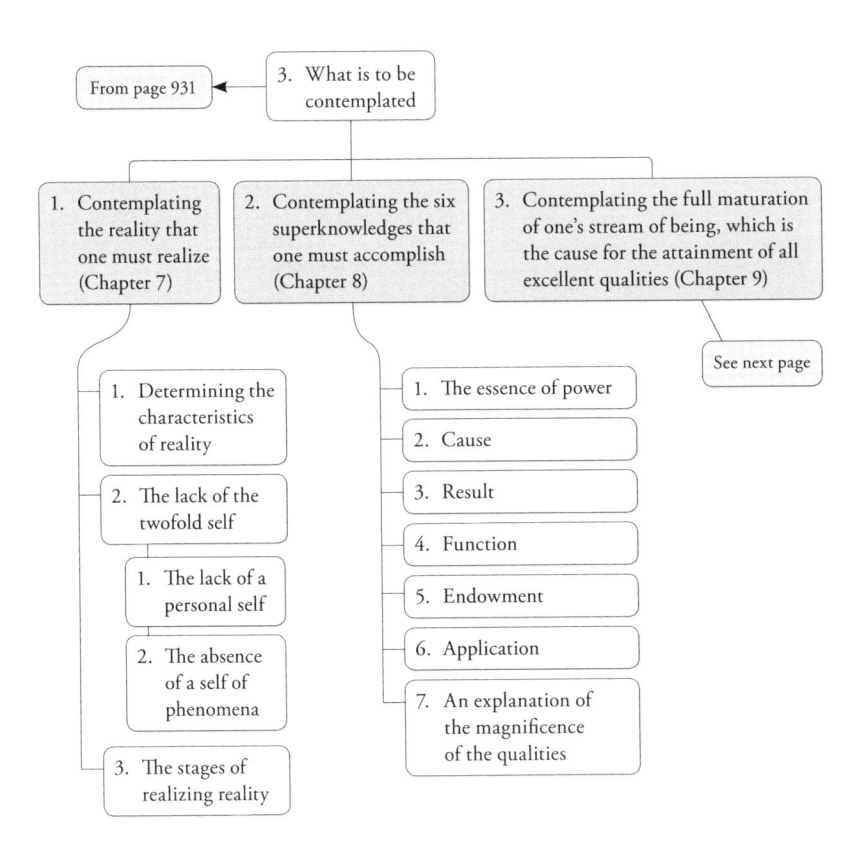

- From page 931 ← 3. What is to be contemplated
  - 1. Contemplating the reality that one must realize (Chapter 7)
    - 1. Determining the characteristics of reality
    - 2. The lack of the twofold self
      - 1. The lack of a personal self
      - 2. The absence of a self of phenomena
    - 3. The stages of realizing reality
  - 2. Contemplating the six superknowledges that one must accomplish (Chapter 8)
    - 1. The essence of power
    - 2. Cause
    - 3. Result
    - 4. Function
    - 5. Endowment
    - 6. Application
    - 7. An explanation of the magnificence of the qualities
  - 3. Contemplating the full maturation of one's stream of being, which is the cause for the attainment of all excellent qualities (Chapter 9)
    - See next page

APPENDIX

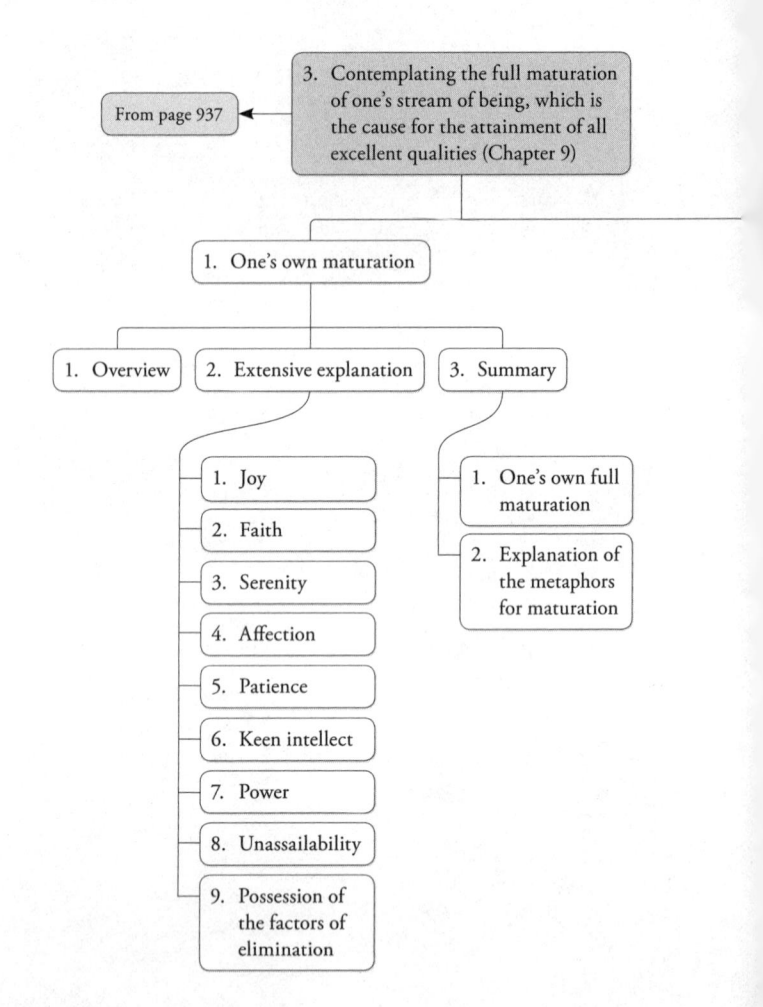

```
From page 937 → 3. Contemplating the full maturation
                 of one's stream of being, which is
                 the cause for the attainment of all
                 excellent qualities (Chapter 9)
                        │
                  1. One's own maturation
           ┌────────────┼────────────┐
    1. Overview  2. Extensive explanation  3. Summary
                        │                      │
                   1. Joy                 1. One's own full
                   2. Faith                  maturation
                   3. Serenity           2. Explanation of
                   4. Affection             the metaphors
                   5. Patience              for maturation
                   6. Keen intellect
                   7. Power
                   8. Unassailability
                   9. Possession of
                      the factors of
                      elimination
```

A VISUAL REPRESENTATION OF MIPHAM'S TOPICAL OUTLINE

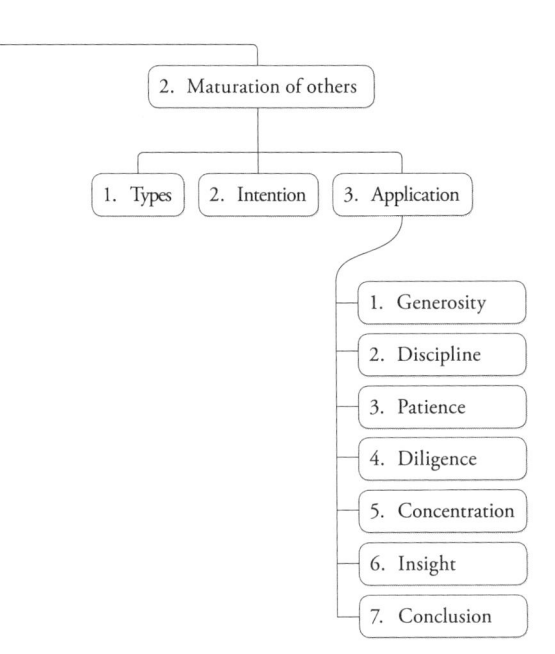

- 2. Maturation of others
  - 1. Types
  - 2. Intention
  - 3. Application
    - 1. Generosity
    - 2. Discipline
    - 3. Patience
    - 4. Diligence
    - 5. Concentration
    - 6. Insight
    - 7. Conclusion

APPENDIX

```
From page 931 ← 4. The inconceivable (Chapter 10)
                   │
       ┌───────────┴───────────┐
1. Overview of how      2. Extensive explanation
   enlightenment is the    of the nature of
   final attainment        enlightenment
                              │
                ┌─────────────┴──────────────┐
         1. General presentation    2. A sixfold presentation of
            of enlightenment by        the enlightenment that          See page
            describing its ten         possesses those qualities        943
            qualities
               │
   ┌───────┬───┴───┬───────────────┐
1. Inconceivability  3. Sublime refuge   4. Transformation

2. Perfection of the
   twofold benefit
```

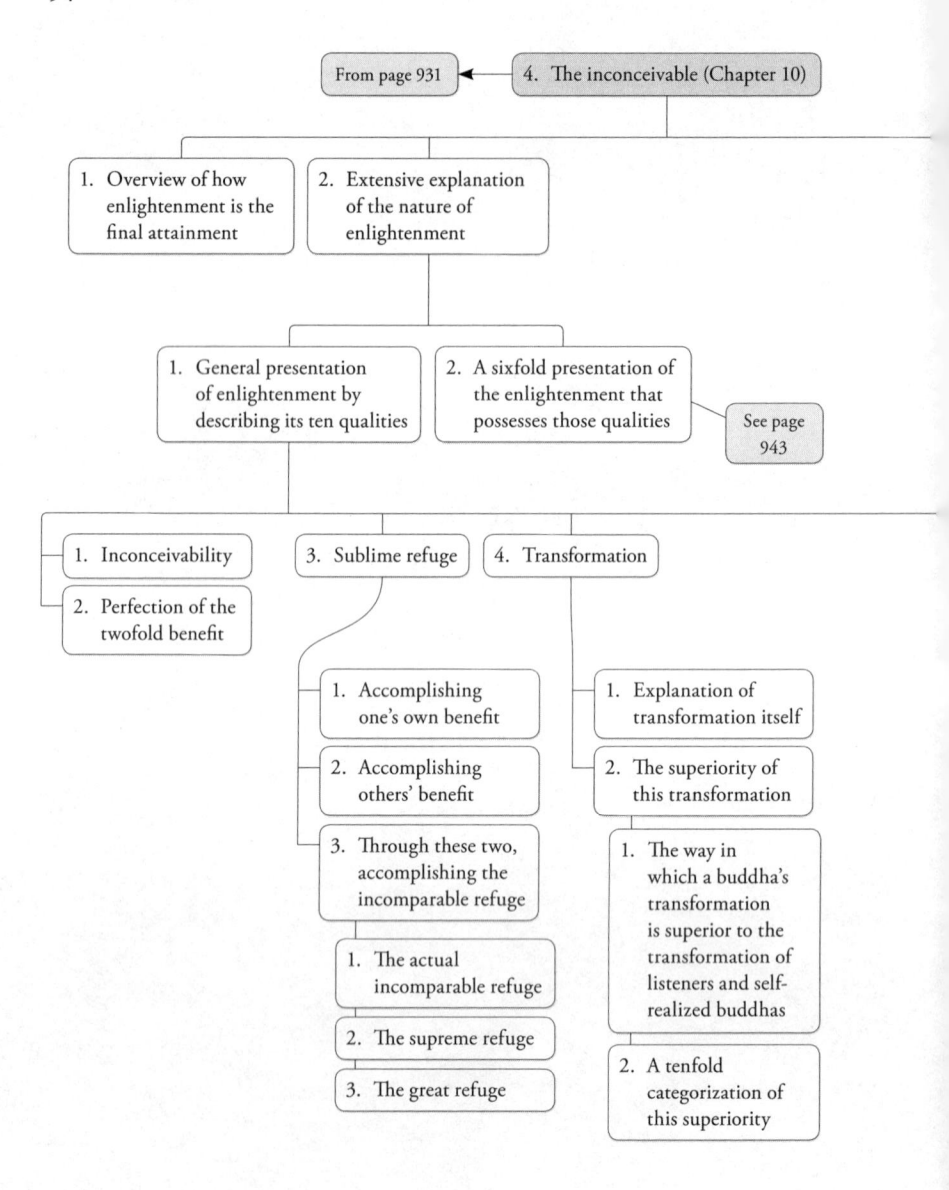

- 1. Accomplishing one's own benefit
- 2. Accomplishing others' benefit
- 3. Through these two, accomplishing the incomparable refuge
  - 1. The actual incomparable refuge
  - 2. The supreme refuge
  - 3. The great refuge

- 1. Explanation of transformation itself
- 2. The superiority of this transformation
  - 1. The way in which a buddha's transformation is superior to the transformation of listeners and self-realized buddhas
  - 2. A tenfold categorization of this superiority

A VISUAL REPRESENTATION OF MIPHAM'S TOPICAL OUTLINE 941

3. Summary that provides advice for cultivating the enlightened mind oriented toward unsurpassable enlightenment

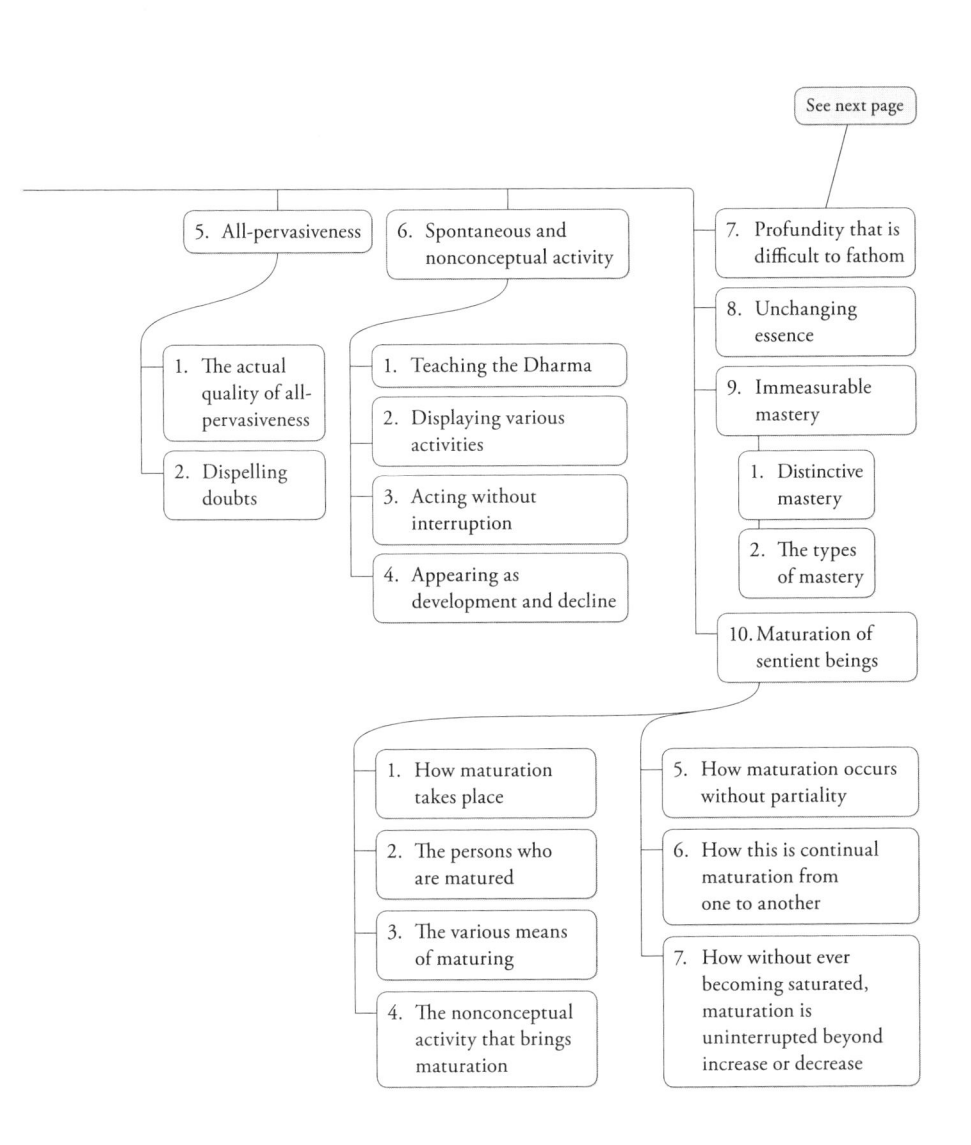

See next page

5. All-pervasiveness
6. Spontaneous and nonconceptual activity
7. Profundity that is difficult to fathom
8. Unchanging essence
9. Immeasurable mastery
10. Maturation of sentient beings

Under 5. All-pervasiveness:
1. The actual quality of all-pervasiveness
2. Dispelling doubts

Under 6. Spontaneous and nonconceptual activity:
1. Teaching the Dharma
2. Displaying various activities
3. Acting without interruption
4. Appearing as development and decline

Under 9. Immeasurable mastery:
1. Distinctive mastery
2. The types of mastery

Under 10. Maturation of sentient beings:
1. How maturation takes place
2. The persons who are matured
3. The various means of maturing
4. The nonconceptual activity that brings maturation
5. How maturation occurs without partiality
6. How this is continual maturation from one to another
7. How without ever becoming saturated, maturation is uninterrupted beyond increase or decrease

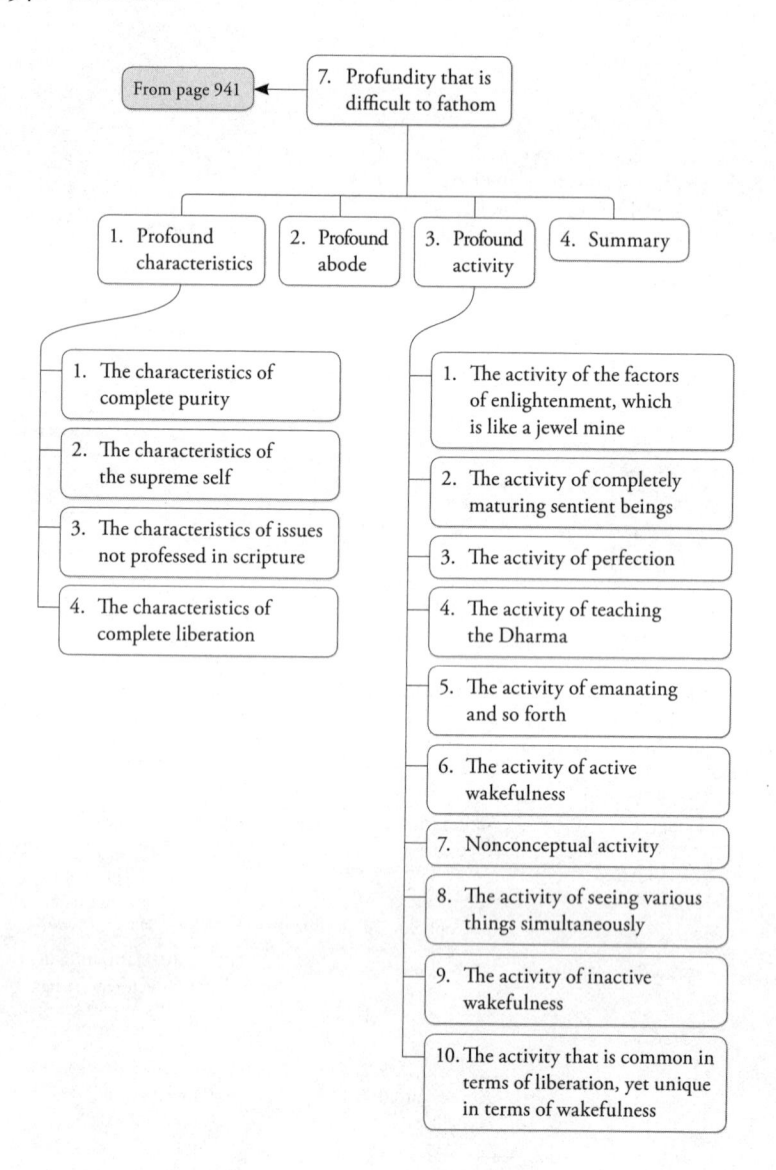

```
7. Profundity that is difficult to fathom
   ├── From page 941
   ├── 1. Profound characteristics
   │   ├── 1. The characteristics of complete purity
   │   ├── 2. The characteristics of the supreme self
   │   ├── 3. The characteristics of issues not professed in scripture
   │   └── 4. The characteristics of complete liberation
   ├── 2. Profound abode
   ├── 3. Profound activity
   │   ├── 1. The activity of the factors of enlightenment, which is like a jewel mine
   │   ├── 2. The activity of completely maturing sentient beings
   │   ├── 3. The activity of perfection
   │   ├── 4. The activity of teaching the Dharma
   │   ├── 5. The activity of emanating and so forth
   │   ├── 6. The activity of active wakefulness
   │   ├── 7. Nonconceptual activity
   │   ├── 8. The activity of seeing various things simultaneously
   │   ├── 9. The activity of inactive wakefulness
   │   └── 10. The activity that is common in terms of liberation, yet unique in terms of wakefulness
   └── 4. Summary
```

A VISUAL REPRESENTATION OF MIPHAM'S TOPICAL OUTLINE 943

- From page 940 ← **2. A sixfold presentation of the enlightenment that possesses those qualities**
  - 1. The actual presentation of enlightenment
  - 2. Specific explanation of its applications
    - 1. Explanation of the three exalted bodies that form the support
      - 1. Brief presentation
      - 2. Extensive explanation
        - 1. Explanation of each of the three exalted bodies
          - 1. The perfect enjoyment body
          - 2. The body of qualities
          - 3. The emanation body
        - 2. Explanation of their inclusion, equality, and permanence
    - 2. Explanation of the four wakefulnesses that are supported thereby
      - 1. Summary
      - 2. Extensive explanation of each wakefulness
        - 1. Mirror-like wakefulness
        - 2. The wakefulness of equality
        - 3. Discriminating wakefulness
        - 4. All-accomplishing wakefulness
      - 3. Demonstration of the cause for attaining such wakefulness
        - 1. The cause of ripening
          - 1. The actual cause of ripening
          - 2. Supplemental topics
        - 2. The cause of attaining complete purity
      - 4. How the wakefulness of the buddhas is the consummation of all paths

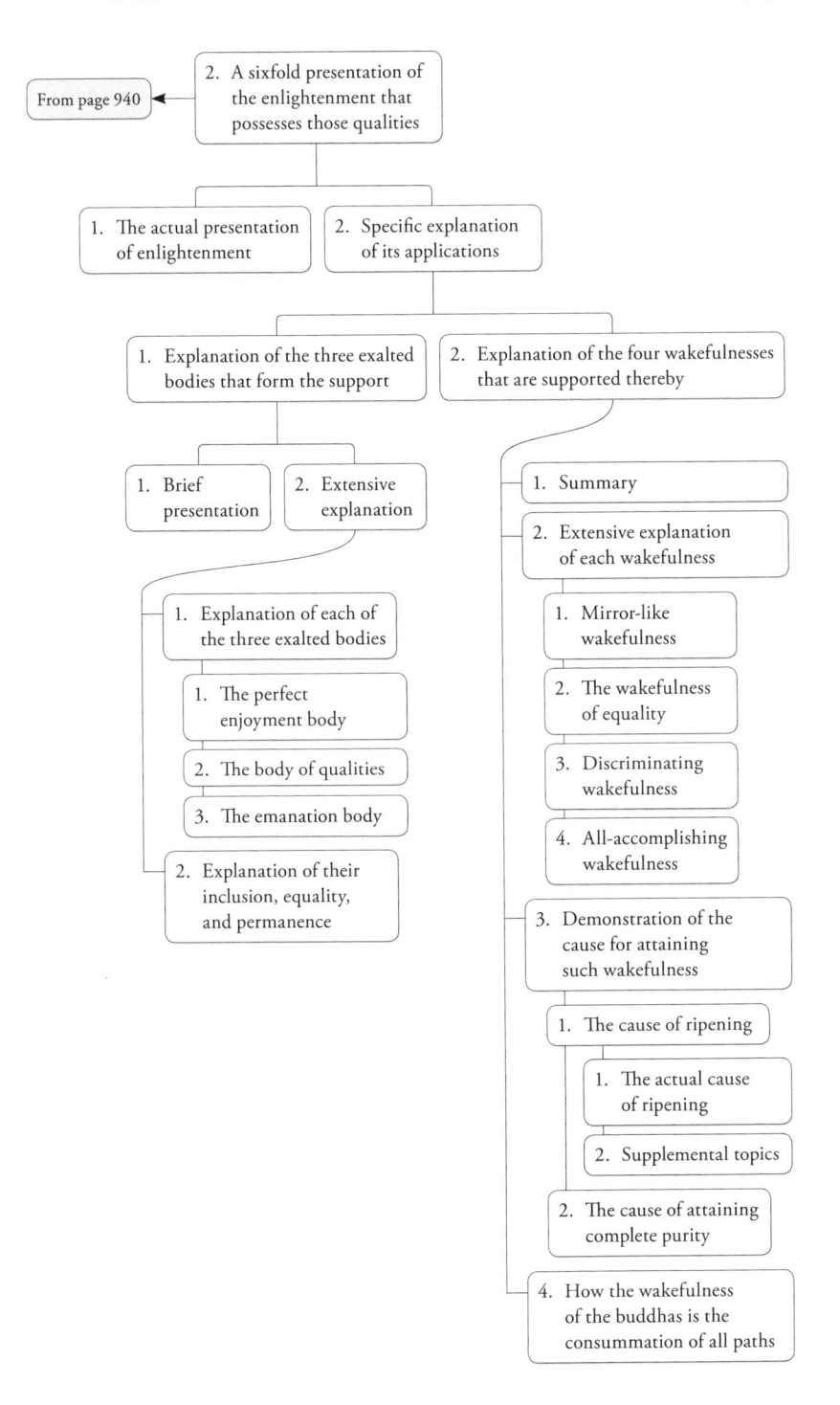

APPENDIX

```
From page 931 ← 5. The essence of the factors that accord with enlightenment
                    ├── 1. The five chapters of the preliminaries, beginning with inspiration
                    └── 2. The actual factors of enlightenment — See page 950

1. The five chapters of the preliminaries, beginning with inspiration
   ├── 1. The chapter on inspiration, which is the cause (Chapter 11)
   ├── 2. Investigation of the Dharma (Chapter 12) — See page 946
   ├── 3. Teaching the Dharma (Chapter 13) — See page 948
   └── 4. Practice of the Dharma (Chapter 14)
```

1. The chapter on inspiration, which is the cause (Chapter 11)
1. The twenty-seven types of inspiration
2. The sixteen obstacles to inspiration
3. The benefits of inspiration
4. Specific explanation of inspiration in the Great Vehicle
   1. A metaphorical teaching on the distinct inspiration that belongs to the Great Vehicle
   2. Advice to embrace the Great Vehicle with delight and without being fainthearted
      1. Entering the Great Vehicle without dejection
      2. Entering it with joy because great merit proceeds from doing so
      3. Entering it based on a demonstration of three qualities

4. Practice of the Dharma (Chapter 14)
1. General presentation
2. Detailed explanation
   1. The conditions for practice
   2. The essence of practice
      1. Short summary
      2. Expanded analysis
   3. The examples that demonstrate the way to practice
3. Summary

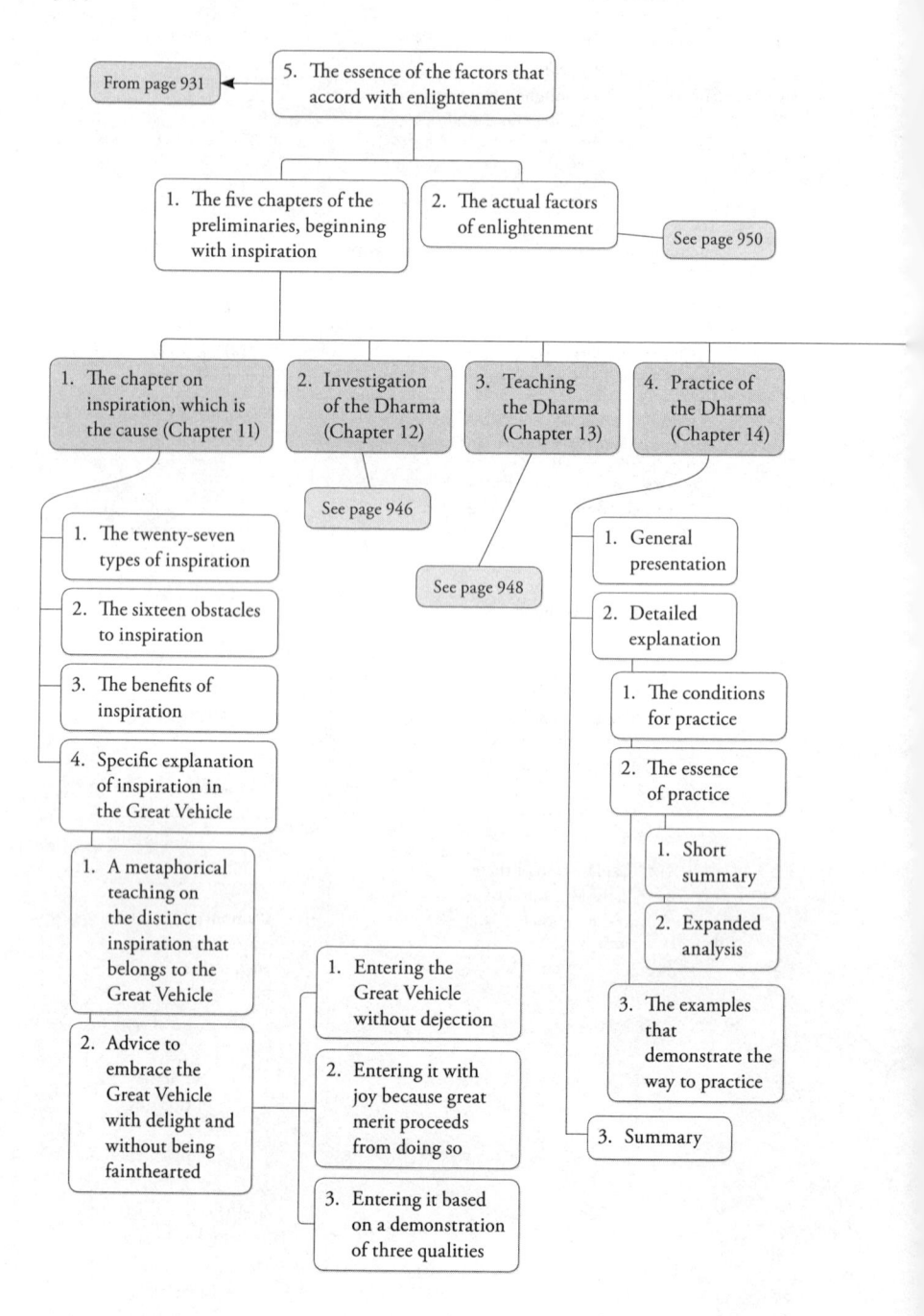

A VISUAL REPRESENTATION OF MIPHAM'S TOPICAL OUTLINE 945

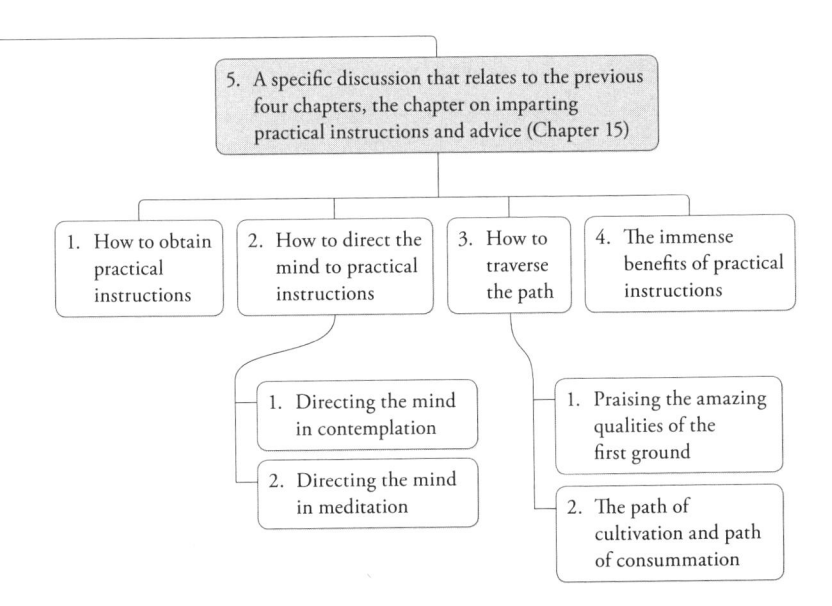

5. A specific discussion that relates to the previous four chapters, the chapter on imparting practical instructions and advice (Chapter 15)

1. How to obtain practical instructions

2. How to direct the mind to practical instructions
   1. Directing the mind in contemplation
   2. Directing the mind in meditation

3. How to traverse the path
   1. Praising the amazing qualities of the first ground
   2. The path of cultivation and path of consummation

4. The immense benefits of practical instructions

946 APPENDIX

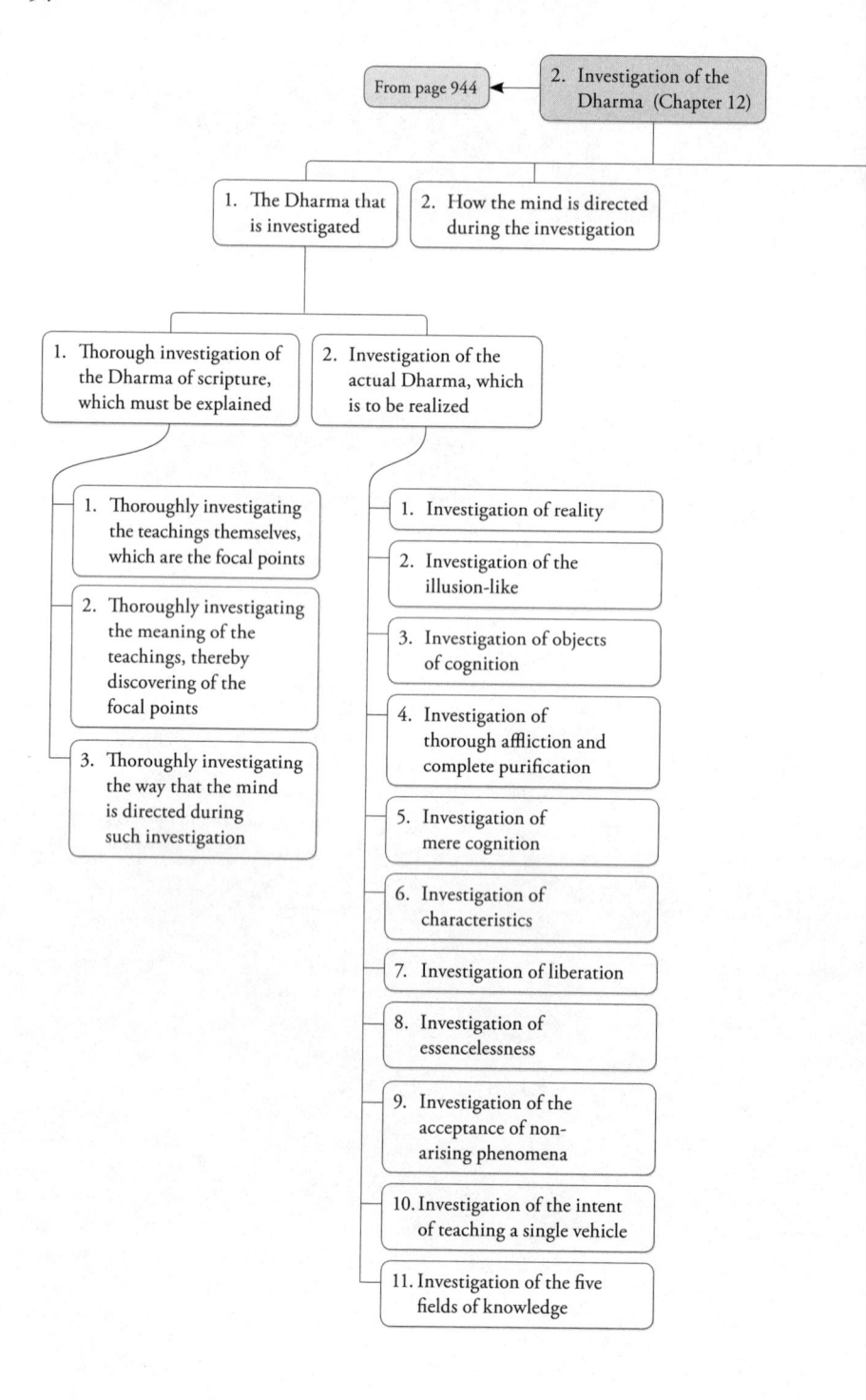

- From page 944 ← **2. Investigation of the Dharma (Chapter 12)**
  - 1. The Dharma that is investigated
    - 1. Thorough investigation of the Dharma of scripture, which must be explained
      - 1. Thoroughly investigating the teachings themselves, which are the focal points
      - 2. Thoroughly investigating the meaning of the teachings, thereby discovering of the focal points
      - 3. Thoroughly investigating the way that the mind is directed during such investigation
    - 2. Investigation of the actual Dharma, which is to be realized
      - 1. Investigation of reality
      - 2. Investigation of the illusion-like
      - 3. Investigation of objects of cognition
      - 4. Investigation of thorough affliction and complete purification
      - 5. Investigation of mere cognition
      - 6. Investigation of characteristics
      - 7. Investigation of liberation
      - 8. Investigation of essencelessness
      - 9. Investigation of the acceptance of non-arising phenomena
      - 10. Investigation of the intent of teaching a single vehicle
      - 11. Investigation of the five fields of knowledge
  - 2. How the mind is directed during the investigation

A VISUAL REPRESENTATION OF MIPHAM'S TOPICAL OUTLINE 947

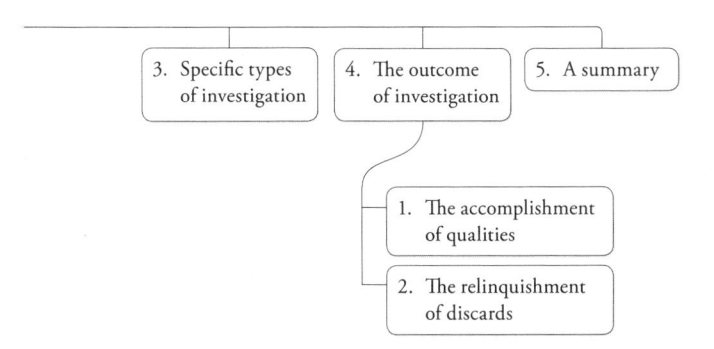

- 3. Specific types of investigation
- 4. The outcome of investigation
  - 1. The accomplishment of qualities
  - 2. The relinquishment of discards
- 5. A summary

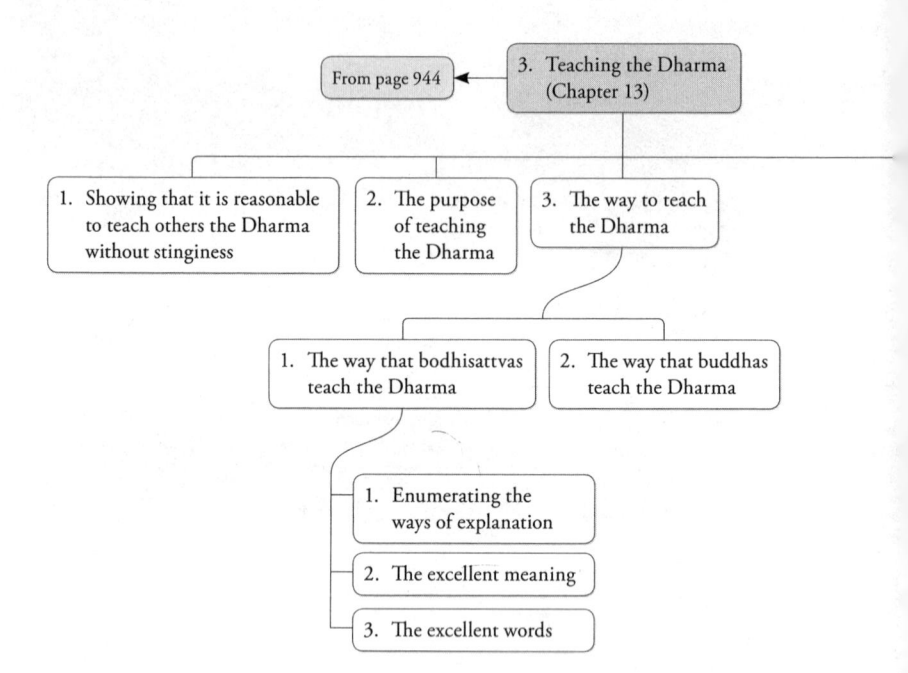

APPENDIX

- **3. Teaching the Dharma (Chapter 13)** ← From page 944
  - 1. Showing that it is reasonable to teach others the Dharma without stinginess
  - 2. The purpose of teaching the Dharma
  - 3. The way to teach the Dharma
    - 1. The way that bodhisattvas teach the Dharma
      - 1. Enumerating the ways of explanation
      - 2. The excellent meaning
      - 3. The excellent words
    - 2. The way that buddhas teach the Dharma

A VISUAL REPRESENTATION OF MIPHAM'S TOPICAL OUTLINE 949

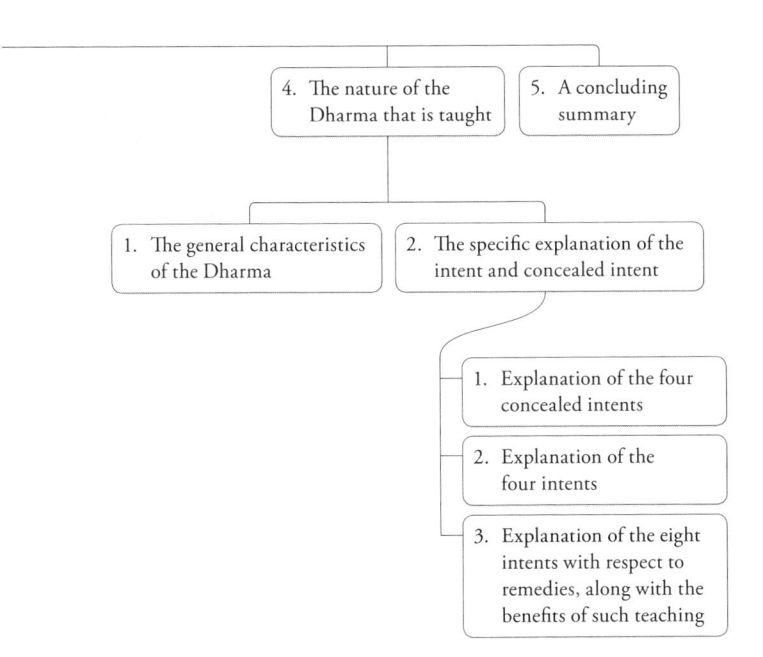

- 4. The nature of the Dharma that is taught
  - 1. The general characteristics of the Dharma
  - 2. The specific explanation of the intent and concealed intent
    - 1. Explanation of the four concealed intents
    - 2. Explanation of the four intents
    - 3. Explanation of the eight intents with respect to remedies, along with the benefits of such teaching
- 5. A concluding summary

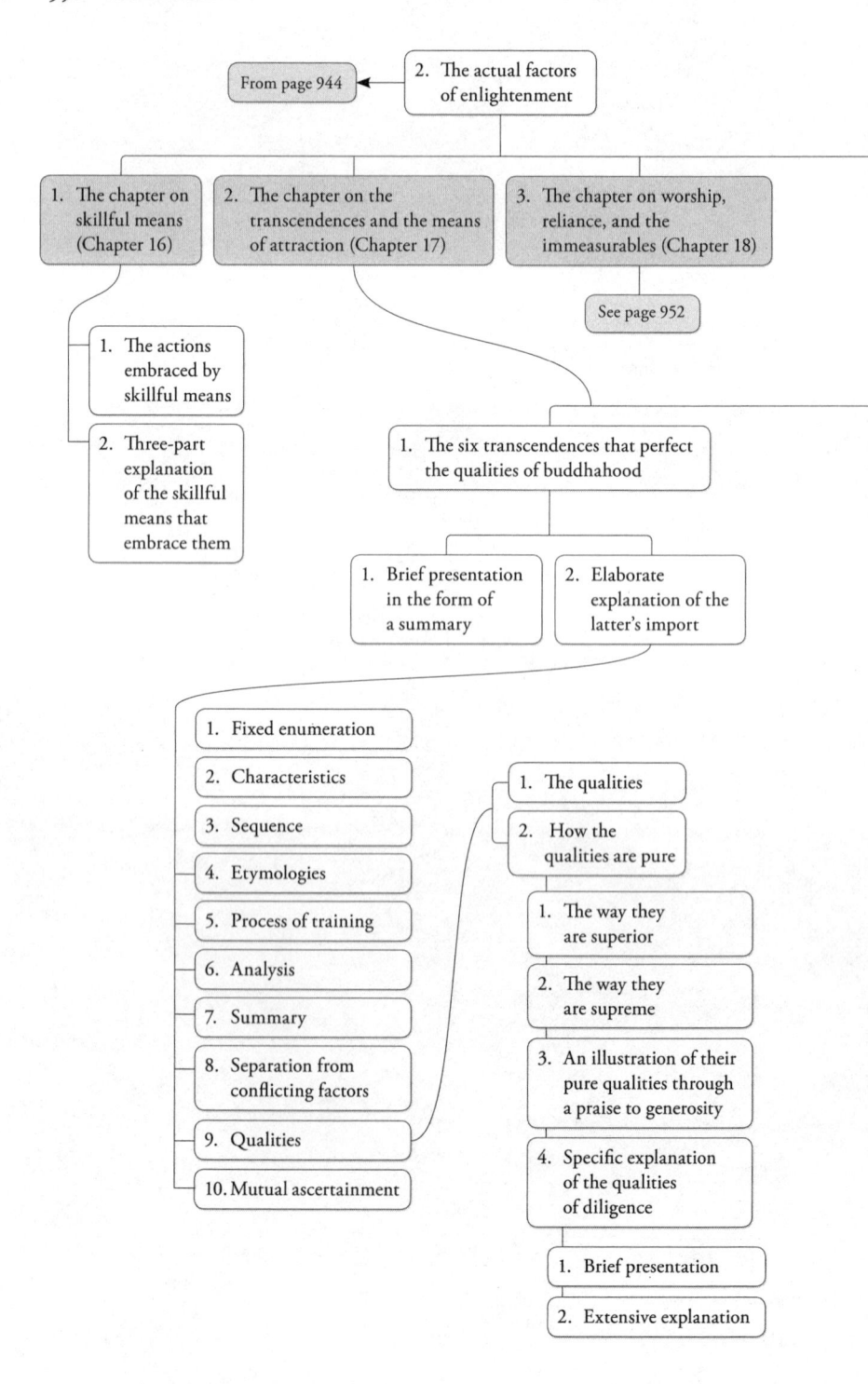

APPENDIX

```
2. The actual factors of enlightenment
├── From page 944
├── 1. The chapter on skillful means (Chapter 16)
│   ├── 1. The actions embraced by skillful means
│   └── 2. Three-part explanation of the skillful means that embrace them
├── 2. The chapter on the transcendences and the means of attraction (Chapter 17)
│   └── 1. The six transcendences that perfect the qualities of buddhahood
│       ├── 1. Brief presentation in the form of a summary
│       └── 2. Elaborate explanation of the latter's import
│           ├── 1. Fixed enumeration
│           ├── 2. Characteristics
│           ├── 3. Sequence
│           ├── 4. Etymologies
│           ├── 5. Process of training
│           ├── 6. Analysis
│           ├── 7. Summary
│           ├── 8. Separation from conflicting factors
│           ├── 9. Qualities
│           │   ├── 1. The qualities
│           │   └── 2. How the qualities are pure
│           │       ├── 1. The way they are superior
│           │       ├── 2. The way they are supreme
│           │       ├── 3. An illustration of their pure qualities through a praise to generosity
│           │       └── 4. Specific explanation of the qualities of diligence
│           │           ├── 1. Brief presentation
│           │           └── 2. Extensive explanation
│           └── 10. Mutual ascertainment
└── 3. The chapter on worship, reliance, and the immeasurables (Chapter 18)
    └── See page 952
```

A VISUAL REPRESENTATION OF MIPHAM'S TOPICAL OUTLINE

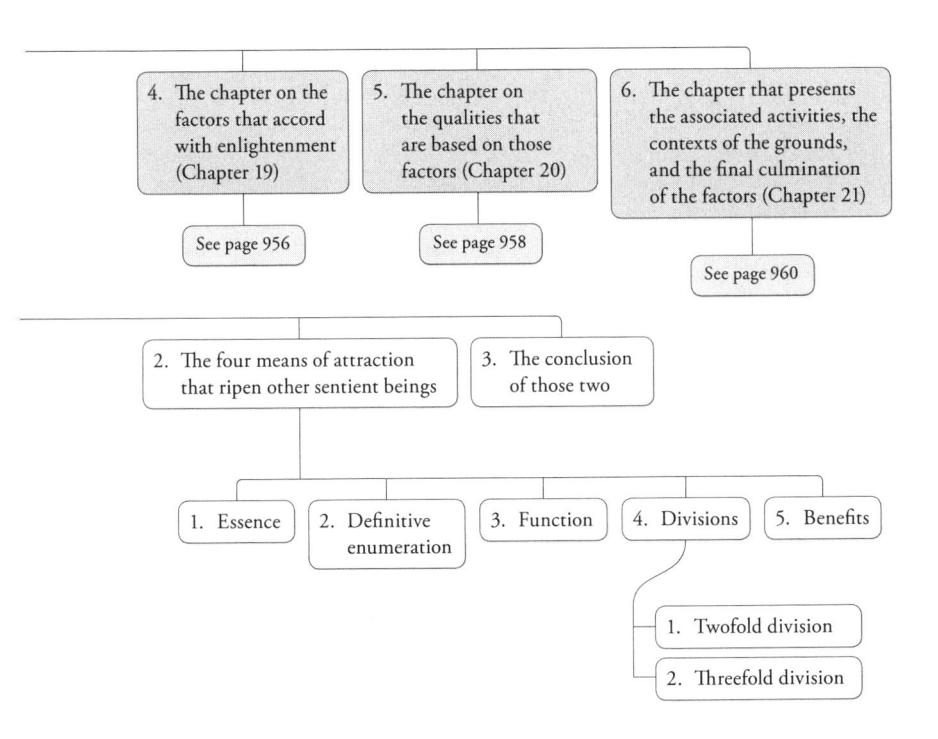

- 4. The chapter on the factors that accord with enlightenment (Chapter 19)
  - See page 956
- 5. The chapter on the qualities that are based on those factors (Chapter 20)
  - See page 958
- 6. The chapter that presents the associated activities, the contexts of the grounds, and the final culmination of the factors (Chapter 21)
  - See page 960

- 2. The four means of attraction that ripen other sentient beings
  - 1. Essence
  - 2. Definitive enumeration
  - 3. Function
  - 4. Divisions
    - 1. Twofold division
    - 2. Threefold division
  - 5. Benefits
- 3. The conclusion of those two

APPENDIX

From page 950 ← **3. The chapter on worship, reliance, and the immeasurables (Chapter 18)**

- **1. Worshipping the buddhas**
  - 1. The nature of worship
  - 2. Types of worship
- **2. Relying on a spiritual teacher**
  - 1. The way to follow a spiritual teacher
    - 1. Brief presentation
    - 2. Elaborate explanation
      1. The characteristics of the support, the spiritual teacher
      2. The bases, or entities, by means of which one follows such a teacher
      3. The marks of reliance
      4. The objectives of the dedication
      5. The causes of practice in relation to the spiritual teacher
      6. The ensuing skill in terms of wakefulness
      7. The purification of the field that consists of the environment and its inhabitants
      8. The abode within which one rests while following the spiritual teacher
  - 2. The relevant divisions
  - 3. The distinctions of supreme reliance

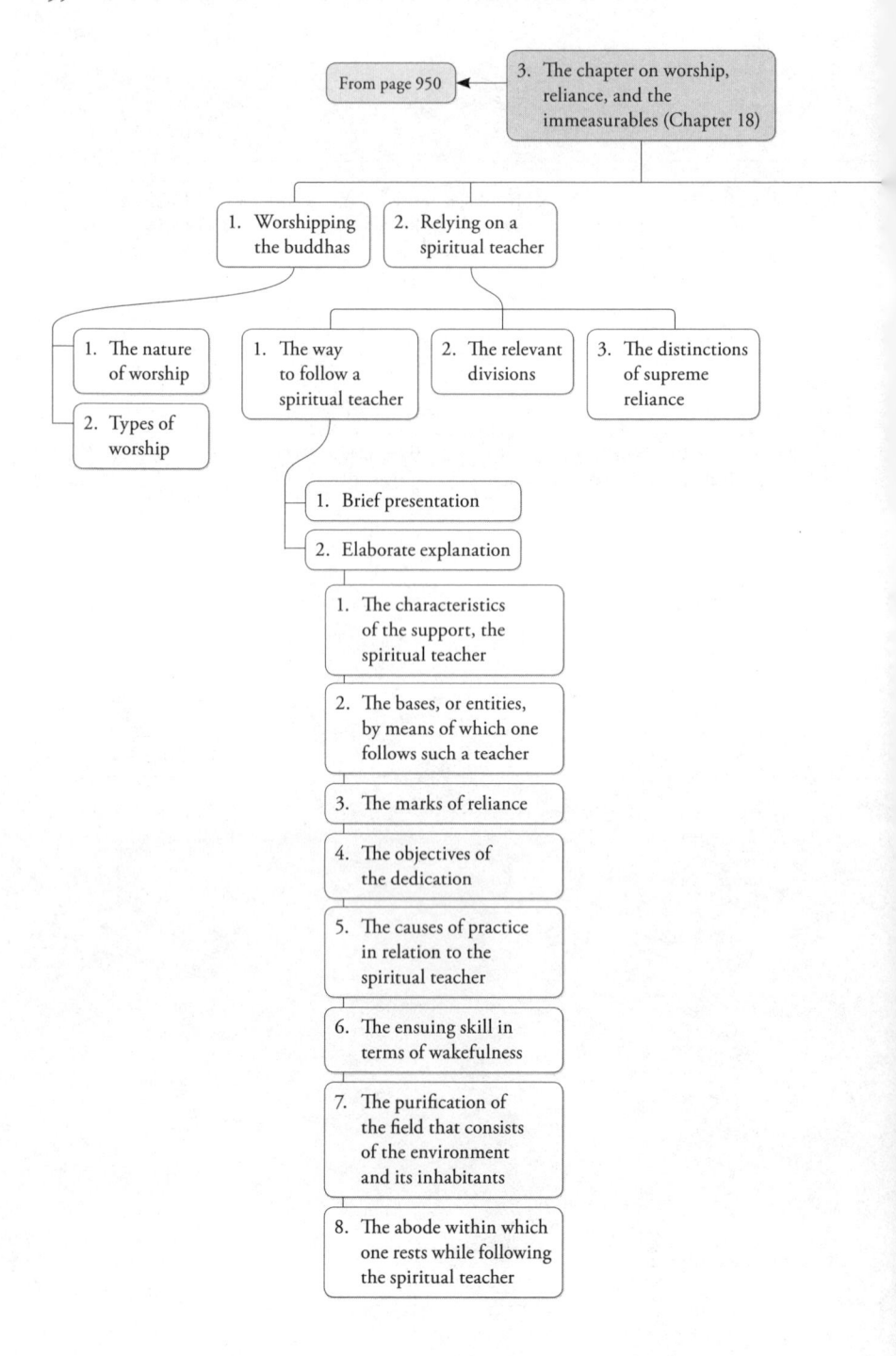

A VISUAL REPRESENTATION OF MIPHAM'S TOPICAL OUTLINE

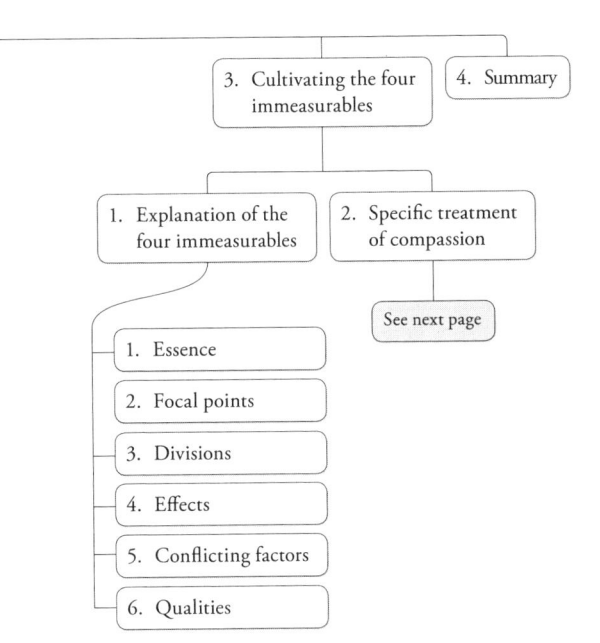

- 3. Cultivating the four immeasurables
  - 1. Explanation of the four immeasurables
    - 1. Essence
    - 2. Focal points
    - 3. Divisions
    - 4. Effects
    - 5. Conflicting factors
    - 6. Qualities
  - 2. Specific treatment of compassion

    See next page
- 4. Summary

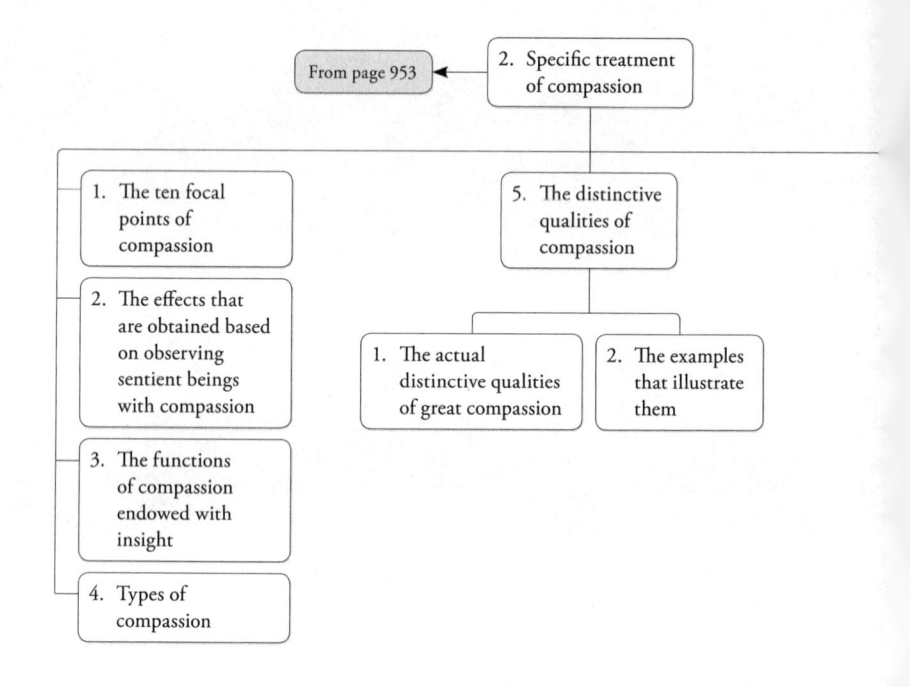

```
                              ┌─────────────────────┐
         ┌─────────────┐ ◄─── │ 2. Specific treatment│
         │From page 953│      │    of compassion     │
         └─────────────┘      └──────────┬──────────┘
                                         │
   ┌─────────────────────┬────────────────────────────────────┐
   │                                                          │
┌──┴──────────────┐                              ┌────────────┴─────┐
│ 1. The ten focal│                              │ 5. The distinctive│
│    points of    │                              │    qualities of   │
│    compassion   │                              │    compassion     │
└─────────────────┘                              └─────────┬────────┘
┌─────────────────┐                                        │
│ 2. The effects that│                     ┌───────────────┴──────────────┐
│    are obtained based│              ┌────┴──────────────┐  ┌────────────┴───┐
│    on observing    │                │ 1. The actual     │  │ 2. The examples│
│    sentient beings │                │    distinctive    │  │    that illustrate│
│    with compassion │                │    qualities of   │  │    them        │
└─────────────────┘                   │    great compassion│ │                │
┌─────────────────┐                   └───────────────────┘  └────────────────┘
│ 3. The functions│
│    of compassion│
│    endowed with │
│    insight      │
└─────────────────┘
┌─────────────────┐
│ 4. Types of     │
│    compassion   │
└─────────────────┘
```

A VISUAL REPRESENTATION OF MIPHAM'S TOPICAL OUTLINE

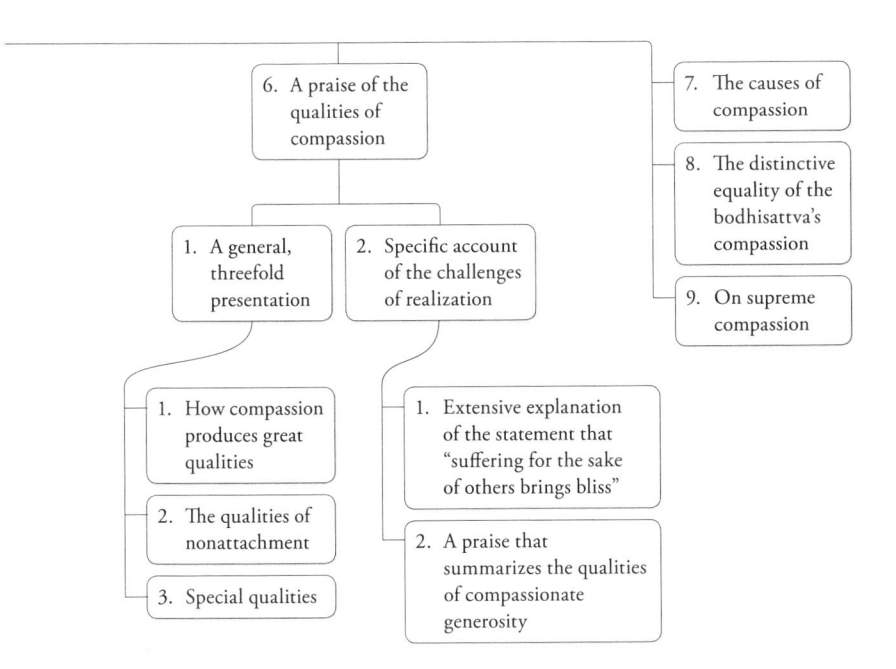

- 6. A praise of the qualities of compassion
  - 1. A general, threefold presentation
    - 1. How compassion produces great qualities
    - 2. The qualities of nonattachment
    - 3. Special qualities
  - 2. Specific account of the challenges of realization
    - 1. Extensive explanation of the statement that "suffering for the sake of others brings bliss"
    - 2. A praise that summarizes the qualities of compassionate generosity
- 7. The causes of compassion
- 8. The distinctive equality of the bodhisattva's compassion
- 9. On supreme compassion

APPENDIX

4. The chapter on the factors that accord with enlightenment (Chapter 19) ← From page 951

- **1. The framework for cultivating the factors of enlightenment**
  - **1. Conscience**
    - 1. The characteristics of conscience
    - 2. The bases of conscience
    - 3. Types of conscience
    - 4. The flaws that ensue from a lack of conscience
    - 5. The benefits of conscience
    - 6. A praise to those who are endowed with conscience
    - 7. The signs of possessing conscience and embarrassment
    - 8. The character of supreme conscience
  - 2. Steadfastness
  - 3. Indefatigability
  - 4. Knowledge of the treatises
  - 5. Knowledge of the world
  - 6. The four reliances
  - 7. The four ways of correct awareness
  - 8. The two accumulations
    - 1. Brief presentation
    - 2. Elaborate explanation
      - 1. Characteristics
      - 2. Types
      - 3. Immutability

- **2. The essence of the factors of enlightenment**
  - **1. Elaborate explanation of the thirty-seven factors of enlightenment**
    - 1. The four applications of mindfulness
    - 2. The four authentic eliminations
    - 3. The four bases of miraculous power
    - 4. The five faculties
    - 5. The five powers
    - 6. The seven aspects of enlightenment
      - 1. Their temporal context
      - 2. The type of knowledge they involve
      - 3. Their own character
      - 4. Their fivefold categorization
    - 7. The eight aspects of the noble path
  - 2. Summarizing discussion of calm abiding and special insight

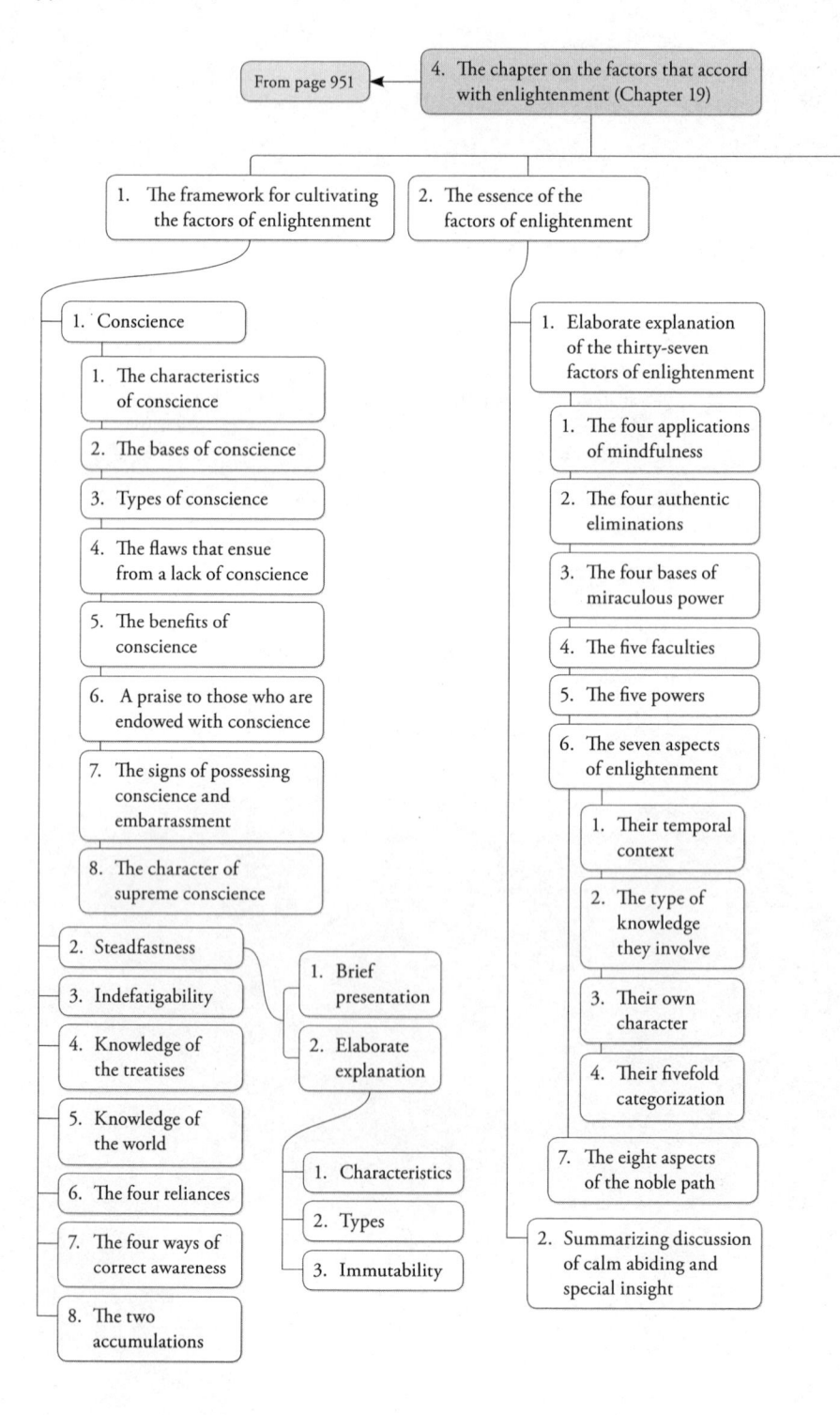

A VISUAL REPRESENTATION OF MIPHAM'S TOPICAL OUTLINE

- 3. The factors that distinguish them
- 4. Summary
  - 1. Skill in means, which allows for the unfailing accomplishment of great aims with little hardship
  - 2. Complete retention of the Dharma teachings that one previously received
  - 3. Aspiration whereby excellent qualities will be attained in the future
  - 4. Meditative absorption and the four summaries that ensure the purity of the path
    - 1. The three meditative absorptions
    - 2. The fourfold summary of the Dharma
      - 1. Concise explanation
      - 2. Proof of impermanence and absence of self
        - 1. Proof of impermanence
          - 1. General presentation
          - 2. Specific explanation
            - 1. All inner conditioned entities are impermanent
            - 2. How the same also holds for outer entities
        - 2. Proof of the absence of self

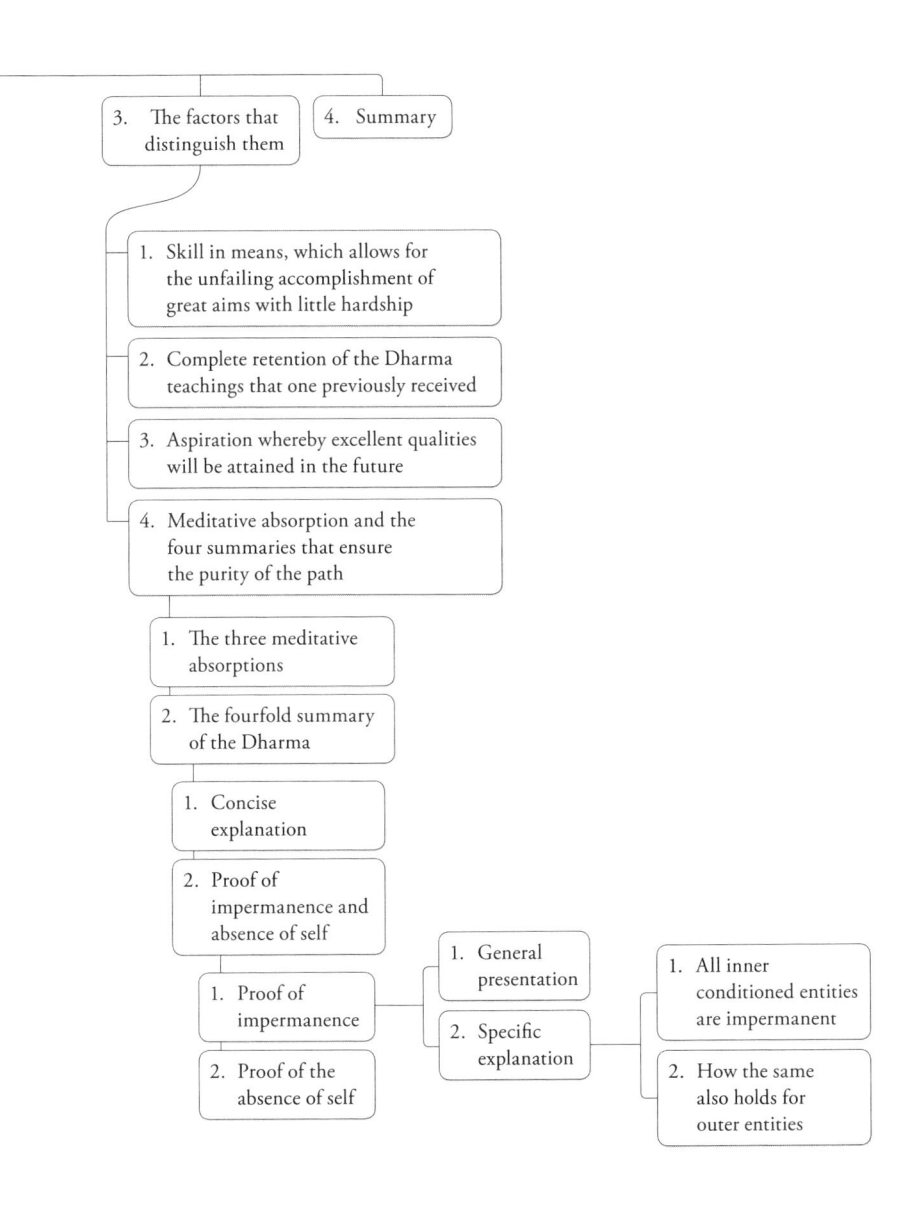

958   APPENDIX

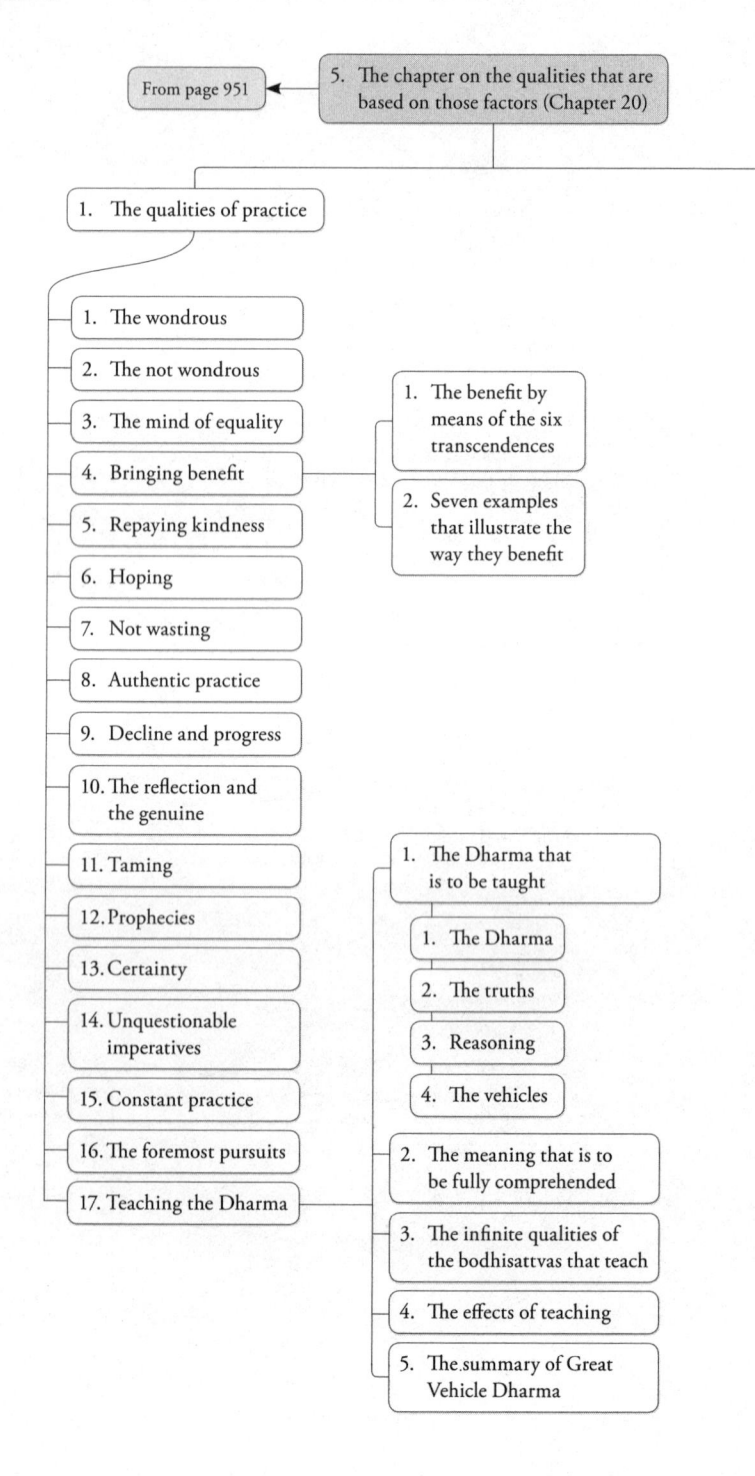

- From page 951 → **5. The chapter on the qualities that are based on those factors (Chapter 20)**
  - 1. The qualities of practice
    - 1. The wondrous
    - 2. The not wondrous
    - 3. The mind of equality
    - 4. Bringing benefit
      - 1. The benefit by means of the six transcendences
      - 2. Seven examples that illustrate the way they benefit
    - 5. Repaying kindness
    - 6. Hoping
    - 7. Not wasting
    - 8. Authentic practice
    - 9. Decline and progress
    - 10. The reflection and the genuine
    - 11. Taming
    - 12. Prophecies
    - 13. Certainty
    - 14. Unquestionable imperatives
    - 15. Constant practice
    - 16. The foremost pursuits
    - 17. Teaching the Dharma
      - 1. The Dharma that is to be taught
        - 1. The Dharma
        - 2. The truths
        - 3. Reasoning
        - 4. The vehicles
      - 2. The meaning that is to be fully comprehended
      - 3. The infinite qualities of the bodhisattvas that teach
      - 4. The effects of teaching
      - 5. The summary of Great Vehicle Dharma

A VISUAL REPRESENTATION OF MIPHAM'S TOPICAL OUTLINE 959

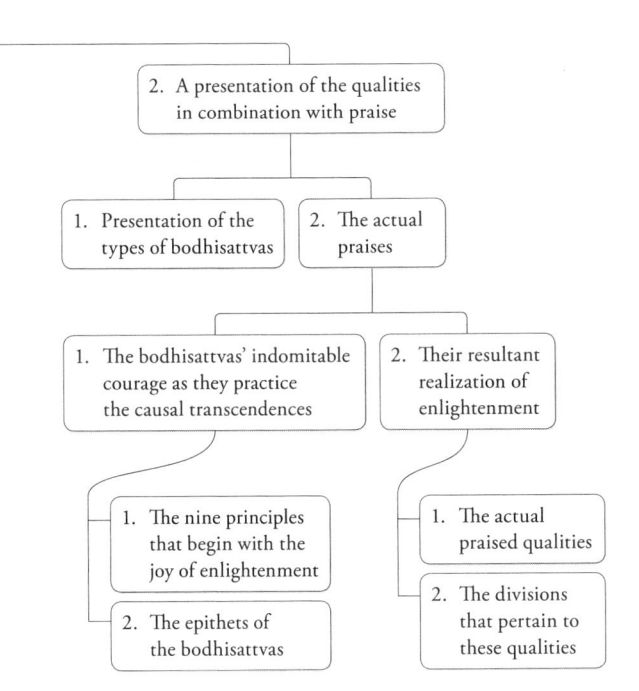

2. A presentation of the qualities in combination with praise
- 1. Presentation of the types of bodhisattvas
- 2. The actual praises
  - 1. The bodhisattvas' indomitable courage as they practice the causal transcendences
    - 1. The nine principles that begin with the joy of enlightenment
    - 2. The epithets of the bodhisattvas
  - 2. Their resultant realization of enlightenment
    - 1. The actual praised qualities
    - 2. The divisions that pertain to these qualities

APPENDIX

- From page 952 → **6. The chapter that presents the associated activities, the contexts of the grounds, and the final culmination of the factors (Chapter 21)**
  - 1. The signs of a bodhisattva
  - 2. The way that the bodhisattvas accept birth
  - 3. Their attainment of the grounds
    - 1. Brief presentation
    - 2. Elaborate explanation
      - 1. Characteristics
      - 2. Persons
      - 3. Trainings
      - 4. Aggregates
      - 5. Accomplishment
      - 6. Marks, or signs
        - 1. The signs themselves
        - 2. The grounds that bear them
      - 7. Etymology
      - 8. Attainment

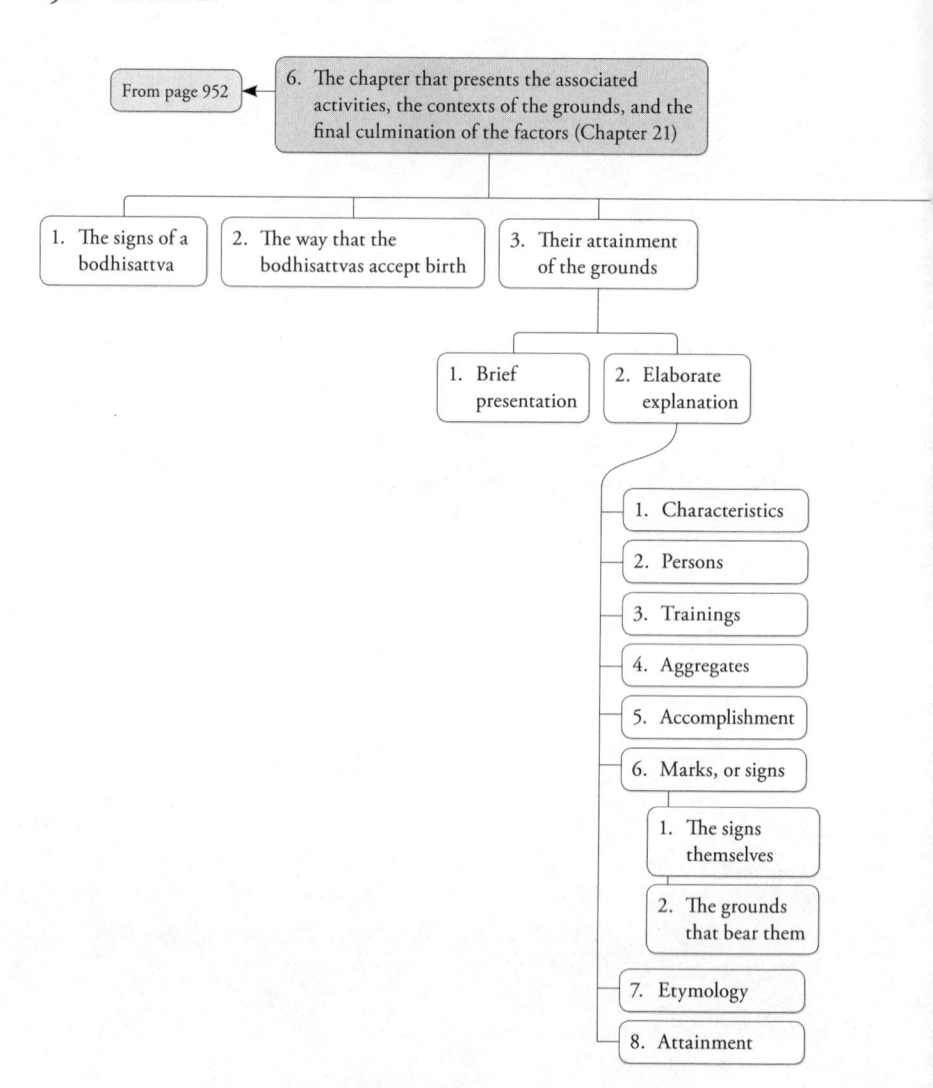

A VISUAL REPRESENTATION OF MIPHAM'S TOPICAL OUTLINE 961

4. Their perfect qualities as presented through praise

1. The four immeasurables
2. Freedoms, commands, and totalities
3. Absence of affliction
4. Knowledge arising from aspiration
5. Correct awareness
6. The six forms of superknowledge
7. The marks and signs
8. The fourfold complete purity
9. The ten powers
10. The four types of fearlessness
11. Nothing to guard
12. Defeating the habitual tendencies
13. Freedom from bewilderment
14. Great compassion
15. The eighteen unshared qualities
16. Omniscience
17. Perfection of the six transcendences
18. Summary of the buddha ground

Notes

Translators' Introduction

1. *'Phags pa shes rab kyi pha rol tu phyin pa khri brgyad stong pa* (Skt. *Ārya-aṣṭadaśasāhas-rikā-prajñāpāramitā*), Tōh. 10, vol. 31, 164b: *ci phyir 'di ni byang chub theg chen bya zhe na // de gang zhon nas sems can thams cad mya ngan zlo // theg pa 'di ni mkha' 'dra gzhal med khang chen te / dga' skyid bde ba mngon par 'thob byed theg pa'i mchog.*
2. The teachings of the Great Vehicle sūtras are typically said to have been communicated by the Buddha to circles of particularly receptive individuals in a way that went unnoticed by other, less gifted disciples. Manuscripts of Great Vehicle sūtras are contained within the world's most ancient extant collections of Buddhist scripture, dating to the first century CE (see Skilling 2013). The scriptural authenticity of the sūtras of the Great Vehicle was contested by *śrāvaka* schools, and the *Ornament of the Great Vehicle Sūtras* hence also devotes its second chapter to "Establishing the Great Vehicle." On this issue, see for example, D'Amato 2000.
3. According to a number of Indian, Chinese, and Tibetan accounts, the *Ornament of the Great Vehicle Sūtras* was among the treatises that the great bodhisattva Maitreya granted to his devotee, the prolific Indian master Asaṅga (fl. fourth century CE). The Chinese canon, however, identifies the author as Asaṅga himself. The origins and authorship of this treatise remain subjects of scholarly debate. For surveys and discussion of the various accounts of the authorship of the treatises that are associated with Maitreya, see Matthes 1996, D'Amato 2000, and Turenne 2010.
4. See, for example, the *Śāli Sprout Sūtra.*
5. See, by way of comparison, stanzas X.41–48.
6. See, by way of comparison, stanza VI.3.
7. See stanzas VII.2–3.
8. See, by way of comparison, stanzas VII.6–10.
9. See p. 698 (commentary on stanza XIX.58).
10. This refers to those who have attained the stage of peace and freedom from suffering through the path of the Lesser Vehicle (Skt. *hīnayāna*). As such, the latter attainment does not involve infinite compassion and omniscient awakening, and hence it is considered undesirable from the perspective of the Great Vehicle.

11. In Buddhist cosmology, "the three realms" is a term for the entire world of existence that is conditioned by karma, up to and including the numerous realms of the gods.
12. The basis for our translation of the core stanzas has been the Tibetan version contained in the Derge (Tib. *sDe dge*) edition of the Tengyur (Tib. *bsTan 'gyur*: the compilation of classical, primarily Indian Buddhist treatises in Tibetan translation). These verses are not extant in Sanskrit as a separate text, but almost all are contained in the three extant Sanskrit manuscripts of the commentary that is ascribed to Vasubandhu. For an overview of the available classical Indian literature associated with the *Ornament of the Great Vehicle Sūtras* in Sanskrit, Tibetan, and Chinese, see D'Amato 2000, 16–22 and Maitreyanātha/Āryāsaṅga 2005, xxxiii–xxxv.
13. For biographies of Khenpo Shenga, see the entry regarding Zhenpen Chokyi Nangwa at the Treasury of Lives website, treasuryoflives.org, and Nyoshul 2005. Biographical details are likewise contained in Thondup 1999, Jackson 2004, and Dreyfus 2005.
14. *Exposition of the Ornament of the Great Vehicle Sūtras* (Skt. *Mahāyānsūtrālaṃkārabhāṣya*). English translation in Maitreyanātha/Asaṅga 2005.
15. The thirteen classics encompass two texts on Vinaya (the *Sūtra on Individual Liberation* and Guṇaprabhā's *Teaching on Vinaya*), two treatises on Abhidharma (*Treasury of Abhidharma* by Vasubandhu and the *Compendium on Abhidharma* by Asaṅga), four works on Madhyamaka (Nāgārjuna's *Root of the Middle Way*, Āryadeva's *Four Hundred Stanzas*, Śāntideva's *Entering the Activity of the Bodhisattvas*, and Candrakīrti's *Entering the Middle Way*), and the five treatises that the Tibetan tradition ascribes to Maitreya (*Ornament of the Great Vehicle's Sūtras*, *Distinguishing the Middle from Extremes*, *Distinguishing Phenomena from Their Intrinsic Nature*, *Ornament of Manifest Realization*, and *Supreme Continuity*).
16. For a biography and an introduction to Mipham's authorship, see Duckworth 2011. Two of the works most central to Mipham's philosophical approach, the *Beacon of Certainty* (Tib. *Nges shes sgron me*) and his commentary on the *Ornament of the Middle Way* (Skt. *Madhyamakālaṃkāra*), are available in English translation (the former in Pettit 1999 and the latter in Mipham 2004a and Shantarakshita and Mipham 2005). Mipham's renowned guide to Buddhist philosophy, the *Gateway to Knowledge* (Tib. *mKhas pa'i tshul la 'jug pa'i sgo*, English translation in Mipham 1997–2012), explains many of the concepts and categories that are contained in the *Ornament of the Great Vehicle Sūtras*. Among the five Maitreya treatises, English translations are available of Mipham's commentaries to *Distinguishing the Middle from Extremes* (Skt. *Madhyāntavibhāga*, in Dharmachakra Translation Committee 2007) and *Distinguishing Phenomena from their Intrinsic Nature* (Skt. *Dharmadharmatāvibhaṅga*, in Mipham 2004b and Dharmachakra Translation Committee 2013). Mipham's philosophical approach has been studied in Pettit 1999, Phuntsho 2005, Duckworth 2009, and Duckworth 2011.
17. The latter approach is the one suggested by Lévi 1907–11 based on his Sanskrit manuscript. The Chinese tradition, in turn, operates with twenty-four chapters. On the enumeration of the chapters in the extant Sanskrit manuscripts, as well as in the Tibetan and the Chinese traditions, see Maitreyanātha/Āryāsaṅga 2005, xxxiii–xxxv.

18. See, by way of comparison, Obermiller 1999 and Chattopadhyaya and Chimpa 1990. Modern scholarship tends to place Sthiramati in the sixth century.
19. *Vast Exposition of the Ornament of the Great Vehicle Sūtras* (Skt. *Mahāyānsūtrālaṃkāra-vṛtti-bhāṣya*). Extant only in Tibetan translation.
20. See p. 3.
21. Maitreyanātha/Āryāsaṅga 2005.

Title and Translator's Homage

22. In transcribed Tibetan, the title thus reads: *Theg pa chen po mdo sde'i rgyan zhes bya ba'i tshig le'ur byas pa*.

1. How the Scripture Was Composed

23. Below, all references to "the commentary" are to this classical work by Sthiramati.
24. In an apparent error, the Tibetan text here reads *mittasapta*.

2. Establishing the Great Vehicle

25. Author's note: "The meaning of 'in accord' is also explained to mean that the Great and Lesser Vehicles emerged together."
26. Unidentified.

4. Potential

27. Stanza X.37.
28. Stanza XIV.19.
29. Ascribed to Maitreya.
30. The Tibetan here also mentions the name of a second person (Tib. *Gyad pakṣi ta*), whose life story likewise serves to illustrate the issue. The name given in Tibetan appears to be a corrupt Sanskrit transliteration, but we have not been able to establish the name of this second person. A similar reference appears on p. 443.

5. Developing the Enlightened Mind

31. Author's note: this line is missing in some manuscripts.

10. Enlightenment

32. As can be seen from the translation on p. 190, this is indeed the case in the *Stanzas Entitled "Ornament of the Great Vehicle Sūtras"* contained in the Derge (Tib. *sde dge*) edition of the Tenjur (Tib. *bsTan 'gyur*) as well as in Shenga's commentary.

33. Author's note: the Sanskrit word *rūpa* denotes both form and nature.
34. Author's note: Sthiramati's commentary states, "They demonstrate great enlightenment."

Summary of Chapters 1 through 10

35. Note that the division of the subject matter of chapters 16 through 21 that is described in this passage differs from the outline that is introduced at the beginning of chapter 16. The latter enumerates chapters 16 through 21 as six distinct topics under the common heading "The Actual Factors of Enlightenment." Since Mipham's commentary relies on the latter structure in its actual treatment of the final six chapters, we have also followed that in the topical outline that is included as an appendix to this book.

12. Investigation of the Dharma

36. As we will see in due course, their elaborate treatment appears elsewhere in the text.

13. Teaching

37. In an apparent error, the Tibetan text here reads *e va ra na*.

14. Practice

38. The Tibetan here also mentions the name of a second person (Tib. *Gyad pa gi ta*), whose life story likewise serves to illustrate the issue. The name given in Tibetan appears to be a corrupt Sanskrit transliteration, but we have not been able to establish the name of this second person. A similar reference appears on p. 69.
39. At this passage, the Tibetan text is corrupt. The translation has been prepared with reference to Sthiramati's commentary.

15. Practical Instructions and Advice

40. Unidentified.

Summary of Chapters 11 through 15

41. This sixfold division of the subject matter of the remaining chapters appears to be an alternative to the one presented at the opening of chapter 11. In the appendix, we have followed the structure that is outlined here.

17. Transcendences and Means of Attraction

42. In an apparent error, the Tibetan text here reads "the benefit for oneself," *rang don*.

43. For obvious reasons, the text here speaks of translations into Tibetan.
44. A traditional reference to the sūtras of transcendent insight.
45. Indian texts speak of the so-called deer that bathes in fire. As the name indicates, this antelope is not harmed by fire but uses it for bathing purposes.

19. The Factors That Accord with Enlightenment

46. The Tibetan text does not state any title of the initial section.
47. Reference to the chapter's summary appears to be missing in the Tibetan text at this point.
48. Stanza XIX.38a–b.
49. In an apparent error, the Tibetan text here reads *sarangarta*.
50. In an apparent error, the Tibetan text here reads "second" (*gnyis pa*).

20. The Qualities

51. Unidentified.
52. In his treatment below, Mipham explains these issues in a simple enumeration of seventeen subdivisions of the "Qualities of Practice." Contrary to his customary practice, he thus does not go by the further divisions and subdivisions of that section, which he otherwise mentions in this prelude. In the appendix, we have followed the structure of the actual commentary with its seventeen subdivisions of the "Qualities of Practice."
53. A traditional reference to the sūtras of transcendent insight.
54. In an apparent error, the Tibetan text here reads "pillar" (*ka ba*).
55. In an apparent error, the Tibetan text here reads "ten" (*bcu*).
56. The Tibetan text here reads *satva*.

21. Activity and Perfection

57. This may be a reference to the *Sūtra of the Inconceivable Secret*.
58. We have not been able to determine how these sixteen marks that are referred to by both Vasubandhu and Sthiramati are to be derived from the root text. Like Sthiramati, Mipham refers to six marks of the first six transcendences and six further marks with respect to the final four transcendences. Nevertheless, he does not explicitly identify the final four marks.

Bibliography

59. Numbering according to the Tōhoku University enumeration of the texts contained in the *sDe dge* edition of the Tibetan cannon.

English-Tibetan Glossary

absence of self	bdag med
absorption	ting nge 'dzin
acceptance	bzod pa
access	'jug pa
accomplishment	'grub pa
accumulation	tshogs
adventitious	lo bur ba
affliction	nyon mongs pa
afflicted mental cognition	nyon mongs pa'i yid
afflictive obscuration	nyon sgrib
agentive cause	byed rgyu
aggregate	phung po
agility	shin tu sbyang ba
agitation	rgod pa
alertness	shes bzhin
all-ground	kun gzhi
appearance	snang ba
application of mindfulness	dran pa nye bar bzhag pa
apprehend	'dzin pa, gzung ba
apprehended	gzung ba
apprehender	'dzin pa
appropriation	nyer len
aspect	cha, yan lag
aspect of enlightenment	byang chub kyi yan lag
aspect of the noble path	'phags lam yan lag
aspiration	smon lam
attachment	chags pa
authentic	yang dag pa

authentic elimination	yang dag par spong ba
awareness	rnam rig
base of miraculous power	rdzu 'phrul gyi rkang pa
basic field of phenomena	chos kyi dbyings
basis	gnas, gzhi
becoming	srid pa
belief	lta ba
bewilderment	rmong pa
bodhisattva	byang chub sems dpa'
body of perfect enjoyment	long spyod rdzogs pa'i sku
body of qualities	chos kyi sku
bond	kun sbyor
brightness	dwang ba
Buddha, buddha	sangs rgyas
buddha nature	bde gshegs snying po
calm abiding	zhi gnas
category	rnam grangs, rnam gzhag
cessation	'gog pa
characteristic	mtshan nyid
classification	rnam grangs, rnam gzhag
coarse	rags pa
coemergent	lhan skyes
cognitive obscuration	shes sgrib
collection of consciousness	rnam par shes pa'i tshogs
command	zil gnon
concentration	bsam gtan
concept	rtog pa
conceptual construct	spros pa
conditioned	'dus byed
conducive	cha dang mthun pa
conducive factor	mthun phyogs
conflicting factor	mi mthun phyogs
consciousness	rnam par shes pa
Consciousness School	rnam rig smra ba'i lugs
construct	spros pa
contact	reg pa
convention	tha snyad
correct awareness	so sor yang dag par rig pa
craving	sred pa

ENGLISH-TIBETAN GLOSSARY 971

cultivation	sgom pa
cyclic existence	'khor ba

dedication	sngo ba
defiling	zags bcas
definitive emergence	nges 'byung
deliverance	nges 'byung
denigration	skur 'debs
dependent [nature]	gzhan dbang
dependent origination	rten 'brel
determination	yongs su gcod pa
development of the enlightened mind	sems bskyed
devotion	mos pa
Dharma, dharma	chos
diligence	brtson 'grus
directing the mind	yid la byed pa
discipline	tshul khrims
discordant factor	mi mthun phyogs
distinction	khyad par
distraction	g.yeng ba
division	dbye ba
doubt	the tshom
downfall	ltung ba
dullness	bying ba

effect	'bras bu
effect of individual effort	skyes bu byed pa'i 'bras bu
effect of ripening	rnam par smin pa'i 'bras bu
effect of separation	bral ba'i bras bu
effect that accords with the cause	rgyu mthun gyi 'bras bu
element	khams
eliminated factor	spang bya
eliminated through cultivation	bsgom spang
eliminated through seeing	mthong spang
elimination	spong ba
emanation body	sprul pa'i sku
emptiness	stong pa nyid
engage	'jug pa
enlightened mind	byang chub kyi sems
enlightenment	byang chub
enlightenment, aspect of	byang chub kyi yan lag

entity	dngos po
equality	mnyam pa nyid
equilibrium	snyoms 'jug
equipoise	mnyam gzhag
error	phyin ci log pa
essence	ngo bo
essential nature	ngo bo nyid
established	grub pa
exaggerated	sgro btags
existence	yod pa, srid pa
experience	nye bar spyod pa, snang ba, myong ba
expert	mkhas pa
external object	phyi don
extreme	mtha'

fact	don
factor of enlightenment	byang chub kyi phyogs kyi chos
faculty	dbang po
faith	dad pa
field	spyod yul, zhing
flaw	nyes pa
focal point	dmigs pa
form	gzugs
formation	'du byed
foundation	gzhi
freedom	rnam thar
freedom from conceptual constructs	spros bral
fruition	'bras bu
fundamental transformation	gnas yongs su gyur ba

generosity	sbyin pa
genuine	yang dag pa
grasping	len pa
Great Vehicle	theg pa chen po
ground	gzhi, sa
ground of inspired conduct	mos spyod kyi sa

habitual tendency	bag chags
heat	dro ba

identification	'du shes
identity	bdag nyid

ignorance	ma rig pa
imaginary	kun brtags
imagination	kun rtog
imputed	kun btags, kun brtags
inference	rjes dpag
innate	lhan skyes
insight	shes rab
inspiration	mos pa
instruction	gdams ngag
intention	'dun pa
interest	mos pa
intrinsic nature	chos nyid
Joyous Realm, the	dga' ldan
karma	las
latency	bag nyal
Lesser Vehicle	theg pa dman pa
liberation	thar pa, rnam grol
linguistic symbol	brda
linguistic universal	sgra spyi
listener	nyan thos
livelihood	'tsho ba
logic	rtog ge
logician	rtog ge
luminous	'od gsal ba
manifest	mngon gyur
mark	mtshan ma
mastery	dbang ba
maturation	rnam smin
meaning	don
means	thabs
meditation	sgom pa
meditative absorption	ting nge 'dzin
meditative equipoise	mnyam gzhag
mental doing	yid la byed pa
mental state	sems byung
method	thabs
Middle Way	dbu ma
mind	blo, sems

mind of enlightenment	byang chub kyi sems
Mind Only	sems tsam
mind stream	rgyud
mindfulness	dran pa
mistaken	phyin ci log pa
mistaken view	log rta
mundane	'jig rten pa

name and form	ming gzugs
nature	don, rang bzhin
negative tendency	gnas ngan len
noble	'phags pa
nonconceptual	rnam par mi rtog pa
nonconceptual wakefulness	rnam par mi rtog pa'i ye shes
nonentity	dngos med
nonexistence	med pa

object	don, yul
object of cognition	shes bya
object of mind	shes bya
object universal	don spyi
obscuration	sgrib pa
observation	dmigs pa
origin	kun 'byung
origination	kun 'byung

path	lam
path of accumulation	tshogs lam
path of cultivation	bsgom lam
path of joining	sbyor lam
path of no more training	mi slob lam
path of seeing	mthong lam
patience	bzod pa
perception, direct	mngon sum
phenomenon	chos
potential [spiritual]	rigs
power	stobs, mthu
practice	sgrub pa, 'jug pa
preparatory stage	nyer ldog
pride	nga rgyal
principle	rnam grangs, rnam gzhag

purification, complete	rnam byang
purity	dag pa

quality	chos, yon tan

rational	'thad pa
real	bden pa, yang dag pa
reality	de kho uddha, don
realization	rtogs pa
realm	khams, gnas
reasonable	'thad pa
relative	kun rdzob
reliable means of cognition	tshad ma
relinquish	spong ba
remedy	gnyen po
result	'bras bu
ripened effect	snam par smin pa'i 'bras bu
ripening	rnam smin
ruled effect	bdag 'bras

tenet	grub mtha'
thoroughly established [nature]	yongs grub
thought	rtog pa, rnam rtog
training	sgom pa, slob pa
transcendence	'das pa, pha rol du phyin pa
transgression	ltung byed
true	bden pa, yang dag pa

ultimate	don dam
unconditioned	'dus ma byed
unmistaken	phyin ci ma log pa

vessel	gnod, sde gnod
view	lta ba
virtue	dge ba

wakefulness	ye shes
weariness	skyo ba
world	'jig rten
world of sentient beings	bcud kyi 'jig rten
world of the environment	gnod kyi 'jig rten
worldly	'jig rten pa

Tibetan-English-Sanskrit Glossary

kun btags	imputed	parikalpita
kun rtog	imagination	parikalpa
kun brtags	imaginary, imputed	parikalpita
kun sbyor	bond	saṃyojana
kun rdzob	relative	saṃvṛti
kun gzhi	all-ground	ālaya
skur 'debs	denigration, depreciation	apavāda
skye mched	sense source	āyatana
skye bu byed pa'i bras bu	effect of individual effort	puruṣakāraphala
skyo ba	disenchantment, weariness	udvega, parikheda
khams	element, realm	dhātu
khyad par	distinction	viśeṣa
khyad par du 'phags pa	distinct, superior	viśiṣṭa, vaiśeṣika
mkhas pa	expert, skilled	kauśalya
'khor ba	cyclic existence	saṃsāra
grub mtha'	tenet	siddhānta

TIBETAN-ENGLISH-SANSKRIT GLOSSARY

dga' ldan	the Joyous Realm	tuṣita
dge ba	virtue	kuśala, śubha
'gog pa	cessation	nirodha
grub pa	accomplishment, establishment	niṣpatti, prasiddha, siddhi
rgod pa	agitation	uddhata, auddhatya
rgyu mthun gyi 'bras bu	effect that accords with the cause	niṣyandaphala
rgyud	[mind-] stream, stream of being	santāna
sgom pa	cultivation, meditation, training	bhāvanā
sgra spyi	linguistic universal	śabdasāmānya
sgrib pa	obscuration	āvaraṇa, āvṛti, chādana, nivaraṇa
sgrub pa	practice	pratipatti, prapatti, prapannatā, sādhana
sgro btags	exaggeration, superimposition	āropa, samāropa
bsgom spang	eliminated through cultivation	bhāvanāheya
bsgom lam	path of cultivation	bhāvanā-mārga
nga rgyal	pride	abhimāna, unnati, māna
nges 'byung	definitive emergence, deliverance	niryāṇa
ngo bo	essence	svabhāva
ngo bo nyid	essential nature	svabhāva, svābhāvikatva
dngos po	entity	bhāva, vastu
dngos med	nonentity	abhāva
mngon gyur	manifest	abhimukhī
mngon shes	superknowledge	abhijñā
mngon sum	perception, direct	pratyakṣa
sngo ba	dedication	nati
chags pa	attachment	sakti
chos	dharma, phenomenon, quality	dharma

TIBETAN-ENGLISH-SANSKRIT GLOSSARY

chos kyi sku	body of qualities	dharmakāya
chos kyi dbyings	basic space of phenomena	dharmadhātu
chos can	subject	dharmin
chos mchog	supreme property	agradharma
chos nyid	intrinsic nature	dharmatā
'jig rten	world	loka
'jig rten pa	mundane, worldly,	laukika
'jig rten las 'das pa	beyond the world, supramundane	lokottara
'jug pa	access, engage, practice	avakrānti, avatṛ-, praviś-, praveśa, pravṛt-, visāra, sāra
rjes thob	subsequent attainment	pṛṣṭhalabdha
rjes dpag	inference	anumāna
nyan thos	listener	śrāvaka
nye bar spyod pa	experience, encounter	upabhoga
nyer ldog	preparatory stage	sāmantaka
nyer len	appropriation,	upādāna
nyes pa	flaw	doṣa
nyon sgrib	afflictive obscuration	kleśāvaraṇa
nyon mongs pa	affliction	kleśa
nyon mongs pa'i yid	afflicted mental cognition	kliṣṭaḥ manaḥ
gnyen po	remedy	pratipakṣa, vipakṣa
mnyam pa nyid	equality	samatā
mnyam gzhag	[meditative] equipoise	samādhā
snyoms 'jug	equilibrium	samāpatti
ting nge 'dzin	absorption, meditative absorption	samādhi
rten 'brel	dependent origination	pratītyasamutpāda

rtog ge	logician	tārkika
rtog pa	concept, thought	kalpanā
rtogs pa	realization	adhigama, anubudhyana, anubodha, praveśa
lta ba	belief, view	darśana, dṛṣṭi
stong pa nyid	emptiness	śūnyatā
stobs	power	bala
brtan pa	steadfastness	
ltung ba	downfall	prāyaścittika
ltung byed	transgression	pāpattikā
tha snyad	convention	vyavahāra
thabs	means, method	upāya
thar pa	liberation	mokṣa
the tshom	doubt	vicikitsā
theg pa chen po	Great Vehicle	mahāyāna
theg pa dman pa	Lesser Vehicle	hīnayāna
thos pa	listening, receiving teaching	śruta
mtha'	extreme	anta
mthun phyogs	conducive factor	sapakṣa
mthong spang	eliminated through seeing	darśanaprahātavya
mthong lam	path of seeing	darśanamārga
'thad pa	reasonable, sound, rational	upapatti
dag pa	purity	śuddhi
dad pa	faith	śraddhā
de kho na nyid	reality	tattva
de bzhin nyid	suchness	tathatā
don	fact, object, meaning, nature, reality, significance	artha, bhāva

TIBETAN-ENGLISH-SANSKRIT GLOSSARY 981

don dam	ultimate	paramārtha
dran pa	mindfulness	smṛti
dran pa nye bar bzhag pa	application of mindfulness	smṛty-upasthāna
dri ma	stain	mala
dri med	stainless	amala, nirmala
dro ba	heat	uṣma
bdag	self	ātman
bdag nyid	identity	uddh
bdag 'bras	ruled effect	adhipatiphala
bdag med	absence of self, selflessness	nairātmya
bde gshegs snying po	buddha nature	sugatagarbha
bden pa	real, true	sat
'du byed	formation	saṃskāra
'dun pa	intention	chanda
'dus byed	conditioned	saṃskṛta
'dus ma byed	unconditioned	asaṃskṛta
'du shes	identification	saṃjñā
brda	linguistic symbol	saṃketa

gnas	basis, realm, state	adhiṣṭhāna, avasthā, āśraya, pratiṣṭhā, sanniśraya, sthāna, sthiti
gnas ngan len	negative tendency	dauṣṭhulya
gnas yongs su gyur ba	fundamental transformation	āśryaparāvṛtti
rnam grangs	categorization, classification, principle, synonym	paryāya
rnam grol	liberation	vimukti, vimokṣa
rnam rtog	concept, thought	vikalpa
rnam thar	freedom, liberation	mokṣa, vimukti, vimokṣa
rnam par dag pa	purity	viśuddhi
rnam par dag pa'i dmigs pa	observation of perfect purity	viśuddhyālambana

982 TIBETAN-ENGLISH-SANSKRIT GLOSSARY

rnam par mi rtog pa	nonconceptuality	avikalpana, nirvikalpa
rnam par mi rtog pa'i ye shes	nonconceptual wakefulness	avikalpana jñāna, nirvikalpa jñāna
snam par smin pa'i 'bras bu	ripened effect	vipākaphala
rnam par shes pa	consciousness	vijñāna
rnam par shes pa'i tshogs	collection of consciousness	vijñānakāya
rnam byang	purification	vyavadāna
rnam smin	maturation, ripening	vipāka
rnam gzhag	category, classification, principle	vyavasthāna, vyavasthāpana
rnam rig	awareness	vijñapti
rnam rig smra ba'i lugs	Consciousness School	vijñāvāda
rnal 'byor	spiritual practice	yoga
snang ba	appearance, experience	darśana, prakhyāna, pratibhās-, pratibhāsa
gnod	vessel	bhājana
gnod kyi 'jig rten	environment of the world	bhājanaloka
spang bya	discarded factor, eliminated factor	prahātavya, heya
spong ba	elimination, relinquishment	tyāga, prahāṇa, vivarjana
spyod yul	field, sphere [of engagement]	gocara
sprul pa'i sku	emanation body	nirmāṇakāya
spros bral	freedom from conceptual constructs	niṣprapañca
pha rol du phyin pa	transcendence	pāramitā
phung po	aggregate	skandha
phyi don	external object	bāhyārtha
phyin ci ma log pa	unmistaken	aviparīta, aviparyasta
phyin ci log pa	error, mistaken	viparyasta, viparyāsa

TIBETAN-ENGLISH-SANSKRIT GLOSSARY

phra ba	subtle	sūkṣma
'phags pa	noble	ārya
'phags lam yan lag	aspect of the noble path	āryamārgāṅga
bag chags	habitual tendency	vāsanā
bag nyal	latency	anuśaya
byang chub	enlightenment	bodhi
byang chub kyi phyogs	factor of enlightenment	bodhipakṣya
byang chub kyi yan lag	aspect of enlightenment	bodhyaṅga
byang chub kyi sems	enlightened mind, mind of enlightenment	bodhicitta
byang chub sems dpa'	bodhisattva	bodhisattva
bying ba	dullness	laya
byed rgyu	agentive cause	karaṇa
bral ba'i bras bu	effect of separation	visaṃyogaphala
dbang po	faculty	indriya
dbang ba	mastery	vaśitā
dbye ba	division, type	bheda
sbyin pa	generosity	dāna
sbyor lam	path of joining	prayogamārga
'bras bu	fruition, result, effect	phala
ma rig pa	ignorance	avidyā
mi mthun phyogs	conflicting factor, discordant factor	vipakṣa
mi slob lam	path of no more training	aśaikṣamārga
med pa	absence, nonexistence	abhāva, asat, asattva
mos pa	devotion, inspiration, interest	adhimukti, adhimokṣa
mos spyod kyi sa	ground of inspired conduct	adhimukticaryābhūmi
dmigs pa	focus, observation	ālambana, upalabdhi, upalambha

rmongs pa	bewilderment	moha, vimoha, saṃmoha
smon lam	aspiration	praṇidhāna
rtse mo	summit	mūrdhāna
brtson 'grus	diligence	vīrya
tshangs pa'i gnas	sublime abode	brahmavihāra
tshad ma	reliable means of cognition	pramāṇa
tshul khrims	discipline	śīla
tshogs	accumulation	kāya, sambhāra
tshogs lam	path of accumulation	sambhāramārga
mtshan nyid	characteristic	lakṣaṇa
mtshan ma	mark	nimitta
mtshan ma med pa	absence of marks	ānimittā, nimittābhāva, nirnimittatā
'tsho ba	livelihood	ājīva
'dzin pa	apprehend, apprehender	grahaṇa, grāha, grāhaka
rdzas	substance	dravya, upadhi
rdzu 'phrul gyi rkang pa	base of miraculous power	ṛddhipāda
zhi gnas	calm abiding	śamatha
gzhan dbang	dependent [nature]	paratantra
gzhi	basis, ground, foundation	ādhāra, nidhāna, vastu
zags bcas	defiling	sāsrava
zil gnon	command, outshine	abhibhavana, abhibhūta
gzugs	form	rūpa

TIBETAN-ENGLISH-SANSKRIT GLOSSARY 985

gzung ba	apprehended	grāhya
bzod pa	acceptance, patience	kṣānti
'od gsal ba	luminous	prabhāsvara
yang dag pa	authentic, genuine, real, true	bhūta
yan lag	aspect	aṅga
yid la byed pa	directing the mind, mental activity	manaskāraṇa, manasikāra, manasikriyā, manaskāra
yul	object	viṣaya
yul can	subject	viṣayin
ye shes	wakefulness	jñāna
yongs grub	thoroughly established [nature]	pariniṣpatti, pariniṣpanna
yongs su gcod pa	determination	pariccheda
yod pa	existence	astitva, bhāva, sadbhāva
yon tan	good quality, quality	guṇa
g.yeng ba	distraction	vikṣepa
rags pa	coarse	udāra, audārika
rang bzhin	nature	prakṛti, svabhāva
rang sangs rgyas	self-realized buddha	pratyekabuddha
rigs	potential	gotra
reg pa	contact	sparśa
lam	path	pratipad, pratipatti, mārga
las	karma	karman
las kyi mtha'	activity	karmānta
len pa	grasping	upādāna
lo bur ba	adventitious	āgantuka

log lta	mistaken view	mithyādṛṣṭi
long spyod rdzogs pa'i sku	body of perfect enjoyment	sāmbhogikakāya
shin tu sbyangs ba	agility	praśrabdhi
shes sgrib	cognitive obscuration	jñeyāvaraṇa
shes bzhin	alertness	saṃprajanya
shes rab	insight	prajñā
sa	ground	bhūmi
sangs rgyas	buddha	buddha
sems	mind	citta, cetas
sems bskyed	development of the enlightened mind	cittotpāda
sems can	sentient being	sattva
sems byung	mental state	caitta
so sor yang dag par rig pa	correct awareness	pratisaṃvid
srid pa	existence, becoming	bhava, sambhava
sred pa	craving	tṛṣṇā
slob pa	training	śaikṣa
bsam gtan	concentration	dhyāna
lhag mthong	insight	vipaśyana
lhag bsam	superior intent	adhyāśaya
lhan skyes	coemergent, innate	sahaja

Bibliography

Canonical Scriptures

Gathering of Precious Qualities (Skt. *Prajñāpāramitāratnaguṇasañcayagāthā*). Tōh. 13.
Great Ornament of the Buddhas (Skt. *Avataṃsaka*). Tōh. 44.
Hevajra Tantra (Skt. *Hevajratantranāmatantrarāja*). Tōh. 417.
Jewel Lamp Sūtra (Skt. *Ratnolkā-nāma-mahāyānasūtra*). Tōh. 145.
Jewel Mound Sūtra (Skt. *Ratnakūṭa*). Tōh. 45–93.
Journey to Laṅkā (Skt. *Laṅkāvatāra*). Tōh. 107.
Long Discourses (Pali *Dīghanikāya*).
Manifest Enlightenment of Vairocana (Skt. *Mahāvairocanābhisaṃbodhi*). Tōh. 494.
Moonlamp Sūtra (Skt. *Sarvadharmasvabhāvasamatāvipañcita-samādhirāja-sūtra*). Tōh. 127.
Noble Ground of Buddhahood (Skt. *Ārya-buddhabhūmi*). Tōh. 275.
Noble Sūtra on Transcendent Insight in Eighteen Thousand Lines (Skt. *Ārya-aṣṭadaśasāhasrikā-prajñāpāramitā*). Tōh. 10.
The Śāli Sprout Sūtra (Skt. *Śālistamba-sūtra*). Tōh. 210.
Śrī Mālā Sūtra (Skt. *Śrīmālādevīsiṃhanāda-sūtra*). Tōh. 92.
Sūtra of Gaya Mountain (Skt. *Gayāśīrṣasūtra*). Tōh. 109.
Sūtra of the Completely Pure Sphere of Activity (Skt. *Gocarapariśuddhi-sūtra*). Tōh. 44:16.
Sūtra of the Great Display (Skt. *Lalitavistara-sūtra*). Tōh. 95.
Sūtra of the Inconceivable Secret (Skt. *Tathāgatācintyaguhyanirdeśasūtra*). Tōh. 48.
Sūtra of the Lord of Retention (Skt. *Dhāraṇīśvararājaparipṛcchā sūtra/ Tathāgatamahākaruṇānirdeśa-sūtra*). Tōh. 147.
Sūtra of the Ornament of the Light of Wakefulness (Skt. *Jñānālokālaṃkāranāma-mahāyānasūtra*). Tōh. 100.
Sūtra on Individual Liberation (Skt. *Prātimokṣasūtra*). Tōh. 2.
Sūtra on Numerous Elements (Skt. *Bahudhātukasūtra*). Tōh. 297.
Sūtra on Repaying Kindness. Translated from the Chinese. Tōh. 353.
Sūtra on the Definitive Explanation of the Intent (Skt. *Saṃdhinirmocana-sūtra*). Tōh. 106.
Sūtra on the Ten Grounds (Skt. *Daśabhūmikasūtra*). Tōh. 44:31.
Sūtra on Transcendent Insight in One Hundred Thousand Lines (Skt. *Śatasāhasrikā-prajñāpāramitā-sūtra*). Tōh. 8.

Sūtra Requested by Brahma (Skt. *Brahmaparipṛchhā*). Tōh. 158.
Sūtra Requested by Ratnacūḍa (Skt. *Ratnacūḍaparipṛcchā*). Tōh. 91.
Sūtra Taught by Akṣayamati (Skt. *Akṣayamatinirdeśa-sūtra*). Tōh. 175.[59]
Vajra Cutter Sūtra (Skt. *Vajracchedikā-sūtra*). Tōh. 16.
The Wheel of Time (Skt. *Kālacakranāmatantrarāja*). Tōh. 362.
White Lotus of the Sacred Dharma (Skt. *Mahākaruṇāpuṇḍarīka*). Tōh. 111.

Classical Indian Treatises

Āryadeva. *Four Hundred Stanzas* (Skt. *Catuḥśatakaśāstra*). Tōh. 3846.
Asaṅga. *Compendium on Abhidharma* (Skt. *Abhidharmasamuccaya*). Tōh. 4049.
———. *Compendium on the Great Vehicle* (Skt. *Mahāyānasaṃgraha*). Tōh. 4048.
———. *Grounds of Yogic Practice* (Skt. *Yogācārabhūmi*). Tōh. 4035–42.
Bhavya. *Precious Lamp of the Middle Way* (Skt. *Madhyamakaratnapradīpa*). Tōh. 3863.
Candrakīrti. *Entering the Middle Way* (Skt. *Madhyamakāvatāra*). Tōh. 3861.
Dharmakīrti. *Commentary on Reliable Means of Cognition* (Skt. *Pramāṇavārttika*). Tōh. 4210.
Dignāga. *Compendium on Reliable Means of Cognition* (Skt. *Pramāṇasamuccaya*). Tōh. 4203.
Guṇaprabhā. *Teaching on Vinaya* (Skt. *Vinayasūtra*). Tōh. 4117.
Maitreya. *Distinguishing Phenomena from Their Intrinsic Nature* (Skt. *Dharmadharmatāvibhaṅga*). Tōh. 4023.
———. *Distinguishing the Middle from Extremes* (Skt. *Madhyāntavibhāga*). Tōh. 4021.
———. *Ornament of Manifest Realization* (Skt. *Abhisamayālaṃkāra*). Tōh. 3786.
———. *Ornament of the Great Vehicle Sūtras* (Skt. *Mahāyānasūtrālaṃkāra*). Tōh. 4020.
———. *Supreme Continuity* (Skt. *Mahāyānottaratantra-śāstra, Ratnagotravibhāga*). Tōh. 4024.
Nāgārjuna. *Root of the Middle Way* (Skt. *Prajñā-nāma-mūlamadhyamaka*). Tōh. 8324.
Śāntideva. *Entering the Activity of the Bodhisattvas* (Skt. *Bodhicaryāvatāra*). Tōh 3871.
Sthiramati. *Vast Exposition of the Ornament of the Great Vehicle Sūtras* (Skt. *Mahāyānsūtrālaṃkāra-vṛtti-bhāṣya*). Tōh. 4029.
Vasubandhu. *Exposition of the Ornament of the Great Vehicle Sūtras* (Skt. *Mahāyānasūtrālaṃkārabhāṣya*). Tōh. 4026.
———. *Treasury of Abhidharma* (Skt. *Abhidharmakośa*). Tōh. 4089.

Tibetan Revelations and Commentaries

'Ju Mi pham 'jam dbyangs rnam rgyal rgya mtsho. *A Feast of the Supreme Vehicle* (*Theg pa chen po mdo sde'i rgyan gyi dgongs don rnam par bshad pa theg mchog bdud rtsi'i dga' ston*). In *Sde-dge dgon-chen Prints of the Writings of 'Jam-mgon 'Ju Mi-pham-rgya-mtsho*. Edited by Dilgo Khyentse. Vol. 2. Kathmandu: Shechen Monastery.

Tantra of Essential Elixir (*bDud rtsi snying po yan lag brgyad pa gsang ba man ngag gi rgyud*). Delhi: Pod kyi lcags po ri'i dran rten slob gnyer khang, 1993.

gZhan phan chos kyi snang ba. *Annotation Commentary on the "Ornament of the Great Vehicle Sūtras"* (*Theg pa chen po'i mdo sde'i rgyan ces bya ba'i mchan 'grel*). Edited by Konchhog Lhadrepa. Delhi: 'Bri gung nyi ma lcang ra'i par khang, 1993.

Modern Research and Translations

Chattopadhyāya, Alaka, and Lama Chimpa. 1990. *Tāranātha's History of Buddhism in India*. Delhi: Motilal Banarsidass.

D'Amato, Mario. 2000. "The Mahāyāna/Hīnayāna Distinction in the *Mahāyānasūtrālaṃkāra*: A Terminological Analysis." PhD diss., University of Chicago.

Dharmachakra Translation Committee, trans. 2007. *Middle Beyond Extremes: Maitreya's Madhyāntavibhāga with Commentaries by Khenpo Shenga and Ju Mipham*. Ithaca: Snow Lion Publications.

———. 2013. *Distinguishing Phenomena from Their Intrinsic Nature: Maitreya's "Dharmadharmatāvibhaṅga" with Commentaries by Khenpo Shenga and Ju Mipham*. Boston: Snow Lion.

Dreyfus, Georges. 2005. "Where Do Commentarial Schools Come From? Reflections on the History of Tibetan Scholasticism." *Journal of the International Association of Buddhist Studies* 28: 273–97.

Duckworth, Douglas S. 2009. *Mipam on Buddha-Nature: The Ground of the Nyingma Tradition*. Albany: State University of New York Press.

———. 2011. *Jamgön Mipam: His Life and Teachings*. Boston: Shambhala.

Jackson, David P. 2004. *A Saint in Seattle: The Life of the Tibetan Mystic Dezhung Rinpoche*. Ithaca, N.Y.: Snow Lion Publications.

Levi, Sylvain, ed. and trans. 1907–11. *Mahāyana-Sūtralaṃkāra*. 2 vols. Paris: Liberairie Honoré Champion.

Maitreyanātha/Asaṅga. 2005. *The Universal Vehicle Discourse Literature (Mahāyānasūtrālaṃkāra)*. New York: American Institute of Buddhist Studies.

Matthes, Klaus-Dieter. 1996. *Unterscheidung der Gegebenheiten von ihrem wahren Wesen ("Dharmadharmatāvibhāga"): Eine Lehrschrit der Yogācāra-Schule in tibetischer Überlieferung*. Swisttal-Odendorf: Indica et Tibetica Verlag.

Mipham, Jamgön. 1997–2012. *Gateway to Knowledge: A Condensation of the Tripiṭaka*. 4 vols. Boston: Rangjung Yeshe Publications.

———. *See also* Mipham, Ju.

Mipham, Ju. 2004a. *Speech of Delight: Mipham's Commentary on Śāntarakṣita's "Ornament of the Middle Way."* Translated by Thomas H. Doctor. Ithaca, N.Y.: Snow Lion Publications.

———. 2004b. *Maitreya's Distinguishing Phenomena and Pure Being with Commentary by Mipham*. Translated by Jim Scott. Ithaca, N.Y.: Snow Lion Publications.

———. *See also* Mipham, Jamgön.

Nyoshul, Khenpo Jamyang Dorje. 2005. *A Marvelous Garland of Rare Gems: Biographies of Masters of Awareness in the Dzogchen Lineage (A Spiritual History of the Teachings of Natural Great Perfection)*. Junction City, Calif.: Padma Publishing.

Obermiller, Eugene. 1999. *The History of Buddhism in India and Tibet by Bu-ston*. Delhi: Paljor Publications. First published 1932.

Pettit, John Whitney. 1999. *Mipham's "Beacon of Certainty": Illuminating the View of Dzogchen, the Great Perfection*. Boston: Wisdom Publications.

Phuntsho, Karma. 2005. *Mipham's Dialectics and the Debates on Emptiness: To Be, Not To Be or Neither*. London: Routledge.

Shantarakshita and Jamgon Mipham. 2005. *The Adornment of the Middle Way: Shantarakshita's "Madhyamakalankara" with Commentary by Jamgön Mipham*. Translated by the Padmakara Translation Group. Boston: Shambhala.

Skilling, Peter. 2013. "Vaidalya, Mahāyāna, and Bodhisattva in India: An Essay towards Historical Understanding." In *The Bodhisattva Ideal: Essays on the Emergence of the Mahāyāna,* edited by Bhikkhu Nyanatusita, 69–162. Kandy, Sri Lanka: Buddhist Publication Society.

Thondup, Tulku. 1999. *Masters of Meditation and Miracles: Lives of the Great Buddhist Masters of India and Tibet*. Boston: Shambhala.

Turenne, Philippe. 2010. "Interpretations of Unity: Hermeneutics in ŚĀKYA MCHOG LDAN's Interpretation of the Five Treatises of Maitreya." PhD diss., McGill University.

Index

Abhidharma, 25, 29, 286–92
abidance, suchness of, 817, 818
absence of marks
  listeners and, 825, 830
  meditative absorption of, 380, 430, 432, 477, 717–19, 721, 905
  seventh ground and, 672, 675, 684, 880–81, 892, 896, 909
absence of self. *See* selflessness of persons
absence of wishes, 380, 430, 432, 477, 717–19, 721
acceptance. *See* stage of acceptance
accumulation of merit and wakefulness
  of bodhisattvas, 46, 47, 791
  directing the mind to, 302
  endowments and, 235, 437
  enlightened mind and, 81–82, 85
  factors of enlightenment and, 671–75
  faith and, 167
  in Great Vehicle, 30, 31, 33, 50, 281–82
  on grounds and paths, 674–75, 901
  inspiration of, 267, 269
  lack of potential and, 72, 73
  maturation of power and, 165
  metaphor for, 92, 96, 209
  perfection of, 75, 139, 140, 209, 217, 252, 347, 408, 454
  three vehicles and, 822
  transcendences and, 374, 379, 672, 673–74
  worship and, 572, 577

activity, authentic, 308, 706, 707
acumen
  correct awareness of, 670–71
  metaphors for, 92, 95–96, 97
affection, full maturation of, 161–62. *See also* love
afflictions
  conquerors of all, 913–14
  elimination of, 141–42, 160–61, 169, 171, 193, 306, 345, 417, 418, 431
  as factors of enlightenment, 440–42
  four eliminations and, 683–84
  freedom from, 103, 704
  habituation to, 67, 68, 156, 345, 348, 441, 806–7
  illusory nature of, 325
  lack of conscience and, 645
  lack of immeasurables and, 597–600
  lack of potential and, 72
  life with seeds and, 740
  listeners' elimination of, 89, 214, 341, 342, 439, 441, 836
  mind as root of, 130, 331–32
  purity of the absence of, 301, 312–13, 315
  remedies for, 23, 391, 426
  scriptures on dispelling, 289–90, 291
  self-liberation of, 440
  steadfastness of no, 655
  supreme protection from, 188–89, 191
  view of self and, 121, 133–34

afflictions (*continued*)
　See also obscurations; thorough affliction
aggregates
　absence of wishes and, 718–19
　bondage of, 828
　complete cognition of nature of, 306
　consciousness and, 667
　cultivating on the grounds, 893–94
　enumeration of, 459
　four applications of mindfulness and, 679–80
　impermanence of, 740–41, 747
　as not the self, 132, 133, 758–59, 762, 764–67
　transformation of, 193–94, 390–91
agility
　as aspect of enlightenment, 307, 696, 702, 704
　bliss of, 469
　meditative absorption and, 689
all-accomplishing wakefulness, 232
　cause for attaining, 249
　explanation of, 246–48
　sense consciousnesses and, 242–43
all-ground consciousness
　afflicted mind and, 222, 332, 338
　dualistic appearance and, 129, 130, 330
　habitual tendencies in, 345, 828, 829–30, 832
　mirror-like wakefulness and, 236, 242, 248
　seeds of transcendences in, 372–73
　transformation of, 142, 220, 223, 233, 321, 345–46, 831
all-pervasiveness, of enlightenment, 198–200
Amitābha, 237, 422
anger
　flaws of, 645
　as predominant tendency, 61
　remedy for, 116, 163, 507, 608
　toward Dharma, 35, 38
　See also hostility and harm

appearance
　all-ground consciousness and, 129, 130, 330
　combined with emptiness, 322
　dependent nature and, 323, 338–39, 476, 817
　fully realizing marks of, 311
　as illusion-like, 315–27
　as mind only, 128, 129, 139, 473–74
　transformation of, 194, 224
apprehended and apprehender. See duality of apprehended and apprehender
arising and ceasing, 724–30, 752–53
arrogance
　conscience and, 643
　of one's view, 290
　of referential views, 255
arts and sciences, knowledge of, 363–64, 658, 660, 811, 815–16
Asaṅga, 129, 130, 442, 666, 803
aspiration
　of bodhisattvas, 44, 45, 120–21
　directing the mind to, 303
　of enlightened mind, 81, 87–88, 93
　factors of enlightenment and, 714–16
　full accomplishment of, 691
　of great compassion, 610, 611, 612
　knowledge arising from, 914
　of listeners to take birth, 359–60
　mastery of, 691, 692
　possessing armor of, 436–37
　steadfastness of, 654
　as support for diligence, 684
　transcendences and, 373, 376, 512
　worship and, 575–76
attachment
　freedom from, 527–28, 552, 615–16
　great love and, 447–48
　remedy for, 426
attainment of qualities, full accomplishment of, 692
attention
　as basis of miraculous power, 307, 687, 688
　to benefiting beings, 610, 611–12

six types of, 456–57, 458–60, 461
Avalokiteśvara, 152
awareness, suchness of, 817, 818

basic field of phenomena
  buddhahood as nature of, 195, 199, 233–35, 250
  direct realization of, 50, 307, 308, 311, 475, 705, 707
  joy of realizing, 704
  mirror-like wakefulness and, 236, 242
  as nonarising, 225
  phenomena as, 439, 440–41
  as single and pure, 257, 258
  stages of realizing, 138–43, 167
  suchness and, 186, 194, 232, 233, 829
  as transcendence of suffering, 830
  unchanging essence of, 215–16
beginning, absence of, 352–53
benefiting others
  attaining enlightenment for, 42–44, 108, 373, 442–43, 576
  by bearing their suffering, 102, 105–6, 111, 112, 480–81, 614–15, 618–27
  delight and joy in, 88, 99–100, 101–2, 156, 377, 624–26
  emanation activities for, 151, 152, 217–18, 239–41, 247
  engagement for, 196, 197
  enlightened mind and, 78, 102–8
  going for refuge for, 42–43, 56
  with loving compassion, 119, 447–48, 541–42, 607–8, 610–14
  maturing activities for, 172–80
  mind of equality and, 85–86, 110–12, 475, 781–82, 788
  nonconceptual activity for, 202
  practice based on, 109–10
  praise of practice of, 846–47
  as reward, 383, 480
  seven examples of, 784–92
  sublime refuge for, 189–92
  supremacy of, 115–17, 312
  taking birth for, 50, 52, 103–5, 327, 596, 600, 610, 612, 655, 680, 779, 868–74, 879
  threefold hope regarding, 383
  through worship, 576
  transcendences and, 501–2, 783
  See also practice for sake of others; twofold benefit
birth and death
  attainment of inconceivable birth, 360
  four applications of mindfulness and, 680
  mastery of, 691, 692
  as nonarising, 353
  by power of aspiration, 691, 872, 873
  by power of mastery, 873, 874, 879
  superknowledge of, 95, 145, 146, 154, 385–86, 690
  wishing for certain, 385, 872
  See also cyclic existence
bliss
  of meditative absorption, 223, 275
  of suffering through love, 623
  of supreme intelligence, 50, 51
bodhisattva vows. *See* vows
bodhisattvas
  acceptance of taking birth, 50, 52, 103–5, 327, 534, 596, 600, 610, 612, 655, 680, 779, 868–74, 879
  aspects of conduct of, 8–9
  commitment of, 45–49
  eleven forms of knowledge of, 860–61
  enduring of hardships, 54, 88, 101–2, 182–83, 280–81, 381–82, 398, 442–43, 493, 534, 793
  epithets of, 850–53
  generosity of, 549–53
  great love of, 101, 106–7, 172, 447–48, 541–42, 616–17
  in lower realms, 69, 105, 442–43, 779
  maturation of, 226, 230
  outshining of, 42, 51–53, 822–23
  praises to, 842–61
  realization of, 49–51, 829–32, 853–61
  with referential views, 255
  signs and marks of, 863–67, 898–905
  stable inspiration of, 269, 278, 279

bodhisattvas (*continued*)
   teaching of, 113–14, 115–16, 402–8
   types of, 9, 841–42
   unbroken lineage and, 46, 47, 712
   of uncertain potential, 358–59, 426–27
   vast meditative absorption of, 535
   See also qualities of bodhisattvas
bodies of the buddhas
   actualization of, 345–46, 858
   as nature of suchness, 206
   omniscience and, 924
   as permanent, 241–42
   profound abode of, 207–8
   as same without distinction, 211, 241
   seeing and not seeing, 199–200, 213
   steadfastness in attaining, 654–55
   three types of, 235–42
   twofold benefit and, 239–41
body of qualities, 235
   absence of distinct arising of, 353
   attainment of, 51, 342, 389, 401, 469, 924
   as basis of form bodies, 236, 240, 241
   continuous activities of, 926
   equality of, 422, 425
   explanation of, 238
buddha fields
   all-ground transformed into, 345–46
   cultivation of, 152–53, 342, 389, 710, 833, 834, 881, 889
   as field of liberation, 346
   obstacles to cultivating, 832–33
   profundity of, 203–15, 230–31, 247–48
   relying on spiritual teacher and, 584
buddha nature, 64, 362
   as noble potential, 341
   unchanging essence of, 215–16
Buddha Śākyamuni, 22, 26, 293, 422, 424–25
Buddha Vipaśvin, 422, 425
Buddha/buddhas
   all-pervasiveness of, 198–200
   being born into family of, 114, 117, 779
   limitless mastery of, 216–24
   limitless maturation of, 229–30
   marks and signs of, 221, 391, 916
   melodious speech of, 410–14, 814
   nature of transformation of, 195–98
   as not one and not many, 249–52
   as perfectly awakened, 325–26
   prophecies of, 802–3
   recollecting qualities of, 302–3
   remedy for disdain and harm of, 424–25, 426
   superior liberation of, 335, 341–42
   supplicating, 375, 711–12, 788
   as supreme protectors, 188–92
   teaching of, 227–28, 398–402, 408–16
   as "thus gone," 195
   wisdom vision of, 23, 27–28, 195, 690
   worship of, 377, 571–78
   See also qualities of perfection
buddhahood
   going for refuge for, 53–54
   ground of, 52, 54, 82, 114, 341, 883–84, 925–26
   as neither existent nor nonexistent, 185, 205–7
   as painting on space, 214–15
   profound abode of, 207–8, 215
   profound activity of, 208–14, 215
   profound characteristics of, 203–7, 215
   See also enlightenment

calm abiding and special insight, 140, 330, 342, 348, 503
   aspects of enlightenment and, 696
   authentic eliminations and, 682–83, 684–85
   cognition and, 304, 306
   eightfold noble path and, 706, 707
   four bases and, 688–89
   grounds and, 694, 709–10, 904–5
   investigation of, 707–10
   marks of, 308, 437, 461–62, 685, 707
   metaphor for, 92, 96–97

nine stages of, 466–70
pride and, 273
unity of, 114, 309, 461
Candrakīrti, 131
causes and effects, 725, 732, 741, 751,
    820–21
certainty
  directing the mind to, 385
  quality of doubtless, 804–5
characteristics
  concealed intent on, 419, 420
  investigation of, 332–43
  suchness of, 817
  of ultimate reality, 126–31
cherishing others, practice of, 110–12
cognition
  characteristics of thorough, 826–28
  directing the mind associated with,
    303–4, 305–6
  investigating objects of, 327–29
  investigation of mere, 331–32
  on path of seeing, 300, 306
  See also objects of cognition
cognitive obscurations, 183
  elimination of, 141–42, 184, 193, 431,
    434
  liberated insight and, 207
  purity of the absense of, 312–13, 342
  remedy for, 27, 707
  See also obscurations
commands, eight, 154–55, 912–13
Commentary on Reliable Means of Cognition, 809
compassion
  benefiting others and, 119, 447–48,
    541–42, 607–8, 610–14
  of buddhas, 921–22
  causes of, 631–33
  conflicting factors and, 598
  directing the mind to, 377
  distinctive equality of, 634–35
  distinctive qualities of, 606–14
  divisions of, 605–6
  effects of, 602–3, 866
  endowed with insight, 604–5
  endowed with love, 612–13, 616–17

enlightened mind and, 80, 81, 87,
    104, 105
  examples and metaphors for, 609–14
  five fields of, 865
  focal points of, 591, 600–602, 635
  generosity and, 624–31, 632
  going for refuge and, 53, 54, 56
  of listeners and self-realized buddhas,
    195–96, 607, 608
  nonattachment and, 615–16
  as sign of a bodhisattva, 119, 864
  as sign of potential, 66
  as source of good qualities, 614–15
  suffering of others and, ix–x, 8,
    106–7, 442, 480–81, 604–5,
    614–15, 618–27
  supreme, 635–36
  transcendences and, 521, 531, 533, 546,
    632–33, 867
  worship and, 576
Compendium on Reliable Means of Cognition, 814
Compendium on the Great Vehicle
  (Asaṅga), 12–13, 130, 143, 251, 422,
    442, 470
complete purification, 127
  illusory nature of, 324, 325
  investigation of, 329–31
  person in possession of, 773–74
  understanding ground of, 308
  See also transcendence of suffering
complete purity
  cause of attaining, 252–55
  characteristics of, 203–4, 342
  of nonabiding transference, 224, 225
  praise of, 916–17
  of thoroughly established nature,
    12–13, 205, 315
concealed intent, of teachings, 419–21
concentration
  accumulations and, 672, 674
  analysis of, 519–20, 522–23
  characteristics of, 506, 507
  compassion and, 633
  conflicting factors and, 374, 527, 529
  constant practice of, 807

concentration (*continued*)
  enlightened mind and, 87
  etymology of, 510
  inclusion of all transcendences in, 559–62
  for maturation of others, 177
  metaphor for, 91, 94
  perfection of, 902
  qualities of, 533, 535, 539, 542
  special training in, 290–91, 504, 892
  superknowledge and, 502, 522
  as support for liberation, 502, 523
  supreme pursuit of, 808–9
  supreme qualities of, 545–46, 549
  See also calm abiding and special insight; meditation
concepts and discernment
  four concentrations and, 460–61
  investigating meaning with, 309–10
  meditative absorption and, 303, 523
  See also discernment
conception, five principles and, 6, 12, 819
Concise Abhidharma Treatise, 477
conditioned things
  as effects of mind, 732–35
  impermanence of inner, 735–47
  impermanence of outer, 747–56
  proof of impermanence of, 722–35
  See also phenomena
confession, 375, 674, 711–12
conscience and embarrassment, 639–50
  basis for, 641–42
  benefits of, 646–47
  characteristics of, 640–41
  flaws from lack of, 644–45
  praise of those possessing, 647–49
  signs of possessing, 649
  supreme cultivation of, 649–50
  types of, 642–44
contemplation, directing the mind in, 455–62
contentment, remedy for, 425–26, 528
continuity of practice, 384, 806–7
continuum of the path, 46, 47, 712

creative emanations, 150–51, 152, 218, 239, 240
cyclic existence
  absence of beginning to, 352–53
  buddhas' pervading of all, 198–200
  definitive emergence from, 146, 147
  disenchantment with, 273
  entering, for benefiting beings, 50, 52, 103–5, 327, 534, 596, 600, 610, 612, 655, 680, 779, 868–74, 879
  as equal to peace, 43–44, 137, 245, 440, 442, 830
  habitual tendencies and, 348, 828, 831–33
  listeners' taking birth in, 359–61
  mind as root of, 130, 330
  as neither decreasing nor increasing, 225
  no fear of, 323
  not wishing to be free from, 64
  process of engaging in, 330, 816, 818
  superknowledge of all, 95, 145, 146, 154
  as trip to pleasure grove, 103–5

dedication, 495, 711–12
  to enlightenment, 249, 375, 660, 674
  to spiritual teacher, 582–83
  transcendences and, 373, 546–47, 548, 630
  worship and, 576, 577
definitive emergence
  diligence and, 704
  discipline of, 521
  on grounds and paths, 89–90, 437
  sevenfold process of, 288, 293–94
  superknowledge of, 146, 147
  transcendences and, 82
Definitive Explanation of the Intent, 884
definitive meaning, 272, 357, 666–67
delight
  in benefiting others, 88, 101–2, 156, 377, 624–26
  directing the mind to, 376–77, 384, 512, 513

in virtue, 161, 167, 522
dependent nature, 13
  absence of wishes and, 430, 432, 477, 718, 719
  of all-ground consciousness, 142, 233
  as basis of appearance, 323, 338–39, 476, 817
  characteristics of, 7, 12, 126–27, 128, 314, 334, 420
  as conventionally existent, 19
  as devoid of essence, 350–52
  elimination of impure, 314–15, 321–22
  false imagination and, 321, 432
  knowledge of, 663
  as nonarising, 353
  as not separate from suchness, 346–47
  of reason, 818
dependent origination, 302
  characteristics of, 338–39, 393
  essencelessness of, 350–52
  ignorance of not seeing, 135, 136–37
  listeners' scripture on, 25
  realization of emptiness of, 888
  realization of reversal of links of, 857
  subtle, inner view of, 130–31
  twelve links of, 130, 352–53, 816, 818
desire
  antidote to, 113, 116, 289
  as predominant tendency, 61, 64
desire realm, 359
  being free from desires of, 360–61
  characteristics of, 119, 278, 279, 465–66
  conscience in, 643
  forms of life in, 737–41
  immeasurables and, 594, 596
developing potential, 63, 64–65, 74, 75
devotion
  directing the mind to, 512
  to Great Vehicle, 427, 454
Dharma
  categories to be taught, 809–23
  characteristics of, 417–18
  engaging in concordant, 431, 433–34

as existent and nonexistent, 320, 324–25
inner knowledge of, 364, 658–60, 811–16
mastery of, 692
metaphors for, 187–88, 209–10, 391
remedy for disdain of, 425
retention of, 248, 380, 712
See also Dharma of scripture; investigation of the Dharma; teaching
Dharma eye, 690, 836–37
Dharma of causal concordance, 340
Dharma of realization
  as direct awareness, 400–402
  investigation of, 313–66
Dharma of scripture
  ascertaining meaning of, 304–5, 309–10, 458–61
  authentic thought and, 707
  Buddha's teaching of, 400, 401
  contemplating, 455–62
  definitive explanation of intent of, 864, 865, 866, 867
  discovery of the focal points, 294–98
  five fields of knowledge and, 810–16
  four qualities of, 417, 418
  investigation of, 285–313
  as like a boat, 430, 433
  reliance on, 666
  summarizing key points of, 304, 459–60
  three vessels of, 286–94
  ways of directing the mind to, 298–313
See also Word of Buddha
difference, remedy for thoughts of, 394–95. *See also* sameness and difference
diligence
  accumulations and, 672, 674
  achieving exceptional, 308
  analysis of, 519, 522
  as aspect of enlightenment, 307, 696, 702, 704
  as basis of miraculous power, 307, 687, 688

diligence (*continued*)
  bodily support for, 167
  characteristics of, 505, 507
  compassion and, 632–33
  conflicting factors and, 374, 527, 528–29
  constant practice of, 384, 807
  divisions of features of, 555–56, 557–58
  enlightened mind and, 77, 78, 105, 107–8
  etymology of, 510
  excellent maturation and, 159, 171
  faculty of, 307, 694
  inclusion of all transcendences in, 559–62
  inspiration and, 267, 269, 272, 273
  for maturation of others, 176–77
  metaphor for, 91, 94
  perfection of, 902
  potential and, 558
  in practice of calm abiding, 684–85
  qualities of, 532, 535, 541–42
  as remedy for four obstacles, 558–59
  steadfastness of, 652, 654
  supreme pursuit of, 808
  supreme qualities of, 545, 549
  as supreme transcendence, 553–59
direct awareness
  attaining wisdom of, 34, 36
  Dharma of realization and, 400–402, 671
  of reality, 126–27, 128, 131
directing the mind, 298–313
  to application of full realization, 310–12
  to aspiration, 303
  associated with cognition, 303–4
  to authentic reception, 309
  in contemplation, 455–62
  with delight, 376–77, 384, 512, 513
  to developing the transcendences, 366–87, 512–13
  to domain of meditative absorption, 303
  to features associated with meditation, 306–8
  to five forms of application, 300–301, 309–12
  to fivefold complete cognition, 305–6
  to the grounds, 896–97
  to induce motivation, 302–3
  to Lesser and Great Vehicles, 313
  to mastery, 312–13
  to meaning of the sūtras, 304–5, 309–10, 458–61
  in meditation, 462–70
  to nature of twofold path, 308–9
  to observing the distinct, 305
  three potentials and, 299, 302
  to twofold benefit, 309
discards, 389
  relinquishment of, 392–95, 476
discernment
  as aspect of enlightenment, 307, 696, 701, 704
  as basis of miraculous power, 307, 687, 688–89
  insight and, 523
  maturation of unassailability and, 166
  meditative absorption and, 303, 467
  transcendences and, 512
  wakefulness of, 164
discipline
  accumulations and, 672, 673
  analysis of, 518, 520–21
  of bodhisattvas, 116, 779, 886
  characteristics of, 505, 506–7
  compassion and, 632
  conflicting factors and, 374, 526, 528
  constant practice of, 806
  etymology of, 510
  five forms of, 174–75
  inclusion of all transcendences in, 559–62
  for maturation of others, 174–75
  metaphor for, 91, 94
  perfection of, 892, 893, 902, 908

qualities of, 531–32, 534, 538–39,
    540–41
results of losing, 598–99
six aspects of, 520–21
special training in, 290–91, 503–4,
    892
supreme qualities of, 544–45,
    548–49
ten virtues and, 540–41
three types of, 81, 548
undefiled vows of, 808
discriminating wakefulness, 232
    cause for attaining, 249
    explanation of, 245–46
    mental consciousness and, 236, 242
disenchantment, 273, 319
*Distinguishing the Middle from
    Extremes,* 323, 676, 678, 818
divine ear, 95, 145, 146, 148, 690
divine eye, 95, 146, 148, 151, 152,
    689–90, 836–37
doubts
    being free from, 159, 166, 307, 795
    dispelling, 114, 199–200, 404
    sūtra as remedy for, 286, 289
downfalls, 288, 289, 292–94
duality of apprehended and
    apprehender
    all-ground consciousness and, 129,
        130, 330
    directing the mind to, 305, 311
    false imagination and, 318, 321, 328,
        432, 446
    focal point of suchness and, 295–98,
        311
    habitual tendencies and, 338–39,
        831–33
    as illusion-like, 315–27, 817
    imaginary nature and, 126, 314,
        337–38, 829
    as obstacle to inspiration, 270, 271,
        275
    relinquishment of, 185, 187
    seeing as equally unestablished, 347,
        474

wakefulness free from, 129, 131, 139,
    141, 142, 194, 243–44, 296, 858
dullness and agitation, 307, 308, 437,
    462, 685, 707

effort, authentic, 308, 706, 707
eight collections of consciousness, 12,
    332, 818, 819
    basis of primary mind and, 335
    as illusion-like, 857
    not relying on objects of, 666, 667
    transformation of, 130, 194, 242–43
    See also six consciousnesses
eightfold noble path, 306, 307–8,
    704–7
eighth ground
    acceptance of nonarising and, 51, 114,
        354, 592, 791, 803, 836
    applications of mindfulness and, 680
    bodhisattvas on, 888–89
    characteristics of, 635, 684, 880–82,
        903, 909
    four masteries and, 346
    single path to be traversed and, 92,
        98, 880
elements
    diversity of, 60, 61
    impermanence of, 749–51
eleventh ground, 483, 883–84
elimination. *See* factors of elimination;
    four authentic eliminations
emanation body, 197, 924
    explanation of, 239–40
    failure to see, 200, 213
    limitless displays of, 150–51, 206, 218,
        223, 239, 240, 247–48
    skillful engagement of, 232, 234–35,
        241
    taking birth by means of, 873
    twofold benefit and, 235, 239–41
emanations
    activities of, 95, 150–51, 152, 210–11,
        342
    all-accomplishing wakefulness and,
        247

emanations (*continued*)
  of god realms, 739
  meditative absorption and, 155, 913
embarrassment. *See* conscience and embarrassment
empowerment, 48, 113, 117, 156, 672, 675, 889
emptiness
  combined with appearance, 322
  determinative affirmation and, 126
  focal points and, 296
  happiness of realizing, 100
  insight realizing, 81–82, 87
  meditative absorption of, 380, 430, 431–32, 477, 717–19, 720–21
  natural luminosity of, 204–5
  nonconceptual wakefulness and, 30, 85
  resolving the nature of, 234
  suchness and, 233
  thoroughly established nature as, 339
  threefold knowledge of, 476
  wrong views of, 393–95
engagement
  directing the mind to, 385–86
  suchness of, 816, 817
  wrong, 817, 818
enjoyment body. *See* perfect enjoyment body
enlightened activity
  of active wakefulness, 211–12
  all-pervasiveness of, 198–200
  of cognizing various things simultaneously, 212–13
  in different world realms, 210, 218, 227–28
  of emanating, 210–11, 223, 234–35
  of inactive wakefulness, 213
  mastery over, 346
  of maturation of others, 170–80, 209
  metaphors for, 208–9
  profundity of, 208–14
  as spontaneous and nonconceptual, 201–3, 212, 228
  of teaching Dharma, 209–10, 225, 249

  ten infinite fields of, 88
  of vivid wakefulness, 213–14
enlightened mind, 42, 46, 47, 259
  attained through intrinsic nature, 82, 83, 84–90
  attained through symbols, 82, 83–84
  as basis of transcendences, 372
  benefits of, 98–108
  blessings of, 234–35
  definitive emergence and, 89–90
  delight of, 88
  diligence of, 77, 78, 105, 107–8
  elevenfold presentation of, 80–82
  essence of, 77–78
  four types of happiness and, 98–100
  as free from fearful aversions, 100–102
  having expertise in what remains, 89
  joyful taking of successive births and, 103–5
  loving compassion of, 106–7
  metaphors for, 90–98
  as never discouraged, 105–6
  never-diminished virtue of, 102
  pure intent of, 88–89
  as resembling birth, 86–87
  stages of the grounds and, 79, 82
  ten great aspirations of, 87–88
  various types of, 78–90
  worship and, 576
enlightenment, 181–259
  all-pervasiveness of, 198–200
  benefiting others and, 42–44, 108, 373, 442–43, 576
  cause of attaining complete purity of, 252–55
  as consummation of all paths, 255–58
  essence of, 233–34
  four forms of wakefulness of, 242–58
  inconceivability of, 15–16, 184–86
  limitless mastery of, 216–24
  maturation of beings and, 224–31
  metaphors for, 15–16, 70–71, 182, 183, 187–88
  overview of attainment of, 181–84
  profundity of, 203–15

resultant realization of, 853–61
seven aspects of, 307, 696–704
sixfold explanation of, 231–35
spontaneous and nonconceptual activity and, 201–3, 212, 228
sublime refuge and, 188–92
three bodies of, 235–42
transcendences as support for, 108, 253, 378–79, 805–6
transformation and, 192–98
twofold benefit and, 186–87
unchanging essence of, 215–16
unsurpassable, 23, 28, 42–43, 52, 75, 78, 110, 258–59
See also qualities of perfection
Enumerators, 350–51
equality
  aspects of enlightenment and, 697–98
  of bondage and peace, 137, 245, 440, 442, 830
  five types of, 475
  of great compassion, 634–35
  mind of, 85–86, 110–12, 199, 781–82, 788, 901
  training in, 248–49
equalizing and exchanging self and other, 112
equanimity
  as aspect of enlightenment, 307, 696, 702–3, 704
  conflicting factors and, 598
  directing the mind to, 378, 382
  focal points of, 591–92
  mark of, 308, 437, 461–62, 685, 707
essencelessness, investigation of, 349–52
establishment, directing the mind to, 378
existence and nonexistence
  buddhahood as transcending, 185, 205–7
  discarding extremes of, 393–94
  as not different, 316, 318, 319–20, 322–23, 324, 339
  as not in conflict, 446

reality as free from extremes of, 126, 127, 128
thorough understanding of facts of, 430, 431–33
expedient meaning, 272, 357, 666

factors of elimination, 166–67, 169
factors of enlightenment, 13, 15, 262–63, 639–776
  activity of, 208–9
  afflictions and, 440–42
  aspiration and, 714–16
  calm abiding and special insight and, 707–10
  conscience and, 639–50
  directing the mind to, 300, 306–8
  eightfold noble path as, 704–7
  essence of, 675–710
  five faculties as, 693–95
  five powers as, 695
  four applications of mindfulness as, 675–81
  four authentic eliminations as, 681–86
  four bases of miraculous power as, 686–92
  four correct awarenesses and, 668–71
  four reliances and, 664–68
  four summaries of Dharma and, 719–75
  framework for cultivating, 639–75
  grounds and, 878, 888, 892, 908
  indefatigability and, 656–57
  knowledge of the world and, 661–64
  knowledge of treatises and, 657–61
  metaphor for, 92, 96, 208–9
  retention and, 712–14
  seven aspects of enlightenment as, 696–704
  skillful means and, 710–12
  steadfastness and, 650–55
  three meditative absorptions and, 717–19
  two accumulations and, 671–75
faith
  benefits of, 265

faith (*continued*)
  displaying miracles and, 113, 151, 153
  factors of elimination and, 167
  faculty of, 307, 693–94
  full maturation of, 160, 170
  See also inspiration
false imagination, 323, 447
  absence of wishes and, 477
  causes of, 334, 337–38
  delusion of duality and, 318, 321, 328, 432, 446
  as neither correct nor false, 327–28
  perceiving all phenomena as, 473, 476
fear
  five sources of, 50, 480
  of Great Vehicle view, 19, 33, 34, 35, 445–46, 789
  of suffering through love, 620, 622
fearlessness
  four types of, 918–19
  freedom from fear, 50, 100–102, 534, 538, 795, 900
  of great compassion, ix–x, 623–24
  magnificent quality of, 156
  transcendences and, 559
Feast of the Supreme Vehicle, A, xii, xiv
fields, mastery of, 346. *See also* buddha fields
fifth ground
  bodhisattvas on, 887
  characteristics of, 878–79, 902, 908
first ground
  acceptance of nonarising and, 354, 836
  aspects of enlightenment and, 697, 701–2, 704
  attainments of, 50–51, 55, 90, 129, 296, 308, 330, 876–77, 901, 902, 908
  bodhisattvas on, 886
  coming to abide on, 114, 117
  directing the mind to, 896–97
  as entry in accord, 433
  genuine faith and, 160
  mind of equality and, 112, 199, 475
  special maturation and, 171

  special qualities of, 475–76, 477–81
  sublime joy and, 85–86, 908
five faculties, 307, 693–95
five fields of knowledge, 362–66, 657–61, 810–16
five powers, 307, 695
five principles, 6–7, 12, 818–19
foe destroyers, 89, 342, 353, 362, 555, 740, 741, 747, 822, 836, 839, 921
Followers of Īśvara, 815
form
  basis of, 335, 336, 338, 343
  as mere imputation, 394, 395
  transformation of, 390–91
form and formless realms, 290, 815
  characteristics of, 119, 278
  conscience in, 643
  forms of life in, 738, 739–41
  immeasurables and, 594, 596
formless absorptions, 149, 522–23, 557
four applications of mindfulness, 300, 306, 675–81
four authentic eliminations, 306–7, 681–86, 688, 694
four bases of miraculous power, 307, 686–92
four concentrations
  calm abiding and special insight and, 708, 709
  conception and discernment and, 460–61
  immeasurables and, 594
  meditative absorption and, 147–48, 468, 694
  miraculous powers and, 688
  realms of, 149, 522, 557, 594, 779
four correct awarenesses, 220, 346, 668–71, 865
  characteristics of, 669–70
  definitive enumeration of, 670–71
  discrimination and, 379
  metaphor for, 92, 95–96
  ninth ground and, 684, 882, 909
  praise of, 915
four immeasurables, 588–636, 867
  characteristics of, 589–90

conflicting factors and, 597–99
directing the mind to, 377–78
divisions of, 593–95
effects of, 595–97
explanation of compassion, 600–636
focal points of, 590–92
metaphor for, 92, 95
miraculous powers and, 688
praise of, 911–12
qualities of, 599–600
sublime abodes of, 149, 523, 589, 596
four inconceivable domains, 159
four means of attraction, 374, 377, 711
benefits of, 567–68
characteristics of, 563–64
divisions of features of, 565–67
functions of, 565
metaphor for, 92, 95
superknowledge and, 153
four obstacles, 558–59
four reliances, 92, 96, 664–68
four summaries of Dharma, 380,
  719–75
concise explanation of, 719–21
metaphor for, 97
proof of absence of self, 756–75
proof of impermanence, 722–56
three meditative absorptions and,
  720–21
four truths, 302, 305, 678, 836
classifications of, 816–19
knowledge of, 306, 662–64
fourth ground
bodhisattvas on, 886–87
characteristics of, 878, 902, 908
freedoms, eight, 154, 155, 741, 912–13
fully accomplished potential, 65

Gathering of Precious Qualities, 562, 631
generosity
accumulations and, 672, 673, 674
analysis of, 517–18, 520
characteristics of, 505, 506
compassion and, 624–31, 632
conflicting factors and, 374, 526,
  527–28

constant practice of, 806
effects of, 866
etymology of, 510
field of, 544, 547–48
first ground and, 90, 902
five bases of, 866
inclusion of all transcendences in,
  559–62
for maturation of others, 173–74
as means of attraction, 563, 564
metaphor for, 91, 94
nonconceptualization and, 506
praise of, 549–53
qualities of, 531, 533–34, 537–38, 540
of relinquishing one's body, 105–6,
  381, 546, 551, 552–53
as sign of a bodhisattva, 865, 902
six aspects of, 376–77
sixfold intention in cultivating,
  513–14
supreme pursuit of, 808
supreme qualities of, 544, 546–48
of teaching Dharma, 397–98
god realms, 361, 690, 739–40
going for refuge. *See* refuge
Great Ornament of the Buddhas, 840,
  898
great refuge, 192
Great Vehicle
benefits of venerating, 18–20
entering with great joy, viii–ix,
  280–83
five rich subjects of, 6–17, 262–63
giving up misconceptions about,
  31–38
going for refuge in, 41–56
listeners' entering, 359–62
listeners' objections to, 24–26
mature joy of upholding, 159
overturning misconceptions about,
  21–31
special qualities of, 358, 838–40
summary of principles of, 840
supremacy of potential of, 62–63
as vast and profound, viii, 24, 30–31,
  33, 35–36, 74–75

Great Vehicle (*continued*)
  vast inspiration of, 267, 269, 276–83
  wandering beings' fear of, 19, 33, 34, 35, 445–46, 789
  as Word of Buddha, 13–14, 22–31
ground, path, and fruition, 131, 254, 305
grounds and paths, 874–911
  as accomplished and unaccomplished, 895–98
  aspirations and, 715–16
  bodhisattva births on, 872–74
  buddha ground, 883–84, 925–26
  calm abiding and special insight and, 694, 709–10, 904–5
  categories of persons on, 884–90
  characteristics of, 875–84
  complete attainment of, 909–11
  cultivating stages of, 16, 79, 82, 340–41, 431–34, 470–83, 779–80, 840
  definitive emergence and, 89–90, 437
  divisions of investigation of, 388–89
  establishing beings on, 114, 116–17
  etymology of names of, 905–9
  forms of knowledge and, 860–61
  four eliminations and, 684
  four masteries and, 346
  gathering accumulations and, 674–75
  great compassion and, 623
  grounds of irreversibility, 871
  immeasurables and, 594–95
  indefatigability and, 657
  inspiration and, 267, 269
  maturation of affection and, 162
  path of accumulation, 473
  path of cultivation, 481–83
  path of joining, 473–74
  path of seeing, 474–77
  progressing maturation and, 171
  qualities of bodhisattvas on, 841–42
  qualities of first ground, 475–76, 477–81
  realizing reality and, 139–43
  signs of attainment of, 898–905
  superior conscience and, 643–44
  superior intent and, 870–71
  superknowledges based on, 147–48
  three special trainings on, 890–92
  undefiled aggregates and, 893–94
  unsurpassed virtues of, 51–53
  wakefulness and, 36, 234
  See also specific grounds and paths
grounds of inspired (imaginative) conduct
  attainments of, 36, 129, 308, 433, 836
  bodhisattvas on, 567, 872, 873
  characteristics of, 841, 896
  fourfold investigation and, 826–27
  practices of, 52, 79, 85, 112, 234, 269, 302, 454
  superior intent and, 871
  twofold absence of self and, 431–33, 820
Grounds of Yogic Practice, 590

habitual tendencies
  all-ground consciousness and, 345, 828, 829–30, 832
  cyclic existence and, 348, 828, 831–33
  defeat of, 469, 920–21
  imaginary nature and, 337
  six appearances and, 338–39
  subtle, 245, 342, 483
  See also obscurations
happiness
  of benefiting others, 99–100, 624–26
  diligence and, 557
  four types of, 98–100
hardships, enduring
  for benefiting others, 398, 442–43, 576, 611, 618–27, 793
  delight and joy in, 88, 101–2, 551
  steadfastness of, 655
  tolerating harm by others, 102, 176, 521, 534
  transcendences and, 182–83, 381–82, 503
  without discouragement, 44, 54, 66, 105–6, 121–22, 280–81, 493, 656

heat. *See* stage of heat
hell realms. *See* lower realms
heroic gait, absorption of, 152, 155, 160, 177, 235, 290, 661
Hevajra Tantra, 440–41
hopes, of bodhisattvas, 383, 793–94
hostility and harm
  elimination of, 603, 606
  lack of immeasurables and, 597, 598
  not feeling dejected by, 121–22, 654
  not retaliating against, 102, 176, 521, 793
  toward the Buddha and Dharma, 424–25, 426
householders, 302, 870
human body, as supreme support, 280

ignorance
  dependent arising and, 136–37, 330
  as essence of enlightenment, 441
illusion-like, investigation of, 315–27
imaginary (imagined) nature, 13, 185
  characteristics of, 126–27, 314, 334, 420, 817
  delusion of duality and, 321, 337–38
  as devoid of essence, 351–52
  emptiness and, 430, 432, 476
  extreme of existence and, 393
  of names, 337–38, 818
  as nonarising, 353
impermanence, 305
  absence of wishes and, 720
  concise explanation of, 721
  of fourteen modes of life, 737–41
  general proof of, 722–35
  of inner conditioned entities, 735–47
  of outer conditioned entities, 747–56
imputed nature, 7. *See also* imaginary (imagined) nature
incarnate emanations, 151, 152, 218, 239, 240
incomparable refuge, 190–92
inconceivable
  Buddhas' teaching of, 411
  enlightenment as, 15–16, 184–86

indefatigability, 656–57
Indra, 152, 202, 413
inner meaning, knowledge of, 364, 658–60, 811–16
insight
  accumulations and, 672, 673
  analysis of, 520, 523–24
  beyond focal point, 439, 440
  as cause of liberation, 253–54, 502
  characteristics of, 506, 507
  compassion and, 604–5, 633
  conflicting factors and, 374, 527, 529
  constant practice of, 807
  enlightened mind and, 81–82, 87
  etymology of, 510
  faculty of, 307, 694
  five fields of knowledge and, 365
  inclusion of all transcendences in, 559–62
  liberated, 207
  for maturation of others, 178
  into meaning of Dharma, 469
  metaphor for, 92, 94–95
  perfection of, 523–24, 902
  qualities of, 533, 535–36, 539–40, 542–43
  special training in, 290–91, 504, 892
  steadfastness of, 652, 654
  supramundane and mundane, 164, 523, 524
  supreme qualities of, 546, 549, 809
  through contemplation, 455–62
  See also calm abiding and special insight
inspiration, 265–83
  benefits of, 265, 274–76
  directing the mind to, 375, 384–85, 548
  of enlightened mind, 80, 81, 87
  free from dejection, 280–81
  for Great Vehicle, 276–83
  obstacles to, 270–74
  of pure grounds, 267, 269
  as sign of potential, 66, 75
  types of, 266–69
  worship and, 575

integration, focal points of, 304–5
intention
  as basis of miraculous power, 307,
    687, 688
  in cultivating the transcendences,
    513–15
  of enlightened mind, 80, 81, 88–89,
    91, 93
  of maturation of others, 171–72
  six types of, 513–15
  See also superior intent
intercourse, transformation of, 220, 223
intrinsic nature
  characteristics of, 128, 321
  direct realization of, 55, 129, 232,
    890–92
  discipline attained through, 175
  enlightened mind attained through,
    82, 83, 84–90
  luminous clarity of, 447
  mind realizing truth of, 131
  of phenomena, 126–28
  potential and, 63, 64
  refuge attained through, 55
  undefiled aggregates and, 893
investigation of the Dharma, 285–396
  of acceptance of nonarising phenomena, 352–54
  accomplishment of qualities and,
    390–92
  of characteristics, 332–43
  of Dharma of scripture, 285–313, 388
  of Dharma to be realized, 313–66, 388
  discovery of the focal points, 294–98
  of essencelessness, 349–52
  of five fields of knowledge, 362–66
  of the illusion-like, 315–27
  of intent for teaching the one vehicle,
    354–62, 426–27
  of liberation, 343–49
  of mere cognition, 331–32
  of objects of cognition, 327–29
  of reality, 313–15
  of relinquishment of discards, 392–95
  of the teachings themselves, 286–94
  thirteen principles of, 387–90

  of thorough affliction and complete
    purification, 329–31
  transcendences and, 366–87
  of ways of directing the mind,
    298–313

Jains, 349
Jambudvīpa, 562, 690, 858, 859
Jewel Lamp Sūtra, 265, 812–13
Jewel Mound Sūtra, 115–16, 450, 673
Jñānaśrī, 13–14
Journey to Laṅkā, 338, 458
joy
  as aspect of enlightenment, 307, 696,
    702, 704
  of benefiting others, 88, 101–2, 156,
    624–26
  conflicting factors and, 598
  of entering Great Vehicle, viii–ix,
    280–83
  of first ground, 85–86, 908
  focal points of, 591
  full maturation of, 158–59, 169–70
  intention of, 514
  meditative absorption and, 466, 467
  transcendences and, 66, 372, 376,
    377–78, 379, 552
Joyful Realm, 93, 98, 151, 152, 335, 740,
  858, 873, 889

karmic action
  bondage of, 156, 806–7, 828
  mastery of, 691, 692
  nondissipation of, 877
  purifying threefold, 707
  undefiled, of listeners, 359, 360
karmic affinity
  for compassion, 633, 635
  for generosity, 512, 547
  for practice, 437
keen intellect, full maturation of,
  163–64
kindness, repaying, 383, 792–93
King Ajātaśatru, 69
knowledge
  arising from aspiration, 914

of bodhisattvas, 860–61
fourfold thorough, 826–28
of treatises, 657–61
of the world, 661–64
See also insight; objects of knowledge

laziness, 270, 271
  remedy for, 425, 507, 528
Lesser Vehicle
  classifications of, 821–22
  going for refuge in, 14, 42, 54, 56–57
  incompleteness of, 23–24, 28, 494, 838–39
  objections to Great Vehicle, 24–26
  response to objections of, 26–31
  tenets of, 23–24, 25–26
  See also listeners and self-realized buddhas
liberation
  as cessation of a mistake, 134
  characteristics of, 206–7
  different forms of, 60, 61–62, 67
  five stages of, 339–43
  investigation of, 343–49, 828–29
  qualities of superior, 335, 341–42
  three vehicles and, 357
  wakefulness beholding, 306
life, fourteen forms of, 737–41
light rays, as activity of superknowledge, 150, 151, 152
linguistics, knowledge of, 363, 413, 658, 660, 811, 814, 815
listeners and self-realized buddhas
  activities of, 202, 214
  attainments of, 89, 311, 523, 688, 822, 829, 836, 839
  bodhisattvas' surpassing of, 51–53, 822–23
  compassion and, 195–96, 607, 608
  conscience and, 641, 643
  deprived of four happinesses, 99–100
  diligence of, 108
  entering the Great Vehicle, 359–62
  fields of knowledge of, 658, 659, 660
  four applications of mindfulness and, 677–81

four means of attraction and, 567
immeasurables and, 595
inferior inspiration of, 269, 278, 279, 312
inferior liberation of, 23, 61–62, 64, 100, 191, 341–42, 439, 441–43, 830
intent of teachings for, 420, 821–22
mastery of, 216–17
peace of, 25, 28, 81, 87, 119, 130, 138, 162, 190
potential of, 61–62, 64, 75, 302, 357, 358, 359, 602
remaining afflictions of, 360
self of phenomena and, 137, 420
view of "mind," 222
See also Lesser Vehicle
livelihood
  authentic, 308, 706, 707
  wrong, 521
logic, of relative domain, 24, 29–30, 36–37. *See also* reasoning
Longchenpa, 495
love
  of bodhisattvas, 101, 106–7, 172, 447–48, 541–42, 616–17
  characteristics of, 589–90
  conflicting factors and, 598
  directing the mind to, 377
  focal points of, 590, 591, 592
  full maturation of, 161–62
  great compassion and, 612–13, 616–17
lower realms
  bodhisattva births in, 69, 105, 442–43, 779
  negative actions and, 68–69, 598
  no fear of falling into, 100–102
  supreme protection from, 189–90, 191
luminosity
  life as, 739–40
  life in absence of, 740

Mahākāśyapa, 293
Maitreya, viii, 6, 10, 128, 666
Manifest Enlightenment of Vairocana, 130

Mañjuśrī, 152
Master Bhavya, 130–31
mastery
  directing the mind to, 312–13
  distinctive, 216–18
  full accomplishment of, 691–92
  of liberation, 346
  seven types of, 218–24
  transcendences and, 515
  of worship, 576
material things
  generosity of, 551, 564
  mastery of, 691, 692
  no concern for, 405, 407, 580, 630, 791
  worship and, 577, 581
maturation of others, 170–80
  classifications of, 170–71
  emanation body and, 236
  four means of attraction and, 563–68, 711
  individuals who are matured, 225–26, 834
  intention of, 171–72
  as limitless and continual, 229–30
  nonconceptual activity for, 228
  superknowledge and, 153
  through transcendences, 173–78, 209
  various means of maturing, 227–28
  way of maturing, 224–25
  without partiality, 229
maturation of self, 157–70
  affection and, 161–62
  enlightened mind and, 79
  factors of elimination and, 166–67
  faith and, 160
  joy and, 158–59
  keen intellect and, 163–64
  metaphors for, 168–70
  nine qualities of, 157–58
  patience and, 162–63
  power and, 164–65
  serenity and, 160–61
  as supreme friend of beings, 168
  transcendences and, 512

  unassailability and, 165–66
medicine, knowledge of, 364, 658, 659, 660, 811
meditation
  cultivating three marks and, 308, 437
  directing the mind in, 462–70
  fourfold features of, 300, 306
  nine stages of, 464–70
  sublime, 253
  teaching the path of, 402
  thirty-seven features of, 306–8
  See also calm abiding and special insight; concentration
meditative absorption, 392–95
  of absence of marks, 380, 430, 432, 477, 717–19, 721, 905
  of absence of wishes, 380, 430, 432, 477, 717–19, 720
  as aspect of enlightenment, 307, 696, 702, 704
  authentic, 308, 706, 707
  bliss and, 223, 275
  diligence and, 557
  directing the mind to domain of, 303
  discriminating wakefulness and, 246
  of emptiness, 380, 430, 431–32, 477, 717–19, 720–21
  faculty of, 307, 694
  five applications pertaining to, 300–301, 309–12
  five fields of knowledge and, 660–61
  fivefold complete cognition and, 305–6
  four bases of, 688–89
  of fourth concentration, 147–48, 694
  free from relishing of, 593–94
  of genuine settling, 466–70
  good qualities associated with, 468–70
  of heroic gait, 152, 155, 160, 177, 235, 290, 661
  of higher realms, 119
  limitless, of enlightenment, 235
  mastery of mind through, 177
  mature faith and, 160

on path of joining, 139, 141
relinquishing mistaken views with, 380
retention of, 714
special training in, 290–91
steadfastness of, 652, 654
of stream of Dharma, 454–55
superknowledge of displays of, 150, 152, 155
of supreme quality. *See* stage of supreme quality
of tenth ground, 883
that dissolves the body, 223
of treasury of space, 152, 155, 220, 223, 235, 548, 560, 576, 588
vajra-like, 71, 184, 482, 483, 894
with and without expression, 303
meditative equipoise
　ensuing attainment and, 194, 232, 233–34, 698, 892, 901
　immeasurables and, 594, 595
mental cognition, 222, 338, 856–57. *See also* cognition
mental consciousness, transformation of, 220, 222–23, 236, 242, 257, 346
mental states, 335, 336
　as basis of delusion, 320, 326
　as momentary, 737–47
Middle Way of Yogic Practice, 131
Middle Way proponents, 64, 128–31, 323
mind
　as afflicted cognition, 222, 332, 338
　basis of, 335–36
　as basis of delusion, 320, 326, 330
　conditioned things as effects of, 732–35
　as luminous clarity, 447
　mastery of, 691, 692
　mere appearance of, 331–32
　Middle Way view of, 130–31
　momentary impermanence of, 737–47
　ninefold method of settling, 464–70
　objects of cognition as, 347, 473–74

realization of nature of, 856
　as root of phenomena, 130, 139, 141, 142, 297
　superknowledge of, 145, 146, 148
　transformation of afflicted, 220, 222–23, 236, 242, 346
　ultimate reality of, 138–43
　unexcelled mastery of, 177
mind only
　abiding in awareness of, 347
　appearance as, 128, 129, 139, 473–74
　three realms as, 476
　view of, 129, 131, 332
Mind Only tradition, 63–64, 128, 129, 130, 131, 357
mindfulness
　as aspect of enlightenment, 307, 696, 697, 701, 704
　authentic, 308, 706, 707
　faculty of, 307, 694
　four applications of, 300, 306, 675–81
　maturation of serenity and, 161
　of meanings of teachings, 164
Mipham, xii–xiv
miracles
　displaying, 95, 104, 146, 148, 150, 151, 152, 177
　mastery of, 691–92
miraculous powers
　four bases of, 307, 686–92
　sixfold accomplishment and, 689–92
mirror-like stage, 335, 340
mirror-like wakefulness, 71, 232
　all-ground consciousness and, 236, 242, 248
　cause for attaining, 248
　explanation of, 243–44
　as source of all wakefulness, 244
　as unmoving, 242
momentariness, 722
　impermanence and, 724–35
　of inner conditioned entities, 735–47
　of outer conditioned entities, 747–56
　of world environment, 832

Moonlamp Sūtra, 458
motivation, directing the mind to induce, 299, 302–3
movement, as momentary, 743–46
mundane wakefulness, 431
  of ensuing attainment, 194, 702, 901
  equanimity and, 702–3
  of subsequent attainment, 328, 434, 476, 482–83, 671

Nāgārjuna, 666, 803
names
  apprehending things based on, 140–41
  directing the mind to, 305, 309–10, 311, 458, 461
  five principles and, 6, 12
  form as, 395
  imaginary nature and, 337–38, 818
  stage of apprehending only, 347
  thorough knowledge of, 826–27
naturally present potential, 63, 64, 65, 74, 75
nature body of qualities. *See* body of qualities
negative actions
  lack of potential and, 72
  lower realms and, 68–69, 598
  refraining from, 81, 161, 175
  Vinaya as antidote to, 289
  See also hostility and harm
negative company
  as obstacle to inspiration, 270, 271–72
  unwholesome influences of, 35, 68
negative tendencies, 309, 348, 469, 685
ninth ground
  bodhisattvas on, 889
  characteristics of, 684, 882, 903, 909
  four masteries and, 346
Noble Ground of Buddhahood, 232
Noble Jewel Mound, 797
Noble Sūtra on Transcendent Insight in Eighteen Thousand Lines, vii
nonarising phenomena, acceptance of
  on eighth ground, 51, 114, 590, 592, 791, 803
  essencelessness and, 351
  investigation of, 352–54
  by means of object universal, 354, 836
nonassociated formations, basis of, 335–36, 343
nonconceptual activity, 201–3, 212, 228
nonconceptual wakefulness, 83, 671
  absence of pride and, 390
  accomplishment of, 51, 52, 193–94, 354, 389, 475, 482, 860–61, 880, 881–82, 909
  conscience and, 640–41, 644, 650
  emptiness and, 30, 85
  ensuing attainment and, 194, 233
  equanimity and, 702
  five principles and, 7, 12, 819
  great compassion and, 608, 635–36
  on path of cultivation, 141–42
  perfection of buddha qualities and, 711
  reliance on, 666–67, 668
  skillful means of, 493, 494
  space-like, 434, 476, 857
  stage of prophecy and, 117
  stages of realizing, 138–43
  superknowledges and, 147, 148
  as supreme observation, 253
  transcendences and, 379–80, 506, 507, 515, 534, 535, 547, 560, 561
nonconceptuality, mastery of, 346, 389
nonobservation of the three spheres, 253, 494
  as not in conflict with observation, 446
  unsurpassable practice and, 451–52
  worship and, 572, 577, 578
nonreturners, 89, 359, 360, 361, 740
Nude, The, 815

objects of cognition
  application of understanding and, 310
  apprehending as mind, 347, 473–74

dependent nature and, 338–39
five bases of, 334, 335–37
illusory nature of, 323–24, 337–38, 395
investigation of, 327–29
subdivisions of, 336–37
thorough knowledge of, 364–65, 826–27
wakefulness that discerns, 476
objects of knowledge
direct perception of, 194, 701
five fields of knowledge and, 362–66, 658
limitless aspects of, 223–24
thorough discernment of, 523
vast insight and, 535
wakefulness comprehending all, 210, 212–13, 244, 245–46
obscurations
as defiled suchness, 233
elimination of, 79, 89, 95, 127, 182, 183–84, 193–94, 701, 829–30, 894
four eliminations and, 683–84
Great Vehicle as remedy for, 62
habitual tendencies of, 193, 342, 345, 348, 483
as infinite and innumerable, 183
of inspiration, 267, 269, 273
teaching on eight remedies of, 423–27
See also afflictions; cognitive obscurations; habitual tendencies
omnipresence, 196, 198
omniscience, 234, 923–24
once-returners, 89, 359, 360, 740
oneness, remedy for thoughts of, 394–95
openhandedness, 865, 866, 867. *See also* generosity
ordination, on the grounds, 869, 870
Ornament of Manifest Enlightenment, 441–42
path of accumulation, 79, 140, 301, 310, 340, 389, 473, 557

path of cultivation, 312, 330
attainment of, 477
characteristics of, 481–83
concordant Dharma and, 433–34
features of cognition on, 305–6
nonconceptual wakefulness and, 141–42
path of joining, 79, 93, 140
application of full realization and, 310–11
four stages of, 389, 473–74
meditative absorption on, 139, 141
realizations of, 129, 340, 347, 354, 454
See also stage of supreme quality
path of no more learning, 16, 131, 142, 483
path of seeing
acceptance of nonarising and, 354
attainment of, 141, 340, 433, 474–77
authentic view of, 311–12, 820
of listeners, 311, 836
realizations of, 300, 301, 306, 307
special insight of, 696
patience
accumulations and, 672, 673–74
analysis of, 518–19, 521–22
characteristics of, 505, 507
compassion and, 632
conflicting factors and, 374, 526–27, 528
constant practice of, 806–7
of enduring harm, 102, 121–22, 176, 503, 521, 793
etymology of, 510
five benefits of, 521
full maturation of, 162–63
great compassion and, 610, 611, 613
inclusion of all transcendences in, 559–62
for maturation of others, 175–76
metaphor for, 91, 94
perfection of, 902
qualities of, 532, 534–35, 539, 541
supreme pursuit of, 808
supreme qualities of, 545, 549

perfect enjoyment body, 235, 924
  explanation of, 237–38
  twofold benefit and, 239, 240, 241
phenomena
  acceptance of nonarising, 114,
    352–54, 590, 592, 791, 803, 836
  buddhas' pervading all, 198–200
  essencelessness of, 18–19, 25, 105, 257,
    349–52, 720, 771
  illusory nature of, 103, 315–27, 446
  as inseparable from intrinsic nature,
    126–28
  mind as root of, 130, 139, 141, 142,
    297, 856
  momentariness of, 747–56
  realizing equality of, 100, 341, 475,
    697–98
  selflessness of, 134–38, 140–41,
    747–56
  special insight into nature of, 708–9
  suchness as nature of, 184–86, 187,
    194, 233, 440–41, 817
  sūtra on characteristics of, 289
  tenfold equality of, 888
  twofold inconceivable wakefulness
    of, 194, 233–34
  See also basic field of phenomena;
    selflessness of phenomena
pleasant speech
  effects of, 866
  five fields of, 865–66
  as means of attraction, 563, 564
  transcendences and, 867
  two aspects of, 865
pliancy, of mind, 468–69
potential, 59–75
  benefits of, 68–69
  characteristics of, 63–65
  classifications of, 66–67
  developing enlightened mind and,
    83–84
  directing the mind based on, 302
  etymology of, 65
  existence of different, 60–62
  explanation of lack of, 72–73
  flaws of inactivated, 67–68

  intrinsic nature and, 63, 64
  maturation of patience and, 163
  metaphors for, 69–71
  prophecy and, 802
  signs of, 65–66
  summary of types of, 59–60
  supremacy of Great Vehicle, 62–63,
    73–75
  teaching in accordance with, 113–14,
    115–16, 201, 202, 407, 422, 791, 834
  transcendences and, 372, 512
powers
  purity of transcendent, 903
  steadfastness of, 654
  ten, 917–18
  See also superknowledges
practical instructions and advice,
    453–88
  authentic reception of, 309
  directing the mind in contemplation,
    455–62
  directing the mind in meditation,
    462–70
  distinctions between, 486
  five forms of application for, 309–12
  how to obtain, 453–55
  immense benefits of, 483–88
  path of cultivation and consumma-
    tion, 481–83
  qualities of the first ground, 477–81
  traversing the path, 470–83
practice, 429–52
  conducive conditions for, 434–37
  diversity of forms of, 60, 61
  essence of, 437–48
  examples demonstrating the way of,
    448–51
  five categories of, 431–34
  purified of the three spheres, 451–52
  qualities of authentic, 796–97,
    799–800
  suchness of genuine, 817, 818
  truth of the path and, 818
  as worship, 578
practice for sake of others, 109–23
  as exalted, 118–20

fourfold magnificence of, 122–23
how to practice, 110–12
inexhaustibility of, 117
mind of equality and, 110–12
supremacy of, 115–17
thirteen categories of, 112–14
twofold benefit of, 109–10
ungrateful beings and, 121–22
as uninterrupted practice, 120–21
See also benefiting others
Pramudita, 152, 239
Precious Lamp of the Middle Way
    (Master Bhavya), 130–31
pride
    absence of conceited, 115, 116
    flaws of, 645
    grounds and paths and, 390, 886, 887, 888
    immeasurables and, 595
    as obstacle to inspiration, 273
    as predominant tendency, 61
    remedy for, 290, 426
    worship with, 578
prophecy
    directing the mind to, 385
    investigation of, 801–3
    stage of, 117
pure conduct, four qualities of, 418
purity
    as not in conflict with impurity, 446–47
    profound character of, 204
    suchness of, 817
    tenfold equality of mind of, 887
    See also complete purity

qualities of bodhisattvas
    accomplishment of, 390–92
    authentic practice, 796–97
    bringing benefit, 782–92
    certainty, 804–5
    constant practice, 806–7
    downfall and progress, 797–99
    epithets of bodhisattvas, 850–53
    examples of, 45–49
    false vs. genuine, 799–800

hope, 383, 793–94
indomitable courage, 843–53
mind of equality, 781–82
not letting go to waste, 794–95
praises to, 842–61
prophecies, 801–3
repaying kindness, 792–93
resultant realization, 853–61
supreme pursuits, 807–9
taming, 800–801
teaching Dharma, 809–40
types of bodhisattvas, 841–42
unquestionable imperatives, 805–6
wondrous and not wondrous, 778–81
qualities of perfection, 911–26
    absence of affliction, 913–14
    complete purity, 916–17
    correct awareness, 915
    defeat of habitual tendencies, 920–21
    eighteen unshared qualities, 922–23
    four fearlessnesses, 918–19
    four immeasurables, 911–12
    freedom from bewilderment, 921
    freedoms, commands, and totalities, 912–13
    great compassion, 921–22
    ground of buddhahood, 925–26
    knowledge arising from aspiration, 914
    marks and signs, 916
    nothing to guard, 919–20
    omniscience, 923–24
    six transcendences, 924–25
    superknowledges, 915–16
    ten powers, 917–18

reality, 125–43
    characteristics of, 125–31
    factors conflicting with realization of, 393–95
    investigation of, 313–15
    lack of personal self and, 132–34
    profound insight realizing, 178
    selflessness of phenomena, 134–38
    stages of realizing, 138–43, 857–58

realization
  application of full, 301, 310–12
  of the array of qualities, 312
  of bodhisattvas, 49–51, 829–32,
    853–61
  divisions of qualities of, 859–61
  praises of qualities of, 854–59
Realm of Bliss, 223
reason, five principles and, 6, 12, 818
reasoning
  classifications of, 819–21
  knowledge of, 363, 658, 660, 811, 815
reflection
  inspiration and, 268, 270, 272–73
  life in form of, 741
refuge, 13, 41–56
  commitment in, 42, 44–49
  directing the mind to, 303
  distinctions of, 41–53
  fruitional aspect of, 54
  great purpose of, 55–56
  incomparable, 190–92
  nature of distinctive, 53–55
  outshining nature of, 51–53
  realization and, 49–51
  six aspects of, 55
  sublime, 188–92
  three vehicles and, 54–55, 56–57
  two categories of, 55
  universality of, 42, 43–44
rejoicing, 375, 512, 548, 674, 711–12
relative mind of enlightenment, 83–84
remedies
  concealed intent on, 420–21
  of suchness free from marks, 678
  teaching on eight, 423–27
remorse, 69, 292, 378, 426. *See also*
    conscience and embarrassment
retention
  of Dharma, 248, 380, 712
  discriminating wakefulness and, 246
  factors of enlightenment and,
    712–14
  five fields of knowledge and, 660–61
  limitless gates of, 235
  metaphor for, 92, 97

  of tenth ground, 883
  types of, 713–14
reveling activity, 150, 152, 691
reward
  benefiting others as, 383, 480
  nonexpectation of, 475, 533–34, 630
root attention, 140, 142, 458, 460

sameness and difference, 126, 764–67
Sammitīyas, 762, 765
Śāriputra, 235
Sarvāstivādins, 293
Saw-Like Sūtra, 38
School of Consciousness, 222
seclusion, delight in, 167
second ground
  bodhisattvas on, 886
  characteristics of, 877, 908
  discipline and, 175, 892, 893, 902
self, view of
  afflictions and, 121, 133–34
  five flaws ensuing from, 771–72
  mental cognition and, 856–57
  proof of absence of, 756–75
  stages of relinquishing, 860–61
  supreme protection from, 190, 191
  as thorough affliction, 763–64,
    773–74
selflessness, twofold, 129, 302
  aspects of enlightenment and,
    697–98, 701
  buddhas' comprehension of, 339–40,
    769–70
  emptiness and, 250, 720–21
  essence of insight and, 523
  liberation and, 346–47, 348, 349
  supreme self and, 204–5
  thorough knowing of, 430, 431–33,
    717–19, 820, 822
  wakefulness realizing, 28, 42, 44, 50,
    99, 494, 856
selflessness of persons
  aggregates and, 758–59, 762, 764–67
  Buddha's teaching of, 190, 771–75
  directing the mind to observe, 305,
    306, 309

INDEX 1015

discards and, 393
establishing, 132–34
listeners' realization of, 100, 130, 311
perceiving equality of, 388, 475, 479–80, 541, 607–8
proof of, 721, 756–75
six consciousnesses and, 767–69, 770–71
selflessness of phenomena, 134–38, 196
bodhisattvas' realization of, 311–12
directing the mind to observe, 305, 306
discards and, 394
proof of, 747–56
See also basic field of phenomena; phenomena
sense sources
all-accomplishing wakefulness and, 243
basis of form and, 335, 336
complete restraint of, 161
illusory nature of, 320, 326–27
as momentary, 732–35, 738, 742, 751–52
naturally present potential and, 63
as source of delusion, 323–24
transformation of, 219–20, 221–23, 236, 243, 345, 346
two types of, 222, 320, 326–27
See also six consciousnesses
sentient beings
bearing ingratitude of, 121–22, 654
diversity of interests of, 60, 61
as object of compassion, 600–602
superknowledge of minds of, 95, 145, 146, 148, 690–91
thorough maturation of, 610, 611
serenity, full maturation of, 160–61
seven aspects of enlightenment, 307, 696–704
characteristics of, 697–703
fivefold categorization of, 703–4
as resembling seven jewels, 700–701
temporal context of, 697
Seven Treatises on Valid Means of Cognition, 814

seventh ground
absence of marks and, 672, 675, 684, 880–81, 892, 896, 909
bodhisattvas on, 888
characteristics of, 880–81, 902–3, 908–9
Shenphen Chökyi Nangwa (Khenpo Shenga), xi–xii, xiv
signs and marks
of attaining the grounds, 469, 898–905
of bodhisattvas, 863–67
of buddhas, 221, 391, 916
praise of, 916
single path to be traversed, 92, 97–98, 880–81, 908
six consciousnesses, 828
impermanence and, 732–35, 742
knowledge of nature of, 857
as not self, 767–69, 770–71
realizing nature of, 311
transformation of, 221–23, 242–43
See also sense sources
six transcendences, 497–562
amazing and unamazing notions of, 370–71, 381–82, 778–81
analysis of components of, 515–24
applications of mindfulness and, 678–79
authentic practice of, 384–85, 796–97, 799–800
bringing benefit with, 501–2, 783
characteristics of, 504–7
compassion and, 521, 531, 533, 546, 632–33, 867
conscience and, 641–42
continuity and diligence in practice of, 384, 386, 806–7
diligence as supreme, 553–59
directing the mind to developing, 366–87, 512–13
etymologies of, 509–10
explanation of enumeration of, 498–504
factors of decline and progress in, 797–99

six transcendences, (*continued*)
   fivefold process of cultivating, 511–15
   four immeasurables and, 377–78
   four powers and, 373–74
   joy and, 66, 372, 376, 377–78, 379, 552
   for maturation of others, 114, 173–78, 209
   mutual ascertainment of, 559–62
   nonconceptuality and, 379–80, 506, 507, 515, 534, 535, 547, 560, 561
   perfection of, 376, 924–25
   praise of generosity, 549–53
   praises of qualities of practicing, 843–50
   qualities of, 529–59
   relinquishing seven distortions of, 380
   separating from conflicting factors, 368, 373–74, 375, 377, 379, 525–29
   sequence of, 507–9
   signs and marks of accomplishing, 863–67, 902–4
   superior purity of, 536–43
   as support for enlightenment, 108, 253, 378–79, 805–6
   supreme pursuits of, 807–9
   supreme qualities of, 543–49
   ten masteries and, 692
   thirty-six aspects of, 376–77, 561–62
   three special trainings and, 503–4
   two accumulations and, 140, 374, 379, 672, 673–74
sixth ground
   bodhisattvas on, 888
   characteristics of, 879–80, 902, 908
skillful means, 491–95
   actions embraced by, 491–92
   directing the mind to, 376
   of embracing, 492–95
   factors of enlightenment and, 710–12
   great compassion and, 610, 611, 613
   metaphor for, 92–93, 98
   nonconceptual wakefulness and, 493, 494
   transcendences and, 515

special insight. *See* calm abiding and special insight
speech
   aspects of melodious, 410–14, 814
   authentic, 308, 706, 707
   enlightened, 234
   immaculate, 6, 8, 10, 11
   superknowledge of, 95, 145, 146, 148, 690
   See also pleasant speech
spiritual practice
   directing the mind to, 379
   five stages of, 334, 339–43
   See also practice
spiritual teacher
   basis for following, 581–82
   characteristics of, 579–81
   dedication to, 582–83
   delighting mind of, 583
   divisions of reliance on, 585–87
   infinite qualities of, 833–35
   irreversible faith in, 160
   marks of following, 582
   pure field and, 584
   relying on, 377, 436, 579–88
   wakefulness and, 583–84
Śrī Mālā Sūtra, 357, 361
stage of acceptance, 301, 311, 340, 472, 474
stage of heat, 141, 311, 340, 347, 472, 473
stage of summit, 141, 296, 301, 311, 340, 347, 472, 474
stage of supreme quality, 129, 472
   attainment of, 454, 455, 474
   directing the mind to, 386
   mindfulness of, 704
   mundane insight and, 524
   realizations of, 141, 275, 311, 340, 347–48
steadfastness, 650–55
   characteristics of, 651–52
   divisions of, 653–55
   five bases of, 866
   immutability of, 655

as sign of a bodhisattva, 865, 866
transcendences and, 867
Sthiramati, xiv, 8, 9, 12, 54, 106, 133,
143, 152, 165, 166, 175, 221, 223,
233, 240, 255, 293, 303–4, 312,
325, 336, 348, 416, 458, 469–70,
612, 670, 702, 746, 827, 847,
848
stream enterers, 89, 359, 360, 740
study, reflection, and meditation
discovery of the focal points and,
294–98
insight arising from, 285, 291, 304,
402
Subhūti, 235
sublime refuge, 188–92
suchness
of basic field of phenomena, 186,
194, 232, 829
complete purity and, 12
defiled, 233
devoid of constructed marks, 253–54
as essence of enlightenment, 233
five principles and, 6–7, 12
focal point of, 295–98, 592
of natural purity, 204, 440–41
as nature of phenomena, 184–86,
187, 194, 233, 440–41, 817
nonexistence of duality and, 339
as present in all, 215–16
profound meaning of, 304–5
as remedy, 678
seven types of, 816–19
stages of realizing, 340
as thoroughly established nature,
817, 818, 819
worship and, 577
suffering
bodhisattvas' compassion for, 8,
106–7, 442, 480–81, 604–5
concise explanation of, 721
of conditioned existence, 118–19,
720
continuous nature of, 134, 135, 136
equality in overcoming of, 475

maturation of affection and, 161–62
for sake of others, ix–x, 102, 103,
105–6, 111, 112, 480–81, 614–15,
618–27
suchness of abidance and, 817, 818
three types of, 633
summit. *See* stage of summit
superior intent
acceptance of birth and, 870
compassion of, 607–8
of enlightened mind, 79, 91, 93
explanation of, 870–72
of five signs of bodhisattvas, 867
grounds and paths and, 841–42
superknowledges, 70, 104, 145–56
cause of, 147–48
classifications of, 154–55
concentration and, 502, 522
endowment of, 153–54
essence of, 145–46
full accomplishment of instruction
and, 690–91
full maturation of, 164–65
functions of, 149–53
of listeners and self-realized buddhas,
822
magnificence of, 155–56
mastery of, 177, 217, 346, 391
mature faith and, 160
metaphor for, 92, 95
praise of, 915–16
result of attaining, 148–49, 468
tenth ground and, 889, 903
supramundane path, 51, 52, 901
supramundane wakefulness, 193, 234,
328, 340–41, 433, 474–75
Supreme Continuity, 64, 362, 814
supreme emanations, 151, 152, 218, 239,
240, 342
supreme mundane quality, 82, 388, 389,
472, 675
supreme quality. *See* stage of supreme
quality
supreme refuge, 191–92
supreme self, characteristics of, 204–5

Sūtra, 25, 29
   definitive and expedient meanings in, 357
   directing the mind to meaning of, 304–5, 309–10, 458–61
   five fields of knowledge and, 811–16
   teachings of, 286–92
   See also Dharma of scripture
Sūtra of Gaya Mountain, 611
Sūtra of the Completely Pure Sphere of Activity, 120
Sūtra of the Great Display, 816
Sūtra of the Inconceivable Secret, 49, 409, 410
Sūtra of the Lord of Retention, 221
Sūtra of the Ornament of the Light of Wakefulness, 185
Sūtra on Numerous Elements, 60, 61
Sūtra on Repaying Kindness, 365–66
Sūtra on the Definitive Explanation of the Intent, 126, 394, 815, 817, 818
Sūtra on the Ten Grounds, 304, 456, 458, 460, 469, 476, 687, 691, 817, 873, 876, 877, 887
Sūtra on Transcendent Insight in One Hundred Thousand Lines, 310, 393, 440, 461, 711, 840
Sūtra Requested by Brahma, 391, 404–5
Sūtra Requested by Ratnacūḍa, 911
Sūtra Taught by Akṣayamati, 590, 610–11, 666, 693, 830
Sūtra That Explains the Secret of the Thus-Gone One's Body, 872
symbols
   enlightened mind attained through, 82, 83–84
   refuge attained through, 55

Tantra of Essential Elixir, 814
Tantra of the Wheel of Time. *See Wheel of Time, The*
teaching, 397–428
   benefits of, 427–28
   of bodhisattvas, 113–14, 115–16, 402–8

   of buddhas, 227–28, 398–402, 408–16
   categories to be taught, 809–23
   classification of Dharma, 810–16
   classification of meaning to be comprehended, 823–33
   classification of the three vehicles, 821–23
   classification of the truths, 816–19
   effects of, 835–37
   eight defects of discourse, 416
   of eight remedies and benefits, 423–27
   enlightened activity of, 209–10, 225, 249
   excellent meaning of, 403–5, 418
   excellent words of, 405–8, 418
   four concealed intents of, 419–21
   four intents of, 421–22
   four types of reasoning, 819–21
   general characteristics of, 417–18
   in harmony with potential, 113, 115–16, 201, 202, 407, 422, 791, 834
   inspiration and, 268, 270, 272
   intelligence of expression and, 378
   of oneness of vehicles, 354–62, 427
   purpose of, 398–402
   qualities of teachers, 833–35
   three ways of explaining, 403
   without stinginess, 397–98
   See also spiritual teacher
ten powers, 917–18
tenth ground, 51, 385
   bodhisattvas on, 889–90
   characteristics of, 48, 114, 483, 883, 903, 909
   four masteries and, 346
third ground
   bodhisattvas on, 886
   characteristics of, 877–78, 902, 908
thorough affliction, 127, 189, 191
   as essence of enlightenment, 441
   habitual tendencies of, 339
   illusory nature of, 324, 325
   insight eliminating, 523

investigation of, 329–31
as nonarising, 353
nonengagement with causes of, 196, 197
person in possession of, 758, 763–64, 773–74
See also cyclic existence
thoroughly established nature, 13
absence of marks and, 430, 432, 718, 719, 721
buddhahood and, 185
characteristics of, 7, 126–31, 314, 334, 339, 420
complete purity of, 12–13, 205, 315
directing the mind to observe, 305
perceiving essence of, 476, 858
as suchness, 817, 818, 819
as ultimate, 19, 321, 352
as unarisen, 353
thought
authentic, 307–8, 706, 707
mastery of, 831
transformation of, 220, 222–23
three bodies. *See* bodies of the buddhas
three excellences, 495
Three Jewels, going for refuge in, 42, 53–54. *See also* refuge
three marks, 461–62
cultivation of, 308, 437, 685, 707
three natures, 6, 7, 13, 314–15
essencelessness and, 349–52
five bases for characteristics and, 337–39
as suchness of characteristics, 817
teaching on, 420
thorough knowledge of, 829–30
See also specific natures
three persons, 6, 7, 13, 57
potentials of, 113–14, 115–16, 302
three special trainings, 29, 306–7, 788
Dharma of scripture and, 290–91
on the grounds, 890–92
practical instructions on, 487
transcendences and, 501, 503–4

three spheres. *See* nonobservation of the three spheres
three vehicles
classification of, 821–23
full maturation and, 171
going for refuge and, 54–55, 56–57
potential and, 60–62, 67
teaching of oneness of, 354–62, 427
universality and, 43
totalities, ten, 155, 912–13
transcendence of suffering
displays of, 240
as equal to bondage, 43–44, 137, 245, 440, 442, 830
illusory nature of, 325
lacking potential for, 72, 73
of listeners and self-realized buddhas, 23, 25, 28, 61–62, 64, 81, 87, 100, 190, 191
mind as root of, 130
no attachment to, 323
nonabiding, 51, 122, 138, 223, 245, 440, 712
as peace, 97, 721
without remainder, 62, 94, 131, 362
transcendences. *See* six transcendences
Transcendent Insight, 325, 393
Transcendent Insight in One Hundred Thousand Lines. See *Sūtra on Transcendent Insight in One Hundred Thousand Lines*
transformation, 192–98
explanation of, 193–94
mastery arising from, 218–24
of mind and thought, 220, 222–23
of sense faculties, 219–20, 221–23
superiority of, 195–98
tenfold categorization of, 196–98
transitory collection, view of, 132–34, 758, 763–64. *See also* self, view of
treasury of space, absorption of, 152, 155, 220, 223, 235, 548, 560, 576, 588
truth body, 208. *See also* body of qualities
truth of cessation, 477, 663, 721, 810, 817, 818

truth of origin, 663, 817, 818
truth of suffering, 663, 818
truth of the path, 477, 663, 810, 817, 818
two truths
  as indivisible, 128
  realization of, 857–58
twofold benefit, 28, 78
  accomplishment of, 50, 856
  aspirations for, 716
  bodies of the buddhas and, 239–41
  patience and, 522
  practice endowed with, 109–10
  skillful means and, 712
  spontaneous accomplishment of, 186–87
  sublime refuge and, 188–92
  transcendences and, 374, 501–2
  See also benefiting others
twofold selflessness. *See* selflessness, twofold

Ultimate Emptiness, 771
ultimate mind of enlightenment, 82, 83, 84–90
ultimate reality, 126–31, 420. *See also* reality
unassailability, full maturation of, 165–66
unconditioned, basis of, 335, 336
Unexcelled Realm, 839
uplifting, mark of, 308, 437, 685

Vairocana, 237
Vajra Cutter. See Vajra Cutter Sūtra
Vajra Cutter Sūtra, 185, 808
Vajrapāṇi, 49
valid proof, reasoning of, 820, 821
variegated awareness, realization of, 857
Vasubandhu, xii, xiv, 11, 13, 312, 746
view, authentic, 307, 705, 706–7
views, wrong
  dispelling, 309
  lack of potential and, 72–73

meditative absorptions for remedying, 380
ten discards and, 392–95
Vimalacandra, 425
Vimalakīrti, 626
Vinaya, 25, 29, 286–94
virtue
  accumulation of immeasurable, 183
  aspirations for, 684
  of bodhisattvas, 51–53, 101, 102, 540–41
  delight in, 161, 167, 522
  diligence and, 557
  engaging in defiled, 73
  establishing beings in, 179
  of Great Vehicle potential, 62–63
  inspiration and, 265, 270, 272
  of sacred Dharma, 417, 418
  of second ground, 877
  threefold basis of all, 491–92
  transcendences and, 114, 173, 175, 524
vision, full accomplishment of, 689–90. *See also* divine eye
vows, 81, 458, 849
  discipline and, 518, 520, 521, 524–25
  undefiled, 521, 808, 870

wakefulness
  of acceptance, 36
  activities of, 208–14
  aggregate of liberated, 894
  aspiration for, 715
  bodhisattva potential and, 70, 71
  of buddhas, 923
  cause for attaining forms of, 248–55
  as consummation of all paths, 255–58
  of ensuing attainment, 194, 233–34, 431, 698, 702, 901
  of exhaustion, 353, 884
  four forms of, 194, 232, 242–58
  fourfold authentic, 827–28
  free from focal points, 347
  mastery of, 156, 222–23, 346, 692
  mundane. *See* mundane wakefulness
  observing suchness, 829, 830

self-luminous, 131
source of all, 244
of subsequent attainment, 142, 321, 434, 476, 482–83, 857
supramundane, 193, 234, 328, 340–41, 433, 474–75
that eliminates obscurations, 431, 434
twofold selflessness and, 28, 42, 44, 50, 99, 494, 856
universal, 43, 44
vividness of liberated, 213–14
See also all-accomplishing wakefulness; discriminating wakefulness; mirror-like wakefulness; nonconceptual wakefulness; wakefulness of equality
wakefulness of equality, 222, 232
afflicted mind and, 236, 242
cause for attaining, 248–49
explanation of, 244–45
weariness
absence of, 88, 374–75, 378, 492, 493, 503, 654, 900
impermanence and, 727
welfare of sentient beings. *See* benefiting others
Wheel of Time, The, 814, 815

White Lotus of the Sacred Dharma, 221
Word of Buddha
Buddha's teaching on distinguishing, 25
defining character of, 24
Great Vehicle as, 13–14, 22–31
words
correct awareness of, 669, 670
directing the mind to, 305, 309–10, 458, 461, 659
excellence of bodhisattvas', 405–8
immaculate, 6, 8, 10, 11
world realms
appearance of buddhas in various, 250, 251–52
basis of appearance of, 832–33
enjoyment body in various, 237–38
enlightened activity in, 210, 218, 227–28, 247
fourteen modes of life and, 737–41
knowledge of, 661–64
purification of, 834
superknowledge and, 146, 150, 151, 152–53
worship, 377, 571–78
nature of, 571–72, 577
supreme, 578
types of, 573–78